AF497686

TRANSACTIONS

OF THE

VIITH INTERNATIONAL CONGRESS OF ARCHITECTS

LONDON 1906

JOHN BELCHER, A R A , *Past President R I B A*

PRESIDENT OF THE CONGRESS

INTERNATIONAL CONGRESS OF ARCHITECTS

SEVENTH SESSION

HELD IN LONDON 16–21 JULY 1906

UNDER THE AUSPICES OF THE ROYAL INSTITUTE OF BRITISH ARCHITECTS

TRANSACTIONS

LONDON
THE ROYAL INSTITUTE OF BRITISH ARCHITECTS
9 CONDUIT STREET, W
1908

THE ROYAL INSTITUTE OF BRITISH ARCHITECTS
INCORPORATED BY ROYAL CHARTERS SEVENTH WILLIAM IV AND FIFTIETH VICTORIA

THE COUNCIL, 1905–06.

JOHN BELCHER, A.R A., **President**

Vice-Presidents.
HENRY T. HARE	LEONARD STOKES
EDWIN T HALL	SIR JOHN TAYLOR, K.C.B.

Honorary Secretary.
ALEX GRAHAM, F S A

Members of Council
W H. ATKIN BERRY	ED. W. MOUNTFORD
J J BURNET, A R.S A	Professor BERESFORD PITE
W D CARÖE, M.A Cantab , F S A	A N PRENTICE
T E COLLCUTT	G H FELLOWES PRYNNE.
A W S CROSS, M A Cantab	JOHN W SIMPSON
ERNEST GEORGE.	JOHN SLATER, B A.Lond
JAMES S GIBSON.	C HARRISON TOWNSEND
J. ALFRED GOTCH, F.S A	PAUL WATERHOUSE, M.A Oxon
E A GRUNING.	ED WOODTHORPE, M A Oxon.

Associate-Members of Council
R. S BALFOUR	W. A FORSYTH
HENRY A CROUCH.	H V LANCHESTER

Representatives of Allied Societies.
A W BREWILL	Nottingham Architectural Society.
G. BERTRAM BULMER	Leeds and Yorks Architectural Society
THOMAS COOPER	Birmingham Architectural Associatn
H L. GODDARD, M.A Oxon	Leicester and Leicestershire Society of Architects.
JOHN KEPPIE	Glasgow Institute of Architects.
W. M. MITCHELL	Royal Inst of the Archts of Ireland
G. H OATLEY	Bristol Society of Architects
P. C THICKNESSE	Liverpool Architectural Society
J H WOODHOUSE	Manchester Society of Architects

Representative of the Architectural Association (London).
E GUY DAWBER

The Secretary of the Royal Institute
W J LOCKE, B A Cantab

CONTENTS

PART I
COMMITTEES, DELEGATES, MEMBERS

PART II

ORGANISATION AND RÉSUMÉ OF PROCEEDINGS

PART III

THE OPENING CEREMONIES, REPORTS OF INTERNATIONAL PERMANENT COMMITTEE MEETINGS, RECEPTIONS, FÊTES, VISITS, EXCURSIONS, FAREWELL BANQUET

PART IV

PAPERS AND REPORTS. DISCUSSIONS RESOLUTIONS

SUBJECT

I. The Execution of Important Government and Municipal Architectural Work by Salaried Officials

II Architectural Copyright and Ownership of Drawings.

III Steel and Reinforced-Concrete Construction — (a) THE GENERAL ASPECT OF THE SUBJECT ; (b) WITH SPECIAL REFERENCE TO ÆSTHETIC AND HYGIENIC CONSIDERATIONS IN THE CASE OF VERY HIGH BUILDINGS :—

Contents

XI

PART I.

COMMITTEE OF PATRONAGE

FOR GREAT BRITAIN AND IRELAND, FOREIGN COUNTRIES, AND THE COLONIES.

Patron
HIS MAJESTY KING EDWARD VII.

Hon. President.
H.R.H. THE PRINCE OF WALES.

President.
JOHN BELCHER, A.R.A , President R I B A.

GREAT BRITAIN AND IRELAND.

Hon. Vice-Presidents

H.R.H. the Duke of Connaught.
His Excellency the Viceroy of India
H.H. the Maharaja of Jaipur.
His Grace the Archbishop of Canterbury.
His Grace the Archbishop of York
His Grace the Duke of Devonshire
His Grace the Duke of Northumberland.
His Grace the Duke of Argyll.
His Grace the Duke of Fife
The Most Hon. the Marquis of Ripon.
The Right Hon. the Earl of Wemyss and March.
The Right Hon. the Earl of Plymouth.
The Right Hon. Lord Esher.
Lord Balcarres, M.P.
The Right Rev. the Lord Bishop of London.
The Right Hon. Lord Curzon of Kedleston.
The Secretary of State for Foreign Affairs.
The Right Hon the Lord Mayor of London.
The Chairman of the London County Council
The Vice-Chancellor of the University of London.
The President of the Royal Academy.
Sir Lawrence Alma-Tadema, O M , R A.

General Committee

NOTE —The asterisk (*) denotes Members of the Permanent Committee of the International Congresses of Architects

*Professor George Aitchison, R.A., Past President R I.B A.
*R. Phené Spiers, F R I.B A
Sir Benjamin Baker, K C.B , F R.S , Hon A R.I B A.
Sir John Wolfe Barry, K.C.B , F R S., Hon. A.R.I.B A
Sir William Richmond, K.C.B , R.A , Hon A R I.B A.
Sir William Emerson, Past President R.I B.A.
W. Q Orchardson, R.A , Hon A.R I B A
Hamo Thornycroft, R.A.
George Frampton, R.A , Hon A.R I.B.A
Solomon J. Solomon, R.A., Hon. A R.I.B.A.
Alfred East, A.R.A., Hon. A.R.I.B.A.
J Macvicar Anderson, F.R.S.E., Past President R.I.B A,

W. E. Riley, F R.I B A
F. T. Reade, Hon A R I B A
F N. Jackson, Hon A R I B A.
A. T. Walmsley, Hon A.R I B.A.
Maurice B Adams, F R.I.B A
E Holmes, President Sheffield Society of Architects and Surveyors.
H. H. Thomson, F.R I.B.A., President Leicester and Leicestershire Society of
    Architects.
J. H. Woodhouse, F R I B A , President Manchester Society of Architects.
J. Milne Munro, F.R I B.A., President Glasgow Institute of Architects.
J. T. Cackett, F R I B A , President Northern Architectural Association.
H. Dare Bryan, F R I B A., President Bristol Society of Architects.
W. D. Pratt, President Nottingham Architectural Society
W M. Mitchell, R.H.A., F.R.I.B.A., President Royal Institute of the Architects
    of Ireland
Edmund Kirby, F R I B A , President Liverpool Architectural Society.
J. L Ball, President Birmingham Architectural Association
H S Chorley, F R I B A , President Leeds and Yorkshire Architectural Society.
Harbottle Reed, F.R I B A , President Devon and Exeter Architectural Society.
P H Thoms, F R I B A , President Dundee Institute of Architecture, Science,
    and Art
Arthur Pollard, F R I B A , President York Architectural Society.
J H Phillips, F R I B A , President Cardiff, S Wales, & Monmouthshire Archi-
    tects' Society
R G. Wilson, F.R I B A , President Aberdeen Society of Architects.
H. O. Tarbolton, F R I B.A., President Edinburgh Architectural Association.
J. J. McDonnell, President Ulster Society of Architects.

INCLUDING THE

Executive Committee, viz.

*John Belcher, A.R.A , P R.I B A., *President.*
*Sir Aston Webb, R.A., Past President R I.B.A.
*Alexander Graham, Hon Sec R.I.B.A.
*T. E. Collcutt, President-Elect R I.B A.
*H T. Hare, Vice-President R I.B.A.
*John Slater, F R 1 B.A.
*Leonard Stokes, Vice-President R.I.B.A
John W. Simpson, F R I.B A.
Thos W Cutler, F R I B A.
H. H. Statham, F R I.B A
Reginald Blomfield, A R A , F R I B.A.
Mervyn Macartney, F R I B A
E. Guy Dawber, F.R I B A
R. S Balfour, F R I B A (President of the Architectural Association).
*W. J. Locke, Sec. R I B A , *Secretary.*

AUSTRALIA.

Harry C. Kent, F.R.I.B A (President Institute of Architects of New South
    Wales).
Cyril Blacket (Past President Institute of Architects of New South Wales).
Ernest A. Scott (Vice-President Institute of Architects of New South Wales).
C. A. D'Ebro, F.R.V.I.A. (President Royal Victorian Institute of Architects).
Francis J. Smart, F.R.V I.A (Vice-President Royal Victorian Institute of Archi-
    tects).

Edward Davies (President South Australian Institute of Architects)
Alan C. Walker, A R I B.A. (President Tasmanian Association of Architects).
R. Flack Ricards, F R V I.A. (Tasmanian Association of Architects).
G T Poole, A R I B A. (President West Australian Institute of Architects)
M. F. Cavanagh, F R I.B A. (West Australian Institute of Architects).

AUSTRIA.

Hon. President.
*Wagner, Otto.

Hon Vice-President
Von Wielemans, A

Members.

*Helmer, H	*Streit, A
*Hodl, T.	*Weber, A
*Peschl, H (*Secretary*).	

BELGIUM.

Hon Vice-Presidents.

Acker, Ernest (professeur à l'Académie royale des Beaux-Arts de Bruxelles,
 membre effectif de l'Académie de Belgique [Classe des Beaux-Arts et de
 la Commission royale des Monuments).
Blomme, Léonard (professeur à l'Institut supérieur des Arts d'Anvers, membre
 effectif de la Commission royale des Monuments).

Members.

*Arnou, Albert.
*Caluwaers, Jean-Joseph (Président de la Sociéte Centrale d'Architecture de
 Belgique).
*Cloquet, Louis (professeur à l'Université de Gand, membre correspondant de
 la Commission royale des Monuments, membre du Conseil de perfectionne-
 ment de l'enseignement des arts et du dessin)
*De Vestel, Franz (professeur à l'Académie royale des Beaux-Arts de Bruxelles)

Nominated by the Societe Centrale d'Architecture de Belgique .

Bosmans, Constant
Van de Veld.
Brunfaut, Jules (membre correspondant de la Commission royale des Monu-
 ments et de l'Académie de Belgique [Classe des Beaux-Arts]).
De Braey, Michel (Président de la Société royale des Architectes d'Anvers)
De Noyette, Modeste (Directeur de la Section de la Flandre Orientale de la
 Société Centrale d'Architecture de Belgique)
Hubert, Joseph (architecte communal honoraire, membre correspondant et
 vice-président du Comité du Hainaut de la Commission royale des Monu-
 ments, Directeur de la Section de Mons de la Société Centrale d'Architecture
 de Belgique).
Janlet, Emile (membre effectif de la Commission royale des Monuments et
 de l'Académie de Belgique [Classe des Beaux-Arts]).
Van Assche, Auguste (membre effectif de la Commission royale des Monuments).

CANADA.

Patrons and Honorary Vice-Presidents.

The Right Hon. Lord Strathcona and Mount Royal, G.C.M.G., High Commissioner for Canada, London.

Hon. Louis A. Jette, Lieutenant Governor, Province of Quebec.

His Honour Mortimer Clark, K.C., Lieutenant Governor, Province of Ontario.

R. Harris, Esq., C.M.G., President, Royal Canadian Academy.

J. S. Archibald, *President.*	Jos. Venne.
*Alcide Chaussé, *Secretary.*	J. O Marchand.
*W. E. Doran.	R. Lacroix.
D. R. Brown.	

DENMARK.

Hon Vice-Presidents.

His Excellency Count Chamberlain F. Raben Levetnau, Minister of Foreign Affairs

Meldahl, F (Chamberlain, Professor in the Royal College of Fine Arts).

Members.

*Berg, A.	Jorgensen, T.
*Dahlerup, V.	Kampmann, H.
Amberg, H. C.	Koch, F.
Borch, M	Nyrop, M.
Clemmensen, A.	Storch, H.
Holm, H J.	Petersen, V.
Jensen, A.	Wenck, H.

FRANCE.

Hon. President.

*Daumet, H. (membre de l'Institut de France).

Hon. Vice-Presidents

*Guadet J.

*Nénot, H. P. (membre de l'Institut de France)

Members.

*Poupinel, J. M.	Duchatelet, E.
*Harmand, G.	Fernoux, H.
*Bartaumieux, Ch.	Laloux, V.
*Bissuel, Ed.	Lefort, H.
*Bonnier, L.	Louzier, St. A.
*Gosset, Ant.	Maillard, G.
*Loviot, Ed.	Mainguet, Th.
*Moyaux, C. (membre de l'Institut de France).	Normand, A. (membre de l'Institut de France).
*Newnham, A.	Olive, G.
*Trélat, E.	Pascal, J. L. (membre de l'Institut de France).
Betolaud, A. (membre de l'Institut de France).	Robert-Fleury, T. (membre de l'Institut de France).
Bonnat, L. (membre de l'Institut de France).	Vaudremer, E. (membre de l'Institut de France).
Blondel, F.	
Choisy, A.	

GERMANY.

*Hinckeldeyn, K. (Ministerial- und Oberdirektor).
*Muthesius, H. M. (Landes-Gewerberat, Dr.).
*Von Schmidt, Freiherr H. (Professor).
*Stubben, J. (Ober- und Geheimer Baurat, Dr.).
*Waldow, Edm. (Geheimer Baurat, vortragender Rat).
*Schonermarck, G. (Doctor).
*Neher, L. (Kgl. Baurat).
 Von Thiersch, F (Professor).
 Wallot, P. (Geheimer Baurat, Geheimer Hofrat, Professor)
 Von Seidl, G. (Professor)
 Schwechten, F. (Geheimer Baurat).
 Hofmann, K. (Geheimer Oberbaurat, Professor).
 Hoffmann, L (Kgl Baurat, Stadtbaurat).
 Licht, H. (Stadtbaurat, Professor).

HOLLAND.

Hon. Vice-Presidents

Son Excellence M. le Baron K. W. P. F. Gericke van Herwynen (Envoyé extraordinaire et Ministre plénipotentiaire des Pays-Bas à Londres)
Royer, J. A. (Ingémeur Civil, Référendaire, Chef de la Section des Arts et Sciences
  au Ministère des Affaires Intérieures)

Members.

*Cuypers, Dr. P. J. H. (Délégué du Gouvernement, Architecte des Musées de
  l'Etat).
*Salm G. Bzn., A. (Président de la Société pour la Propagation de l'Archi-
  tecture).
*Berlage, H. P. (Président d'Architecture et Amicitia).
Klinkhamer, Professor J F.
Weeldenburg, P. A (Président de la Société Bouwkunst en Vriendschap).
Rieber, C. T. J. L. (Secrétaire de la Société pour la Propagation de l'Architecture).

HUNGARY.

Hon. President

Hauszmann (Professor).

Hon. Vice-Presidents

Alpár (Vice-President of the Society of Engineers and Architects).
Ney (President of Section for Architects).
Pucher (President of Section for Architects).
Quitner (President of the Society of Private Architects).

Members.

Aigner.	Pecz.	Hultl.
Fellner.	Schannen.	Jámbor.
Freund.	Schickedanz.	Kabdebó.
Gerster, K.	Schmahl.	Kertész.
Kauser, J.	Schulek.	Sàndy.
Korb.	Nágy, V. (Professor).	Szabó.
Lechner, Ö.	Hópfner.	Töry.
Pártos.		

ITALY.

*Basile, Ernest (Professeur à l'Ecole d'application pour les Ingénieurs, Palerme).
*Betocchi, A. (ancien Président du Conseil des Travaux Publics).
*Breglia (Professeur à l'Ecole d'application pour les Ingénieurs, Naples)
*Cannizzaro, M. E. (Président de l'Association pour la Culture de l'Architecture).
*Manfredi, Manfredo (Directeur de l'Institut des Beaux-Arts, Venise).
*Boito, Camille (Directeur de l'Académie de Brera, Milan).
Timoschi, Luigi, Cav. (Président du Collège des Ingénieurs et des Architectes de Gênes)
Allievi, L , *Presidente* (Presidente della Società degli Ingegneri e degli Architetti Italiani, Roma)
Albanese, A (Presidente del Circolo degli Ingegneri ed Architetti liberi esercenti in Palermo).
Casini, G. (Presidente del Collegio Toscano degli Ingegneri ed Architetti, Firenze).
Cavani, F (Presidente della Società degli Ingegneri di Bologna)
Colombo, G. (Presidente del Collegio degli Ingegneri ed Architetti di Milano)
Francesetti di Mezzenile, C (Presidente del Collegio degli Ingegneri e degli Architetti di Torino)
Magni, G (Presidente dell' Associazione fra i Cultori di Architettura, Roma)
Marullo, G (Presidente del Collegio degli Ingegneri ed Architetti di Messina).
Miglioncio, M. (Presidente del Collegio degli Ingegneri ed Architetti Pugliesi, Bari)
Romanin, Jacur L. (Presidente del Collegio Veneto degli Ingegneri, Venezia).

MEXICO.

*De Heredia, G. | *Mariseal, N
*Rivas Mercado, A.

NEW ZEALAND.

Hon Vice-President.
The Lord Bishop of Wellington.

Committee.

The Hon the Minister of Public Works.
The Hon. the Minister of Railways.
The President of the New Zealand Academy of Fine Arts.
The President of the New Zealand Institute of Architects
The President of the Wellington Association of Architects.
The President of the Canterbury Association of Architects.
The President of the Otago Association of Architects.
The President of the Southland Association of Architects.
The President of the Wellington Chamber of Commerce.
The Director of the Wellington Technical School.
Alfred Atkins, F.R I B A
Thomas Turnbull, F R.I B.A.
William Turnbull, F.R.I B.A.
John Campbell, F.R I B.A.
Joseph C. Maddison, F R.I B.A.
F. de J. Clere, F.R.I B A (Hon. Secretary R.I.B.A. for New Zealand)

NORWAY.

Christie, Christian. | Due, Paul

PORTUGAL.

Hon. Vice-Presidents.

His Excellency the Minister for Foreign Affairs.
His Excellency the Minister for Public Works.
His Excelleney the Marquis de Soveral, Portuguese Minister in London.

Members

His Excellency Counsellor Augusto José da Cunha (President of the Royal Association of Portuguese Architects and Archæologists).
His Excellency the Vicomte d'Athouguia (President of the National Society of Fine Arts).
Soares, J. A. (Delegate of the Society of Portuguese Architects)
Parente, F C. (Delegate of the National Society of Fine Arts).
Do Couto, A. (Delegate of the Royal Association of Portuguese Architects and Archæologists).
*Monteiro, J. L. (Professor).
*Bermudes, A R. Adães.
*Terra, M. Ventura.
*Carvalheira, R G A

RUSSIA.

*Bykofsky
*De Suzor, Comte P.

*Rutnez.
*Soultonoff.

SOUTH AFRICA.
Cape Colony.

Members

George Ransome, A.R.I.B A
Arthur H Reid, F R I B A (Hon. Secretary R.I B.A for South Africa).

F. G Green, A R.I B A.
J. C. Tully, A.R.I.B A.
E. J Bridges, A R.I B A
Herbert Baker, F R I.B A

Natal.

Members

W. Lucas, F.R G S., F.R I B.A. (President Natal Institute of Architects)
A. E. Dainton
F. J. Ing
C. W. Methven, M.I.C E , F R.S.E., F.R I.B.A.
A. M. Ritchie.

Transvaal.

Members

J. Waterson, F R I B A (President Transvaal Institute of Architects)
G. A H Dickson, F.R I.B.A (Past President Transvaal Institute of Architects)
G. S. Burt Andrews, A M I.C.E. (Vice-President Transvaal Institute of Architects).
Walter Reid, F.R I B A (Vice-President Transvaal Institute of Architects).
Herbert Baker, F.R I B.A.
J. F. Beardwood.
G. Granger Fleming
H. Seton Morris.
G. St. J. Cottrill (Hon Secretary Transvaal Institute of Architects),

SPAIN.

President

Aparici y Soriano, Son Excellence Federico (Directeur de l'Ecole supérieure d'Architecture, Conseiller de l'Instruction Publique).

Vice-Presidents

*Velasquez Bosco, Son Excellence Ricardo (Président Section d'Architecture de l'Académie Royale des Beaux-Arts et du Conseil des Constructions Civiles).
*Urioste y Velada, Son Excellence José (Académicien des Beaux-Arts)
*Repullés y Vargas, Son Excellence Enrique M (Académicien des Beaux-Arts)
*Arbos y Tremanti, Son Excellence Fernando (Académicien des Beaux-Arts).
*Le Président de l'Association des Architectes de Cataluña.

Secretary

*Cabello y Lapiedra, Luis M (Architecte du Ministere de l'Instruction Publique des Beaux-Arts)

Members

Le Président de la Société Centrale des Architectes.
Le Président de l'Association des Architectes de Vizcaya.
Le Président de l'Association des Architectes de Navarra.
Adaro y Magro, Son Excellence Eduardo (Membre de la Société Centrale des Architectes, Académicien des Beaux-Arts)
Abreu y Barreda, Gabriel (Architecte du Ministère des Affaires Etrangères Professeur de l'Ecole des Arts et Métiers)
Agapito y Revilla, Juan (Architecte de la Municipalité de Valladolid).
Amoroso, Manuel Anibal Alvarez (Professeur de l'Ecole supérieure d'Architecture de Madrid).
Argenti y Herrera, Luis (Architecte de la Députation provincial)
Bellido y Gonzalez, Luis (Secrétaire de la Société Centrale des Architectes, Architecte de la Municipalité de Madrid).
Bertran y de Quintana, Miguel (Secrétaire de l'Association des Architectes de Cataluña, Professeur de l'Ecole supérieure d'Architecture de Barcelona)
Contreras, Mariano (Architecte Conservateur de l'Alhambra de Granada).
Le Directeur de l'Ecole supérieure d'Architecture de Barcelona
Esteve y Fernandez Caballero, Luis (Professeur de l'Ecole supérieure d'Architecture de Madrid)
Casanova, Adolfo Fernandez (Professeur de l'Ecole supérieure d'Architecture de Madrid, Académicien des Beaux-Arts).
Valdés, Fernandez y Menendez (D Joaquin) (Architecte Diocésain de Madrid-Alcala).
Fort y Guyenet, Enrique (Professeur de l'Ecole supérieure d'Architecture de Madrid, Architecte du Ministère de l'Instruction Publique et des Beaux-Arts).
Acebo, Tomas Gomez (Membre de la Société Centrale des Architectes).
Lamperez y Romea, Vicente (Professeur de l'Ecole supérieure d'Architecture de Madrid).
Landecho y Urries, Son Excellence Luis (Académicien des Beaux-Arts, Membre de la Société Centrale des Architectes).
Sallaberry, José Lopez (Architecte de la Municipalité de Madrid, Académicien des Beaux-Arts)
Magadalena y Tabuenca, Ricardo (Architecte de la Municipalité de Zaragoza).
Repullés y Segarra, Son Excellence Enrique (Mayor de la Real Casa, Professeur de l'Ecole supérieure d'Architecture).

Roji y Lopez Calvo, Joaquin (Membre de la Société Centrale des Architectes, Directeur de la Revue *Arte y Construccion*).
Terreros, Luis Sainz de los (Membre de la Société Centrale des Architectes, Directeur de la Revue *La Construccion Moderna*)
Saavedra y Moragas, Son Excellence Eduardo (Membre des Académies de l'Histoire, de la Langue, et des Sciences, Conseiller de l'Instruction Publique, Membre de la Société Centrale des Architectes).
Vega y March, Manuel (Directeur de la Revue *Arquitéctura y Construccion*).
Zabala y Gallardo, Manuel (Membre du Conseil des Constructions Civiles, Professeur de l'Ecole supérieure d'Architecture et Membre de la Société Centrale des Architectes).
Zavala y Alvarez, Daniel (Président de la Société Centrale des Architectes)

SWEDEN.

*Clason, I. G. (Professor).	Sahn, K.
*Möller, C.	Dahlander, M.
*Wickman, G.	Thorburn, E.
Améen, G	Thurdin, A
Lallerstedt, E.	Wahlin, Th.

SWITZERLAND.

*Fulpius, F. | *Geiser, E. | *Bluntschli (Doctor and Professor).

TURKEY.

*Aposthohdhis.

UNITED STATES.

Hon Vice-Presidents.

The Honourable the Secretary of State.
The Honourable the Secretary of War.
His Excellency the American Ambassador to Great Britain.
The Honourable Francis G. Newlands, U S. Senator.

Members.

Carrere, John M.	Mowbray, Henry Siddons.
Choate, Hon Joseph H.	Peabody, Robert S.
Day, Frank Miles.	Post, George B.
French, Daniel C.	Saint-Gaudens, Augustus.
Gilbert, Cass.	Stillman, James
La Farge, John.	Taylor, J. Knox.
McKim, Charles F.	Walters, Henry.
Millet, Francis D.	Ware, Professor W. R.
Morgan, J. Pierpont.	

The Presidents of the following Societies :

American Institute of Architects.	National Academy of Design.
Architectural League of America.	National Sculpture Society.

Society of American Artists.

Members ex officio

*Allen, Francis R.	*Eames, William S.
*Brown, Glenn.	*Jenney, William le Baron.

*Totten, George O., Jun.

COMMITTEES OF THE EXECUTIVE &c.

Exhibition Sub-Committee.	*Visits and Entertainments Sub-Committee.*	*Literary Sub-Committee.*
Belcher, J.	Belcher, J.	Belcher, J.
Stokes, L.	Blomfield, R.	Slater, J.
Statham, H. H.	Simpson, John W.	Graham, A.
Cutler, Thos. W	Hare, H. T	Macartney, M.
Macartney, Mervyn.	Collcutt, T. E.	Locke, W. J.
Gotch, J A	Locke, W. J.	
Townsend, C. Harrison		
Bond, F		
Millard, Walter.		
Prior, Edward S		
Forsyth, W A		
Wonnacott, W.		
Locke, W. J.		
Straus, Ralph (*Secretary*).		

Ladies' Committee

Lady Webb	Mrs. Slater (*Hon Sec*).	Mrs. Dawber.
Mrs. Belcher (*President*).	Mrs. Cutler.	Mrs. Statham.
Mrs. Hare (*Hon Sec*)	Mrs Blomfield.	
Mrs Stokes	Hon Mrs Macartney.	

Steward-Interpreters.

Plunkett, Count G N.	Lacy, H A	Adlersparre, C von.
Plunkett, Countess.	Vermont, J.	Fleming, Owen.
Campbell, A. N.	Curtis, S C	Rowe, Miss E.
Ward, W. H.	Ferrier, C. W.	Bollag, Gustav
Westbye, Jos. W.	Jackson, F. N.	Bourdon, E.
Maynard, D. C.	Wood, E.	Chaussé, A
Roscoe, E G.	Sayer, C E	English, C. W.
Fletcher, J. B.	Poynter, Ambrose	Lanchester, H J.
Fletcher, H M.	Warren, E P	Triggs, H. Inigo.
Pope, Reginald.	Newton, Mrs	Ryan-Tenison, A. H.
Hardcastle, W.	Hudson, E. W.	Horsfield, Mrs. Nixon.
Sachs, E. O	Brown, Prof G Baldwin.	Bayard, Louis
Favarger, H	Stannus, H.	Bayard, J
Favarger, Mrs	Bryan, Mrs Dare.	Castello, M N.

STAFF

Herbert G Tayler, Assistant-Secretary.
Rudolf Dircks, Editor of Handbook.
G Northover, Editor of *Comptes-rendus* and other Papers.
J C Tanner, Bookkeeper and General Chief Clerk.
F. G. Baker, Assistant Chief Clerk.

DELEGATES.

FOREIGN GOVERNMENTS.

BELGIUM.

J J. Caluwaers (Président de la Société Centrale d'Architecture de Belgique).

DENMARK.

Etatsraad Vilhelm Dahlerup.

FRANCE.

H Daumet	J M. Poupinel.
H P. Nénot.	

GREECE.

Nicholas Balanos.	Anastase Metaxas

HOLLAND.

Joseph Theodore Cuypers.

HUNGARY.

Julius Berczik.	Alexandre d'Aigner

ITALY.

Mariano Edoardo Cannizzaro	Commendatore Alfredi d'Andrade

RUSSIA.

ACADÉMIE IMPÉRIALE DES BEAUX-ARTS.

M. le Comte Paul de Suzor.	Léon Bénois

SPAIN.

Richard Velasquez Bosco	E M Repullés y Vargas
Luis Mª Cabello y Lapiedra.	F Arbos y Tremanti.

SWEDEN.

Professor J. G. Clason.	Kaspar Salim.

UNITED STATES OF AMERICA.

Frank Miles Day

Francis R. Allen	William S Eames.
Glenn Brown.	W L B Jenney
George O Totten, Jun.	George B. Post

SOCIETIES AND CORPORATIONS.

BRITISH.

CORPORATION OF THE CITY OF LONDON.

Alexander Ritchie, J.P.	W. H Pitman.

ROYAL ACADEMY.

Sir W. B. Richmond, R.A.	Sir Aston Webb, R.A.

UNIVERSITY OF CAMBRIDGE

J W Clark, Registrary. | W M Fawcett.

UNIVERSITY OF LONDON.

Sir Aston Webb, R A.

VICTORIA UNIVERSITY, MANCHESTER.

Professor S H Capper.

UNIVERSITY OF LIVERPOOL.

Professor C. H Reilly

SURVEYORS' INSTITUTION.

George Langridge | H W D. Theobald.

ROYAL SANITARY INSTITUTE

Thomas W. Cutler. | A. Saxon Snell

THE ROYAL INSTITUTE OF PUBLIC HEALTH,

Thomas W Aldwinckle.

ARCHITECTURAL ASSOCIATION

Walter Cave. | Henry Tanner, Jun

SOCIETY OF ARCHITECTS

Albert E. Pridmore | Ellis Marsland.

DISTRICT SURVEYORS' ASSOCIATION.

Edward Dru Drury | Frederick Wallen

INCORPORATED ASSOCIATION OF MUNICIPAL AND COUNTY ENGINEERS

J W. Cockrill. | J. Patten Barber

SOCIETY FOR THE PROTECTION OF ANCIENT BUILDINGS

Professor W. R Lethaby | F W. Troup.

BRITISH FIRE PREVENTION COMMITTEE.

E O Sachs. | Max Clarke.

INSTITUTE OF BUILDERS

Benjamin I Greenwood. | Frank May.

THE SHEFFIELD SOCIETY OF ARCHITECTS AND SURVEYORS.

E M. Gibbs | J. B. Mitchell-Withers

LEICESTER AND LEICESTERSHIRE SOCIETY OF ARCHITECTS.

S Perkins Pick. | H Langton Goddard

MANCHESTER SOCIETY OF ARCHITECTS.

J H. Woodhouse. | J. W. Beaumont.

GLASGOW INSTITUTE OF ARCHITECTS

James M. Monro. | Horatio K. Bromhead.

NORTHERN ARCHITECTURAL ASSOCIATION

J. T. Cackett. | A. B. Plummer.

BRISTOL SOCIETY OF ARCHITECTS.

G. H. Oatley. | H. Dare Bryan.

ROYAL INSTITUTE OF THE ARCHITECTS OF IRELAND.

William M. Mitchell, R.H.A | R. Caulfeild Orpen.

LIVERPOOL ARCHITECTURAL ASSOCIATION.

Edmund Kirby. | Professor C. H. Reilly.

BIRMINGHAM ARCHITECTURAL ASSOCIATION

J. L. Ball | A Dennis Thacker.

LEEDS AND YORKSHIRE ARCHITECTURAL SOCIETY
H. S. Chorley | H A. Chapman.

DEVON AND EXETER ARCHITECTURAL SOCIETY.
Harbottle Reed. | R Priestley Shires.

DUNDEE INSTITUTE OF ARCHITECTURE, SCIENCE, AND ART
P. H. Thoms | J Donald Mills.

YORK ARCHITECTURAL SOCIETY.
S. Needham. | F Raney.

CARDIFF, SOUTH WALES, AND MONMOUTHSHIRE ARCHITECTS' SOCIETY.
J. H. Phillips. | Edwin Seward.

ABERDEEN SOCIETY OF ARCHITECTS
Robert G. Wilson. | John Rust.

EDINBURGH ARCHITECTURAL ASSOCIATION
J. Hippolyte Blanc, R.S.A. | H. O. Tarbolton

ULSTER SOCIETY OF ARCHITECTS.
J J. McDonnell. | W J Gilliland

AUSTRIA.

OESTERREICHISCHER INGENIEUR- UND ARCHITEKTEN-VEREIN
A. von Wielemans. | Hans Peschl
Hermann Helmer.

BELGIUM.

ACADÉMIE ROYALE DE BELGIQUE
Jacques Winders

SOCIÉTÉ CENTRALE D'ARCHITECTURE DE BELGIQUE.
Gustave Maukels | Maurice van Ysendyck

CHAMBRE SYNDICALE DES ARCHITECTES DE BRUXELLES.
Fernand Isidore Alphonse Symons. | Louis van Langendonck

ASSOCIATION DES ARCHITECTES DE LIÉGE.
Arthur Snyers. | Alphonse Caganus.
Armand Piron.

FRANCE.

SOCIÉTÉ CENTRALE DES ARCHITECTES FRANÇAIS.
H. P. Nénot. | Alfred Besnard.
Gustave Olive. | C. Nizet.

SOCIÉTÉ DES ARCHITECTES DIPLÔMÉS PAR LE GOUVERNEMENT.
J M. Poupinel. | A. C. Danne.
J. Bourdon.

ASSOCIATION PROVINCIALE DES ARCHITECTES FRANÇAIS.
Réné Martin

CAISSE DE DÉFENSE MUTUELLE DES ARCHITECTES.
H P Nénot. | G. Rozet.
Gustave Olive. | Georges Harmand.

SOCIÉTÉ NATIONALE DES ARCHITECTES DE FRANCE.
H. Fernoux. | A. Lecavalé.
J. Giboz. | A. Marchand.
F. Nanteuille.

SYNDICAT DES ARCHITECTES DU DÉPARTEMENT DU RHÔNE
F. Clermont.

SOCIÉTÉ DES ARCHITECTES DE LA BASSE-NORMANDIE.
J. Sandret.

SOCIÉTÉ RÉGIONALE DES ARCHITECTES DU NORD DE LA FRANCE
Alphonse Dubuisson | Georges Antoine.
Alfred Newnham

SOCIÉTÉ DES ARCHITECTES D'ANJOU.
Adrien Paul Dubos.

SOCIÉTÉ ACADÉMIQUE D'ARCHITECTURE DE LYON.
Pierre Richard.

SOCIÉTÉ DES ARCHITECTES DU DÉPARTEMENT DE LA MARNE.
Jules Alard

SOCIÉTÉ DES DIPLÔMES DE L'ECOLE SPÉCIALE D'ARCHITECTURE.
Eugène Chastel. | Camille Porat.
Eugène Quentin. | Paul Ricadat.

GERMANY.

VERBAND DEUTSCHER ARCHITEKTEN- UND INGENIEUR-VEREIN
Dr. Ing. Muthesius.

ARCHITEKTEN-VEREIN ZU BERLIN.
Julius Habicht. | Dr. Ing Hermann Muthesius.
Fritz Korte. | Dr. Ing. J. Stübben.

VEREINIGUNG BERLINER ARCHITEKTEN.
Bodo Ebhardt.

FRANKFURTER ARCHITEKTEN- UND INGENIEUR VEREIN.
Max Berg.

ARCHITEKTEN- UND INGENIEUR-VEREIN MANNHEIM.
G A Karch.

HOLLAND.

MAATSCHAPPIJ TOT BEVORDERUNG DER BOUWKUNST.
A. Salm G. Bzn

GENOOTSCHAP "ARCHITECTURA ET AMICITIA."
H. P. Berlage.

HUNGARY.

MAGYAR MÉRNOK- ÉS EPITÉSZ-EGYLET.
Virgil Nágy.

ITALY.

MUNICIPALITY OF ROME.
G B. Giovenale.

ASSOCIAZIONE ARTISTICA FRA I CULTORI DI ARCHITETTURA.
G. Magni Rem-Picci. | Filippo Galassi.

ACCADEMIA DI S LUCA.
Filippo Galassi

COLLEGIO TOSCANO DEGLI INGEGNERI ED ARCHITETTI
Comm. Giovanni Pini.

JAPAN.

INSTITUTE OF JAPANESE ARCHITECTS.
S. Chujo.

PORTUGAL.

SOCIÉTÉ DES ARCHITECTES PORTUGAIS.
José Alexandre Soares.

SOCIÉTÉ NATIONALE DES BEAUX-ARTS.
Francisco Carlos Parente.

ASSOCIATION ROYALE DES ARCHITECTES ET ARCHÉOLOGUES PORTUGAIS
Ventura Terra | Antonio do Conto

RUSSIA.

SOCIÉTÉ IMPÉRIALE DES ARCHITECTES RUSSES.
M. le Comte Paul de Suzor | M Robert Boker.

SPAIN.

DIRECCIÓN DE OBRAS DEL REAL PATRIMONIO
Francisco Perez de los Cobos

MUNICIPALITÉ DE MADRID
Joseph Urioste y Velada

ACADÉMIE DES BEAUX-ARTS DE MADRID
Joseph Urioste y Velada

SOCIÉTÉ CENTRALE DES ARCHITECTES ESPAGNOLS
E M Repullés y Vargas | Francisco Perez de los Cobos
Luis M' Cabello y Lapiedra | J B Lazaro de Diego
Anibal Alvarez y Amoroso

ACADÉMIE PROVINCIALE DES BEAUX-ARTS DE CATALOGNE
Joseph Artigas y Ramoneda.

ASSOCIATION DES ARCHITECTES DE CATALOGNE
Pelayo de Miquelerena y Noriega | Salvador Oller y Padrol

SWEDEN.

SVENSKA TEKNOLOGFORENINGEN.
Gustave Wickman.

SWITZERLAND.

SCHWEIZERISCHER INGENIEUR- UND ARCHITEKTEN-VEREIN
Fritz Stehlin.

UNITED STATES.

AMERICAN INSTITUTE OF ARCHITECTS
Frank Miles Day. | Cass Gilbert.
Wm Bryce Mundie

THE ARCHITECTURAL LEAGUE OF AMERICA.
Ernest John Russell. | N. Max Dunning.
Albert Kelsey. | William B. Ittner.

CHICAGO ARCHITECTURAL CLUB.   CHAPTER AT LARGE A I.A.
John Devereux York.   W. Churchill Noland.

NEW JERSEY CHAPTER A.I.A.
Robert Campbell Dixon, Jun. | Hugh Roberts.

St. Louis Chapter A I A
Theodore Carl Link.

Michigan Chapter A.I.A.
Frank C. Baldwin.

T. Square Club, Philadelphia.
Albert Kelsey.

Boston Chapter A I.A.
C. Howard Walker.

Baltimore Chapter A I.A.
William M. Ellicott.

South Californian Chapter A.I.A.
August Wackerbath.

Philadelphia Chapter N I.A
Thomas Nolan.
Albert Kelsey

New York Chapter A I.A.
John M. Carrère.

Brooklyn Chapter A.I.A
Isaac E. Ditmars

Central New York Chapter A.I A
J Foster Warner.

Buffalo Chapter A I A
Edward A. Kent.

Washington Architectural Club
George Oakley Totten, Jun

Washington Chapter A I A
Joseph C Hornblower.
E W Donn, Jun.

Minnesota Chapter A I A
W. Channing Whitney

Illinois Chapter A.I A.
Morrison H. Vail

San Francisco Chapter A.I.A.
William Curlett

Cincinnati Chapter A I A
George M Anderson

BRITISH COLONIES.

Province of Quebec Architects' Association
John S. Archibald. | Alcide Chaussé
Andrew T Taylor

The City Council of Montreal.
Alcide Chaussé.

Royal Victorian Institute of Architects
Christopher A Cowper.

Institute of Architects of New South Wales
Sir Charles Nicholson, Bart. | H. C. Corlette.
A W. Anderson.

South Australian Institute of Architects.
Albert Selmar Conrad.

West Australian Institute of Architects
J Talbot Hobbs | J. C. Cavanagh.

Tasmanian Association of Architects.
Alexander North

Cape Colony Society of Architects.
Frederick G Green | E J. Bridges.
W White Cooper

Transvaal Institute of Architects.
Walter Reid. | Gilbert St. John Cottrill
Ernest Willmott.

Natal Institute of Architects.
A. E Dainton. | F. J. Ing.

Orange River Colony.
J. D. Clarke.

MEMBERS

THE UNITED KINGDOM.

*(The asterisk * prefixed to a name indicates Donors to the Congress)*

ABERDEEN SOCIETY OF ARCHITECTS, The
Adams, Cole A , 66 Victoria Street, Westminster, S.W.
Adams, Mrs , 66 Victoria Street, Westminster, S.W
Adams, Henry, 60 Queen Victoria Street, E C
Adams, Mrs , 60 Queen Victoria Street, E C
Adams, Maurice B , 1 Marlborough Crescent, Bedford Park, Chiswick, W
Adlersparre, Christopher, 25 Royal Crescent, Holland Park Avenue, W
Adlersparre, Mrs , 25 Royal Crescent, Holland Park Avenue, W
Agius, Mrs., 3 Upper Park Road, Hampstead, N W
Aickman, William Arthur, 34 Gresham Street, E C
*Aitchison, Professor George, R A , 150 Harley Street, W
Aldwinckle, Thos W , 20 Denman Street, London Bridge, S E
Aldwinckle, Mrs , 20 Denman Street, London Bridge, S E
Allen, George P , Dacre House, Arundel Street, Strand, W.C
Allfrey, Edward W., 2 St Michael's Chambers, Oxford
Allison, Richard John, H M Office of Works, Westminster
*Alma-Tadema, Sir Lawrence, R A , 34 Grove End Road, N W
Ambler, Louis, Temple Chambers, Temple Avenue, E C
*Anderson, John Macvicar, 6 Stratton Street, Piccadilly, W
Anderson, Mrs , 6 Stratton Street, Piccadilly, W.
*Anderson, Henry Lennox, 6 Stratton Street, Piccadilly, W
*Anderson, Sir R Rowand, LL D , Allermuir House, Colinton, Midlothian, N B.
Angel, Robert John, Town Hall, Spa Road, Bermondsey, S E
Angel, Mrs , 125 Jamaica Road, Bermondsey, S E
Ansell, William Henry, 18 Guilford Street, Russell Square, W C
Ansell, Mrs , 18 Guilford Street, Russell Square, W C
Anthony, Miss Gertrude, 8 Lansdowne Road, Holland Park, W
*Architectural Association, The.
Arnaud, Miss Cecile, 38 Bolton Gardens, S W
Ashbee, Charles Robert, 37 Cheyne Walk, Chelsea, S W
*Ashbridge, Arthur, 17 York Place, Portman Square, W.
*Atkinson, R. Frank, 8 Sackville Street, W
Atkinson, Mrs., 8 Sackville Street, W
*Ayrton, Maxwell, 3 Verulam Buildings, Gray's Inn, W C
Bacon, Francis (jun), 10 Lincoln's Inn Fields, W C
Baggallay, Frank Thomas, 3 Bloomsbury Street, W C
Bailey, Percival Henry Ashby, Fountain Chambers, Market Place, Dudley,
    Worcestershire.
Baillie, James Thomas, 34 St Andrew Square, Edinburgh
Baker, Fred G , 9 Conduit Street, W.
Baker, Sir Benjamin, K C B , 2 Queen Square Place, Queen Anne's Mansions,
    Westminster, S W
Bale, Mrs. Edmund, The Empress Club, Dover Street, Piccadilly, W.
Balfour, Colonel Eustace, 32 Addison Road, Kensington, W.
*Balfour, Robert Shekleton, 28B Albemarle Street, W
*Ball, Joseph Henry, 2 Clement's Inn, Strand, W.C.
Ball, Mrs , 2 Clement's Inn, Strand, W C.
Barber, J. Patten, Boro' Engineer, Town Hall, Islington, N
Barbour, James, 53 Buccleugh Street, Dumfries, N B.
Barbour, Miss Jane McKay, 53 Buccleugh Street, Dumfries, N.B.
Bare, H. Bloomfield, The Red House, 142A Islington, Liverpool.
Barlow, W. Tillott, Arcade Chambers, Bognor.

Barrow, Ernest R., Amberley House, Norfolk Street, Strand, W C
Barrow, Mrs , Amberley House, Norfolk Street, Strand, W C
Barry, David J , High Street, Reigate, Surrey
Bartlett, Arthur, 11 Adam Street, Adelphi, W C.
Bartlett, Mrs , 11 Adam Street, Adelphi, W C
Bartlett, James, 8 Breams Buildings, Chancery Lane, W C.
Barton, John I , 1 St Thomas's Street, Ryde, Isle of Wight
Barton, Mrs , 1 St Thomas's Street, Ryde, Isle of Wight
Batchelor, Frederick, A R H A , 86 Merrion Square South, Dublin
Batchelor, Mrs , 86 Merrion Square South, Dublin.
Bateman, Chas Edward, 83 Edmund Street, Birmingham
Bates, Ernest, 2 Imperial Buildings, East Croydon.
Batley, Claude, 115 Gower Street, W C
Baumer, Mrs Lewis, 30 Abbey Gardens, St. John's Wood, N W
*Beale, Sydney B , Sutton House, Brighton Road, Sutton, Surrey.
Beale, Mrs., Sutton House, Brighton Road, Sutton, Surrey
Beaumont, James W , 10 St James's Square, Manchester
Beck, Frederick T , Wulfrun Chambers, Darlington Street, Wolverhampton.
Beck, Mrs , Wulfrun Chambers, Darlington Street, Wolverhampton.
Belcher, Arthur Herbert, 8 & 9 Martin's Lane, Cannon Street, E C
Belcher, Mrs , 8 & 9 Martin's Lane, Cannon Street, E C
*Belcher, John, A R A , 20 Hanover Square, W
Belcher, Mrs , 20 Hanover Square, W
Bennett, Mrs E Layton, c/o John Belcher, A R A , 20 Hanover Square, W.
Berrington, Adrian, Bon Accord, Prenton Hill, Birkenhead
Berrington, John Arthur, Bon Accord, Prenton Hill, Birkenhead
Berry, William H Atkin, 23 Old Broad Street, E C
Besant, Ernest George, Willowsmere, Great Shelford, Cambs
Betenson, Frederick Roger, 13 Great James Street, Bedford Row, W C
Bevis, Charles William, Elm Grove Chambers, Southsea.
Bevis, Mrs , Elm Grove Chambers, Southsea.
Billerey, Fernand, 9 King's Bench Walk, Temple, E C.
Bird, William F , The Island, Midsomer-Norton, Somerset.
Bishop, Miss A , c/o H J Snell, 11 The Crescent, Plymouth
Bishop, Miss L , c/o H J Snell, 11 The Crescent, Plymouth
Birkenhead, George Alfred, Caledonian Chambers, Cardiff
Birkenhead, Mrs , Caledonian Chambers, Cardiff
Birkenhead, Miss, Caledonian Chambers, Cardiff
Blacka, John Richard, Mayfield House, Garden Street, Todmorden
Blackwood, William Blackwood, 41 Donegall Place, Belfast
*Blanc, Hippolyte J , R S A , 25 Rutland Square, Edinburgh
Blomfield, Arthur Conran, 6 Montagu Place, Baker Street, W
Blomfield, Charles James, 6 Montagu Place, Baker Street, W
*Blomfield, Reginald, A R A , 1 New Court, Temple, E C.
Blomfield, Mrs., 1 New Court, Temple, E C
Blow, Detmar, 9 King's Bench Walk, Temple, E.C.
*Boardman, Edward Thomas, Town Close House, Norwich
Boardman, Mrs , Town Close House, Norwich
Boehmer, Edward, 11 Spring Gardens, S.W.
Boehmer, Mrs , 11 Spring Gardens, S W
Bollag, Gustave, 18 Norfolk Square, Lancaster Gate, W.
Bolton, Arthur Thomas, Victoria Mansions, 28 Victoria Street, S.W.
Bond, Alexander G , 115 Gower Street, W C
*Bond, George Edward, St. Ronans, Rochester
Bond, Wilfrid, 11 Elmer Street, Grantham
Bone, Charles Belfield, 59 St Mary's Mansions, Paddington, W.

Bone, Mrs , 59 St Mary's Mansions, Paddington, W.
Borrowman, John, 10 Serjeants' Inn, Fleet Street, E C
Boulting, Percy A , 29 John Street, Bedford Row, W C
Boulting, Mrs , 29 John Street, Bedford Row, W C
Bourdon, Professor Eugene, 27 La Crosse Terrace, Hillhead, Glasgow.
Box, Stephen, Eldon, Eldon Road, Eastbourne
Box, Mrs , Eldon, Eldon Road, Eastbourne.
Brace, Henry George, 66 Wood Vale, Forest Hill, S.E.
Brace, Mrs , 66 Wood Vale, Forest Hill, S.E.
Brand, Walter, 33 Bowling Green Street, Leicester
Brewerton, Joseph Henry, Richmond Chambers, Bournemouth
Briggs, Robert Alexander, 12 Norfolk Street, Strand, W C
Briggs, Mrs , 12 Norfolk Street, Strand, W C
British Fire Prevention Committee, The
*Brodie, Charles Henry, 17 Sydenham Road North, Croydon
Brodie, Mrs , 17 Sydenham Road North, Croydon
Bromhead, Horatio K , 243 St Vincent Street, Glasgow
Brooks, Charles William, 58 Boundary Road, N W.
Brooks, Mrs. C. W., 58 Boundary Road, N.W.
Brooks, Miss, 58 Boundary Road, N W
Brown, Mrs E Charles, 52 Fitzjames Avenue, West Kensington, W.
Brown, Professor G. Baldwin, 50 George Square, Edinburgh
Brown, Mrs. Baldwin, 50 George Square, Edinburgh.
Brown, Philip Ernest, 74 High Street, Sheffield
Brown, W. L. Trant, 332 High Road, Kilburn, N W.
Browne, Flint, 30 Watling Street, E C
Bruce, James, Emerson Chambers, Blackett Street, Newcastle-on-Tyne.
Browne, Miss.
Bruton, Edward Henry, 119 Queen Street, Cardiff
Bryan, Henry Dare, 4 Unity Street, College Green, Bristol.
Bryan, Mrs., 4 Unity Street, College Green, Bristol.
Bunney, Michael, 23 Queen Anne's Gate, Westminster, S W.
Bunney, Mrs , 23 Queen Anne's Gate, Westminster, S W
Burnell, A Burnell, Effingham House, Arundel Street, Strand, W C
Burnell-Burnell, Mrs , 48 Aldridge Road Villas, W.
*Burnet, John James, A R S A , 239 St Vincent Street, Glasgow.
Burnet, Mrs , 239 St Vincent Street, Glasgow
Burnett, Alfred Andrew, 2 High Street, Southampton.
Burnett, Mrs , 2 High Street, Southampton
Burr, Alfred, 85 Gower Street, W C
Burr, Mrs , 85 Gower Street, W C
Burrell, William, 11 King William Street, E.C.
Burt, William Henry, 14 Southampton Street, Strand, W C
Butler, Charles McArthur, The Society of Architects, Staple Inn Buildings,
    Holborn, W C.
Butler, Mrs , Staple Inn Buildings, Holborn, W C.
Butler, Rudolph M., Dawson Chambers, 12 Dawson Street, Dublin.
Byng, Miss, c/o L G. Summers, 15 George Street, Nottingham.
*Cackett, James Thoburn, Pilgrim House, Newcastle-on-Tyne
Cackett, Mrs., Pilgrim House, Newcastle-on-Tyne.
Caine, Charles Quane, Grosvenor Chambers, Deansgate, Manchester.
Caldwell, Oliver, Elmsdale, Alexandra Road, Penzance.
Caldwell, Mrs , Elmsdale, Alexandra Road, Penzance.
Caple, William Henry Dashwood, Church Street Chambers, Cardiff
Capper, Professor S Henbest, Victoria University, Manchester.
Caroe, William Douglas, 94 Cheyne Walk, Chelsea, S W.

Caroe, Mrs , 94 Cheyne Walk, Chelsea, S.W
Cart, Henry Philip, 59 Lancaster Gate, W.
Cart, Henry Thomas, 49 Albert Court, S W.
Castello, Manuel Nunes, 35 Norfolk Street, Strand, W C
Cave, Walter, 8 Old Burlington Street, W
Chalk, Miss G M , 8 Buckingham Gate Gardens, S W.
Chapman, Henry Ascough, Prudential Buildings, Park Row, Leeds.
Chappell, Henry, The Grove, Newtownards.
Charles, Mrs. Nugent, 69 Palace Court, W
*Charles, Miss, 49 York Street Chambers, Bryanston Square, W
Cheers, Henry Arthur, 25 Waldegrave Park, Strawberry Hill, Twickenham.
Cheers, Mrs , 25 Waldegrave Park, Strawberry Hill, Twickenham.
Chisholm, Robert F., 10 John Street, Adelphi, W C
Chorley, Harry Sutton, 16 Park Place, Leeds
Chubb, John Burland, Foundling Hospital, W.C
Chubb, Mrs , Foundling Hospital, W C
Clapham, F Dare, 3 Overbury Avenue, Beckenham
*Clarke, Howard Chatfeild, 63 Bishopsgate Street Within, E C.
Clarke, Mrs Chatfeild, 63 Bishopsgate Street Within, E C
Clarke, Miss Chatfeild, 63 Bishopsgate Street Within, E C.
*Clarke, Max, 4 Queen Square, Bloomsbury, W C
Cleaver, Albert William, 54 & 55 London Wall, E C
Cobb, Edmund Farley, 20 High Street, Rochester.
Cochrane, Robert, I.S.O , Office of Public Works, Dublin.
Cochrane, Mrs , 17 Highfield Road, Dublin
Cockrill, John William, Municipal Buildings, Great Yarmouth
Cole, Arthur, " Mogok," 34 Thurlestone Road, West Norwood, S.E
Coles, Frank Alleyn, 7 Carteret Street, Westminster, S W.
Coles, Miss A J , 7 Carteret Street, Westminster, S.W.
Collard, Allan Ovenden, 8 Buckingham Street, Strand, W C
*Collcutt, Thomas E., 36 Bloomsbury Square, W C
Collinson, George Frederick, 81 Hallam Street, Portland Place, W
Conder, Alfred, Palace Chambers, 9 Bridge Street, Westminster, S.W
Connon, John Wreghitt, 16 Park Place, Leeds.
Conzelman, John E , Queen Anne's Chambers, Westminster, S W.
Cooper, Thomas, 19 Temple Street, Birmingham.
Corby, Joseph Boothroyd, 15 All Saints Place, Stamford, Lincs.
Corlette, Hubert Christian, 2 New Square, Lincoln's Inn, W.C
Corlette, Mrs , 2 New Square, Lincoln's Inn, W.C
Cosway, Reginald Wentworth Alfred James, 68 Buckingham Gate, S.W
Crace, John D , 15 Gloucester Place, Portman Square, W
Crawford, A Hunter, 10 Randolph Place, Edinburgh
Crawford, Mrs , 10 Randolph Place, Edinburgh
Crawfurd, Miss E , 71 Sussex Gardens, W
Crawshaw, Herbert, 13 Regent Street, Barnsley, Yorks
Crawshaw, Mrs., 13 Regent Street, Barnsley, Yorks.
Cresswell, Herbert Osborn, 17 Buckingham Street, Strand, W C
*Cross, Alfred William Stephens, 46 New Bond Street, W.
Crossland, Robert E., St Martin's House, 29 Ludgate Hill, E C
Crossland, Mrs , St Martin's House, 29 Ludgate Hill, E C
Crouch, Henry Arthur, 12 Gray's Inn Square, W.C
Crowley, Walter St. Leger, Mosley Chbrs., 30 Mosley St , Newcastle-on-Tyne
*Currey, Percivall, 37 Norfolk Street, Strand, W.C.
Curtis, Spencer Carey, 11 Bermondsey Square, S E
*Cutler, Thomas W , 5 Queen Square, Bloomsbury, W.C.
Cutler, Mrs., 5 Queen Square, Bloomsbury, W.C.

Cutler, Miss, 5 Queen Square, Bloomsbury, W C
Cuxson, G A Pryce, Mead House, Chislehurst, Kent.
Cuxson, Mrs. Pryce, Mead House, Chislehurst, Kent
Dakin, Miss Ellen, 17 Thurloe Square, South Kensington, S W.
Daniell, G F Blackburne, c/o Post Office, Cairo.
Dashwood, Miss Maud, 71 Sussex Gardens, W
Davey, J Sydney, Boehym, Cury Cross Lanes, R S O , Cornwall
Davis, William Edward, 13 John Street, Adelphi, W C
Davis, Mrs , 13 John Street, Adelphi, W C
*Davidson, James, 6 Academy Street, Coatbridge, N.B.
Davidson, Miss Jessie, 6 Academy Street, Coatbridge, N B
Davison, T Raffles, " Kingshaw," Woldingham, Surrey
Davison, Mrs Raffles, " Kingshaw," Woldingham, Surrey
Davison, Thomas, 28 Great Ormond Street, W.C
*Dawber, E Guy, 22 Buckingham Street, Adelphi, W.C
Dawber, Mrs , 22 Buckingham Street, Adelphi, W C
Dawson, Charles James, East Street, Barking
Dawson, Owen, c/o A T Taylor, Esq , 21 Lyndhurst Road, Hampstead, N.W.
Day, Ernest, 6 Sansome Place, Worcester
Day, Mrs , 6 Sansome Place, Worcester
Deakin, Walter Scott, 25 Berwick Road, Shrewsbury
Delves, Stanley W W , 23 Mount Sion, Tunbridge Wells.
Denham, Geoffrey, City Road, Winchester.
Detmar, Lionel G , 1A St Helen's Place, E C
Dewes, Walter, 4 Bloomsbury Place, W C
Dick, David B , Winona, Horsell Rise, Woking, Surrey
*Dick, R Burns, Pilgrim House, Newcastle-on-Tyne.
Dircks, Rudolf, 9 Conduit Street, W.
District Surveyors' Association
Dobson, Walter E., 3 Victoria Street S W
*Doll, Charles Fitzroy, 5 Southampton Street, Bloomsbury, W C
Doll, Mrs., 5 Southampton Street, Bloomsbury, W C.
Dore, William C H , " Gosforth," Sandy Hill Road, Wallington, Surrey
Dore, Mrs., " Gosforth," Sandy Hill Road, Wallington, Surrey.
Douglas, Miss, Langlands, Dumfries, N B
Douglas, James Wightman, 1 St Nicholas Buildings, Newcastle-on-Tyne.
Douglas, Miss Jessie M , 18 Petherton Road, Highbury, N.
Downing, H P Burke, Avalon, Merton, Surrey
Downing, Mrs , Avalon, Merton, Surrey
Drew, Sir Thomas, P R H A , 22 Clare Street, Dublin
Driver, David G , Architectural Association, 18 Tufton St , Westminster, S W
Drury, Edward Dru, 25 Queen Anne's Gate, Westminster, S W.
Dunch, Charles, St Clement's House, Clement's Lane, E C.
Dunkerley, Frank Brookhouse, Graythwaite, Hale, Cheshire
Dunkerley, Mrs , Graythwaite, Hale, Cheshire
*Dunn, Archibald, The Wood House, Branksome Park, Bournemouth
Dunn, Mrs , The Wood House, Branksome Park, Bournemouth
Dunn, Edwin Thomas, 7 Roding Street, Ilford, Essex
*Dunn, James Bow, Victoria Chambers, 42 Frederick Street, Edinburgh
*Dunn, William, 35 Lincoln's Inn Fields, W.C.
Dunstall, Herbert Henry, Bank Chambers, Railway Street, Chatham
Dunstall, Mrs , Bank Chambers, Railway Street, Chatham
Duquesne, Marcel, 6 Dorville Road, Ravenscourt Park, W
Durrans, Thomas, 1 Cornwall Terrace, Regent's Park, N.W.
Dyson, H Kempton, 4 Southend Road, Beckenham.
East, Alfred, A R A , 2 Spenser Street, Westminster, S.W.

Eastwood J H , 42 Cheniston Gardens, Kensington, W.
Eastwood, Mrs., 42 Cheniston Gardens, Kensington, W
Ebbetts, Walter J , Savoy House, 115 Strand, W C
Edwards, Frederick E Pearce, Whitaker Buildings, Victoria Square, Bradford
*Edwards, Robert Clarke, 55 Buckland Crescent, Hampstead, N.W.
Edwards, Miss, 55 Buckland Crescent, Hampstead, N W
Edwards, William, 25 Darlington Street, Wolverhampton.
Egerton, William, 12 Queen's Road, Erith, Kent
Elgood, Frank Minshull, 98 Wimpole Street, W.
Elkington, George, Norfolk House, 7 Laurence Pountney Hill, Cannon Street, E C .
Elkington, Mrs , " St Aubyns," Woodborough Road, Putney, S W
*Emerson, Sir William, 2 Grosvenor Mansions, 76 Victoria Street, S W
Emerson, Lady, 2 Grosvenor Mansions, 76 Victoria Street, S W
Emerson, Miss, 2 Grosvenor Mansions, 76 Victoria Street, S W.
English, Charles William, Staple Inn Buildings, 335 High Holborn, W.C
Errington, Charles Septimus, Victoria Buildings, Grainger Street West, New-
    castle-on-Tyne
Favarger, Henri, 2 Balfour Place, Park Lane, W
Favarger, Mrs , 2 Balfour Place, Park Lane, W
Fawcett, Miss, c/o Mr A Womersley, 16 Warwick Mansions, Cromwell Crescent,
    Kensington, W
Fawcett, William Milner, 4 Trumpington Street, Cambridge.
Ferguson, Godfrey W , Dunedin, Belfast
Ferguson, Mrs , Dunedin, Belfast
*Ferrier, Claude W , 11 Waterloo Place, Pall Mall, S W
Fetissoff, Peter Paul, 20 Montague Street, W C.
Field, Alfred W , Norfolk House, Norfolk Street, Strand, W C.
Field, Miss A M A 12 Norfolk Street, Strand, W C
Figgis, T Phillips, 28 Martin's Lane, Cannon Street, E C
Figgis, Mrs , Twirton, Warwick Road, Margate
Fitzsimons, Nicholas, 13 Lombard Street, Belfast
*Fleming, Owen 14 Cheyne Walk, Chelsea, S.W.
Fleming, Mrs., 14 Cheyne Walk, Chelsea, S W
Fletcher, Banister Flight, 29 New Bridge Street, E C
Fletcher, H Phillips, 29 New Bridge Street, E C.
Fletcher, Henry Martineau, 10 Lincoln's Inn Fields, W C
Fletcher, Walter John, County Surveyor's Office, Wimborne, Dorset
*Flockhart, William, 180 New Bond Street, W.
Flockhart, Mrs , 180 New Bond Street, W
Ford, George McLean, 10 Walbrook, E C
Ford, P , Burton Tower, Gresford, North Wales
Forsyth, J Dudley, The Studios, 335 Finchley Road, Hampstead, N W
Forsyth, William A , 16 Great Marlborough Street, W.
Foster, Frank, 8 Duke Street, Adelphi, W C
Frampton, George, R A , 32 Queen's Road, St John's Wood, N W
Frampton, Mrs , 32 Queen's Road St John's Wood, N W
Franck, J Ernest, 11 Pancras Lane, Queen Street, E C.
Fraser, Percival Maurice, 10 Basinghall Street, E C
Gabriel, Edward, 42 Old Broad Street, E C
Gabriel, Miss Lilian, 42 Old Broad Street, E C
*Garbutt, Matthew, 95 Howards Lane, Putney, S W
Garbutt, Miss, 95 Howards Lane, Putney, S W
Garbutt, Miss Bessie, 95 Howards Lane, Putney, S.W
Gass, John Bradshaw, 19 Silverwell Street, Bolton.
Gass, Mrs , 19 Silverwell Street, Bolton.
*George, Ernest, 18 Maddox Street, Regent Street, W.

George, Miss, 18 Maddox Street, Regent Street, W
George, William Henry, Warrington Street, Ashton-under-Lyne.
George, Mrs , Warrington Street, Ashton-under-Lyne.
*Gibbs, Edward Mitchel, 15 St James's Row, Sheffield.
*Gibson, James Sivewright, 5 Old Bond Street, W.
Gibson, Mrs , 5 Old Bond Street, W.
Gill, Frederic John, 236 Rolfe Street, Smethwick, near Birmingham
Gilliland, William John, 9 Howard Street, Belfast.
Glover, William, 68 Tyrwhitt Road, Brockley, S E
Goddard, Henry Langton, 8 Market Street. Leicester
Goddard, Mrs , 8 Market Street, Leicester
Godsal, Mrs , 11 Buckingham Gate Gardens, S W
Goldsmith, Francis Thomas Wilberforce, 1 Verulam Buildings, Gray's Inn, W.C
Goldsmith, Mrs , 1 Verulam Buildings, Gray's Inn, W C
Gordon, Robert Clifford Turner, 395 Romford Road, Forest Gate, E
Gotch, John Alfred, Bank Chambers, Kettering, Northants
Gourlay, Professor Charles, 30 Hamilton Drive, Hillhead, Glasgow
*Graham, Alexander, Carlton Chambers, 4 Regent Street, S W
Graham, Charles C , 6 Manor Mansions, Belsize Park Gardens, N W
Grant, Spencer William, 63 Finsbury Pavement, E C.
Graves, Walter, Winchester House, Old Broad Street, E C
Grayson, George E , Egerton Park. Rock Ferry, Cheshire.
Grayson, Hastwell, 31 James Street, Liverpool
Green, T Frank, Carlton Chambers, 12 Regent Street, S W.
Green, Mrs , Carlton Chambers, 12 Regent Street, S W.
Greenop. Edward, Falcon Court, 32 Fleet Street, E C
Greenop, Mrs , Falcon Court, 32 Fleet Street, E C.
*Greenwood, Benjamin I , Loughborough Park Works, Brixton, S W
Grellier, William, 6 Queen Anne's Gate, Westminster
Griffiths, Rhys Samuel, Tonypandy, Rhondda Valley
*Grunning, Edward Augustus, 25 Gresham House, Old Broad Street, E C
*Gutteridge, Alfred Fowler, 9 Portland Street, Southampton
Gutteridge, Mrs , 9 Portland Street, Southampton
Guy, Albert Lewis, 4 Verulam Buildings, Gray's Inn, W C
Guy, Mrs , 4 Verulam Buildings, Gray's Inn, W C
Hale, William J , 13 St James's Row, Sheffield
*Hall, Edwin Thomas, 54 Bedford Square, W C
Hall, Herbert Alfred, 13 South Square, Gray's Inn, W C
Hammond, Frederic, 150 Finchley Road, Hampstead, N W
Hamp, Stanley, 36 Bloomsbury Square, W C
Hamp, Miss, 36 Bloomsbury Square, W C
Hanson, Septimus Charles, 10 Basinghall Street, E.C
Hardcastle, Frederick Henry Appleton, 11 Clyde Street, South Kensington, S W
Hardcastle, Miss Ida Mary, 11 Clyde Street, South Kensington, S W
Hardcastle, Wilfred John, 130 Temple Chambers, Temple Avenue, E C.
Hardcastle, Mrs , 130 Temple Chambers, Temple Avenue, E C
*Hare, Henry Thomas, 31 Cumberland Terrace, Regent's Park, N W
Hare, Mrs , 31 Cumberland Terrace, Regent's Park, N W
Hare, Miss, 31 Cumberland Terrace, Regent's Park, N.W
Harper, Ewen, Ruskin Chambers, 191 Corporation Street, Birmingham.
Harper, Mrs , Ruskin Chambers, 191 Corporation Street, Birmingham.
Harris, Francis E L , 1 Balloon Street, Manchester
Harrison, Arthur, Council Chambers, 109 Colmore Row, Birmingham.
Harrison, Mrs , The Croft, Moseley Wake Green, Birmingham
Harrison, Miss Beatrice, The Croft, Moseley Wake Green, Birmingham
Harrison, Stockdale, St. Martin's East, Leicester.

Harvey, Frederick Milton, 48 Lowestoft Road, Gorleston, Gt. Yarmouth
Harvey, Miss F , c/o H. J. Lanchester, Southlea, Lindfield, Surrey.
Haswell, Francis Robert N., Monkseaton, near Newcastle-on-Tyne
Hawkins, Edgar A , 21 Northumberland Avenue, W C.
Hawkins, Percival W , 42 King's Hall Road, Beckenham
Hayes, Louis A , 1 Brook Street, Hanover Square, W
Hayes, Mrs , 1 Brook Street, Hanover Square, W
Hayes, Reginald, 93 Cornwall Gardens, Queen's Gate, S W
Hayward, Arthur Baldwin, 20 John Street, Adelphi, W C
Hayward, Mrs C Forster, 20 John Street, Adelphi, W.C
Heathcote, Charles Henry, 64 Cross Street, Manchester
Heathcote, Mrs , 64 Cross Street, Manchester
Heazell, Arthur Ernest, Burton Buildings, Parliament Street, Nottingham.
Heazell, William Arthur, Burton Buildings, Parliament Street, Nottingham
Helhoar, Evelyn, 10 Serjeants' Inn, Fleet Street, E C
Henman, William, 19 Temple Street, Birmingham.
Henry, James Macintyre, 7 South Charlotte Street, Edinburgh.
Hesketh, Robert Lempriere, 110 Cheapside, E.C
Hewitt, Edward, 33 Brazennose Street, Manchester.
Hewitt, Mrs , 33 Brazennose Street, Manchester
Hewitt, Edwin Richard, 3 Brent Villas, Hendon, N W
Hewitt, Mrs , 3 Brent Villas, Hendon, N W
Hewitt, Walter Ernest, 22 Buckingham Street, Strand, W C
Hewitt, Mrs , 22 Buckingham Street, Strand, W.C
Hicks, Frederick G , 86 Merrion Square, Dublin.
Hicks, Mrs , 86 Merrion Square, Dublin
Hill, Arthur, 22 George's Street, Cork
Hill, Mrs , 22 George's Street, Cork
Hills, Gordon P. G , 7 New Court, Carey Street, W.C.
*Hills, Osborn Cluse, Hamilton House, 149 Bishopsgate Street Without, E C
Hills, Mrs , Hamilton House, 149 Bishopsgate Street Without, E.C.
*Hine, George Thomas, 35 Parliament Street, Westminster, S.W.
Hine, Mrs., 35 Parliament Street, Westminster, S.W
Holbrook, Alfred J , Wilford Lane, West Bridgford. Nottingham
Hooper, Francis, 27 Albemarle Road, Beckenham.
Hooper, Mrs , 27 Albemarle Road, Beckenham
Hooper, T Rowland, Station Road, Redhill, Surrey
Horsburgh, Victor D , 23 Rutland Square, Edinburgh
Horsfall, Jesse, Todmorden.
Horsfall, Mrs , Todmorden.
Horsfield, J Nixon, Summit Cottage, Surbiton Hill, S W
Horsfield, Mrs , Summit Cottage, Surbiton Hill, S W.
Horsley, Gerald, 2 Gray's Inn Square, W.C.
Howard, Edward Page, 39 Cursitor Street, Chancery Lane, E.C
Howell, W Roland, 17 Blagrave Street, Reading.
*Hubbard, George, 112 Fenchurch Street, E.C.
Hubbard, Mrs , 112 Fenchurch Street, E.C
Hudson, Edward William, 76 Fellows Road, South Hampstead, N.W.
Hulbert, Maurice C., Ingleside, Edge Hill Road, Ealing, W.
Hulbert, Mrs , Ingleside, Edge Hill Road, Ealing, W.
Hummel, Miss, Fermoy, Kelsey Park Road, Beckenham
Humphreys, George Alfred, Mostyn Estate Office, Llandudno, N. Wales.
Hunt, Leonard Vincent, 34 Queen Street, E C
Hunter, Percy, 53 Clapham Road, S W.
Hunter, Mrs , 53 Clapham Road, S.W.
Hunter, Miss, 53 Clapham Road, S W.

Hutchinson, Charles Edward, 29 John Street, Bedford Row, W C
Ibberson, Herbert G , 28 Martin's Lane, Cannon Street, E C
Ince, Howard, 53 Berners Street, W.
Ingelow, Benjamin, Carlton Chambers, 4 Regent Street, S W
Jackson, A. Blomfield, 3 New Square, Lincoln's Inn, W C
Jackson, Mrs. Blomfield, 3 New Square, Lincoln's Inn, W C.
Jackson, Frank Newton, 26 Bedford Row, W C
Jackson, Thomas Graham, R A , 14 Buckingham Street, Strand, W C.
James, Cholton, Charles Street Chambers, Cardiff.
James, Mrs , Charles Street Chambers, Cardiff
James, Thomas Egbert Lidiard, Lonsdale Chambers, 27 Chancery Lane, W C.
James, Mrs., Lonsdale Chambers, 27 Chancery Lane, W C
James, William H., 4 Bloomsbury Place, W.C.
*Jarvis, Henry, 29 Trinity Square, Southwark, S E.
Jenkin, Mrs. Bernard, 64 Bedford Gardens, Campden Hill, W
Jerman, James, 1 Bedford Circus, Exeter.
Jerman, Mrs , 1 Bedford Circus, Exeter
Joass, John James, 18 Blenheim Road, St. John's Wood, N.W.
Joass, William C , Dingwall, N.B.
Joass, Mrs , Dingwall, N B
Johnson, A L , Queen Anne's Chambers, Westminster, S.W.
Johnson, Mrs., Queen Anne's Chambers, Westminster, S W
Johnson, Henry Winter, Bank Chambers, Market Harborough.
Johnson, Mrs., Bank Chambers, Market Harborough.
Johnson, Joseph, 47 Mark Lane, E C
Johnson, Mrs , 47 Mark Lane, E.C
Johnson, Richard, 58 Wood View, Manningham, Bradford.
Johnston, Mrs , Yeatton, Abbey Wood, Kent
Jones, Elijah, 10 Albion Street, Hanley, Staffs.
Jones, Mrs., 10 Albion Street, Hanley, Staffs
*Jones, Ronald Potter, King's College, Strand, W C
*Jones, W. Campbell, 32 Bedford Row, W C
Jones, Mrs Campbell, 32 Bedford Row, W.C.
Joseph, Delissa, 98 Inverness Terrace, Hyde Park, W.
Joseph, Mrs , 98 Inverness Terrace, Hyde Park, W.
Judge, Max, 7 Pall Mall, S W
Kaye-Parry, William, 63 Dawson Street, Dublin.
Keats, Walter Osborn, 8 Brandreth Road, Mannamead, Plymouth
Keen, Arthur, 4 Raymond Buildings, Gray's Inn, W C.
Keen, Mrs , 4 Raymond Buildings, Gray's Inn, W C
*Keppie, John, 140 Bath Street, Glasgow.
*Kersey, Alex. Henry, Moorgate Station Bldgs., 21 Finsbury Pavement, E C
Kersey, Mrs , Moorgate Station Buildings, 21 Finsbury Pavement, E C.
King, Vivian H., 11 New Court, Carey Street, W C
King, Mrs., 11 New Court, Carey Street, W.C.
Kirby, Edmund, 5 Cook Street, Liverpool.
Knight, James E , 33 College Street, Rotherham.
Koch, Alexander, 58 Theobald's Road, W.C.
Lacey, Albert Edward, Ashford, Kent.
Lamont, Alexander Hay, 24 Millar Crescent, Morningside, Edinburgh.
Lanchester, Henry Jones, Southlea, Lindfield, Sussex.
Lanchester, Mrs , Southlea, Lindfield, Sussex.
*Lanchester, Henry Vaughan, 47 Bloomsbury Square, W.C.
Lander, H. Clapham, Effingham House, Arundel Street, Strand, W.C.
Langridge, George, The Broadway, Tunbridge Wells.
Langridge, Mrs., The Broadway, Tunbridge Wells.

Lawton-Brown, George, Spencer Chambers, Leicester
Lawton-Brown, Mrs , Spencer Chambers, Leicester
Laycock, Edward Renard, 4 Bloomsbury Place, W C
Laycock, Mrs., 10 Lancaster Road, West Norwood, S E
Leaning, H J , 28 John Street, Bedford Row, W C
Leaning, Mrs , 28 John Street, Bedford Row, W C
Lees, Ernest William, 35 Mecklenburgh Square, W C
Leest, Edgar May, 14 St Aubyn Street, Devonport
Leighton, Arthur George, 26 Elsworthy Road, South Hampstead, N W
Leighton, Mrs , 26 Elsworthy Road, South Hampstead, N W.
Lenny, Miss Violet, c/o J H. Eastwood, Esq , 42 Cheniston Gardens, Kensington, W.
Lethaby, Professor William Richard, 111 Inverness Terrace, W
Leverton, Walter John Hopkins, 10 Lancaster Place, Strand, W.C
Leverton, Miss, 10 Lancaster Place, Strand, W.C
Lindsay, James, 248 West George Street, Glasgow
Locke, John, 70 Ashworth Mansions, Elgin Avenue, W
Locke, William John, 9 Conduit Street, W.
Lockie, W , Haxells Hotel, Strand, W C
Lohr, Charles Henry, 11 Maldon Road, Acton, W
*Lonsdale, H. Walter, 3 John Street, Bedford Row, W C
*Lorimer, Robert Stodart, A R S A , 54 Melville Street, Edinburgh
Lorimer, Mrs , 54 Melville Street, Edinburgh
Loveday, Arthur, North Collingham, Newark, Notts.
Lovegrove, Henry, 18 Foxgrove Road, Beckenham
Lovell, Richard J., 46 Queen Victoria Street, E C
Lucas, Geoffry, 16 Hart Street, Bloomsbury, W C
Lucas, R Macdonald, Bargate Chambers, Southampton
Lucy, Hubert A , 4 Albert Street, N W
*Lutyens, Edwin L , 29 Bloomsbury Square, W C
Lynam, Charles, Stoke-on-Trent
Lynam, Mrs , Stoke-on Trent
Lynam, Miss Mary, 8 Montague Street, Russell Square, W C.
Macartney, Mervyn, Silchester Common, near Reading
Macartney, Hon. Mrs , Silchester Common, near Reading
MacDonald, R Falconer, 4a Cork Street, Bond Street, W
MacDonald, Mrs , 4a Cork Street, Bond Street, W
McDonnell, J J , 27 Chichester Street, Belfast
McGibbon, Alexander, 109 Hope Street, Glasgow
Mackenzie, A G R , 13 Waterloo Place, Pall Mall, S W
Mackenzie, A Marshall, A R S A , 13 Waterloo Place, Pall Mall, S W
McMullen, James Finbarre, 30 South Mall, Cork
Maidman, Edward C H , 13 South Charlotte Street, Edinburgh
Maidman, Mrs , 13 South Charlotte Street, Edinburgh.
*Mallows, Charles E , 28 Conduit Street, Hanover Square, W
Mallows, Mrs , 28 Conduit Street, Hanover Square, W
Mansell, Edward, 47 Temple Row, Birmingham.
Mansell, T Gildart, 47 Temple Row, Birmingham
Marks, Miss Constance, 10 Matheson Road, W.
Marks, Frederick William, 3 Staple Inn, Holborn, W C
Marks, Mrs , 3 Staple Inn, Holborn, W C
Marks, Percy L , Albert Buildings, 49 Queen Victoria Street, E C.
Marshall, Alfred, Craven Bank Chambers, Otley, Yorks
Marshall, Charles John, Parliament Mansions, Victoria Street, S.W
Marshall, Mrs., Parliament Mansions, Victoria Street, S W.
Marshall, Miss E D , Parliament Mansions, Victoria Street, S.W.
Marshall, Ernest William, 139 Oxford Street, W.

*Marsland, Ellis, 73 Sydenham Hill, S.E.
*Martin, Leonard, Charing Cross House, 29A Charing Cross Road, W C.
Martin, Mrs., Charing Cross House, 29A Charing Cross Road, W C.
Marwick, Miss, c/o Mr. J. J Burnet, 239 St. Vincent Street, Glasgow.
Mason, C., Chiswick, W.
Mathews, J Douglass, 11 Dowgate Hill, E C
Matthews, Herbert William, Institute Chambers, Terrace Walk, Bath
Matthews, Mrs , Institute Chambers, Terrace Walk, Bath.
Maule, Hugh P G , 16 Great Marlborough Street, W
May, Edward John, 21 Hart Street, Bloomsbury, W C
May, Mrs , 21 Hart Street, Bloomsbury, W C.
*May, Frank, Hyde Street, Bloomsbury, W C
Mayell, Alfred Young, 76A Westborne Grove, W
Maynard, D Christopher, 20 John Street, Adelphi, W C
Maynard, Mrs , 20 John Street, Adelphi, W C
Mayston, Arthur Richard, 11 Great James Street, Bedford Row, W C.
Medlicott, Walter Barrington, 75 Newman Street, W
Medlicott, Mrs , 75 Newman Street, W.
*Menzies, Duncan, 39 York Place, Edinburgh
Middleton, George Alexander Thomas, 19 Craven Street, Strand, W.C
Milburn, Thomas Ridley, 20 Fawcett Street, Sunderland.
Milburn, William, 20 Fawcett Street, Sunderland
Millard, Walter J N , 10 Gray's Inn Square, W.C.
Millard, Mrs , 10 Gray's Inn Square, W C
Mills, Alfred Henry, 33 Brazennose Street, Manchester.
Mills, Mrs., 33 Brazennose Street, Manchester   .
Mills, J Donald, 10 Tay Street, Dundee
Mitchell, William M , R H A , 10 St Stephen's Green North, Dublin
*Mitchell-Withers, John B , Millgrove, Millhouses, Sheffield
Money, Mrs. E Kyrle, c/o Mr John Belcher, 20 Hanover Square, W
Monkhouse, Miss Bella, c/o Maxwell Ayrton, 3 Verulam Bldgs , Gray's Inn, W C
Monro, James Milne, 28 Bath Street, Glasgow
Monro, William Ernest, 46 Lincoln's Inn Fields, W C
*Moore, Albert Walter, 131 Fenchurch Street, E C
Moore, Mrs., 131 Fenchurch Street, E C
Moore, Harry Wilkinson, 6 Beaumont Street, Oxford
Morgan, David, Charles Street Chambers, Cardiff
Morgan, Mrs , Charles Street Chambers, Cardiff
Moscrop-Young, Frederick Charles, Waldorf Chambers, Aldwych, W C
*Mountford, Edward William, 11 Craven Hill, W
Mountford, Mrs , 11 Craven Hill, W
*Moxham, Glendinning, 39 Castle Street, Swansea.
Moxham, Mrs , 39 Castle Street, Swansea
Mullins, Arthur Ernest, 48 Peckham Road, S E.
Mullins, Mrs , 48 Peckham Road, S E.
Mullins, Miss, 13 Gt James Street,, Bedford Row, W C
Murray, Albert E , A R H A., 37 Dawson Street, Dublin.
Murray, Mrs , 37 Dawson Street, Dublin
*Murray, John, 11 Suffolk Street, Pall Mall, S W
Murray, John C T., 35 Old Queen Street, Westminster, S W
Nash, W Hilton, 18 Kensington Park Gardens, W.
Neale, James, 10 Bloomsbury Square, W C.
Needham, Samuel, 18 Coney Street, York.
Newcombe, William Lister, 89 Pilgrim Street, Newcastle-on-Tyne.
Newcombe, Mrs , 89 Pilgrim Street, Newcastle-on-Tyne
Newton, Ernest, 4 Raymond Buildings, Gray's Inn, W C

Newton, Mrs , 4 Raymond Buildings, Gray's Inn, W.C.
Nicholson, Sir Charles, Bart , 2 New Square, Lincoln's Inn, W C
Nield, H. Krauss, 20 New Bridge Street, E.C.
Niven, David Barclay, Gwydir Chambers, 104 High Holborn, W C
Northover, George, 9 Conduit Street, W
Oakley, Harold, 14 Henrietta Street, Covent Garden, W C
Oakley, Mrs , 14 Henrietta Street, Covent Garden, W C
Oatley, George H., Edinburgh Chambers, Baldwin Street, Bristol.
O'Connor, George L , 198 Gt. Brunswick Street, Dublin
O'Connor, Mrs , 198 Gt Brunswick Street, Dublin
Oldrieve, William Thomas, H M Office of Works, Edinburgh.
Oliver, Andrew, 5 Queen's Gardens, Hyde Park, W.
Oliver, Miss M , 5 Queen's Gardens, Hyde Park, W
Oliver, Miss K , 5 Queen's Gardens, Hyde Park, W
Orpen, R Caulfeild, 13 South Frederick Street, Dublin
Osborn, Arthur William, 90–91 Queen Street, Cheapside, E C
Osborn, Mrs , 90–91 Queen Street, Cheapside, E.C.
Oswald, Joseph, 33 Mosley Street, Newcastle-on-Tyne.
Packer, H H., Dovercourt Bay, Essex.
*Paine, George Henry, 62 Moorgate Street, E C.
Parker, R Barry, Baldock, Herts
Passmore, Herbert, 3 Great College Street, Westminster, S W
Paterson, Alexander Nisbet, 266 St Vincent Street, Glasgow
Paterson, Mrs , 266 St. Vincent Street, Glasgow
Paxton, James, 12 Paddenswick Road, Ravenscourt Park, W
Payne, E Harding, 11 John Street, Bedford Row, W C
Pearson, H Dighton, 27 Chancery Lane, W C
Pearson, James Montgomerie, 51 John Finnie Street, Kilmarnock, N B
Pennington, T Frederick, Tivoli House, Hounslow Heath, W
Perks, Sydney, City Surveyor, Guildhall, E C
Phillips, John H., Clive Chambers, Windsor Place, Cardiff
*Pick, S Perkins, 6 Millstone Lane, Leicester.
Pick, Mrs , 6 Millstone Lane, Leicester.
*Pilditch, Philip Edward, 2 Pall Mall East, S W
Pite, Professor Beresford, 2 York Gate, Regent's Park, N W
Pite, William Alfred, 116 Jermyn Street, St James's, S W
Pither, Francis Leon, 91 Tollington Park, N.
Pitman, Walter Hayward, 30 Newgate Street, E C
Plummer, Arthur B , 13 Grey Street, Newcastle-on-Tyne
Plunkett, Count George Noble, Kilternán Abbey, Co Dublin
Plunkett, Countess, Kilternan Abbey, Co Dublin.
*Pollard, Arthur, 1 Burton Stone Lane, York
Ponting, Charles Edwin, Marlborough, Wilts
Pope, Reginald, 17 Cheriton Place, Folkestone
Powell, Frederick Atkinson, 344 Kennington Road, S E
Powell, Mrs., 344 Kennington Road, S E
Poynter, Ambrose Macdonald, 8 Southampton St , Bloomsbury, W C
Pratt, W Dymock, Cauldon Place, Long Row, Nottingham.
Prendergast, Colonel Lenox, 14 Thurloe Square, S W
*Prentice, Andrew N., Hastings House, 10 Norfolk Street, Strand, W C.
Prideaux, Miss Edith R , c/o Mr. J Henry Ball, 2 Clement's Inn, Strand, W C.
Pridmore, Albert E., 2 Broad Street Buildings, E C
Pridmore, Mrs , 2 Broad Street Buildings, E C.
Prosser, Howell, Education Committee Offices, Walthamstow, N.E
Pryce, Thomas Edward, 10 Gray's Inn Square, W C
*Prynne, George H. Fellowes, 6 Queen Anne's Gate, Westminster, S.W

Prynne, Mrs Fellowes, 6 Queen Anne's Gate, Westminster, S.W.
Prynne, Miss Fellowes, 6 Queen Anne's Gate, Westminster, S W.
Prynne, Charles Fellowes, 6 Queen Anne's Gate, Westminster, S.W.
Pugh, Miss Alice, 74 High Street, Sheffield.
Punnett, William Henry, 63 Moorgate Street, E.C.
Punnett, Mrs , 63 Moorgate Street, E.C.
Randall, William Edward Rendell, Jun., Elm House, Chatham.
Randall, Mrs , Elm House, Chatham.
Raney, Frank, 50 Stonegate, York
Read, Herbert, 4A Cork Street, Bond Street, W.
Read, Mrs , 4A Cork Street, Bond Street, W.
Reade, Frederick Thomas, 10 Gt Ormond Street, W.C
Reavell, George J. Thrift, H M Office of Works, Storey's Gate, S.W.
Reed, Harbottle, 12 Castle Street, Exeter
Reilly, Charles, 23 St Swithin's Lane, E.C.
Reilly, Professor Charles Herbert, Dingle Bank, Liverpool.
Reilly, Mrs , Dingle Bank, Liverpool.
Reilly, Miss, High House, Upminster, Essex
*Richards, Francis Augustus, 36 Victoria Street, Westminster, S W.
Richmond, John, 22 Buckingham Street, Adelphi, W.C.
Richmond, Mrs , 22 Buckingham Street, Adelphi, W C
*Richmond, Sir William, B , K C B , R A , Beavor Lodge, Hammersmith, W.
Richards, Thomas Robert, Bedford Row Chambers, 42 Theobald's Road, W C.
Richards, Mrs., Bedford Row Chambers, 42 Theobald's Road, W.C
Rickards, Edwin Alfred, 47 Bedford Square, W C.
*Rickman, Thomas M , 8 Montague Street, Russell Square, W C.
Ridge, Lacy W , 5 Verulam Buildings, Gray's Inn, W C
Riley, William Edward, County Hall, Spring Gardens, S W
Rippon, Herbert, 55 Lincoln's Inn Fields, W.C
Ritchie, Alexander, J P , C C , 12 and 13 Upper Thames Street, E C
Ritchie, Mrs , 12 & 13 Upper Thames Street, E.C.
Robbins, Rev. John, St. George's Vicarage, 25 Campden Hill Square, W.
Robbins, Miss, St George's Vicarage, 25 Campden Hill Square, W
Robinson, Miss Fothergill, c/o W B. Medlicott, Esq , 75 Newman Street, W
Robinson, John Barrett, 1 Lombard Street, Belfast.
Robinson, Miss, 1 Lombard Street, Belfast.
Robinson, Percy, 53 Albion Street, Leeds.
Robinson, Mrs., 53 Albion Street, Leeds
Rollo, Andrew, 11 Hammersmith Terrace, W.
Ross, James MacLaren, 9 Doughty Street, Mecklenburgh Square, W.C.
Rowe, Miss Eleanor, 46 Pembroke Road, Kensington, W
Rowell, Reginald B , Triangle Corner, East Sheen, S W
Rowell, Mrs , Triangle Corner, East Sheen, S W
*Royal Institute of British Architects, The.
Royal Sanitary Institute, The
Ruddle, Alan Wilfrid, Cathedral Gateway, Peterborough
Ruddle, Miss, Cathedral Gateway, Peterborough
Runtz, Ernest, 10 Walbrook, E C.
Rust, John, 224 Union Street, Aberdeen
Ryan, Wm Patrick, 1 Metal Exchange Buildings, Whittington Avenue, E C
Ryan, Miss, 1 Metal Exchange Buildings, Whittington Avenue, E.C.
*Sachs, Edwin O , 7 Waterloo Place, Pall Mall, S W.
Sachs, Mrs , 7 Waterloo Place, Pall Mall, S.W.
Satchell, Herbert Arnold, 3 Staple Inn, Holborn, W C.
Sayer, Charles Edward, 17 Soho Square, W
Schultz, Robert Weir, 14 Gray's Inn Square, W.C.

Scorer, George O , 22 Surrey Street, Strand, W C
Scorer, William, Bank Street Chambers, Lincoln
Scott, Anthony, 34 Lower Sackville Street, Dublin
Scott, Augustine Alban Hamilton, 10 Basinghall Street, E C
*Scott, W. Gillbee, 25 Bedford Row, W C
Searles-Wood, Herbert Duncan, 157 Wool Exchange, Coleman Street, E C.
Searles-Wood, Mrs , 157 Wool Exchange, Coleman Street, E C
Serrailher, Lucien, Queen Anne's Chambers, Westminster, S W
Serrailher, Mrs , 15 Babington Road, Streatham, S.W.
*Seth-Smith, W Howard, 46 Lincoln's Inn Fields, W C
Seward, Edwin, Queen's Chambers, Cardiff
Seward, Mrs., Queen's Chambers, Cardiff
Shardlow, John Thomas. 61 Carlton Road, Worksop, Notts.
Shepherd, Herbert, 120 Kensington Park Road, W
Shepman, Miss Rose, c/o R C Edwards, 55 Buckland Cres , Hampstead, N W.
Sheppard, James, 61 Threadneedle Street, E C
Shewbrooks, Edward, Bank Chambers, 24 Grainger St West, Newcastle-on-Tyne.
Shewbrooks, Mrs , Bank Chambers, 24 Grainger St West, Newcastle-on-Tyne
Shires, B Priestley, Old Town Chambers, 104 Old Town Street, Plymouth
Sills, Francis, Donington House, Norfolk Street, Strand, W C
Sills, Mrs , Donington House, Norfolk Street, Strand, W C
Simon, Frank W , 64 Devonshire Road, Prince's Park, Liverpool
Simon, Mrs , 64 Devonshire Road, Prince's Park, Liverpool
Simpson, Miss, Prudential Buildings, Park Lane, Leeds
Simpson, Miss Clare, Twentieth Century Club, Stanley Gdns , Ladbroke Sq , W.
Simpson, Professor Frederick M , 3 Brunswick Place, Regent's Park, N W
Simpson, Mrs , 3 Brunswick Place, Regent's Park, N W
Simpson, Jonathan, 14 Acresfield, Bolton, Lancs
Simpson, Miss S M , 14 Acresfield, Bolton, Lancs
*Simpson, John W , 3 Verulam Buildings, Gray's Inn, W C
Skipper, George J , 7 London Street, Norwich
*Slater, John, 46 Berners Street, W
Slater, Mrs., 46 Berners Street, W
Slater, Miss, 46 Berners Street, W
Slater, William Ford, Burslem, Staffs
Smallman, Henry R G S , 8 Queen Street, Cheapside, E C
Smith, Professor Elsey, 130 Temple Chambers, Whitefriars, E C
Smith, Mrs Elsey, 130 Temple Chambers, Whitefriars, E C
Smith, Miss Roger, 130 Temple Chambers, Whitefriars, E C
Smith, F Adams, 35 New Broad Street, E C
Smith, Mrs Adams, 35 New Broad Street, E C
Smith, J Osborne, 7 Old Queen Street, Westminster, S W.
Smith, Mrs Osborne, 7 Old Queen Street, Westminster, S W
Smith, Miss Osborne, 7 Old Queen Street, Westminster, S W
Smith, William Auger, 138 Holme Road, West Bridgeford, Nottingham
Smither, James George, 1 Allison Grove, Dulwich, S E
Snell, Alfred Saxon, 22 Southampton Buildings, Chancery Lane, W C.
Snell, Mrs Saxon, 22 Southampton Buildings, W C
Snell, Miss, 22 Southampton Buildings, W C
Snell, Henry John, 11 The Crescent, Plymouth.
*Society of Architects, The
Solomon, Lewis, 21 Hamilton Terrace, N W
Solomon, Mrs , 21 Hamilton Terrace, N W
Solomon, Solomon J , R.A., 60 Finchley Road, N.W.
Solomon, Mrs , 60 Finchley Road, N.W.
Spencer, Mrs., c/o A. H. Mills, 33 Brazennose Street, Manchester.

Spiers, Walter L , 13 Lincoln's Inn Fields, W C.
Spiers, R Phene, 21 Bernard Street, Russell Square, W C
Spurrier, William James. 22 High Street, Birmingham.
Squire, J H , 69 Palace Court, W
Stannus, Hugh, 24 York House, Highbury Crescent, N
Stannus, Mrs , 24 York House, Highbury Crescent, N.
Stanton, Stephen James Bridges, 47 Cavendish Road, Brondesbury, N W
Statham, Henry Heathcote, 1 Camp View, Wimbledon Common, S W.
Statham, Mrs , 1 Camp View, Wimbledon Common, S W
Statham, Miss, 1 Camp View, Wimbledon Common, S W.
Stevens, Joseph Wallace, Belph, Whitwell, near Mansfield
Stevens, John William, 21 New Bridge Street, E C
Stevens, Mrs , 21 New Bridge Street, E C
Stevenson, John James, 4 Porchester Gardens, W
*Stewart, William, " Ecclesbourne," The Avenue, Wanstead, Essex
Stewart, Mrs , " Ecclesbourne," The Avenue, Wanstead, Essex.
Stock, Henry W., Rutland Lodge, Petersham, Surrey
*Stokes, Leonard, 2 Gt Smith Street, Westminster, S W
Stokes, Mrs., 2 Gt Smith Street, Westminster, S W.
Stokes, Walter, 110 Cheapside, E C
Strahan, Thomas Francis, 61 Drumcondra Road, Dublin
Strange, Charles Hilbert, 20 Dudley Road, Tunbridge Wells.
Stranson, John Clark, 13 Gray's Inn Square, W C
Stratton, Arthur, 16 Hart Street, Bloomsbury, W C.
Stratton, Mrs , 16 Hart Street, Bloomsbury, W C
Straus, Ralph, 58 Bassett Road, North Kensington, W.
Style, Arthur James, 3 Victoria Street, S W
Summers, Lawrence George, 15 George Street, Nottingham
Swan, James A , 56 Newhall Street, Birmingham
Swarbrick, John, 30 St Ann Street, Manchester.
Sykes, Arthur, 45 Finsbury Pavement, E.C.
Tanner, Charles, 9 Conduit Street, W
Tanner, Sir Henry, I.S O., H M Office of Works, Storey's Gate, S W.
Tanner, Lady, Rothbury, Beckenham
*Tanner, Henry, Jun., Carlton Chambers, 12 Regent Street, S W
*Tarbolton, Harold Ogle, 12 Queen Street, Edinburgh
Tayler, Herbert Godfrey, 9 Conduit Street, W
Taylor, Andrew Thomas, 21 Lyndhurst Road, Hampstead, N W.
Taylor, Mrs , 21 Lyndhurst Road, Hampstead, N W
*Taylor, Sir John, K C B , Moorfield Langley Road, Surbiton Hill, Surrey
Taylor, Miss Agnes H , Moorfield, Langley Road, Surbiton Hill, Surrey
Taylor, Miss Mary A , Moorfield, Langley Road, Surbiton Hill, Surrey.
Taylor, J Walton, St John Street, Grainger Street West, Newcastle-on-Tyne
Tenison, Arthur H Ryan, 12 Little College Street, Westminster, S W
Tenison, Mrs Ryan, 12 Little College Street, Westminster, S.W.
Theobald, H W D , 110 Gt. Russell Street, W.C
*Thomas, Sir Alfred Brumwell, 5 Queen Anne's Gate, Westminster, S.W
Thomas, Miss, 5 Queen Anne's Gate, Westminster, S.W
Thomas, Walter William, Commerce Chambers, 15 Lord Street, Liverpool.
Thoms, Patrick Hill, 46 Reform Street, Dundee.
Thomson, Howard Henry, Halford Chambers, Leicester
Thornycroft, Hamo, R A , 2A Melbury Road, Kensington, W.
Tickle, Miss Dorothy, 3 Wilbury Avenue, Hove, Sussex
*Tickner, Thomas Francis, High Street Chambers, Coventry.
Tickner, Mrs , High Street Chambers, Coventry.
Tiltman, Alfred Hessell, 39 Frognal, Hampstead, N.W.

Tiltman, Mrs , 39 Frognal, Hampstead, N.W
Tinney, Miss, 10 Albert Road, St. Johns, S E.
Townsend, C. Harrison, 32 Gt. George Street, Westminster, S W.
Tree, Philip Henry, Leckhampton, St. Leonards-on-Sea
Triggs, H Inigo, 4 South Parade, Bedford Park, W
Triggs, Mrs., 4 South Parade, Bedford Park, W
Triggs, Miss Edith, 4 South Parade, Bedford Park, W.
*Tubbs, Percy Burnell, 68 Aldersgate Street, E.C
Tubbs, Mrs , 41 Campden Hill Court, Kensington, W
Tucker, Benjamin Roper, 41 Sisters' Avenue, Clapham Common, S.W.
Tucker, Miss A J , 41 Sisters' Avenue, Clapham Common, S W.
Tulloch, Frederick H , 77A Victoria Street, Belfast
Turner, Philip John, Parliament Mansions, Victoria Street, S.W
Turnll, Vivian Edward, 41 Broad Street House, E.C.
Tyler, Henry Bedford, Gippeswyck, Linden Road, Bournville, near Birmingham.
Underwood, Edgar S , 3 Queen Street, Cheapside, E C.
Underwood, Mrs , 3 Queen Street, Cheapside, E C
Unwin, Raymond, St Jude's Cottage, Spaniards Road, Hampstead Heath, N W.
Unwin, Mrs., St. Jude's Cottage, Spaniards Road, Hampstead Heath, N.W
*Vallance, Robert Frank, The Ridge, Mansfield, Notts.
Vallance, Miss, The Ridge, Mansfield, Notts.
Vaughan, E M. Bruce, 21 Dumfries Place, Cardiff.
Vickers, Arthur Edward, 60 Queen Victoria Street, E C
Wade, David, Hazel Mount, Daisy Hill, Bradford
Wager, Jasper, 17 Elsham Road, Kensington, W
Wager, Mrs , 17 Elsham Road, Kensington, W
Wakley, Horace Magemss, 11 Adam Street, Adelphi, W C
Walker, Benjamin, Hillsborough, Gravelly Hill, Erdington, near Birmingham.
Walker, John Wilson, 181A Union Street, Aberdeen
Walker, Robert, 17 South Mall, Cork.
Wallen, Frederick, 96 Gower Street, W.C
Walhs, Charles Edward, 38 Queen Anne Street, Cavendish Square, W
Walmisley, Arthur Thomas, 9 Victoria Street, Westminster, S.W.
Walmisley, Mrs., 9 Victoria Street, Westminster, S W.
Ware, Alfred George, Observer Chambers, Albert Road, Bournemouth
*Warren, Edward Prioleau, 20 Cowley Street, Westminster, S W.
Warren, Mrs., 20 Cowley Street, Westminster, S W.
Warwick, Septimus, 13 South Square, Gray's Inn, W C
*Waterhouse, Paul, Staple Inn Buildings, Holborn Bars, W C
Watson, Arthur Maryon, 9 Nottingham Place, W
Watson, Mrs Arthur, 9 Nottingham Place, W
*Watson, Thomas Henry, 9 Nottingham Place, W
Watson, Robert, 35 Lincoln's Inn Fields, W C
*Webb, Sir Aston, R.A., 1 Hanover Terrace, Ladbroke Square, W
Webb, Lady, 1 Hanover Terrace, Ladbrooke Square, W
Webb, Miss D , 1 Hanover Terrace, Ladbrooke Square, W
Webb, Maurice E., 1 Hanover Terrace, Ladbroke Square, W.
Webb, Philip E , 1 Hanover Terrace, Ladbroke Square, W.
Webb, Miss, Redstone Manor, Redhill, Surrey
Wells, R. Douglas, 61 Chancery Lane, W C
Westbye, Johannes Thorvaldsen, 4 Nassington Road, Hampstead, N W
Weston, Thomas Harry, 44 Corn Street, Bristol
Weymouth, Richard Henry, 3 Victoria Street, S W
White, William B , 219 St. Vincent Street, Glasgow.
*White, W. Henry, 14A Cavendish Place, Cavendish Square, W.
White, Mrs , 14A Cavendish Place, Cavendish Square, W.

Wigfull, James R , 14 Parade Chambers, Sheffield.
Wigglesworth, Herbert Hardy, Gwydir Chambers, 104 High Holborn, W C.
Williams, E. Jenkin, 29 John Street, Bedford Row, W C
Williams, J Leonard, 3 Staple Inn, W C.
Williams, John, Northampton Institute, Clerkenwell, E C
Williams, Mrs , Northampton Institute, Clerkenwell, E C
Williams, Robert, Westfield, Odiham, Hants
Williams, Mrs , Westfield, Odiham, Hants
Williamson, James Anderson, 11 Royal Exchange, Edinburgh.
Williamson, Mrs., 11 Royal Exchange, Edinburgh
Willmott, Ernest, 14 South Square, Gray's Inn, W C
*Wills, Frank William, 8 St. Stephen Street, Bristol.
Wilson, Butler, Greek Street Chambers, Leeds
Wilson, Robert G , 181A Union Street, Aberdeen
Wilson, William G., 5 Bloomsbury Mansions, Hart Street, W C
Wilson, Mrs , 5 Bloomsbury Mansions, Hart Street, W.C
Wilson, Miss, 5 Bloomsbury Mansions, Hart Street W C
Wilson, William S , 290 Mount Pleasant Road, Tottenham, N.
Womersley, Alfred, 16 Warwick Mansions, Cromwell Crescent, Kensington, W
Womersley, Mrs., 16 Warwick Mansions, Cromwell Crescent, Kensington, W
Wonnacott, William, 199 Piccadilly, W
Wonnacott, Mrs , 199 Piccadilly, W.
Wood, Edgar, 78 Cross Street, Manchester
Wood, Frederick James, County Hall, Lewes, Sussex
Woodhouse, John H , 100 King Street, Manchester
*Woodward, William, 13 Southampton Street, Strand, W C
Wornum, Ralph Selden, 26 Bedford Square, W C.
Wornum, Mrs Selden, 26 Bedford Square W C
Worsley, Arthur Henry, St Stephen's House, Westminster, S W
Yates, Thomas Charles, 20 Sloane Street, S W
Yates, Mrs , 20 Sloane Street, S W
Yeates, Alfred Bowman, 18 Maddox Street, Regent Street, W.
*Young, Clyde, 6 Lancaster Place, Strand, W C
Young, Mrs , 6 Lancaster Place, Strand, W.C.
Young, George Penrose Kennedy, 42 Tay Street, Perth, N.B.
Young, Jas R., Scottish Provident Buildings, Belfast.
*Young, Keith D., 17 Southampton Street, Bloomsbury, W C
Young, Mrs , 17 Southampton Street, Bloomsbury, W.C.
Young, Robert M , Scottish Provident Buildings, Belfast.
Young, Miss, Scottish Provident Buildings, Belfast

AUSTRALIA.

ANDERSON, Arthur William, 9 Bridge Street, Sydney, N S W.
Burwell, Frederick William, Town Hall, Freemantle, Western Australia
Burwell, Mrs , Fremantle, Western Australia.
Cavanagh, James Charles, Eagle Chambers, Hay Street, Perth, West Australia
Conrad, Albert S , Broken Hill Chambers, King William Street, Adelaide, South
  Australia
Conrad, Mrs , Adelaide, South Australia
Cowper, Christopher A , Melbourne
Hobbs, J Talbot, Perth, West Australia
Hobbs, Mrs , Perth, West Australia.
Jackman, Sydney, Adelaide, South Australia

AUSTRIA.

HELMER, Hermann, 7 Servitengasse, Vienna IX
Kammerer, Marcell, 1 Kreindlgasse, Vienna XIX/1.
Kammerer, Frau, 1 Kreindlgasse, Vienna XIX/1
Peschl, Hans, Magdalenenstrasse 38, Vienna VI
Schaumann-Fürstenburg, Franz Edler von, Kornenburg
Wagner, Otto, 3 Schillerplatz, Vienna
Wagner, Frau, 3 Schillerplatz, Vienna
Wielemans, Alexander, 39 Laudongasse, Vienna VIII/1

BELGIUM.

ACKER, Ernest, 94 Chaussée de Charleroi, Brussels
Anciaux, Emile, 31 Rue Wiertz, Ixelles, Brussels
Bécasseau, Lucien, 4 Rue Laruelle, Liége, Belgium
Benoît, Joachim, 19 Rue de la Limite, St Josse-ten-Noode, Brussels
Benoît, Madame, 19 Rue de la Limite, St Josse-ten-Noode. Brussels
Blomme, Henri, 37 Rue de la Princesse, Antwerp
Blomme, Léonard, 17 Rue du Roi, Antwerp
Braey, Michel de, 282 Rue de la Province (Sud), Antwerp
Buls, Charles, 40 Rue du Beau-Site, Brussels
Caluwaers, Jean-Joseph, 40 Rue du Taciturne, Brussels.
Caluwaers, Madame, 40 Rue du Taciturne, Brussels
Cloquet, Louis, 9 Boulevard Léopold, Gand
Cloquet, Madame, 9 Boulevard Léopold, Gand
Comblen, Paul, 33 Rue des Augustins, Liége.
Crespin, Professor Adolphe, 31 Rue de l'Artichaut, Brussels.
Crespin, Madame, 31 Rue de l'Artichaut, Brussels
Defontaine, William, 34 Rue de Hongrie, Brussels
Defontaine, Madame, 34 Rue de Hongrie, Brussels
Delpy, Adrien, 63 Rue Belliard, Brussels
Delpy, Madame, 63 Rue Belliard, Brussels
Denoyette, Modeste, Rue de l'Eglise, Ledeberg-Gand
Detournay, Mademoiselle, 13 Rue du Boulet, Brussels.
De Vestel, Franz, 13 Rue de la Grosse Tour, Brussels
De Vestel, Madame, 13 Rue de la Grosse Tour, Brussels
De Vreux, Emile, Charleroi.
De Vreux, Mlle Emilie, Charleroi
De Vroye, Jean, 2 Rue du Stuyvenberg, Berchem, Antwerp
Didier, Charles, 89 Rue Armand Campenhout, Brussels
Dumont, Alexis, 17 Rue d'Ecosse, Brussels
Gaspar, Doctor Edouard, Rue du Collège, Verviers
Geefs, Eugène, 10 Rue St -Vincent, Antwerp.
Ghysels, Gustave, 113 Avenue Besme (St -Gilles Parc), Brussels.
Gilson, Jean, 114 Rue des Deux Tours, Brussels
Gosschalk, J , 25 Rue de Belle-Vue, Brussels.
Groef, Pierre de, 11 Rue des Echevins, Brussels.
Hubert, J , 17 Rue de la Terre du Prince, Mons.
Jaspar, Marcel, 61 Rue Beeckman, Liége.
Jaspar, Paul, 149 Boulevard de la Sauvenière, Liége
Jaspar, Madame, 149 Boulevard de la Sauvenière, Liége.
Jaspar, Mdle Jeanne, 149 Boulevard de la Sauvenière, Liége.
Keersmaeker, Gustave de, Hamme, par Jette-Saint Pierre
Ladon, Auguste, Fosse Ste -Elisabeth, Gand
Langendonck, Louis van, 15 Avenue des Arquebusiers, Brussels
Latière, Jules, 60 Rue de Ter, Namur.

Le Clerc, Paul, 9 Avenue du Midi, Brussels.
Maukels, Gustave, 5 Rue Ortélius, Brussels
Piernay, Clément, 10 Rue Renoz, Liége
Piron, Armand, 34 Avenue l'Observatoire, Liége.
Piron, Léopold, 14 Rue Vautier, Ixelles, Brussels
Puchot, Ernest, Rue de Nimy, Mons
Rooms, Remi, 36 Rue de l'Ecole, Gand
Rosschaert, Jean, 15 Rue d'Allemagne, Brussels
Rosschaert, Madame, 15 Rue d'Allemagne, Brussels
Saintenoy, Professor Paul, 119 Rue de l'Arbre Bénit, Brussels.
Simon, Oscar, 1 Place Armand Steurs, St Josse-ten-Noode, Brussels.
Simon, Madame, 1 Place Armand Steurs, St Josse-ten-Noode, Brussels.
Snyers, Arthur, 40 Pont d'Ile, Liége.
Soubre, Professor Ch., 15 Rue Raikem, Liége
Staadt, Franz, 53 Rue Stévin, Brussels
Symons, Fernand, 35 Rue Souveraine, Brussels.
Thirion, Charles, 14 Rue Tranchée, Verviers.
Thirion, Carlo fils, 14 Rue Tranchée, Verviers.
Tourdon, Léon, 11 Rue Gerard-Dubois, Ath
Van de Voorde, Oscar, 39 Cour du Prince, Gand.
Vaes, H., 36 Rue de Comines, Brussels.
Van Dyck, Professor François, 48 Avenue du Sud, Antwerp
Van Houtte, Professor Cyril, 22 Rue du Gouvernement, Courtrai
Van Houtte, Mlle Julia, 22 Rue du Gouvernement, Courtrai
Van Mansfeld, J , 70 Rue Jourdan, Brussels
Vanvarenbergh, Joseph, 41 Rue des Eburons, Liége
Van Ysendyck, Maurice, 109 Rue Berckmans, Brussels
Winders, Jean Jacques, 85 Rue du Péage, Antwerp

CANADA.

Archibald, John S , 59 Beaver Hall Hill, Montreal
Archibald, Mrs , 59 Beaver Hall Hill, Montreal
Baker, Francis Spence, Mail Building, Toronto
Builders' Exchange, The, 204 St James Street, Montreal
Chaussé, Alcide, 1051 St Hubert Street, Montreal
City Council of Montreal.
Graham, Miss G., c/o Mr. J. S. Archibald.
Lacroix, R , 5 Beaver Hall Square, Montreal
Nobbs, Professor Percy E , McGill University, Montreal
Province of Quebec Association of Architects, 5 Beaver Hall Square, Montreal,
    Canada

DENMARK.

Bjerre, A , Town Hall, Copenhagen
*Dahlerup, Etatsraad Vilhelm, Farimagsgade 30, Copenhagen
Dahlerup, Madame Etatsraadinde, Farimagsgade 30, Copenhagen.
Dalherup, Mlle Marie, Farimagsgade 30, Copenhagen
Holsoe, Poul, 18 Rahbeks Allée, Copenhagen
Kietz, Mlle Louise, Farimagsgade 30, Copenhagen
Kofoed, Jens Christian, 18 Frederiksborggade, Copenhagen
Lorenzen, Vilhelm, Copenhagen
Mathiesen, Aage, Sct. Jorgensborg, Copenhagen. B
Novi, Cajus Theophilus, 42 Vodrofsvey, Copenhagen.
Nyebolle, Victor, 161 Gothersgade, Copenhagen
*Nyrop, Martin, 4 Gyldenlóvesgade, Copenhagen.
Nyrop, Madame, 4 Gyldenlóvesgade, Copenhagen

Nyrop, Mdle. E., 4 Gyldenlóvesgade, Copenhagen
*Wright, Hans, Raaduset, Guildhall, Copenhagen.
Wright, Madame, Raaduset, Guildhall, Copenhagen

FINLAND.

Brunila, Birger, 5 Petersgatan, Helsingfors
*Petterson, Lambert, Tammerfors..
Tavaststjerna, Alarik Axel, Helsingfors
Sandelin, Karl, Finland.
Stålström, Mlle Agda, Helsingfors
Strengell, Gustaf, 5 Mikaelsgatan, Helsingfors

FRANCE.

Alard, Jules, 35 Rue Courmeaux, Reims.
Andouin, Maurice, 32 Avenue du Trocadéro, Paris.
Antoine, Georges, 2 Rue d'Alger, Amiens
Arnaud, Charles, 6 Rue Blatin, Clermont-Ferrand (Seine)
Baert, Albert, 7 Passage de la Fontaine-Delsaux, Lille
Barrias, Paul, 9 Avenue des Chasseurs, Paris (XVIIᵉ)
Barrias, Madame Ernest, 9 Avenue des Chasseurs, Paris (XVIIᵉ)
Barrias, Mlle., 9 Avenue des Chasseurs, Paris (XVIIᵉ)
Barrilhet, Henri, 7 Rue Torricelli, Paris
*Bartaumieux, Charles Victor, 66 Rue La Boëtie, Paris (VIIIᵉ)
Bayard, J , 33 Rue Poussin, Paris
Bayard, Louis, 33 Rue Poussin, Paris
Berard, André, 11 Rue Edmond-Valentin, Paris.
Berard, Madame, 11 Rue Edmond-Valentin, Paris
Bertin, Paul Henri, 53 Rue de Courcelles, Levallois Perret (Seine)
Bertrand, Paul, 109 Rue de Sèvres, Paris
Besnard, Jean Alfred, 54 Rue des Abbesses, Paris.
Blanc, Louis Adrien, 6 Rue des Beaux-Arts, Paris
Blanc, Madame, 6 Rue des Beaux-Arts, Paris.
Bobin, Prosper Etienne, 16 Rue le Verrier. Paris.
Bonnier, Louis, 31 Rue de Berlin, Paris
Bornoil, Albert de, 13 Avenue Bosquet, Paris (VIIᵉ)
Bougoüin, Joseph, 10 Rue du Calvaire, Nantes (Loire-Inférieure)
Brizon, Joseph Eugène, 23 Rue Masséna, Lyons
Brizon, Mlle. Else, 23 Rue Masséna, Lyons
Brizon, Louis, 23 Rue Masséna, Lyons
Chastel, Eugène, 3 Rue de Bagneux, Paris
Chastel, G , 22 Avenue du Maine, Paris.
Clermont, François, 14 Place de la Martinière, Lyon (Rhone).
Clermont, Madame, 14 Place de la Martinière, Lyon (Rhone).
Clermont, Mlle., 14 Place de la Martinière, Lyon (Rhone)
Closset, Charles, 6 Rue du Renard, Paris (IVᵉ).
Comment, A , 26 Rue des Prés hauts, Châtenay, Seine
Comment, Madame, 26 Rue des Prés hauts Châtenay (Seine)
Comment, Mlle. Suzanne, 26 Rue des Prés hauts, Châtenay (Seine)
Comment, Mlle. Marguerite, 26 Rue des Prés hauts, Châtenay (Seine).
Constant-Bernard, François, 28 Avenue Carnot, Paris.
Dailly, Edouard, 3 Rue Léonie, Paris (IXᵉ).
Danne, Charles, 4 Rue Mariotte, Dijon
*Daumet, Honoré, 28 Rue du Luxembourg, Paris (VIᵉ).
Daumet, Madame. 28 Rue du Luxembourg, Paris (VIᵉ).
Daumet, Georges, 28 Rue du Luxembourg, Paris (VIᵉ).

*Davoust, Léon Louis, 5 Rue des Saints Peres, Paris (VIe).
Debrie, Georges, 20 Rue de Tournon, Paris.
Deglane, Henri Adolphe Auguste, Grand Palais, Avenue d'Antin, Porte C., Paris.
Deglane, Madame, Grand Palais, Avenue d'Antin, Porte C , Paris
Demerlé, S , 11 Rue du Regard, Paris (VIe)
Deperne, Charles, 27 Place Sébastopol, Lille.
Deperrière, Gilles, 4 Rue Talot, Angers, Maine-et-Loire
Deperrière, Madame, 4 Rue Talot, Angers, Maine-et-Loire.
Descrières, Georges, 73 Rue des Batignolles, Paris
Dubuisson, Alphonse, 93bis Rue des Stations, Lille
Dubuisson, Mlle. Marguerite, 93bis Rue des Stations, Lille.
Dubuisson, Mlle Madeleine, 93bis Rue des Stations, Lille
Dujardin, Mlle Frédérique, c/o H. Daumet
Dupard, René, 418 Rue Saint Honoré, Paris
Dupuy, Charles, 32 Avenue du Trocadéro, Paris
Duval, Ch , 12 Rue de Berlin, Paris
Farochon, Paul, 80 Rue Vanneau, Paris
Flageul, Georges, 14 Place de la Nation, Paris
Flageul, Madame, 14 Place de la Nation, Paris.
Garot, Emile, 1 Boulevard St.-Martin, Paris
Gasse, Paul, 9 Rue Buffon, Tours (Indre-et-Loire).
Gasse, Madame, 9 Rue Buffon, Tours (Indre-et-Loire)
Gaté, Paul Louis, 10 Rue de Bellechasse, Paris
Gautier, Charles Albert, 49 Rue Madame, Paris
Gautier, Mlle Sabine, 49 Rue Madame, Paris
George, Léopold, 109 Boulevard Beaumarchais, Paris
Giboz, Jules, 122 Avenue de Wagram, Paris
Giboz, Madame, 122 Avenue de Wagram, Paris
Gonse, E., 12 Rue de Berlin, Paris
Gontier, Alphonse Jules, 34bis Rue Vignon, Paris
Gottereau, P , 7 Avenue Fitz-James, Marly-le-Roi, Seine-et-Oise
Guadet, J., 240 bis Boulevard St -Germain, Paris
Guadet, Paul, 240 bis Boulevard St.-Germain, Paris.
Guedes de Queiroz, José, 38 Boulevard Emile Augier, Paris.
Harmand, Georges, 5 Rue Montaigne, Paris.
Henard, Eugène, 58 Rue St.-Lazare, Paris
Henner, Madame Jules, c/o H Daumet
Hess, Emile, 8 Rue du Collège, Albi (Tarn)
Huot, Joseph Lazare, 32 Allées des Capucines, Marseilles.
Janty, Ernest, 24 Rue St. Denis, Colombes (Seine).
Jasson, Albert, 4 Rue de Glacis, Nancy
Lafont, Georges, 17 Rue Rosiere, Nantes, Loire-Inférieure.
Lasneret, Alfred, 30 Rue Chaptal, Paris.
Le Foll, Victor Auguste, 136 Avenue Victor Hugo, Paris.
Le Foll, Madame, 136 Avenue Victor Hugo, Paris
Lenoble, Henri, 4 Carrefour de l'Odéon, Paris (VIe)
Leroyer, Mlle Mary, Alençon (Orne).
Lesage, Robert, 164 Avenue Parmentier, Paris
Lieutier, Alfred, 28 Boulevard du Muy, Marseilles
Longfils, Emile Louis, 18 Avenue Trudaine, Paris
Maigrot, Emile, Villers-Allerand (Marne) par Rilly-la-Montagne.
Maillet, André, 4 Rue Monge, Paris
Mallet-Stevens, Robert, 148 Boulevard Haussmann, Paris (VIIIe).
Marcel, Alexandre Louis Auguste, 86 Rue de Lille, Paris.
Marcel, Madame, 86 Rue de Lille, Paris.
Marchand, A., 112 Faubourg Saint-Denis, Paris.

Marie, Eugène Alfred, 21 Rue des Carrières, Suresnes (Seine), France
Mayeux, Henri, 55 Rue de Rébeval, Paris
Méguelle, Costerousse, 9 Rue d'Alençon, Paris
Méguelle, Madame, 9 Rue d'Alençon, Paris.
Messiah, Aron, 1 Rue du Lycée, Nice (Alpes-Maritimes).
Mollet, Victor, 133ᵇⁱˢ Rue Jacquemars-Giélée, Lille.
Mollet, Madame, 133ᵇⁱˢ Rue Jacquemars-Giélée, Lille.
Mongeaud, Paul, Niort
Mongeaud, Mlle. Yvonne, Niort
*Moyaux, Constant, 10 Rue Bellechasse, Paris
Navarre, Edouard, 64 Rue des Martyrs, Avenue Trudaine, Paris
Navarre, Madame, 64 Rue des Martyrs, Avenue Trudaine, Paris.
Navarre, Didier, 64 Rue des Martyrs, Avenue Trudaine, Paris
Nénot, Henri Paul, 17 Rue de la Sorbonne, Paris
Nénot, Mlle Antoinette, 17 Rue de la Sorbonne, Paris.
Nénot, Mlle Geneviève, 17 Rue de la Sorbonne, Paris.
Newnham, Alfred, 5 Rue de Valmy, Lille.
Newnham, Madame, 5 Rue de Valmy, Lille
Nizet, Charles, 7 Avenue de Breteuil, Paris (VIIᵉ)
Normand, Paul, 51 Rue des Martyrs, Paris
Olive, Gaston, 8 Rue Danton, Paris.
Olive, Mlle Suzanne, 2 Rue de Berne, Paris
Parent, Gaston, 83 Boulevard St.-Michel, Paris
Parent, Madame, 83 Boulevard St.-Michel, Paris
Pater, P., 45 Rue Falguière, Paris
Paumier, Félix, 4 Place Possoz, Paris
Perat, Camille, 23 Boulevard Barbès, Paris
Pergod, Ernest, 9 Rue de Lancry, Paris
Peyron, Lazare, 42 Rue St.-Bazile, Marseilles
Peyron, Louis, 42 Rue St.-Bazile, Marseilles.
Pfeiffer-Depré, Madame, 83 Boulevard St.-Michel, Paris.
Piat, Emile Jules, 78 Rue d'Anjou (VIIIᵉ)
Poupinel, Jacques Maurice, 45 Rue Boissy d'Anglas, Paris.
Poupinel, Mlle Jeanne, 45 Rue Boissy d'Anglas, Paris
Quentin, Eugène, 22 Rue Fabert, Paris
Quentin, Madame, 22 Rue Fabert, Paris
Rey, Adolphe Augustin, 119 Rue de la Faisanderie, Paris (XVIᵉ)
Rey, Madame, 119 Rue de la Faisanderie, Paris (XVIᵉ).
Ricadat, Paul, 8 Rue St.-Denis, Asnières (Seine)
Rich, Victor, 73 Rue du Cardinal Lemoine, Paris (Vᵉ).
Richard, Albert, 2 Rue d'Oron, Lyon.
Richard, Pierre, 2 Rue d'Oron, Lyon
Rivière, Jules, 15 Avenue Vauban, Toulon
Roth, Germain, 9 Place des Ternes, Paris (XVIIᵉ).
Roth, Madame, 9 Place des Ternes, Paris (XVIIᵉ)
Roussi, Georges, 2 Rue de Berne, Paris (VIIIᵉ)
Roy, Lucien, 50 Rue du Rocher, Paris
Roy, Madame, 50 Rue du Rocher, Paris
Rozet, Gaston, 178 Rue du Faubourg St.-Honoré, Paris
Salard, Germain, 72 Avenue de la Grande Armée, Paris
Salard, Madame, 72 Avenue de la Grande Armée, Paris.
Sandret, Jean, Alençon (Orne).
Sandret, Madame, Alençon (Orne)
Sandret, Mlle Jeanne, Alençon (Orne)
Sargant, Lionel, 27 Rue Faidherbe, Lille.
Schaeffer, Mlle. Bertha, c/o H. Daumet

*Société Centrale des Architectes Français
Société des Architectes diplomés par le Gouvernement.
Sortais, Louis, 80 Rue d'Assas, Paris
Soudée, Antoine, 136 Boulevard Saint-Germain, Paris
Tixier, Jules, 33 Rue Pétinaud-Beaupeyrat, Limoges, Haute-Vienne.
Tixier, Mlle., 38 Rue Pétinaud-Beaupeyrat, Limoges, Haute-Vienne.
Tondu, Victor François Adrien, 13 Rue de Douai, Paris (IXᵉ).
Trélat, Gaston, 2 bis Avenue des Gobelins, Paris
Vogüé, Marquis de, 2 Rue Fabert, Paris.
Wallon, Charles, 1 Rue de Lille, Paris.
Wallon, Madame, 1 Rue de Lille, Paris
Wernel, Madame, 51 Rue St. Lazare, Paris.

GERMANY.

ARCHITEKTEN-VEREIN zu Berlin.
Armknecht, Fraulein Olga, c/o P Knobbe
Arntz, Ludwig, 19B Rothgerberbach, Cologne
Arntz, Frau, 19B Rothgerberbach, Cologne
Behr, Professor Hugo, 2 Schutzenstrasse, Gorlitz
Berg, Max, 203 Roderbergweg, Frankfurt-a/M.
Berg, Frau, 203 Roderbergweg, Frankfurt-a/M
Berlepsch-Valendàs, Hans, Maria Eich, Planegg, bei Munich, Bavaria.
Booz, Josef, 22 Volksgarten-Strasse, Cologne.
Brachmann, Raymund, 23 Leibnizstrasse, Leipzig.
Brachmann, Frau, 23 Leibnizstrasse, Leipzig
Buhring, Carl James, 18 Albertinenstrasse, Weissensee, bei Berlin
Burckner, Adolf, 3 Königin Augusta Strasse, Berlin, W 9.
Claussen, Fraulein, Magdeburg.
Ebhardt, Bodo, 28A Jagowstrasse, Grunewald, Berlin
Elkisch, Robert, 5 Giesebrechtstrasse, Charlottenburg.
Faesch, Emil, 26 Sommergasse, Basel.
Felisch, Bernhard, 31 Wangenheimstrasse, Grunewald, Berlin.
Felisch, Frau, 31 Wangenheimstrasse, Grunewald, Berlin
Felisch, Fräulein, 31 Wangenheimstrasse, Grunewald, Berlin
Fruhwirth, Alfred, 19 Holbeinstrasse, Frankfurt-a/M
Gause, Carl, 105 Koniggratzer Strasse, Berlin, S W
Gause, Frau, 105 Koniggratzer Strasse, Berlin, S W.
Gerhardt, Fraulein Martha, 10 Marchstrasse, Charlottenburg
Gerlach, Friedrich, 153 Hauptstrasse, Schoneberg, Berlin.
Gessner, Hans, 69 Hasenhaide, Berlin, S 59
Geusen, Carl, 5 Thiergartenstrasse, Dusseldorf.
Geymuller, Baron Henry von, 3 Louisenstrasse, Baden-Baden
Giesecke, Albert, 8 Strasse 17B, Charlottenburg
Goecke, Theodor, 17 Neue Winterfeldtstrasse, Berlin, W 30.
Habicht, Julius, 57 Joachim Friedrichstrasse, Halensee, bei Berlin ii.
Hagedorn, Julius, 10 Bremerstrasse, Bremerhaven
Hagedorn, Frau, 10 Bremerstrasse, Bremerhaven.
Hehl, Christoph, 10 Marchstrasse, Charlottenburg.
Hehl, Fraulein, 10 Marchstrasse, Charlottenburg
Hehl, Johannes, 13 Goethestrasse, Wetzlar.
Heilmann, Albert, Munich
Heinrich, Alfred, 24 Promenadenstrasse, Leipzig.
Hemming, Carl, 36 Capellstrasse, Dusseldorf
Hensen, Alfred, 9 Windthorststrasse, Munster i W
Hensen, Fraulein Maria, 9 Windthorststrasse, Munster i W

Hercher, Dr. Ludwig, 68 Cordestrasse, Munster i W.
Hochgrassl, Johann, 4 Thierschplatz, Munich
Hochgrassl, Frau, 4 Thierschplatz, Munich
Hofmann, Albert, 104 Koniggratzer Strasse, Berlin, S.W 11
Hopfner, Adolf, 41 Schonhauser Allee, Berlin, N. 5 ₹.
Huber, Paul, Sonnenburg, bei Wiesbaden
Kafer, Carl, Radebeul, Dresden
Kafer, Frau, Radebeul, Dresden
Karch, G Anton, Mannheim
Karch, Dr. Robert, Heidelberg
Kempe, Otto, 34 Mattigstrasse, Bautzen, Saxony
Knobbe, Paul, 20 Parkstrasse, Gelsenkirchen.
Knobbe, Frau, 20 Parkstrasse, Gelsenkirchen
Kohnke, Richard, 31 Rickertstrasse, Zoppot.
Korte, Fritz, 7 Hafenplatz, Berlin, S W
Krah, Franz, 15 Herzog-Albrecht Allee, Konigsberg
Krahe, Wilhelm, 191 Neuerweg, Braunschweig
Lange, Carl, 17 Winklerstrasse, Grunewald, bei Berlin
Lundt, Werner, 25-26 Glockengiesserwall, Hamburg
Mackowsky, Dr Walter, 2 Zinzendorferstrasse, Dresden.
Magens, Heinrich, 73 Osestrasse, Hamburg.
Manchot, Professor Wilhelm, 60 Holzhausenstrasse, Frankfurt-a/M
Manchot, Frau, 60 Holzhausenstrasse, Frankfurt-a/M.
Moritz, Carl, 37 Kamekestrasse, Cologne.
Muller, Carl, 1 Rathenowerstrasse, Berlin, N W
Muller, Frau, 1 Rathenowerstrasse, Berlin, N.W
Muller, Fraulein E , 1 Rathenowerstrasse, Berlin, N W
Muthesius, Dr Ing Hermann, Nikolasse, bei Berlin.
Neher, Ludwig, 24 Goethestrasse, Frankfurt-a/M.
Ott, August, 40 Esplanade, Hamburg
Peiffhoven, Carl, 25 Goethestrasse, Dusseldorf
Pieper, Hugo, 12 Stolzestrasse, Hannover
Possenbacher, Heinrich, 55 Briennerstrasse, Munich
Possenbacher, Frau, 55 Briennerstrasse, Munich
Radke, Johannes, 72 Graf Reckestrasse, Dusseldorf.
Rambatz, Johann Gottheb, 36 Ferdinandstrasse, Hamburg
Rehorst, Carl, 3 Lafontainestrasse, Halle a/Salle
Reinboth, Friedrich, Eylau, West Prussia.
Richter, Ernst, 19 Lindenufer, Spandau, bei Berlin
Riessbrodt, Moritz, Koslin
Rolffs, Juhns, 12 Blucherstrasse, Bonn
Rueff, Eugen, 5 Wilhelmstrasse, Stuttgart
Rueff, Julius, 5 Wilhelmstrasse, Stuttgart.
Rueff, Frau Julius, 5 Wilhelmstrasse, Stuttgart.
Ruppel, Friedrich, 7 Lenaustrasse, Hamburg.
Schade, Ernst, c/o W Boche, 92-93 Wilhelmstras e, Berlin, W.
Schmidt, W A , 5 Von Werthstrasse, Coblenz.
Schmitz, Jean, 1 Bismarck-Strasse, Cologne
Schulze, Bruno, 3 Lützeroderstrasse, Hannover
Schuppan, Paul, 14 Schillerstrasse, Wandsbek, Hamburg.
Schuppan, Frau, 14 Schillerstrasse, Wandsbek, Hamburg.
Schuster, Helmuth, 33 Schaperstrasse, Berlin, W.
Schuster, Frau, 33 Schaperstrasse, Berlin, W.
Siebel, Werner, Rath, Dusseldorf.
Siedler, Eduard, 18 Ottilienstrasse, Ruttenscheid, Essen a d. Ruhr
Sonnenthal, Hugo, 66 Kurfurstendamm, Charlottenburg.

Stieler, Adolf, 14 Leonhardtstrasse, Charlottenburg, Berlin
Stubben, Dr Ing H J , 10 Gneiststrasse, Grunewald, bei Berlin
Sturm, Otto, 54 Myliusstrasse, Frankfurt-a/M.
Sucksdorf, Willy, 18 Ackermannstrasse, Hamburg.
Süssenguth, Georg, 5 Wielandstrasse, Charlottenburg
Verlohr, Carl, 1 Theodorstrasse, Hannover
Volcker, Friedrich, Landau in der Pfalz.

GREECE.

Métaxas, Anastase G , Rue Alexandre-Sontzo 4, Athens.
Métaxas, Madame, Rue Alexandre-Sontzo 4, Athens.

HOLLAND.

Arkel, Gerrit van, 760 Keizersgracht, Amsterdam
Beirer, Loderoyk, 37 Alexander Boersstraat, Amsterdam.
Berlage, Hendrik Petrus, Nz , 117 Verhulstsstraat, Amsterdam
Beyderwellen, B H , Rotterdam
Cuypers, Eduard, 2 Jan Luykenstraat, Amsterdam
Cuypers, Dr Pierre Joseph Hubert, Roermond, Amsterdam
*Cuypers, Joseph Theodoor Jan, 77 Vondelstraat, Amsterdam
Goor, C N van, 126 Jonker Fransstraat, Rotterdam
Lehman, J H W , 559 Keizerzgracht, Amsterdam
Povel, Mlle Jeanne, 77 Vondelstraat, Amsterdam ,
Rieber, C T. J Louis, 402 Marnixstraat, Amsterdam
Roosing, J., Jun , Zomerzorgerlaan, A 80, Bloemendaal, North Holland
Royer, J A , The Hague
*Salm. A G. Bzn, 26 Weesperzyde, Amsterdam
Stok, J. P. Wzn, 93 Schiedamschesingel, Rotterdam.
Straaten, J. A. Van, jun , 463 Heerengracht, Amsterdam.
Stuyt, Jan, 296 Keizersgracht, Amsterdam.
Van den Ban, Jacob, 70 Kampersingel, Haarlem.
Weeldenburg, P. A., 18 Middensteiger, Rotterdam ,
Weissman, A William, 44 Raamsingel, Harlem, Holland
Weissman, Madame, 44 Raamsingel, Harlem, Holland.

HUNGARY.

Aigner, Alexander de, 55 Josefsring, Budapest.
Aigner, Madame de, 55 Josefsring, Budapest.
Bartok, Ferencz, 95 Király-utcza, Budapest.
Benes, Imre, 1B Nágy Janos-utcza, Budapest, vi.
Berczik, Jules de, Budapest
Berczik, Madame de, Budapest.
Fellner, Alexander de, 1 Pármán Street, Budapest.
Fellner, Madame de, 1 Pármán Street, Budapest
Fóthi, Vilmos, 6 Karmelita-uteza, Budapest, iii
Francsek, Imre, 11 Kerepesi-ut, Budapest, viii.
Hubschl, Kálmán, Vác
Kakusz, Béla, Eperjes.
Kommer, Jozsef, 3 sz. Baross-utca, Budapest, viii
Kommer, Madame Lenke, 3 sz Baross-utca, Budapest, viii
Kommer, Mlle. Paula, 3 sz Baross-utca, Budapest, viii
Kommer, Mlle. Irma, 3 sz Baross-utca, Budapest, viii.
Krisztinkovich, Bela de, 20 Kerepesi-ut, Budapest, vii
Nágy, Virgil, 11 Mész-utcza, Budapest
Nágy, Madame, 11 Mész-utcza, Budapest.

Pauer, John, 17 u. Realtanoda, Budapest, iv
Podhradszky, Olivier, 63 Jozsef-Korut, Budapest, viii
Rerrich, B , Royal Hungarian Polytechnic, Budapest
Sándy, Gyula, 20 Toldy Ferencz-utca, Budapest, 11
Sándy, Madame Paulin, 20 Toldy Ferencz-utca, Budapest, 11.
Steiner, József, 7 sz. Szent László-u, Arad
Steiner, Madame, 7 sz Szent Laszlo-u, Arad.
Tafler, Imre, 7 Lonyay-utca, Budapest, ix
Torley, Jos. de, 16 Sándor-utca, Budapest, viii
Tscheuke, Herman Ernest, 39 Nagy Janos-utcza, Budapest, vi

INDIA.

FRITCHLEY, Edwin Wolleston, Canada Building, Hornby Road, Fort, Bombay
Gwyther, William Banks, Public Works Department, Bengal Secretariat,
  Calcutta

ITALY.

ALLIEVI, Ing Lorenzo, 379 Corso Umberto, Rome
Baldi, Rodolfo, 24 Via della Pace, Rome
Baldi, Madame, 24 Via della Pace, Rome
Baldini, Arturo, 14 Via Maria Adelaide, Rome.
Baldini, Madame, 14 Via Maria Adelaide, Rome
Barontini, Cav. Cesare, Corso Principe Amedeo, Genoa
Barontini, Madame, Corso Principe Amedeo, Genoa
Benucci, Prof Com F S , 12 Via Margana, Rome
Breglia, Nicola, Naples
Cannizzaro, Mariano Eduardo, 89B Via Panisperna, Rome
Cervelli, Raffaele, 79 Amilta, Rome
Collegio degli Ingegneri e Architetti, The President of, Florence.
Coltellacci, Cav. Costantino, 72 Via Panisperna, Rome
D'Andrade, Commendatore Alfredo, Palazzo Madonna, Torino.
Ferrua, Edoardo, 42 Via Maria Vittoria, Torino
Galassi, Filippo, 45 Via del Quirinale, Rome.
Giovenale, Cav. Giovan Battista, 18 Via Testa Spaccata, Rome
Magni, Giulio, Rome.
Moretti, Ing Costantino, 243 Via Nazionale. Rome
Pini, Commendatore Giovanni, 26 Via Pietrapiana, Florence
Pini, Mario, 26 Via Pietrapiana, Florence
Rapisarda Rizzo, Cav Pasquale, 6 Via Carlo Alberto, Rome.
Rem-Picci, Pietro, 4 Vicolo del Collegio Capranica, Rome
Riem, Roberto, 18 Via Nazionale, Rome
Rinaldi, Giorgio, 20 Sette Sale, Rome
Società degli Ingegneri ed Architetti, The President of, Bologna

JAPAN.

CHUJO, S , Tokio

MEXICO.

ANGUIANO, A , c/o N Mariscal.
Boari, A , c/o N. Mariscal
Campos, M , c/o N Mariscal.
Heredia, G , c/o N Mariscal
Mariscal, F , c/o N Mariscal
Mariscal, N , 4 Estampe de Jésus Maria, Mexico
Mercado, A R , c/o Mariscal

POLAND

SZANIOR, Thadeus, 4 Hortensya Street, Warsaw

PORTUGAL.

BARBOSA, Philinto Elysio Pinto, 85 Rua Mousinho da Silveira, Oporto.
Barbosa, Madame, 85 Rua Mousinho da Silveira, Oporto
Bermudes, A R Adães, 69 Rua Novo do Almada, Lisbon.
Bermudes, Madame, 69 Rua Novo do Almada, Lisbon.
Cerqueira Machado, João Maria, Ponte da Barca
Costa Campos, Alfredo Maria, 10 Calçada do Desterro, Lisbon
Gomez, J P de Souza, 20 Largo da Bibliotheca, Lisbon
Guimarães, Antonio Peres Dias, 56 Rua do Bomfim, Oporto
Lino de Carvalho, João, 33 Rua do V do S^{to} Ambrosio, Lisbon.
Lopes, Professor Joaquim Carlos d'A Graveiro, 335 Rua de S. Bento, Lisbon.
Lopes, José Teixeira, 72 Rua da Batalha, Oporto
Lopes, Madame, 72 Rua da Batalha, Oporto.
Lopes, Professor Teixeira, Villa Nova de Gaya, Oporto
Mendes Guerreiro, Jean Verissimo, 14 Calçada do Sacramento, Lisbon
Parente, Francisco Carlos, 38 C do Marquez d'Abrantes, Lisbon.
Rato, Arthur Manoel, 306 Rua 24 de Julho, Lisbon.
Ribeiro, Frederico Augusto, 145 Rua de D^n Estephania, Lisbon.
Salgado, José Velloso, 99 Rua da Quintinha, Lisbon
Salgado, Madame, 99 Rua da Quintinha, Lisbon
Smart, Alexander Y , Grand Hôtel de Paris, Oporto.
Soares, José Alexandre, 17 Rua da Conceição da Gloria 3', Lisbon.
Terra, Ventura, 149 Rua Alexandre Herculano, Lisbon.
Terra, Madame, 149 Rua Alexandre Herculano, Lisbon.
Verde, Jayme, Avenida Ressano Garcia, J.M., Lisbon

RUSSIA.

BENOIS, Louis Léon, 3 Ligne No 20, St Petersburg, W ost
Benois, Madame, 3 Ligne No. 20, St Petersburg, W ost.
Boker, R , 81 Moika, St Petersburg.
Mehlbart, Harry, 18 Saulenstrasse, Riga
Reinberg, August, 46 Muhlenstrasse, Riga
Reinberg, Madame, 46 Muhlenstrasse, Riga
Schousseff, Alexis, 4 B Grebetskaia, St Petersburg
Suzor, Count Paul, 21 Ligne des Cadets, St. Petersburg
Tchijof, Professor N , 12 Quai Anglais, St Petersburg.

SOUTH AFRICA.

BRIDGES, E J , The Castle, Cape Town.
Cottrill, G St John, Rand'Club, Johannesburg
Clarke, John Daniel, Bloemfontein
East, Hubert S , P O Box 120, Cape Town
Green, Frederick G., Hiawatha, Alma Road, Rosebank, near Cape Town.
Green, Mrs. F G , Hiawatha, Alma Road, Rosebank, near Cape Town
Hitchin, Thomas Henry, Savings Bank Bldgs , St George's Street, Cape Town.
Lucas, William, Lyles Chambers, Pietermaritzburg, Natal.
Pitts, Davidge, c/o Mr A H. Reid
Reid, Arthur Henry, P O Box 120, Cape Town
*Reid, Walter, Box 746, Johannesburg, Transvaal Colony
Reid, Mrs., Box 746, Johannesburg, Transvaal Colony
Sladdin, Thomas Arthur, 100 St. George's Street, Cape Town
*Transvaal Institute of Architects
Walker, Hubert, P.O Box 555, Port Elizabeth.
White-Cooper, William, Grahamstown, Cape Colony.
White-Cooper, Mrs , Grahamstown, Cape Colony.

SOUTH AMERICA.

Acosta y Lara, Horacio, 223 Calle Arapey, Monte Video, Uruguay Republic.
Carrique, Domingo, Obras del Puerto, Rosario, Argentine Republic

SPAIN.

Alvarez y Amoroso, Anibal, Ballesta 9, Madrid
Aranda y Sanchez, Pablo, Princesa 42 pral dra , Madrid
Aranda, Madame, Princesa 42 pral dra , Madrid
Arbos y Tremanti, Fernando, 20 Luis Velez de Guevara (antes Urosas), Madrid
Arroyo, Jerónimo, Palencia, Madrid
Barandiaran, Antonio, 2 Plaza Circular, Bilbao
Bassegoda y Amigo, Joaquin, 7 Lauria, Barcelona
Bastida, Ricardo de, Ercilla, S M , Bilbao
Beck, Carlos, 21 Calle Génova, Madrid
Beraza y Farraga, Raimundo, 4 Torre, Bilbao
Bertran de Quintana, Miguel, 4 Canuda, Barcelona
Cabañes y Rabassa, 6 Emilio S José, Barcelona
Cabello y Lapiedra, Luis M., 5 Calle Columela, Madrid
Cobos, Francisco Perez de los, Cuartel de la Montaña, Madrid
Currill y Montobbio, Buenaventura, 46 Paseo de Gracia, Barcelona.
Elizalde, Luis, 3 Avenida, San Sebastian
Escalera y Amblard, Alfredo de la, 17 Velasco, Santander.
Farrés y Aymerich, Antonio, 29 Carrera de San Jeronimo, dupᵈᵒ, Madrid.
Fort, Enrique, 9 Calle Jorge Juan, Madrid
Frexe y Mallore, Ramon, Balmes 57, Principal, Barcelona.
Garnelo y Alda, José, 5 Paseo de Recoletos, Madrid
Gomez Acebo y Retortillo, Tomas G , 4 Calle Serrano, Madrid
Guitart Trulls, Benito, 4 Calle de la Libertad, Madrid
Jalvo Millan, Mauricio, 40 Calle de la Magdalena, Madrid
Lavin Casalis, Valentin P Ramon, Calle de Castelar, Hotel L , Santander.
Lázaro, Juan Bautista, 23 & 25 Lope de Vega, Madrid
Massera y Ladico, Captain Honorato, 37 Paseo Recoletos, Madrid
Mathet y Rodriguez, G. Pedro, 20 Arenal, Madrid
Maymo y Cabanellas, Juan, 48 Calle Ronda de S Pedro, Barcelona
Mercader y Sacanella, Eduardo, 99 Claris, Barcelona
Miquelerena, Pelayo, 10 Vidrio, Barcelona
Miquelerena, Madame. 10 Vidrio, Barcelona.
Oller y Padrol, Salvador, 592 Córtes, Barcelona
Palacio, Alberto de, 99 Rue Hortaleza, Madrid
Polles y Vivó, Buenava, 72 Rambla Cataluña, Barcelona
Repulles y Vargas, Enrique, 3 Calle San Agustin, Madrid
Roca y Carbonell, Valentin, Columela 5, primero, Madrid
Roca, Madame, Columela 5, primero, Madrid
Roncal, Joaquim, 7 Calle Factor, Madrid
Saldana y López, Joaquin, 31 Carretas, Madrid
Saldana, Madame, 31 Carretas, Madrid
Salvat Espasa, Pablo, 46 Rue Universidad, Barcelona
Santarromana. Madame Isabel, 29 Calle Hermosilla, Madrid
*Sociedad Central de Arquitectos
Urcola, Francisco de, 15 Calle Hernani, San Sebastian
Urioste y Velada, José, 37 Carrera de San Jeronimo, Madrid
Urioste, Madame, 37 Carrera de San Jeronimo, Madrid
Urioste, Mdle , 37 Carrera de San Jeronimo, Madrid
Valeri y Pupurull, Salvador, 17 Alta S Pedro, Barcelona.
Vega y March, Manuel, 272 Cortes, Barcelona.

Velazquez Bosco, Ricardo, 4 Plaza de Santa, Barbara, Madrid
Vilaseca y Casanovas, José, 2 Plaza Urquinaona, Barcelona
Villar y Carmona, Franco del, Jefe Superior de Administracion Civil, Barcelona.
Yanguas y Santafé, Jesús, Hotel de Francia, Cartagena
Zavala, Daniel, 3 Conde de Aranda, Madrid

SWEDEN.

BODIN, Victor, 98 Drottninggatan, Stockholm.
Clason, Professor Gustav, Kammakaregatan 10, Stockholm
Dahlander, Magnus, Oerebro
Dahlander, Madame, Oerebro.
Enblom, Rudolf S , Djursholm, Stockholm
Enblom, Madame, Djursholm, Stockholm.
Ericson, Sigfrid, 26 Sodra Vageu, Gothembourg
Ericson, Madame, 26 Sodra Vageu, Gothembourg
Frykholm, Madame Nils, c/o Mr. R S Enblom
Gellerstedt, Nils, Sverige, Stockholm
Hahr, Erik, Sweden.
Hahr, Madame, Sweden
Hellerström, Alfred, Helsingborg
Klemming, Wilhelm E , 88 Drottninggatan, Stockholm
Salin, Kaspar, Drottninggatan 38, Stockholm
Tengbom, Ivar, 22 Berzelugatan, Gothembourg.
Thorburn, Eugen Jacobi, Gothembourg
Thurdin, Albert N., Hernosand.
Thurdin, Madame, Hernosand.
*Wickman, Gustave, 27 Biblioteksgatan, Stockholm
Wickman, Madame, 27 Biblioteksgatan, Stockholm
Zettervall, Folke, 81 Linnégatan, Stockholm.
Zettervall, Madame, 81 Linnégatan, Stockholm.

SWITZERLAND.

STEHLIN, Fritz, 69 St. Alban Vorstadt, Bâle.

TASMANIA.

NORTH, Alexander, Launceston
North, Miss, Launceston.
North, Miss Adeline, Launceston

UNITED STATES OF AMERICA.

ALLEN, Francis R , 6 Beacon Street, Boston, Mass., U.S.A.
Allen, Mrs , 6 Beacon Street, Boston, Mass., U S.A
Allen, Miss Dorothy, 6 Beacon Street, Boston, Mass., U.S A
*Anderson, George Mendenhall, Ingalls Building, Cincinnati, Ohio.
Anderson, Mrs. Lary, Ingalls Building, Cincinnati, Ohio
Anderson, Mrs William P., Ingalls Building, Cincinnati, Ohio.
Baldwin, Frank Conger, 1103 Union Trust Building, Detroit, Michigan, U S A.
Baldwin, Mrs , 1103 Union Trust Building, Detroit, Michigan, U S A.
Beaumont, George, 115 Dearborn Street, Chicago, U S.A.
Brown, Glenn, The Octagon, Washington, D C , U S A.
*Carrère, John M , 28 East 41st Street, New York, U S A.
Cook, James B , Randolph Building, Memphis, Tennessee, U.S.A.
Day, Frank Miles, Mount Airy, Philadelphia, U.S A
Day, Mrs., Mount Airy, Philadelphia, U S A
Ditmars, Isaac E., 111 Fifth Avenue, Brooklyn, New York, U.S.A.

Dixon, Robert Campbell, jun., 148 Bull's Ferry Road, Weehawken, New
    Jersey, U.S A
*Eames, William S., 711 Lincoln Trust Building, St Louis, U.S.A.
Ellicott, William M , 1101 Union Trust Building, Baltimore, U S A
Frost, Charles S., 184 La Salle Street (Room 806), Chicago, U S.A
Gilbert, Cass, 11 East 24th Street, New York, U.S.A.
Goodrich, E P , 1170 Broadway, New York, U S A.
Goodrich, Mrs , E P , Brooklyn, New York, U S A.
Ittner, William B , St Louis, U S A
Ittner, Mrs , St Louis, U S A
Kelley, James T , 57 Mount Vernon Street, Boston, U.S.A.
Kelley, Mrs., 57 Mount Vernon Street, Boston, U S A.
Kelsey, Albert, 931 Chesnut Street, Philadelphia, U S A
Kelsey, Mrs , 931 Chesnut Street, Philadelphia, U S A
Kent, Edward A , 512 Delaware Avenue, Buffalo, N Y , U S A.
Lafarge, John, 51 West Tenth Street, New York, U.S.A
Link, Theodore Carl, 1000 Carleton Building, St Louis, U.S A.
Link, Mrs. T. C , 1000 Carleton Building, St Louis, U.S.A.
Maginnis, Charles Donagh, 100 Boylston Street, Boston, Mass , U S A.
Millet, Frank Davis, 6 East 23rd Street, New York, U S A.
Mundie, Wm Bryce, 1406 New York Life Building, Chicago, U.S A
Nolan, Thomas, University of Pennsylvania, Philadelphia, U.S A
Noland, Wm Churchill, Chamber of Commerce Building, Richmond, Virginia,
    U S A
Parsons, Wm Barclay, 60 Wall Street, New York, U S A
Pennington, Josias, 311 North Charles Street, Baltimore, Maryland, U S A
Post, George B , 347 Fifth Avenue, New York, U S A
Roberts, Hugh, New Jersey, U S A
Rogers, Arthur Durand, 85 Water Street, Boston, Mass , U S A
Rogers, Mrs , 85 Water Street, Boston, Mass., U S A
*Russell, Ernest John, 1620 Chemical Building, St Louis, U S A
*Rutan, Charles Hercules, 122 Ames Building, Boston, Mass , U S A
Rutan, Miss Eleanor, 122 Ames Building, Boston, Mass , U S A
Rutan, Miss Elizabeth, Boston, Mass , U S A
Thomas, John Downey, 1501 Commonwealth Trust Building. Philadelphia, Pa.
Thomas, Mrs , 1501 Commonwealth Trust Building, Philadelphia, Pa
*Totten, George Oakley, Jun, 808 17th Street, Washington, D.C , U.S.A.
Totten, Miss Ada S., 808 17th Street, Washington, D C , U S A
Vail, Morrison Huggins, Dixon, Illinois, U S A
Vosbury, Charles Edward, Binghamton Savings Bank Building, Binghamton,
    New York, U S A
Walker, Charles Howard, 15 Beacon Street, Boston, Mass , U S A
Walker, Mrs C H , 15 Beacon Street, Boston, Mass , U S A
Walker, Harold D , 15 Beacon Street, Boston, Mass
Wallace, Miss Helen, 15 Beacon Street, Boston, Mass
Wallingford, C A , 54 and 55 Central Trust Building, Indianapolis
Wallingford, Mrs , 54 and 55 Central Trust Building, Indianapolis, U S A
Warner, J Foster, 1036 Granite Building, Rochester, New York, U S.A.
Whitney, Wm Channing, 313 Nicollet Avenue, Minneapolis, Minn , U.S A.
Wight, Peter Bonnett, 1112 Chamber of Commerce Building, Chicago, U S A.
Willis, B F., York, Pennsylvania, U.S.A.
York, John Devereux, 524 North Clark Street, Chicago, U.S.A.

FRONT OF BANQUET MENU CARD.

Designed by Sir Lawrence Alma-Tadema, O.M., R.A.

[To face p. 49.

PART II.

ORGANISATION AND RÉSUMÉ OF PROCEEDINGS

FACE OF MEMBER'S CARD OF IDENTITY.
DESIGNED BY MR. JOHN W SIMPSON

ORGANISATION AND RESUMÉ OF PROCEEDINGS.

Origin of the Congress.

At the closing meeting of the Bureau of the Sixth International Congress, Madrid, 1904, the Royal Institute of British Architects was entrusted with the task of organising the Seventh Congress in London, and some members of the Royal Institute were added to the British Section of the Permanent International Committee to form the basis of an Executive Committee. The Royal Institute of British Architects added other members, and thus formed the Executive Committee The Institute also appointed a Committee of Patronage and a General Committee. Foreign countries and British Colonies were invited to appoint their Committees of Patronage, and a complete list of the various Committees is given in preceding pages All that was possible to do without the intervention of the British Foreign Office, which does not take official cognisance of Congresses, was done with regard to inviting Foreign Governments to appoint official delegates

At the invitation of the Executive Committee, British and Foreign and Colonial Societies, and various other bodies interested, appointed delegates. A list of delegates is given in preceding pages.

Membership.

There were three classes of members—viz ·
Donors, who contributed £4 and upwards to the funds of the Congress.
Subscribing Members, who paid a minimum subscription of £1.
Lady Members, who paid a subscription of 10s. Ladies had the same privileges as Donors and Subscribing Members with regard to card of identity, badge, &c., all meetings, receptions, visits, and the Farewell Banquet.

Meeting Places of the Congress.

The headquarters of the Congress were the Grafton Galleries, Grafton Street, W.
The Inaugural Meeting took place at the Guildhall, E.C
Meetings were held both at the Grafton Galleries and the premises of the Royal Institute of British Architects, 9 Conduit Street, W., for the discussion of the subjects of the programme.

Opening Day

The Grafton Galleries were open at 10 o'clock on the morning of Monday, 16th July, when the President held an informal reception till 11.30
Badges, tickets for visits, &c , cards of invitation, were obtainable at the Congress Bureau, Grafton Galleries, from 10 to 1.30, and from 5 to 6 30;

At 11.30 a meeting of the Permanent International Committee was held at the Rooms of the Royal Institute, 9 Conduit Street

At 3 o'clock the Inaugural Meeting of the Congress took place at the Guildhall, E C, kindly placed at the disposal of the Congress by the Corporation of the City of London.   H R H the Princess Louise honoured the meeting by her presence, and the Duke of Argyll took the Chair.   The Lord Mayor and Sheriffs were present officially.

Receptions &c.

The Royal Academy of Fine Arts entertained the Congress at a Soirée at Burlington House on the evening of Monday, 16th July.

The Right Hon the Lord Mayor of London entertained the Congress at a Conversazione at the Mansion House on the evening of Tuesday, 17th July.

The Royal Institute of British Architects entertained the Congress at a Garden Fête at the Royal Botanic Society's Gardens on the evening of Thursday, 19th July

The Art Workers' Guild entertained a small party of members on the evening of Friday, 20th July.

The Chairman and Directors of the London Exhibition, Ltd., put five hundred invitations to visit the Imperial Royal Austrian Exhibition at Earl's Court at the disposal of the Executive Committee

The Zoological Society of London gave to foreign members admission to their Gardens on Sundays, 15th and 22nd July—days that are closed to the public—on presentation of their cards of identity

The Royal Botanic Society offered members free admission to their Gardens during the Congress week on presentation of their cards of identity

The Athenæum, the Arts Club, and the National Liberal Club elected all the foreign delegates to honorary membership

The Lyceum Club (for ladies) constituted Hon. Members of the Club lady members of the Congress visiting London.

The Lyceum Club also held a reception of Members of the Congress on the afternoon of Wednesday, 18th July.

The Ladies' Committee, recognisable by the Committee badge, arranged for the comfort and convenience of ladies.

Time=Table of Visits.

A. *Hatfield House* —By the kind consent of the Marquis of Salisbury. Tuesday, 17th   Rendezvous, King's Cross Station, main line booking office, 2 10 P M   Departure, 2 25   Arrived Hatfield, 2 50.   Tea at the Red Lion and Salisbury Hotels, 5 30   Departure from Hatfield, 6.10. Arrived King's Cross, 6 33   Col Eustace Balfour met the party at Hatfield.   In charge of visit, Mr D. G. Driver.   Price of ticket, including railway and tea, 5*s* 6*d*

B *Hampton Court Palace*, on the Thames —Tuesday, 17th   Rendezvous, Waterloo Station (South Station), 2.15 P M.   Departure, 2.25. Arrived Hampton Court, 2 53   Tea at the Greyhound Hotel, 5 0. Departure from Hampton Court, 5.50   Arrived Waterloo, 6.22.   In charge of visit, Mr. H P. G Maule.   Price of ticket, including railway fare and tea, 3*s* 6*d*.

N.B.—Visits A and B were alternative and simultaneous.

C *Buckingham Palace Gardens* (by the gracious consent of His Majesty King Edward VII) *and Westminster Abbey* —Wednesday, 18th. Rendezvous, Gate, Grosvenor Place, W., at 2 20 P.M.   Admission by card of identity at gate   Left at 3.30 by motor omnibus for Westminster

Abbey, arriving at 3 45. Rendezvous at west front. In charge of visit, Mr. Maxwell Ayrton

D. *Messrs. Holloway's Works (large building contractors).*—Wednesday, 18th. Left Westminster Abbey by motor omnibus at 4 45 P M Arrived at Messrs. Holloway's, 5 0. Left by motor omnibus at 6.0. Omnibus set down members on the way to Oxford Circus. In charge of visit, Mr. J. Maclaren Ross.

E. *Messrs Doulton's Works (Earthenware and Pottery).*—Wednesday, 18th. Left Westminster Abbey by motor omnibus at 4.45. Arrived at Messrs. Doulton's at 5 0 Left by motor omnibus at 6 0. Omnibus set down members on the way to Oxford Circus In charge of visit, Mr. A. Maryon Watson.

N.B.—Visits D and E were alternative and simultaneous.

F. *Windsor Castle*—By the gracious consent of His Majesty King Edward VII. Thursday, 19th Rendezvous at Paddington Station, No 4 platform, at 2 15 P.M. Departure, 2 25 Arrival at Windsor, 3.0 Tea at the White Hart Hotel at 5.0. Departure from Windsor at 5 45 Arrived London, 6 20 In charge of visit, Mr George Hubbard, F.S A. Price of ticket, including railway fare and tea, 4s.

G. *St Paul's Cathedral, the Temple, St. Bartholomew's, and the Institute of Chartered Accountants*—Thursday, 19th Rendezvous on the steps of St Paul's (west front), 2 20 P M The visit began at 2.30 The Ven. the Archdeacon of London received the visitors. Met motor omnibuses outside at 3.20. Arrived at the Temple, 3 30. The Rev the Master of the Temple received the visitors. Left the Temple by motor omnibus at 4.15. Arrived at St. Bartholomew's, 4.30. Left St. Bartholomew's at 5.0, passing by Electra House and Winchester House, and arrived at the Institute of Chartered Accountants at 5 30 In charge of visit, Mr C. E Hutchinson.

H *Kensington Palace and Dorchester House* (the latter by the kind consent of His Excellency the American Ambassador)—Thursday, 19th Rendezvous outside the Palace in Palace Gate at 2 30 P M Left the Palace, 3 30 Met motor omnibus in Kensington High Street (end of Broad Walk), and arrived at Dorchester House at 4 0 In charge of visit, Mr. Septimus Warwick.

N.B.—Visits F, G, and H were alternative and simultaneous.

J *Oxford*—Friday, 20th. Rendezvous, Paddington Station (No. 3 platform), at 9.50 A M Departure from Paddington, 10 5 Arrival at Oxford, 11.25. Luncheon, 1.30. Departure from Oxford, 5 35. (Tea at the station if desired) Arrival at Paddington, 6 35 In charge of visit, Mr. C. B. Bone. Price of ticket, including railway fare, luncheon, and brake, 14s 6d. Special programme distributed.

K *Cambridge.*—Friday, 20th. Rendezvous at St. Pancras Station (main line booking hall) at 9.30 A M. Train at 9.45. Arrival at Cambridge, 11 5. The party received at the Senate House by the Master of Trinity, acting Vice-Chancellor. Luncheon, 1 30. Departure from Cambridge, 5 5 (Tea at the station if desired.) Arrival St. Pancras, 6 20. In charge of visit, Mr. G. F Blackburne Daniell. Price of ticket, including railway fare, luncheon, and brake, 10s. Special programme distributed.

N B—Visits J and K were alternative and simultaneous.

L. *Tower of London.*—Friday, 20th. Rendezvous at Tower Gate, 11 0 A M. Tower left at 12 30 to see working of Tower Bridge. In charge of visit, Mr. T. P. Figgis

M. *Victoria and Albert Museum, and Royal College of Science.*—Friday,

20th.   Rendezvous at 3.0 P.M at the central entrance, Royal College of
Science, Imperial Institute Road, S.W   Sir Aston Webb, R A., the
architect of the building, received visitors.   In charge of visit, Mr.
Maurice E. Webb.

N.B.—Visits L and M were arranged for those members who did not
visit Oxford or Cambridge.

N *Bridgewater House.*—By kind permission of the Right Honourable the
Earl of Ellesmere.   Saturday, 21st   Rendezvous at Bridgewater House,
St. James's, W , at 11 30 A M.   In charge of visit, Mr. G F Collinson.

O. *Greenwich Hospital.*—Saturday, 21st.   Rendezvous, Charing Cross
Pier, Thames Embankment, at 2.20 P.M   Boat left pier at 2.30.   Arrival
at Greenwich, 3 10   By kind permission of the Director of Works of the
Admiralty, Mr. A. L. Perfect, C E , of the Greenwich District, and Mr.
E. A. Hawkins, A R I B.A , Architectural Assistant of the Admiralty,
accompanied and gave explanations to the visitors.   Tea at the Ship
Hotel, 4 40   Left Greenwich, 5 15   Arrived Charing Cross, 6 0   In
charge of visit, Mr F Darc Clapham   Price of ticket, including boat
and tea, 1s 9d.

P. (i) *Houses of Parliament* —Saturday, 21st.   Rendezvous, Victoria
Tower, Old Palace Yard, Westminster, at 3 50 P M.   Captain Butler,
Secretary to the Lord Great Chamberlain, and Sir Henry Tanner, I.S.O ,
of H M Office of Works, met the visitors.   In charge of visit, Mr.
Sydney Beale

P. (ii) *New Westminster Cathedral.*   Saturday, 21st.   Rendezvous,
outside west front at 4 15 P M

N.B.—Visits O, P (i), and P (ii) were alternative and simultaneous.

Farewell Banquet.

The Farewell Banquet, at which many lady members were present,
took place on the evening of Saturday, 21st July, at the Hôtel Cecil,
at 7 30   Price of ticket (wines included) 21s.

Sir Lawrence Alma-Tadema, O.M., R.A , kindly designed the menu card.

Exhibitions

The following exhibitions were held in the Congress premises, Grafton
Galleries .—

An exhibition of photographs of buildings executed by living British
architects.

A chronological exhibition of British architecture from the Norman
Conquest (1066) to the death of Sir Charles Barry (1860).

Oil paintings and water-colour drawings of English architecture

A few choice specimens of British furniture and silver work.

A Catalogue of the Exhibition, with Preface by Mr. Ralph Straus,
Secretary of the Exhibition Sub-Committee, is appended to this volume.

At the premises of the Architectural Association, 18 Tufton Street,
Westminster, S W , were exhibited a selection of Viennese students'
drawings arranged by Professor Otto Wagner (Vienna).

Subjects Discussed.

Communications on the questions of the programme were received from the various corporations and members mentioned below :—

(1) THE EXECUTION OF IMPORTANT GOVERNMENT AND MUNICIPAL ARCHI-TECTURAL WORK BY SALARIED OFFICIALS

    Society of Austrian Architects
    Gaston Trélat (France)
    Oscar Simon (Société Centrale d'Architecture de Belgique)

(2) ARCHITECTURAL COPYRIGHT AND THE OWNERSHIP OF DRAWINGS

George Harmand (France)	H H Statham (England).
Gaston Trélat (France).	D. Pablo Salvat (Spain)

(3) STEEL AND REINFORCED-CONCRETE CONSTRUCTION—(*a*) The general aspect of the subject ; (*b*) With special reference to æsthetic and hygienic considerations in the case of very high buildings.

    The Joint-Committee on Reinforced Concrete (England).
    Herr Wielemans (Austria)
    Professor Henry Adams (England)
    E P Goodrich (America).
    Louis Cloquet (Société Centrale d'Architecture de Belgique).
    Joaquin Bassegoda (Spain).
    Aug Rey (France)
    Gaston Trélat (France).
    Peter Wight (America).

(4) THE EDUCATION OF THE PUBLIC IN ARCHITECTURE.

John Belcher. A.R.A. (England).
T. G Jackson, R.A (England)
Arthur Hill (Ireland)
Othmar von Leixner (Austria).
Herr Muthesius (Germany).
Banister F. Fletcher (England).
Jean Gilson (Belgium).
Francisco del Villars y Carmona, Manuel Vega y March, Eduardo
    Mercador y Saccanella (Spain)
Society of Austrian Architects
Gaston Trélat (France).
Gaston Anciaux (Société Centrale d'Architecture de Belgique).
Albert Mayeux (France).

(5) A STATUTORY QUALIFICATION FOR ARCHITECTS.

Robert Walker (England)	Gaston Trélat (France)
John S. Archibald (Canada).	Virgil Nágy (Budapest).
L. Bonnier (France).	A. North (Tasmania).
Society of Austrian Architects.	

(6) THE ARCHITECT CRAFTSMAN . HOW FAR SHOULD THE ARCHITECT RE-CEIVE THE THEORETICAL AND PRACTICAL TRAINING OF A CRAFTSMAN ?

Reginald Blomfield, A R.A. (England).
Professor W. R. Lethaby (England).
J M. Poupinel (France).
Fr. van Gobbelschroy (Société Centrale d'Architecture de Belgique).
Society of Austrian Architects.
Gaston Trélat (France).
Robert Lesage (France).

(7) THE PLANNING AND LAYING-OUT OF STREETS AND OPEN SPACES IN CITIES

Raymond Unwin (England)
Herr Stübben (Germany).
E. Hénard (France)
B. Polles y Vivo, J. Majo y Ribos, M Bertrand de Quintana (Spain).
C H Buls (Société Centrale d'Architecture de Belgique).
Aug Rey (France).
Gaston Trélat (France).

(8) TO WHAT EXTENT AND IN WHAT SENSE SHOULD THE ARCHITECT HAVE CONTROL OVER OTHER ARTISTS OR CRAFTSMEN IN THE COMPLETION OF A NATIONAL OR PUBLIC BUILDING ?

Sir W. B. Richmond, K C B , R A (England).
H P Nénot (France)
C. B Muller (Germany)
Association of the Architects of Catalonia (Spain)
Society of Austrian Architects.
Gaston Trélat (France)
P J. H Cuypers (Amsterdam).
Modeste De Noyette (Belgium).

(9) THE RESPONSIBILITIES OF A GOVERNMENT IN THE CONSERVATION OF NATIONAL MONUMENTS

Professor G. Baldwin Brown (Scotland)
A. Besnard (France)
Tuscan College of Engineers and Architects.
Professor W R Lethaby
Gaston Trélat (France).
Joseph Artegas y Ramoneda (Spain).

(10) THE ORGANISATION OF PUBLIC INTERNATIONAL ARCHITECTURAL COMPETITIONS

J. Guadet (France).
Society "Architectura et Amicitia" (Holland)
Gaston Trélat (France)

A communication on the Method for the Reconstruction of Architectural Monuments by Metrophotography was received from M. Marcel le Tourneau, of Paris.

Monsieur Honoré Daumet (Paris) read a communication on the Château de Saint-Germain

Mr Cecil Smith (Keeper of Greek and Roman Antiquities, British Museum) read a Paper on The Tomb of Agamemnon.

Abstracts of the Papers and Communications were issued by post to members in the United Kingdom, and were obtainable by other members in the Congress Rooms both at Grafton Street and at the Institute

The reading of the Papers selected for delivery was limited to fifteen minutes. Speakers in the discussions were limited to five minutes.

Railway Facilities.

Great Britain and Ireland.—The British railway companies issued return tickets from the 11th to the 25th July inclusive at the rate of a *single fare and a quarter* to members on *presentation of voucher* at booking office.

France—The Compagnie du Chemin de Fer du Nord, in conjunction with the South-Eastern and Chatham Railway, issued return tickets to London (*via* Calais-Dover or Boulogne-Folkestone), on *presentation of card of identity*, at the Gare du Nord, Paris, at the following rates .—First class, 72 85 francs.   Second class, 46.85 francs.   For French Congressists travelling by the Chemin de Fer du Nord, and not starting from the Gare du Nord, Paris, a corresponding reduction was made *on presentation of card of identity*   Congressists were required to inform Monsieur J. M. Poupinel, 45 Rue Boissy d'Anglas, Paris, of the station they proposed to start from   Validity of ticket, one month.

The Compagnie du Chemin de Fer de l'Ouest, in conjunction with the London, Brighton and South Coast Railway, issued return tickets to London on presentation of card of identity at the Gare Saint-Lazare, Paris (*via* Dieppe-Newhaven) at the following rates ·—First class, 49 15 francs.   Second class, 37.90 francs.   Validity of ticket, 14 days

The Compagnie des Chemins de Fer de l'Est offered men Congressists (not ladies) a reduction of 50 per cent on their system on presentation of a voucher to be obtained from M Poupinel, 45 Rue Boissy d'Anglas, Paris   Members were required to inform M Poupinel of their route over the Eastern system.

Holland and Belgium.—The Great Eastern Railway Company of England arranged for the issue of return tickets, on presentation of voucher at Cologne, Brussels, Antwerp, Hook of Holland, from Antwerp and Hook of Holland to London at the following rates ·—

Hook of Holland.—First class, 37*s*. 6*d*   First-class steamer and second-class train, 32*s*. 6*d*

Antwerp—First class, 32*s* 6*d*   First-class steamer and second-class train, 27*s*. 6*d*.

Italy—The Italian railway companies, through the intermediary of M Cannizzaro and a Committee of Italian architects, granted a reduction of 60 per cent on the ordinary rates to members of the Congress travelling over their system.

Spain.—The Spanish railways offered a reduction of 50 per cent on presentation of voucher signed by M. Luis M Cabello y Lapiedra, 5 Columela, Madrid   M Cabello received from London the cards of identity of all Spanish Congressists, and forwarded them personally with voucher

Portugal.—The Portuguese railway companies, through the good offices of the Portuguese members of the Permanent Committee, granted to members of the Congress travelling on their lines a reduction of 50 per cent. on the ordinary fares.

General Information.

The languages of the Congress for Papers and Discussions were English, French, German, and Italian

The notices issued during the Congress week were in English and French.

The steward-interpreters wore coloured ribbons to indicate the languages with which they were conversant

The Congress badge, together with the various invitations, final programme, &c., were issued to members at the Congress Bureau, Grafton Galleries, on presentation of their cards of identity

The badge designed by Mr. John W. Simpson was in bronze. Members desiring the badge in gold were supplied with it at a cost of £2 by giving early notice to the Secretary.

Members of the Executive Committee wore a silver-gilt badge with blue ribbon, and the members of the Ladies' Committee were distinguished by a red ribbon attached to a similar badge.

Members not residing in London were requested to notify their temporary addresses to the officials at the Congress Bureau, Grafton Galleries.

A post and telegraph office was established at the Grafton Galleries for the convenience of members, who were also at liberty during the Congress week to have their letters addressed "VIIth International Congress of Architects, Grafton Galleries, Grafton Street, London, W."

Handbook.—A handbook was issued giving descriptions, with plans, of the buildings on the Programme of Visits, and information concerning various places of interest in London; together with a list of hotels recommended by the Executive Committee, tariffs, cab fares, &c.

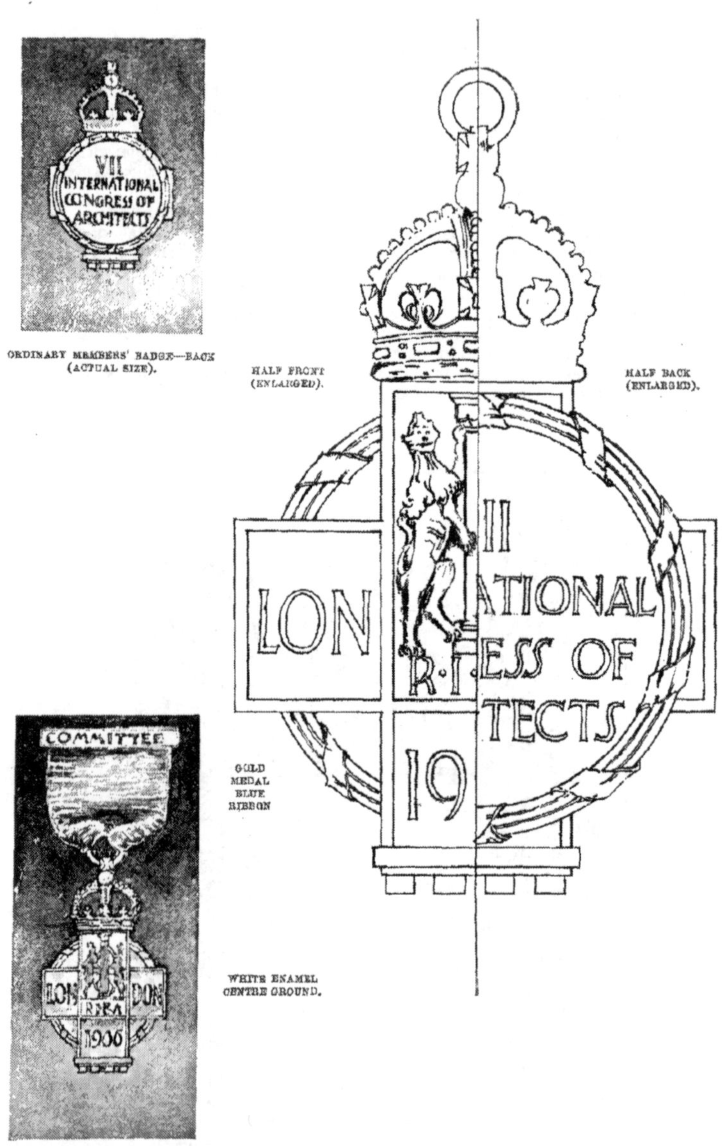

ORDINARY MEMBERS' BADGE—BACK
(ACTUAL SIZE).

HALF FRONT
(ENLARGED).

HALF BACK
(ENLARGED).

GOLD
MEDAL
BLUE
RIBBON

WHITE ENAMEL
CENTRE GROUND.

COMMITTEE BADGE—FRONT
(ACTUAL SIZE).

THE INTERNATIONAL CONGRESS BADGE, 1906.

Designed by JOHN W. SIMPSON, and reproduced from his Drawings.

[To face p. 58.

PART III.

THE OPENING CEREMONIES

INTERNATIONAL PERMANENT COMMITTEE MEETINGS

RECEPTIONS, FÊTES, VISITS, EXCURSIONS

FAREWELL BANQUET

OPENING CEREMONIES

President's Informal Reception.

THE Congress opened at the Grafton Galleries at ten o'clock on Monday morning, the 16th July. The President, wearing the Institute Presidential insignia of office, and supported by most of the members of the Executive Committee, awaited members in the great central hall in readiness for the first item on the Programme, the President's Informal Reception A Master of the Ceremonies was in attendance to announce the names of members as they advanced to be presented to and welcomed by the President

To minimise the confusion that would probably attend the sudden ingress of some hundreds of members, a large number of whom were unacquainted with the English tongue, every member on entering was handed a paper giving directions in English, French, German, and Italian as to the exact course to follow in order to have his requirements in the way of badge, cards for entertainments and visits, railway tickets, &c , at once attended to. By this means endless questions were anticipated and answered without need for reference to anyone Placards conspicuously placed on the walls indicated the counters where members could be attended to in their own language, and interpreters, distinguishable by the coloured ribbons they wore, were posted about the rooms ready to lend their services where required The machinery for dealing with this preliminary part of the business worked so smoothly that in less than three hours after the opening of the doors the wants of the thousand or more members who had put in an appearance had been met After being presented, the visitors passed through the Galleries and inspected the various exhibits.

International Permanent Committee: First Meeting.

At 11 30 the International Permanent Committee held a meeting at the Institute Rooms, 9 Conduit Street, at which the following members were present :—

Members of the Executive Committee.

MM. John Belcher, A.R A., President. MM. Leonard Stokes.
Sir Aston Webb, R A. Alexander Graham, F.S A.
Henry T Hare. W. J Locke, *Secretary.*

Members of the International Permanent Committee

Austria.—MM. Otto Wagner, H. Helmer, H Peschl, A. von Wielemans.
Belgium.—MM J Caluwaers, F. de Vestel.
Canada.—M. Alcide Chaussé.
Denmark.—M V Dahlerup
France.—MM. H. Daumet, J. M. Poupinel, C. Moyaux, Ch. Bartaumieux, G. Harmand, H. P. Nénot.

Great Britain.—[See members of Executive Committee above]
Germany.—MM. J. Stubben, H M. Muthesius
Holland.—M A Salm
Italy —M. M. E. Cannizzaro.
Portugal.—M. Venturo Terra.
Spain —MM Fernando Arbos y Tremanti, Enrique M Repullès y Vargas,
    J. Urioste y Velada, R Velasquez Bosco
Sweden.—MM Gustave Clason, G Wickman
United States.—MM George O. Totten, jun , Wm S. Eames.

The following report of the proceedings at the Meeting has been kindly
contributed by M Poupinel, Secretary of the Permanent Committee —

M Daumet, Président du Comité permanent, prend place au Bureau,
avec M. John Belcher et M Alex Graham à sa droite, et MM. J. M.
Poupinel et W. J. Locke, secrétaires, à sa gauche

M. Daumet (Président) : J'ai l'honneur de représenter ici tous mes
confrères et je suis tout ému en vous présentant en leur nom et du fond
du cœur mon salut confraternel Je suis très fier de l'honneur qui m'est
dévolu de prendre la présidence en cette circonstance ; mais pour mener
ma tâche à bonne fin, je crois devoir compter sur votre bonne volonté
Je commence par souhaiter la bienvenue aux délégués des différents
Gouvernements et je vous prie de vous joindre à moi pour remercier M
le Président de l'Institut Royal des Architectes britanniques, qui est
à ma droite, d'avoir bien voulu mettre à profit son influence pour obtenir de hauts patronages. (*Applaudissements.*) Il devrait se trouver ici à
ma place, car il y a plus de droits que moi, et si j'ai le privilège de diriger
la séance de ce jour je ne le dois qu'à mon âge Je prie maintenant
M. Locke de vouloir bien vous dire quel est l'ordre du jour de la réunion
de ce jour
M. W. J Locke (Secrétaire) Le Comité général désire uniquement que
le Comité international règle la tenue des réunions du Congrès. Comme
plusieurs de nos collègues ne parlent ni français ni allemand, le Comité
pense qu'il y a lieu de désigner un président d'honneur pour chaque
séance, ainsi que deux secrétaires d'honneur—un Anglais et un étranger.
Nous vous proposons d'arrêter comme suit la composition des bureaux
pour chaque séance ·—

—	—	Présidents d'honneur	Secrétaires d'honneur
Lundi, 11 30–1*	Comité permanent	H Daumet (France) John Belcher, A R A (Angleterre)	J M Poupinel (France) W J Locke (Angleterre)
Mardi, 10–1 †	Sujet 3	F M Day (États-Unis) J J. Caluwaers (Belgique)	P Rapisarda-Rizzo (Italie) F. N Jackson (Angleterre)
„ 10–11 *	H Daumet ' Le Château de Saint-Germain "	Reginald Blomfield (Angleterre) Mariano Eduardo Cannizzaro (Italie)	C V Bartaumieux (France) Harbottle Reed (Angleterre)
„ 11–1 * .	Sujet 1 . .	Repulles y Vargas (Espagne) J Slater (Angleterre)	Hans Peschl (Autriche) G H Fellowes-Prynne (Angleterre)
„ 10–1 †	Sujet 6	Otto Wagner (Autriche) R S Balfour (Angleterre)	H O Tarbolton (Écosse) Gustave Wickman (Suède)
„ 8 30 † .	Sujet 7 .	Charles Buls (Belgique) Sir W Emerson (Angleterre)	S Perkins Pick (Angleterre)

* Lieu d'Assemblée Salle des Réunions de l'Institut, 9 Conduit Street.
| Lieu d'Assemblée Grafton Galleries, Grafton Street

—	—	Présidents d'honneur.	Secrétaires d'honneur
Mardi, 10–12 * .	Sujet 10	Dr Ing Hermann Muthesius (Allemagne) H T Hare (Angleterre)	E Guy Dawber (Angleterre) Ventura Terra (Portugal)
Mercredi, 12–1 *	Sujet 2 . .	H P Nénot (France) W S. Eames (États-Unis)	Urioste y Velada (Espagne) Walter Reid (Transvaal)
„ 8 30 *	Sujet 9	E V Dahlerup (Danemark) A Graham (Angleterre)	C A Cowper (Melbourne) Franz de Vestel (Belgique)
Jeudi, 10–1 †	Sujet 4	Dr Ing H. J. Stubben (Allemagne) Sir Aston Webb, R A (Angleterre)	A G Bzn Salm (Pays-Bas) W M Mitchell (Irlande)
„ 10–11 *	Sujet 2 (*continui*)	H P Nénot (France) W S Eames (États-Unis)	Urioste y Velada (Espagne) Walter Reid (Transvaal)
„ 11–1 *	Sujet 8 .	R Boker (Russie) Leonard Stokes (Angleterre)	E Kirby (Liverpool) G O Totten (États-Unis)
Vendredi, 8 30 †	Cecil Smith "Le Tombeau d'Agamemnon"	R Phenè Spiers (Angleterre) Alexander Wielemans (Autriche)	Alcide Chaussé (Canada) H Blanc (Edinburgh)
Samedi, 10 *	Séance du Comité permanent	H Daumet (France) J Belcher, A R A (Angleterre)	J M Poupinel (France) W J Locke (Angleterre)
„ 11 30 †	Sujet 5	Prof 1 G Clason (Suède) E T Hall (Angleterre)	E Chujo (Japon) J T Cackett (Newcastle)

* Lieu d'Assemblée Salle des Réunions de l'Institut, 9 Conduit Street
† Lieu d'Assemblée Grafton Galleries, Grafton Street.

M le Président S'il n'y a pas d'opposition, cette liste est adoptée.

M. Locke (Secrétaire) : J'ai le regret de vous annoncer que la conférence de M le Professeur Meydenbauer ne pourra pas avoir lieu. En ce qui concerne la séance d'inauguration de cet après-midi, au Guildhall, il a été décidé par le Comité que les délégués étrangers répondraient par ordre alphabétique à l'allocution du Président.

M. Cannizzaro . J'ai apporté au Congrès, de la part du Gouvernement italien, les livres contenus dans ce coffre Je désirerais savoir au cours de quelle séance je serai autorisé à les présenter au Congrès

M Locke (Secrétaire) : Je pense qu'il conviendra de les déposer au cours de la séance dans laquelle nous discuterons le point auquel ces publications se rapportent, c'est-à-dire au No. 9, qui se discutera mercredi soir.

Adopté

M. Poupinel Gentlemen, allow me to remind you that at a meeting of the International Congress of Architects a proposition was brought forward suggesting that the Committee of Organisation should become the real and sole Board of the Congress. This proposal was a well-deserved act of courtesy. It is only fair that those who have done the work should receive the honour.—Messieurs, dans les Congrès précédents nous avons prié les membres du bureau de la Commission d'organisation de vouloir bien accepter les fonctions de membres du bureau du Congrès Je pense qu'il y a lieu de persévérer dans cette habitude parce que c'est le seul moyen de donner aux membres du Bureau permanent un témoignage de gratitude pour tout le mal qu'ils se sont donné et aussi parce qu'on dit généralement qu'il est juste que ceux qui ont été à la peine soient aussi à l'honneur. (*Applaudissements.*)

M. le Président . Si personne ne demande la parole sur la proposition je la déclare adoptée.

M. John Belcher (Président de l'Institut Royal des Architectes britanniques, Président du Congrès) [*en anglais*] : Messieurs, je vous remercie de l'honneur que vous me décernez, je ferai de mon mieux pour faire valoir le grand intérêt que présente le Congrès pendant la durée de mes fonctions. Je puis vous assurer que c'est un grand plaisir pour moi de voir présents tant de confrères, tant de distingués délégués officiels et autres, et je suis certain qu'avec votre aide je pourrai remplir ma tâche de façon satisfaisante. Je vous souhaite la bienvenue à Londres.

M. Poupinel · M. Locke a donné connaissance de la composition des bureaux des sections, mais il se pourrait que quelques membres n'aient pas été désignés parce qu'ils n'étaient pas présents ou bien parce qu'ils ont été suppléés Par simple courtoisie je désire vous donner les noms des membres du Comité permanent qui, de fait, se trouvent devoir venir à la suite des bureaux que nous avons composés .

> M. Daumet, *Président*, MM John Belcher, M E Cannizzaro, J Guadet, J Stubben, *Vice-Présidents* du Comité permanent
> *Secrétaires*.—MM. J M Poupinel, Caluwaers, G Harmand, W. J Locke, H. Muthesius, G. O. Totten, jun , R. Velasquez Bosco, présents au Congrès , et les absents, pour mémoire, MM T J H Cuypers, W L. B Jenney, A Weber, qui pourraient peut-être arriver pour la dernière séance

De cette façon notre organisation sera complète. Je désire exposer la raison simple pour laquelle nous n'avons pas de délégué hongrois · c'est parce qu'en 1904 la Hongrie n'était représentée par personne au Congrès Si elle se faisait représenter au présent Congrès, nous en serions très heureux

M. W J Locke [*en anglais*]: La Hongrie n'est pas représentée au Comité permanent le nombre des membres du Comité permanent est limité ; L'Autriche est déjà représentée par six membres, mais jusqu'à présent la Hongrie n'a pris aucune part aux Congrès internationaux. Voilà pourquoi la Hongrie n'a pas de représentant au Comité permanent. C'est maintenant la première fois que la Hongrie a des rapports avec notre organisation. La question qui se pose est celle-ci Voulez-vous formuler une demande de représentation de la Hongrie dans le Comité permanent ?

M. Virgil Nágy (Hongrois) Je cherchais précisément la liste des noms des architectes que notre club avait désignés pour le Comité permanent, mais je ne la retrouve pas Je ne sais si on a envoyé leurs noms au Comité d'organisation de Londres.

M. Locke . Il y en a tant et tant. On vous expliquera cela au Bureau et on réglera la question ultérieurement Faites une demande formelle de la constitution d'une section hongroise. C'est ce qu'il y a de mieux à faire pour l'instant.

M. Nágy. M. le Président, je vous demande officiellement d'admettre la Hongrie à faire partie du Comité permanent

M Cannizzaro · Ne serait-il pas préférable de traiter cette question des représentations au Comité permanent à la séance du Comité international de samedi ?

M. le Président : La question devrait être traitée à cette séance-ci parce que le temps manquera à la dernière séance dont l'ordre du jour est toujours très chargé. D'ailleurs nous sommes en nombre aujourd'hui et nous pourrions donc prendre une décision

M. Cannizzaro : Je serais très heureux de voir la Hongrie représentée au Comité permanent ; mais nous avons cependant le droit en ce qui concerne l'Italie d'en référer d'abord à nos compatriotes. Il serait donc préférable de remettre la chose à samedi.

M. LE PRÉSIDENT   M. Poupinel me dit qu'il n'y a pas d'inconvénient à remettre à samedi.

M. CANNIZZARO . Dans ce cas je renonce à la parole sur cette question. Je désire cependant ajouter quelques mots en anglais [*La suite en anglais.*] Nous autres en Italie formons une sorte de parlement   Nous sommes élus par le Congrès ; moi et M d'Andrade sommes les délégués du Gouvernement ; il y en a ici qui ne sont pas délégués du Gouvernement , il y en a d'élus par le Congrès ; ils représentent le peuple ; ils représentent les architectes de leur pays, mais ne sont pas réellement élus par les architectes de leur propre pays   Je suis chargé de présenter la décision de notre Comité italien d'abandonner nos fonctions pour l'avenir et de demander au Comité central de faire procéder à des élections régulières, élections dans tous les pays, mais spécialement dans notre pays. Nous vous demandons de donner toute autorité au Comité italien pour remplir sa tâche à l'avenir parce que nous sommes là réellement sans les moyens de faire de bonne besogne, n'étant pas élus par nos collègues compatriotes Dans la situation actuelle nous ne pouvons plus travailler et nous serons obligés de renoncer à l'honneur d'être membres du Comité permanent

M G. HARMAND   Et les statuts ?

M. CANNIZZARO   Je connais bien les statuts sous lesquels existe le Comité central, aussi dans le cas où ma motion ne serait pas admise la seule chose que nous puissions faire est de renoncer à en faire partie. [*La suite en français*]   Si la proposition n'était pas admise, nous serions obligés de renoncer à faire partie du Bureau, parce que nous ne sommes pas investis d'un mandat par nos collègues architectes italiens   Nos membres veulent que les délégués au Comité international représentent tous les architectes du pays. Ils désirent donc prendre part à l'élection des délégués. Nous n'avons pas en Italie une société centrale, mais on pourrait charger une des sociétés du pays de faire procéder à l'élection dans chaque région du pays

M. C. MOYAUX · Est-ce que la carrière est libre en Italie comme chez nous ?

M. CANNIZZARO . Oui.

M. BARTAUMIEUX   Dans ce cas ce sera le suffrage universel, car tout le monde peut se dire architecte.

M. HARMAND   Je voudrais répondre quelques mots à M Cannizzaro, qui n'est pas au courant de la question parce que nous n'avons pas eu le plaisir de le voir à Paris

M CANNIZZARO   Les délégués italiens ne peuvent prendre aucune résolution sans s'être adressés d'abord aux architectes

M HARMAND : C'est une difficulté spéciale à l'Italie. Le programme du Congrès a été envoyé et on avait le temps de faire des observations Or, je constate que personne n'avait soulevé cette question jusqu'ici Nous ignorions donc cette situation qui cependant ne doit pas être réglée internationalement. Elle est tellement nationale et spéciale à l'Italie que je pense que les Italiens se mettront facilement d'accord d'ici à la réunion de samedi. Statutairement, c'est dans l'année qui suit le Congrès qu'il faut que nous ratifiions les nominations ; l'Italie aura donc le temps d'ici un an d'étudier cette question

M CANNIZZARO . Il vaudrait mieux qu'à cette séance les délégués italiens puissent assister et voter réglémentairement.

M HARMAND : Voici la difficulté qui se présente. Pour ne pas remettre toujours en discussion les questions réglées en décembre 1905 à Paris, on a décidé que les modifications aux statuts ne pourront être proposées que par les deux tiers des membres du comité. Je crois que vous n'obtiendrez pas cette majorité pour soumettre la question que vous soulevez Mais il a été entendu à Paris que chaque pays réglerait sa délégation comme il l'entend et que le Congrès se bornerait à prendre acte de la décision. Il

F

suffira donc que le Congrès ratifie la nomination des délégués italiens au Comité pour que ceux-ci puissent voter et délibérer réglémentairement

M. CANNIZZARO . Tout cela devra donc se faire pour samedi et je ne puis pas prévoir quelle personne sera déléguée en Italie par les Italiens.

M. HARMAND Vous ne m'avez pas compris Il suffira, dans un ou deux mois, d'écrire à M. Poupinel que telle personne a été désignée, pour que le Bureau permanent prenne acte de cette désignation, et celle-ci est alors ratifiée au prochain Congrès , mais quant au Comité, il est complet par la présence volontaire des Italiens

M. LE PRÉSIDENT · Je pense que ces explications donneront toute satisfaction à M. Cannizzaro

M. CANNIZZARO Mais les désignations devront être ratifiées par le prochain Congrès

M HARMAND Mais en attendant, les délégués peuvent siéger au Comité et celui-ci peut fonctionner régulièrement Il n'est pas douteux que le Congrès prochain ratifiera les désignations italiennes.

M. CANNIZZARO . Cette explication satisfait les membres actuels, qui pourront abandonner leur mandat en faveur de ceux qui seront désignés ultérieurement par les architectes italiens.

M LE PRÉSIDENT . Ce seront peut-être les mêmes, car on peut les réélire.

M CANNIZZARO On pourrait laisser les noms en blanc jusqu'à samedi , en attendant l'arrivée des désignations italiennes, s'il est possible de les obtenir d'ici là, ce dont je doute fort.

M. HARMAND C'est peut-être un procédé parlementaire, mais il est en tout cas irrégulier, car il suffirait que vous n'obteniez pas les désignations pour samedi pour que nous restions sans délégués italiens Or, nous ne voudrions pas manquer de membres italiens jusqu'à ce que cette notification des désignations nous soit parvenue Veuillez donc rester provisoirement au Comité. Vos remplaçants éventuels viendront plus tard.

M LE PRÉSIDENT . C'est régulier. S'il n'y a pas d'opposition, il en sera donc ainsi

M HARMAND · Je désire faire une courte motion. Nous aurons mercredi une discussion concernant la propriété artistique des dessins architecturaux et, à cet égard, j'essayerai de vous donner l'état actuel de la législation sur la matière. En ma qualité de juriste, je reconnais cependant qu'il est très difficile de se faire une idée saine de cette législation, car on a beau lire une loi avec grand soin, c'est l'application qu'en font les magistrats qui en fait la vraie valeur. Il est donc très difficile de dire quels sont vos droits en cette matière. Je proposerai samedi de prier chaque nation représentée de vouloir envoyer au Comité permanent, dans un délai rapproché, l'état de la législation dans chaque pays, de façon à nous renseigner d'une manière exacte Les travaux condensés pourront alors être insérés au bulletin officiel Ce travail prouvera que, dans beaucoup de pays déjà, vos œuvres sont protégées.

M LE PRÉSIDENT . Cette proposition a un intérêt considérable, car elle formera en quelque sorte une législation internationale. Si plus personne n'a de propositions à faire, je lève la séance.

[*La séance est levée à midi et demi*]

The Inaugural Meeting at the Guildhall

The formal inauguration of the Congress took place at the Guildhall, kindly placed at the disposal of the Congress for this purpose by the Lord Mayor and the Corporation of the City of London   H R H. the Princess Louise (Duchess of Argyll), sister of His Majesty King Edward VII, graciously honoured the meeting with her presence ; and the proceedings were presided over by the Duke of Argyll, one of the Vice-Presidents of the Congress.

The meeting took place at three o'clock, and was very largely attended, the great historic hall being filled to overflowing   Her Royal Highness and the Duke were awaited at the door of the side gallery by the President and members of the Executive Committee and by the Lord Mayor and Lady Mayoress and the Sheriffs of the City   On their arrival Mrs Belcher, on behalf of the Ladies' Committee, presented the Princess with a beautiful bouquet of flowers   The whole party then proceeded up the staircase and through the picture gallery on to the dais of the Great Hall   Among those assembled on the dais were the United States Ambassador, the Greek Minister, and the various delegates from foreign countries who were subsequently to address the meeting ; Sir L. Alma-Tadema, O.M., R.A , Sir W. B Richmond, R A , Sir Aston Webb, R A , Sir. Wm. Emerson, Sir John Taylor, Professor Aitchison, R A , Mr Alfred East, R A , Mr. Reginald Blomfield, A R A , the Hon. Nona Kerr and Captain Geoffrey Robert, in attendance on the Princess ; the members of the Executive Committee, the Secretary, and several members of the Institute Council.

The Lord Mayor, having addressed from the Chair a few words of welcome to the Princess Louise and the Duke of Argyll, surrendered the Chair to the Duke, who then called upon Mr Belcher, the President, to deliver his Address of Welcome.

ADDRESS BY THE PRESIDENT, MR JOHN BELCHER, A R A

Your Royal Highness, my Lord Duke, your Excellency, my Lords, Ladies, and Colleagues,—As President of the Royal Institute of British Architects I have the honour of being invited to preside over the work of this the Seventh International Congress of Architects , and on behalf of the Executive Committee I take the earliest opportunity to heartily welcome the distinguished Delegates and Architects who have honoured this country by their presence, and to assure them of our high regard and esteem

I feel sure that the members of the Congress will be gratified to know that His Majesty King Edward VII. has been graciously pleased to be the Patron of the Congress, that the Prince of Wales has consented to be its Honorary President, and that the Royal Family have in other ways shown an interest in our proceedings which has been, and will continue to be, a great incentive and encouragement to us.

The Royal Princess whose kindly and gracious presence we welcome amongst us to-day is not only herself a distinguished sculptor, but has shown also a keen and discriminating appreciation of Art in all its forms   The artistic tastes and interests of the Princess Louise are as well known to our confrères from other lands as they are to us.

Gentlemen, I have every hope that our deliberations will prove of great interest and value, and will tend to the advancement of our beloved art throughout the world   It is by interchange of ideas, comparison of methods, and the statement of experiences under new and changing conditions that that advancement will be assured   These Congresses, therefore, may be expected to bring in their train fresh life and vigour, increased enthusiasm, broader views, and new ideas which cannot fail to benefit the community at large.

I say " community " advisedly, because the fact is beginning to be recognised that Architecture as a fine art is not, or must not any longer be, one of the luxuries of the rich, but is of vital importance to the physical and moral well-being of all sorts and conditions of men, especially in cities and large towns Environment is a tremendous factor in education and development A man's surroundings have enormous power over him, whether for good or for evil, a power that acts continuously, without cessation—almost, we may say, by day and by night This fact is being more and more clearly recognised every day, and efforts, we hope, will be made to introduce a stricter supervision over buildings of every kind, that a better order of things may gradually be created

But here, at the very outset, we are confronted by a popular mis-conception concerning the true nature of Architecture.

In past years public interest has been almost limited to the scientific side of the question, viz , that houses and other buildings should be well built, sound, and wholesome, that drainage and ventilation should be carefully attended to, and other so-called " practical " matters Occasionally, and more frequently of late, a certain amount of ornament and so-called style has been demanded, and this has been thrown in or daubed on afterwards, and the result dignified with the name of Architecture

Such work is not true Architecture at all It is mere building—sound and good perhaps, but still mere building—plus certain ornamental and decorative features Now, if our architecture is to be an elevating and refining influence , if it is to be an enduring power for good , still more, if it is to be a witness to coming generations of earnest purpose and high aspirations, of moral power and intellectual greatness, the artistic element must not be something merely added ; it must interpenetrate and blend with scientific knowledge and experience from the very first.

Architecture is both a science and an art, and the mathematical symbol of the relation between the two is not that for mere addition (+), but for multiplication (×) In other words, Science supplies the facts and the laws which Art takes and presses into the service of noble ideals The scientific and artistic elements in a good building may perhaps to a certain extent be distinguished, but they cannot be separated , they are as inseparably connected as mind and body

The primary motive for all building lies in the practical needs of life, in the demand for shelter and comfort ; but the architect's work calls for a much wider range of thought and purpose than is necessarily implied in such provision If the task entrusted to him is to be honourably as well as adequately fulfilled he must be an artist, with an artist's motives, aspirations, and ideals, as well as a man of practical skill and scientific knowledge. In this way the elementary necessities of life may be made to serve high and noble ends, and much that is elevating and refining may be brought into the lives of the people as a silent but continuous power for good. Their homes, the streets they traverse, and the buildings they work in may all be made, as Lord Leighton once observed, to contain " the fire-germ of living beauty," quickening and invigorating the deep springs of health and joy.

The proceedings of this Congress and the publicity attaching to them will help, we trust, to bring this important subject into greater prominence , and we shall, I am sure, find, as we have often before found, the public Press most ready and most powerful in helping on anything that concerns the common weal

It may perhaps be as well here to inform those of our honoured guests who are not yet aware of the fact that in this country we have no Minister of Fine Art or similar authority to watch over the interests of the public in this respect of the art, as distinguished from the science, of building. We have a " First Commissioner of Works," it is true , but, however able and enlightened he may be, tradition and custom limit his activity and his authority within certain fairly well-defined lines.

There has been, however, of late, amongst the educated portion of the public, a wonderful awakening to the interest and value of Architecture as a fine art. On all hands we discover a receptive spirit, a disposition to inquire, and a readiness to learn something of the mystery of our art— not merely to admire and study its past achievements, but, treating it as a living art, to ascertain its true functions and vital principles   Every- where intelligent men are asking how they may distinguish between good and bad , and asking, too, *why* this is good and that bad

We are taking steps to supply the public with some simple criteria of a general character which may serve as a basis for the formation of a critical taste and sound judgment , and the question of how best to carry this out is a subject that will come before the Congress for consideration and discussion

If we can thus give the public an insight into some of the living prin- ciples of our art—and here I beg to emphasise the word " living "—we shall unlock to them a veritable storehouse of interest and information For no man has a richer field lying before him for exploration and research than the man who takes an intelligent interest in Architecture, who can appreciate its points, and decipher its meaning   Everywhere, at every turn, he finds a new " subject " to exercise his perceptive and reflective faculties upon   Every truly good work will be to him a fund of infor- mation as well as a revelation of character and purpose   He will read the mind of a people in their buildings and understand the social condi- tions that prevailed in each age.   For all true Architecture is instinct with life, the life of its people and of its age.   We may study the thoughts and purposes of past generations, not only in their poetry and their prose, but also in the architectural work that they leave behind them   No historian's verdict is more reliable than that which is written as with a pen of iron in brick and in stone   How much have we learnt of the brilliance of Greece and the majesty of Rome from the monuments of their Architecture that have survived !

So also our buildings tell of our daily life and doings, of our noble aims or our sordid interests, of our broad, large-hearted views or of narrow- minded selfishness   A private residence is an index to the character, tastes, and disposition of its owner   So, too, our public buildings will declare aloud to after generations the ideals and sentiments that govern our municipal and national life.

The educational value and historical interest and importance of Architecture are enhanced by the fact that, unlike Literature, Architecture is cosmopolitan and universal in its language   its great works, its priceless treasures, are open to be known and read of all

Every nation, it is true, has its own accents and its peculiar idioms even in Architecture ; but this is to be counted for a gain rather than a hindrance by the man who visits other lands.   As he travels from one country to another, or even from one city to another, he finds an infinite diversity of expression, throwing an ever-shifting light upon the various aspects and sides of human life and thought and feeling   Many a record of the past, too, is opened to his eyes, speaking of men and manners that have passed away

The study of Architecture may indeed be made one of the most entran- cing of pursuits , but if it is to be delivered from that touch of pedantry, that archæological flavour, that so often clings to it, the student must be brought into contact with living principles   The monuments of the past, as well as the work of to-day, must be read and judged in the light of those principles that hold good for every age and for every nation.

In addressing my brother architects from other lands—and I am proud to see so many distinguished men amongst them—I may venture to point out that our Architecture, like that of other nations, has a distinctive character of its own, being of a severer and graver type than is found elsewhere.

This is partly accounted for by the dull grey atmosphere which so constantly wraps us round, by the comparative rareness of clear and sunny skies, and our generally unfavourable climatic conditions; but I am afraid we must not throw all the responsibility upon Nature.

We are insular in character and disposition—there is no doubt about it—and more so perhaps as individuals than in our corporate life. Every man is his own island—a sort of moated grange, in fact, with the drawbridge habitually raised. We are reserved and apt to shut ourselves up within ourselves In our railway trains, and even in our clubs, we sit apart in silence, or merely throw remarks at one another over the top of the morning paper. We habitually repress our emotions and hide our feelings Naturally, therefore, our buildings also are often stolid, even grim and forbidding in appearance · they lack the charm and brightness which distinguish the Architecture of other and sunnier lands. We hide them away too—in back streets or (if they be in the country) behind high walls and as many trees as we can press into the service

But let me hasten to add that I have a purpose in speaking of these external characteristics of British Architecture, and that is to beg my illustrious confrères from abroad not to stop at the external features, but to pursue their researches a little further, and they will find set forth in our buildings another characteristic of the people of the land they are honouring with a visit. Under a somewhat grave and sedate appearance it will be found that our people possess warm hearts ! Once within the doors of their houses there will be no lack of a heartiness of welcome and a sincerity of goodwill which may be firmly relied upon. The many mansions and other beautiful residences with which our country abounds reflect this deeper element of our hearts and lives, and will be found worthy of your notice

I believe it is generally agreed that our modern domestic buildings present a noteworthy development of our art, and one that is almost peculiar to this country. We cannot show you streets leading to public buildings of such stately character as may be seen and admired in other great cities of Europe, and our public buildings themselves are consequently at a disadvantage.

The new Approach to Buckingham Palace and the Memorial to Queen Victoria—designed by Sir Aston Webb—show what might be done if only such opportunities were more frequently given.

Had Sir Christopher Wren been allowed to carry out his plans for laying out the City after the Great Fire, there would have been no lack of fine streets to show you, or of splendid vistas opening up to view every building of importance. But there was no Minister of Fine Art to turn the scales in favour of an enlightened policy !

Having drawn attention to some of the features and conditions of British Architecture, let me acknowledge, on behalf of my countrymen how much we have learnt from, and how much we have profited by, the many splendid examples of Architecture which are to be found and admired in your respective countries We naturally and instinctively turn to the South for that which is bright and beautiful The warmer temperament of the southern artist is favourable to productive fancy.

We see that the nations amongst whom the love of beauty is a national trait, instinctive and inherited, seek it in all their works, and set forth their national greatness in their public buildings—an element in the education of the people which no Government can afford to despise.

The union of the arts in which we believe the secret of your success to lie is not so advanced amongst us as with you ; but signs are not wanting even here of the growth of a closer bond between them, and architects and sculptors will be found collaborating on a building to present its distinctive purpose with greater clearness and beauty before the eyes of men.   The utilitarian cast of mind, running ever in its one groove, may laugh or even sneer at this , but from a national as well as humanitarian standpoint there can scarcely be a greater mistake than to overlook and neglect the emotional side of man's nature   The greater the advance in civilisation, the more pressing the claim of the emotions of the people to due recognition and well-balanced development on true and right lines   Feats of engineering, appealing to the intellect, astonish but do not move us , but works of beauty, buildings of graceful proportion and appropriate design lift the beholder above the vulgar and commonplace into a higher region, and fill the heart with lofty ideals and pleasurable emotions

The aim and purpose of the Congress is the welfare of the people   This can only be accomplished by raising the ideal both of architects and the public, by setting a higher tone and proposing a nobler end for all work, and thus lifting that which would otherwise be blankly material, utilitarian, and commonplace into the region of the beautiful, the elevating, and the inspiring.

In conclusion, permit me once again to offer you all a heartfelt and most cordial welcome.   I trust that the Congress will be a great success, and that your visit to London will prove both a profitable and an enjoyable one

Vote of Thanks to the Lord Mayor and Corporation

Sir Aston Webb, R A , asked to be allowed to propose a vote of thanks to the Lord Mayor and the Corporation for their great kindness in lending that noble hall in which to hold the inaugural meeting of the Congress   The Guildhall, as many of them knew, was first built in 1211 , it was rebuilt in 1326, and once again in 1411.   It suffered severely from the Great Fire of London in 1666, and once again it was restored.   The building suffered again somewhat severely when George Dance, the architect, added a Gothic front to it.   George Dance was an architect who did most admirable work at the Mansion House, and who also designed Newgate Prison, which had recently ceased to exist and given place to the new buildings of the Central Criminal Court.   The Guildhall had been the scene of many historic ceremonies, the greatest sovereigns of the world and many of England's most distinguished sons having been received in it—and Gog and Magog had looked on at all these ceremonies unmoved !   There was a tradition—he did not know how true it was—that when once Gog and Magog heard the clock strike the hour of one they would come out into that hall ; but at present they remained where they were. It was because of the great traditions and the great associations that the Guildhall had, and with which no modern building could possibly vie, that the Congress had been asked to meet there that day, and he asked the Meeting to pass a most hearty vote of thanks to the Lord Mayor and Corporation for their great kindness and courtesy in allowing them to do so

The vote of thanks having been unanimously agreed to, the Lord Mayor, responding on behalf of the Corporation, said that it was a great pleasure to them to place the hall at the disposal of the Institute for the admirable work which had been inaugurated   He, the Lady Mayoress, and the Sheriffs had unhappily to take their leave in order to attend to other duties, but he hoped to meet many of them at the Mansion House the following evening.

The Lord Mayor and the Sheriffs then retired.

REPORT OF THE SECRETARY OF THE CONGRESS.

Mr W. J. LOCKE, Secretary of the Royal Institute of British Architects and Secretary of the Congress, then read the following report

Your Royal Highness, your Excellencies, my Lord Duke, my Lords,
Ladies, and Gentlemen,—

The Executive Committee has the honour to present to you the
official report of their labours in the form of this programme, supple
mented by a brief summary which it is my duty and privilege to lav
before you as their executive officer

The Permanent International Committee at their meeting in Madrid
at the close of the Sixth International Congress of Architects decided
that the Seventh Congress should take place in London, and that the
Royal Institute of British Architects be invited to undertake the task of
its organisation. Nine representatives of the Royal Institute were
appointed as members of the Permanent International Committee, and
the Royal Institute, having accepted the invitation, appointed six other
representative architects to join the nine and thus form the Executive
Committee of the Congress

The work of organisation began by the Executive Committee asking
the premier architectural societies of the world to issue circulars of pro-
paganda to the architects practising in their respective countries.   By
their generous and loyal help over 25,000 circulars were distributed, the
invitation to join the Congress was printed in every architectural journal.
with the result that practically every practising architect the world over
had the Seventh International Congress brought to his notice

The Executive Committee have departed from tradition in according to
ladies practically full privileges of the Congress at a special subscription

The Committee are proud to record the fact that the number of
members has reached the figure, unprecedented in these Congresses, of
nearly 1,700   Of these, 700 are from foreign European countries, America,
and the British colonies.

The Executive Committee have to mention to their colleagues from
other countries the fact that the British Government stands aloof from
participation in the organisation of Congresses of this kind   It neither
subventions them nor invites foreign Governments to appoint official
delegates   The guarantor of the Congress is the Royal Institute of
British Architects, and foreign Governments have been approached semi-
officially through the independent action of the Executive Committee
acting under the authority of the Royal Institute

The foreign Governments who have in these circumstances appointed
delegates are as follows ·—Belgium, M J J Caluwaers (Président de la
Société Centrale d'Architecture de Belgique) ; Denmark, Etatsraad
Vilhelm Dahlerup ; France, H Daumet, H P. Nénot, and J. M. Poupinel ,
Greece, Nicholas Balanos and Anastase Metaxos; Holland, Joseph Theodore
Cuypers , Hungary, Julius Berezik and Alexandre d'Aigner ; Italy, Mariano
Edoardo Cannizzaro and Commendatore Alfredi d'Andrade , Russia
(Académie Impériale des Beaux-Arts), M le Comte Paul de Suzor and
Léon Bénois , Spain, Richard Velasquez Bosco, Luis Ma Cabello y
Lapiedra, E. M Repulles y Vargas, and F Arbos y Tremanti , Sweden,
Professor J. G Clason and Kaspar Salim ; United States of America, Frank
Miles Day, Francis R Allen, Glenn Brown, George O. Totten, jun ,
William S. Eames, W. L B Jenney, and George B Post. Besides these
Government delegates there are 101 bodies in Great Britain and abroad
who have appointed 159 delegates, and these range from the Teckno-
logforeningen in Sweden to the Institute of Architects of Japan   The
list, whose recital would be tedious, is given in the official programme

The programme of the Congress can be divided into two sections—
work and social intercourse

There are ten subjects to be discussed, carefully chosen by the Executive Committee as subjects of universal importance to architects, without regard to conditions peculiar to any one nation   Over seventy reports on these subjects have been contributed by representatives of every country in Europe and America   The time at the disposal of the Congress will not allow the whole of these papers to be read, and the Executive Committee have had to make a careful selection.   Printed abstracts, however, of all communications are in the hands of every member, and those which are not read will be printed *in extenso* in the *Compte-Rendu* There will be discussions after the reading of the selected papers, and the Committee hope that the result will be an invaluable exchange of thought between the members of the architectural profession of the civilised world.

The opportunities for social intercourse afforded by the Congress are numerous   The following may be specially mentioned.   The Royal Academy are generously giving a reception to the Congress in their galleries to-night at Burlington House   The Lord Mayor is kindly receiving the Congress to-morrow evening   The Royal Institute of British Architects are entertaining the Congress at an evening garden party on Thursday

The Executive Committee have organised visits to many places which they think will be of interest.   The Athenæum, the Arts Club, the National Liberal Club, the Lyceum Club (for ladies), the Art Workers Guild, the Zoological Society, the Royal Botanic Society, the directors of the Austrian Exhibition at Earl's Court, have all offered in their several ways their hospitable welcome to members of the Congress.   There will also be a farewell banquet on Saturday, the 21st.

The Executive Committee therefore venture to hope that the arrangements they have been privileged to make for the instruction and entertainment of the Congress will meet with your approval

In conclusion, I have the honour, on behalf of the Executive Committee, to call upon the representatives of the various countries to reply briefly to the President, after which His Grace the Duke of Argyll will deliver his Inaugural Address.

Replies of Foreign Representatives

Replies by the delegates were made in the alphabetical order of the countries represented *

Herr Otto Wagner, Government Delegate for Austria, said he felt it an honour to greet that august assembly, and on behalf of himself and his fellow-countrymen he expressed his pleasure at the opportunity afforded by his English *confrères* for the discussion of interesting questions, both artistic and scientific, relating to the art of architecture.

Monsieur J J Caluwaers, Government Delegate for Belgium —Votre Altesse Royale, vos Excellences, Monseigneur, mes Lords, Monsieur le Président, Mesdames et Messieurs   J'ai le grand honneur de vous exprimer, au nom du Ministre des Beaux-Arts de Belgique, les vœux les plus sincères pour le succès de ce Congrès   Je salue les membres de la Famille royale, et les différentes autorités qui ont bien voulu donner leur appui aux organisateurs de cette réunion. La haute protection que votre Roi et les membres de la Famille royale ont voulu accorder à nos travaux est une preuve éclatante de l'intérêt porté aux arts et en particulier à l'art architectural   L'histoire est là—et les monuments dont votre beau pays est sillonné parlent pour elle—pour nous prouver que de tout temps, pour la gloire la plus pure du pays, le culte des Beaux-Arts a trouvé le meilleur appui auprès de la Couronne.   Je salue aussi

---

* Verbatim reports of the foreign speeches are given only in those cases where the MS. of the speeches was handed in by the speakers

les eminents confrères de tous pays, accourus ici dans un même but, et je suis persuadé que l'effort réuni de nous tous produira des résultats fructueux pour le plus grand bien des corporations d'architectes et pour le public Au nom de la Société centrale d'Architecture de Belgique, au nom de tous les architectes belges, je formule le vœu le plus cordial, le plus affectueux pour nos confrères du Royaume-Uni ! Nous n'avons dû faire aucun effort pour accourir vers vous, pour répondre à votre appel, et je suis vraiment heureux de dire que les Belges sont nombreux parmi vous, et qu'ils pourront témoigner toute la sympathie qu'ils éprouvent pour vous, et toute l'admiration qu'ils ont pour vos travaux. Avant et après nos séances, nous parcourrons votre belle métropole et une partie du pays , nous pourrons admirer vos palais royaux, vos palais des corporations, vos puissants collèges d'instruction et d'éducation , nous parcourrons vos quartiers neufs, où s'étale avec fierté la prospérité du pays, et où nous pourrons constater que les architectes anglais de nos jours continuent les nobles traditions de leurs devanciers, et que l'art moderne a gardé toute sa beauté, tout son cachet propre, tout son caractère national ! Nous parcourrons aussi vos admirables musées où se trouvent réunies les plus belles créations du monde et où le travailleur peut venir se recueillir, se retremper, dans une atmosphère de sereine beauté !—Au nom de la Société centrale d'Architecture de Belgique, j'adresse un souvenir ému à la mémoire de Waterhouse Nous étions fiers d'avoir son nom inscrit sur la liste de nos membres d'honneur Ses œuvres sont particulièrement connus parmi nous, et nous avions pour son génie, pour sa grande puissance de travail, une réelle admiration.

M. Joseph Th. J Cuypers, Government Delegate for the Netherlands — Votre Altesse Royale, vos Excellences, Monseigneur, Mesdames, Messieurs S'il m'est permis d'occuper votre attention pendant quelques instants, ce n'est que pour donner expression aux sentiments de vive sympathie que nous portons aux Pays-Bas dans l'organisation si vaillamment entreprise de ce VIIe Congrès International des Architectes. Le Gouvernement néerlandais, d'une part, en voulant bien me charger de le représenter dans vos conférences et débats ; les confrères de Hollande, d'autre part, comprennent toute la valeur des liens réciproques qui depuis le seizième siècle ont influencé sur le développement des arts architecturaux et décoratifs dans les Îles Britanniques et dans les Pays-Bas , le caractère des meubles, l'aspect des maisons de campagne, le dessin des jardins en sont la preuve évidente Encore dans le dernier quart du dix-neuvième siècle nous voyons les meilleurs éléments de notre activité architecturale constamment en rapport intellectuel avec l'esprit de renouvellement dans l'art anglais. Voilà autant de points qui nous rapprochent Puissent les auspices sous lesquelles cette noble assemblée si dignement présidée dans le Guildhall de Londres—une des merveilles de l'Europe, la même salle dans laquelle en l'année 1885 notre Roi Guillaume III reçut comme monarque une adresse d'honneur de la Cité—aujourd'hui, le troisième centenaire de la naissance de notre grand Rembrandt—puissent tous ces heureux présages nous stimuler à entreprendre avec ardeur et confiance les travaux artistiques, dans les sentiments d'une bonne confraternité internationale !

Monsieur H Daumet, Government Delegate for France.—Votre Altesse Royale, Votre Grâce, My Lord Maire, Mesdames, Messieurs Après l'honorable Mr. John Belcher, Président de l'Institut royal des Architectes britanniques, et les confrères qui m'ont précédé, en qualité de président des Congrès internationaux des architectes, pour M Nénot, délégué comme moi par M le sous-secrétaire d'État des Beaux-Arts de France et pour M Poupinel, délégué du ministre du commerce et de l'industrie, j'adresse de respectueux hommages à S M. le roi Édouard VII qui a bien voulu accorder son haut patronage au VIIe Congrès international de notre corporation C'est un grand honneur pour les architectes d'obtenir cette nouvelle et royale marque de sollicitude pour l'art qu'ils exercent, ils en sont profondément reconnaissants Modestie à part, ils la croient justifiée : car partout où la civilisation a pénétré et à toutes les époques, de grandes œuvres ont été conçues par les architectes, afin de témoigner de la puissance des États, éterniser les hauts faits de l'histoire, élever des temples, fortifier et embellir les villes, y construire des palais, des édifices pour la diffusion des lettres, des arts et des sciences Depuis les époques les plus reculées, rien de monumental n'a pu être édifié sans le concours des architectes, et avec quelles perfections dans l'antiquité il suffit de visiter le Musée britannique pour le constater On reste frappé d'admiration pour ces immortels maîtres de l'art architectural au temps de Périclès Ils peuvent compter parmi ceux dont les œuvres honorent l'humanité

Herr H MUTHESIUS, Government Delegate for Germany, said that in the name of German architects he returned sincere thanks for the kind invitation which had brought them there and the kind words of welcome addressed to them German architects attached considerable importance to the transactions of the Congress, and they looked forward to getting a greater knowledge of English work and art, and that had induced some of them to accept the invitation to the Congress. They all knew that English architecture was full of interest and merit and of great international importance They knew especially how much the world had to learn from England in domestic architecture, from which ideas were emanating and revolutionising the whole world of architecture, and if he might be allowed to express a wish at the beginning of the Congress, it would be to suggest that foreign representatives should be shown specimens of the best English domestic architecture of the day. He hoped that the Congress would be as great a success in the architectural sense as in the sense of establishing a cordial feeling between all the nations represented there that day.

Monsieur A METAXAS, Government Delegate for Greece.—Permettez-moi de vous exprimer tous les remerciements de mon Gouvernement pour l'honneur qui lui a été fait en l'invitant à se faire représenter à ce Congrès C'est un honneur pour moi d'avoir été chargé de cette représentation. Au nom du Gouvernement hellénique, je souhaite grand succès à ce Congrès international.

Monsieur J. BERCZIK, Government Delegate for Hungary, expressed his appreciation of the honour the Hungarian Government had conferred upon him in appointing him its representative at the Congress, and his heartiest wishes for its success

Professor D'ANDRADE, Government Delegate for Italy, brought the greetings of the Italian Government, and expressed his sense of the honour conferred on him as its representative. He said that the compatriots of Michelangelo and Bramante were looking forward with much pleasure to seeing the work of the English masters. He hoped that the Congress would contribute to the increase of friendship between the nations, no less than to the advancement of art and science

Mr. S CHUJO, Government Delegate for Japan, said it was a great honour to be present and to address the Congress. The Congress was international, and it showed the necessity for the common brotherhood of the art and of the human happiness of the world Japan, like other nations, had its own national architecture, which was very different from the architecture of Western nations, but Western civilisation had brought a change in Japan in many respects, and architecture had to play its part in that change They would watch the growth of architecture in their country, and would strive to influence it in the proper direction. He hoped to see a future Congress in Japan, and to see there all the members of the present Congress !

Senhor VENTURA TERRA, representing Portugal —C'est pour moi

un grand honneur et un grand plaisir de pouvoir prendre la parole dans cette assemblée remarquable et distinguée parce que cela me permet de saluer respectueusement S.A R la Princesse Louise, et Son Excellence Monsieur le Duc d'Argyll. Cela me permet encore de saluer tous les confrères qui prennent part aux travaux du Congrès   Il est toujours agréable d'exprimer ces sentiments et de se trouver parmi vous pour manifester publiquement l'admiration que j'éprouve pour les hautes qualités de ce grand et beau pays qu'est l'Angleterre   Je suis heureux d'espérer que les discussions du Congrès auront pour résultat de propager à l'étranger les bienfaits de la haute civilisation que nous admirons dans ce beau pays   J'espère aussi que les délibérations auront pour résultat de faire bénéficier la civilisation des solutions qui seront données aux questions que votre Congrès se propose d'étudier.

Monsieur ROBERT BÖKER, representing Russia, said he had the honour to convey to the Royal Institute of British Architects the cordial greeting of the Imperial Society of Russia and to return thanks to the Institute for the invitation to attend the Congress   Most respectfully he expressed their profound gratitude to His Majesty the King for consenting to become the President of the Congress, which showed the interest the King took in the progress of their art   He (the speaker) personally appreciated the privilege of meeting so many distinguished architects assembled from all parts of the world to discuss architectural questions of universal importance and interest   He knew from past experience how warm-hearted and sympathetic was the welcome hospitable Englishmen invariably extended to all foreigners, and he could not help feeling impressed by the cordial reception in this the greatest city the world had ever seen   He wished prosperity and long life to the Royal Institute of British Architects

Señor DON VELASQUEZ BOSCO, Government Delegate for Spain, said he found it a most agreeable task to bring the greetings of his society in particular and of his *confrères* in general   He expressed a hope that the Congress would increase the friendship and kindliness which had so long existed between the two countries

Professor CLASON, Government Delegate for Sweden —Délégué par le Gouvernement suédois, je désire, en son nom, au nom de mes confrères, aussi bien qu'en mon nom personnel, remercier l'Institut Royal des Architectes britanniques d'avoir bien voulu nous inviter à ce Congrès international   Je ne puis laisser passer ce moment exceptionnellement favorable sans exprimer à l'architecture britannique les sentiments de sympathie et d'admiration pour l'habilité artistique et la probité parfaite avec lesquelles les architectes anglais savent exercer leur métier   En disant cela, je suis certain de résumer les sentiments de tous mes confrères de Suède. L'architecture britannique moderne porte l'empreinte d'études profondes de l'architecture ancienne   Elle est frappée au coin de la science et de l'art historiques   Je n'hésite pas à dire qu'un congrès organisé par des architectes animés d'un pareil esprit ne peut manquer d'être un grand succès et que les décisions qu'il va prendre auront une portée vraiment internationale

INAUGURAL ADDRESS BY THE DUKE OF ARGYLL

The DUKE OF ARGYLL   Your Royal Highness, Your Excellencies, Ladies, and Gentlemen,—I shall emulate the brevity of the foreign delegates, whom—and the Princess associates herself with me—I most cordially welcome, and I hope they will spend a very pleasant time in England. The Princess has never been so greatly daring as to make designs and become the architect of any great building, but it has been her pride to interest herself in the sister art of sculpture.   It is a very great pleasure to converse with an architect, for in doing so one has a feeling as if one

were building a house—one of the joys of this life. It is a joy if we build
it with our own gold, and so much the greater joy if we can build it with
one's friend's gold; and if we can dip our hand into the Treasury and
build it with the money of the public purse, that is the supremest joy of
all! Architecture is a great art, one which allows of no shirking. There
is no such thing as impressionist architecture It is an art which is
thorough, real, and earnest. I do not think we need be ashamed of what
we can show our friends from abroad in the shape of English architecture,
notably perhaps in church architecture One of the greatest of American
generals, when asked what he liked best in his recollections of the old
country, said, after a pause : " The seven lancet windows of York Minster "
But in other buildings I think we can hold our own, as we do in this
Guildhall, and under the shadow of the fabrics erected by Wren and by
Barry We must, however, remember the country from which so much
of our inspiration comes—namely, Italy It is, after all, not so very
long since we were a province of Rome, and beneath the surface of this
country, if we were to dig down, there would be found numerous fragments
of Samian pottery and other indications of the Italian people from whom
we get our inspirations The Romans, on their side, were indebted to the
colonists who came to them from Egypt and also from Greece When
we think of Italy, we must think of the magnificent mediæval fortresses
and fortress-houses in Genoa, in Florence, and in Rome And then,
again, when we think of France, let us think of those marvellous châteaux
on the Loire and elsewhere Let us think, again, of the triumphs of Spain,
of the Escurial, and of other magnificent buildings, not to speak of those
in the Low Countries nearer home. In the future it may be surmised
that in our domestic architecture we shall be compelled by our motor-
omnibuses and our traction-engines to go back to a more ancient system
of architecture—namely, rooms within a court. And there is another
great development which I do not think has been alluded to—in
buildings which could not strictly be called architecture—viz in
the curious fabrics arising here and in America—buildings in a steel
cradle We have had experience of the disastrous effect of earthquakes
on buildings recently in San Francisco These iron-frame structures
seem to stand earth tremors better than others , it may be that buildings
will be built like the earth itself, with rock and with steel running through
it, and buildings of this kind may become a feature of future architecture.
In conclusion I should like to express the hope that we shall meet the
present company again—in another country if not in this.

Mr BELCHER then proposed a vote of thanks to H.R H the Princess
Louise and His Grace the Duke of Argyll for their kind interest in the
Congress. They were grateful, he said, to the Princess for her thought
and interest and sympathy in architecture as a fine art, they were
also grateful to the Duke for presiding, and for the address which
he had just delivered
The vote of thanks having been heartily agreed to,
The DUKE replied, and mentioned that, by the courtesy of the Lord
Mayor and Corporation, the Guildhall Art Gallery, containing a valuable
collection of works of Belgian painters, was thrown open to members of
the Congress
The proceedings then terminated.
At the close of the proceedings the foreign representatives were
successively presented to the Princess, who shook hands with each of
them.

EVENING RECEPTIONS AND FÊTE.

Soirée at Burlington House.

At the reception held in honour of the Congress by the President and members of the Royal Academy at Burlington House on the evening of the opening day some three thousand guests were present, and were afforded the opportunity of viewing under the most agreeable conditions the Royal Academy Exhibition of the year's paintings, sculptures, &c The staircases were beautifully decorated with palms and flowers, and the band of the Royal Artillery, under Cavaliere Zavertal, was in attendance, and played in the Lecture Room. The guests were received by Sir Edward Poynter, P R.A. The Duke of Argyll again honoured the Congress with his presence at the function

Conversazione at the Mansion House

On Tuesday evening, 17th July, members of the Congress were the guests of the Right Hon the Lord Mayor of London, Sir W. Vaughan Morgan, Bart, at the Mansion House The guests on arriving were received and welcomed by the Lord Mayor and Lady Mayoress, attended by some of the principal City dignitaries in their robes of state. A numerous and distinguished company had been invited to meet the visitors, and the scene presented in the noble Egyptian Hall and Ball-room was a strikingly brilliant one Some vocal music was excellently rendered by Misses Macleod and Cook, and Messrs. Sidwell Jones and Rainger, and selections of instrumental music were performed at intervals during the evening by Herr Stanislaus Wurm's Orchestra.

The Institute Garden Party.

On Thursday, 19th July, the Institute entertained the Congress at an evening fête held in the Gardens of the Royal Botanic Society The President, supported by several members of the Institute Council, received the visitors at the entrance of the large conservatory, near the Broad Walk, from 9 to 10 P M. The gardens were brilliantly illuminated with limelights and beautifully decked with Chinese lanterns swung from tree to tree Particularly effective were the innumerable tiny lamps glittering amidst the dark foliage of the trees.

By kind permission of Colonel Fenwick, the magnificent band of the Royal Horse Guards Blue played in the gardens throughout the entire evening under the direction of Mr. Manuel Bilton. A compliment much appreciated by the foreign guests was the performance by the band of the National Anthems of the various countries represented at the Congress In the Conservatory a selection of music was rendered by the "Ladies' Salon Quintet," a piano and a quartet of strings played by lady artists led by Miss Maud Aldis A further attraction in the gardens was the pastoral play "A Midsummer Night's Dream," performed by Mr. Patrick Kirwan's troupe of "Idyllic Players," the Singing Fairies being personated by Messrs Bellew and Stock's Choir. Refreshments were served in the marquees on the East Lawn of the Gardens.

During the evening a pleasing little ceremony took place in the Committee-room of the Gardens. Assembled in the room were Mr Belcher and some members of the Institute Council, when M Bonnier (President of the French "Société des Architectes diplômés par le Gouvernement"), attended by several distinguished colleagues, advanced and presented

Mr Belcher with a replica of the beautiful medal of the Société, as a gift from that body to the Institute in memory of the occasion   On the obverse of the medal was inserted a small panel bearing the inscription: " A l'Institut Royal des Architectes Britanniques —VII· Congrès International des Architectes à Londres 1906 "   The gift was accompanied by a graceful little address in French , and in conclusion M. Bonnier, having referred to Mr Belcher's services to architecture and to the debt of gratitude they owed him for his presidency of the Congress, went on to ask his acceptance of the position of Corresponding Member of the Société des Architectes diplômés, to which the Société had unanimously elected him   Mr Belcher replied, thanking the Société and accepting the medal on behalf of the Institute, and expressing his gratification and high appreciation of the honour the Société had conferred upon him in electing him Member of their distinguished body

---

VISITS AND EXCURSIONS

The various excursions arranged for the Congress included visits to Hatfield House, by the kind consent of the Marquis of Salisbury ; Hampton Court Palace ; Windsor Castle and Buckingham Palace Gardens, by His Majesty's gracious consent ; Westminster Abbey , the works of the building contractors, Messrs. Holloway, and the potteries of Messrs Doulton , St. Paul's Cathedral, the Temple, St. Bartholomew's, and the Institute of Chartered Accountants , Oxford and Cambridge (all-day visits), the Tower of London, Victoria and Albert Museum and Royal College of Science, Bridgewater House, Greenwich Hospital, the Houses of Parliament, and the Roman Catholic Cathedral of Westminster.   The following reports are mainly contributed by the gentlemen in charge of the various visits.

HATFIELD.—Tuesday, 17th July.

A large party of members, numbering between 500 and 600, journeyed to Hatfield by special train from King's Cross.   Brilliant weather favoured the visit.

The party was received at the entrance of Hatfield House by Colonel Eustace Balfour, who very kindly gave a short historical account of the mansion, pointing out various features of interest   The members were then divided into batches of about thirty and conducted through the principal rooms

The beautiful gardens were seen to great advantage, and were probably appreciated quite as much as the house

Other points of interest were the old banqueting hall with its fine open-timber roof, now used as a stable ; and the adjoining church, &c.

An ample tea was provided in two or three of the hotels and inns in the town, after which the party returned to town, arriving about 6 30.

HENRY T. HARE.

HAMPTON COURT —Tuesday, 17th July.

The Hampton Court visit was attended by nearly 300 members, and, under the able guidance of Messrs. Maule and Chart and their assistants, the party were enabled to see a very great deal of the beautiful building in a short time, also to have tea at the riverside hotels in time to catch the train back   The visitors seemed most to enjoy the splendid collection of pictures in the Georgian rooms and the grounds with their charming vistas and well-kept beds and lawns.   HENRY TANNER, JUN.

BUCKINGHAM PALACE GARDENS —Wednesday, 18th July.

This visit seemed to be one of the most popular of all, as between 450 and 500 members of the Congress were present, and the crowd waiting in Grosvenor Place for the opening of the gates must have been a surprise to passers-by, who no doubt thought that a royal procession was about to pass.

The King was not at the Palace, but the Queen was in residence, though nobody was fortunate enough to see her. The members were not admitted into the building, but all seemed to enjoy the stroll through the gardens very much, to judge by the amount of urging that the tail-end of the party needed to get them to the exit, which was at the front of the Palace, where 'buses were waiting to take them to Westminster Abbey.   HENRY TANNER, JUN

MESSRS DOULTON & Co's WORKS —Wednesday, 18th July

The works of Messrs Doulton & Co., Limited, are on the southern bank of the Thames, adjoining Lambeth Palace, the seat of the Archbishop of Canterbury They cover an area of some acres, the different sections being devoted to the separate manufactures of architectural terra-cotta, sanitary stonewares, sanitary fittings in metal and wood, crucibles, household pottery, &c The section of the Lambeth Works open for inspection comprised the showrooms, the studios, and the factories for stoneware and architectural terra-cotta

The visit was attended by some 350 members of the Congress, including many ladies, and great interest was shown in the various processes which were seen in operation. Here was the bench where the potter working at his wheel takes a shapeless lump of clay and, with a dexterity more wonderful than any sleight-of-hand, moulds the material to the shape of close-necked jug of sturdy proportions or slender vase with delicate rim , while in another part of the building were women applying moulded ornament in relief or laying on the pigments that when burnt produce those rich and varied colours which distinguish the " Doulton " ware

To architects not the least attractive part of the visit was the opportunity afforded of not only seeing the methods adopted in the design and execution of wall decorations such as painted tile-panels, but also some of the latest refinements in the application of sanitary science to hospital and domestic uses

In the course of the route taken through the factories, a certain number of ware kilns were seen, some being filled and others emptied of their contents. The largest kilns take about fourteen days to " set and draw " Here each week some thirty miles of stoneware pipes are turned out, 2,000 tons of clay used, and 1,700 tons of coal consumed.

Messrs. Doulton, not unmindful of the comfort of their visitors, had provided tea and light refreshments, which were much appreciated on that hot afternoon in July. The members returned by motor omnibus to the northern side of the river, the visit being completed at about 6 P M
                                                        A MARYON WATSON

MESSRS HOLLOWAY BROTHERS (LIM.) —Wednesday, 18th July.

The inspection of these premises at Belvedere Road, despite simultaneous attractions at Lambeth, was well patronised, and the members who availed themselves of Messrs Holloway Brothers' hospitality were amply rewarded.

Entertained to tea on arrival the visiting party split up into small sections, and under the leadership of the members of the staff made a tour through the shops and yard In some cases, oblivious of the surrounding industry, the guests wandered along the wharf and admired the beautiful river prospect, with perhaps a thought for municipal palaces In the yard itself the moulding machines, rubbing tables, and powerful stone-cutting saws attracted much attention , while as far as the shops were concerned it was interesting to observe how the foreign members crowded round an example of a sash-window, which was repeatedly lowered and raised for their edification, and before leaving its fascinations quite a number of window-cords were chopped up for presentation purposes and removed as souvenirs

The complete lesson in building construction to be learnt on these works accounted for the difficulty in persuading the members to leave at six o'clock, and it was only on the positive assurance that the last motor was beginning to throb its departure that they reluctantly submitted to the kind offices of a gentleman armed with a clothes-brush !

J MacLaren Ross

Windsor Castle —Thursday, 19th July

So great was the gathering at Paddington Station that a relief train, in addition to the special train, was required to convey the members of the Congress to Windsor. The two trains arrived at Windsor within a few minutes of each other, and the party proceeded at once to the Castle

The admirable arrangements which had been made at the Castle to deal with so large a gathering made the visit a particularly enjoyable one

The members of the Congress were conducted through the gorgeous State apartments, where the valuable collection of old masters was much appreciated and the beautiful carvings by Grinling Gibbons greatly admired In rapt attention and interest the party were conducted from the State Ante-Room through the Rubens Room, the Council Chamber, the King's Closet, the Queen's Audience Chamber, the Queen's Presence Chamber, and through the Great Library into the Guard Chamber, and thence on to the Terrace The gorgeous sumptuousness of these royal and historic apartments has a living interest which apparently appealed most strongly to the representatives of our Colonies and republican countries

After the lovely view had been admired from the Terrace the company proceeded to St. George's Chapel The fascination of the choir was irresistible It is here that Divine service is held at the ceremony of installing the Knights of the Garter, and the helmets and banners of the living knights hang over the stalls

The visit here, as perhaps elsewhere in the Palace, was too hurried

Most managed to get some tea before returning to London, which was reached in time to allow members to prepare for the reception at the President's party at the Royal Botanical Gardens in the evening.

George Hubbard.

St. Paul's Cathedral, the Temple, St Bartholomew's, and the Institute of Chartered Accountants —Thursday, 19th July.

The party, which numbered about thirty, assembled at the west steps of St. Paul's Cathedral at 2.30 p m , and were received by the President Archdeacon Sinclair conducted us round the Cathedral, and gave a lucid description of the various features, including the Crypt and the Whispering Gallery, the latter being of exceptional interest

After spending an hour in the Cathedral we proceeded by motor 'bus to the Temple Church, where we were received by the Master of the Temple, who gave an interesting account of the history of the church, and afterwards conducted us over the halls of the Temple.

The next visit was to the Church of St. Bartholomew the Great, Smithfield, where the party were met by Mr. Alfred Webb, one of the churchwardens, and brother to Sir Aston Webb, R A., who recently restored the church

G

On the way to the Institute of Chartered Accountants we stopped for a few minutes at Winchester House and Electra House, both of which were designed by the President, who explained any details upon which information was asked

Finally we arrived at the Institute of Chartered Accountants, where Mr. Belcher conducted the party over the building. This proved to be one of the most interesting and instructive visits of a very busy afternoon

An expression of thanks is due to the Chief Commissioner of City Police, who provided the services of Detective Constable Nicholls, whose assistance was most useful with regard to the traffic.

C. E Hutchinson

KENSINGTON PALACE AND DORCHESTER HOUSE.—Thursday, 19th July.

Sir John Taylor met the members in the Broad Walk, Kensington Gardens, and on the way to the Palace conducted them through the Orangery, which is a perfect specimen of garden architecture designed by Sir Christopher Wren, with some internal wood carving by Grinling Gibbons.

The party were then taken over the Palace by Sir John, whose remarks were very interesting, particularly so as all the restoration was done under his superintendence some seven years back   After going though the various rooms (which in some instances were perhaps more interesting from an historical than an architectural point of view, although there is some very fine oak panelling and more of Gibbons's excellent carving) the party proceeded through the quaint courtyard past that portion of the Palace in the occupation of the Duke and Duchess of Argyll, round the exterior of the building   A little garden alcove, evidently Wren's work, was much admired, as was also the statue of our late Queen, designed by her talented daughter H R H. Princess Louise

Thence the party proceeded in motor omnibuses to Dorchester House, where they had a most enjoyable time   The American Ambassador and Mrs Whitelaw Reid kindly received the members, and their Excellencies' hospitality was greatly appreciated. The marble staircase and fine suite of rooms, with their priceless collection of pictures and furniture, were greatly admired, including the Caryatid chimney-piece designed by the late Alfred Stevens.

The members were able to take their own time looking through this mansion, which was designed by Lewis Vulliamy in the style of the Italian Renaissance   Its collection of pictures includes examples of the work of Rembrandt, Rubens, Paul Potter, Cuyp, Claude, Hobbema, and other eminent masters

SEPTIMUS WARWICK.

ROYAL COLLEGE OF SCIENCE AND VICTORIA AND ALBERT MUSEUM, Friday, 20th July.

Some fifty members visited these buildings, assembling at 3 o'clock at the College of Science, where they were met by Sir Aston Webb, R A , under whose guidance the various buildings were inspected   Sir Aston Webb first took the party round the College of Science, explaining the special points of construction for ensuring freedom from vibration in the physics laboratories, and pointing out that, while chemical students as they advanced in proficiency moved higher up in the building for the sake of better light, physics students began at the top of the building and descended to the ground as they advanced in the classes, as what they required above all things was a solid foundation and freedom from disturbance by vibration. The upper story of the physics department showed the only wooden roof in the building, steel being avoided here on account of its disturbance of experiments in electricity and magnetism   The roof is of sequoia wood, which has been largely used in the building,

and looks very well A gallery has been constructed along the centre
of the roof framing, to afford an opportunity for pendulum experiments.
In regard to the main staircase, the architect drew attention to the fact
that the centre well had been floored over at each level, instead of leaving
the staircase hall open to the ceiling , the architectural effect might suffer,
but the open staircase hall would have been noisy, whereas the construction
of a floor at each level not only prevented this, but also gave the students
a convenient place on each floor to assemble when necessary. After
looking at the exterior of the building from the opposite side of the road,
the party proceeded down Exhibition Road and round by Thurloe Square,
in order to get a view of the portion of the front of the Victoria
and Albert Museum from which the scaffolding is now uncovered. The
architecture from that point looks very bright and sparkling in effect,
and the portrait sculpture in niches comes out admirably. The niches
in the east portion of the building are filled with portrait statues of eminent
architects ; those in the corresponding position on the other side of the
façade are to represent sculptors , statues of painters are to fill the centre
portion, and statues of craftsmen are to occupy the niches on the return
front towards Exhibition Road On these works sixteen among the
most able of the youngest sculptors of the day have been employed,
each sculptor taking two figures. An important point in regard to these
statues is that the stone out of which they are carved has been built
into and bonded to the walls, and the carving then executed *in situ*,
so that there will never be any trouble from the failure of cramps and the
possible danger of the falling-out of a figure in consequence The party
then entered the building, which of course is at present only in a shell
state inside , but by reference to a large plan displayed in the centre hall
Sir Aston explained the arrangements of the new portion of the building.
On entering the central hall the spectator has the whole length of the
building visible to him to right and left along the western and eastern
courts. The original fan shape of the plan had been departed from when
the architectural courts were built with an axis placed at right angles to the
line of Cromwell Road at that point , and this occasioned the special
treatment of the plan of the front façade, in order to keep the western
portion at right angles with Exhibition Road, and at the same time
to have the eastern portion at right angles to the axis of the architectural
courts. Care had been taken, in setting out the plan, to provide for
vistas which might lead up to important works of art The West Central
Court and the East Central Court have been planned in a basilica form,
with side aisles divided off by columns, the aisles being finished with a
cross-vault ceiling, the intention being to place here works of ecclesiastical
art in a surrounding somewhat suggestive of a church. There will be
no elaborate decoration, however, as the principle throughout the treatment of the interior is that the exhibited works are to be the decoration,
and that the building is only, as it were, a case to contain them. The
walls are all to be lined internally with Cranham bricks, which, while
sufficiently hard, will admit nailing into for the fixing-up of such smaller
works or cases as may be hung to the wall. In passing through the
building, Sir Aston pointed out that the large arches which form partial
architectural divisions, such as those across the western and eastern courts,
and those in the entrance-hall, are all of the same centres and dimensions
so as to give a note of unity to the principal features of the interior After
traversing the principal parts of the building, the visitors were invited
to a tea provided in the room adjoining the main refreshment-room of the
old buildings, when a member expressed, on behalf of those present,
their thanks to Sir Aston Webb for his invitation and for his lucid and
interesting descriptions.

G 2

Tower of London —Friday, 20th July

Notwithstanding the counter-attractions of Oxford and Cambridge, a fair number of members visited the Tower of London on Friday morning to take advantage of the special privileges the occasion afforded of being shown over various parts of the buildings not usually open to the public

Every facility for this purpose had been provided by the Chief Con stable, to whom grateful thanks are due

The party, having inspected St John's Chapel, assembled on the roof of the White Tower   Here Lord Dillon, the Curator of the Tower Armouries, delivered a short but very interesting address, and by the aid of plans and sections explained the buildings, tracing their history and use, especially of the White Tower   After his Lordship had drawn attention to the chief specimens of armour to be seen in the Tower, and the various characteristics of each, the party divided into groups, and each group, accompanied by a Yeoman warder, made a tour of inspection of various parts, ending up with the Wakefield Tower and Crown Jewels

The Tower Bridge was then visited, and proved a highly satisfactory ending to the morning's sight-seeing

Through the courtesy of the City Surveyor, Mr Sidney Perks, a minute inspection of the machinery for working the bascules was possible Accompanied by the resident engineer, Mr Gass, a complete tour was made of the bridge, not only to the high level, but also as low down as the bed of the river   The various operations for lifting the bascules, each of which weighs some 1,100 tons, were described and seen at work—an object-lesson in hydraulics those present are not likely to forget

T P Figgis

Oxford —Friday, 20th July

On Friday the programme for the Congress included visits to Oxford and Cambridge Universities   Fortunately the weather continued to be most favourable   About five hundred gathered at Paddington, where a special train was in readiness at ten o'clock   Oxford was reached by 11 35, and here the four sections into which the large party were divided separated.   Each group was provided with a separate programme showing its own special route   The sections were led—one by Messrs Reginald Blomfield, A R A , and H C Corlette, and the others by Messrs. E P Warren, C Barry Cleveland, Paul Waterhouse, and Charles Bone   These were helped very much in every way by the unfailing courtesy of all the visitors

After a pleasant morning spent among the various colleges, luncheon was provided in the halls of Magdalen, Exeter, and Balliol, and at the Randolph Hotel   In each case the visitors were most hospitably entertained

The entire party assembled at Magdalen afterwards, where there was a reception by the Provost   After being shown through the more interesting parts of the college the visitors saw the gardens, which are at their best at this season   These latter seemed greatly to delight the foreign guests, and altogether this typical college excited great admiration

After this the several sections proceeded to the brakes, and continued the visits as arranged on their respective programmes

In every case the kindness with which the visitors were received at the various colleges, and shown over the buildings and gardens by some members of the college, was most keenly appreciated.   This ready hospitality was acknowledged with many hearty thanks in the speeches made before the several luncheon parties separated, and by individual acknowledgment on every hand during the day   To Mr. Charles Bone is especially due the thanks of the whole party, for it would have been impossible to arrange for the comfort of so many had it not been for the skill in detail of organisation and the great amount of time and energy he devoted to the success of the Oxford visit   H C Corlette

CAMBRIDGE —Friday, 20th July

On Friday a large party from the Congress visited Cambridge   Though the morning was dull and threatening, the first arrivals made their appearance at St Pancras nearly an hour before the train was due to leave, and until the moment of departure—nearly twenty minutes late—more members continued to arrive   Luckily for us, the weather cleared during the journey, and we drove down to the Senate House in bright sunshine. Here we were received by the Master of Trinity, acting for the Vice-Chancellor, who was unfortunately away from Cambridge.   The foreign delegates were presented to him, and he then delivered a short but characteristic address of welcome   We then proceeded down Trinity Street, where one or two old house-fronts came in for a good deal of notice, to the great gate of Trinity   Dr. Cunningham received us here, and conducted the party over the college, showing us, among other things, the early front of the buildings facing the bowling green, lately discovered and restored, the chapel, kitchens, and hall, and so along the famous lime tree avenue to the Fellows' Garden, looking its best in the sunshine   Then the party drifted towards lunch, a large number visiting Caius *en route* , and divided into three, the largest number, with the President and the Master of Trinity, going to King's, and smaller parties to Clare and Trinity Hall

After lunch we reassembled in King's Chapel, where the Provost explained the history and origin of the building and the college   Speaking in French for the benefit of the numerous French and Belgians among the party, the Provost said —

"La Chapelle de King's College est le seul de nos bâtiments qui ait été achevée en conformité avec les projets de notre fondateur, le roi Henri VI.   C'est le roi même qui a posé la première pierre de cet édifice, le jour de la fête de S. Jacques, 25 juillet 1446 (il y a juste 460 ans)   Grâce aux guerres civiles si désastreuses qui désolaient notre pays, la maçonnerie du bâtiment n'a pu être achevée avant l'an 1515   Encore vingt ans et les vitraux et les boiseries étaient en place   Le roi Henri VI a donc commencé la construction   Le roi Richard III y a contribué   Le roi Henri VII à la fin de ses jours a repris l'ouvrage interrompu , c'est lui qui a complété la construction en pierre   C'est au roi Henri VIII que nous devons nos vitraux et la plupart des boiseries   La chapelle ne devait pas être isolée comme on la voit   Elle aurait dû être liée avec des bâtiments constituant une grande cour quadrangulaire, de sorte que, vue aujourd'hui, sa régularité est excessive. Quelques mots seulement sur autant de pointes frappantes.   Comme construction on trouve des ressemblances entre la chapelle et la magnifique basilique de Sainte-Cécile d'Albi   Même absence de bas-côtés, même disposition de chapelles entre les contreforts   Les blasons qu'on voit sur les contreforts et qui revêtent les murs de la nef sont ceux d'Henri VII, non pas d'Henri VI. La grande voûte selon le projet du fondateur était destiné à recevoir un coloris très éclatant   les nervures dorées, les clefs de voûte peintes, le fond bleu.   Les vitraux datent des années 1515 à 1534   Quatre étaient l'ouvrage d'un certain Barnard Flower, peintre-verrier du roi.   On compte parmi ce nombre le deuxième, au-dessus de la porte du nord, et celui aussi qui est maintenant sous réparation   Les ouvriers des autres étaient domiciliés à Londres   Les noms de quelques-uns paraissent être flamands, mais la plupart en sont anglais   L'ouvrage tout entier fut fait à Londres.   Les sujets des vitraux sont tirés de l'histoire de la Sainte Vierge, de notre Seigneur et des Apôtres   Dans la plupart des fenêtres on voit en bas les événements du Nouveau Testament et en haut des scènes typiques tirées du Vieux Testament.   La série rappelle vivement les tapisseries de la Chaise-Dieu en Haute-Loire

" *Les Boiseries* —Le jubé qui porte le monogramme de la malheureuse

reine d'Henri VIII Anne Boleyn date de 1532 à 1536. Le soubassement
des stalles est de la même époque Les armoiries furent ajoutées en 1633.
Les dais, exceptés ceux du côté du jubé, étaient faits environ 1675–1680.
Le buffet d'orgues est en partie du temps d'Henri VIII, mais la plupart
fut posée en 1606 "

Then occurred the one variation from the printed programme that
had been distributed , instead of picking up the brakes again at the gate
of King's, the party walked along Queen's Lane, and through Queen's
College, where the delightful Cloister Court came in for a full measure
of praise, and so over the geometrical bridge to the garden gate, where the
brakes were waiting to drive us along the Backs. Coming to the back
gate of St. John's, we walked through the courts, and were shown the
library, combination room, and chapel, and so came again to the brakes,
which were waiting for us at the Round Church The first two or three
brakes, getting away rather ahead of the others, made a round through
Downing Street to see the new science buildings ; the others went straight
up St Andrew's Street and Regent Street to the station, where the refresh-
ment rooms coped more or less successfully with the heavy demands for
tea   That the arrangements worked so smoothly throughout was mainly
due to Mr. W. M. Fawcett, who managed all the preparations at Cambridge ;
to Messrs. Cook's representative, and to the co-operation of a large number
of the English members, who were always ready to help in any way that
was necessary.   G. F. Blackburne Daniell.

Greenwich Hospital.—Saturday, 21st July

About 250 members paid a visit to Greenwich Hospital   The journey
was made by river, and a special steamer conveyed the party to Greenwich

They were met by Mr. A. L. Perfect, Civil Engineer for the Admiralty
in the Greenwich District, and Mr. Edgar A Hawkins, A R I B A., of the
Admiralty, who had most thoughtfully provided a large-scale site plan of the
Hospital.   Mr. Hawkins, before proceeding to conduct the members round,
gave them a very interesting description of the buildings and their history

A visit was first paid to the chapel ; after this the Queen Anne's quarter
was seen, where the visitors were most interested in the old crypt to the
church of the Palace of Placentia   After walking round the buildings
and through the courts to see the elevations of the various blocks, the
Painted Hall was visited, the members being especially interested in the
paintings and the pictures.   By the courtesy of the authorities, the party
were allowed to inspect the collection of original architectural drawings,
some of them being by Sir Christopher Wren   They then visited the
School with its various buildings, and also the Queen's house.   The old
Ship in the Forecourt was viewed with great interest

Time did not allow the visitors to walk through the park to the Obser-
vatory, and after partaking of tea at the Ship tavern the party returned
again by boat to Charing Cross.   Not the least interesting part of the
afternoon was the journey up and down the river, which enabled our
visitors to see many buildings of interest and also the busy life of the river
                                                   F Dare Clapham

Houses of Parliament and Westminster Hall.—Saturday, 21st July.

On the occasion of the visit to the Houses of Parliament the buildings
were closed to the general public—a circumstance peculiarly favourable
for the inspection by a body of architects The members of the Congress—
some 300 in number—assembled at the Victoria Tower, and, passing into
the Palace, were met at the head of the broad stairway from the Norman
Porch by the State and Office of Works officials. An announcement

was made that Captain Butler, Yeoman Usher of the Black Rod, was present on behalf of the Lord Great Chamberlain, by whose permission the visit had been arranged, also that Sir Henry Tanner, I S O, principal architect of H M Office of Works; Mr. J. B. Westcott, M V.O, architect in charge of the Houses of Parliament, Mr Patey, resident engineer, and the Clerk of Works, Mr. Ridge, each with a staff of assistants, were there to render any services that might conduce to the usefulness and interest of the visit   After a formal introduction of the Congress the visitors entered upon the tour of the Palace.   Captain Butler, assisted by Mr Williams, Superintendent of the House of Lords, explained the many interesting features of the various chambers and apartments   The visitors passed through the King's Robing-room to the Royal gallery, the scene of many now almost historic pageants, thence through the Princes' Chamber, in which the portraits of the wives of Henry VIII were seen   Entry was then made to the House of Lords   The Upper Chamber appeared to have a piquant interest for our republican and democratic visitors.   The Throne was uncovered, and the "Woolsack" and the various sections of the chamber occupied by the princes and peers of the realm were pointed out, and then a move was made to the Central Hall. The famous "Moses" fresco by Herbert and those not less beautiful by Cole, in the Commons' corridor were viewed *en route* to the Commons' Lobby, and then the "House" itself was entered.   The seating accommodation for 670 members was evidently a matter of much wonderment to our foreign visitors, in view of the fact that one section of those present, some 150 in number, alone appeared to fill the House   After a tour of the division lobbies a move was made to the interesting fan-vaulted corridors, used as cloak-rooms by the members of the House, thence to the crypt of St Stephen's Chapel, and the Congress had at last come upon the much-looked-for "antique."   The crypt, originally known as the Chapel of St Mary in the Vaults, many years in building, was finished about 1350, in the reign of Edward III.   All that now remains of the original St. Stephen's Chapel is still in excellent preservation, the decoration, of course, is modern   Westminster Hall now demanded the attention of the Congress, full as it is of its own grandeur and of many historic associations. Here Sir Henry Tanner sketched a short history of Westminster Hall, drew attention to interesting features, and recalled the dates of building There now remained to be accomplished a visit to the cool shades of the Terrace by the river, and the route thereto through the many internal courts disclosed abundant evidence of the skill that Barry bestowed on every part and detail of his great work   Throughout the visit Captain Butler and all officially connected with the Palace of Westminster afforded the Congress every reasonable facility and the fullest information   The work of interpretation to the foreign delegates was effected by the willing help of Mr C L Veale and Mr. W H. David, of H.M. Office of Works It seemed to be the opinion of the members of the Congress that the visit to the Palace of Westminster had proved most interesting and successful, certainly it was evident that the foreign delegates had found much to admire in the national monuments of which all English-speaking races are very proud. SYDNEY B BEALE

BRIDGEWATER HOUSE.—Saturday, 21st July

The visit to Bridgewater House, by the kind permission of the Earl of Ellesmere, proved to be a very popular one, upwards of three hundred members and others going over the house in the course of the morning. Bridgewater House, erected in 1848, from the designs of the late Sir Charles Barry, is in itself interesting as a good specimen of modern English architecture   In the centre of the house is a large hall, surrounded, on the upper floor, by an arcaded and richly decorated gallery.

The chief attraction, however, is the fine collection of pictures by
Raffaelle, Titian, Nicholas Poussin, Rembrandt, Velasquez, and many
others   By the extreme kindness of Lord Ellesmere, the members of
the Congress were enabled to see everything, even in the private rooms.

G   F.   COLLINSON

International Permanent Committee : Second Meeting.

THE final meeting of the International Permanent Committee was held
on Saturday, 21st July, in the rooms of the Institute, 9 Conduit Street
The following report of the proceedings has been kindly contributed by
M Poupinel, Secretary of the Permanent Committee .—

Présidence de M   H Daumet, Président du Comité permanent,
assisté de M John Belcher, Vice-Président, Président du VIIᵉ Congrès.

Ont signé la feuille de présence MM Francis Allen, Ch Bartaumieux,
John Belcher, Louis Bonnier, Caluwaers, M Cannizzaro, Alcide Chaussé,
Gustave Clason, Dahlerup, H Daumet, W. S Eames, Alex. Graham,
Georges Harmand, A Helmer, W. J Locke, H Muthesius, H P Nénot,
H Peschl, J. M Poupinel, Repullès y Vargas, Salm G Bzn, John Slater,
J. Stubben, V Terra, G O Totten, Urioste y Velada, R. Velasquez Bosco,
F de Vestel, Otto Wagner, J Wickman, von Wielemans, C. Moyaux,
Phenè Spiers

M. DAUMET (Président) . En ouvrant la séance je tiens à présenter
tout d'abord nos remerciements aux architectes anglais qui tous ont été
pour nous si obligeants et si aimables   Je donne la parole à Monsieur le
Secrétaire-Général du Comité permanent

M J M POUPINEL (Secrétaire-Général)   Messieurs, je dois vous
rendre compte des travaux du Comité permanent depuis le dernier Congrès
qui a été si réussi à Madrid en 1904   Je vais le faire de la façon la plus
courte possible. Vous savez que le Comité permanent des Congrès Internationaux des Architectes se compose à l'heure actuelle de membres appartenant aux promotions du 2 septembre 1897 (Bruxelles) ; d'août 1900
(Paris) ; 13 avril 1904 (Madrid), et des membres proposés depuis par leurs
sections nationales et qui sont à ratifier au Congrès de Londres

    La promotion de 1897 comprenait 22 membres , cinq d'entre eux nous
      ont quitté à jamais

    La promotion de 1900 n'a été que de 5 membres ; nous les avons tous
      conservés

    La promotion de 1904 a ajouté 61 membres , huit d'entre eux nous ont
      déjà quittés.[2]

    Le Congrès de 1906 en a neuf à ratifier sur présentation de leur section
      nationale [3]

    Ces 84 membres se répartissent entre 17 nations —Allemagne, Autriche,
Belgique, Canada, Danemark, Espagne, Etats-Unis, France, Grande-Bretagne, Italie, Mexique, Pays-Bas, Portugal, Russie, Suède, Suisse, Turquie

---

[1] Les membres de la promotion de 1897 décédés sont MM Charles Garnier,
Adrien Chancel, Charles Lucas (de France), Valère Dumortier (de Belgique), Pedro
d'Avila (de Portugal)

[2] Les membres de la promotion de 1904 décédés sont MM. Fenger (Danemark),
Ernest Paugoy (France), Vivanet (Italie), Juvet (Suisse)   ont démissionné MM Th
Höd (Autriche), Helleputte, Lagasse (Belgique), Axel Berg (Danemark)

[3] Les nominations à ratifier sont celles de MM Neher et Schönermark (Allemagne),
de Wielemans (Autriche), C Moyaux (France), Clemmensen et Klein (Danemark),
A Graham (Grande-Bretagne), J L Monteiro (Portugal), Bluntschli (Suisse).

Le nombre des membres par nation est inscrit à l'article 5 des statuts dont vous avez tous reçu un exemplaire le nombre maximum n'étant pas atteint nous pourrons admettre des adhésions d'autres nationalités.

Les membres du Comité permanent des Congrès Internationaux des Architectes présents à Madrid se sont réunis le 13 avril 1904 et ont aussitôt décidé de fixer le siège du Comité permanent à Paris , ils ont examiné un avant-projet de statuts, élu un bureau et un comité provisoires chargés de l'élaboration des statuts, et décidé que le Septième Congrès International des Architectes aurait lieu à Londres en juillet 1906 selon la proposition de l'Institut royal des Architectes britanniques.

Le Bureau provisoire s'est adjoint les membres de la section française et a tenu à Paris des séances les 29 juin et 9 décembre 1904, 2 et 17 février, 4 mars, 26 mai 1905, au cours desquelles un projet de statuts a été présenté par M GEORGES HARMAND, étudié, remanié Ce projet de statuts et les procès-verbaux des séances ont été imprimés et distribués , ils ont fourni les éléments d'une Assemblée générale du 15 décembre 1905 Le projet de statuts y a été discuté article par article, sensiblement modifié, enfin voté, tel qu'il vous a été distribué en brochure La comparaison est facile, grâce au 1er Fascicule, et aux annexes des deux fascicules parus et envoyés en décembre 1904 et novembre 1905

Entretemps le Bureau provisoire a eu à s'occuper du concours international ouvert par M CARNEGIE pour l'édification du Palais de la Paix de La Haye vous vous souvenez qu'il a obtenu une extension libérale du programme de ce concours qui a été récemment jugé

Il ne s'est pas désintéressé davantage de l'étude des modifications en cours de la Législation d'Italie et d'Allemagne sur la propriété littéraire et artistique Il a prêté une aide bienveillante à la section anglaise à laquelle incombait la plus lourde tâche, celle de l'organisation du Septième Congrès International des Architectes ; enfin des réponses ont été envoyées aux demandes de renseignement sur les expropriations et servitudes à Paris, sur l'organisation et le fonctionnement du Conseil des Bâtiments civils et Palais nationaux de France, et des questions de bibliographie

Le Bureau a rencontré beaucoup de bonnes volontés, du dévouement même, permettant de bien augurer du développement de l'action du Comité permanent et de l'influence qu'il acquerra peu à peu. Vos statuts rédigés dans l'esprit le plus libéral, respectueux des usages et du tempérament de chaque nation, permettront à tous de collaborer à l'œuvre commune, de lui apporter leur dévouement et de lui faire produire son plein effet.

Le Bureau définitif nommé le 15 décembre 1905 a été composé avec la préoccupation d'attribuer au moins une fonction à chaque section nationale . nous avons réparti entre elles le Président, six Vice-Présidents, un Secrétaire-Général, sept Secrétaires, un Trésorier, onze membres Voici la liste du

Bureau du Comité Permanent des Congrès Internationaux des Architectes élu le 15 Décembre 1905 pour sept ans, Décembre 1905 à Décembre 1912.

Président.—M H Daumet, France.

Vice-Présidents —MM John Belcher, Grande-Bretagne , M E. Cannizzaro, Italie , P J H. Cuypers, Pays-Bas , J Guadet, France ; W L B. Jenney, Etats-Unis , J Stubben, Allemagne

Secrétaire-Général —J. M Poupinel, France

Secrétaires —MM J Caluwaers, Belgique ; G Harmand, France , W J. Locke, Grande-Bretagne , H. Muthesius, Allemagne , G O. Totten, Etats-Unis , R Velasquez Bosco, Espagne , A Weber, Autriche.

Trésorier.—Ch Bartaumieux, France

Membres —MM Apostolidhis, Turquie , A Betocchi, Italie , A Chaussé, Canada , G Clason, Suède , W Dahlerup, Danemark ; E Geiser, Suisse ,

N. Mariscal, Mexique ; J. L Monteiro, Portugal , E M. Repullès y Vargas, Espagne ; P. C de Suzor, Russie , F de Vestel, Belgique

Conformément à l'article des statuts il reste disponible un poste de secrétaire, un poste de membre   L'article 7 des statuts fixe la durée du mandat à sept années qui courront donc du quinze décembre mil neuf cent cinq pour finir le quinze décembre mil neuf cent douze

 , Nous espérons que toutes les sections nationales se sont constituées quoique nous n'ayons reçu de nouvelles à ce sujet que de dix d'entre elles , en tous cas le présent Congrès les y poussera puisqu'elles auront à transmettre à leur Gouvernement les vœux du VIIᵉ Congrès International des Architectes et à faire tous leurs efforts pour en assurer la prise en considération et la réalisation (Article 1ᵉʳ de nos statuts).

Nous venons de vous dire, Messieurs, ce qu'a fait la section française constituée sous la présidence de M H Daumet , nous allons maintenant passer la parole successivement à un représentant des nationalités prenant part au Congrès, leur demander ce qu'a fait leur section depuis avril 1904 et inscrire avec soin les renseignements qu'ils vont nous donner   je pourrai au fur et à mesure vous indiquer la composition de chaque section, les modifications qu'elle a subies, la promotion de ses membres, et quel membre du bureau elle comprend

Suivons si vous voulez bien l'ordre alphabétique   D'abord

Allemagne,

comprenant sept membres, deux de la promotion de 1897, MM Hinkelden et J. Stübben ; trois de la promotion de 1904, MM Muthesius, von Schmid, Waldow , deux encore, MM L Neher et Schonermark, présentés par la section en 1905, approuvés par l'Assemblée générale du comité du 15 décembre 1905, qui devront être ratifiés pendant ce Congrès

Nous ne connaissons pas encore la composition du Bureau de la section allemande qui cependant compte un Vice-Président et un Secrétaire du Bureau du Comité permanent, MM J Stubben et Muthesius

Cette section s'est je crois occupée spécialement de la question de la propriété artistique ce qui lui a occasionné beaucoup de besogne.

M J Stübben : Je dois demander au Comité permanent de vouloir bien remplacer M le Dr Schonermark par M K Hofmann, Geheimer Oberbaurat à Darmstadt , M le Dr Schonermark s'est retiré du comité de la section allemande pour raison de santé ; tout travail lui est interdit. Je dois aussi vous prier d'augmenter le nombre des membres et de le porter pour l'Allemagne à dix si possible   Les statuts le permettent et, de plus, toutes nos sociétés ne sont pas représentées au Comité permanent   Nous désirons apporter aux futurs Congrès une collaboration plus importante. Les nouveaux membres que nous proposons sont MM H. Keyser, Geheimer Baurat à Berlin , Gabriel Seidl, professeur à Munich , Schmitz Bruno, professeur à Charlottenburg

M J M Poupinel · Nous prendrons tout à l'heure une décision sur toutes les demandes de modification des comités nationaux, en examinant si elles sont compatibles avec les statuts   Bonne note est prise de votre désir.

Autriche.

Cette section comprend un membre nommé en 1897, M Otto Wagner ; quatre de la promotion de 1904, MM H Helmer, J Peschl, A Streit, A Weber, M Theodor Hodl, s'est retiré pour raisons de santé , la section autrichienne a proposé M A de Wielemans Monteforti pour le remplacer Elle a constitué son bureau · Président, M Otto Wagner ; Vice-Président, M. A. de Wielemans ; Secrétaire, H ᵣPeschl.   M. A. Weber est secrétaire du Comité permanent

Cette section a effectué tout le travail qui lui a été demandé. J'ai reçu la lettre suivante où la constitution de la section est indiquée , elle se termine ainsi "Notre section s'est résolue de faire une invitation au VII⁰ Congrès International des Architectes à Londres pour que le VIII⁰ Congrès International des Architectes soit réuni à Vienne , cette invitation a été déjà envoyée au Secrétariat du Congrès à Londres, et aussi d'autres démarches dans ce but sont déjà faites à Vienne " La lettre est du 12 juillet 1906 et signée de M H Peschl

M Otto Wagner a annoncé cette invitation dans une séance tenue aux Grafton Galleries   •

M H Peschl   La section demande qu'au cas où le Comité permanent déciderait que le prochain Congrès aura lieu à Vienne, on voudrait bien lui adjoindre cinq nouveaux membres en vue d'assurer l'organisation du Congrès

M Daumet (*Président*)   L'article 16 des statuts a prévu le cas   Le voici

"Article 16 —Le Comité permanent s'adjoindra pour la durée de l'année pendant laquelle aura lieu un Congrès International, et dans le pays où le Congrès se tiendra, cinq membres adjoints ayant voix consultative.   Ces membres seront choisis par le Comité sur la présentation des délégués du pays où se tiendra le Congrès   Ces membres devront être désignés au moins six mois avant l'ouverture du Congrès   Leurs pouvoirs continueront de durer jusqu'à l'expiration de l'année dans laquelle aura lieu le Congrès "   Vous avez ainsi satisfaction

M J. M. Poupinel : Je dois vous rappeler, Messieurs, qu'à la réunion du Comité permanent du 15 décembre 1905 j'ai annoncé que j'avais reçu du Dʳ Muthesius une lettre demandant à prendre date pour que l'Allemagne soit proposée comme lieu de réunion du VIII⁰ Congrès International.   Cela fait deux invitations.

Belgique.

La section belge comprend quatre membres : MM A Arnou, J. Caluwaers, L Cloquet, F. de Vestel, tous de la promotion de 1904, ceux de 1897 étant décédés ou s'étant retirés   Cette section s'est constituée en désignant M J Caluwaers comme Président, Frantz de Vestel comme secrétaire . tous deux font partie du Bureau du Comité, M Caluwaers comme secrétaire, M de Vestel comme membre.   M Caluwaers voudra bien vous faire part des travaux de sa section.

M. Caluwaers . Les membres de la section belge se sont réunis le 19 février 1905 pour arrêter les termes de la protestation à adresser au Comité Carnegie relative au programme dressé en vue du concours pour la construction d'un Palais de la Paix à La Haye   On décide d'appuyer la lettre émanant de M. Daumet, président de la section française, et réclamant un concours public et international.

Une réunion a eu lieu le 1ᵉʳ décembre pour examiner le projet de statuts du Comité permanent des Congrès Internationaux des Architectes, et soumis par la section française.   A la même séance on a constitué la section belge de la façon suivante. *Président* . J Caluwaers (Bruxelles) ; *Secrétaire :* Frantz de Vestel (Bruxelles)   *Membres :* L. Cloquet (Gand) et Arnou (Anvers)   Plusieurs séances ont été consacrées à l'organisation de la participation belge au VII⁰ Congrès

Aucune autre question n'a motivé de réunion

Canada.

M J M. Poupinel   Il y a peut-être eu confusion dans cette section entre les qualités de membre du Comité permanent et de membre du Comité de Patronage du présent Congrès   Cette section ne comprend officiellement que deux membres, MM Alcide Chaussé et Doran, qui se font assister de huit autres   Cette situation doit être régularisée. Nous n'en apprécions pas moins pour cela le précieux concours fourni au VIIᵉ Congrès International par les membres du Comité de Patronage Canadien, MM the Right Hon. Lord Strathcona and Mount Royal, G.C M G., High Commissioner for Canada, Londres ; Hon. Louis A Jette, Lieutenant-Governor, Province of Quebec , his Honour Mortimer Clark, K.C., Lieutenant-Governor, Province of Ontario ; MM. R Harris, C.M G., President, Royal Canadian Academy , J S. Archibald, *President* , Alcide Chaussé, *Secretary* , W E Doran, D. R Brown, Jos Venne; J O Marchand, R Lacroix. et A T Taylor

M. A. Chaussé . Le Canada n'est pas resté en arrière . le rapport que M Archibald doit lire tantôt aux Grafton Galleries le prouvera surabondamment   Je prie le Comité d'ajouter le nom de M Archibald à la liste de la section canadienne

M. le Président . Nous prenons note de votre demande ; il sera statué tout à l'heure.

Danemark

M J M. Poupinel La section danoise a perdu deux de ses membres sur trois, et le troisième, M. Dahlerup, déclare vouloir se retirer aussi MM. Clemmensen et Klein ont été désignés en 1905 , M Nyrop est proposé maintenant en remplacement de M. Dahlerup Nous tenons à remercier les trois premiers membres de la section danoise pour la part qu'ils ont prise aux travaux de début du Comité permanent Vous aurez, messieurs, à ratifier ces propositions

Espagne.

Cette section s'est occupée activement du présent Congrès. Elle a obtenu des réductions de tarif des chemins de fer en faveur des congressistes espagnols et portugais : elle a présenté des rapports à peu près sur toutes les questions discutées   Elle se compose de six membres, dont trois désignés en 1900 : MM Repullès y Vargas, Urioste y Velada, R. Velasquez Bosco; et trois nommés en 1904. MM Arbos y Tremanti, Cabello y Lapiedra, le président Mercader. La section a pour président M R. Velasquez Bosco et pour secrétaire M Cabello y Lapiedra. MM. Velasquez et Repullès y Vargas sont membres du Bureau du Comité permanent

Etats-Unis.

Cette section s'est également occupée du Congrès et a proposé des questions : il en a été admises   M G. O. Totten paraît désirer l'adjonction d'un sixième membre

M. G. O Totten Je demande l'inscription de Monsieur George B Post, qui est venu au Congrès et prend part aux travaux

M. J. M. Poupinel : La section des Etats-Unis d'Amérique comprend déjà cinq membres, deux de la promotion de 1897, MM. W. L B. Jenney et G. O Totten , trois de la promotion de Madrid (1904), MM F. R Allen, W S. Eames, Glenn Brown ; alors M G B Post serait de la promotion de 1906. La section s'est constituée en désignant MM. W. L. B. Jenney comme président, W S Eames vice-président, G. Totten, secrétaire. MM Jenney et Totten sont membres du Bureau du Comité permanent.

France

Cette section est nombreuse, à cause de l'initiative des Congrès Internationaux des Architectes, qui se sont réunis à Paris en 1867, 1878, 1889, 1900. Elle a perdu un nombre important de ses membres de la promotion

de 1897 (Bruxelles) ; il ne reste que MM E. Loviot, A Newnham, J M
Poupinel , de 1900 nous avons encore MM. A. Gosset et Georges Harmand,
légistes ; de 1904 restent MM Ch Bartaumieux, Ed Bissuel, L Bonnier,
H. Daumet, J. Guadet, H P Nénot, Emile Trélat. En remplacement nous
avons proposé en 1905 M C Moyaux , nous proposons en 1906 MM Frantz
Blondel et Gustave Olive, occupant des situations identiques à celles de
deux des membres que nous avons eu la douleur de perdre

La section française s'est constituée dès 1904 en choisissant comme
président M Daumet, vice-présidents MM. J. Guadet et H. P. Nénot,
secrétaires MM C. Lucas, décédé, Poupinel et Georges Harmand, trésorier
M Bartaumieux Elle compte cinq membres dans le Bureau du Comité
permanent.

Grande-Bretagne.

Ici nous n'avons que de chaleureuses félicitations à adresser aux
membres du Royal Institute of British Architects pour l'activité et le
dévouement dont il a été donné tant de preuves dans l'organisation du
Congrès et la réception aimable et grandiose qu'ils nous ont réservée.
(*Applaudissements.*)

La section anglaise comprend promotion de 1897, MM. G. Aitchison,
Phenè Spiers , de 1904, MM John Belcher, Th E. Collcutt, H. T Hare,
W J Locke, John W. Simpson, J. Slater, Leonard Stokes, Sir Aston Webb ;
de 1905, Alexander Graham.

Italie.

Nous demanderons à M. Cannizzaro des détails sur la section qui
comprendrait sept membres un de la promotion de 1897, M A Betocchi ;
cinq de 1904, MM E Basile, C Boito, E Cannizzaro, G. Kock, M.
Manfredi , un de 1905, M. Vivanet, décédé la même année. Quatre autres
noms ont été aussi proposés, mais sans solution La section italienne n'a
pas constitué de bureau à notre connaissance

M Cannizzaro : Je crois que M Betocchi et moi nous sommes les
seuls qui avons payé la cotisation. Les autres membres délégués n'ont
pas accepté la mission. M. Betocchi, âgé de 87 ans, n'a pas pu entreprendre
le voyage, de sorte que c'est moi seul qui représente à la fois les membres
et le Gouvernement italiens En Italie nous n'avons pas de société
centrale Il n'y a qu'une société d'ingénieurs et d'architectes, mais qui
ne s'occupe que des questions professionnelles et non de questions artistiques. Certaines sociétés, celle de l'Académie de Saint-Luc et d'autres,
sont très anciennes Elles ne s'occupent jamais de questions pratiques
La seule société qui s'en occupe date d'il y a quinze ans et a été créée à
Rome. J'ai été longtemps président de cette société. Elle a des
membres correspondants dans toutes les provinces d'Italie et a une
influence réelle. Mais les architectes italiens exigent que le comité
italien soit élu par eux-mêmes Le comité qui a préparé la participation italienne au présent Congrès ne peut être considéré que comme
provisoire, car il n'a fait que m'assister et a obtenu, avec moi, la réduction de 60 % du prix du transport des congressistes sur les chemins de fer
et d'autres facilités encore. Le Gouvernement a voulu en quelque sorte
reconnaître le comité en me chargeant, avec M d'Andrade, de le représenter au Congrès Quant au concours pour le Palais de la Paix, nous
nous sommes réunis à Florence et nous avons admis les propositions
françaises à la condition que nous aurions au Jury autant de représentants
que les autres pays, ce qui ne nous a pas été accordé

M. J. M. Poupinel : A la suite du Congrès de Madrid, l'Italie comptait
déjà sept membres Combien vous en faut-il pour une bonne répartition
entre les différentes régions de l'Italie ?

M. Cannizzaro : Ce nombre doit être porté à huit pour pouvoir
répartir le travail dans toute l'Italie Je vous demande donc de nous

maintenir provisoirement, M. Betocchi et moi, qui vous donneront plus tard la liste de tous les membres qui seront élus en Italie par les architectes eux-mêmes.

Le Président : Il est évident que MM Betocchi et Cannizzaro, n'étant pas démissionnaires, restent membres du Comité et peuvent régulièrement transmettre au secrétaire général les noms de leurs nouveaux collègues nous les attendrons donc

M Cannizzaro Avant de me rasseoir je dois vous communiquer la lettre suivante que l'ambassade d'Italie a reçue du Gouvernement italien (*Lecture en italien*) .   .   .   .
Le Gouvernement dit donc qu'il sera enchanté si le Congrès décide de se réunir à Rome. Ce n'est pas encore une invitation mais un espoir de vous voir à Rome (*Applaudissements*) Si cette décision est prise nous demanderons que le Congrès tienne des séances alternativement à Venise, Rome et Florence.

Mexique.

M. J. M Poupinel Je continue par le Mexique La section mexicaine comprend trois membres de la promotion de 1904 · MM. de Heredia, M Mariscal, Rivas Mercado Nos rapports ont été les plus fréquents avec M Mariscal, qui est membre du Bureau du Comité permanent ; il n'a pu venir à cause de la grande distance, mais s'intéresse aux travaux du Comité et à ce Congrès

Pays-Bas

La section des Pays-Bas compte trois membres, MM P J H Cuypers et A. Salm G. Bzn, nommés à Bruxelles en 1897, et M. H. P Berlage, nommé à Madrid en 1904 M. P J H. Cuypers est un des vice-présidents du Comité permanent , il est le président de la section hollandaise et a M Salm comme secrétaire

Ces messieurs se sont efforcés de faire de la propagande pour le VIIe Congrès, d'obtenir des réductions de tarif des chemins de fer et bateaux, de faire connaître les thèmes à traiter et obtenir des rapports , enfin et très activement il se sont occupés spécialement du concours du Palais de la Paix. Nous tenons à leur adresser des remerciements tout particuliers (*Applaudissements.*)

M le Président Daumet Ce sont les efforts de nos confrères hollandais qui ont abouti à l'admission de tous les pays au concours Nous devons les en remercier du fond du cœur (*Applaudissements*)

Portugal

M J M. Poupinel Cette section a perdu M. Pedro d'Avila, nommé en 1897 , il a été remplacé en 1905 par M. J. L Monteiro MM Adacs Bermudez, R Carvalheira, V Terra sont de la promotion de 1904 ; seul ce dernier a pu venir à Londres

Cette section voudrait s'adjoindre M Alexandre Soarès : nous en prenons note Elle a travaillé très sérieusement elle nous a fourni des études et proposé certaines questions intéressantes à discuter mais qu'il a fallu d'un commun accord écarter à cause de la longueur du programme du Congrès

M V Terra : Je désire ajouter que nous avons obtenu en faveur des congressistes une réduction de 50 % sur le prix du transport en chemin de fer. Plusieurs membres qui ne faisaient pas partie du Comité nous ont puissamment aidés. Je voudrais vous demander de nous les adjoindre.

M J M Poupinel · Je prends note de la demande.

Russie

La section russe se compose de quatre membres M. P. de Suzor nommé en 1897, que nous connaissons tous, et MM Bykofsky, Rutner,

Soultonoff, ajoutés en 1904   Cette section a beaucoup travaillé et échangé avec nous une correspondance très active au sujet de nos statuts et du concours de La Haye

Suède

La section suédoise compte trois membres, MM G Clason, Moller et Wickman ; le premier, de 1897, est membre du Bureau du Comité permanent et préside à la section suédoise

Suisse.

La section suisse se compose de MM. Fulpius et Geiser de 1904, et M Bluntschli, remplaçant M Juvet, décédé , il est à confirmer   Ce pays devra, à raison de la situation particulière, avoir une organisation différente : M Fulpius nous a écrit qu'il croyait nécessaire que la désignation des membres suisses du Comité permanent soit faite par les sociétés les plus importantes.   Nous rappellerons que les statuts ne s'y opposent pas du tout

M. Cannizzaro   Voilà, c'est comme chez nous, où il n'y aura jamais de président

M. le Président · Ne pouvez vous, par exemple, donner la présidence aux principaux groupements successivement ?

M. Cannizzaro . Un des membres est chargé de la présidence.

Turquie

La section, composée d'un seul membre, est tout constituée et a répondu aux diverses communications qui lui ont été adressées

Hongrie.

M. J M Poupinel . La Hongrie a demandé à être représentée au Comité permanent , elle avait organisé un comité de patronage important pour le présent Congrès qui a fait inscrire avant le 4 juillet vingt-huit adhérents au Congrès   Y a-t-il de l'opposition ? (*Non, non !*) Dans ce cas nous nous mettrons en rapport avec ces Messieurs , on pourrait attribuer trois noms à la section hongroise.

M. le Président Daumet   Cette demande est justifiée par l'importance géographique du pays   Le délégué présent, M Virgil Nágy, nous fera parvenir les noms

M. Looke : J'ai reçu une lettre de l'association de Buda-Pesth qui demande la nomination de six membres. (*Protestations.*)

M Nágy : On se contentera de cinq membres

M Poupinel · Vous pouvez en avoir trois seulement , veuillez nous donner les noms

M. Nagy : Nous désirons être autorisés à les choisir nous-mêmes (*Adhésion.*)

Un Membre   Dans le cas où le Comité décide d'aller à Vienne, en 1908, nous demanderons que le Congrès aille aussi à Buda-Pesth.

M. le Président : Vous demandez que le Congrès y tienne séance ?

Un Membre : Au moins que les congressistes puissent aller à Buda-Pesth , la ville est très intéressante et pas trop loin de Vienne.

M Nagy : La Hongrie recevrait avec la plus grande joie les congressistes à Buda-Pesth, mais vous n'ignorez pas que les affaires politiques sont très tendues entre nos deux pays   Or, l'on ne peut pas faire de politique ici.   Permettez-moi donc de ne pas insister sur cette proposition.

M. le Président : Nous architectes nous formons une grande république dans laquelle chacun à les mêmes droits, mais nous sommes tout prêts à déférer à votre désir et nous ne voulons pas nous immiscer dans des questions politiques   Nous travaillons pour notre art et notre profession, sans préoccupations politiques. (*Bravos !*) Nous laisserons donc ces Messieurs décider entre eux ce qu'il convient de faire et nous déférerons à leur cordiale invitation. (*Applaudissements.*)

M POUPJNEL . Il reste à ratifier les propositions et les désignatio1
Nous étions quatre-vingt-quatre au Comité permanent. Si l'on accor
toutes les ratifications et adjonctions, nous serons quatre-vingt-dix-sept,
qui n'est pas encore le maximum. Mais il faut réserver quelques sièges
faveur des nouvelles adhésions qui nous parviendront aux Congrès suivan1
　　　M CANNIZZARO : Je demande de fixer simplement le nombre de plac
pour l'Italie, mais non de désigner les titulaires, qui seront élus par nou:
　　　M LE PRÉSIDENT . Cela a déjà été entendu   Mais il faudra admett
les noms proposés, sauf à les ratifier plus tard, car sans cela le Comité 1
pourrait pas se réunir au complet.
　　　M. POUPINEL   Je demande de voter par nationalité.

(Votes)

Allemagne

Messieurs L Neher (de Francfort) et Dr G Schónermark (de Berlin
proposés en 1905 par la section allemande, sont ratifiés , ensuite, suivant
demande de M. Josef Stubben, 1°, M C Dr G Schonermark démissionnai
est remplacé par M. K. Hofmann (de Darmstadt)   2°, Il est nommé tro
membres en plus à la section allemande, MM H Keyser (de Berlin),
Prof Seidl (de Munich), le Prof Schmitz Bruno (de Charlottenburg
Ces propositions mises aux voix sont adoptées

Autriche

Monsieur Th Hodl s'étant retiré, la section autrichienne a propo:
en 1905 M A de Wielemans Monteforti , il est à ratifier
La proposition mise aux voix est adoptée.

Canada.

La section canadienne demande un membre en plus : M. J. S Archibal(
La proposition mise aux voix est adoptée

Danemark.

La section danoise a présenté en 1905 MM Clemmensen et Klein (d
Copenhagen) en remplacement d'un membre décédé et d'un autre d(
missionnaire : ils sont à ratifier.   En outre M Dahlerup déclare se retir(
et la section propose de le remplacer par M Nyrop
Les propositions mises aux voix sont adoptées

Etats-Unis.

La section américaine demande l'adjonction de M George B. Post.
La proposition mise aux voix est adoptée.

France.

La section française demande la ratification de MM. C Moyaux (1905
Frantz Blondel et Gustave Olive en remplacement de membres décédés
La proposition mise aux voix est adoptée

Grande-Bretagne.

M. Alexander Graham (de 1905) est à ratifier.
La proposition mise aux voix est adoptée

Italie.

La section italienne serait composée dorénavant de huit membr(
dont M. Cannizzaro nous donnera ultérieurement les noms
La proposition mise aux voix est adoptée.

Portugal.

La section portugaise demande l'adjonction de M. Alex. Soarès.   Il y a
aussi à ratifier M Monteiro.

Les propositions mises aux voix sont adoptées.

Suisse.

La section suisse présente M le Prof Bluntschli en remplacement de
M. Juvet, décédé.

La proposition mise aux voix est adoptée.

Hongrie

A la demande du Prof Virgil Nágy, la section hongroise est admise et
se composera de trois noms.

La proposition mise aux voix est adoptée

M. J M POUPINEL · A la suite de ces votes voici la composition du
Comité permanent des Congrès internationaux par nationalité —

Allemagne	10	Hongrie.	3
Autriche	6	Italie	8
Belgique	4	Mexique	3
Canada	3	Pays-Bas	3
Danemark	3	Portugal	5
Espagne	6	Russie	4
Etats-Unis	6	Suède	3
France	15	Suisse	3
Grande Bretagne	11	Turquie.	1

Au total, quatre-vingt-dix-sept membres   Le maximum prévu par
les statuts étant de cent membres, il ne reste plus que trois places pour
les nationalités qui voudraient adhérer , ce n'est pas beaucoup

M. CALUWAERS Je désire faire une proposition. Je désirerais voir le
comité examiner pour le prochain Congrès la possibilité de n'avoir que
des réunions dans une seule et même salle. On ne peut assister à la fois
à deux discussions intéressantes dans différentes salles. (*Très bien !*)

M LE PRÉSIDENT Nous devons certes rendre hommage à l'expérience
de nos confrères anglais, mais je crois aussi qu'il serait préférable de
réduire le nombre de questions à traiter et de n'avoir qu'une seule réunion
par jour dans un seul local

M. BONNIER Je demande que, dorénavant, dans l'intérêt général,
on puisse échanger ses idées d'une façon pratique Aujourd'hui nous
sommes obligés de voter après avoir entendu un certain nombre de communications qui ne nous permettent pas de nous rendre compte de ce
qui se fait dans les différents pays en matière d'architecture Il faudrait
qu'on nous initie le plus possible à la vie intime dans ces pays
Nous visitons de beaux monuments qui, sous réserve de l'architecture
spéciale au pays, présentent toujours des caractères généraux Une
cathédrale ou un palais de justice se ressemblent dans tous les pays.
J'estime qu'il serait intéressant pour nous de pénétrer dans la vie intime
particulière à chaque pays Nous verrions ainsi de plus près les détails
de la vie même du pays Ce serait profit pour tout le monde.

M LE PRÉSIDENT : Si j'ai bien compris, il faudrait des mémoires
expliquant cette question.

M BONNIER . Mais non. Je demande qu'on étudie le moyen pratique
pour nous de pénétrer la vie intime du pays. Des bâtiments comme
Westminster et autres, tous ceux qui ont un peu voyagé les connaissent,
mais nous ne connaissons pas la vie intime du pays dans lequel se tient

H

le Congrès, nous ne connaissons pas les petits détails de la construction.
Ainsi, la façon de construire un "home" · les Anglais ont fait des choses
admirables dans ce genre. Il y a avantage pour nous à voir cela dans la
mesure où cela est compatible avec le respect de la vie intime de la famille

M le Président · Cette idée est certainement réalisable à propos
de constructions en cours d'exécution

M. Bonnier Ma proposition vise aussi les maisons habitées pour
autant qu'on ne gêne pas les habitants Ainsi, en France, on ne parvient
pas à faire convenablement la fenêtre guillotine que les Anglais font si
bien De même, les serrureries anglaises et américaines sont très intéres
santes et nous aurions beaucoup à y apprendre. (*Applaudissements*)

M. Nagy . Je voudrais qu'au prochain Congrès on nous remette un
rapport sur les conditions de bâtir dans chaque pays. Il est très difficile
pour un étranger de comprendre les explications qu'on donne, parce
que nous ne connaissons pas la valeur réelle des termes employés et parce
que ces termes ne sont pas les mêmes dans chaque pays J'ai eu d'ex
périence de cette difficulté, ayant été chargé par le Gouvernement hongrois
de dresser un projet de loi concernant les qualifications des gens de métier
Cela a été pour moi une tâche très difficile, parce que je ne comprenais
pas les termes usités dans les autres pays. Ainsi, l'architecte anglais ne
fait que les plans et non les devis , mais, dans notre pays, il doit tout
faire et doit donc aussi tout connaître.

M le Président : Ce vœu sera communiqué aux organisateurs du
prochain Congrès.

M Harmand Je me permets de rappeler ce que j'ai dit à la séance
de lundi au sujet de la législation en matière d'architecture Je demande
que chaque pays communique l'état de la jurisprudence, de façon à
pouvoir, pour le prochain Congrès, vous présenter un travail complet sur
cette question si importante. (*Applaudissements*)

M. le Président Il est dans l'intérêt de notre art, de notre profession, d'admettre ce vœu (*Adhésion.*)

M Locke : Il y a encore lieu d'adopter les vœux émis dans chaque
séance des sections

M. Cannizzaro Nous ne pouvons pas les changer ; nous avons donc
simplement à les enregistrer, en adoptant la rédaction

M. le Président . C'est bien dans ce sens que nous les adoptons

M Poupinel Nous avons reçu la lettre suivante qui nous embarrasse
un peu. (*Lecture*)

" Au Bureau du VIIe Congrès International des Architectes, à Londres

" La société Architectura et Amicitia a l'honneur de fixer votre
attention sur les considérations suivantes .

" Sans doute tous nos collègues auront suivi avec suprême intérêt *le
Concours du Palais de la Paix*, et auront lu avec stupéfaction le rapport du
Jury Ce qui nous a frappé surtout dans ce rapport si sobrement motivé
c'est que le Jury ne s'est pas rendu compte de *l'article* 5 du programme
qui dit · 'Le projet d'un concurrent qui n'a pas rempli exactement les
stipulations du programme ne sera pas pris en considération pour obtenir
une distinction '

" Nous mentionnons que le Jury en décernant les récompenses s'est
éloigné des conditions du programme sur quelques points cardinaux,
dont nous citons par exemple, 'La somme fixée pour la construction,
l'exécution des dessins, la superficie de l'enceinte indiquée sur le plan, et
la superficie avec la situation des pièces '

"Et pourtant *l'article* 8 du programme dit : 'En acceptant leurs
mandats, les membres du Jury seront censé avoir adhéré complètement
aux stipulations du programme,' etc.

" Ces considérations nous forcent de faire appel à votre sentiment
d'équité et de justice , et, si vous partagez nos sentiments sur ce point,

nous vous prions de bien vouloir prendre tels mesures que vous jugeres bons, et d'en faire part à *la fondation Carnegie* à la Haye

> "La Société Architectura et Amicitia.
> H P. BERLAGE, *Président*
> PAUL J. DE JONGH, *Secrétaire*"

Amsterdam, juillet 1906

M DAUMET . Nous ne pouvons que renvoyer cette lettre à l'examen du comité Carnegie. Nous n'avons pas droit de contrôle sur ce concours qui, à notre demande, a été rendu universel C'était tout ce que nous pouvions obtenir

M. NÉNOT · Je crois que je suis le seul membre du Jury ici présent Vous savez tous qu'en matière de concours il est très difficile de calculer exactement le coût de réalisation de chaque projet soumis au Jury Il y a eu, à ce sujet, au sein du Jury des discussions laborieuses à cause de la question des langues parlées par les différents membres Cela allongeait considérablement les discussions sans les rendre plus claires D'ailleurs, vous savez qu'en matière de travaux ceux qui sont bon marché sont en général mauvais et que ceux qui sont bons coûtent cher. Il est donc difficile de dire si un projet coûtera deux ou trois millions. Aussi avons-nous demandé l'avis du comité de la fondation Carnegie On a répondu qu'on ne pouvait pas nous donner les éléments d'appréciation nécessaires pour vérifier et nous avons finalement décidé que nous ne pouvions pas nous occuper de la question du coût Nous nous sommes bornés à décider quel était le plan le meilleur C'était tout ce qu'il était humainement possible de réclamer de nous

M LE PRÉSIDENT Ce que nous cherchons, dans les concours publics, c'est l'éclosion d'une œuvre d'art, mais nous ne pouvons entrer dans l'examen des menus détails Dans l'occurrence nous devons nous incliner devant la décision du Jury composé d'hommes compétents Cette réclamation ne pouvant pas aboutir, je propose de passer à l'ordre du jour.

M CANNIZZARO Je désire qu'il soit donné acte que l'Italie s'abstient parce qu'elle n'a pas obtenu au Jury la représentation à laquelle elle avait droit.

M LE PRÉSIDENT Nous ne pouvons pas suspecter l'impartialité de nos collègues et nous ne pouvons que mentionner cette réclamation. (*Adhésion*) Il reste une dernière question à résoudre le lieu de réunion du prochain Congrès C'est un honneur pour nous d'être invités à la fois à New-York, à Vienne, à Rome N'oublions pas que Berlin nous a déjà invités antérieurement Il semble que la proposition de siéger à Vienne rencontrera toutes les sympathies à raison surtout de la facilité du voyage La perspective d'une extension du Congrès à Buda-Pesth nous permettrait d'aller voir deux belles capitales. Nous serons reçus, je n'en doute pas, avec la cordialité avec laquelle nous avons été accueillis jusqu'ici

M J STÜBBEN (Allemagne). Nous renonçons au profit de Vienne (*Applaudissements*)

M CANNIZZARO (Italie): Nous demandons qu'on prenne acte de notre proposition (*Applaudissements*)

M. G. B. POST (Etats-Unis) J'insiste pour qu'on accueille notre invitation.

M CANNIZZARO Faisons d'abord le tour d'Europe (*Hilarité.*)

M LE PRÉSIDENT Nous apprécions toute la courtoisie de nos collègues d'Allemagne, des Etats-Unis et d'Italie. Leur demande sera prise en sérieuse considération pour un prochain Congrès Voulez-vous décider d'aller à Vienne en 1908 ? (*Oui, oui*) Vous savez dans quelles vues nous émettons ce vote Toutes les invitations nous sont également sympathiques, mais vous reconnaissez que les réunions en Europe sont plus faciles, plus commodes à réaliser

M OTTO WAGNER: Je remercie le comité d'avoir décidé de tenir la prochaine réunion du Congrès à Vienne, où vous serez accueillis avec la plus vive sympathie   (*Applaudissements*)

M   BARTAUMIEUX · Je demande, maintenant que les sections sont constituées partout, de vouloir bien prier celles-ci de s'occuper elles mêmes des rétributions et de correspondre seules avec le trésorier général

M   LE PRÉSIDENT   Il sera fait mention de cette proposition au compte rendu.

[*La séance est levée à midi*]

Les Secrétaires généraux,
J. M. POUPINEL,
W   J. LOCKE.

THE FAREWELL BANQUET

THE Farewell Banquet was held in the Victoria Rooms of the Hôtel Cecil on Saturday, the 21st July.   Covers were laid for some five hundred guests   This being about as many as the dining-hall could comfortably accommodate, the dinner-list had to be closed some few days beforehand and numerous applications for tickets had to be refused.   The foreign delegates were all accorded places of honour, and among other guests at the high table, besides the President and Mrs Belcher, were the Duke of Northumberland, the Netherlands Minister, the Greek Minister, M   and Mme. Metaxas   Sir Lawrence and Lady Alma-Tadema, Sir William and Lady Emerson, Sir Henry Tanner, Sir John Taylor, Sir Aston and Lady Webb, Commendatore d'Andrade, M Daumet, Mr George B Post, Herr Otto Wagner, Dr. Muthesius, M. and Mme. Caluwaers, M. and Mme Benois, &c

Presiding at the lower tables were Mr Alexander Graham, *Hon. Sec R I.B A.*, Messrs John Slater, Edwin T Hall, J S. Gibson, Reginald Blomfield, A R A , M. Nénot, H Heathcote Statham, Maurice B Adams H V Lanchester, W. A. Forsyth

The cover of the menu card, very kindly designed for the Congress by Sir L Alma-Tadema, O.M., R A., represented Architecture with her sister arts Painting and Sculpture   A reproduction to somewhat smaller scale forms the frontispiece to this volume

Grace was sung and a selection of glees rendered during the evening by "The Westminster Singers."   The toasts were limited to the usual loyal toasts, the Foreign Delegates, and the Royal Institute of British Architects

The President, in proposing His Majesty the King, said that the toast was always received by Englishmen with enthusiasm, and he antici pated that on this occasion it would be doubly honoured, for not only had His Majesty accorded the honour of his patronage to the Congress, but he was held in esteem, he believed, by all the guests   His Majesty had done a great deal in the interests of peace, and peace was a necessary condition if the arts were to flourish   "Long may we all enjoy the blessing of peace," the Chairman concluded, "and may the reign of His Majesty be distinguished by a great advance in the art of architecture ! "

The President then proposed the toast of " Queen Alexandra, the Prince and Princess of Wales, and the other members of the Royal Family. The Prince of Wales, he reminded the assembly, was the Honorary Presi dent of the Congress, and no doubt but for his many duties he would have taken a more active part in the Congress, for all the members of the

Royal Family had inherited a love of art, and many of them were accomplished artists.

Sir William Emerson, in proposing "The Foreign Delegates," said that the toast placed in his hands, and which he had the distinguished honour and pleasure to propose, was that of the delegates accredited to the Congress by foreign Governments   Their presence in England had afforded infinite satisfaction and pleasure   The result of the Congress, the success of which had been greatly due to their friends from other countries, could be only good—that is to say, good in the highest sense of the word , not only to the architectural profession—for that would be benefiting only a small portion of the community—but good to humanity at large.   This Congress had been a great cosmopolitan meeting, and the questions discussed affected all nations   The wide scope of the discussions could be gathered from a glance at the subjects of the papers   They ranged from the conservation of ancient monuments and the planning and laying-out of towns and streets, to the statutory qualification of architects, the collaboration with and control by architects of artists and craftsmen, the question of competitions, the ownership of drawings, and to reinforced concrete   All these were questions not only of importance to architects, but affecting the health and happiness, the convenience and comfort, and the pleasure of the public, to whatever country they might belong   It was clear that on the proper laying-out and extension of towns and construction of houses and buildings the sanitary welfare of the public depended, as well as their convenience and comfort in transit and transport, and also their happiness by the pleasure that beautiful and artistic structures would afford to their æsthetic sense   These papers, contributed by various members of the Congress, were invaluable , they all showed such care, research, and thought in their preparation that it would be invidious to mention any names in particular   They had learned much from their foreign friends, and such meetings impressed both on the public at large and themselves as a profession the necessity to consider architecture not merely as an art, nor merely as a practical and useful science.   It must be looked at from both points of view; for without the artistic element it was not architecture, and without a careful consideration of the practical and scientific questions of building, rendering it useful for its particular purpose, however beautiful it might be to the eye, it was a failure.   The history, habits, and customs, the loftiness of the ideals and the civilisations of people who had long passed away, were judged of most accurately in after ages by the remains of their architectural monuments and buildings which had outlasted the memory of those who erected them   Hence the importance of such questions as had been under discussion to all great nations of the earth if they would leave behind them noble and enduring records of their aspirations, endowments, and governments   The Congress had also had the effect of bringing together and creating intimate acquaintance and friendship with many men of many countries, and in relation to the widespread feeling of a universal *entente cordiale,* it must be greatly encouraging to such a sentiment , for we learn by such meetings as these that in every country, no matter what it might be, there were equally thoughtful, unselfish, good, clever, and kindly personalities ; in fact we found them one and all to be what in common English parlance we should call "jolly good fellows."   It was only to be regretted that with so many various schemes for our mutual edification and for the entertainment of our visitors during the week the time had been far too short for them to see much of the interesting old and historic architectural monuments of the country.   Many beautiful old country mansions and halls would have been well worth a visit, and, of course, only a few of our castles, cathedrals, and abbeys could possibly be inspected   Still, the best possible had been done to show the most in the shortest time. One thing at least we had as Englishmen learned from our distinguished visitors, and that was how great a charm there was in the felicitous expression of nice feeling and sentiment as conveyed in their many charming short speeches The British did not, as a rule, express themselves with ease and felicity at a moment's notice, whilst our Continental friends invariably did so in the happiest manner , nevertheless, the inner feeling of the Britisher was no less warm He could only repeat that it had been a source of the greatest pleasure to them to see their brethren of other countries, and he trusted they would take away with them a reciprocal feeling of the sincere, truly cordial sentiments of respect and esteem which Englishmen entertain for them, and he was sure he was right in saying that all would endorse his expression of these sentiments

The toast was enthusiastically honoured, and as each of the Delegates successively rose to respond his compatriots rose also, and were warmly cheered by the united assembly The speeches which follow are reported where possible in the language of their utterance

Monsieur J. J. CALUWAERS, Government Delegate for Belgium —Monsieur le Président, Mesdames, Messieurs et chers Confrères. Au nom de la Société Centrale d'Architecture de Belgique, au nom des architectes et les dames belges présents, je félicite la Commission d'organisation du Congrès pour les brillants résultats de ses travaux. Je ne parlerai des résolutions votées à la suite des discussions auxquelles ont pris part les plus éminents confrères de tous pays que pour vous dire que c'est avec confiance que je les présenterai à mon Gouvernment et que j'insisterai pour que des résolutions soient prises en s'inspirant de vos délibérations C'est pour moi une agréable mission d'exprimer à Monsieur le Président J Belcher, au Secrétaire W. J Locke, et à tous nos confrères anglais notre profonde reconnaissance pour l'accueil qui nous à été réservé, et pour les jouissances artistiques qu'ils nous ont procurées. Nous garderons de notre séjour parmi vous un souvenir ineffaçable, nous nous souviendrons toujours des splendeurs des œuvres merveilleuses de l'art architectural anglais que vous nous avez fait visiter D'autre confrères, plus habitués que moi de parler en public, vous diront d'une façon plus éloquente les sensations que nous avons tous éprouvés, laissez-moi tout simplement vous dire, mais je le dis de tout cœur Merci à tous! Nous sommes particulièrement reconnaissants envers les dames anglaises, qui ont bien voulu se trouver parmi nous pendant nos séances et pendant nos excursions et ont donné à ces réunions un vrai caractère familial Nous vous quitterons avec regret, mais avec le vif désir de revenir Nous nous embarquerons en poussant un triple " Hurrah " pour l'Angleterre

Monsieur H. DAUMET, Government Delegate for France —Mesdames, Messieurs et chers Confrères . Les architectes congressistes venus à Londres à la réunion du Congrès international de 1906 ont passé ici une semaine mémorable ; elle laissera un profond souvenir à ceux qui ont eu l'heureuse chance d'assister aux réunions si bien préparées par nos confrères de l'Institut royal des Architectes britanniques, et combien nous devons en savoir gré au Président, M. John Belcher, et ceux qui l'ont secondé, à M. Locke, secrétaire du comité d'organisation, qui, avec un zèle inlassable, a contribué à donner à notre séjour à Londres un charme particulier Quelle belle séance que celle d'inauguration dans cette salle célèbre de Guildhall ! Quel brillant accueil au Mansion House, au palais des Académies, et quelles excursions que celles de Hatfield et du palais Windsor, le grandiose et pittoresque ensemble, où, depuis des siècles, s'accumulent les beautés de notre art et les œuvres des maîtres de la peinture ! Quel lieu magnifique dominant un paysage riant, enchanteur ! Et ces villes d'Universités où des traditions savantes ont préparé les lumières des lettres et des sciences ! Quelle quantité d'édifices caractéristiques par leur architecture ! On reste charmé de la variété des aspects de ces salles somptueusement construites, de la poésie des parcs, avec ces arbres plusieurs fois centenaires qui ont abrité tant d'illustrations de ce beau pays   Il est impossible d'analyser toutes nos impressions sans louer ceux qui les ont fait naître, les fondateurs des collèges d'Oxford et de Cambridge   Il reste au président des Congrès internationaux à remercier de tout cœur une nation amie, comme nous pénétrée d'émulation pour la grandeur de la civilisation, l'exaltation des arts, les progrès de celui que nous pratiquons, l'architecture ! Messieurs, je me permets de porter un toast à l'éternelle concorde et amitié des artistes, aux architectes que représentent nos délégués, en la faisant remonter au Roi, aux augustes princes et princesses de sa famille, aux protecteurs de notre art, qu'ils ont bien voulu honorer en acceptant de patronner la réunion internationale qui se clot ce soir dans des agapes confraternelles

M Boker, representing Russia, speaking in English, said that, on behalf of the Russian members of the conference, which had been brought that day to so successful a termination, he begged to offer their most hearty thanks for the warmth and cordiality of the recep tion which had been accorded them in England, the memory of which would never fade from their mind. They would have much pleasure in telling their friends in Russia of the kindness that they had met with in England, and of the magnificent productions of architectural art, both ancient and modern, which they had had the pleasure of admiring   It was difficult for him to find words eloquent enough to express the gratitude they felt, but he trusted that their thanks might make up by their depth and sincerity what they lacked in eloquence of expression   He was sure he was rightly interpreting the feeling of the Russian members of the Congress in proposing the very good health of their kind and hospitable English friends

M Gustav Wickman, Government Delegate for Sweden, and Mr Chujo, Government Delegate for Japan, both replied in English, and expressed their thanks for the hospitality of the welcome they had received.

Speeches in acknowledgment of the toast were also delivered by the following Delegates, either in French or in the language of their respective countries · Professor Otto Wagner (Austria), M Etatsraad Vilhelm Dahlerup (Denmark), M J T Cuypers (Holland), Dr Ing. H. J. Stubben (Germany), M. J. Berczik (Hungary), Signor Cannizzaro (Italy), Senhor Ventura Terra (Portugal), Señor Fernando Arbos y Tremanti (Spain)

Mr G Oakley Totten, Government Delegate for the United States, said that, on behalf of the Delegates of the United States, the members of the American section of the Permanent Committee, and the American architects present, he desired to express to their cousins of Great Britain their sincere appreciation and thanks for all the courtesies which had been so graciously and cordially extended to them   The debt America owed their mother-country, from whom they had inherited their customs, literature, laws, and the language which they were said to speak indifferently well, was almost beyond measure   It was to her, too, they owed the best they had in art, that which came to them by inheritance at the time of George III —which the English called colonial—which the Americans called their own. For the inspiration of their monuments they must ever turn to the glories of Athens and the splendour of Rome , but for the inspiration of that which was most near and dear to their hearts, the home, they must look to good old England, the creator and builder of the home. There had ever been a kindliness between the two nations with kindliness would come interest, with interest knowledge. Kindliness, interest, knowledge—these were the strands which would form the cord of union that might ever bind them closer and closer together   The next Congress was to be held in Vienna   On behalf of his countrymen he had the honour to extend to them a most cordial and hearty invitation to hold the following one in

America. In extending this invitation he begged to assure them that they would endeavour to the utmost to make the meeting equal to and, if it were possible, an even greater success than the great Congress just closing.

Mr. Cass Gilbert, of the American Institute of Architects, said he had to propose the toast of " The Royal Institute of British Architects and its President." He, the representative of the youngest nation, had been selected to lay this tribute of homage at their feet in the country to which they looked for representative government It had been said in his country that they should have a national art, and the feeling had grown that they should express themselves in their own way , but while they had no apologies to make for what they had done, humble as might be their own opinion of it, they thought the time had not yet come for them to have an art of their own They had unusual conditions in their practice, and perhaps they met those unusual conditions with a certain ingenuity, but there was also a certain lack of that quality which made a great art Americans came to Europe to study in France, Germany, Greece, Italy—to all the great nations of the world They might go as far as Japan for inspiration in that personal art which was so beautiful Seventy-two years ago the Royal Institute of British Architects was founded : the time therefore approximated to their time as understood in a little story that he would venture to tell One of their landscape artists, Mr Armstead, having planned a great estate, visited the owner, who said to him " Mr Armstead, this is a beautiful thing you have done, but there is one defect in it. That knoll over there is a little barren. What would you do with it ? " Mr Armstead's reply was " I would plant it with oaks " " But," said the owner, " that is a matter of sixty years " Said Mr Armstead " I was looking sixty years ahead." It was that sentiment which inspired them They were looking sixty years ahead. Those who founded the Institute were looking sixty years ahead, and could they see them that night—in all the glory of that assembly, with all Europe represented there , and see some of the finest men of the Continent and elsewhere who had come to do honour to their profession—he thought their pleasure would be very great. An eminent Archbishop once said : " There is a time when the truth should be told let us praise ourselves " He (the speaker) had come to praise the Royal Institute of British Architects He ventured to hope that the Institute would go forward in the great work it had started. They had laid the foundations in America at least of that tradition of practice which made for equity between man and man Upon the Statute of the Practice and Charges of American Architects had appeared for twenty-five years the scale adopted by the Royal Institute of British Architects, and that American architects had followed. To the Institute they looked, and he begged them to go forward in their great work—work of which they had seen ample evidence in England Might the future bear out the promise of the past !

Mr Belcher, responding to the toast, thanked the assembly on behalf of the Institute The kind words, he said, spoken by Mr. Cass Gilbert and the way in which he had referred to the Institute, as well as the like references of so many of the Delegates who had spoken that evening, made it necessary that he should thank them very sincerely for the expression of their goodwill It was gratifying to the Institute to know that the Congress had been successful, and that all had derived some pleasure by their visit to London This was mainly due to the admirable work of the Secretary and to the unremitting labours of the Staff of the Institute. As to the Institute, it might interest visitors to know that they (the Institute) showed in a practical way their union with their brother architects of every country by nominating as a recipient of the Royal Gold Medal—which the King annually bestows— an architect of eminence, or one who had furthered the art, irrespective of nationality   They also showed their close relation with their colleagues everywhere in that they possessed over sixty honorary corresponding members—men of eminence in their respective countries of whose association with them they were justly proud.   Thus they recognised that *Art is one*, and on occasions like the present were they not made to feel that artists were also *one* ?   They might speak different languages, but architecture was a language which every man could read in his own tongue   They could therefore claim to be a great fraternity, enjoying the same privileges, possessing the same treasures, with hearts filled with the same joy and pride, as they contemplated the *chefs-d'œuvre* scattered over the face of the earth.   And as they realised that they shared these treasures in common, they would unite in the endeavour to preserve them for the benefit of posterity.   He wished to thank the members on his own behalf for the kindness and consideration that had been extended to him during the Congress, and for all the kind things which had been said of him   It had been a great pleasure to him to preside on this memorable occasion, and to find himself surrounded by such distinguished Delegates and brother architects   It was an honour of which he should cherish the memory.   He could truly say in conclusion on behalf of every British architect, whether members of the Institute, of its Allied Societies or others, that their hearts had gone out to their colleagues   The ties of brotherhood had been strengthened by their visit, and though they now had to part they were constrained to say *Au revoir, à bientôt !*

PART IV.

PAPERS AND REPORTS

DISCUSSIONS

RESOLUTIONS PASSED BY THE CONGRESS

·

PAPERS AND REPORTS, DISCUSSIONS; RESOLUTIONS

SUBJECT I.

THE EXECUTION OF IMPORTANT GOVERNMENT AND MUNICIPAL ARCHITECTURAL WORK BY SALARIED OFFICIALS.

Tuesday, 17*th July* —*Institute Meeting Room*

Chairmen Señor E M Repullés y Vargas (Spain), Mr John Slater (England)
Hon. Secretaries Herr Hans Peschl (Austria), Mr Harbottle Reed (England).

(1) By OTTO WAGNER, Imperial and Royal Superintendent of Works, Vienna; Professor of the Imperial and Royal Academy of Plastic Arts.

(On behalf of the Society of Austrian Architects.)

" *Ausführung wichtiger Regierungs- und städtischer Bauten durch besoldete Beamte* "

Es empfiehlt sich, vorerst die Begriffe Architekt und dessen Werdegang möglichst klar zu stellen, da alle Meinungsdifferenzen in der mehr oder minder richtigen Auffassung dieser Begriffe wurzeln

Was den Werdegang des Architekten betrifft, so ist in Betracht zu ziehen, dass künstlerische Fähigkeiten, also manuelle Fertigkeit, Phantasie, Geschmack, Individualität und eine gewisse Findigkeit Dinge sind, welche der Architekt als Künstler besitzen muss, welche aber nicht erlernt werden können Dem entgegen sind humanistisches, bautechnisches und konstruktives Wissen, Fähigkeiten, welche der Architekt besitzen soll, diese aber sind zu erlernen

Das vom Architekten aufzunehmende wissenschaftliche Material hat sehr grosse Dimensionen erreicht, so dass es in Teile zerlegt, also in Fachwissenschaften aufgelöst werden musste Schon aus diesem Grunde ist es dem werdenden Architekten nicht möglich, sich die volle Kenntnis dieser Spezialfächer anzueignen; ist doch die verfügbare Zeit und die geistige Aufnahmsfähigkeit des Individuums eine begrenzte

Da der Architekt während seiner gesamten Schaffenszeit, das heute sogar literarisch sehr ausgedehnte Gebiet der Kunst in erster Linie pflegen wird, aber gleichzeitig von allen technischen Neuerungen Kenntnis haben soll, kann es sich für den Baukünstler nur darum handeln, dass seine technisch-wissenschaftliche Bildung soweit reiche, dass er das Wesen all dieser Wissenschaften und ihre Fortschritte verstehe und dieses Verständnis ihn bei seinem Schaffen befähige, die menschlichen Errungenschaften in den Dienst der Kunst zu stellen

Seine technische Bildung muss ihn ferner in den Stand setzen, die richtigen Konstruktionen und die geeigneten Materialien für seine Herstellungen wählen zu können, ja sein Wissen soll es ihm, im Vereine mit seiner angeborenen Findigkeit ermöglichen, neue Konstruktionen zu ersinnen oder bestehende soweit abzuandern, dass sie ganz seinen Zwecken entsprechen   Hieraus geht hervor, dass Praxis und Erfahrung, welche sich der Architekt im Laufe seiner Tätigkeit aneignet, auf ausreichendem Wissen basiert sein mussen

Erst nach reifer, technischer Ausbildung ist die Frage zu losen, ob der Kandidat des kunftigen Architekten-Berufes jene angeborenen Qualitaten besitzt, welche einen Erfolg beim Betreten dieser Laufbahn voraussetzen lassen

Es gibt also im Werdegang des Architekten eine stark markierte Grenze   Diese Grenze liegt wie erwahnt und naturgemass zwischen der erreichten, reifen, technischen Bildung und dem Ubertritte an eine Akademie fur bildende Kunst

Die Akademie, respektive die an einer solchen wirkenden Meister haben zu prufen und festzustellen, ob der Kandidat die eingangs erwahnten angeborenen Eigenschaften besitzt oder nicht.

Es ist den Meistern nicht genug ans Herz zu legen, bei dieser Prufung die grosste Strenge walten zu lassen, da das Resultat dieser Prufung einen grossen Einfluss auf die allgemeine kunstlerische Qualitat des Standes haben wird und nur so jene Kategorie von Scheinarchitekten, welche heute zum Nachteile von Kunst und Kunstlern ihr Wesen treiben, vom Schauplatze verschwinden kann

Jenen Kulturstaaten, deren Schulen es jedem absolvierten technischen Hochschuler ermoglichen, den Beruf des Architekten zu ergreifen, auch ohne dass er die kunstlerische Eignung hiezu besitzt, sei hiermit der wohlmeinende Rat gegeben, mit dieser Praxis zu brechen

Ganz besonders soll noch bemerkt werden, dass es fur Baukunstler nur eine Kunstschule geben kann und diese kann nur eine Akademie der bildenden Kunst sein , eine Akademie deshalb, weil Kunst nicht gelehrt, also nicht als wissenschaftliches Fach in einen Lehrplan aufgenommen werden kann und die kunstlerische Ausbildung nur darin besteht, dass der Meister dem Kunstjunger den richtigen Weg zur Vollkommenheit weist und ihn durch seine eigene Tatigkeit zum Betreten dieses Weges anregt.

Es ist daher vollig unrichtig. wenn technische Hochschulen und auch Kunstgewerbeschulen baukunstlerisches Heranbilden in ihren Lehrplan aufnehmen, da durch das ungesichtete Schulermaterial bedingt minderwertige baukunstlerische Qualitaten entstehen

Aus dem bisher Gesagten geht hervor, dass der Architekt ein Kunstler mit wissenschaftlicher Bildung ist.

Mit den, vom Individuum mit Erfolg absolvierten technischen Studien und der akademischen Lehrzeit ist aber der Begriff Architekt noch immer nicht erschopft   Es fehlen ihm noch die praktische Betatigung und die aus derselben resultierende Erfahrung

Ist die Lehrzeit des Architekten schon eine uberaus lange, so wird sie durch die Periode, in welcher er sich in einem Atelier die Praxis aneignet, sicherlich noch erheblich ausgedehnt

In diesem Abschnitte der Lehrzeit eines Architekten (seine Lehrzeit endet erst mit seinem Tode) steht derselbe abermals vor Teilungen seiner Werdebahn, das heisst, Veranlagung Verhaltnisse etc bringen ihn dahin, entweder den Kampf ums Dasein aufzunehmen, oder in den sicheren Hafen einer Stellung einzulaufen.   Seine kunstlerische Qualitat spielt hiebei die Hauptrolle, denn je grosser diese ist, umso leichter wird er die verlockende Fessel einer Anstellung mit Ausnahme der Lehramtstatigkeit zuruckweisen konnen

Der bisher skizzierte Werdegang des Architekten ist der normale ; es soll aber sofort bemerkt werden, dass er sicher nicht der einzige ist, und dass es genugend Fälle geben wird, bei welchen die angeborenen Fahigkeiten des Architekten, also seine Talente so gross sind, dass ein Minus wissenschaftlicher Bildung kaum in Betracht kommt

Dieser Umstand, so wie der, dass es eine Talentgrenze nach oben und unten nicht gibt, ferner die nicht zu bestreitende Tatsache, dass die ersten Architekten der Welt sich in vielen Fallen daruber nicht einigen wurden, wer ist Architekt, wer nicht, geben den sicheren Beweis, dass der Titel Architekt nicht zu schutzen ist, und dass eine Beurteilung kunstlerischer Qualitaten nur durch die Kunstler selbst, also durch Gruppierung der Kunstler untereinander moglich ist

In letzterem Umstand liegt wieder der Beweis, dass Staats- und Stadtverwaltungen nicht einmal in der Lage sind, die richtige Wahl eines Kunstlers fur die Einreihung in ein Amt zu treffen

Noch ein wichtiger Faktor kommt bei einer solchen Einreihung in Betracht. Der in ein Amt berufene Architekt wird im Amte sicherlich nicht die erste Rolle spielen , seine Individualitat, sein Geschmack etc mussen sich daher diesen Eigenschaften seines oder gar seiner Vergesetzten unterordnen   Die im Amte zur Ausfuhrung gelangenden Werke wurden also nicht die Fähigkeiten, den Geschmack und die Individualitat des schaffenden Kunstlers, sondern die sicherlich minderwertigen seiner Vorgesetzten zeigen, und da solche Vorgesetzte in den meisten Fallen sogar kunstlerische oder gar technische Laien sind, so bedarf es kaum der weiteren Begrundung, dass aus solcher Kombination nie Gutes entstehen kann

Zu erwähnen ist noch, dass die kunstlerischen Eigenschaften des unter das Amtsjoch gedruckten Kunstlers, nie die unbedingt notige Entfaltung erhalten konnen   Diese Erwagungen bestatigen zur Genuge, dass eine Staats- oder Stadtverwaltung nicht in der Lage ist, erstklassige Kunstler als besoldete Beamte zu acquirieren.

Staats- und Stadteverwaltungen haben aber sicher die heilige Verpflichtung der Kunstpflege, das heisst, bezuglich der Baukunst, die von ihnen hergestellten Bauten sollen mustergiltig und vorbildlich wirken. Solche Bauausfuhrungen sind nur von grossen Kunstlern und nicht von kunstlerisch minder befahigten Beamten zu erwarten.

Aus denselben Grunden darf sich auch die Befugnis von Beamten nur auf die zweckliche, technische und okonomische, nie aber auf eine künstlerische Kontrolle von Bauausfuhrungen ausdehnen. Wird endlich erwogen, dass durch die Eruption, die auf dem Kunstgebiete entstand, ein heftiger Kampf allerorts tobte und die offentliche Meinung sich heute daruber kaum beruhigte, daher nicht in der Lage ist, mit unbeeinflusstem Kunstempfinden uber Kunstwerke aburteilen zu konnen, so ist damit eine so grosse Anzahl von Begrundungen angefuhrt, dass uns die richtige Beantwortung der Frage 1 leicht wird , sie kann nur lauten :

Wichtige Regierungs- und städtische Bauten konnen nur durch bedeutende Kunstler und nicht durch besoldete Beamte ausgefuhrt werden

Die bisherigen Betrachtungen werden die Losung der kommenden Fragen wesentlich erleichtern und die jetzt zu beantwortende.

(2) Par Oscar Simon

(Pour la Société Centrale d'Architecture de Belgique)

*" De l'exécution des édifices importants destinés à l'État et aux Municipalités
par des fonctionnaires salariés (agents voyers, etc)"*

La Société Centrale d'Architecture de Belgique estime qu'aucun
avantage ne peut résulter de l'exécution des édifices publics par des fonctionnaires salariés (agents voyers, etc),

Ni pour l'administration qui couvre son agent et endosse sa responsabilité civile ,

Ni pour le public qui paie et pâtit de l'imparfaite ordonnance des
locaux destinés à son usage et dont trop souvent le sens esthétique est
péniblement impressionné par la vue journalière d'édifices généralement
dépourvus de caractère artistique

Nous gardant de faire des personnalités ou de vouloir léser des intérêts
privés ; n'ayant en vue que la prépondérance de l'art architectural et pour
but que le meilleur devenir de la corporation des architectes ;—considérant
que ceux-ci ont un domaine artistique et des intérêts à défendre ,—qu'il est
abusif que certains fonctionnaires (agents voyers, etc) offrent aux particuliers en quête d'autorisations administratives des services que les
règlements interdisent, constituant une concurrence illicite, hautement
préjudiciable aux architectes libres vivant uniquement de leur art professionnel ,

Souhaitant qu'une action plus énergique des architectes tende à obtenir
des pouvoirs législatifs ·

1º. La mise en harmonie avec les besoins modernes de la vie du taux
des tarifs surannés imposés encore aux architectes.

(*Donner une consécration juridique à ce principe :* " *À un talent plus
grand doivent être attribués des honoraires plus élevés* ")

2º. La cessation de l'envahissement du domaine architectural par des
personnes ne pratiquant pas exclusivement la profession d'architecte

3º. La révision des lois du bâtiment, là où le texte, *ou l'interprétation
qui en est faite,* attribue à l'architecte des obligations et des responsabilités
incompatibles avec sa mission d'artiste et disproportionnées avec les
honoraires qui s'y rattachent.

(*Appliquer juridiquement à l'architecte et à l'entrepreneur le principe
de droit commun* " *À un profit plus grand doit correspondre une responsabilité plus étendue* ")

4º La Société Centrale d'Architecture de Belgique, persuadée que dans
un cadre même modeste le concours de l'architecte aura encore pour
effet de faire exécuter les travaux, dans des conditions de prix, de durée
et d'aménagement avantageux, sans exclure un cachet artistique qu'il y a
toujours lieu de rechercher, est d'avis que s'il est essentiel que l'exécution
des édifices publics soit confiée à des architectes privés, il faut ardemment
souhaiter voir confier exclusivement aux professionnels de l'art architectural *tous les travaux, quelle qu'en soit l'importance,* de construction
et d'aménagement de bâtiments à usage du public

Il y a là des considérations d'intérêts corporatif, économique, éducatif
et artistique, auxquelles les mandataires publics ne peuvent rester indifférents.

C'est la consécration normale de l'enseignement public artistique,
un encouragement professionnel et une reconnaissance officielle des
droits et des prérogatives qui sont légitimement dûs à notre corporation

Mû par un sentiment de solidarité corporative, le *Septième Congrès
International des Architectes réuni à Londres en* 1906,

Voulant affirmer de tout son pouvoir les revendications et les justes aspirations des architectes, en vue de l'amélioration des conditions économiques de leur existence,

Émet le vœu :

Qu'à l'avenir les administrations gouvernementales, départementales ou provinciales, municipales ou communales, de même que les administrations de bienfaisance qui en ressortissent, chargent des projets de travaux ou d'édifices à exécuter dans leur juridiction des architectes professionnels à désigner par voie de concours publics ou restreints, ou dont les aptitudes spéciales ou la notoriété sont incontestables ,

Qu'une interdiction radicale mette fin à l'ingérance des agents salariés par les administrations publiques, dans l'obtention par les particuliers d'autorisations à accorder par les pouvoirs publics ,

Que dans la mesure de leur influence dans les assemblées législatives nos mandataires veuillent prendre l'initiative de réformer les lois en vigueur, là où les obligations et les responsabilités imposées à l'architecte sont incompatibles avec sa mission d'artiste et disproportionnées avec les émoluments qui s'y rattachent

(3) Par Gaston Trélat (Paris)

" De l'exécution des édifices importants destinés à l'État et aux Municipalités par des fonctionnaires salariés (agents voyers, etc) '

Les termes, dans lesquels cette première question se pose, attirent immédiatement la pensée sur deux points de vue essentiels . d'une part, *l'idéal* que les agents en question auraient à considérer, pour assurer une direction judicieuse de leurs capacités à la conception et à l'exécution des édifices publics, tout en restant d'accord avec les besoins des collectivités, nationale ou municipale ; d'autre part, le caractère spécial aux *cérébrations d'architectes*, quand ils ont à aborder la complexité des services qu'ils ont à rendre en pareil cas   Le titre d'architecte, en effet, s'imposait ici pour caractériser la fonction et la dénommer comme il convient.

Ce début entraîne une pensée primordiale   Son *idéal* une fois déterminé, l'artiste se trouve dans la nécessité de montrer *ipso facto* toutes les aptitudes que l'exécution peut bien susciter   Ces aptitudes sont les mêmes, qu'il s'agisse de l'état ou qu'il s'agisse des municipalités   Dans les deux cas, ce sont des services collectifs qui demandent les mêmes capacités et les mêmes aptitudes   Ils exigent toujours une étude préalable de la localité prise dans son ensemble

Et cette étude s'applique à la généralité des emplacements qui repèrent la circulation , elle se poursuit en tenant le double compte des dispositions existantes et des prévisions que l'édification projetée entraînerait.   C'est là une source de méditations abondantes, présentant un intérêt considérable   Il s'ensuit donc une extension de pensées, où les dispositifs à envisager rencontreraient une orientation qui accroîtrait encore l'ampleur des aménagements de détail, dans la mesure où l'étude pourrait être poussée.

Le plan même de l'édifice se trouve donc subordonné partiellement à l'ensemble de la localité, dont l'étude sera du moins amorcée, dès les premières esquisses.   On voit dès lors ce que devrait être l'influence des localités sur la disposition des services et des galeries de circulation, leur permettant de communiquer entre eux.   A son début, l'étude est une émanation des compréhensions d'ensemble   Peut-être même, celles-ci doivent-elles être considérées comme servant toujours de base à la recherche du *parti*. Après semblable élaboration, sans négliger, bien entendu, la *dominance* revenant toujours aux services principaux, il serait enfin loisible d'aborder les aménagements de détail

Toutefois il ne faudrait jamais oublier que ceux-ci constituent une étude complémentaire en vue d'une réalisation toujours en rapport avec les nécessités sociales

A l'appui de ce qui précède, on serait conduit, malgré soi, à signaler des exemples Mais ils seraient vraisemblablement empruntés aux agglomérations, avec lesquelles nous sommes en affinité plus particulière Et il semble que, dans une réunion internationale comme celle qui sert de mobile aux idées émises, il y ait avantage à se garder de tout exclusivisme d'application nationale, pour s'attacher de préférence aux idées et aux souvenirs que l'on pourrait susciter dans les esprits des collègues, suivant leurs différents pays d'origine. Nous nous en tiendrons conséquemment à l'exposé de notre pensée, avec l'espoir qu'elle évoquera, chez les personnes ayant bien voulu nous suivre, des rappels de mémoire qui soient de nature à contrôler ce que ces lignes avancent

Elles se sont attachées surtout jusqu'ici aux prodrômes des études relatives au *parti* de plan. Si l'on passe maintenant au *parti plastique*, on a devant soi l'ambiance visuelle, dont la reconnaissance impose une certaine analyse Tous les éléments qui s'offrent à l'œil, qui se laissent percevoir des différents points de vue, peuvent devenir des sources de beauté qui soient de nature à inspirer l'esprit de la silhouette qu'il faut déterminer. Pour le motif plastique présenté par l'édifice, la silhouette est la ligne d'enveloppement où se résume notre sentiment par rapport à l'ambiance que nous envisageons. Et cela montre bien la portée que de telles conditions initiatrices pourraient assigner à cette silhouette. On ne saurait oublier que les édifices publics doivent répondre à des exigences de beauté Les peuples y deviennent de jour en jour plus sensibles ; on a donc de moins en moins le droit de négliger la *beauté publique*. Contrairement à une époque dont le souvenir reste présent à l'esprit des hommes de mon âge, il n'y a pour ainsi dire plus d'objet qui n'ait à revêtir un caractère *plastique* La mentalité en est à prendre un tour différent qui excède la satisfaction du bien être matériel, auquel l'industrie du siècle précédent avait dû s'attacher exclusivement. Aujourd'hui que la solution des besoins immédiats peut être considérée comme généralement assurée à tous les échelons qu'elle comporte, une société, plus éduquée dans sa masse, demande à *l'art public* des joies et des contentements imprévus jusqu'ici Des aspirations nouvelles s'ensuivent. Elles veulent que la beauté soit mise à la portée du grand public, alors qu'une élite était seule autrefois à en réclamer les faveurs

Mais il convient sans doute de serrer un peu plus le sujet. Grâce aux esquisses d'ensemble, les *partis* finissent par s'arrêter d'eux-mêmes Ils comprennent · 1°, relativement aux dispositifs du plan, l'examen de toutes les conditions d'arrangement et de commodité des services , 2°, au point de vue plastique, la silhouette de l'édifice qui présente un intérêt capital en fait de beauté On en arrive enfin à pousser l'étude des différents aménagements figurés en plan Et le travail se poursuit, sans jamais négliger les caractères plastiques du relief monumental qui vient affirmer l'art en architecture.

Cette suite d'études prendrait autant d'étendue que les loisirs disponibles pourraient le permettre Elles ont pour objectif : l'unité et l'ampleur ménagées à la disposition des services dans l'édifice ; la beauté et la richesse sous lesquelles il se présente aux regards Tout cela comporte une élaboration d'autant plus généreuse et d'autant plus étendue que le tempérament de l'homme répond à un *idéal* plus personnel. L'artiste s'attache alors à la *maestria* de tenue dans le plan, à l'ordonnance éloquente de la matière, sous tous les aspects où l'on peut en juger et que les divisions de l'atmosphère permettent de réaliser

Voilà ce que nous étions conduits à rappeler à propos de l'œuvre architecturale, lorsqu'elle prend le caractère d'un édifice public. On voit, comme on le sait de reste, la variété d'aptitudes et le nombre de connaissances auxquelles ses applications multiples peuvent faire appel.

Ce sont des élaborations qui mettent en jeu toute l'expérience acquise.
L'évocation scientifique s'y transforme par la méditation sincèrement
approfondie de tous les éléments que la composition proprement dite fait
intervenir Et, lorsque l'exécution est ainsi préparée, l'esprit entre dans
une douce quiétude C'est là une source d'apaisement considérable,
que le génie de l'art saurait déduire de la science après bien des tourments,
sur lesquels les lignes précédentes ont peut-être ouvert les yeux quelque
peu

Telles sont en partie les pensées que nous avions à rappeler ici, à
propos du premier point de vue que la question soulevait dans notre esprit.
Elles se lient d'une façon absolue à *l'idéal* qui oriente les exécutions de
demain, quand il s'agit d'édifices publics Maintenant, voyons donc le
second point qui se rapporte au caractère intellectuel à mettre au service
d'une exécution suffisament déterminée par ce qui précède

Comment créera-t-on ces compétences spéciales ? Comment s'y
prendra-t-on pour éduquer les esprits en vue de conceptions accomplies,
eu égard aux exigences qu'il est possible de pressentir pour l'avenir ?
On connaît trop l'inconvénient d'erreurs en pareille circonstance Il
s'agit donc avant tout de ne pas exposer les intérêts publics à ce préjudice
Et la précaution n'est pas à négliger, puis qu'il s'agit de travaux en général
dispendieux, dont il faut subir assez longtemps les incorrections, quand
elles ont été commises. Comment faudrait-il donc s'y prendre pour armer
les esprits de façon spéciale aux circonstances qui nous préoccupent ici ? Il
y aurait urgence à éviter des écoles malencontreuses qui sont une épreuve
redoutable pour les collectivités de divers ordre, alors que le courant
engagé de notre temps voudrait les servir plus effectivement. En effet, le
grand phénomène social de la démocratie, qui est bien caractéristique de
notre âge, est là pour pousser à la solution qui s'impose chaque jour
avec une énergie nouvelle

Plaçons nous donc sur le vrai terrain et abordons la question psychologique avec une franchise aussi directe que possible Nous rencontrons
devant nous l'instruction technique d'une part et d'autre part l'éducation si abondante que le *grand laboratoire de la société elle-même* tend
à développer incessament A côté de l'instruction, il y a donc une
éducation qui est le fruit de l'expérience et qui repose sur *l'hypothèse
en science et l'idéal en art* L'un comme l'autre doivent être considérés
comme des nécessités par rapport au service des besoins contemporains
C'est grâce à une initiation première de la science que *l'idéal et l'hypothèse* peuvent surgir et assurer la vie ou les applications opportunes que les
lendemains réclament Il y a là un vaste problème de psychologie Le
passé assurait en partie la solution, au moyen de l'apprentissage qu'on ne
saurait plus songer, dit-on, à reconstituer aujourd'hui Toutefois il doit
encore servir de base et éclairer l'opération intellectuelle, par laquelle il
y a lieu de chercher à assouplir les esprits présentement Il n'est pas
douteux que, vu le degré de connaissances qui caractérisait l'époque
où l'usage des apprentissages était couramment répandu, l'éducation
prenait facilement une importance qu'elle n'a plus, proportionellement
à l'instruction répandue de nos jours Et, si l'on rapproche ce qui est
de ce qui existait antérieurement, la proportion est toute à l'avantage
du passé. Cependant il conviendrait peut-être de puiser une leçon dans
la constatation du rapport allégué en ce moment. Alors, l'instruction,
toujours croissante, deviendrait précisément motif à éducation supérieure
des esprits. Il y a là un équilibre à rétablir. Il s'agit seulement de
retrouver, entre l'éducation et l'instruction, le rapport qui existait autrefois,
à l'époque où l'apprentissage était florissant.

Mais, pour reconquérir les bienfaits de l'apprentissage et de cette
éducation personnelle qu'il entraînait, l'idée vient immédiatement de
développer, à côté des enseignements collectifs de la science, les travaux
d'atelier ou de laboratoire. Il n'y a que leurs mises en œuvre, qui

permettent aux personnalités de s'accuser par des solutions originales répondant au tour individuel des intelligences Alors des conceptions plus larges suivraient les *hypothèses* et *l'idéal* que le présent arriverait à suggérer à des cerveaux tourmentés des exigences du lendemain

Les idées, qui viennent d'être évoquées, mettent en évidence l'inanité d'une proposition souvent entendue : qu'il y aurait trop de science, par le temps qui court A quoi bon se plaindre ainsi d'une trop grande abondance, d'une trop grande richesse ? Vraiment, cela ne pourrait jamais se soutenir dans une pensée sérieusement conduite. Car cette abondance n'est en réalité qu'une source de suggestions plus variées et appelées à prendre forme d'*idéal* et d'*hypothèse*, qui préparent à l'action du lendemain comme aux satisfactions de l'avenir On ne saurait assez répéter que, grâce à ces suggestions, s'accuse l'utilité de nos efforts ou de nos travaux, d'accord avec les besoins nouveaux Et c'est bien le cas des édifices publics, tels que l'Etat ou les municipalités les voudraient voir

Nous n'avons encore rien dit de l'hygiène et de la salubrité que notre temps a dû mettre à l'ordre du jour Nous ne devons pourtant pas nous soustraire à la question. Les édifices publics ont, par les services qu'ils comprennent, le caractère d'habitations collectives Et les solutions, qu'elles réclament, engagent directement la responsabilité des techniciens appelés à donner leur concours Or, les architectes, chargés d'installations de cet ordre, songeront toujours que leurs intérêts personnels, comme leurs intérêts professionnels, restent subordonnés à cet autre grand intérêt de la collectivité qui a nom *santé publique*. L'architecte n'a donc pas le droit de se désintéresser de la salubrité ambiante de l'homme, qu'on le considère individuellement ou en collectivité. Mais ces questions d'hygiène font toujours penser à l'action développée de longue date par la Grande-Bretagne. Car elle a toujours été à la tête du mouvement en fait de santé publique A ce propos je me rappelle que ma première jeunesse fut nourrie des préceptes‘ de Miss Nightingale, et je ne parle pas de toutes les initiatives dont l'écho venait, déjà à cette époque, intéresser le continent. Elles visaient particulièrement les questions de salubrité appliquée d'après Douglas Galton, dans les grandes habitations collectives représentées par les hôpitaux ou par les casernements. . Mais il ne serait point permis aujourd'hui de passer sous silence un fait plus récent : la ville de Londres a su donner au monde un bel exemple, en procédant à la démolition de quartiers entiers dont la défectuosité avait été reconnue en égard à la santé Le fait est bien simple il s'agissait d'épidémies régnantes. L'insalubrité, une fois constatée, fut signalée par un *groupe d'autorités compétentes* dans un amoncellement suranné de bâtiments infectés et conséquemment favorables à la propagation des épidémies En suite de quoi, des projets furent conçus pour répondre aux exigences actuellement reconnues en fait de santé, cela sans oublier l'ancienne clientèle à laquelle étaient assurés des logements à bon marché. Et c'est ainsi que les sujets du Royaume-Uni savent comprendre la mission que leur assigne notre époque et répondre aux exigences de plus en plus pressantes de la salubrité à maintenir dans les habitations des masses

C'est bien là une compréhension qui honore un pays et qui montre la puissance de ses activités

Je veux ajouter un mot en ce qui touche l'entretien d'édifices anciens représentant des traditions que nous devons respecter . . Cependant, tout en apportant dans les travaux de conservation et d'entretien une attention respectueuse, il convient de reconnaître qu'il faudra généralement s'attacher aux exigences modernes d'hygiène et de confort . par rapport à l'évacuation des usures de la vie, à l'aération ou à la ventilation, comme au maintien de l'air au degré de température convenable à l'habitant Cela peut toujours se réaliser par l'étude, dont le jugement intellectuel apprécie la mesure

Et maintenant je crois que c'en est assez pour établir le cadre des opérations telles qu'on les entrevoit et auxquelles l'architecte doit faire face, quand il s'agit d'*édifices importants* destinés à l'Etat et aux municipalités.

Résumé —Il en est temps, je résume ma pensée Les édifices, qu'on peut avoir à édifier ou à aménager, répondent aux besoins présents ou d'avenir Il y faut des connaissances et de l'expérience

L'enseignement ne suffit pas au développement des aptitudes nécessaires. Elles demandent encore autre chose qu'un emmagasinage de faits caractéristiques de l'instruction Celle-ci doit être complétée par une éducation personnelle de métier. Il convient de ne pas s'attarder et d'assurer la simultanéité des deux opérations L'éducation intellectuelle et technique comporte un agrandissement notable de la pensée. Il peut être infini , même il n'est pas rare qu'il dure autant que la vie Il y a là comme un excitant à acquérir de nouvelles connaissances, dont le besoin s'accentue en intensité, du fait des idées personnelles Mais, par-dessus tout, c'est la vraie source des points de vue originaux en opposition avec les recettes apprises.

Dans les exercices que comportent l'atelier, le laboratoire ou bien cet autre grand atelier social qu'est la nation, l'éducation agit toujours et donne une allure particulière à l'esprit. Alors s'affirment les aptitudes à *l'hypothèse* et à *l'idéal*, en fait de *science* et en fait *d'art*. Et ne faut-il pas dire qu'ils sont une base d'opération pour l'étude et la solution des exigences du lendemain, qu'elles sont même seules à préparer les réalités en rapport avec les besoins nouveaux ? A l'atelier comme au laboratoire, où le maître respecte toujours, quand l'occasion le permet, le point de vue directeur de l'élève, cette éducation se fait et se parfait Elle prend des formes inattendues et infinies, que les valeurs personnelles sont seules à mesurer

Ces aperçus nous conduiraient donc à émettre le vœu que, en art comme en science, le même mode fût employé à la mise au point intellectuelle Les travaux de laboratoire et d'atelier accuseraient la variété initiatrice des esprits. Mais, en tenant compte bien entendu de l'ampleur contemporaine de la science, c'est le mode d'action individuelle, et caractéristique de l'apprentissage au temps passé, qui devrait guider à présent

De nos jours, après Claude Bernard, après Pasteur—pour ne citer que des noms empruntés à la nationalité que je représente—*l'art* et la *science* finissent par se rapprocher l'une de l'autre, au point d'affirmer une parenté plus effective que jamais. En effet, du fait d'aptitudes imaginatives que représentent également *l'idéal* et *l'hypothèse*, il semblerait qu'il faille tendre à les confondre, pour le moins, dans les aptitudes initiatrices qui ouvrent un champ inexploré à des travaux nouveaux. Toujours est-il que *l'art* et la *science* sont aujourd'hui notablement plus rapprochés qu'ils ne l'étaient. Ce sont deux branches directrices de l'activité humaine, chacune d'elles n'ayant plus aucun droit à se désintéresser de l'autre

Conclusion.—L'étude des édifices publics soulève bien des questions intéressant nos sociétés C'est là un trait général de la mission inhérente à l'architecte. Il doit donc suivre son temps et l'interroger constamment sur les exigences qu'il peut bien manifester.

La science et l'art lui permettent un choix de solutions étendues. S'ensuivent des connaissances et une expérience dont les différents modes signalés ici seraient le développement. Il y a intérêt à en propager la coutume.

Mr G OAKLEY TOTTEN, Jun. (U.S.A.), said that this was one of the few subjects of the Congress of which it was possible to see the material effect. A great many matters were to be discussed, that it would be impossible to press to any final or definite conclusion. During the Congress of 1897 at Brussels he suggested, as one interested in the Government Office at Washington, quite informally, a subject which was similar in nature to that under discussion   The Congress took the matter up seriously, and appointed a committee to consider it and to report on what they thought the best method of obtaining designs for Government buildings. The Committee concluded that competition was the best method. It might be of interest to members of the Congress to know in a general way what was being done in this matter in America. Every possible method was being tried, in every possible combination. Government architecture in America is divided broadly into three classes · (1) That for the general Government, known as Federal architecture, including the U S Capitol and its accessories, all post-office buildings, the Federal court buildings, custom houses, mints, naval and military academies, army barracks, &c , buildings owned by and for the use of the general Government. (2) State buildings, which correspond in a general way with the Federal buildings, but are owned and controlled by the individual States , these include the State capitols and their accessories, county courts, hospitals, and asylums of various sorts, &c   (3) Municipal buildings—buildings owned by the municipalities, such as municipal office buildings, courts, schoolhouses, fire departments, hospitals, &c   Speaking first of city buildings, the municipal work in many of the large cities is in charge of a city architect. His work, however, is usually confined to school buildings and engine houses, and when larger municipal buildings are to be erected a competition is held for the selection of the architect. The same might be said to be true in regard to the architectural work in the various States. In Washington they have no city architect. A few of the smaller buildings are designed in the office of the Inspector of Buildings   The major part of the work is apportioned out to private architects of standing, usually by direct appointment, but in case of larger buildings by competition   The largest general bureau, that under the Treasury Department, is known as the Supervising Architect's office. The work of this office is largely confined to the designing of post-office buildings and Federal courts and custom houses, but it also includes quite a variety of other buildings. The bureau employs a varying number of draughtsmen and clerks, from 125 to perhaps 250, depending on the work in hand. Congress this year appropriated $39,000,000 for Federal buildings, which would go through this office. It was in order to try to place this enormous amount of work in the hands of the private architects that the Tarsney Act was passed. Mr Totten spoke of having brought up the subject, at the Brussels Congress in 1897, of the "Best Methods of Obtaining Designs for Government Buildings"   The Congress appointed a special committee to consider the matter, and presented the following resolution, which was adopted by the Congress . "It is desirable that the construction of public buildings shall be confided to private architects, chosen by public or private competition, or otherwise, and that the architects superintend the erection of the works, but under the direction of the Government." This was after the passing of the Act, but before any work was given out under it. As a delegate from the Government, recommended by Mr. Lyman J. Gage, Secretary of the Treasury, Mr Totten had the honour of presenting the conclusions of the Congress of 1897 to Mr Gage, and was informed that it helped to influence him to put into effect the Tarsney Act as proposed and urged by the American Institute of Architects   A *résumé* was given of the work done under this Act ; a more detailed account, prepared by Mr Brown, would be found in the *Brick Builder* for this year.   The American Institute of Architects, as far back as 1875, formulated a Bill to regulate and improve the Federal practice , modifications were made to this until 20th February 1893, when it became law.   In brief, it gave to the Secretary of the Treasury the power, at his discretion, to obtain designs for Federal buildings by competition, stipulating that at least five competitors should be selected in each competition, and that the general super- vision should be under the office of the Supervising Architect.   This Act was passed in 1893, but through some misunderstanding with Mr Carlisle, then Secretary, it was not put into effect until after his successor, Mr Lyman J. Gage, held the first competition in August 1897.   It is interesting to note that since that date twenty-two competitions have been held for buildings, varying in cost from £100,000 to £4,000,000   It is a great gratification to the profession at large in America that these competitions have always been fairly and unbiassedly judged, and that in perhaps every case the best scheme submitted was selected.   In con- clusion Mr. Totten requested that a list of the regulations of the com- petitions might be printed in the Proceedings of the Congress [1]   The Bill had had a salutary influence upon other departments of the Govern- ment and municipal authorities, and was bringing about better results

Professor VIRGIL NÁGY (Hungary) said he was a professor of archi- tecture, and he felt that unless a young architect had an opportunity of cultivating his talents after leaving school much of his ability would be lost.   If the young designer who entered an office had no opportunity of acquiring that knowledge of his art which was necessary to make a good architect, though he might become a superior in time so far as position was concerned, he would remain what he was as regards matters of art and construction · he would be fitted to do only the work of the office   He agreed with Herr Wagner's conclusion, that important Government buildings should be the work of eminent architects only, and not of officials   There was a danger of young architects entering a municipal office becoming indifferent to art   He agreed that officials should not make designs for public works

Mr F E P. EDWARDS (Bradford) said it seemed to him that the title of the subject was just a little wrong.   The title barred the way altogether to the possibilities of any good coming out of the work done by salaried officials as such   He understood that the real intention and the real ground upon which this subject was founded was the question of important municipal and public work being carried out by engineers and surveyors   He should like that to be made clear from the Chair—i e as to whether that was really the basis of the subject they were discussing or not.   He might say at once that he was a salaried official, but, before all, he hoped he was an architect, and with regard to work done by official architects in this country as such he ventured to think that a number of instances could be quoted, without being personal in the matter, of most excellent work done by official architects.   In the north, east, south, and west of their country, and in the metropolis itself, there was excellent work being done by official architects, and therefore he asked that the subject should be put upon a little clearer basis   They all knew that the style of work and the style of design and plan which was carried out by the municipal engineer and surveyor with a staff of two or three archi- tectural draughtsmen was not at all what was aimed at   They aimed at something very different   He had written to the Secretary of the Institute before, asking that when this matter was discussed at the Institute these

---

[1] The regulations referred to are printed in an Appendix to this discussion . see page 125.

two points should be clearly differentiated. He ventured to go a little further and to say that he thought that at the bottom of the whole thing was the fear that their living was being taken away from them   If the experience of a large body like the Architectural Department of the London County Council was that their work could be carried out at less cost than by the usual commission paid to an architect, that was a strong inducement to the employer when making such an appointment   He thought himself that the whole evil arose from the fact that there were too many young fellows taken into architects' offices as premiumed pupils, who, after two or three or five years, were turned loose and had to get their living somehow   Up north there were so many of these young men about that private firms who had architectural work to be done, and who did not care about the artistic side of such work, saw that their work—mills, boiler-houses, &c.—could be done cheaper by employing these young men. He knew numerous instances in Yorkshire where private firms employed architects on the staff, he did not know what salaries they paid , he presumed it was a living salary, and it might be a good salary   All this proceeded from the fact that there were too many pupils, and that parents did not properly realise the responsibility which attached to them in putting their sons into a profession for which they had not the slightest aptitude   It was too late to reconsider the matter when the young man was twenty-two or twenty-three, and the result was that there were too many architects—good, bad, and indifferent—and they had to make a living. He put that forward with all deference for their consideration, for he thought that the question they were discussing was intimately bound up with the present system of pupilage

Mr. A W. WEISSMAN (Holland) said he was once an official architect, but now he was a private architect, and he did not know that it made much difference whether a man was an official or a private architect   It depended on the gifts a man possessed   If a private architect had no gifts, and if the official architect had, then he should prefer the official architect. There were architects in Holland who did not put a line on paper ; their young pupils did that, and he hoped such practices did not prevail in England. Perhaps they did, but in any case they did elsewhere   The fact was, if a man had talent it made no difference whether he was an official or a private architect   They could not say in general that no official architect should carry out great and important buildings , it all depended on whether he had the capacity to carry them out.

Mr. A B PLUMMER (Newcastle-on-Tyne) said that as hon secretary of an Allied Society to the Institute he might say that they in the provinces, at all events in England, felt that the subject was most important. While he agreed with the last speaker that he would prefer an official architect with ability to a non-official architect without ability, he would still more prefer a non-official with ability to an official with ability. In many of our large centres we had non-official architects with ability who had very little opportunity of carrying out municipal work. He did not know whether the discussion was limited to important municipal buildings, but in the provinces it seemed to them that official architects and engineers and surveyors, who had no one to criticise or supervise them, and who took private practice, could practically pass their own work , whereas the practising architect was criticised and had his work rejected by the gentlemen in question   In the provinces it was a temptation to people wanting to employ an architect to go to the official architect to do their work when they knew that that official would be able to pass that work   If the Congress could do something to make it illegal for salaried officials, clerks of works, and sanitary inspectors to practise as private architects in their own districts it would do a great deal of good. The matter required serious consideration   They did not object to an able architect acting as a city architect, for example, but they objected to the salaried official competing, in his private capacity, with private practitioners   That was what they complained of.   As to its being cheaper for a large municipality or Government to carry out work with a large staff, that might be so in some cases, but in the provinces it was not so.   Say an architect carried out a Council school , when the work was completed the expense to the municipality ceased , whereas a municipality keeping up a staff had to keep that staff going when the work was finished, and whether there was work or not   Often a practising architect was an expert in some municipal work, and the municipal architect was not an expert in that work, and it was to the interest of the ratepayers that the various corporations and other public bodies should be able to obtain the best advice.   There were architects who had made a special study of special work, and to put such special work into the hands of salaried officials because they were officials could not be to the advantage of the ratepayers   He hoped the question would be pressed forward   In the provinces the practising architect was suffering severely, and increasingly severely, in the matter

Mr G H. Fellowes Prynne said the subject was one of the most important which could be brought before the Congress   It was a subject which touched every practising architect in these days, when there were so many public bodies in England and abroad   In England we suffered from the disadvantage of not having a Minister of Fine Arts, nor had we any sort of Jury of Fine Arts, and therefore in England perhaps more than on the Continent—and he trusted more than in the United States— we suffered from officialism.   The matter had been so clearly dealt with in the three papers that it did not need much debating to show how detrimental the present system was.   M Oscar Simon summed up the whole matter when he said that there were two good reasons against the giving of important municipal architectural work to salaried officials—viz that it was neither for the good of the administration nor for the good of the public.   Those two reasons were very distinct, and they were absolutely sound   There was a large amount of work which was good, and must be good, coming as it did from good men who had been appointed to official positions, and who often had means of obtaining expert experience that could not easily be got by others   At the same time, as Mr. Plummer had said, these officials not only acted in their official capacity, but were allowed to take private work in addition   They also had a large staff of clerks who were paid by the municipality by whom they were employed , and, as had been said, a large amount of the work turned out was done by salaried clerks and not by the architects themselves.   An official was too often taken up by his official duties   Think of the enormous amount of official work which had to be got through before the official architect could touch the artistic side of the work of architecture !   And think of the amount of time one gave to one's designs when interested in even a small work, let alone a work of national importance !   One's whole time was taken up in throwing oneself into the design, and this was utterly inconsistent with the carrying-out of official duties of an important and complex character in addition   He would go even further   In large corporations in England, and he supposed elsewhere— take such a body as the Ecclesiastical Commissioners, for instance— where a man had the power of criticising and altering other men's plans, or even of throwing them aside (often rightly so and with great advantage) , it was a dangerous thing to give this power where the official had the power also of taking private work as well as the work connected with the body with which he was associated.   It became a danger to the whole profession generally that it should be accepted as the right thing for salaried officials, by right of their position to take up large public works of national importance.   Beyond that, it was surely bad for their art that the designs of an artist, of any high instinct at all, might be pulled about

and altered by a number of men who, however willing to save the public
purse, were not in the least authorities on art , and it could not be denied
that officials, however good their designs might be in the first place, were
terribly handicapped by the criticisms of this, that, and the other perfectly
ignorant man as to the artistic ideas in that design.   He therefore hoped
that the Congress or that meeting would not end without passing some
definite resolution—a resolution put forward by that International Congress
of Architects, and sent to the various Governments, expressing the opinion
of the Congress.   But, as had been said, it was all very well to pass such
resolutions ; they must go a little further and let it be known that these
were the honest opinions of men working for the highest end—viz. the
advancement of the art of their country.

Mr MAURICE B. ADAMS said that the majority of architects interested
in this discussion would realise that the salaried officials aimed at were
the engineers and road surveyors employed throughout the country by
County Councils and smaller bodies   If there happened to be a fully
qualified architect at the head of affairs of a big bureau or big central
office such as must be associated with a large County Council, and if
these public bodies found it was cheaper on behalf of the ratepayers to
have such a bureau, it was useless for practising architects to protest
against such an arrangement, except of course to point out in this regard
to such authorities that it was scarcely possible, however great a man's
artistic ability when he originally accepted such a chief official position,
for him to retain that architectural ability or to develop it ; it was bound
to be deteriorated by the various clerical and administrative detail work
of such an office   There was so much clerical work to do that the
original power as an architect or artist must necessarily be very much
curtailed and injured by the process   Even if the salaried architect was,
or might to some degree be still, an artist, it was scarcely possible for him
to produce such work as the man who was engaged as an independent
architect, and who had produced works which would justify a Government or any other authority in inviting him to take part in a limited competition, or commission him to do the work, as it was generally more
often done in America   What the Institute desired to impress upon the
public was that it was not economical or good in any sense or form—quite
apart from their individual interests as architects—for the ratepayers as
well as architects—that men trained as engineers and road surveyors
should—in fact, by virtue of the very power they had to carry out
those duties—do the strictly architectural work such as they were constantly called upon to do.   He thought that the Royal Institute of
British Architects and the Congress should in the most unqualified way
say that in the interests of architecture as a fine art and in the interests
of the ratepayers it was a bad thing for them to go on in this hugger-
mugger way.   Everywhere buildings done in this fashion were in evidence.
The most expensive buildings were thus often erected by men for whom
otherwise and personally they might entertain the greatest regard.   Judged,
however, as architects, they were not architects at all ; such men employed,
and were obliged to employ, young men who had a certain amount of
artistic ability, but who had no practical capacity, and had failed to get
into practice themselves.   They were artistic ne'er-do-wells, who were
employed from month to month, being kept on a long time at great public
expense until all the details of payment &c. were cleared up, because the
engineer or the surveyor did not personally know anything about the
matters in question.   The extent of the expense was never known ; it was
impossible to know what the office and establishment charges were.   These
" temporary " assistants were kept on until the whole work was cleared
up, so that they could consult with the quantity surveyors as to extras and
so on, whereas when a private architect was employed he was always available, and the expense was curtailed.   This question was, as a matter of fact,

mixed up with municipal trading ; some public bodies could manage large establishments, labour bureaux, &c., but the rank and file could not , they kept on large staffs, and actually created work at the expense of the ratepayers in order to keep the works department going.   They must not, in considering the question, forget that there was a general tendency at the present time—at all events in England, he did not know how it was abroad—for municipalities to take on work which should more properly be done by private enterprise.   He suggested that the meeting should clear up a little more definitely what they meant by "salaried officials," but he entirely sympathised with what Mr. Weissman had said—if they possessed a good man, wherever they found him his personality would show itself   But he would go further and say that an architect in an official position with a personality was obliged to over-concern himself with some work which did not rightly belong to an architect as such, and that work would curtail his artistic work and hamper him to a considerable degree, preventing his designing good architecture.

M. JULES DE BERCZIK (Budapest) said that there seemed to be a hostile tendency towards architects occupying official positions.   It would be undesirable if, in discussing the question, they were so unfortunate as to give currency to a view calculated to depreciate the general artistic ability and personal fitness of architects occupying official positions.   It was well known that the artistic training of architects occupying official positions was the same as that of architects in private practice, and seeing, as had been pointed out, that artistic ability was a purely personal gift, it would be scarcely justifiable to deny all Government and municipal architects the right to take part, as a private venture, in artistic works. Nor, indeed, was this at all necessary in order to attain the object which he believed they all had in view.   For it was not solely on administrative and economic grounds that the construction of important buildings by Government or municipal departments was to be objected to   It was eminently to the educational interest of the Government or municipality that monumental building should be as perfect as possible from an artistic standpoint, and should give expression to the educational progress as well as to the artistic education of the country.   This object could, however, only be attained if all the best ability of the country were permitted to co-operate in the construction of these buildings.   From this open competition no architect possessing formal and personal fitness should be excluded. He would therefore (in order to eliminate all personal considerations from the question) venture to propose that the Congress should pass the following resolution—viz that " important municipal and Government buildings should not be constructed by municipal or State administration."

Mr JOHN SLATER (Chairman) said that Mr. Edwards wished the particular wording of the question to be altered, but it was impossible, he was afraid, to do so, for Herr Wagner had submitted it as printed.   But, as had been said, it was the principle they were fighting for, and it would be absurd to deny that in some, perhaps in many cases the municipal architect was a man of knowledge and training and competent to carry out architectural work , but it was folly—and Herr Wagner had brought that out very clearly in his paper—to think that under ordinary circumstances an official architect could possibly have the time at his disposal for dealing with large municipal buildings, which required an amount of thought and consideration in planning and arranging which his other duties made it impossible for him to give   It was with that view that they were promulgating this question now, and he certainly agreed with Mr. Prynne when he said that they ought to endeavour to get an actual resolution passed and carried which might have weight not only in this country, but in all the countries represented at the Congress   He called upon M. Poupinel to propose, and Mr. Plummer to second, such a resolution.

M Poupinel then proposed the following resolution —"That, in the future, in the interests of administrative bodies and the public, and in the higher interests of the art of architecture, public bodies, whether Government, provincial, or municipal, should entrust architectural works only to professional arch tects who may have special aptitude for the particular work or may have a renown which is incontestable, and that they should put an end to the employment of their own salaried officials in private works "

Mr Totten said that the subject under discussion was not put forward at the Brussels Congress, in 1897, as an official subject, but he presented it personally on behalf of his Government, and the conclusions adopted at that Congress, it seemed to him, were quite applicable to, and exactly followed, the lines of Herr Wagner's resolutions, and in accordance with what they should adopt that day He suggested that the resolution adopted at the Congress of 1897 be accepted as the sense of the present meeting The resolution was that it was desirable that the erection of public buildings should be confided to private architects chosen by public or private competition or otherwise, and that the architects superintending the erection of the work should be under the direction of the Government.

Mr. Slater asked if Mr Totten could accept M. Poupinel's resolution.

Mr. Totten said not altogether The two might be combined

Mr Plummer seconded M Poupinel's resolution He said they were agreed as to the character of the resolution.

Mr. Adams suggested that the last line would be better as an expression of opinion. The part as to officials engaging in private practice would come rather badly in connection with the previous part They were all agreed about it, but he thought it would be better put separately.

Mr. W E Riley said they were not all agreed about it by any means They wanted to hear what it meant.

A speaker said that in that case it would be better to put the latter part separately It would only come as an expression of opinion

M. Poupinel agreed to separate the resolution as proposed, ending the first resolution at the word "incontestable "

Mr. Prynne said the resolution was not quite happy yet. He thought they might accept as an addition " by competition or otherwise," for they did not want to shut out the genius who might not be known and men who were really clever, otherwise men would not come forward at all

Mr Riley moved that the words "by qualified architects " be inserted

Herr Bodo Ebhardt (Berlin) said that Germans had had long wars on this subject It was found impossible to say that an official architect could not have genius because he was an official, and they had agreed that a competition should be the way to find the man to plan a work, and that all big works should be submitted to competition among architects generally.

Mr Riley said that he would be disposed to accept that if it was the sense of the meeting, but he should like it made quite plain that officials should not be excluded He did not know what the official had done to be treated in the way proposed. The official was what he was by circumstances. He was there in that way as was any architect in the same circumstances in the position he occupied. He begged the Congress not to come irrationally to the conclusion that because a man was an official he should be excluded from the proper discharge of his work He moved that the resolution should not exclude the qualified official.

Mr Leverton seconded.

M. Poupinel said that his resolution did not exclude the official if Mr. Prynne's addition were agreed to.

Mr Riley said that if that were so he would accept it

Mr. Slater then read the resolution again, with Mr Prynne's addition —viz. " by competition or otherwise."

Mr. RILEY said he had no objection to that.

Mr TOTTEN said that they had lost sight of the main question—viz the method of executing public works of architecture   One side had presented that it might be done by salaried officials quite as well as by private architects, and the other side had maintained that public officials were occupied too much by other duties to have the time to spare for designing works of art   According to what was now proposed, anyone could do these works so long as he had some reputation.

Mr. RILEY . Only architects

Mr TOTTEN . The general broad question is, What is the best way, from the point of view of architecture, of having work executed—is it by entrusting the work to men who occupy positions as officials, or to men who have some authority in art ?   He did not think the resolution covered that, and he did not think the question should be settled by a small meeting such as the present had become   He moved that the matter be referred to a small committee to formulate the resolution, and that it be dealt with later on

Mr RILEY asked if the motion was in order.

Mr SLATER said it was in order, but he did not see how the motion could be given effect to for want of time

Mr. TOTTEN said the matter could be disposed of in half an hour the following morning if the proposed committee dealt with the form of resolution

Mr PRYNNE said that if they had to give a vote then, the words " salaried officials " ought to be included in the resolution

Mr. E. HARPER moved that the discussion be adjourned until the following morning at 9 15

Mr TOTTEN seconded

Mr. FAWCETT said that if they adjourned they would not get half the present audience who had heard the arguments

Mr SLATER   Quite true, but half the audience have left who have heard

The motion to adjourn was then put and lost

Mr SLATER then put the original resolution, as amended—viz

" That, in the future, in the interests of administrative bodies and the public, and in the higher interests of the art of architecture, public bodies, whether Government, provincial, or municipal, should entrust important architectural works only to professionally qualified architects. either by competition or otherwise "

The motion was agreed to, and the proceedings terminated

REGULATIONS AS AMENDED FEBRUARY 24, 1903, FOR THE ENFORCEMENT OF THE ACT OF CONGRESS (U S A) APPROVED FEBRUARY 20, 1893, TO ENABLE THE SECRETARY OF THE TREASURY TO OBTAIN, BY COMPETITION AMONG ARCHITECTS, DESIGNS AND SPECIFICATIONS FOR PUBLIC BUILDINGS TO BE ERECTED UNDER THE SUPERVISION OF THE TREASURY DEPARTMENT

FOR the enforcement of the Act approved February 20. 1893, to enable the Secretary of the Treasury to obtain, by competition among architects, plans, drawings, and specifications for public buildings to be erected under the supervision of the Treasury Department

By virtue of the authority contained in the Act of Congress approved February 20, 1893, entitled " An Act authorising the Secretary of the Treasury to obtain plans and specifications for public buildings to be erected under the supervision of the Treasury Department, and providing for local supervision of the construction of the same," the Secretary of the Treasury hereby declares his purpose to enforce said Act with reference to such buildings as may be hereafter selected by him, subject to the following regulations .

COMPETITORS

1. At least five architects of good professional standing, who are citizens of the United States, shall be invited by the Secretary of the Treasury to submit plans, drawings, and specifications in accordance with the conditions set forth in these regulations ; and such plans, drawings, and specifications shall be passed upon as to merit by the commission herein provided for

COMMISSION OF AWARD

2 A commission shall be appointed by the Secretary of the Treasury consisting of the Supervising Architect of the Treasury Department, and four well-known architects, to judge and report to him as to the relative merit of the designs and plans submitted

3. No member of the commission herein referred to shall have any interest whatever, direct or indirect, in any design submitted in the competition, or any association with, or employment by, any of the competitors : and no employee of the Treasury Department shall be allowed to enter any competition held under these regulations.

DATA FURNISHED.

4 The office of the Supervising Architect will furnish full data and information as to cost and general requirements of the buildings placed in competition under these regulations, and the successful architect will be awarded a commission to prepare complete plans, drawings, and specifications, and to locally supervise the buildings won in any competition

UNSUCCESSFUL COMPETITORS

5. It must be understood that no claim shall be made upon the United States by any unsuccessful competitor for any fee, percentage, or payment whatever, or any expense incident to, or growing out of, his participation in the competition

REJECTED DESIGNS

6 The department agrees to make selection from the designs submitted if, in its opinion, one suitable in all respects as to design, detail, and cost be submitted, but expressly reserves the right to reject any and all plans, designs, and specifications submitted, and to reopen the competition if, in the opinion of the commission herein referred to, or of the Secretary of the Treasury, no design suitable in all respects has been submitted.

MISCONDUCT

7 It must be understood that a competitor will forfeit all privileges under these regulations who shall violate any of the conditions governing a competition, or who shall seek in any way, directly or indirectly, to gain advantage by influencing in his favour any of the commission

COMPETITIVE DRAWINGS

8 Each set of drawings, with its accompanying description, must be securely wrapped and sealed, and addressed to the " Secretary of the Treasury, Washington, D C.," plainly and conspicuously marked with the name of the building under competition, and without any distinguishing mark or device which might disclose the identity of the competitor

9. There must be inclosed with each set of drawings, &c , a plain, white, opaque envelope, within which the competitor will place a card bearing his name and address The envelope must be securely sealed with a plain wax seal having no impression, legend, device, or mark upon it which might disclose the identity of the competitor

OPENING OF DRAWINGS.

10. Upon opening the packages containing the drawings, the commission will number the envelope containing the name and address of the competitor, and will place the same number upon each drawing, plan, specification, &c , submitted by him, and will preserve unopened the envelope containing such name and address until final selection shall be made

FINDING OF COMMISSION

11. The commission shall place out of competition any set of drawings as to which the conditions of these regulations have not been observed, and examine those remaining, giving to each the rank to which, in their judgment, its merit entitles it, and submit their findings to the Secretary of the Treasury.

FINAL SELECTION

12 The selection of one of the designs by the Secretary of the Treasury, and its subsequent approval by him, the Postmaster-General, and the Secretary of the Interior, shall be final and conclusive.

SUCCESSFUL COMPETITOR MAY BE REJECTED

13 In the event that the architect to whom the commission is awarded should prove to be an incompetent or improper person, the Secretary of the Treasury expressly reserves the right to remove him, to revoke the commission awarded him, and to annul the contract entered into with him, but such architect shall receive equitable compensation for the work properly performed by him up to the time of his removal, to be fixed by the Secretary of the Treasury

RETURN OF COMPETITIVE DRAWINGS

14. Upon the award of the contract to the architect, all designs of unsuccessful competitors will be returned to them, and no use will be made of any of the drawings not accepted, or of any part that may be original, without the consent of the author thereof

DRAWINGS AFTER AWARD.

15. The architect to whom the commission is awarded shall revise his competitive drawings to meet the further requirements of the Secretary of the Treasury, and upon the basis of these revised preliminary drawings shall prepare full detailed working drawings and specifications for said building; and shall thereafter, from time to time, make such changes in the plans, drawings, and specifications as may be directed by the Secretary of the Treasury, for which just compensation shall be allowed, but no changes in the plans, drawings, and specifications shall be made without written authority from the Secretary of the Treasury.

16 Alterations in the working drawings and specifications which may be necessary to keep the cost of the building within the limit furnished by the office of the Supervising Architect shall, when required by the Secretary of the Treasury, be made by the architect in charge at his own cost.

17. The architect is to provide for the use of the Treasury Department one set of tracings of all working drawings, one copy of the specifications, and one copy of detailed estimate of cost of entire building, which, with the competitive drawings or revised competitive drawings as may be necessary, shall remain in the custody of the Department, and to be and remain the property of the United States and not of the architect; but such drawings and specifications shall not be used for any other building.   The office of the Supervising Architect will furnish for the use of intending bidders all necessary duplications of plans and specifications.   All detail and full-size drawings and sketches necessary for the use of the contractors during construction must be furnished by the architect, and copies supplied by him both to the contractors and the Government " Superintendent of Construction " at the building The architect shall also furnish the " Superintendent of Construction " with copies of all letters addressed by him to the contractors relative to the work

ARCHITECT'S FEE

18 The architect (or architects) to whom said commission shall be awarded will receive in compensation for full professional services, including local supervision of the building, a fee computed at the rate of 5 per cent. upon the cost of the work executed from his drawings and specifications and under his superintendence.   The sum upon which the architect's commission is to be computed shall be the actual construction cost of the building as ascertained from the net amount of contracts awarded and proposals accepted for additions or deductions.

19. The architect's commission shall be paid as the work progresses in the following order :

One-fifth of fee when preliminary drawings are completed and approved in the manner herein provided, three-tenths of fee when general working drawings and specifications are completed and copies delivered to the Supervising Architect; and balance of percentage monthly upon the basis of payments for work performed as of record on the books of the office of the Supervising Architect

20. Until the actual cost of the building can be determined the fee of the architect will be based upon the proposed cost of the work as above indicated, or as may be readjusted from time to time, and will be paid as instalments of the entire fee, which will be finally computed as per paragraph No. 18

21. The compensation herein stipulated to be paid to said architect shall be in full payment of all charges for his full services, inclusive of all travelling and other

expenses necessary to his proper superintendence of the work.   Expenses incurred in travelling under orders from the Department may be reimbursed on approval of the Secretary of the Treasury

WORK NOT INCLUDED

22 The services of the architect will not be required, or paid for, in connection with the supply of furniture, gas, or electric fixtures, or electric light plants, unless specially ordered in writing by the Department

GOVERNMENT SUPERINTENDENT OF CONSTRUCTION

23 The Department will appoint and maintain on the work as its local repre sentative a " Superintendent of Construction " This officer will act under orders from the Department and solely as its representative, and not at all as the representative of the architect in charge, who will not be relieved in any particular from his responsibility for the actual superintendence of the work by the presence of the " Superintendent of Construction," who will not give orders to contractors or their employees

ARCHITECT'S CERTIFICATE OF WORK DONE

24 Payments upon the work of construction under contract will be made upon vouchers certified by the architect in charge and countersigned by the " Superintendent of Construction " representing the United States Government, which will be paid by a disbursing officer appointed by the Secretary of the Treasury

CONTRACTS FOR CONSTRUCTION

25. The Supervising Architect of the Treasury Department will receive the proposals for contracts to be awarded, and shall likewise determine the manner in which the various branches of the work are to be contracted for

26. All further details necessary properly to carry out these regulations may be arranged by the Supervising Architect from time to time, provided they do not conflict herewith

27 The foregoing regulations shall be subject to modification and change at the pleasure of the Secretary of the Treasury

July 3, 1897

As amended February 24, 1903

LESLIE M SHAW,
Secretary of the Treasury

ARCHITECTURAL COPYRIGHT AND OWNERSHIP OF DRAWINGS

Wednesday and Thursday, 18th and 19th July —Institute Meeting Room

Chairmen M H P Nénot (France); Mr W S Eames (United States)
Hon Secretaries Señor Oriosto y Velada (Spain), Mr Walter Read (Transvaal).

1 —THE OWNERSHIP OF ARCHITECTS' DRAWINGS

By H HEATHCOTE STATHAM.

The fact that this subject has been put down for discussion along with two papers on architectural copyright may, I fear, tend to confirm the confusion of mind which, as I had occasion to observe at a recent discussion at the Institute of Architects, seems to exist with some members of the profession in regard to these two subjects   It is therefore as well to point out at the outset that the question as to the ownership of drawings made by an architect for the carrying out of a building has nothing whatever to do with the question of copyright in an architectural design , it is a different question entirely, resting on a different basis of argument The question of copyright is concerned with the right of an architect to prevent the copying or reproducing of his design by another person The subject of the ownership of drawings turns on the question whether the drawings and specification made by the architect for the purpose of carrying out a building are his property, or whether he is bound to hand them over to his client on the completion of the building.

To French or German architects the very existence of such a point of dispute will probably seem absurd, for in those countries architects are not trampled on and ridiculed by the law as they are in England   An architect practising in Paris informs me that in France the law gives the architect the absolute right to keep his drawings, and that the ruling of the English Courts on this subject would be regarded in France as absurd , that " the architect owes to the client a complete building, and not any of the papers, drawings, &c , which he prepared for his own use for carrying out the building " I am informed that it is not infrequently the custom for the architect to give the client a copy of the general elevations and plans , but that this is merely a matter of custom or courtesy, and cannot be enforced by law

The evidence of a German architect on the point is as follows :—

" Architects keep all their original drawings, specifications, papers, and correspondence relating to a job   They are, however, bound to provide a client with one copy (tracing, lithograph, or process copy) of all drawings, if called upon to do so, without extra charge. [I am in some doubt, however, whether by " all drawings " my correspondent means to include all the various detail drawings, or whether he only means the plans and elevations]   On the other hand, the client is not allowed in any way to use these drawings for any further building operations, the arrangement being that the fee for the architect's services is for design and supervision for the specific job, and that if his copies of drawings be refused by the client, he is entitled to a fresh set of fees for the design as distinct from supervision "

This last seems an exceedingly unsatisfactory arrangement, since, in the case of a client disposed to make an unfair use of the copies of the architect's design, it leaves on the architect the *onus* of finding this out, and the expense of taking legal steps to prevent it or to obtain compensation for it   The latter is only a question of money and inconvenience, but the first part of the business, the discovery of the illegal proceeding, may never come to pass at all if the client chose to carry out a building on the same lines in some distant situation.   However, by the German practice the architect, at all events, remains the custodian of his own drawings

This has also been the almost universal and recognised custom in England for many years—I believe one might say for some generations past.   In every office I have been in since I was an articled pupil the custom has been that the drawings of each building that had been carried out in the office were filed and labelled for reference if required, and in the office in which I was for seven years a pupil I remember on many occasions clients calling who wished to add to or alter a building previously carried out, and the plans being taken out and consulted, and I never knew any case in my experience of a client claiming, or even appearing to think of claiming, the right to have the drawings handed over to him, and I have no doubt that any amount of evidence in the same direction would be forthcoming if asked for.   My reason for emphasising this point will appear just now.   It is sufficient for the moment to note that practically we have always in England gone on the principle that the drawings were our property, and that the immense majority of our clients have always acquiesced in that view ; in fact, I only know of two instances to the contrary.   In my office it was always the custom to give the client a complete plan of the drainage of his building, that being given as a right and useful thing to do, and not under legal compulsion   That would be of use to the client in a legitimate manner.   Copies of the general drawings could only be of use to him in an illegitimate manner, or what ought to be considered so

Thus stood the case in England till the law got its finger in the pie. But before going into that story, let us consider for a moment what is the abstract equity of the matter   What is an architect paid for ?   Not, surely, for making drawings of buildings, but for producing a building of a special type of design and with special arrangements of plan.   He cannot do this with his own hands, as a painter produces a picture, he has to give his instructions to a number of people, for which purpose he must in most cases make drawings and write a specification.   But those are not the building, they are his instructions for producing the building. He may also find it necessary in many cases to show to his client a sufficient representation on paper of the proposed plan and appearance of the building to satisfy the client that he is going to get what he wants, if he knows what he wants—many clients do not.   But that, again, is not what the client pays him for; that is only an intimation of what he proposes to produce, the client pays him for what he produces.   A third reason for making a plan in the case of large buildings for multifarious uses is that the architect himself could not otherwise arrange it with the best regard to economy of space and simplicity of working ; that is a motive in which he himself alone is concerned.   On the top of all that there is the abominable contract system, the bane of modern architecture, in accordance with which it is necessary to have complete drawings made beforehand in order to get quantities and estimates of cost   But for that the architect might in many cases, if he chose, and if he had time to be on the ground a great deal, dispense with formal drawings altogether , some people think that would be to the advantage of architecture. That may be utopian , but all these considerations go to show that the drawings are not what the client pays for, and that there is no logical reason why his payment of the architect's commission should be supposed to entitle him to them   And there are two very important reasons why the architect should keep them   The first is, that an architect's method of working, in drawing and in designing details, is a matter of interest to him just as much as a sculptor's or painter s first sketches for a statue or a picture are of interest to him   The second and perhaps more important reason is that plans and specifications, of a large building especially, embody a great deal of knowledge gained by long experience , the specification of a large building is a kind of summary of the architect's practical experience, acquired, perhaps, through many years , why is he to give that knowledge and experience for permanent use to his client ? He is paid for applying that experience to the carrying out of one particular building , he is not called upon to sell it in perpetuity for the use of another person.

Such was the generally accepted position until, as before observed, the law got in its finger. The beginning of this was the case of *Ebdy* v. *M'Gowan* in 1870, when the architect had made the drawings, but the building had not been carried out, and the architect claimed payment for the work done on them, but declined to give them up   In this he was morally right, but wrong according to professional custom, since it has been the custom to hand over the drawings when the matter had not gone beyond drawing, on the ground, apparently, that otherwise the client got nothing for his money , and the plaintiff could not get evidence, therefore, of professional custom in his favour, and had to give way. But it was never supposed in the profession that this judgment amounted to anything more than a legal sanction of the custom of giving up the drawings when the building had not been proceeded with   But two years ago came on the case of *Gibbon* v *Pease*, in which the client was the plaintiff and sought to obtain the drawings from the architect   In this case the work had been carried out, but, to the astonishment of all but the lawyers, the judges ruled that the precedent of *Ebdy* v *M'Gowan* applied in every case as to the ownership of drawings , they refused to hear any evidence as to professional custom , they spoke of the architect, in an almost insulting manner, as " a person who was trying to break the law," and inquired what an architect wanted with the drawings , a point on which they might have had ample information if they would have condescended to hear the evidence which was forthcoming, but which they resolutely refused to hear

The law of this country, as established by our wonderful system of going by precedent and not by the rights of the case, therefore now stands thus   Any client, after he has paid the architect's fees, may demand that the whole of the drawings and specification should be handed over to him, although he has already got what he really paid for, viz. the building. And as there is no provision in our law to prevent him making any use of them that he pleases, he can, if he chooses, apply them to the carrying-out of a similar building elsewhere, without the architect having the slightest legal redress or compensation of any kind.

How has this preposterous state of things come about ?   There are four main reasons for it, and it will be seen that the architects themselves, and the Institute as their representative body, have in some degree contributed to it   The four reasons, as they appear to me, are :—

1. The general inability of lawyers to understand what an architect is and what architecture means.

2 The refusal of judges to listen to evidence

3. The unfortunate and mistaken wording of Clause 1 in the Institute Scale of Professional Charges of Architects

4 The suicidal and totally illogical custom of consenting to give up the drawings when the building has not been carried out.

As to the first, I have had various talks with lawyers on the subject, and it is impossible to make them understand that an architect is not paid for making drawings, or understand why his drawings should be of any value to him   I told one man—a solicitor—that he might just as well expect that a man who paid a sculptor for a marble statue should require also to have handed over to him all the sculptor's clay studies and sketches for the work   He coolly replied   " If it came into Court, I expect the law would rule that he must hand them over ! "   What is one to say after this ?   The writer of an able letter in *The Builder* said in relation to this extraordinary remark :—

> Let him inquire whether the purchaser of a piece of ordnance obtains with it all the experimental and completed drawings and specifications, all the calculations, particulars, and tests, and all the patterns, foundry-plant, and tools as well , or let him ask himself whether such firms as those of Armstrong or Krupp would have even come into existence had every purchaser of a new form of gun been able to claim as part of the bargain and without payment the brains which, had the purchaser himself possessed them, would have rendered an Armstrong or a Krupp a superfluity.

That is to the point, I think

2 The refusal of judges to hear evidence, upon which it is useless to say anything.   When judges have once got it into their heads that the law as settled by precedent is so and so, the offer of any evidence to show that the sacred precedent was founded on a misconception of facts is only regarded as an attack on the majesty of the law, and all that the plaintiff gets is that—

> He has his judge's joke for consolation.

3 The wording of the first clause in the Institute Scale of Charges is most unfortunate   It states that the commission is, among other things, " for the necessary general and detailed drawings and specifications," which a lawyer would undoubtedly interpret into an admission that the drawings were the things paid for, and were therefore the property of the person who paid.   It was certainly not intended so, but it is a most unfortunate piece of wording   It ought to have run   " Furnishing the contractor and other workmen with such drawings and directions as are necessary for the accurate carrying-out of the work "   That would have put the case in the right manner

4. The custom, which has been acquiesced in generally in the profession, of consenting to give up the drawings of a building not carried out on the payment of the $2\frac{1}{2}$ per cent commission on the estimated cost, although it arises from a perfectly virtuous motive, viz the feeling that the client ought to have something for his money, is a most foolish and illogical one, and has done a great deal to play into the hands of the lawyers   It is really to a great extent giving away our own case   Why, because a client did not know his own mind, and intended to build and then gave it up—why on that account is he to obtain permanent possession of the architect's professional knowledge to make use of as he pleases ?   Cannot architects see that in that case an unscrupulous person has only to say he has changed his mind, get possession of the drawings and specification, and carry out the building with a clerk of works of his own, and save himself half the architect's fees ?   I have heard of a case in which a public body actually adopted that policy, and one of their number let the cat out of the bag in a confidential conversation in which he showed how cleverly they had saved the ratepayers' money.   It is a thing always possible to an unscrupulous person   The proper and logical course would

be, if the drawings had been made and building abandoned, for the architect to send in a charge for time expended A charge based on that consideration might be, probably would have to be, considerably less than the orthodox 2½ per cent. would be , but both the individual architect and the profession at large would be in a far better position, which would be well worth the sacrifice of something in immediate £ *s d*. They would put themselves in a logical position, and would prevent the public from despoiling them in a very unfair manner. Why is a client to claim all your drawings and specification, the concrete body of your experience, for his own use, because he has changed his mind ? Let clients learn to know their own minds If he complains that he has to pay for your time and gets nothing for it, whose fault is that ? People who do not know their own minds generally have to pay for it in this world in one way or another ; I see no reason why an architect's clients should be an exception

What is the remedy for the present state of things ? Of course it has been suggested by the judges, in both the cases referred to, that an architect can make a special stipulation that the drawings are to remain his property before undertaking a commission. But that is a most unsatisfactory solution In the first place it is acquiescing in a state of the law which is entirely wrong and unjust. In the second place, it is simply providing or suggesting a ground of dispute between architect and client. As soon as you begin to make a special stipulation of that kind, you put it into the head of a cantankerous client (and we all know there are plenty of them) to dispute the point It ought to be an understood thing without any necessity for special stipulations at all. The law is wrong, and the law must be altered. The first thing to be done is for the Institute of Architects to amend the first clause of its " Professional Practice as to Charges," and put it in a form that will properly express the position. That will be paving the way so far. As to getting the law altered, there are, I believe, only two ways of doing that one by getting a new precedent established in case another action similar to that of *Gibbon* v *Pease* should arise , the other by getting a Bill passed in Parliament. In the present opinion and disposition of English judges on the subject it would be of no use to hope to get a new precedent except by carrying a case to the House of Lords, which is what the Institute ought to have done in the case of *Gibbon* v. *Pease*, when they found that the defendant in the case could not afford to do so It is, I believe, too late for that now ; but I must say that I think the Institute has been most remiss, and has failed in its duty to the profession in not taking up that case and fighting it out, as Messrs Colls & Sons took up the ancient lights case and fought it out. The Institute have, I believe, established a Board of Defence , I should like to know what it defends if it cannot defend the interests of architects in such an important matter as this I shall be told, I suppose, that they took the advice of their lawyer, who told them they had no case. Then they should have made a case What is the use of going to a lawyer in regard to a matter in which the law itself is in the wrong ? Of course he will tell you that you have no case , all that a lawyer can ever see is—the law · that the law is wrong and wants altering is a matter beyond his sphere But I am not satisfied, and I should hope there are many others who will not be satisfied with being told that we must lie down submissively and be trampled on by the law. And I beg, in conclusion, to move the following resolution —

That, in the opinion of this Meeting, the Royal Institute of British Architects, having revised the wording of its paper on the Professional Practice as to the Charges of Architects in the sense indicated above, should as early as possible take steps to get a Bill introduced into Parliament for securing the adoption of their scale of charges, so amended, as part of the law of the land

2.—DE LA PROPRIÉTÉ ARTISTIQUE DES ŒUVRES D'ARCHI-TECTURE

Par M GEORGES HARMAND (Avocat à la Cour d'Appel, Paris),

Membre des Conseils judiciells de la Société Centrale des Architectes Français et de la Caisse de Défense Mutuelle Membre Correspondant honoraire de l'Institut Royal des Architectes Britanniques

I. BASES DE LA PROPRIÉTÉ ARTISTIQUE.

Nous pensons qu'il peut être utile, en commençant un rapport sur le droit de propriété artistique, d'expliquer brièvement le but de cette propriété, sa source juridique, et l'extension des droits qu'elle comporte.

Tout d'abord à quoi se réfère le droit de propriété artistique et comment se justifie-t-il en *droit naturel* ?

Le droit de propriété artistique se réfère à la personnalité de l'auteur, au respect de sa personne, disons même plus, de sa pensée—c'est là une source de droit, infiniment légitime, trop justifiable pour que nous insistions, surtout ici en Angleterre où le respect de la personne a pris dans la législation une place si importante, qu'elle a fait école dans toute l'Europe

Voici donc un architecte, qui dessine et trace les plans d'un édifice, d'après ses goûts, ses sentiments artistiques, ses études et ses conceptions soit des avantages d'un terrain sur lequel il pense élever son œuvre, soit des besoins de son client. Que cela soit bon ou mauvais, puisqu'il s'en déclare l'auteur, il en prend la responsabilité devant ses contemporains, ses confrères, et les critiques d'art. Parcequ'il affirme que cela est son œuvre, il a par suite le droit d'empêcher un tiers de copier cette œuvre et de la reproduire sur le terrain, ou simplement à l'aide d'un autre procédé des arts graphiques ou plastiques Son œuvre peut plaire ou ne pas plaire, être bonne ou mauvaise, malheureuse pour sa notoriété ou géniale, cela n'importe en rien *en droit*, quant à l'importance des droits que l'on doit lui reconnaître. Si l'œuvre qu'il a conçue, dessinée, puis édifiée, est de lui, il a le droit de défendre cette œuvre, de s'en réserver les mérites aussi bien que les rémunérations ∶ de même qu'il lui faudra évidemment subir les désagréments des critiques que cette œuvre peut lui attirer.

Ses contemporains ne seront pas gênés par l'exercice de ses droits, pour exercer légitimement, eux-mêmes, les droits qu'il revendique pour lui Ils peuvent s'inspirer de son œuvre, comme il s'est inspiré des œuvres des artistes du passé, ou de ceux du temps présent

Si son œuvre a un caractère personnel et original, elle est à lui, si les autres s'inspirent de son œuvre, aussi bien que de celles des autres architectes, ils doivent produire une œuvre ayant un caractère personnel et original, pour jouir des droits que votre confrère réclame pour lui

Tel est et doit être le raisonnement de l'architecte-artiste, c'est d'ailleurs celui des autres artistes, des littérateurs, et de tous les penseurs

Telle est la justification du droit de propriété artistique elle ne diffère guère de la justification du droit de propriété Aussi bien on a pu dire que la propriété artistique était *une propriété.*

Ceci expliqué, il sera plus facile d'entrer dans l'étude du droit de propriété artistique, et en particulier du droit de propriété artistique des œuvres d'architecture

II PRINCIPES DE LA PROPRIÉTÉ ARTISTIQUE

Le droit de propriété artistique est, pour l'artiste, plus particulièrement le droit de reproduire l'œuvre qu'il a conçue, et de la rendre publique. A ce droit, qui est l'un des principaux éléments du droit de propriété artistique, s'ajoutent différents autres droits, comme le droit de décider si l'œuvre sera publiée en entier ou en partie, à quelle époque, et aussi moyennant quelle rémunération l'auteur en autorisera la reproduction par des tiers.   Enfin, l'auteur a seul le droit de décider quelles modifications, corrections ou remaniements peut subir l'œuvre dont il est l'auteur L'auteur a le droit aussi de décider si l'œuvre qu'il a créée sera signée, et s'il la signera de son nom ou d'un pseudonyme, ou s'il la laissera anonyme Personne, sans son consentement, ne peut modifier ces diverses conditions de la publication de son œuvre.

Il faut de suite indiquer que tous ces droits, dont on constate depuis un siècle l'existence, n'avaient pas jusqu'à ces dernières années de source juridique très nettement déterminée ; en équité l'on sentait bien que toutes ces affirmations du droit de l'auteur étaient judicieuses · la vraie raison juridique n'a été déterminée que lorsqu'on a dégagé ce que l'on appelle *le droit moral*.

Le Droit Moral de l'auteur repose sur la responsabilité qu'il prend, ayant créé l'œuvre, de s'en affirmer l'auteur : en échange, ainsi que nous l'avons déjà dit, il s'expose autant aux critiques des autres artistes, ses pairs, ou des esthéticiens, des critiques d'art et du public qu'à leurs éloges Le corollaire de cette responsabilité et de cette affirmation de créateur est, que seul il a le droit de signer l'œuvre, et que personne ne peut porter atteinte à sa signature, pas plus qu'à l'œuvre, sous forme de modifications ou de corrections.   A plus forte raison, a-t-il seul droit aux honoraires ou rémunérations que les tiers peuvent donner pour jouir de l'œuvre ou en obtenir des reproductions , et il est évident que tous les moyens d'obtenir une rémunération de l'œuvre sont, quelqu'intérêt qu'ils présentent, d'ordre moral infiniment moins important que ce droit à la signature de l'œuvre, à la détermination de ses modes de publication D'où il résulte que le Droit Moral de l'auteur est en même temps que la base du droit d'auteur, la justification du droit de reproduction sous lequel pendant si longtemps le droit d'auteur a été seulement envisagé.

III Historique Sommaire de la Protection de la Propriété Artistique

Ces principes sont communs à tous les artistes, aux dessinateurs, aux peintres et sculpteurs   Ceux-ci jouissent depuis longtemps de l'exercice de leurs droits d'auteur d'une manière infiniment étendue.   Les dessinateurs et les peintres ont évidemment les premiers bénéficié, avec les graveurs, des premières dispositions législatives qui, à partir du xviiiᵉ siècle, ont mentionné et reconnu le droit d'auteur   Dans les siècles précédents, il semble que ce soient, en même temps que les littérateurs, les graveurs, qui aient obtenu, les premiers, des protections temporaires, plus ou moins développées , et l'on cite au xviᵉ siècle les privilèges accordés notamment par la République de Venise à Albert Durer.

Ce qu'il y a d'intéressant, c'est que la Grande-Bretagne est la première de toutes les nations européennes, qui ait accordé aux dessinateurs et aux graveurs de sujets d'architecture un monopole, qui était bien la proclamation d'un véritable droit d'auteur, comme nous l'entendons aujourd'hui. C'est ensuite la France qui, dans sa loi de propriété artistique des 19-24 juillet 1793, a affirmé le plus complètement le droit de l'auteur

Il importe de retenir les termes dans lesquels, en France, en 1791 Chapelier, membre de la Constituante, et en 1793 Lakanal, membre de la Convention, invoquant l'exemple de l'Angleterre, demandèrent à l'Assemblée de reconnaître le droit d'auteur "*La plus sacrée, la plus légitime, la plus inattaquable et, si je puis parler ainsi,*" disait Chapelier, "*la plus personnelle de toutes les propriétés est l'ouvrage fruit de la pensée d'un écrivain.*" Et Lakanal ajoutait que "*de toutes les propriétés la moins susceptible de contestations, celle dont l'accroissement ne peut donner d'ombrage à la liberté, c'est sans contredit celle des productions du génie.*"

En 1793 en France comme en Angleterre en 1735 et 1766, le législateur songeait particulièrement aux dessinateurs et aux peintres et graveurs, qui feraient graver ou reproduire leurs œuvres

Bien que la loi française fut muette à l'égard des sculpteurs et des architectes, des sculpteurs bientôt réclamèrent la même protection que les peintres et les dessinateurs elle leur fut accordée sans difficulté , et, en 1855, pour la première fois, en France, un architecte réclama cette même protection : elle lui fut également accordée

En 1886, un architecte belge, M Beyaert, réclama, tandis que la Belgique était régie par la loi française de 1793, la protection de la propriété artistique, à l'encontre d'une revue belge, qui avait publié des reproductions de la Banque, l'un des principaux édifices d'Anvers dont il était l'auteur Cette protection lui fut accordée

Depuis, la France a, par la loi du 11 mars 1902, ajouté expressément les architectes et les sculpteurs au nombre des artistes bénéficiant de la loi de 1793 sur la propriété artistique.

Nous dirons tout à l'heure, dans une revue de la législation du globe sur la propriété artistique des architectes, combien de pays protègent l'architecture, et dans quelle limite les architectes sont protégés dans ces pays.

IV Quelles Œuvres d'Architecture doivent être Protégées

Il nous paraît maintenant indispensable de faire connaître les raisons par lesquelles l'architecte doit être protégé de la même manière que les peintres, les sculpteurs et les autres artistes.

L'architecte a les mêmes moyens d'expression, les mêmes règles de dessin, de perspective ou de figuration, que les dessinateurs et les peintres. Et dans l'exécution sur le terrain de son œuvre dessinée, de ses plans, de l'ensemble de ses dessins, que nous appellerons en terme général " LES DESSINS D'ARCHITECTURE," l'édifice, dont il dirige la reproduction, emprunte l'expression de ses reliefs aux procédés de la sculpture, ainsi que les règles de cet art

On chercherait donc vainement une raison de ne pas accorder aux architectes, la protection que l'on donne aux peintres et aux sculpteurs Il ne s'agit d'ailleurs de protéger que les œuvres ayant un *caractère original et personnel*, de même que pour les peintres et les sculpteurs ; et, comme pour les peintres et les sculpteurs, il est juste d'admettre que les œuvres originales et personnelles peuvent être composées, soit d'idées personnelles, soit d'éléments ordonnés d'une manière originale et personnelle, d'après ce que nous ont transmis les siècles passés (ce que l'on appelle LE DOMAINE PUBLIC).

LE DOMAINE PUBLIC, c'est ce bagage considérable que nous ont légué les Grecs, les Romains, les Égyptiens et toutes les civilisations passées ainsi que les siècles qui nous précèdent, où d'éclatantes périodes artistiques se sont manifestées, au temps de la Renaissance, sous la reine Anne comme sous Louis XIV, sous Louis XV, sous Louis XVI, etc.

Les peintres, comme les sculpteurs, se sont inspirés de l'œuvre des artistes de ces mêmes époques, et il est aussi difficile en peinture, en sculpture qu'en architecture de faire une œuvre *entièrement et absolument* NOUVELLE Aussi, pour les peintres et les sculpteurs ne discute-t-on pas qu'ils aient le droit de s'inspirer des œuvres du passé pour produire une œuvre personnelle, que la loi protégera aussi complètement qu'une œuvre absolument nouvelle.

V Objections contre la Protection des Œuvres d'Architecture
Réponse à ces Objections

Nous avons essayé dans une conférence lue en avril 1898 à l'Institut Royal des Architectes Britanniques [p. 285 du JOURNAL R I B A , 9 avril 1898] de donner un résumé des objections que l'on faisait à la protection des architectes, objections, qui avaient été principalement accueillies par le législateur allemand dans la loi de 1876 [1]

On a proposé d'écarter les architectes de la propriété artistique parce que, dans leur œuvre, la partie matérielle l'emportait considérablement sur la partie intellectuelle. On leur refusait aussi le droit d'auteur parce que leur art tendait avant tout à satisfaire un besoin de leurs contemporains, celui d'être couverts et à l'abri des intempéries, encore plus qu'il ne contribuait à la décoration des villes ou des habitations.

Nous avons en 1898, comme d'ailleurs en 1892 et 1893, dans *L'Architecture*, le journal de la Société Centrale des Architectes Français, tenu à répondre à ces objections Nous ne voulons y revenir que d'un mot Est-ce que pour la sculpture, le poids matériel du marbre, du bronze ou de la pierre, qui compose l'œuvre de sculpture, n'est pas, proportionnellement au volume, aussi pesant que le poids du marbre, des pierres ou du fer dans l'œuvre d'architecture ? Et, dès lors que le sculpteur est protégé, il n'y a pas d'exception à faire pour l'architecte Est-ce que la valeur d'utilité d'une œuvre d'art, que ce soit un vase, une coupe ou un édifice, n'est pas une qualité qui subsiste avec autant de mérite, que l'œuvre rende un service réel ou serve seulement à la décoration ? Est-ce que cela n'est pas aussi vrai pour une œuvre sculptée que pour une maison ?

Keats a dit qu'une belle chose était une joie pour toujours , et, qu'elle rendît un service réel, ou qu'elle servît à la décoration, il est évident que Keats n'eut rien changé à sa formule. Il est bien juste qu'en échange de cette joie perpétuelle que l'œuvre d'art doit procurer, on donne à l'artiste une protection qui n'est, sous une forme légale, que le respect de sa personnalité En vertu du *droit moral*, l'auteur a droit incontestablement à cette garantie ; le législateur ne pourrait manquer d'ajouter au Droit Moral le *droit de propriété artistique* qui, nous l'avons vu, s'y rattache si étroitement

Il importe essentiellement aux architectes de bien se persuader qu'ils ne demandent que ce dont jouissent déjà les peintres, sculpteurs ou dessinateurs, et qu'ils ont le droit d'affirmer qu'il serait singulièrement injuste que l'une des catégories d'artistes soit exclue, quand toutes les autres sont protégées Si l'on pense qu'il est juste d'affirmer comme tant de fois cela a été affirmé par des critiques éminents, par des philosophes, par des artistes, que *c'est par l'architecte que l'expression primitive de l'art a été formulée*, et qu'à ces débuts L'Architecte a associé à l'expression de ses idées le Peintre et le Sculpteur, il serait singulièrement injuste qu'à notre époque civilisée, le Peintre et le Sculpteur *se trouvent mieux protégés que* L'Architecte.

On a ensuite prétendu que l'œuvre de l'architecte, lorsqu'elle est placée en façade des rues et des places publiques, perdait le droit à la protection, parceque cette exposition impliquait de la part de l'auteur, une sorte d'abandon au public de la jouissance de son œuvre, et partant, de son droit de propriété artistique [2]

Nous avons déjà répondu que le sculpteur ne devait pas être plus tôt présumé avoir abandonné son droit d'auteur pour les statues exposées sur les places publiques que l'architecte sur ses façades . or dans un certain nombre de pays où les sculpteurs sont déjà protégés il n'est fait aucune différence entre leurs œuvres placées dans des galeries ou des maisons particulières et celles qui sont placées dans les rues à l'extérieur des maisons

---

[1] Nous sommes heureux d'apprendre que le 9 janvier, 1907, il a été promulgué en Allemagne une loi accordant la protection de la propriété artistique des œuvres d'architecture Cette loi constitue, malgré certaines insuffisances de protection, un réel progrès et une protection déjà importante des œuvres d'architecture Voir *l'Architecture*, journal de la Société Centrale des Architectes Français, 1907

[2] C'est malheureusement la théorie du législateur allemand dans la loi du 9 anvier 1907

Mais encore pour l'architecte, il faut rappeler que son œuvre originale consiste dans ses dessins d'architecture, ceux-ci ne sont jamais placés dans les rues, ce n'est que la reproduction de ses dessins, *l'édifice*, qui s'y trouve. Il paraît inadmissible *en droit*, que les droits, que l'auteur peut avoir sur l'original, puissent être diminués par des circonstances propres à la reproduction

Enfin comment admettre que le fait même de laisser apparent l'original, objet du droit, puisse entraîner pour l'auteur une diminution des droits, dont il peut bénéficier ? *Ira-t-on soutenir que le fait de tenir en évidence votre portefeuille autorise le voleur à vous en dépouiller ?* À cette considération de droit incontestable, nous ajouterons volontiers que ce serait gravement nuisible à la décoration des villes, à leur esthétique, que de décider que ce qui fait l'ornement des villes, de leurs places publiques, de leurs rues, entraînera pour les artistes une diminution de droit artistique, et qu'ils perdront le profit matériel des œuvres, dont la création leur aurait rapporté la gloire et la notoriété ils perdraient ainsi le bénéfice de leurs meilleures œuvres, de celles dont le succès serait le plus répandu ! ! !

Et dès-lors, au profit de qui ? de quelques éditeurs qui vendront les reproductions par la gravure ou la phototypie, de ces œuvres ! et qui n'en feront en réalité qu'un commerce fructueux aux dépens de l'architecte, sans profit pour le public Un pareil résultat justifie-t-il une atteinte à la *propriété* et au *respect de la personnalité* ? nous n'hésitons pas à répondre *non* En fait il suffit que l'éducation publique soit développée . nous verrons que la satisfaction de ce besoin peut être aisément assurée sans nuire à l'artiste, sans le dépouiller indûment En effet, les édifices, les constructions se partagent en deux groupes : ceux qui sont la propriété des particuliers, et ceux qui sont la propriété de l'Etat, des services publics ou des communes

Or pour ceux qui sont la propriété des particuliers, nous avons déjà indiqué que les édifices ne sont que la reproduction sur le terrain des dessins d'architecture, œuvre de l'auteur. C'est à l'œuvre originale que s'attachent les droits de propriété artistique, ils naissent dès que l'original est créé ; le droit de reproduction existe avant qu'il soit pratiqué par l'auteur: le sort de la reproduction ne modifie pas le droit né avant qu'elle ne soit exécutée.

Rien ne peut donc diminuer le droit de propriété artistique, à moins que l'auteur n'en fasse, par convention formelle, abandon partiel ou total A défaut d'abandon consenti par l'auteur, celui-ci conserve le droit de reproduire sur un autre terrain ou à l'aide d'un autre procédé que la construction, l'œuvre originale qu'il a créée et exprimée dans ses dessins d'architecture.

En est-il différemment à l'égard des monuments publics ? Non, l'État n'est qu'une collectivité de particuliers les communes, les autres parties de l'Etat sont de même. La collectivité des particuliers n'a donc pas de formes de droit différentes de celles des simples particuliers. Aussi ne ferons-nous aucune différence.

Toutefois, ainsi que nous l'avons dit, il est désirable que les monuments publics servent à l'éducation nationale, et jamais architecte ou artiste ne souhaitera s'opposer à l'éducation nationale · ils seront au contraire heureux d'y contribuer

Il suffirait donc d'admettre que les élèves d'art, les élèves architectes pourront librement dessiner d'après les édifices publics, pour que cette objection ait sa complète satisfaction , et que par suite aucune dérogation ne soit apportée à la pleine protection des architectes et des autres artistes. Ces élèves d'art n'ont, en effet, pas besoin de tirer un profit matériel de leurs dessins, ni de les réaliser sur le terrain ou de les reproduire Ils devront créer à leur tour après avoir librement étudié les œuvres de leurs aînés

VI. Conséquences de la Propriété Artistique des Œuvres d'Architecture

Quelles seront, particulièrement pour l'architecte, les conséquences de la protection artistique que nous venons d'exposer ? Les voici en quelques lignes

Tout d'abord l'architecte manifeste ses idées dans un ensemble de dessins et de plans, coupe, élévation, détails des façades extérieures et intérieures, détails décoratifs et autres en général, ensemble que nous exprimerons à l'aide de ces mots, LES DESSINS D'ARCHITECTURE

Les dessins d'architecture constituent la première manifestation de l'idée de l'architecte, L'ORIGINAL DE L'ŒUVRE L'architecte a droit de signer cet ensemble de dessins

L'architecte est maître de publier, quand il lui convient, l'œuvre qu'il a tracée Il a droit de la reproduire par les procédés qu'il lui convient de choisir, et de la manière qu'il l'entend

L'exécution des dessins d'architecture sous la forme d'un édifice élevé sur le terrain, est un des modes de reproduction des dessins d'architecture

Nul ne peut reproduire l'œuvre sans l'assentiment de l'auteur

L'architecte est maître de déterminer les honoraires qu'il lui convient de fixer, pour consentir à la reproduction de son œuvre.

Sauf stipulation contraire, l'architecte, en donnant son consentement, ne concède à son client que le droit de faire exécuter une seule reproduction de son œuvre.

Nul ne peut apporter, sans l'assentiment de l'auteur, des corrections, modifications ou remaniements à l'œuvre originale ou aux reproductions consenties par l'auteur.

VII. De la Protection de l'Œuvre de l'Architecte après sa Mort.

Il est presque constant que les législations, qui ont organisé la propriété littéraire ou artistique, concèdent pour un temps déterminé, qui, le plus souvent, comprend la vie de l'auteur et une période de 30, 50 ou 80 ans après sa mort, le monopole de propriété artistique. Pendant la durée de cette période, l'auteur, puis après lui ses héritiers ou ses cessionnaires, ont seuls le droit de publier, de reproduire l'œuvre.

En examinant attentivement les éléments du droit moral, on a vite constaté que les héritiers n'avaient pas absolument autant de droits que l'auteur sur l'œuvre.

Il y a en effet quelque chose de choquant à ce que l'on puisse admettre que les héritiers puissent détruire l'œuvre, ou la modifier dans *des conditions inesthétiques*. On n'admettrait pas non plus qu'ils se refusent systématiquement à reconnaître que l'œuvre a été produite par l'auteur. De là, on en est venu à penser que, lorsque le délai de protection est accompli, et que l'œuvre, ainsi qu'on le dit, est tombée dans le *domaine public*, on devait envisager que le public n'avait pas plus de droits que les héritiers de l'auteur. Et c'est là un des plus importants résultats du droit moral, que de produire des conséquences au-delà du délai de protection de l'auteur. Si, après l'expiration du délai de protection, tout le monde peut reproduire l'œuvre, néanmoins tout le monde trouvera naturel que l'on puisse interdire de faire de déplorables reproductions de l'œuvre, et de donner cependant ces reproductions comme représentant l'œuvre de l'auteur.

Il est évident qu'il serait profondément honorable pour les nations civilisées, de faire respecter la mémoire de l'auteur aussi bien dans ses œuvres que dans les reproductions de ces œuvres · et l'on admettrait volontiers que les grands corps ou instituts, existant dans toutes les nations civilisées, puissent se constituer les défenseurs de la mémoire des artistes qui ont appartenu à ces grandes sociétés ou instituts En tous cas, l'Etat, la collectivité, à laquelle l'artiste a appartenu et que son souvenir contribue à honorer, sont intéressés à défendre la mémoire des artistes après que la période, pendant laquelle la loi organise la protection, est accomplie

Ce sont là des considérations d'ordre moral le plus élevé, de nature à justifier, non seulement l'aspiration qu'ont les architectes à obtenir la protection de la propriété artistique, mais encore à justifier l'intérêt que tous les architectes ont à s'unir pour obtenir du législateur une protection, qui leur est aussi légitimement due qu'aux autres artistes, dessinateurs, peintres et sculpteurs.

VIII De la Répression de la Contrefaçon

Il est admis par toutes les législations sur la propriété artistique que le fait de reproduire, sans le consentement de l'auteur, une œuvre, constitue un acte répréhensible que l'on appelle la contrefaçon , et l'une des conséquences de la contrefaçon reconnue par le juge est le droit pour l'auteur soit de faire prononcer la destruction des contrefaçons, soit de se faire remettre les objets contrefaisants pour en disposer à son gré Sans doute, ces principes pourront subir de légères exceptions.

Pour l'architecte, lorsque la contrefaçon est faite à l'aide de planches gravées, d'estampes tirées à l'aide de ces planches ou de photographies, la répression de la contrefaçon se fait comme pour le peintre, le sculpteur ou le graveur : il peut se faire remettre les planches et les épreuves tirées avec ces planches : ou bien le juge peut en ordonner la destruction.

Mais, a-t-on dit, est-il possible qu'un architecte puisse exiger la destruction d'une maison élevée pour le compte d'un propriétaire de bonne foi, au profit de qui on aurait abusé des plans d'un architecte et pour qui on les aurait contrefait ? La situation s'est déjà présentée ; les magistrats, dans ce cas, sans ordonner la destruction de la maison, ont accordé une réparation—que nous estimons satisfaisante—en accordant à l'architecte contrefait des dommages-intérêts, égaux au moins aux honoraires qu'il eut obtenus pour consentir à l'exécution de son œuvre sur le terrain, et aussi en ordonnant que l'exécution contrefaisante ne porterait aucune signature d'auteur Ces solutions, absolument équitables, respectent le principe de la propriété artistique, et sont de nature à prouver que rien ne s'oppose à la protection complète de l'œuvre de l'architecte de même qu'à celle *des autres artistes*, peintres ou sculpteurs

IX. Rapports de l'Architecte avec son Client

Si l'on envisage la propriété artistique de l'architecte, on voit de suite que la convention, qui intervient entre l'architecte et son client, a pour but l'exécution sur un terrain d'une reproduction de l'œuvre de l'architecte L'édifice, nous l'avons dit, est une reproduction des dessins d'architecture.

En vue de cette reproduction, pour le cas où l'architecte la dirige en personne, il ne lui est nécessaire de remettre à son client qu'une série de copies des plans, soit des calques, soit des lithographies, soit des tirages en bleu S'il arrive que l'architecte ne soit pas chargé de diriger la construction, il doit remettre à son client les copies des plans utiles à cette construction.

Mais de ce qu'il conserve tous les droits de reproduction de son œuvre originale, et de ce que le client, dans aucun des deux cas examinés, n'a besoin des dessins originaux de l'architecte, nous pouvons affirmer au surplus, que le client n'a aucun droit à ces dessins originaux, puisqu'il est bien entendu, par ce que nous avons déjà dit que la convention n'a pour but qu'une reproduction sur le terrain ou la remise des moyens de cette reproduction.

Est-ce une conséquence exagérée ? Nous ne le pensons pas. Voyons ce que le musicien remet à celui qui traite avec lui d'une reproduction musicale de son œuvre L'amateur, qui désire exécuter ou faire exécuter chez lui l'œuvre du musicien, cherche à se procurer une reproduction manuscrite ou imprimée de l'œuvre : il la joue lui-même ou la fait jouer chez lui, grâce à cet exemplaire

Est-il arrivé que cet amateur réclame le manuscrit de l'auteur ? On peut affirmer que non Ce n'est qu'entre l'auteur et l'éditeur que la remise du manuscrit est l'objet du contrat, mais en ce cas une convention détaillée et spéciale intervient, qui sort de notre sujet

Il en est de même pour l'acheteur d'une reproduction en bronze, ou en toute autre matière, d'une sculpture La remise de l'exemplaire en bronze satisfait l'amateur il ne lui est jamais arrivé de réclamer l'original fait par le sculpteur Sauf au cas, tout spécial, où l'acquéreur convient qu'il achète le marbre original ou un bronze en épreuve unique, il lui est remis en ce cas un exemplaire original. Mais en ce cas, à bien examiner ce qui se passe en sculpture, on peut dire que l'original de l'œuvre peut exister en dehors de l'épreuve originale en marbre ou en bronze, ou en toute autre matière

Voilà donc qui nous conduit à regretter qu'une décision judiciaire récente soit intervenue, qui ait obligé un architecte anglais à remettre à son client ses minutes, ses dessins originaux et toutes les lettres et documents relatifs à la convention intervenue entre l'architecte et le client, alors que ce dernier n'avait pas donné suite à son projet de confier à l'architecte la direction de la construction.

C'est en vertu des principes du mandat que le juge anglais est arrivé à ordonner la remise, au client, des minutes de l'architecte

À l'abri des principes que nous avons exposés sur les rapports du client de l'architecte, et aussi que des principes de la propriété artistique, nous pouvons affirmer que l'architecte a droit de conserver tous ses dessins et plans originaux En effet la convention, analysée plus haut par nous, ne saurait produire d'autre solution plus ample que celle par nous indiquée

Dès lors qu'il est admis que la convention de bâtir laisse à l'architecte l'exercice de ses droits de propriété artistique et n'a trait qu'à la convention de reproduction que nous avons indiquée, rien ne peut enlever à l'architecte ses dessins et ses plans originaux.

Aussi bien, est-il légitime que l'architecte garde ses plans et dessins en minutes ou en original, surtout s'il a dirigé la construction, car au cas d'exercice contre lui de l'action en responsabilité, c'est dans ses dessins et ses plans originaux qu'il trouvera la justification de la direction, des ordres qu'il a donnés S'il est bien convenu que cette privation n'a pas été convenue, comment serait-elle imposée à l'architecte par déduction du seul contrat de mandat de diriger la construction ? Comment en effet, s'il se dépouille de ses dessins originaux, l'architecte pourrait-il exercer les autres droits de propriété artistique qui lui restent, comme celui d'exposition de ses dessins originaux, notamment ? Par suite de quoi l'architecte devrait-il être privé de ces droits bien différents, alors qu'il n'a consenti qu'à une convention de reproduction sur le terrain ?

L'avantage de l'existence d'un droit de propriété artistique, reconnu par le législateur, se trouve donc démontré à l'évidence par notre rapport.

X État de la Législation Contemporaine dans les divers États du Globe

Dans certains pays le législateur n'a pas nommé dans la loi de propriété artistique l'architecture, mais les termes généraux dans lesquels il indique les œuvres bénéficeant de la protection légale permettent d'y comprendre l'architecture

Aussi la Roumaine (loi de 1862, art 1), l'Italie (loi de 1882, I), la Belgique (loi de 1886, I)

Dans d'autres pays l'architecture est désignée par le législateur parmi les arts du dessin, qui sont protégés. Principauté de Monaco (loi de 1889, 2), Tunisie (loi de 1889, 3).

L'architecture est encore désignée et assimilée pour la protection aux œuvres du dessin à la peinture et à la sculpture en France (loi de 1793 et de 1902, I), en Espagne (loi de 1879, 37).

En Hongrie (loi de 1884, 67), l'architecture est protégée : toutefois il est licite de reproduire dans un autre art les œuvres se trouvant à demeure dans les rues et places publiques et autres lieux publics du même genre (62)

En Suède, l'architecte est protégé pour les plans qu'il a publiés (loi de 1877, I) Est autorisée la reproduction des œuvres d'art appartenant à l'Etat, ou aux communes, ou exposées dans les lieux publics ou apposées à l'extérieur des édifices (loi de 1867).

En Suisse, les dessins d'architecture sont protégés (loi de 1883, 8) sauf pour les édifices n'ayant pas un caractère artistique (11, § 8). D'autre part la reproduction des objets d'art qui se trouvent dans les rues ou sur les places publiques, lorsque la reproduction n'a pas lieu dans la forme de l'original, est licite (7) Enfin l'acquéreur de plans architecturaux a le droit de les faire exécuter, sauf stipulation contraire (6).

En Russie, l'architecture est protégée (L 1886, 30 et 32). Toutefois l'auteur ne jouit d'un droit que s'il a fait enregistrer son œuvre (31), mais il ne conserve son droit d'auteur sur les œuvres commandées par les particuliers que s'il a fait des réserves (36). Sauf dans le cas où il comprendrait ses œuvres dans une édition de ses œuvres complètes

Au Vénézuéla, l'architecte est protégé (loi de 1887, 3) à charge de faire un dépôt de son œuvre (31)

Au Danemark, l'architecte ne conserve ses droits que jusqu'à la publication de ses dessins ou de ses plans (loi de 1864, 4) Un projet de loi de 1891 concéderait à l'architecte la protection complète.

En Norwège (loi de 1896, 25), l'architecte est protégé Il est interdit d'utiliser pour une œuvre architecturale les dessins originaux de l'auteur, ni les dessins modèles qui ont été exécutés d'après ses dessins originaux (25)

En Finlande, le législateur réserve un droit exclusif à l'architecte jusqu'à la publication de ses plans (L 1880, 2)

Au Mexique (loi 1884, art 1191), l'auteur d'un plan d'architecture et l'architecte sont protégés. Cependant l'architecte n'est protégé que pour la partie intérieure des maisons particulières. La reproduction des édifices publics ou de la partie extérieure des constructions particulières est licite (1207 xvi) Cependant le propriétaire de la maison n'a le droit de la reproduire que s'il a stipulé formellement à cet égard

En Angleterre, le dessinateur ou le graveur d'un sujet d'architecture est protégé par un Act de 1766 (I), et un Act de 1852 (14) protège les croquis d'architecture Les dessinateurs sont protégés d'une façon assez générale dans ces Acts pour que l'on puisse admettre que l'auteur des dessins d'architecture serait protégé.

En Allemagne, les plans édités sont protégés (loi de 1870, 43), mais une loi de 1876 a déclaré que les dispositions qu'elle contenait ne s'appliquaient pas à l'architecture (art 3) D'où il suit que, la reproduction d'après un édifice exécuté est licite Un projet de loi, qui est venu en discussion en janvier 1906, admet pour l'architecte une protection à peu près équivalente à celle de la loi suisse.[1]

L'Autriche, dans la loi de 1846 (4, § 4) protégeait l'architecture, mais

---

[1] Cette loi a été votée le 9 janvier 1907 Voir la note, p 187.

dans la loi de 1895 le législateur n'a accordé que la protection des parties intérieures de l'édifice, laissant licite la reproduction dans un autre art, des édifices artistiques en façade des rues et des places publiques.

XI   Convention Internationale de Berne

Une convention internationale, signée à Berne en 1886, unit pour la protection de la propriété artistique un nombre considérable des États du globe : ce sont l'Allemagne, la Belgique, le Danemark, l'Espagne, la France avec l'Algérie et ses colonies, la Grande-Bretagne avec ses colonies et possessions, Haïti, l'Italie, le Japon, le Luxembourg, Monaco, le Monténégro, la Norwège, la Suède, la Suisse, la Tunisie

Aux termes de cette convention (art 4) les plans croquis et ouvrages plastiques relatifs à l'architecture sont protégés   Mais par suite des différences entre les législations des pays adhérents (voir ces différences dans notre exposé) il en résultait que divers pays entendaient ne pas protéger les édifices construits et la reproduction de ces édifices.

En 1896, à une conférence diplomatique tenue à Paris, il a été décidé que les pays adhérents à l'Union, qui protégeraient non seulement les plans des architectes mais encore les œuvres d'architecture, pourraient admettre ces œuvres au bénéfice de la convention.

C'est là un pas considérable accompli, mais il faut maintenant faire des efforts pour que le plus grand nombre des Etats adhérents, et même tous ces États, accordent une protection complète aux architectes

Il y a entre les pays unionistes un argument très fort pour donner aux architectes une prompte satisfaction, c'est que les architectes des pays unionistes, qui ne sont pas encore suffisamment protégés, fassent observer à leur Gouvernement, que, puisqu'il a signé un article de la convention de Berne impliquant que les œuvres d'architecture pourront être protégées, c'est qu'il trouve logique que l'architecture bénéficie d'une telle protection, et que dès lors il est juste qu'il l'accorde à ses nationaux. D'autre part il est aussi juste que les architectes de ces pays fassent observer à leurs Gouvernements qu'il est digne de leur préoccupation de ne pas obtenir des autres plus qu'on ne leur donne soi-même   et comme dans certains pays adhérents à l'Union la protection est accordée même sans réciprocité, il y a donc des pays où l'architecte non protégé chez lui, pourrait l'être en vertu de la convention de Berne et de l'Acte de Paris de 1896

L'Union internationale produira, un jour, ce résultat admirable d'une unification des législations sur la propriété artistique.   Déjà l'Union de Berne a pour effet d'accorder, dans les pays adhérents, la protection aux nationaux des autres pays adhérents, après accomplissement seulement des formalités prescrites au pays d'origine   De la sorte, l'architecte n'a plus à se préoccuper que des formalités du pays, où il publie son œuvre ou bâtit son édifice, pour être protégé ensuite sans autres formalités dans les autres pays adhérents il s'en suit une grande simplification de formalités, une grande tranquillité pour l'artiste, qui peut ne se préoccuper d'aucunes frontières : sa loi nationale l'accompagnera partout où il se rendra pour dessiner ou bâtir dans l'intérieur de l'Union.

XII.   Conclusion et Vœu

Nous pensons avoir réussi à montrer les avantages de la propriété artistique, ses bases logiques et juridiques : enfin ses avantages moraux et pécuniaires.   Nous terminerons ce travail en indiquant que de nombreux congrès de propriété artistique, et les 3e, 4e, 5e et 6 Congrès Internationaux des Architectes, ont dans leurs vœux demandé la protection de la propriété artistique des architectes

Tant qu'il restera des pays dont la législation ne protégera pas complètement l'architecte, il faut répéter ces vœux, et les conserver aussi semblables que possible aux vœux précédents, afin que l'affirmation de la même idée vienne enfin forcer l'attention du législateur.

Dans cette intention nous vous proposons de voter le vœu suivant, que nous avons eu le grand plaisir de faire voter à l'unanimité le 23 juin 1906 par le XXXIVe Congrès des Architectes Français.—

Vœu

Le VIIe Congrès International des Architectes, réuni à Londres en 1906
Rappelant, d'une part, les vœux émis depuis vingt-huit ans dans les
    Congrès Internationaux des Architectes et de la Propriété Artistique,
    ainsi que dans les Congrès Internationaux de l'Association Littéraire
    et Artistique Internationale, et notamment à Madrid en 1904, et
    rappelant d'autre part le Protocole de clôture de la Conférence
    diplomatique tenue à Paris en 1896, lequel consacre le principe de la
    protection complète des œuvres d'architecture,
Rappelant enfin la loi espagnole de 1879 et la loi française de 1902, lesquelles
    protègent expressément les œuvres d'architecture,
Est d'avis
1°. Que les dessins d'architecture comprennent les dessins des façades
    extérieures et intérieures, les plans, coupe et élévation, et constituent
    la première manifestation de la pensée de l'architecte et l'œuvre
    d'architecture,
2° Que l'édifice n'est qu'une reproduction, sur le terrain, des dessins
    d'architecture ; ·
Et renouvelle le vœu que les œuvres d'architecture soient protégées
    dans toutes les législations et dans toutes les conventions inter-
    nationales, à l'égal de toutes les autres œuvres artistiques

---

3—LA PROPRIÉTÉ ARTISTIQUE DES ŒUVRES D'ARCHITEC-
TURE ET LA PROPRIÉTÉ DES DESSINS D'ARCHITECTURE

Par Gaston Trélat (Paris)

La propriété artistique une fois admise, il est impossible de ne pas être frappé par l'extension qu'elle tend à prendre. On voit le champ de son action s'accroître de plus en plus, dans la mesure du besoin que ses défenseurs ont de servir les idées se rattachant à une doctrine, sur laquelle bien des doutes pourraient cependant surgir.

Dois-je l'avouer ? C'est là une question que je n'ai encore pu bien comprendre. Il semble qu'elle conduirait à vouloir réglementer l'usage des idées, leur utilisation. De ce fait, elle nous apparaîtrait facilement comme un danger En effet je ne sache pas que ce puisse être autre chose, qu'une question de *morale personnelle*, qui s'oppose à ce que nous nous emparions d'une idée d'autrui Cette morale se résout dans une élégance du geste Et il s'en suivrait des caractères accusés qu'on apprécierait dans leurs réserves Et même le respect signalerait les scrupules frappants de certaines personnalités Mais c'est seulement le mot d'élégance—élégance morale !—qui conviendrait en la circonstance

Au contraire ce serait par vulgarité qu'on en arriverait à jouer avec les idées d'autrui, à s'en servir pour édifier l'œuvre dont on s'attribuerait la création personnelle Et ce ne serait ni bon, ni même avouable.

Mais, pour cela, il ne faudrait pas oublier que toute idée, même des plus originales, s'édifie sur une autre idée prise on ne sait où, n'importe où. Et, le travail de la pensée se poursuivant inconsciemment, si par hasard les choses étaient engagées de façon tant soit peu démesurée dans la voie de sauvegarde—qu'autoriserait le service de *la propriété artistique*—on courrerait grand risque d'aboutir à une entrave de la liberté des esprits en fait d'échanges intellectuels Ce serait une atteinte au progrès d'affinement qui marque la civilisation contemporaine.

Il y a peut-être urgence à objectiver la question davantage et à serrer de plus près la *propriété artistique en ce qui regarde les œuvres d'architecture.* Si nous interrogeons notre expérience comme artiste, nous voyons qu'en art l'élaboration n'est jamais terminée. On peut toujours y apporter le fruit de méditations nouvelles, leur succession visant la perfection. C'est l'objectif de la vie et des activités d'un artiste. Pour lui, le travail est sans fin ; l'exécution seule en arrête les recherches, sans cela l'étude se perpétuerait L'idéal, que l'artiste doit servir, fait passer son esprit par bien des idées Quelle pourrait donc bien être celle de ces idées à laquelle s'attacherait *la propriété artistique* ? On n'en sait trop rien. En supposant l'une des idées prise et utilisée sous forme de plagiat, il est difficile de voir là un tort bien déterminé et de nature à permettre d'établir un droit lésé Je n'y vois, pour ma part, qu'une faiblesse intellectuelle Elle s'accuse dans le ridicule du plagiat lui-même. Et tout plagiaire tend à se diminuer moralement et socialement. Mais je ne puis constater le mal qui aurait été fait à qui que ce soit, en dehors de lui-même L'idée, dont il s'est emparé, correspond simplement à une étape de la pensée en travail de composition, pour l'artiste Sa valeur et son effort se mesurent par une suite d'essais intellectuels semblables à celui-là

L'œuvre d'art est donc une résultante des apports successifs d'un esprit en production Du reste, il me semble facile de s'en rendre compte d'une autre façon. Ce que je vais dire a pour origine une longue expérience d'éducation artistique, que la vie d'atelier caractérise essentiellement C'est dans ce *laboratoire* que se forme l'esprit des artistes, avec leur tournure originale résultant de points de vue personnels que les applications de l'enseignement scientifique suscitent dans les compositions élaborées sur programmes spéciaux. Mais il y a encore l'échange d'idées entre maître et élève. Outre le contrôle intellectuel dont les jeunes gens profitent, il en découle un stimulant artistique auquel le maître lui-même ne saurait échapper En somme, c'est un champ d'observations psychologiques Voyons donc ce qu'elles permettraient de déduire en ce qui concerne la deuxième question.

En fait d'art, la vie de l'atelier suppose un échange d'idées qui porte en général sur des indications plastiques. Des dessins ou des croquis y complètent toujours la parole Et bien, j'ai remarqué, que toutes les fois qu'on s'adressait à des hommes doués intellectuellement, ces indications figurées subissaient une transformation en rapport avec le développement des idées que permettait la durée de l'étude. A tel point que l'idée première devient à peine reconnaissable.

Et, s'il en est ainsi pour les débutants, que serait-ce *à fortiori* pour l'artiste consommé, dont la valeur soustrait aux liens de choses apprises et dégage pleinement la liberté de pensée ? Cela reste bien une marque caractéristique des différentes idées par lesquelles on passe, avant d'arriver à l'œuvre accomplie que l'art fait entrevoir.

J'ajoute que toute copie est bête. Mais alors qui faudrait-il donc protéger ? Serait-ce le copiste contre sa bêtise ? On n'y songe pas. Qui donc alors ? . Dois-je dire ma pensée ? Lorsque je m'interroge en conscience, je ne sais si l'homme qui se sent atteint dans sa *propriété artistique* a jamais pu s'interroger sur la portée de *l'art.*

A ce propos, je veux citer un exemple qui montre bien l'art tel qu'il faudrait arriver à le concevoir. Un ami statuaire de grand mérite me contait un jour un incident remontant à sa première jeunesse. Le maître, avec lequel il travaillait alors, avait à exécuter un monument commémoratif comprenant quatre figures allégoriques. Son œuvre représentait déjà plusieurs années de travail, lorsque le grand artiste en vint

L

à prier mon ami de refaire une des figures. Il donna donc des indi
cations initiatrices des changements qu'il convenait d'apporter à l'éla
boration antérieure   Le jeune sculpteur travailla et la figure fut exécutée
conformément à la volonté du maître.   Une fois la figure construite et
suffisamment poussée, le maître l'examina et dit que ce n'était pas encore
ce qu'il désirait.   Il détruisit de nouveau la figure, mais il ajouta.
" *Voilà assez de temps que je consacre à cette étude, maintenant il faut
l'arrêter. Je vais donc écrire au mouleur pour lui donner rendez-vous dans huit
jours* "   Étonnement du jeune homme qui, huit jours plus tard, voyait la
figure refaite et prête à être moulée.   C'est ainsi que plus de quatre années
de recherches inquiètes montraient leurs résultats effectifs dans le travail
d'une semaine.   Cet incident revenait à mon esprit, en conséquence du
tour pris ici par mes pensées

Mais la voie, où je me trouve engagé, veut que je conte encore une
histoire   Cette fois l'ami est peintre ; comme il me montrait deux photographies représentant deux figures, je fus frappé du caractère et de la
valeur que l'une d'elles prenait à mes yeux ; je le lui dis timidement dans
la crainte de froisser le sentiment ou l'intérêt de l'artiste . . . alors celui-ci
de s'écrier " *Mais cette figure-là est seule à être de ma composition, l'autre
en est une copie par le statuaire X, et je veux lui faire un procès* "   De mon
côté, je gardai le silence, heureux du compliment que j'avais pu faire et
qui venait à point, tout en restant en accord avec la conscience de mon
sentiment   Mais les bras me tombèrent d'entendre parler de procès ;
car je ne compris pas, je ne comprends pas encore, comment une mauvaise
figure statuaire, inspirée par une bonne figure peinte, pourrait léser l'auteur
de cette dernière et donner lieu à un procès   Rien de plus naturel, semble-
t-il, que la figure peinte inspirant la figure statuaire.   Et, si l'inspiration
ne réussit pas, il n'y a qu'un regret à avoir, en admettant qu'on s'en occupe

Après ces exemples de statuaire et de peintre, je reviens naturellement à l'architecture : voici un *parti* de plan qui répond à un terrain donné
et que j'ai longuement médité   Je suppose qu'un confrère, l'ayant apprécié,
veuille l'appliquer à un terrain différent.   S'il copie réellement, il n'aboutit
qu'à une solution détestable, vu la différence de *terrain donné*, et je
plains l'auteur d'une telle maladresse   Au contraire, si une transposition
intelligente permet finalement une bonne œuvre, j'applaudis et je suis
honoré d'une collaboration inconsciente et inattendue.

L'architecte poursuit son œuvre, en commençant toujours par des croquis,
des esquisses.   C'est bien, quand ces esquisses répondent à un point de vue
personnel et intéressant par l'utilité du service qu'elles font entrevoir
ou par tout autre avantage dont elles donnent la pensée   Mais, somme
toute, étant donnée l'œuvre finale qui est en vue, les considérations sur-
gissent en abondance, se succédant et se contrôlant les unes les autres
Lorsqu'elle est bien comprise, l'étude consiste donc en élaborations successives   Par transposition d'un art à l'autre, il faut donc appliquer
à l'architecte l'exemple du maître statuaire   Et nous répéterons que,
pour l'artiste à portée réelle, les études sont infinies   Elles ne sont comprises dans leur ensemble que par l'auteur qui les résume dans la per
fection d'une œuvre accomplie.

Résumé —En résumé, je ne crois pas qu'il y ait propriété artistique en
dehors de la possession des objets eux-mêmes ; ce qui est précisément
le cas pour la propriété des dessins d'architecture . leur valeur est en
rapport avec ce que l'artiste en déduit, lors de l'exécution   En fait d'art,
en fait d'élaborations architecturales, il n'y a pas de *propriété artistique.*
Nous avons vu que la question était de nature à intéresser la *morale*, en ce
sens qu'elle règle nos actes personnels vis-à-vis d'autrui   Mais le *droit*, qui
s'attache aux actes d'autrui vis-à-vis de nous-même, n'a pas à intervenir
en l'espèce

En architecture, les proportions d'un terrain, le site, l'ambiance sont

autant d'éléments qu'il faudrait envisager dans les études que commande
une composition.   L'esprit de l'artiste est hanté par trop d'idées également
déterminantes dans l'orientation de son œuvre, pour qu'aucun autre esprit
puisse jamais en arriver à surprendre la pensée directrice de sa conception.
Les dispositifs et les ordonnances s'y rattachent tous   C'est une loi, à
laquelle l'artiste ne se soustraira jamais, sous peine de faire de mauvaises
choses, et par conséquent de desservir sa personnalité.

Conclusion —La *propriété artistique*, telle que j'ai pu arriver à la comprendre, ne repose pas sur un examen suffisant de la question , elle ne
saurait résister à une analyse suivie en conscience.   Il en résulte donc,
suivant moi, une action sans profit et une perte de temps regrettable.

La sociologie voudrait que l'on distinguât toujours la *morale* et le
droit

Et l'on verrait ici un objet de mesure ou de procédé regardant seulement la *morale*, en tant que protection d'autrui.   Mais, d'autre part, je
ne vois pas que le *droit* ait à intervenir comme protection personnelle

---

4.—LA PROPRIÉTÉ DES DESSINS D'ARCHITECTURE.

Par D. PABLO SALVAT (Barcelona)

1° La propriété, en matière d'art architectonique, doit être reconnu
et jouir de droits identiques à ceux de la propriété intellectuelle en
général.

2°. Chaque pays doit fixer, en ce qui le concerne, les limites de la
durée de la propriété ; mais dans aucun cas ces limites ne pourront être
inférieures à vingt-cinq ans, à compter du décès de l'auteur

3° Dans aucun cas le projet, c'est-à-dire l'idée, en matière d'art
architectonique ne doit être reproduit sans autorisation préalable de son
auteur.

4°. L'œuvre architectonique ne doit jamais être reproduite, ni dans
son ensemble ni dans aucun de ses détails, pour n'importe quel usage
ayant rapport à la construction, sans autorisation préalable de son auteur

5° On pourrait reproduire l'œuvre architectonique par la sculpture,
le dessin, la peinture, la photographie ou la gravure, pourvu que son
auteur n'en aurait pas manifesté expressément, en un endroit apparent,
la prohibition absolue

6° Le droit de propriété est inhérent à l'œuvre artistique · il est
constitué de fait et sans besoin de faire aucun enregistrement ni dépôt
d'aucune sorte   Pour que tous les droits de propriété soient complètement garantis, la signature et la date suffiront

7° Les transmissions de propriété doivent se faire dans la même
forme que pour la propriété mobilière et au gré des deux contractants.

8°. L'auteur doit spécifier dans la transmission les points sur lesquels
il se réserve le droit de propriété.

9°. Tout traité sans restrictions indique une transmission aussi sans
restrictions

10° La cession sans restrictions ne prive pas l'auteur de la faculté
de reproduire ses propres œuvres, mais l'acheteur peut, par condition
expresse, demander le droit de s'y opposer.

DISCUSSION ON SUBJECT II.

Ownership of Architects' Drawings.

Mr. W. S. EAMES (United States) succeeded Dr. Muthesius in the chair when this subject was discussed.

Mr. E. W. HUDSON having seconded the resolution moved by Mr. Statham (see page 133), a discussion arose as to whether the question of the ownership of architects' drawings and that of artistic copyright should be taken together or separately

M. HARMAND thought it would be a mistake to separate the questions, for copyright gave a right to keep the drawings. What Mr Statham said as to this being an English question was very true, but they all hoped that the British Parliament would pass a law which would settle the copyright question

THE CHAIRMAN thought they had better consider the question of the ownership of drawings apart from the question of copyright. The resolution of Mr. Statham would not interfere with any similar resolution with regard to copyright law, but while one measure might pass and have a good result, a combination of the two subjects might result in the failure of both

Dr. H. MUTHESIUS (Germany) said that the question raised by the reader of the paper was not one which concerned England only, but was of international importance. He would rather like to have the matter put in such a way that the Congress might be concerned with it as an International Congress, and not as an English Congress To his knowledge the circumstances were entirely the same in Germany, where in any law case this uncertainty arose as to whom the drawings belonged. Their judges, however, were inclined to take the conclusion arrived at by professional bodies, and if an International Congress gave as its firm opinion that the charges of architects did not refer to any drawings, but only to the executed building, that would help them forward in any country This would state the case that the client did not pay for the drawings, and if he changed his mind during the course of the erection of the building, he would have no right to get the drawings from the architect In their German Schedule of Charges they had a clause to the effect that the drawings did not belong to the client, but were the property of the architect, but it was stated that the client must be provided with copies of the drawings if he desired to have them That clearly showed that the original drawings belonged to the architect, but at the same time he believed they would have difficulties in any law case over the point. Therefore he would like the present International Congress to give its opinion that an architect was only paid for the actual carrying-out of the building as a work of art, and that the drawings had nothing to do with the design, and were the property of the architect himself.

Mr. G. A T MIDDLETON said he would like to move an amendment. He was very sorry to find himself in opposition to Mr. Statham on the matter, because he thought that generally on the whole ground he was in the right; but, further than that, he thought that even if the resolution were carried it could not be carried out until Architecture, like Law or Medicine, was a definitely legalised profession; which was a course of policy on which Mr Statham and he differed. There was another question as to the Institute Scale of Charges being legalised—that is, not only this portion of the Scale of Charges, but the whole of it He felt that if the Scale of Charges were once taken into the House of Commons, Parliament would consider it from the point of view of the public, and not from the point of view of the architects, and they would prevent architects charging too much as against the public. They would certainly not make a scale in favour of architects They would make the present scale a maximum scale, while now it was the minimum scale, and architects would probably get just the reverse of what they wanted   He felt that a legal scale would be very harmful to architects.   The only profession which had a legal scale was the law, and that scale was forced upon the lawyers to prevent them from robbing the public   The scale was not given to the legal profession to enable them to obtain their charges, but to prevent them from overcharging   He felt that this was the view Parliament would take in regard to architects' charges, and he moved as an amendment —" That in the opinion of this meeting the Royal Institute of British Architects should revise the wording of its paper on the professional practice as to the charges of architects in the sense indicated above "   He thought the resolution should stop there.   That would do away with the question of forcing it on the House of Commons or the House of Lords as matter of law, and would only be asking the Royal Institute of British Architects to revise its scale   That scale was very well accepted as the general custom when cases came before the Courts at the present time, and if they altered it in the sense indicated, he thought it would become very generally recognised.

Mr ALEXANDER NORTH, in seconding the amendment, said he fully believed with the last speaker that if the matter were brought before Parliament an endeavour would be made to make the Scale of Charges and the ownership of drawings in the interests of the public rather than in the interests of architects.   He was a delegate from Tasmania, and in that country they felt very keenly upon this subject   He might say that in conversation with one of the vice-presidents of the Royal Institute of Victorian Architects before he left the desire was expressed that everything possible should be done so far as legalising the retention of drawings by the architect was concerned.   In the old Scale of Charges they had a clause which definitely set out the minimum charge of 5 per cent, and it was stated that all drawings prepared by the architect should remain the property of the architect, and were simply to be used for the particular work for which they were produced.   Now, in spite of that, he had had clients who had really claimed the drawings, and more particularly of works which had not been carried out, and he had felt that it was so problematical whether or not the law would support what was stated on the printed matter placed before the client with the charges that he had never felt disposed to fight it in a court of law   On one occasion he was compelled to give up the working drawings, but in other cases he had endeavoured to appease the client by giving him such tracings as would meet the requirements of the case   Under those circumstances he thought it would be a wiser course to follow the amendment, and let the Institute alter the wording of its paper rather than to take it to Parliament, where he was afraid they would have a verdict against them

Mr. A. H. KERSEY said that he had another amendment in his mind, but he thought they were losing sight of the nature of that meeting   This was an International Congress, and, as Dr. Muthesius had suggested, they ought to consider the matter from an international point of view   Mr. Statham's resolution was one distinctly affecting English architects only, but he (the speaker) asked the Congress to follow rather the suggestion of Dr Muthesius.   The English architects were quite capable of passing a resolution themselves with regard to what they wanted, but what was required was for the Congress to give a sign manual that the architect's drawings were his own, and that the architect was not merely a workman for providing so many sheets of paper, but that his business was to produce an architectural building.   It had been pointed out there and elsewhere that the architect had to spend laborious hours and much money, and have the natural gift, before he could do this   He would read the resolution he intended to move, and then if it were carried Mr. Statham would no doubt move that the Institute should do what was wished.   He proposed — " That this Congress is of opinion that the architect is paid for the production of a building, and that the drawings and paper prepared by him to that end are undoubtedly the property of the architect, and that this is the universal practice in other countries." He proposed that, but would be prepared to accept any alterations which would carry out the object they had in view.

Mr MIDDLETON appealed to Mr Statham to withdraw his resolution in favour of that of Mr. Kersey, and then he would withdraw his amendment

Mr E. W HUDSON asked if Mr. Kersey would substitute the words "should be" for "are undoubtedly the property." There was no doubt at present the judges were against them

Mr. KERSEY said he was speaking universally, but he was quite prepared to accept the suggestion. His only desire was to get a strong resolution by the Congress which would show English people that theirs was the only country where the architect was not entitled to retain his drawings.

Mr. STATHAM said he would withdraw his resolution, and Mr. Middleton then withdrew his amendment.

Mr READ suggested that they might get the foreign delegates to say what the law was in their countries, so that they might have the weight required in the resolution.

Mr KERSEY moved his suggested amendment as a resolution

Mr. W. H. ATKIN BERRY, in seconding the resolution, said he was very glad that it had been substituted for the original one He quite agreed in sentiment and theory with all that Mr Statham had stated, but they had a very much sterner law than theory and sentiment, and the law had laid it down emphatically that they had not the right to the ownership of their drawings. It was no use their standing there and saying what they wished, or what they believed, or what they liked They were in the position of the men in the stocks, and must get out as best they could. He thought the resolution proposed by Mr Kersey was an excellent one, as it would enable them to express what they would like without fighting against the laws that be. He took that opportunity of deprecating most strongly any attempt to alter or tamper in any way with the existing schedule of charges of the Institute until the law was amended. That schedule of charges was now used as their sheet-anchor in this matter. It was the only ground upon which they could stand, and they had always based their contention with regard to charges upon the fact that it was the custom They had no stronger ground, and that schedule of charges showed their custom Immediately they began to tamper with it and turn it about they lost the value of that plea of custom, and he thought it would be a most dangerous precedent They had for many years past recognised the fact that they had no ground to stand upon in claiming the ownership of drawings They used to have on their schedule of charges a footnote stating that it was not law, but it was the custom They were advised to withdraw that note because it was misleading their professional members, and it was withdrawn accordingly That was a very significant fact The profession recognised that under the law as at present they were not entitled to the ownership of drawings, and it was no use their attempting to enforce it Mr Statham had made some remarks deprecating the inaction of the Royal Institute of British Architects in the case of *Gibbon v Pease* He (the speaker) contended that the Institute were perfectly justified in the course they pursued, for if they had taken the matter further they would have landed themselves in a great deal of expense for nothing at all. He had much pleasure in supporting the resolution, and trusted it would get such unanimous support as would show the feeling of architects not only in this country but in all other countries

Mr. E W. FRITCHLEY (India) asked to be allowed to say a word from the point of view of the client. It was, he thought, well to put themselves in the client's position, and see how the thing affected him   An architect might have put up a building for the client, and at some future time the client might want to make an extension of the building   Well, the architect who had prepared the original drawings might have died, or he and the client might have fallen out over the erection of the first building, and the client might not want to retain him again   It certainly seemed rather hard upon the client that he should have to break away portions of the construction in order to find out what the construction was like, which he might have to do if the architect retained the drawings.   Therefore he would suggest some alteration of the resolution to the following effect : "That all drawings shall be the property of the architect except such constructional drawings as are necessary to give an idea of the original construction."

Mr. STATHAM said it was perfectly open for the architect to give copies of these drawings without parting with the originals

Mr. KERSEY said it was almost a universal practice with London architects when a job was finished to supply the client with a drawing which gave him all the details he wanted to know, such as the positions of the drains, bells, hot water and other pipes, and all information which was likely to be required to prevent the pulling about of the building.

M. HARMAND pointed out that it would be a most dangerous thing for them to say that they were paid for putting up a building, for the natural question would be, if they did not build, "What are you going to be paid for ? "   He thought they would all agree that the drawings should be the property of the architect, but he thought that they ought first to deal with the question of copyright, and then come back to this matter

THE CHAIRMAN, in reply to M. Harmand, said the opinion of the members present seemed to be in favour of the separation of the two questions, and the discussion must be confined to the ownership of drawings.

Dr. MUTHESIUS said he hardly liked the wording of the proposition, saying that this was the universal practice in other countries   In the first place it made it a purely English matter, whereas they wanted to make it an international question, and in the second place it was not quite true.

Mr. KERSEY said he would delete the last words of the resolution.

Mr HUDSON suggested that the resolution should read —" That in the opinion of this meeting the architect is paid for the building or for the opportunity of building, &c "

Mr. KERSEY said if that were done the client would certainly claim the drawings.   The lawyer would arrive at once at the conclusion that the client should have the drawings

Mr. FRITCHLEY said that according to this wording of the amended resolution the client would not be entitled to any drawings, and his clients would greatly object to that.

THE CHAIRMAN pointed out that Mr. Kersey had explained that the usual practice was to supply drawings showing the location of the drains and wires, hot water, and other pipes, &c.

The resolution was then put and carried as follows —

" That this Congress is of opinion that the architect is employed to produce a building, and that all drawings and papers prepared by him to that end are undoubtedly his property."

[Discussion of the question of " Artistic Copyright " was adjourned to the following day.]

Artistic Copyright

The discussion of this question was proceeded with on Thursday morning, July 19.

M GEORGES HARMAND (Avocat à la Cour d'Appel, Paris) went through Señor Salvat's propositions (p 147), commenting as he proceeded

With No 1 he fully agreed With regard to No 2, he queried the limit of twenty-five years. Considering that literary copyright in Spain extends over a period of eighty years, why should artistic copyright be given a lower limit ? Nos. 3 and 4 he fully endorsed With regard to No 5, he said, why demand that this prohibition be explicitly expressed ? It should rather be implicitly understood With regard to No 6, M Harmand considered the optional addition of the signature as an excellent sugges-tion, though he would not make it obligatory. No. 7, he observed, referred to a purely Spanish legal aspect concerning the transfer of pro-perty. With regard to No. 8, instead of the author specifying, in the assign-ment, the points as to which he reserved copyright, M Harmand sug-gested that the author reserved his absolute copyright, except in so far as the client had specified the direction (if any) in which he (the client) wished to acquire a copyright Clause 8 should reserve to the artist the right of specifying restrictions as to the reproduction of his work. Clause 9 was negatived by M Harmand, who would maintain the in-violability of copyright, even without explicit mention. With regard to No. 10, M Harmand approved of the first half of the clause, but considered that the second half contradicted the first.

M SALVAT (Barcelona), the author of the propositions, suggested that it would be as well to lay stress on the inherent difference between the drawing and the executed work. He would give to the drawings them-selves every copyright that could be claimed, but he would leave full liberty to reproduce the executed building, whether by photographs, drawings, or engravings

M HARMAND amplified his preceding remarks, and quoted a regula-tion which is in force in both France and Italy In the case of a street, for instance, while an ordinary general sketch is allowed, in which perhaps several houses appear, with no undue preponderance of one over the others, yet it is not allowable to make a careful drawing or a detailed sketch of one single house without the permission of the architect.

M HARMAND moved the following resolution ·

" *This Seventh International Congress of Architects assembled at London in 1906, recalling on the one hand the resolutions passed during the past twenty-eight years by the International Congresses of Architects and the Inter-national Congress of Artistic Copyright, as well as by the International Congresses of the Association Littéraire et Artistique Internationale, notably at Madrid in 1904 ; recalling, on the other hand, the Protocole de Clôture of the Diplomatic Conference held at Paris in 1896, which upholds the principle of complete protection of works of architecture ; recalling, finally, the Spanish law of 1879 and the French law of 1902, both of which expressly protect works of architecture,*

" *This Congress is of opinion*

" *1. That architectural designs comprise designs of façades, exterior and interior, together with the plans, sections, and elevations, and they constitute the first manifestation of the architect's idea and the work of architecture.*

" *2 That the building is but a reproduction, on the site, of the archi-tectural drawings.*

" *And this Congress again expresses the desire that works of architecture be protected in all legislative enactments, and in all international conventions, equally with every other kind of artistic work.*"

Mr KERSEY, in seconding the resolution, said he agreed absolutely with all that was contained in it, but he would like to have a little clearer understanding of what had taken place at the Conventions and what was the nature of the resolution of 1886 He would like to know if the convention was signed by representative delegates to bind all countries to adhere to the protection of all artistic productions

M HARMAND said that in 1886 delegates of the countries met at Berne to consider the protection of literary works, paintings, sculpture, and maps and plans of architects, and there was a meeting again in 1896. The delegates of Belgium, France, Italy, and Spain reported that they had protection for architectural work, and promises were made by Germany and Great Britain The Conference had not since met, but it was hoped to meet in 1907. Germany had got a project before its Parliament to protect architecture fully, but Great Britain so far had done nothing

Mr KERSEY said that if they passed the resolution great service would be rendered in strengthening everybody's hands with the English Government. If they were able to show the English Government that Great Britain was practically the only civilised country in the world which was standing outside the Convention for the Protection of Artistic Productions they might get something done

M. SALVAT criticised the wording of the resolution, and M. Harmand replied. After some further discussion, M Salvat expressed himself satisfied by the remarks of M Harmand

The resolution [see p 152] was then put to the meeting and agreed to

Subject III

STEEL AND REINFORCED-CONCRETE CONSTRUCTION

(*a*) The General Aspect of the Subject.—(*b*) With Special Reference to Æsthetic and Hygienic Considerations in the Case of very High Buildings.

Tuesday, 17th July.—Grafton Galleries.

Chairman Messrs Frank Miles Day (United States) and J J. Caluwaers (Belgium)
Hon. Secretaries Messrs Rapisarda-Rizzo (Italy) and F N Jackson (England)

1.—REINFORCED CONCRETE

Communication from the Joint Reinforced Concrete
Committee (London)

The great and increasing use of reinforced concrete in buildings and other structures, and the need for having some authoritative pronouncement on the proper conditions of its use, has led the Royal Institute of British Architects, with the co-operation of other bodies, to appoint a Committee to inquire into the subject

The members of the Committee are as follows

Nominated by the Royal Institute of British Architects.—Sir Henry Tanner, H.M. Office of Works , Professor W C Unwin, LL.D., F.R.S. , Charles F. Marsh, M Inst C E , A T Walmisley, M Inst.C E. ; Max Clarke, F R I B A , William Dunn, F R I.B.A ; H. D Searles-Wood, F R I B A. ; Colonel C. F Winn, late R E.

Nominated by the War Office.—Colonel C. B. Mayne, R.E., Assist. Director of Fortifications and Works, War Office , Major E M Paul, R E , Instructor in Construction, School of Military Engineering, Chatham

Nominated by the Admiralty —C H Colson, M Inst C.E.

Nominated by the Incorporated Association of Municipal and County Engineers.—A. E. Collins, M.Inst.C.E. , J W. Cockrill, A.R.I.B.A., M Inst.C E

Nominated by the District Surveyors' Association.—E. Dru Drury, F R.I.B A , T H Watson, F R I B A

Nominated by the Institute of Builders Benjamin I Greenwood , Frank May, J P

The Committee has appointed Sir Henry Tanner as Chairman, Professor Unwin and Col Mayne as Vice-Chairmen, and Mr. H. D Searles-Wood as Hon Secretary

It has appeared desirable to the Royal Institute that some statement be made before the International Congress of Architects in London as to the general scope and aim of the Committee, and the following outline is made with their approval

The aim of the Committee's deliberations is to prepare a report, stating their recommendations and conclusions as to ·

1. What drawings and details should be prepared before work is commenced.

2. The nature of the materials which may be employed, and the standards to which these should comply, *i.e* (*a*) The metal in reinforcement; (*b*) The matrix; (*c*) The sand, (*d*) The gravel, stone, clinker, or other aggregate, (*e*) Water

3 What are the proportions for concrete to be used in different cases

4. How the ingredients for concrete are to be mixed and deposited on the work.

5. The distances to be allowed between the reinforcing bars, and what covering of concrete is necessary.

6. What precautions are necessary in the design and erection of centering and false work, and how long the whole or portions of centering and false work should remain in position

7. The rules which should be used in determining the dimensions of the several parts necessary for security, and what safe stresses should be allowed.

8. The supervision necessary and the special matters to which it should be directed.

9. The fire-resisting properties of reinforced concrete.

10 Its adaptability for structures where resistance to liquid pressure is essential, and what special precautions may be advisable under these conditions.

11. What are the necessary conditions for its permanence ; resistance to rusting of metal, disintegration of concrete or effects of vibration.

12. The testing of the materials employed and of the finished structures

13. What provisions are desirable in Building Laws or Government Regulations relating to buildings and other structures, so far as these affect the use of reinforced concrete.

The Committee having been recently constituted, and only two meetings having been held, no conclusions have been arrived at, and members of the Congress are invited to send communications, either the results of experiments or other information or suggestions that may be of use.*

In December 1905 Messrs. William Cubitt & Co, of Gray's Inn Road, made a number of beams of concrete reinforced in various ways, and very kindly invited the members of the Science Committee of the Royal Institute of British Architects to witness the making of them Those who attended were exceedingly interested in the process of mixing the concrete by machinery, the types of reinforcement adopted, and the laying and punning of the concrete By desire of the Chairman of the Science Committee a beam of plain concrete without reinforcement was also made

At a later date, when the Committee on Reinforced Concrete was formed, Messrs. Cubitt & Co placed these beams at the disposal of that Committee for testing in order that the members might have the opportunity of observing and discussing the behaviour of the materials in the presence of actual beams tested to destruction.

The Reinforced Concrete Committee deputed Professor W. C. Unwin to take charge of the tests, and the results are set out in the following notes.

In addition to the tests here rendered, one beam of each of the types illustrated was kept for testing at six months Unfortunately, by a regrettable accident, these beams were broken, and though they were put in the testing machine the results are of no value The drawing shows the construction of each type of beam, the photographs show two beams of each type in the testing machine taken after breaking.

The Royal Institute is greatly indebted to Messrs Cubitt & Co for the opportunity of making these tests and for the use of their testing machinery, and to Professor Unwin for so kindly undertaking the conduct of the work

RESULTS OF TESTS OF REINFORCED-CONCRETE BEAMS MADE BY PROFESSOR W. C UNWIN, F R S

The beams with various types of reinforcement were made by Messrs Cubitt   They had been hardening for three months before being tested They were broken in an Amsler-Laffon testing-machine

To protect the concrete from crushing at the knife-edges, a steel plate, ½ inch thick and 12 inches long, was placed below the upper knife-edge, and plates 6 inches long and ½ inch thick over the under knife-edges

The beams showed considerable elasticity when the load was removed until the breaking load was nearly reached

At the end the breaking down was very gradual   This is largely due to the action of the Amsler machine, for when a deflection occurs the load is automatically diminished till the pressure is pumped up again   The load given as the breaking load in the tables is the maximum load which could be got by pumping, and was generally reached some little time after the beam was for all practical purposes broken

NOTE.—The bars were marked A, B, C, D to correspond with the figures, and in addition those marked P had steel rods with plain ends   Those marked S had steel rods with split ends   The ultimate deflection given is that at the greatest load at which the deflection was steady enough to be observed   With a little more load the deflection went on increasing

Mark, No Iron   314 lb
Beam 12 3 inches deep, 4 08 inches wide at one end and 3·98 inches at other, span 5·12 feet.

Load tons	Deflection ins	
0 0	0 000	
0 25	0 000	
0 50	0·001	
0 75	0 001	
1·00	0 002	
1·25	0 003	Vertical crack at centre.
1 30	0 063	Broke vertically across at centre

Mark, A P.   306 lb
Beam 12 3 inches deep, 4 0 inches wide , span 5 12 feet.

Load tons	Deflection ins	
0 0	0·000	
0 5	0 006	
1 0	0 013	
1 5	0 014	
2 0	0 018	
0 0	0 010	
2·0	0 018	
2 5	0 026	
3 0	0 034	
0 0	0 014	
3 0	0 034	
3 5	0 037	Cracks on left of centre.
4 0	0 049	
0 0	0 014	
4 0	0 050	
4 5	0 054	Small cracks on right of centre.
5 0	0 060	
5·5	0 074	More cracks.
6 0	0 090	
6 2	—	Broke The chief crack was diagonal.

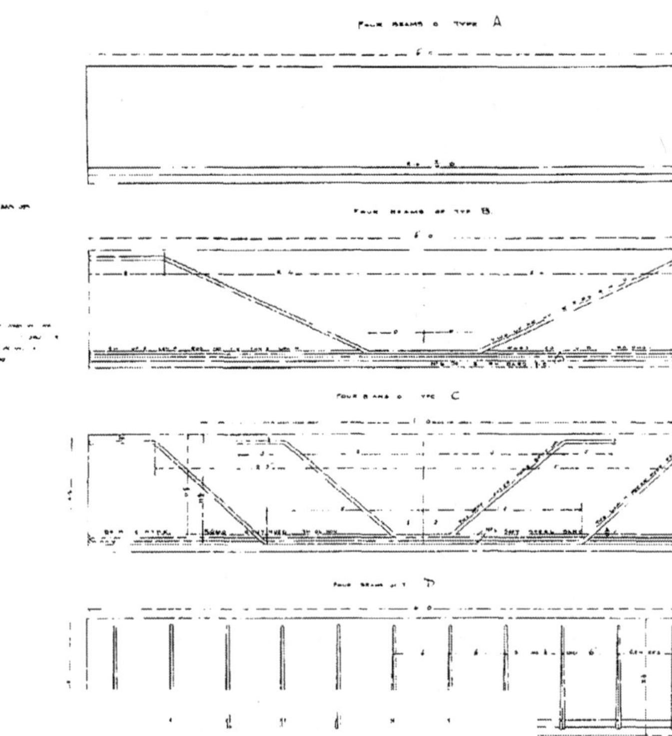

FOUR BEAMS o TYPE A
FOUR BEAMS of TYPE B
FOUR BEAMS o TYPE C
FOUR BEAMS of TYPE D

Mark, A S.   303 lb
Beam 12·2 inches deep, 3·98 inches wide ; span 5 12 feet.

Load tons	Deflection ins	
0·0	0 000	
0 5	0 000	
1 0	0 002	
1 5	0 005	
2 0	0 008	
2 5	0 010	
3·0	0 012	
3·5	0 018	
4·0	0 030	
4 5	0 035	Cracks started
5 0	0 040	Further cracks
5 8	—	Broken

Mark, A S.   311 lb. (No. 2).
Beam 12 3 inches × 4 0 inches , span 5 12 feet.

Load tons	Deflection ins.	
0·0	0·000	
0·5	0·000	
1·0	0·002	
1 5	0 008	
2 0	0 018	
0 0	0 000	
2·0	0·018	
2 5	0 020	
3 0	0 021	
3 5	0 028	
4 0	0 036	
0 0	0 002	
4 0	0 036	
4 5	0 038	
5 0	0 042	Diagonal crack left of centre.
0·0	0 003	
5·0	0 050	
5 5	0 060	
5 8	—	Broken.

Mark, B. P   306 lb
Beam 12·35 inches × 4 0 inches , span 5·12 feet.

Load tons	Deflection ins	
0 0	0 000	
0 5	0 002	
1 0	0 003	
1 5	0 003	
2·0	0 005	
0 0	0 003	
2·0	0 009	
2 5	0·015	
3 0	0·021	
0 0	0 003	
3 0	0 022	
3 5	0 023	
4 0	0 025	
0 0	0 005	
4·0	0 026	
4·5	0 027	
5 0	0·029	
0 0	0 005	
5 0	0 029	
5·5	0 035	
6 0	0 042	
0·0	0·005	
6·0	0·043	

Load tons	Deflection ins	
6 5	0 044	
7 0	0 046	
0 0	0 013	
7 0	0 053	
7 5	0 062	
8 0	0 063	Cracks chiefly diagonal
8 5	—	Soon after vertical crack near centre.
9 5	—	Broken

Mark, B P   307 lb (No 2).
Beam 12·25 inches × 4 0 inches ; span 5 12 feet.

Load tons	Deflection ins	
0 0	0 000	
0 5	0 002	
1 0	0 003	
1·5	0 010	
2 0	0 015	
0 0	0 000	
2 0	0 016	
2 5	0 020	
3 0	0 020	
3 5	0 023	
4 0	0 030	
0 0	0·003	
4 0	0 032	
4 5	0 039	
5 0	0 040	
5 5	0 042	
6 0	0 050	
0 0	0 008	
6 0	0 050	
6·5	0 056	
7 0	0 060	Diagonal crack on left of centre.
7 5	0 063	
8 0	0 080	Second crack on left also on right.
0 0	0 021	
8 0	0 080	
8·5	0 098	
9·0	0·100	Vertical crack near centre
9 3	—	Subsiding
10 0	—	Broken after much yielding

Mark, B. S.   310 lb.
Beam 12 3 inches deep, 4 inches wide ; span 5 12 feet.

Load tons	Deflection ins	
0 0	0 000	
0 5	0 009	
1 0	0 018	
1 5	0 026	
2 0	0 028	
2 5	0 034	
3 0	0·046	
3 5	0 049	
4·0	0 053	
4 5	0 063	
5 0	0 068	
5 5	0 070	
6 0	0 072	
6·5	0 084	
7 0	0 093	
7·5	0 100	
8 0	0 108	
8 5	0 126	Diagonal cracks near ends and after at centre
9 2	0 488	Broke.

MARK: No Iron.

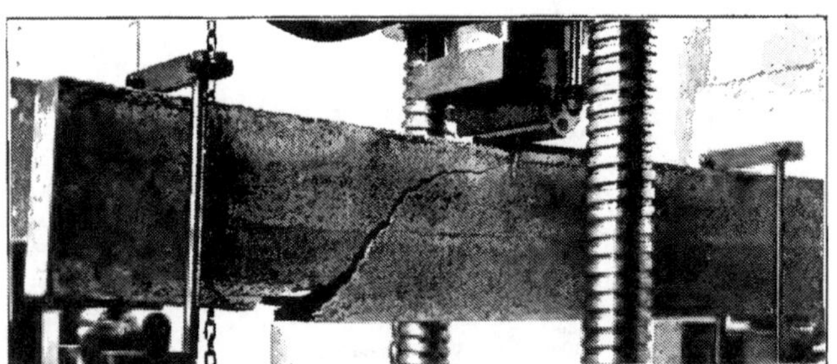

MARK: A. P. 306 LB.

MARK: A. S. (2) 311 LB.

TESTS OF REINFORCED CONCRETE BEAMS.

[To face p. 158.

Mark, C P. 316 lb.
Beam 12·3 inches × 4 00 inches , span 5·12 feet

Load tons	Deflection ins	
0·0	0 000	
0 5	0 001	
1 0	0 006	
1 5	0 009	
2 0	0 010	
0 0	0·002	
2 0	0 010	
2 5	0 012	
3 0	0 020	
3 5	0 024	
4 0	0 030	
0 0	0 009	
4 0	0 030	
4·5	0 032	
5 0	0 040	
5·5	0 046	
6 0	0·050	
0 0	0 010	
6 0	0 050	
6 5	0 052	
7 0	0 060	
7 5	0 068	
8 0	0 070	
0 0	0 022	
8 0	0 074	
8 5	0 089	Diagonal cracks
9 0	0 100	
9 5	0 150	Diagonal cracks both sides of centre
9 6	—	Broken Some crushing at top near centre

Mark, C. P   307 lb (No 2).
Beam 12·3 inches × 4 0 inches ; span 5 12 feet

Load tons	Deflection ins	
0 0	0 000	
0 5	0 000	
1·0	0 002	
1 5	0 006	
2 0	0 016	
0 0	0 002	
2 0	0 016	
2 5	0 022	
3 0	0 025	
3 5	0 032	
4 0	0 036	
0 0	0 002	
4·0	0 036	
4 5	0 040	
5 0	0 042	Very small crack left of centre.
5·5	0 045	
6 0	0 054	Two small cracks on right.
0 0	0 002	
6·0	0 060	
6·5	0 062	
7 0	0 064	
7·5	0 074	
8·0	0 082	
0 0	0 008	
8 0	0 085	
8 5	—	Subsiding and broken , some crushing at top

Mark, C S   306 lb.
Beam 12 3 inches deep, 3·98 inches wide ; span 5 12 feet.

Load tons	Deflection ins
0 0	0 000
0 5	0 004
1·0	0 008

Load tons	Deflection ins	
1 5	0 015	
2 0	0 020	
2 5	0 022	
3 0	0 030	
3 5	0 039	
4 0	0 042	
4 5	0 046	
5·0	0 054	
5 5	0 059	
6 0	0 061	
6 5	0 066	
7 0	0 078	Cracks near ends
7 5	0 080	
8 0	0 086	Cracks near centre.
8 5	0 102	
9·0	0 118	
9 5	0 460	Gradually sunk with this load; crushing at top just where reinforcing bent from diagonal to horizontal Many cracks over centre half of beam

Mark, D S.   309 lb

Beam 12¼ inches deep, 4 inches wide ; span 5 12 feet

Load tons	Deflection ins	
0 0	0 000	
0 5	0 000	
1 0	0 002	
1 5	0 006	
2 0	0 015	
2 5	0 020	
3 0	0 026	Small cracks left side of centre.
3 5	0 038	
4·0	0 040	
4 5	0 044	
5·0	0 058	Cracks on right of centre.
5 5	0 066	
6 0	0 080	
6 5	0 100	
6 9	0 460	Broke The cracks in this beam were nearly vertical, and the worst crack was at a stirrup.

Mark, D P   310 lb

Beam 12 3 inches × 4 0 inches , span 5 12 feet

Load tons	Deflection ins	
0 0	0 000	
0 5	0 000	
1 0	0 001	
1 5	0 002	
2 0	0 006	
0 0	0 000	
2 0	0 008	
2 5	0 019	
3 0	0 020	
3 5	0 024	
4 0	0 034	
0 0	0 003	
4 0	0 039	
4 5	0 040	
5 0	0 044	
5 5	0 056	Two nearly vertical cracks
6 0	0 061	
0 0	0 020	
6 0	0·064	
6 5	0·080	Subsiding
6·9	—	Broken.

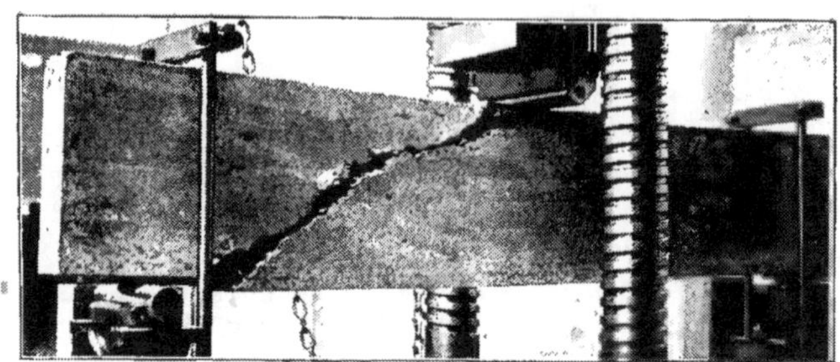

MARK: B. P. 306 LB.

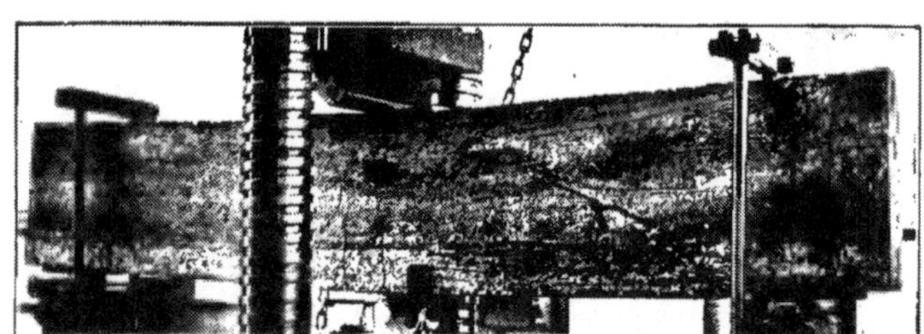

MARK: B. S. 310 LB.

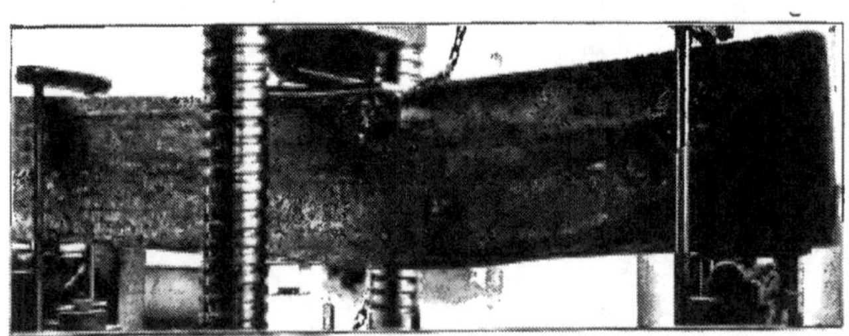

MARK: C. P. 318 LB.

TESTS OF REINFORCED CONCRETE BEAMS.

[To face p. 160.

Mark, D S   312 lb   (No 2).
Beam 12 4 inches × 4 00 inches , span 5·12 feet.

Load tons	Deflection ins	
0 0	0 000	
0 5	0 000	
1 0	0 002	
1 5	0 004	
2 0	0 016	
0 0	0 002	
2·0	0 019	
2 5	0 020	
3 0	0 022	
3 5	0 031	
4 0	0 040	
0 0	0 013	
4 0	0 040	
4 5	0 046	
5 0	0 058	
5 5	0 060	Cracks nearly vertical
6 0	0 075	
0 0	0 030	
6·0	0 080	
6 5	0 090	
7 0	0 260	
7 1	0 660	Subsiding.
7 3	—	Broken.

SUMMARY.

No of test	Mark on Beam	Maximum Load	Load at which the last deflection was taken	Ultimate Deflection	Deflection with 5 tons load	Set with 6 tons Load
		Tons	Tons	Inches		Inches
1	No iron	1 30	1 30	0 063	—	—
2	A P.	6 20	6 00	0 090	0 060	—
3	A S	5 80	5 00	0 040	0 040	—
4	A S (2)	5 80	5 50	0 060	0 050	—
5	B P.	9 50	8 00	0 063	0 029	0 005
6	B P (2)	10 00	9 00	0·100	0 040	0 008
7	B S	9 20	9 20	0 488	0 068	—
8	C P	9 60	9 50	0 150	0 040	0 010
9	C P (2)	8 50	8 00	0 085	0 042	0 002
10	C S	9 50	9 50	0 460	0 054	—
11	D P	6 90	6 50	0 080	0 044	0 020
12	D S	6 90	6 90	0 460	0 058	—
13	D S (2)	7 30	7 10	0 660	0 058	0 030

RESULTS OF TESTS MADE BY WILLIAM CUBITT & CO. AT 258 GRAY'S
INN ROAD, LONDON, W C , ON A SAMPLE OF PORTLAND CEMENT

Received from Grays, Essex, on November 28, 1905, being a sample of 50 tons of cement supplied by the Associated Portland Cement Company, on November 27, 1905, by barge   The sample contained in a sack

Temperature of air in the test-room 57° F.
    „   , water „ „ 54° F
Apparent density of the cement 1·025 ; specific gravity 3 1

Fineness.

Residue on 50 × 50 standard sieve (2,500 meshes per square inch), nil %
   „   76 × 76   „   (5,776   „   „   ), „ „
   „ 180 × 180   „   (32,460   „   „   ), 9 4 „

Setting Time

Final in air $5\frac{1}{4}$ hours, water used 25 % by weight
 ,,   water $7\frac{1}{2}$,,   ,,   ,,   ,,   ,,

Soundness.

Pats set in air   sound, and after being in boiling water 6 hours sound
 ,,   water ,,   ,,   ,,   ,,   ,,   ,,   ,,

Expansion —Le Chatelier's Test

Cylinder set in air nil, m/m, and after being in boiling water 6 hours 1 m/m.
 ,,   water ,,   ,,   ,,   ,,   ,,   ,,   nil.

Tensile Tests (in lb per square inch)

3 of standard sand and 1 of cement

7 days	28 days
248	470
312	470
255	508
248	460
310	490
280	450
1,653	2,848
$275\frac{1}{2}$	$474\frac{2}{3}$

Percentage of water used in gauging the sand briquettes 10 % by weight.

RESULTS OF TESTS MADE BY WILLIAM CUBITT & CO. AT 258 GRAY'S INN ROAD, W C, ON CONCRETE MADE FROM THE SAME MATERIALS AS THOSE USED FOR THE BEAMS TESTED BY PROFESSOR UNWIN, F R S, ON MARCH 7, 8, AND 9, 1906

Compression tests on 4-inch cubes in tons. Proportions, one of cement and five of aggregate, the latter made up of two parts gravel and one part sand

The cubes three months old.

1–4 inch cube (weight 2,630 grammes), $29\frac{1}{8}$ tons
1–4   ,,   (,   2,530   ,, $30\frac{1}{2}$,,

          5,160   60

Average   2,580 grammes   30 tons

Specific gravity of the concrete cubes 2·46

For making each cube there was used

1 litre ballast
$\frac{1}{2}$,,   sand
330 grammes of cement
180 c c clean water

For the quality of cement see test-sheet above

The actual apparent density was 1·025, but to allow a good margin it was assumed to be 1 1, which gives 330 grammes for the proportion of one to five, as above.

MARK: C. P. (2) 307 LB.

MARK: D. S. 309 LB.

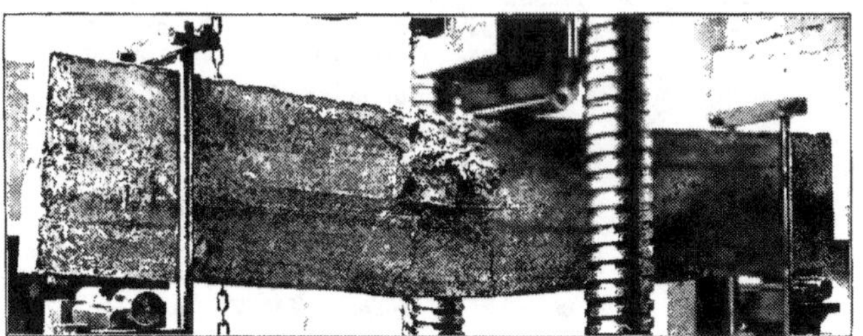

MARK: D. P. 310 LB.

TESTS OF REINFORCED CONCRETE BEAMS.

[To face p. 162.

2 REINFORCED CONCRETE AND ITS RELATION TO FIRE PROTECTION.

By E P GOODRICH (New York City, U S.A)

In choosing the subject of " Reinforced Concrete and its Relation to Fire Protection," the writer had in mind the dual conditions necessary to the greatest immunity from fire in large building construction, particularly where such has varied types of occupancy, together with correspondingly different manufacturing fire hazards.

The requisites are . First, the employment of the most incombustible building materials and the assembling of these elements in such manner as will most effectively limit the spread of fire Secondly, the equipment of the building with such protective and extinguishing apparatus as a wide experience has determined most effective Either of these essentials alone will accomplish a large measure of result, but to secure the maximum the combination is necessary

The writer makes no apology, therefore, for dwelling at some length on the details of protective equipment, and confining the description of the concrete construction to such points as are more or less novel, assuming his audience to be familiar with the ordinary practice of the art.

For general purposes, no other type of construction combines flexibility of application with fireproof property so completely as reinforced concrete, and for this reason it was selected for the construction of the sixteen great factory buildings now in progress or prospect for the Bush Terminal Company of Brooklyn, New York

The progress in popularity and importance characterising concrete construction in the United States in the past decade has been enormous, and it is only necessary to point to the great Manchester Ship Canal Docks as evidencing its wide employment in this country

The Bush Terminal Company owns and operates in New York Harbour a steamship and railroad terminal which handles nearly one-quarter of the total tonnage of that harbour In connection with this terminal are certain affiliated enterprises which serve as feeders for the terminal Their development at present consists of seven piers 150 feet wide, and approximately 1,300 feet long , together with nearly one hundred storehouses of various dimensions and designs, and of a series of tenant factory buildings. Added to these are the usual miscellaneous items, such as a power-house, central office building, railroad tracks, pavements, water supply development, sewerage system, &c

When this development was originated, slow-burning mill construction was the type adopted for most of the buildings. At the present time, however, reinforced concrete has been so far decreased in cost and increased in facility of construction, that it has even surpassed the old type of heavy timber construction for many structures as far as first cost and maintenance go. All of the newer construction work carried out by the Bush Terminal Company has been of this type, and it is the purpose of this paper to describe the latest of the tenant factory buildings and the special reasons which led to the adoption of the several features which characterise its design.

The structure last designed is to be the type in accordance with which fourteen similar factory buildings are to be erected. It is 600 feet long, 75 feet wide, and approximately 100 feet high, divided into six stories with a basement. The building was arranged with special reference to its being leased to tenants who would require blocks of space ranging from 20,000 square feet upward The buildings thus far constructed have proved so attractive that the one now occupied was wholly leased three months before it was completed, and the one now under construction is over 75 per cent leased, while only the foundations have been constructed up to the present date

In length, the building was limited by the size of the property. The breadth was largely limited by the possibility of securing good light along the centre line of the building. The height of the building was to some extent limited by the number of elevators and other appliances which would be necessary to handle the crude and manufactured materials incidental to the operations on the several floors, and to a greater extent by the increased insurance rate which is exacted of such buildings if they exceed a height of six stories above grade   The buildings are arranged in pairs, back to back, and are so designed that deliveries can be made to trucks on the streets at the fronts of the buildings, and to railroad cars which can be placed on tracks between the backs of the buildings   Special loading platforms, &c , are provided for facilitating these deliveries

The arrangement of stairs, elevators, windows, skylights, parapets, water supply, fire escapes, dividing walls, floor covering, light, heat, &c , was largely determined by the effects they would have upon the insurance rates for the building structure, to some extent, but particularly with regard to the contents rates which would be exacted from tenants of the building   A little later it will be shown exactly to what extent insurance rates thus became factors determining the writer as the designing engineer in making his lay out.

In the United States the insurance companies have become affiliated to a great extent   One of the effects of this closer relationship is that in several of the large cities " Exchanges," so called, have been established, which have to do with all matters with regard to building inspection, determination of rates, &c., for all the affiliated companies   Thus, in New York City, the Insurance Exchange issues a schedule from which the rate of any building can be computed.   These schedules have been made up after an extended study of the causes of fires and of the damage which has been found to take place with different kinds of construction, different devices employed in fighting fire, different fire prevention methods, &c. With regard to fireproof buildings constructed of reinforced concrete, the following items enter to make up the schedule :

A base rate

A factor depending upon the areas between fireproof walls.

The number of stories in the building.

Character of the doors opening into halls, elevators, &c

Whether or no all structural steel is fireproofed.

Whether or no floors are watertight and water shedding

Whether or no stairways extend entirely from top to bottom of building

Whether or no a special tank with risers and hose is installed, and elevators are always in readiness to carry the fire department hose to any floor

In addition to these several items which are specifically included in the schedule, there is a very broad factor called " exposure," which often determines almost completely the actual rate charged for a building This item is determined by numerous features largely external to the building, but to some extent also by the structure itself   The distance which separates any building from the adjacent ones obviously should enter this item   The character of construction of such adjacent buildings also largely influences it.   Consideration is also given to the installation of special devices looking toward a reduction of the risk from fires in adjacent buildings, such devices taking the form of water curtains, or wire glass in all light openings, &c.

The rates on factory buildings were at one time so excessive that numerous owners combined to form mutual companies which would underwrite fire risks more cheaply than the line companies were doing Eventually a large number of these mutual companies combined, and now have a strong standing, especially in the New England and Southern

Examples of Hollow Metal Window Frames Glazed with Wire Glass.

Interior View, showing Standard Metal-covered Fire-doors.

BUSH TERMINAL COMPANY'S FACTORY BUILDING, NEW YORK.

[To face p. 164

States Because of the mutual character of these organisations the actual rates are very low, when all rebates are considered. These companies maintain regular engineering inspectors, and have established well-formulated regulations to which all prospective insurants must accurately conform. The principal requirement exacted by them is the installation of a sprinkler system with all necessary appurtenances, including fire pumps, automatic alarms, large supply tank, specified sizes of underground and overhead mains, approved sprinkler heads, &c

In addition to the organisations named, there exists a National Board of Fire Underwriters. This board has developed numerous standard designs for doors, windows, &c. Experience has proved the advantages, from a fire-resisting point of view, of structures built in accordance with these designs, and the underwriters allow lower insurance rates where such standard designs are carried out

In designing the work herein particularly described, special regard was constantly maintained for all insurance regulations of both the mutual and the regular companies, and the consideration given to each of the several items follows .

As stated above, the length of the building could not well be varied.

The clear height of floors was determined by an inspection of a very large number of factory buildings to ascertain what were the actual requirements in this regard for all kinds of machines, when run by shafting and by individual motors ; to what height it was economical to pile goods kept in storage ; what height was required for proper heating and ventilation in manufacturing operations of various kinds, &c After consideration had been given to all these items, it was determined that a height from floor to floor of 13 feet 6 inches should be adopted Once having determined this point, consideration was given to the possibility of carrying windows up to within a few inches of the ceiling on each floor, so as to secure light from as great an elevation as possible

Having secured a proper design with regard to this point, the required width of window was determined to supply good illumination at the centres of buildings of different widths. Of course, the wider a building could be constructed, the more economical it would be from the landlord's point of view, since relatively less money would be expended for walls which do not pay dividends, and relatively more would be invested in floor space which would be directly remunerative. In determining a proper width for the buildings, consideration was also given to the requirements in this regard of various small manufacturing industries such as the shoe trade, clothes manufacturers, &c. A width of 75 feet outside walls was finally determined upon. While the matter of width was not directly determined by any insurance considerations, still it was to some extent influenced by them, because the insurance schedule dictated an increase of one unit in the rate for each one thousand square feet above five thousand which was found between fire walls This meant that a narrow building could profitably be divided into longer open spaces than could a wide one, and the possible length of open space is often a consideration to manufacturers.

With regard to the longitudinal division of the building, two schemes have been worked out. The first building was constructed with a single fire wall at the centre of the 600 foot length The other buildings will probably be constructed with two fire walls, each 150 feet from an end of the building. These walls, however, are so designed that a manufacturer can take space on each side of one of them, and even then he will be hampered only by the necessity of communicating between the two sections through two fairly large openings in the walls. The latter are of reinforced concrete 12 inches thick, and are carried through the roof, and to a height of 3 feet above it. This is in conformity with the regulations of the insurance companies governing this point. If these walls were omitted or were not constructed so as to secure the advantage of the decreased insurance rate, the ratio between the rate for the 600 foot building without walls, and with one wall at the centre, would be as 51 5 is to 29, a saving of 43 5 per cent for this item alone, other items being of standard design throughout for the purpose of this comparison

The combining of all stairways and elevator shafts at particular points in the building and enclosing them by thoroughly fireproof walls is another important item in the securing of low insurance rates Structural advantages also dictate such a course, and as finally arranged for the latest of the Bush factory buildings, four stairways were constructed, two at the front and two at the rear in pairs, and each pair located about 150 feet from an end of the building. Additional outside steel stairways to serve as fire escapes are provided, so as to secure ample egress in case of panic even with large numbers of employees   Of course, all structural work of inside stairs was built in reinforced concrete with patent safety treads and with metal balustrades, newels, &c. Ignoring this point would add 7 per cent to the insurance rate for the building

In order to secure all possible insurance reduction with regard to waterproofing of floors, care was first taken that concrete work should be made as impervious as possible by the use of a relatively large amount of cement After the floor had been installed, a coating of coal tar and asphalt was applied hot over the whole surface of the concrete. Nailing strips were then laid down and properly wedged to grade, and a poor quality of cinder concrete was installed between them to give a good bearing surface for the wooden floor surface. The latter consisted of maple. The boards were $1\frac{1}{4}$ inches thick by $3\frac{1}{2}$ inches wide, were tongued and grooved at sides and ends, and were bored for nailing, so as to obviate all possibility of splitting Maple, like almost all other kinds of wood, when wet will swell so as to make a surface which is practically impervious to water, and on which large amounts can be thrown, and remain for considerable periods, without penetrating through so as to cause damage to occupants below Construction of this kind secured a reduction of over 5 per cent in the insurance rate. Several compounds besides asphalt were experimented with as an impervious coating, and some were found fully as effective and as economical   In connection with the asphalt, a felt strip, tarred top and bottom, was laid over the joints which occurred in the floor concrete between different days' work

With the narrow width of the building, and because of the difficulty in installing machinery on a floor which was not absolutely level, it was decided not to give the floors a grade   Numerous doors were provided in the length of the building on each floor, with outriggers over them at the level of the roof, so that larger pieces of machinery, cases of goods, &c., could be hoisted than could be accommodated by the elevators. These doors, opening as they did at the floor level, provided ample waterways for getting rid of water which might be discharged by sprinklers, used in washing down floors, or employed in the extinguishing of fires. Other than these door openings no special devices, like scuppers, were provided

All doors throughout the building were designed in accordance with the requirements of the National Board of Fire Underwriters for the special cases encountered. The principal items involved are the following.

Usually three thicknesses of 1-inch boards placed at different angles and clinch nailed

A galvanised iron or tin covering, the parts of which are fastened together by locking of joints, without the use of solder or nails, which might be melted off in a conflagration.

All doors fastened to brick or concrete work, or to special metal frames

All doors supplied with weights or other devices so as to close them automatically unless particularly prevented by approved devices.

PILE OF COLUMN REINFORCEMENT WIRE CYLINDERS
AND ROW OF CINDER SHELLS.

VIEW OF TYPICAL GIRDER REINFORCEMENT "UNIT."

BUSH TERMINAL COMPANY'S FACTORY BUILDING, NEW YORK.

[To face p. 166.

The latter consist essentially of a fusible link with necessary appurtenances capable of being severed at low temperature (160° F), and allowing doors to close automatically.

Special track, hangers, stops, hinges, guides, metal sills, &c., such as have proved satisfactory under trying circumstances.

The majority of the smaller doors for stairways, &c., were swinging doors. Some large doors were horizontally sliding doors, while all elevator doors were vertically sliding doors, divided so as to open at the centre and allow one half to slide upward and the other half downward. The large doors which opened on to shipping platforms were designed as horizontally cross folding doors This class has the special advantage of opening without occupying floor space, and when opened, of forming a sort of hood which protects the door opening to a considerable extent from the weather. Large doors were provided with panes of wire glass, so that the same ratio of light surface was secured in each bay throughout the full length of the building.

The window sills are placed 3 feet 6 inches above the floor, so that benches or small machines can be installed close to the walls without interfering with the glass surface. The specifications for the window frames, sash, &c., were drawn in accordance with the requirements of the National Board of Fire Underwriters The hazard of exposure always exists, and is independent of the nature of the building construction, however incombustible The window area in the Bush factory buildings is very large, 42 per cent. of the total wall area, and with such window openings unprotected, the possibility is large of a hot fire on a single floor being forced out of the windows on that floor, and drawn in again at windows above or below This danger is generally termed " auto-exposure," and is most pronounced when floors are entirely segregated There still exists, though in milder form, by reason of the wide spacing, a danger of fire being communicated from building to building through these same window openings. For window openings, efficient protection against fire may be had in two forms shutters, and wire glass mounted in metal frames. Shutters are of two types, sheet iron and tin-clad wood. Both have the same serious defects—liability to rapid corrosion, necessity for daily opening and closing, likelihood of being found open in moments of emergency, and, in the case of the Bush factories, their absolute inadmissibility from an architectural point of view. With wire glass, however, an ideal solution was effected. The openings are 13 feet in width and 8 feet in height The window frames and sashes are hollow, and constructed of 22 and 24 galvanised iron, in the double mullion form The upper sashes are stationary, while those of the lower row are pivoted. The brass pivots are slightly above the centre of each sash, the sash being held open by a chain with fusible link placed near the top, where the first attack of heat is most likely to occur. Upon the fusing of the link, the sashes close and lock by gravity. The sashes are glazed with ¼-inch Mississippi wire glass in either rough or ribbed surface, depending upon the distribution of light required. This glass is cast solid, and is the only type in the United States recognised for fire-retardant purposes by the National and Local Boards of Fire Underwriters. It may be of interest to note that wire glass made under this process was used throughout the Manchester Ship Canal work already referred to

In spite of the practically fireproof quality of the building, erected as it is of reinforced concrete, sprinklers were installed throughout. About 42 feet above the roof a 30,000 gallon tank was constructed in accordance with the specifications of the Factory Mutual Insurance Companies. Stand pipes with standard hose outlets, and at least one length of hose with nozzle at each floor, were installed in each stairwell, and in connection with sprinkler mains at other points in the building. Some distance from the building, but connected to it by a water main of large size, were installed two 1,000 gallon underwriters' fire pumps   The piping for the sprinkler system was of ample size throughout, all built in accordance with the specifications of the same insurance companies   The heads were placed so as to protect a space of approximately 100 square feet.   All heads within the building were of the automatic type   Because the distance between buildings was approximately 55 feet, and because of the fact that all buildings in the vicinity were to be of the same practically fireproof type, it was not deemed necessary to provide special outside open sprinklers to prevent possible damage in one building due to fire in adjacent ones.   On the piers belonging to the Bush Terminal Company such precautions were taken, however, and open sprinkler heads have been installed so as to provide a water curtain of considerable volume over the full length of each side of each pier whenever necessary.   Such a contrivance would not be necessary where wire glass is used for light openings. With its use the only necessity is a sprinkler head of very small size, just sufficient to provide water which would cool the glass surface so that it should not become sufficiently hot to ignite inflammable goods stored close to window openings, from the radiant heat which would be given off by the glass itself if heated sufficiently high by an adjacent conflagration

The most important among the specifications laid down by the factory mutual insurance companies for tanks, pumps, &c., are as follows ·

Tanks may be of wood or steel, as local conditions dictate.

If of wood, they are to be built with a taper, and be hooped with round steel rods, spaced according to special tables

Special pipes for filling, discharging, overflow, &c., must be provided.

Special arrangements must be made to prevent freezing of discharge pipe and tank in cold climates.

The pumps must be duplex, built for 45 lbs. steam pressure

Sizes of all parts are to be in accordance with standard specifications

Only approved manufacturers are to build pumps, and same are to be subject to special test at any time by regular inspectors

In the United States great strides have been made during the past two years in the use of reinforced concrete for all classes of construction work.   Its costs have been rapidly decreased, through increased familiarity with that class of work and the invention of labour-saving devices

On the other hand the costs of timber have increased rapidly, so that in numerous instances concrete buildings actually cost less than they would do if built of timber   In the case of several mill buildings with which the writer is familiar, bids were received both for concrete and for timber construction   The concrete was found to cost only about half what the timber would do

In the case of the first Bush factory building, bids were received for steel frame structures with reinforced concrete floors, as well as for a building constructed of reinforced concrete throughout   The latter was found to cost almost exactly 10 per cent. less than the steel frame structure.

In fireproofing qualities, furthermore, concrete has been proven superior to all others, in the opinion of most engineers and architects. A fire and water test, conducted before the Building Department of New York City by one of the earliest advocates of concrete for floors, was of a small building in which one half was built with concrete and the other half with segmental hollow tile   The result of the test was a clear demonstration of the superiority of the concrete.   The Baltimore conflagration also gave a more or less emphatic proof of the better qualities inherent in concrete, and the tendency at the present time in the United States seems strongly toward that material   The San Francisco catastrophe further added strength to the movement

Among the various ingredients usually employed, the latest tests, both in England and the United States, show a slight superiority for hard coal cinders as producing the best fireproofing material.

Interior View, showing Sprinkler Piping, Columns built with
Cinder Shell Fireproofing, &c.

General View of First Completed Building.

BUSH TERMINAL COMPANY'S FACTORY BUILDING, NEW YORK.

[*To face p.* 168.

It was a careful consideration of these points which determined the use of reinforced concrete for the structural part of the Bush factories.

The exterior was given a special treatment, to give it a considerable artistic effect for advertising purposes, and the subject was worked up in a modified Florentine style with red and buff bricks. The exterior treatment of all sixteen of the buildings will not be uniform, and it is probable that many will be constructed entirely of concrete.

Special study was given to the subject of the type of reinforcement to be used in the building, in order to realise the highest degree of efficiency. None of the then existing systems were adopted, but a new one was worked out, which might be called an "Eclectic." Another designating name often given is that it is a "Unit" system. During the same period at two other points in the United States similar systems were being developed   The distinctive point about the work is that all the steel reinforcing bars are combined and rigidly fastened together so as to form a frame or truss, very similar to a bridge truss   This truss can be constructed in a special factory, can be transported from the factory to the work without damage, can be placed in the work with small expense, and will maintain its position in the centering with a perfection which discrete members cannot be made to attain

The points claimed are summed up as follows

Designed as a "Unit"

Built as a "Unit."

Delivered as a "Unit."

Supported as a "Unit"

Erected as a "Unit."

Acts as a "Unit"

It is carefully designed for each span.

Each member is the necessary size.

It is the proper shape.

Tension and shear members scientifically spaced

All parts securely held.

No part can be forgotten.

Nor omitted.

Entire frame is placed at once

A system in which the concrete can be thoroughly tamped without disturbing the reinforcing members.

Adapted for use with every conceivable system of slab reinforcement.

Another feature of the system adopted for the Bush factories is in the use of a multiplicity of stirrups which practically hoop the entire beams   Actual tests have proved that with such stirrups a special fireproofing material can be employed around and below the tension rods, if so desired   By this means a special grade of concrete can be employed and installed in the bottom of beams and girders, composed of hard coal cinders, pumice stone, or other fire-resisting material.

All beams and girders, as far as possible, were designed so as to take advantage of reverse moments over points of support   Great care was exercised to give such members ample strength where they were joined to columns, so that the weakest point of the beam or girder (the point at which failure would be likely to occur) would not be where it would involve the destruction of the column, and thus endanger the whole of the building above that special point   While this point has no reference to insurance requirements, still it was duly considered in drawing up the design for the building, because of the possibility of fire doing enough damage to make possible the failure of a small section of a floor which might happen to be excessively loaded above the conflagration

Another device looking to the protection of columns against possible damage, as well as proving advantageous from other points of view, was the use of cinder concrete shells as column moulds. It is a well-known fact that rock concrete, when heated to a high temperature and suddenly cooled by the application of water, will spall, so that some tested concrete floors have been so far disintegrated as to fail in consequence The cinder moulds designed for the columns of the Bush factories were cast in a special yard arranged for the purpose, and were taken to the building and erected in place by common labourers The shells were about 1½ inch thick, and carried on their inside surfaces a coil of high carbon steel wire which was designed as a column reinforcement, very similar to that devised by Considère in France and Jamieson in Canada. When set up in place, the shells formed the centering for the columns, and were filled with rock concrete to make a thoroughly first-class construction One column which had to be demolished, and a sample which was tested to over 4,000 lbs per square inch, proved conclusively the value of the method.

In view of the result, it is but fair to say that the scope of accomplishment anticipated in the design has been achieved The building now completed is pleasing to the eye, has more applications for space than can be accommodated, and is accorded the very lowest fire insurance rate by the most critical body of underwriters in the United States— The Associated Mutual Factory Fire Insurance Companies of Massachusetts. It seems a fact hardly possible of controversy that the use of reinforced concrete for building work, viewed solely from the fire underwriter's standpoint, is of small value unless all other parts of the structure are equally fireproof.

---

3 L'EMPLOI DU BÉTON ARMÉ EN ARCHITECTURE.

Par le Professeur CLOQUET.

[Présenté par la Société Centrale d'Architecture de Belgique]

POINT DE VUE CONSTRUCTIF

L'édifice ancien était caractérisé par la séparation entre deux parties distinctes, les murs et le comble Il y a défaut de solidarité entre elles Au point où les fermes de charpente s'appuient sur les murs existe comme une articulation A ce défaut caractéristique des édifices aux murs en pierre et aux combles en bois l'introduction des charpentes métalliques n'a d'abord pas remédié On s'est longtemps borné à combiner des fermes en fer analogues aux fermes en bois. La solution du problème des grands halls n'a fait un progrès décisif, que lorsqu'on inaugura les fermes cintrées ayant leur naissance sur le sol, comme les fermes du type de Dion Désormais la solidarité fut assurée entre les parties verticales et inclinées Toutefois ce sont les fermes seules qui sont indéformables La solidarité des parties verticales et inclinées n'est pas réalisée dans les surfaces enveloppantes , il y a manque d'homogénéité entre les deux parties de l'édifice, à savoir son ossature et sa paroi. La logique réclame une solution plus radicale qui consisterait à solidariser non pas seulement les montants et les fermes, mais plutôt le mur et le toit C'est ce que permet de réaliser l'emploi du béton armé La paroi-mur peut même disparaître ou se confondre avec la voûte L'ensemble présentera des surfaces à peu près continues au dehors et au dedans, avec suppression des encombrantes saillies internes des charpentes Le dispositif nouveau revient donc à économiser les fermes, et à ne maintenir qu'une enveloppe qui se soutient toute seule Or, l'expérience prouve que des constructions ainsi conçues ne coûtent pas plus cher que celles construites en grosse maçonnerie avec combles métalliques et qu'elles sont durables.

S'il s'agit d'une construction à étages, le plancher en béton armé se substitue avantageusement aux anciens systèmes La conséquence la plus caractéristique de l'emploi du béton armé est la suppression du toit, le dernier plancher-haut pouvant servir de couverture et constituer une terrasse habitable   Ce genre de construction se prête en outre aux porte-à-faux les plus hardis

Ce système, appliqué de manière rationnelle, peut transformer les formes architectoniques   Il simplifie les formes, il fait disparaître les complexités encombrantes des charpentes et gîtages ; il réalise simplement toutes les surfaces enveloppantes ou séparatives   Il efface toute distinction entre le mur et le toit   Il inaugure une architecture faite de parois enveloppantes si souples, qu'elles peuvent être circonscrites à toute capacité quelconque qu'il est utile d'enclore   Les habitations prendront la forme de parallélipipèdes terminés en terrassons et les grands édifices celle de voûtes bombées à extrados apparents   Il faut s'attendre à voir disparaître la sculpture et les reliefs modelés et prévaloir les revêtements colorés   Un changement radical des formes internes et externes des édifices sera la conséquence de la substitution d'une structure concrète, solidaire, homogène, à notre ancien organisme architectonique.   Toutes les formes propres à un assemblage de pierres appareillées et ravalées, désormais supprimé, seraient ici dénues d'expression et de valeur esthétique   Il faut les sacrifier et en chercher des nouvelles

Point de Vue Esthétique

Nous distinguons trois sortes de formes   les formes de *convenance, de structure* et *d'expression*

Les formes de convenance, par lesquelles l'édifice reçoit sa complète utilité et un caractère adéquat à sa destination, satisfont l'esprit sans délecter la vue   Ces formes de convenance qui sont excellentes, sinon les plus agréables, peuvent être réalisées à merveille à l'aide des procédés si souples du béton armé

Les formes d'expression sont celles par lesquelles l'architecte et ses aides mettent un peu de leur imagination et de leur âme dans l'édifice, afin de lui donner l'éloquence d'aspect. L'idéal est, qu'elles fassent partie intégrante et inséparable de la construction   Dans les édifices en béton armé il reste peu d'emploi pour le talent des artistes, surtout des sculpteurs. Il ne subsiste guère que le décor superficiel de la peinture et des revêtements polychromes, céramiques ou autres : mais pour les artistes de la couleur il reste tout un vaste champ qui convient à leurs créations

Les formes de structure, réelles ou fictives, sont le principal ornement des édifices de l'ancien régime   Ce sont ces formes organiques qui rendent vivant l'aspect des constructions en maçonnerie d'appareil

Dans la conception ancienne un bâtiment est comparable à un organisme vivant où se lit une ossature, une membrure et comme une anatomie   Le béton armé n'offre pas les éléments d'intérêt et de charme , il donne l'impression d'ouvrages exécutés avec des matériaux trop dociles, où le labeur sacré de l'ouvrier et ses procédés traditionnels n'ont pas laissé l'empreinte de la noble lutte entre l'artisan et la matière.   On ne trouve pas la même beauté dans ces ouvrages coulés d'un bloc en une matière morte et terne, sans appareil, sans organisme, qu'on ne peut mieux faire que de dissimuler sous un décor superficiel

Pour conclure, les procédés nouveaux, économiques et puissants, sont précieux au point de vue de certaines réalisations hardies ou complexes   Il leur manque le charme de l'expression artistique   D'ailleurs l'économie n'est qu'une loi relative et d'ordre secondaire, et la hardiesse de la structure n'est pas toujours requise   Un procédé qui prévaut à ces deux points de vue ne s'impose nullement à l'exclusion des autres   On pourra y recourir pour la satisfaction économique de programmes utilitaires, la réalisation du confort et la solution de problèmes hardis.   Jamais il n'éliminera de la pratique architecturale les combinaisons nobles et artistiques de la maçonnerie appareillée, moulurée et sculptée, des charpentes en bois et en métal, des superstructures voûtées, etc

4. CONSTRUCTIONS EN ACIER ET EN CIMENT ARMÉ.

Par Gaston Trelat (Paris)

Les constructions en acier et en ciment armé ont pour trait distinctif de réaliser une économie appréciable du fait de réduction dans l'épaisseur des murs. Relativement au capital représenté par l'immeuble, on y trouve l'avantage d'une augmentation de superficie utilisable, en conséquence du peu de volume que prennent les éléments constitutifs de l habitation. C'est déjà une considération qui a sa valeur, elle est due au caractère mécanique de l'ossature des bâtiments, par le fait même de l'élément de construction que réalisent l'acier et le ciment armé Le caractère original de ce dernier mode d'installation est de réunir à lui seul les résistances à la flexion du métal et à la compression des matériaux lourds et encombrants De là une étendue d'applications, que l'expérience encore nouvelle permet déjà d'entrevoir, mais elles sont loin d'avoir dit leur dernier mot

L'emploi est encore assez nouveau. On lui a surtout demandé des services utilitaires. Mais, pour répondre à la question, telle que le programme du VIIe Congrès a entendu la poser, croyons-nous, il conviendrait d'aborder les solutions qui pourraient être atteintes en allant plus loin, jusqu'à envisager l'esthétique et l'hygiène, sans négliger les constructions à grande hauteur, que la question vise également.

Si l'on se place au point de vue esthétique, on ne peut douter que l'acier et le ciment armé ne puissent devenir des sources de beauté par leur mariage tout indiqué avec des matériaux destinés à constituer une enveloppe plastique

En la circonstance, il n'y aurait pas de placage, à proprement parler, rien qui rappelât ce dont on trouverait un exemple dans la variété et la richesse de marbres que montrent notamment les parois de Santa Maria Novella à Florence. Elles y sont obtenues par apposition à l'élément constructif de maçonnerie et restent par trop indépendantes pour n'avoir pas froissé la logique du constructeur à certaines époques. Mais le grès, par exemple, est un matériel, que sa constitution et sa structure préparent au mariage avec le métal La figure de ses différentes unités pourrait répondre aux nécessités de liens ou d'attaches suffisamment solides avec l'ossature d'acier ou avec les éléments métalliques du ciment armé Sans s'attacher à une discussion mécanique des résistances spéciales, intervenant dans l'ensemble pour assurer la solidité de l'abri, on comprend que les éléments métalliques pourraient s'étendre à un revêtement de beauté et continuer l'homogénéité des résistances mécaniques de l'œuvre

Le grès et l'émail dont il est apparemment revêtu, permettent d'envisager des beautés infinies, eu égard aux applications déjà connues La variété des émaux s'inspire déjà des anciens produits d'extrême-orient, elle est destinée à aller bien au-delà de ce que l'on voit aujourd'hui avec les moyens industriels dont on dispose et qui s'accroissent journellement. On n'essaierait donc pas de prévoir à quelle ampleur d'harmonies et d'aspirations plastiques ils sont destinés à répondre. La liberté de conception permettra de réaliser les imaginations décoratives qui sont de nature à enrichir l'horizon offert aux regards de la foule, comme l'exige, du reste, le courant auquel nous assistons.

Considérant enfin l'hygiène, les parois de grès, aménagées à l'intérieur des habitations, sont favorables à la salubrité de l'ambiance offerte à la vie humaine. Avec le grès, rien n'est plus facile que d'en assurer l application à toutes les parois, aussi bien horizontales que verticales. Ces parois deviennent toutes faciles à laver, à désinfecter et ne présentent aucun refuge à la poussière. Tous les angles s'arrondissent, en suite des prévisions qui seraient commandées par une étude bien conduite, eu égard à la salubrité.

Alors les constructions à grande hauteur deviendraient bien moins défectueuses, au point de vue sanitaire, qu'elles ne l'étaient avec les autres modes de construction antérieurement répandus Car une désinfection générale des locaux habités serait facile à répéter dans un semblable aménagement. Son ensemble prendrait un caractère essentiellement réfractaire à toute contamination, par suite des parois émaillées, aussi bien horizontalement que verticalement.

Toutes les habitations collectives, visant spécialement l'assistance, verraient leur salubrité notablement accrue, par suite des facilités d'entretien aseptique et antiseptique de tous les éléments de construction. De même pour les habitations à bon marché

Ajoutons que l'étude pourrait aboutir à une ordonnance décorative de ces parois planes, et charmer la vue par leur expression décorative, tout en ménageant la santé Elles deviendraient pour les enfants une source d'élévation vers l'élégance morale ou mentale , elles créeraient même une atmosphère spécialement heureuse pour l'esprit des parents et reposante pour leurs âmes, après les fatigues et les âpretés d'une lutte inclinant souvent à toute autre chose. Il en découlerait une distinction relative à l'éducation du goût Elle apparaîtrait comme un contrepoids bienfaisant pour les cerveaux. Et ce serait tout profit pour l'ensemble social, dont il n'y a aucun droit de se désintéresser, aujourd'hui que tout le monde sans exception peut concourir à la formation des élites

Résumé.—En résumé, l'acier et le ciment armé sont appelés à voir leurs applications se généraliser. Ils sont aptes à un mariage facile et commode avec d'autres matériaux comme la terre cuite et surtout le grès Et de la sorte peut se créer un corps matériel pourvu de solidité et de nature à assurer la beauté, qui entre dans l'ordre des préoccupations courantes

De plus, les parois ainsi constituées sont excellentes relativement à l'hygiène des habitants par suite de l'absence de poussière inhérente au grès flammé et de toute espèce de retraite occupée par les germes, auxquels il faut toujours penser, pour lutter contre eux.

Les avantages de ce mode d'installation particulièrement salubre sont surtout appréciables lorsqu'il s'agit d'habitations hospitalières ou d'assistance, et de logements à bon marché.

Par suite de la désinfection facile des parois, le nombre des habitations, superposées dans des bâtiments à grande hauteur, se trouve sensiblement dépourvu d'inconvénients, en lui-même tout au moins

Conclusion.—L'acier et le ciment armé sont des éléments qui permettent de construire à grande hauteur, tout en réduisant l'épaisseur des organes, tels que murs et planchers. Grâce au caractère mécanique de ces matériaux, ils se trouvent pourvus de résistances à la compression et à la flexion qui permettent de gagner des espaces utilisables par rapport à l'ensemble couvert.

Au point de vue plastique, ils peuvent faire corps avec le grès émaillé formant des parois au charme séduisant pour le regard

Relativement à l'hygiène les avantages ne sont point inférieurs à ceux que les émaux permettent d'envisager, en fait de beauté, avec leur finesse de tonalité. L'émail du grès flammé permet la constitution de parois impénétrables aux germes. Il crée finalement une ambiance dont on ne saurait assez recommander la salubrité.

Solidité, économie des espaces, beauté plastique, salubrité, voilà donc quatre qualités résolues en l'espèce.

5 FERRO-CONCRETE CONSTRUCTION.

By Henry Adams, M Inst C E

So much has been written during the last four or five years upon the use of concrete and steel in combination that there is practically nothing new to be said. Those who have studied the literature of the subject will probably have been struck with the number of different terms used to express this mode of construction   "Béton armé," and the English equivalent, "armoured concrete," are perhaps the least appropriate "Reinforced concrete" gives undue prominence to one element to the total exclusion of the other , "concrete-steel" is less open to objection, but the writer prefers the term "ferro-concrete" as being self-explanatory of the intimate combination between the two materials, the more important one coming first. A superficial criticism might allege that *ferrum* is iron, and therefore not applicable to steel, but steel is generically iron, and the term is therefore quite appropriate

In early designs no provision whatever was made to resist the shearing stresses, which were either overlooked or ignored, and it is interesting to observe the gradual recognition these stresses obtained in the hands of the designers, until in recent construction they receive nearly as much consideration as what are called the "direct" stresses of tension and compression   The importance of considering shear was brought prominently under notice by the failure of experimental beams which had no special provision for meeting the shear stress towards the ends, where of course it is greatest   Various methods are employed in the different systems, but the Kahn trussed bar seems peculiarly suitable, the fin on either side of the core being left attached throughout the middle portion where the tension is greatest, and separated and bent upwards towards the ends to take the shear where the tension is least

The question of adhesion between the concrete and the steel at one time caused some anxiety   It was naturally supposed that with increase of temperature the steel would expand more than the concrete, and it was thought that this would be sufficient to impair, if not to destroy, any adhesion that might be otherwise obtainable   As a matter of fact the linear change for a given variation of temperature is about 15 per cent less for concrete than for steel, but when the actual figures are compared the difference is very trifling   Taking the range of temperature between summer and winter as seventy degrees Fahrenheit, the change of length in 100 feet produced by this variation of temperature will be for steel $0\cdot546$ inch and for concrete $0\ 464$ inch, the difference between the two materials in a length of one foot being less than a thousandth of an inch

With equal care in mixing the concrete the adhesion varies with the condition of the surface of the steel   When coated with red oxide paint it is extremely slight, and even a bituminous paint reduced the adhesion below that due to a clean unprepared surface   It is, however, found that the best adhesion occurs when the steel is rusted all over before being embedded in the concrete   This appears to be due to the formation of some chemical compound, or salt of iron and lime, which may not be detrimental in the absence of further moisture, but the final result is doubtful in such cases as reservoir walls, tanks, and dams   Painting the steelwork over with cement wash is a simple method of commencing the contact, and this would seem to prevent further rusting, on the principle of the pail of limewater into which the Sheffield grinders dip their small-goods to resist the tendency to rust when left wet.

Professor Bauschinger found the ultimate adhesion to be from 569 to 668 lb. per square inch, but Mr J S Costigan found it not to exceed 65 lb per square inch   Probably in the former case it was measured

by the resistance of a rod to withdrawal, and in the latter by the insertion
of small plates in a briquette.   At any rate it is not safe to reckon upon
more than 50 lb per square inch as a working load for adhesion   Allowing
16,000 lb per square inch as the working load on steel, the embedded
length that would make the strength and adhesion equal would be 16,000
times the sectional area of steel in square inches divided by fifty times
the surface area per inch in length, or, briefly, 320 $a-s$, so that a quarter-
inch square bar embedded for a length of twenty inches would be equally
strong against tearing or slipping, and similarly a one-inch square bar
would need to be embedded for a length of eighty inches   There are many
different constructions in which this fact may be of importance ; for
instance, in a simple beam, if the span is less than twice the above lengths,
there will be a tendency for the rod to draw before the tensile strength
is utilised, unless the ends are turned up to form cleats   In the edge of
a circular ferro-concrete tank, instead of overlapping the ends of the
rods, for which the above distance would be a minimum, it would clearly
be more economical to turn up the ends and slip a welded link over them.
There are several specially prepared bars giving greater resistance to
withdrawal, *e g* the Ransome twisted bar, the square corrugated bar,
and the Columbian bar, which relies for efficiency upon its large surface
area compared with its sectional area , but plain rods which can be obtained
everywhere should be adopted whenever possible, on the score of economy
and avoidance of delay

Ferro-concrete does not at first sight lend itself readily to architectural
effect ; the warehouses and coal stores constructed of it can hardly be
called visions of beauty , but some of the recent arched bridges have a
decidedly pleasing effect, and when the adaptability of the compound
material becomes better known we may confidently look forward to the
expression of taste as well as utility in the designs.

Perhaps the greatest departure from existing models occurs in the
construction of ferro-concrete retaining walls.   Hitherto we have looked
upon weight as the essential element of such walls, and stability has been
secured by leaning this weight against the bank of earth to be supported
We are now confronted with a new type in which added weight bears no
part ; the only weight employed is that of the earth itself   The construction consists of a skin of concrete reinforced with steel rods, securely and continuously attached to a similar base and forming with it two sides of a
triangle   The face wall is then kept in position by rods protected by concrete, tying the inner edge of the base at intervals to the face at one or more
points of the height.   It does not follow because the centre of effort of
the thrust occurs at one-third of the height that that is the proper place
for the connection to be made ; it would be if the wall were disconnected
at the bottom , but being firmly secured there the point of attachment
should certainly be higher than one-third.   If the stiffness throughout
the height be uniform the point of attachment should be about 58 per cent.
of the height.   There are some other rather nice points of calculation
about these walls which the writer does not propose to go into now ; he
would only point out that, apart from strength, the stability is obtained
by the weight of earth resting on the base.   Other examples of these walls
have reinforced counterforts six to nine inches thick extending to the
whole height at intervals of eight to ten feet, in the length, and others
again have reinforced buttresses at similar intervals, and in one case the
writer has seen the base of the wall extended in the front instead of at
the back, so as to react by pressure at a considerable leverage ; but this
method does not appear to be so economical as that previously described

There are, no doubt, many other uses to which ferro-concrete systems
may be applied   Englishmen are naturally conservative ; they like to
feel that in their adoption of any new system they are not running too
great a risk, and a novel form of construction such as this must undoubtedly

have some failures, but, paraphrasing the old saying, the writer would urge that "nothing succeeds like failure" It is from failures that the greatest knowledge of true principles can be obtained, and, therefore, we should be grateful to those pioneers who do venture to take risk, even at the sacrifice of some reputation.

---

6 DER BETONEISENBAU IN DER MONUMENTAL-ARCHITEKTUR.

By A von WIELEMANS (Architect), Vienna

Die hervorragenden Leistungen des Betoneisenbaues in den Gebieten der Ingenieurbaukunst, in welchem derselbe bewundernswerte, grossartige Werke geschaffen hat, regen die Frage an, inwieferne diese moderne Konstruktionsart, fur welche in den alteren Bauweisen kein Vorgänger vorhanden ist, in der monumentalen Baukunst Eingang finden konne

Und zwar in anderer Weise, als nur blosser Ersatz von Gewolben, von Deckenkonstruktionen oder von Pfeilerbildungen, welche in derselben Form und Gestaltung auch in anderen Materialien herstellbar sind und auch früher so hergestellt worden sind Es ist vielmehr zu untersuchen, ob die Eigenart dieser Konstruktion und die besonderen Eigenschaften der hiebei verwendeten Materialien nicht auch Anhaltspunkte bieten, welche zu einer dieser Konstruktionsart eigentumlichen, keine andere Konstruktionsart nachahmende Formenbildung fuhren konnten

Bei dem Umstande, als es bei dieser Konstruktionsart moglich ist, nicht blos Gewolbe oder gewolbeahnliche Baukorper, flache Decken verschiedener Art, sowie Trager und Pfeilerbildungen herzustellen, ware derselben das gesamte Gebiet der monumentalen Architektur, welches Deckenkonstruktion, Trager und Pfeilerbildung umfasst, eigentlich erschlossen, d.h. sobald es moglich wird, mit dieser Konstruktionsart derartige Formen zu verbinden, welche derselben so spezifisch eigentumlich sind, dass die Erscheinung dieser Baukorper als solche, schon den Gedanken an eine Imitation von aus andern Baumaterialien hergestellten Bauteilen ausschliesst.

Inwieferne solche Formbildungen bereits moglich geworden sind, soll durch die nachfolgenden Untersuchungen klar gestellt werden, oder dabei doch wenigstens ein Weg angedeutet werden, welcher in dieser Richtung betreten werden konnte.

Durch die Ausfuhrung von zwei grossen Gebauden (den Gerichtsgebauden in Salzburg und Brunn) war es moglich, fur einen Teil der in nachfolgenden entwickelten Anregungen zur kunstlerischen Verwendung der Betoneisenkonstruktion die praktische Durchfuhrung folgen zu lassen

Ueber deren Umfang und die hiebei erzielten Resultate wird hier zu dem Zwecke berichtet, um weiteren Kreisen als Anregung zu dienen und zu erfahren, ob der hier betretene Weg auch anderwarts betreten worden ist.

Die natürliche Gliederung der Frage in Betreff der Verwendung der Betoneisen-Konstruktion ist gegeben durch die Teilung in die Elemente der Architektur als : Deckenkonstruktion, Trager und Pfeilerbildung.

1 Betoneisen-Konstruktion als Deckenkonstruktion, d.h. mehr oder weniger flache ebene Decke und Gewolbeformen ;

2 Betoneisen-Konstruktion als Trager ,

3. Betoneisen-Konstruktion als Pfeiler ;

wobei zu bemerken ist, dass die Punkte 2 und 3 vielfach im Zusammenhange zu betrachten sein werden, da bei der kombinierten Herstellung

von Betonpfeilern und ebensolchen Tragern dieselben nicht als getrennte
Baukorper hergestellt werden, und deshalb auch einheitlich in die Erscheinung treten sollen.

I. DECKENKONSTRUKTIONEN UND GEWOLBEFORMEN.

Die gewohnliche Art, in welcher bei den jetzt gebrauchlichen Deckenkonstruktionen oder Gewolbeformen vorgegangen wird, besteht darin,
dass dieselben auf einem, die gewunschte Form genau zeigenden Geruste
hergestellt werden, nach erfolgter Erhartung wird nach Entfernung des
Gerustes die Fertigstellung der Decke mit Verputz und den weiteren
kunstlerischen Ausstattungen genau in derselben Weise vorgenommen,
wie dies bei anderen Herstellungsarten ublich ist

Die Schwierigkeit bei Herstellung dieser Arbeitsgeruste andere als
die primitivsten Formen zu bringen, verhindert die Eigenschaft des
Betons (jede gewunschte Form anzunehmen, wenn eine geeignete Unterlage, d i Model[1] fur diese Form geschaffen ist) vollkommen auszunutzen

Es wurde ganz wohl moglich sein auf diesen primitiven Gerusten
weitere Formen in Holz oder Metall auizubringen und dadurch der Betondecke oder Gewolbe eine entsprechende plastische Gliederung der sonst
ungebrochenen Untersichten zu geben.

Durch diese Model ist nicht blos eine belebende zweckmassige Einteilung der Flache, sondern insbesondere bei Gewolbeformen konnte damit
auch eine zweckmassige konstruktive Verteilung starkerer und schwacherer
Teile und eine gewisse zulassige Erleichterung der Konstruktion erzielt
werden. Die Untersicht wurde damit eine sonst im Gewolbebau nicht
ubliche plastische Gliederung erhalten, welche der weiteren kunstlerischen
Dekorierung die Wege weist.

Die Aufbringung flacher schusselartiger Model, in Eisen oder Holz auf
dem Stampfgeruste, ware als ein Versuch in dieser Art zu bezeichnen

Bei Tonengewolbeformen wurden immer gleiche, bei kuppelformigen
Herstellungen aber verjungte Auflagen notwendig werden.

In statischer Beziehung ist keine Einwendung dagegen zu erheben, da
die regelmassige Verteilung der Model- oder Muldenformen die technisch
richtige Lage der Eiseneinlagen ermoglicht.

Einzuwenden gegen diese Art der Herstellung waren nur die bei
grosseren Bauten wesentlichen Kosten der Beistellung vieler solcher
Model, deren weitere Verwendung bei anderen Bauten fraglich bleibt—
wenn es nicht vorgezogen wird, eine Art von Typen herzustellen, welche
von der kleinsten Form ausgeht und durch Umlagen dieselben vergrossert,
so dass eine mehrfache Verwendung derselben Model erzielbar ware

Die Verwendung glatter solcher Model aus hartem Holz oder Metall
wurde gestatten, den Verputz auf diesen Stellen wegzulassen

Auch durch Auslassung von Offnungen in der Mitte der Mulden zur
spateren Einbringung eines ebenfalls in Betonguss herzustellenden Knaufes
oder einer Rosette, ware ein weiterer Schritt zur konsequenten
Durchbildung einer derartigen Baukonstruktion.

Eine andere Art der dekorativen Ausstattung von auf Stampfgerusten
erzeugten flachen oder gewolbten Decken ist die Einbetonierung von
vorher erzeugten ornamentalen Zierstucken in die Decke Es sind dann
diese Stucke durch schwalbenschwanzahnliche Ansatze fest mit der zu
erzeugenden Decke verbunden. Das charakteristische Merkmal dieser
Art von Dekoration wird darin zu finden sein, dass lange zusammenhan-
gende Formen nicht erzeugbar sind, und nur Einzelstucke in Verwendung
kommen konnen.

Auf dem Schalgeruste ist, je nachdem diese Zierstücke vortreten oder
vertieft in der allgemeinen Flache angebracht sind, eine entsprechende

---

[1] Model = Negativ-Form

N

Auffütterung oder Ausschneidung der Schalung vorzusehen. Diese Art
der Herstellung wird sich dann als zweckmässig erweisen, wenn die Decke

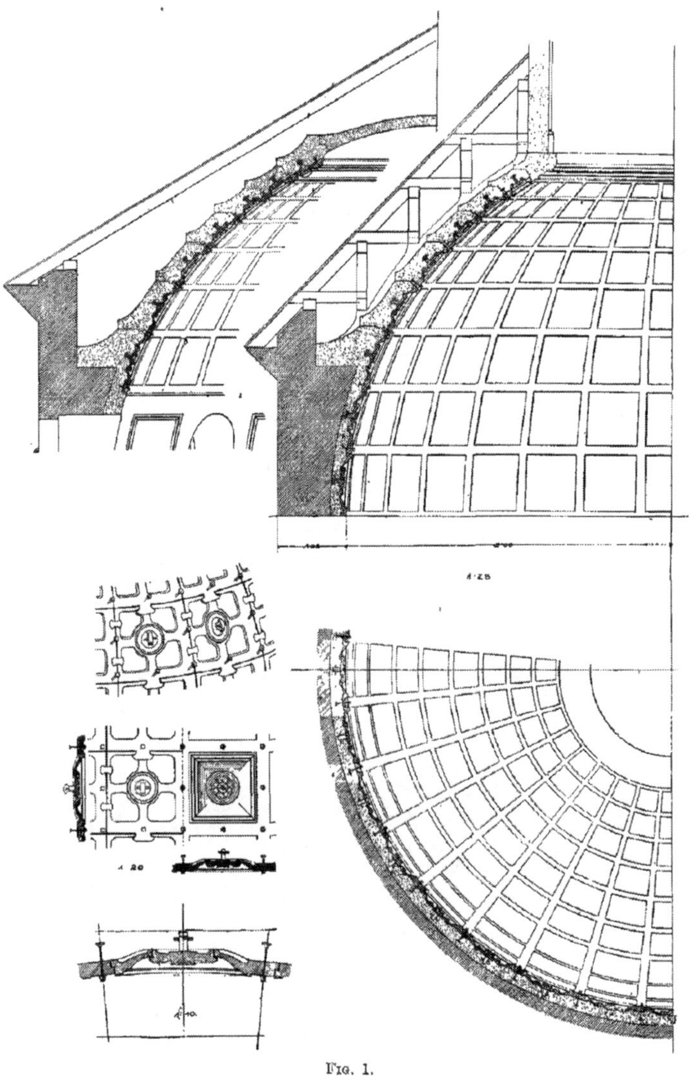

Fig. 1.

in Verbindung mit Hennebiqueträgern gleichzeitig hergestellt werden
soll.

Zu anderen Resultaten gelangt man, wenn die Eigenschaft des Betons
in geeignetem Model, jede auch die feinste Form wiederzugeben, ausnutzt,
und die so erzeugten Bauteile fertig auf die Baustelle bringt   Es entfallen dann die Stampfgeruste, die fertiggestellten Teile der Deckenkonstruktion werden in gewohnlicher Weise zwischen den Tragern versetzt.
Da die Betonteile vollig glatte Oberflache bezw. Untersichten zeigen,
entfällt die Herstellung eines Verputzes und kann sofort die weitere
Fertigstellung der Decke durch Malerei u s.w erfolgen.

Fig 2

Die unerlässliche Bedingung ist dabei aber die Aufstellung solcher
Formen, welche die Technik des Betongusses gestattet und als solche
zum Ausdruck bringt—und vermieden wird, dass diese Herstellung den
Charakter einer Imitation, einer Holz- oder Gipsdecke trage
      Bei den vorgenannten Bauten war es moglich solche Decken zur
Ausfuhrung zu bringen, und zwar als Kassettendecken zwischen Traversen

in einfacheren und reicheren Formen, fur die Kapelle des Gefangenhauses und den Schwurgerichtssaal in Salzburg

Ausgegangen wurde von der Herstellung einer Decke mit quadratischen Kassetten zwischen Traversen, von 122 cm Seitenlänge in der Form von Spiegelgewolben mit 3 cm. bis 7 cm. Dicke und 9 mm. Eiseneinlagen. Eine unter Kontrolle des Stadtbauamtes in Salzburg vorgenommene Probebelastung zweier Kassetten ergab, dass eine Belastung von 1180 kg. per m² noch keinerlei Veranderung in den Kassetten bewirkte

Ebenso hat eine Probe mit dem Herabfallenlassen eines 14 5 kg. schweren Granitpflastersteines aus 5 m Hohe keine anderen als die lokalen Beschadigungen der Aufschlagstelle gezeigt

Diese Kassetten bestehen aus je 5 Teilen, welche durch Falze untereinander verbunden sind und mit verstarkten Auflagern auf den unteren Flanschen der Traversen ruhen

Zur Erzeugung der geringen Zahl an Stucken fur diesen ersten Versuch wurden Model aus Gips benutzt, fur eine weitere umfangreichere Verwendung werden Model aus Zinkguss benutzt werden

Das Ergebnis der vorerwahnten Probebelastung gestattet eine weitere Verringerung der anfanglich angenommenen Minimalstarken der Konstruktion, insbesondere dann, wenn es sich blos um Deckenkonstruktionen ohne weitere Belastung handelt.

Entsprechend der in Osterreich ublichen Bauweise mit beschutteten Decken (Schlacken, Sand oder Bauschutt) sind diese Decken projektiert In Landern, in welchen Beschuttungen weder ublich, noch vorgeschrieben sind, konnen noch geringere Starken angenommen werden

Die gewahlte Form der Kassettendecke als flaches Spiegelgewölbe ist, sowie die bei der Plattendecke von unten sichtbare Höhlung charakteristisch fur ein aus lockerem Materiale in einer Negativform erzeugtes Produkt, so dass keinerlei Ahnlichkeit mit einer aus gehobeltem Holze oder Gyps hergestellten Decke mehr besteht.

Die fur Beton festgestellte Zugfestigkeit gestattet einen weiteren Versuch zur Herstellung einer segmentformigen Kassettendecke in einem Vestibule ebendort Werden quadratische aus einem Stuck bestehende Kassetten mit schwalbenschwanzformigen Verbindungen untereinander in die Richtung des Druckes des Gewolbes aufgebaut, so ist klar, dass es keines weiteren Gerüstes als der zur Einhaltung der gewunschten Bogenform erforderlichen Lehrböger bedarf, um durch derart verbundene Teile eine Schale zu erzeugen, auf welcher die weiters erforderliche Betomerung aufgetragen werden kann

Ein derartiges Vestibul-Gewolbe soll im nächsten Herbste zur Herstellung gelangen—den erwarteten Erfolg vorausgesetzt, wäre damit auch die Moglichkeit eroffnet, grosse Kuppelgewölbe ohne besondere Tragergerüste herzustellen. Die Nachbetomerung ist in ringformigen Zonen vom Widerlager aufwärts aufzubringen. Die bei Kuppelbauten notwendige Verjungung des Seitenmasses der Kassetten bedingt aber ein Model fur jede Zone. Vereinfacht kann die Herstellung der Model dadurch werden, dass jede Rosette selbstandig eingesetzt werden kann, wodurch das Eigengewicht der Kassette, was bei der Aufstellung von Bedeutung ist, verringert wird. Auch bei der Einteilung der Kassetten ist es zweckmassig, darauf zu achten, dass das Gewicht der einzelnen Stucke 50-60 kg. nicht uberschreitet, damit zwei Arbeiten ohne Zuhilfenahme von Hebezeugen dieselben verlegen können

Die Verbindung der Kassetten respective der spater einzusetzenden Rosetten mit der Nachbetomerung erfolgt durch schwalbenschwanzahnliche Ansatze an denselben oder durch in die einzelnen Teile einbetomerten Metalldubel

Fur grosse Raume, beziehungsweise Spannseiten ergibt sich die Moglichkeit einer weiteren Gliederung der Decke dadurch, dass eine die

FIG. 3.— Landesgerichtsgebaude in Salzburg   Kleines Vestibul

Wandfläche abschliessende Hohlkehlenkonstruktion oder Schrägfläche
angebracht wird, an welche sich dann die Kassettendecke anschliesst.

Steht jedoch die Deckenkonstruktion in unmittelbarer Verbindung
mit der Dachkonstruktion, wie es bei Kirchen, Konzertsälen und der-

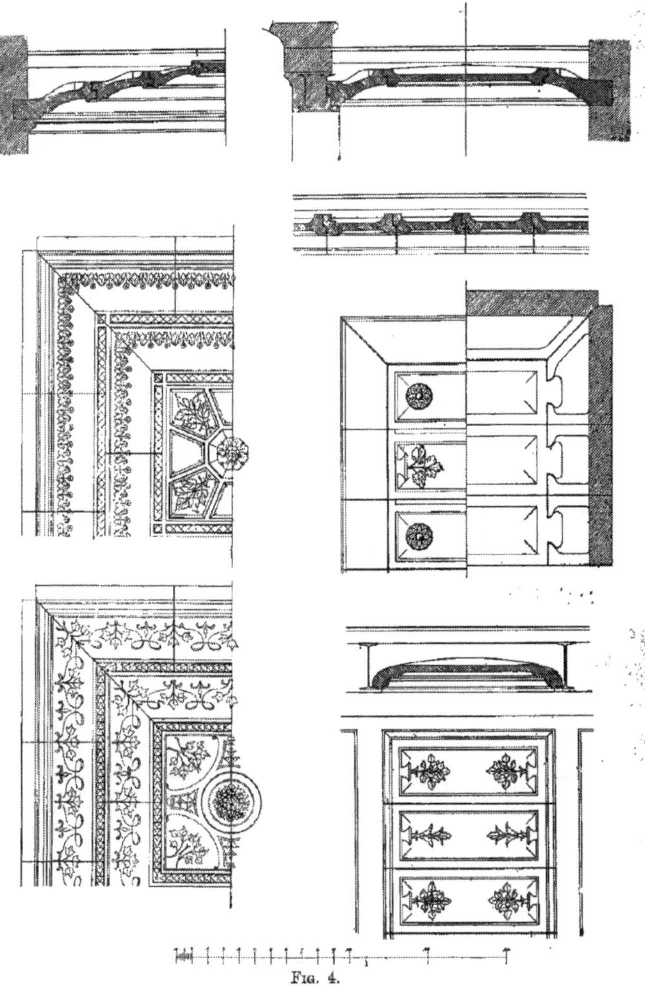

Fig. 4.

gleichen möglich ist, so führt diese Art von Deckenkonstruktion zu einem
trapezförmigen Querschnitt des Raumes, oder auch zu einer bogenförmigen
Ausgestaltung desselben, durch segmentförmige, halbrunde oder spitz-
bogige Tonnen ; es kommt hiebei der Vorteil in Betracht dass durch die

Verwendung derselben Kassette eine einheitliche Raumdekoration ermöglicht wird Eine solche Decke zeigt ein Projekt für eine grosse stadtische Pfarrkirche mit 20 m breitem Mittelschiff und einem Fassungsraum für 3000–4000 Personen, welches bereits 1890 aufgestellt worden ist

Fur Raume geringeren Hohenmasses ist es notwendig eine Abänderung des Kassettenprinzipes in der Weise vorzunehmen, dass mehr flache Streifen von 30–60 cm. Breite zwischen den Trägern zu liegen kommen. Um die Fugen, welche zwischen den durch Falze verbundenen Platten sich bilden, nicht sichtbar zu machen, sind dieselben mit vortretendem Rande versehen, sonst aber als flache Mulden gebildet, in welchen die weitere ornamentale Verzierung sich befindet Insbesondere zur Anwendung abwechselnder architektonischer Motive eignet sich diese Art der Herstellung, ebenso für Podeste in Stiegenhausern, bei denen selten grossere Spannweiten als 1.60 m. vorkommen werden

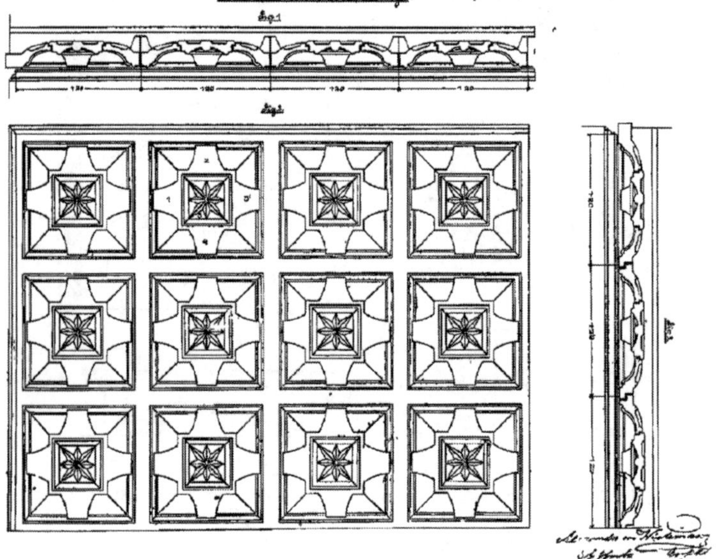

Fig 5

Die Preise dieser verschiedenen Arten von Kassettenherstellungen, bei welchen die Untersicht der Traversen-Unterflansche mit oder ohne Verputz bleiben können, stellen sich so gunstig, dass die Herstellung keine grösseren Kosten verursacht, als eine gewohnliche Betondecke und deren weitere Verzierung mit einer Holzdecke oder Stuckarbeit, es ist somit die Aufgabe der Herstellung einer mehr oder weniger reich ausgestatteten Betondecke, welche keiner weiteren Ausstattung mehr als durch Malerarbeit bedarf, als gelöst zu betrachten

Die Tragfähigkeit der früher geschilderten Betonhohlkehlen, bei entsprechendem Widerlager, gestattet durch Aneinanderreihung zweier oder dreier solcher Hohlkehlen, welche untereinander durch loffel- oder schwalbenschwanzartige Verbindungsstücke verbunden sind, auch Bildungen von Decken anzustreben, wie solche ähnliche in der italienischen mittelalterlichen Kunst (in Holz) vorkommen (Rimini, " St Zeno in Verona " u s w.). Eine weitere Kombination ergibt sich durch die Verwendung von selbständig erzeugten, an der Untersicht dekorirten Betonbalken, welche zur Unterteilung der Längsfelder zwischen die Traversen eingelegt werden, der weitere Abschluss erfolgt dann durch flache dekorierte Platten wie vor.

II. Tragerformen

Die Tragerformen in der Betoneisen-Konstruktion sind meistenteils gebunden durch den Umstand, dass deren Erzeugung auf der Baustelle erfolgen muss, da nur kleinere Trager zweckmassig fertig an Ort und Stelle gebracht werden konnen, und sind daher abhangig von den Formen welche sich durch die Schalung erzielen lassen Die Untersicht der Trager kann durch die Einbetonierung vertiefter Zierstucke aus Beton verziert werden.

Durch beiderseitig anzuordnende Tragefalze ist das Auflager der Kassettendecken erzielt. Bei geringeren Belastungen oder geringeren Dimensionen werden durch aufstehende Rippen oder Hohlräume in den Trägern weitere Gewichtsverminderungen der Trager sich erzielen lassen.

Zur Formbildung von Trägern, welche nicht wie die oben geschilderten eigentlich nur Deckentrager sind, sondern von Pfeiler zu Pfeiler gehend, die daruber herzustellenden Mauerkorper tragen sollen, ist selbstredend nur die Erzeugung auf der Baustelle in Betracht zu ziehen.

Die notwendige Einfachheit der Form, welche hiedurch bedingt ist, gestattet nur jene Detailbildungen in Betracht zu ziehen, welche durch Einlagen in die Stampfbetonschalung hergestellt werden konnen

In ahnlicher Weise, wie bei der Erzeugung von Formsteinen fur den Ziegelrohbau, wo durch Einlagen in die einfache landesübliche Ziegelform Façon-, Kehlen- und Rundstabziegel erzeugt werden, kann auch hier vorgegangen werden. Es ist dabei anzustreben, dass diese Einlagen aus solchem Materiale hergestellt werden, die eine moglichst ebene Flache des Betons ergeben, so dass der Verputz entfallen kann, was am zweckmassigsten durch Einlagen aus Eisenblech oder Zinkguss erreicht wurde und welche immer wieder verwendbar waren.

Eine weitere Ausgestaltung der Trager ist durch die Einbetonierung vorher erzeugter Zierstucke zu erzielen. Durch die Art der Erzeugung der Trager ist derselbe nicht so an die gerade und rechtwinkelige Form gebunden, wie dies bei Stein- oder Holztragern der Fall ist Es sind die notwendigen Verstärkungen gegen das Auflager in Form von schrägen Teilen oder Hohlkehlen leicht herstellbar und es wird damit die organische Verbindung des Tragers mit dem Pfeiler zum Ausdruck gebracht.

Bei Besprechung der Pfeilerbildung wird hierauf zurückgegriffen werden

Sind grössere Spannweiten zu ubersetzen, und namentlich dann, wenn die zu tragenden Mauerkorper sichtbar sind, wie z B. bei einer dreischiffigen Anlage mit uberhohtem Mittelschiff, so wird mit der oben angefuhrten Formgebung des Tragers das Auslangen nicht gefunden werden konnen, da sowohl das ästhetische Bedurfnis als die konstruktive Notigung zu anderen Formen, die sich mehr oder weniger der Segment- oder Polygonalform nähern, hinführen.

Durch kräftige seitliche Ausweitung der Konsolen ähnlichen Formen am Anlaufe ist die zweckmassigste Lagerung vorzubereiten, aus welcher die geradlinig-trapezformige oder gebrochen segmentformige Hauptform des Trägers sich entwickelt, wobei die Brechungspunkte durch eingelegte Zierstucke zu betonen sind (Rosetten, Scheiben, Kreuze u.s.w.), durch

welche der Uebergang der einzelnen Teile gebildet wird und wobei auch
die wiederholte Verwendung derselben Model erzielbar wird. In dieser
Formgebung können sowohl die Tragerkonstruktion der Seitenschiffwande,
als die Ueberspannung des Mittelschiffes gemacht werden, wenn nicht die

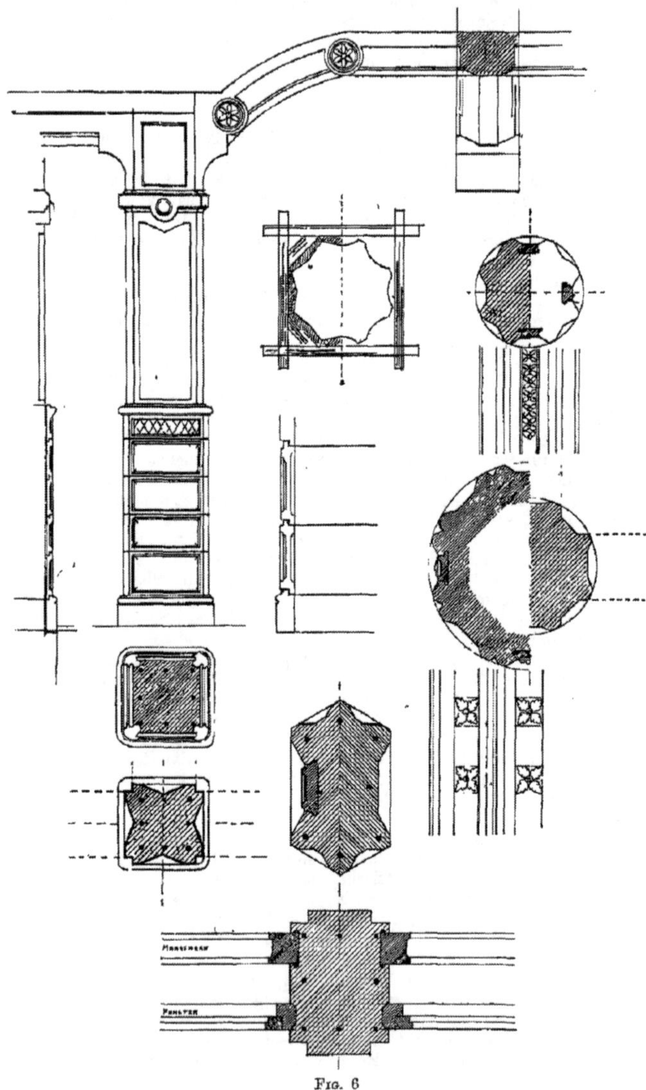

Fig. 6

Deckenkonstruktion einheitlich, ohne Querteilung und mit der Dachkonstruktion zusammenhängend hergestellt wird.

Im Falle, als es sich als zweckmässig erweist, die Querteilung des
Mittelschiffes nach den Pfeilerstellungen vorzunehmen, kann mit der

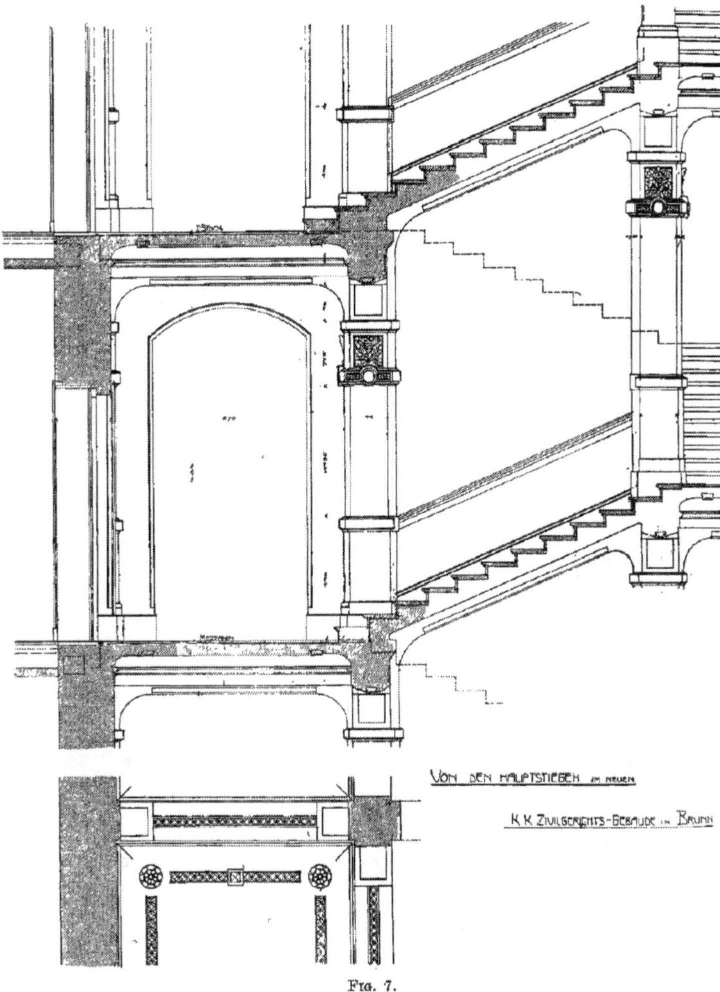

Fig. 7.

Tragekonstruktion der Decke auch die Unterlage des Daches, besonders
bei flachwinkeligen Dächern durch kurze Betonpfeilerstellungen geschaffen
werden.

III. Pfeilerbildungen.

Von der Pfeilerbildung durch vorher fertiggestellte Beton-Körper ware abzusehen, da hiedurch nichts anderes als der Ersatz der Stein- oder Ziegelpfeiler durch Betonsteine erzielt ware, ohne dass besondere Eigenschaften der Betoneisen-Konstruktion zur Geltung gebracht wurden Es sind daher die Pfeilerbildungen auf Grundlage der Erzeugung an der Baustelle aus Stampfbeton im Schalgeruste in Betracht zu ziehen.

Von der einfachsten Form des quadratischen oder reckteckigen Schal- oder Stampfkastens ausgehend, ist es ähnlich wie bei der Erzeugung von Tragern, die Verwendung von formgebenden Einlagen in den Stampf- kasten, welche in Betracht kommt.

Durch rechteckige Einlagen, durch Viertelstucke, welche Hohlkehlen erzeugen u s w, werden Gliederungen, und durch Einlage grosserer Form- stucke sind ebene und hohle Polygonalformen fachgemass zu erzeugen. Auch der allseitige freien Form, einer Paraphrase der Rundsaule oder Pfeilers kann naher getreten werden

Zur weiteren Ausgestaltung der Betonpfeiler, fur welche die Gliederung in Fuss, Schaft und Kapital oder Gesimse nicht mehr die konstruktive Bedeutung der Markierung selbstandiger Bauteile besitzt, kann die Befriedigung des asthetischen Bedurfnisses nach einer Gliederung uber- langer Formen, durch bandartige flache Unterbindungen erzielt werden.

Ferner ist durch Mitbetonierung einzelner Zierstucke eine Ornamentie- rung zu erzielen

Eine andere Art der Gestaltung der Betonpfeiler ware zu erzielen, wenn aus vorher fertiggestellten Formstucken mit verzierter Aussenseite, welche eines uber das andere aufgebaut und untereinander fest verbunden sind, der Hohlraum fur den Stampfbeton hergestellt wird, und dadurch das Stampfgeruste entbehrlich gemacht wird

Die Fahigkeit des Stampfbetons und des Betongusses jede Form der Negativ-Model getreu wiederzugeben, gestattet, auch fur den Aussen- und Innenbau, jener Form der Zierweise wieder näherzutreten, welche als "à jour"-Architektur in der gothischen Stylweise und noch später so glanzende architektonische Effekte geschaffen hat.

Selbstverstandlich kann es sich hiebei wieder nicht um die Imitation von Stein-Masswerken handeln, sondern es muss durch Verwendung von vorher hergestellten Zierstucken, bei kombinatorischem Gebrauche desselben Models eine Dekoration erzielt werden   Namentlich durch die Verbindung mit schmalen aber tiefen Betonpfeilern, so bei Erkern, Kirchen- oder Hallenfenstern werden eigenartige Bildungen von prachtiger dekora- tiver Wirkung geschaffen werden können

Aber auch die Flachendekoration von Mauerkorpern, im Aussern sowohl als auch im Innern der Gebaude, ist in den Formenkreis des Beton- baues einzubeziehen   Abgesehen von der Verkleidung mit kachelahn- lichen Zierstucken, kann die Erzeugung dekorirter Wandflachen durch Aufstellung der Model auf dem Geruste in Anwendung kommen.

Bei den obenerwähnten Bauausfuhrungen wird eine oder die andere Art der hier skizzierten Herstellungsarten in Anwendung gebracht werden konnen

Es ware von Interesse zu erfahren, inwieferne ähnliche Versuche oder Bestrebungen auf anderem Wege vorzugehen, gemacht worden sind. Bei der Bedeutung, welche die Betoneisen-Konstruktion im Allgemeinen und auch bei Hochbauten erlangt hat, wird die Frage nach einer kunst- lerischen Gestaltung derselben immer mehr nach einer Losung drangen, als einen Versuch dieser Frage naher zu treten, sollen diese Mitteilungen betrachtet werden.   Ein wohlbekanntes englisches Sprichwort sagt.

Where there's a will there's a way

7 LES CONSTRUCTIONS EN ACIER ET EN CIMENT ARMÉ

Par A.-Augustin Rey, Architecte de la Fondation Rothschild, Paris.

Table des Matières

Considérations générales.
Le surpeuplement des villes Causes—Effets—Remèdes
Le logement des familles nombreuses
Application du ciment armé aux bâtiments économiques
Principes généraux d'aération et d'éclairage des bâtiments urbains.
Bâtiments économiques. types pour familles nombreuses
Avantages du ciment armé sur les méthodes de construction courante.
De l'économie pouvant résulter de l'emploi judicieux du ciment armé
Renseignements généraux sur prix de bases

Table des Dessins

Principes d'Aération et d'Éclairage des Bâtiments

Bâtiments Economiques Types pour Familles Nombreuses

Les constructions en ciment armé sont destinées à être de plus en plus employées dans nos immeubles urbains à étages.

Les avantages considérables que donnent ces procédés de construction, et dont les preuves ne sont plus à fournir lorsqu'ils sont judicieusement employés, nous ont depuis quelques années incités à l'étude très approfondie de l'application du ciment armé aux constructions de maisons à loyers réduits.

Nous présentons au Congrès quelques résultats d'une des études à laquelle nous nous sommes livrés et qui concerne la construction de maisons ouvrières contenant exclusivement des logements pour familles nombreuses. On sait à quel point toutes nos grandes agglomérations souffrent de ne pouvoir loger convenablement les familles ayant plus de quatre enfants *La plaie sociale du surpeuplement des logements est une des plus graves à l'heure actuelle.* Les plus grandes villes d'Europe et d'Amérique en sont toutes plus ou moins atteintes et tout porte à penser que le mal est encore dans sa période de croissance

C'est donc un devoir social de première importance d'en établir les causes, d'en constater les effets, de chercher des remèdes.

Les causes du surpeuplement des villes sont étudiées depuis plus de trente ans par nos plus éminents sociologues et Hommes d'Etat. Elles sont complexes On peut indiquer comme cause principale cependant l'attirance presque invincible que produisent les grands centres urbains sur les habitants des petites agglomérations et des campagnes Ce déracinement a comme conséquence directe de produire dans la classe populaire, devenue ouvrière, une sorte d'indifférence, presque de désaffection, à posséder de la terre. Pour l'observateur ce phénomène est plus profond qu'on ne se le figure et aboutit à ce besoin d'accaparement collectif qui hante tant de cerveaux exaltés

Les effets produits par le surpeuplement sur la santé publique sont dénoncés de toute part. La natalité, la mortalité, comme la moralité dans tous nos pays en sont gravement atteints

Ce surpeuplement qui peut se définir . la cohabitation dans une même pièce (de 36 mètres cubes en moyenne) de plus de deux personnes, a été mis en lumière d'une manière saisissante dans toutes les statistiques officielles.

Toutes nos grandes villes d'Europe et d'Amérique ont publié sur ce point des chiffres décisifs

Grâce aux travaux remarquables du Dr Jacques Bertillon, chef du Service statistique de la Ville, nous avons pour Paris des chiffres dont la rigueur est presque absolue

La totalité, à Paris, du nombre des logements de 860,800 comporte 209,550 occupés par une seule personne et 651,250 occupés par deux personnes et plus—constituant des ménages Si nous défalquons, du nombre de pièces de chaque logement occupé par ces 651,250 familles, la cuisine, qui ne peut et ne doit être comprise parmi les pièces habitables, nous trouvons que 266,000 *familles de deux personnes et plus*, soit 41 % des logements occupés par des ménages, *sont surpeuplés.*

Le nombre de familles formées de 3 à 15 personnes occupant pour tout logement une seule et unique chambre constituant en même temps cuisine est de 37,200.

Pour celles occupant au minimum une chambre distincte de la cuisine et plus, dans des conditions de surpeuplement, voici les constatations résumées dans le petit tableau suivant

Composition des Familles	Composition des Logements (Cuisine non comprise)			
	1 chambre	2 chambres	3 chambres	4 chambres
4 personnes .	34,850			
5 personnes	15,260	16,600		
6 personnes .	6,640	7,930		
7 personnes	2,850	3,330	2,370	
8 personnes	1,160	1,500	1,970	
9 à 10 personnes	660	850	630	370
11 à 15 personnes	65	160	120	80

Donc indépendamment des familles entassées dans une pièce unique servant à tout, les familles ayant des logements surpeuplés mais avec cuisine sont au nombre de :

66,600 ayant de 2 à 3 enfants.
23,100 ayant de 4 à 5 enfants
7,100 ayant de 6 à 8 enfants.

Comme chiffre global Paris a 132,000 personnes constituant les 37,200 familles de 3 à 15 membres vivant dans une pièce unique servant à tout, et 528,000 personnes formant les 96,800 familles de 4 à 10 membres vivant dans des logements surpeuplés

Au total 660,000 *habitants sont mal logés, soit* 24 % *de la population totale de Paris.*

Pour la France entière nous serons au-dessous de la vérité en évaluant à *quatre millions* le nombre d'habitants de nos agglomérations urbaines notoirement mal logés, et dont l'entassement est un danger permanent pour la santé publique

Ces constatations ne sont pas spéciales à la France. Elles sont soit en partie atténuées, soit aggravées dans presque toutes les nations où l'industrie a pris un large essor.

On commence à se rendre compte de l'étendue du mal, et les calculs, bien imparfaits cependant, sur les progrès de la tuberculose urbaine en sont la preuve   Mais un des aspects vraiment poignants qui ressort de ces statistiques sur l'habitation est que plus la famille aura d'enfants plus elle sera mal logée

Les Remèdes —Ils sont de deux catégories · les uns d'ordre général, visant à l'organisation toujours plus rationnelle de la société, les autres spéciaux à l'Architecte touchant au développement de toutes les méthodes de construction propres à diminuer le coût de l'habitation urbaine à étages et ses frais d'entretien.

Sans sortir des limites de notre sujet disons brièvement pour les uns

(*a*) La société doit viser avant tout à rendre à la hauteur des besoins modernes les conditions de crédit qui permettent la réunion des capitaux destinés aux constructions populaires à prix réduits.

(*b*) Sur une échelle tou-

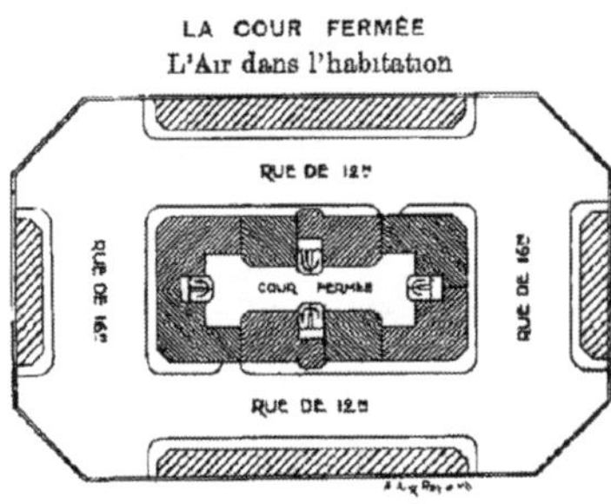

Fig 1 —Plan d'ensemble.

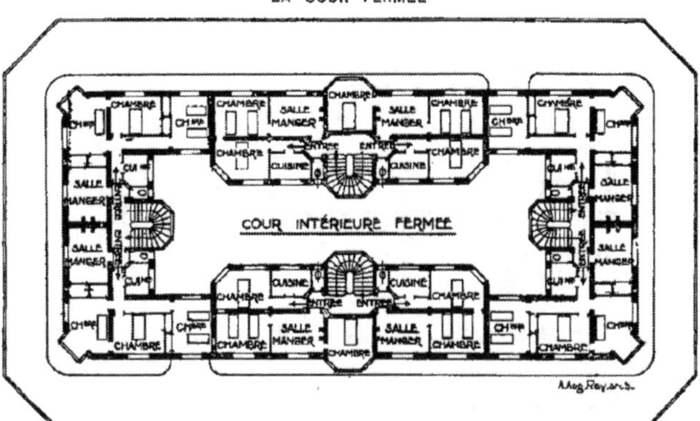

Fig 2 —Plan de distribution

jours plus vaste doivent être faites l'application des formes de baux emphytéotiques avec promesse de vente—de terrains à bas prix—terrains appartenant soit à l'État, aux communes, ou aux particuliers.

(*c*) Le devoir d'hygiène sociale qui s'impose étant de dégorger nos villes encombrées, il devient de nécessité impérieuse pour les pouvoirs publics de multiplier avec une intensité croissante les moyens de transports rapides et à bon marché de la population *extra muros*. La conséquence sera pour les habitations économiques de fuir les terrains chers des villes pour les terrains bon marché de leurs banlieues

Quant aux immunités fiscales de tous ordres, elles seraient d'un faible résultat sur le coût final des constructions à loyer réduit. Qu'elles revêtent la forme de suppression partielle ou totale de certains impôts ou taxes, frais d'emprunts, d'hypothèques, d'héritage, elles doivent être considérées comme des encouragements précieux par leur côté moral Elles sont le gage des dispositions favorables de l'État et de la Société toute entière, gardiens des devoirs d'humanité dont ils ont avant tout la charge.

Quant aux remèdes qui incombent aux Architectes dans notre état social, ils sont d'un ordre très élevé   Il faut qu'ils fassent appel de plus en plus aux procédés de construction qui, tout en abaissant le prix de revient de l'habitation, réduisent ses frais d'entretien Ces deux facteurs interviennent au même titre dans la *réduction du loyer du logement populaire.*

**

Après bien des études et des travaux, nous sommes arrivés, dans cet ordre d'idées, à préconiser l'emploi rationnel du ciment

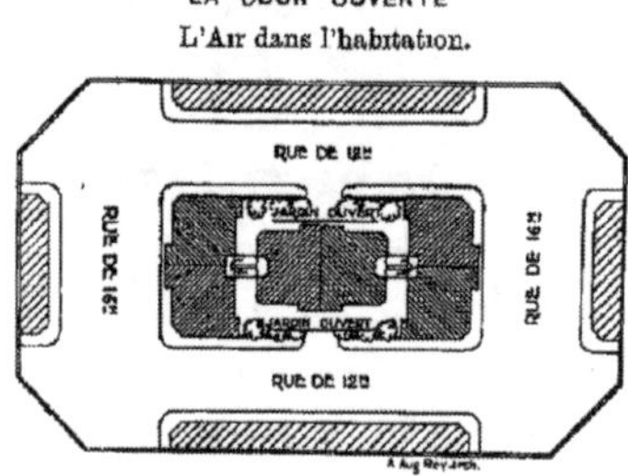

FIG 3 —PLAN D'ENSEMBLE.

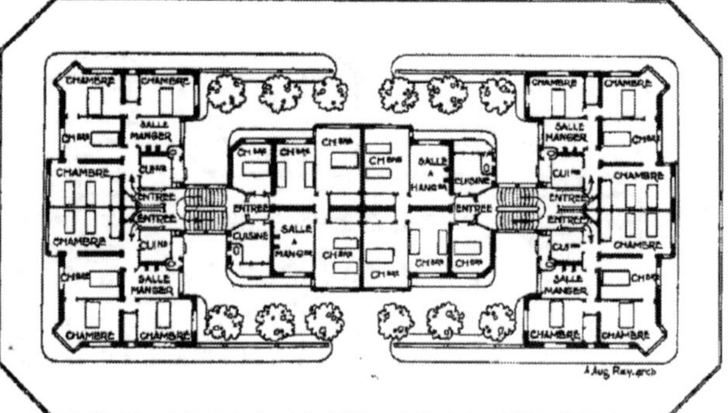

FIG. 4.—PLAN DE DISTRIBUTION.

armé comme ossature pour les maisons à étages pour logements populaires.

Qu'il nous soit permis de nous arrêter quelques instants avant d'entrer dans les détails d'aménagements et de construction sur l'aération et l'éclairage de l'habitation.

La large aération, comme l'abondante pénétration de la lumière dans l'habitation, reste, on peut le dire, de plus en plus à améliorer, dans la création de nos bâtiments qui deviennent tous les jours plus complexes Les problèmes accumulés sont en effet dans les grandes cités, en ce qui les concerne, toujours plus difficiles à résoudre.

Nos villes modernes ayant une tendance à manquer d'air et de lumière, il semble essentiel de chercher à entourer les bâtiments d'habitation de conditions qui facilitent dans la plus large mesure leur hygiène au lieu de l'aggraver

La rue est un réservoir intarissable d'air, l'habitation doit y puiser largement, car là est pour elle, en réalité, l'espace libre par excellence. Un autre espace limitant l'habitation est la cour, dont l'action sur la santé publique est indéniable. Des enquêtes faites dans le monde entier ont prouvé trop souvent que l'insalubrité de l'habitation urbaine venait de la cour cachée derrière de hautes façades, vrai puits, où ni l'air, ni la lumière ne peuvent pénétrer librement.

Si l'on songe que dans certains quartiers surpeuplés de nombre de villes, plus des deux tiers de la population vit sur des cours fermées, on se rendra compte de l'étendue du mal et des efforts considérables qu'il y a à faire.

La cour fermée est un réservoir stagnant, où l'air confiné, déversé par toutes les ouvertures des chambres qui s'ouvrent sur elle, ne peut s'écouler. Cet air est d'autant plus malsain qu'il n'a pas été soumis à l'action régénératrice des rayons lumineux

Dans la Figure 1 qui accompagne ce travail, nous avons réprésenté en plan de masse, un immeuble dégagé de toutes parts, où des logements, établis pour la classe populaire, sont groupés autour d'une cour centrale fermée

La Figure 2 en indique les dispositions de détail.

C'est la solution en usage pour les immeubles à nombreux étages, et qui utilise le terrain dans des conditions de revenu satisfaisantes.

La grande réforme que nous préconisons, et dont nous avons été l'initiateur, à la suite de patients travaux, est la suppression des cours fermées et leur remplacement par les cours ouvertes

Nous en avons montré une application dans le Concours International de la Fondation Rothschild en 1905, qui, en classant au premier rang nos plans, a indiqué d'emblée toute la valeur technique et pratique de cette grande révolution dans nos méthodes de construire le bloc d'habitation urbaine

Les bases que nous avons données ont servi depuis à fixer les lignes générales des plans actuellement en voie d'exécution à Paris

Il est, en effet, impossible de considérer comme hygiénique un bâtiment dont l'une des façades est située sur une rue de largeur supposée suffisante, et l'autre sur ce tronçon de rue fermé au deux bouts qu'est la cour fermée, réduite parfois au tiers de la largeur de cette rue, quand ce n'est pas davantage Le traitement auquel sont condamnées ces deux façades opposées d'un bâtiment, et cela souvent même sur les plus somptueuses avenues, *doit aboutir fatalement à la maladie incurable de l'habitation*

Nous établirions volontiers une comparaison entre cet état de choses et la santé d'un homme, dont un des poumons respirerait de l'air pur et l'autre de l'air vicié

Par la cour ouverte, l'habitation reprendra une intensité d'aération qui constitue sa vie même

En rejettant au dehors les cours, qui se sont installées peu à peu, par des habitudes séculaires, au sein même de l'immeuble, en les faisant revenir au devant de nos blocs habités, on assurera, comme automatiquement, le renouvellement constant de l'air pur sur toutes leurs façades sans exception, air qui leur est aussi nécessaire qu'à la voie publique elle-même.

Où veut-on en effet que la cour prenne de l'air, si ce n'est sur la voie publique ?

La Figure 3 nous montre sur la même surface de terrain et dans les mêmes conditions de construction générale un immeuble occupant, construit le même nombre de mètres carrés que le précédent, dans lequel se trouve supprimé tout espace non en communication directe avec la voie publique.

Le même nombre de pièces y est ménagé, suivant les détails de dis-

tribution donnés dans la Figure 4, par conséquent le même revenu. Ce
plan en cours ouvertes nous permet d'économiser la moitié des escaliers
nécessaires au plan à cour fermée   Nous pouvons donner à ces escaliers
un espace en pleine lumière, ce qui est essentiel à l'hygiène de l'habitation
Le plan à cour fermée à moins de perdre de l'espace ne nous permet pas
d'obtenir un emplacement aussi favorable.

Les logements que nous avons ainsi transformés ont une ventilation
transversale, que le plan en cour fermée interdit

Dans cette nouvelle disposition, il n'y a plus de façades intérieures,
toutes fonctionnent comme de véritables façades extérieures balayées

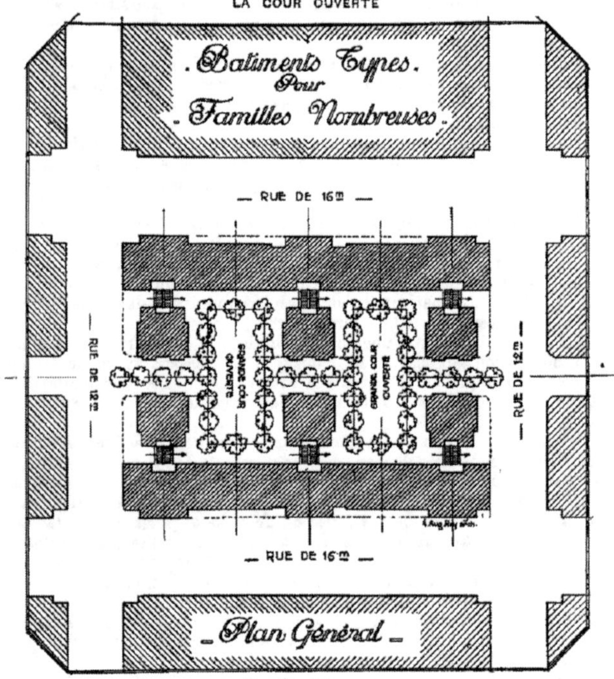

Fɪɢ 5.—Aᴇʀᴀᴛɪᴏɴ

dans toutes leurs parties par l'air constamment renouvelé des voies
publiques.

*Dans le plan à cour fermée, un grand nombre de pièces ne sont pas
ventilables dans des conditions acceptables*

*Dans le plan à cour ouverte, au contraire, pas une pièce, si petite soit-elle,
ne s'ouvre sur un espace fermé, toutes prennent air sur un espace libre, largement balayé par l'atmosphère*

Par ce plan type notre but est de montrer les bases qui permettent,
en modifiant les formes générales surannées de nos blocs habités actuels,
d'entamer une lutte sans merci à l'air confiné, ce poison lent, mais inéxor-
able, qui atteint à un si haut degré, à l'heure actuelle, nos populations
urbaines

C'est, en effet, à l'air confiné et au manque d'éclairage des lieux habités que la science médicale actuelle attribue le plus lourde part de responsabilité dans la propagation de la tuberculose.

*
* *

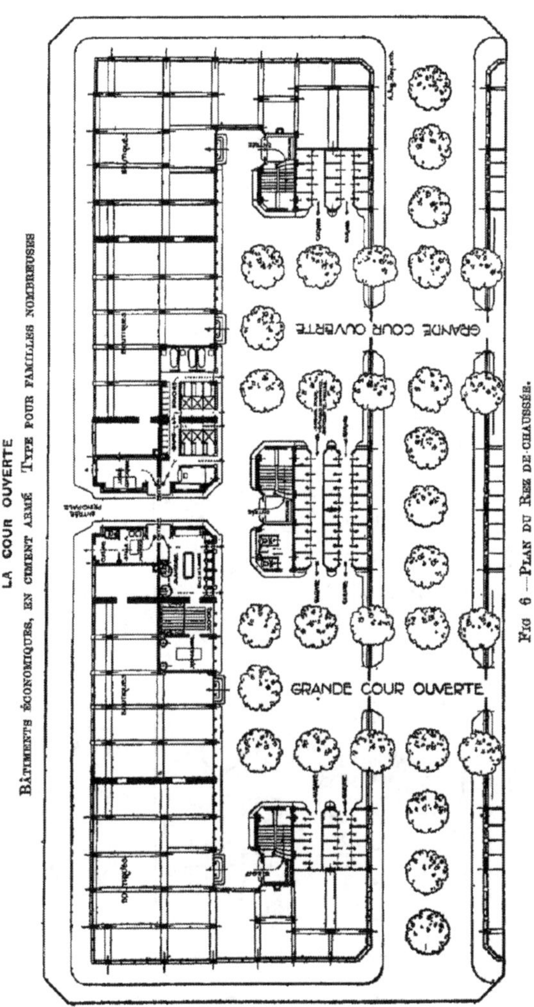

Fig 6 —Plan du Rez de-chaussée.

Nous avons l'honneur de présenter au Congrès, comme application des principes de ventilation que nous venons d'établir, et qui sont en même temps souverains pour obtenir le bon éclairage de nos maisons, un projet type dont les lignes générales très simples, en font d'emblée saisir l'économie. Nous avons tracé ces bâtiments dans le but de loger des familles nombreuses.

Sur un îlot de forme rectangulaire en façade sur les deux plus larges

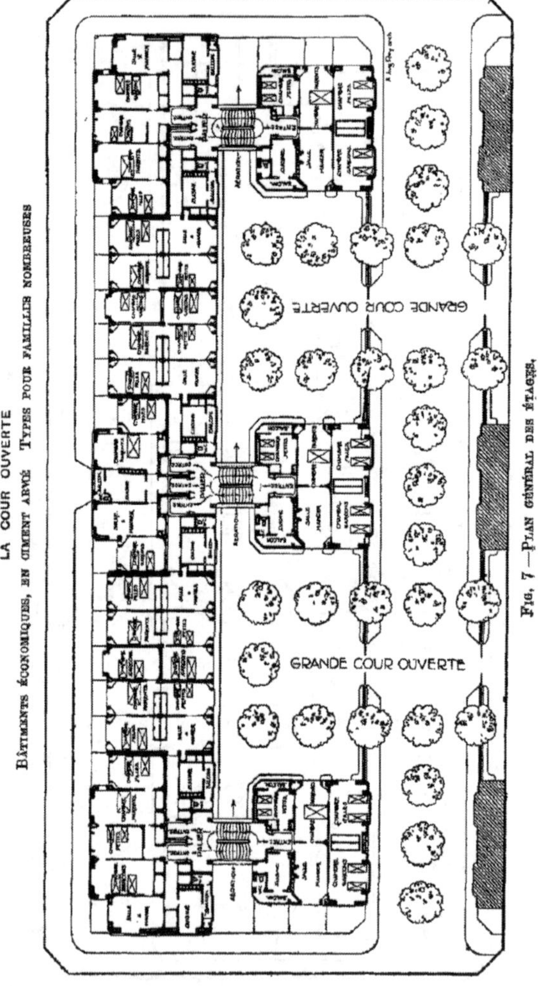

voies, s'alignent les deux bâtiments principaux. Perpendiculairement sont construites les ailes, reliées par des escaliers.

Ces ailes, laissant entre elles de larges espaces plantés d'arbres, sont séparées par une voie également plantée, qui permet à l'air en mouvement de venir baigner sans exception toutes les surfaces des bâtiments

Cette disposition a permis l'aération et l'éclairage parfaits des logements, jusque dans leurs plus minutieux détails.

Nous donnons Figure 5 le plan général de la masse des bâtiments qui montre à quelles lignes simples cette disposition se réduit.

Les logements de quatre chambres sont pour familles de quatre enfants et éventuellement cinq La lumière et l'air sont très largement répandus partout, puisque suivant le tracé général, il n'existe aucune cour intérieure fermée.

L'intérieur de chaque logement peut être ventilé dans la perfection, car toutes les pièces sont aérables transversalement, ce qui constitue un des grands avantages des plans à cours ouvertes

Ainsi qu'on peut s'en rendre compte dans le tracé des plans, Figures 5, 6, 7, 8, et par la coupe générale des bâtiments, Figure 9, les escaliers sont établis en pleine lumière, et pour ainsi dire à l'air libre.

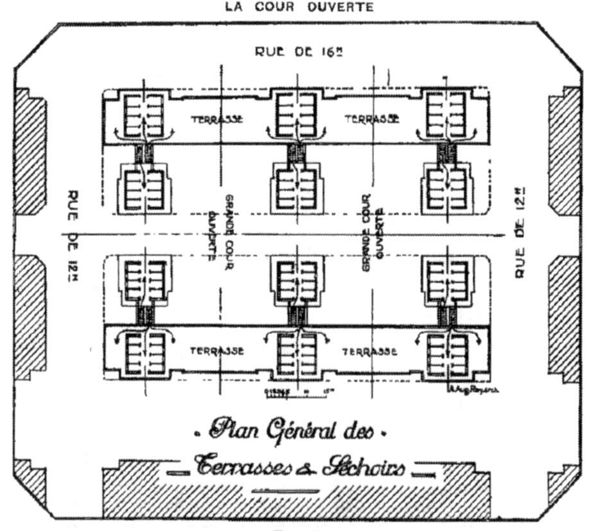

Fɪɢ 8

Leur ventilation peut être considérée comme aussi active que s'ils étaient situés au beau milieu d'une voie publique

La Figure 10 donne le plan type de l'escalier reliant les bâtiments principaux aux ailes ; le tracé des détails de construction des marches est indiqué à la Figure 11.

Si l'on veut bien y réfléchir, l'escalier est le prolongement naturel de la voie publique Nous en avons maintes fois expliqué la haute importance dans l'habitation en disant : "l'escalier est une rue verticale." Ces principes d'aération et d'éclairage exceptionnels de l'escalier sont, à notre avis, des plus importants si l'on songe que ce chemin vertical d'accès au logement est public à tous les locataires et dans des conditions pour ainsi dire analogues à celles de la voie extérieure

Au rez-de-chaussée, dont la Figure 5 donne le détail, sont disposés les services généraux communs buanderie, séchoir d'hiver, repassage, douches, bains et cases privées pour voitures d'enfant, bicyclettes et malles, annexés à chaque logement. ..

La suppression de tous les combles et leur remplacement par des terrasses en ciment avec cases formant séchoirs privés, attachés à chaque logement dont le plan Figure 8 et les coupes Figure 12 et 13, constitue un perfectionnement.   Les murs de refends en maçonnerie séparent seuls les groupes entre eux et forment pignon contre le roulement général des bâtiments   Il nous semble en effet essentiel que le contreventement soit assuré de deux manières   par le chaînage naturel du ciment armé et par cette maçonnerie qui en cas d'incendie peut former un écran d'isolement.

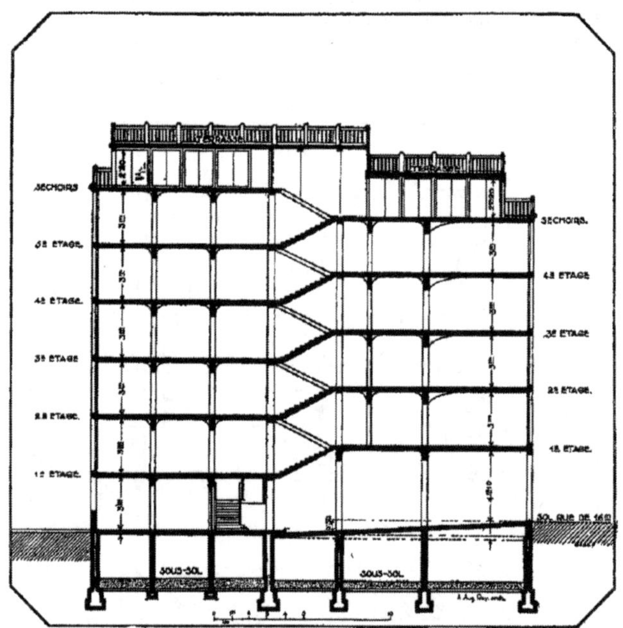

FIG. 9 —COUPE GÉNÉRALE SUR L'ESCALIER CENTRAL

L'ossature générale en ciment armé est formée de poteaux reliés par des poutres horizontales, formant les caches des chambres.   Les planchers sont constitués par des dalles d'une seule portée, ne laissant dans les plafonds aucune poutre apparente.

Tous les murs extérieurs sont creux—vrais murs du pauvre—les moins déperditeurs de chaleur et de fraîcheur.   Ils sont en briques d'agglomérés recouvrant sans exception tous les poteaux en ciment armé et enduits au ciment crépi tyrolien et peints à la chaux.   Les cloisons intérieures sont en agglomérés de plâtre, chaux et mâchefer, scories ou autres produits similaires   Les cloisons des logements sont traitées de même.   Les fenêtres montent au ras des plafonds et arrivent à 0m 150 du plancher. Elles sont calculées au 1/3 de la surface des planchers des pièces qu'elles éclairent.

Suivant le type de la chambre habitable modèle, dont les parois murs et plafonds sont exposés directement à la pleine lumière, et dont nous avons exposé les principes au Congrès International de la Tuberculose de 1905, tous les poteaux extérieurs en ciment armé sont noyés dans les placards ménagés dans chaque pièce Les poteaux intérieurs sont revêtus aux angles de pièces, d'un treillis métallique s'opposant aux fissures longitudinales

Pour les conduits de fumée, nous en avons fait une étude spéciale. La hauteur de chaque étage habitable de plancher à plancher étant de 3m 150, soit 3m. de vide pour chaque étage, nous constituons nos conduits en poteries enrobées dans une ossature extérieure en ciment armé ou analogue ayant d'un seul bloc 3m.150 de hauteur. De ce fait à 0m.800 au-dessus de chaque foyer se trouve le seul joint disposé pour être vu et visité de chaque colonne de tuyaux de fumée Nous avons ainsi assuré l'étanchéité pour ainsi dire absolue de ces conduits, ce qui est un perfectionnement dont on appréciera l'importance La figure 14 en donne le schéma.

*
* *

Si nous résumons en quelques mots les avantages des méthodes de construction en ciment armé, nous dirons :

Le ciment armé assure à un ensemble de bâtiments à étages une indéformabilité remarquable.

L'homogénéité de l'ossature générale donne à tout son squelette un liaisonnement intime Sans vouloir rien exagérer, il n'est pas téméraire d'affirmer que les méthodes couramment employées pour l'édification de nos maisons à étages sont plutôt défectueuses à cet égard.

Les matériaux de petit échantillon constituant les œuvres vives de nos édifices courants—les planchers n'étant trop souvent qu'un assemblage incohérent de matériaux à dilatation des plus variables—que peut représenter comme efficacité le chaînage dans son ensemble et l'ancrage ? La plupart du temps il est absolument illusoire

Si nos villes sont, pour l'instant, loin de présenter les dangers du sol qui vient de ruiner l'admirable cité de San Francisco, dans l'état de nos connaissances sur les secousses et les cataclysmes qui doivent venir bouleverser tôt ou tard l'écorce de notre globe, ne semble-t-il pas prudent de donner sans hésiter la préférence à une construction homogène ?

Nos éminents confrères des Etats-Unis nous répondront à cette question par les solutions qu'ils vont adopter pour les reconstructions de leurs

ESCALIER
À DOUBLE PALIER D'ENTRÉE.

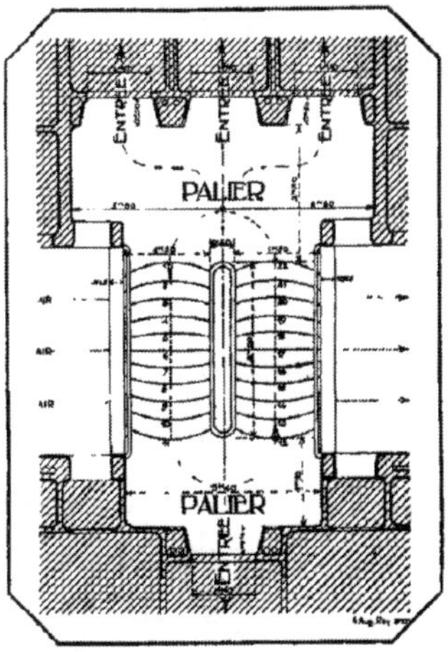

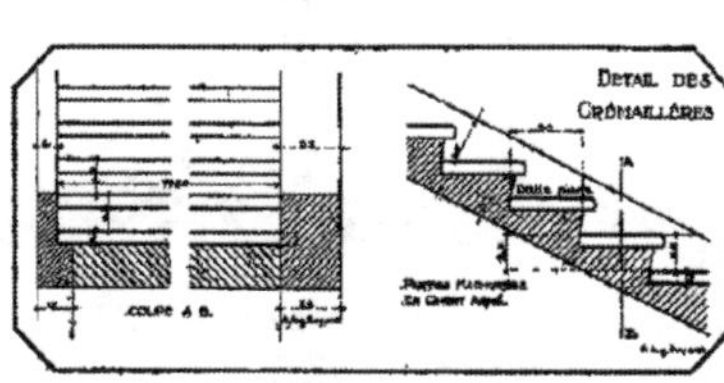

Fig 10 —Les deux paliers desservent 4 logements.

Fig 11 —Détail des Marches

villes détruites, mais sur la question générale que nous venons de poser, nous appelons l'attention de tous nos confrères

Il est indiscutable qu'une construction exécutée dans ses parties essentielles en ciment armé est un bloc solidaire dans tous ses éléments, aucun ne fonctionnant sans intéresser l'ensemble. C'est non seulement à la compression mais à l'extension et à la flexion que toutes ses parties peuvent travailler—ce qui leur permet de faire face aux actions les plus complexes que nous appelons actions secondaires et qui peuvent se présenter à chaque instant dans un bâtiment.

Il serait donc très imprudent, à notre avis, de n'employer ce procédé que partiellement en constituant par exemple les planchers en ciment armé reposant sur des murs en construction ordinaire Pour donner tous les précieux résultats constructifs que nous attendons de ces procédés, il est indispensable que de la base au sommet, dans toute sa structure vive, la maison collective à étages soit en ciment armé.

*
* *

Sans nous étendre sur les points acquis favorables et qui sont : résistance aux charges statiques, extrême raideur, faible volume, résistance aux effets dynamiques, protection du fer assurée contre l'oxydation et les liquides, résistance au feu, imperméabilité assez grande, disons quelques mots sur deux défauts du ciment armé, son pouvoir de transmission de la température et des sons.

Comparé au fer, le ciment armé a un coefficient de conductibilité beaucoup moindre Il suffit de citer un de ses emplois les plus répandus : la construction de réservoirs préservant l'eau des variations de température. Il est par conséquent précieux pour l'établissement de terrasses, aux lieu et place de charpentes et couvertures métalliques, et permet d'éviter le surchauffement des locaux

Mais s'il faut le comparer aux maçonneries à épaisseur égale il a un pouvoir de conductibilité moindre que celui de la pierre naturelle La brique conduit plus mal la chaleur que le ciment armé Il faut donc logiquement conclure que le ciment armé ne vaut pas la maçonnerie courante comme isolant contre les changements de température extérieurs.

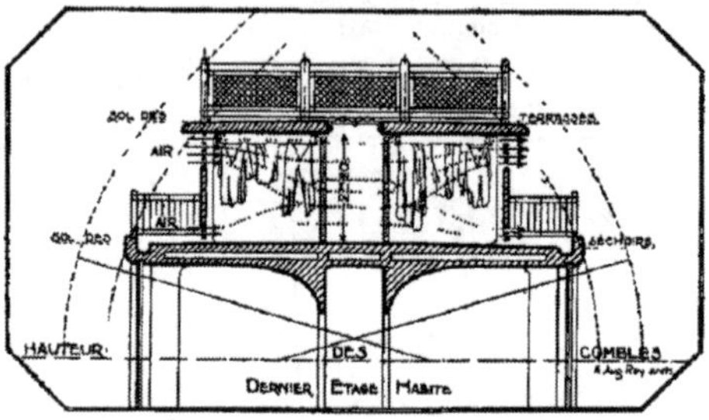

FIG 12 —COUPE GÉNÉRALE DES SÉCHOIRS ET TERRASSES.

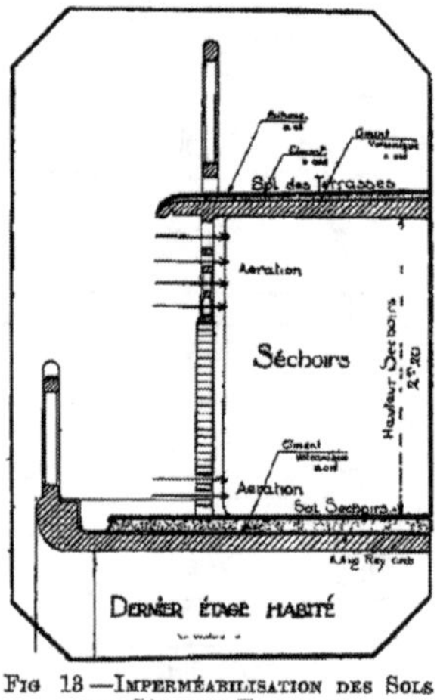

FIG 13 —IMPERMÉABILISATION DES SOLS DES SÉCHOIRS TERRASSES

Mais ce défaut peut être très facilement supprimé par l'emploi de murs creux laissant des vides formant matelas isolant d'air C'est ce que l'on verra dans nos plans. Ceci a une importance considérable si l'on songe au chauffage général de l'immeuble que nous avons assuré par un système de chauffage central pendant l'hiver.

Le ciment armé a une facilité assez grande à propager les sons Une pile, formant épine continue d'un bâtiment à étages, frappée à une hauteur de 15 mètres, transmet à sa base le son avec une grande précision La raison de cette résonnance est dans l'extrême cohésion de ses molécules. et à la présence de l'ossature métallique intérieure, conducteur naturel du son Comment entraver cette sonorité ? Nous nous sommes livré à cet égard à plusieurs recherches que nous soumettons ici à l'étude de nos confrères, dont quelques figures annexées à ce travail donneront l'idée

Nous avons noyé tout poteau, que nous appellerons ' transmetteur du son,' dans des doublures de la construction, de manière à ce qu'aucune de ses faces ne soit en communication avec l'air vibrant des pièces habitables Les poutres reliant ces poteaux verticaux et supportant les dalles formant planchers sont noyées de même dans les gorges des angles des plafonds existant dans toutes les pièces Voilà pour les poutres de tous ordres formant squelette de l'édifice La Figure 15 donne le détail de ces dispositions.

Pour les planchers, nous avons dit qu'ils sont constitués par des dalles continues formant au-dessous plafonds unis et reportant leurs poids propres et leurs surcharges sur les poutres transversales servant à tous les croisements, de chaînages C'est ici un des avantages inappréciables du ciment armé, qui permet de réduire les planchers à des épaisseurs totales variant de 0m 100 à 0m 150 tout compris, suivant les portées courantes des chambres Nous avons pu ainsi obtenir le vide de 3m.000 net, qui est, selon nous, la formule rationnelle de hauteur des étages des maisons servant à l'habitation La Figure 16 donne le détail de cette structure si simple et rationnelle.

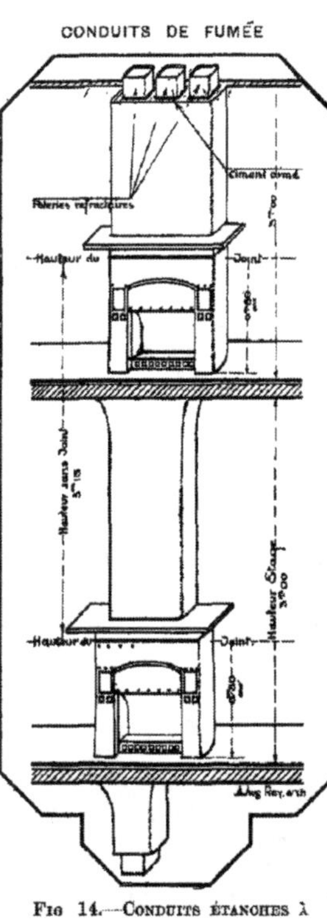

Fig 14.—Conduits étanches à doubles enveloppes

Pour obvier à la sonorité de ces dalles, nous avons écarté la solution coûteuse, du plancher creux, et qui ferait, par conséquent, perdre une partie des avantages d'économie que nous recherchons avant tout. Nous avons adopté la couche d'amiante devenue d'emploi industriel et économique. Étendue avec un mélange au lait de ciment, sur une épaisseur de 0m.020, elle assourdit les sons d'une manière considérable et arrive aux résultats d'insonorité des meilleurs planchers en usage. Si nous ajoutons l'emploi d'agglomérés de fibre de bois cimentés par divers produits, dont le principal est la magnésie, et que nos confrères d'Allemagne

emploient avec tant de succès—pour remplacer les parquets en bois
dont les inconvénients hygiéniques ne peuvent plus être énumérés, tant
ils sont nombreux—nous aurons constitué les planchers les plus résis-
tants, les moins épais, très insonores, et rationnellement économiques.

* * *

Nous arrivons à la dernière question . celle qui doit en réalité les
contenir toutes, car sans elle rien ne se fait dans le domaine de la construction—la question d'économie dans la dépense générale et dans
les frais d'entretien des bâtiments construits avec ces méthodes

Le ciment armé est une matière dont l'essor commence à peine. Il est
d'une telle souplesse qu'il permet l'adaptation, par des formes souvent
inattendues, des programmes les plus complexes La construction en
maçonnerie est trop souvent vouée aux formes lourdes et pesantes. Celle
en métal, à la structure si sèche et si rébarbative ne permet, si l'on veut
rester dans l'économie la plus sévère, aucune complication dans la conception des plans et dans l'exécution.

Le ciment armé se prête au contraire aux solutions les plus imprévues, tout en restant dans l'économie la mieux observée Il se joue
des encorbellements les plus invraisemblables—des parties suspendues
sur des appuis réduits à leur extrême limite,—des berceaux de voûtes dont
les flèches sont diminuées à l'extrême, et qui permettent couramment
la voûte biaise. Sa raideur, sa cohésion sont là pour répondre à tout
imprévu, là où succomberait tout autre mode de construction C'est
dans cette souplesse jointe à la rapidité d'exécution, lorsque les conditions
climateriques sont favorables, que nous trouvons le secret de son économie.

Nous pouvons établir dès aujourd'hui, d'une manière générale, que
le ciment armé peut, s'il est judicieusement employé, et dans des travaux
d'ensemble, donner de 20 à 40 % d'économie sur la construction par les
méthodes courantes

Pour donner quelque précision, supposons le béton de ciment à 50
francs le m.c., compris coffrages, et 25 francs les % k° de fer Nous
atteindrons les prix suivants du mètre cube de ciment armé .

> 60 f. si le C.A. contient au m c 0,5 % de fer
> 90 f. si le C A. contient au m.c. 2 % de fer
> 150 f. si le C A contient au m c 5 % de fer

Pour le compare au fer, supposons un pilier en ciment armé de 0,5 %
de fer. Il aura pour résistance égale un volume 23 fois plus fort qu'une
colonne en fer Si cette colonne coûte 35 frs les % k° le béton armé
sera moitié moins cher

Le ciment armé est d'une économie réelle si on sait proportionner
rationnellement la quantité de matière aux résistances fixées par le calcul.

Il faut ici rendre hommage à un des calculateurs les plus éminents
d'Europe—un des précurseurs qui a rationnellement appliqué le calcul
au ciment armé—à M de Tedesco. C'est à la ténacité et la persévérance
de ses travaux que nous devons la mise au point de bien des questions
obscures, qui ont eu sur l'évolution des méthodes de calcul la plus décisive
influence.

L'emploi judicieux de la matière est des plus difficile pour les constructions faites en matériaux courants et l'on peut affirmer, sans hésitation, que ces matériaux sont trop souvent employés en excès par suite
du manque d'homogénéité des masses qui nous font toujours craindre
les ruptures sous des efforts secondaires

Par rapport aux constructions courantes, le ciment armé présente
de plus l'avantage de réduire et presque de supprimer l'entretien extérieur.
Dans les plans que nous présentons, les terrasses, les balustrades, les enduits
extérieurs en ciment, quel entretien nécessitent-ils comparés aux couver-

tures, même les mieux établies, aux appuis balustrades en métal, jointoiements des constructions courantes ?

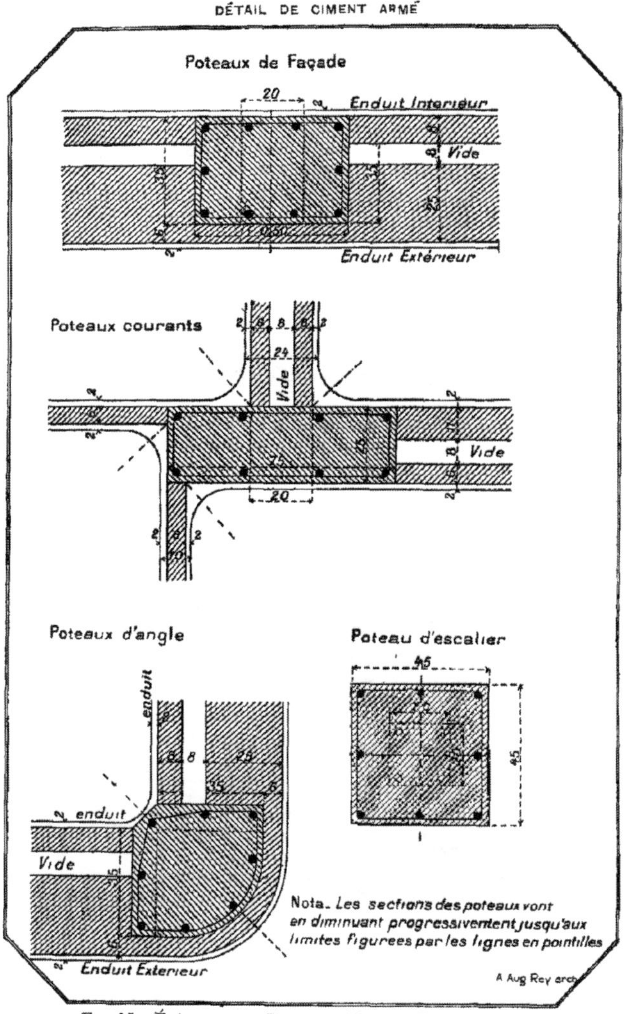

Fɪɢ 15 —Éʟéᴍᴇɴᴛs ᴅᴇs Pᴏᴛᴇᴀᴜx Mᴜʀs ᴇᴛ Cʟᴏɪsᴏɴs ᴄʀᴇᴜsᴇs

Pour nos constructions économiques nous préconisons, pour des raisons
d'hygiène de la lumière, la première des hygiènes et la plus agissante
de toutes, le badigeon à la chaux sur tous les extérieurs, une ou deux
fois par année

En tons clairs en hiver, plus sourds en été ils constitueront une des véritables réformes à opérer dans nos immeubles urbains, si rapidement

DÉTAIL DE CIMENT ARMÉ.

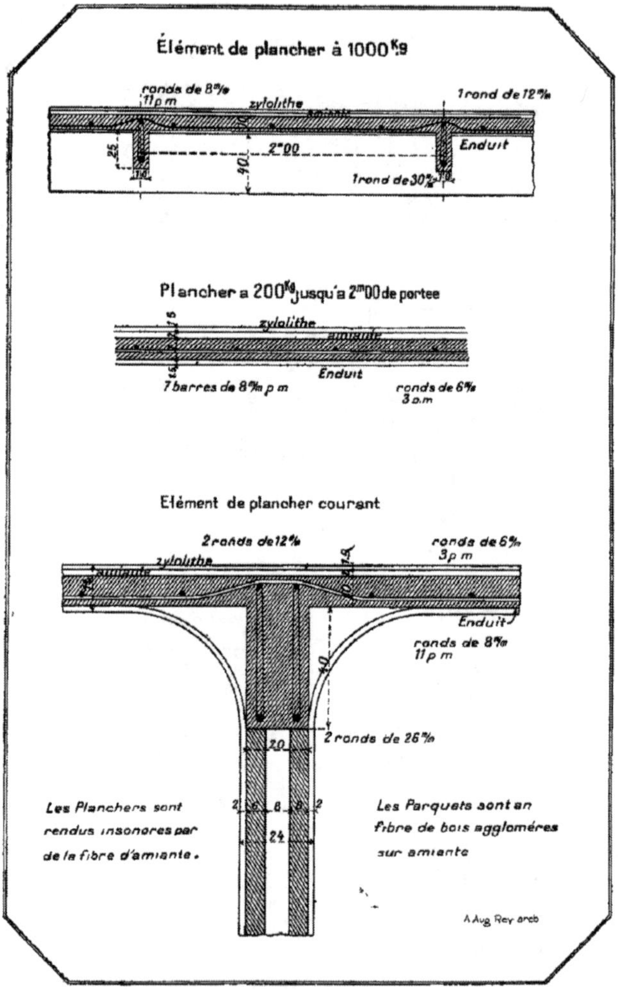

FIG 16 —ELEMENTS DES PLANCHERS POUTRES—PLANCHERS DALLES—PARQUETS INSONORES

noirs, si vite tristes et maussades. Ne devons-nous pas être artistes aussi par la couleur ?

***

Pour clore cette étude, voici un tableau sommaire donnant quelques renseignements de principe sur des prix généraux de base de ciment armé
à Paris, et dans les banlieues de grandes villes, comparés à ceux de Londres

Nous avons établi ces chiffres d'ensemble avec M. L. Coignet,
l'ingénieur constructeur auquel on doit en Europe des travaux d'une
grande hardiesse, et à l'expérience si reconnue duquel nous avons fait si
souvent appel.

PRIX BARÉMES.
(*Moyens.*)

	Paris.	Banlieue de Grandes Villes	Londres.
Aciers Ronds, prix de base, la tonne	230 f.	10 % en plus pour octroi, le cas échéant.	250 f.
Ciment, la tonne	60 f.	48 f. + 8 f. d'octroi, le cas échéant.	38 f.
Sable et Gravillon, le m c	8 f	8 f.	10 f. (6 shellings le yard cube)
Béton. Prix de revient des matières, le m c.	28 f.	26 f. 80	21 f. 40
Main-d'œuvre (le prix à Paris, étant 100)	100 f.	80 f.	120 f.

Ces prix montreront à nos confrères Anglais que le ciment armé peut
entrer résolument dans la pratique journalière de leurs importants travaux
Notre but aurait été rempli si nous avions pu, par ce trop rapide exposé,
les engager à expérimenter pour des maisons à étages pour la classe populaire urbaine ces méthodes de construction si intéressantes, si utiles et présentant, au point de vue de l'économie de construction première et
d'entretien future, de si sérieux avantages.

— — — · · · —

8   THE USE OF BURNED CLAY PRODUCTS IN THE FIRE-PROOFING OF BUILDINGS IN THE UNITED STATES OF AMERICA.

By PETER B WIGHT, F A I A. (Editor of *Fireproof Magazine*, Chicago, U S A.)

IT is proposed in this paper to treat of the actual use of burned clay in
building construction as employed in the United States of America in
the erection of fireproof buildings   In nearly every country on the face
of the earth clays of various qualities may be obtained, and burned clay
is the most ancient of building materials so far as the remains of the
earliest examples of architecture that have yet been discovered have
revealed to us.   Stone may have been used earlier, but if so no remains
of wrought stone have been discovered which antedate brick   Natural
clays vary in hardness and fire-resisting qualities, from the soft clays
which can only be burned to the consistency of a porous flower-pot, to
the refractory clays which resist a temperature of nearly 4,000° F. in the
open hearth furnace   Nothing else will stand the latter test. Hence it
is within the reach of anyone who can get the right kind of clay to employ a
fire-resisting material of higher efficiency than any other known substance.

In this connection it may be stated that, in practical use, it has been
found that no two clays are exactly the same, and therefore no standard
of efficiency can be established except that peculiar to each country

or locality. The highest efficiency of clays in any country, therefore, must be determined by tests and experiments But a general classification of clays may be made everywhere. It concerns us, however, to consider only the use of refractory clays, which in their turn even have different degrees of efficiency. It is not, therefore, assumed that the proper clays have always been used in fire-resisting constructions. The commercial factor enters very strongly into the fireproofing problem, and it must be admitted that there have been failures in the use of clays for fireproofing purposes because unsuitable ones have been used in the manufacture of material where better ones could have been procured It is mainly a question of paying for the best, and using it judiciously. Proper clays have been used and have stood the test of destructive fires , and, what is more, the best of clays are never so costly or so difficult of fabrication that their use is in any sense prohibited.

Burned fireclay is only a medium non-conductor of heat ; but it can be fabricated in cellular form admitting air spaces which are the best non-conductors , or its structure may be made porous by mixing combustible materials with it, and eliminating them by the process of firing. In the latter condition it becomes one of the best non-conductors Then, again, both qualities may be obtained in the same piece. Different clays admit of different degrees of porosity in fabrication , but as strength is an important element, it has recently been found that the best form of manufactured fireclay for fire-resisting purposes is a semi-porous body made in cellular form, which has lightness and toughness to resist shock, as well as sufficient non-heat-conducting property to resist the action of heat in all possible exposures in burning buildings.

The extensive use of burned clay other than in the form of bricks in the interior of buildings in the United States dates from about the year 1878 But it had been used in a few instances at earlier dates Primitive forms of incombustible floor construction with iron beams were used as early as 1850 A brick arch was used to span the space between the beams, but gave no protection to the beams. Rolled I beams were first used in 1855, and the filling of the floor was made also with brick arches. The first perfected flat arch of hollow bricks for spanning spaces between I beams was made by Garçin in France in 1868 Similar flat hollow arches were used to a limited extent in New York, Chicago, and St Louis from 1871 to 1878, and at the same time hollow bricks for partitions were introduced

It is hardly necessary for me to give a detailed account of the numerous inventions of this nature that were patented between 1870 and 1880. The records of the French, British, and American Patent Offices are full of them. A great impetus was given to the invention of forms for hollow bricks and newly suggested uses by the invention of the various kinds of clay presses for the manufacture of drain and sewer pipes by pressing the prepared clay through dies or mandrils Most of them were impracticable, and very few were ever used ; but the number of inventions was so great as to destroy the value of nearly all the patents taken out after this period. Hence there are now very few fireproofing materials or processes in which burned clay is used that are covered by patents At the present time the direct-action vertical sewer-pipe steam press is the most important agent for making the present extensive use of hollow burned clay products practicable and economical for building purposes.

It was during the experimental period above referred to that porous tiles were first made. A clay was mined at Brazil, Indiana, which had such great toughness that it was possible to mix equal quantities in bulk of clay and sawdust, so that after burning the weight was reduced 50 per cent., and still great strength retained. This was manufactured at Chicago, first for tiles 16 inches square and two inches thick, to be set between T irons for roof constructions. They were covered by slates laid in cement and secured with wire nails driven into the tiles. These were first used in the roof of one of the pumping-houses of the Chicago Waterworks and the roof of the State Capitol Building at Des Moines, Iowa. The tiles were cast by hand in plaster moulds

Porous terra-cotta tiles were first used by the writer in fireproofing the cast-iron stanchions of a building in Chicago in 1873, and another in Milwaukee. The stanchions were cast with projecting webs, and gores of terra cotta were set in cement between them, also covering the webs, and fastened to the iron by screws tapped into it   This method of protecting iron stanchions proved so effective in one building, not otherwise fire-proof, which was badly damaged by fire, that the finished stanchions were taken out of the ruins with all the fireproofing attached   These gores were hand-made in plaster moulds. The stanchions in a large number of buildings were fireproofed in this manner between 1879 and 1885   They have been subjected to several fires, and have never failed; but I have not seen them constructed for fifteen years past. During this time porous terra cotta was manufactured for flat floor arches and partitions at factories near New York, being made hollow through mandrils on presses working horizontally. They were used for the new roof of the Patent Office at Washington, a part of which, of unprotected iron con-struction, had been destroyed by fire. About the same time the writer executed in porous terra cotta the protection of all the roof trusses of the Chamber of Commerce at Milwaukee, covering every member and using mechanical fastenings, which had never before been done. When called upon, also, he covered all the truss work and girders supporting the roof of the reconstructed Patent Office at Washington. Since those times porous terra cotta has been made through dies or mandrils in various parts of the United States for all purposes for which burned clay was required for fireproofing the interiors of buildings. I regret to be obliged to say, however, that much of it that was made between 1885 and 1890, during a great demand for new buildings, was of very inferior quality, even red-brick clay being used in some localities.

In referring to the use of porous terra cotta for fireproofing purposes as distinguished from construction purposes I have somewhat anticipated the thread of my subject. I have not yet stated the reason for the ex-tensive use of burned clay hollow and porous fireproofing materials after 1875, and especially after 1880   This was found in the discussions and investigations which followed the great fire at Chicago in 1871. Up to that time the incombustible systems of building which had been the result of the introduction of rolled I beams in France and Belgium in 1854, and in England and the United States in 1855, were thought by most architects to be sufficiently fireproof for practical purposes   Cast and rolled iron were used with brick for interior constructions, with indiffer-ence to the effects of heat upon iron   There had been few destructive fires in such buildings until attention was attracted to the destruction of a cotton mill at Oldham in England. But the Chicago conflagration gave evidences everywhere of the unreliability of iron in a severe fire , for quite a number of incombustible buildings were destroyed, and none were saved which had been directly exposed   Experiments in pro-tecting iron construction with clay products slowly followed this revela-tion, and it was several years before they received recognition.

In 1880 there commenced at Chicago a building revival of great extent, which was followed in New York and other cities   There was a demand for buildings not only incombustible but fireproof, and a large number of buildings which had been erected at Chicago during the re-building after the fire in great haste were replaced by fireproof structures. In these hollow and porous clay products were used almost exclusively for all the constructive parts which were not of iron, and for covering all the exposed iron of both kinds that had been employed. In 1888

the steel skeleton had been fully developed, and called for still greater
care in its protection , for it had become the vital part of the new constructions, and cast iron, before used for stanchions, had gone almost
entirely out of use in such buildings   Steel was believed to have greater
liability to distortion than cast iron. This soon became the experience
in all the other large cities.

But the erection of tall office buildings, generally denominated " sky
scrapers," of ten stories or more, had preceded the introduction of rolled
steel, which dates from 1885   The first one was erected in 1881, and in
it the two most serious questions of construction involved in buildings of
this class began to find solution   At the bottom of all was the foundation question. This building was to be ten stories high. It had not been
found safe before that time to place a weight of more than 4,000 lb.
per superficial foot on the clay which underlies nearly the whole of the
site of Chicago, or to excavate more than thirteen feet deep where there
was a crust somewhat harder than at any point below this depth. So
on account of the number of floors the weight was such as to require an
excessive spread to the footings. Messrs. Burnham & Root were the
architects, and the writer was engaged as consulting architect. The
building was to be fireproof and all iron protected with burned clay.
The problem of building very light floors had to be solved. Girders
were so placed as to reduce the spans of I beams to 18 and 16 feet, placed
from three to four feet from centres, and a section of hollow tile flat floor
arch was devised whose net weight was only 25 lb. per superficial foot
It was made of a hard fireclay, with walls only half an inch thick.
No such light tiles had ever before been made, but they proved to be a
great success as far as construction goes. They were tested up to 500 lb.
to the superficial foot, but not to destruction, though intended to carry
only 70 lb   Knowing the full weight of the floors the spread of the footings
could now be ascertained. When the calculation had been made it was
found that some of the foundation piers of bridge masonry with safe allow-
ance for offsets would reach above the basement floor. The bottom course
of the piers was to have been of concrete, 18 inches thick, on which it
was intended to set back the first course of bridge masonry 12 inches
But if the tops of the piers were to be kept below the basement floor,
the offsets on the concrete must be increased to two or more feet   It
was to prevent the possible shearing off of this offset that the writer
introduced iron rails imbedded in the upper part of the concrete in two
directions   This experiment is what led to the general use of so-called
"grille" foundations, which ultimately were reduced to nothing but
concrete and steel, very shallow, but sufficiently strong. Thus it will
be seen how the hollow tile became a factor in solving the high building
question

But now neither the light floor tile nor the " grille " foundations are
necessary. Foundations of concrete piers built in tub-like caissons,
with hoops on the inside, to a depth of 60 to 100 feet have made us
indifferent to great weight, and we are able to use floors of any weight
that satisfy the demand for a fireproof construction that will resist the
greatest conflagrations. The thin-walled, hard tiles have been found to
be insufficient for the purpose. They are required to be with thick walls
and round-cornered in the cells, and in the best work are neither of hard
tile nor porous tile, but of hollow tiles, which are semi-porous, yet strong,
tough, and not subject to sudden expansion or contraction, or to damage
by shock when struck by heavy falling bodies

The Montauk Block is no more. It has been torn down to be replaced
by a still larger and higher building in which are embodied all the improvements of twenty years in foundations, steel construction, and semi-
porous terra-cotta fireproofing. The first National Bank is its successor—
a building many times larger and just ten times as costly—the architect

of which is the head of the firm which designed the first building, Mr Daniel H. Burnham.

With this object lesson illustrating only a few incidents in the development of fireproof building construction in the United States, we will now proceed to as brief a description as possible of the details of the systems now in use, leaving out all further mention of its early history

All fireproofing with clay is now done with machine-made material pressed through mandrils, and most of it is made in the vertical steam press originally invented for making sewer pipe. This has proved to be the most economical method of forming the tiles after the clay has been ground in dry pans and mixed in its proper proportions and tempered in wet pans. Hand-made porous terra cotta is no longer used on account of the expense   Hard hollow tiles, made without mixture of combustible ingredients, are no longer used for first-class work on account of their brittleness and hability to expansion on exposed sides, the built-in parts being subject to less expansion in a fire   The two standard materials, therefore, are denominated porous terra cotta and semi-porous terra cotta   All clays that are sufficiently refractory to be used in fireproof construction may be manufactured into one or the other of these materials There is a limit, however, to the thickness of the walls in tiles of porous terra cotta, which is two inches, on account of the danger of the combustible ingredients being only charred and not completely reduced to ash.   If solid blocks are made thicker than this they must be run with frequent holes to facilitate uniform burning   The walls of a semi-porous tile may not exceed an inch and a half   The best practice is to make the walls of the semi-porous tile from three quarters to one inch thick, and the porous tile from one inch to one and a half inch.

There are two classes of use for burned clay in fireproof buildings— one when used constructively under pressure, and the other when used as a non-conducting and structure-protecting material.   In the first case it must sustain strains and at the same time resist heat for its own protection, and in the other it acts only for the protection of the steel members of the building   In some it performs both offices, as in the case of floors and roofs ; in others it is inert, as used in protecting-steel columns and girders

The principal uses of clay products for construction are in floors, roofs, and partitions   For use in floors I will give only a few typical illustrations   Floors are arched between I beams with either flat or segmental arches.   Flat arches were formerly made with joints radiating from a common centre.   They are now made with all joints parallel to the sides of the key   Repeated tests have shown that both are equally strong, and that the mechanical action of a flat arch is that of a beam with fixed ends.   The illustration given (fig. 1, p. 213) is a diagram showing eight depths and minimum lengths of tiles used for flat arches with the weights of each per superficial foot   The lengths of these spans may be increased 25 per cent for some classes of buildings   In the best practice the soffits of these arches when set are two inches below the beams, and the tops are one inch below the tops of the beams, so that each arch shown on the diagram is for a beam one inch less in depth than the size figured on each   These are for " end pressure " arches—that is, for those in which the cells run in the direction of the arch.   In some of the arches keys are shown for illustration on the side-pressure principle, and such keys are generally used when required less than eight inches wide at the top, because they can be bedded more perfectly than if they were cut from the voussoir section of tile   The skewback tiles are cut out to fit the beams and hold the protecting soffit tiles   Soffit tiles are made two inches thick, and the width of the flanges of the beams, with a hollow space of one half inch in the centre of each. , They are set longitudinal with the beams   They are for the protection of the beam from heat, and if the arch tiles are bedded perfectly add greatly to the strength of the arch, as tests have demonstrated, in comparison with arches similarly set without soffit tiles.   (See section across beams, fig 2, and also fig. 3, pp 213–14)

The original flat arch was made on the " side pressure " principle— that is, the hollow spaces in the tiles were parallel with the I beams But as the end pressure arch was shown to have greater strength, the side-pressure arch is no longer used for standard work, and therefore will not be illustrated.

Segment arches in hollow tile are made both on the side-pressure and end-pressure principle   The greatly superior strength of this arch, and its capacity for use in long spans, do not militate against the use of side-pressure tiles   It has been found in practice that there is no necessity for breaking joints in the end-pressure arches, for in them the whole strength of the material is brought in play.   But there is a certain advantage in breaking joints in long-span segment arches , hence side-pressure tiles are preferably used.   The illustration given (fig 4, p. 215) is a section of a segment arch of 18 feet 6 inches span used in the Brown Block, St. Louis, Mo   This shows the method of covering the flanges of the beams, and the form of the skewbacks.   The cross-section at A B through the crown of the arch shows how the tie-rod is protected by special tiles cramped together.   On top of these protecting tiles partition tiles are set in courses and fitted up close under the arch, thus dividing the ceiling into panels.   Both flat and segment arches are used for roofs as well as floors.   (See also figs. 3 and 6 for side-pressure segment arch and fig. 5 for other details of flat and segment arches.)

Several systems of floor construction are used with hollow tiles in which steel-tension materials are used, and concrete is combined with the tiles to resist pressure, making it possible to introduce very long spans.   These are not arches, but lintels

In the Johnson system (patented by E. V. Johnson, see figs. 7 and 8) the tension is taken up by a steel fabric laid in a bed of cement between the tiles.   The tiles are then laid on the end-pressure principle on this bed of cement, and placed an inch or more apart, after which the spaces are filled with cement, and it is spread over the top of the tiles.   This is then ready for whatever finish is put on to form the floor   This system of construction is laid so as to form a continuous floor over the whole building, crossing the girders, and entering a certain distance into the exterior walls.   It has been extensively used in hotels, asylums, and manufacturing buildings (see also figs. 6 and 8)   The most perfect piece of work done in this manner is in the floors and roof of the underwriters' laboratories at Chicago.   These floors are built in the manner above described, but, in addition, a ceiling of two-inch porous tiles is set under them and wired to the tension fabric before the bed of cement is spread.   They are set herring-bone fashion and left without plastering, cleaned off, and the joints in the ceiling scraped out and carefully pointed (see fig. 9).

The Bevier system (patented, see fig. 10) is built with straight tiles from beam to beam, the bottoms of which are two inches below the beams, as in end-pressure arches, but the joints are vertical   The same soffit tiles, as in that last described, are used for the protection of the beams   There is introduced between the courses of tiles from beam to beam a wire truss reinforcement bedded in the joint.   In very long spans two and sometimes three of these reinforcements are built in the joints and turned up at the ends to provide against shearing.   This system of floor construction was recently successfully tested by the British Fire Prevention Committee, which published a detailed description of it (see fig. 11, p 221):

A third patented tile floor with tension member is known as the Kahn system   This combines some of the features of the Johnson and Bevier systems.   The tiles are laid in the same position as in the Bevier floor, but somewhat wider apart, so that three or four inches of concrete are filled in between them   In this concrete are set tension bars of a special pattern of rolled steel, which are cut and bent so as to apportion them to the true strains   The illustration I will give (fig. 12) is from a detailed drawing of a modification of the Kahn system as used by Captain John S. Sewell, Corps of Engineers, U.S.A., in charge of the erection of New War College at Washington, D.C., where it is used in all the floors.   The special tiles used were designed by Captain Sewell

The last three systems involve the same principles of construction as the reinforced concrete floors of Monier, Hennébique, and the many different kinds that have recently been introduced into the United States. The main difference is in the weight of the floors, which is very much less (at least 30 per cent.) than that of reinforced concrete of equal strength.

Hollow-tile partitions not only fulfil constructional conditions, as they are miniature walls, and often weight-bearing, but act as fire-stops   In the full-steel skeleton buildings there are no brick division walls, and hollow tiles are depended upon to provide all stops against the horizontal spread of fire   The Baltimore and San Francisco conflagrations revealed the weakness of hollow-tile partitions as formerly used, but did not betray any fault in the material itself   They were found to be insecurely placed in many ways, and filled with wooden frames, sashes, and doors. This defect is now being rectified   Partitions are made heavier, frames are of steel, doors incombustible, and sashes of metal glazed with wired glass   With these precautions any other means for stiffening hollow-tile partitions are unnecessary.   They vary in thickness from three inches to eight, according to the length and height, and porous terra cotta is preferable because it can be penetrated by screws and sometimes by nails. But a very excellent metallic wall plug is also used in the joints, making a perfect nailing device.   The best examples of model partitions are found in the new Underwriters' Laboratories at Chicago (see fig. 9).   I confidently believe that it is to-day the most thoroughly fireproof building in the world for business purposes

For bearing purposes extraordinary strength has been developed in hollow-tile partitions.   In the Underwriters' Laboratories partitions were built of two courses of three-inch tiles, tied together, which took the place of iron columns in carrying the ends of steel girders.   A specially burned heavy, hard, hollow tile has been made which has developed a crushing strength of from 6,000 lb. to 8,000 lb. per square inch in the net section of clay used   A test was made, 29th November 1905, of these tiles set as a section of a partition three feet long, twelve feet high, and four inches thick, which sustained 130 tons before it buckled or showed any fracture, or 43 tons per lineal foot (see fig. 13)   These tiles have also been built into the form of 8 by 8 inch square stanchions, 33 inches high, for testing purposes, and one of them sustained a load of 228 tons before crushing, or 8,142 lb per square inch of sectional area of the material tested (see fig. 14).   Tests of large stanchions built of these blocks without reinforcement will soon be made at the University of Illinois, from which even better results are expected.

While preparing this paper a very remarkable test has been made of a 4 by 8 inch column tile built into a section of partition   This test was made in the presence of the officials of the Department of Buildings of the city of Chicago, who have signed the test sheet, a copy of which is shown as an illustration (see fig 15, p. 224).   Half-tone prints from photographs of this test are also shown, marked figs. 16 and 17.

Of the uses of burned clay as a fire-protecting material for covering steel members of construction the most important are stanchion fireproofing and girder fireproofing The most vital points in buildings are to be found when steel stanchions are required to be used. Cast-iron stanchions are now seldom used in fireproof buildings except in those of four to six stories in height. Fireproofing of cast-iron stanchions with porous terra cotta was brought to great perfection between 1875 and 1890 ; in fact, attention was first directed to the importance of fireproofing the ironwork of buildings by several disasters from fire which had occurred in buildings in which cast-iron stanchions were used. The first statutory regulation to prevent such accidents was in the building law of the city of New York thirty-five years ago, which required that all cast-iron stanchions supporting brick walls should be double, one within the other, and each of sufficient strength to carry the load. Now all stanchions, whether of iron or steel, are required to be made fire-resisting with outside coverings by the building laws of all our large cities It is held in all of these that the stanchion must first be covered with pure cement, leaving no air space between steel and tile

The illustrations here given (figs 18, 19, and 20) are horizontal sections of steel stanchions showing different sections of steel and methods for covering them as now used. I desire also to call attention to the sections of steel stanchions shown in fig. 3 [p. 215] with their fireproof coverings, which are known as " plate-and-angle columns " (in the United States all stanchions used in construction are called "columns," whether they have architectural form or not) This is the section which has recently been most favoured by engineers and architects, because of its economy and other advantages in facilitating the best connections, and the rapid construction of the steel frame There are several other simple forms evolved from the commercial products of the steel mills which have been gradually superseding the patented sections In fig 18 will be seen the common method now used in protecting round cast-iron stanchions The tiles should be held together with metallic cramps as well as cement.

Next in importance to the protection of steel stanchions comes the matter of girder protection ; and for a better understanding between us allow me to say that the word " girder " used herein is intended to refer to the beams resting directly upon stanchions, whether the latter be of steel or brick. Girders are of various form and size, from the single I beam used in ordinary mercantile structures to the great box girder such as is used in the proscenium wall or the roofs over the stages of theatres. The flanges of girders always admit of tiles being very firmly secured between them by cement joints, being forced into place between the flanges. But soffit tiles for the exposed bottoms of girders often require mechanical fastenings if the girders are wide These fastenings, however, are never left exposed, but the sections are such that any metal used is covered with a tile. Approved sections of fireproofed girders are shown in figs. 2, 5, 7, 8, and 9.

The above-described details cover only a few of those now in regular use, but it is hoped that they may serve to illustrate the main features of the system The illustrations are mostly copies of working drawings of executed work, showing many other details of construction which I will not attempt to describe.

A system of burned clay fireproofing, which is used to a large extent in the United States, but not so generally as that before described, is that known as the Guastavino system. It was introduced by Raphael Guastavino, an architect who came to America from Barcelona, Spain, in 1878. It would take more time than I have to spare to describe the principles involved, or the details of this construction. It is called by him " cohesive construction," and all the work is done with laminations of small flat tile about six by ten inches in size and seven eighths of an inch thick, laid in as many courses as may be necessary in Portland cement, breaking joints, and seldom more than four courses in thickness. It dispenses very largely with steel, and except where used in place of a steel girder all flat surfaces are spherical, no barrel arches being used. It is therefore monolithic and homogeneous. The ultimate and highest expression of this system of construction has been shown in the building of large and often very flat domes , but it is principally used for floors and roofs

In all tests that have been made its fireproof qualities have been proved, and in the conflagration at Paterson, N.J., a few years ago it went successfully through several actual tests in buildings. The architects of the United States feel greatly indebted to Mr Guastavino for introducing and practising his system, for it has made possible many accomplishments in novel design which might not otherwise have been carried out. It has been in use for twenty-eight years without failure or accident. Though not now protected by patents, no one else has even attempted to do similar work that I know of, except in one instance of a vaulted church ceiling. It is a method that requires trained and expert workmen as well as an accomplished head to direct them. Mr. Guastavino and his son plan and direct the work. He was an architect of reputation in his native country, but gave up his practice shortly after he came to the United States   The illustrations herewith presented are half-tones from photographs of floors in the Tiffany and Gorham Buildings, New York City, figs. 21 and 24

The principles embodied in the Guastavino system have been put in practice in one of the largest storage warehouses in the world—that of the Pittsburg Terminal Warehouse and Transfer Company at Pittsburg, Pa. In this building the unit of floor construction is a panel 20 by 22 feet, the floors being supported by steel stanchions at these distances The short spans between the stanchions are supported by 18-inch I beams, and the long ones by 24-inch I beams. Short 8-inch I beams set diagonally near the stanchions form diagonal square platforms, from which are sprung four arches of 6-inch hollow tiles to the centre, with a rise of only 17 inches. The four sections meet at joints where 8-inch cambered I beams are set as guides, these being sprung from the girders, and meeting at the crown of the arch. This makes a domical construction the haunches of which are filled with concrete to make a level floor, which is finished with cement (see figs. 22 and 23)

I have only to refer to one more of the many uses made of hollow-clay tiles in this country, and that is an extensive one, though it dates only about six years back. This material is causing a revolution in the method of building grain storage houses, called in the United States "elevators." The reason for the use of that name is not generally understood, and can be explained in a few words   All the grain that enters these structures is carried by machinery to the house on top, called the "cupola," and there distributed to the bins, which hold from 20,000 to 80,000 bushels each. When it is removed it is taken out at the bottom and then "elevated" again to the top, to be delivered through chutes to boats or cars. Hence it is all "elevated" twice. Formerly the bins were built of solid wood by nailing two by six inch scantlings on top of each other on the flat sides, like bricks in a wall.

The first engineer to plan these elevators in the United States was Geo. H. Johnson, now deceased. Though he was a native of England his inventions were all made when he was in America   The old form of grain elevator, surrounded by brick walls and sometimes only with sheet iron, and bins enough to hold from 500,000 to 2,000,000 bushels, was his invention. The system was introduced at Manchester about eight years ago, long after his death   He had in two cases built the bins of brick, and circular, reinforced with iron insertions, but they were too expensive to repeat

[*Text continued at p* 138

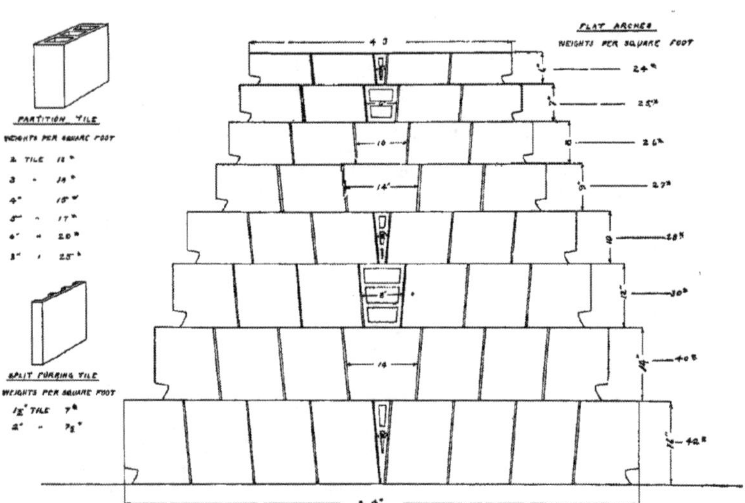

FIG 1—ELEVATIONS OF (HOBART) NATIONAL FIREPROOFING COMPANY'S POROUS TERRA COTTA END-PRESSURE FLAT ARCHES

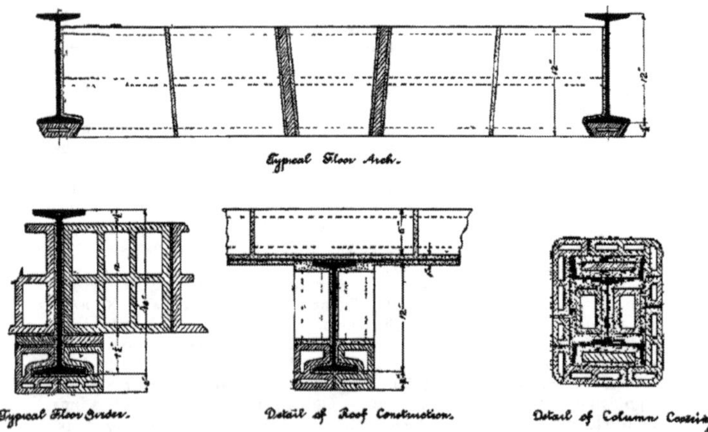

FIG 2—DETAILS OF FIREPROOF CONSTRUCTION. END-PRESSURE FLAT ARCH, ALSO GIRDER, STANCHION AND ROOF FIREPROOFING, CARDILLAC AUTOMOBILE FACTORY, DETROIT

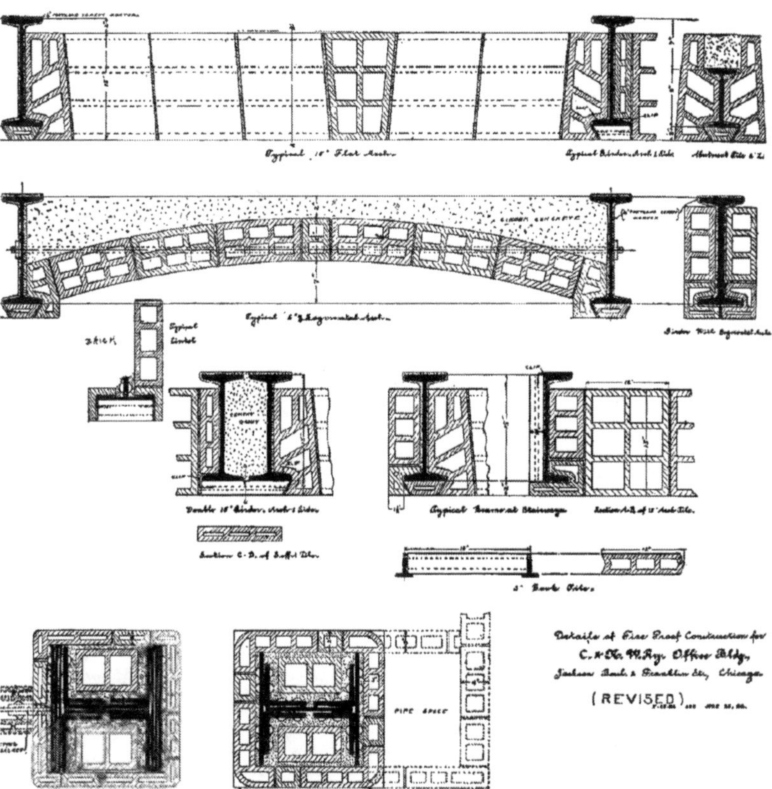

FIG. 3.—END-PRESSURE FLAT ARCH WITH SIDE-PRESSURE SKEWBACK, ALSO SEGMENT SIDE-PRESSURE ARCH AND STANCHION COVERING, CHICAGO AND NORTH-WESTERN RAILWAY OFFICE BUILDING, CHICAGO.

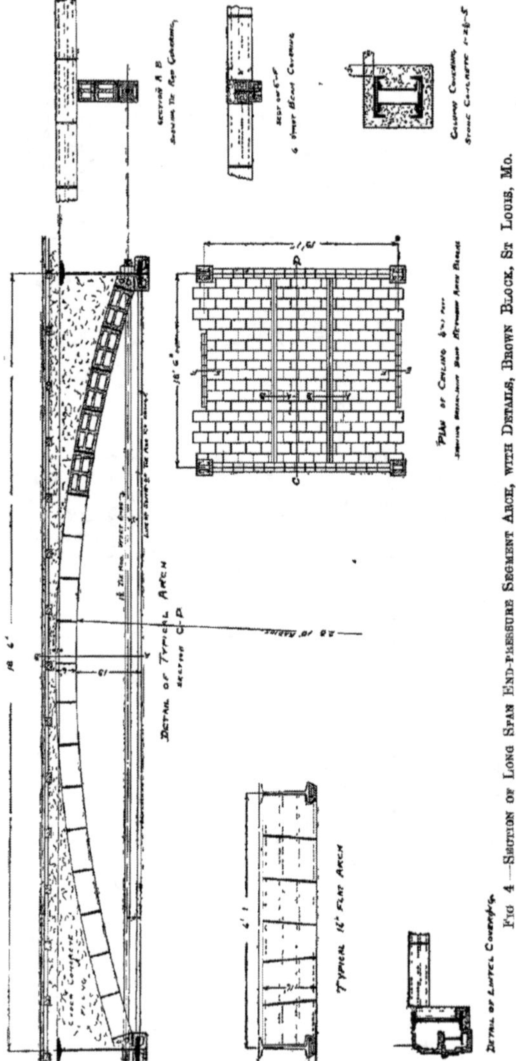

FIG. 4.—SECTION OF LONG SPAN END-PRESSURE SEGMENT ARCH, WITH DETAILS, BROWN BLOCK, ST. LOUIS, MO.

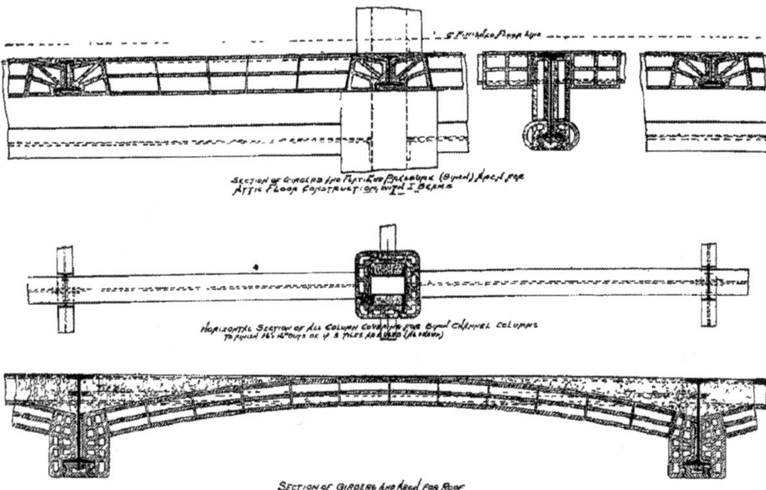

FIG 5—SECTIONS OF END PRESSURE FLAT ROOF ARCH AND GIRDER, ALSO END-PRESSURE SEGMENT ARCH SAME ALSO SHOWS SECTION OF STANCHION COVER CRAMPED WITH STEEL AND FILLED WITH CONCRETE DESIGNED BY THE AUTHOR

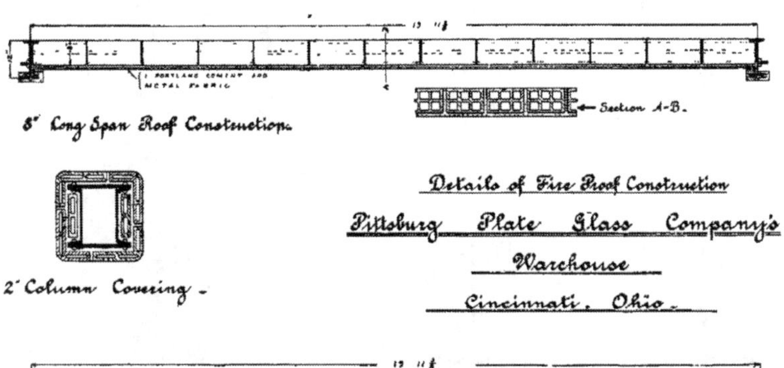

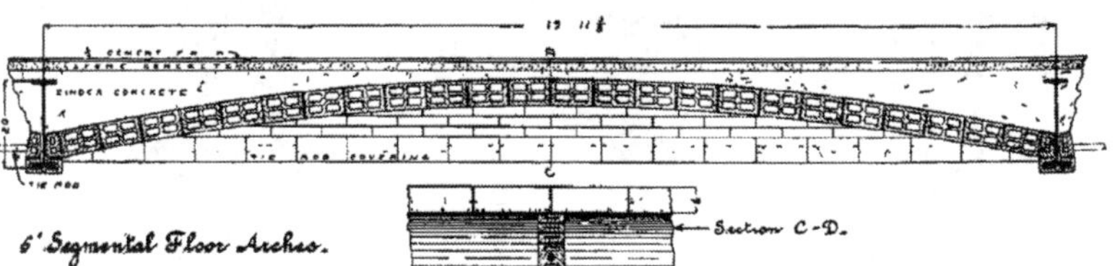

FIG 6—SECTION OF LONG SPAN SEGMENT, SIDE-PRESSURE ARCH, ALSO LONG SPAN ROOF CONSTRUCTION WITH STEEL TENSION (JOHNSON SYSTEM)

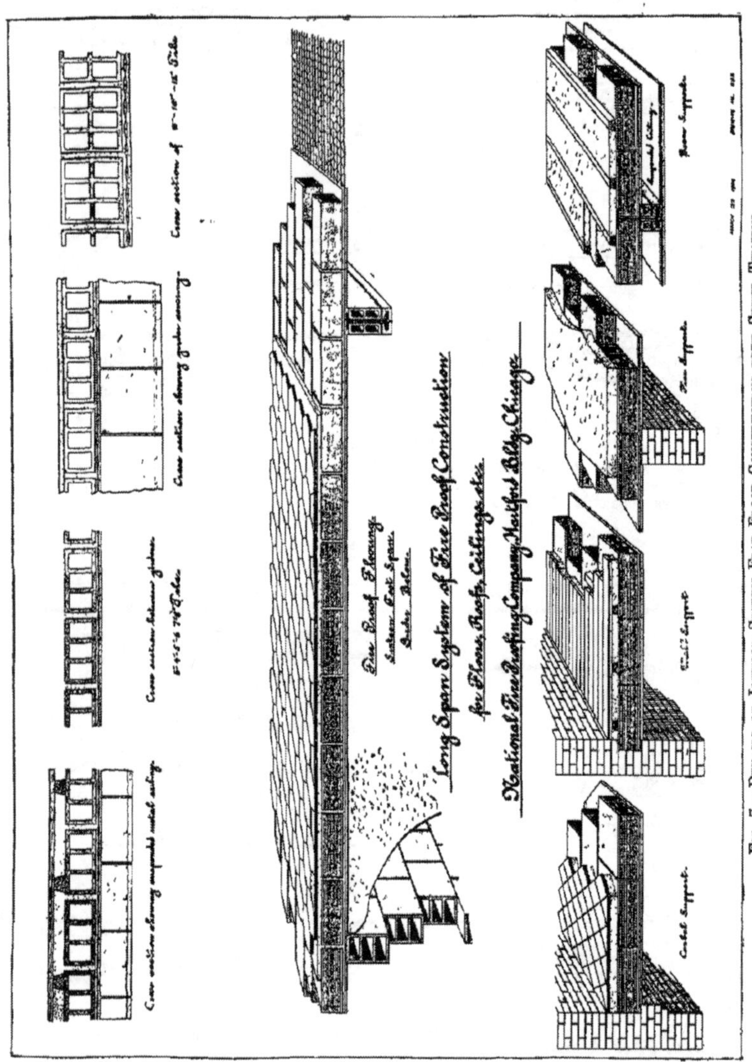

Fig. 7.—Details of Johnson System Flat Floor Construction with Steel Tension.

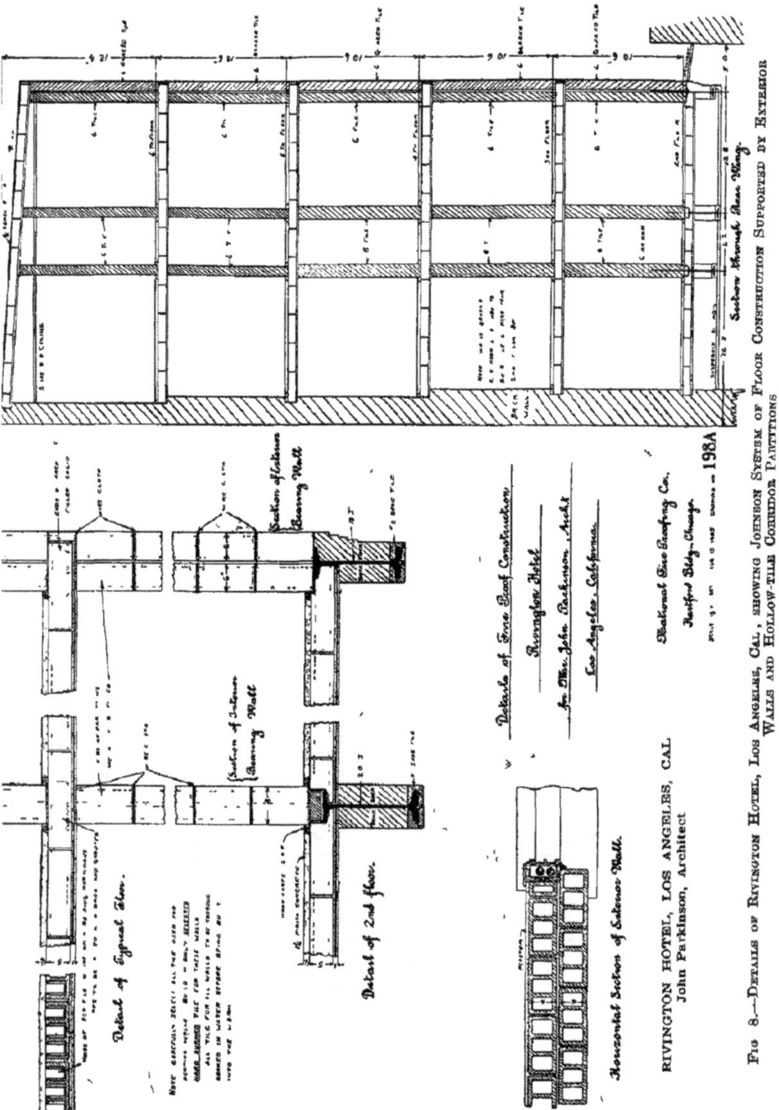

RIVINGTON HOTEL, LOS ANGELES, CAL
John Parkinson, Architect

Fig. 8.—Details of Rivington Hotel, Los Angeles, Cal, showing Johnson System of Floor Construction Supported by Exterior Walls and Hollow-tile Corridor Partitions

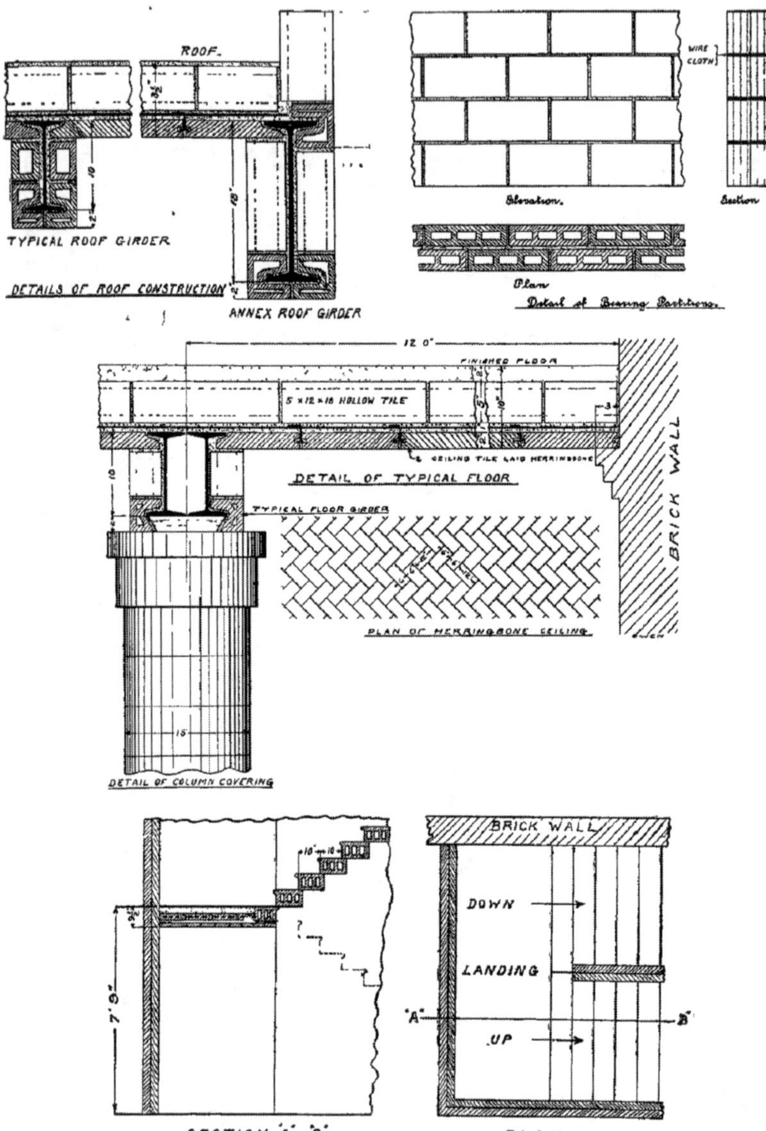

Fig. 9.—Details of Fireproofing and Construction in Underwriters' Laboratories at Chicago showing Johnson System Floor Construction with Tile Ceiling under and Supported by Steel Tension and Cement

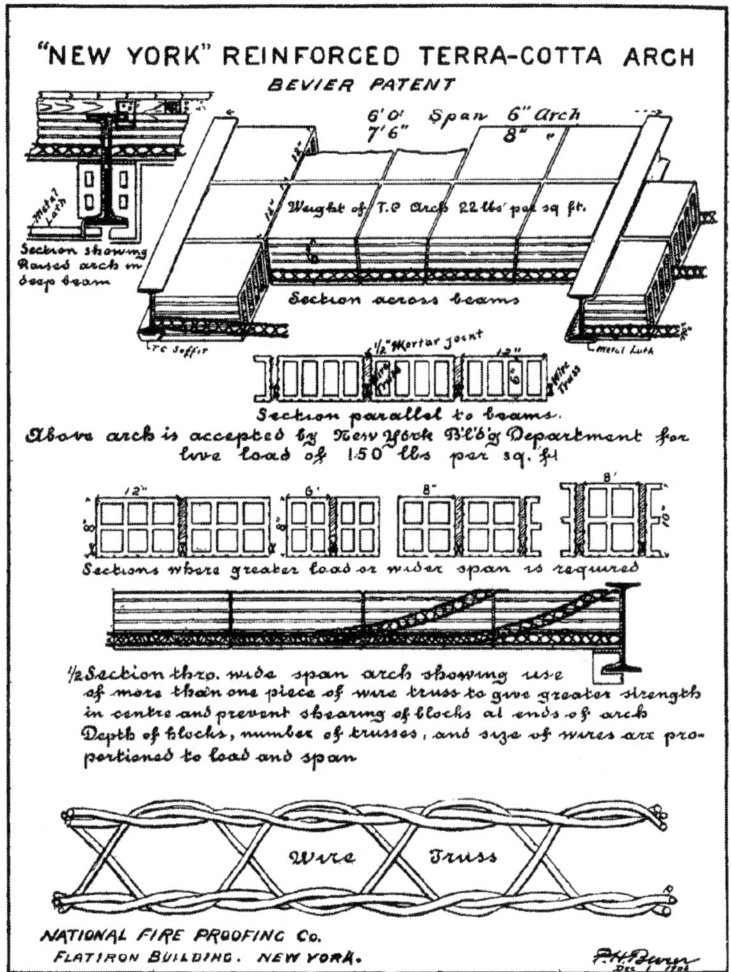

FIG 10 —BEVIER SYSTEM FLAT HOLLOW-TILE TENSION FLOOR

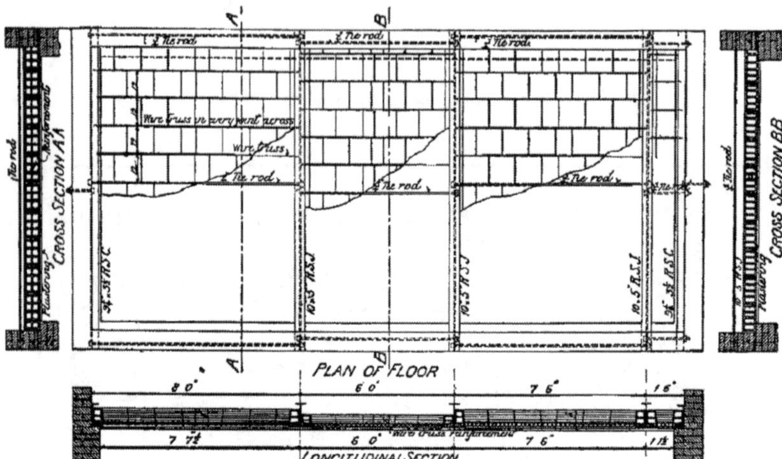

FIG 11—PLAN AND SECTIONS OF BEVIER FLOOR TESTED BY THE BRITISH FIRE PREVENTION COMMITTEE, FOR FULL PROJECTION

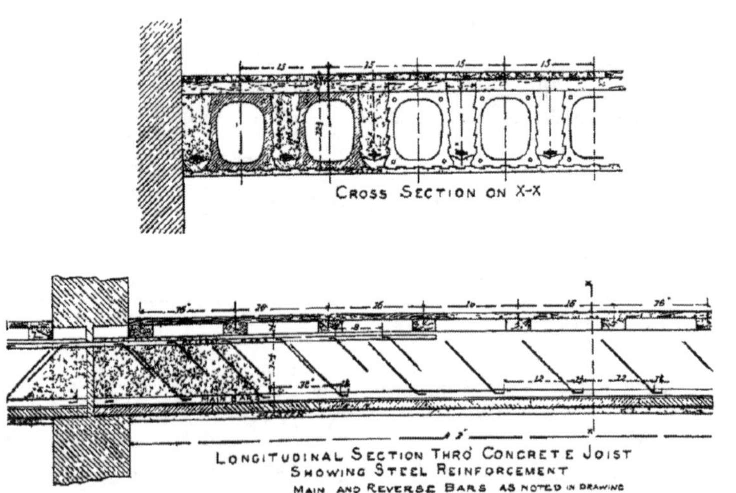

FIG 12—FLOOR SHOWING COMBINATIONS OF REINFORCED CONCRETE WITH HOLLOW-TILE SEPARATORS, FLAT CONSTRUCTION, KAHN SYSTEM, AS USED BY CAPT. JOHN S SEWELL, U S CORPS OF ENGINEERS

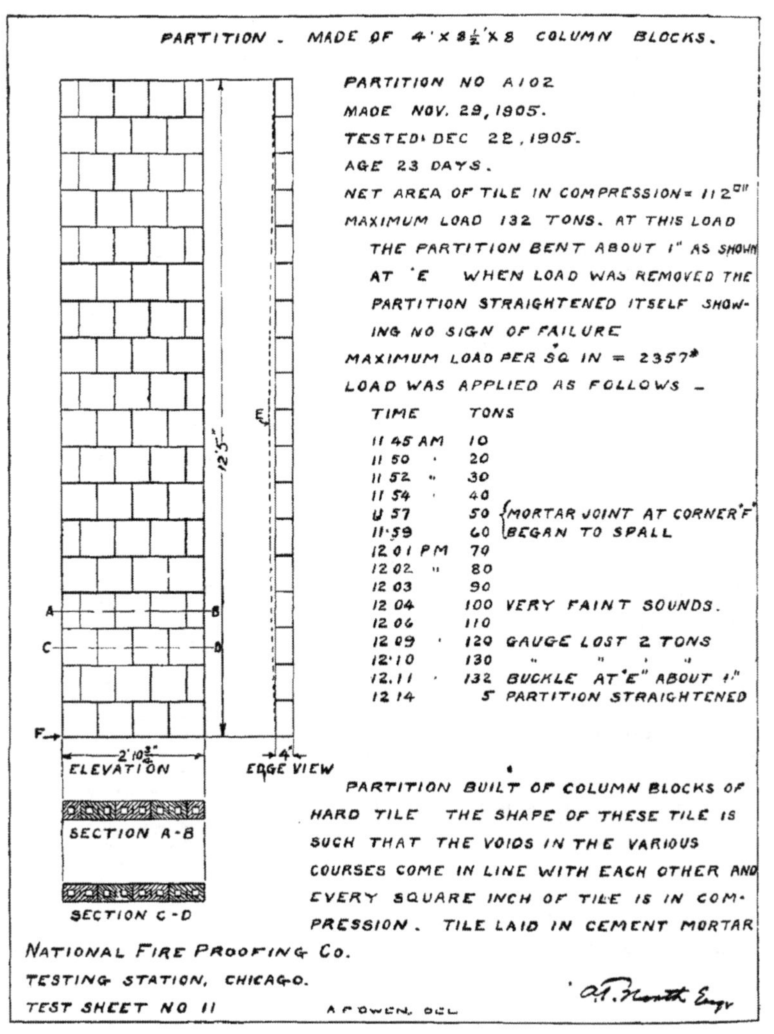

Fig 13.—Test Sheet No. 11, N. F. P. Co., showing Four-inch Heavy Tile Partition

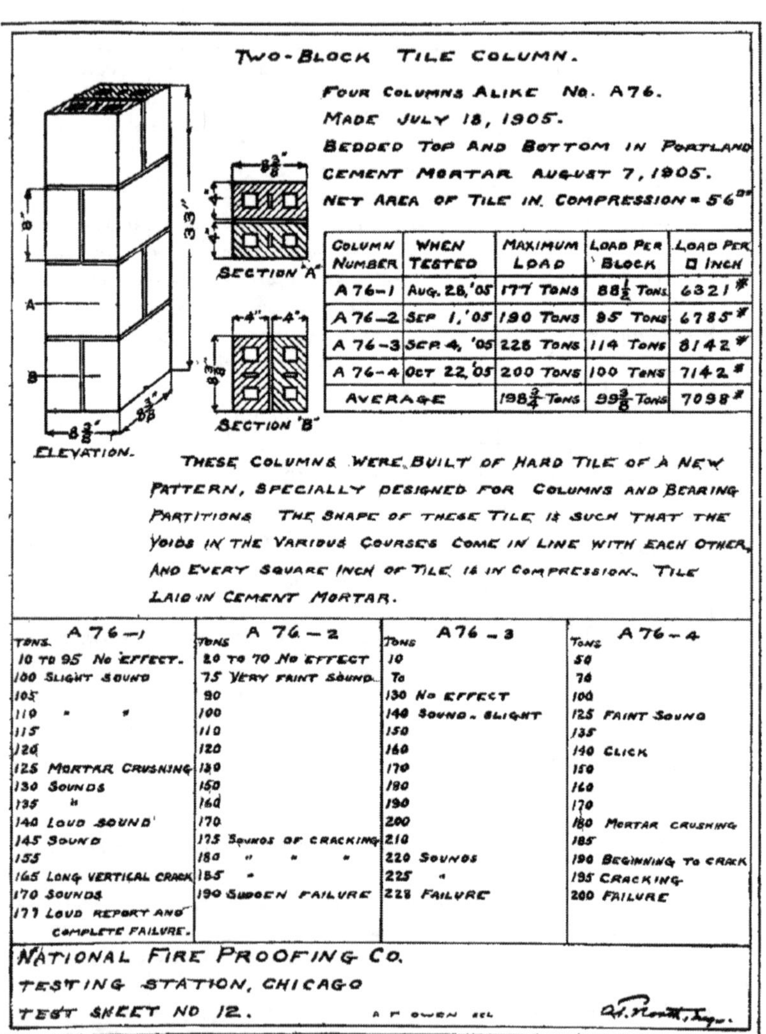

Fig 14—Test Sheet No 12, N F P. Co A Short 8 by 8 inch Stanchion Built of Heavy 4 by 8 inch Hard Burnt Tiles

PARTITION. OF 4" X 8½" X 8' JOHNSON BLOCKS. PLASTERED

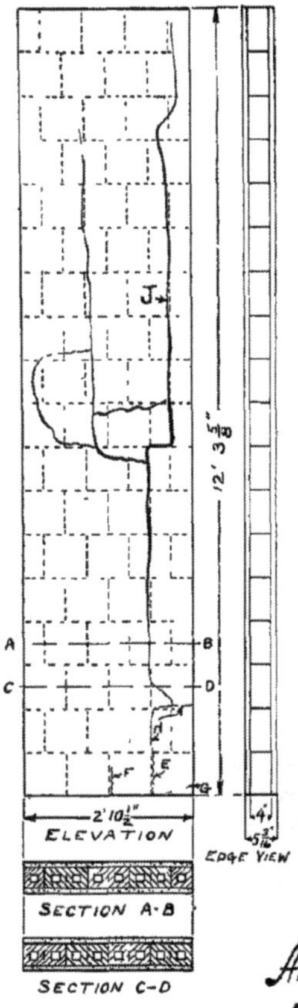

PARTITION NO A 103

MADE JAN 31, 1906.

PLASTERED WITH ACME PLASTER FEB 5, 1906

TESTED MAY 15, 1906

NET AREA OF TILE IN COMPRESSION - 112 □"

MAXIMUM LOAD - 185 TONS

MAXIMUM LOAD PER SQUARE INCH = 3303#

LOAD APPLIED AS FOLLOWS —

3 46 PM	4¼ TONS.	LOAD GRADUALLY INCREASED TO
4·09 "	90 "	NO APPARENT EFFECT
4 11	100 "	HAIR CRACK "E" IN PLASTER
4 16 "	110	" "F" " "
4 19	120	PLASTER SPALLING AT "G"
4 25 "	130 "	DULL THUD. PLASTER SHEARING.
4 29 "		GAUGE LOST 1 TON
4 31 "	135 "	PLASTER GIVING WAY AT "H" AND G"
4 36 "	140	NO SIGN OF BUCKLE
4. 37	145	GAUGE LOST 1 TON IN 2 MINUTES
4 40 "	150 "	GAUGE HOLDS
4 43 "	160	CRACKING SOUNDS FROM PLASTER
4 45 "	170 "	SOUNDS. PLASTER LOOSENING NEAR TOP. GAUGE LOST 2 TONS IN 2 MIN
4 48	180 "	NO BUCKLE
4 49 "	185 "	SOUNDS CRUSH ON EAST SHELL OF TILE AT CENTER POINT IN HEIGHT, EVIDENTLY RESULTING FROM THE WALL BUCKLING, AND VERTICAL RUPTURE "J".

NO BUCKLING WAS APPARENT DURING TEST.

PARTITION BUILT OF JOHNSON COLUMN BLOCKS OF MEDIUM HARD TILE. THE SHAPE OF THESE TILE IS SUCH THAT THE VOIDS IN THE VARIOUS COURSES COME IN LINE WITH EACH OTHER, AND EVERY SQUARE INCH OF TILE IS IN COMPRESSION. TILE LAID IN CEMENT MORTAR, (1 TO 3)

TEST WITNESSED BY

Peter Bartzen — COMMISSIONER OF BUILDINGS, CITY OF CHICAGO.

Andrew F. Hughes, — DEPUTY COMMISSIONER OF BUILDINGS, CITY OF CHICAGO

Henry E. Cordell — ARCHITECTURAL ENGINEER, BUILDING DEPARTMENT, CITY OF CHICAGO

Charles Brooks — ENGINEER, LOS ANGELES, CALIFORNIA.

A. T. North — ENGINEER, WESTERN DEPT NATIONAL FIRE PROOFING CO

NATIONAL FIRE PROOFING CO.
TESTING STATION, CHICAGO
TEST SHEET NO. 15.

FIG 15.—TEST SHEET NO 15, N F P CO, SHOWING 4-INCH HEAVY TILE PARTITION WITH CEMENT FINISH ON BOTH SIDES

APPEARANCE OF EAST SIDE WHEN CRUSHED BY 185 TONS.

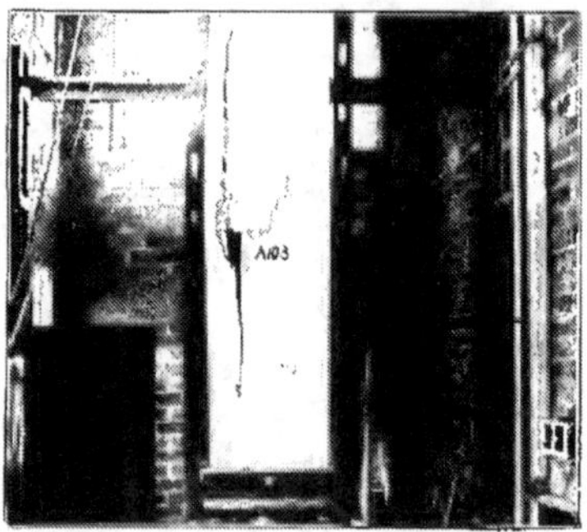

APPEARANCE OF WEST SIDE WHEN CRUSHED BY 185 TONS.

FIGS. 16 AND 17.—FROM PHOTOGRAPHS OF TEST NO. 15 AT INSTANT OF FAILURE UNDER LOAD OF 3,303 POUNDS PER SQUARE INCH.

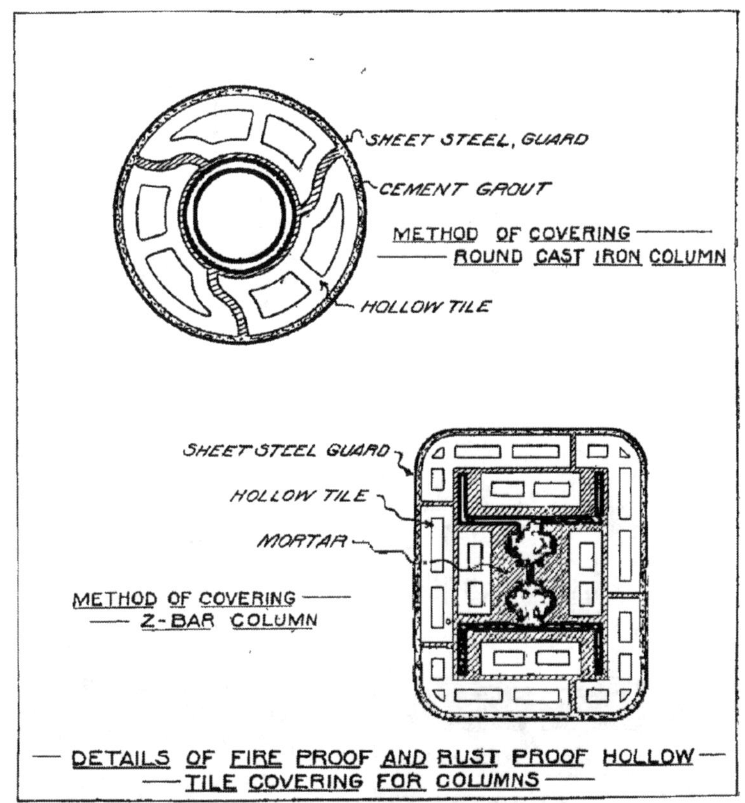

WESTERN ELECTRIC BUILDING

Fig 18—Sections showing Methods of Covering Cast-iron and Z-bar Steel Stanchions in Western Electric Company's Buildings, Chicago

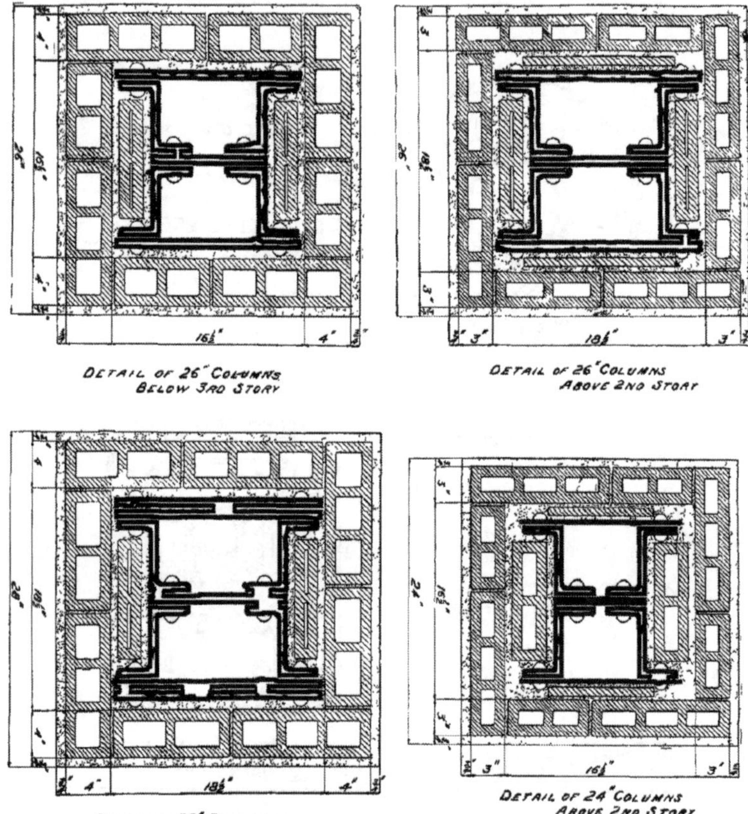

Fig 19 —Sections showing Z-bar and-plate Steel Stanchions and Methods of Fireproofing
in U S Government Building, Chicago

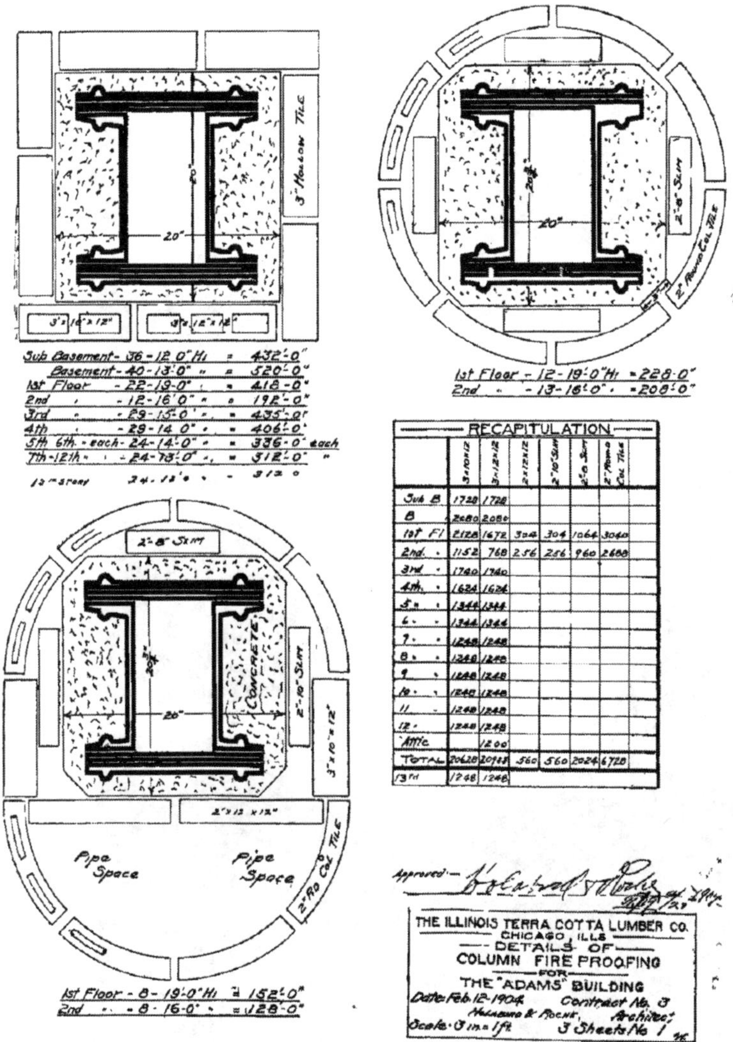

FIG. 20.—SECTIONS SHOWING CHANNEL-AND-PLATE STEEL STANCHIONS AND METHODS OF FIREPROOFING STEEL IN THE "ADAMS" (NOW THE REPUBLIC) BUILDING, ADAMS AND STATE STREETS, CHICAGO.

Fig. 21.—Interior of the Exhibition Room, Covering the Entire Top Story of the Tiffany Building, New York City. Guastavino System. Executed in Enamelled Tiles.

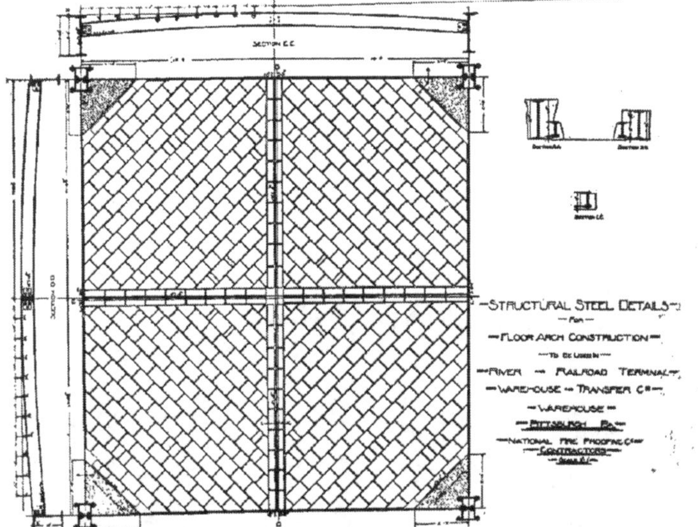

FIG. 22.—PLAN AND SECTIONS OF ONE FLOOR PANEL, SHOWING CONSTRUCTION OF THE PITTSBURG TERMINAL WAREHOUSES, PITTSBURG, PA.

FIG. 23.—INTERIOR OF TEST-CHAMBER AFTER A FIRE TEST OF 2,200° F., SHOWING UNDER SIDE OF FIG. 22.

FIG. 24.—INTERIOR OF ONE OF THE UPPER FLOORS OF THE GORHAM BUILDING, NEW YORK CITY. GUASTAVINO SYSTEM. NO PLASTERING WAS USED.

FIG. 25.—FROM A PHOTOGRAPH OF PART OF THE GRAIN TANKS OF THE ST. ANTHONY ELEVATOR CO., MINNEAPOLIS, MINN. BUILT ON THE JOHNSON SYSTEM. EACH OF THESE TANKS HAS A CAPACITY OF 80,000 BUSHELS OF GRAIN.

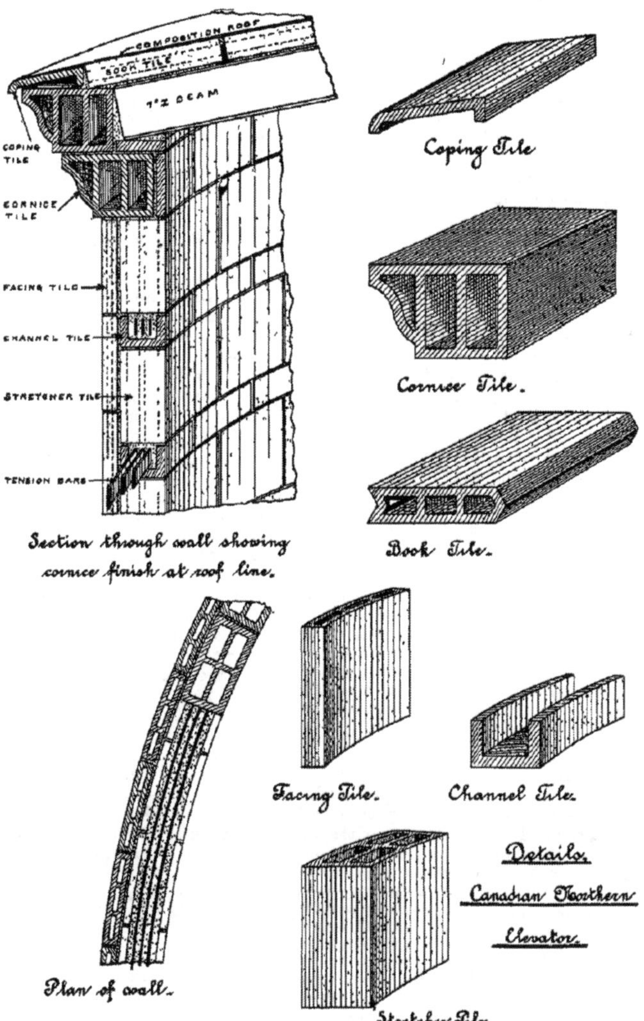

FIG. 26.—DETAILS OF HOLLOW-TILE GRAIN TANKS AS BUILT BY E V JOHNSON, ENGINEER

It is therefore natural, in the course of events, that Mr Johnson's only son, Mr E V Johnson, should have perfected in permanent fireproof materials the elevator construction that his father initiated The first test was on a single bin at Minneapolis, to contain 20,000 bushels He built it of hollow-clay tiles, reinforced with steel bands set edgewise within the tile wall, filled it with wheat, and tried to destroy the grain by building a fire against it. He did not succeed in the latter purpose, and the result has been that up to the present time there is probably one hundred million bushels of grain stored in tanks of similar kind which have since been built, and nearly all of it is uninsured. It is hoped that a few illustrations will show how these " elevators " are constructed (figs. 25 and 26).

It must now be evident to the reader, as it is to the writer, that the subject of this paper is such a vast one that it is impossible to comprehend more than an outline of it in this effort. I have not troubled my hearers with statistics, or told of the great and costly structures in which the American system of fireproof construction has been used for the past twenty-five years, nor have I descanted upon its effectual saving of the structural parts in the Baltimore conflagration, or the part which it has borne even more effectively in the recent San Francisco disaster, notwithstanding much that has been said to the contrary , those are matters of history ; nor have I claimed for it absolute perfection. Like all the other efforts of mankind, it is still in evolutionary development It is an art which is not practised with equal conscientiousness by all. The material of which I speak has too often been used as a sham and pretence to mislead the victims of the greedy impostor into a sense of security for which there is no reason More than one burned building has proved this , but more than a hundred others have been saved from fires in their early stages that would have been wholly destructive in buildings of the ordinary class.

I venture also to say that the fireproofing with clay products is in no country impracticable on account of added cost The fact that the earliest inventions in this material in Great Britain and on the Continent were not developed and put in practice in those countries, but in one across the sea, is no argument that they have been tried and found wanting If the manufacture should be more expensive at first than in the United States, this would only show that improved methods and machinery there used are here unknown. In my opinion the fireproof material as made in the United States could, after less than one year's experience, be made cheaper in England or France than on the other side of the sea, with its high-priced labour and coal. It is a large product, and must be made on a very large scale. It must also find cheap transportation. I do not think that the American manufacturers are anxious to send their product to England, though I know that it has been shipped from New York at less cost than it could by a short railroad line in England. I think the American contractors, whose spirit and enterprise know no bounds, would much prefer to buy or make their materials in the countries in which they find contracts to execute than to carry it away from home where they have plenty of use for it. It is matters like this which seem to me to be especially pertinent to an International Congress of Architects. We are here to learn what others are doing , and, while we learn from others, we are endeavouring to impart that information which we happen to possess to our brothers in other lands, which we hope will be useful to them It is for such reasons that I have endeavoured to contribute what little I can to the fund of information to be here accumulated for the benefit of our *confrères* throughout the world.

9. LES CONSTRUCTIONS EN ACIER ET EN CIMENT ARMÉ.

Par Joaquin Bassegoda.

I.

De toutes les questions se rapportant à la construction moderne il n'en est point qui éveille autant d'intérêt que la question du ciment armé. Le succès obtenu par ce système de construction depuis vingt ans, c'est-à-dire depuis que M. Monier commença à l'employer d'une manière scientifique, est vraiment extraordinaire. Lorsqu'à cette époque on voyait recouvrir de ciment des cercles et des tringles de fer pour en former des tuyaux de conduite pour les eaux, il était fort difficile de prévoir les nombreuses et importantes applications que l'on ferait de ce procédé, surtout dans les ponts grandioses récemment construits et dans les vastes édifices dont l'ossature est exclusivement formée de ce nouveau matériel

Ce fait oblige les architectes, surtout ceux qui, comme nous, ont regardé dès le principe avec une certaine prévention le ciment armé, à l'étudier consciencieusement mais avec impartialité, afin de constater si son application dans les travaux architectoniques présente ou non les grands avantages que lui attribuent ses défenseurs en le comparant aux autres systèmes de construction employés jusqu'ici. Ce thème a été amplement discuté dans le dernier Congrès International tenu à Madrid en 1904 , néanmoins en le remettant de nouveau en discussion le Comité organisateur du Congrès actuel de Londres démontre d'une manière positive la grande importance qu'il lui accorde   Comme nous partageons en cela l'opinion du Congrès nous ne croyons pas inutile de présenter dans la discussion ce petit exposé dont le but n'est point de traiter à fond la matière, mais de soumettre quelques courtes considérations d'un caractère pratique, dont les unes sont le fruit de la lecture des lumineux ouvrages publiés jusqu'à ce jour, et les autres de notre longue expérience professionnelle.

II.

Le plus éminent des architectes archéologues, M Viollet-le-Duc, a dit dans un de ses ouvrages que la construction au Moyen Age était parvenue jusqu'à la subtilité à force d'individualiser les organes constructifs suivant la fonction que chacun remplit dans la structure   Comme déduction de cette même idée nous dirons que la subtilité est ce qui caractérise le mieux la construction en ciment armé   en effet ce ne sont point seulement ici, comme dans l'exemple cité, les membres ou organes formant partie intégrante de la construction qui s'individualisent, mais bien les plus petits éléments de chacun d'eux. Former une structure concrétionnée à l'aide d'éléments de nature et de propriétés distinctes mais agencées de telle sorte que chacun d'eux puisse développer l'effort qui lui correspond suivant sa nature et le mode de travail de la masse, est à notre avis l'idée la plus subtile qui ait jamais été mise en pratique dans l'art de la construction   L'idée primitive de l'emploi du ciment armé n'est point due aux progrès de la Mécanique à l'époque actuelle, mais bien à l'intuition du constructeur pratique, car la preuve scientifique basée sur les calculs et venant confirmer pleinement ses assertions n'a été faite que plus tard.

L'invention du béton et du ciment armés fut bien modeste au principe. Appliqués tout d'abord, dans les parterres, à la fabrication d'objets de pur ornement, pouvant résister à l'influence de l'humidité atmosphérique, employés plus tard dans les tuyaux de conduite pour les eaux, ils servirent ensuite à la construction de grands réservoirs. Mais la nécessité de recouvrir ces réservoirs au moyen de voûtes fit naître l'idée de construire des voûtes plus résistantes pour plafonds et toitures   Ce problème qui offre toujours les plus grandes difficultés dans toute construction une fois résolu, on vit qu'il n'y avait aucun motif qui s'opposât à l'emploi du nouveau système pour les éléments soutenants d'un édifice comme les murs et les piliers   Cette innovation ayant donné un résultat satisfaisant on en vint à former les éléments soutenants entièrement horizontaux, plafonds et couvertures, avec la même concrétion armée que le reste de l'édifice.   C'est ainsi qu'on arriva à soumettre avec un égal succès aux efforts de flexion une matière dont on n'avait utilisé jusqu'alors que les efforts d'extension et de compression

De même que le fer à son apparition dans les constructions commença à remplacer quelques éléments de maçonnerie et de bois, et en vint même, dans certains cas, à les substituer totalement, ainsi en advint-il du ciment armé et nous avons vu en peu de temps des édifices entièrement construits d'après ce nouveau principe.   Mais, comme il est logique et naturel, cette substitution de matériaux n'a produit aucune forme ou disposition nouvelle   Ceci est tellement vrai que si nous pénétrons dans un édifice fait de ciment armé, pour peu que le constructeur l'ait revêtu de quelques motifs de décoration, nous ne pourrons nous rendre compte de l'économie interne de cette construction.   Ce n'est point que l'architecte ait résolu un nouveau problème ou introduit un nouveau principe il n'a fait que changer le matériel qui n'est ni pierre naturelle ou artificielle, ni bois, ni fer, mais du ciment armé dont les propriétés diffèrent notablement de celles des matériaux cités.

L'introduction d'un nouveau matériel dans la construction moderne est donc un fait indéniable.   Faisons abstraction pour le moment des éloges plus ou moins exagérés que lui prodiguent ses partisans et des censures plus ou moins justifiées de ses détracteurs—ce qui est certain c'est que ce nouveau matériel a servi à la construction de nombreux édifices que nous pouvons admirer   les uns destinés à une fin utilitaire et dépourvus de tout caractère et d'autres qui offrent un cachet vraiment artistique   d'où l'on peut conclure que le nouveau système s'adapte à tous les genres.   Si dans ces travaux le constructeur ne développe aucun nouveau principe et ne pare à aucune nécessité négligée jusqu'alors, il n'en est pas moins vrai que le fait d'employer un nouveau matériel oblige l'architecte à se fixer sur sa nature propre et ses propriétés afin d'étudier les formes qu'il doit lui donner pour accomplir la loi inéludible à toutes les époques qui dit qu'à tout matériel nouveau correspondent des formes nouvelles dans une même civilisation.

<h1 style="text-align:center">III</h1>

Le principe que deux éléments aussi hétérogènes entre eux que le sont le mortier et le métal peuvent s'unir pour constituer un nouveau matériel, ayant été admis aussi bien au point de vue théorique que pratique, et le succès de ses applications ayant été sanctionné par une longue expérience, celles-ci se multiplièrent de jour en jour   Cela donna naissance à une foule de nouveaux systèmes dont quelques-uns n'avaient de nouveau que ce qui est strictement requis pour l'obtention d'un brevet d'invention, tandis que d'autres avaient un vrai caractère scientifique   Des hommes de science et d'éminents ingénieurs se sont dédiés à l'étude théorique et expérimentale de la mécanique de la nouvelle construction avec une sollicitude et une diligence qui n'ont jamais été mises au service des travaux de maçonnerie qui malheureusement sont encore en grande partie soumis aux lois de l'empirisme.   C'est vraiment une anomalie tout au moins apparente, de voir qu'en peu d'années on a mis en concordance avec les formules générales de la résistance de matériaux une multitude de faits observés pendant le travail d'une masse de béton armé, tandis que dans le calcul des voûtes concrétionnelles non armées nous devons nous contenter d'appliquer aux formules générales quelques coefficients numériques d'une approximation fort douteuse   À notre avis cette anomalie est due à la raison primordiale de la faveur dont jouit le ciment armé qui n'est autre que *l'économie.* Nous admettons certainement quelques-uns des avantages qu'offre le système, tels que · la facilité de donner à la construction des formes variées, l'obtention d'une grande solidarité entre les éléments qui le composent, une plus grande résistance aux actions atmosphériques et au feu que ne la possède le fer · mais pour nous on pourrait résumer tous ces avantages dans un seul mot : l'économie , car c'est elle en effet qui les domine tous   L'économie dans cette nouvelle structure ne dépend pas cependant du bas prix des matériaux composants qui sont chers relativement à ceux qu'emploie la maçonnerie, mais dans la juste combinaison des deux éléments de manière à pouvoir réduire à leur limite extrême les dimensions de chaque partie de la construction. Lancé dans cette voie, l'empirique n'a point osé de lui-même arriver à la ligne de démarcation entre l'économique et le périlleux, et il a fait appel à l'homme de science pour qu'il lui indiquât par le moyen du calcul la limite qu'il pouvait atteindre.

Pour le béton armé la stricte économie est une question vitale laissant de côté les subtilités de la théorie pour rester dans le terrain de la sécurité absolue, comme nous avons coutume de le faire dans les constructions en maçonnerie, l'économie disparaîtra en bien des cas et par le fait la structure armée n'aura plus sa raison d'être.

De là cette concurrence entre les constructeurs pour réduire les dimensions de l'œuvre et par conséquent le devis, et de là aussi ce caractère de légèreté exagérée que présentent plusieurs constructions. A notre avis quelques-uns des accidents qui malheureusement ont eu lieu dans ces constructions n'ont point d'autre cause, quoique officiellement on ne l'ait pas reconnu ainsi   Dans certains cas on attribue la chute au manque de lavage du sable, dans d'autres à un décintrage prématuré ou à la dilatation thermique des matériaux , sans rejeter absolument l'influence de quelqu'une de ces causes dans les accidents, nous croyons que la vraie cause pour la plupart a été la lutte pour l'économie par l'amincissement excessif de quelques membres et la suppression totale de quelques autres   Il est vrai qu'en faisant usage de matériaux de première qualité pouvant travailler à des coefficients élevés, supérieurs aux courants, on peut arriver à produire des travaux économiques, mais il faut observer qu'en ce point on est aussi tombé dans des abus   En effet dans la nouvelle construction on a adopté quelquefois des équivalents qui n'avaient jamais été si élevés dans les constructions en maçonnerie   De là est venue la comparaison peu équitative entre les anciens systèmes et les modernes au point de vue de l'économie, car si dans les premiers on avait admis des coefficients aussi élevés que dans les seconds on aurait obtenu des résultats très avantageux pour la légèreté et l'économie sans sortir du domaine d'une absolue sécurité. Si dans les voûtes en pierre de taille elles-mêmes, qui offrent un si frappant contraste avec les arcs métalliques et en ciment armé, on avait mieux tenu en compte les excellentes qualités du matériel, on aurait produit des effets surprenants de légèreté selon l'opinion autorisée du savant ingénieur M Resal.

Néanmoins puisqu'il s'agit d'une concrétion dans laquelle le mortier joue un rôle très important, il est nécessaire de ne point exagérer le travail de cet élément moins encore que celui du fer   En effet il est très difficile d'en assurer les propriétés qui dépendent de la qualité du ciment, de la nature, forme et grosseur des sables et graviers, de la nature de l'eau, des proportions entre ces composants et de la manipulation et emploi des mortiers et des bétons

Ce point est la cause principale de la grande variété qui existe entre les divers systèmes qui se mettent en pratique. Les uns laissent au béton le soin de résister aux efforts de compression soit directe soit produite par la flexion   tels sont entre autres les systèmes Coignet, Hennebique, Piketty, Boussiron, Cottancin et autres. Quelques-uns, au contraire, sacrifiant l'économie ou la cherchant autre part, veulent que le métal soit seul à résister aux différents efforts, considérant ainsi le ciment ou le béton comme un simple revêtement protecteur du métal mais qui ne l'aide à résister ou tout au plus augmente sa rigidité. Tels sont les systèmes Matrái, Bonna, Chaudy, Canovetti, etc.

Dans le premier groupe il y a des constructeurs comme Vallière et Minich, qui, confiant entièrement dans le travail du ciment, placent une simple armature de fer à la partie inférieure des pièces sujettes à flexion, tandis que d'autres formant la grande majorité, veulent que le béton soit aidé par le métal, soit pour le travail à la compression, soit pour les efforts de tension qui se font sentir à l'extrémité supérieure de la poutre par l'effet des encastrements   Il faut déduire de là que la composition du congloméré doit varier énormément suivant le rôle qu'on lui confie. Quand il doit résister à de grands efforts, surtout de compression, il requiert des mortiers riches en ciment, préparés avec du sable fin, battus et gâchés avec soin.   Pour les systèmes où l'on réserve au fer toutes les résistances on peut employer des mortiers plus pauvres   et même dans les systèmes qui font abstraction complète du travail du ciment, comme ceux de Matrái et Cottancin, on forme un béton de mâchefer qui offre, en même temps qu'une économie considérable, une plus grande légèreté

Le fer, comme matériel de construction, étant mieux connu que le ciment, peut être employé à des coefficients assez élevés , il y a cependant une grande différence quant à la forme suivant laquelle on l'emploie dans les divers systèmes.   La grande majorité préfère et utilise exclusivement le fer rond, tandis que les autres, quoique peu nombreux, comme Matrái, Bonna et Golding, se servent de préférence des fers spéciaux et encore dans le système Matrái combine-t-on d'une façon très ingénieuse les fers ronds et les spéciaux.

Cette question est des plus importantes, car le profil et la section du fer influent sur le degré de contact et d'adhérence du métal avec le béton plus que n'influe sa résistance intrinsèque   C'est un fait prouvé par l'expérience que les fers ronds de petite section sont ceux qui facilitent le plus l'adhésion, tandis que les fers trop gros ou de section spéciale la rendent difficile et obligent pour atténuer cet inconvénient à employer des mortiers plus riches en ciment, d'un sable plus fin et gâchés avec un léger excès d'eau, en un mot, des mortiers parfaitement plastiques

L'évaluation de l'effort que représente l'adhérence du fer et du ciment est plus difficile à déterminer que la résistance et le coefficient d'élasticité des deux composants.   Nous savons par la pratique de tous les jours que le ciment et le fer adhèrent parfaitement tant que les charges qu'ils sup portent ne dépassent pas les limites ordinaires. Les expériences con-cluantes de M Considère nous ont même démontré que dans les pièces armées les conglomérés peuvent supporter des allongements vingt fois supérieurs à ceux que l'on considère comme devant produire la rupture dans les pièces non armées ; ce qui prouverait que le mortier et le fer continuent d'adhérer dans ce mouvement d'allongement   Mais la théorie de M Planat, appuyée sur des faits observés, tend à démontrer que dans les parties étirées, lorsque l'effort arrive à une certaine limite, le fer et le mortier se séparent et il se produit une désagrégation partielle de ce dernier dans la section correspondant au plus grand travail d'extension. Ce fait peut se prouver facilement par la formation de petites fissures, bien avant d'atteindre la charge de rupture   Cette séparation une fois produite, il est évident que le mortier ne réalise plus aucun effort d'exten-sion et le fer reste seul à résister à cet effort, et comme le travail du métal peut encore augmenter beaucoup, les fissures du mortier n'indiquent point la proximité du moment de la rupture.

L'observation des fissures qui a donné lieu à cette théorie a été combattue et MM Tedesco et Maurel disent à ce sujet que l'observation aura été sans doute mal interprétée, car si le ciment se crevassait réellement un dépôt en ciment armé ne serait pas imperméable

Ces divergences d'appréciation s'étendent, comme il est naturel, aux applications : quelques constructeurs sont partisans de faire entrer dans le calcul cet effort d'adhérence des deux matériaux, tandis que d'autres au contraire ne le font point entrer en ligne de compte. S'il s'agit d'une poutre soumise à un travail à la flexion, les premiers admettent la force d'adhérence du ciment et du fer comme moyen d'unir les parties étirées aux parties comprimées · ils arrivent à fixer comme équivalent de cette force huit kilogrammes par centimètre carré Les seconds, quoique en plus petit nombre, ne font aucun cas de cette adhérence ; l'un d'eux, M. Hennebique, dit même que si cet effort se démontre clairement dans les expériences de laboratoire il décroît notablement lorsqu'il s'agit de grandes masses Un autre constructeur, M. Cottancin, reconnaît que dans la pratique l'adhérence disparaît fréquemment pour des causes difficiles à prévoir , il assure même que le béton se désagrège lentement sous l'action du temps et des efforts répétés. Si cela est certain (et il nous semble assez difficile de prouver le contraire) il faut s'attendre tôt ou tard à des résultats désastreux pour les œuvres exécutées d'après quelques-uns des systèmes actuellement en vogue

IV.

Le principe économique auquel obéit l'emploi du ciment armé est énoncé par MM Tedesco et Maurel de la manière suivante : Une unité de résistance à la compression coûte de 3 à 6 fois moins en employant le béton qu'en employant le fer   et inversement une unité de résistance à l'extension coûte deux ou trois fois moins avec le fer qu'avec le béton Il est donc évident que si l'on peut disposer les matériaux de telle sorte que dans la même poutre on fasse travailler le béton à la compression et le fer à l'extension on parviendra à réaliser pour une résistance donnée le maximum d'économie qu'il soit possible d'obtenir dans l'emploi des deux matériaux. Ce raisonnement admis, nous demandons en généralisant davantage la question : Pouvons-nous dans la structure armée remplacer le béton par un autre matériel qui travaille plus économiquement à la compression ? Oui, sans aucun doute et ce matériel, c'est la brique. Il faut observer néanmoins que la résistance de la brique varie considérablement suivant les lieux d'origine, et son prix modique ne permet pas le transport à de grandes distances. L'application de la brique ne peut donc avoir lieu que dans les endroits qui en possèdent de première qualité et où la maçonnerie de ce matériel avec le mortier de ciment soit plus économique que la maçonnerie en béton ou en ciment Il est évident que l'économie provenant de cette substitution sera très appréciable dans les pays qui, comme le nôtre (Barcelone), réunissent les avantages indiqués plus haut. En effet le mètre cube de béton coûtant 50 francs et travaillant à la compression à 20 kilogrammes par centimètre carré, l'unité de résistance revient à 2 fr 50, tandis que si nous employons la brique au ciment, dont le prix au mètre cube est de 30 francs, quoique le travail soit seulement de 15 kilos, l'unité de résistance reviendra à 2 francs.

L'idée d'armer la brique avec des fers soutenus au moyen de tirants est d'une date fort ancienne et il est singulier qu'elle ait été mise en pratique à une époque antérieure à la généralisation du ciment armé En effet nous pouvons citer comme preuve de ce que nous avançons que M. Torras, architecte, professeur de l'Ecole de Barcelone, employa, il y a plusieurs années, des poutres de forme parabolique construites d'après ce principe et quoique l'idée se prêtât à de notables et originales applications et surtout à une plus grande économie, son auteur n'essaya pas de généraliser le système.

Mais par la force même de la logique, après le béton armé devait venir
la brique armée. et c'est ce qui est arrivé.   Un constructeur français,
M. Cottancin, est celui qui met en pratique ce système du mode le plus
rationnel, mais avec une différence essentielle par rapport à l'essai pratiqué
par M. Torras , celui-ci l'employa dans les poutres, tandis que le premier
l'utilise seulement pour les murs et les cloisons.   Les briques peuvent
être pleines ou creuses ; si elles sont pleines on les arme de fils de fer qui
passent par les joints de façon à ce que chaque brique occupe une maille
du filet , si elles sont creuses, les fils passent par les trous qui doivent
à cet effet être placés verticalement et se remplissent ensuite de ciment.
M Cottancin préconise les cloisons doubles de ce système pour la construction des murs extérieurs , il dit qu'avec des cloisons de cinq centimètres d'épaisseur simples ou doubles, renforcées de leur armature qu'il
appelle arêtes-contreforts, on peut construire la façade d'une maison
de six étages   Le même constructeur a bâti les murs d'une église de
35 m. de hauteur, avec des briques armées de 11 centimètres d'épaisseur
seulement   Ces résultats sont réellement notables au point de vue
économique, mais nous craignons fort que l'on n'entre par là dans le
domaine de l'exagération qui a causé et cause encore tant de préjudices
à la construction armée.

Mais là où nous croyons que la brique peut offrir les plus grands avantages, c'est dans la construction des voûtes   Celles que nous construisons
en Catalogne avec de légères briquettes posées à plat (tradition romaine),
grâce à leur résistance et à la bonté du ciment employé, acquièrent des
résistances considérables qui permettent de leur donner des épaisseurs
qui paraissent invraisemblables qui ont pour limite non l'effort à la compression mais la déformation produite par la flexion de la voûte   Les
armatures de fer, dûment calculées, permettraient d'empêcher cette
déformation et par conséquent de diminuer encore l'épaisseur   Le
résultat pratique obtenu par cette innovation ne serait pas précisément
l'économie, car le métal des armatures coûterait passablement plus cher
que la maçonnerie supprimée par la réduction de l'épaisseur , mais on
pourrait augmenter la limite actuelle quant à la portée donnée aux voûtes,
ce qui, en dernier terme, contribuerait à l'économie générale de la construction

Finalement l'emploi du système armé est parfaitement indiqué pour la
construction des hourdis en briques pleines dont on fait un si grand
usage en Catalogne, lesquels travaillant à la flexion, exigent une épaisseur
assez considérable proportionnée à la faible résistance du ciment à l'extension   Le placement convenable de quelques fers à la partie inférieure
du hourdis permettrait d'en diminuer l'épaisseur, ou bien, comme dans
les voûtes, on pourrait augmenter considérablement la distance entre les
appuis et par conséquent diminuer le nombre des poutres

La considération du prix élevé du béton et du mortier de ciment
Portland a donné lieu de chercher l'économie par d'autres moyens que la
brique . nous avons déjà vu que quelques constructeurs confiant presque
toute la résistance à l'armature métallique employaient des mortiers ou
bétons de bas prix parmi ces derniers on peut utiliser avantageusement
le mâchefer

V.

Traitons maintenant la question au point de vue qui nous intéresse
davantage comme architectes, je veux dire, au point de vue de l'esthétique
En donnant une plus grande importance à ce point qu'aux autres, nous ne
prétendons pas mettre de côté l'aspect mécanique et constructif qui
évidemment doit accompagner l'esthétique dans tout œuvre architectonique : mais tout ce qui regarde le côté purement scientifique du ciment
armé ayant été longuement et minutieusement étudié par un grand
nombre d'hommes de science et en particulier d'ingénieurs, nous osons

affirmer qu'il serait difficile de rien ajouter d'essentiel à ce qui a été étudié jusqu'ici

Par contre ce n'est que depuis peu que les architectes ont commencé à s'occuper sérieusement de l'emploi artistique de cette nouvelle construction, et la question a été lumineusement discutée dans le dernier Congrès International de Madrid   Comme il fallait s'y attendre, deux tendances se manifestèrent alors   les partisans à outrance du ciment armé, qui trouvaient en celui-ci tous les avantages possibles et ceux qui l'admettent avec de nombreuses restrictions dont la principale est précisément le manque de caractère artistique.

Un simple raisonnement suffit, croyons-nous, pour circonscrire la question en la plaçant dans ses justes limites.   La construction en béton ou ciment armé est-elle assujettie à une forme déterminée ?   Evidemment non.   Au contraire, comme toute concrétion ne peut affecter d'autre forme que celle du moule qu'on lui applique, il est en notre pouvoir de lui donner la forme qui nous paraît convenable.   Mais si cela est certain, nous ne devons pas oublier cependant que toutes les formes ne sont pas également logiques et économiques   En effet la forme doit être en rapport avec la nature et le mode de travail du matériel , et comme, dans le cas présent, au lieu d'une concrétion homogène nous en avons une formée de deux corps absolument distincts, comme le ciment et le fer . .   de là un dualisme de principes qui fait qu'on s'incline de préférence à donner à la construction la forme du matériel dominant . le simple examen d'un bon nombre d'édifices construits ainsi nous en est une preuve.   Dans la plupart des systèmes de plafonds, dans lesquels le travail du mortier à la compression est très important, on adopte les formes droites et les profils rectangulaires, dans les poutres et poutrelles, comme dans le hourdis, c'est-à-dire les mêmes formes que nous adoptons dans une construction en bois.   Mais supposons maintenant qu'il s'agisse d'une construction de dimensions extraordinaires, un pont par exemple, lorsque son amplitude arrive à une certaine limite, le travail à la compression du mortier atteint un coefficient excessif et il faudra augmenter considérablement sa section et par conséquent le poids mort qui chargera les armatures métalliques, ce qui obligera à augmenter la quantité de fer   Quand cette quantité sera sensiblement égale à celle que réclame la construction d'un pont homogène métallique de mêmes dimensions, la raison d'être du ciment armé au point de vue économique aura disparu   C'est pour cela que lorsque dans cet ordre de travaux les constructeurs se rapprochent de cette limite, comme le fer a beaucoup plus d'importance que le béton, ils donnent à la construction les mêmes formes que ses analogues en fer, ce que nous pouvons voir dans les ponts construits à l'aide de cette nouvelle concrétion

Mais, hors ces cas extrêmes, et concrétant la question aux constructions architectoniques de grande élévation, il est certain que, grâce au ciment armé, nous pouvons employer une grande variété de formes droites et courbes dans les ouvertures, les plafonds, toitures, etc , avec très peu de différence quant au prix, si ce n'est pour la confection des moules   En outre les formes obtenues par ce procédé sont susceptibles d'embellissements à peu de frais, ce qui plaide en faveur de l'économie du système mais c'est justement contre ce procédé que nous ferons quelques objections.   Peut-on admettre le moulage comme principal moyen d'obtenir les formes décoratives ?   Nous nous adressons à un Congrès d'Architectes et si notre humble travail méritait les honneurs de la discussion nous sommes sûrs que toutes les opinions seraient unanimes sur ce point.   Il n'est pas possible que l'architecte accepte de plein gré cette ingérence trop accentuée du moulage sur la forme, et s'il l'accepte ce ne sera que par circonstance, mais jamais comme moyen systématique.   C'est pour cela que nous n'admettons point au nombre des avantages du ciment armé la facilité d'obtenir les formes décoratives.   Celles-ci doivent s'étendre jusqu'à appliquer à la concrétion des matériaux d'un autre caractère, pierres naturelles ou artificielles, qui laissent à l'architecte plus de liberté d'action que le ciment seul.

En architecture la couleur est inséparable de la forme : ce sont les deux facteurs constituants de la beauté. Si, comme nous venons de le voir, la forme s'adapte docilement à la volonté de l'architecte, il n'en est pas de même de la couleur. Des deux éléments constitutifs de la concrétion dont nous parlons seul le ciment est apparent, le métal reste caché. et la couleur des ciments n'est certes ni assez agréable ni assez variée pour servir de base à une décoration monochrome ou polychrome A ce point de vue le béton est en infériorité évidente sur les autres travaux de maçonnerie. Si donc le ciment armé doit entrer dans la catégorie des constructions architectoniques il est de toute nécessité que, à l'instar de toutes les concrétions employés dans les diverses périodes de notre art, il soit revêtu de matériaux dont l'aspect et la richesse fassent oublier la pauvreté de la concrétion. Inutile même d'indiquer la voie à suivre pour atteindre ce résultat, car c'est le désir de tous et nous avons déjà de très beaux exemples de ce principe heureusement appliqué par d'éminents architectes, parmi lesquels M de Baudot occupe le premier rang

Résumé

La structure en ciment armé ne résout aucun nouveau problème d'art ou de construction , c'est une structure mixte composée de matériaux pierreux et métalliques, au moyen de laquelle, mettant à profit les propriétés des deux composants, on résout plus économiquement les difficultés qu'on ne pourrait le faire avec chacun d'eux en particulier

L'économie dans le ciment armé ne dépend pas du bas prix des matériaux qui le composent et qui sont relativement chers, mais de leur juste combinaison qui permet d'en réduire la quantité L'économie a par conséquent une limite dans le coefficient maximum du travail du fer et du béton

Il n'y a pas de raison pour que ces coefficients, surtout celui du béton, soient plus élevés que dans les constructions homogènes, car il y a une foule de circonstances, toutes difficiles à prevoir, qui peuvent produire des résistances inférieures à celles qui ont servi de base dans le calcul telles sont · la qualité du ciment, la nature et la grosseur des sables et des graviers, la manipulation et l'emploi des divers matériaux

Cette considération a produit divers systèmes dans lesquels on fait abstraction presque complète du travail du ciment, ou tout au moins on ne le fait pas entrer en ligne de compte dans le calcul il est dès lors considéré comme une simple enveloppe extérieure destinée à protéger le métal contre les agents qui tendraient à le détruire, comme l'oxidation et le feu.

La sécurité arrive à son maximum dans ces systèmes, mais par contre l'économie diminue il peut se faire que ces maçonneries deviennent moins économiques que d'autres homogènes, comme par exemple la brique posée au ciment

Dans les pays où l'on a de la brique excellente que l'on emploie par une coutume déjà ancienne, en épaisseurs très réduites soit dans les éléments servant de soutien soit dans les éléments soutenus (voûtes et planchers horizontaux), on pourrait introduire le système d'armer ces constructions, obtenant ainsi une plus grande économie que dans les maçonneries homogènes et celles en béton armé

Dans les endroits où la construction en brique ne réunit pas les conditions indiquées l'emploi du ciment armé présente une économie réelle et effective sur tous les autres systèmes de construction économie qu'il ne convient pas d'exagérer en admettant des coefficients de travail très supérieurs à ceux que l'expérience a reconnus comme étant d'une sécurité

absolue , on peut recommander comme tels les systèmes dont l'armature
en fer est calculée pour pouvoir résister à tous les efforts extérieurs

Quant au point de vue artistique de la question, le ciment armé n'a
pas de forme exclusive ; au contraire, comme toute concrétion il s'accommode à celle qui lui est imposée   L'élément soutenant, couvrant un vide,
peut être droit (poutre) ou courbe (arceau) ; le premier a dans sa longueur
une limite relativement restreinte ; le second l'a beaucoup plus étendue,
comme cela a lieu d'ailleurs dans les constructions homogènes.

Dans la forme droite comme dans la courbe la limite théorique du
ciment armé exige, à cause du poids propre du béton, l'emploi dans les
armatures d'un plus grand volume de fer que celui qui est exigé dans les
constructions métalliques homogènes   La relation ou le rapport entre
les unités de résistance et de poids est treize fois plus grand dans le ciment
que dans le fer   Il s'ensuit qu'à mesure qu'augmentent les dimensions
absolues des travaux en ciment armé l'importance du fer sur le ciment
augmente aussi et en conséquence les formes sont alors les caractéristiques
des constructions métalliques, comme on peut le remarquer dans les
grands ponts.

En revanche, dans les travaux architectoniques où l'on ne prétend
presque jamais atteindre le maximum des dimensions possibles, le caractère artistique doit résulter des lignes, des saillies et de la coloration
dans les premiers l'architecte peut choisir librement, sans restriction
aucune , les seconds, quels qu'ils soient, moulures, embellissements, d'ornementation, etc , peuvent s'obtenir aussi avec facilité et économie relative,
mais avec l'inconvénient de devoir pour leur exécution recourir au moulage,
ce qui indique une limitation de l'effet artistique ce à quoi ne peut se
résoudre l'art architectonique.   Quant à la couleur on ne peut admettre
comme unique celle du ciment, mais il faut au contraire traiter cette concrétion moderne comme on traitait celles de l'antiquité, c'est-à-dire en
les revêtant en tout ou en partie d'autres matériaux dont la coloration
variée permette d'obtenir l'effet désiré, et comme le pratiquent déjà
certains architectes et ingénieurs qui ont réussi à employer dans leurs
travaux le ciment armé avec un cachet tout à fait artistique

DISCUSSION ON SUBJECT III

The CHAIRMAN, in opening the proceedings, said that the subject for
discussion was one of life interest   It was one which appealed to them
from many points of view—from the economic view, from the purely
constructional view, and from the view of the appropriate expression
of the material in the design   He was sure they had so many speakers
who would be able to treat the subject from the various points of view
that it would indeed be curious if they did not carry away with them much
light upon the subject

The following discussion ensued upon the reading of Mr. Goodrich's
Paper (p 163), which was one of the first read —

Mr E O. SACHS asked to be allowed to make a few remarks on Mr
Goodrich's very valuable Paper   In the first place, he wished to thank
the author for coming over and telling them about one of the biggest
buildings in reinforced concrete erected in the United States recently.
In the course of the Paper the word " cinder " had been used constantly,
and he would like to know the definition of that term in the United States.
Did it come within the term " coke-breeze " as used in this country,
or was it more used in the definition of " clinker " ?

Mr GOODRICH replied that " clinker " was the more synonymous word.

Mr SACHS said that reference had been made to the fact that the fire

insurance companies' regulations specified the aggregate to be used.
One heard constantly of rock and stone aggregates, but experiments
had been made showing that clinker aggregates and slag aggregates had
a far higher fire resistance than these aggregates.

Mr. GOODRICH said that the experiments in the United States, as in
this country, showed that clinker and coke-breeze had a higher resisting
point, but the insurance companies thought the rock and stone aggregate
was equivalent.

Mr. SACHS asked where the aggregate was defined The fire-office
regulations in this country required, he believed, that every part of the
aggregate should pass a 1-inch mesh That was of the utmost importance,
as they found in tests and in actual cases of fire that aggregates split and
the larger pieces fell off, with the result that the metal became red-hot
and the beams deflected.

Mr GOODRICH said the rules did not define the aggregate, except that
it should be able to pass between the bars, and in no case be larger than
2½ inches.

Mr SACHS said that the object of primary importance so far as fire
resistance was concerned was the protection of all metal-work The metal-
work should be protected by a certain number of inches The number of
inches could not be exactly defined by the present state of science, but
it would certainly be 2 inches or more. He would say, however, that it
was of equal importance on this question of the thickness of the protecting
covering that the aggregate should be defined Further, as safeguards
for the actual construction and the additional protection, which could
be obtained at practically no expense, was the rounding-off of external
angles. He offered those three points as being most important in relation
to fire protection and reinforced concrete

Mr MAX CLARKE said he would like to ask the reader of the Paper
what was the definition of "clinker." Mr. Goodrich had told them
that this was one of the aggregates which applied, and that cinder was
another, but he wanted to get a hard-and-fast definition of "clinker " He
thought the material to form the aggregate of concrete was one of the
subjects which were going to be considered by the Joint Committee on
Reinforced Concrete, and it appeared to him that very serious investigation on the point was needed, and it could not be too thorough, as it was
now fairly well known, from the experiments conducted by the British Fire
Prevention Committee, that light and porous materials were generally
the best in case of the outbreak of fire, but not the most satisfactory for
strength-giving in construction For the latter purpose most people
would admit that gravel would be used from choice, but it was almost
the worst from a fire point of view Whether some happy combination
could be thought of remained to be evolved from the deliberations of
those who had the matter in hand, and he would ask Mr. Goodrich whether
such combinations had been worked out at all in America The Fire
Offices Committee in London excepted coke-breeze from their list of
materials for the aggregate of reinforced concrete, and he understood the
regulations of New York were on the same lines It was not used as one
of the materials, but cinder was He would like Mr Goodrich to give a
hard-and-fast definition as to what coke-breeze was, and also as to what
cinder was contrasted with clinker With regard to coke-breeze, he
knew the Fire Offices Committee objected to it on account of its having
a small proportion of unburned coal in it , but, as a matter of fact, they had
discovered from experience that unburned coal in the concrete, subjected
to 1,800 degrees of heat for three hours, came out just as it was put in,
and anyone present wishing to see the specimens was at liberty to do so.

Mr. GOODRICH said the definitions differed. They tried to exclude
materials which were poor. Some engineers allowed soft bituminous
coal ash or clinker to be used. Others required the use only of anthracite

material   His personal opinion was that anthracite only should be used
In some cases he had required screening and washing of materials. so as to
exclude the fine material, which would be nothing more than sand of poor
quality, and which would serve to bring the cement into a hard material
which would take the place, primarily, of gravel, except that it was more
porous.   It was almost impossible to exclude unburned coal, and in some
cases where tests had been made the unburned coal was 50 per cent. of
the clinker, and this was found to be very little affected, except on the
surface which was close to the fire   The use of 2 or 3 inches of covering was well where it could be done, but it seemed unnecessary in many
cases, especially with small material   In any case the use of a certain
amount of unburned coal was almost necessary, and, in all probability,
was not detrimental.   Whenever the unit system was employed, if it was
thought worth while, the lower portion of the aggregate could be made of
fireproof material, and the compression part on the top could be made of
rock aggregate   This had actually been used in some cases, and he himself
had made such a beam before Captain Sewell brought up the matter in a
Paper before the American Society of Engineers

M AUGUSTIN REY (Architecte de la fondation Rothschild, Paris) ·
Messieurs, nous venons d'entendre, de M. E P Goodrich, de New-York, la
plus intéressante communication.   Il vient de nous montrer comment, par
la Fédération créée entre les Compagnies d'assurances contre l'incendie,
des méthodes uniformes de construire certains éléments ont été adoptées
Résoudre de cette manière si ingénieuse l'abaissement des primes est
une des solutions les plus élégantes qu'il soit possible de rêver.   Amener
à un haut degré de perfection la construction des murs, des planchers,
des escaliers, des cages d'ascenseurs, multiplier les portes automatiques
isolant les différents blocs de l'édifice, de manière à circonscrire dès le
début un foyer d'incendie, sont des résultats remarquables et dont nous
remercions hautement le Rapporteur de nous avoir fait connaître le détail
Aussi non seulement la prime du bâtiment lui-même baisse à un niveau
inconnu jusqu'ici, mais tout ce que contient ce bâtiment est assuré à des
primes notablement inférieures à celles appliquées aux bâtiments construits avec les vieilles méthodes.   Si, en Europe, nos Compagnies
d'assurances sur l'incendie, venaient à dresser le chapitre des modifications à faire subir à certains points de nos constructions dans le
but d'abaisser les primes, ce serait une voie nouvelle, plus rationnelle,
à laquelle seraient conviés tous les constructeurs et qui permettrait
de développer d'une manière vraiment rationnelle la construction de nos
grandes cités.   Il y a là une conception du rôle de nos Compagnies d'assurances qui mérite une attention toute spéciale de leurs Conseils d'Administration   Nous demanderons à M. Goodrich, qui vient de nous ouvrir
par ses déclarations des aperçus tout nouveaux comme renseignement
technique, de nous indiquer à quelle température sont faits aux Etats-
Unis les essais de résistance au feu

Mr G. B. POST said it might be of interest to the gentlemen present to
know that those in large practice as architects in the United States used
ferro-concrete with considerable trepidation, from the fact that there
were no established constants which could be employed in computing the
strains.   They did not know, under different conditions, even, what the
position of the neutral axis of the beams should be under different loadings.
The material itself must be most carefully mixed, and all the ingredients
must be perfect, as it was subject to failure   In fact, their opinion of the
material was very much like that of the distinguished Mr Weller with
regard to veal pies—they were "werry good things when you know'd
the lady as made them"   They all looked to the time when they would
know more with regard to the subject   Those who were putting up work
with enormous rapidity, and who were required constantly to build eight,
ten, twelve, or twenty story buildings in eleven months, were looking

forward to the time when they would have more scientific data which would enable them to use the material in a more scientific and less amateurish way   His object in speaking was to say that he had had the honour to be appointed, with Mr. Eames, by the President of the United States a member of an Advisory Board which had been instructed to make extensive tests of all building materials, as well as coal and fuel and various things of that kind. He had urged the Commission that very careful experiments should be made with regard to reinforced concrete, so that the same error would not be found in the calculations with regard to reinforced concrete which was found in the constants for wood which were determined from experiments and tests carried out on small sections   Fortunately for their country the errors in the loads required by the building laws almost exactly compensated for the deficiency in the constants in the building materials. He did not know whether Congress had made the necessary appropriation for the continuance of those experiments in the last session or not, but if the appropriation had been made he believed that before the next Congress assembled America would be able to furnish them with valuable information with regard to the whole subject   There was one other point which was to have most careful and thorough investigation, and that was the question as to whether cement was or was not an efficient protection of steel from corrosion   He had seen steel in small sections in the form of expanded metal used in tabular floor construction which was exposed twelve months to the atmosphere, and which was absolutely destroyed by corrosion   Thus, of course, might have been an exceptional defect due to some curious ignates which could not be determined either by physical or chemical tests ; but it was necessary for the safe use of the material that they should know how to protect steel.   Another matter not mentioned in the regulations of the Committee which had been brought before them that morning, and which he thought should receive attention, was the danger of electrolysis from the huge free current of electricity in all their great cities

Mr. Goodrich, replying to the question asked by M. Rey, viz. " To what temperature have the experiments as to the fireproof qualities been pursued ? " said that the actual temperatures found by the use of the melting-point of building materials varied from 1,400 deg to 2,000 deg. In the Baltimore fire the temperature varied from 1,400 deg. to slightly over 2,000 deg   It was between these limits that the tests had been made   He believed that the United States Building Department required that a temperature of 1,800 deg should be maintained for eight hours   In some cases the temperature was raised and had been maintained at over 2,000 deg., but the usual temperature was from 1,700 deg. to 1,800 deg Fahr. for several hours. Then the question was asked whether the methods of construction referred to were applied to buildings several stories high, such as working-class dwellings, and so on, and he might say that he had at the present time an office building of eleven stories high, and also several dwellings from three to six stories high, and in San Francisco nearly $1,000,000 worth of work of buildings from one to six stories high.

Mr. A. W. Ruddle (Peterborough) said he had been rather troubled by the statements of the speakers from America. He did not know whether he had made a mistake, but he understood Mr. Goodrich to say that it was unnecessary to use two rods in the reinforcing of steel work

Mr. Goodrich   Under certain conditions

Mr. Ruddle said he took it that there was no necessity to obtain any greater external area of the steel, because he understood that the concrete adhered to the steel work, and that the reinforcing in the members which were to give additional strength against tensile strains was given by the adhesion of the concrete to the steel   However, another speaker had raised a point as to whether cement was an adequate protection of steel, and if they coated their steel with any paint they lost at once the adhesion of the concrete to the steel which was to be of so much assistance.

The following discussion took place after the reading of the other Papers brought before the Meeting —

Mr. SACHS thanked the readers of the Papers, and said they had each brought out points which were of the utmost importance to them as architects if they were going to keep the building of reinforced concrete structures in their own hands. He meant chiefly the effect of these buildings upon the public Reinforced concrete buildings at the present moment were being utilised, many for utilitarian purposes of the factory and warehouse class, and if the material was to come forward it was necessary for the architect to settle down and think how reinforced concrete buildings put up in cities were going to be dealt with from the architectural point of view—that is to say, how it should be clothed. It was surely one of those things which should come before their architectural societies and before the students of those societies The problem was how to deal with these large flat surfaces, which must necessarily form a reinforced concrete building, and anything which could be done to bring that before architects in the future would be most valuable to the profession, because it would mean that architects would be able to retain buildings of that material in their own hands, instead of such buildings being erected by the engineer

Mr F E. HARRIS (Manchester) said that, having been instrumental in putting up a few reinforced-concrete buildings in this country, it had been frequently asked him what were the qualities of the external walls in relation to non-conductibility. This was, of course, a matter which did not largely apply in connection with manufacturing premises, and up to the present reinforced concrete had been mainly used for such buildings only. If they were to use reinforced concrete for any purpose other than manufacturing buildings they would want to know among other things whether the walls were good non-conductors Their colleagues from America and from the Continent would probably have used armoured concrete for domestic buildings, and would perhaps be able to tell them what the qualities of the walls were in this connection. One other point struck him The walls were all right, and the effect was all right for manufacturing premises They could get sufficient effect from using armoured concrete purely and simply, but if any real architectural effect was desired they wanted something more than they got in manufacturing premises The only way in which they could get that, so far as he had been able to weigh the matter up at present, was by the wasteful use of the material they had, or, as an alternative, to simply use the armoured concrete for the columns and floors His view at present was that they must simply use armoured concrete for walls and floors, for he did not see how they could get any architectural effect such as would be agreeable to clients unless they limited their use of the materials for the purposes he had mentioned. There was a flatness about armoured concrete which would be objectionable unless they used an excessive amount of material, and that, of course, would not be an economical thing to do. He would personally like to have an expression of opinion from their Continental visitors on two points . (1) As to the qualities of reinforced concrete walls for resisting heat and cold, and (2) whether they found they got a good architectural effect not merely by decorating the outside of the surface ; and if so, could they get it economically ?

Mr E. WARREN said he would like to introduce a second question with regard to the possibilities of architectural effect, for he was much struck by Professor Cloquet's conclusion dealing with the æsthetic side of the subject It seemed to him that if they were to deal with plain surfaces in which construction in the architectural sense was absent, they must resort to some merely plastic form of decoration or applied decoration. To be honest, in dealing with this form of construction, he would like to ask those who had considered the use of the material whether any serious attempt had been made to give it a real constructive or architectural expression, because if there was no constructive or architectural expression in the building, it was not architecture at all   There could be no architectural inspiration, and no architectural enthusiasm could be aroused by dealing with a structure in which they could not give any external expression whatever, and in which no constructive problem arose. If any of the distinguished architects from the Continent would inform them as to what experiments had been made in the direction of the real architectural use of this material, they would all be very much the gainers.

M. Louis Cloquet (Belgium) · Je crains de ne pas avoir bien compris ce qui a été dit, car j'ignore, j'en suis honteux, la belle langue anglaise, mais un confrère a bien voulu me dire en deux mots l'objet de la discussion   D'abord, on a demandé si on peut s'opposer à la transmission de la chaleur à travers les parois, et si on peut revêtir d'un relief les édifices en ciment armé.   J'ai indiqué tout à l'heure, précisément comme une chose inévitable, que les édifices en ciment armé seront construits à doubles parois.   La membrure de ces surfaces, quoique de même largeur, est assez développée, et comme elle n'est pas décorative, on aura souvent intérêt à les cacher dans les interstices dont j'ai parlé   Cela est d'ailleurs intéressant au point de vue de la résistance.   En effet, à l'aide de ces interstices, on a réalisé une merveille architecturale qui a vraiment étonné le monde   Je crois que ce même procédé nous donnera à la fois la solidité et l'étanchéité, car entre les deux parois il restera un air confiné réfractaire à la chaleur.   En ce qui concerne la décoration, il est entendu, me semble-t-il, que le décor architectonique auquel nous sommes familiers est un décor ayant un caractère intellectuel , mais il n'est pas permis de dire que nous sommes en présence de la faillite de la plastique   Quant à moi, j'attends la solution du problème, et dans les constructions en béton armé je suis persuadé que nous allons voir resplendir à nouveau la peinture et les arts plastiques, qui s'accommoderont très facilement à un nouveau système. La question est posée et il faut bien qu'elle soit résolue.   Vous ne m'en voudrez pas, à cet égard, si je triche un peu pour le temps accordé aux orateurs en vous lisant la fin de mon rapport qui précisément traite cette partie de la discussion   [*M. Cloquet read part of his Paper printed at* p 170.]

Replying to Mr E. O Sachs, the Chairman said he would be prepared to entertain any resolutions which might be proposed

Mr Max Clarke said that in the Papers which had been read before the Congress and elsewhere it seemed to have been accepted that the material, or combination of materials, now known as reinforced concrete was satisfactory in every respect, and the only remark he saw bearing on this particular point was that by Mr. Henry Adams where he spoke of failures   No doubt they would all like to learn something by failures, but they were naturally anxious that such failures should occur, if at all, in other people's buildings, and not in their own. Where they did take place they were not made as public as they ought to be.   Of course it was quite natural for a man not to let his failures be more widely known than he could help ; but, on the other hand as Mr Adams observed, it was only by such failures that they learned something about a full-sized experiment. They had a very large number of minor experiments, but not of the failures in a full-sized experiment, and that was exactly what they wanted   In Switzerland last month he heard a great deal of conversation with regard to the failure of a building at Basle, but he could not learn from anybody what the actual facts of the case were, and he did not suppose that if he went there now he would be able to find out the cause of this particular upset.   Bearing all this in mind, it seemed to him that an inquiry in the direction of what failures had taken place and

their causes would be desirable   Another matter to which he thought
the attention of members connected with this class of construction should
be called was whether any data existed as to the life of the steelwork in
combination with concrete.   Most people knew that it was a most difficult
thing to make concrete sufficiently close or homogeneous, so that it would
not allow the passage of air or moisture.   If not consolidated enough to
make it impervious to these two agents, deterioration might take place
in the reinforcing bars, and the structure would lose all the qualities on
which its stability depended, and on which the calculations had been
based.   He took it that this deterioration might also damage the concrete
itself, not only the steel rods for once the steel rods began to rust the rust
on them would damage the concrete by expansion, and it would be quite
impossible to ascertain the nature and effect of the damage (assuming
his premisses were correct) before the building was so seriously damaged
as to collapse   People talked in a light and airy manner about adhesion,
Portland cement, concrete, and steelwork.   They also said that they had
seen pieces of hoop-iron and other sorts of iron and steel taken out of buildings
where they had been for twenty-eight years, and that they could see the
original blue on them   That he had done himself , but, on the other hand,
he had seen a considerable amount of experimental reinforced concrete,
and he had observed that this concrete did not close itself up to the metal,
and that there were a number of interstices which had never been filled.
They must presume that they were filled with something, and, if it was not
with liquid, it was with some vapour, and this vapour, he took it, would
be either damp or dry, according to the state of the weather.   This
particular phase of this particular type of construction seemed to be the
one which should be thoroughly gone into   If they erected a building
two stories high, suitable for an agricultural labourer's dwelling, it did not
make much difference whether it lasted fifty years or not , but if they
erected a building of the monumental type which was supposed to represent
a very considerable sum of money, he took it that it was the duty of those
who designed the building, or, at any rate, who advocated the use of
this material, to be prepared to show what its life would be   So far as
he had been able to ascertain, no sufficient inquiry had been devoted to
this particular point   They were talking about reinforced concrete because
a certain number of gentlemen, whom he called " patentees," and other
people called experts, had put the thing on the market.   He thought, as
architects, they should not be carried away too rapidly.   With regard to
the architectural treatment of the material under discussion, he would like
to add that it was quite possible to apply decorative details to concrete,
and he had seen it done abroad   They could cast ornaments and place
them on buildings, but it was not architecture.   It was merely sticking a
lot of stuff on to a concrete wall   If they were going to descend to that
sort of thing in their architecture it would be very much better if they had
nothing to do with reinforced concrete at all, for they were going to lose
something.   One other question he would like to ask, and that was on
the subject of cost   No one was able to tell him what the cost of a reinforced-concrete building was   If Mr Goodrich would append to his Paper
the cost of the building he had described they would have an idea as to
whether it was worth their while to depart from their present methods
He moved   " That it is the sense of this Meeting that an inquiry into
the cases of failure in reinforced concrete and their causes would be most
desirable."

The CHAIRMAN formally seconded the resolution.

Mr E O SACHS, in supporting the resolution, said it was really of
the utmost importance that they should know what the failures were   He
was with the mover of the resolution in Switzerland a few weeks ago when
the accident at Basle formed the subject of much discussion, and he made
what effort he could to get hold of the actual facts of the case   The facts

of that case were available in the form of a report by three borough surveyors of three of the principal Swiss cities. It was in the form of a confidential report to the Basle authorities, but, although confidential at the time (for the accident occurred in 1901), the authorities were good enough to say that for the object of scientific research the report could be seen   He had a copy of the report, and he had no doubt but that copies of all such reports would be at the service of a committee dealing with the subject.   There was a similar case in Alexandria, Egypt, and two or three cases in the United States, and if real independent reports, and not *ex parte* reports, could be put before an independent committee, such as the Reinforced Concrete Committee which had been formed by the Royal Institute of British Architects, or any similar body, and the causes of failure arrived at and the results summarised, they would be the most valuable lessons they could learn from

Mr. HENRY ADAMS said that, as one who had suggested a new reading of an old proverb, he would like to support the resolution   They were all agreed that ferro-concrete to be satisfactory should be solid, but they had been told, in the first place, that the American practice allowed $2\frac{1}{2}$ inches for the aggregate, while the English practice wisely brought them down to 1 inch   But neither of these took account of what seemed to him to be the most important matter of all—viz the grading of the material to various sizes   This was brought home to him very closely a short time ago, when, after the Fire-prevention Committee had discovered that broken brick was one of the best materials if not the best which could be adapted, a firm in London commenced to manufacture broken brick and screened it to pass a 1-inch mesh.   All the smaller material was done away with.   They thus threw away what was the most valuable part.   If they had simply removed the dust and retained the particles, from $\frac{1}{4}$ inch to 1 inch, he believed they would have obtained a sounder material.   When there were alterations and pulling down of buildings and ferro-concrete was exposed, they all knew that spaces did show in the material, and they should not show   If they wanted proper adhesion to the steel they had the concrete solid   He believed that more than one of the failures would be found to arise from the improper mixing of the aggregate, and he looked upon the grading of the material as one of the most important points in connection with it.

Mr. HORATIO K BROMHEAD (Glasgow) asked whether it was possible to really know the actual material under discussion   Steel was well known from tests   Cement was partially known from tests   But when reinforced concrete was named, there was no knowing exactly what was referred to   Concrete was made by many different dilutions or adulterations, not one of which was by a standard or even generally recognised formula   All that can be said of concrete is that its strength is *generally* more than one-tenth of its bulk of Portland cement, and sometimes a great deal more , with its adulteration composed according to fancy   Before a scientific discussion of reinforced concrete could be valuable there must be at least one (or more) definite formula for the manufacture of the concrete, with some tests of its strength in the proposed forms of its use, and further tests showing its increase of strength when certain known and indicated reinforcers are added in the same forms of concrete and conditions

The CHAIRMAN remarked that from something which had been said it might be in the minds of those present that good practice in America justified the use of $2\frac{1}{2}$ inch stone in armoured concrete. It was perfectly true that certain building laws and certain underwriters' rules might permit of such construction, but it was very far from proof that the best architects in America permitted any such construction. The building laws in many States and cities were diverse, but in the principal cities the building laws were coming rapidly to a form in which they prescribed

1 inch or smaller and $\frac{3}{4}$ inch and smaller of those portions of the concrete which were reinforced with iron. Naturally, in massive concrete, larger stones were permitted In his own practice, and he thought in that of the majority of architects in America who used armoured concrete, it was the absolute rule that in the portions that were reinforced in the girders especially the size of the concrete should be 1 inch or less and preferably $\frac{3}{4}$ inch and less. It was not at all to be assumed that because certain building laws permitted the use of other materials they were generally employed. It always seemed to him that there were so many sources of possible failure in the use of reinforced concrete that it ought only to be employed under the most favourable conditions—that is to say, it must be designed by an expert very capable of calculating the strains, and knowing as much about these strains and the way of meeting them as it was possible to know in the present state of the art. In the second place, the drawings and specifications must be of the most rigorous character, and designed in as great detail as was possible before actual construction In the third place, the materials must not only be wisely chosen, but they must be submitted to rigorous tests; and, in the last place, the depositing of these materials must be done by persons under the most skilful direction and careful supervision. Only under such conditions could they hope to secure a structure in which they could have faith, and with regard to which they could rest with the assurance that it would be what they hoped it would

The resolution was then put from the Chair and carried

Mr SACHS said that, as the subject of fire-protection and reinforced concrete had been so frequently touched upon in the course of the previous discussion, he would propose a resolution which might perhaps seem a little out of place to those who were conversant with the failures of reinforced concrete in fire, but which he thought might serve as a safeguard to many architects in practice It was · "That where reinforced concrete is intended to be fire-resisting the greatest possible care must be taken in the selection of the aggregate, its size, and in the protection of the steel , further, that the aggregate does not exceed what will pass through a 1-inch mesh, and that the thickness of the protection should never be less than 2 inches." The size of the aggregate was of importance—more important to his mind sometimes than the actual mixture of the aggregate. The protection also was of importance, and the reason why he suggested that 2 inches should be put in the resolution was because so many tried to scamp that protection, and they came across reinforced concrete buildings in which the protection to the steelwork was supposed to be $\frac{1}{2}$ inch, but where they could scrape it off and find that there was not $\frac{1}{4}$ inch covering He would like to add one word as to fire tests It had been mentioned that 1,400 to over 2,000 degrees were the conflagration temperatures That was right in America and on the Continent It was further stated that in the New York rules the test required was 1,700 degrees People had asked why it should be 1,700 degrees The standard arrived at in this country at the Congress held about three years ago was 1,800 degrees, and in arriving at this figure the point brought out was this—that in all test-pieces great care was taken to make the test-piece an excellent piece , but in ordinary practice the work could not be of the same quality as the work carried out for a distinct purpose, so both in temperature and time there must be a margin for bad work. There was a consultation between London and New York on the subject, and that was why the high temperatures and long hours were hit upon

Mr. EDWIN SEWARD (Cardiff), seconding the resolution, said his more particular object in rising was to speak to a portion of the subject which did not seem to have been touched upon. While a good deal of reference had been made to the failure of reinforced concrete, he did not know whether any real experience of such failures had been given If not, he would like to give an experience of his own of failure in the use of reinforced concrete. He might preface his reference by the statement that it was a very happy failure and did nobody any harm. In that sense it might tend to illustrate what seemed to him very important possibilities in connection with the use of reinforced concrete by the architect. But first he might say he recognised that a very important disadvantage in using it was, that most methods of reinforced concrete seemed to be surrounded by the difficulties of royalties and patents. No doubt these were very excellent rewards to those whose ingenuity had devised the methods, but, at the same time, one could not help feeling that in practice they were restrictions upon the free, extensive, and applicable use which any building material should have in the architect's mind and on his drawings. To refer more particularly to this question of failure, he might say he had to deal with a building where there was an ordinary street frontage He decided to use reinforced concrete for the main construction for one reason, which was that the party-walls belonged on each hand to the neighbours, and, owing to active business uses, it was impossible to interfere with them. He found the convenience very great of being able to construct the girders within his own building instead of having to swing long steel girders and cut into the party-walls This was his first experience of reinforced concrete, and he did not think it would be a proper thing to put the front on to a main street of this material. There were chances, architecturally speaking, in the immense advantage they got from the great cantilever methods, and the reinforced concrete cantilever and its treatment might possibly in the future become a feature for architects to give their serious attention to, but in this case he had nothing of that chance , and simply dealing with a flat frontage he came to the conclusion that the frontage of the building must be of hard stone Then came the question of how the whole of the floors and a great deal of the side walls and the girder construction should be legitimately united to the front portion of the building, and he decided to have some steel anchors and anchor the frontage of hard stonework into the reinforced concrete They found one morning that the reinforced concrete had taken care of itself. They had finished their reinforced concrete 8 inches or 10 inches from the front itself, and the anchor was to unite it. But on this particular morning the new concrete floors got heavily loaded. A very zealous foreman had removed a certain number of struts in the front, and the whole mass was in just that state that it exerted a pressure towards the front. On examination he found it something like 8 inches or 9 inches out of its true plane. The whole of the girders and concrete floor had swelled forward into the cavities ready prepared in the backing of the hard stone front of the building This happy accident had the effect of throwing the end sections of the floor right into the cavities, and so quite accidentally they got a united building. It suggested to him that there might be great possibility in the architectural adaptation of the material. It was in that sense waxy, they could alter its contours; and he thought by the use of vertically curved surfaces there were architectural chances. He did not think that at this stage of its development reinforced concrete was sufficiently mobile for their requirements, but it was a great field for architectural study. The application of surface decoration was, of course, quite easily done, and the fact that reinforced concrete was made in wooden sheeting might lead to the sheeting containing incised designs or some relief which might become decorative

Mr E W. FRITCHLEY (Bombay) said that in India he had used armoured concrete and crushed-stone concrete for the last three or four years They sieved their stone It was crushed basalt, and when powdered was as good as sand They had three or four grades—one between 1 inch and $1\frac{1}{4}$ inch, another between $\frac{1}{2}$ inch and $\frac{3}{4}$ inch, and a third was almost a powder , and in no case had he had a failure They had used it in reinforcing girders, and for three years had used nothing else for floors, because the rat had to be considered, and they found that rats' teeth would not go through armoured concrete.

A delegate suggested that it would be better if the resolution was taken under two heads.

The CHAIRMAN said he would accept the suggestion and divide the resolution

Another delegate expressed the opinion that, as there was a Committee sitting dealing with points such as those discussed, it would be better if both this and the first resolution were referred to that Committee to deal with

Mr SACHS said that if the suggestion in the resolution of the 1-inch mesh was not accepted, he would suggest that the motion be taken on general lines, and therefore he amended it so as to read —" That, where reinforced concrete is intended to be fire-resisting, the greatest possible care must be taken as to the nature of the aggregate and its size, and also as to the protection of the steel "

The resolution, as amended, was then put to the Meeting and carried

In answer to a suggestion that the resolutions should be referred to the Reinforced Concrete Committee of the Royal Institute of British Architects, Mr Sachs said the Committee would be dealing with that, and a special resolution was not needed.

Mr ELLIS MARSLAND remarked that the Romans reinforced with brick and tile, but they did not leave the brick-concrete bare   They covered it up with stone and marble and other materials   He thought they were going away from the fact that reinforced concrete was a constructional material, like ordinary steelwork used for building, which was, as a rule, covered up, and he felt that it would be perfectly legitimate to cover up this reinforced concrete by either stone, or brick, or concrete.

M AUGUSTIN REY, asking permission, before the Meeting separated, to make a few remarks on a subject he considered of great importance in connection with reinforced concrete, said —Messieurs, nous avons entendu, au début de cette séance, une déclaration faite par nos Confrères Anglais nous informant qu'une commission importante, dans laquelle entrent à la fois les délégués du Gouvernement intéressé et les représentants des grandes Sociétés d'Architectes et de Constructeurs, venait d'être constituée   Cette commission est destinée à faire des recherches sur tout ce qui concerne le ciment armé   Nous devons faire remarquer au Congrès que depuis plus de vingt ans tous les grands pays étrangers ont fait des expériences officielles sur ce genre de construction   Les Gouvernements se sont fait représenter plusieurs fois dans ces expériences qui revêtent, par conséquent, un caractère presque officiel   Nous pensons donc que nos Confrères Anglais, qui sur la question d'application du ciment armé ne sont pas encore arrivés à des conclusions à l'égal des Etats-Unis, de la France, de l'Allemagne, de l'Espagne, de Belgique et d'autres pays, feront leur profit des grandes expériences faites   Dans une question de cette importance, et devant les spécialistes éminents qui sont dans cette salle, il est opportun de relever que si des travaux considérables ont été faits dans des pays autres que l'Angleterre, c'est que le ciment armé y a été étudié d'une manière approfondie depuis de très longues années et a permis des travaux considérables qui ont eu un plein succès   Certains organes de la presse technique anglaise cherchent à créer un mouvement d'études sérieuses.   Des travaux originaux, des dessins très complets, des calculs basés sur les dernières méthodes, tout particulièrement celle de M. N de Tedesco, ce précurseur et cet infatigable chercheur, auquel nous tenons ici à rendre hommage, ont été publiés en Angleterre   Nous souhaitons à nos Confrères Anglais, qui n'ont pas eu le périlleux honneur de faire ce long apprentissage de plus de vingt ans, soit en Europe soit en Amérique, pour les constructions en ciment armé, de rattraper à larges enjambées le temps perdu et de nous montrer bientôt des travaux dignes de leur audace et de leur science. Le temps nous a manqué pour donner lecture du Rapport que nous avons présenté au Congrès [p 188] Qu'on nous permette d'indiquer à larges traits, d'une manière brève, ce qui nous semble le plus interessant au point de vue social dans l'application de ces procédés de construction *La grande plaie dont nous souffrons—et cela dans tous les pays sans exception— est le surpeuplement invraisemblable dans lequel vivent nos populations urbaines* Pour Paris, dont nous avons fait une étude toute spéciale, les chiffres sont effrayants. La définition du surpeuplement est la cohabitation dans une même pièce (de 12 m. environ de surface) de plus de deux personnes. Paris a sur 651,250 familles, 260,000 d'entre elles qui vivent dans des conditions de surpeuplement Si nous prenons le chiffre global de personnes, nous voyons que 660,000 habitants sont mal logés, soit 24 % de la population totale de Paris Pour la France entière, près de quatre millions d'habitants de nos villes peuvent être considérés comme mal logés Or, *les nouvelles méthodes de construction qui ont pour base le ciment armé, qui, comme le dit si justement M. Cloquet de Gand, ne peut constituer que l'ossature, le squelette, peuvent nous apporter, par l'économie de ces procédés, le plus grand secours pour solutionner la grave question du surpeuplement urbain* Nous estimons que dans tous les cas où le ciment armé pourra être appliqué judicieusement à des constructions à étages, il diminuera le prix total de la construction d'une manière appréciable Toutes ces populations mal logées nous avons le devoir de les mieux loger à l'avenir, *tout ce qui nous permettra de réduire les frais de l'habitation constituera un bien inappréciable pour nos sociétés.* Nous convions tous nos Confrères à examiner dans ce sens et dans tous les pays où la question se pose, l'emploi du ciment armé dans l'habitation populaire ; il y va de la santé de nos grandes cités et de l'avenir social des nations Dans notre Rapport on trouvera l'étude d'une question palpitante entre toutes, celle du logement des familles nombreuses *On verra, par la disposition spéciale, et toute nouvelle, que nous avons créée, supprimant d'une manière radicale toutes les cours intérieures, quelles qu'elles soient, et les remplaçant par des cours ouvertes, largement balayées d'air et baignées de soleil, une application pratique des méthodes de construction en ciment armé.* Nous tenons à ajouter que de distance en distance nous avons conservé de grands pignons en maçonnerie destinés à résister aux pressions latérales et à constituer un rigide contreventement dans le sens longitudinal des grands corps de bâtiment On verra comment nous avons disposé les cages d'escalier, à la fois séparation et liaisonnement des corps de bâtiments Ces cages d'escaliers, dans les climats où cela est possible, sont ouvertes en plein air et constituent ce que nous appellerons *la rue verticale.* Il est, en effet, de la plus haute importance pour avoir un minimum de contamination par cette voie commune à tous les locataires, de la laisser largement ouverte à tous les vents et baignée abondamment de lumière *Loin d'être un véhicule certain de contamination, l'escalier doit être un espace aussi sûr au point de vue de l'hygiène publique que la rue.* Il est donc naturel qu'il soit entièrement ouvert. De cette manière l'air viendra frapper aux portes mêmes de chaque logement Chaque fois que la porte d'entrée du logement sera ouverte un appel d'air s'y fera, la ventilation y trouvera un surcroît d'action. Ces escaliers, construits en ciment armé, présentent presque une durée indéfinie. Ils n'ont aucun inconvénient aux intempérées extérieures. La lumière pénétrera ainsi jusqu'à l'entrée du logement et ce ne sera pas un des moindres bienfaits de cette disposition toute nouvelle. Nous pensons que cette transformation de l'escalier, dont nous sommes l'initiateur, surtout lorsqu'il s'agit d'immeubles populaires, est précieuse On verra dans la disposition des plans annexés à notre Rapport la suppression presque totale des couloirs intérieurs, véritable plaie des immeubles populaires, lorsqu'ils sont mal étudiés. Divers autres perfectionnements sont visibles dans les dessins, nous y renvoyons ceux de nos Confrères que cela pourrait intéresser Un dernier mot *Nous estimons qu'une réforme nécessaire est la suppression de la toiture surtout dans les immeubles populaires et leur remplacement par des terrasses.* Les combles, tels qu'ils sont actuellement compris, sont funestes à la santé de ceux qui les habitent Nos médecins savent à quel point l'habitation dans une maison à étages, déjà défectueuse par elle-même, devient déplorable sous les combles Nous ne parlons pas ici de leur suppression dans des bâtiments où, au point de vue artistique, ils ont une place marquée, il ne s'agit ici que de l'habitation du plus grand nombre *Tout est pour ainsi dire défectueux dans leur construction, lorsqu'il faut loger sainement des êtres humains ; l'aération ni l'éclairage ne peuvent y être assurés d'une manière complète. L'entretien de ces combles est de plus une des lourdes charges du budget, leur construction constitue une dépense importante, il n'est pas admissible que nous continuions à les maintenir lorsque tout nous permet de les modifier* L'habitation moderne doit, à notre avis, tenir compte des conditions sanitaires auxquelles doit répondre cet étage à l'égal de toutes les autres de l'habitation *Couverte en terrasses, dont les procédés les meilleurs sont à notre disposition depuis de longues années, tous ces inconvénients disparaissent L'étage des combles devient un étage carré à parois verticales extérieures permettant l'ouverture de baies à surfaces verticales. L'hygiène aura ainsi reconquis ce dernier étage et en aura fait un des plus sains, un des plus ensoleillés.* Il y a là une formule bien moderne qu'il était utile de signaler. Au Congrès International de la Tuberculose (Paris, octobre 1905) nous avons sur ce point attiré l'attention de ce Congrès ; car, ne l'oublions pas, tout ce qui intéresse l'habitation, tout ce qui l'améliore, et régénère ses formes est une attaque directe contre la tuberculose, le fléau terrible qui décime nos grandes cités Le ciment armé est donc un des procédés de construction de l'avenir, on ne saurait trop le répéter. Au point de vue social il peut jouer dans le logement des classes populaires un rôle considérable Si l'on vient nous dire qu'à certains égards c'est un rêve, nous dirons : " Rêve d'aujourd'hui sera la réalité de demain."

Subject IV

THE EDUCATION OF THE PUBLIC IN ARCHITECTURE.

Thursday morning, 19th July—Grafton Galleries.

Chairmen Sir Aston Webb, R A (England), Herr Stubben (Germany)
Hon. Secretaries. Messrs. A G Bzn Salm (Holland) ; W. H Mitchell (Ireland).

---

(1) By John Belcher, A R A , *President R.I B.A.*, President of
the Seventh International Congress of Architects

The increasing interest taken in architecture as a fine art is causing lovers
of art and the public generally to search for the principles which govern
what is universally recognised as good architecture

Hitherto the attention of the educated public has been chiefly directed
to ancient buildings as specimens worthy of admiration They have
also been shown by comparative methods how the different periods can
be recognised, and have learnt to pick out with accuracy and intelligence
the characteristic features of each " style."

Such knowledge, however valuable, is purely archæological, and does
not profess to explain *why* the buildings thus selected and pointed out for
admiration are good, nor what it is that distinguishes them from bad or
inferior work of the same period.

Moreover, the exclusive study of " styles " under which buildings have
been catalogued has proved detrimental to the advance and development
of architecture , since it has resulted in a demand for the reproduction of
some " style " of the past, which has been most admired and best understood by those desiring to build

I am, therefore, of opinion that what is now needed for the education
of the public generally is to point out in simple language, free from technicalities, the true functions of architecture and those essential qualities
which distinguish good art from bad.

Having thus briefly stated the direction in which such an educational
scheme should proceed, permit me to set forth more in detail those principles, qualities, and factors which must be more generally understood
and appreciated if a sound public taste and judgment in matters of architecture is to be created and fostered.

In any popular exposition of the principles of architecture the importance of the " plan " of a building must be emphasised at the very outset.
It must be shown that no really fine building is possible without a good
plan ; that the latter is, as it were, the root from which excellence springs ;
that though it is possible to " graft " ornamental features on to a bad
plan, and so deceive the untrained eye, such work can never attain to
high and enduring merit

It will also be necessary to make plain that architecture is not simply
an art. It is an art based upon science, and should be a perfect combination of the two

In a good work the scientific and artistic elements are so blended that they may perhaps, to a certain extent, be distinguished, but they cannot be separated.

Science lends itself to exact rules, and therefore admits of logical and precise explanations ; but art does neither

Nevertheless we can judge results, and may justly require that every work which claims our approval should exhibit certain qualities which are distinctive of good architecture   These qualities spring from two great principles which we may now proceed to consider.

Truth.

The first great principle that must be sought and required in architecture is *truth*

Good architecture never deceives the eye even for a moment.

Nothing must appear to be other than it is.   There must be no false statement or suggestion either in regard to the purpose or construction of the building, nor any hiding under one external feature that which is usually expressed by another.

A church must not be like a town-hall nor a town-hall like an assembly-room   The character of the building must be true to the purpose for which it is designed

There is a principle of truth also in the use and treatment of material Each kind has its true place and its true form or forms, corresponding with natural qualities.   There is a " sense of fitness " which instinctively recognises the proper disposition of materials, and knowledge and experience teach the best forms.

Again, not only must the relative position of the different materials be appropriate, but the methods of support and resistance of the different parts of the building amongst themselves should be clear and well defined. It is not sufficient that the building be strong and solid , it must have the *appearance* of strength and solidity.

This element of fitness and satisfaction of the eye, which is always present in good architecture, is the essential difference between engineering and architecture   Engineering is purely scientific, but architecture should be artistic as well as scientific   Its work represents science *plus* art   The engineer is satisfied with the minimum of material for a given end, whereas the architect must provide more than that , for every building has not only to be true in fact, from the scientific and practical side, it has also to be true to the eye ; it must satisfy the spectator's sense of truth and fitness

The engineer may know by exact mathematical calculation that a small steel column or stanchion is quite adequate support for a heavy brick wall or for several stones ; but such a triumph of exact science is apt to make the beholder shudder

In architecture—where science is allied with art—there are other considerations to be taken into account   Not only must the materials in use be sound and capable of supporting one another, but their relative positions must be appropriate, and their combination must express the purpose of the structure

Above all, the essential element of truth must be exhibited   It cannot be said that a slight steel structure, however safe it may be, covered externally with a thin shell or casing in a material intended to appear like solid masonry complies with this requirement   Nor are the conditions truthful which make a building appear to be standing on a sheet of plate glass, as if it were suspended in the air without adequate support !

In all the elements of good architecture it is truth which must be paramount , and in proportion as this is faithfully presented will the building impress the beholder.

Beauty.

The spirit of beauty which Shelley describes as "dear and yet dearer for its mystery" is the second great principle of architecture.

It is a very elusive quantity, and, despite the many efforts which since the days of Lessing have been made to analyse its constituent elements, it still remains "dearer for its mystery"

It is protean in its many shapes, yet so far as it can be made to take a concrete form it leads to the highest excellence.

Its power is to kindle the imagination and rouse the emotions.

A noble building of imposing mass and stately outlines strikes deep and solemn chords in the human heart.   The eye rests with delight upon the subtle lines and curves, the pure and refined detail of some beautiful home, because of the lofty thought and tender sentiment that they arouse to activity

Beauty of form is, perhaps, less generally appreciated than beauty of colour, but neither may be ignored as a well-spring of powerful emotion. Both kinds of beauty should be looked for and required in any work that claims to be good architecture

The two great fundamental principles—truth and beauty—will find expression in and be recognised by the following qualities :—

    (1) Strength.
    (2) Vitality.
    (3) Restraint
    (4) Refinement
    (5) Repose.
    (6) Grace.
    (7) Breadth.
    (8) Scale.

1. *Strength.*

It was Sir Christopher Wren who said that "a good building ought certainly to possess the attribute of eternal." Truly a building should be constructed to endure and survive the shocks of time   It must also have the appearance of strength. Like the everlasting hills (or man's counterpart, the Pyramids of Egypt) it must appear to be solidly planted in the soil, and must seem to take hold of it.   The strength of a tree is in its roots, and the width of its trunk as it rises from the ground is proportional to the branches it has to support   So a building which presents an appearance of vitality will suggest a growth from a strong base.   The largest and firmest parts and details will be seen in the lowest stage, while the upper stages will be found to increase in lightness and delicacy.

In addition to the largeness of form and detail in the lower stages, the idea of strength is also conveyed by the use of the strongest material. Granite, for instance, is suggestive of strength and solidity, and the fact that this building material is obtained in large blocks adds to the sense of security and firmness   When used with judgment it renders most effectual aid in convincing the eye that everything placed on it is secure and most fittingly supported.

2. *Vitality.*

Good architecture should show evidence of life, and the methods of construction should be such as are expressive of vitality and growth This element or quality will make itself felt in many subtle ways

The conventional treatment of the evidence of life in the world of nature around us furnishes the necessary architectural symbols.

The most striking suggestions of vitality and growth in architecture seem to follow the analogy of trees or plants, which, rising from a base rooted in the soil, lift up tapering branches to the skies and clothe them with the luxuriance of leaf and flower

This figure or form of life is easily recognised in Gothic work, in cathedrals and churches whose shafts and ribs rise perpendicularly from base to vaulting, and externally lose themselves, as it were, heavenwards in pinnacles and crocketed terminals   The wonderful Palais de Justice at Rouen may be cited as a most beautiful illustration of this quality of vitality

Architecture should be seen following nature in these indications and evidences of life and growth   Moreover, in nature there is to be observed an endless variety of expression by the same means   No two trees, though consisting of trunk, branches, twigs, and leaves, are alike   Again, nothing is more wonderful than the human countenance, which, consisting of the same features, presents infinite differences in form and expression

So in architecture there should be found ever new combinations and effects presented by accepted forms and materials. Occasionally there may be small tentative departures—variations from type—such as are found in nature.   This also is an evidence of vitality seeking to assimilate and adapt some means to meet a special need, or to put forth fresh powers where a strange environment insists upon a new development

3. *Restraint.*

By restraint in architecture is meant the limitation of means to an end, and the suppression of all unnecessary parts, lines, or details.

Whatever be the purpose of a building, there should be no feature, ornament, or line which has not a definite end and meaning.

As simple language is always the most powerful, and is only weakened by qualifying adjectives or undue emphasis, so in architecture the unrestrained use of ornament rather detracts from than increases the beauty and effect of the building

4 *Refinement.*

Refinement is impossible without restraint, but it means more than mere restraint.   It includes absolute purity of form and perfection of material

It excludes anything approaching to the frivolous, gaudy, or extravagant.

Everything must be the best of its kind, and at the same time so suited to its purpose and place that it appears inevitable.

Undue costliness of material and excess of ornament are both alike inconsistent with refinement.

5. *Repose*

Repose is the especial gift of the well-bred amongst men.   So in architecture every really good work is clothed, as it were, in an atmosphere of repose   As may be readily understood, this quality is not possible where there is a profusion of ornament or the crowding together of fussy details.

Architectural forms should be regarded as symbols intended to convey some specific meaning.   They must be used with restraint and refinement, for if these features appeal too loudly or insistently to the emotions then the beholder is wearied.

Any excess or vulgar exuberance must inevitably destroy repose ; and while there is abundance of life in repose, yet it is quiet and unassuming.

6. *Grace.*

A dignified seriousness of purpose should be observed in the appearance of all public buildings, but an expression of the " grace " of life should not be lacking.

This is effected by refinement of detail, by ornamental enrichment of constructive features, by beauty of line and finish.

This quality of "grace" must figure largely in the composition of all domestic buildings, and is often an index to the character and spirit of the owner

The mansion of the rich man and the cottage of the labourer may both alike present an appearance of either vulgar display or modest reticence, of grim inhospitality or cheery welcome

7 *Breadth*

This somewhat technical term is used to denote a certain comprehensiveness of form and firmness of line which is to be seen in every great architectural work.

It has reference to the treatment of the subject *as a whole* in a simple grand manner, to the proper massing of the several parts, the subordination of detail to the larger forms of the composition, and the bringing of the whole design into unity.

A building may be large in extent and size without being broad in treatment.   For instance, we cannot expect breadth in a building which has been enlarged by small additions made from time to time and linked together as circumstances or convenience dictated   The result of such a process may be picturesque and possess a charm of its own, but the whole, as a whole, would probably be quite lacking in breadth.

8 *Scale*

What is known as scale in architecture may be described as the right relation of the several parts to one another and to the whole in point of size

It is a technical term which may be easily understood by those who are familiar with the principles of music.

Scale is like a "measure" which regulates the division of parts in a building, and it is by the proper use of the subdivisions (as with the gamut in music) that perfect harmony can be produced.

The scale may be large or small, but the intervals are in proportion.

The key-note is set and the others are in relation to it.

The architect, like the musician, should so adapt every part of his work that it may synchronise and take its place in due proportion to the leading or dominant motive.   The different scales in architecture are as powerful and as distinct in their effects on the eye as the various keys in music are in their effects on the ear

The scale which is set will depend upon the purpose and character of the building   The scale suitable to an important or monumental building should be large, and each part and every moulding should be proportionate the one to the other   For a smaller building of a lighter character the scale may be smaller, but the relative proportions would be the same.

Factors.

Having thus briefly enumerated the qualities which should be found in good architecture we may next proceed to show that there are certain means by which these "qualities" are obtained   They may be subdivided as follows ·

1. Proportion.
2. Light and shade
3. Solids and voids.
4 Balance and symmetry.

These are matters of the right use and adjustment of architectural forms necessary for the purpose of the building—such as window and door openings, floor divisions, chimneys, projections and recesses, cornices, stringcourses, &c.

All these architectural forms serve a definite end in the constructional needs of the building, and must not for artistic purposes be employed in a way which is inconsistent with their practical use. They play a most important part on the artistic side, but this part must grow out of their original purpose.

1 *Proportion*

We have seen that scale and harmony are essential qualities in good architecture   To obtain these the architect avails himself of proportional divisions which must be in true relation to one another

Proportion is a matter of relation , it is not the actual size, but the relative size of one part to another, that is of so much importance   There are certain divisions which, when used with, and in relation to, each other, please the eye much in the same way as certain divisions of sound in combination charm the ear

It must be understood that the human figure is the standard or scale by which the eye insensibly measures everything   When Michael Angelo desired to represent his sibyls and prophets in the Sistine Chapel as giants, he obtained the effect by comparison, introducing into the composition smaller and subordinate figures.

In a similar way an apparent greater size is given to some parts of a building by smaller but relative subdivisions

To obtain horizontal proportions and divisions cornices, large or small as their position or purpose demands, may be employed   The primary use of these is the protection of the part of the building below them from rain, or sometimes in sunny aspects to afford necessary shade   In the South of Europe the overhanging cornices and projections are on this account much larger

Another method by which horizontal divisions are effected is by a change of material from, say, a stage or story in granite to one in stone above, or from stone to brick over

Again these divisions may be formed by a change in the texture of the material , as, for instance, from a base of rough-hewn stone to a finely worked surface over it.

The comparative width of horizontal divisions is a matter depending upon special technical knowledge, and must be subject to a variety of circumstances as well as to the character of the design

The same remark applies to the perpendicular divisions and their relative proportions. These, like the horizontal divisions, are secured by the disposition of architectural forms necessary to the construction of the building and the requirements of the plan. The breaking forward or recessing some parts of the building and the use of columns, pilasters. or buttresses provide the means for perpendicular subdivisions, and are made to subserve the purpose of rhythm in the composition.

2. *Light and Shade.*

For the subdividing and contrasting of perpendicular masses effects of light and shade must be taken into account, for they play a not unimportant part in the harmonious treatment of a building

The amount of projection or the exact depth of a recess will depend upon the " aspect " of the building, for it is obvious that the effects both of light and shade will be stronger on the south side than the north   A recess on the south side may look cool and inviting, while a similar recess on the north would only produce an impression of gloom

Every projection must have its distinct purpose arising out of the plan and the constructional needs of the building, but be used also in emphasising the lines which make the composition both true and good.

It is the artistic employment of means for the realisation of specific ends that differentiates architecture from mere building

3. *Solids and Voids.*

The adjustment of solids and voids is a matter of great consequence in good architectural work.

Like other factors in design, they grow out of the architectural needs of the building, the "voids" being the window and door openings, and the solids the constructional supports and walls of the building.

It will be readily understood that if the openings for light are unduly large a false "scale" is set up, the size of the building apparently diminished, and the composition otherwise spoilt.

4. *Balance and Symmetry*

These factors give a distinctive character to a building, and aid in setting forth its special purpose

An orderly and well-balanced arrangement of parts is suggestive of official and public life   A wide central entrance with dominating tower or dome invites attention to an important official centre.

Buildings of a public or semi-public character will generally be treated in the same symmetrical way—with a central block and flanking wings and an orderly array of columns and windows—with, however, modifications and variations in which there will generally be found balance and rhythm.

For there can be rhythm in the parts of a building as in the lines of poetic verse   Moreover, to continue the simile, there is a kind of blank verse in building as in poetry—irregular parts, not tallying, yet rhythmic all the same.

Materials.

Materials, which are, of course, the primary factors in all building, may be roughly divided under the four heads :

1. Stone
2 Wood.
3 Metal
4. Brick, cement, &c.

In each class will be found varying degrees of hardness, of coarse and fine texture, and other special characteristics, all of which, rightly understood, are guides to the true use and proper place of the material.

The finer and more delicate kinds are out of place where strength and hardness should be the primary consideration.

For purposes of ornament also there are certain species of material which lend themselves more readily to beautiful work   The treatment which is quite suitable in one material is not necessarily so in another, even if the latter admits of it.   Materials which can with advantage be cut or shaped by tools should differ in form from those cast in mould ; and so on.

Bearing this in mind it will easily be understood that there are certain architectural forms suitable to each material and its varieties

I may not occupy your time by expanding this most prolific theme. I have in hand a more extended form of the whole subject, but I must be content here with having indicated the broad lines on which, as it seems to me, any attempt to educate the public in matters of architecture should be carried out.

The subjects I have so briefly dealt with would, I believe, be appropriate for popular lectures, and might also be useful to teachers in schools —ordinary and technical—art classes, and similar institutions.

It may thus be possible by inculcating right "principles," by teaching and illustrating the special "qualities" which distinguish good architecture from bad, and by explaining the right use of the "factors" at hand, not only to develop and extend popular interest, but also to create a true critical appreciation on the part of the public of all that is best, most worthy, and most enduring in our beloved art.

(2) By T. G. JACKSON, R.A.

The subject of the education of the public in architecture is by no means a new one   It has been discussed often enough, and by many people.   Its importance will be obvious to any one who considers the conditions under which works of art can be produced.   It is for the public that art exists : without public demand for it art at the most could only exist as a private amusement of individuals   It is on the public that artists depend for employment, and it is ultimately on their power of pleasing the public taste that they have to rely for getting a living. Consequently it is of paramount importance that the public taste should be correctly educated to appreciate what is good and reject what is bad It is then, and only then, that a high standard will be reached by the average work of art in any age   The supply will correspond to the demand. As the late Lord Leighton said at the first National Congress for the Advancement of Art, " you cannot too strongly print this on your minds, that what you demand that you will get, and according to what you accept will be that which is provided for you " [1]

In none of the arts, if we come to think of it, is a correct judgment on the part of the public more necessary than in that of architecture. We need not raise the question which is the greatest of the arts, or whether one is greater than another   I prefer to regard all art as one, of which architecture, sculpture, and painting are only different modes of expression.   But we may claim this for architecture, that it is most necessary, one may almost say the only necessary one of the three   for while we may do and often have to do without painting and sculpture, we must have houses to live in and churches to worship in and markets and exchanges to trade in.   In order to see works of painting or sculpture, we may have to go out of our way to find them in galleries or museums, but architecture meets the eye at every turn indoors and out   One cannot walk down the next street without being vexed or pleased with the buildings that line it. To have to pass a hideous structure or a row of ugly houses in their daily walk is a penance that the neighbours have to put up with whether they like it or not   A man may buy a bad picture or a rubbishy piece of sculpture, and no one but he will be the worse for it , but he may put up a detestable house next door to us without our being able to stop him, and in that way inflict an injury on his neighbours which they are powerless to prevent and equally powerless to remedy   For the mental torture which we are thus obliged to suffer no doubt we have in justice and in the first place to thank the architect , but ultimately the blame must rest with his employer, who approved the design and paid for its realisation in brick and stone.   Had he not been ignorant of the elements of good design in architecture and careless about them, we should not have been called upon to suffer.

Considering, then, that private buildings will be naturally such as please the individual, and public buildings such as are approved by councils or committees or boards that have to do with them, surely we have a right to demand, in the interest of public happiness, that those who are to judge the design which the public will have to endure, whether they like it or not, should have some knowledge of the subject about which they are to adjudicate.   We leave the decision to them and are at their mercy, and if they fail us, " *quis custodiet ipsos custodes ?* " We must give up in despair all hope of better things

The desirability of diffusing a general knowledge of architecture was insisted upon from a different point of view by another speaker at the same Congress in 1888. Professor Roger Smith claimed a place for

[1] *Transactions of the National Association for the Advancement of Art, &c &c , at Liverpool,* 1888.

architecture as part of a liberal education.[1]   He said that " the man who is in other ways cultivated but is no artist and no lover of art has one side of his nature undeveloped," and that a knowledge of art which leaves out architecture is necessarily incomplete   "Architecture," he goes on to say," is the historic art, far more historic than painting or sculpture The most the painter can do for us is to suggest events in the past as he is able to imagine them   The works of architecture *are* the past "

But in order to get all the pleasure out of works of architecture which they are capable of affording it is imperative that the observer should to some extent at all events understand their meaning   The ignorant observer, though he may be stirred with admiration as he regards a fine building, " will with his untutored eyes barely see even half of what is before him, a fact of which," says Professor Smith, " any one who will endeavour on the spot to explain a building which he knows well to visitors not familiar with architecture soon becomes aware "

To consider this personal. aspect of the matter still further, one may point out how much the pleasure of travel would be increased if the traveller were capable of taking an intelligent and instructed interest in the buildings that he sees.   I say an intelligent and instructed interest, because it is patent that the number of people who do take interest of a certain kind in fine works of architecture is a very large one.   For, after all, it is to see architecture that most people visit strange places   Why else do they throng to Venice or Florence or Rome ? why do they visit in crowds the great cathedrals of England or France ? what else takes them to Knole or Haddon, Hardwick or Burghley ?   Why do they haunt the ruined abbeys of Yorkshire or the *châteaux* on the Loire, or the castle at Heidelberg ?   If architecture thus draws them by an irresistible attraction, surely it is strange that so few should take the trouble to understand what they see, and that the majority should rest content with the modicum of pleasure which is all that a mere casual and superficial observation can afford.

It is, however, not so much with the effect on the individual of ignorance or carelessness, or of deficient and shallow acquaintance with the subject, that we are concerned to-day, as with its effect on the progress and condition of contemporary art   If it rests ultimately with the general society of any age to say what shall be the character of the art of their day, surely it is of the utmost importance that there should be as wide a diffusion as possible among all educated men and women of the right canons of judgment in matters artistic   How is this to be effected ? What can we do to spread the knowledge of true principles of art among an unenlightened generation ?

There are, perhaps, few more difficult questions to answer than this It is no new one , it has been asked over and over again, and various methods of solution have been tried already, with varying measures of failure or success   How far any of them have found a satisfactory answer to the question is another matter   Let us consider some of them and see what result has followed their application.

First of all there has been the literary method.   This at all events has had a fair trial.   The bibliography of architecture is enormous , the number of books that have been written about it would fill a library by themselves   Every style has been systematised, classified, analysed, and described.   Almost every building of note, if not every one that much matters, has been visited, measured, and illustrated in expensive works by competent and learned writers, and that is true of buildings not only in Europe but in Asia and Africa as well   Their dates have been accurately fixed, their authors discovered, if they are discoverable, and there is little left to be found out about them by future industry

[1] *Transactions of the National Association for the Advancement of Art, &c &c at Liverpool*, 1888, pp 159–160

Of these books many are on a monumental scale, and therefore can never be generally studied . many more are technical and only fitted for the use of professional architects. But there is an enormous amount of literary work of a less abstruse kind in the form of handbooks, guides, glossaries, and popular descriptions of well-known buildings which is within the scope of every ordinary intelligence and within the reach of the most slender purse Scarcely a month passes without the announcement of some new book on architecture, for which it would seem the public appetite is insatiable : for there would not be this abundant supply were it not that there is a constant and even a growing demand for works on this subject. In the face of this apparent craving on the part of general readers it is impossible not to admit that there is a very wide interest taken in architecture It would seem to be recognised by most educated persons that Professor Smith was right in claiming a place for architecture in the scheme of a liberal education Most people of any pretence to cultivation have a smattering of knowledge enough to enable them to distinguish the various styles more or less correctly, and to have an approximate idea of their chronology So far as a literary acquaintance with the subject goes they are fairly well equipped, and have plenty of sources of information open to them We shall see how far this is of use to them in their judgment of the merits or demerits of works of architecture in their own day, which is, of course, a very different matter

Another method of diffusing the knowledge of architecture has been by popular lectures Many of these in this country have been given under the management of the Societies for the Extension of University Teaching. They have been attended by large classes of interested students, and have been found very attractive Modern facilities for illustration by lantern slides have done much to popularise them. Many of these lectures have been followed up by visits, under the guidance of the lecturer, to ancient buildings, which have been explained on the spot.

The same plan has been followed by the various antiquarian and archæological or architectural societies which exist in every county, and which make periodical excursions to famous buildings within their respective districts. These societies also publish their transactions, and so contribute very largely and usefully to the stores of literary wealth at the disposal of the architectural student, whether professional or amateur

After a survey of this vast literary and educational effort one may well imagine the question being asked, What more can be done for the education of the public in architecture than has been done and is being done already ? If there is that general hunger for instruction in architecture on the one hand, and on the other this apparently inexhaustible supply of provender which is greedily devoured and digested, what more would one have ? What is there left to be done further for the architectural education of the general mass of educated people ?

The answer to such a question will depend on what we mean by the architectural education of the public. We began by saying that since it rests with the public, who are the employers, to approve or condemn the designs of the buildings which are provided for them by the architects, who are the employed, it is of the utmost importance that the employers should be able to tell good work from bad, and fresh and living work from work that is stale and commonplace Will study of the architecture of the past, such as has just been described, however patient and careful it may be, suffice to qualify a man for pronouncing with certainty on the merits or demerits of the design for a modern building ? It will probably be replied that there is no better way of forming a correct taste than the study of fine examples Very true ! but they may be studied in many ways and from many points of view, and it is important that they be regarded in the right aspect if the study of them is to be of any use to us for future practice of our art.   For it is obvious that to study fine architecture of the past and to look no further is one thing, and to study it with the view of catching the spirit of it which may inspire our own work, and enable us to produce something as good as the work of our forefathers, and possibly better than theirs, is another thing altogether.   The former line of study is more or less antiquarian and archæological.   Not that it excludes a high degree of appreciation of the artistic element in what we see   But it is quite possible to enjoy that extremely ; to be moved by the beauty of minster or manor-house, townhall or village church, and to rest in that without further application of the lesson they teach to anything we ourselves are doing.

Let us imagine the case of an educated gentleman interested in architecture, who has visited and carefully examined every cathedral in the kingdom and every old mansion that came within his reach, who has travelled and seen the most famous buildings in France and Italy, who has read his Ruskin and diligently studied his guide-books, and who has the chronology of the principal European styles at his fingers' ends   Above all let him have a genuine love for his subject, and not be a mere perfunctory sightseer who goes about to see what fashion makes it necessary for him to see and be able to talk about.   Imagine this man sitting as member of a committee to build a townhall for the place where he lives, and called upon to decide between the relative merits of a number of competitive designs of which he is to choose the best.   Will his architectural studies suffice to save him from making a mistake and guide him to the right choice ?   I venture to say that if he has no other qualifications for deciding correctly than those we have described he will be as much at sea as the veriest tiro, and his opinion will be only that of the ordinary amateur.   Something more than literary study or even personal knowledge of the works of architecture in the past is wanted to enable a man to deal successfully with the creation of new architectural work in the present.   Something more than University extension lectures, or the multiplication of handbooks and architectural illustrations, is necessary to save a man from overlooking meritorious work and being caught by designs of mere mediocrity or even worse

What then is this something more, and what is it that is wanting in such studies as those to which I supposed our committee-man to have devoted himself ?

Let us consider the mental process through which he will pass in forming his decision   The designs he has to judge are those of a townhall Naturally his mind will fly back from the designs before him to the designs of the past with which he has familiarised himself.   All the townhalls of Belgium, Ypres, Brussels, Ghent, Bruges and Louvain will rush in upon his memory, or the Broletto of Como, or the Palazzi Comunali of Brescia, Cremona, or Siena, or the Classic palaces of Rome, Vicenza, and Florence, by Sangallo, Michelozzi, Bramante, Palladio, and other great masters of the Renaissance   From these he forms his standard   From them he learns to look for certain conventional forms and features, and if they are not there the design seems to him faulty and defective.   If, on the other hand, they are present he is content whether or no they are wanted and whether or no there is a reason for them   If, again, the design has anything for which his memory furnishes no precedent he is offended, for there is no purist so rigid and fastidious as the cultivated amateur.   Thus it is that in forming his judgment he falls back on convention and precedent. All his studies predispose him to require authority in ancient example for everything that is done nowadays   If he can trace the origin of something in the design to an ancient model with which he is familiar he is pleased, and approves the new imitation of it as satisfactory and orthodox.   No experience is more common for an architect when sub-

mitting a design to his employer than to be asked what it is taken from.
The same question put to a poet or an author, or to a painter or a sculptor,
would be resented as an insult   But in dealing with an architect it comes
naturally to the lips of most people   The majority of architectural con-
noisseurs seem to think that all modern architecture must be imitated
from something that has been done in antiquity or in the Middle Ages
They cannot understand how it can be produced on any other terms
Should you reply with befitting modesty that you are not aware of there
having been anything done before like what you have designed, and that
you are not a copyist, you are met with a look of surprise and perhaps
incredulity; and you may perhaps be told, as I have been, that it is
impossible but that there must have been something somewhere on which
your performance is modelled   One wonders how such people suppose
architecture ever came first into being

Here then we have the result of all this elaborate study of our art from the
literary and antiquarian standpoint.   The mistake has been that it regards
architecture mainly from the historical side and takes no account of the
practical aspect which has to do with our use of it as a living and working
style for everyday life   It ignores the difference between architecture
and archæology, and confuses one with the other   Archæology is a
most entrancing and delightful science, and it forms an invaluable element
in all historical research, in which it now plays a much more important
part than it has ever done in the past.   But archæology will never teach
us to build up a design sensibly and beautifully in such a way as to justify
its claim to be held a work of art   To do this requires that other faculties
be called into play with which mere archæology has nothing to do.   Not
that we are to shut our eyes to what has been done before by other people
Far from it   All science and art is progressive, and every fresh step in
advance must be taken from the vantage ground that has been won by
those who preceded us   Without the example of the men of old we
should be nowhere—mere explorers and beginners—whereas with their
experience behind us we are the heirs of all the ages, and it will be our
own fault if we fail to advance our work to fresh and ever fresh developments   But while we study with all the ardour it deserves the art of
the past we must not forget that we are to study it not to copy and reproduce it, but to take from it the lessons in style that it can teach us
When Michel-Angelo on his way to Rome to build the dome of
St. Peter's looked back on Brunelleschi's cupola at Florence, he ex-
claimed, "Come te non voglio, meglio di te non posso."   So we in looking
at the great works of our forefathers may well doubt our ability to do
better, but we must nevertheless, if we have any faith in the vitality
of our art, cry with the mighty master that we will not be mere copyists
The work of the past will be our tutor rather than our model

The fault, then, of the way in which people in general have learned
to study architecture is that it is almost exclusively archæological   And
not that alone, but, what is worse, archæological only on one side of the
subject   It has been uniformly with the externals of the various styles
that all the popular books on the subject have concerned themselves
So far as the mere account of phase after phase through which the art
passed successively is concerned the literary record is fairly complete.
The amateur student soon learns to know style from style and to assign
each example to its proper class and its approximate date.   And this, so
far as it goes, is all very well, the mistake is that, having reached this
standard of knowledge, he thinks he understands architecture, whereas
he has only acquainted himself with the outside of it   Such knowledge of
the subject is only like that of a man who, after turning over a collection
of shells and learning the names of the principal specimens, should think
he understands conchology, or still more exactly that of one who, after
mastering the list of kings and the dates of battles and revolutions of any

particular period, should think he understands its history   If we estimate
the value of any opinion one student might express on conchology and
the other on the true historical aspect of the period with which he thinks
he has acquainted himself we shall be able to appreciate the value of the
judgment the mere archæologist is qualified to express on any problem
of modern architecture   His only standard is that of resemblance to
ancient example, faithful imitation, and close adherence to precedent ;
and the natural result is that from his point of view it is the business of
modern use to accommodate itself to ancient habit rather than that the
lessons of the past should show the way to the right practice of architecture at the present day

I have said that archæological study itself in the case of most people
only deals with one side of the subject, and that the outside   The true
inner reason which underlies and inspires the development of all healthy
architectural growths is hidden from them. It is not enough to acquaint
yourself with the outward details of any style of architecture if you wish
to understand it , you must look deeper and follow them up to their
origin, and in that way arrive at their meaning   It will be found that
they are all to be traced ultimately, so far at least as their general features
go, either to accidents of race and social condition, or to necessities and
conveniencies of construction, all of which influences have combined
to give the current style a certain direction, and in fact to make it what it
is   All these elements in its constitution are discoverable, and if the
style is to be really understood they must be discovered and their effects
traced and recognised.   It is not, of course, to be expected that difficult
problems of construction should be puzzled out, except by professional
students of architecture, but there is no great mystery about the elements
of construction, and some acquaintance with them is within the reach of
every one ; for, whether they know it or not, all men are influenced by them
to some extent   From the time when as children they constructed
their house of cards, or played with their box of bricks, to that when they
build or buy or only hire a house in which to live securely, ideas of stability
and the rudiments of good building will have been present to all men.
A man's first question will be whether his house is well built, and he will do
his best to detect any faults of construction long before he thinks of its
external claims to architectural beauty   What he wants in order to
qualify himself for the right understanding of the architecture of the
past is to connect the two ideas together , to get some knowledge of the
constructional problems which the builders in former times had to face
and conquer, and to trace in their architecture the adaptation of the
means to the end ; to see how the several characteristic features of the
style are based upon constructional necessities and are outwardly expressive of them—to see, for instance, in looking at a Gothic minster, how
from first to last the construction has ruled the design—how the wish
for clearer floor-space, combined with increasing skill in craftsmanship,
has evolved the lightness and airiness of the nave of Salisbury from the
ponderous piers and heavy arches of the Norman work at Winchester ;
how this development was made easy by the adoption of the pointed
arch, and how it had been retarded by the conservatism which clung to
the round one , how the difficulty of applying the cross groining of the
Roman to any but square bays led step by step to the perfection of rib
and panel vaulting , how cross vaulting, by relieving the curtain walls
from pier to pier, allowed the expansion of the window space into the
glorious clerestories of Amiens or York   I might, did time allow, pursue
this into all the main features of Gothic construction ; but I will only
point out how greatly the interest which the mere superficial admirer
of architecture feels would be increased if he grasped even imperfectly
something of the meaning of what he saw , how much the pinnacle would
gain in dignity if he understood that it was not a mere flourish to look well

against the sky, but a valuable equipoise to steady the piers below , if he saw in the flying buttress not merely a gracefully leading outline but a working member without whose aid the structure would fall , if he were reassured as to the stability of such buildings as the Sainte Chapelle at Paris or the Abbey at Bath or King's College Chapel, which seem mere lanterns of glass, by understanding the distribution and concentration of the disruptive forces of the vaulting or isolated points of support and resistance All the beauty of a design is enhanced by knowledge of its fitness to its purpose, by the intelligence that it has a meaning, that there is a reason for it, and that it is not the creation of mere idle fancy and artistic caprice.

It is in this direction, then, that I would have the education of the public turned as regards their study of the architecture of the past; but it is still more important from our point of view as architects that they should apply the same principles of reason to the architecture of to-day We are not a congress of archæologists, but of architects, and the great thing for us to consider is how we are to ensure the right appreciation of what is good and true and the rejection of what is false and bad in the art of the day on the part of the general public who are our judges and employers. I have ventured to show what I think is wanting in the way the subject is now generally presented to the unprofessional student, and, if I may say so, not only to him but very often to the professional architect as well. So long as people think that classic architecture is a matter of columns and round arches and capitals and the five orders, and Gothic a matter of pointed arches and quatrefoils and trefoils, so long will the architecture of the day be condemned to the mere faithful repetition of stale examples. Till it is understood that architecture must above all the arts be logical, and that every design ought to be required to give a reason for its existence in the form it has taken, we shall get no further. Till then it is inevitable that the imitation of familiar details will be demanded by the generality of men and accepted as a warrant of orthodoxy. And, further, so long as it is only the outward features of bygone styles that are generally associated with it, it follows that it will be in the ornamental details that the essence of the style is considered to reside With most people it is not too much to say that architecture means ornament Take a plain building and plaster on or pin on some ornamentation, and you make it at once a work of architecture There is no more fatal fallacy than this It lies at the root of all the debased gaudy work that disfigures our streets Till the public are enlightened as to the difference between ornamenting buildings and building beautifully, which is quite another thing, and till they learn that to be artistic it is not necessary to be smart, it can hardly be said that their education in architecture has even begun.

What, then, is the best way of bringing these elementary truths home to the unprofessional lover of our art? Something may be done by persuading those who write or lecture on the subject to look at it and treat it from the rational point of view rather than from that of a shallow æstheticism—to get them to think less of " the styles " and more of "style , " to show the common basis of all architecture in sound construction, and from that foundation to build up the knowledge of the various forms into which different peoples and different ages cast their art, though obeying the same sound general principles.

But, after all, art of any kind is a thing to be done rather than something to be talked about It is for us, the architects, to teach the world what good work is by doing our best to produce it We are the real missionaries, and not the writer, however brilliant, or the lecturer, however attractive Every good, honest building we put upon the ground is in itself a better sermon than any that can be read or preached, and will do more to convert an unbelieving or mistaken world than a score of University Extension lectures or a whole shelf full of guide-books or text-books on the styles.

It is for us to show the outside public that our art is still alive , that it is not to be studied as a dead language , that archæology and architecture are not inseparable, still less synonymous, and that interesting—overpoweringly interesting—as the styles of the past must always be to all sensible minds, still there is before us the problem of how to do our own building work, and that surely has even a greater claim on our attention.

How little attention this great problem receives is too well known to need remark.   There is a room full of fresh architectural designs yearly at the Royal Academy, but it is resorted to mainly for a nap or a quiet *tête-à-tête*   There are rarely more than three or four people in it at once, while the picture galleries are crowded   In the newspaper critiques of the year's exhibition architecture and sculpture are dismissed with at most a few closing paragraphs in the "fourth and concluding notice"   I do not complain of this, and scarcely wish it otherwise   Art is in my opinion a great deal too much written about and talked about   It is not criticism, but work that is wanted   It may be doubted whether it would not be better for art if all literature or talking about it could be suppressed for a generation.   Instead of listening to the critics and thinking about what they see at secondhand, as most people are in the habit of doing, they might then get into the way of looking at the works of art and thinking for themselves , and instead of making critical studies of them simply sit down and enjoy them, which is now often the very last thing they think of doing   It was, I believe, Canova who said, "You English see with your ears," and it is the case with most people that before they dare admire or enjoy a work of art they wait to hear what the critics say about it, so that they may be sure they are doing right and not committing themselves to a heterodox opinion on which the self-constituted arbiters of taste would frown   In literature criticism is on a different footing : there the critic is at all events a fellow craftsman with those whom he reviews . but in art it is different   There the critic is generally an amateur, for every man is an amateur in respect to those arts to which he does not himself put his hand , and the only difference between him and other amateurs is that he makes his amateurism a profession   To artists criticism from this source is of little or no use.   The general experience is that from the mere professional critic one has never got anything helpful. The criticism that really does us good is that of our brother-craftsmen, who know the difficulties and have struggled with them themselves, and whose candid and not always flattering remarks are salutary and invigorating even when they are least complimentary.

If, then, the public, who are our masters and our judges, are to qualify themselves for a right judgment in matters of architecture, and to bring a wholesome influence to bear on the practice of the art to-day, they must learn that architecture is not archæology ; that the study of an old building is a very different thing from designing a new one , that the essence of architecture lies not in its outward details, least of all in its ornament, but in the expression of its vital principles of construction They must dare to think for themselves instead of waiting to be told by the critics what they may or may not admire   They must accustom themselves to regard architecture not as a subject for learned disquisition and antiquarian research, but as something to be enjoyed, as the citizens of Venice or Florence or our own towns in the Middle Ages enjoyed the lovely buildings that they watched their brother-burghers raising for them, in those happy days when art criticism was as yet unknown.

And, lastly, we architects must remember that it is from us that the public can really learn most, and that if we work conscientiously and do what we feel to be right, even if it leads us to defy convention, we shall be doing more than any literary crusade to convert the public, with whom, of course, it rests, in the final resort, to say whether the art of their age shall be honest, true, and noble, or the reverse.

(3) By Arthur Hill, B E., M.R.I.A. (Lecturer on Architecture, Queen's College, Cork.)

For the intelligent appreciation of any art or science some knowledge of that art or science is indispensable   It is not to be expected that the ordinary non-professional observer will take an interest in what he does not understand   To many people a new building represents nothing more than the money it cost, that being the only scale they are capable of applying to the object.

The value of university training for professional purposes does not now need an argument ; the principle has been already adopted in some of the modern universities of this country   But why should the teaching be limited to professional students ?   Why should not the history of architecture, taught by a professional architect, be included as a branch of general history available to students specialising in history for the B A degree ?

Several universities admit lectures on classic art and archæology, but the " mother of all the arts " scarcely receives adequate treatment in lectures of this kind   Why limit the subject to the classic period ? Does not architecture, taken as an historical study, reflect the social conditions of a people in one century as well as in another ?   Taken from its own standpoint as an art, how can an artistic sense be better cultivated or acquired than by a critical review of the best buildings of all time that have survived to the present day ?

Lectures on the history of architecture, showing its true basis of evolution, delivered by trained architects, and with the prestige of the " university," would exercise an important and beneficial influence on the public appreciation of our art   For, in addition to the students who would take the university course, it may safely be assumed that through the medium of the University Extension System, which is bound to follow the example of the parent university, lectures would be given and considerable interest aroused among a number of people in many parts of the country

There can be no doubt that the criticism of those who have had the necessary training on which to form an opinion would be a valuable aid to the development of good architecture throughout the kingdom, and a stimulating influence both to the architect and his client

This is not the only way, but perhaps one way, in which the public may be brought to take more interest in our professional work.

---

(4) Von Othmar v Leixner, Architekt (M d G), k k Professor

" Zur Frage der Baukunstlerischen Bildung des Publikums '

Es durfte wohl sehr wenige Fragen allgemeiner Natur geben, die wie diese fur die internationale Architektenschaft von allergrosster Bedeutung.   Leider wurde aber gerade diese Frage, die man kann es ruhig sagen heute zu einer Cardinalfrage der kunstlerisch gebildeten Architektenschaft geworden, noch sehr wenig in den Kreis allgemeiner Beratungen gezogen.   Abgesehen von einigen modernen Kunstforschern und schriftstellernden Architekten die durch hochwertvollen Arbeiten die Baukunst dem Publikum naher zu bringen suchten, weiter abgesehen von einigen ruhrigen Architektenvereinigungen Suddeutschlands vor allem Bayerns die die Pflege der Heimatkunst den Massen naher zu bringen suchen, ist wenig oder besser gesagt gar nichts geschehen. In vollkommener Abgeschlossenheit arbeiten die meisten Architektenvereinigungen, Fachfragen von allgemeinstem Interesse werden immer nur am grünen Tisch, respektive in den Fachjournalen die ja dem Publikum unbekannt zur Austragung gebracht.

Hier Wandel zu schaffen gilt für die internationale Architektenschaft als Pflicht, ich möchte sagen der Selbsterhaltungstrieb, die Freude am eigenen Beruf zwingt alle dazu, ihr Möglichstes zu einer Besserung der Verhältnisse beizutragen   Heute steht das grosse Publikum der Baukunst beinahe vollständig indolent gegenüber.   Diese allgemeine Indolenz des Publikums in Baufragen, die durch dieselbe bedingte kritiklose oder flächliche Behandlung der Baukunst und ihrer Meister hat es mit sich gebracht, dass heute der Architekt weitaus nicht jene Rolle im offentlichen Leben spielt, wie im Mittelalter und in der Renaissance   Und doch sind die Aufgaben des modernen Architekten viel grössere und schwierigere geworden, stellt doch die unaufhaltsam vordringende Cultur der Baukunst immer grossartigere und schwierigere Probleme   Die Meinung des heutigen Publikums, ich sage des kunstverständigen Publikums, geht schon so weit den Architekten aus dem Kreis der Künstler überhaupt auszuschalten   Das moderne Publikum versteht unter Künstler einen Maler, Bildhauer, einen berühmten Geiger oder Pianisten, sehr selten , denkt es aber an den Architekten   Man betrachtet eben heute nicht die Baukunst als vollwertige Kunst und gerade sie ist ja die Mutter der Künste. Von diesem Standpunkte aus betrachtet die grosse Menge den Architekten, begreiflich dass damit jenes zweifellos internationale Scheinarchitektentum sagen wir besser Hochstaplertum gross gezogen wird, der Kunst und ihren wahren Künstlern zum Schaden   Die Architektur ist für dem Durchschnittsbauherrn eine Preisfrage, nicht der Kunst, der Billigkeit gilt der Erfolg.   Wie viele stolze selbstbewusste Künstlernaturen müssen heute sehen wie dieses Kunstparasitentum dass ja um jeden Preis arbeitet, geschäftsmännisch annonciert und für sich Reklame gewöhnlichster Art treibt mit Bauaufträgen reich versehen, während sie selbst warten können bis allenfalls eine Konkurrenz ein ungewisses Etwas bietet.   Betrachten wir die Bauten der grösseren und kleineren Städte, wieviel Geschmacklosigkeit ist da überall zu finden   Ware das Publikum baukünstlerisch gebildet, ware damit auch diesem Kunstparasitentum der Boden ihrer Thätigkeit entzogen.   Wir wollen nun den Versuch machen dieser so ernster Frage nach drei Punkten hin näher zu treten

1. Wie verhalt sich das heutige Publikum der Baukunst gegenuber ?

2 Wo sind die Gründe zu suchen für die heutige Anschauung des Publikums ?

3. Welche Mittel und Wege stehen der Architektenschaft zur Verfugung eine Besserung der Verhältnisse herbeizuführen ?

1. *Wie verhalt sich das heutige Publikum der Baukunst gegenuber ?*

Um dieser Frage näher zu treten müssen wir das sogenannte kunstverständige Publikum aus dem sich ja auch zum Theil unsere Bauherrn rekrutieren genauer betrachten.   Begleiten wir dieses Publikum in die Kunstausstellungen, begleiten wie dasselbe auf der Reise, und wir werden sehen, dass die Grundanschauungen dieses ganz internationalen Publikums vollkommen gleichartig sind.   Wie schon erwähnt, steht das Publikum der Baukunst entweder vollkommen indolent oder aber äusserst zaghaft gegenuber.   Achtlos zieht das Publikum an den historisch wertvollen Bauten voruber, ganz momentanes Interesse bringt es irgend einem monumentalen Neubau entgegen, nur kurze Zeit lasst sich dasselbe von einer aktuellen Baufrage fesseln, wenn eine unsachgemässe Zeitungskritik die Frage öffentlich aufgegriffen.   Dieses Publikum, dass in baukünstlerischen Hinsicht so indolent und unwissend, zeigt sich aber in den

Kunstausstellungen und Museen weit reifer , wenn auch diese Reife sehr
einseitiger Natur genannt werden kann.   Daheim und auf der Reise
werden wir immer die gleichen Erscheinungen wahrnehmen   Verhalt-
nismassig richtiges Verstandnis fur Bild und Farbe, fur Linie und Gesammt-
wirkung, bei oft reicher Heranziehung von Vergleichstucken historischer
oder moderner Art da und dort grosse Kenntnisse auf dem Gebiete der
historischen Malerei, insbesondere in Frauenkreisen.   Die Kritik sehr
oft gut und dabei haufig vollkommen individuell und unbeeinflusst von
der Tageskritik   Interesse und gutes Verständnis für kleinere halb-
plastische Arbeiten, wie Plaquetten, Reliefs und allenfalls auch fur kleine
Vollplastiken   Verhältnismässig geringes Interesse fur 'grossplastische
Arbeiten   Vollste Unsicherheit auf baukunstlerischen Gebiete, kritische
Bemerkungen lassen beinahe durchwegs auf eine Beeinflussung von
anderer Seite schliessen   Von vornherein ist es ganz auffallig, dass fur
die Plastik und Architektur, ein so vermindertes Interesse einerseits und
eine so zaghafte Beurtheilung anderseits konstatiert werden kann
Abgesehen von einer ganzen Reihe anderer spater zu erorternden
Grunden fur dieses Verhalten des Publikums, wollen wir hier schon auf
die Schwierigkeit des dreidimensionalen Sehens das Augenmerk lenken
Die Flache ist fur den Laien begreiflicher Weise verständlicher wie der
Korper, wie der Raum   Zeigt sich diese Schwäche beim Publikum schon
in der Plastik, um wie viel schwerer muss es demselben werden Baumassen
in ihren Verhältnissen richtig eingeschatzen, richtig in ihrer beabsichtig-
teten und auch erreichten Wirkung zu verstehen.

Dasselbe Publikum, dass über Rubens, Rembrandt, Botticelli, Rafael,
Markart und Lenbach ganz trefflich Bescheid weiss, ein Publikum dass
uber Worpswerder und Dachauer Kunstler spricht wird ratlos den
historischen und modernen Baudenkmalen der Heimatstadt gegenuber
stehen und nichts, gar nichts zu sagen wissen   Begleiten wir dieses
Publikum in die Kunstausstellungen so ergibt sich uberall das gleiche
Resultat das Hauptinteresse gilt den Bildern, daneben finden noch die
Kleinplastiken allgemeinere Beachtung, wie wenig Menschen sehen wir
aber jenen Salen wo grössere plastische Arbeiten ihre Aufstellung gefunden.   Da muss schon ein Meunier eine Spezialausstellung erhalten um
auf grosseres Interesse des Publikums rechnen zu können.   Prufen wir
aber diese Besichtigungen auf ihren inneren Wert, so werden wir finden,
dass viele der Besucher mehr des guten Tones halber, um auch mitreden
zu konnen hierher gekommen.   Schreiten wir dann weiter durch die
Raume der Kunstausstellungen und finden wir da und dort auch einen oder
den anderen kleinen Raum der der Baukunst gewidmet so konnen wir
bestimmt darauf rechnen dort nur Kollegen anzutreffen.   Mit einer
heiligen Scheu weicht unser Publikum diesen Räumen aus.   Ah, da sind
Plane, komm gehen wir, davon verstehen wir ja so nichts kann man an der
Thure ofters horen.   Welche Muhe hat es aber gekostet, wie viel Energie,
wie viel Kunst steckt aber oft gerade hier in diesen Arbeiten.   Ich glaube
annehmen zu konnen, dass solche Erfahrungen nicht nur in Wien sondern
auch in Paris, London, Berlin, etc., gesammelt werden konnen.   Doch
prufen wir das Publikum weiter, ziehen wir mit ihm hinaus in die Ferne,
folgen wir der Gesellschaft nach den Lagunen Venedigs, an dem Arnostrand,
nach Brüssel, auch hier konnen wir bald zu ahnlichen Resultaten gelangen.
In auffallender Weise zeigt sich dieser Zug des Publikums auch bei der
alljahrlich   an den Kunsthochschulen veranstalteten Ausstellungen.
Fur diese akademische Ausstellungen gilt das Gleiche wie fur die Kunstausstellungen   Der Hauptzulauf bei den Malern, veringerte Besucher-
zahl bei den Bildhauern   Und in den Architekten-Schulausstellungen ?
Dort trifft man nur die junge Architektenschaft die heftig kritisierend
über die Kollegen zu Gericht sitzt   So wie die Alten singen, so zwitschern
die Jungen   Ab und zu verirrt sich das Familienmitglied eines Ausstellers
in diese Raume, um die Arbeiten eines Verwandten in Augenschein zu

nehmen   Die Kritik lautet dann immer   Sehr schon muss viel Arbeit
kosten, sehr hubsch gezeichnet, nur so weiter   Der nebenstehende
Kunstjunger steckt die freundliche Kritik ruhig ein, die meist in diametralen
Gegensatz zur Ansicht seiner verehrten Kollegen steht, nun hat er wenigstens ein freundliches Wort auch gehort

Wie schon erwähnt ist das Publikum auf der Reise nicht anders.
Wandern wir durch die prachtigen Raume der Uffizien in Florenz, folgen
wir dem baedeckerbewaffneten Publikum durch die herrlichen Samm-
lungen.   Bald konnen wir zwei Gruppen von Menschen klar unterscheiden,
die eine die nur die mit Sternchen markierten Bilder betrachtet und die
Zeitdauer der Betrachtung abhangig macht von der Anzahl der Sternchen.
Die zweite Gruppe, feiner empfindend und selbstständiger, wird da und
dort auch ein Bild in Augenschein nehmen, langer vor diesem verweilen,
obwohl sein Meister ein unbekannterer Quattrocentist, ein kleinerer
Meister des Cinquecento   Gehen wir hinuber in den anderen Flugel wo
die herrliche Niobidengruppe ihre Aufstellung gefunden, da ist es meist
recht sparlich besucht   Wie sich das Interesse des Publikums so einseitig
der Malerei zuwendet, konnen wir noch auffalliger in jenen Raumen
sehen wo Handzeichnungen ausgestellt.   Die Maler werden eingehend
besichtigt, die hoch interessanten Architekturhandzeichnungen beinahe
keines Blickes gewurdigt   Man versuche einmal die mediceische Venus
aus der Tribuna zu entfernen und in einem Plastiksaal aufzustellen, mit
der allgemeinen Beruhmtheit ware es bald aus   In Brussel und anderen
beruhmten Museumsstadten kann man ganz gleiche Erfahrungen machen
Wie wenig das Publikum im Allgemeinen mit der Plastik anzufangen
weiss zeigt uns ein Gang durch das Nationalmuseum von Athen   Das
Hauptinteresse wendet sich dem mykanischen Saal zu, die reichen Gold-
funde von Mykane und Tiryns sind es die das Auge des Publikums fesseln.
Als zweiter Anziehungspunkt jene Schranke wo die Tanagrafiguren ihre
Aufstellung gefunden.   Die herrliche attische Grossplastik wird rasch
absolviert, da und dort allenfalls ein Grabrelief vom Dipylon das einige
Minuten Beachtung verlangt   Wir haben hier das Publikum auf sein
Verstandnis der Malerei und Plastik gegenuber etwas gepruft , begleiten
wir es jetzt vor die monumentalen Bauschopfungen, sehen wir zu wie
die herrlichen Werke der Baukunst vom Publikum aufgenommen   Ich
sehe hier ganz ab von antiken Ausgrabungsfeldern, wo es ja selbst dem
nicht geubten Kollegen schwer wird sich ein Bild der alten Anlage vorzu-
zaubern.   Betrachtet ein Laie eine grossere Monumentalschopfung so
werden wir nie von ihm horen, dass der Bau in seiner Gesammtheit schon
immer wird er nur auf Detaile hinweisen   Da ist es ein reizvolles Fruh-
renaissanceportal mit schönen Pilasterfullungen und reichen Lunetten-
schmuck, dort ein schones gothisches Masswerksfenster dass sein Interesse
besonders in Anspruch nimmt.   Die Gesammtkomposition bleibt fur ihn
fremd   Je reicher der Stil mit ornamentalen Beiwerk desto klarer
verständlich wird fur ihn die Façade.   Der Palazzo Ca'doro mit seiner
reichen Loggienbildung und reizvollen Details wird dem Laien weit
verstandlicher sein, wenn wir das Wort Verstandnis uberhaupt anwenden
dürfen, wie die Front der Kirche Redentore in Venedig   Fur diese
einfach classische Strenge fehlt dem Laien der Massstab vollkommen
Hier hat er kein Einzeldetail, dass sein Auge fesseln konnte, hier ist ja
nur die Gesammtfront in ihrer Proportion massgebend.   Interessante
Studien gibt auch der Vergleich zwischen dem Eindruck der Redentore
Palladios und der S M Salute Longhenas in Venedig   Das Publikum
steht ausschliesslich auf Seite Longhenas.   Die reiche Architektur wird hier
wohl noch unterstutzt durch das schone Bild der unmittelbaren Umgebung, kunstlerisch objektiv genommen steht doch trotz der grossen
Kälte die Redentorekirche hoch über der Salute, ein Bach dort, ein
lustiger Italiener da wenn wir einen musikalischen Vergleich ziehen wollen.
Im Innenraum der Kirchen zeigt sich der Laie wieder voll und ganz als

T

Freund der Malerei Der Raum mag noch so schon in seinem Verhaltnis,
das Interesse gilt den Altarbildern, den Grabdenkmalen. Auch hier ein
Beispiel aus Venedig Der Innenraum von S. Zaccaria gehort zu den
schonsten die Venedig aufweisen kann Diese elegante Vermischung
von Fruhrenaissance und Gothik, diese keuschen Detaile, diese prachtigen
Raumverhaltnisse Der Laie tritt ein, bleibt einen Augenblick stehen,
um dann mit Musse wieder seine Galleriestudien fortzusetzen Das
Bellinische Madonnenbild ist der Anziehungspunkt des Laien, vor diesem
bleibt es lange in Betrachtung stehen Wohl ist das Bild ein herrliches, soll
aber nicht dem Raum auch der Tribut gebracht werden Die italienische
Kirchenraume betrachtet aber der Laie beinahe durchwegs nur vom
Standpunkte der vorhandenen Altarbilder Eine Kirche wird ihm
umsomehr in Erinnerung bleiben, je mehr beruhmte Altarbilder
darinnen Tritt die Malerei uns als Gewolb- und Wanddecoration auf
so bleibt das Interesse schon zuruck. Hier wird es dem Laien eben
schon schwer die Wand- und Gewolbflachen im Ganzen zu betrachten.

Trotz aller Schonheit wird die Kirche S. Francesco in Assisi, mit den
herrlichen Werken eines Giotto, keinen sonderlichen Eindruck bei den
meisten Laien hinterlassen Wir haben fruher einen musikalischen
Vergleich versucht und Palladio mit Bach, Longhena mit einem Bellini
verglichen. Hier die lustige wenn auch oberflächliche gut komponierte
Architektur, dort die strenge Ruhe, die mathematische Ausdrucksform,
die unbedingte Logik Der Laie soll nicht allein diese leichte Architektur
verstehen lernen, er soll auch tiefer empfinden, wie er es ja in der Musik
auch tatsachlich gelernt hat. Der Laie betrachtet eine grossere Architektur
nur nach dem einzelnen Detail, damit ist es ihm aber schon unmoglich
den Kunstler des Baues zu verstehen Das Erinnerung an einen zarten
Andantesatz, wenn ein Allegro und andere Satze verstandnislos an den
Ohren des Zuhörers vorubergerauscht, wird kein Interesse an einer sym-
phonischen Komposition wach erhalten. Unser heutiges Publikum, dass
bei Beethoven aufgezogen, dass in Wagner aufgeht, hat aber musikalisch
schon ein so tiefes Verstandnis, dass Gesammtkunstwerk halbwegs
verstehen zu können. Warum sollte dies in der Baukunst, die ja einst
gefrorene Musik genannt wurde, nicht moglich sein? Es fehlt nur die
Erziehung.

2 *Wo sind die Grunde zu suchen fur die heutige Anschauung des Publikums ?*

Wie haben gesehen wie sich das Hauptinteresse des Publikums der
Malerei zuwendet Als Grunde fur diese Erscheinung sind anzufuhren,
die viele Kunstausstellungen selbst in kleineren Provinzstädten, die das
Publikum mit der modernen Bildkunst vertraut machen und die damit
verbundene Besprechung derselben in den Tagesjournalen Die reich
vorhandene Literatur gemeinverstandlicher Art uber moderne und
historische Malerei, endlich noch die derzeitige Schulerziehung im Freihandzeichnen. Die vielen grosseren und kleineren Kunstausstellungen
erwecken das allgemeine Interesse des Publikums Die Tagesblatter
sorgen dafur durch eine mehr oder weniger gute Kritik das Publikum
mit den Kunstansichten der Maler vertraut zu machen Das besser
situierte Publikum kauft ein oder das andere Bild fur seine Sammlung
oder nur als Schmuckstuck fur das eigene Heim Eine grosse Anzahl von
Kunstjournalen, wie der " Studio," " Kunst für Alle," etc., liegt heute schon
in den Kaffeehausern auf, die vorzüglichen Einzelarbeiten über Kunstler-
gruppen, die kleineren Monographien in diesen Journalen regen das Publikum
zur Betrachtung an, Tagesblatter und Kunstblatter dieser Art halten
das Publikum immer auf dem Laufenden. Soweit die moderne Malerei
Auf dem Gebiete der historischen Malerei sehen wir auch vorzugliche
literarische Kleinarbeit, gemeinverständlicher Art. Vor allem angefuhrt seien hier die Kunstlermonographien von Knackfuss, die in vor-

zuglicher Art die grossen Meister der Malkunst, bei reichem Illustrations-
material und billigen Preis behandeln Daneben finden wir auch das
Museum, Handzeichnungen aller Meister, Kupferstichkabinet, etc ,
vielfach in Laienkreisen abonniert. Hier wird das Beste gebracht, was
die internationale Galerien aufweisen können, der Preis ist verhaltnis-
mässig ein sehr billiger.

Betrachten wir die Vortragsprogramme der gemeinverstandlichen
Vortrage, wie sie von einzelnen Professoren und Dozenten in diversen
Vereinen gehalten, ein weiter Raum ist hier der Malkunst eingeraumt. An fruherer Stelle haben wir bereits darauf hingewiesen, dass
beim Bild das nur zweidimensionale Sehen dem Laien die Betrachtung erleichtert Der Laie ist durch die Schulerziehung an die Flache
und Farbe gewohnt   In welcher Weise wurde der Unterricht im Zeichnen
bisher gepflegt? Mit der Flache beginnt der kleine Knirps an der Elemen-
tarschule sein Freihandzeichenstudium, mit der Fläche beendet er
dasselbe am Gymnasium, an der Realschule.   Die kurze Zeit die dem
Modellzeichnen gewidmet spielt in dieser langen Studienzeit gar keine
Rolle   Vom einfachsten Maanderband bis zu den reichen Grotteskorna-
menten der Renaissance lernte der Schuler die Fläche und Farbe kennen,
ja selbst das Kopfstudium; das figurale Zeichnen wurde nach Vorlagen
gelernt.   Wie soll da ein Verstandnis fur Raum und Korper geweckt
werden? Der Unterricht in Projektionslehre wie er an oberen Klassen
gelehrt wird, tragt fur unsere Zwecke sehr wenig bei, da hier meist akademische Lösungen schwierigster Art verlangt werden, die zwar den
Geist anregen, aber einer vergrosserten Raumvorstellung in unserem
Sinne nicht zu Gute kommen   Wohl ist es heute besser geworden, da ja
an einzelnen Schulen uber hoheren Auftrag bereits dem Korperzeichnen
nach der Natur von fruhesten Anfang ein breiter Raum eingeraumt
Heute wird das Kind bereits von vornherein zum dreidimensionalen
Sehen gezwungen.   Die Erfolge dieser neuen Unterrichtsmethode wird
man gar bald zu fuhlen bekommen   Als grosser Fehler erscheint auch
die weitaus zu grosse Ignorierung des theoretischen Perspektivstudiums
an den niederen und hoheren Schulen

Wie sieht es nun auf dem Gebiete der Baukunst aus ? Was wurde hier
bisher fur das Publikum geleistet ? Sehr, sehr wenig   Ist die Literatur
uber Plastik schon eine sehr kleine, so fehlt sie auf architektonischem
Gebiete beinahe ganz   Erst in allerneuester Zeit zeigen sich die Ansatze
zu einer Besserung zu mindest was die Frage des modernen Heims, des
modernen Landhauses anbelangt   Wo sind die Ausstellungen die das
Publikum der Baukunst naher bringen konnten, wo die fachmannische
Kritik, ich betone fachmannische Kritik in den Tagesblättern, die das
Publikum aufklart. wo die gemeinverstandliche Literatur uber moderne
und historische Baukunst ?

Wie selten hort man etwas von gemeinverstandlichen Vortragen uber
Baukunst. Die prachtigen Arbeiten die in den Fachjournalen zu finden,
bleiben dem Publikum fremd, sie sind auch meist viel zu fachmännisch
gehalten   Die Kritiken in den Tagesblättern sind meist so unsachgemäss
und leiden gewöhnlich an einer entsetzlichen Unkenntnis   Auf diesem
Gebiete kann aber doch nur der technisch gebildete Kunstler sprechen. Der
Journalist, er mag noch so kunstverstandig, bringt durch seine Arbeiten meist
nur Unheil ins Publikum. Da und dort Phrasen die vom Publikum ohne
Verstandnis aufgenommen werden zum Schaden der Kunst, zum Schaden
der Architektur   Hier kann nur der Architekt selbst helfend eingreifen.
Das heutige Publikum, dass sich fur Malerei, Musik und Literatur so
interessiert, wurde auch der grossen Baukunst ihr volles Interesse zu-
wenden, wenn sich die Architektenschaft selbst als Lehrer und Erzieher
hergeben wurde. Ich habe schon bei Laien vorzügliche Erfahrungen
gemacht, da und dort eine Anregung, eine Aufklärung und das Interesse
ist schneller erwacht als man glauben sollte. Dazu gehort wohl vor

allem ein möglichst objektives Empfinden, dass leider unseren Kreisen
vielfach abgeht Bei aller individuellen Eigenart ist ein objektives
Behandeln der Baukunst und ihrer Schonheit möglich So lange aber die
Architektenschaft so zersplittert, so lange immer nur eine Clique gegen
die andere kampft, das schlecht heisst, was die andere gut und schon
nennt, so lange wird von einer Besserung der Verhaltnisse keine Rede sein
Nirgends herrscht eine solche Zersplitterung wie in unseren Kreisen,
nirgends so wenig collegiales Zusammenhalten Wie anders bei den
Arzten, bei den Juristen Werden moderne Architekturfragen sagen
wie Fehden moglichst offentlich ausgetragen hier zum Schaden des Publikums, sehen wir in anderen akademischen Kreisen zwar ebenso heftige
Fehden, die aber immer im engen Zirkel der Fachkreise zur Austragung
kommen Was soll sich das Publikum dabei denken, wie soll das Publikum uber Baukunst urtheilen, wenn die Meinungen der Architekten
selbst so diametral ? Selbst als strengster Moderner kann man soviel
Objektivität bewähren auch anderes gut zu finden. Man darf das Publikum nicht einseitig fur eine Sache interessieren, das Publikum soll nur
die Schonheit der Baukunst fuhlen lernen Allein seligmachende Kunst
gibt es nicht, zu allen Zeiten von den Agypten an wurde Grosses und
Schones geleistet, zu allen Zeiten auch schlechte Architektur gemacht
Hier konnen wir alle zusammen arbeiten zum eigenen Nutzen und zum
Frommen der Laien. Zum Schlusse noch ein wesentlicher Punkt Der
Architekt soll durch seine Bauten, das Publikum an Architektur, sagen
wie wahre Architektur gewohnen, das Publikum fur das Schone erziehen.
Die Aufgaben der kunstlerischen Architekten beschranken sich aber meist
nur auf kleinere Arbeiten wie Zins- und Landhauser Grosse Kunst kann
aber nur an Monumentalbauten gezeigt werden. Hier soll der Staat als
Erzieher auftreten Wer macht nun meist diese monumentalen Amtsbauten, die jedem Staat zur Zierde gereichen konnten ? Der Architekt ?
Der Kunstler ? Meist sind es die grossen Bauamter, die durch ihre
Ingenieure, diese Arbeiten zur Ausfuhrung bringen lassen Abgesehen von
einigen Landern, wo erste kunstlerische Krafte fur diese Bauten Verwendung finden, sehen wir normal die sogenannte Amtsarchitektur die nach
Bureau riecht Diese Amtsarchitektur kann kaiserlich, kaiserlich koniglich, grossherzoglich, koniglich, etc , sein, sie bleibt im Genre immer
gleich Kalte, seelenlose, schablonenhafte Architektur, ohne Individualitat,
ohne Kunst, sie tragen meist den Charakter von schlechten Schulaufgaben
aus dem Entwerfen an sich.

Wir sehen also dass der Staat die erste Pflicht hatte erziehlich auf das
Publikum einzuwirken, meist aber sehr wenig fur dieses thut, hie und da
könnte man eher sagen er erzieht das Publikum zur Geschmacklosigkeit
Auch hier kann es nur eine zielbewusste völlig geeinte Architektenschaft
sein, die Wandel schaffen kann, die Wandel schaffen muss. Wäre das Publikum zu einer wahren Kunst erzogen, wurde es sich viele dieser immer
neu erstehenden Amtsbauten nicht bieten lassen Blicken wir zuruck zur
Antike, sehen wie uns die Zeit der Renaissance an welch herrliche Pracht-
bauten entstanden hier, Staat und Fursten setzten ihren Stolz darein in
ihren Bauten wurdig reprasentiert zu werden. Heute steht der Staat,
genau so wie das Privatpublikum, auf dem Standpunkt der Billigkeit
Fur Staat und Gemeinde gilt heute der Grundsatz je billiger der Bau
desto besser , die Kunstler haben damit das Nachsehen

Wir haben damit die Gründe besprochen die das Publikum auf jenen
indolenten Standpunkte der Baukunst gegenüber bringen mussten
Im nachfolgenden soll versucht werden, auf Grund der bisher am Publikum selbst wahrgenommenen Erscheinungen ein Programm aufzustellen
dass einer Erziehung des Publikums im baukunstlerischen Sinne ent-
spricht.

3 *Welche Mittel und Wege stehen der Architektenschaft zur Verfugung eine Besserung der Verhaltnisse herbeizufuhren ?*

(*a*) Aufgaben des Staates

Die internationale Architektenschaft hat allen ihren Einfluss aufzubieten, dass neuzuerrichtende Staatsgebaude von Baukunstlern, nicht von Bauingenieuren ausgefuhrt werden   Eine offentliche Konkurrenz strengster Art hat hier zu entscheiden

In jenen Schulen wo der Freihandzeichenunterricht noch in alter Weise gepflegt wird ist von Seite der Architektenschaft, sagen wir der Kunstlerschaft uberhaupt bei den Unterrichtsbehorden auf das neue Unterrichtsprogramm in Freihandzeichnen hinzuweisen   In diesem neuen Programm muss dem Zeichnen nach der Natur der grosste Spielraum eingeraumt werden   Weiters ist darauf hinzuarbeiten dass der Unterricht in der darstellenden Geometrie weniger akademisch spitzfindig behandelt wird, da ja die Projektionslehre vor allem bei richtiger Behandlung des Stoffes berufen wäre die Jugend zur Raumvorstellung zu erziehen.   Ebenso notwendig ware es dem Perspektivunterricht selbst an den Burgerschulen ein kleines Augenmerk zuzuwenden.   Losungen einfacher perspektivischer Aufgaben von Gebaudetheilen, etc , wurden die Jugend zum Zeichnen und zum Studium der Baukunst anregen Die Architektenschaft hat bei den Unterrichtsbehorden dahin zu arbeiten, dass selbst an Volks- und Burgerschulen in den oberen Klassen Baugeschichte wenn auch im gedrangter Form gelehrt wird.   Dieser Unterricht hat Hand in Hand mit dem Geschichts- und Geographieunterricht zu gehen An Stelle der Geschichte wie sie heute meist vom kriegsgeschichtlichen Standpunkte gelehrt wird soll die Culturgeschichte treten, die fur den praktischen Menschen weit mehr erziehliche Bedeutung   Die Vaterlandskunde hat auch die heimatliche Baukunst einzuschliessen   Bei der Geschichte des Heimatlandes soll chronologisch die Bauentwicklung des Landes besprochen werden, im Geographieunterricht ist auf die Vertheilung dieser Bauten hinzuweisen   Skioptikonbilder, Ansichtskarten sind zur Unterstutzung des Unterrichts heranzuziehen   Man rege die Jugend zum Sammeln von Ansichtskarten, die Bauten der Heimatskunst wiedergeben, an , Material ist genugend da   Auf diese Weise kann schon beim Kinde die Freude an der heimischen Baukunst geweckt werden Heute, wo die Frage der Denkmalpflege in allen Landern akut geworden, ist dies von grosster Bedeutung.   Lehrt der Jugend die Liebe zur herrlichen Kunst und damit ist der beste Hort fur die Erhaltung unserer Denkmaler gegeben.   So wurde sich der Staat in Massen Leute erziehen die die Denkmale ihrer Heimat schatzen wurden und manches Objekt wurde damit vor Verfall gerettet werden konnen

Als Nothwendigkeit stellt sich damit ein obligater Unterricht in allgemeiner Kunstlehre mit besonderer Berucksichtigung der Heimatkunst an den Lehrerseminaren ein   Auch dies ware nicht undurchfuhrbar Solange die Massen nicht fur die Baukunst Interesse gewinnen solange bleibt die Denkmalpflegefrage eine illusorische   Soweit die Aufgaben der Regierungen in dieser Frage.

Als Aufgaben der Architektenvereinigungen sind anzusehen .

(*a*) Veranstaltung von Ausstellungen moderner Bauten und Ausstellungen historischer Bauwerke der Heimat

(*b*) Damit in Verbindung Vortrage die allgemein zuganglich und als Themen zu behandeln hatten.   Moderne Bedurfnisse im Wohnbau, der moderne Innenraum, Bedeutung des Architekten fur den Bauherrn, offentliche Besprechungen uber akute Städtebaufragen, Monumentalbauten, Konkurrenzen   Veranstaltung von Vortragscyklen gemein verstandlicher Art uber historische Baukunst mit besonderer Berucksichtigung der Heimatskunst   Grossere und kleinere Excursionen fur das Publikum, unter Fuhrung von Vereinsmitgliedern   Ausschreibungen kleiner Konkurrenzen fur Bauanlagen auf dem Lande, wie Kirchen, Gemeindebauten, etc   Empfehlungen pramnerter Arbeiten von Seite der Vereine, unter Umstanden kostenlose Uberlassung der Plane an arme Gemeinden   Diese Aufgaben waren den Hauptvereinen und den kleineren Bezirksvereinen zuzuweisen

Dem Architekten als Einzelnen fallen folgende Aufgaben zu Moglichst objektive Behandlung jeder Baufrage Laien gegenuber, moglichste Betheiligung literarischer Art bei Kunstfragen. Der Architekt muss selbst zum Wort kommen wenn er verstanden werden soll   Einsendung von Beitragen uber heimatliche Baukunst an grossere Tagesblatter Architekten von grosser historischer Bildung fallt endlich die Aufgabe zu in gemeinverstandlicher Art kleinere oder grossere Gebiete der Baukunst in Einzelarbeiten zu behandeln. Reichere Vereinigungen konnten hier viel dazu beitragen solche Monographien unter nicht zu teuren Preis dem Publikum zuganglich zu machen

Zum Schlusse der Arbeit sei noch einmal erinnert, dass ein einiges Vorgehen hier zum Ziele fuhren kann. Hier muss jedes Privatinteresse, jede vorgefasste kunstlerische Ansicht zuruckstehen, gegen den grossen idealen Gedanken, der Baukunst jene Stellung einzuraumen, die ihr seit den Uranfang der Cultur zukommt

Wien 3 Marz 1906

---

(5) ARCHITECTURE AND ITS PLACE IN A GENERAL EDUCATION

By Banister F. Fletcher, F R I B A

Part I.—Architecture.

As we glance along the perspective of past ages, we can find in the buildings of each period a lithic history which indicates conditions of existence far more truthfully than that written by men in more perishable materials   Thus architecture has been the mirror of the history of each period, and has been an index of the social and political condition of the people, swayed by those great religious and historical events which serve as landmarks in the history of mankind.

Architecture, then, may be said to be the result of, and inseparable from, history, because the work of man in each period is before us as we look upon the mighty structures of past civilisations   By the study of architecture we learn of the condition, hopes, fears, and the very thoughts of the peoples of bygone days as certainly as, if not more surely than, by the contemporary written chronicles

The advancement of civilisation is made manifest in architecture, which presents so noble a field for the display of the grand and the beautiful, and which at the same time is so intimately connected with the essentials of life

In creations of surpassing excellence the painter and the sculptor may display their individual genius, but it is in the great monuments of architectural taste and magnificence that the genius of a nation is unmistakably stamped   The Egyptian, the Greek, the Saracen, the Mediævalist—what a key their respective styles afford to the character and conditions of the people !

In prehistoric days man in his savage state required but shelter from the elements, wild beasts, and human enemies, and this he obtained by means of the natural cave, the hut of twigs and " wattle-and-daub," or the tent. The evolutions of form which took place during the period between that far-off time and the earliest historic architecture have not yet been bridged by any discovery

Architectural history can be divided into two main groups—viz historical, i e styles evolved from a parent stem and influencing other styles, and non-historical, which were developed mainly on their own account, and have little direct influence on other styles

In dealing with this subject let us take the former, which mainly comprises Egyptian, Assyrian, and European architecture, and ascertain what it tells us of history, leaving aside the second group, which includes Indian, Chinese, Japanese, Peruvian, Mexican, and Saracenic, as these have only exerted a limited influence on European architecture

Egypt is the first to claim our attention, and there we find, dating from about B.C 5000, the first and greatest attempts at permanent constructions   Appropriately is the Sphinx at Ghizeh placed as a sentinel forbidding us, as it were, to know by what long stages of evolution historic architecture has come to life   Built nearly B C. 4000, the Pyramids represent the governing idea of the Egyptian faith—viz that immortality could be insured by the preservation of the mummy, secured in such everlasting mounds of masonry, the secret of whose construction even in these days of engineering skill is a wonder to the world   We glean from the pyramids, mastabas, and rock-cut temples the Egyptian's strong belief in a future state, the existence of a powerful priesthood, and the significance of the traditional, unchangeable, and mysterious religious rites.   Herodotus informs us that the dwelling-house was regarded as a temporary lodging, the tomb being the permanent abode of the spirit   The temples, with entrances made imposing by splendid avenues of sphinxes, alike in their mysterious planning, forbidding aspect, and painted hieroglyphics, tell us of the exclusiveness of the Egyptian religion, for they were not places of worship for the people, but rather sanctuaries for the kings and priests

These massive buildings would have been impossible without a despotic government and the forced labour of a vast and submissive population of slaves and captive foreigners, who probably received no other reward than their food

We next turn our attention to the architecture of Western Asia, which tells us that the Assyrians and Persians were a nation of warriors to whom warlike deeds or the conquest of surrounding countries were more congenial than the erection of stupendous tomb houses.

Temples are wanting, sacrifices having been conducted in the open air, but the thousands of prisoners taken in battle were employed in raising those enormous mounds or elevated platforms on which the palaces of Nineveh, Nimroud, Khorsabad, Susa, and Persepolis were constructed, a small space being reserved for those temple observatories built in receding coloured stages, from which the astrologer-priests could consult the signs of the heavens.

We now come to a more definite period—viz that of the Greeks, whose architecture reflects each stage of their history with remarkable accuracy, rising to its fully developed artistic height after the battles of Marathon and Salamis

The buildings of the Pelasgic and Mycenæan periods indicate the ruggedness and severity of the earlier inhabitants , but the Hellenic period introduces us to the most refined architecture the world has ever seen, which has been a pattern to, and has exerted so great an influence on, all subsequent art, that Greece must be regarded as the primary source of the best artistic inspiration, which corresponds in a marked degree with her literary pre-eminence   In a climate remarkable for the clearness of its atmosphere, and in a country rich with marble (the most beautiful and monumental of all building materials), the Greeks evolved a type of architecture whose purity of outline and perfection of proportion has never been equalled.   National games and religious festivals united them in reverence for their religion, engendered a desire to erect stately temples, gave them that love for music, the drama, and literature, and inspired that emulation in manly sports and contests which distinguished the race   The national exaltation of the Greeks when they finally defeated the Persians was accountable for the fact that all the more important temples now found in Greece were built in the "fifty years" which succeeded the overthrow of their enemies.

The most famous and the most refined of these were erected during the rule of the great Athenian, Pericles (B C 444–429), which marked the climax of Athenian prosperity, art, and culture.   This is reflected in those world-famous structures on the Athenian Acropolis, in which the most delicate optical refinements were introduced, and the most perfect sculpture known in the history of mankind was employed in their adornment

The principal Greek buildings are the temples, and these are directly in contrast to those of Egypt, being public as opposed to royal monuments   Instead of the high inclosing wall and mysterious halls of the priest-ridden Egyptian, we find the small "cella" for the statue of the god, while on the exterior is lavished all the beauty of column, entablature, sculptured metope, frieze, and pediment, brightly treated in many colours.

The open-air unroofed theatres, in which the plays of the great Athenian dramatists were produced, the palæstra, with their lecture recesses, and the stadia are the practical evidences of the Grecian love for the drama, philosophy, and outdoor sports.

The power of Macedonia was made paramount by Philip and his son Alexander the Great, and the latter in B C 334 set out on his great expedition for subduing Egypt, Persia, and Northern India   His influence on these countries and the dissemination of Hellenic civilisation far and wide throughout Asia are made manifest in the architecture of Northern India, which is specially remarkable for its Grecian purity and for the influence it exerted on subsequent Saracenic styles of art which a thousand years later were introduced there

When in B C 146 Greece became a Roman province, her architecture as a national style died with her nationality, although, like her civilisation, it continued for a long period to exert its influence upon Roman art

The architecture of Rome then displaced that of Greece, as did also her civilisation, and we pass from the simple trabeated style to a complex type of arch, vault, and beam

Roman development was influenced largely by the older Etruscan civilisation of Central Italy, so that in Roman architecture we find the blending of the beam of the Greeks with the arch of the Etruscans.   The character and history of the Romans is well shown in their architecture and the number and variety of their buildings

Temples were still erected, but of a different type from those of the Greeks, and were rendered necessary as much for the protection of accumulated Greek spoils as for worship.   In addition to the stately temples, finished and adorned with the finest sculptures, we now find buildings designed for many purposes, and of complicated construction   Stately palaces laid out on an immense scale tell us of the magnificence and luxury of the Roman court, while the superbly decorated private houses of Rome and Pompeii indicate the important character of the "patria potestas"—the basis of Roman law   The Romans' love of justice is also displayed in their numerous basilicas or courts of law, while their theatres indicate quite a different idea of the drama and its representation from those of the Greeks   The amphitheatres and the *circi* were the natural results of that love for brutal sports between men and wild beasts, and that coarseness yet boldness of character which enabled the Romans to bring the whole of the then known world under their domination, while the great thermæ of the later empire indicate the indolence and love of luxury which led to the final decline and fall of the empire. The conquering legions of Rome were utilised during the periods of peace as unskilled workmen in the formation of the great Roman roads, and the triumphal arches, which are to be met with in various parts of Europe, form the permanent expression of Roman power and dominion.

Further, by the universal use of the newly invented material, concrete, and the employment of the arch, vault, and dome, the original architecture of imperial Rome was reproduced in all parts of the empire Thus the Roman style of building, ever the faithful mirror of Roman civilisation, became the foundation of all later European architecture.

The most magnificent period of Roman art synchronised with the Augustan age of literature, and it was the boast of Augustus that he had found Rome of brick, but would leave it of marble.

From this period began the decline of the Roman Empire, and the life of ease and luxury led by the Romans is amply illustrated in their later architecture, which is often over-decorated and coarse in detail

But a climax was at hand, and with the fall of the Roman Empire came the end of a great chapter in architecture and civilisation

The new force in the world's history was Christianity, and, as all roads led to Rome, the very highways which formed the connecting links of the empire could be used for the propagation of the new faith. As Tennyson has said

A fuller light illumined all,
A breeze thro' all the garden swept

The new religion resulted in the construction of over thirty churches of the basilican type in Rome alone   This form of building was preferred by the early Christians for reasons too numerous even to touch upon here   These churches, by the retention of pagan Roman architectural features and arrangements, modified by degrees to meet the requirements of the new religion, clearly indicate that the new faith was slow in developing.

An impetus was given to the new development by the transference of the capital from Rome to Byzantium (Constantinople), resulting in a new style known as Byzantine.   Away from the influence of " old Rome," the architecture of " New Rome " developed features which were undoubtedly of Eastern origin, although carried out largely by Greek workmen, and of these the dome on pendentives was the most important. This style reached its culmination in St Sophia, Constantinople, and became the official architecture of the Eastern or Greek Church, which, like the orthodox faith it represents, has remained strangely conservative even to the present time.

Not so the architectural development in Western Europe outside Italy.   Here during the Dark Ages architecture was dormant, for from the break-up of the Western Empire till the time of Charlemagne, in the eighth century, building was at a standstill   Charlemagne, however, in a great measure restored the arts to Western Europe, and his magnificent tomb house at Aix-la-Chapelle is one of the finest examples of the period. The rise and cohesion of the Gothic nations was a matter of time, but the changes and progress of the Roman Church throughout the mediæval period were faithfully exemplified in the great monastic establishments erected.

Till the Western European nations could get out of leading-strings they looked to Rome, and for three centuries—tenth, eleventh, and twelfth—cathedrals and churches were erected all over Europe, bearing distinct resemblance to the later Roman architecture, although carried out by the new nations which had been spreading over Europe from the north and east, the style being known to us as Romanesque.   This is exceedingly interesting, for it shows us how far-reaching and how settled Roman civilisation was   The Romans themselves, however, were eventually driven by the Goths into their native country, and as time went on the nations of Western Europe developed their own styles.   The formation of the European States, and the religious enthusiasm of the period manifested in the Crusades, were most important factors in giving the necessary impetus to the introduction of that type of architecture known as Gothic

The architecture of the Middle Ages was an evolution of the Romanesque style derived from the universal *concrete* of the Romans, and was an architecture of *stone in small pieces*, representing the disintegrated state of European society, and symbolising as it were the breaking up of the Roman Empire into small independent States.

The Gothic masons heaped up their small stones in towers that rose on open archways through the lofty roofs of the surrounding naves, and, pointing heavenward, tapered away in lofty spires, embroidered in a fretwork of elaborate tracery

The prominence of the clergy, consequent upon their learning and the wealth and power of the monastic orders, caused the Church to be the one great avenue for advancement in the Middle Ages, and this, aided by the religious fervour of the times, was responsible for the great outburst of church building at the commencement of the thirteenth century Hence the pointed-arch architecture of the thirteenth, fourteenth, and fifteenth centuries in Europe was in great measure an ecclesiastical one, causing the construction of an immense number of important cathedrals, to say nothing of innumerable parish churches   Throughout this period, although militarism was an important factor in the social *régime*, the builder's art caused the employment of a large section of the community, while the Church was the chief profession.   The historic development is shown very clearly in these Gothic churches   The *priest* is exemplified in the plain and somewhat ascetic character of the Early English or thirteenth-century style, the *noble* in the more florid treatment of the Decorated period, and the *merchant* in the matter-of-fact yet occasionally showy character of the fifteenth century—characteristics which were surprisingly similar in all the countries of Europe

Gothic cathedrals are very faithful exponents of mediæval civilisation and Church history   Their place in the national life was all-important, for, in the absence of printed matter, they formed the history-books of the period, their sculptures and beautiful stained-glass windows reflecting incidents of Bible history from the Creation to the Redemption.   They took the place now occupied by the school, free library, museum, and picture-gallery   Here also is to be found the grand chronicle of secular history, in which kings and nobles, knights and commoners were represented   The worship of relics, of local saints (as St. Thomas at Canterbury), the periodical pilgrimages, the introduction of Mariolatry, the necessity of aisles for processional purposes, the introduction of chantry chapels for masses for the dead, and other changes of ritual, had their influence on church plans and on their ornamentation

The great size and beauty of the mediæval cathedrals was in a large measure due to the concentration of the artistic energy of the period on these works, instead of its being employed, as so often happens nowadays, on a variety of buildings.

Militarism, on the other hand, is expressed in the fortified and frowning castles of the nobles, which form an eloquent though silent testimony to the feudal system of the mediæval period, as also the comparatively unsettled condition of the country

Gothic architecture closed with the mediæval period at the commencement of the fifteenth century in Italy, and of the sixteenth century in the rest of Europe.   It had, like the mediæval civilisation which accompanied it, run its course, and was overturned by a succession of historical events which in the succeeding centuries were to alter the face of Europe.

We can, by a retrospective view, see the influences which slowly paved the way for that great upheaval of literature and art which we know as the "Renaissance," and which, aided by national enthusiasm and the uncovering of classical buildings buried for centuries, caused a desire for the revival of old Roman architectural forms and ornamentation.

As was to be expected, the return to classic ideals naturally commenced in Italy, where the Gothic art had never been followed as in Northern Europe   The first town to be affected by the revival was Florence, due in large measure to its commercial prosperity and the enlightenment of the Medici family.   The way was paved by the writings of Dante, Petrarch, Boccaccio, and, later still, by Erasmus, who helped to crystallise the revolt against mediæval thought and art.   This revolt was also aided by the newly discovered MSS. of Greek and Latin authors, of which the books of architecture by Vitruvius, who lived in the time of Augustus, were most important.   Other facts, such as the invention of printing, which aided the spirit of inquiry and the diffusion of thought, the discovery of gunpowder, which changed the whole method of warfare, and the mariner's compass, which led to the discovery of the New World, were important factors in the propagation of that freedom of thought and action characteristic of the period.   The influx of Greek scholars and artists to Europe, consequent upon the capture of Constantinople by the Turks in 1453, had an important influence in an age ripe for an intellectual change, and in which it became, for a time, the fashion to talk in Latin—an evidence of the close connection between the architecture and literature of this period.

All these influences might have been futile if they had not been sown on fruitful ground, but fortunately such artists as Della Robbia, Ghiberti, Brunelleschi, Alberti, Donatello, Bramante, Peruzzi, Sangallo, Raphael, Vignola, Michael Angelo, Sansovino, the Lombardi, Palladio, and a host of others, were as giants in the arts   Vasari, in his writings on the lives of different architects and artists, shows us the personal influence exercised by them on the arts and crafts of the Renaissance period   The character of the architecture, as represented in the new churches and palaces, faithfully reflects all these great changes in favour of the ancient Roman traditions by the banishment of the Gothic pointed arch, pointed intersecting vault and vertical features, and the employment in a modified form of the Roman orders of architecture, clothing plans derived from the Roman circular dome supported on a square base by means of the Byzantine pendentive

This wave of Roman rejuvenation was felt in France, England, Germany, Spain, and north-western Europe, though the effect in each country was delayed by the distance from the fountain-head, and was influenced by various social and political events

In France, rich with splendid piles of Gothic architecture, the new style did not entirely displace the old, but was drafted upon it in a most delightful and picturesque fashion.   It was mainly utilised in the palaces of the kings and the town halls and large country houses of the nobility, the immense number of churches of the Middle Ages long sufficing for the spiritual needs of the people   We cannot justly trace the influence of Italy upon France unless due notice is taken of the invasions of the former

country by Charles VIII. and Francis I., in vindication of their claims to
the thrones of Naples and Milan, because their return to France marks the
distribution over Europe of Italian artists and workmen, such as Leonardo
da Vinci, Cellini, Serlio, Vignola, Rosso, Primaticcio, and others who
followed in their train

The Renaissance in England, which synchronised with the Reformation, was brought about by many historical events, such as the meeting
of Henry VIII with the French king on the Field of the Cloth of Gold, and
the consequent introduction into England of Italian and French architects.
Again, the suppression of monasteries in 1536 caused the diffusion of vast
revenues, which were distributed amongst the courtiers of Henry VIII ,
and this led to the erection of residences for the new favourites which
displaced the obsolete castles of the old nobility, a large proportion of whom
had been killed in the Wars of the Roses. A further result was the building
and endowment of grammar schools and colleges, which played an important part in the movement, and paved the way for the great literary
activity of the Elizabethan era, rendered famous by the writings of Spenser,
Shakespeare, Burleigh, and Sir Philip Sidney

The Elizabethan period, when church-building was at a standstill,
is notable for the influx of Flemish and German workmen and the immigration of Huguenot craftsmen, due to the Massacre of St. Bartholomew in
1572, and is remarkable for its numerous domestic mansions, the design
of which was influenced very largely by this immigration The newly
introduced classical details were used with such caution and delayed by
such conservatism as we should expect of the English character, and the
buildings still retain many special features, such as the great hall, long
gallery, broad staircase, and large mullioned windows, all inherited from
the previous periods These mansions are generally found in a perfect
setting formed by a beautiful formal garden, indicative of the Englishman's
love of country life, and they are designed on generous lines, illustrating
the scale of hospitality which obtained in the spacious times of Queen
Elizabeth.

The later Renaissance period felt more strongly the classical influence,
which was introduced in its purer state by Inigo Jones, and by Sir
Christopher Wren in the latter half of the seventeenth century

Owing to the Great Fire of London, when many places of worship were
destroyed, numerous churches were erected in the city for the Protestant
religion, which gave prominence to preaching, and demanded galleries
and congregational planning in place of the long-drawn processional aisles
of the mediæval period

In North-West Europe the Reformation accompanied, or rather
preceded, a fresh building era, but with the exception of the period of
Charles V. the existence of a number of independent petty states occasionally at war, each having its own government and capital, prevented any
such national effort as was possible in France. On the other hand, ecclesiastical, commercial, and municipal buildings tell of the flourishing condition of some of the principal towns of this part of Europe

In Spain the Renaissance followed the fall of Granada in 1492, when the
country became consolidated under Ferdinand and Isabella ; but the new
style was much influenced by the Moorish craftsmen, who gave a special
ornamental character of richness, intricacy, and refinement to the architecture of the country

Until the nineteenth century, which was the era of revivals of all styles,
architecture was generally traditional. These revivals were brought about
by numerous causes, among which the facility of travel, the ease of illustration, and the break-up of traditional schools of craftsmen were important
Nevertheless, architecture still continues to reflect the thought of the day,
the social needs and aspirations of the people, and is an index of the civilising
forces at work. This is shown in the erection of numerous types of build-

ings, such as museums, board schools, public libraries, public markets, hospitals, swimming baths, drill halls, colleges, picture and art galleries, and scientific and benevolent institutions to meet modern requirements. Architecture is hardly likely to develop into a systematised style in the future, because architects, having eaten of the tree of knowledge of all past periods, will continue to be swayed, as regards mere decorative forms, by passing fancies helped by literature and accentuated by sentiment

In the foregoing I have endeavoured to elucidate that a study of the history of architecture enables us to interpret the moral, artistic, and religious character of humanity, and that a closer insight into the profoundest characteristics of a nation is to be obtained by a study of the buildings erected in different periods, so that the thoughts, habits, and instincts of the times are more clearly and more truthfully presented to us without the possibility of being misled as by the writings of an inaccurate historian

`Part II.—Architecture. Its Place in a General Education.`

The petrified history, *i e* the architecture of the past, having thus been outlined, let us look at its place in the present educational system, first considering some reason why a detailed study of the art has not hitherto been included in educational curricula.

Its absence has doubtless been largely due to its technical nature, and to the misconception formed by many that the lay mind could not embrace its forms or the constructive principles of which it is the outcome. There does not appear to be any other valid reason that would account for the fact of the educational door having been shut so long upon such an important and entrancing subject   A stronger reason may probably have been the inability to discuss the subject from the educational point of view, because of the absence of readily available illustrations   To expound architecture to the layman without adequate views and plans is like reading a play instead of witnessing it upon the stage, and this lack of illustration must obviously have been a great deterrent, which nowadays no longer exists.

Notwithstanding that architecture has been entirely omitted from educational codes of the past, there have always been *dilettanti* who have been worshippers at her shrine, and among modern writers it is well to remember that many, like Ruskin, Freeman, and Fergusson, have had no professional education in the art   Many of the world's greatest men and rulers of the past were builders, or at least patrons of architecture, *e g* the kings of Egypt, Darius, Xerxes, Pericles, Alexander, Augustus, Hadrian, Trajan, Constantine, Theodoric, Theodosius, William of Wykeham, William the Conqueror, Charlemagne, the Medici, Wolsey, Elizabeth, Francis I , Louis XIV , Philip of Spain, and Napoleon III.   Owing, however, to the march of democracy and the wider distribution of wealth, the patronage and protection of great men have been wanting in recent times, and, the people not being educated up to the value of art as a national system, the study of architecture has fallen into a state which is not likely to promote either the production of good building or national interest therein   The art cannot thrive without these protecting influences so necessary for its production

Architecture has no place assigned to it in the present educational schemes on account of the apathy of directors of education.   This is scarcely their own fault, since, being brought up on a scientific code, they naturally clamour for the inclusion of geology, mineralogy, astronomy, and other sciences

The fact that music and singing are also included (although taught in an elementary sense only) accounts for the greater general interest taken in these arts by the public, and justifies music being termed, as it was by

Symonds, the truly modern art   History and literature are also included
in modern education, but they lack much human interest, because their
joint production, architecture—or the petrified history of the past—is
scarcely ever mentioned   Surely the work of human hands is worthy of
study, since it gives us an insight, not obtainable in other ways, to the
thoughts, feelings, and aspirations of the men who produced it

It is regrettable that architecture has as yet no seat within the portals
of the ancient universities, and I submit that the time is now ripe for the
establishment of a special faculty of architecture, to advance its general
study apart from its adoption as a profession.   If anywhere, these centres
are essentially the places where we might reasonably expect that the
history of the humanities should be welcomed, and that the student
should be able to obtain instruction in the elementary principles of the art
of past ages.

All over the country at the present time scientific and strictly technical
education, helped by large grants of money from the public purse, is
advancing with rapid strides, and schools in business and other centres
are being erected in furtherance of the forward policy of national education.
This being so, at such universities as Oxford and Cambridge the wider
aspect of life, ancient and modern, should be cared for, and their curricula
ought to include the culture and art of all ages   Architecture is much
more worthy of inclusion in a general education than a score of subjects
one might mention that have secured recognition and protection.

Architecture, and the kindred arts of painting and sculpture, are
unique, as they represent not only the thought of each period, which is
likewise expressed in its literature, but they exhibit also the work of
human hands, the buildings of all kinds which are the results of brain
power or thought and hand-power or construction

As regards the technicalities of the subject, there seems no reason why
these, which are much simpler than in many of the sciences above referred
to, should not be easily learnt by the average student of history, and why
a lecturer, imbued with the absorbing nature of the subject, should not
invest it with sufficient human interest and explain the necessary technical
details so as to make it intelligible to the ordinary general student

The possibilities of the inclusion of architectural history in any scheme
of liberal education seem to be facilitated and indeed rendered more necessary for many reasons, a few of which can be enumerated briefly   Courses
of lectures on various periods of architectural history have already been
provided through the progressiveness of certain modern educational
authorities, of which the London University is an example, and from the
attendance at these the authorities must now be alive to the fact that what
they have provided was greatly needed and is much appreciated, in spite of
the fact that the lectures are given without much relation to or co-ordina-
tion with the general history of the period, which detracts from their mutual
interest

Modern facilities for travel have also done much to arouse a genuine
interest in the architectural works of the past in different countries   The
personally conducted educational expeditions which have been popular
during later years are also largely responsible for the desire among travellers
to know something of the forms of art which are thus brought prominently
before them   Photography, too, has been an important factor in interesting
a large section of the community, especially of the travelled and educated
public and *dilettanti*, in matters of art and architectural history, and has
caused a thirst for knowledge of the subject which can best and most
easily be obtained by attendance at lectures in which it is systematically
dealt with   The general spread of education in matters of art has caused
a yearning for some knowledge of architectural forms not provided by any
educational scheme yet in vogue

Further, the use of lantern slides, the importance of which must not be overlooked, rendering possible the adequate illustration of the various forms and features of each period to large audiences, has given an added interest to such lectures, and has awakened an enthusiasm for the subject which could have been brought about by no other means

Photographs in conjunction with lantern slides enable the art history of any period of which examples remain to be shown and dealt with *seriatim*, because by means of photographs of detail and ornament the subject can be illustrated and the process of evolution and design thus made clear, so as to be entirely comprehensible to the least imaginative

The inclusion of art in the new scheme of the humanities initiated by the University Extension Board of London University is an important step, for true art is the grandest work of which man is capable, and the history of any period is incomplete without it   The whole scheme of work is arranged solely from the point of view of a liberal education, and not for professional or technical purposes

We have seen in the general history of European architecture how its various forms resulted from the social, political, and industrial condition of the people, and how through this intimate connection art was swayed by it

We have also seen why its study has not been included in past schemes of so-called liberal education, and why its inclusion is not easily rendered possible   Let us now consider the probable result of such inclusion, and the benefits which the general community will derive thereby.

I plead on behalf of every person to whom a liberal education is desirable, not as a means of enabling him to gain a living, but as fitting him to enjoy to the greatest extent his daily existence by inculcating a special interest in the history of past ages   Travelled and cultured people are included in this class, and for them each type of architecture must be bound up with the causes—geographical, geological, climatic, religious, social, and historical—of which it is the result, and its intimate connection with all these must be shown more clearly than is possible in a technical course for young students

At present most people who wander amongst the most beautiful and most soulful creations of the past are unable to appreciate either their meaning or their qualities, owing to their ignorance of architecture   To them form has no meaning, and a Grecian temple, a Roman amphitheatre, or a Gothic spire fails to recall any of the conditions which render each a reflection of its own period in history.

The inclusion of architecture therefore in any systematic course of instruction seems essential, and will give to those who study it, even in a superficial way, a general outline of the arts of form, and a clearer perception of the trend of humanity in past ages, which is very necessary to a thorough and complete understanding of history   It will also give an additional pleasure in travelling, through awakened interest in the great works of architecture, and because of the knowledge acquired of the place of each work in the evolution of art

To know something about pictures, to talk with an air of knowledge about the various schools of painting and sculpture, and to show an acquaintance with the galleries in which they are found has long been fashionable, but has it been realised that with a knowledge of architecture each street is a picture gallery where everyone may enter without so much as the payment of an entrance fee ?

The late Bishop Creighton once said at an architectural gathering that " architecture is the most democratic of the arts, that it goes literally into the market place, that it is for everybody, and that rich and poor alike may enjoy it." How essential, then, it is for the production of well-designed buildings that the patrons of architecture—the public—should have a desire for good buildings ! Then consider the individual buildings ; have not a great number of them been erected by the general mass of the community in past ages ?   Are they not in the highest degree human, for can we not see the marks of saw and chisel, made maybe hundreds of years ago, but still telling us of the methods of construction, craftsmanship, and design of the time ?   Again, our free gallery of buildings varies with the day and time of year , we may see them in the haze of early dawn, in the full flood of noonday sun, in the dimness of twilight, or in the weirdness of moonlight, while in the change of seasons we get that variety which gives them life   No special lighting is necessary for the works of the architect, which form a setting in their highest flights for the work of sculptor and painter

The sense of environment, and the effect of the weather, which gives colour and texture to the walls and lichen-covered roofs, add to the enjoyment obtainable from the study of an old cathedral, and the good influence of a beautiful building upon all who pass and repass it daily.   By environment we mean not only the position of the building on some specially interesting spot, but the environment of the period in which the building was erected, viz. the history of the time and of the people who helped to erect the structure   If we study either architecture or history aright, we must get into the " atmosphere of the period."   It may be said with some truth that history has been to architecture what steam is to machinery, the grand propelling power , while, on the other hand, architecture has been the printing press of all periods.

Architecture is more particularly entitled to the attention of the general student than any other of the fine arts, because it calls into action so many and such varied branches of mechanical labour, and because, operating thus extensively upon industry, it also promotes national prosperity   Hence the dissemination of a taste for it among the middle as well as the more opulent classes of the State is to be recommended, no less as sound policy than with regard to more direct and more obvious results.

Therefore, in these days of enlightenment, and in the interests of true as against superficial education, is it not expedient to provide for the study of architecture and its connection with history in the curriculum of the education necessary for every individual ?   Is it not the art that shelters us from the elements, and with which we are brought into daily contact , the art which gives us " home , " the art that enshrines and illuminates the most sacred of our associations, forming and fashioning the ornamentation of religion, which it aids by the mystery of its light, shade, and colour , the art that has been and is the outcome of conditions intimately bound up with the history of the human race ?   Finally, is it not the art which is the mother of all arts ?   For from it sprang painting, sculpture, and all the arts and crafts of succeeding ages of development

The time spent in the study of such an enthralling subject will not be regretted, for every ruin will then tell of the history of other days, and will enable the character of the men of the period in which it was erected to be understood.   It will also open up the enjoyment of the contemplation of forms of which the meaning will be appreciated, and will also enable us to realise more fully the truth of the poet Longfellow's lines

To build,

That is the noblest art of all the arts
Painting and Soulpture are but images,
Are merely shadows cast by outward things
On stone or canvas, having in themselves
No separate existence   Architecture,
Existing in itself, and not in seeming
A something it is not, surpasses them
As substance shadow

(6) By OTTO WAGNER, Imperial and Royal Superintendent of
Works, Vienna, Professor of the Imperial and Royal Academy
of Plastic Arts.

(On behalf of the Society of Austrian Architects.)

Baukunstlerische Bildung des Publikums kommt durch die Erorterungen uber die Frage 1 schon in jenes Gebiet, von welchem aus eine
richtige Beantwortung zu erhoffen ist.

Werden die besten Vorbilder durch hervorragende Kunstler geschaffen,
so wird das kunstlerische Empfinden der Allgemeinheit sicher dadurch
wachgerufen, oder das Bestehende verstärkt

Freilich bleibt es dabei immer Hauptbedingung, dass diese Vorbilder
auf sehr hoher kunstlerischer Stufe stehen, also von ersten Künstlern
geschaffen sind   Erstklassige Kunstler werden jedes Werk dem Zwecke
vollig anpassen ; sie werden sich des geeigneten Ausfuhrungsmateriales
und der richtigen Konstruktion bedienen, um die Kunstformen daraus
zu bilden   Nur so wird die erwünschte Charakteristik und Schönheit
des Werkes entstehen und nur diese werden imstande sein, den Beschauer
zu befriedigen   Sicher wird dann auch die Erkenntnis im Beschauer
aufleuchten, dass der Kunstler in allgemein verstandlicher Sprache spricht.
Ist aber das Kunstwerk dem Beschauer verständlich, so schwindet der
bestehende Widerwille, sich in ein Werk zu vertiefen, und die Moglichkeit und der Wille, es zu beurteilen, tritt ein

Gewiss ist, damit mustergiltige Bauausführungen entstehen, die Staatshilfe notig, da der Staat in erster Linie berufen ist, die Kunst, den Kultur-
messer der Menschheit zu fordern

Diese Staatshilfe ist, wenn sie wirksam sein soll, nur dadurch moglich
dass sich der Staat, das Land oder die Stadt, da ihnen das Kunstver
ständnis mangelt, zur Losung aller Kunstfragen eines geeigneten Organes,
eines Senates bedienen, welcher Senat nur aus sich betätigenden Kunstlern zu bestehen und daruber zu wachen hatte, dass nur Gutes geschaffen
wird

Die Antwort auf Frage 4 muss daher lauten

Die baukunstlerische Bildung des Publikums kann nur durch das
geschaffene Gute richtig beeinflusst werden, denn nichts ist so siegreich
wie eben das Gute

---

(7) By FRANCISCO DEL VILLAR Y CARMONA, MANUEL VEGA Y MARCH,
and EDUARDO MERCADER Y SACANELLA.

The want of architectonic education among the masses of the public
is everywhere a general fact. Owing to local circumstances and to the
various shades of the phenomenon it is generally attributed to different
causes, there is in reality, however, but one, and this is the most pitiful
ignorance of what constitutes and characterises our art

The reality and importance of the subject are of course evident, as
well as the necessity for affording concrete solutions that may modify
the actual state of things for the benefit of the public, whose education
will increase ; of architects, whose status will improve in proportion as
their efforts are duly appreciated ; of art, by means of which it will ensure
the respect of everybody, and will henceforward be free from sacrilegious
attacks by the ignorant masses.

Public architectonic education includes two problems : first, to teach
people what architecture is ; secondly, to direct their taste, so that knowing

what art is they may point out the best models   This second problem is only an aspect of the general one of artistic education, which nowadays one tries to solve in all art manifestations.

It is necessary to educate public taste in architecture as we educate it, for instance, in music or in painting   In reference to the first, it must be said that, though almost everybody knows, instinctively at least, what music is and what painting is, yet very few know what is meant by architecture   Therefore it is necessary to teach it; without such teaching it would be losing one's time to pretend to educate public taste in art

In order to solve the first problem it is necessary to make the public understand that architecture is all that realises art in a building   There is, or there ought to be, art in the selection of a site , in the distribution of a building ; in its situation , in the selection of materials , in the silhouette of the whole building , in the composition of the façade ; in the decoration of the inside , in the distribution of light and shade ; in the sanitary arrangements ; in comfort ; in the cleverness with which inside and outside aspects, diversified or uniform, are brought about , in the whole impression of the building upon its dweller or upon the spectator , in colour , in relief ; in proportion , in material security , in a word, in everything which reveals the thought of the artist-architect and the influence of his soul on the work   Art is to be displayed in buildings, gardens, towns, and even in the country.   By architecture is meant the construction of a cathedral, of a bridge ; the planning of a mansion, as well as the laying out of a village , the outlining of a road, the hollowing of a canal, if there is art in them

To solve the second problem it is necessary to feed the public imagination with examples, as well as by teaching them what in the present and in the past has been best produced in architecture , and, in addition, to keep them free of all exclusive preference of school, giving them to understand that only what is true, sincere, direct, and spontaneous is good in art   What really stands against beauty is untruth , and everything, whether poor or sumptuous, little or great, transitory or permanent, may be artistic if it be sincere.   But what is architectonic sincerity ? It is the essential quality of beauty, viz harmony.   If there is harmony between the aim and character of a building, between its wants and its aspect, between its style and distribution, between the forms and distances, between the impression of the whole and every one of its inherent parts, between its materials and the use made of them and its appearance, between the moral and material aspects within the order of the purpose which the building is to fulfil ; if there is harmony between the immanent logical conception of the building conceived and its corporeal realisation, in the whole and in its parts, beauty then really exists.   If there be anything, however trifling, contrary to this harmony, no beauty can exist That is the measure which must be made clear to the public, so that they may formulate their judgment with accuracy, and be enabled to give their assent only to what is a good æsthetic theory

To obtain these ends we recommend the adoption of the following means .—

1. All Governments should order to be placed in every primary school photographs or drawings showing the specimens of classical works of architecture, with an indication of its style and epoch

2. The teaching of æsthetics and of the history and theory of the fine arts should be included in the general curriculum of schools

3 Schools of every kind should be compelled to teach elementary architecture

4 All countries should promote permanent exhibitions of architectonic works, conveniently classified, represented by drawings or photographs or models, and illustrated with short descriptive explanations

5. Governments should encourage all kinds of publications for the

divulgation of art, instituting for the purpose rewards and bounties.
They should also purchase a considerable number of them for distribution among all public libraries, and their price should be such as to place
them within the reach of persons of small means.

6 Free chairs should be endowed for the divulgation of the history and
theory of architecture.

7 It would also be expedient to arrange cheap excursions to the
most renowned buildings of all countries, the parties to be presided over
by an architect who would lecture on the monuments visited.

8. Money bounties should be awarded for the best collections of
buildings or architectonic works exhibited in cinematographs and theatre-
sceneries, &c., of which municipalities should afford gratuitous displays.

9. Artistic educational associations should be organised for the propagation everywhere, and with all the means at their disposal, of the teaching
of art, more especially of architectonic art.

(8) Par GASTON TRELAT (Paris).

La question est complexe par suite de l'extension que la répartition des
activités finit par assigner à l'architecture En se plaçant au point de
vue exclusif des avantages réalisés dans l'habitation, le public devient
de plus en plus exigeant , et ses exigences reposent sur des connaissances
ou sur des sentiments qui se sont développés avec l'époque où nous vivons
C'est bien là une éducation réelle.

L'explication, qui viendrait tout d'abord à la pensée s'appuierait sur
le grand phénomène de la société tout entière et quelle que soit l'étiquette
dont elle soit revêtue ; je veux parler de la démocratie. Elle marque le
mouvement social, caractère distinctif de notre temps. Il ne connaît
point de frontières , c'est une manifestation universelle Elle s'étend à
tous les peuples, sans exclusion d'organisation sociale, de régime politique
servant de titre à la discipline que le Gouvernement entretient En conséquence on peut dire que, partout aujourd'hui, la démocratie remplit
son rôle—et que personne ne songerait à discuter !—d'étendre le champ
dans lequel les élites ou les aristocraties devront se recruter. C'est là
une définition qui n'est pas pour déplaire aux sujets de la Grande-Bretagne ; car elle entrerait plutôt dans la doctrine que sert sa grande aristocratie, en restant ouverte aux nouvelles recrues qui peuvent l'honorer.
Peut-être même l'analyse scientifiquement conduite trouverait-elle, dans
l'expérience que le Royaume-Uni nous montrerait là, un exemple de
nature à inspirer la solution hiérarchique du problème que la démocratie
contemporaine à soulevé dans le monde   Elle n'en est qu'à ses débuts,
à la période transitoire qui précède l'ordonnance vers laquelle nous
nous efforçons et qui n'existe pas encore

Voilà pour les conditions sociales qui caractérisent l'époque Elles
concourent sans doute à répandre dans le public un état de réceptivité . .
pourrais-je dire, des esprits. Le phénomène psychologique comprend à la
fois et les choses de goût et les conditions de confort ou de salubrité
que la science actuelle tendrait à développer de plus en plus, sans que
nous en prissions nous-mêmes conscience Et c'est pour la quatrième
question deux points importants qui en résument les parties objectives.

On ne pourrait suffisamment insister sur certains *desiderata* du grand
public, notamment en ce qui a trait à la salubrité de l'habitation Avec
leurs beaux travaux, Pasteur, Koch, bien d'autres sont des initiateurs
auxquels l'histoire fera une place à part. Ils ont changé la face des
choses quant à la santé de l'homme et des milieux qui l'avoisinent Le

U 2

courant, qu'ils ont créé dans les idées, dans les sentiments humains, incline à se généraliser, à développer le confort et la santé dans des habitations de plus en plus salubres

La satisfaction des besoins revêtait jusqu'ici un caractère que je qualifierai de *terre à terre bourgeois* Elle s'attachait exclusivement aux besoins matériels, parce que les personnalités, à qui la conception en incombait, n'étaient hantées par aucune idée plus médiate et répondant à des visions plus élevées Tandis que, maintenant, il n'y a plus de milieu humain où l'on ne rencontre des aptitudes à la compréhension des ordonnances que revêt la matière, pour satisfaire à la beauté et aux impressions plastiques qui en découlent C'est un tour nouveau qu'il faut noter Il est des personnes, pour ainsi dire sans préparation spéciale, qui montrent un sentiment incontestable et très accusé de la beauté plastique D'où cela viendrait-il donc ? Peut-être bien la beauté comporte-t-elle une sérénité que les intelligences, en s'éduquant elles-mêmes, rechercheraient à leur insu et dont elles subiraient le charme involontaire, découvrant un nouveau monde aux esprits. Tandis que, en raison de l'affinement que nos civilisations tendraient à revêtir aujourd'hui, la laideur équivaudrait à une contorsion intellectuelle. Et pourtant, dans tous les mondes, il y a des esprits attachés au service incessant de la laideur ; ils s'essayent à montrer leur valeur personnelle par les habiletés qu'ils dépensent à côté ou en dehors de la rectitude. . . . En fait d'art, c'est un déchet qu'il faut bien reconnaître . Jamais il n'aboutira à conquérir l'assentiment général parmi les gens simples qui nous occupent ici Cela tient à leur goût directement en rapport avec la simplicité. Et celle-ci fait naturellement penser à l'art, qui, par la force des choses, aboutit à la grandeur. Car la simplicité est le caractère que l'œuvre prend, toutes les fois qu'elle est étudiée en conscience, c'est-à-dire lorsqu'on prend le temps d'user toutes les causes de trouble et de confusion, dont la réalisation idéale ne se ressent jamais Alors apparaît une rectitude voulue, sous l'impression de laquelle on reste. Et c'est toujours le fruit de l'étude et de la méditation

Résumé —Le phénomène contemporain de la démocratie caractérise le monde où nous sommes appelés à développer nos activités Il tend à créer l'équilibre entre les classes et les hommes Il en résulte des compréhensions et des sentiments qui se généralisent de jour en jour. Et voilà pour la nature d'esprit caractéristique du public à notre époque.

Les découvertes, qui sont dues aux grands initiateurs du temps, ont éclairé des voies nouvelles en fait de salubrité des habitations D'où résulte aujourd'hui cette angoisse à laquelle nous assistons, eu égard à la santé publique Aucun milieu n'échappe à cette inquiétude, qui semble être une marque de notre temps et qu'on peut qualifier d'initiation heureuse.

. De même l'ordonnance plastique de la matière a fini par être une cause impressionnante pour tous les milieux sociaux, en suite d'une éducation peut-être inconsciente mais très réelle Tout au moins y rencontre-t-on des gens d'un goût indiscutable et sensibles à une rectitude dans la forme, celle-ci étant toujours en accord avec le mode des réalisations entrevues.

Conclusion —L'architecture touche à bien des sciences qui sont d'un intérêt vivant pour le public. Elle est pour ces sciences l'objet d'applications courantes Il s'ensuit une cause immanente d'intérêt pour la masse grandissante du public intelligent

Mais encore, la beauté publique voit le nombre de ses admirateurs croître journellement. Et, comme l'architecture en est un élément considérable, on y constate le témoignage d'une éducation toujours croissante.

(9) Par Gaston Anciaux

[Pour la Société centrale d'Architectes de Belgique]

D'après Mr. Morris " L'Art doit être fait pour le peuple, et par le peuple." Cette dernière idée semble, dans l'état actuel des choses, plutôt utopique S'il faut pourtant se garder de la rejeter absolument comme trop idéaliste, il convient aussi de reconnaître qu'aujourd'hui, malgré les énormes progrès réalisés en tous les domaines, nous sommes non seulement bien loin de l'Art par le peuple, mais très éloignés aussi de l'Art pour le peuple. Et cela pour quelle raison ?

Camille Mauclair vient, dans un de ses récents articles de la Revue Bleue, de nous le dire d'une façon mordante, mais caractéristique " Il ne s'agit pas, dit Mauclair, de placer un être qui jure, qui crache, qui hurle, qui ne se lave pas, devant un chef d'œuvre, et de croire qu'on a fait envers lui son devoir Il s'agit de conduire cet être par un enseignement persuasif à l'idée que toute créature doit s'affiner , et c'est ainsi qu'on le rendra capable de comprendre et de reconnaître dans une belle chose, l'héritage indivis de sa race En un mot il sied de former le caractère du peuple pour le préparer à l'Art, et non pas d'escompter qu'en le mettant en contact direct avec l'art on lui fournira un caractère

" Un ouvrier peut se rendre digne des chefs d'œuvre, mais les chefs d'œuvre n'ont pas pour vertu et pour raison de dégrossir un ouvrier "

Et ce que Mauclair exprime de façon si incisive pour le peuple proprement dit, ne s'appliquerait-il pas assez exactement aussi à nos foules ? à la grosse masse du public ?

Sans vouloir aller jusque là, sans pousser les choses au noir, il faut reconnaître pourtant qu'il y a fort à faire sous ce rapport. Aussi, est-ce avec beaucoup de raisons que la question d'éducation du public en fait d'architecture a été portée à l'ordre du jour du présent Congrès International des Architectes   De longs développements sur ce point seraient donc, pensons-nous, assez superflus, aussi courrons-nous directement aux conclusions que nous vous proposons en ce sens.

Conclusions.

L'éducation du public en architecture ne peut être obtenue que par de longs, de patients, et d'incessants efforts

Les moyens les plus propres à faire l'éducation architecturale du public sont d'ordres très multiples et des plus variés

Parmi ceux-ci, les suivants nous semblent plus particulièrement propres à donner de bons résultats.

(*a*) Pour l'avenir :

Dans le plus bref délai possible . établir ou développer aux différents degrés de l'enseignement des cours spéciaux propres à former le goût architectural , ou mieux encore, surtout dans l'enseignement inférieur et moyen, infuser cet élément dans l'enseignement général sans en faire l'objet d'un cours particulier

À cet effet notamment, faire évaluer plus sensiblement l'enseignement de l'histoire guerrière et politique des peuples vers celui des civilisations, en caractérisant celles-ci par leurs stades en architecture, sans isoler toutefois cet élément caractéristique des mœurs, des coutumes, des institutions sociales les plus marquantes de chacune d'elles

Faire évaluer également l'enseignement de la géographie dans un sens similaire. Dans ce but faire excursionner les élèves dans leur ville, leur province, leur pays et même à l'étranger si possible Illustrer dans le même but les ouvrages classiques de vignettes comprenant non seulement des sites typiques mais des vues de monuments ou d'intérieurs (de préférence encore existants)   Encadrer les textes de fragments ornementaux, d'allure architecturale et décorative des meilleurs maîtres des époques traitées, et ne prendre de celles-ci que les plus caractéristiques

Réformer l'imagerie scolaire actuelle dans un sens plus artistique en ayant recours aux artistes de valeur et en utilisant les procédés modernes de reproduction parfaite et à bon marché ; phototypie, chromolithographie, etc

Ne mettre toutefois en mains des élèves que des éléments de première valeur, et viser à la qualité plutôt qu'à la quantité, à la synthèse plutôt qu'au détail.

Pour l'enseignement supérieur, créer des chaires spécialement affectées à l'Art Architectural et à sa philosophie.

Ne faire donner cet enseignement délicat que par un personnel particulièrement apte et spécialement compétent, les résultats en cas contraire ne pouvant être que désastreux et diamétralement opposés au but visé.

(*b*) Pour le présent

Agir de façon propre à obtenir la réalisation des désiderata suivants .

1º La création de Musées d'Architecture non seulement centraux, dans les capitales, mais aussi régionaux dans les villes de moindre importance

Ces musées seraient accolés, soit aux musées de peinture et de sculpture, soit plutôt adjoints aux musées de moulages et d'art décoratif qu'ils primeraient.

Ces musées comportant, à côté des graphiques d'exécution des maquettes, des photographies et des aquarelles plus suggestives et plus attrayantes pour le public que les dessins techniques.

Ces musées comportant aussi des ensembles décoratifs des intérieurs meublés, où le cadre architectural proprement dit, largement traité, serait accompagné de la documentation graphique y afférente.

2º. L'organisation dans ces musées de conférences publiques nombreuses et attrayantes, d'expositions temporaires d'œuvres architecturales récentes ou de projets d'architecture, celle-ci comprise dans le sens le plus large du mot.

3º. Le soin pris par les pouvoirs publics de n'ériger que des constructions, qu'elles soient importantes ou accessoires, temporaires ou définitives, propres à former le goût du public.

---

(10) Par Albert Mayeux (Paris)

De tous les arts l'architecture est celui qui touche ou doit toucher le plus l'humanité, puisqu'il a trait à un besoin immédiat de la vie—l'habitation.

De tous les arts l'architecture est celui qui a le plus exercé le génie humain, par le raisonnement nécessaire à la conception de projets d'une infinie variété, à leur réalisation et à la recherche d'une sensation esthétique pour la plupart

C'est aussi le seul art créé, pour ainsi dire, de toutes pièces par l'homme Tandis que la peinture et la sculpture ne font qu'envisager diversement la nature, prise comme modèle, l'architecture transforme celle-ci, crée des formes nouvelles, et pour y arriver même des produits nouveaux.

D'autre part les peintres et les sculpteurs n'ont que peu ou point de collaborateurs , l'architecte, au contraire, en possède une légion, depuis le terrassier qui fait la fouille jusqu'au couvreur qui termine les combles, et cela pour le programme le plus simple, parfois un modeste hangar

L'architecture est donc un produit éminemment collectif qui doit intéresser quand même le public, si on sait lui expliquer les raisons de l'intérêt qu'il doit y porter.

Les œuvres d'architecture, depuis les plus simples bâtiments jusqu'aux monuments somptueux, peuvent être considérées comme des immeubles formant une des sources principales de la fortune publique. En dehors même de la question de pure utilité, que de monuments, pour ne pas dire même de constructions intéressantes—sont des sources de richesses pour le pays Chartres, Reims, Amiens avec leurs cathédrales, Versailles avec son palais, Rouen avec son palais de justice, Nancy avec ses places et Carcassonne avec ses remparts apportent aux villes qui les possèdent un profit moral et matériel indéniable

C'est-à-dire que les productions de l'architecture ont droit, non seulement à l'intérêt, mais aussi au respect de tous.

Il faut apprendre, au public, lui dire et lui redire la valeur des choses édifiées, pour prévenir la mutilation et la destruction totales ou partielles des œuvres d'architecture, en faisant appel non seulement aux sentiments de morale et d'esthétique, mais aussi à ceux d'économie sociale

L'architecture étant, de tous les arts, celui qui réflète le plus intimement l'état moral d'une époque, au point qu'on a dit qu'un monument était un *livre* de pierre où l'histoire se lisait en pages ineffaçables, on doit comprendre combien son enseignement peut être intéressant pour le public au point de vue de la seule curiosité

C'est à-dire que les faces où l'on peut envisager cet enseignement sont nombreuses et variées, mais pour réussir il faut qu'il soit forcément à la portée des auditeurs, suivant les milieux et le genre de public

Or le public à qui l'on peut donner une éducation architecturale est de deux sortes

1 Les élèves et les soldats.

2 Le public libre.

L'enseignement aux élèves peut se faire naturellement dans les écoles, lycées et collèges, et celui des soldats dans les casernes, tandis que l'enseignement au public peut se faire par des conférences et des visites collectives.

Un complément d'instruction existe à peu près pour tout le monde par les livres et les bibliothèques, mais c'est un moyen qu'il faut savoir employer et qui, en tous cas, sort d'un programme d'études spéciales comme celui que nous proposons au Congrès.

L'Enseignement aux Elèves.

Dès l'école primaire le maître peut déjà ouvrir l'esprit de son jeune auditoire en lui parlant, très succinctement, bien entendu, des beautés générales des édifices qui sont à la portée de tous Mais ne se bornant pas à un élan d'admiration en face d'œuvres supérieures, il ramènera l'attention sur une construction modeste, si c'est à la campagne en face d'une *grange*, par exemple, en s'efforçant d'analyser l'œuvre dans une mesure à la portée de ses auditeurs

Il dira, par exemple, d'abord, son utilité, le pourquoi de sa forme particulière, les raisons de ses murs, de sa charpente, de sa couverture, des matériaux mis en œuvre, etc., de manière à laisser dans l'esprit autre chose qu'une impression vague et conséquemment fugitive. Une autre fois il mènera ses élèves devant une maison d'école, une chapelle, etc , les préparant ainsi à une éducation plus étendue dans la suite

Quelques visites à des chantiers en construction, ou dans des ateliers où l'on pourra leur faire voir les matériaux ouvrés, seront un complément excellent d'éducation

Enfin il les pénétrera d'une sorte de respect pour l'effort collectif que représentent déjà ces modestes bâtiments, ce qui leur donnera l'intuition de l'effort gigantesque qu'il a dû falloir pour la grande église ou le grand hôtel de ville de la région, dont on n'a pas parlé, mais qu'ils ont pu déjà apercevoir. Inutile de dire qu'à la ville les exemples seront plus nombreux, mais la méthode sera la même du simple au composé.

Pour les lycées, collèges, les maîtres, plus instruits, pourront développer la même thèse en s'aidant de gravures, dessins et photographies d'œuvres architecturales, plutôt simples que complexes, où toujours l'esprit d'*analyse* et de *critique* suivra la phase plus ou moins vive l'admiration qui doit forcément précéder en attirant l'attention de l'auditoire.

Quant à l'enseignement de l'architecture dans les écoles normales d'instituteurs, elle peut être beaucoup plus développée sous forme de conférences spéciales où un architecte érudit et causeur serait mieux à sa place qu'un professeur de lettres. Là, en effet, où des maîtres sont à former, il faut dire et surtout expliquer plus

La généralité sur les monuments ne suffisent plus ; il faut entrer dans le vif du sujet, parler de la donnée du programme, de la composition des formes, des proportions, des rapports, de la silhouette et de la décoration ; insister sur la nécessité d'organes particuliers à l'œuvre qui n'existent pas à d'autres monuments, tels des contreforts, des grandes portées, des piliers multipliés, des baies larges ou réduites, des toitures plates ou à pentes rapides, etc.

Enfin la partie historique, archéologique, nulle ou restreinte à l'école primaire, au collège et au lycée, devient ici très importante.

L'étude du style, ses tendances, complètent dans la mesure du possible l'enseignement en question.

L'Enseignement aux Soldats

C'est naturellement à la caserne que peut s'effectuer l'enseignement aux soldats ; mais comme il est rare que les garnisons ne soient pas dans une ville de quelque importance, les officiers pourront organiser des visites aux monuments et aux usines de la région, sous la conduite d'hommes dont les professions dans la vie civile se rattachent à celles du bâtiment.

A la caserne des officiers, portés par leurs goûts aux choses de science pratique et d'art, pourraient faire quelques conférences sur des monuments visités et si, au cours des manœuvres, les cantonnements se font dans un pays possédant un ou plusieurs monuments de quelque intérêt, ces officiers pourraient, dans les moments de liberté, expliquer ce qu'ils savent à ce sujet à leurs hommes, historique des édifices, caractère de leur construction, emploi judicieux des matériaux, etc., et finalement expliquer le respect qui doit découler non seulement pour une belle œuvre, mais pour une œuvre collective réunissant tant d'efforts d'artistes, d'artisans et d'ouvriers. Enfin insister sur la conséquence morale de l'amour du travail manuel, la ténacité et la conviction dont ont fait preuve les gens de métiers qui ont collaboré à ces monuments admirés

L'Enseignement au Public libre.

Une fois sorti de l'école ou du collège, et libéré du service militaire, l'homme devient libre, et si ses goûts se portent vers l'étude de l'art ou de l'archéologie, il peut, sans être un spécialiste, augmenter ses connaissances en architecture. Il faut pour cela qu'il le veuille, car rien ne l'y oblige, et si on l'y incite il faut le faire adroitement et sagement

Pour cela, la meilleure des manières pour attirer le public libre est encore la conférence, et la conférence agréable et attirante

Le conférencier devra donc commencer d'ordinaire, après avoir exposé son sujet, à montrer par des dessins préparés ou des photographies les monuments qu'il va étudier ; s'il est en état de faire de bons croquis au tableau cela peut être excellent , enfin s'il lui est possible d'avoir recours aux projections à la lumière oxhydrique il fera bien de s'en servir, car la lanterne magique de nos pères, surtout avec ses perfections

modernes, a toujours le plus grand attrait Voir, étant bien assis, sans
seulement avoir la peine de tourner la tête ni le feuillet d'un album,
s'entendre expliquer en même temps l'edifice en cause, ne faire aucun
autre effort que celui de comprendre, c'est l'idéal du public le plus nombreux des conférences S'il apprend, tant mieux, s'il ne retient rien il
s'est amusé Aussi ne l'amusez-vous plus qu'il cesse de venir aux conférences suivantes

A côté de ces auditeurs simplement curieux s'en trouvent quelques-uns
qui veulent apprendre, aussi pour ceux-là le conférencier fera-t-il bien
de compléter les descriptions générales, marquées au sceau de l'admiration
des œuvres architecturales présentées dans le but d'échauffer l'enthousiasme du public, par des explications sur le côté technique des
dispositions et de la construction. En sus de la beauté des proportions et
de la décoration qui séduisent d'ordinaire seules le public amateur, il
parlerait de la structure, des organes essentiels, des données pratiques
ayant présidé à la conception de l'édifice, assaisonnant de temps à autre,
pour corriger l'aridité de la démonstration, une anecdote, un fragment
d'histoire, une légende. S'il fait rire ou sourire, cela vaudra mieux,
s'il veut trop faire penser et réfléchir il obtiendra bientôt un vide relatif
dans sa salle de cours Ce genre de conférences demande de l'esprit et
du tact

Un conseil que le conférencier pourra donner fructueusement pour
ses auditeurs convaincus, c'est le recours aux bibliothèques en indiquant
immédiatement les ouvrages traitant du sujet dont on vient de faire l'étude,
de manière à permettre de compléter les lacunes d'une description forcément sommaire et hâtive, car l'attention soutenue et prolongée est une
fatigue qu'on veut bien supporter dans une certaine mesure. Le public
libre, c'est-à-dire qui n'est obligé à rien, est très difficile à contenter, et les
auditeurs convaincus sont plus exigeants qu'on le croit généralement
par la raison qu'il est rare qu'un but immédiat les pousse, c'est plutôt
une vague et saine curiosité qui motive leurs déplacements.

Instruire en amusant, même pour un sujet grave tel que l'architecture,
telle est, à notre avis, la ligne de conduite à suivre en face du public libre.

On ne peut tracer ici un programme positif d'enseignement, les professeurs ou conférenciers étant de tempérament et d'aptitudes variables ;
c'est une ligne de conduite générale qu'il est seul possible d'esquisser

Des visites collectives de monuments et même de villes intercalées
dans des excursions à prix réduits, et tout l'agrément qui découle de ces
promenades en compagnie, sont encore à noter parmi les meilleurs moyens
d'enseigner l'architecture, car la vue sur place en dit plus que la meilleure
des photographies, avec un bon conférencier-cicérone le résultat, qui
est en somme d'arriver au développement de l'intérêt et du respect des
monuments et de la nécessité de leur conservation, est alors amplement
obtenu.

Vœu

La question posée par le Congrès, à laquelle nous venons de répondre,
semble d'un intérêt primordial, nous émettons donc le vœu que les sociétés
telles que la notre étudient l'élaboration de *Manuels types* à l'usage des
conférenciers.

Paris le 15 mai 1906

(11) Par JEAN GILSON (Bruxelles), Architecte, Professeur de
Dessin à Boitsfort

"L'Art procède d'un homme et s'adresse à des hommes. Il est la flamme
d'un esprit, son rayonnement ; il ne peut manquer d'affecter d'abord,
l'être même d'où il émane, puis, de proche en proche, d'autres êtres,"
affirmait M Sertillanges

Il en est ainsi de l'Architecture, Reine-Mère de tous les Arts, appelée,
avant tout, à frapper et à retenir l'attention du public

Pour atteindre ce but hautement désirable et qui devrait être l'objet
d'une noble émulation, sans cesse en éveil, il importerait, au préalable,
de viser à provoquer graduellement, au sein des masses, l'éclosion de ce
sentiment esthétique qui, chez bon nombre, existe à l'état latent, semblable à ces feux dormants, couvant sous la cendrée, que le moindre
souffle avive.

Une objection, maintes fois colportée, et contre laquelle il convient
de réagir, est celle qui tend à faire croire que l'Architecture est un Art
trop au-dessus de la compréhension de la grande majorité du public !

Cette objection, à première vue, peut paraître vraisemblable Cependant, je ne crains pas de déclarer, qu'à mon sens, si le public n'est
pas plus impressionné par la beauté ou la grandeur des créations architecturales, cela ne veut pas dire qu'il y soit tout-à-fait insensible et qu'il faille
désespérer, si pas s'immobiliser dans l'ornière où, momentanément, la
question artistique se meut péniblement

Bien au contraire, j'estime que *les convaincus*, les vaillants qui ont le
culte et, partant, l'enthousiasme de l'Art, doivent sans faiblesse, de même
que sans découragement, lutter contre le mal, né en grande part de
l'envahissement, lent et progressif, du domaine de l'Inspiration, par le
pédantisme qui prétend régenter, "mathématiser" le génie créateur !

L'affirmation osée, que je viens d'émettre hardiment, provoquera—
je le présume—la surprise, pour ne pas dire . . . la raillerie ! Je ne
m'inquiéterai guère plus de l'une que de l'autre et, croyant sincèrement
être dans le vrai, n'ayant en vue que la défense d'une cause, belle entre
toutes, je tiens à m'exprimer en toute liberté de penser !

A notre époque, où l'instruction est donnée à profusion et poussée à
un haut degré, trop élevé même pour l'immense majorité des gens de
métiers, un mouvement puissant, véritable emballement, a porté au
pavois nos instituteurs : corps évidemment des plus méritants—je me
fais un devoir de le reconnaître—mais qui, malheureusement, par le
fait de l'importance acquise, en est arrivé à croire posséder l'omniscience ?

C'est ainsi que l'on constate, trop souvent, des cas où la mission d'initier
à cette chose immatérielle, dénommeé Art, est postulée et confiée à des
instituteurs au détriment de professionnels ayant fait de l'esthétique et
de ses multiples applications, l'étude et la pratique constantes de leur
existence, toute de recherches

En raison de ce choix peu judicieux, justifié uniquement par la croyance
que la pédagogie doit primer toutes les autres branches intellectuelles, il
arrive que l'initiation de l'enfance et de la jeunesse, aux délicates et
sublimes beautés de l'Art, est, trop souvent, dévolue à des *théoriciens* ne
possédant incontestablement pas—quoiqu'ils prétendent—la même compréhension ni la même vision que des hommes *spéciaux*, ayant fait des
études *spéciales*, qui leur permettent de définir et d'expliquer la raison
d'être, la formation de telles ou telles géniales créations !

Il est indubitable que l'instruction est une admirable et superbe
chose , mais, je ne cesserai de le répéter, ainsi que je l'ai fait, l'an dernier,
au Congrès de Liége, parmi ces admirables artisans qui furent nos aïeux

et qui nous ont légué ces purs chefs-d'œuvre aussi bien comme tapisserie, que comme orfèvrerie, ferronnerie, ébénisterie, etc , etc., pièces, de haut mérite, conservées jalousement dans nos Musées, combien, parmi ces gens de métiers, n'y en avait il pas d'*illettrés* ? . .

Leur ignorance, en matière scientifique, ne les a pas empêchés de produire ces immortels morceaux de maîtrise que, de nos jours, nombre d'artisans *instruits, très instruits* même, documentés et outillés comme ne l'étaient pas nos anciens, parviennent difficilement à surpasser, si pas à égaler !

Et, cependant, le progrès constant, apporté dans le perfectionnement des outillages, procure, aux artisans modernes, des facilités d'exécution que, certes, ne possédaient pas les merveilleux gens de métiers des siècles disparus

Il est évident qu'à ces époques évanouies—néanmoins toujours présentes au souvenir, grâce au précieux héritage de leurs créations géniales incomparables—habitations, mobilier, bijoux, vêtements, etc , le tout concourait à former un ensemble décoratif portant, nettement, une date dans l'Histoire de l'Art et ayant eu une influence prestigieuse sur la vision des populations vivant dans un milieu, pour les besoins duquel d'admirables créateurs mirent à profit les ressources de leur talent professionnel.

Qui oserait soutenir que ces merveilleux artisans devaient à l'instruction pédagogique la magistrale inspiration s'affirmant dans leurs œuvres ?

Et cette constatation ne démontre-t-elle pas, éloquemment, que le soin de l'initiation, de l'enfance et de la jeunesse, aux radieuses beautés de l'Art, devrait être réservé aux hommes d'élite, dont la compétence irrécusable est la résultante de l'étude des maîtres et d'une *pratique* de tous les instants

Ces gens *compétents*, chargés de l'enseignement de l'*Art appliqué à l'Industrie* et qui ont à cœur l'importance et la grandeur de leur mission, feraient valoir, auprès de l'élève et de ses proches, les avantages à tirer des métiers s'inspirant de l'Art

Se tenant au courant des besoins que, journellement, l'homme se crée, ces instructeurs, ces guides de l'artisan annoteraient soigneusement les progrès réalisés au point de vue des conceptions nouvelles et des matières employées.

Ce qui doit préoccuper, avant tout, c'est le début de l'éducation artistique

Le goût raisonné est la chose qui doit intéresser toute société bien constituée.   Le goût, tel que nous le comprenons ici, qui forme un sixième sens, le *Sens du Beau*, doit servir de base à toute éducation , il aidera, plus tard, au succès de la carrière que l'élève ou l'apprenti se propose de suivre, ou bien, encore, il le mettra à même d'apprécier la valeur d'un travail vraiment artistique lorsque, par la suite, il fera une acquisition quelconque.

Ne remarquons-nous pas que les peuples grands eurent leur imagination, leur sensibilité portées vers les œuvres magistralement grandioses qui, après des centaines et des milliers d'années, nous parlent encore et continueront à parler d'eux ; œuvres prodigieuses démontrant éloquemment ce que peuvent accomplir les efforts combinés d'artisans d'élite, aux métiers divers, mais qui étaient animés de l'enthousiaste et unanime désir d'arriver, par une noble émulation, à se survivre dans leurs créations

J'ai cité, plus haut, le sixième sens : celui du *Beau*. La beauté n'est-elle pas ce qui, caressant et charmant délicieusement la rétine, s'y incruste et nous fait apprécier la jouissance de la vue, cet autre sens ?

Ici, ne peut-on affirmer que la vue est la faculté la plus capricieuse chez l'homme ?

En raison d'une éducation spéciale, actuellement encore insuffisamment propagée, l'œil arrive à saisir la forme des objets placés dans la nature et à se rendre compte de leur coloration

Et, cependant, ce qui démontre nettement les diversités des sensations produites par un même objet, c'est de rencontrer, dans un groupe de personnes, le contemplant, des divergences de vision amenées par la perception personnelle de la silhouette ou de la tonalité

Ces impressions dérivent de l'éducation reçue par l'individu, et la reproduction de l'objet, sur lequel se porte son rayon visuel, se ressentira de la délicatesse de la perception la main n'étant que l'esclave de la pensée, de la conception, tout comme chez l'écrivain.

Il importe donc de développer le goût chez l'enfant , de faire éclore le tempérament artistique qui sommeille en lui ou qui pourrait s'y faire jour.

Dès le jardin d'enfants, on devrait mettre sous les yeux des élèves des tableaux, des modèles aux formes simples, pures et gracieuses, que l'œil saisit aisément.

On veillerait soigneusement à proscrire certains modèles aux contours lourds, disgracieux, ainsi que ces tableaux au dessin manquant de pureté et d'élégance, dont le coloris, sous prétexte de simplicité, n'est que grossièrement criard.

Dès lors, l'enfant s'habituerait, même inconsciemment, à voir des objets bien proportionnés, aux belles lignes, harmonieux de couleurs, et il en conserverait, dans la rétine, un souvenir vivace, qui, forcément, lui fera la vision saine et juste

Et non seulement pendant les premières années, mais encore par la suite, il conviendrait de continuer, toujours et quand même, à leur mettre sous les yeux des reproductions graphiques ou plastiques des belles créations dont nos ancêtres furent les inoubliables auteurs.

En même temps, des leçons-conférences tendraient à faire saisir, à faire comprendre par l'élève ٠ *pourquoi* ces œuvres sont belles , *pourquoi* la ligne en est pure et délicate ; *pourquoi* la silhouette en est originale ; et, comme corollaire, lui feraient *voir* l'harmonie des couleurs.

Je le sais . une pareille méthode, toute d'intuition, se heurte aux conceptions dogmatiques "Mais"—dit le docteur Lebon—"l'enseignement ne doit jamais l'être (dogmatique), et l'élève *ne doit pas s'habituer à croire une chose parce que le maître le lui a dit, mais parce qu'il a reconnu que c'etait ainsi* , on conçoit qu'il y ait un grand avantage à commencer l'éducation par un ordre de connaissances où la preuve soit toujours facile."

Qui veut la fin, veut les moyens ! Pour obtenir une génération d'artisans d'élite, au goût éclairé, il faut—on ne pourrait assez le répéter— inculquer progressivement, à l'enfant, les notions du Beau

Lorsqu'il sera à même de se faire la compréhension des choses, son goût personnel pourra se développer Amélioré par des principes inculqués avec patience et persévérance, l'adolescent, poursuivant ses études d'art appliqué à l'industrie, pourra arriver à créer des œuvres vraiment fortes et belles.

Il parviendra à concevoir une architecture rationnelle, en rapport avec les progrès prodigieux accomplis par la science depuis les siècles derniers

L'artisan saura en tirer profit en évitant la routine vulgaire et, par des efforts constants, arrivera à la réalisation d'un programme répondant aux exigences modernes, dans ce qu'elles ont de grand et de beau.

Indiscutablement, les principes erronés, inculqués à l'enfant, influent sur son imagination et, bien souvent, dans le cours de sa carrière, l'obsession se fera jour malgré tout.

Les idées, illogiquement préconçues, auront ainsi paralysé son élan, enrayant sa carrière et réduisant à néant l'originalité et l'individualité de ses conceptions

Il importe donc que l'artisan d'Art arrive à se mettre à la hauteur de son époque et porte ses aspirations vers le noble et le beau, s'en inspirant pour produire des conceptions sortant de la banalité.   Il faut, en un mot, qu'il répudie résolûment les créations bâtardes basées sur les époques de décadence

Le travailleur d'Art contribuera ainsi à améliorer une situation déplorable qui n'est que la résultante naturelle du désastreux laisser-aller paraissant être devenu la règle admise de nos jours

Pour atteindre ce but de rénovation du goût, il est donc nécessaire que l'enseignement soit, dès le début, intuitif.   A cette fin, il est indispensable que des modèles en relief, choisis avec compétence et discernement, soient mis constamment sous les yeux de l'élève, afin d'aider à rendre plus compréhensibles les explications du professeur.

L'enfant, dont l'imagination vierge s'ouvre aux choses de la vie et dont le cerveau, pareil à de la cire molle, garde l'empreinte des émotions ressenties, se plaira insensiblement, si pas à admirer, du moins à contempler une décoration expressive dont la belle ordonnance lui fera éprouver une jouissance d'Art

Toujours dans ce même ordre d'idées—*l'éducation par la vue*—il serait souhaitable que les matières ou matériaux employés ne soient pas dissimulés sans raison : ceci afin de conserver l'effet que l'œuvre demande, et obtenir une sincérité d'aspect constituant une des conditions primordiales de la Beauté

Et afin que les artisans soient bien imprégnés de ce sentiment esthétique, ils devraient pouvoir le puiser aux sources si pures de l'Art grec et du Gothique, deux éléments fondamentaux dont on doit s'inspirer dans l'enseignement parce qu'ils sont, en réalité, la base de l'Ecole-mère dont la pureté et le caractère de grandeur ne peuvent qu'ennoblir et élever le sentiment.

L'interprétation des modèles devrait aussi être l'objet d'une attention spéciale autant qu'éclairée et se faire d'une façon correcte et raisonnée.

Un pareil enseignement, de première importance, est à confier, *non pas à des théoriciens*, mais à des hommes entendus ayant acquis une pratique indiscutable et *sachant expliquer et faire comprendre le pourquoi* des diverses applications d'un modèle et ce d'une façon claire, compréhensible et judicieuse !

Si ce modèle représente un motif décoratif où la flore fournit l'élément essentiel, il est logique de comparer la structure naturelle de la plante interprétée, son caractère particulier, et de faire remarquer, à l'élève, le parti que l'artisan, amoureux de son art, sait tirer de la nature, dans la formation des différents styles

A chaque époque de l'Histoire, l'artiste, par sa vision personnelle de son époque et l'ambiance du milieu dans lequel il vivait, exprimait un sentiment différent et, toujours, il arrivait à la forme la plus simple, la plus expressive, la plus géométrique de l'élément emprunté à la nature, dont il s'était inspiré tout en lui conservant le caractère et la forme qui lui sont propres

Il s'ensuit qu'il est nécessaire, pour ne pas dire indispensable, de mettre à portée de la vue des élèves des produits naturels de la végétation qu'ils auraient à dessiner, abondant ainsi dans le sens de *Senel*, lequel affirmait que " *l'observation devant diriger le crayon de l'artiste.*"

Ce qui tend à dire qu'il faut viser à émouvoir les cœurs, qui se sentent, tout naturellement, attirés vers l'œuvre d'Art !

L'artiste, ayant conçu une œuvre, ayant exprimé avec noblesse et conviction une pensée, ne devrait se trouver satisfait que lorsqu'il est parvenu à faire comprendre, à faire partager son sentiment par autrui.

Selon E. Barberot, " le Beau absolu est celui qui s'impose à toutes les intelligences justes et rationnelles et que tout homme, bien organisé, est forcé de reconnaître."

Cette éducation de l'œil serait éminemment salutaire, et l'enfant, devenu homme, comprendrait que si l'Art n'est peut-être pas indispensable à la vie prosaïquement matérielle, terre-à-terre, il est, par contre, impérieusement nécessaire à la vie intellectuelle.

L'Art et l'Histoire se confondent, et l'Art c'est l'homme. Dans les créations produites, à chaque époque, par le génie, on voit s'épanouir, pour la Postérité, tout ce qui caractérise la créature humaine la pensée, le sentiment, la vie morale et sociale, en un mot, les divers échelons de la civilisation

Le Beau apparaît, dans l'univers, avec l'être moral, et de prime abord, comme attribut de l'être supérieurement doué

En effet, l'homme se caractérise par sa personnalité, par son "moi," c'est-à-dire par sa conscience et sa tendance à s'individualiser

Sa personnalité commence à s'affirmer à la transition de l'enfance insouciante à l'adolescence. Elle se manifeste d'une façon quelque peu gauche, timide, hésitante, comme entravée dans sa spontanéité, par une gêne qui vient de la conscience indécise

Par la suite, et tout naturellement, l'homme se révèle et aime ce que les autres admirent en lui, il arrive ainsi à prendre souci de l'opinion d'autrui et à travailler, sans cesse, afin que cette opinion lui soit favorable et louangeuse

C'est à ce sentiment, absolument humain, que nous devons la création d'œuvres immortelles, patiemment conçues et exécutées, qui marquent les glorieuses étapes de l'Histoire de l'Art.

M S. Perès le définit en d'autres termes

"Une œuvre d'Art ne peut viser à l'éternité que parce qu'elle n'est pas l'œuvre d'un jour."

Telle est bien la caractéristique de notre art, à nous, architectes !

Nous avons vu, par ce qui précède, que, pour arriver à impressionner le public, il fallait commencer par l'intéresser au moyen d'œuvres qui soient à la portée de sa compréhension

L'œil se plaît à s'arrêter complaisamment sur ce qui le flatte . en un mot, sur une chose quelconque, complète, pondérée, qui lui donne à comprendre le but pour lequel elle est créée, évitant ainsi, à celui qui la contemple, un travail de recherches toujours fatigant pour celui insuffisamment initié pour arriver à saisir le pourquoi de la chose créée

Que faut-il faire pour atteindre ce but essentiel ?

Il convient de mettre sous les yeux du public des créations qu'il peut voir dans leur ensemble ; œuvres qui soient à une échelle humaine et qui représentent nettement la pensée ayant guidé la main de l'auteur dans l'élaboration de sa conception En un mot, il faut que ces œuvres soient en rapport direct avec le milieu où elles sont installées et l'usage qu'on doit en faire.

La forme artistique d'une création devrait parler, avec éloquence, à l'œil du contemplateur comme le développement expressif de la pensée inspiratrice

Par des formes exagérées on provoque incontestablement l'attention , mais cette attention n'est éveillée que par l'étrangeté, la bizarrerie de la conception, que je ne crains pas de qualifier d' "*Acrobatie de l'Art !*" Aussi l'attention ne s'y attache que momentanément et se désintéresse bien vite.

Certes, il convient de traduire son sentiment par une expression originale Mais, pour obtenir cette originalité, il ne faut pas, toutefois, que ce soit au détriment d'une esthétique saine et raisonnée, ni de son caractère décoratif

Et de fait, la Décoration a pour effet de faire resplendir l'expression et de donner à l'œuvre la clarté et l'intensité voulues , elle doit être expressive et doit accentuer, sans exagération, l'effet des éléments essentiels de la structure, en faisant dominer son influence, développant ainsi l'expression d'ensemble

Le décor appliqué ne peut donner satisfaction à l'œil quant à l'impression d'ensemble ; il est sans expression et le plus souvent irrationnel

Il est également incontestable que tous les arts décoratifs, indistinctement, doivent marcher de pair avec l'Architecture afin de ne former qu'une seule et même conception, un tout homogène, complète et entière manifestation de la pensée en travail

C'est, en réalité, ce qui constitue l'idéal de nos conceptions architecturales.

A moins d'être doués exceptionnellement, gardons-nous de verser dans l'erreur de ceux qui visent à produire du "neuf quand même " ¡

Evitons de vouloir innover dans le but d'étonner, d'ébahir le public. Surtout, abstenons-nous d'être des *plagiaires*, imitant maladroitement les innovateurs

Visons, avant tout, à faire œuvre saine et expressive.

Le "neuf," que l'on cherche avec tant de persistance, apparaîtra par la force des choses, en raison des besoins de notre état social et par l'utilisation des produits nouveaux que la Science et l'Industrie, mises au service de l'Art, créent sans cesse

Cependant, si la Science apporte son aide puissante à l'Art, il serait néfaste qu'elle arrive à le dominer, ce qui amènerait, pour conséquence, quasi la paralysie de l'imagination enfantant les œuvres.

A ce propos—il y a vingt ans—Mr. Stevens écrivait ces lignes prophétiques

"Aujourd'hui "—c'était en 1886—" la science est dogmatique et toute-puissante, et toutes les formes de la pensée humaine sont soumises à ses lois ; l'atmosphère, que nous respirons, est saturée de vapeurs scientifiques , et l'on voudrait que, dans un pareil milieu, l'Art, qui vit d'esprit et de quelque chose de supra-humain, fleurisse et se développe !

"Mais cela est impossible !

"Les mélanges de races, la perte de caractères spéciaux, des coutumes et des mœurs, la diversité des opinions philosophiques ont produit une société hétérogène et hétéroclite à laquelle manque nécessairement l'essence artistique ; et si la Science a détruit la superstition et l'hypocrisie, si elle a créé la Presse et réuni les nations, si elle a produit le développement industriel qui fait la richesse des peuples, elle a, dans la même proportion, abaissé leur niveau artistique, en leur enlevant les conditions de vitalité nécessaire aux progrès de l'Art.

"Il est de toute évidence que l'Art s'adresse aux sentiments et la Science à la raison

"Or, l'Architecture, étant, avant tout, un Art, doit premièrement obéir aux lois du Beau ; elle doit ensuite être vraie et répondre à nos besoins. Mais il ne faut pas renverser l'ordre de ces principes . *placer l'utile au premier rang pour reléguer le Beau au troisième.*

"Nous ne combattons pas la Science, ce serait absurde "—concluait Mr Stevens—" mais *nous repoussons un système d'instruction qui, se basant principalement sur des études techniques, produirait, peut-être, d'excellents constructeurs, mais de bien misérables artistes ! "*

Je le répète : ceci fut écrit en 1886, et ces appréciations, qui dénotent une vision étonnamment juste des événements survenus, ne définissent que mieux *l'empiétement graduel,* incessant, des *théoriciens* dans le domaine des *praticiens.*

De nos jours, dans l'octroi des fonctions de *Professeur d'Art appliqué,* on a une tendance prononcée à faire choix de *pédagogues,* incontestablement très intelligents, mais qui, cependant, ne devraient pas avoir la prétention, suffisamment osée, d'enseigner, de façon entendue, un Art qu'ils ne pratiquent que peu ou point

Leur enseignement, en tout cas, ne peut être comparé à celui des hommes *spéciaux* ayant consacré leur vie à l'étude de la question qui nous occupe.

J'aborde mes conclusions, dans lesquelles je me plais à définir le but auquel nous devons tendre pour arriver à faire l'éducation esthétique du public et, en même temps, nous faire comprendre par lui.

Ces conclusions, les voici, nettement exprimées ·

Il importe, tout d'abord, chose essentielle, que *l'Architecte ait le respect de son Art et de lui-même*

Malgré les difficultés, souvent bien ardues, de la vie, lorsque l'on a l'honneur de se prévaloir du titre d'Architecte, on devrait ne pas s'oublier au point de compromettre sa dignité et celle de la Corporation aux yeux du public—autrement dit, la clientèle—en laissant marchander les honoraires dûs au talent, soit le prix d'un travail purement intellectuel, ainsi que la marée se marchande aux Halles !

Ce respect de notre Art, partant de nous-mêmes, est d'autant plus nécessaire à la défense de notre cause, qu'actuellement on est enclin à confier l'éducation des masses, en matière esthétique, à des gens, intelligents certes, mais dont la valeur est, avant tout, scientifique !

Une protestation, ferme, résolue, convaincue, de tous ceux qui ont le culte et le respect des nobles et impérissables traditions d'Art, se légitime de plus en plus.

J'ajouterai, ne fut-ce que pour enhardir les timorés, que, depuis les protestations de nos groupements professionnels, froissés à la longue par certains agissements attentatoires à la dignité corporative et à notre amour-propre de nationaux, un courant, favorable à notre cause, s'est dessiné dans l'opinion publique.

La Presse s'aperçoit que la cause des Architectes est tout aussi intéressante, tout autant digne d'attention que celle des peintres, des sculpteurs, des musiciens, etc.

Si la Presse voulait seconder nos efforts quel superbe rôle *d'éducatrice* ne remplirait-elle pas ?

Elle intéresserait et instruirait le public en faisant paraître des articles judicieusement conçus, commentant et mettant en valeur les qualités des œuvres dignes de ce nom

Il serait donc souhaitable de voir *la Presse* reporter, sur des Architectes, un peu de l'intérêt qu'elle prodigue aux peintres, aux sculpteurs, aux musiciens ou aux littérateurs.

De même que les Muses sont sœurs, les Arts ne sont ils pas frères ?

L'intérêt vital du pays, notre dignité de disciples de l'Art, ainsi que nos intérêts professionnels, nous obligent donc à nous élever courageusement, sans défaillance, en une confraternelle union, contre des tendances néfastes, qui, finalement, empêcheraient l'Architecture, ce grand Livre de la Tradition, d'augmenter encore, de merveilleuses pages, les glorieuses annales de l'Art Belge !

---

(12) ARCHITEKTUR UND PUBLIKUM.

Von Dr. Ing HERMANN MUTHESIUS (Berlin).

Es ist häufig, und zwar auch von Architekten hervorgehoben worden, dass die Werke der Architektur heute in Hierolgyphen geschrieben werden, dass die Architekten eine Geheimsprache reden, die nur von den Eingeweihten verstanden wird. Die Architektur ist im weitesten Sinne unpopulär, sie ist die am wenigsten verstandene der bildenden Künste. Die Bauzäune, die den Verkehr in den grossstädtischen Strassen einengen, rufen beim Vorübergehenden kaum den Wunsch hervor, zu wissen, was hinter ihnen entstehen wird. Und wenn ein neues Werk der Architektur dem Gebrauch übergeben wird, so pflegt das Interesse des Publikums mit der Frage erledigt zu sein, " in welchem Stil " das Haus gebaut ist.

Der Mangel des Interesses an Architektur fallt besonders auf, wenn man ihn mit der enormen Wertschatzung vergleicht, deren sich heute die Malerei erfreut. Ueber Malerei spricht, streitet und spintisiert jeder. Die Tageszeitungen sind gefullt mit Berichten uber Malerausstellungen, ein ganzes Heer von Kunstschriftstellern widmet sich ausschliesslich der Aufgabe der Beurteilung der Malerei und irgend ein konstruierter "Fall" kann die Gemuter eines ganzen Landes aufregen. So sehr ist das Interesse fur Malerei angeschwollen, dass das heutige Publikum den Begriff "Kunst" durch das Oelgemälde fur erschopft halt Kunst ist ihm bemalte Leinwand. Es ist kein Zweifel daruber : Unsere Kultur leidet an einer Wucherung der Malerei und einer Verschrumpfung der Architektur

Handelt es sich nun aber um eine Untersuchung, welche Abhilfe hier wohl geschaffen werden konnte, so scheint es notig, sich vor allem erst einmal die Grunde zu vergegenwartigen, welche zu diesen Zustanden gefuhrt haben Die Entfremdung zwischen der Architektur und dem Publikum ist da, aber wer tragt die Schuld daran ? Von vornherein kann man annehmen, dass jede Unpopularität ihre Grunde hat und haufig liegt bei einem Feindschaftsverhältnis die Schuld an beiden Teilen Daher scheint es gewagt, von vornherein davon auszugehen, dass es nur einer sogenannten "Erziehung des Publikums zur Architektur" bedurfte, um die Popularitat der Architektur wieder herzustellen, dass das heutige Missverhaltnis lediglich dem Publikum in die Schuhe zu schieben sei. Es fragt sich vielmehr, ob die Unpopularität der Architektur nicht in den Zeitverhältnissen wurzelt und ob nicht die heutige Architekturausubung selbst zum guten Teil fur den Umstand verantwortlich zu machen ist, dass sie bei den Zeitgenossen nicht das Interesse entfesselt, das die Architektur in fruheren Zeiten erweckte und dessen sich die anderen Kunste heute erfreuen

Es verlohnt der Muhe, zunachst einmal einen Blick auf vergangene Kunstzeiten zu werfen, um den heutigen Stand der Architektur gegen den damaligen abzumessen.

In allen grossen Kunstzeiten stand die Architektur an der Spitze der Kunste, ja sie war der Inbegriff der Kunst uberhaupt Malerei und Plastik leisteten ihr Dienste, sie waren Teile der Architektur. Weder in der griechischen Antike noch der romischen Bauglanzzeit, noch der byzantinischen Kunst, noch der Gothik war es denkbar, dass die Architektur hinter ein so kleines Spezialgebiet, wie es die heutige Tafelmalerei ist, hätte zurucktreten konnen Diese Zeiten, die eine wirkliche massgebende Kunst produziert haben, waren ganz und gar Zeiten der Architektur. Die Architektur war der Ausdruck der Zeit und die uberkommenen Architekturdenkmaler tragen noch jetzt wesentlich zu dem Bilde bei, das wir uns heute von ihnen machen Das Interesse, das diese grossen Kunstzeiten an der Architektur hatten, erklärt sich daraus, dass die Architektur die Gestalterin gewisser grosser Ideen war, die diese Zeiten beherrschten Vorwiegend war sie berufen, die religiosen Vorstellungen der Zeiten zu verkorpern, Vorstellungen, die von einer Wucht und Bedeutung waren, dass sie das gesammte Geistesleben beherrschten Die religiosen Vorstellungen haben die Menschen stets zu den hochsten Leistungen in der Baukunst begeistert. Man braucht nur an die griechische Antike und die Gothik zu denken, um sich das zu vergegenwartigen Nachst den religiosen waren es beispielsweise die sozialen Stromungen, die in der romischen Zeit zu riesigen baulichen Werken fuhrten, wie wir sie in den Cirken, Thermen und Basiliken bewundern Im europaischen Mittelalter waren die Rathauser der Ausfluss des Selbstbewusstseins wohlorganisierter ortlicher Korporationen. Und mit dem Begrunder der absolutistischen Konigsgewalt Ludwig XIV. erstand eine alles beherrschende hofische Baukultur, die fur die letzten drei Jahrhunderte der markanteste Ausdruck des Zeitgedankens geblieben ist

Welche Gedanken beherrschen nun in ahnlichem Sinne die Gegenwart ?

Niemand wird behaupten wollen, dass dies die religiosen seien. Trotz der sich breit machenden kirchlichen Parteibestrebungen hat unsere Zeit aufgehort, von religiosen Ideen fortgerissen zu werden   Die heute bestehende kirchliche Baukunst ist in ihrer Kunstlichkeit und ihrem Formalismus der rechte Ausdruck fur das Scheinleben, das die religiosen Gedanken weiter fuhren.   Auch die aristokratische Baukunst ist in den Hintergrund getreten   Die Wunsche der Fursten vermogen der Zeit nicht mehr das Geprage zu geben   Eine grosse stetige Masse, das Burgertum hat sich heute an die Oberflache gedrangt und sie ist es, die heute das Wesen der Zeit bestimmt.   Ihr gegenuber ist selbst der Ausdruck des staathchen und stadtischen Korporationsgedankens nicht mehr stark genug, sich in hervorstechender Weise bemerklich zu machen.

Mit dem Erstarken der burgerlichen Bevolkerungsschicht sind diejenigen Ideale in den Vordergrund getreten, die diese Schicht heute beherrschen. Die Wunsche und Bestrebungen des Burgertums drucken auch dem baulichen Leben den Stempel auf   Der Kaufmann, der Industrielle, der Ingenieur sitzen am Webstuhl der Zeit   Sie haben nichts zu tun mit alten Privilegien und arbeiten nicht mit abstrakten Ideen   Sie drangen auf den Ausbau des Lebens auf moderner Basis, auf der Grundlage der enormen Fortschritte der technischen Wissenschaften, auf der Errungenschaft eines Heeres von weltbewegenden Erfindungen.

Einer der wichtigsten Gedanken, die die heutige Gesellschaft bewegen, ist die Ausgestaltung der Verkehrsmittel.   An ihr arbeitet ein grosser Teil der Intelligenz der Zeit und sie ist unzweifelhaft einer der unsere Zeit bewegenden Gedanken, die heftig nach baulichem Ausdruck ringen. Sie gehoren unserer Zeit allein, sie sind der Ausdruck eines wesentlichen Inhaltes unserer Zeit und sie sind popular

Mit dem Ausbau der Verkehrsmittel in Verbindung steht ein vollig neues, unserer Zeit eigentumliches Gestaltungsgebiet, das der Maschinen und Werkzeuge.   Auch in ihm spricht sich ein ganz moderner Gedanke aus, der der streng wissenschaftlichen Durchdringung aller Einzelgebiete der menschlichen Tatigkeit.   Verkehrsmittel und Maschinen stehen heute im Mittelpunkt des baulichen Interesses   Eisenbahnen, Brucken, Dampfschiffe, elektrische Maschinen, wissenschaftliche Instrumente, sind das Neue, das unsere Zeit gesucht hat   Die Gestalter auf diesem Gebiete dringen frisch und frei, unbeengt durch die Ueberlieferung und ledig aller Sentimentalitat vorwarts, sie schliessen keine Kompromisse mit unsachlichen Gesichtspunkten, sie konnen ihre ganze Tatkraft und Intelligenz in den Dienst der einen Sache stellen.   Und in diesem Sinne sind sie modern und popular.

Ganz anders liegen die Verhaltnisse auf dem Gebiete der heutigen eigentlichen Architektur   Jenes freie unbeengte Gestalten ist hier langst nicht mehr vorhanden.   Wir finden es zuletzt zur Zeit der Gothik, der letzten Phase jugendkraftiger selbstandiger Architekturausubung.   Mit der Renaissance zogen unsachliche, aus fremden Geistesbezirken und Kulturen hergeholte Gesichtspunkte in die Architekturausubung ein.   Es wurde zwar infolge des gesteigerten geistigen Lebens ein grosser baulicher Aufschwung hervorgerufen, allein, bei Lichte betrachtet, handelte es sich in der Architektur der Renaissance um abgeleitete Werte, um Werke, die nicht mehr eine kunstlerische Originalidee verkorperten.   Sie waren alle im Hinblick auf die Antike gebaut, und nur die beschrankte Kenntnis der Antike hat die damaligen Baumeister davor bewahrt, Imitationen zu erzeugen

Je weiter die Erkenntnis der Antike in Laufe des Jahrhunderts vordrang, um so unselbststandiger wurde die Architektur vom Standpunkt der Zeit aus   Den letzten Stoss erhielt sie durch die Fulle von Erkenntnismaterial, das die Mitte des achtzehnten Jahrhunderts brachte   Jetzt verkehrten sich die Leistungen der Architekten fast in einen antiken Mummenschanz. Man hat die Empfindung, dass niemand mehr daruber

nachdachte, wie eine Aufgabe sachlich zu losen sei, sondern dass das
einzige Ziel war, jede nur irgend vorliegende bauliche Aufgabe in das
Schema eines antiken Gebäudes zu drängen   Die Gottin Architektur
verfiel in einen hypnotischen Zustand   Aus diesem Zustande heraus
machte sie im Verlauf des 19. Jahrhunderts die mannigfachsten Bewe-
gungen, ohne aber jemals das Gegenwartsbewusstsein wieder erlangen zu
konnen   Auch heute noch ist sie in dem Wahn befangen, dass ihre
Leistungen vor allem so auszusehen hatten, als gehorten sie irgend einer
vergangenen Kultur an.

Der Stilgesichtspunkt ist auch heute noch nicht aufgegeben, ja er
giebt haufig in erster Linie den Ausschlag   Waren wir nicht bis zur
Urteilslosigkeit in den Vorurteilen unserer Zeit befangen, so wurde uns
das Bestreben, moderne Aufgaben in historische Formen zu kleiden,
genau so lächerlich vorkommen, als wenn sich ein Mensch verschiedene
Maskeradenkostume hielte und heute als gothischer Ritter, morgen als fran
zosischer Hofmann, ubermorgen als alter Grieche einherzuschreiten unter-
nahmen.   Denn die Stilbestrebungen sind nichts anderes als Verkleidungs-
kunststucke, hervorgegangen aus einer gewissen Charakterlosigkeit und
Haltlosigkeit der Architektur

Man hat die architektonische Ueberlieferung mit einer Sprache verglichen, die sich fort und fort bis auf die Gegenwart weiter entwickelt hat
Das würde zutreffen, wenn wir in der architektonischen Ausdrucksweise
nicht fortlaufend von einer toten Sprache auf die andere gesprungen
waren, so dass wir uns heute in einem Sprachbabel befinden, aus dem es
kein Entrinnen zu geben scheint   Aber blosse Sprachbetatigung kann
uberhaupt nicht bis zu dem Masse Selbstzweck sein, wie es der heutige
Stilgesichtspunkt in der Architektur ist.   Die Sprache hat vielmehr stets
nur dazu gedient, Gedanken auszudrucken   Der Wunsch aber, einen
Gedanken klar, scharf und logisch auszudrucken, schliesst es aus, sich
heute dazu etwa der Sprache des Nibelungenliedes zu bedienen, man kann
froh sein, wenn man ihn in seiner eigenen Sprache uberzeugungsfähig
darstellen kann.   Zu welchen grotesken Erzeugnissen die Stilmanover in
der heutigen Architektur zu fuhren pflegen, konnen wir auf Schritt und
Tritt beobachten   Lasst sich eine grossere Ungereimtheit denken als
eine romanische Ausstellungshalle oder ein byzantinisches Bierlokal ?
Und doch bietet unsere Architekturausubung willig die Hand zu solchem
unwurdigen Maskeradenspiel.   Die Werke der Stilarchitektur konnten im
allerbesten Falle als erheiternde Spasse gelten, etwa wie Arnold Holz
seine Gedichtsammlung ' Dafnis " betrachtet, die die Alluren der Dichter
des siebzehnten Jahrhunderts nachahmt.   Wer sich aber allen Ernstes
zu solchen Spielereien hergibt, kann weder beanspruchen als Kunstler
betrachtet zu werden, noch kann er damit rechnen, von den verstandigen
Zeitgenossen anerkannt und gewurdigt zu werden   Mussen nicht derartige
Uebungen die Besten unserer Zeit zu dem Schlusse fuhren, dass die Architektur aus der Reihe der lebendigen Kunste verschwunden sei und heute
nicht mehr mitzahle ?   Und ist es denn wirklich noch erstaunlich, dass
die heutige Welt uberhaupt die Architektur als ein ihr fernliegendes
Spezialgebiet betrachtet, in dem eine Gilde von merkwurdigen Leuten
ein unverstandliches Wirken entfaltet ?   Kann nicht der Mensch der
Gegenwart verlangen, dass die Leistungen einer Berufsklasse, die er aner-
kennen soll, auch den Geist der Gegenwart tragen ?   Wer hat heute Zeit
zu Mummenschanz und sentimentalen Spielen ?   Die Gegenwart drangt
und stellt Probleme, die unsere ganze Kraft erfordern   Alles arbeitet
fieberhaft, um sie zu bewaltigen, nur wir Architekten stehen abseits und
träumen Marchen.

Nicht minder bedenklich als unser architektonisches Wirken in der
Nachbildung alter Stile ist unsere Tatigkeit auf dem Gebiete der sogenannten Denkmalpflege.   Dieselben Verirrungen, dieselbe Verkennung der
einfachsten Tatsachen hier wie dort !   Die alten Bauten wurden dem 19

Jahrhundert in einem Zustande überliefert, der ihrem natürlichen Lebens-
prozess entsprach, z T gebrechlich infolge ihres Alters, z T durch die
aufeinanderfolgenden Menschengenerationen durch Anbauten und Eingriffe umgestaltet und ausgebaut Zu ihnen nahm nun die Architektenschaft des 19 Jahrhunderts eine ganz neue Stellung ein. Sie fühlte das
Bedürfnis in sich, sie auf Neue zu komplettieren, ähnlich wie die Leute der
Renaissance zerbrochene aufgefundene antike Statuen durch Ansetzen
von Beinen, Armen und Nasen ergänzten Und wenn die Ergänzung
wenigstens noch im Sinne und mit den Ausdrucksmitteln unserer Zeit
erfolgt wäre ! Die Architekten verfielen aber auf die Idee, sie im
Sinne längst vergangener Jahrhunderte zu bewerkstelligen Sie gaben
vor, sich so haarscharf in das Denken und Fühlen des 12 oder 13 Jahrhunderts versetzen zu können, dass sie das Werk des damaligen Baumeis-
ters fortsetzen konnten Und viele von uns glauben noch heute daran,
dass sie es konnten Nun ereignet sich bei Wiederherstellungen zwar
stets das Eigentümliche, dass nach einem Jahrzehnt die fremde Hand,
die die Eingriffe in den alten Bestand vollführt hatte, deutlich sichtbar
wird Jede folgende Generation erkennt, dass die vorige sich in dem
Einfühlen in den Geist des alten Baus gründlich geirrt hat Aber keine
Generation ist bisher auf den naheliegenden Gedanken gekommen, dass
auch sie sich wie alle Vorgänger irren könne und dass vielleicht schon zehn
Jahr später das Unzulängliche ihrer Nachahmung des Alten offen zu Tage
liegen werde. Der Irrtum grassiert weiter, obgleich sich in neurer Zeit
der Widerspruch eines grossen Teils des gebildeten Publikums gegen die
Wiederherstellungsbestrebungen gewendet hat Noch heute stellen
Architekten-Versammlungen Programme und Anweisungen auf, wie man
sich ganz genau in den Geist der alten Baumeister versetzen könne und
noch heute fälschen und vernichten sie weiter Es ist nicht zuviel
behauptet, dass alle vorhergehenden Jahrhunderte mit ihren Kriegen,
Feuersbrünsten und Revolutionen weniger vernichtend in den Bestand
an historischen Bauten eingegriffen haben als das Wirken derjenigen, die
sich im 19 Jahrhundert als deren Hüter ausgaben, der Architekten

Das Bestreben, aus der Empfindung vergangener Zeit heraus zu
bauen, treibt noch andere Blüten Man glaubt den künstlerisch geschlossenen Charakter eines alten Marktplatzes, einer alten Patrizierstrasse
dadurch zu erhalten, dass man dafür sorgt, dass etwa entstehende Neu-
bauten in denselben Formen errichtet werden, die die alten Bauten zeigen
Städte mit reichlicher Ueberkommenschaft alter Baukunst schreiben
Konkurrenzen für Fassaden im alten Stil aus und die ganze Architektenschaft beteiligt sich an dem unmöglichen Beginnen, das Kulturbild einer
uns fern liegenden Zeit zu imitieren Die Fassaden in alten Formen
mögen sich abmühen wie sie wollen, sie kommen mit den alten Originalwerken nicht in Einklang und auch hier ereignet sich wieder der Fall,
dass die nachstfolgende Generation erkennt, wie gänzlich daneben der
Imitator gehauen hat. Die Imitation steht jetzt wie ein plebejisches
Surrogat zu einem noblen alten Original Was der gesunder Menschen-
verstand schon von vornherein hätte lehren müssen wird jetzt offenbar
dass es keine grössere Torheit giebt, als eine Imitation, die an irgend
einer anderen Stelle vielleicht noch erträglich sein würde, in unmittelbarer Nachbarschaft zum Original zu stellen Echtheit und Nachahmung
stehen zueinander wie Oel und Wasser Dagegen werden echt empfun-
dene Kunstwerke, mögen sie stammen aus welcher Zeit sie wollen, stets
eine gute Nachbarschaft bilden Die Einheitlichkeit wurde daher viel
weniger durch Stilimitation, als dadurch erzielt werden, dass man dafür
sorgte, dass nur gute, von wirklicher Künstlerhand herrührende neue
Bauten neben die alten traten

So bewegt sich unser heutiges architektonisches Wirken noch in
mannigfachen Irrtümern, die alle darauf zurückzuführen sind, dass wir
nicht freudig und unbefangen vorwärts blicken, sondern sentimentalen

oder archaologischen Ideen folgen   Jede neu auftauchende " Stromung "
ist bei dieser unserer Gemutsstimmung eine neue Gefahr. Der Anschluss
an das Bauernhaus und die Wiederaufnahme heimischer Bauweise klingen
als Programm ausgezeichnet, aber man muss bange fragen wohin
werden Sie uns fuhren ? Immer handelt es sich um Anpassungen und
Wiederaufnahmen   Unser Blick ist nicht auf das Ziel vor uns, sondern
auf irgend etwas hinter uns oder seitlich von uns gerichtet, wir versuchen
mit dem Rucken nach vorn gewendet vorwarts zu schreiten   Dass wir
dabei keinen geraden Weg verfolgen konnen, sondern gehemmte Zick-
zackgange machen, ja, eine Reihe von Fehltritten begehen, ergiebt sich
daraus von selbst   Unser Gestalten wird nicht so sehr geleitet von
sachlichen oder kunstlerischen Beweggrunden, als von sich kreuzenden
Reminiscenzen. Zum Unterschiede von allen anderen kunstlerischen
Gestaltern haben wir Architekten heute keine einheitliche Kunstuber-
zeugung mehr   Wir sind im Stande, fur jede neue Aufgabe eine neue
Ueberzeugung anzuziehen, fur eine Kirche, die gothische, fur ein Ver-
waltungsgebaude die der absolutistischen Konigszeit, fur ein Landhaus
die der Bauernkunst. Das ist ein ganz neuer Zustand. Die Architekten der Vergangenheit waren stets der festen Ueberzeugung, dass der
gerade herrschende Geschmack der richtige wäre. Das gab ihnen die
Kraft, sich ihren Aufgaben mit voller Hingabe zu widmen, ein Stuck
starker personlicher Ueberzeugung in ihnen niederzulegen   Wie kann
man als Kunstler eine Richtung schopferisch vertreten wollen, die man
selbst nur fur unbedingt richtig halt ! Das Resultat mussen Verwasse-
rungen sein. Der Kunstler kann, wenn er sich uber das Niveau des
Maskenschneiders erheben will, nur eine einzige Ueberzeugung haben.
Das Wirken in heterogenen Kunstrichtungen ist geistiger Selbstmord.

Die Architektur wird ihre Starke nicht wieder erlangen, sie wende
sich denn von ihren sentimentalen und archaologischen Zielen ab. Die
Archaologie ist eine schatzenswerte Wissenschaft, aber sie hat nichts mit
der kunstlerischen Schopfung zu tun und kann diese stets nur in verhang-
nisvoller Weise beeinflussen   Fur die schaffende Architektur konnen,
wie fur die angewandte Kunst uberhaupt, nur zwei Gesichtspunkte massgebend sein, und zwar erstens ein realer . der der exakten Deckung des
Bedurfnisses, und zweitens ein idealer der der Erzeugung einer kunstlerischen Stimmung   Die exakte Deckung des Bedurfnisses ist die
klare Richtung im Wirken des Ingenieurs, Maschinenbauers, Sanitats-
technikers u.s w   Die vollige Klarheit in ihrem Ziele hat es zu den
erfreulichen und auch nach neuerer Ansicht kunstlerisch völlig befriedigenden Leistungen des Ingenieurs gebracht   Die Verwirrung tritt erst
ein bei dem Versuche, ein Mehr zu geben als die exakte Deckung des
Bedurfnisses   Dieses Mehr kann nur aus einem kunstlerischen Geiste
heraus gegeben werden, und wer diesen nicht hat, stehe fuglich davon ab.
Keinesfalls kann eine mangelnde kunstlerische Befahigung ersetzt werden
durch ein Anlernen archaologischer Brocken, mit dem Zwecke, damit
die baulichen Gebilde aufzuputzen   Das verhangnisvolle Spiel, das
wir heute in der Architektur mit leeren Begriffen und toten Floskeln
treiben, setzt uns in schroffen Gegensatz zu einer im ubrigen freudig und
kuhn vorwartsdrangenden Zeit, die auf allen anderen Gebieten der menschlichen Geistestatigkeit einen so enormen Aufschwung zu verzeichnen hat

Nur eine lebenskräftige, vorwärtsblickende, im besten Sinne moderne
Geistestatigkeit kann in einer solchen Zeit das Interesse fesseln   Das
Hauptmittel, die Architektur dem Publikum wieder naher zu bringen,
ist das, eine gute, sachliche, von archäologischen Gesichtspunkten freie
Architektur zu schaffen   Dass das Publikum an Kunstausserungen dieser
Art Anteil nimmt, zeigt der ungeheure Aufschwung, den das moderne
Kunstgewerbe in den letzten zehn Jahren genommen hat. Die neuzeit-
lichen Bestrebungen im Kunstgewerbe haben es vermocht, die gesamte
gebildete Welt zu fesseln. Das Interesse begann hier in dem Augen-

blicke, als das Kunstgewerbe anfing, nicht mehr ruckblickend, sondern
vorwartsblickend zu gestalten   Die Stilmatzchen der alten Art unter
halten aber auch in der Architektur nicht mehr, und die Bauten in historischen Verkleidungen erringen selbst dann, wenn sie ausgezeichnet
gemacht sind, nur noch einen Achtungserfolg   Wie sehr dagegen ein
wirklich moderner Bau im Publikum Anklang findet, das zeigt am besten
der Bau Wertheim in Berlin   Jeder Gebildete hat hier die Empfindung,
dass es sich um ein Bauwerk handelt, das in das Gegenwartsleben eingreift
und an der Losung der Aufgaben der Gegenwart teilnimmt.   Von dem
Augenblicke an, wo wir alle von einem solchen modernen Geiste beseelt
sein wurden, wurde sich die Kluft zwischen der Architektur und dem
Publikum zu schliessen beginnen   Wir brauchten nicht mehr auf Mittel
zu sinnen, das Interesse des Publikums kunstlich zu wecken, unser Schaffen
wurde wieder in ein naturliches Verhältnis zu unserer Zeit treten, die
Architektur hatte Aussicht wieder populär zu werden

Es ist nicht zu leugnen, dass wir heute bereits auf dem besten Wege
sind, zu einem solchen Lauterungsprozesse der Architektur zu gelangen
Allerorten regt und ruhrt es sich im Sinne einer neuen Architektur-
auffassung, hier und da sind schon ausgezeichnete Resultate zu verzeichnen.   Hier nun gilt es einzusetzen und das Werk der Gesundung vorwarts
zu treiben   Das Interesse, das das gebildete Publikum an den Architekturwerken dieser Art nimmt, bildet die Handhabe, die Popularisierung
fortgesetzt und mehr und mehr zu steigern   Alle diejenigen Mittel, die
bisher schon mit mehr oder weniger Erfolg versucht worden sind, um
dem Publikum die Architektur naher zu bringen, werden an der Hand
dieser Werke doppelt und dreifach wirken.   Als solche schon bisher
versuchte Mittel sind zu erwahnen . Einreihung von architektonischen Darstellungen in die Kunstausstellungen und Belehrungen durch die Presse

Der Erfolg der Architekturabteilungen in den Jahreskunstausstel-
lungen hat nicht immer den Erwartungen entsprochen   Die Architektur
ist eine raumliche Kunst und Abbildungen von Werken der Architektur
sind fast noch schaaler als Abbildungen von Bildwerken   Die zeichnei-
ischen und malerischen Darstellungen von Architekturwerken haben die
Ausstellungsbesucher haufig nur durch die an ihnen entfaltete Aquarell-
technik oder die Flottheit der Federzeichnung interessiert.   Wenn man
Interesse an der Architektur selbst erwecken will, so bleibt fur Ausstellungen eigentlich nur die verkleinerte raumliche Nachbildung, das Modell,
ubrig.   An Modellen von Bauwerken hat jeder Ausstellungsbesucher
Freude und bis zu einem gewissen Grade erwecken sie einen Widerhall
der raumlichen Wirkung, die das Bauwerk selbst ausuben wurde. Freilich
ist das nur in Bezug auf die aussere Architektur moglich, weil hier der
beim wirklichen Bauwerk mögliche ferne Standpunkt einen Vergleich
mit einer Verkleinerung erlaubt.   Die Wirkung von Innenraumen durch
Modell zu ubermitteln, stosst immer auf sehr grosse Schwierigkeiten.

Allzuviel Hoffnungen wird man aber auf das Erwecken des Interesses
durch Ausstellungen uberhaupt nicht setzen durfen   Kunstausstellungen sind nur fur Tafelbilder und graphische Werke das richtige, nur
diese konnen sich dort im Original präsentieren   Neben den Vorfuhrungen
von Originalwerken werden aber Vorfuhrungen von verkleinerten Nach-
bildungen immer im Nachteile sein, weil sie erst durch Uebersetzung ihren
Eindruck erreichen sollen

Viel wichtiger als das kunstliche, durch Ausstellungen erregte Interesse
an der Architektur ist jedenfalls das naturliche Interesse an der Architektur selbst.   Am meisten und reinsten wirkt in der Erziehung zur
Kunst immer die Weckung eines personlichen Verhältnisses zu ihr.   Ein
solches personliches Verhaltnis ist aber gerade bei der Architektur von
selbst vorhanden, denn jeder Mensch lebt in den raumlichen Gebilden,
die sie schafft.   Die Wohnung ist das Bindeglied, das jeden Menschen mit
der Architektur verknupft.   Wurde nun das Interesse der Menschen an

ihrer Wohnung gestiegert, so ware die Brucke zur Architektur bald geschlagen.   Und hier treffen wir auch auf den Punkt, an dem die neue Bewegung im Kunstgewerbe mit so grossem Erfolg eingesetzt hat : es begann mit der fur jeden einzelnen Menschen hochst interessanten Aufgabe, die nachste Umgebung des Menschen, die Raume, in denen er täglich lebt, neu zu gestalten

Die Fortsetzung des Weges ist in der Gestaltung des Einzelhauses zu erblicken   Es ist von vornherein anzunehmen, dass, wenn die Sitte im Einzelhause zu wohnen wächst, auch das Interesse an Architektur wachsen wird   Naturlich hängt die Möglichkeit des Wohnens im Einzelhause mit der Wohlstandsfrage zusammen, aber immerhin muss auch beim Reichen zunächst der Wunsch vorhanden sein, dem Leben im Einzelhause, und das heisst fast in allen Fallen, dem Leben ausserhalb der Grossstadt den Vorzug zu geben vor dem Leben in der Stadt.   Augenblicklich geht nun ein solcher Zug durch die Menschheit.   Die Stadtbewohner drängen aufs Land und wir befinden uns in einem Aufschwung der landlichen Baukunst   Von ihr ist das Meiste in der Richtung zu erhoffen, das Interesse des Publikums an der Architektur zu heben.

Freilich ist auch hier zunachst noch ein grosses Werk der Reinigung zu vollbringen.   Die unsachlichen Gesichtspunkte, die in das ganze Gebiet der Architektur durch das Stilgetriebe des 19. Jahrhunderts gekommen sind, uberwiegen auch noch im Bau des Einzelhauses   Auch hier irrt das Publikum noch, gefuhrt von einem Heere unverstandiger Versorger in allen moghchen Nebensächlichkeiten umher, ohne auf die Hauptsache genugend zu achten   Die rein sachlichen Gesichtspunkte, von denen man doch annehmen musste, dass sie die einzigen seien, die das Publikum etwas angehen, stehen noch im Hintergrunde.   Die beste Lage des Hauses, die Beziehungen des Hauses zum Garten, die Lage der Raume zueinander, die zweckentsprechende Ausgestaltung der einzelnen Raume   das alles pflegt beim Bau des Hauses eine weit geringere Rolle zu spielen, als die Gesichtspunkte der sogenannten architektonischen Gruppierung   So lange wir Architekten das Publikum noch mit solchen Aeusserlichkeiten unterhalten, werden wir auf ein wirkliches Verstandnis fur das Wesen der Architektur noch nicht rechnen können.

Das Beispiel Englands zeigt uns, wie eingreifend gerade das Wohnen im Einzelhause nach der Richtung des Verständnisses und des Interesses an Architektur wirken kann.   Denn die hausliche Baukunst erfreut sich dort einer Popularitat, wie in keinem anderen Lande der Welt.   Was dabei aber wohl zu beachten ist, ist der Umstand, dass es hauptsachlich die sachlichen Gesichtspunkte sind, die in England gelaufig sind und unter deren Verstandnis das Interesse an der hauslichen Baukunst gedeiht. Die Vorstellungen uber die gesundheitlich beste Anlage der Wohnung, uber die behaghche Gestaltung der Innenräume und uber die zweckentsprechende Anordnung der Raume zu einander, namentlich der Bedienungs- und Wirtschaftsraume, sind in England die geklartesten, und sie stehen so stark im Vordergrunde, dass irgendwelche Stilgesichtspunkte gegen sie nicht aufkommen können.

Belehrung uber diese wichtigsten und das Publikum am meisten angehenden sachlichen Fragen in der Architektur tate dringend not, und in ihnen wurde ein weiteres Mittel gefunden werden konnen, das Interesse an der Architektur in vernunftiger Weise zu steigern.   Es ist zu bedauern, dass so wenig Architekten bereit sind, diese Gesichtpunkte vor der breiteren Oeffentlichkeit zu erortern   Die Erorterungen uber Architektur spielen sich fast lediglich in Zeitschriften ab, die Niemand ausser den Fachgenossen in die Hand bekommt   Was hat es aber fur Zweck, gewisse Dinge immer und immer wieder lediglich vor den Fachgenossen zu erortern, wenn man wunscht, dass sie die Oeffentlichkeit interessieren sollen ?   Der Weg, die Oeffentlichkeit zu erreichen, ist nur der, das Feld der allgemeinen Presse, vorwiegend das der Tagespresse und Zeitschriftenpresse, zu betreten

Die Einwirkung der Zeitungs- und Zeitschriftenlitteratur auf die Vorstellungen des modernen Publikums ist ungeheuer, und gerade hier liegen hoffnungsreiche Möglichkeiten einer Steigerung des Interesses an Architektur. Es würde für gehaltreiche und allgemein verständlich geschriebene Aufsätze über architektonische Fragen gewiss nicht an Lesern fehlen. Aber es fehlt vorläufig an den Schriftstellern Die grosse Mehrzahl von Kunstschriftstellern, die das Publikum täglich mit Unterhaltungsstoff über Gemälde versorgen, versagt, wenn es sich um Werke der Architektur handelt. Die Architektur ist ihnen ein Buch mit sieben Siegeln, sie stellen sich irgend etwas Geheimnisvolles darunter vor und tappen, wenn sie an die Erörterung architektonischer Fragen gehen, nicht selten in Irrtümern, die unter Umständen mehr Verwirrungen als Klärungen hervorrufen. Vielleicht bildet auch hier das jetzt im Vordergrund des Interesses stehende Kunstgewerbe, dessen Sinn und Bedeutung viele Tagesschriftsteller erfasst und dem grösseren Publikum dargelegt haben, die Brücke, um auch die Architektur allmählich mit mehr Verständnis zu durchdringen und in geeigneter Weise vor das Publikum zu bringen. Denn so erwünscht es auch wäre, dass sich praktische Architekten der Aufgabe unterzogen, schriftstellerisch für die Hebung des Interesses an Architektur zu wirken, so aussichtslos erscheint dieser Weg angesichts des Umstandes, dass die im praktischen Leben stehenden Architekten meist völlig von ihrem Beruf absorbiert sind, ganz abgesehen davon, dass ihnen die Routine der schriftstellerischen Darstellung meistens abgeht.

DISCUSSION ON SUBJECT IV

Mr ALBERT KELSEY (Philadelphia), in opening the discussion, said he had listened with great interest to the papers that had been read Considerable interest had been awakened in architectural matters among the people of the United States, due not so much to the points that had been referred to by the readers of the papers as to the great object-lessons that had sprung up, as it were, in a night in the form of their exhibitions There was no time for him to explain why it was thought expedient to make those buildings more or less archæological, but it had had a tremendous influence, and had done a great deal more than all the reading and all the teaching in their various institutions to awaken an interest in architecture The Dewey Arch, for instance, which was a work of love, had created a tremendous furore throughout the entire country, and for days and days dozens of people might be seen photographing it The T-Square Club delegate to the Brussels International Congress of Architects said that in the United States among their reproductions of Continental architecture they had already in Florida specimens of the Spanish Renaissance as fine as any in Spain At Philadelphia they had very high buildings, occupied by bureaux of commerce, where the ground floor and the first floor were in the style of François I , as fine as any examples of that epoch in France At New York they had a "Tour Giralda de Seville," and at Boston a Sainte-Geneviève library, a perfect example But a modern spirit, national, indigenous, and inspired by their epoch, a spirit which represented that epoch instead of those servile copies of old-world monuments, had yet to come, and they awaited its advent with impatience That was nine years ago, and they were still impatient Since then twentieth-century life had created twentieth-century problems Since then architecture had passed through the experimental stage, and was now recognised as one of the learned professions. This fortunate state of affairs had been brought about primarily by the creation of an educational system which stretched from the Atlantic to the Pacific, a system so liberal in its interchange of courtesies between the architectural societies and the architectural schools of their universities that it was now possible for any talented and ambitious draughtsman (either college or office trained) to procure the advantages of foreign travel, as well as a course at the Ecole des Beaux-Arts, without cost to himself   Moreover, a complimentary arrangement had even been made by the French Government whereby the winner of the Paris prize in the final competition of the New York Beaux-Arts Society was admitted to the first class upon his arrival in Paris, thus eliminating an exacting entrance examination and all the work of the lower class required of other architectural students at the French National School of Fine Arts: Their educational system, however, was not alone responsible for progress and prosperity   They had had unusually lavish opportunities to build , and, lastly, their endeavours had been loyally seconded by an Architectural Press which had done much to raise standards and to diffuse knowledge. And now the domestication or nationalisation of their architecture was the next problem confronting them   The florid oyster ornament so common on the inferior new buildings of Paris—and its architectural suburb, New York—was a manifestation of ignorance which they were combating, many contending that in a search for indigenous sources of inspiration their traditions led to England rather than to France   For instance, within one hundred miles of his home, they had ancient customs still in vogue, carried out under the shadows of good old Georgian buildings   At Lancaster and York the ancient rivalries were perpetuated by the emblematic use of the red and white roses of the Royal Houses, after which those towns were long ago named.   At Bethlehem a trombone choir ascended to the lofty belfry of the old Moravian church, and there by playing familiar chorals announced to the people below the death of a member of their congregation   At Bird-in-Hand a church debt was solemnly discharged annually by the payment of a single red rose   At Ephrata the old monastery still stood where Protestant monks and nuns lived   Thus in the United States more than anywhere else their architects were entitled, both on account of diverse historical associations and because of the constantly increasing mixed population, to come to a reunion like this, prepared to learn something from every delegate that might be turned to appropriate and practical use.   Naturally their thoughts turned first to the Mother Country, and with gratitude to the Royal Institute of British Architects for the magnificent entertainments they were enjoying, and for the many expressions of cordial goodwill they had listened to   They fully recognised how vitally and intimately related their work was to the work of the English architect , they recognised the manifold advantages to be derived from an international *entente cordiale,* and in consequence they proposed to do all in their power to strengthen, fortify, and buttress those fraternal ties

Herr BERNARD FELISCH (Berlin) having spoken,

Mr HUGH STANNUS said that, as Mr Jackson had remarked in his very thoughtful paper, the public whom they wanted to educate in architecture were their masters, and naturally their clients   If architecture be combined of three elements—firstly, the plan, that accumulation of cells which together made the building, the cells themselves, and the conglomeration of those cells arising from the function that they expected the building to perform , secondly, the walling or the inclosing of those cells when they had put them together , and, thirdly, the decorating in a fitting and logical manner of the building—they had got to educate the public to recognise those three elements , and they could do it in the way Mr Jackson had pointed out   They might build large buildings by way of educating the public, and he believed that the majority of them would be only too glad to educate the public in that manner , but unfortunately the public went to others besides architects. He quite granted Architects were the salt of the earth,-and that wisdom would

die with them , but the public was not content to come to them, only ;
it went to others , and thus it was that bad buildings were made as well
as good buildings. If they, were to educate the public while they were
waiting for the buildings to be made, it must be done by lectures, and
their lectures must be made more interesting   They must interest the
public and get them to attend before they could induce them to accept
their *dicta* on the subject. Then, in the second place, their, lectures
must be clear and convincing with regard to the *Plan*. Too much
had architecture been considered to be merely a matter of the outside—
of the perspective , for they knew how competition committees were
swayed by Perspectives of the outside of buildings.   They ought to
recognise that architecture governs the inside as well as the outside—
that a building should grow from the inside, and that the inside must be
considered and planned first. That led him to the suggestion that
more and more they should try to persuade competition committees
that, in addition to the perspectives, there should be sections and plans
in *Perspective*. That was one of their methods at South Kensington—
when they had a plan of a building it was put into perspective, with
the walls showing a certain height all through   In that manner the
public understood a building much better than if they merely had the
plans drawn geometrically. He wanted to see perspective sections
required by competition committees, and in that way the public could
understand the inside of a building much better than by the mere ordinary
elevation. Those of them who were old enough to recollect the first
publication of Choisy would remember that it was from those beautiful
perspectives with which he enriched his book that they were able to
learn more about the construction of Gothic architecture than from a
mere plan or elevation   The first point, therefore, he wanted to make
was that they should " think in Perspective," as Alfred Stevens said
Secondly, he wanted to say something about the use of Models. Their
brethren in the engineers' craft made very much of models in the teaching
of engineering   Of course, they had models of complete machines, but they
also had, in an engineering class, models of portions of machinery—models
of pulley-blocks, pedestal-blocks, cranks, &c.—portions of machinery
which were capable of being put together to construct machines   They
as architects might very well take a lesson from them , and he believed
the more models they employed in the teaching of architecture—models
which were capable of being taken to pieces and recombined to make
further designs—the better for the student and the more they would be
able to interest the public. If they had lectures accompanied by models
which could be taken to pieces, instead of lantern-slides, he thought they
would be able to interest the public more. He would further suggest
that the teaching should not end when the last echo of the speaker's
voice had died away , but that every lecturer, whether lecturing before
the public or before a class of students, should allow half an hour for
Questions and Conversation, and perhaps for practical Demonstration on
the subject   In that way he ventured to think that they would interest
the public, and by interesting them they would be also educating them
Architecture was essentially the art of putting together, and if they
desired to interest the Public he ventured to think that their method of
teaching should rather be synthetic, reserving the analytic method for
their Students

M. AUGUSTIN REY (Architecte de la fondation Rothschild, Paris) —
Messieurs, les rapports les plus intéressants viennent de nous être résumés
Il se dégage, à notre avis, des différents points de vue auxquels se sont
placés nos confrères une idée générale, celle que le public ne comprend
pas la plupart du temps l'idée directrice qui se dégage de nos monuments   Nous pourrions, à cet égard nous étendre longuement et expliquer
que, si cette opinion générale est si ancrée dans la foule, c'est que le monu-

ment est un simple décor plat et par conséquent n'intéresse qu'à l'égal
d'un décor de theâtre.   Un des moyens les plus indiqués serait de chercher
à éduquer ce public par un enseignement approprié.   Certes des conférences
faites par nos maîtres dans l'art de l'architecture et présentées d'une manière
attrayante pourraient exercer quelque influence   Nous estimons cependant
que là n'est pas le moyen principal. *Les Concours Publics sont d'une
action autrement plus pénétrante dans la grande foule.   Il faut intéresser
les citoyens d'une ville comme ceux d'une nation à la création de nos
grands monuments, en leur faisant aussi fréquemment que possible
l'agréable surprise de les convier à l'examen public de projets*   Comment
voulez-vous, dans une matière, comme l'architecture, qui est parfois
si abstraite, intéresser seulement par la simple image ce grand public
que nous constatons être si indifférent à nos efforts ?   Nous ne pouvons
le secouer de sa torpeur qu'en faisant intervenir l'élément moral de son
jugement , en écartant systématiquement de tous nos grands Concours
Publics l'opinion du grand nombre, nous nous aliénons sans nous en
douter l'action puissante que peut avoir cette opinion publique à laquelle,
en dernier ressort, est remis tout jugement définitif   Pourquoi voyons-
nous si souvent un monument de grande valeur passer au milieu de
l'indifférence générale pendant les premières années qui succèdent à sa
terminaison ?   Pourquoi la foule n'est-elle nullement impressionnée
par la beauté plastique des formes, par les masses monumentales, par
l'idée morale qui se dégage et que l'auteur y a souvent comme incrustée
par un travail parfois génial ?   Simplement parce que *le public a été
tenu à l'écart soit de l'élaboration du concours, s'il y en a eu un, soit de
l'étude successive des plans qui ont précédé l'exécution définitive   Pour
ma part, je crois trouver là la véritable cause de l'indifférence parfois
hautaine du public vis-à-vis de nos plus grands monuments.* Il faut
bien nous convaincre que si nous voulons reprendre la haute situation que
nous possédions dans les siècles précédents au point de vue de l'art,
l'Architecte doit soumettre volontiers, dans toutes les occasions où cela
sera possible, au jugement de tous ses études et ses projets   *A cet égard
les Concours Publics, et surtout les Concours Publics Internationaux,
peuvent nous apporter une solution pratique   Qui n'a vu de ces concours
dans lesquels aucune part n'était réservée au jugement du public ?   Les plus
grands monuments furent décidés parfois en petit comité, sous le manteau
de la cheminée.*   Au jury que nous nous donnons dans ces concours
devraient être intéressés intimement des représentants de l'opinion
publique   La presse, si indifférente vis-à-vis de nous, lorsqu'elle ne va
pas jusqu'à la malveillance, devrait, lorsqu'il s'agit d'un monument
d'une grande importance pour un ville, être représentée.   De nos jours
c'est la presse quotidienne qui remue et brasse les idées, c'est elle qui
renseigne quotidiennement des millions de nos citoyens, c'est à elle que
nous devons faire appel. Il y a là, il nous semble, une idée raisonnable
à mettre en pratique   Il est bien certain que nous devons faire aussi
une certaine part à la vanité humaine   *Si les citoyens d'une ville se
considéraient comme ayant participé, si peu que ce soit, à la création de tel
ou tel monument public, ils en seraient fiers et sauraient manifester cet
orgueil si naturel et si profitable à tous*   C'est en exaltant ces sentiments de la foule que nous ressaisirons le sceptre que nous avons peu
à peu laissé tomber de nos mains, celui de maître de l'œuvre, de chef
dont on doit sentir la puissante action   Tous autres modes d'éducation
du public peuvent certes ne pas nuire au but que nous cherchons à réaliser,
mais ils sont d'ordre secondaire.

Herr H P. BERLAGE (Amsterdam) said he agreed with what Mr.
Jackson had said in his paper, that after all the best means of educating
the public in architecture was by the production of well-designed buildings

On the motion of Mr. KELSEY, a vote of thanks was accorded to the
Chairman for presiding.

SUBJECT V

A STATUTORY QUALIFICATION FOR ARCHITECTS

Saturday Morning, 21st *July —Grafton Galleries*

Chairmen   Professor I G Clason (Sweden), Mr Edwin T. Hall (England)
Hon Secretaries   E. Chujo (Japan);
J T Cackett (Northern Architectural Association, England)

(1) By JOHN S ARCHIBALD (Montreal, Canada)

The question of the advisability or not of demanding a statutory qualification for architects has been engaging the attention of the profession
for some time   Much has been said and written on the subject on all
sides, and from all points of view; but I venture to think that the basic
principles underlying the argument have often been misunderstood, and
the point of view cramped and ill-taken.

We grant it is a delicate subject for the profession to agitate—motives
can be so misrepresented and arguments appear biassed and prejudiced,
but, for want of uninterested advocates, we needs must take up the
cudgels in our own behalf, fortified with the conviction that we are not
fighting the battle of the "select few," but the wider field of humanity
and public interest   Opposition is even met with in our own ranks
from men and influences compelling respect even if they be against us,
whilst laymen look upon it as another species of "trades unionism" and
"incorporated tyranny"   It should be needless to point out that the
principles underlying the formation of "trades unions" are wholly different
from those which actuate us   Trades unionism is purely a movement to
regulate the compensation and earning powers of the individual amongst
a limited number of persons, whilst the latter is a movement to raise
the standard of professional practice and to safeguard public interests
without limitation (other than that set by competence) of the number
who wish to practise the profession of architecture   Trades unionism is
a combination for offensive and defensive purposes, of the weaker against
the stronger, statutory qualification for architects is a voluntary movement of the stronger (represented by the profession) in the interests of
the weaker (represented by the public—and who are often entirely ignorant
of the responsibilities inherent in the practice of our profession).

Generally speaking, there are two sides to architecture, viz the
æsthetic and the utilitarian—the former appeals to the senses, whilst
the latter is the practical · the application of theory to the requirements
of mankind.   The former may, or may not, have a good or bad influence
on humanity, this being dependent upon whether we are prepared to
admit that without beauty we cannot have goodness, and ugliness usually
leads to depravity, but, as regards the latter (utilitarian), especially in
its constructional aspect, there can be no division of opinion as to the
necessity for the most careful examination before being permitted to
design and erect structures.   The object of an architect's labour is to

prepare, generally speaking, for habitation by humanity Human life
has, under civilising influences at any rate, always been looked upon as
valuable, beyond price and compensation It is recognised in the practice of medicine, all countries demanding a most rigorous examination
before one is allowed to administer to the corporate ills of mankind. It
is recognised in the practice of law, where even the civil life of man must
be guarded by specially trained individuals. Why should it not be
recognised in the practice of architecture, where requirements are demanded combining science, chemistry, and law, all individually and
collectively of the greatest importance, and fraught with serious conse-
quences to the public ?

It has been said that a statutory qualification is only necessary in
countries where the standing of the profession is not as high as it ought
to be We would infer from such an argument that as soon as it was
decided that the professional standing had reached a certain height the
statutory qualification would be withdrawn ; and, on the other hand, it
would be fair to assume that the elevation attained by the profession
in such circumstances, in the public estimation, was due to that
very statutory qualification If the statutory qualification was the means
of elevating the profession, why remove it ? Will the profession remain
stationary after such a procedure, or will it not naturally enter on a
retrograde movement ? The argument is illogical

To me it is a surprise that the question has not been taken up by
the Governments of the respective countries long ere this We are hedged
about by legislative enactments which, at their root, must have emanated
from the conviction that the practice of architecture was a responsible
one, calling for particular training and study In the Province of Quebec
we work under the Napoleonic Code, which attaches to an architect the
responsibility of the stability of his buildings for ten years after completion. The only inference to draw from such an enactment is that the
practice of the profession is of such a nature that the individual cannot
throw off all responsibility the moment a contract is complete, but that
he must have exercised such caution that a building in all its inherent
and constructional parts must be perfect for at least a period of ten years
after completion, else the responsibility devolves upon the shoulders of
the architect Of course, a certain and individual responsibility pertains
also to the contractor, but such side issue does not affect the general
argument Architects are compelled to erect buildings under the direct
superintendence and dictates of law The logical sequence would be
that the law would make provision that all who enter on the practice of
the profession would be found fully competent to carry out the spirit
and dictates of such enactments

How can such an end be attained ? Obviously the only answer is,
by a system of examinations True, this is not always the most satisfactory method, but for want of a better we needs must adopt it We
grant that the mere passing of an examination does not ensure a competent practitioner, but at least, for want of a better method, it obviates
the fear that he may be altogether incapable It is certainly far ahead
of present conditions, which are almost universal to-day, where any
irresponsible individual may clothe himself with the title " architect "
and no one has the right to say " Yea " or " Nay "

The public require to be protected. At present they are indifferent
How are they to know whether an architect is qualified or competent
to be entrusted with the erection of buildings ? As a rule, " time " is
the judge; but ere " time " has passed his verdict the trouble has been
done, structural weakness becomes apparent, or, what is sometimes even
worse, another abortion is raised before the eyes of an unsuspecting
public, to wield its baneful influence, unwittingly it may be, over the
moral temperament of its unhappy beholders A man should not be

permitted to endanger lives and property, neither should he be permitted to offend the higher senses of mankind

I have already said that competence can only be ascertained by a system of examinations Such examinations must be all-embracing, and wielded by powers beyond the faintest tinge of suspicion, and removed, in the public eye, from all question of self-interest

There are at present several architectural societies working under private or legislative enactments where entrance can only be obtained after passing a series of examinations Such examinations are, as a rule, conducted by professional practitioners, men who, in the public eye, are particularly interested in the number entitled to all the benefits of such associationship. Now, I do not want to be misunderstood in this connection I am not impugning the motives underlying the formation of such an examining board, neither am I questioning the motives influencing such examiners , far from it   Those of us who belong to such associations know that the question of the *number* presenting themselves for examination has no influence whatever on the minds of the examiners or associations when it comes to the question of how many shall they pass ; but in this connection we must take our view-point from that of the public, from those outside who are apt to misconstrue an undesirable necessity into an intentional stumbling-block.

I use the word " undesirable " advisedly.

If "statutory qualification" is to become a fact, we must not forget that it can only be obtained by proving to the general public that we are not acting from selfish motives, that we do not desire to bar the profession to all, irrespective of ability, that we are not endeavouring to form another "close corporation," but that we are actuated simply by our interest in the public good, and by the desire to elevate, not merely the profession, but the moral temperament of the community. Therefore, to enlist public opinion on our behalf, the power to admit to the practice of the profession must be put in the hands of men who, even to the eye of the professionally illiterate, shall be above the cry of self-interest   Such a board must be composed of men eminent in their respective spheres, and who are not engaged in the actual practice of the profession, and their appointment must come from authority outside the ranks of the profession. They should be appointed by the Government that grants the necessary legislation   Only by such means may we expect to get any measure of legislative enactment looking toward statutory qualification

Such examinations would, of course, cover the whole ground of architectural practice. The advisability of a thorough examination on the constructional or utilitarian side of the profession can hardly be denied. An architect erects not things of beauty only to be admired in the abstract. His genesis is utility. Utility leads to construction. His works must not endanger the lives of the public, and he must exhibit a certain knowledge of scientific and physical laws. Vitruvius elaborates on this point, and what he wrote then is just as applicable, and, indeed, is more so, to-day   He points out the complexity of the professional requirements of those days ; how much greater is it to-day ! All cities require the obtaining of "permits" previous to building , these are required in order that certain hygienic constructional and scientific regulations be complied with. The inference is that a certain standard of plan and construction is desired and made compulsory by the powers that be The logical sequence of such action would be to set a standard of qualification for all who design buildings. A standard is made compulsory for the building; why should a standard not be made compulsory for the designer ?

All countries deem it necessary and advisable to hedge architects around with a large amount of legal responsibility, such responsibility usually being more exacting in countries where the standard of the profession is high.   In fact, investigation will prove that the higher the standard of the profession in a country the greater the responsibility attached by law to the profession   This is as it should be, for it recognises the importance of the subject, and, by inference, points to the necessity of some qualifications being set.   This is recognised from earliest times   In the earliest known code, that of the Babylonian, compiled by Hammurabi 2250 B.C., provision is made for due compensation to be paid by the architect to the owner in the event of any disaster happening to the building during construction or after it is completed (see Edicts Nos. 238–233 inclusive)   All our present laws on the subject are built more or less on the edicts of Hammurabi, and the only inference we can draw is that the erection of a building has been considered at all times as an occupation of importance which should only be exercised by properly qualified individuals

With respect to the æsthetic side of the professional practice we meet with a more difficult proposition.   We are told it is almost impossible to make a standard for design.   We are told it is a question of appropriateness, that there is great room for difference of opinion, that it is purely a matter of "taste," and that "good taste" is simply a question of fashion.   Such arguments are mere nonsense

There is a basis of design which no one should be permitted to evade.

A badly designed building architecturally may not be a physical danger to the public; but who can say what its effect may be on the moral temperament ?   We are all influenced, to a greater or less extent, by our environment   True, some surmount all circumstances and influences of environment, but the majority are swayed by its all-pervading presence If in such an environment beauty is absent and ugliness predominant, depravity and a low moral condition will usually be found amongst the people.   On the other hand, beauty is always accompanied by refinement, higher state of civilisation, and, as a rule, a higher moral condition amongst the people.   It is therefore incumbent upon our legislators to recognise such influences.   It is a truism that the social condition of a country is reflected in its architecture   This is borne out by history, past and present , and, whilst the architecture is merely a reflection of the social life of the people, it is fair to suppose that good architecture, typical of the beautiful, would have an elevating influence on the people and reflect back those beneficent rays of goodness and truth.

Such influences have been recognised from times immemorable.   Plato calls the "beautiful" the "child of the good," and argues that it should not be weighed by any other standard than the good   In his "Republic" he goes into the argument more fully, and holds therein that State superintendence should be extended over sculpture and building so that they may be prohibited from exhibiting all forms of vice, intemperance, meanness, and ugliness.   He argues, further, that those who cannot design accordingly should be prevented from practising the art "lest the taste of our citizens be corrupted"   He would not have them grow up among images of moral deformity " as in some noxious pasture, and then feed upon harmful herbs until they silently gather a festering mass of corruption in their own souls.   Let our artists rather be those who are gifted to discern the true nature of the beautiful and the graceful ; then will our youth dwell in a land of health and fair sights and sounds, and receive the good in everything ; and beauty, the effulgence of fair works, shall flow into the eye and ear like a health-giving breeze from a purer region, and irresistibly draw the soul from earliest years into likeness and sympathy with the beauty of reason."

A sense or perception of the beautiful is to be found within the soul of every human being.   In a few it is overpowering, enthusiastic striving at all times for opportunities of action ; in some it is handicapped and fettered with influences, overcome occasionally, but sometimes made subservient to them   In a great many it is lying dormant, almost dead, but yet with that spark of life which only requires the gentle breeze of encouragement to break out into flames of activity   It should be our pleasure to encourage it at all times, to influence our community with its leaven of goodness, and it should be the duty of the State to recognise such influences and to grant a statutory qualification to prevent influences other than that of the good to be over her people

A beneficent Providence has set us down in a world where beauty reigns supreme   We see it in the grass, in the tender bud, in the full-blown flower , we see it in earth and sky, it is above us, it is at our feet— "the universe is its temple"   Man only is the disturbing element   He is permitted to create and thrust before the gaze of his fellow men creations of ugliness and untruth, and we stand aside, not lifting a finger to prevent it   Is it neglect or indifference, or both ?   The work of a painter may not inspire us with healthy moral sentiments—it may be typical of ugliness and souring to the soul , but whereas it is viewed by a very limited number of people, its baneful influence is restricted and confined to a few.   On the other hand, the work of an architect is thrust before all, whether they desire it or not , it is there to stay as long as the stone and mortar endure   Is it not therefore incumbent upon the State to foster all influences that make toward beauty, and to restrict the practice of the art to those who prove themselves capable of teaching the lesson of "sweetness and light" ?

The standard should not be difficult to set ; the basic principles underlying good design are well known.   If the principles are sound the application should be comparatively easy.

So far so good, as regards the question from the theoretical standpoint, and I trust I shall not be considered too illusionary or utopian; And now a few words from the practical side of the question, based on actual experience

The Province of Quebec Association of Architects, to which I have the honour to belong, is the pioneer—on the Western side of the Atlantic, at any rate—of statutory qualification for architects.   During the year 1890 several architects in the Province banded themselves together and formed the P Q A A., and on December 30 of the same year an Act of Incorporation was granted them by the Lieutenant-Governor in Council. According to the preamble of the Act, incorporation was granted as it was "deemed expedient for the better protection of the public interests in the erection of public and private buildings in the Province of Quebec, and in order to enable persons requiring professional aid in architecture to distinguish between qualified and unqualified architects, and to ensure a standard of efficiency in the persons practising the profession of architecture in the Province, and for the furtherance and advancement of the art of architecture."

The passing of this Act merely gave the right to those who belonged to the Association to designate themselves as "Registered Architects." There still remained a large number practising the profession outside the ranks of the Association

In 1898 the Act was amended, compelling all who were practising, or intended practising, to become members of the Association   The amendment reads ·   "No person can take or make use of the *name* or title of *architect*, either singly or in connection with any other word, name, title, or designation, giving it to be understood that he is an architect, under this Act, unless he is registered under this Act as a member of the said Association."

In the preamble above quoted the whole argument in favour of a statutory qualification is concisely set forth, and it says much for the legislators of the Province of Quebec that they thereby recognise the importance of the question. The enactment was granted because, *first,* it is deemed expedient for the better protection of public interests ; *secondly,* to ensure that any persons requiring the services of an architect shall be given duly qualified professional advice ; *thirdly,* to ensure a standard of efficiency in the persons practising the profession , and, *lastly,* for the advancement of the art of architecture in our community. The Association is given power to pass by-laws in accordance with the Act for admission to the study and practice of the profession.

A system of examinations has therefore been inaugurated, consisting of preliminary and final , the former being for those who intend entering upon the study of architecture as students, and the latter for final registration giving the right to practise. The examinations are held twice a year, and the final covers all phases of practical and theoretical architecture.

It will be noted that the protection and qualification provided for in this Act is merely in the right to designate oneself as an " architect," and therein lies the strength or weakness of our case. Much has been said on both sides. It has been argued that the " practice " of the profession should be the basis of such enactments and not the name   The difficulty in connection with this is obvious , it would prohibit the designing and erecting of any construction by an individual even for his sole use , it would be difficult to discriminate between a building which might, with safety, be designed by even a layman and one calling for professional assistance, and as even an individual may administer drugs to himself on his own initiation without laying himself open to prosecution at law, it is evident that the law will always recognise the right of an individual to design a structure for himself under certain limitations. On the other hand, by giving to the public and profession the qualifications based on the *name* of the profession, a broader view is taken of the subject, and the ground, as far as the public is concerned, is equally well covered.

From our limited experience, so far, it seems to be working out well. Eight years is a short time whereon to base any definite conclusions, but even in that short space of time evidence is not wanting to prove that the aims of the profession are being gradually realised and 'the public interests conserved and fostered.

In conducting our examinations, the point I endeavoured to make in the beginning of this paper with respect to the formation of the board of examiners has, consciously or unconsciously, been influencing its composition ; for, as a rule, two out of the board of five are men of professional standing outside the ranks of our Association

Of course, all laws require power of enforcement, and this is no exception. Any infraction of the law is met by a heavy fine for each and every conviction, and although some difficulty was encountered at first, by a recent amendment to the charter on this point the necessary machinery is now at hand to compel obedience.

It has been exercised on very few occasions, and only when all other means failed. We recognise that, as members of a liberal profession, prosecutions should only be resorted to as a last resource.

In spite of what has been said to the contrary, we do not endeavour to keep our Association wholly as a " close corporation." We welcome to our ranks *confrères* from other countries whose professional standing has been gained either as a result of his work or as a member of a recognised sister association. Our charter particularly stipulates that " the Council may also admit to membership all members of associations of architects in the sister provinces, also members of the Royal Institute of British Architects, and of foreign associations of architects of equal standing, on their presenting their credentials "   We are proud to count in our ranks architects of eminence from countries other than our own,

Y

and more especially our cousins across the line. Architecture must not
be bound in by any artificial boundaries. Architecture belongs to no
particular country , it is universal, and all associationship must be based
on such a conception. We raise no barrier against competence ; we act
from a sincere desire to perform our duty in the public interests, to protect the good name of the profession against incompetency, to set up a
standard which we fain would hope will eventually reflect itself in improved conditions of environment, and to advance our art in our province. If by setting up a statutory qualification such desires may be
attained, we seek for no further justification

---

(2) Par Louis Bonnier (Paris)

Le Titre et le Diplôme d'Architecte

La science n'est pas une richesse individuelle . elle est le résultat sans
cesse renouvelé des acquisitions antérieures   Si certains individus plus
heureusement doués, ou arrivant au moment précis de l'éclosion d'une
idée parvenue à maturité, augmentent brusquement cette richesse, illu-
minant leur époque du rayonnement de leur intelligence, la régularité de
son évolution est tellement nécessaire que les novateurs à vues trop
lointaines ne sont souvent pas compris de leur entourage.   De même, les
réactions ne parviennent à produire qu'un retard passager.

Dans l'art même, où l'individualité s'expliquerait plus facilement, si
quelques artistes des arts plastiques semblent parfois pouvoir se passer
d'enseignement, ces exceptions ne se produisent que pour ceux qui cultivent
spécialement et exclusivement une partie de leur art, vibrations de la
lumière, mouvements des lignes, etc   Et encore n'échappent-ils pas à
l'hérédité artistique, à l'enseignement de l'ambiance

Les sociétés organisées cherchent donc légitimement à transmettre et
à accroître ces richesses, les résultats acquis, matières premières des
progrès futurs   C'est alors, en art comme en science, l'enseignement
méthodique.

Dans l'architecture qui procède à la fois de l'art et de la science, plus
que partout ailleurs, l'enseignement est indispensable   Enseignement
technique : étude approfondie des besoins, connaissance raisonnée des
matériaux, application judicieuse des procédés, et enseignement artistique .
groupement des masses, harmonie des lignes, saveur des détails.

Ces deux enseignements qui n'en font qu'un ne peuvent être, bien
entendu, que théoriques   Ils ne peuvent se séparer sans donner des
résultats incomplets   ou des dessinateurs, ou des bâtisseurs , pas d'architectes. Pas d'architectes, c'est-à-dire pas d'artistes dont l'esprit, fait
d'idées logiques et de sentiments décoratifs, est prêt à toutes les études, à
toutes les adaptations, à tous les progrès, sachant, entre plusieurs solutions propres à satisfaire l'ingénieur, choisir la meilleure, c'est-à-dire la
plus harmonieuse, la plus belle

Si l'enseignement est nécessaire à la transmission des résultats acquis,
il ne peut être vraiment efficace et utile que s'il est accompagné d'une
sanction désignant nettement celui à qui, entre tous, on peut, en toute
sécurité, confier la fortune des particuliers et le budget de l'Etat, la santé
des individus et l'hygiène des foules, la conservation du domaine artistique
d'un pays, l'amélioration du décor de la vie familiale et sociale

Cette sanction, c'est le diplôme.

Le diplôme, consécration de longues études scolaires, préparant l'architecte à toutes les éventualités, ne peut et ne doit pas être obligatoire dans

un pays de liberté ; il est seulement une indication et, comme on l'a dit
justement, une présomption puissante de valeur artistique et professionnelle

Il correspond naturellement à un besoin qui, depuis de très longues

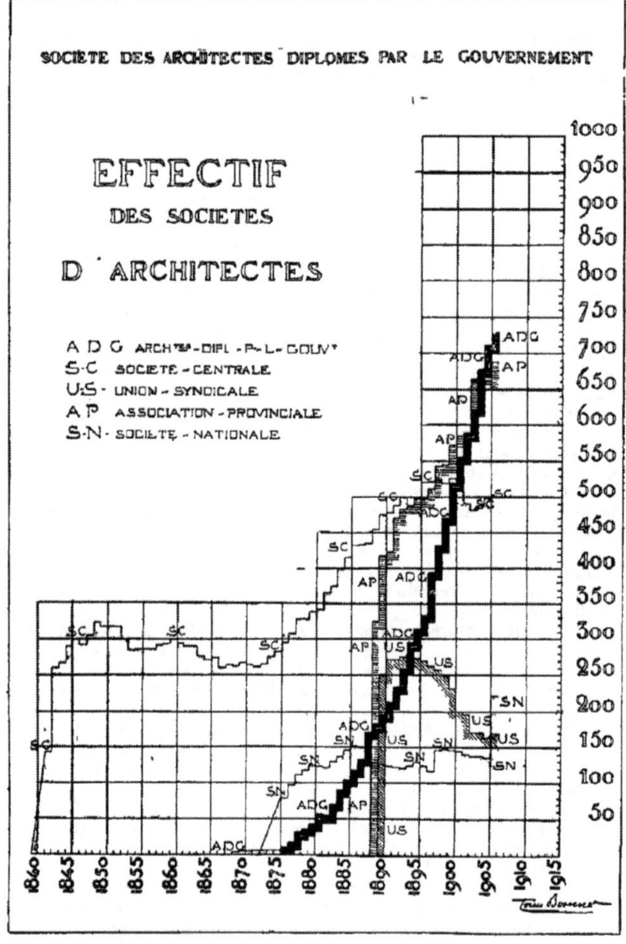

années, tourmente l'esprit des architectes et figure au programme de tous
les congrès

Ce besoin a reçu, en France, pleine et entière satisfaction.   Les faits
sont là pour le prouver, évidents.

La campagne a commencé dès 1840.

Dès cette époque lointaine, la Société Centrale des Architectes Français en prit l'initiative, et, pendant plus de vingt années, par des controverses, des rapports, des démarches, elle combattit le bon combat jusqu'au jour où, en 1863, Monsieur Eugène Guillaume obtint du Gouvernement le décret créant le diplôme

Après une période modeste et obscure où les premiers titulaires du diplôme, sans lien, sans force et sans appui, traités en intrus, sont l'objet d'attaques aussi furieuses qu'inintelligentes de la part d'architectes à courte vue, les diplômés se réunissent en association en 1877.

Pendant de longues années, ils cherchent seulement à vivre, à durer Peu à peu leur nombre augmente. Ils sont 200, les hostilités s'atténuent ; ils sont 500, on les accepte.

Ils sont aujourd'hui 750 répartis en France, à l'Institut, dans toutes les grandes administrations de l'Etat, des départements, des grandes villes, constituant des groupes spéciaux dans les colonies et à l'étranger, en Suisse, aux Etats-Unis, lauréats des concours publics, propageant de leur mieux, dans l'intérêt général, et suivant leur programme, le culte des hautes études d'architecture

En 1912 ils seront 1,000 ; le graphique annexe [*v.* p 323] à cette note l'indique clairement

Ce développement foudroyant et cette prospérité incontestée du diplôme en France montrent à quel impérieux besoin a répondu sa création. Nous pensons que, pour le bien de tous, il faut entourer de garanties le titre d'architecte et le sanctionner par le diplôme.

---

(3) Par GASTON TRÉLAT (Paris).

Titre et *diplôme* répondent à deux ordres d'idées. Pour préciser leur différence, il faut procéder par définitions :

Le *titre* vise exclusivement la fonction que déterminent les applications de métier Ce *titre* comprend et couvre toutes les activités pouvant être suscitées, au cours d'une vie dirigée dans la même voie

Le *diplôme*, au contraire, vise les personnalités et les préparations dont elles ont été pourvues au début de la vie, avant même que la carrière ne fût engagée effectivement.

Comme on le pense sans doute, le *titre* d'architecte modifie incessamment son acception réelle et les aptitudes qu'il en vient à exiger. En cela, il se relie aux caractères successifs que la société peut bien arriver à prendre et au tour nouveau qu'elle donne aux activités qui se partagent le champ social.

Aujourd'hui, par exemple, avec les nouvelles allures que l'intelligence doit revêtir pour répondre aux exigences de la santé publique d'une part, et de la beauté publique d'autre part, l'architecte est appelé à accroître et à multiplier les compétences qui lui étaient suffisantes antérieurement. Il en découle un nouvel intérêt de l'action sociale qui lui appartient. Or, il est incontestable que le temps présent est caractérisé par la continuité des transformations Elles devront aboutir à des solutions qui étaient imprévues, il y a moins de dix ans. Hier encore, le cadre des opérations, que comprenait l'architecture, ne dépassait pas la conception et la construction des édifices ; ce qui réclamait déjà des capacités très appréciables et qu'on se trouve conduit à respecter encore maintenant, lorsqu'on examine avec quelqu'attention ce qu'elles nous ont laissé. L'homme, dont la pensée montre tant soit peu d'inquiétude relativement à ce que demande l'époque actuelle, n'a pas le droit de négliger l'extension du champ qui lui appartient. Sans vouloir entrer dans aucun détail, nous

rappellerons ici que la salubrité de l'habitation doit répondre au chapitre
de la santé publique et que le service plastique des ensembles doit s'accorder
avec la beauté publique ; une extension de compétences s'ensuit, et elle est
considérable

Le *diplôme*, qui est une marque d'études, ne saurait avoir d'autre
valeur que celle de l'enseignement qui lui sert de fond.   Est-ce une bonne
chose ?   Je n'en puis rien savoir   Cependant il est un stimulant appréciable dans les études dont il contrôle la suite régulièrement éprouvée.
Ce qui du reste entraîna sa création précisément à l'Ecole Spéciale d'Architecture où fut inaugurée la transformation des études qu'on a pu constater
dans l'enseignement de cet art, vers la fin du siècle écoulé.   Un diplôme
deviendrait détestable, s'il arrivait à conférer un privilège ; ce qui n'est
heureusement pas.   Ce privilège aurait pour résultat d'entraver les
développements et les grandeurs d'esprit que recherchait précisément
l'enseignement contrôlé   Recherche qui reste infime et exclusive de
tout privilège.   Cet enseignement, il faut y songer, se double, pour l'architecte, d'une éducation, sorte de théorie pratique   Elle se poursuit dans le
laboratoire qu'est l'atelier.   Cette éducation fait partie de ce qu'il appartient
au diplôme de constater au début de la carrière ; mais c'est bien peu de
chose relativement aux activités que permettra une compréhension
approfondie de la société ; on peut même affirmer que ce n'est rien par
rapport à la valeur que montrera avec l'expérience un artiste mûri,
quand une envergure suffisante assure sa capacité effective.   L'artiste
se développe, toute sa vie durant, par le fait d'un autre grand atelier
que la société elle-même vient offrir aux observations comme aux comparaisons de l'homme expérimenté, ainsi qu'aux exercices incessants, par
lesquels il est amené à contrôler, avec une compétence toujours grandissante, le fruit de ses méditations.   Et l'ampleur, dont elles témoignent
souvent, est en général refusée aux débutants.   Il y faut les activités
d'une vie personnellement conduite.   Vraiment, il n'est pas contestable
que, pour un esprit entraîné, les hantises ultérieures de la vie courante
dominent de très haut le *diplôme* exclusivement attaché à des épreuves
satisfaisantes d'écolier.   Pour quiconque sait réfléchir, ce n'est donc
pas autre chose qu'un *certificat* d'études   A vouloir assigner une autre
portée au diplôme, on risquerait fort de s'écarter du cadre que le bon sens
permet de considérer.

Idéalement ce serait réduire le champ de travail offert à la pensée
que de s'attacher trop exclusivement au service toujours amoindrissant
d'un petit groupe

Effectivement, ce petit groupe serait substitué à l'intérêt général,
dont jamais on n'a le droit de se désintéresser, quand on a le souci d'une
carrière subordonnée à l'utilité de l'œuvre poursuivie.   C'est d'une façon
toute différente que l'humanité et les diverses sociétés qui en sont nées
grandissent les civilisations, leur faisant honneur d'un affinement toujours
nouveau

Je m'étends peut-être longuement sur ces considérations d'ordre
sociologique.   Cela tient sans doute à ce que, dans ma pensée, le sujet
s'y rattache par tous les côtés

De plus, et pour parler cette fois du pays que je représente, voilà
plusieurs années de cela, Spuller, alors Ministre de l'Instruction Publique
et des Beaux-Arts, fit faire une étude approfondie de la question par une
commission nommée à cet effet.   Il s'agissait de décider s'il convenait
d'imposer un diplôme aux architectes.

Au début l'opinion était partagée dans la commission : les partisans
de l'affirmative étaient au moins égaux en nombre aux partisans de la
négative.   Mais l'échange des idées aboutit à la solution négative.
La question s'impose aux méditations d'esprits indépendants, par un
temps comme celui que nous traversons, où l'esprit syndical tendrait
souvent à prendre la place d'inquiétudes intellectuelles, celles-ci envi-

sageant les questions pour elles-mêmes, à l'exclusion de tout autre intérêt troublant la raison des solutions.

Et, dans la circonstance, on peut affirmer que les progrès généraux restent essentiellement liés à l'action personnelle Il n'y a pas de syndicalisme qui puisse intervenir utilement en la matière. L'autorité légitime se mesure seulement aux services que la collectivité humaine commande. Il y aurait à redouter, en conséquence, la création de petites *églises*, où des *diplômés* symboliseraient le ralliement. Elles n'aboutiraient qu'à une sorte d'action syndicale ruinant, dans son développement, toute personnalité à cause de son action trop énergique et trop indépendante. Plus d'initiative personnelle librement éclose Rien autre que l'intérêt d'un petit groupe. Ce qui est opposé à la puissance que prépareraient les développements intellectuels, pour répondre à l'intérêt de la société ou de l'humanité L'architecture, prise dans son objectivité, veut être abordée en plein , mais cela n'empêche de reconnaître l'influence des considérations avoisinantes, quand on veut éviter l'abîme attaché à toute erreur sociale.

Cette cinquième question était intéressante à soumettre à une assemblée internationale, soustraite *ipso facto* à toute étroitesse d'influences locales. Elle est fatalement dominée par la recherche de solutions intéressant l'humanité en général dans les besoins de sa mentalité aussi bien que des satisfactions économiques. L'œuvre, que nous avons à poursuivre, se résume en conséquence dans un point de vue spécialement technique et dans un point de vue d'art pur

Pour être bien servies, les activités qui s'ensuivent auront toujours avantage à ce que le champ de leur recrutement soit aussi étendu que possible.

Il y a donc lieu d'éviter tout ce qui pourrait aboutir à une restriction du mouvement que l'Ecole Spéciale d'Architecture a créé, il y a plus de quarante ans.   L'exemple qu'elle a donné tend de plus en plus à se propager ; c'est une conséquence de l'évolution rapide à laquelle nous assistons. Pour y répondre effectivement, il faut une instantanéité que les procédés officiels ne comportent point. Leur caractéristique est l'immuabilité. Tandis que l'expérience apprend combien il faut de liberté aux initiatives. Elles seules peuvent répondre aux nécessités changeantes d'un enseignement professionnel et d'art comme celui de l'architecture

L'état ou les municipalités organisent fort bien l'enseignement élémentaire qu'il convient d'imposer à tout le monde. Mais il n'en saurait être de même pour les préparations d'ordre technique et artistique qui ont à faire face aux exigences d'applications nouvelles, que la science autorise sans cesse. Il n'y a que la liberté et les initiatives conséquentes, dont l'action ne saurait être assez étendue, pour répondre aux besoins toujours renaissants de la société.

Les organisations officielles présentent souvent des perfections, qui sont à l'honneur des états auxquels elles ressortissent. Mais, par cela même, elles sont dépourvues de toute souplesse, que les choses du jour nécessiteraient. Ce qui conduit ma pensée à concevoir le spectacle lamentable d'une collectivité nationale ou municipale, qui n'aurait, pour satisfaire ses besoins multiples, que des services officiellement organisés ; on se rend compte des inconvénients qui en résulteraient. Nos organismes comportent des besoins qui n'autorisent aucune des lenteurs que l'expérience nous montre comme inhérentes aux délégations collectives Ainsi se figure-t-on une ville comme Londres, comme Paris alimentée uniquement du fait d'administrations officielles. Il est bien clair que, pour satisfaire des besoins généraux aussi complexes, il n'y a que l'initiative privée avec le ressort et le stimulant de l'intérêt direct Elle s'impose donc au premier chef. Et, si l'on se place au point de vue intellectuel, l'instantanéité des solutions ne s'impose pas avec moins de vigueur. Autrement ce serait courir les risques de diminution et d'infériorité par rapport au mouvement général des esprits dans des sociétés obéissant à une meilleure discipline mentale ou sociale   Ce serait la fatalité d'un abaissement d'autant plus rapide que la société humaine comporte une intensité encore inconnue dans ses activités.

S'il y a solidarité reconnue parmi les intérêts humains, les sciences sont également solidaires, par le mouvement qu'elles créent dans les esprits, par l'influence qu'elles exercent toutes sur les applications de l'art   Et l'architecture, par suite de la variété des connaissances auxquelles elle fait appel, par suite de l'étendue de son champ intellectuel, tient une place des plus importantes, relativement à cette solidarité, dans la série des arts ou applications qui se partagent la production de l'homme.

Si nous nous attachons plus directement à l'enseignement professionnel et d'application, le moment présent fournit bien des exemples à l'appui de ce qui vient d'être dit, en regardant la puissance des initiatives libres et le rôle forcément ineffectif de ces grandes synthèses d'intérêts généraux que les états représentent.

De notre temps, en effet, si nous élargissons le cadre, et en respectant la chronologie, nous citerons en France : *L'Ecole Centrale des Arts et Manufactures, l'Ecole Spéciale d'Architecture, l'Ecole des Sciences Politiques, l'Institut Pasteur, l'Ecole d'Electricité, l'Ecole de Chimie Appliquée*, et j'en passe, tant le mouvement est dirigé dans ce sens, en conséquence des exigences sociales que les Etats ne peuvent solutionner par suite des longueurs inhérentes à la perfection des rouages administratifs.   Et pourtant je ne puis passer sous silence l'exemple que donne encore la Faculté de Médecine : on y assiste maintenant à des enseignements dus à l'initiative privée voulant répondre précisément à l'urgence des besoins nouveaux, tels qu'ils résultent notamment de notre extension coloniale et des idées que peut suggérer la solidarité déjà évoquée

D'ailleurs il n'y a jamais eu d'utilité qui se soit résolue autrement que du fait des efforts individuels   Cette constatation, qui résulte d'une analyse sociale assez élémentaire, montre le champ que l'avenir lui reserve en suite de la rapidité dont les évolutions donnent un spectacle si intéressant et si curieux à observer de nos jours   Les Etats n'ont donc le droit de décourager aucune des initiatives ; et je ne sais si cette assurance de la liberté dans les efforts des intelligences n'est pas pour eux une fonction prédominante.

En voilà assez, je pense, pour établir que tout diplôme peut être intéressant comme marque d'études.   Il est donc désirable qu'il y en ait beaucoup qui entrent en concurrence les uns avec les autres   Et ce serait à l'honneur de la vie sociale, en ce qui concerne les intérêts largement compris des collectivités humaines.

Pour un homme de valeur, le diplôme, dont il est pourvu, n'est jamais, dans la vie, rien autre chose que l'incident d'un instant   Y penser ultérieurement, c'est se montrer au-dessous de la fonction sociale à laquelle astreindrait l'avenir dans sa marche en avant   Il faut ouvrir l'œil sur les services qu'il exige et s'attacher à un idéal, seule inspiration précise des activités de demain, en un temps aussi évoluant que le nôtre.   C'est seulement en sachant orienter ces inspirations et ces conceptions qu'il nous est loisible d'honorer nos diplômes ou, ce qui est l'équivalent, la période originelle de nos carrières

En dehors de là, rien que le service étroit de petits intérêts se résumant en petites *églises*, à l'exclusion de tout ce que la société et le progrès peuvent attendre d'une compréhension plus élevée d'intérêts sociaux

Résumé.—Je me résume

Les *diplômes* sont une bonne chose, dans la mesure ou les études qu'ils représentent, grandissent et élèvent le titre d'architecte à la hauteur que commande la société, pour en comprendre les aspirations. Mais on en viendrait facilement à une cause d'abaissement ou, ce qui est équivalent d'incapacité à pouvoir comprendre autre chose que les connaissances et les applications dont un enseignement particulier serait le détenteur Alors un diplôme, pris comme *criterium* de toute application d'art ou de tout savoir utile, serait un comble d'inanité humaine

Les efforts individuels sont aujourd'hui plus nécessaires que jamais par suite du mouvement que l'on peut constater partout, et qui est de nature à susciter les initiatives, de tous côtés à la fois. En tant que synthèses des intérêts collectifs, il appartient aux Etats d'assurer le libre épanouissement du travail et de s'opposer en conséquence à tout ce qui ressemblerait à un privilège. Par un temps ou les lumières tendent à se généraliser de jour en jour, la concurrence doit être plus libre que jamais Les intérêts, étroitement compris, amènent souvent les hommes à vouloir, dans un aveuglement intéressé, créer de petits états artificiels dans le grand état qui est soumis au contrôle de la délégation parlementaire Il y a là un danger, sur lequel les hommes de pensée n'ont pas le droit de fermer les yeux Ces petits états artificiels sont toujours des causes de désordre dans les activités. Ce sont des calamités, en regard du développement de l'intelligence humaine comme de l'organisation même de la société. Des autorités factices se manifestent, grâce à ces petits états d'intérêts opposés à celui de la collectivité. Dans leurs préoccupations exclusives de personnes ou de clans, ces simulacres autorisés ne sauraient répondre aux exigences de l'évolution contemporaine. Ce sont des puissances trompeuses qui deviendraient des obstacles à la rectitude voulue des efforts, que les initiatives individuellement dirigées seraient naturellement conduites à produire.

Conclusion —Quand ils se bornent à être des excitants au travail de la jeunesse, les diplômes sont peut-être une excellente chose Mais ils deviendraient détestables, s'ils devaient entraver la libre activité du technicien, au cours de sa vie ultérieure Alors restriction de conscience et appauvrissement de l'action

Le champ n'est jamais assez largement ouvert aux aptitudes que comprend ou soulève la société. Les civilisations avancées de l'Europe sont souvent cause de faiblesse dans la production individuelle Pour s'en rendre compte, il suffit de jeter les yeux sur des peuples plus jeunes où l'organisation sociale assure des valeurs individuelles qui pourraient nous servir d'exemples

Je répète cette pensée : si le diplôme est pour l'homme d'études un contrôle de ses efforts, il devient, dans la suite, un incident sans influence sur la carrière d'une personnalité de valeur

Il faut aller de l'avant sans jamais regarder en arrière.

---

(4) By Otto Wagner, Imperial and Royal Superintendent of Works, Vienna, Professor of the Imperial and Royal Academy of the Plastic Arts.

(On behalf of the Society of Austrian Architects)

Gesetzmässige Befähigung des Architekten, hiezu sei Folgendes erwähnt

Allerorts tritt das Bestreben der Künstler, die Kunst zu fördern, stark hervor Ja, sie sind tatsächlich die einzigen Förderer, denn die von Erwerb und Politik ganz erfüllte Menschheit hat für die Kunst nahezu jede Empfindung verloren. Es ist daher begreiflich, dass das Verlangen zutage tritt, die Kunst zu schützen und glaubt man dies dadurch zu erreichen dass man dem Titel Architekt eine gesetzmässige Kraft verleiht.

Diese gesetzmässige Kraft ist, wie fruher gezeigt wurde, nicht moglich
Sie ist aber auch gar nicht nötig.   Denn nicht darum handelt es sich,
dass amtlich bestätigte Baukunstler zur Ausfuhrung von Werken zuge-
lassen werden, sondern darum, dass nur das Allerbeste geschaffen werde.
Wenn sich also Staat, Land und Stadt, respektive ihre Verwaltungen
eines Kunstsenates bedienen, so tritt dieserart eine kunstlerische Kontrolle ein, welche das anzustrebende Ziel am ehesten erhoffen lässt.

Bei einer gesetzmassigen Befahigung des Architekten kann es sich
daher nicht um die kunstlerische Qualitat des Architekten handeln.
sondern nur bezuglich seiner fachwissenschaftlichen Qualitat ist eine
amtliche Kontrolle zulässig   Diese aber ist sehr einfach, da alle Behorden
ihre wohlgeschulten Bauamter haben, welche sich mit dieser Kontrolle
bei der Baubewilligung beschaftigen konnen.

Der gesetzmässige Vorgang hat demnach darin zu bestehen, dass der
Architekt für die von ihm verfassten Plane die Haftung durch seine
Unterschrift ubernimmt und sich durch die Unternehmer der einzelnen
Arbeiten, welche wieder die von ihnen gefertigten, statischen Berech-
nungen beizubringen haben, deckt

Die Beantwortung der Frage 5 hat daher zu lauten

Der Architekt ist zu jeder Bauherstellung durch die von ihm verfassten und gefertigten Plane berechtigt wenn dieselben die künstlerische
und bautechnische Kontrolle passiert haben.

---

(5) By Robert Walker

1. In calling the attention of the Congress to subject No 5 on the
programme, it will be convenient to say here that there is parliamentary
precedent to be found in the Statute Books of the House in which Registration Bills have passed into Acts with a view to conserving the interests
of the profession and the public in their relations each to the other.

2. Without giving a long list of the professions so dealt with, it will
be sufficient to name the cases of solicitors, barristers, physicians, and
surgeons.   The Medical Act is apposite to the requirements of the Architects' Education and Registration Bill

3. The words "statutory qualification for architects" are consonant
with the interests and well-being of the communities and peoples throughout His Majesty's vast jurisdiction, from the peasant in his cottage to
the dwellers in royal palaces

4. From the small cottage industries to the hives of industry covering
many acres, teeming with busy workers labouring to provide for requirements and necessities of the rich and the poor.

5. The housing of commercial enterprises, the meeting of the demands
of municipal, social, and religious life

6. All buildings should be designed suitably to their purposes in
fitness, strength, and beauty, and our homes made healthy as well as
beautiful by observing the laws with which scientific research, applied
with experience, has made us acquainted

7 It will be seen, therefore, that this subject is in touch with the
interests of the whole community, and is so far-reaching in its common
interests that it extends to all the countries of the earth.

8. It is pre-eminently a subject of international interest, and is fittingly
placed on the programme of this Congress

9 The word "architect" is derived from the two Greek words ἀρχός
and τέκτων, and signifies "chief constructor," which would appear to
involve complete control and guidance from the inception of the design
to its final completion in fitness, strength and beauty

10. The word "qualification" signifies that the architect (or the chief constructor) should be duly qualified to undertake those responsible duties by the acquisition of an irreducible minimum of general and expert knowledge, and technical education and equipment in accordance with a curriculum laid down by the General Council, when appointed by Parliament, under the stipulations of a Bill which, when it passes, becomes law, making compulsory "statutory qualification for architects " by placing the Bill on the Statute Book as the " Architects' Education and Registration Act."

11. The procedure in the case of Bills of this nature is according to precedent. The promoters deposit the Bill, making it as perfect as possible, accompanied by a memorial showing its necessity, and those who oppose its passing petition against it, stating their objection, and should it reach the Committee stage both parties have an opportunity of arranging clauses and agreeing to amend its provisions

12. The necessity for such an Act appears to be conceded generally owing to the consideration that has been given to the subject during the last twenty years.

13. The members of recognised architectural bodies should be registered on their proving their membership, or on verified lists being sent to the registrar by the secretaries of those bodies.

14. The stumbling-block which has chiefly and ostensibly retarded the progress of such a measure for all these years, coupled with apathy, indifference, and jealousies, is precisely the same as that which blocked the Medical Act for thirty years from 1828 to 1858—namely, that Parliament declined to pass a measure which made no provision for the vested interests of the unqualified men who assumed the functions of medical practitioners and were accepted by the public in ignorance of their want of expert and technical equipment.

15 It may be possible to come to some arrangement on this matter by way of compromise with the Select Parliamentary Committee.

16 A time limit of, say, five years may be agreed upon, during which practitioners could prove that they were in practice prior to the passing of the measure.

17. There appears to be no doubt but that the trend of opinion is in the direction of obtaining " statutory qualification for architects," which will protect the members of the profession and the public, in the prescribed parliamentary form of an Education and Registration Act having the short title " Architects Act."

18. The sooner such a measure is placed on the Statute Book the sooner will the evil complained of disappear. It will not impair the status, privileges, or invade the membership of existing architectural bodies

19. The placing of the names of persons having what the Legislature denominates vested rights does not confer the right to membership in any of the existing bodies.

20. " Statutory qualifications " are qualifications enjoined and required by a curriculum prepared by a competent authority, made compulsory by statute, and tests applied by competent examining bodies whose functions commence when the competent teaching bodies have completed their work. The result of the tests is then recorded and published in a book called the " Register."

21 The whole scheme, in all its details and departments fully equipped and governed by a Council, should be stipulated and set forth in a Bill which would be fittingly designated in an extended title as " The Architects' Education and Registration Bill."

22 The parliamentary draughtsmen would see that precedent be complied with.

23 When the Bill reached the Committee stage, memorialists in

favour of it and petitioners against it would be heard at length, when clauses may be amended, struck out, or new clauses inserted by agreement. Should the Committee find that the preamble was proved, it would be sent back by them to the House; and if passed it would then become law, and be placed on the Statute Book as the "Architects Act."

24. Want of qualification on the part of persons employed as architects may result in injury to life or health, discomfort, pecuniary loss, lawsuits, embarrassments, and much loss and damage without a remedy.

25 Any means that can be devised to even tend towards guarding the public against the evils attendant on incompetency will be hailed with satisfaction by the profession and the public alike   Reforms should come from within, and it is clearly the duty of the profession to initiate and work out this movement.

26. The education and training of an architect should be special and technical, theoretical and practical, as it is in other professions.   It is not consistent with the scope of this paper to do more than refer to it incidentally   The drawing-up of a curriculum satisfactorily can only be done by, and examinations instituted under, the auspices of a competent Central Council, appointed under a Registration Act, which will give force and authority to its decision

27. The public not only suffer from ignorant practitioners, but the profession suffers from the absence of confidence on the part of the public .engendered by their experience of unqualified practitioners.

28 If the public were assured that the guarantee of previous special and technical study was possessed by the members of the profession being registered as duly qualified, there is no doubt but that the confidence which is now extended by some to individual members of the profession would be extended in varying degrees to all duly qualified practitioners.

29 The modern system of competition and the rivalries of private practice bring into undue prominence individual interests, until the members of the profession may be described as a number of fortuitous atoms with a strong tendency to develop the antithesis of *esprit de corps*.

30 A Registration Act should be obtained without disturbing any of the recognised bodies, whether they exist with or without charters. Their powers should not be impaired in the slightest degree , the Act should deal with their members only by way of recognition, and not with the bodies, as such, by way of abrogating their functions or curtailing their powers of expansion   On the contrary, it is but reasonable to suppose—and it is a result looked forward to with great confidence— that all existing bodies throughout the kingdoms would be greatly increased in membership and efficiency.   This latter result has followed the discussion of the measure.

31. Provision should be made for preserving the rights, privileges, and status of existing bodies, and for enlarging and varying their charters as they may approve.   The passage of this Act presents an opportunity for such enlargement, which may be availed of without adding to the cost of the Bill.

32. There is a class of practitioners who do not possess the minimum qualifications that it is desired in future to secure in all who seek to enter the profession, and it becomes a most important consideration as to what position they should occupy.   There is no doubt they must be dealt with, as well as those who have given proof of undoubted qualifications

33. These men have acquired a vested interest, and have established a position with, perhaps, an indiscriminating and a too confiding public, which has enabled them to make a living   It is clearly and absolutely just that such men should not be excluded from registration, and in this

the policy observed in the passing of the Medical Act forms a precedent worthy of following.   We must succeed if we only attempt what is reasonable and just.

34 Let it be borne in mind, also, that registering under the Act will not either confer or withhold any distinction not already possessed, or which may be acquired outside the Act.   It is not a question of granting diplomas to, or the measuring of the attainments or abilities of, the present practitioners.   It is rather the building-up into a legally constituted body, with the special object of raising the standard of attainments and due qualification, to the manifest advantage of the profession and the public   It is the erection of a platform to which in future all must attain before any will be recognised   It confers no ability, but it ensures a minimum of attainments in professional aspirants.

35 Men will still rise above their fellows in proportion to their possession of natural gifts, fitness, and industry, their opportunities and their attainments   The presence of any of the qualities or acquirements which without the Act bring distinction and pre-eminence will still confer the same advantages on their possessors under the Act

36 It will, however, confer a legally recognised status which will command the respect and confidence of the public.

37. Chairs of architecture should be established in every college similar to the chairs of engineering and the chairs allocated to medicine and surgery.

38 Also teaching and examining bodies should be established under the provisions of the Bill.

39. A special committee should be appointed to investigate and report on the education and training necessary to fully equip aspirants for the architectural profession with the minimum of general, special, and technical knowledge and training as statutory qualification for architects.

40 If the holding of the Seventh International Congress of Architects in London at this juncture should help to bring about a consensus of opinion in favour of all practitioners uniting in promulgating a Bill in this present Parliament, with the R.I.B.A. taking the premier position, , which position for the past twenty years the Registration Bill Committee recognised as of right it doth belong

41 It will prove an epoch-making event, marking a new departure for the practice of our noble art, in which evils long deplored will be gradually and considerately removed, to the great benefit of the public and the profession, but, above all, to the art and science of our noble architecture

42. Twenty years ago a Bill was drafted and read a first time   It was petitioned against with great vigour, was withdrawn and amended, and again presented the following year and read a first time.   This process has been repeated from time to time since, keeping the Bill " alive " by the parliamentary method of hanging it up.

43 A distinct stream of tendency has latterly set in, which probably is due to its having a basis of sound principle underlying it.   There is a quality in our people which is attracted by persistent effort, which has led them to examine the scheme, which was all that was necessary to change apathy and indifference into approval, which has developed in great measure into advocacy and support

44 Should the ardent hopes of those in favour of the Bill be realised this year, and its preamble be proved in Committee, and the Bill pass the House, next year it would attain its majority by coming into force as an Act, no doubt to be amended from time to time as blemishes are discovered and as experience and developments suggest.

45. Such a Bill is commended to your favourable consideration and approval.

46. Suggested clauses may perhaps be arranged as follows :—

Clause

1. Short title.
2 Commencement of Act
3 General Council
4. Members of General Council.
5. Branches of the Council for England, Scotland, and Ireland.
6 Qualification.
7 Resignation or death of member of General Council
8 Time and place of meeting of General Council
9. Election of president of General Council
10. Revision of constitution of General Council.
11. Existing charters remain in force.
12 Appointment of registrars and other officers.
13. Appointment of registrars and other officers by Branch Councils.
14 Fees for attendance at Councils
15 Application of fees.
16. Accounts to be published
17 Duty of registrars to keep the registers correct
18. Removal of name from register by Councils. Restoration of name to the register.
19 Persons qualified to be registered.
20. Annual renewal fee
21 Penalty on unregistered persons using title &c.
22. Qualifying examinations
23. Registration of branch registers.
24 Evidence of qualification to be given before registration.
25 Register to be published.
26. Registered persons may have titles of distinction added.
27. None but registered persons to recover damages.
28. None but registered persons to hold public appointments.
29. Meaning of term " legally qualified practitioner."
30. No certificate to be valid unless persons signing be registered.
31. Penalty on wilful falsification of register.
32. Penalty for obtaining registration by false representations.
33 Recovery of penalties and fees.
34 Notice of death of practitioners
35. By-laws
36. Services of notices by post.

Colonial and Foreign Practitioners

37 Registration of colonial practitioner with recognised diploma.
38 Registration of foreign practitioner with recognised diploma.
39 Diploma of colonial and foreign practitioner when deemed to be recognised
40. Separate lists of colonial and foreign practitioners in register
41 Power of His Majesty in Council to define colonies and foreign countries to which this part of the Act applies
42. Default of General Council and Examining Body or Bodies. Exercise of powers of Privy Council.
43 Orders evidence
44. Definitions

47. The supreme authority will in all such cases be His Majesty's Most Honourable Privy Council.

48 The word " profession " means the practitioners who profess to be duly qualified. When the Bill passes it will mean practitioners duly qualified by conforming to the terms of the Architects Act.

(6) By A. NORTH (Tasmania).

I have been instructed by the Royal Victorian Institute of Architects, to which I belong, to support the proposals made for registration, and in doing so I cannot do better than read the instructions which have been given me : " The following *résumé* of the work of the R V I.A. is compiled by resolution of the Council of the Institute   I am directed to forward a copy to you, as a member of the Institute, in order that, when the respective subjects are dealt with in the Congress, you may be able to cite the action of the Institute in its endeavours (*a*) to place the members of the profession upon a legal status by registration, (*b*) to further the education of the architect by university and other teaching, and (*c*) to modernise the building regulations of our cities in order that iron, steel, and other modern construction may be adopted

" *Registration.*—A Bill was prepared in 1891 by the R.V I A. and the general body of practitioners.   It was submitted to the Legislative Council in 1892, but was then rejected   It has not been re-introduced since   The need of registration, however, remains as great as ever During the past fourteen years registration has been made compulsory in many of the professions, and before long it will be necessary for the Institute to move again in this direction, both in the interests of the public and the profession   The demand for registration is shared by all competent members of the profession, whether members of the R V I A. or not

" *Education.*—In addition to awarding prizes for the best work done yearly in the building construction and architectural classes at the Working Men's College, Melbourne, the Council arranges annually R V.I.A competitions for subjects in design, measured work, and sketching, and awards medals and substantial money prizes and certificates for the best work in each division   This year, however, the new regulations for the Diploma of Architecture at the Melbourne University have been issued (a copy being forwarded to you herewith).   The scheme was prepared by a joint committee of the Faculty of Engineering at the University and by the Council of the R V I A.   Mr. A Henderson (one of our past Presidents) has been appointed lecturer on the subject, and Mr Percy Oakden (also past President) represents the Institute upon the Faculty of Engineering for 1906.   The work is thus directly in touch with the Institute.

" *Modern Methods of Construction.*—In order that modern methods of construction may be applicable to our larger cities, the Institute is (at the request of the Melbourne City Council) preparing a list of suggestions for improving the building by-laws of the city.   Copies of the building regulations of the principal cities in Great Britain and America have been courteously forwarded for our guidance, and the first interim report was forwarded to the City Council last September   We ask that provision be made in the revised by-laws for the erection of iron and steel structures and for buildings composed wholly or in part of reinforced concrete.   We further request that in the new regulations a clause be inserted whereby any method of construction in use in the cities referred to in an annexed schedule, although such construction be not provided for in the Melbourne Building Regulations, may, with the sanction of the official referees, be adopted in Melbourne   It will necessarily be some time before the amendment of the proposed regulations can be effected, as the work of revision is by no means an easy task. Signed, JOHN NITTLE, *Hon Secretary* "

Although we have failed as yet to obtain legislation in Australia on the subject of registration, we have been successful in obtaining a Chair of Architecture at the Melbourne University, which was an official recognition of architecture by the Government.   So far as testimony is concerned, the Victorian Institute is absolutely unanimous in favour of registration

---

(7) By VIRGIL NÁGY (Budapest).

(On behalf of the Association of Hungarian Architects and Engineers)

The enormous quantity of technical work done in our age and the great development of technical arts have produced in many countries unsatisfactory conditions, because the quantity of work and the wide fields of occupation have caused undesirable competition between well-trained people—in our case architects—and people who are not well trained.   The public the world over, which is more or less ignorant in matters of our art, often thinks that its interests are best or at least as well served if the cost of the architect's work is the smallest possible, and, in consequence, it often spoils the ship for the proverbial half-pennyworth of tar   The result is, besides deficiency of art work, badly and unpractically laid-out buildings, resulting in the loss of private and national wealth   On the other hand, a reasonably remunerative practice for the well-educated architect has become very difficult on account of unsuitable competition.

These unfavourable conditions have resulted in many countries, as in Hungary, in a movement to protect the architect's interest as well as that of the public, in a similar way as has been done in the case of solicitors, teachers, physicians, etc , *i e.* to demand, at least to a certain degree, compulsory qualification for the practice of architecture   The last National Congress of Hungarian Architects and Engineers decided to bring forward a motion in favour of legal regulation of *the titles and practice* of engineers, mechanical engineers, and architects.

The Association of Hungarian Architects and Engineers were commissioned by the Congress to prepare a Bill providing for the compulsory qualification and practice in the different technical branches. This has been done.   The Bill has been accepted by a majority of the Congress and transferred to the Government, and we hope will soon be brought before Parliament.

According to this Bill, the right of bearing the *titles* and engaging in *practice* as engineers, mechanical engineers, and architects would be reserved to individuals of proper *qualification*, acquired by polytechnic or academic studies.   Appropriate considerations are prepared, which answer to the conditions of architecture as an art.   Only qualified individuals could act as official *experts, designers,* and *directors* of buildings of importance.

To assure proper control, to obtain proper evidence, and to repress unsuitable practice are proposed to be done by autonomic institutions—namely, by constituting as the *Technical Chamber* a legally constituted Union of Engineers, Mechanical Engineers, and Architects.

The Bill, with explanations and part of the discussion, has been published by our Association.   It is in Hungarian ; but I am sure our Association will answer with pleasure a request to have it translated, in whole or in part, in one of the languages of this Congress.

DISCUSSION ON SUBJECT V

M. Augustin Rey (Architecte de la fondation Rothschild, Paris).—
Messieurs, la société nous accuse d'aggraver la santé publique par la
mauvaise construction de l'habitation Cette audacieuse affirmation
n'est pas l'expression de la vérité C'est la société, au contraire, qui
nous tue en laissant la profession ouverte sans barrière aucune au premier
venu. Voyez les déclarations si fortes faites par nos principaux Rapporteurs Notre Confrère M. J. S Archibald (du Canada) "*Donner
le moyen au public de reconnaître entre les Architectes qualifiés et les Architectes non qualifiés !*" Notre Confrère M Bonnier : "*L'enseignement de
l'architecture ne peut être vraiment efficace que s'il est accompagné d'une
sanction désignant celui à qui, entre tous, on peut en toute sécurité confier
la fortune des particuliers, le budget de l'Etat, la santé des individus et
l'hygiène des foules !*" Je tiens tout particulièrement à citer en dernier
lieu notre Confrère M Robert Walker d'Irlande "*Il y a le plus grand
intérêt à ce que les Architectes dignes de ce nom prennent l'initiative d'un
mouvement s rieux et qu'en Angleterre, notamment, ce mouvement aboutisse
au vote par le Parlement d'une loi qui s'appellerait la Loi des Architectes*"
De ces déclarations, dont nous n'avons cité que les plus typiques, il ressort
nettement la nécessité de créer un mouvement d'opinion dans tous les
pays du monde *Est-il équitable que plus notre profession demande un
ensemble de connaissances étendues—celles-ci ne font qu'augmenter de jour
en jour—moins le public s'en doute ? Aussitôt qu'il apprendrait qu'un
examen seul peut autoriser à porter le titre d'Architecte et pratiquer la profession, il est absolument certain qu'il saurait le reconnaître immédiatement.*
Nous ne pouvons rien obtenir du public sans cela. Dans cet
intérêt professionnel, qui a de si hautes visées, et "qui n'a pas
de frontières," comme l'a dit si justement notre vaillant confrère M.
Archibald—les Architectes du monde entier doivent se mettre avant tout
d'accord entre eux pour mener avec vigueur cette campagne. Cette
loi, si elle est reconnue nécessaire pour nous, et il semble que cette opinion
se dégage nettement de la discussion qui vient d'avoir lieu devant ce
Congrès, *protègera d'abord ce public, qui est si facilement trompé et qui est
mineur dans les questions techniques avant que de prot ger les membres de
la profession* La question est donc d'intérêt général Il ne s'agit pas
de créer une caste fermée, dans une profession qui constitue un des rouages
sociaux de la plus grande importance, par un examen trop difficile qui
demanderait de trop nombreuses années d'études. Il s'agit d'instituer
un examen comprenant les principaux éléments de la construction,
joints à ceux artistiques qui sont la base même de l'architecture. Si
je ne craignais par le terme " d'examen minimum " de rabaisser notre
grande et magnifique profession au rang d'une carrière ne nécessitant
que des efforts insuffisants pour être exercée, c'est ce terme même que
j'emploierais Tout est une question de nuances et d'appropriation
aux circonstances, aux mœurs, et aux pays. *Dans cette pensée, nous
devons grouper tous nos int rêts professionnels dans une puissante fédéra
tion. Tous les pays du monde doivent s'y faire repr senter.* Nous
demandons que dans notre prochain Congrès International, en 1908,
cette question soit examinée avec toute l'attention qu'elle mérite et en
lui consacrant plus d'une simple séance. C'est en appliquant ces idées
que nous parviendrons à relever la profession de l'Architecte dans la
société moderne.

M. BONNIER, in answer to an English questioner, explained that the course of study at the Ecole des Beaux-Arts in Paris may extend over a period of eight years or longer   There are examinations in mathematics, art subjects, &c   The courses of the second or elementary course cover a period of two or three years, and the courses of the first class three to five years   There is an oral examination on the laws relating to building &c., on professional practice, and other subjects.   And this, together with the written examination, secures the diploma given by Government

Mr. GEORGE HUBBARD said that the question of registration was one which had become of increasing importance to architects in England. There was no doubt that they were all anxious to do the best they could to raise the status of the profession, and it was only a question as to the best means to adopt.   It had been suggested that it was the duty of the architects to teach the public.   No doubt that might be the duty of architects, but, if he might suggest it, he thought that their first duty was to teach themselves before they could be in a position to teach the public At the present time the doors of the profession were thrown wide open , all might enter, and a formidable adversary had entered the ranks, viz the limited liability companies   The large art decorators came in, and by their system of advertisement—a system which was precluded to the legitimate architect—they were in a better position than architects to " educate " the public   Their view of the whole question was absolutely opposed to the view of qualified architects   They catered to supply the public with what they wanted, and whether the public wanted good or bad architecture they were ready to supply it, and would continue to supply it unless architects took some active means to keep them out of the profession   It was one of those cases in which they must all work together in order to protect themselves and raise the status of the whole profession.

Mr ROBERT WALKER (Cork) said that the object of holding International Congresses was to exchange views upon and deal with matters of common interest.   He felt honoured to be called on to represent England on Subject V.   It was an international congress question of pre-eminent importance to architects and the public in all countries alike, and he recognised, from the enthusiastic approval with which this view was received by the assembled delegates of all countries represented, that this was an epoch-making Congress, where hands joined hands over seas and oceans, across continents and frontiers, to support the peaceful common interests of all civilised nations by the promulgation of a measure framed in the best interests of the arts and crafts throughout the world.   He therefore called for a resolution from this assembly approving of the principle of the subject under discussion, and urged the delegates not to be deceived by a mere name, because "Statutory Qualification for Architects " and " Architects' Education and Registration Bill " meant one and the same thing.   The designations were synonymous.   He called upon the delegates to recommend the proper authorities or departments of Government in the countries which they represent to promulgate a measure to give force and effect to the principle by adapting it to the special requirements of each nationality.

Mr. ELLIS MARSLAND said he wished to enter a friendly protest that a subject of this importance should have been relegated to the last day of the Congress, when a counter-attraction had been provided—an arrangement which was not made on any other morning of the week This subject was of much greater importance than the subject discussed on Thursday, *i.e.* the education of the public, as until they had educated

* z

the architect it was quite impossible to educate the public   If they endeavoured to educate the public at the present time he was quite sure they would be in the position of the blind leading the blind, or they would be divided into two parts, and they would hear that Codlin was the friend, not Short   The great point in this matter of the registration of architects, or the statutory qualification of architects—they were both identical—was public confidence   They must secure public confidence, which at the present time was wanting   They found men boasting that they could do without architects—not men unable to afford architects, but men who were in a high position in the country. A case occurred recently when a party of architects went to a noble lord's residence   Unfortunately for the noble lord, he did not know that they were architects, and in showing them what he had done and what additions he had made to his building, he made the proud boast that he had done without architects   That showed that there was a certain amount of public confidence in the architect. But few people knew what the architect was, and they did not care very much   Architects wanted to counteract this tendency and feeling by making it compulsory for any architect or anyone who practised the profession of architecture to be properly qualified before he did so   What had been said in favour of the subject had been said over and over again, and he desired to move   the following resolution, viz   "That it is desirable in the interests of the public and the profession of architecture that all practitioners should have a statutory qualification."

Mr W. W Thomas seconded.

Mr C A Cowper (Melbourne) said he entirely approved of the resolution   As the delegate of the Royal Victorian Institute of Architects of Australia he had been instructed to support any such resolution   As they had heard from Mr North, a Bill had been introduced into the Australian Parliament some time ago, and a smaller Bill would shortly be introduced with a view to bringing about compulsory registration   When the syllabus of the Congress reached them in Australia, they were glad to see that this subject was to be discussed, and he could assure the meeting that his Institute would be very glad indeed to hear that this resolution was carried, if it should be carried   It would very much strengthen their hands in bringing about what they believed was a very necessary reform—a reform which would do both the profession and the public a great deal of good.

Mr G A T. Middleton said that as one who, like Mr. Walker, had taken a great interest and part in the matter for full twenty years, he should like to express his extreme pleasure to hear that morning the unanimous expression of opinion on the matter. There had not been a single dissentient voice from any country represented there   All were agreed that there should be a statutory qualification for architects   It might be brought about in one country by one means and in another country by another, but the principle remained the same in each case, and it was the principle they were there to affirm that morning, and he hoped that they would do so

Mr D Morgan (Cardiff) said that as one who came from South Wales and Monmouthshire he was entirely in sympathy with the proposition made, having to come into competition, as he did, with an outfitter, who was developing the profession of architecture and getting the full percentage. That was proof that in that part of the country they needed legislation very badly.

Mr F G GREEN (Cape Colony) said that as delegate from Cape Colony he had very great pleasure in supporting the motion. Some of them might have noticed that at the opening of the new City Hall and Municipal Buildings at Cape Town he brought the matter forward, referring also to the question of the education of the public. He thought the public were to a large extent to blame Very often gentlemen about to build houses left it to the ladies, and often accompanied them to certain districts to look at houses already erected They liked this or that, but they did not inquire who the architect was, but who was the builder, and they went to the builder and asked him to erect a building like the one they had seen and admired In addition to registration of architects, there should be some security against the multiplication of buildings done by an architect in the first place and then copied by builders afterwards.

THE CHAIRMAN said he did not wish to curtail discussion, but a late hour had been reached, and he should like to know what the pleasure of the meeting was as to continuing the discussion or not. He would put the question to the meeting

It having been agreed to discontinue the discussion,

THE CHAIRMAN said he was placed in a difficulty as to the resolution There had been several gentlemen present who had come prepared to speak against such a resolution, but as the time had gone on they had departed. Moreover, the subject of the statutory qualification of architects was an abstract one, and if the question were, Is it desirable in the interests of architecture all over the world ? it could be dealt with. But, as far as he understood, the papers read dealt with the question of the statutory qualification of English architects, which was not the subject before them

Mr WALKER said that the whole of his paper was written at short notice for the purpose of submitting his views to the Congress, and the observations he made afterwards were for the purpose of uniting the various countries represented

Several members called upon the Chairman to put the resolution

THE CHAIRMAN said he was in control of the meeting, and he should put the resolution in due course, but for the time being he wished to address the meeting Mr Walker's paper dealt simply with the procedure by which a Bill should go to the British Parliament, whereas the subject for discussion was whether statutory qualification for architects would be desirable for all countries, not for England alone They had had a discussion dealing with the application of such a qualification to England, and a comparison had been made between that qualification and the Diploma of Architecture in France. The latter diploma, which it was a great honour to hold, was however an entirely different thing, and did not bar other people from practising in architecture They had heard that the architects of Hungary had decided to put forward a Bill, but it had not yet passed, and therefore there was no evidence as to the working of such a measure M. Rey also made a speech on the subject, in which he said, not that statutory qualification for architects was essential to the practice of architecture, but that it was desirable to show that men practising architecture had a minimum of knowledge That was a good thing, though a very different thing. There was a difference, and it was an essential difference. As they all knew, the subject had, from the English standpoint, been gone into thoroughly by a committee of the Royal Institute of British Architects He did not want to worry the International Congress with the matter, but he would point out that the investigations of that committee had been very thorough, and had

been taken part in by eminent men all over the country   What was
said was this · If statutory qualification were found to be desirable
years hence, there was no reason against resorting to it then , but in
the meantime it was desirable to try the method of the French diploma
first   He was bound to put the resolution, but he suggested that the
phraseology be varied so as to refer to the public of all nations, seeing
that the present was an international congress.   In his opinion it was
an impropriety to ask an international congress to agree to such a resolution applying to England alone

Mr WALKER : It is evidently intended to mean all the countries represented

THE CHAIRMAN . That is what it should do.

It being understood that the resolution should apply to all the countries
represented, a vote was taken, and the meeting

> *Resolved, That it is desirable in the interests of the public and the pro-
> fession of architecture that all practitioners should have a statutory
> qualification.*

Subject VI.

THE ARCHITECT-CRAFTSMAN: HOW FAR SHOULD THE ARCHITECT RECEIVE THE THEORETICAL AND PRACTICAL TRAINING OF A CRAFTSMAN?

Wednesday Morning, 18th July —Grafton Galleries.

Chairmen · Herr Otto Wagner (Austria) , R S. Balfour (England)
Hon Secretaries · H O Tarbolton (Scotland) , Gustave Wickman (Sweden)

1 ARCHITECTURE AND CRAFTSMANSHIP

By Reginald Blomfield, A.R A , M.A Oxon., F S A.

The idea of the architect-craftsman has been much in the air in recent years, and, owing to misunderstandings and some confusion of ideas, a good deal of uncertainty prevails as to the degree in which craftsmanship is necessary to an architect, and to what extent a training in the handicrafts should form part of his education   In this paper I shall endeavour to clear up these points, by tracing the historical development of this idea in modern thought, and by a consideration of the actual function of architecture.

In the earlier days of the Italian Renaissance the architect was almost invariably a craftsman of some sort, or rather it would be more correct to say that, as an artist, he practised architecture among other arts, turning his hand indifferently to architecture, sculpture, or painting The names of Bramante, Raphael, the Sansovinos, Baldassare Peruzzi, and others of that time, will at once occur to you, and it was not till the middle of the sixteenth century that the architect detached himself from his brethren and specialised in architecture, as, for example, Serlio, Palladio, Vignola, Bullant, and Delorme   The result was that inferior men, such as Giulio Romano, usurped the control of the decorative arts   In France, for example, the architects were utterly routed by Primaticcio. In England, Inigo Jones was the only architect of the seventeenth century who went outside architecture in his remarkable designs for the Court masques ; and the last of the Italians who retained the ambidextrous ability of the Renaissance was Bernini, an artist to whom less than justice has been done   I think that, as a general rule, by the end of the seventeenth century architects had ceased to trouble themselves with anything beyond their buildings ; and such was the admirable workmanship to hand, and so strong was the vitality of their tradition, that they were able to dispense with much of the detail drawing which is inevitable in the case of a modern architect who cares to see his work properly done. The loss in certain directions was more than counterbalanced by greatly increased skill in architectural design   The best work of Wren is more mature than that of Inigo Jones ; and the design of such men as Mansard and De Cotte is far above the level reached by Lescot and Delorme, or

even by their able successors in the first half of the seventeenth century.
The French architects, it is true, took a wider view of their duties than
their contemporaries in England.   Boffrand's decorative work at the
Hôtel de Soubise is famous, and De Cotte, besides being first architect of the King, director of the Academy of Architecture, and vice-
president of the Academies of Painting and Sculpture, was also superintendent of his gardens and buildings, arts, and manufactures.   But the
architects practically limited themselves to architectural decoration, and
so matters continued till the latter part of the eighteenth century, when
architects again took it into their heads to embark on multifarious design
The solid tradition of Neo-classic architecture was breaking up, the dilet-
tante was so much interested in the art that he was beginning to lay down
the law on architecture, and, for the first time in the history of the art, architecture became a matter of literary fashion   Robert Adam devoted his
inexhaustible fertility to the design of anything and everything, and in
1812 Percier and Fontaine produced their collection of designs for decoration, including everything necessary to the furnishing of a house ˙ vases,
buffets, candelabra, chairs, tables, sofas, all in the severest classical manner
of the first Napoleon   The superb skill of French workmen will always
give value to this furniture, but it is depressing stuff, showing little care
for the materials, and no sort of appreciation of the limitations they
impose   Design of this kind—design, that is, which was mainly a matter
of draughtsmanship without regard to materials—might have multiplied
itself indefinitely, but by the nature of the case it could have no vitality,
because it was, so to say, always in the air, and never went back to the
materials it dealt with   Accordingly, it died the death it deserved, and
left the way open for all the fads and revivalisms of the nineteenth century.

In England, at any rate, architecture went plunging down the slope of
sham mediævalism, with Augustus Welby Pugin leading the way like
the Pied Piper of Hameln.   Where it still clung to the last foothold of
tradition, it dared not go outside the limits of a frigid and unimaginative
scholarship   I would not for one moment underrate this last stand of
the Old Guard , men such as Decimus Burton, or, a little later, Barry and
Cockerell, maintained the last tradition of architecture as well as they
were able in an age of rapidly spreading sentimentalism.   Except for the
stand they made, we of to-day should be floundering about in a quag-
mire of scrap-book fashions, without a clue to any ideal, however
remote   Such a clue, faint as it is, they left us, though they failed in the
struggle, and English art sank to the lowest depths of degradation it is
ever likely to reach at a date fixed for us, with curious irony, by the
Great Exhibition of 1851

Pugin died in 1852.   Whether it was his enthusiasm, or the sight of
so much accumulated ineptitude at that Exhibition that stirred some
latent feeling for better things it is now difficult to say, but the Exhibition
marked a turning-point, and about this time there appeared on the scene
that most interesting group of men, the Pre-Raphaelite Brotherhood.
With the significance of the Pre-Raphaelite movement in regard to painting
I am not here concerned , the aspect of it to which I would call your attention is one that has received less notice, but is not less important, and that
is, the influence of this movement on current ideas of architecture and
craftsmanship   Before doing so, I must ask you to remember that this
movement, which began among artists, was promptly collared by the
literary man, and that at an early date its inspiration and its impact on
opinion became literary, politico-philosophical, ethical, anything rather
than artistic   The more one reads of the early days of the Pre-Raphaelite
Brotherhood, the more evident it is that these young men were very
much in earnest about something, but the precise shape of their aspirations it is not very easy to fix   On the one hand there was that ardent
and half-mystical mediævalism which inspired the best of Rossetti's

work both in poetry and design ; on the other an almost fanatical anxiety
to get at what the artist conceived to be the actually visible facts of
Nature.   The latter seems to have been the principal motive of Mr.
Holman Hunt's work, *plus* his personal temperament.   The two ideals
seem to me to have been like oil and vinegar, in immediate juxtaposition,
but never in fact in touch with each other.   If Rossetti was a poet and a
dreamer, Mr. Holman Hunt was a revolutionary, aspiring to do away with
conventions of every kind, and that not only in painting, but in the
other arts.   To Mr. Hunt, as a young man, this appeared to be quite a
possible ideal   Writing of 1847, he says · " I had grown to regard all
decorative design as part of a true artist's ambition, and I declared that
until our craft again employed itself in designing beautiful forms, taste
in furniture, in costume, and even in architecture, would remain as bad
as, or grow worse than, it had been for the last fifty years, during which
the practice of design had been left to tradesmen only "   (It will be noted
that by " artist " Mr Hunt means " painting artist ")   Further on in
the same volume he makes the astounding pronouncement of himself and
Rossetti that " we agreed that architecture also came within the proper
work of a painter, who, learning the principles of construction from
Nature herself, would apply them by shaping and decorating the material
he had to deal with."   I shall return to this passage again.   At present I
refer to it only as evidence of the mental attitude of the young men of
movement towards the art of architecture fifty years ago   Mr Ruskin,
not to be left behind in zeal for the reformation of architecture, urged in
his *Seven Lamps* that it was useless for an architect to study his art
in cities.   " Send him," he said, " to our hills, and let him study there
what Nature understands by a buttress, and what by a dome."   He
might, indeed, but it would be something very different from what an architect has to understand by a buttress and a dome.   But that would have
made no sort of difference to Mr. Ruskin, who ended a prodigious flight
of eloquence with a reference to " the old power of architecture," which
" gives the Temple gate the depth and darkness of Elijah's Horeb cave "
One should perhaps be thankful that he did not throw in Zeba and Salmana
as well ; for after Mr. Ruskin set the fashion, no one had a chance of
getting a hearing on architecture who did not pepper his discourse with
abundant references to the Eternal Hills and the pebble stones by the
seashore   That such views would lead to greater knowledge or skill in
architecture was improbable , and the art itself ceased to be regarded,
except as occasional material for copy.   Rossetti went off into strange
visions, Mr. Hunt into desperate wrestlings with ethical ideas and the
simulation of Nature , but there were others to follow of equal ability
and enthusiasm   Ford Madox Brown had, indeed, preceded Rossetti
and Holman Hunt, and seems to me, in his strong grasp of the actualities
of emotion, to have been the only genuine Mediævalist of them all.   It
was he who inspired the Morris group and was one of the founders of
the famous firm   Morris meanwhile had tried architecture and given it
up in disgust, and thereupon, with characteristic energy, had formulated
a theory of architecture which boldly cut the knot.   Architecture in his
mind was to be the occasion of a great assemblage of the arts in which,
if one may so put it, none was to be before or after other, and architecture itself should disappear, or rather voluntarily efface itself, and be
content with the part of a vehicle for carving, and ornament, and storied
tapestry, and beautiful glass.   To the realisation of this view Morris
devoted half his life, and he adhered to it to the end   There is no doubt
that, as handled by Philip Webb, the realisation of this theory was sometimes beautiful and always profoundly interesting.   Morris, at any rate,
was no half-hearted advocate.   In the lecture that he gave to the Arts
and Crafts Society in 1893, he stated as an axiom that " Architecture is
the art of ornamental building "   " A true architectural work is a building

duly provided with all necessary furniture, decorated with all due ornament" He contrasted the freedom of Gothic with "the iron rule of
Classic," and in regard to the latter spoke of " the acknowledged slavery
of everyone but the great man "; why "slavery" does not appear,
unless there is slavery in the fact that one man has brains and another
has not But Morris never approached architecture from the standpoint
of an architect His brief apprenticeship in an architect's office disgusted
him with the drudgery of the art, and to his fervid imagination a short
cut to beauty seemed possible by omitting architecture When he did
deal with the art, it was from the point of view of the craftsman and the
Socialist Gothic was to him the art of arts and the art of the future,
because it was supposed to be the work of the Guilds, because no man
stood a head and shoulders above the rest, because it gave infinite room
for a riot of the handicrafts Neo-Classic, on the other hand, was hateful
and unintelligible, wicked even, and without a soul. In the same lecture
you will come upon this remarkable statement · " St. Paul's was not
built to be beautiful, to be the home of the citizens in their moments of
exultation, their surprise, grief, and hope, but to be proper, respectable,
and therefore to show the due amount of cultivation .   ," and so on.
The writer of this passage can never have witnessed a nation's grief under
the dome of St Paul's, or, if he did, must have been a singularly unim-
pressionable man. But apart from this the criticism is irrelevant. Morris
had his eye so firmly fixed on detail that he never rose to the conception
of an art of architecture which is concerned with the rhythm of building,
with thought in great spaces, an art in which detail takes its proper
place in reinforcing a dominant idea.

But the genius of Morris, his personality, his enthusiasm, his lofty
integrity of purpose, were irresistible to those who came within his range
We younger men sat willingly at his feet ; two architects of ability
relinquished architecture for the pursuit of the handicrafts, and in due
course the Arts and Crafts Society came into existence, for the dual purpose of exhibiting work not otherwise to be seen, and of advocating
definite views (which were, in fact, the views of William Morris) in regard
to the decorative arts Morris wrote the preface to a volume of essays
issued by the Society in 1893, in which he dwelt on the increasing ugliness
of modern life, and the necessity of a deliberate stand for beauty being
made in the handicrafts , architecture was, as usual, left out in the cold.
Thus the all-embracing revolution in the arts contemplated by the Pre-
Raphaelite Brotherhood had, I will not say consciously, but rather as the
result of the personal temperament of one man, narrowed itself down to
a half-despairing championship of the handicrafts—a championship that
sought to promote its end by proclaiming the Liberty, Fraternity, and
Equality of the Arts, and has left us looking each other in the face, with
all sorts of pretty things in hand and little or no idea what to do with them.
It is out of these conditions and from these intellectual antecedents that
the idea of the architect-craftsman has been evolved.

I need hardly dwell on the inestimable value of the work done by
William Morris in the arts that lie round architecture His strenuous
example did away with much that was foolish in all sorts of design He
taught people again to value good workmanship, good material, good
colour, to dislike all empty-headed art, and to aim high. Nor. again, do
I underrate all that has been done by the Arts and Crafts Society to
regenerate the minor arts, the stimulus and encouragement it has given
to handicraftsmen, the resolute stand it has made against commercialism,
and the undue preponderance of the middleman in matters which ought
to lie directly between artists on the one hand and the public on the other
But by the nature of its crusade the Society has had to concentrate its
attention on the handicrafts, and with the wheat has grown up a most
plentiful crop of tares The result has been that the sense of proportion

between architecture and the crafts has been lost. The architectural sense has disappeared under a prolific growth of cheap accomplishment. It would not be fair, however, to lay this solely at the door of the Arts and Crafts Society. I have come to the conclusion that architecture as the art of building did not enter into the serious consciousness of the Pre-Raphaelite Brotherhood and their successors. They never realised it as an art in itself; and they, with Mr. Ruskin, are to a large extent responsible for the failure of the public to recognise it as such. How else is it possible to account for Mr Holman Hunt's astonishing words which I quoted above ? That distinguished artist is perhaps only referring to views which he held nearly fifty years ago. Without some such gloss on the text I do not hesitate to say that the words " learning the principles of construction from Nature herself " have no meaning, and show a total ignorance of the actual problems of architecture. Titian, or Velasquez himself, might look at Nature for a thousand years and not discover the principle of such a rudimentary piece of construction as a king-post truss. But Mr. Hunt never, in fact, meant architecture, for he added that the painter was to " apply the results of his studies to architecture by shaping and decorating the material he had to deal with." In other words, he conceived of the whole business of architecture as an affair of decoration only, and we find ourselves again face to face with that ingrained fallacy, that architecture is the application of ornament, a fallacy which was sedulously taught in the nineteenth century, and is at the root of half our difficulties at the present moment. It cannot too often be insisted on, in the present state of the public taste, that architecture is not mere decoration or ornamented building, but that it is something outside and beyond the various crafts which it calls into play.

If this is so, we have at least arrived at one stage in our inquiry ; and that is, that the architect is not a craftsman in the sense that a cabinet-maker is, with the corollary that the training necessary to an architect will differ from that necessary to the cabinet-maker But we have still to aim at clearer ideas on the province of architecture before we can discuss the question of the kind and amount of training in craftsmanship necessary to an architect. We were taught in our youth that architecture is both a science and an art Having little aptitude for science, I can well recollect the alarming vista of scientific study that this suggested. Chemistry, geology, higher mathematics, and so on, all would be necessary before we could hope to master the mysteries of this intractable art, and how was one also to study its forms and perfect oneself in the actual *mécanique* of design ? I am not underrating the value of scientific knowledge to architects ; we should, all of us, design more boldly if we had full scientific knowledge of statics and dynamics, and could handle the calculus as freely as our T-square ; but the fact was that the conception presented by this formidable combination, " science and art," was a mere bogey. Architecture is not a science in the same sense that chemistry, botany, or geology is a science. It is bound to recognise the facts and laws of Nature ; but then, so does the art of sculpture in conforming to the facts of anatomy ; and the real science of architecture is that knowledge of the effect to be aimed at, and of the means of realising it, which is the hall-mark of the competent artist. I confess to having little sympathy with the amiable view that bad workmanship is atoned for by excellence of intention This may be well enough for amateurs, but we architects are, or should be, expert artists in building To architects the study of actual buildings is on the same footing as the study of anatomy to the sculptor. When enthusiasts and others urge us to study Nature, they are only urging us to beat the air. Possibly they have still in the back of their minds the ingenious theory of forest trees and Gothic vaulting ; perhaps they are only repeating a piece of cant. It is only by prolonged and intimate study of buildings—not merely of details, not only of the physical laws which govern construction and the conduct of materials, but by the study and analysis of the effects obtained in noble buildings, and by the search after the principles that govern their disposition—that we can hope to attain to mastery in architecture.

For what is it that architecture sets out to do ?   Let me quote to you the words of our distinguished colleague, M. Guadet: "Architecture is not an art of pure theory or of doctrinaire ideas.   Its object is to construct, its means the knowledge of construction, the design of its plan and façades is made up of sacrifices "   Its end is to produce buildings which not only answer their varied purposes as inclosed and covered-in spaces, but also appeal to the æsthetic sense and to the imagination by the beauty and fitness of their forms, by their disciplined design, by rhythmical combinations which appeal to some such instinct within us as is touched by great orchestral music.   Architecture is differentiated from craftsmanship or decoration, however beautiful, by its greater scope, by the sense it inspires of organic thought moving in orderly sequence through particulars to the total effect   I can only compare a fine architectural composition to some stately concerto of Bach   In both there is the deliberate restraint, the selection and interweaving of motives, the definite and consecutive construction in which each detail falls into its place,.and the masterly handling of these varied phrases so that they all combine for one great effect   This I believe to be the essential quality of architecture, the quality which alone justifies its claim to be the most intellectual of the arts.   It is a quality which can only be reached by the perfect use of the technique of the art itself—that is, however much architecture may be enhanced by union with sculpture and painting, it is yet independent of those arts in producing its peculiar impact on the senses   The Panthéon, for instance, would not cease to be impressive if shorn of all its ornament. The proportions of the Parthenon are not dependent on its sculpture. Space composition, space music, are the artistic aims peculiar to architecture, aims beyond the reach of any other art

Now, this aspect of architecture is one that seems to have dropped out of view in the last fifty years or so.   It formed no part of the Gothic revival, a revival that concerned itself almost entirely with details, cusps and crockets, mouldings and tracery, tiles and vestments, and all the other knicknacks and gewgaws of that preposterous anachronism   Neither, as I have ventured to suggest, did it occur to the Pre-Raphaelite Brotherhood or their successors.   Morris did, indeed, attack detail in genuine earnest ; but the view of architecture as the architectonic art, the art that controls and orders the crafts, was not compatible with the Socialistic ideal of art , and it was only the logical, if unconscious, result of that ideal that this view should be repudiated, that in its place we should be offered the noble army of craftsmen, all tumbling over each other in their haste to invest our ineffectual efforts with artistic merit   I cannot think the results have justified the enthusiasm of twenty or thirty years ago Hell, they say, is paved with good intentions , so is much of our modern decorative art in England, work done with laudable zeal, but with inadequate technique   Amongst other things, we find "l'Art Nouveau" confronting us as a monstrous result of mere craftsmanship divorced from architecture.   The Socialistic ideal of art, the ideal of unalloyed craftsmanship, has been tried and found wanting   The future, in architecture at any rate, is not with the Socialist, but with the individual master mind

It is time that the architect reasserted himself, and took his stand on the true function of his art.   What that is I have endeavoured to suggest to you ; and if we realise that conception we shall have some standard to which to appeal in considering how far craftsmanship is necessary to an architect   I have suggested that architecture, broadly speaking, plays a part analogous to that of the art of orchestral music   It presupposes in its exercise full knowledge of the resources of the art in detail.   If a composer is hung up for a phrase, if technical difficulties of expression are constantly in his way, he cannot express himself freely, he is likely to lose the thread of his idea in the struggle with details   This stage must be passed before an architect begins, as one may say, to rank , that is, he must be acquainted with his materials and with the laws that govern their behaviour—he must know, in short, what he can fairly get out of them

Brickwork, for example, has different properties from masonry, and wood from metalwork , and to learn what these are the student must study actual work   He should see actual bricks being laid, actual masonry set out and worked, the essential methods of lead, steel, and iron work in operation.   These studies should be systematically pursued in the workshop and in buildings , but it is of the first importance that the student should keep steadily before him the end in view   He is not there to qualify himself as a bricklayer, or a plumber, or whatever it may be, but in order that he may learn to know his way about among those crafts when he himself comes to deal with buildings.   All this practical training is simply the groundwork and foundation of that higher art which is ultimately to express itself with easy mastery in the plenitude of its knowledge   Mr Walter Crane said truly in the volume of essays I have referred to above, " The true root and basis of all arts lies in the handicrafts," but it does not follow from this unexceptionable premiss that the handicrafts constitute the whole of art

We are not to suppose that architecture can be taught in any given period of years, its range is so great, the study and observation required so intimate   The career of Wren, for example, shows how slow the process must be even in a man of his extraordinary aptitude for the art   A critical study of his work shows that he started practice as an amateur, that it was not till early middle age that he brought himself abreast of his time, but that from this time forward to the end of his long career he advanced, far ahead of his contemporaries, to that admirable attainment in the art which no other Englishman has reached   It is not so with painters   They arrive early, sometimes they advance, more often they pursue their calling at a steady equable level   It is doubtful, for example. if Millais ever painted anything more searching than " The Blind Girl," painted as long ago as 1854   But great architects have not, as a rule, reached the maturity of their powers till, at any rate, early middle age , and the reason is that it is impossible in any short space of time to cover the immense amount of minute observation, of analysis and reflection, that are necessary to any skill in this most difficult art

All, therefore, we can hope to do in the training we offer to our students is to lay a good foundation, to familiarise them with the use of their tools and materials, and to give them some insight into the means available for architectural expression.   In doing so it is essential to keep before the student the ultimate end of all this training—namely, skill, not in draughtsmanship or in craftsmanship, but in architecture.

It is because this point of view has been lost sight of in the crosscurrents of thought of the last fifty years that I have ventured to criticise the distinguished men to whom I have referred in this paper   No one can be more sensible than I am of all that we owe to the genius of William Morris, and, indeed, to the ability and enthusiasm of the younger generation who started the Arts and Crafts Society

But the unintentional effect of that movement has been to substitute craftsmanship for architecture, to depose architecture from her proud position as the mistress of the arts, and allow her to exist only on the sufferance accorded to the man who blows the bellows   Architecture is, indeed, very much under a cloud at present.   A recent French critic has formulated the theory that nothing is more disastrous to the arts than the hegemony of architecture, and he points with pride to the exploits of Primaticcio   Anyone who has seen Giulio Romano's work in the Palazzo del Tè will find in it a sufficient answer to the contrary.   I only call attention to this new attack on architecture, proceeding as it does from a very different standpoint from that of the Morris school, in order to show the danger in which the art stands at this moment, and to insist that the position into which some would thrust it is one which we, as architects, cannot for one moment accept.   We must stand for the higher view of our art.   Admirable work, of which we are justly proud, has been done by English architects.   Mr Norman Shaw has shown that there are still men among us who worthily maintain the great traditions of our art ; and the steady development of his genius shows how the real architectural instinct draws away from the narrower standpoint of the crafts, and concentrates on the rarer and more subtle qualities to be won from the planes and masses of buildings   We may be permitted to hope that there are signs of improvement here and there ; but we cannot yet feel certain that the art is back on the lines of true development ; and there is little hope of its being so till we ourselves take our art seriously, and place it on an intellectual and imaginative level beyond the reach of fashions and beyond the range of the copyist.

We have finished with the nineteenth century, its cross-purposes, its sentimentalisms, its confusion of thought.   Let us admit once for all the debt that we owe it in breaking up ground, in stimulating thought and enthusiasm, and then let us turn our back on it and set our face toward the future   If architecture is to hold up her head again in this country, it will be through the unwearied efforts of architects to realise and make others realise that there is such a thing as the art of architecture, and that it is worth our devotion on its merits.

April 1906

<hr>

2. THE RELATION OF MODERN ARCHITECTURE TO CRAFTSMANSHIP

By W. R Lethaby.

The practice of modern architectural design is, for the most part, based on custom, and in some countries customary methods are so widely accepted that, continuously followed, they seem to produce a characteristic style ; a style, however, which has little depth of meaning, and, I think, no possibility of life such as existed when art was nearer to the sources of inspiration.   In other countries, of which I fear England is one, there is little of this essential agreement, and sudden changes of fashion preclude all chance of a process of growth.

We are probably all agreed as to many of the necessary conditions for the existence of a school of architecture ; but beyond these what are the possibilities by which modern architecture may enter on a true development, a development not founded on mere caprice, but on the nature of things ?   How can it gain that reality which we feel gives life to old buildings ; and how can we compel that unanimity of effort which is so essential a force ?

All great schools of art have been shaped by a growing mastery of craftsmanship   There were ideas, too ; but of these we should argue long, while of the development of craftsmanship there is no doubt.   When I speak thus of executive power, I do not mean the mere ability to compel materials into preconceived forms, but I mean a sympathetic relation and reaction between the artist and his materials by which he explores their nature, and in so doing discovers art. Art, indeed, cannot be created at will, it must be a discovery.

The forms which run so readily from the point of an architect's pencil are decayed and degraded memories of the discoveries once made by ancient craftsmen Whence, then, is new energy in modern architecture to be derived ?

In part it may come from the investigations of science applied to the solution of the compelling forces of civilisation, and in the main I think it will come from this source in the immediate future; but even so, we want a vital and resourceful craftsmanship which shall be able to deal with such new ideas and interpret them in proper terms.

As at present conducted, however, the profession of architecture is shut away almost completely from any direct relation with workmanship. While this is the case there is, so far as I can see, small possibility of healthy and intelligent growth. Confess it as little as we may, we are imprisoned within a limited sphere of ideas, which causes modern practice to be directed to making new combinations with known, and in many cases entirely outworn, elements, so that no reasonable explanation can be given of a great number of the secondary forms with which even our most successful buildings are covered

Some of our most gifted architects, feeling the workmanlike interest of old architecture, that is, its truly artistic quality, but perhaps understanding its source incompletely, have tried to give their buildings the *appearance* of interested handiwork and masterly ease ; they have designed roughnesses, and even accidents ; they have tried to bring back the semblance of old ways of doing things; but such a procedure is but one more partition between us and the veracities of art, and one more burden to the labour thus called in to parody labour.

I cannot, then, too strongly urge the view that all fine work must for ever be the result of a growing tradition, not too far removed from the shaping forces of necessity.

The possibilities before us of such growth are · the *force majeure* of civilisation, whatever that may have in store for us, the scientific exploration of material and constructive facts which should be as thorough as the most rigorous method will allow, and a renewed contact with craftsmanship. All the rest, if not an outcome of these—call them by what names we will, proportion, design, invention—are but arbitrary, and sometimes capricious, exercises of the will, having no root of poetry. A work of architecture must be as real as a ship ; that is, shaped by the primal facts of existence. Contact with labour may mean several things besides the one that we have more particularly now to consider. We need, for instance, to be in closer touch with the executants of our buildings, and to be anxious to learn from them what *they*, the artists, think is good work, and what improvements of method they can suggest. It is, I believe, a fact that most of the improvements in detail applied to progressive arts, like machine construction, spring from suggestions made by the workers. We need, I am sure, to open out a way for promotion from the ranks ; we need to arouse an interest right down through the whole body of those engaged in building ; and we must recognise that at present, so far as the initiation of art is concerned, modern architecture is the result of practically servile labour, and of course bears its mark.

In the second place, contact with craftsmanship may mean the acceptance by the scientifically trained directing architect of the help of independent expert assistance, from workmen of a high order—painters, sculptors, metal-workers, modellers, and the like—and the sloughing-off of the ordinary wrappings, shrouds even, of office-designed ornamentation. It will, I think, be necessary to come to some form of Home Rule

in the arts associated with architecture, so that a metal-worker shall
be responsible for the design of metal-work, and a glazier for glass, as
well as a painter for paintings, and a sculptor for sculpture. It is as
absurd for an architect to design ornamental metal-work as it would be
for him to design oil paintings to be carried out by hireling labour.

To come to our immediate subject—" How far should the architect
receive the theoretical and practical training of a craftsman ?"—the idea
underlying this inquiry is, I have found, liable to misinterpretation in at
least two ways It is laughed at as a mere whim, as though it were
proposed that the architect should make his own mortar and lay his
own bricks , or, secondly, it is received as a sort of new gospel, and then
immediately the initiate is likely to show his interest in craftsmanship
by taking up enamelling, gesso-work, or wood-carving.

The craftsmanship I have in view is a course of workshop training in
masonry and carpentry, so long as they remain the principal factors in
construction. So understood, craftsmanship should form the basis of
architectural education The student wants at an early time to deal
less with paper and more with things having weight and volume I
would have him play, if only we could be reasonable enough, with
elaborate boxes of wood bricks, and so acquire for himself an instinctive
sense of balance in walls and arches I would have him actually taught
to cut stone, to frame up wood, and to handle bricks

Of course the youth, in training for the work of a modern architect,
cannot afford much time for such manual practice, and could hardly
acquire more than the rudiments of craft knowledge But surely there
cannot be a doubt that practical contact with materials and tools would
be of the greatest value in starting him on his way in what must ever
be a calling continually dependent upon experiment, initiative, and
decision An hour's demonstration in stone-cutting would be better
than none at all, and to have worked at it for a month would make the
questions of bedding, of tooling, of moulding, and the like ever after
have a different significance. A short course of craft demonstration
and practice should be essential in the training of even one who is to
become the most highly specialised of modern architectural practitioners.
Other students, once having come into close relations with the materials
and tools of a builder, would become more and more interested in the
practical work of building, and as a result we might hope to train architects
of varying gifts and capacities for works of different classes. It is the
mistake of all systems to turn out men of one pattern fitted for one and
the same end, whereas in the enormous mass of work which modern
building comprises it is surely evident that many different aptitudes
are needed.

However desirable it may be to train some men to the highest degree
of academical skill, administrative ability, and draughtsmanship who
may be able to deal with the complicated problems of practice in a big
city, it must be remembered that a far vaster volume of building work
consists of tasks of a humbler nature, tasks which a highly trained expert
is too refined to deal with satisfactorily Such works need the intimate
handling of those who perhaps have rougher faculties. I hold it for
certain that the more we elaborate (and possibly of necessity elaborate)
the education of architects who are to practise in large cities, the more
we are making it difficult to supply the everyday needs of the country
I see, then, in a basis of craftsmanship, not only a necessary part of the
education of all who are to be architects, but a way of opening out
channels for diversities of gifts which may correspond with the diversities
of requirement.

3. Par Fr. van Gobbelschroy, Architecte, Directeur de l'Ecole
professionnelle de Menuiserie de Bruxelles.

[Pour la Société Centrale d'Architecture de Belgique]

*De l'Architecte-Artisan   jusqu'à quel point l'architecte doit-il recevoir
l'éducation théorique et pratique de l'artisan ?*

Quoique souvent déjà l'importance du mandat de l'architecte ait été
démontrée, il ne sera pas hors propos d'exprimer ici, en quelques mots,
ce qu'on est en droit d'attendre de lui et ce que lui-même doit avoir
conscience de pouvoir faire pour mener à bonne fin une mission délicate,
sans crainte de voir jamais s'ébranler la confiance qu'on doit avoir dans
son art et dans sa science

Ces conditions ne sont malheureusement pas toujours remplies, d'abord,
grâce à ceux qui s'arrogent les droits que confère la qualité d'architecte
—mais que fort heureusement bientôt une loi leur contestera—grâce à
ceux, disons-nous, qui ravalent les connaissances de l'architecte au
niveau de l'intellect d'un vulgaire faiseur de plans qui, souvent encore,
n'est qu'un maladroit homme d'affaires , ensuite et surtout parce que, en
général, les connaissances sont incomplètes

A beaucoup de jeunes architectes, trop impatients des jouissances que
procure au maître de l'œuvre la matérialisation de son projet, inconscients
aussi du poids de la responsabilité qu'ils encourent et ignorants des devoirs
qui les attendent, à ceux-là manque—comme à d'autres malheureusement
aussi—cette grande masse de connaissances et d'expérience indispensables
pour inspirer cette confiance absolue que toutes les industries du bâtiment
devraient avoir dans l'auteur de l'œuvre qu'elles érigent ensemble

En un mot, sauf de rares exceptions, l'éducation intégrale manque
généralement à l'architecte, car il ne devrait pas seulement pouvoir composer des plans ingénieux ayant une valeur artistique, et être capable
de les faire exécuter dans leur ensemble en toute conformité avec ses
projets, mais il devrait ne pas devoir compter, exclusivement pour cette
exécution, sur l'entrepreneur et ses sous-traitants qui sont actuellement
seuls à connaître les difficultés de leurs métiers respectifs et à en posséder la
technique

L'architecte devrait être en état de juger, en réel connaisseur, des
plus petits détails de sa construction, il devrait pouvoir en commander
l'exécution complète et posséder les connaissances générales techniques
de tous les métiers, au point de pouvoir faire rectifier, sans crainte ni
hésitation, toutes les incorrections qui peuvent s'y glisser, soit par la
négligence, soit par l'incompétence de ceux qu'ils emploient

Ces multiples connaissances que nous avons rencontrées et que nous
rencontrons encore, à un certain point, chez certains éminents confrères,
manquent au grand nombre d'entre nous, non pas par dédain de la connaissance de la partie manuelle de l'exécution des projets, mais parce que
nous n'avons pas eu, au cours de nos études, ni le temps ni l'occasion
de les acquérir pratiquement et complètement.

Nous ne voulons pour preuve de cette lacune regrettable que nous
signalons que certains détails de menuiserie que nous avons eus récemment sous les yeux   Il n'eut pas été possible d'exécuter l'ouvrage comme
les plans le renseignaient, et, de l'étude laborieuse qui en avait été faite,
on n'a pu respecter que la composition artistique et les profils.

C'était bien la technique du métier qui faisait complètement défaut
au dessinateur qui avait voulu combiner le travail de menuiserie en question

Cette lacune dans l'éducation de l'architecte doit disparaître; il ne
faut pas que l'entrepreneur ou les sous-ordres puissent constater que

l'auteur des plans ignore comment s'exécutent pratiquement et conformément à la technique spéciale du métier en cause les détails des travaux qu'il commande   Il faut, au contraire, qu'ils aient la conviction, la preuve matérielle qu'on ne peut jamais lui faire admettre ce qui est mal exécuté, et qu'il sait tout commander et tout apprécier.

Et alors, sachant que rien, même dans les parties cachées de la bâtisse, ne peut échapper à la surveillance éclairée du maître de l'œuvre, aucun entrepreneur ne risquerait d'exécuter des travaux contraires aux règles de l'art, et la science qu'il serait forcé de lui reconnaître contribuerait énormément à ramener le prestige de l'architecte au niveau qui ne lui serait plus contesté ni par les propriétaires, ni par les entrepreneurs.

D'ailleurs, cette connaissance parfaite de la technique des métiers que nous réclamons de l'architecte n'est pas une innovation.   En effet, beaucoup d'architectes du moyen-âge et d'autres hommes de science tels que Galilée, Newton, Leibnitz, Stephenson et tant d'autres encore, n'étaient-ils pas, en même temps, des travailleurs manuels ? La plupart ont été des hommes qui savaient manipuler la matière pour réaliser leurs conceptions, et leur esprit trouvait un aliment autant dans leurs doigts que dans leurs connaissances théoriques

Certes, il ne faut pas pousser l'exigence pour les connaissances techniques de l'architecte au point de lui imposer un maniement irréprochable des outils de tous les métiers, comme on l'exige d'un ouvrier d'élite, mais il ne faut pas qu'il ignore comment s'exécute un ouvrage pour qu'il soit conforme aux règles de l'art ; il ne faut pas qu'il adopte cette indifférence, lourde de responsabilités, à l'égard des procédés de construction employés par les différents métiers sans jamais ressentir le désir, le devoir de connaître et de pouvoir apprécier ces travaux spéciaux

Il est indispensable que l'architecte possède la technique de tous les métiers du bâtiment, c'est à dire qu'il sache, pour les avoir faits lui-même et pour en avoir suivi toutes les phases en détail sous l'œil d'un maître exercé, comment s'exécutent les ouvrages qu'il rencontrera plus tard dans l'exécution de ses projets.

Ces connaissances lui ouvriront encore un autre vaste champ d'action, car non-seulement il sera en état de faire exécuter tous les détails aussi parfaitement qu'ils peuvent l'être, mais, connaissant les nécessités, les particularités et les difficultés inhérentes à chaque métier, il sera à même, grâce à l'instruction supérieure qu'il a reçue dans d'autres branches, non seulement de perfectionner rationnellement et pratiquement les procédés d'exécution adoptés par tel ou tel métier, mais encore d'en découvrir d'autres qui seront exécutables et meilleurs

Bref, dans ces conditions, l'architecte, au cours de ses visites sur les travaux, pourra donner toutes les instructions qu'exige un travail d'exécution parfaite, et, au point de vue de sa dignité et de son prestige, il ne sera plus jamais exposé à convaincre, malgré lui, ses sous-ordres de son manque de savoir dans la technique de certains travaux qui, quoique mal exécutés —moins par inaptitude que par lucre—n'eut pas attiré son attention, soit involontairement, soit aussi par prudence.

Certes, cette feinte de ne pas avoir remarqué est un moyen d'éluder les questions pour la critique desquelles on ne se sent pas de force, mais il est non moins vrai que cette tactique n'échappe pas à l'ouvrier qui, sachant fort bien lui-même ce qu'il a mal exécuté dans son ouvrage, taxera comme il convient l'architecte qui ne se sera pas aperçu de la malfaçon

Grâce aux connaissances techniques que nous désirerions voir posséder par l'architecte on verrait bientôt disparaître ces velléités de gains incorrects manifestées par une certaine catégorie d'entrepreneurs, et dont la réalisation compromet non-seulement la valeur et la solidité de la construction, mais augmente encore la responsabilité, déjà suffisamment grande, de celui qui en a fait les plans.

Voilà jusqu'où l'architecte, c'est à dire celui qui, selon l'acception propre du mot, dirige des constructions suivant les règles de l'art de bâtir, qui en dresse les plans et les devis, voilà jusqu'où "le maître de l'œuvre "—comme il était si justement appelé au moyen-âge—doit être artisan. Il faut, somme toute, que l'architecte réalise en tous points cette sentence si vraie : " On ne commande bien que ce que l'on sait bien faire soi-même."

Cette éducation, comme nous venons de la présenter, serait intégrale et, bien que très-complexe, ne nécessiterait, de la part des candidats, qu'un supplément de deux années d'études

L'élaboration d'un programme approprié, orienté dans un ordre pratique, demanderait une étude assez minutieuse et exigerait un remaniement complet des programmes d'études de l'architecture existants, car l'indécision de ceux-ci est démontrée par le fait qu'ils attirent actuellement deux espèces d'élèves . les ouvriers exerçant réellement une profession dans l'industrie du bâtiment, et les personnes qui étudient l'architecture par pur dilettantisme dans le but de s'assimiler la culture artistique préparant à la carrière d'architecte.

Or, c'est à ces derniers que le programme, le matériel de l'enseignement et son esprit, sont surtout adressés.

Dans ces écoles, le niveau des études—beaucoup trop conventionnelles pourtant—est généralement trop élevé pour les artisans, mais, d'un autre côté, il ne prévoit rien qui puisse donner à l'architecte-artiste ce qui lui manque de l'architecte-artisan

L'enseignement de l'architecture, qui applique des principes si élevés et si divergents, nécessite de la part des élèves, pour être suivi avec succès, des connaissances très-vastes et une maturité d'esprit qu'on ne trouve pas chez la moyenne des ouvriers   Ceux-ci ne pourront jamais, pendant le temps dont ils disposent, acquérir le savoir nécessaire pour combiner des ensembles, pour composer enfin, car ses connaissances de la construction et la subtilité de sentiment pour le faire avec discernement et avec goût leur manquent

C'est pourquoi le caractère de nos écoles d'architecture ne convient guère aux ouvriers, qui ne font qu'y entraver la marche normale des études et abaisser le niveau de l'enseignement des architectes

Il faut, pour commencer des études sérieuses d'architecture, posséder d'abord le programme complet de l'enseignement moyen, et c'est ce qui manque aux ouvriers

Les cours pour les métiers du bâtiment, spécialement destinés à former des artisans seulement, devraient exister isolément, autant que possible en dehors de l'influence des académies, afin que l'ouvrier ne soit pas sollicité par les cours brillants d'architecture et puisse s'attacher à des études bien appropriées à la profession qu'il veut exercer.

Seulement, des cours spéciaux pour les métiers du bâtiment, organisés en rapport avec les connaissances que possède l'élève-architecte qui a fait des études complètes d'architecture, devraient être créés dans les académies, comme complément obligatoire d'études

En somme, ces études se feraient dans des ateliers, où l'architecte apprendrait à mettre en pratique une partie des études qu'il a terminées, et où il s'initierait à toutes les difficultés techniques des métiers qu'il aura à conduire au cours de sa carrière.

Quant aux professeurs, ils devraient être choisis parmi des spécialistes capables d'exécuter, dans la perfection, les métiers qu'ils seraient appelés à enseigner, être pédagogues et en état de répondre pratiquement à toutes les questions qui lui seraient certainement posées par ceux qui déjà posséderaient, non seulement la théorie des métiers, mais qui auraient déjà des vues très-étendues comme architectes-constructeurs

Bref, dès le début, ces professeurs pourraient entrer dans le cœur du sujet, vu que leurs élèves posséderaient la terminologie de la profession et une connaissance complète des méthodes de construction et des matériaux à employer

A A

En Allemagne et en Autriche sont organisés des établissements qui forment des ouvriers et des techniciens des industries du bâtiment. Ce sont les seuls pays qui aient consacré des écoles spéciales d'entrepreneurs à l'étude des métiers divers

Cet important groupe d'écoles, qui jouit de grandes faveurs et qui rend de grands services, comprend deux degrés :

(*a*) Les écoles du bâtiment du degré inférieur pour apprentis.

(*b*) Les écoles du second degré pour contre-maîtres, patrons et entrepreneurs

Toutes les deux ont leur but et leurs méthodes propres. Elles enseignent les sciences concrètes rattachées à l'objet de la profession et le dessin relatif à des sujets empruntés au bâtiments.

Les méthodes et l'enseignement sont adaptés au degré de culture des élèves, et les programmes nettement déterminés, d'après le but spécial de l'école

C'est la seconde catégorie d'écoles qui nous intéresse surtout ici, car c'est elle qui, en beaucoup de points, serait applicable à celle qui devrait être créée pour nos jeunes architectes.

Ces écoles ont pour but de former des techniciens ayant une connaissance parfaite des matériaux, science qui constitue la point de départ des études techniques   Les élèves y apprennent à distinguer les matériaux de bonne et de mauvaise qualité et à se rendre compte de leurs propriétés afin de pouvoir faire un choix judicieux   Ils étudient l'agencement et le fonctionnement de l'outillage employé par l'ouvrier et par l'entrepreneur, soit pour le transport et l'élévation des matériaux, soit pour d'autres travaux.   Ils exécutent tous les ouvrages qui peuvent se présenter en se servant de tous les outils spéciaux qui doivent intervenir dans l'achèvement d'un même travail.

L'école d'éducation architecturale complète dont nous voudrions voir la création chez nous nécessiterait la combinaison des principes adoptés chez nos voisins avec notre enseignement artistique et scientifique, en basant toutefois l'enseignement technique sur celui des écoles techniques anglaises, qui est essentiellement pratique, et où les cours oraux, les manipulations aux laboratoires et le travail manuel dans les ateliers—enseignés d'après des méthodes qui développent chez l'élève l'esprit de recherche, la décision et l'initiative—constituent les moyens d'éducation.

Il est incontestable que le résultat de ces éléments dans un programme d'études serait, au bout de quelques années, décisif dans la compétition de plus en plus grande entre les architectes, parce qu'il contribuerait à faire disparaître la routine et l'empirisme qui mettent en infériorité réelle un nombre considérable de nos jeunes confrères.

Cet aperçu, forcément rapide, ne nous permet pas d'entrer dans le détail des programmes des cours—ces détails appartiennent au projet d'organisation même—mais nous espérons avoir pu laisser l'impression que cette école serait conçue dans un esprit caractéristique très-moderne.

Étant donné la tendance à la fois supérieure et pratique des études qui s'y feraient, nous sommes persuadés que les jeunes artistes, porteurs du diplôme de sortie de l'école, posséderaient des connaissances et des aptitudes qui seraient appréciées par le monde artistique, scientifique et industriel   Notre travail apportera, nous l'espérons, quelques éléments à la solution de la question si importante de savoir jusqu'à quel point l'architecte doit recevoir l'éducation théorique et pratique de l'artisan, et aura établi la connexité indéniable d'une éducation complète—toujours tenue à la hauteur des besoins nouveaux—avec le relèvement de la carrière d'architecte au niveau auquel elle a le droit de prétendre.

4 By OTTO WAGNER, Imperial and Royal Superintendent of Works,
Vienna ; Professor of the Imperial and Royal Academy of Plastic Arts.

(On behalf of the Society of Austrian Architects)

Wie weit ist ein Architekt in theoretischer und praktischer Beziehung
als Handwerker auszubilden , hiezu sei bemerkt ·

Wiederholt wurde im Vorhergehenden auf die wissenschaftliche
Bildung des Architekten verwiesen und betont, dass er ein sehr reiches
Material in sich aufzunehmen habe, und dass diese Aufnahme aus den
eingangs erwähnten Grunden keine vollständige sein kann   Es handelt
sich also bei Absolvierung der technischen Studien des Architekten um
eine gute Basis, welche es ihm ermoglicht, wahrend seiner spateren
Schaffenszeit sich das weiter Erforderliche anzueignen

Das Schaffen des Architekten und eine Anzahl kunstlerischer Dinge
wie die Pflege der so nahe verwandten Malerei und Bildnerei, das Verfolgen der Fachliteratur etc. werden ihn sicher veranlassen, mit der Zeit,
welche er fur all diese Arbeiten aufwenden kann, recht haushälterisch
zu sein, auch wird er sicher fur die Beaufsichtigung der durch ihn auszufuhrenden Arbeiten einen ganz erheblichen Zeitaufwand zu reservieren
haben   Man wird also nicht fehlgehen, wenn man behauptet, dass diese
Leistungen schon aus Zeitmangel kaum mehr zu bewaltigen sind   Hiezu
kommt noch jener Zeitverlust, der dadurch entsteht, dass Schaffenslust
und daher Schaffensfähigkeit Eigenschaften sind, uber die der Kunstler
nicht jederzeit verfugen kann

Eine weitere Aufburdung durch Erlernung eines oder mehrerer Hand-
werke (alle sind uberhaupt nicht zu erlernen), fallt daher sicher uber
jenes Mass von Zeit, welche dem Architekten fur seine Arbeitsleistung
uberhaupt zur Verfugung steht   Wird noch erwogen, dass derartige
handwerksmassige Leistungen einen ziemlichen Grad von physischer
Kraft in Anspruch nehmen und daher die Ruhe und das Feingefuhl der
Hand schadigen, so ist davon abzuraten, so weit in das Handwerksmassige
des bautechnischen Schaffens einzudringen. Die Kenntnis, wie ein
Bauteil gemacht wird, gehort in das Gebiet der Praxis, die sich der Architekt wahrend seiner Schaffenszeit umso leichter aneignen wird, weil seine
angeborene Findigkeit ihm hilfreich zur Seite steht.

Die in Rede stehende Frage 6 kann also nur in dem Sinne beantwortet
werden, dass der Architekt jedes Handwerk und die Eigenschaften der
Materialien, welche er bei seinen Herstellungen verwendet, in theoretischer
Beziehung und in Bezug auf Anschauung kennen muss, es aber unnötig
ist, dass er sich die manuelle, zum Handwerk gehorige Fertigkeit aneigne.

---

5 Par ROBERT LESAGE (Paris)

[Rapporteur de la Commission de l'Enseignement de la Société des Architectes
diplômés par le Gouvernement].

Sous ce titre "*de l'architecte-artisan*," nous avons pensé que les organisateurs du Congrès voulaient considérer *l'architecte dans l'application*
de ses connaissances techniques et théoriques. Nous avons limité notre
étude à la préparation de l'architecte à son rôle de praticien , nous avons
cherché à définir ce que pourrait être une *Instruction strictement pratique*,
en opposition à une éducation générale et particulièrement à l'enseignement
théorique de l'art d'architecture. Enfin, nous avons essayé d'établir
le programme d'une *école d'application* des arts et métiers du Bâtiment.

La création d'écoles techniques, pratiques et professionnelles est à
l'ordre du jour un peu partout en Europe. En France, jusqu'aujourd'hui,
l'objet visé par les maîtres de nos écoles, lycées et facultés a été surtout,

presque exclusivement même, la "*culture intellectuelle*" de leurs élèves dans un sens purement esthétique et aristocratique : *former des esprits distingués*. Les contingences ordinaires de la vie n'existent plus, notre sphère est idéale, nous ignorons la lutte pour la vie.

Il y a quelques années encore, l'homme qui exerçait une profession dite "libérale" pouvait rester dans sa tour d'ivoire, la concurrence ne l'avait pas terriblement soumis à son joug ; sa fortune dépendait d'une aristocratie dirigeante à laquelle son devoir était surtout de plaire.

Aujourd'hui, la démocratie, dirigeante à son tour, lui demande autre chose et davantage, elle est indifférente aux élégances, *trop peut-être*, elle ne s'attache qu'aux services réels, facilement tangibles et qu'elle compte par les profits qu'ils lui procurent La "culture intellectuelle" lui importe moins, la connaissance et l'habileté professionnelle développées grâce à la spécialisation l'intéressent plus. Elle ne demande pas à ses enfants d'être des sujets remarquables, mais d'être des serviteurs réellement utiles à la collectivité.

Elle a déjà créé des écoles pour des ouvriers, des ateliers professionnels où l'ancien apprentissage est remplacé par l'enseignement méthodique il faut maintenant que pour les *chefs du travail*, ingénieurs, architectes, entrepreneurs même, elle en institue de nouvelles où sera complétée, dans le même sens, l'instruction qu'ils reçoivent actuellement dans les écoles théoriques et idéales Il ne sera pas parlé, dans ce rapport, des écoles professionnelles *ouvrières*, mais seulement de celles qui conviendraient à des *chefs* dans les professions du Bâtiment et particulièrement à des architectes

Nous voulons dire tout de suite que nous sommes trop attachés aux élégances passées pour signer leur condamnation et que, si nous reconnaissons la nécessité impérieuse d'un enseignement exclusivement professionnel, c'est à la condition que celui-ci soit donné *à côté de l'école d'art et qu'en rien il ne puisse la diminuer*. L'école professionnelle doit être *complémentaire* ; elle doit donner *ensuite* à l'artiste les moyens de mettre son *intelligence améliorée* au service des *besoins* de la société

Avant d'aborder le programme général d'une école professionnelle d'architectes, nous devons dire quelques mots de plusieurs essais qui ont été faits, déjà en France, par l'initiative privée comme pour montrer le chemin à l'Etat.

Parlons, d'abord, de certains cours professés le soir de huit heures à dix heures sous les auspices d'associations d'enseignement post-scolaire · les associations philotechniques, philomathiques, polytechniques, et sous ceux des chambres syndicales. Malheureusement ces cours sont généralement isolés et ne font partie d'aucun corps qui puisse donner l'idée d'une École , ils sont irrégulièrement suivis ; leur auditoire est formé surtout de jeunes ouvriers ou de jeunes employés ; les élèves architectes ne les fréquentent guère. Le corps enseignant, ouvert à toutes les bonnes volontés, n'offre pas toujours des garanties scientifiques suffisantes.

Depuis quelques années, une école créée à Paris par l'ingénieur Eyrolles pour préparer des jeunes gens aux examens de conducteur des ponts et chaussées a ouvert un cours de métré et vérification des travaux du bâtiment, et tout dernièrement un cours de construction. Ces deux cours ont eu un succès réel, prouvant que le besoin auquel ils doivent répondre existe véritablement ; des architectes les suivent

Enfin, pendant ces deux dernières années, plusieurs membres de la Société des architectes diplômés par le gouvernement ont fondé deux nouvelles écoles · l'École du Bâtiment et l'École d'Enseignement mutuel des Arts La première a franchement abordé le programme professionnel ; elle s'est strictement limitée à l'étude détaillée et précise des métiers du Bâtiment et à leur comptabilité spéciale. Les cours professés par des spécialistes de chaque corps d'état sont complétés par des exercices et des travaux pratiques sur des chantiers , c'est une école complémentaïre, elle ne touche pas à l'art d'architecture. La seconde, dans un superbe ensemble de conférences de vulgarisation sur ce que l'on pourrait appeler la technologie des Arts, a réservé une place particulière aux arts du Bâtiment , ces conférences généralement isolées sont professées par des architectes, des médecins, des ingénieurs, des entrepreneurs. . . . Les élèves ne sont astreints à aucun exercice

Abordons maintenant l'étude du programme général de notre école, sans tenir compte des conditions particulières et nationales.

Nous avons dit que notre école préparera l'architecte à son rôle d'artisan, c'est à dire à appliquer ses connaissances théoriques et techniques.   Elle sera donc une *école spéciale d'application* et une *école complémentaire* ; l'élève n'y sera admis que s'il possède déjà ces connaissances qu'il va apprendre à appliquer, s'il sait dessiner, s'il a étudié la composition des édifices et les règles de leur construction ; en somme, s'il a déjà acquis l'instruction générale qui est au programme de nos écoles des beaux-arts et de nos écoles d'architecture

Cette éducation générale, elle pouvait à l'école théorique lui être donnée à l'amphithéâtre où, attentif, il n'avait qu'à recevoir de son maître des principes, des règles, des idées.   A l'école d'application où il devra maintenant s'attacher à l'étude analytique du travail, s'arrêter à des détails, à des réalités, l'enseignement " ex cathedra " ne lui suffira plus. Il faudra qu'il sorte de la salle des cours, qu'il aille sur le tas, qu'il voie l'ouvrier travailler et même peut-être, quelquefois, qu'il travaille avec lui   Il étudiera les matériaux isolément, il les comparera, les essayera, les travaillera , ce n'est qu'après avoir vécu quelque temps avec eux qu'il les connaîtra bien   Ensuite, en suivant le travail des ouvriers, il se rendra compte des moyens employés, des ressources offertes par les outils et les machines, des "tours de main," des difficultés d'exécution, du temps dépensé, des déchets

Au point de vue pédagogique un enseignement aussi varié, aussi vivant peut sembler impossible à réaliser.   Il le serait peut-être, en effet, pour une école privée, mais non pour une Institution d'État

Du reste nous avons déjà en France une école analogue et qui a eu un succès considérable ; je veux parler de l'internat des hôpitaux, pour les étudiants en médecine , il nous donnera, je l'espère, par analogie la solution de notre problème.

Notre école d'application devra donc donner à l'élève-architecte

1º. Les moyens de faire des études personnelles sur les matériaux et des essais de travail manuel

2º. Un champ d'expérience

D'où, deux divisions bien distinctes , *une division intérieure* et *une division extérieure*

A la division intérieure devront correspondre des cours de technologie et de comptabilité, des ateliers de travail et des laboratoires d'essai, un musée des produits des industries du bâtiment et une bibliothèque industrielle   Parmi les exercices et travaux pratiques qui seront imposés aux élèves, il semble que les exercices de dessin (détails d'éxécution, attachements figurés) et de comptabilité devront avoir une place plus importante que celle des travaux purement manuels   Il ne faut pas, en effet, oublier que notre école *n'aura pas à former des ouvriers,* mais seulement *des chefs d'ouvriers,* et que s'il peut être extrêmement intéressant pour ces derniers de s'essayer à quelques travaux manuels afin d'acquérir une connaissance plus complète des matériaux, des outils et du travail, il leur est absolument inutile de devenir des ouvriers experts Notre programme, déjà extrêmement chargé, deviendrait absolument irréalisable, faute de temps nécessaire pour l'accomplir   Ces travaux manuels ne devront donc être, à notre avis, pour l'élève-architecte que de *simples essais pour voir*

Notre *division extérieure* paraîtra peut-être plus difficile à organiser

Nous avons dit que l'internat des hôpitaux pouvait nous offrir un modèle à suivre.   Comme l'assistance publique a ouvert les portes de ses hôpitaux aux étudiants en médecine, l'administration des bâtiments civils ouvrirait celles de ses chantiers aux étudiants en architecture.   Comme les externes et les internes suivent la visite du docteur chef de service, les élèves-architectes suivraient celle de l'architecte en chef.   Comme l'interne donne son assistance au médecin, nos élèves seconderaient l'architecte

Mais il faudrait que cette école des chantiers fût rigoureusement organisée, et non considérée comme une suite de visites récréatives, un moyen d'enseigner en amusant, une simple promenade de vulgarisation. Il faudrait que le service des élèves fût exactement déterminé, obligatoire et constaté , il faudrait que l'architecte pût compter sur son élève-inspecteur, comme le médecin sur son interne.

Ce projet d'une *école d'application des métiers du Bâtiment* absolument indépendante de l'école d'architecture proprement dite, et aux élèves de laquelle elle serait accessible soit pendant les dernières années de leurs études d'art, soit après l'achèvement complet de celles-ci, nous semble être une solution convenable partout où il existe déjà une école d'art architectural spécialisée comme l'est notre École nationale des Beaux-Arts   Partout ailleurs, cette école d'application pourrait être simplement considérée comme l'une des sections de l'école d'architecture et peut être même devenir un simple stage d'apprentissage qui précéderait l'enseignement théorique.   La forme de l'école dépendra évidemment des conditions particulières et nationales de l'enseignement déjà existant, et devra varier suivant les pays , mais ce qui nous semble devoir être permanent c'est le caractère strictement pratique que nous voudrions donner à une période au moins de l'instruction professionnelle de l'architecte

Tel est le programme général.

Est-il réalisable ?   Nous croyons pouvoir répondre qu'au point de vue français il l'est sous la forme même que nous venons de proposer

L'École des Beaux-Arts n'est pas une école d'architecture, mais une *école spéciale des Beaux-Arts* où l'art d'architecture tient une place analogue à celles qu'y tiennent les arts de la peinture, de la sculpture et de la gravure.   Le but de l'École des Beaux-Arts est *d'éduquer l'esprit* de l'architecte, de le pousser vers l'art, et *non* de lui *apprendre un métier*, de le préparer à *l'exercice de sa profession.*   L'instruction technique de l'architecte, la préparation du praticien à son rôle social, n'est point de son domaine

Les examens et concours de mathématiques et de construction qu'elle impose à ses élèves dès le début de leurs études d'art n'ont point d'autre raison d'être que celle d'éliminer immédiatement parmi eux ceux qui seraient absolument inaptes à l'étude des sciences de la construction, et par conséquent à devenir de véritables maîtres d'œuvre   Mais les connaissances techniques, ses élèves doivent aller les chercher ailleurs et les demander surtout à l'expérience des chantiers.

Il est aujourd'hui hors de doute que cette instruction, laissée au hasard de l'expérience, devrait être faite d'une façon méthodique et donner lieu à un véritable enseignement, ainsi, assurément, nos architectes seraient plus tôt et mieux préparés à défendre les intérêts dont ils ont la charge.

Dans de précédents Congrès, Monsieur le Professeur J. J. Pillet a déjà proposé une solution à ce problème   Pour lui l'enseignement technique devrait être limité chez nous à *des écoles provinciales* et former *l'enseignement secondaire* de l'architecture , l'École des Beaux-Arts représentant l'enseignement supérieur, accessible seulement à une élite très limitée.

A l'époque où ce projet fut présenté, il aurait pu être facilement réalisé par la création d'écoles régionales d'architecture, bien autonomes et absolument provinciales   C'eût été de la bonne décentralisation.

Aujourd'hui les circonstances ont changé   Le Gouvernement français vient de créer en province des écoles régionales qui sont des succursales de l'École des Beaux-Arts   Les mêmes cours, les mêmes examens, les mêmes exercices, s'y font en même temps qu'à Paris, où les travaux des élèves sont expédiés et jugés par le jury ordinaire de l'École des Beaux-Arts   Ces écoles décernent le même diplôme que l'École de Paris

Devant cet épanouissement de l'École des Beaux-Arts, il ne semble plus rester qu'une seule solution au problème de l'enseignement technique : c'est la création, à côté et indépendamment d'elle, d'une *école d'application de la construction* sur le programme général que nous venons de tracer. Sa situation serait, à côté de l'École des Beaux-Arts, absolument analogue à celle qu'ont à côté de notre École Polytechnique les écoles d'application de l'artillerie, du génie, des mines, des ponts et chaussées   Comme celles-ci, elle recevrait quatre catégories d'élèves

1°. Des élèves-architectes, anciens élèves de la première classe de l'École des Beaux-Arts

2°. Des élèves-externes, admis par voie d'examen ou de concours.

3° Des élèves étrangers

4°. Des auditeurs libres.

Pour conclure, nous proposons le vœu suivant

Vœu.

Le Congrès, considérant que l'architecte, maître d'œuvre ayant sous sa direction immédiate les ouvriers et les artisans des corps d'état les plus différents et utilisant les services des industries les plus diverses, ne saurait prétendre à acquérir en chacun de ces métiers et en chacune de ces industries les connaissances approfondies d'un spécialiste ; considérant qu'il existe déjà dans la plupart des états européens des écoles d'apprentissage pour les ouvriers, des écoles d'application et des laboratoires pour les ingénieurs (où sont formés des spécialistes), exprime le vœu qu'il soit créé *spécialement pour les architectes* et pour les *entrepreneurs généraux* des écoles où, dans l'espace restreint de deux années, ils pourraient embrasser, d'une façon générale mais précise, la technique des différents métiers et industries du bâtiment sans prétendre à l'exercice de ces métiers et industries.   Il émet aussi le vœu qu'entre ces écoles s'établissent des rapports internationaux et suivis.

―――――――

6 Par Gaston Trélat (Paris).

Non ! je ne vois pas l'utilité qu'il y aurait à ce que l'architecte devînt artisan.   Mais est-ce bien le point de vue que veut soulever la question ainsi libellée, de l'architecte-artisan ?   Ces mots rappellent une pensée qui a souvent hanté l'esprit de l'artiste et du professeur que je puis représenter, par le fait d'une pratique déjà longue.

Je me suis souvent demandé comment les artisans, appartenant aux différents métiers de la construction, ne tournaient pas davantage leurs vues du côté de l'architecture   Alors ce serait *l'artisan-architecte* qui ne répondrait pas à la même idée que *l'architecte-artisan.*   En tant que technicien, j'ai parfois rencontré, parmi les collaborateurs ouvriers que l'exécution des travaux entraîne, des hommes encore jeunes, montrant une intelligence ouverte et largement préparée aux compréhensions excédant le cadre de leurs spécialités.   Le travail manuel, on ne peut en douter, comporte sa philosophie comme toute autre activité   La conscience approfondie d'un métier servirait de fond, base excellente aux études qui prendraient un tour intéressant du fait d'un *criterium* spécial.   L'artiste trouverait, dans cette connaissance de la matière, un soutien intéressant à la variété de points de vue caractéristiques des applications de l'architecture.   Parmi les étudiants et les hommes de la profession, cela jetterait une source d'élaborations nouvelles et originales

Un échange de pensées s'ensuivrait qui serait fertile en conséquences heureuses   Je m'étonne que la chose n'ait pas été plus souvent tentée   Il semble pourtant que ce serait bien dans l'ordre d'idées que l'époque actuelle est conduite à envisager.

Autrefois, c'était une croyance courante que l'art voulait être abordé dès la première jeunesse, pour que les études produisssent des résultats. Or, une expérience, remontant déjà loin, m'amènerait à une conviction différente, sinon opposée

J'ai eu des élèves sortant des écoles primaires supérieures ; j'en ai eu qui avaient fait de hautes études classiques ; d'autres avaient déjà derrière eux des carrières—en tant qu'instituteur, ingénieur, militaire, officier du génie, etc   Toutes ces catégories m'ont montré parfois des intelligences ouvertes et des esprits distingués.   Mais il ne faudrait pas croire que ceux qui avaient déjà l'expérience intellectuelle plus avancée d'une carrière fussent moins aptes à l'éducation d'art.   Des exemples sont présents à mon esprit qui contrediraient semblable opinion

Mais il n'est que temps d'aborder la vraie question, celle de *l'architecte-artisan*.   Les connaissances, que l'architecture comprend et qui lui servent de point de départ, ouvrent déjà les yeux sur tous les procédés à l'aide desquels les projets, dont nous concevons les éléments, pourraient se réaliser   Plus tard, le contact avec les différents métiers jette des clartés plus vives sur les modes d'exécution en usage.   Il s'ensuit des points de vue spéciaux pouvant devenir une source de vivacité d'esprit dans la manière de traiter différents points de détail qui concourent à la totalité de l'œuvre

Je crois que, étant donné le caractère que prend cette œuvre totale, il est bon qu'une première éducation s'attache à en concevoir tous les éléments, afin d'assurer une concordance particulière à la mise au point générale de l'ensemble   C'est déjà une grosse étude pour l'artiste et pour le technicien   Et même, en se plaçant à ce double point de vue, on pourrait craindre qu'il y eût un danger à pousser ces études jusqu'à la théorie et la pratique spéciales aux différents travaux manuels , on risquerait d'aboutir à une dispersion regrettable des facultés, à un usage déplacé du talent.   La qualité, qu'on s'attacherait à donner aux parties élémentales de l'ensemble, en viendrait à tirer l'œil, à distraire de l'idée générale, que l'ordonnance a pour condition première de servir et de représenter.   La mise au point, voulue par l'intelligence de la conception, serait certainement compromise. L'unité du parti se perdrait dans la multiplicité des détails dépourvus de concordance.

Nous voudrions donc mettre en garde contre la doctrine que l'architecture gagnerait quelque chose à ce que ses agents reçussent, au début de leur carrière, une éducation spécialement attachée à la théorie pratique de l'artisan   Il en résulterait, croyons-nous, une perte de temps considérable et une confusion dans les idées d'expression plastique   Ainsi la netteté comme la rectitude, caractéristiques de ce que nous nommons en art *le parti*, en souffriraient   Son éloquence se perdrait du fait d'un talent dépensé hors de propos.   Ce serait contraire à l'esprit d'ensemble que voulait une conception bien conduite, il n'est pas permis d'en douter.

Dans notre pensée, l'architecte doit développer en lui l'éducation théorique et pratique de l'artisan dans la mesure de sa *pratique* professionnelle ou d'artiste   Mais il ne conviendrait pas de débuter par une éducation qui détruirait la mise au point des intelligences de l'art   Cette éducation appartient essentiellement à l'expérience professionnelle qui dure autant que la vie active.   Elle résulte pour l'architecte d'une affinité continue avec tous les artisans qui lui apportent leur concours.   Elle se poursuit sans exclusion aucune de spécialités   Il s'ensuit des idées de mieux en mieux établies sur ce qu'il est permis de demander à chacune d'elles.

Pour en revenir au terme usité du programme, il y a là une véritable *éducation*.   Seulement elle dure toute la vie de l'artiste.   Elle tient

compte des changements incessants dans la science, dans son influence
sur les applications de l'art

Cette éducation se confond donc avec la vie elle-même de l'artiste.
Et il lui assigne toujours la place qui lui convient dans ses inquiétudes et dans ses préoccupations, s'il se montre à la hauteur du rôle
que lui attribue son activité bien comprise.

Mais je ne crois pas qu'elle doive prendre une place particulière dès
le début de la carrière.

Résumé.—L'éducation théorique et pratique des artisans peut certainement devenir une source abondante de développement en art. Mais il
faut alors qu'elle soit judicieusement conduite. Autrement elle aurait
des dangers qui ne tarderaient pas à se manifester dans les œuvres.

Je tiens à dire tout de suite qu'elle doit être conséquente du tour
que prend la vie professionnelle. Et celle-ci entraîne l'affinité générale
avec tous les métiers qui peuvent concourir à l'exécution des œuvres de
l'architecte. Il en résulte une vraie éducation *théorique et pratique*, qui,
celle-là, se résume toujours en extension de *conscience* chez l'artiste.
D'où une vivacité d'esprit qui se manifeste dans le caractère particulier
des éléments concourant à l'harmonie d'ensemble, à laquelle ils restent
subordonnés. Sans quoi, seraient excédés le goût et la mesure que nous
enseigne certaine *philosophie* tirée des ordonnances que la matière peut comprendre. On le voit, c'est là une éducation à laquelle la vie est consacrée.

Mais il n'y aurait pas lieu de compter, pour cela, sur une initiation
du début de la vie. Elle doit, avant toute autre chose, s'attacher à dévoiler
les inconvénients de faire dominer trop effectivement, dans une œuvre,
les différents éléments que la variété des métiers représente. Car ce
serait s'exposer à une cause de disparates à éviter dans la conception et
dans l'exécution architecturales. Certains maîtres, dont la mémoire est
entourée du respect qui leur est dû pour l'ensemble de leur vie, et certaines
écoles en fourniraient au besoin des témoignages, si la chose demandait à
être appuyée de preuves matérielles. Mais ce n'est pas le cas.

Cette éducation, pour ne pas jeter le trouble dans les esprits, se pour-
suivra donc par le fait de la carrière elle-même. Elle résultera pour
l'architecte exclusivement de l'expérience que lui donneront tous les
métiers auxquels l'exécution de ses édifices fait appel.

Conclusion —L'éducation d'architecte-artisan se fait suffisamment
d'elle-même par le courant d'une vie pratiquement absorbée dans les
applications de l'art

Pour ce qui serait d'une éducation théorique et pratique au début
de la carrière, les avantages ne répondraient point au temps consacré,
les inconvénients en seraient même prédominants

---

7. Par M. Poupinel.

Jusqu'à quel point l'architecte doit-il recevoir l'éducation théorique
et pratique de l'artisan ?

Les questions de l'enseignement de l'architecture et de l'éducation
de l'architecte ont été traitées à peu près sous tous les points de vue dans
les congrès internationaux de 1867, 1878, 1889, 1897, 1900 et 1904.

L'intitulé a été varié avec soin ; précisant le sujet à traiter spécialement,
différant du thème actuel , et cependant en se reportant aux ouvrages
parus sur ces congrès on s'aperçoit qu'à chaque instant rapporteurs,
conférenciers, orateurs se sont laissés entraîner à des questions tangentes,
et en y réfléchissant on découvre que leurs raisonnements s'étendent
bien au delà des limites tracées par le titre de leur communication et s'appli-
queraient à la pratique comme à la théorie scientifique et à l'art.

Il y a encore profit à tirer des thèses sur l'enseignement pratique du personnel du bâtiment, traitées par MM. Douillard, Duvert, Lehman, Ch. Lucas, à Paris en 1889 , de nos confrères de Belgique en 1897 ; de nos confrères d'Espagne en 1904.

Puisque des noms viennent d'être prononcés, énumérons encore les Baltard, Rohault de Fleury, César Daly, Charles Garnier, Guillaume, Emile Trélat, Bourdais, de Baudot, Gout, Wallon, MM Phenè Spiers, G Aitchison, A Mélida, Stier et Otzen de Berlin, Geymuller, Otto Wagner, Pedro d'Avila, Bénouville, Pillet, et j'en omets involontairement qui au cours de leurs discours nous ont fourni des aperçus et des critiques, ou des conseils dont nous pourrions faire notre profit encore aujourd'hui.

Je ne crois pas du reste devoir me lancer dans les détails, sachant que des confrères français l'ont fait, que des confrères étrangers ont étudié à fond la question actuellement à l'ordre du jour

Lorsqu'il est question de bon sens on se rencontre, fatalement les redites sont à craindre.

Je me bornerai pour éviter toute perte de temps à vous dire quelle conclusion me paraît à tirer de l'œuvre de nos devanciers

De même que pour l'art et la science, nous n'arriverons jamais à connaître la fin de la pratique, tant l'architecte a de problèmes artistiques, scientifiques et pratiques à résoudre plusieurs existences seraient nécessaires Madame de Sévigné a écrit · " Je dis toujours, que si je pouvais vivre seulement deux cents ans, je deviendrais la plus admirable personne du monde." C'est le temps qu'il faudrait, croyons-nous, à une élève-architecte pour recevoir une teinture suffisante de toutes les sciences qui lui sont nécessaires et les mettre en pratique.   Aussi constatant que, malgré les progrès des sciences médicales et de l'hygiène, les générations actuelles et futures n'ont guère de chance de longévité pareille, nous ferons peut-être bien de borner notre ambition. et dans l'intérêt même de nos jeunes confrères et successeurs de limiter notre vœu et de le formuler ainsi, sans nous perdre dans les détails ou les programmes compliqués —

" Que l'architecte reçoive un enseignement pratique sommaire lui permettant de faire le meilleur usage des forces humaines, des ressources matérielles, mis à sa disposition par la nature et l'industrie."

DISCUSSION ON SUBJECT VI

At the conclusion of the papers M. LESAGE proposed his resolution (p 359), which, translated, is as follows :—

This Congress, considering that the architect, the master of the works, having under his immediate direction workmen and artisans of the most varied bodies of the State, and utilising the services of the most varied industries, has no means of acquiring in each of these trades and in each of these industries the complete knowledge of a specialist , considering that there exist already in the majority of European countries training schools for artisans, schools for practical application and laboratories for engineers where specialists are trained, expresses the desire that there should be created *specially for the architects* and for the *general contractors* schools in which, in the limited space of two years, they could acquire in a general but exact manner the technical part of the various trades and industries of the building trade, without claiming to practise these trades and industries.   It also expresses the wish that between these schools international and continuous relations may be established.

Dr JOSEPH CUYPERS (Amsterdam) · J'ai écouté, avec grand intérêt, les trois rapports lus ce matin   Il ne reste pas grand' chose à dire sur cette question après la lecture de ces rapports.   Je voudrais cependant poser deux questions d'intérêt général. Les vues du professeur Lethaby expriment bien le sentiment qui a cours en Hollande concernant cette question importante de l'éducation de l'architecte, au point de vue technique. Je voudrais toutefois demander l'avis de l'assemblée sur la question de savoir à quel moment de cette éducation il doit commencer l'étude de la technique. Est-ce entre 14 et 18 ans ou bien à un âge plus avancé ? Si j'ai bien compris, il faut que le futur architecte apprenne à bien distinguer les caractères distinctifs des différents métiers, ce qui veut dire qu'il ne faut pas se borner à des connaissances purement théoriques. A ce point de vue, il serait suffisant qu'un élève-architecte suive des cours généraux des différents métiers En Hollande des écoles spéciales ont été fondées par des particuliers réunis en association L'Etat leur accorde des subventions, mais il désire ne pas restreindre l'initiative privée, lui laissant le soin de donner aux études l'orientation qui paraît la plus convenable. Le Gouvernement préfère ne pas imposer de modèle et laisser à chaque association la liberté la plus complète Il accorde des subsides qui atteignent quelquefois 90 pour cent de la dépense annuelle L'on obtient ainsi des types d'écoles indépendantes Nous espérons pouvoir continuer dans cette voie et ne pas nous voir imposer un type général, comme on l'a fait, je crois, en France, avec un résultat désastreux. Les institutions anglaises sont les plus indépendantes et en concurrence l'une avec l'autre Elles montrent que les idées qui président à leur organisation sont les meilleures. En Belgique on se propose d'avoir des cours de métiers pour les élèves-architectes, cours à suivre par eux lorsqu'ils sont déjà en stage. Il me semble que ces cours-là, donnés d'une façon permanente, sont encore moins nécessaires parce que les intéressés peuvent suivre des cours de vacances, ce qui est amplement suffisant. Mais ceci sort du cadre de la discussion actuelle. Le futur architecte doit avoir des idées pratiques des différents métiers qui concourent au bâtiment, et pour cela il doit suivre les écoles d'artisans où l'on apprend à manier le bois et le fer. Ceux qui s'intéressent à la bonne éducation des futurs architectes devront suivre cette orientation.

Mr MAURICE B ADAMS said he was entirely in sympathy with many of the views Professor Lethaby had expressed in his Paper. But much as he admired what Professor Lethaby advocated, the difficulty with architectural students was comprised in the vast field their labours covered. The art or arts which the modern architect had to supervise had been multiplied in a most enormous degree during his (the speaker's) own time, and although he realised the necessity of architects handling materials, as materials were handled by the practical artificer, he did not see how the architect could spare the time to devote to such a purpose. He (Mr. Adams) had himself worked at the joiner's bench for some two or three years before he was articled, and though he had never regretted it, he was not quite sure whether that was the sort of thing they ought to advocate nowadays with the material advantages which had accrued from the various schools recently brought into existence. It seemed to him that in dealing with a question of this kind they had to realise the exacting conditions under which the architect had to work, and not only the architect, but the builders, and also the whole system of building which was now adopted. Professor Lethaby's advocacy seemed to refer to a more elementary stage of existence than that which we enjoyed to-day If an architect had one or two small, or even large, country houses to build, he could devote a great deal of time to them; but the remuneration was somewhat limited when it was restricted to a small amount of work of that kind. The architect had to compete for commissions very largely nowadays Very few men came into the world favoured by circumstances which enabled them to depend on private clients, and therefore the architect had to fight his way by competition, very often against adverse circumstances for a long time, and then when he had succeeded in his work he was bound to fall into line with the ordinary methods of competition amongst builders and contractors, and it would be an extremely difficult thing for any individual architect to interfere with the progress of an undertaking once commenced and carried out on those lines Further than that, there seemed to be a growing disposition to go in for direct labour by large municipal authorities, while others insisted upon employing their own men, thereby emphasising to an enormous degree the amount of labour each architect had to devote to his business as supervisor or architect-in-chief. It seemed to him they must recognise the conditions under which architects had to work, and, looking at the schools that were at present existing, in his opinion the Schools of the Architectural Association went about as far as they could reasonably and practically go in the matter of enabling the student to acquire a more practical and technical knowledge of building operations, and that method was carried on by enabling the pupil to go on to buildings in progress and to make reports to his master of what he saw there   One of the first necessities of an architect was observation—that he should observe and note all the things on a building; that he should state his difficulties to his master and have them explained to him. Of course, if they assumed, as Professor Lethaby appeared to assume, that the modern architect's position was radically wrong from beginning to end—that there should in fact be no such thing as the professional architect at all—then one was able to follow his argument more closely, but he (the speaker) took it that we were obliged to take the world pretty much as we found it, and, of course, all agreed that the architect's work could only be appreciated by the amount of mind which he was able to put into it. No work of art could possibly be a work of art unless it had the full individual impression of the person who conceived it. If they could rely on the various arts and crafts to conceive the various parts of the building—the brick and roof work, the masonry, &c.—much on the lines that the old mediæval work was done, that might be extremely good; but he could not see how it could be done nowadays, and he did not understand what object there was in utilising the student's time for so long a period as would be necessary to teach him to do those things personally   He noticed that Professor Lethaby in one part of his paper spoke of a very short time being devoted to craftsmanship as being better than no time at all. His (the speaker's) own experience was that the main advantage in going to work at the bench was that it enabled him to realise how builders handled materials—how they cut up the stuff and utilised materials, but as to architects becoming expert joiners or expert metal-workers, that was impossible   It seemed to him that they might take up some of those things as a hobby, and have a smithy or a small furnace and go in for enamels and carry on metal-working to a higher form   It was undesirable to shape all architects exactly in the same mould, in his opinion, they must deal with that question in a general broad way. He understood from the resolution that it was proposed that there should be some sort of school arranged with contractors or builders. In that connection they must remember that builders were ceasing to be builders; they were gradually becoming mere financiers   A builder in the old acceptation of the word was a man that studied, as they wished architects to study, every branch of the building business, but nowadays it was a very rare thing to find a builder that had served his time at the bench as they used to do, and had acquired a knowledge of the minutiæ of the various trades   Under the present contract system—whether it was good or bad, there it was, and it had been brought about by modern circumstances—the custom was to appoint a manager of each department, and to look to the manager of each department to show a profit on that department's working. So they could not rely on the co-operation of the builder in the sense that they used to have it, and he thought he was correct in saying that there were very few builders—unless they remained in the country in quite a small way of business—who could afford to devote the time, or did devote the time, in the course of their apprenticeship to the business of acquiring that technical knowledge which was advocated as so necessary for all architects.   Therefore it seemed to him that what they should do would be to multiply schools like those of the Architectural Association—the various schools might well take that as a basis of their operations—and they should bring the students more into contact with the actual work, and if a man was articled to an architect he should afford the pupil every possible facility of visiting buildings in progress, and possibly in some cases becoming clerk of the works—although he was not quite sure that it was a fair thing to the owners of the buildings that a pupil should be employed as a responsible clerk of the works   He thought, moreover, that they should do something not only to exclude students who had no natural ability for architecture more rigidly than they had done from their schools, but, having got the right type of men in the schools, one of the best things they could do was to take them as much as possible on to buildings in the way he had advocated.

Professor V Nagy (Budapest) said it seemed to him that it was very difficult to talk about a question of this kind from an international point of view, as the conditions of things varied in different countries.   In his opinion an architect ought to be a man of wide technical knowledge, one who was able to construct everything that his fancy conceived, and he must be an artist to give a pleasing form to that which he was able to construct.   The knowledge and requirements of the architect covered such a vast field that they, as professors, knew that it was only possible in a short time or a few years to give an architect the foundation of the theoretical as well as the technical education in his profession   He thought that the resolution which had been proposed by their French friends went too far in many respects   It was like sending a wanderer from home and charging him with so many things that he would be obliged to drop, as it were, necessary things in order that he might be able to go on his way   What he meant was—let them confine themselves to teaching the necessary things, and other things the student could pick up on his way as he went along through life   What he personally felt was that the architect's work was endangered by something else than a lack of exact knowledge of the different crafts   It was the engineer's work which endangered the architect's work.   The progress of technical studies, especially in iron buildings, had, he considered, not only in his own country but all over the world, taken architecture out of the hands of the architects, and the result would be that the architect would no more be the conceiver or the constructor of his ideas, because he could not follow them out.   Therefore, if there was time to be spared on the education of architects, he would rather that it should be spent in acquiring a knowledge of those things which could not be picked up on the road when he was in practice   On the other hand, as regarded the crafts, it was easier to pick them up by practice rather than at a school.   His idea was that two years was far too long to devote to acquiring a technical knowledge of the different crafts.   The architectural student was already overcharged, and a short time, just to get a fundamental knowledge of the different crafts, would be sufficient   He would therefore propose that the resolution read as follows :—" This Congress, considering that the architect, the master of the works, having under his immediate direction workmen and artisans of the most varied bodies of the State, and utilising the services of the most varied industries, has no means of acquiring in each of these trades and in each of these industries the complete knowledge of a specialist, expresses the desire that opportunity should be given to architectural students to acquire in a general but exact manner the technical parts of the various trades and industries of the building trade without claiming to practise those trades and industries. It also expresses the wish that international and continuous relations may be established between these schools "

Professor Lethaby asked Professor Nágy if he would consider two years too long if it was understood that the student was to be instructed in his profession from the highly scientific and engineering point of view That was his (the speaker's) idea of the meaning of the resolution as it stood. The school he had in his mind should not merely concern itself with handicrafts, but should be a technical polytechnic

Professor Nágy said that if the idea was to include theoretical and technical studies then he was quite satisfied

Professor Lethaby said that was his meaning.

Mr Reginald Blomfield, A R A, remarked that such a school as outlined by Professor Lethaby would meet a want which was much felt in England—viz. the want of training in expert building. Professor Nágy had pointed out that there was a tendency towards the engineer taking charge of the work of the architect The right way to meet that was to train the architect to obtain some knowledge of those problems of engineering which at present were handed over too much to the engineer. The resolution seemed to him to deal with that difficulty, because both M. Lesage and Professor Lethaby had made it plain that their idea was that the two years' training should be devoted to those higher problems of building to which he had referred He should therefore support the resolution.

Professor Nágy said that what he understood by craftsmanship was the handling of tools, and therefore he thought two years was too long to devote to such an object He would rather the resolution were carried as he had proposed to amend it, because under it each country could teach what trades it liked England could take up the science of engineering if so desired, but in France perhaps that would not be necessary, because there arch tects were trained in engineering work, and in Austria and Hungary it would simply mean that the students would get a certain training in the material part of their crafts.

M. Lesage En France et ailleurs il y a actuellement des écoles professionnelles très bien organisées pour l'apprentissage des différents métiers, et nous demandons, en France, que les jeunes architectes puissent acquérir une teinture générale de la technique des différents métiers du bâtiment Il me semble que, dans la forme proposée, le vœu est bien conforme à ce qui a été dit ici Ce que nous disons est très précis Nous ne demandons pas de faire de l'architecte un homme manuel, un ouvrier, mais bien qu'il étudie suffisamment la technique des différents métiers, afin qu'il les connaisse le jour où il aura à les surveiller. Ce qui caractérise l'école que nous avons créée en France, c'est précisément que ce n'est pas une école formant des spécialistes, mais bien des hommes ayant une idée générale sur tout ce qui concerne leur future profession Il nous semble qu'un terme de deux ans est conforme à ce qu'on pense être nécessaire pour arriver à cette teinture de la technique du bâtiment. Il ne faut pas rester dans des généralités Il faut préciser dans un vœu. Il faut donc dire que l'architecte ne doit pas devenir un ouvrier, mais qu'il doit avoir des idées des détails de chaque métier employé au bâtiment Nous voulons voir faire de l'architecte non un homme manuel, mais bien un chef, un directeur de travaux

M. Virgil Nágy Je trouve que nous devons nous placer ici au point de vue international On a parlé ici d'écoles spéciales. Je ne sais si, en France, en Angleterre et en Belgique, les programmes de ces écoles comprennent des études grapho-statiques Quoi qu'il en soit, nous ne pouvons pas, dans un congrès international, imposer le programme de tel ou tel pays. Nous devons nous borner à émettre des idées générales. Dans

mon pays les élèves-architectes apprennent la grapho-statique.   Mais
il ne faut pas deux ans pour acquérir des notions générales des différents
métiers.   D'après moi, l'architecte doit aussi avoir quelques connaissances
de l'ingénieur.   C'est pourquoi il faut se borner dans le vœu à émettre
des idées générales

M. Lesage : En France l'enseignement de notre Ecole des Beaux-Arts
est incompatible avec celui de notre École d'Architecture.   En tous cas
j'accepte la nouvelle rédaction proposée par M. Nágy, à condition qu'on
ne précise pas non plus en disant que les notions spéciales doivent
s'acquérir à l'école même

Dr. Cuypers remarked that, in his opinion, instruction in practical
work should be at the beginning of every architect's education, and his
theoretical education would come afterwards

Mr C Walker (Boston, U.S.A.) said that their custom in America
was somewhat different from that of other countries.   He was a director
of the Massachusetts Institute of Technology and a director of the Department of Design of the Museum of Fine Arts, and it was his experience, from
having pupils in his office and in each of those departments, that where
there was marked specialisation in any one thing, the pupil became so
enamoured of that particular thing that it hampered him in his after-
work.   The general education—both theoretical and practical—should
run side by side, and it should always be recognised that the architect
was primarily a man of affairs, and one who planned, he was essentially
a man who planned if he was to be an architect of ability and of large
work, and to control a large number of men   Every attention paid to
small details crippled him, to a certain extent, in the carrying-out of
his large work, and while it was absolutely essential that he, as the chief
builder, should understand the general manipulation and character [of
his material, any special attention paid to that for any length of time
was certainly, in his (the speaker's) opinion, and in the opinion of the
schools that he represented, work which it was not wise to undertake.
They should be carried on correlatively, and special attention should
always be paid to the larger project—viz the handling of men and the
beautifying of the plan   In his office he had had men educated in different
ways, those who were educated in technical perfection were inefficient in
the larger problems, those who were educated in technical perfection of
any kind, whether it was in engineering or in any of the crafts, did not
in their later life become men of affairs—they did not become the leaders
of the profession in America.   Therefore, in his opinion, it was inadvisable
to name any definite period for the instruction of architectural students
in technical matters

Mr H G P Maule said that his knowledge was derived from practical
experience of seeing how much students were capable of taking in.   He
agreed with every word Mr. Blomfield had said in his paper   It seemed
to him that one point had been entirely forgotten in the discussion,
and that was that an architect was always a student—he remained a
student as long as he lived—and if they remembered that, and if they
took into consideration the very few years in which he could be definitely
trained, it seemed to him that they must confine themselves during
those years to a great extent to principles, and not go into a great
mass of detail   They must, he thought, endeavour, during that short
period of training, to instil into the student principles which would guide
him all his life, and by which he could go on improving his education   It
seemed to him that if they bore in mind the principles Mr. Blomfield
had enunciated, and if they also bore in mind the great advantage of
knowing something of the crafts, it only rested with the student or the
young architect to go on adding to and completing his knowledge for
many, many years.   If they attempted to overburden the student in his
early years, they would simply confuse him.   There was no greater danger

in education than confusion, and if they confused a student they ruined him.   Therefore, keeping in mind the international point of view, he would ask them always to remember that they had to train in principle rather than in detail, and if they endeavoured to do that he thought they would raise the whole status of architecture throughout the world— they must teach the student to educate himself by his own initiative and his own observation

Dr CUYPERS (Amsterdam) observed that they wanted to get back to the practical principles of every-day life in regard to the education of the architect.

Professor LETHABY said that, as there seemed to be considerable difference of opinion as regarded details, it occurred to him that the needs of the case would be met if they were to pass a resolution merely agreeing to the principle that architectural education should be founded on the basis of practical construction in the building trades   If some such general proposition could be agreed upon, without entering into details, he thought that would be sufficient

Mr. REGINALD BLOMFIELD said it seemed to him that the proposition of Professor Lethaby that training in architecture should be founded on a training and knowledge of the building crafts was unassailable, and he would be very pleased to support that proposition provided it was understood that that was not supposed to be the whole of the training of an architect.   He thought they would all agree that no man could claim to be a competent architect who had not got more than an amateur knowledge of the building trade.   He was rather inclined to question the view of their American colleague respecting the architect.   They did not consider that the man who would be called a leader in the profession was the ideal to which they should direct the attention of architectural students   They heard very constantly that the architect was an artist—he might be successful or not—they could not control the future   What they wanted was to turn out the best architects, and by the best architect they understood an artist in bricks and mortar and stone and wood in building forms   Before they could arrive at that they must understand those forms, and that knowledge could only be gained by the handling of the tools and the materials   He agreed with what Mr. Maule said, that, after all, what they gave to the student was only the groundwork of his training. They endeavoured to give students the real rudiments of the technique of the work, and the student himself must add to that the transformation of his work into beautiful forms, and get into it some of the quality that they all admired in great architecture   That was the point of view he had endeavoured to put before them in his paper, and he thought that his paper and that of Professor Lethaby should be taken together.   He very rightly insisted on training in what he might call a building sense, and he (Mr Blomfield) wanted it to go still further, and to continue it in the sense of architecture.

THE CHAIRMAN then put the resolution as amended by Professor Nágy, and it was unanimously

> RESOLVED,—*That this Congress, considering that the architect, the master of the works, having under his immediate direction workmen and artisans of the most varied bodies of the State, and utilising the services of the most varied industries, has no means of acquiring in each of these trades and in each of these industries the complete knowledge of a specialist, expresses the desire that the opportunity should be given to architectural students to acquire in a general but exact manner the technical part of the various trades and industries of the building trades without claiming to practise these trades and industries   It also expresses the wish that international and continuous relations may be established between the schools.*

SUBJECT VII.

THE PLANNING AND LAYING-OUT OF STREETS AND OPEN SPACES

Wednesday Evening, 18th July —Grafton Galleries

Chairmen   Sir Wm Emerson (England) and M Ch Buls (Belgium)
Hon. Secretary   Mr. Perkins Pick (England)

---

1 Par M. CH. BULS.

De la Disposition et du Développement des Rues et des Espaces libres dans les Villes.

Le tracé des rues et des places d'une ville est un problème très compliqué à raison des facteurs nombreux dont il y a lieu de tenir compte.

Pour aborder sa solution d'une façon méthodique, il faut d'abord déterminer, d'une façon précise, dans quels termes le problème est posé. S'agit-il :

1 D'UNE VILLE NOUVELLE A FONDER COMME LE FUT ALEXANDRIE D'EGYPTE, ZEEBRUGGE EN BELGIQUE OU CERTAINES VILLES AMÉRICAINES ?

2' D'UN QUARTIER DE VILLE ANCIENNE A TRANSFORMER, POUR SATIS-FAIRE AUX EXIGENCES DE LA VIE MODERNE ?

3' D'UN FAUBOURG NOUVEAU A AJOUTER À UNE CITÉ ANCIENNE, DEVENUE TROP PETITE ?

Les solutions varieront suivant les données de chacun de ces trois problèmes.

Nous croyons pouvoir négliger le premier de ces problèmes qui ne trouve guère d'application en Europe.

§ 1' CRÉATION D'UNE VILLE ENTIÈREMENT NOUVELLE.

Cependant, pour ne pas laisser un blanc sous ce paragraphe, nous exposons le plan de Zeebrugge, qui sera fondé à l'embouchure du Canal reliant Bruges à la mer, et nous citerons les exemples classiques de Washington, de Carlsruhe et de Mannheim, dont les plans sont bien connus.

2° QUARTIER DE VILLE ANCIENNE A TRANSFORMER.

Motifs invoqués   il faut dégager le centre de la cité congestionné par une circulation intensive, lui fournir des dégagements plus larges et plus directs, assainir des ruelles sans air, tirer parti de terrains ayant acquis une trop grande valeur pour servir à des habitations médiocres, mettre le centre d'affaires de la ville en communication avec les gares et les quartiers nouveaux.

Facteurs à considérer . Beauté monumentale ou pittoresque à conserver ; souvenirs historiques, caractère national, traditions civiques à préserver ; exigences d'une circulation facile et rapide, éviter les causes d'accidents et d'insalubrité.

Beaucoup de municipalités sont encore trop disposées à négliger ces facteurs et à se laisser uniquement entraîner par les motifs invoqués en faveur de la modernisation absolue d'une vieille ville. *Causes :* Manque

B B

de goût, d'attachement aux souvenirs du passé , ignorance, cupidité, indifférence.

En général, les villes anciennes sont nées sans plan préconçu Attirés par des facilités de communication au croisement des deux routes, comme à Tournai, au confluent d'une rivière et d'un fleuve, comme à Termonde, des marchands se groupent d'abord autour d'un champ de foire qui devient ensuite un marché permanent. Le lieu est en même temps un site stratégique qui a amené le seigneur de la contrée à y ériger un burg , son intérêt est de protéger les marchands qui le paient et l'approvisionnent

Le grand développement de la cité finit par rendre cette protection insuffisante ; les bourgeois clôturent alors leur ville de solides murailles Les chemins sinueux conduisant au grand marché, où se dressera la maison commune et la cathédrale, pénètrent par les portes et rayonnent autour du centre civique. La population croissant toujours, les secteurs triangulaires entre ces rues se bâtissent et l'on y a accès par des rues annulaires parallèles aux remparts circulaires.

On reconnaît là le plan des vieilles villes qui nous plaisent par leur caractère naturel et rationnel ; il constitue le charme pittoresque de Bruges, Louvain, Gand, Malines.

C'est cette formation spontanée, découlant de la vie même de la cité, qui donne l'aspect d'un organisme vivant au réseau complexe des rues d'une ville ancienne. De là naissent des effets pittoresques, familiers, qui nous séduisent si fort quand nous arrivons d'une ville moderne banalement cristallisée en son plan géométrique. C'est là ce qu'il faut s'efforcer de conserver en conciliant le respect du passé avec les exigences de la vie moderne

Les utilitaires répondront que nous menons un genre de vie absolument différent de celui de nos pères, que pas plus que nous n'avons conservé leurs fraises incommodes et leurs costumes si longs à revêtir, nous ne pouvons continuer à habiter leurs villes Le marché n'est plus un centre d'approvisionnement, les grandes voies de communication s'arrêtent aux gares placées en dehors des remparts transformés en boulevards La population est devenue trop nombreuse pour former encore une famille agrandie, dont tous les membres se connaissent, et pour se réunir au forum et y discuter les intérêts publics Il n'y a plus un centre unique vers lequel doivent rayonner les rues principales. Il est remplacé par des ganglions stations, postes, télégraphes, théâtres, banques, bureaux, parlement, ministères, reliés par des rues qui s'anastomosent entre elles. Nous n'habitons plus le centre affairé et bruyant, il nous faut des tramways et des chemins de fer élevés ou souterrains pour nous conduire chaque soir à notre villa ou pour nous permettre d'aller chercher l'air pur à quelque parc de la périphérie.

Cependant nous ne pensons pas qu'une ville humaine doive être uniquement une usine, combinée mécaniquement pour satisfaire aux seules exigences matérielles de la circulation, aux seuls besoins du commerce, de la finance et de l'administration.

Ce sont là des moyens de vivre, ce n'est pas le but de la vie.

L'existence sans aspiration vers un idéal, sans une recherche de beauté, sans satisfactions intellectuelles désintéressées, mène droit à l'égoisme, à la sécheresse, au spleen et au suicide.

Les administrateurs d'une ville ne sont pas uniquement les directeurs d'une usine où l'on boit, mange, circule en vue de gagner de l'or. Ils ont à se préoccuper, non seulement de la santé physique de leurs administrés, mais encore de leur hygiène morale, sentimentale et intellectuelle.

Et l'un des moyens qu'ils pourront employer pour cela c'est d'éveiller l'amour de la cité en préservant son caractère, en conservant les témoins du passé, évocateurs d'anciennes mœurs, d'époques glorieuses, de souvenirs historiques. La beauté d'une ville étendra son irradiation sur ses habitants. Leurs mœurs se ressentiront du respect pour le passé, du culte admiratif pour ses monuments, et leur inspireront la fierté d'être les citoyens d'une ville admirée et le désir de l'illustrer. L'estime de soi-même, quand elle prend sa source dans une haute idée des devoirs qu'imposent de glorieux ancêtres, incite aux vertus N'était-ce pas ce sentiment qui animait le Romain ?

COMMENT RÉALISER LA CONCILIATION ENTRE LE POINT DE VUE PRATIQUE ET LE POINT DE VUE ESTHÉTIQUE ?

Commençons par déterminer les rues insuffisantes pour les besoins de la circulation, puis les points qui doivent être reliés entre eux par des voies plus directes, ensuite les centres de dispersion de la foule. Traçons un plan schématique de ces desiderata et appliquons-le sur un plan de la ville ancienne Gardons-nous bien de résoudre le problème en perçant des boulevards rectilignes, en remblayant des ravins, en bouleversant l'orographie primitive, en éventrant de vieux quartiers.

Cherchons, au contraire, à élargir les rues sinueuses parallèlement à l'ancien alignement, tirons parti des différences de niveau, des accidents du sol, des rues existantes en reliant celles qui ont à peu près la direction désirée par des tronçons, ne reculons pas devant le tracé d'une courbe pour adoucir une pente, contourner un vieil édifice, ménager une vue sur un groupe pittoresque d'habitations et partout où il restera un coin inutilisé, plantons-y un arbre, un bosquet, un monument décoratif.

3° PLAN D'UN FAUBOURG A ANNEXER À UNE VILLE ANCIENNE.

Ici le programme des exigences à satisfaire sera beaucoup plus complexe. Il faudra d'abord se demander quelle sera la destination du nouveau quartier : commercial, industriel, administratif, universitaire, populaire, bourgeois, aristocratique, mixte ?

Il y aura l eu de tenir compte de son étendue Si elle est considérable il faudra y réserver une place pour des succursales de certains services publics · mairie, bibliothèque, postes, télégraphes, commissariats de police, postes de pompiers, écoles de différents degrés, édifices du culte ; ménager des promenades, des parcs, des places des jeux, un théâtre, des salles de concerts, de conférences

Puis on tracera les courants de circulation Ceux qui partent du noyau central devront être prolongés pour aboutir à un village voisin, à un pont, un port, un lieu de villégiature, de récréation champêtre.

Si quelque vieille route traverse le quartier projeté, conservons en le plus possible les méandres. Cette ancienne chaussée, bordée d'arbres, constituera l'épine dorsale du nouveau faubourg. Adaptons ensuite ce premier schéma à la topographie des lieux, en tenant compte des dénivellations qui peuvent obliger à faire des déblais, des remblais ou des voies abordant les hauteurs par la moindre pente.

Gardons-nous du procédé trop commode qui consiste à créer une vaste plaine artificielle dans laquelle nous tracerons un plan rectangulaire comme dans l'île de Manhattan à New-York, ou un plan rectangulaire semé d'étoiles, comme à Washington , ou un plan formé d'une série de carrés inscrits les uns dans les autres et coupés de diagonales, comme à Henrichemont , ou un plan en forme de toile d'araignée, comme à Carlsruhe. Ces conceptions artificielles peuvent donner des plans fort beaux sur le papier, mais ils ne correspondent à aucune réalité, à aucun besoin, ils sont morts-nés

Quartier Commercial.—A part deux ou trois artères de grande communication assez larges pour recevoir des lignes de tramways, les rues ne devront pas avoir une largeur exagérée, l'expérience ayant démontré que les rues étroites sont plus favorables aux magasins et plus fréquentées par les acheteurs. Eviter la direction nord-sud.

Quartier Industriel.—Orienté de manière que les vents dominants ne chassent pas la fumée vers les quartiers d'habitation. Communications faciles par rail avec la gare de marchandises, le canal, le port, suivant le cas.

Réserver des blocs de terrains à bon marché, pour habitations ouvrières, pour écoles primaires et places de jeux.

Quartier Administratif —En atténuer la froideur par des plantations, des squares fleuris.

Quartier Universitaire.—Comme à Strasbourg, disposer les instituts dans un parc, les entourer d'air et de lumière, éloigner tout trafic bruyant.

Quartier Populaire.—Traversé par une large voie à tramway pouvant conduire rapidement les ouvriers à leur travail. Lotir les terrains de façon à faciliter la construction de maisons à bon marché, répartir des places de jeux dans le quartier, et des emplacements pour jardins d'enfants et pour écoles, clubs-ouvriers, bibliothèques populaires, bains publics, gymnase, soigner spécialement la salubrité publique

Quartier Bourgeois.—A côté d'une grande voie de circulation, ménager des rues sinueuses avec des lots de terrains de prix moyen pour maisons isolées, précédées ou entourées d'un jardinet ; squares, parc avec kiosque pour musique.

Quartier Aristocratique —Avenues avec allées de cavaliers, bordées d'arbres, entourant des blocs assez vastes pour y créer des parcs.

On peut, si l'étendue est suffisante, réunir ces différents quartiers dans un faubourg mixte. Ce sera alors dans les secteurs compris entre les grandes voies de communication qu'on tracera des rues secondaires qui répondront aux exigences indiquées plus haut.

Moyens de réalisation —Mais si l'on veut conserver leurs avantages à ces divers quartiers, il faudra frapper une partie de ces terrains d'une servitude de non-bâtisse pour assurer la conservation des jardins, des jardinets

Ce résultat ne peut être obtenu et on ne fera du nouveau quartier une œuvre d'art qu'à la condition que la commune acquière elle-même le terrain et impose aux acheteurs les servitudes qui doivent assurer la conservation du caractère qu'elle a entendu lui donner

L'entreprise peut aussi être concédée à une société immobilière qui se chargera de l'opération moyennant l'observation des conditions imposées par la commune pour obtenir le résultat désiré.

Un troisième moyen a été employé, à Bruxelles, pour la création du quartier du Nord-Est

Après avoir arrêté le plan de ce quartier et déterminé les servitudes décoratives dont il serait frappé, la ville a laissé le choix aux propriétaires des terrains ou d'être expropriés, ou de payer la plus-value résultant des travaux projetés et de partager ainsi avec la ville les risques de l'opération immobilière

En résumé, la création de quartiers nouveaux ne doit pas être livrée aux hasards de la spéculation privée, mais être conçue, par les autorités municipales, comme une œuvre sociale, scientifique et esthétique.

Nous avons indiqué les principes généraux qui doivent présider au tracé du plan des quartiers nouveaux, examinons maintenant les détails de son exécution.

Le cas ordinaire en Europe est celui d'une ville primitivement entourée de remparts qui brise sa ceinture trop étroite pour déborder au dehors.

A Bruxelles à Anvers, à Louvain, à Bruges cela a permis de ceindre ces villes de larges boulevards plantés d'arbres

Mais Bruxelles fournit un excellent exemple de la nécessité impérieuse de l'intervention officielle pour la préservation des intérêts public et des beautés naturelles dans les parties suburbaines d'une grande agglomération La ville n'ayant pu obtenir l'annexion à son territoire des communes rurale, les faubourgs furent construits sans aucun souci de beauté, sans prévoyance même au point de vue de la viabilité ; on n'y poursuivit que la mise en valeur des terrains à bâtir. Aussi le résultat fut déplorable ; ces faubourgs forment une masse incohérente agglomérée aux flancs de la capitale.

Le mal a heureusement été enrayé par l'initiative du Roi Léopold II ; grâce à lui l'agglomération bruxelloise s'est entourée de la deuxième ceinture du boulevard circulaire, le long duquel on a eu soin de ménager des parcs qui constituent des oasis de verdure au milieu de la marée montante des maisons.

C'est un plan analogue que la ville de Vienne se propose de réaliser dans des proportions plus grandioses.

FORME DES RUES.

En vertu de principes établis précédemment, nous aurons à tracer un quartier traversé par quelques grandes artères de circulation intense ; elles limiteront des îlots parcourus par un réseau de veines qui conduiront aux habitations.

Ces artères et ces veines seront-elles droites, courbes, sinueuses ou brisées, d'égale largeur ou lenticulaires ?

Les artistes et les esthètes ont beaucoup médit des rues droites, et non sans raison, à cause de l'abus qu'on en a fait. On ne saurait cependant les bannir d'une ville moderne.

Une rue droite ne se voit pas. La fuite perspective des façades en confond toutes les lignes. Si elle est trop longue, l'extrémité se perd dans la brume de l'éloignement. Une demi-heure à l'avance le piéton aperçoit son point d'arrivée et le trajet est ennuyeux par son uniformité. Les trombes de neige, de pluie, de poussière n'y trouvent pas d'obstacles et assaillent le passant. Si la rue est dans la direction Nord-Sud, elle n'a pas un coté ombré au moment le plus chaud de la journée.

Cependant la rue droite a quelques avantages ; elle est le plus court chemin entre deux points ; elle facilite la circulation des voitures et l'établissement de tramways ; dans certains cas elle est l'élément indispensable d'un quartier monumental

Bannir absolument les rues droites dans une ville moderne serait donc exagéré, comme l'est toute solution absolue

Il faut concilier les exigences de la circulation et de la beauté, en conservant les avantages de la ligne droite, tout en corrigeant son uniformité, soit en limitant sa longueur, soit en variant sa largeur La longueur peut être limitée par un détour de la rue, par un monument : église, palais, arc de triomphe, fontaine monumentale ou square planté.

Toute construction devra présenter une silhouette qui se lise clairement à distance.

A quel point de la rue rectiligne faut-il placer cet écran interrupteur ?

On ne peut pas le déterminer par un rapport entre la largeur de la rue et sa longueur ; c'est plutôt la limite de la vue normale qui doit servir de guide.

Des observations faites dans deux rues trop longues de Bruxelles—la rue Royale terminée par l'église Ste-Marie, la rue de la Loi fermée par l'Arc du Septantenaire—me font estimer que dans ces rues le monument aurait dû être placé à environ 1000 mètres de l'œil du spectateur stationnant à leur commencement

Si on se décide à interrompre la longueur d'une avenue par un square, il faut se garder de la faute commise au rond-point de l'avenue Louise à Bruxelles. Sa forme circulaire est une sérieuse entrave à la circulation des voitures. Elle peut être évitée en donnant au square une forme ovoïde allongée.

L'uniformité fatigante d'une avenue peut encore être atténuée en ne maintenant pas un parallélisme absolu entre l'alignement des façades

opposées, et en y creùsant, de distance en distance, des concavités   Elles
pourraient être alternantes ou opposées, et l'espace ainsi gagné serait orné
de parterres   Mais ce système ne peut être employé que dans des avenues
à maisons fermées , dans une rue commerçante les magasins placé dans la
partie concave auraient une moindre valeur.

La solution la plus heureuse sera toujours de dévier une rue très longue
de la droite inflexible, et il est très rare que quelque disposition locale
n'en offre le prétexte.   Nous aimons mieux deviner qu'une rue continue
au delà d'une inflexion que de la voir trop brusquement arrêtée par un
monument que l'on aperçoit longtemps à l'avance.   Ce monument lui-
même aurait produit un plus grand effet si brusquement nous nous étions
trouvé devant lui à bonne distance, soit trois fois sa hauteur.

Les rues sinueuses des vieilles villes ont un charme qui a été signalé
plus d'une fois   Dans notre *Esthétique des Villes* nous avons indiqué
comment le hasard a merveilleusement disposé les habitations le long de
la vieille chaussée serpentante qui est devenue le Marché aux Herbes et la
rue de la Madeleine à Bruxelles.   Grâce à ses sinuosités les maisons ne se
cachent pas dans les perspectives effacées de la ligne droite, des pans de
façades apparaissent successivement.   A mesure que la pente se gravit,
l'œil perçoit des blocs superposés, et les déchiquetures des toits découpent
le ciel en zigzags étranges   Le même effet pittoresque peut s'observer à
Bruges, rue des Pierres ; à Lubeck, Breitstrasse.

Le dessinateur d'un plan de ville ne peut négliger ces enseignements.
Seulement, s'il courbe une rue, il doit justifier cette fantaisie par la nécessité
d'adoucir une pente, le désir de respecter un vieil édifice, l'obligation de
joindre deux rues qui ne sont pas dans le même axe, mais dans la même
direction désirée.

Car un effet pittoresque artificiel manquera de naturel et ne satisfera
pas notre sens esthétique.   Les irrégularités des rues anciennes ne sont
pas le résultat d'une pure fantaisie, mais découlent de nécessités pratiques,
de l'existence d'anciens chemins, de la constitution orographique du sol,
de l'obligation de multiplier les rues dans une enceinte étroite limitée par
les remparts.

Ce sont ces causes, obscures mais réelles, qui ont doté les rues anciennes
d'une individualité que nous ne parvenons pas à donner à des rues modernes,
dont l'unique destination est de mettre en valeur des lots de terrains.

D'autres fois, une fausse conception de l'esthétique d'un plan nous
a fait dessiner un ensemble symétrique de rues qui n'est appréciable que
vu à vol d'oiseau, mais qui laisse absolument insensible le promeneur qui y
circule.   Pour éviter cette faute, on a établi une maquette en relief du
quartier projeté ; photographiée convenablement, elle peut donner une
idée de l'effet que produira son exécution.

INTERSECTION DES RUES.

Le croisement des rues est une question qui est une transition naturelle
de la rue à la place publique dont l'origine est souvent la rencontre de
plusieurs voies de communication

Il n'y a pas de plus mauvaise solution que la convergence d'un grand
nombre de rues vers un point commun, comme à la Place de l'Etoile à Paris,
à la Place Victor-Emmanuel à Turin.   M. Camillo Sitte a condamné
avec d'excellents arguments ce système aussi peu pratique qu'anti-
esthétique

Il faut, au contraire, chercher à répartir la circulation de manière à
éviter la création de carrefours où les véhicules sont exposés à se heurter
et les piétons à être écrasés.

Si paradoxal que cela paraisse, M. Sitte a démontré qu'il vaut mieux
que deux rues ne se traversent pas en croix, car ce système présente 54

chances de rencontre des voitures, avec 12 intersections de trajectoires.
Des déviations sinueuses de ces rues permettent d'éviter ces inconvénients
et fournissent en même temps l'occasion de tirer parti de la beauté d'une
rue courbe.

Profil en Longueur et en Largeur des Rues, leur Nivellement, Établissement de leur Sol, Hauteur relative des Maisons

L'étude de ces questions complexes nous entraînerait dans trop de
détails. Nous croyons d'autant plus inutile de la traiter ici que M. J
Stubben l'a magistralement exposée dans son beau livre *Der Stadtebau*,
publié dans le *Handbuch der Architektur*, Darmstadt 1890, pp. 77 et
suivantes

Espaces libres dans les Villes

Les places publiques des villes anciennes avaient deux destinations
le forum et le marché. Nettement séparés dans l'antiquité, ils furent
souvent confondus dans le nord, au moyen âge
Aristote (Politique, L. IV C. XI 2) recommande que la place de la
Liberté ne soit jamais souillée de marchandises et soit interdite aux artisans,
aux laboureurs et à tout autre individu de cette classe.
Le marché doit être établi loin de cette place et bien séparé d'elle ;
il sera d'un accès facile à tous les transports venant de la mer ou de l'intérieur du pays
Dans le Nord de l'Europe, au contraire, sauf le parvis devant l'église,
la place principale devant l'hôtel de ville était le grand marché. Toutes
les anciennes places de Bruxelles conservent encore dans leur nom le
souvenir de leur destination spéciale : marché au bétail, marché aux
chevaux, marché au bois, marché aux porcs, marché au fromage, marché
aux peaux, marché aux herbes, marché aux poulets
Les villes modernes présentent une bien plus grande variété de places,
si bien qu'on a pu les classer sous quatre rubriques :
1.—Place de circulation.
2 —Places utiles { a —Marchés. b.—Garages
3.—Places ornées.
4.—Places monumentales

1° *Place de Circulation.*

On est amené à créer ces sortes de places quand on fait converger un
grand nombre de rues vers un même point, comme à Paris, où douze rues
se dirigent vers l'Arc de l'Etoile.
Nous avons déjà condamné ce système au point de vue de la facilité de
la circulation, et malgré l'autorité d'un homme aussi compétent que M. J
Stubben (*Der Stadtebau*, p 147) nous nous rallions absolument à la critique
de M C Sitte (*Der Stadtebau*, p 103). 'Sur le papier une telle place en
impose sans doute par sa belle régularité, mais quel est son effet réel ?
La possibilité de voir des perspectives infinies de rues que les anciens ont
su éviter avec art est élevée ici à son maximum   Le point central de la
circulation est en même temps le lieu d'intersection de tous les rayons
visuels.'
De sorte que si l'on veut jouir de ce spectacle, en pivotant sur ses
talons, on risque fort d'être écrasé
Personne ne nie que la perspective montante des Champs-Elysées se
termine admirablement par l'Arc de Triomphe de l'Etoile, mais on recon-

naîtra en même temps que les douze rues rayonnantes ne contribuent en rien à sa beauté.

Cependant au centre d'une ville on ne peut toujours éviter que quatre ou cinq rues convergent vers une même place En ce cas, au lieu de les diriger vers un point central, il vaut mieux allonger la place en ellipse et les faire aboutir à ses deux foyers afin de diviser la circulation.

A la place de Brouckère, à Bruxelles, par exemple, le boulevard de la Senne et le boulevard du Nord s'engagent latéralement à la place ; le boulevard Anspach est dans l'axe de celle-ci, et le Fossé aux Loups en traverse un des petits côtés On peut constater que la circulation des trams et des voitures y est facile malgré le croisement. Les rues secondaires doivent être traitées comme les affluents d'un fleuve et y verser leur circulation dans le sens du courant principal. C'est ordinairement le désir de produire un ensemble décoratif sans le souci des exigences pratiques qui a amené l'ingénieur à créer les places, belles mais incommodes, de même que, trop souvent, les architectes ne rêvent que de construire une superbe façade sans s'inquiéter de la commodité des habitants du palais.

Si à la place de Brouckère un bon résultat a été obtenu, il est probable qu'il n'en faut pas faire de mérite à l'auteur du plan. Sans la nécessité de ne pas bâtir sur le lit voûté de la Senne il est probable que, comme un empereur de Russie, l'ingénieur aurait tracé une ligne droite entre la gare du Nord et la gare du Midi, qu'il s'agissait d'unir par un boulevard central. Cela démontre une fois de plus que l'obligation de tenir compte de la topographie naturelle du lieu produit une solution esthétique.

2° *Places utiles.*—(a) *Marchés.*

Les marchés ayant une autre destination que les places de circulation, la partie centrale y est réservée à l'étalage des denrées mises en vente

Quoique les marchés aient perdu leur ancienne importance parce que les denrées alimentaires se vendent dans des magasins à portée des consommateurs ou sont livrées à domicile, on en trouve beaucoup encore fort achalandés.

A Bruxelles, à la Grand' Place, se tient tous les jours un marché matinal (Vroeg markt) très pittoresque, surtout en hiver, quand il s'étale sous la clarté lunaire des lampes électriques, dans le cadre grandiose des maisons de gildes Les légumes qu'on y vend, destinés à alimenter les halles et les magasins, doivent avoir disparu à 8 heures du matin. Un stationnement de voitures et un petit marché aux fleurs y prennent ensuite place ; une ligne diagonale de circulation principale y est alors laissé libre. La Grand' Place sert aussi en été, le soir, à des concerts populaires, aux fêtes nationales, à des déploiements de cortèges. Mais le Bourgmestre n'y proclame plus, à son de trompe, de la bretèche de l'Hôtel de Ville, les arrêtés communaux. Ceux-ci sont affichés dans toute la ville.

Signalons que sur cette place presque quadrangulaire, les rues aboutissent en turbine à chaque angle, de façon que le spectateur qui y arrive n'a pas le vide d'une rue opposée devant lui, mais une partie du cadre de la place ; disposition à recommander pour toutes les places encadrées. Le riche cadre de la place célèbre est formé de l'Hôtel de Ville, de la Maison du Roi, des anciennes maisons de corporations. Il est jalousement préservé de toute mutilation aux frais de la ville.

Bruxelles, malgré plusieurs marchés en plein vent toujours fort fréquentés, a cependant sacrifié à la tendance moderne d'abriter les marchés. La ville a construit dans ces conditions un marché aux poissons, une boucherie, deux halles centrales. Mais à raison de la faveur dont jouissent les marchés découverts, une de ces halles a été transformée en café-concert l'été, en skating l'hiver.

Les marchés du Grand Sablon et le Vieux Marché aux Grains ont un terre-plein central encadré d'arbres et bordé de quatre rues.

C'est la seule disposition qui nous paraisse à préconiser pour les marchés qui durent toute la journée.

Les foires, les kermesses, les concours de bétail, les marchés aux chevaux, exigent de vastes emplacements encadrés d'arbres, et sont généralement placés le long d'un boulevard.

Les parades, les exercices militaires et gymnastiques réclament la même disposition de place. Cette plaine est ordinairement située au confins de la ville.

(b) *Garages.*

Nous comprenons parmi les places de garages, celles qui s'étendent aux abords des stations de chemin de fer pour le stationnement des fiacres, automobiles et omnibus. Pour diviser la circulation on y sème souvent des squares, des fontaines, des statues, et on s'efforce d'impressionner favourablement le voyageur par une entrée de ville majestueuse.

Nous comprenons encore dans cette catégorie les lieux de stationnement des fiacres disséminés en ville Les auteurs de places oublient souvent de les prévoir, et c'est un tort. Car les autorités communales ont quelqu fois beaucoup de peine à trouver des emplacements suffisants qui ne soient pas incommodes pour les habitants voisins.

Il faut toujours, à cet endroit, disposer des moyens énergiques de lavage, pour éviter les mauvaises odeurs, garantir la salubrité publique. Un dallage imperméable qui ne permette pas la contamination du sol est à recommander

3° *Places ornées*

Les places ornées de plantations furent inventées par les Anglais, quand la disparition graduelle des jardins privés à l'intérieur des villes leur firent sentir la nécessité de reconstituer des réserves d'air en faveur de l'hygiène publique.

Nous attribuerons encore leur création à l'amour des arbres bien plus développé chez les peuples du Nord que chez les méridionaux.

Cependant les villes provençales possèdent généralement un *cours* ombragé de vieux platanes, et dans les villes espagnoles la population va, au coucher du soleil, se promener à *l'alameda*, plantée de peupliers, comme l'indique son nom.

Les *corso* où flânent les Italiens sont à l'intérieur de Rome, de Palerme, de Naples, et sans plantations. Il est vrai que leurs belles villas (Borghèse, Flora, Reale) leur offrent une compensation.

Les *squares* anglais ont encore souvent pour objectif de permettre la construction d'un quartier paisible en dehors de la circulation fiévreuse de la Métropole D'ordinaire ces squares ne sont accessibles qu'aux habitants du pourtour qui possèdent la clef de la porte. D'autre fois, ils sont placés au centre d'un bloc bâti et servent de jardin commun à ses occupants Les squares, malgré leur nom, outre carrés, peuvent être circulaires, ovales, polygonaux, rectangulaires, semi-circulaires, triangulaires, ornés de bassins, de fontaines, de monuments, d'exèdres, de nymphées, de termes; la plus grande fantaisie y peut être déployée puisqu'en dehors de leurs bienfaits hygiéniques, ils n'ont qu'une destination d'agrément Il appartient à l'architecte de la ville de tirer un heureux parti des terrains disponibles et de se garder d'une uniformité monotone dans son plan (voir Stübben, *Stadtebau,* p. 439).

4° *Places monumentales.*

Nous ne comprendrons pas sous cette rubrique des places devenues monumentales, comme notre forum communal de Bruxelles, comme la place de la Signoria de Florence, comme l'Altstadtmarkt de Braunschweig,

parce que les citadins, par orgueil civique, y ont successivement concentré
l'église, l'hôtel de ville, des maisons de corporation, un corps de garde.

Nous donnerons ce nom à des places conçues d'un jet pour obtenir
un ensemble monumental, comme la Place Royale à Bruxelles, la Place
de la Concorde à Paris, la Belle-Alliance Platz à Berlin, le Capitole et la
Piazza del Popolo à Rome, la Place Stanislas à Nancy.   Nous y joindrons
aussi les parvis, en étendant toutefois cette appellation à toute place
s'étendant au devant d'un édifice, qu'il soit civil ou religieux

Ce sont donc des places de luxe et d'apparat comme quelques Américains, admirateurs des Forums européens, voudraient en créer, sous le
nom de centres civiques, à New-York, Boston, Chicago, San Francisco,
afin d'atténuer un peu la laideur et la mortelle monotonie de leurs villes

PROPORTIONS DES PLACES

Le premier problème dont ait à se préoccuper l'architecte d'une pareille
place, c'est de déterminer une proportion harmonieuse entre les dimensions
de la place et la hauteur des maisons qui doivent l'encadrer.   Si la place
est trop grande par rapport aux édifices, ceux-ci perdent leur importance,
si elle est trop petite, on ne peut se placer à une distance convenable pour
les admire .

On admet généralement que les règles établies par H. Maertens (*Der
Optische Massstab*, Berlin 1884), n'ont pas été contredites

Placé à une distance égale à la hauteur de l'édifice, le spectateur en
distinguera les détails et il le verra sous un angle de 45°,

Placé à une distance égale à deux fois la hauteur, le spectateur embras-
sera l'ensemble de l'édifice et le verra sous un angle de 27°,

Placé à une distance égale à trois fois la hauteur, le spectateur ne
distinguera plus les détails, apercevra les contours de l'édifice unis aux
constructions voisines, et le verra sous un angle de 18°,

Placé à une distance égale à quatre ou cinq fois la hauteur de l'édifice,
le spectateur n'apercevra plus qu'une silhouette pittoresque.

FORMES DES PLACES

Le plus souvent elles sont rectangulaires et la proportion entre les
petits et les longs côtés est comme 1 · 3.   Pourtant il est des places carrées
qui ne font pas mauvais effet (Grand' Place à Furnes) ; d'autre part une
place trop longue, comme la Place Navone à Rome et la Place de Meir à
Anvers, devient en réalité une rue.

La Place St.-Marc à Venise montre qu'une forme trapézoïdale n'est
pas déplaisante.   Il faut cependant tenir compte du campanile et des
trois mâts qui remplissent le vide du côté le plus large

La Place St.-Johannis, à Copenhague, fait admettre une forme trian-
gulaire, grâce à la bonne disposition du square entourant l'église

Les places circulaires sont trop régulières et trop géométriques, elles
nous laissent froids   Le Bernin, pour atténuer ce mauvais effet, a donné
à la Place St.-Pierre à Rome la forme d'une ellipse dont le grand axe est
parallèle à la façade de l'église.   Nous inclinons à croire que si le grand axe
de l'ovale avait continué celui du dôme, l'effet eût été meilleur, le regard
du spectateur aurait été mieux amené vers le temple, et, comme l'extrémité de l'ellipse aurait été plus éloignée de l'église, le spectateur
aurait aperçu le pied du tambour du dome, qui disparaît derrière le
fronton de la façade

Deux demi-cercles combinés avec deux côtés droits et des rampes
plantées d'arbres, comme à la Place du Peuple à Rome, constituent un bel
ensemble décoratif.

Une place ovale, comme la Place de la Croisée à Verviers, est d'un effet agréable et n'a pas les défauts du cercle, tant au point de vue de la circulation que de l'aspect monumental

La place octogonale est aussi peu à recommander que la place circulaire et pour les mêmes motifs.

Encadrement des Places

Tous les esthètes qui se sont occupés du décor des villes réclament l'encadrement des places   Ce système était appliqué aux forums antiques Au moyen âge on obtenait ce résultat en faisant aboutir les rues d'accès aux grand'places en bras de turbine.

En Italie, et lorsque dans le Nord on adopta le style italien, ce fut à l'aide d'arcades qu'on dissimula les ouvertures qui interrompaient le cadre de la place.   Citons les exemples suivants : à Vérone, le cadre de la Place des Signori est complété par des portes à une arcade , à Nancy, la célèbre Place Stanislas montre le débouché des rues dissimulé par les belles grilles de Lamour, deux fontaines dans les angles et une rue coupée par la Porte Royale en forme d'arc triomphal , à Bruxelles, Place Royale, les quatre ouvertures angulaires sont formées par une arcade surmontée d'une balustrade et percée de trois portes

Ces exemples sont à recommander , il y a lieu de les imiter sous peine de faire perdre à une place monumentale son caractère d'ensemble

L'objection que ces arcades forment obstacle à la circulation ne tient pas devant le principe déjà énoncé plus haut à propos du tracé des rues il faut répartir convenablement la circulation afin de ne pas en faire croiser les lignes sur une place.   A la Place Royale de Bruxelles ce résultat pourrait facilement être obtenu

Groupement des Places

Le groupement de deux ou trois places d'inégale grandeur est très fréquent dans les villes anciennes, soit qu'on ait voulu séparer deux places de destination différente : le marché et le parvis, comme à Ypres , soit qu'on ait voulu faciliter la circulation en la divisant; soit qu'on ait voulu obtenir le maximum d'effet des édifices   Dans ce système chaque façade a sa place, chaque place son édifice, comme à la Piazza et à la Piazzetta de St -Marc, à Venise   On connaît l'admirable combinaison des trois places qui forment à Florence la Place de la Signoria.   Des groupements analogues se rencontrent à Brunswick, à Lubeck et à Brême

Nous pourrions nous étendre sur la nécessité de respecter le cadre resserré des vieilles églises gothiques et le caractère fermé des anciennes places, mais je pense que ce rapport ne doit pas être consacré à la conservation des monuments anciens , son objet principal est de fixer les principes à la fois pratiques et esthétiques à suivre pour la construction de quartiers nouveaux

Si nous avons cité tant d'exemples anciens, c'est surtout pour attirer l'attention sur leur beauté, souvent obtenue inconsciemment par leurs auteurs, et pour engager les dessinateurs de plans à s'en inspirer.

Décor des Places

Le décor des places monumentales est souvent conçu d'une façon symétrique à l'imitation de certaines places de Rome, ou de la Place de la Concorde à Paris   Cette dernière est l'une des plus belles du monde, quoiqu'elle manque de cadre et que les dimensions en soient telles que l'ensemble décoratif n'en peut être embrassé en une fois.

Cependant on peut y constater que la disposition des principaux monuments l'obélisque et les deux fontaines sur le grand axe de la place, rétrécis par les terre-pleins clôturés de balustrades et ornées des statues des quatre grandes villes de France, entrave sérieusement la circulation intense qui se fait, à certaines heures, entre l'Avenue des Champs-Elysées et la Rue de Rivoli et la Rue Royale Si ces éléments décoratifs avaient été reportés vers le jardin des Tuileries, l'effet n'aurait pas été moindre, la circulation eût été rendue plus facile et la symétrie n'en aurait pas été trop troublée.

La symétrie absolue est le moyen le plus banal et le plus commode d'obtenir du succès auprès de la foule insensible aux délicatesses de l'art.

La même observation s'applique à l'absurde manie moderne de placer toujours les statues au centre des places. Les anciens les disposaient en dehors des courants de circulation, laissaient le centre des places libre et plaçaient les monuments aux points morts

Nivellement des Places

Ici encore inspirons-nous de l'exemple des anciens. Ils donnaient généralement à leurs places un nivellement concave, alors que nous le rendons convexe. Voyez le Forum romanum, le marché de Furnes, le Römerberg à Fran fort, la Place St.-Pierre à Rome, le Mercato Vecchio à Sienne, etc On constate à ces places qu'au point de vue perspectif les lignes verticales se soudent plus normalement à une pente s'élevant vers elles qu'au profil convexe d'une place. Le profil convexe enterre la base des maisons, le rofil concave leur donne de l'élancement et une base. Au point de vue pratique la forme en cuvette des places favorise l'écoulement des eaux de pluie

Conclusion

Les principes que nous venons d'exposer découlent de la recherche des moyens pratiques qui peuvent rendre une ville moderne commode et hygiénique et la doter d'une beauté qui en fasse un séjour agréable. Une ville ne doit pas seulement être un entrepôt commercial et une usine industrielle, mais aussi un *home* humain

Depuis que les villes ne sont plus formées par la lente alluvion des siècles, elles ont perdu leur charme pittoresque et leur caractère national. Au travail inconscient de l'ancien constructeur doit se substituer l'œuvre consciente du constructeur mod rne.

La mission de nos architectes de villes doit donc être de les parer d'une beauté nouvelle dont les éléments seront fournis par les besoins d'une circulation intense, d'une vie saine, par des principes esthétiques dérivés de l'étude des lois de la jouissance artistique.

Résumé —7ᵐᵉ Question —Rues

Quand on veut établir les règles à suivre pour la création de rues et de places, il faut envisager les trois hypothèses suivantes :

1º *Ville nouvelle a créer de toutes pièces* . Cas rare en Europe, exemple de Zeebrugge en Belgique ;

2' *Quartier de ville ancienne à transformer en quartier moderne* : Il faut respecter l'aspect pittoresque du quartier, conserver les monuments historiques, tout en cherchant à donner satisfaction aux besoins modernes ;

3º *Faubourg nouveau à ajouter à une ville ancienne* . Etablir le schéma des principales directions de la circulation, l'adapter à la topographie du lieu, déterminer le caractère du quartier, suivant qu'il est destiné à être commercial, industriel, administratif, universitaire, populaire, bourgeois, aristocratique.   Servitudes à établir pour lui conserver le caractère qu'on a entendu lui donner.   Expropriation par zones ou participation des propriétaires de terrains dans les frais d'aménagement.

Formes des rues.—Artères principales droites ou presque droites, rues secondaires sinueuses.

Les rues droites ne doivent pas être trop longues ; tous les mille mètres elles doivent être déviées ou se terminer par un monument.   Les squares disposés dans ces rues ne doivent pas être ronds mais ovales.   On peut encore les varier en ne donnant pas une largeur uniforme à toute la rue.

Intersection des rues.—Ne pas faire converger la circulation au même point, la répartir au contraire dans toute la ville   Eviter l'intersection en croix.

Espaces libres.—Dans l'antiquité les places publiques étaient le forum, centre politique, et le marché, centre commercial.   Dans le Nord, au moyen âge, il y avait le parvis devant l'église et le grand marché devant l'hôtel de ville

1 *Les places de circulation*—Les places étoilées à condamner ; elles amènent l'encombrement dans la circulation et forment un cadre trop déchiqueté.   Les rues doivent déboucher dans les angles de la place.

2. *Marches*—Le centre de la place doit être dégagé, les rues peu nombreuses doivent y aboutir en bras de turbine

3. *Garages.*—Places devant les gares, la circulation doit y être divisée par des squares, des fontaines, des statues ; vers la ville ménager une entrée monumentale.   En ville réserver des lieux de stationnement pour les fiacres.

4. *Places ornées*—Squares plantés d'arbres.   Ils peuvent affecter toutes les formes.

5. *Places monumentales.*—Places créées pour produire un effet d'apparat.

A. Proportions des places.   Rapport entre la hauteur des maisons et les dimensions de la place   Règles établies par M. H. Maertens.

B. Forme des places   rectangulaires dans la proportion comme 1 : 3, trapézoïdales, triangulaires.   Formes circulaires et octogonales condamnées.   Forme ovale admissible.

C. Encadrement des places à recommander, en dissimuler les ouvertures par des grilles, des arcades, des débouchés en bras de turbine.

D. Groupement des places, produit un effet pittoresque.   Ces places peuvent entourer un édifice

E. Décor des places   Quelquéfois symétrique, mais en général l'asymétrie est préférable   Il vaut mieux ne pas placer les statues, les fontaines au centre de la place

F. Nivellement des places   La surface concave doit être préférée pour des motifs esthétiques et pratiques.

Conclusion générale

Les constructeurs de villes, administrateurs et architectes doivent s'inspirer du beau vers de Térence :

Homo sum   humani nihil a me alienum puto.
Je suis homme, et rien d'humain ne m'est indifférent

2 Par Eugène Hénard, Architecte diplômé par le Gouvernement, Membre de la Société Centrale des Architectes à Paris

La facilité des échanges, la rapidité des communications, et, par suite, le développement méthodique d'un réseau commode de voies publiques, comptent parmi les facteurs les plus importants de la prospérité d'une grande ville D'un autre côté, la création de grands parcs ou de jardins pouvant servir au repos ou à la promenade en plein air, contribue de la manière la plus efficace au bien-être et à la santé de tous les habitants

En outre, la bonne disposition de ces éléments a une influence décisive sur la beauté et le charme des perspectives urbaines.

Malheureusement, les tendances de la spéculation moderne et les intérêts privés des propriétaires de terrains, sont en contradiction constante avec le maintien des espaces libres existant déjà, et, à plus forte raison, avec la création de nouveaux parcs ou jardins de surface suffisante. De plus, la disposition générale des villes, qui est l'œuvre de nos ancêtres, n'est plus en rapport avec les nécessités de la circulation moderne et rend très difficile l'amélioration de la voirie Je parle ici des villes ayant déjà de longues années d'existence, comme nos vieilles cités d'Europe, et non de villes créées de toutes pièces comme on en trouve dans les pays neufs Toute grande ville, en effet, commence par être une simple bourgade, un modeste village, et ce n'est que par un accroissement très lent qu'elle augmente d'abord sa surface, puis, si sa position géographique est favorable, si son commerce est florissant, si son rôle politique prend de l'influence, son mouvement d'expansion se précipite, sa force d'attraction augmente avec sa masse ; les habitants affluent de toute part, les maisons se construisent de plus en plus nombreuses, et la largeur des rues primitives devient dès lors insuffisante. Il en résulte que la partie centrale des grandes villes, qui devrait être la plus dégagée, la mieux desservie par le réseau des voies publiques, est toujours la partie la plus tassée, la plus compacte de la cité, mais comme c'est cette partie qui contient les monuments les plus anciens de son histoire, monuments qu'il faut à tout prix conserver et respecter, l'élargissement des anciennes voies, l'ouverture des voies nouvelles, la création de nouveaux parcs, soulèvent des problèmes très délicats que les municipalités ne résolvent pas toujours conformément aux règles d'une bonne esthétique, d'une bonne hygiène, et d'une bonne circulation C'est donc au triple point de vue de la facilité des communications, de la santé des habitants et de la beauté des aspects que nous allons essayer de dégager les principes essentiels qui doivent guider, de nos jours, les travaux édilitaires. Nous n'avons certes pas la prétention dans ce rapport de traiter complètement ces questions si complexes, qui exigeraient de longs commentaires ; nous nous contenterons d'en donner un aperçu sommaire, d'en esquisser le tableau d'ensemble.

Des Diverses Espèces de Circulations dans les Grandes Villes

Avant d'aborder l'étude du réseau des voies de circulation, il importe tout d'abord de définir celle-ci Or, ce que l'on appelle la circulation d'une ville se compose d'une série de mouvements très complexes ; elle n'est que la somme d'un certain nombre de circulations particulières que nous allons analyser

La circulation individuelle d'un habitant qui se dirige soit à pied, soit en voiture, vers un but déterminé et qui, une fois ce but atteint, rentre chez lui, se divise en deux phases un mouvement d'aller et un mouvement de retour, à première vue ces deux mouvements paraissent identiques, puisque la trajectoire parcourue est toujours fermée ; il y a cependant une différence notable entre le mouvement d'aller et celui de retour , le premier est presque toujours plus rapide, car il tend, dans la plupart des cas, à la réunion d'un certain nombre de personnes à une heure déterminée ; le second, au contraire, est plus lent, parce qu'il peut se faire à loisir , le premier fait converger plusieurs individus vers le même point, le second les disperse. C'est l'ensemble des mouvements d'aller qui définit le vrai sens de la circulation générale Ainsi, quand nous dirons d'une circulation qu'elle est convergente, nous entendrons exprimer cette idée que les buts qui attirent les passants, dans leur premier mouvement, sont groupés vers le centre , quand nous parlerons d'une circulation divergente, nous admettrons que les attractions motrices sont à la périphérie, quoique, dans les deux cas, un mouvement exactement inverse doive ramener les passants à leur point de départ. Nous ne nous occuperons, bien entendu, que des mouvements généraux et nous laisserons de côté les cas particuliers, celui, par exemple, des immigrants ou des émigrants dont le parcours n'est pas fermé.

Quant à la circulation des voitures ou des marchandises, nous la considérerons comme une conséquence de la circulation des individus, puisque tout mouvement de voitures ou de marchandises implique le mouvement correspondant d'un conducteur, d'un porteur ou d'un livreur

Ceci posé, on peut subdiviser en six espèces, suivant leur nature, les diverses circulations qui sillonnent une grande ville.

La première espèce comprend les mouvements de tous les individus, hommes ou femmes, agissant pour leur propre compte ou pour celui des autres, qui sortent de leurs logis pour assurer la vie matérielle de la population C'est la *circulation ménagère* Elle a pour objet les achats quotidiens d'aliments, de boissons, de combustibles, etc , dont chaque famille, même la plus pauvre, a besoin pour sa subsistance , elle se renouvelle chaque jour, aux mêmes heures, comme la nécessité à laquelle elle répond Elle a pour but parfois un emplacement spécial, le marché, mais, le plus souvent, un grand nombre de magasins qui se répartissent à peu près également sur toute la surface de la ville, car ces magasins doivent desservir chaque habitant isolé ou chaque famille avec la moindre dépense de temps et d'efforts Tous ces établissements, boulangeries, crémeries, boucheries, épiceries, débits de boissons, fruiteries, petits restaurants, pharmacies, herboristeries, débits de combustibles ou d'objets de ménage, etc , font généralement bien leurs affaires dans chaque quartier, car leur clientèle est toujours identique

Cette circulation représente des mouvements de va-et-vient courts et uniformément répartis sur toute la surface de la ville Elle est surtout pédestre, et, sauf de rares exceptions, n'use pas des moyens de transport à longue distance, car chacun se loge, selon ses ressources, dans les quartiers riches ou pauvres, et dans tous ces quartiers s'établissent les magasins de denrées répondant, pour les prix et la qualité, aux ressources des habitants.

La seconde espèce de circulation est la *circulation professionnelle.* On peut y faire entrer tout individu isolé ou chef de famille que sa profession appelle tous les jours, sauf les dimanches et fêtes, au même établissement où il passe la journée, pour revenir le soir au logis. Elle comprend les trajets, aller et retour quotidiens, des fonctionnaires ou employés des administrations publiques ou privées, de tous les ouvriers ou commis se rendant à leurs ateliers, à leurs usines ou à leurs magasins, de tous les étudiants se rendant à leurs cours Cette circulation comporte un réseau de trajets toujours identiques, partant généralement de la périphérie pour aller vers le centre, là où se trouvent la plupart des établissements administratifs ou des grandes écoles. La plupart de ces passants, n'ayant que des ressources limitées, doivent se loger à bon marché, dans les quartiers périphériques , ce qui fait que, dans la majorité des cas, les trajets à parcourir sont assez longs. C'est à cette circulation que les

transports en commun, omnibus, tramways, métropolitain, bateaux, etc,
rendent les plus grands services

La troisième espèce de circulation, que nous proposons d'appeler
circulation économique ou d'affaires, a trait à tout mouvement ayant
pour but l'achat, la vente ou la mise en œuvre d'une matière première
ou d'un produit fabriqué, ainsi que l'échange de paroles, de conventions,
d'opérations financières, judiciaires ou autres qui en sont l'origine ou
la conséquence. Dans cette circulation on peut faire entrer le financier
qui court à la Bourse, le commerçant qui reçoit ou expédie une marchandise, le camionneur qui la transporte, l'acheteur ou l'acheteuse de cette
marchandise, l'avocat qui va plaider une cause, l'industriel qui engage
une affaire, etc C'est la circulation vraiment active et spontanée, source
de la richesse de la cité. Elle est imprévue, variable, suivant l'intensité
des transactions ou la nouveauté des idées motrices, mais elle est la plus
grande possible là où se trouvent les divers lieux de réunions, ou d'échanges.
Elle est donc essentiellement convergente, car c'est vers le centre que
les habitants d'une ville trouvent les édifices sièges de leurs principales
associations, et l'outillage économique qui leur est nécessaire, Bourse,
Banque, Chambre de Commerce, Tribunaux, Hôtel des Postes, Marchés,
grands magasins, etc , etc Elle emploie tous les moyens de transport .
 mnibus, tramways, métropolitain, fiacres, voitures particulières, voitures
de commerce, camions, etc

La quatrième espèce de circulation est la *circulation mondaine* ou de
plaisir , elle comprend tous les déplacements provoqués par les relations
sociales, des plus modestes jusqu'aux plus luxueuses, provoqués aussi
par les visites, réceptions, représentations théâtrales, concerts, expositions,
banquets, conférences, promenades des étrangers et, en général, par toute
réunion ayant pour objet la satisfaction d'un plaisir matériel ou intellectuel Elle prend tout son développement dans les quartiers habités
par la classe aisée ou riche, et surtout vers le centre de la ville, où se
pressent les salles d'expositions, les théâtres, les restaurants, les cafés et
attractions diverses

Cette circulation est donc, comme la précédente, essentiellement
convergente Elle emploie presque exclusivement les voitures.

La cinquième espèce de circulation n'est pas journalière, comme les
quatre premières. C'est la *circulation fériée.* Elle a lieu exclusivement
les dimanches et jours de fêtes ; toutes les autres circulations, sauf la
ménagère qui subsiste encore dans la matinée, sont très réduites ou tout
à fait interrompues La grande majorité de la population, pour peu
que la saison le permette, s'évade de la ville et prend d'assaut les chemins
de fer et les tramways suburbains. C'est donc une circulation divergente, un exode qui, périodiquement, vide en partie les rues, du commencement du printemps à la fin de l'automne

La sixième et dernière espèce de circulation est la *circulation populaire*
ou exceptionnelle. Elle est intermittente et ne bat son plein que lors
d'évènements imprévus ou annuels, ouverture d'une grande Exposition,
visite d'un souverain, cortège, solennité hippique, revue militaire, etc
Une partie plus ou moins importante de la population se porte alors sur
un espace restreint ou sur parcours défini et l'encombre pour un jour
ou pour une heure. Cet espace ou ce parcours est très variables. Cette
circulation est essentiellement pédestre et elle arrête complètement le
mouvement des voitures partout où elle se produit.

Nous résumerons les caractères principaux de ces six espèces de circulation de la manière suivante ;

Circulation ménagère · constante et uniformément répartie.

Circulation professionnelle . constante et convergente.

Circulation économique . constante et convergente.

Circulation mondaine : constante et convergente.

Circulation fériée : périodique et divergente

Circulation populaire . exceptionnelle et variable,

Cette classification n'a évidemment rien d'absolu. Beaucoup de passants pourraient être classés à la fois dans l'une ou l'autre espèce.

Nous ne prétendons pas dire, non plus, que les circulations professionnelle, économique et mondaine soient exclusivement convergentes, car il existe, loin du centre, nombre d'usines, de magasins, d'écoles, de lieux de réunions ; nous voulons dire seulement, que, dans le fourmillement total de la ville, il y a un important excédent de piétons et de voitures se dirigeant vers le centre ; et cela suffit amplement pour provoquer l'encombrement du noyau et justifier l'élargissement des voies qui y conduisent , car c'est cet excédent qui constitue la force vive, le moteur réel et puissant de la vie et de la richesse de la cité.

Les Voies de Circulation

A ces six espèces de mouvements correspondent ou devraient correspondre des types de voies publiques appropriées à leur destination.

A la circulation ménagère, qui est comme la circulation capillaire de l'organisme, les plus petites rues, les moindres passages de piétons suffisent , les vieux quartiers en sont la preuve. Cette circulation, ayant existé depuis l'origine même de la ville, a toujours su se frayer un passage à travers les ruelles les plus étroites du moyen âge. Elle n'a donc aujourd'hui encore aucune influence sur l'élargissement des rues, que réclament, à des points de vue différents, l'hygiène publique ou les nécessités du trafic général.

La circulation professionnelle, qui est surtout celle des travailleurs modestes, s'accommode également de toutes les voies qui lui sont offertes. Chacun des éléments qui la composent suit tous les jours un même itinéraire différent de celui du voisin ; tous ces itinéraires se croisent, s'entremêlent, mais sans encombrement ni confusion, car tout encombrement produisant une perte de temps modifierait immédiatement les itinéraires qui en seraient affectés. Cette circulation, n'employant que les moyens de transport en commun, omnibus, tramways et métropolitain, est particulièrement intéressée par le tracé des lignes nouvelles et des stations à créer. Mais, de même que la ménagère, elle n'a pas ou elle n'a que peu d'influence sur la largeur des voies.

A la circulation ferrée, il faut, au contraire, des accès faciles aux gares de chemin de fer. De toutes ces gares doivent partir de larges rues en éventail, pour drainer la population et l'amener au grand canal d'évacuation, qui est la voie ferrée. Pour la circulation exceptionnelle populaire, aucune prévision ne peut être faite. Nous sommes ici dans le domaine de l'imprévu. Toutefois, lorsqu'il existe dans une ville un emplacement spécial destiné aux grandes réunions ou aux grandes fêtes, il est du devoir de l'édilité d'étudier un réseau complet de voies d'accès et de dégagement, en vue d'assurer, sans accidents de foule, l'envahissement et l'évacuation facile de la place.

Restent les deux plus importantes circulations, la circulation économique et la circulation mondaine, qui constituent pour ainsi dire la vie même de la cité. Ce sont elles qui provoquent le mouvement du plus grand nombre de véhicules de toutes formes et de toutes grandeurs et qui exigent des chaussées carrossables de plus en plus larges. C'est pour elles surtout que les progrès du cyclisme et de l'automobilisme vont bouleverser dans un avenir prochain la disposition d'ensemble de nos voies publiques et provoquer la création de nouvelles avenues plus en rapport avec la vitesse des nouveaux engins de transport.

Il y a dix ans, au moment de la naissance de l'automobilisme, la largeur des rues actuelles des villes d'Europe paraissait à peine suffisante.

Déjà les rues de 10 à 15 mètres, avec des chaussées de 7 à 8 mètres, offraient souvent le spectacle d'encombrement de voitures. Cette largeur moyenne de 8 mètres de chaussée peut bien, en effet, donner passage à

quatre voitures de front, deux dans un sens, deux dans l'autre, lorsque
ces voitures sont des coupés à deux places de 1m 60 d'encombrement,
mais elle n'admet plus de trois voitures de front, lorsqu'un omnibus, un
tombereau, une voiture de commerce de plus grande largeur entre dans le
courant de la circulation. Dès lors, il suffit qu'une voiture s'arrête et
stationne le long d'un trottoir pour qu'aussitôt un ralentissement se pro-
duise, entravant tout le mouvement commercial de la rue

C'est pourquoi, dans le tracé des voies plus récentes, on a porté leur
largeur à 20 et 22 mètres, avec une chaussée de 12 mètres Ces rues sont
suffisantes pour une circulation intensive ordinaire, elles admettent
facilement le passage de cinq voitures de front, et, à la rigueur, de six
coupés, ou le stationnement de deux lignes de voitures, le long des trottoirs,
avec une circulation double, parallèlement à l'axe de la chaussée.

Les avenues et boulevards créés par Haussmann à Paris ont presque
tous 30 mètres de largeur et 14 mètres de chaussée ; ce sont de belles voies,
mais qui s'encombrent rapidement lorsqu'une double ligne de tramways
occupe la partie médiane et ne laisse à droite et à gauche de la voie ferrée
que le passage de deux voitures

Mais il ne faut pas oublier qu'avec l'automobilisme toutes ces dimensions, résultat d'une expérience acquise, vont devenir insuffisantes ; la
tendance moderne est d'augmenter la vitesse, car augmenter la vitesse c'est
économiser le temps.

Avec plus de vitesse, le jeu, qui autrefois existait entre les files de
voitures et qui permettait aux piétons de se garer, devra nécessairement
être augmenté, les chaussées de 12 à 14 mètres devront être élargies

Nous admettrons, pour les voies maîtresses à établir dans l'avenir,
une largeur de 40 à 50 mètres avec une chaussée de 20 à 30 mètres, et
encore en proposant de tels chiffres ne sommes-nous pas bien sûr de
n'être pas trop timides ?

Réseaux des Voies Publiques

Il s'agit de grouper les éléments que nous venons d'examiner suivant
un plan d'ensemble qui puisse donner satisfaction aux divers courants de
circulation. Il faut que leur réseau forme un système complet et raisonné
de grandes artères, se ramifiant jusqu'aux points les plus reculés de
l'agglomération urbaine.

Dans les vieilles villes, les rues représentent la direction des courants
naturels résultant de la disposition topographique primitive des lieux
Ces courants eux-mêmes avaient déterminé le tracé des routes sur le bord
desquelles s'élevèrent les premières maisons.

Les quartiers neufs qui s'ajoutent à la périphérie des quartiers anciens
sont généralement tracés sans aucune préoccupation de développer une
disposition d'ensemble, ce sont des fragments de villes nouvelles, juxta-
posés à l'ancienne ville, sans qu'une idée directrice en coordonne les divers
éléments

Les voies créées récemment sont ou trop nombreuses, ou trop larges,
ou trop uniformes ; les voies à ouvrir dans la vieille ville sont tracées
souvent sans nécessité Cela se fait pour réunir deux points plus ou
moins importants, sans raison péremptoire, pour redresser tel ou tel
parcours.

Comment doivent être disposés ces 'réseaux d'artères, de veines, de
vaisseaux capillaires ? Existe-il des principes bien définis pour dresser
ces projets de grande voirie, principes tirés de l'observation des faits ou
appuyés sur une théorie sérieuse ? C'est ce que nous allons rechercher.

Pour les villes neuves, construites d'emblée comme en Amérique, il
existe deux systèmes principaux, le système en damier et le système
rayonnant, plus un système mixte essayant de combiner les deux premiers,
mais ces systèmes par trop primitifs donnent au point de vue esthétique

de si piètres résultats que nous ne nous arrêterons pas longtemps à les
discuter

On sait en quoi existe le système en damier Presque toutes les
villes des États-Unis en ont adopté le principe La ville entière est
divisée, suivant deux directions à angle droit, en une série d'îlots de forme
rectangulaire, et souvent de surfaces identiques , les îlots sont séparés
parallèlement à l'une des deux directions, par des avenues, parallèlement à
l'autre, par des rues plus étroites

Pour se rendre d'un îlot quelconque à un autre îlot, il suffit de suivre
une avenue longitudinale jusqu'à la rencontre de la rue transversale qui
contient la maison cherchée Ce système remonte à la plus haute antiquité, c'est le plan du camp romain, et Turin, en Europe, en offre un
vieil exemple Toutefois, il faut reconnaître que les municipalités américaines ont su le perfectionner jusqu'à lui donner la rigidité d'un dogme.

Lorsque le réseau rectangulaire est coupé par un accident topographique,
la direction des voies n'en est pas déviée d'un centimètre À New York,
par exemple, en face de Ward's Island, plusieurs avenues longitudinales
sont interrompues par une courbure du rivage. Elles repartent imper-
turbablement au délà ce l'échancrure, suivant les mêmes alignements

Ce système n'a qu'un seul mérite, celui de la simplicité Il ne peut
s'appliquer qu'à des villes entièrement neuves , il ne peut nous donner
aucune indication sur les grands travaux de voirie à exécuter dans nos
anciennes villes d'Europe

Le système rayonnant, également très simple, consiste à faire converger les rues principales vers une place ou un monument unique La
Nouvelle-Orléans, en Amérique, la ville de Carlsruhe, en Europe, peuvent
être considérées comme des types de ce système Ces villes ressemblent
à de vastes éventails La disposition générale, quoique moins monotone,
ne semble pas meilleure que la disposition du damier En effet, lorsque
ces voies rayonnantes sont trop multipliées, comme à la Nouvelle-Orléans,
les îlots formés par les rues s'amincissent, et leur forme, en secteurs aigus,
n'est ni agréable ni commode

À Washington, on a essayé de combiner les deux dispositions Le
Capitole, siège du Gouvernement des États-Unis, est le centre de rayonnement de douze belles avenues groupées, par trois, coupant régulièrement, de leurs quatre faisceaux, le quadrillage des rues secondaires. Le
quatrième faisceau, du côté de l'ouest, encadre un grand parc qui s'étend
jusqu'au Potomac

L'ensemble du plan a grande allure, et sa composition presque symboli-
que, qui a pour soutien une symétrie parfaite dont le Capitole, siège du
Gouvernement, est le centre, ne manque pas de grandeur ; mais la monotonie du canevas persiste et ce n'est pas encore dans cette conception
purement géométrique que nous trouverons un principe général de circulation rationnelle

On peut chercher dans les mémoires d'Haussmann la pensée directrice
de ses grands travaux pour le rajeunissement de Paris , malheureusement,
cette pensée est presque entièrement masquée par une préoccupation
d'intérêt dynastique Les questions stratégiques dominent les questions
de circulation

Haussmann paraît surtout pénétré de la nécessité d'éventrer les
anciens amas de maisons insalubres, de faire pénétrer l'air et le soleil dans
les îlots malsains, en quoi certainement il n'avait pas tort, sous la réserve
cependant qu'il eût mieux fait de ne pas détruire aussi complètement le
pittoresque savoureux du vieux Paris

La comparaison des plans des grandes capitales modernes va nous
ouvrir d'autres aperçus et apporter à la solution du problème de nouveaux
éléments que l'étude d'une seule ville ne pourrait dégager

Plans Comparatifs des Grandes Capitales

Nous aurions beaucoup désiré faire porter notre travail sur un grand nombre de villes, toutes très intéressantes, telles que Vienne, Rome, Madrid, Bruxelles, Genève et tant d'autres, mais la tâche eût été trop lourde pour nos seules épaules, et cet examen aurait démesurément allongé notre rapport. Nous nous sommes donc limités à quatre grandes capitales et nous avons choisi les plans de Berlin, de Londres, de Moscou et de Paris parce que leurs situations au bord d'un fleuve, à l'intérieur des terres, leurs étendues, leurs populations, leurs rôles politiques sont analogues et laissent prévoir pour elles une extension continue Nous avons laissé de côté les villes maritimes telles que Saint-Pétersbourg, Constantinople et New York, parce que leurs conditions d'existence sont très différentes

Dans les quatre plans que nous donnons, Planche I , nous avons seulement figuré par des traits noirs les voies principales de circulation, dont l'importance est proportionnelle à la largeur de ces traits.

Nous avons indiqué, en outre, les grands espaces libres, parcs et jardins et l'emplacement des gares, mais nous avons supprimé toutes les autres indications, notamment celles des lignes de chemins de fer, qui auraient compliqué inutilement le dessin, puisque dans ce Rapport nous ne nous occuperons que de la circulation urbaine au niveau du sol

Berlin

La figure 4 de la Planche I représente Berlin réduit à son réseau essentiel   Le plan de cette capitale a une grande qualité   la clarté de sa disposition d'ensemble

On distingue nettement un noyau central limité par des voies à peu près concentriques, dont les principales sont la Neue Friedrichstrasse et la Dirksenstrasse. au milieu de laquelle se trouve la gare centrale métropolitaine, non loin de l'Alexander Platz

Ce premier noyau, dans lequel se trouvent réunis un grand nombre de monuments publics, Hôtel de Ville, églises, Bourse, Halles, etc , est traversé par la Spree. Celle-ci entoure une grande île qui contenait la ville primitive, la Kölln, où se dressent actuellement le Château impérial, le Dôme et le Musée, avec le Lustgarten

De la place du Château part en droite ligne, sur une longueur de 1200 mètres environ, jusqu'à la porte de Brandebourg, la large avenue Unter den Linden, bordée d'édifices remarquables l'Opéra, l'Université, l'Arsenal, l'Académie et plusieurs palais

Au-delà, et dans la même direction, commence la Chaussée de Charlottenbourg, qui traverse le magnifique parc de Tiergarten et se prolonge, toujours en ligne droite, jusqu'à la forêt de Spandau

Perpendiculairement à Unter den Linden, et en son milieu, passe la Friedrichstrasse, qui s'étend du Nord au Sud et forme, avec Unter den Linden, la grande croisée de Berlin.

À son passage dans le Tiergarten, la Chaussée de Charlottenbourg est traversée par l'allée de la Victoire (Sieges-Allee) , entre ces deux voies, mais avec une légère obliquité, est tracée la Wilhelmstrasse, qui aboutit, au sud, à la place de la Belle-Alliance, et au nord, à la place Neue Thor De la ceinture de rues qui limite le noyau central de la vieille ville, rayonnent dix grandes voies, les unes directement, les autres par des détours de peu d'importance   On trouvera leurs noms sur le plan   Ces dix voies sont reliées par une grande ligne circulaire partant de Neue Thor pour aboutir à Belle-Alliance. Assez régulière, sauf au coude formé par la gare de Stettin, mais de largeur variable, cette boucle va rejoindre les deux extrémités de Sieges-Allee, par Invaliden-Strasse au nord, et Königgratzerstrasse au sud

De chacune des extrémités de Sieges-Allee partent deux autres voies

PLANS COMPARATIFS DES VOIES PRINCIPALES DE CIRCULAT
DANS LES GRANDES CAPITALES

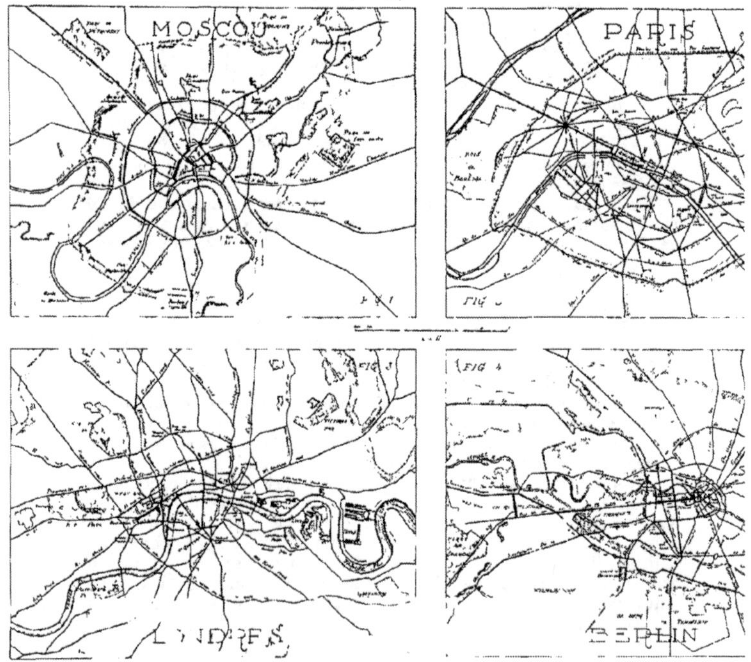

rayonnantes, d'un dessin plus irrégulier ; ce sont . Heidestrasse et Alt Moabit, au nord , Tiergartenstrasse et Potsdamstrasse, au sud.

C'est entre ces quatre voies que se développe, vers l'ouest, les nouveaux quartiers de Berlin, soit du côté de Charlottenbourg, soit du côté de Wilmersdorf ou de Schöneberg

De ce réseau simplifié on peut, en redressant les irrégularités du tracé, tirer un schéma purement théorique, qui donne le caractère général du plan de Berlin

Nous donnons ce schéma figure 4, Planche II   Ainsi réduit, le plan de la capitale allemande est un plan décentré, mais sensiblement symétrique par rapport à son grand axe   D'un noyau très dense se dirige vers l'ouest la chaussée de Charlottenbourg, droite comme une lame d'épée, dont Unter den Linden serait la poignée et le Lustgarten le pommeau

Autour de ce noyau central et reliées entre elles par une voie courbe rayonnent quatorze voies, qui régularisent et amènent de la périphérie au cœur de la cité les courants de circulation. C'est bien là le siège du Gouvernement d'une grande puissance militaire, où tout converge vers le chef unique

En examinant cette disposition générale, on ne s'étonne plus de la croissance extrêmement rapide de Berlin, car ce réseau de circulation a contribué, de la manière la plus efficace, à l'expansion économique de la capitale de l'Allemagne, rien ne s'opposant à la création des nouveaux quartiers autour de la vieille ville , aucun d'eux n'étant sacrifié, tous, au contraire, possédant une voie directe pour les relier au centre

Londres

La figure 3 de la Planche I. représente les lignes principales du plan de Londres.

Ce plan est beaucoup moins clair que celui de Berlin   A première vue, il paraît inextricable. C'est un lacis confus de voies irrégulières, présentant le caractère d'anciennes routes rurales, sur les bords desquelles se sont élevées des maisons   Les Anglais ne perdent pas leur temps à rectifier au cordeau les rues que l'usage a créées, et, du moment que la circulation est assurée, ils se tiennent pour satisfaits , en quoi ils n'ont pas tout à fait tort, car si leur bourse y gagne, le pittoresque de la ville n'y perd rien.

Cependant, à examiner de plus près ce plan, on ne tarde pas à distinguer trois grands carrefours, ou plutôt trois groupes de carrefours d'où rayonnent presque toutes les voies, et qui forment les trois sommets d'un triangle presque régulier ; c'est, sur la rive gauche, Trafalgar Square et le carrefour de la Banque, et, sur la rive droite, Saint George's Circus

Trafalgar Square est relié à la Banque par le Strand, Fleet Street, Ludgate Hill, Cannon Street et Queen Victoria Street, dont la ligne forme la base du triangle ; du sommet opposé Saint George's Circus, partent cinq voies en éventail qui viennent rejoindre cette base, en traversant la Tamise, sur cinq grands ponts   London Bridge, Southwark, Blackfriars, Waterloo et Westminster.

De chacun de ces trois groupes de carrefours, partent des voies rayonnantes qui sillonnent la ville dans toutes les directions

Au groupe de Trafalgar Square s'attachent Regent Street qui conduit à Regent's Park, Piccadilly qui mène à Hyde Park, le Mall qui forme l'avenue d'honneur du Palais de Buckingham, Whitehall qui aboutit au Parlement et à l'abbaye de Westminster, etc.

Tout autour, s'étendent les quartiers riches et aristocratiques de la grande ville.

Du carrefour de la Banque, où, avec la Mansion House et la Bourse, se trouv concentré l'outillage financier, divergent les grandes artères commerciales, et vers l'est, les voies qui desservent les docks de la Tamise

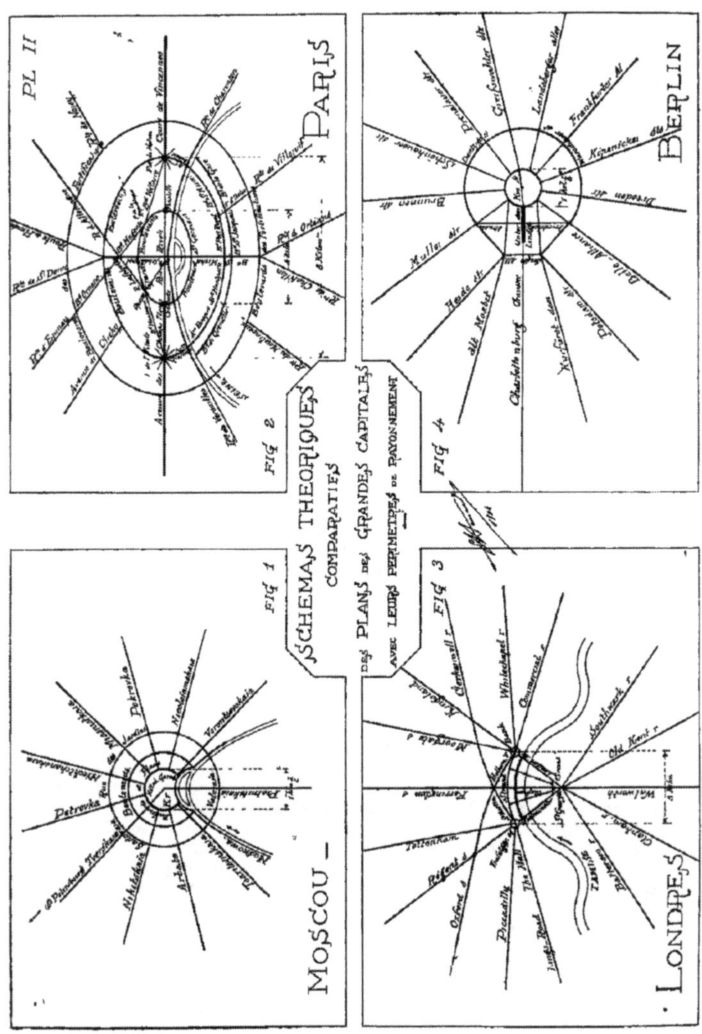
PL II
PARIS
FIG 2
BERLIN
FIG 4
SCHEMAS THEORIQUES
COMPARATIES
DES PLANS DES GRANDES CAPITALES
AVEC LEURS PERIMETRES DE RAYONNEMENT
FIG 1
MOSCOU
FIG 3
LONDRES

Ce groupe-là, c'est la Cité, le centre par excellence des affaires, du commerce maritime, de la richesse de l'Angleterre

Du troisième groupe, Saint George's Circus avec " l'Elephant et Castle," se disperse vers le sud le réseau des voies qui s'étendent sur la rive droite, à travers les quartiers industriels

L'ensemble du plan apparaît composé de voies enchevêtrées, tortillées, parmi lesquelles la voie droite est l'éxception rare   On dirait un paquet de cordages, avec trois nœuds principaux   Mais tirez légèrement sur ces lignes distendues, redressez-les dans leur direction moyenne, et immédiatement le plan s'éclaire et se traduit par le schéma théorique que nous donnons fig. 3, Planche II.

Le triangle central n'a pas plus de trois kilomètres de côté. De ces trois sommets, autour desquels se concrètent le commerce maritime, l'aristocratie terrienne et la production manufacturière de l'Angleterre, rayonnent seize voies principales, allant porter partout le mouvement et la richesse.   On saisit là le secret de la prodigieuse extension de la ville. Comme dans le plan de Berlin, la circulation convergente est admirablement organisée   Il n'y a pas dans ce plan de boulevards circulaires

Moscou.

Le plan de Moscou (Pl I, fig 1) est encore plus clair que celui de Berlin.

C'est une ville semi-orientale qui a eu à lutter contre l'invasion des hordes d'Asie, et qui n'a pu maintenir son existence qu'à la condition de s'entourer, à plusieurs reprises, de fortifications permanentes.

Comme Paris, elle s'est développée par anneaux concentriques , aussi, est-elle riche en boulevards circulaires.

Au centre, au bord de la Moskowa, se dresse le Kremlin, citadelle militaire, religieuse et politique, enfermant dans son enceinte des palais, des églises, des couvents, un arsenal, un tribunal, des casernes

À l'est du Kremlin, dont elle est séparée par la place Krasnaïa ou place rouge, s'étend la vieille ville (Kitaigorod), qui contient l'église Saint-Basile, d'un art à la fois si barbare et si pittoresque, la maison des Romanow, la cathédrale de Kasan, les grands bazars (Riady) et la Bourse

Le premier noyau central est entouré de larges avenues, de jardins et de places dont la plus importante est la place des théâtres

De cette ceinture partent onze voies rayonnantes, parmi lesquelles la Tverskaïa prolongée par la route de Saint-Pétersbourg, qui conduit au grand parc de Petrowsky.

Les onze voies rayonnantes sont reliées entre elles par deux ceintures circulaires, distantes l'une de l'autre d'environ un kilomètre ; la première est formée d'une série de très larges boulevards, coupés de portes et de monuments, et au milieu desquels s'étendent des squares allongés , la seconde est constituée par la Sadowaïa ou rue des jardins laquelle, sous divers noms, entoure la ville d'un cercle presque parfait.

Au delà de la rue des jardins les faubourgs se développent plus ou moins régulièrement : au nord, jusqu'au parc Sokolniky , au sud-ouest, jusqu'au parc Neskoutchny.

La schéma théorique du plan de Moscou s'établit facilement, comme l'indique la figure 1, Planche II. C'est une disposition régulière formée de trois cercles concentriques et dont tous les rayons s'attachent sur un noyau de 1,500 mètres environ de diamètre. L'ensemble du système est d'une netteté parfaite , tout converge vers le Kremlin, cœur triplement cuirassé, en qui se résume l'autorité unique, politique religieuse et militaire du Tsar   Ce plan de l'ancienne capitale de la Russie offre tous les caractères du siège gouvernemental d'un empire absolu

PÉRIMÈTRES DE RAYONNEMENT

De la comparaison de ces trois plans qui ont chacun leur physionomie bien spéciale, il est possible maintenant de dégager une notion nouvelle Malgré des différences considérables de forme et de disposition intérieure, on remarque ce trait qui leur est commun . Toutes les voies d'expansion et de pénétration convergent bien vers le noyau central, mais non toutes au même point, ni vers le même monument   Toutes ces voies, au contraire, s'attachent à une sorte de circuit fermé ou collecteur, que nous proposons d'appeler *périmètre de rayonnement,* et qui est tracé à une certaine distance du centre mathématique de la ville

Ce périmètre joue un grand rôle dans le plan des trois capitales , il est, pour ainsi dire, le régulateur de la circulation convergente, qui n'aboutirait qu'à un inextricable chaos, si les voies concouraient toutes à la même place   C'est lui qui reçoit les courants affluents et qui les distribue ensuite, à l'aide des petites rues secondaires, jusqu'à l'édifice ou la maison qui est le but du mouvement individuel de chaque élément de la circulation

Pour que le périmètre de rayonnement soit efficace, il faut, non qu'il enserre, dans un noyau trop grand, tous les édifices principaux, tous les points d'attraction de la cité, mais plutôt qu'il passe à travers le semis irrégulier de ces édifices, les laissant tantôt d'un côté, tantôt de l'autre de son parcours fermé

Nous regrettons que les limites forcément restreintes de notre rapport ne nous aient pas permis d'étudier le plan de Vienne dans les mêmes conditions que les plans précédents , nous aurions montré comment une initiative intelligente avait transformé les anciens remparts de cette ville en une superbe promenade, la Ringstrasse, bordée de palais, de monuments, et de jardins, promenade qui donne à la capitale de l'Autriche un magnifique périmètre de rayonnement.

Paris

On trouvera, Pl 1, fig 2, les voies principales de Paris, abstraction faite, comme dans les trois plans précédents, du réseau des rues secondaires

Il y a, dans le plan de Paris, deux parties de qualités très différentes , l'une, qui comprend les quartiers bâtis du côté de la convexité du fleuve, représente les deux tiers de l'agglomération, comme à Londres, et à Moscou , son tracé est clair et bien conçu , l'autre, située dans la concavité de la Seine, est caractérisée par un enchevêtrement de boulevards et de grandes voies aussi inutiles que mal conçues.

Parmi les lignes maîtresses, on distingue d'abord la grande croisée actuelle composée des deux transversales est-ouest (cours de Vincennes, rue de Rivoli, avenue des Champs-Elysées) et nord-sud (boulevard de Sébastopol, boulevard Saint-Michel)   Ces deux transversales constituent, au point de vue de la circulation, quatre voies rayonnantes partant d'un même point   On peut considérer comme deux autres rayonnantes les lignes des quais qui partent de la place du Châtelet en deux sens opposés Une septième voie rayonnante, l'avenue de l'Opéra, part de la place du Palais-Royal, mais s'arrête au boulevard Haussmann   On peut y ajouter la rue Turbigo et la rue Montmartre, qui, malgré leur étroitesse, jouent un rôle considérable dans la circulation parisienne

Ces neuf voies sont reliées par la ceinture elliptique des grands boulevards et du boulevard Saint-Germain. La place de la Concorde et la place de la Bastille sont placées aux extrémités du grand axe.

Sur la rive droite, de grandes voies obliques (boulevard Voltaire, boulevard Magenta, boulevard Haussmann et rue Lafayette), sont menées tangentiellement à l'ellipse. Sur la rive gauche, la rue Monge et la rue de Rennes s'arrêtent également sur cette ellipse sans la pénétrer, si ce n'est par des prolongements de largeur insuffisante

À deux kilomètres environ de distance, se déroule une seconde ceinture de forme plus irrégulière, constituée par les boulevards extérieurs, dont l'Arc de Triomphe et la place de la Nation forment les deux points extrêmes. Sur la rive droite, les lignes des boulevards extérieurs est franche et nette , sur la rive gauche, elle se dédouble, se brise, se disloque en fragments mal ajustés

C'est seulement sur cette seconde ceinture que s'amorcent de nouvelles voies rayonnantes . l'avenue de Clichy, l'avenue d'Orléans, l'avenue des Gobelins, l'avenue d'Italie, etc.

Enfin, une troisième ceinture ovale, la série successive des boulevards des fortifications, relie entre elles toutes les voies qui sortent de l'enceinte.

Paris possède donc trois grandes ceintures fermées ; c'est un luxe qui lui donne un caractère spécial qu'il faut conserver, et dont nous sommes loin de nier le charme , mais les voies rayonnantes sont peu nombreuses ou s'amorcent trop loin du centre. Le périmètre de rayonnement actuel est constitué par l'ellipse des grands boulevards intérieurs dont le grand diamètre a un longueur de 4 kilomètres, et dont le développement atteint 10 kilometres, ce qui est tout à fait exagéré.

Ainsi limité, le noyau central a une superficie trop vaste Il est trop tassé et n'est coupé que par deux grandes voies, le boulevard de Sébastopol, déjà très encombré, et l'avenue de l'Opéra. Plusieurs rues très passantes, mais trop étroites, la rue de Rivoli, la rue Montmartre, la rue de Richelieu, la rue Dauphine, la rue du Bac, etc., dégagent difficilement ce noyau Plusieurs voies de pénétration ou d'expansion ne commencent qu'à la seconde ceinture, dont le plus grand diamètre est de 8 kilomètres.

Aux deux extrémités de ce diamètre, nous possédons bien deux magnifiques centres de rayonnement. l'un présente douze voies rayonnantes c'est l'Arc de Triomphe de l'Étoile , l'autre en offre dix . c'est la place de la Nation Ces deux centres de rayonnement symbolisent, par deux œuvres très belles, le génie militaire et l'apothéose de la République ; mais malheureusement, ils ne desservent aucun courant important de circulation

Le schéma théorique du système des voies de Paris est représenté Pl **II** , fig 2 On y trouve figurées toutes les voies que nous venons de citer. Ce schéma a la forme d'une ellipse, dont les deux foyers sont représentés par des monuments glorieux et artistiques, mais purement décoratifs

Résumons en quelques lignes les résultats de cet examen

Nous avons trouvé ·

Pour Berlin, un noyau central de 1 kil 5 de diamètre ; un périmètre de rayonnemment développant 4 kil 5 et 14 voies rayonnantes ,

Pour Londres, un noyau central de 3 kilomètres de diamètre ; un périmètre de rayonnement développant 9 kilomètres et 16 voies rayonnantes ;

Pour Moscou, un noyau central de 1 kilomètre de diamètre ; un périmètre de rayonnement développant 4 kil 5 et 11 voies rayonnantes ,

Pour Paris, un noyau central de 4 kilomètres de diamètre , un périmètre de rayonnement de 10 kilomètres et seulement 9 voies rayonnantes.

Villes Modernes

Cette disposition de voies rayonnantes s'attachant à une voie circulaire ou polygonale fermée, qui entoure elle-même un noyau central, est donc un fait d'expérience. Nous en concluons que cette disposition répond à un besoin général, puisque nous la trouvons réalisée par le labeur de plusieurs générations, dans le plan de quatre grandes villes assez éloignées les unes des autres, et appartenant à des nations très différentes.

Nous pouvons nous appuyer sur cette observation pour définir ce que doit être une ville moderne, et pour prévoir son évolution dans l'avenir.

Une ville moderne n'est plus, comme au moyen âge, un simple assemblage de maisons serrées les unes contre les autres pour permettre aux habitants de se défendre contre une agression possible c'est un lieu de réunion où se trouvent concentrées toutes les ressources d'une civilisation très avancée

L'avantage que les hommes recherchent dans les capitales ou dans les centres commerciaux c'est d'avoir, sous la main, et dans le minimum d'espace tout l'outillage du progrès, et de pouvoir utiliser cet outillage avec la moindre dépense d'efforts et de temps. Mais comme cet outillage est contenu dans un certain nombre de locaux dont le volume ne peut être réduit à un point mathématique, il faut s'efforcer de grouper dans un noyau central les édifices nécessaires au développement de l'activité matérielle et intellectuelle.

D'un autre côté les hommes qui prennent part à cette activité, sous peine de trop étendre la surface de ce noyau et de perdre ainsi le bénéfice de leur concentration, sont amenés à rejeter plus loin leurs propres habitations, celles de leurs familles, de leurs enfants , leurs lieux de repos et d'agrément

Une grande ville moderne doit donc se composer de deux parties la première partie sera le centre des affaires et du mouvement intellectuel et artistique   Là, se trouveront réunis les agences, les halles, les grands magasins, les bourses, les banques, les tribunaux, les organes administratifs, les musées, les bibliothèques, les théâtres, les lieux d'études et de plaisir

La seconde partie sera périphérique par rapport à la première ; l'activité y sera moins grande , elle sera presqu'entièrement occupée par les maisons d'habitation dont la superficie, le confortable et le bon marché varieront avec la distance au centre   Ces deux parties, d'ailleurs, se pénétreront, et l'on passera de l'une à l'autre par des transitions peu sensibles.

Une ville moderne représente donc une agglomération d'édifices dont la densité et l'importance augmentent de la périphérie au centre

Par suite, les voies de circulation et d'échange ne doivent pas être uniformément réparties , les voies maîtresses doivent être de plus en plus larges, à mesure qu'elles se rapprochent du centre, et leur direction doit tendre vers le noyau d'activité, absolument comme les veines et les artères d'un organisme vivant, qui augmentent d'importance à mesure qu'elles se rapprochent du cœur. Elles doivent donc présenter une disposition rayonnante

Mais il serait imprudent de faire tendre toutes les voies vers le même point ou vers la même place, car on ferait naître sur cette place un encombrement inextricable ; il faut qu'elles s'attachent sur un grand collecteur circulaire ou polygonal, plus large que la plus large d'entre elles C'est ce collecteur que nous avons appelé périmètre de rayonnement , il ne doit pas embrasser une trop grande surface, et doit passer à distance moyenne des principaux édifices de la cité

Voies Rectilignes et Voies Sinueuses

Nous avons dit précédemment que les vieilles villes européennes, formées par une lente accumulation séculaire, se trouvent, au point de vue de la circulation, dans une situation anormale, puisque les voies du noyau central sont les plus anciennes et les plus étroites, et que les voies de la périphérie sont les plus nouvelles et les plus larges , c'est précisément le contraire qu'il faudrait réaliser

C'est de cet état de choses ainsi que de la présence des anciens monuments groupés toujours au centre, que provient toute la difficulté de la transformation d'une grande ville. Aussi, lorsqu'il devient nécessaire d'ouvrir une voie nouvelle, il est rarement possible de l'ouvrir en ligne droite, et il ne faut pas hésiter à recourir à des lignes courbes et brisées, afin de ménager les richesses artistiques de la cité. Cela, d'ailleurs, ne présente aucun inconvénient sérieux lorsque les courbes sont suffisamment allongées, et lorsqu'on évite les changements brusques de direction , la perte sur la longueur du parcours est, en ce cas, presque toujours négligeable

Il est très difficile de faire pénétrer cette idée dans les bureaux administratifs chargés des alignements. Dans ces bureaux, la ligne droite semble la seule solution acceptable pour le tracé d'une voie nouvelle. Rien n'oblige cependant à recourir, quand même, au tracé rectiligne. Il n'est pas douteux, lorsqu'il est possible de l'appliquer, que l'on n'obtienne des effets de perspective grandiose, quoiqu'un peu monotone. Mais il n'est pas douteux non plus que le tracé courbe ou sinueux ne donne, d'autre part, des effets plus pittoresques et plus imprévus Le Grand Canal de Venise est l'un des exemples les plus typiques et les plus fameux de la beauté que peut offrir une voie sinueuse.

Nous dirons donc, et ce sera l'une des premières conclusions à tirer de cette étude sur la disposition et le développement des rues dans les villes, que toutes les fois qu'une municipalité se trouve en présence de la nécessité d'ouvrir une voie nouvelle, elle ne doit, sous aucun prétexte, accepter un tracé qui aurait pour conséquence de détruire un monument présentant un intérêt historique ou esthétique , qu'il est toujours possible de trouver un tracé respectant ce monument ; et qu'enfin ce tracé devrait toujours être étudié par une Commission d'Architectes, ou, tout au moins, approuvé par cette commission.

Les Espaces Libres—Parcs et Jardins.

Nous venons de décrire ce que l'on pourrait appeler l'appareil circulatoire de ce grand organisme vivant constitué par une ville moderne , il nous reste à examiner ce que l'on pourrait appeler son appareil respiratoire. Cet appareil respiratoire est composé de ses espaces libres, parcs ou jardins

Avant d'aller plus loin il est nécessaire d'aller au-devant d'une objection que ne manquent pas de faire les spéculateurs, lorsqu'on leur parle de développer dans les villes ces espaces si utiles à l'hygiène publique

"A quoi servent ces jardins et ces parcs ?" disent-ils. "Croyez-vous que la qualité de l'air qu'on y respire soit bien différente de celle de la rue ou de la maison que vous habitez ? C'est la même atmosphère qui baigne ces jardins et cette maison , à quoi bon laisser improductifs de revenu, de larges espaces qu'on pourrait si fructueusement couvrir d'immeubles ? "

Il est facile de répondre à cette objection l'air que l'on respire dans la maison et dans la rue est continuellement mélangé de toutes les poussières microscopiques, plus ou moins nocives, que soulève le passage incessant des piétons et des voitures ; l'air d'un jardin ou d'un parc, à condition toutefois que sa superficie soit suffisamment grande, est beaucoup plus sain et plus épuré Mais pour que cette épuration soit certaine, il faut que le parc soit entouré de massifs épais, et de hauts arbres, dont le feuillage constitue un filtre très efficace contre l'envahissement des poussières urbaines Enfin, le soleil, qui est le grand agent d'oxydation, y brûle les miasmes, et l'action chimique des végétaux sur la composition de l'air contribue à assainir ces espaces

Les parcs et jardins publics doivent donc être composés de vastes pelouses ensoleillées, coupées par des écrans ou des rideaux d'arbres, et bordées de haies épaisses, de véritables murailles de verdure.

"Mais," objectent encore les adversaires des espaces libres, "est-il bien utile de créer, à grands frais, de pareilles enceintes, à l'intérieur des villes, alors que les moyens de transport modernes, chemins de fer ou tramways,

permettent à tout habitant de s'évader de sa maison et, en quelques
minutes, de gagner la plaine campagne ? " Cette objection serait exacte,
si la distance à laquelle on peut trouver la campagne n'augmentait
d'une façon constante Or, le phénomène de l'extension des grandes
villes ne s'arrête pas ; leur périphérie se bouche de plus en plus Il faudra
donc aller toujours plus loin, et le temps qu'il faudra dépenser pour trouver
la zone de verdure, en rendra l'accès de plus en plus difficile

Enfin, il existe une raison péremptoire qui exige l'aménagement des
parcs à l'intérieur des agglomérations urbaines c'est la santé des enfants
Depuis sa naissance jusqu'au moment ou commence son instruction,
l'enfant, pour se développer et se bien porter, a besoin de prendre l'air
toutes les fois que le temps le permet Il doit pouvoir profiter de la
plus petite éclaircie pour respirer au dehors. Demanderez-vous aux
meres de famille qui ont plusieurs enfants en bas âge de prendre à chaque
in tant le chemin de fer ou l'omnibus pour aller chercher un coin d'air
pur, et de perdre, par des déplacements coûteux multipliés, le temps
précieux dont elles peuvent disposer ? Trouver un lieu favorable aux
jeux et aux ébats de leurs enfants, voilà un problème que toutes les
mères de famille connaissent bien et dont les municipalités n'apprécient
pas toujours la haute importance. Il faut donc, dans une grande ville,
que les parcs et jardins soient convenablement répartis et espacés de
telle sorte que tout enfant soit certain de trouver, non loin de sa demeure,
un espace libre pour jouer et respirer à l'abri de la poussière des rues et
des miasmes des maisons surhabitées On peut estimer cette distance
maxima à 500 mètres pour un jardin ou à 1,000 mètres pour un grand
parc

D'ailleurs, si les espaces libres sont indispensables aux enfants, ils
sont également d'une grande utilité aux vieillards, aux femmes, aux
convalescents. Il n'est pas jusqu'aux hommes valides eux-mêmes qui
ne trouvent plaisir à s'y promener. La vue des arbres, des pelouses, des
fleurs provoque chez les plus agités, les plus enfiévrés de la vie moderne
une détente physique et morale qu'on ne saurait nier C'est un élément
incontestable de calme et d'apaisement

A un autre point de vue, qui vous intéresse tout particulièrement,
au point de vue esthétique, la présence des parcs et jardins joue un rôle
des plus importants dans l'aménagement des villes Quelle que soit la
beauté architecturale des monuments, la ontinuité des masses de pierre
provoquerait bientôt un ennui intolérable, si la monotonie de leurs aspects
n'était coupée et égayée par des masses de verdure Ces deux éléments
se font valoir réciproquement , et de leur opposition naissent des sites
pittoresques d'une grande beauté.

SURFACES DES PARCS ET JARDINS.

Nous allons essayer maintenant de comparer entre elles, au point de
vue des espaces libres, les quatre grandes villes que nous avons choisies
Nous commencerons par donner les chiffres bruts des surfaces de ces
espaces, puis nous examinerons quelle est leur répartition. Il doit être
entendu que nous faisons toute réserve sur la précision des résultats
obtenus , les documents et plans que nous avons eus entre les mains étant
à des échelles trop petites pour permettre une appr.ximation complètement satisfaisante. Ils suffiront toutefois à donner une idée de l'ordre
de grandeur des espaces considérés Nous prendrons pour unité de
surface l'hectare, qui peut être représenté par un carré de cent mètres de
côté, et qui contient 10,000 mètres superficiels

Voici ces chiffres ·

Londres.

Surface totale de l'agglomération bâtie	34,000 hectares
Population, environ	4,500,000 habitants

Parcs Intérieurs.

	Hectares
Hyde Park	240
Regent's Park	160
Battersea Park	80
Victoria Park	90
Clapham Common	80
Greenwich Park	74
Blackheath	94
Crystal Palace Park	53
Wandsworth Common	52
Finsbury Park	35
Green Park	35
St. James's Park	25
Autres parcs, jardins et squares divers, ensemble	2,200

Parcs Extérieurs ou Périphériques

Richmond Park	780
Putney Heath	360
Old Deer Park at Kew Gardens	272
Hampstead Heath et Parliament Hill	200
Total	4,830

Berlin

Surface totale de l'agglomération bâtie	6,360 hectares
Population	1,750,000 habitants

Parcs et Jardins Intérieurs

	Hectares
Tiergarten	290
Humboldhain	40
Friedrichshain	57
Jardin Botanique	10
Victoria Park	14
Autres parcs et jardins, ensemble	142

Parcs ou Forêts Extérieurs ou Périphériques.

Parc de Treptow	90
Grunewald et Forêt de Spandau } plus de	5,000
Total	5,643

Moscou.

Surface totale de l'agglomération bâtie	7,440 hectares
Population	1,200,000 habitants

Parcs et Jardins Intérieurs.

	Hectares
Jardin du Kremlin	17
Parc Catherine	25
Parc de l'Intendance	90
Parc Neskoutchny	66
Jardin Zoologique	34
Jardins des boulevards intérieurs	19
Autres parcs et jardins, ensemble	346

Parcs Extérieurs ou Périphériques.

		Hectares
Parc Petrowsky.	.	156
Parc Sokolniky .	.	520
Total . .		1,273

Paris.

	Hectares
Surface totale comprise dans l'enceinte précise des fortifications .	7,800
Surface bâtie immédiatement attenante aux fortifications	10,200
Surface totale de l'agglomération bâtie	18,000

Population .

	Habitants
Enceinte des fortifications	2,700,000
Communes attenantes	800,000
Population totale, environ	3,500,000

Parcs ou Jardins Intérieurs

	Hectares
Champs Élysées	30
Tuileries . .	21
Luxembourg	26
Jardin des Plantes .	21
Champ de Mars	44
Trocadéro	14
Esplanade des Invalides	10
Buttes Chaumont	24
Parc de Montsouris	16
Parc Monceau	8
Autres jardins ou squares, ensemble .	49

Parcs ou Bois Extérieurs ou Périphériques.

Bois de Boulogne	750
Bois de Vincennes	730
Parc de St Cloud	240
Total . . .	1,720

Parcs Extérieurs.

Dans les tableaux précédents nous avons divisé les parcs et espaces plantés en deux catégories . les parcs et jardins intérieurs, ceux qui sont entourés d'habitations , et le parcs extérieurs ou périphériques, qui sont situés en dehors de la ville ou qui ne la touchent que par un de leurs côtés

Il est bien rare, en effet, qu'une grande ville n'ait pas à sa proximité des bois ou des forêts, résidus des forêts primitives qui l'entouraient à son origine. Quand l'on examine les chiffres ci-dessus, on voit que les quatre grandes capitales sont bien pourvues de parcs excentriques, et que leurs habitants peuvent y trouver, les jours fériés, des promenades suffisantes. Berlin, qui est entouré de tous les côtés par des forêts, arrive en tête de la liste, sans contestation possible

Mais, ainsi que nous l'avons dit plus haut, les parcs trop éloignés du centre des villes, quoique d'une utilité incontestable, sont incapables de rendre à la population les services journaliers qu'elle est en droit d'attendre. Nous citerons à ce sujet l'opinion d'Haussmann, le grand

préfet de Paris, qui créa de toute pièce le parc des Buttes Chaumont et
le parc de Montsouris ; et qui aménagea et agrandit d'une façon si heureuse
notre Bois de Boulogne. Dans le tome III de ses mémoires, voici ce
qu'il dit relativement au Bois de Boulogne et au Bois de Vincennes

"Malgré tous mes efforts pour rendre aisément accessibles à la population de Paris ces deux splendides promenades extérieures, je ne pus réussir
à l'en faire profiter généralement, sinon les dimanches et jours de fête,
à cause de la distance, du temps pour la franchir à l'aller et au retour,
et des frais de transport qui, fussent-ils des plus économiques, finissent
par être onéreux lorsqu'ils se répètent souvent "

C'est donc pour la création et l'augmentation des parcs intérieurs
que les municipalités doivent redoubler leurs efforts

Ici se présente une grave difficulté Comment comparer les espaces
libres dans les quatre grandes villes qui sont si différentes, tant par leurs
surfaces que par leurs formes et par la disposition même de leurs parcs ?
Considérerons-nous tous les parcs compris dans les limites administratives ? Mais ces limites sont purement fictives Prendrons-nous tous les
parcs compris dans un cercle de rayon donné ? Mais où placerons-nous
le centre de ce cercle et quel rayon lui donnerons-nous ? Prendrons-
nous la surface réellement bâtie de chaque ville ? Mais cette surface est
bien peu précise, où s'arrête-t-elle ? Où commence-t-elle ? Londres
et Berlin passent par des transitions peu sensibles de l'agglomération serrée
à la pleine campagne

PARCS INTÉRIEURS—PLANS COMPARATIFS

Pour obtenir une relation un peu nette, nous choisirons comme
surface de comparaison commune la surface de Paris qui est la mieux
définie puisqu'elle est limitée par une ceinture continue de fortifications
réelles qui contient exactement 7,800 hectares Nous prendrons donc
le périmètre de Paris, et nous découperons dans la partie la plus dense
de Londres, de Berlin et de Moscou des surfaces identiques, de même
périmètre. Si dans ces surfaces nous faisons figurer seulement les parcs
et jardins existant dans chaque ville, nous aurons là un moyen frappant
de mettre en évidence la proportion relative des parcs et jardins intérieurs
des quatre capitales. Nous obtenons ainsi la Planche III. Totalisons
maintenant les surfaces des espaces libres de chaque ville existant dans
ce même périmètre, nous obtenons les chiffres suivants ·

Pour une même surface de 7,800 hectares

	Hectares
Londres possède 200 parcs ou squares d'une surface totale de	752
Berlin possède 20 parcs ou squares d'une surface totale de	553
Moscou possède 35 parcs ou jardins, d'une surface totale de	483
Paris possède 46 parcs ou squares, d'une surface totale de	263

Nous rendons ici hommage à l'immense supériorité de Londres sur
les autres villes, au point de vue des jardins intérieurs Cette surface
de 752 hectares n'est, en effet, que la moindre partie de la superficie totale
de ses parcs et jardins Car si dans le périmètre ci-dessus, Hyde Park
figure avec Regent's Park, ni Battersea Park, ni Clapham Common, ni
Crystal Palace Park, ni Greenwich Park, ni Hampstead Heath ni Parliament Hill n'ont pu y trouver place.

Aussi, est-ce avec une véritable admiration que nous constatons la
prévoyance des édiles de Londres Lorsqu'on examine un plan de
Londres, on trouve dans la périphérie de la ville, dans les parties non
encore construites, des réserves déjà préparées pour devenir plus tard les
parcs et jardins du plus grand Londres.

Quand on compare les anciens plans des villes avec leurs plans modernes,
on s'aperçoit toujours qu'un certain nombre de jardins ont disparu, ou

ont été plus ou moins diminués La constatation est frappante pour
Paris Depuis cent ans, Paris a perdu les deux tiers de ses jardins

À quoi donc tient ce déplorable état de choses qui empire tous les
jours un peu plus ? A ce simple jeu de la spéculation qui s'appelle la
mise en valeur d'un terrain

Ce n'est pas que l'opération en elle-même ne soit parfaitement légitime
et même désirable dans la plupart des cas , mais son défaut est dans son
outrance même, à laquelle aucune édilité n'a encore essayé de trouver
un contrepoids. Car ici, il faut y insister, l'intérêt particulier est opposé
à l'intérêt général, et l'on peut poser en principe que toute mise en valeur
d'un grand parc réalisée dans un intérêt privé, et qui donne une fortune
au propriétaire, apporte une moins-value à l'ensemble de la ville Il
faudrait alors, lorsque s'élève un nouveau quartier de pierre, qu'un espace
libre, un jardin proportionné à son importance, en formât le centre d'agrément et de bonne hygiène. Cet espace, il serait de l'intérêt, bien entendu,
des propriétaires de le ménager, mais ce serait trop demander à la spéculation que d'abandonner le principe d'un rendement intensif et immédiat pour
le remplacer par celui d'un rendement plus solide et de plus longue durée.
C'est donc aux municipalités à prendre l'initiative d'une mesure qui
est au-dessus des forces des particuliers Bien plus, les anciens quartiers
du centre devraient, eux aussi, être pourvus de grands jardins qui leur
manquent totalement et dont ils sentiront d'autant plus le besoin, que
le diamètre de l'agglomération urbaine augmentera davantage.

D'autre part, il devrait être interdit aux municipalités de spéculer
sur les espaces libres, et de vendre la moindre parcelle du patrimoine
commun pour augmenter leurs ressources budgétaires La conservation
intégrale des parcs ou jardins et espaces libres doit être considérée comme
un principe absolu n'admettant aucune dérogation.

On peut chercher quelle est la proportion la plus favorable à maintenir
entre les espaces libres et les espaces bâtis dans les grandes villes Pour
déterminer cette proportion nous manquons de données précises , nous
ne pouvons que nous appuyer sur les faits d'expérience. Nous admettrons
donc que c'est un dixième de la surface totale de la ville qu'il faut affecter
aux espaces plantés d'arbres Cette proportion est sensiblement la même
que celle que nous avons trouvée pour Londres dans nos quatre plans
comparatifs. Pour une surface donnée de 7,800 hectares, Londres possède
752 hectares de parcs et jardins. C'est dans cette ville qu'on trouve la
proportion la plus favorable

D'après la théorie précédente les grands parcs et jardins devraient
être répartis, sinon d'une manière uniforme, du moins de telle sorte que
toutes les parties d'une ville jouissent du même bienfait, et qu'aucune
habitation ne fût à moins de 500 mètres d'un jardin ou à 1,000 mètres
d'un parc

Malheureusement, à ce point de vue, aucune ville ne possède une
répartition satisfaisante des parcs et jardins Il y a toujours une partie
de la ville où la concentration des maisons a détruit les espaces plantés
si nécessaires à l'hygiène publique À Londres, à Paris, à Berlin, le
centre du noyau primitif est presque dépourvu de jardins, et certains
quartiers en manquent totalement

Il serait donc nécessaire de tracer un programme d'ensemble dans
chaque grande ville, afin de créer, entre les parcs déjà existants et partout
où cela serait nécessaire, des parcs intermédiaires d'au moins 10 hectares
de superficie. Cela coûtera incontestablement très cher, mais la dépense
sera largement compensée par une amélioration de la santé publique.

CITÉS-JARDINS.

Quelques esprits généreux ont poussé à l'extrême la conception des
espaces libres dans les villes, et ont préconisé la création de cités-jardins,
c'est-à-dire de villes dont plus de la moitié de la surface totale serait

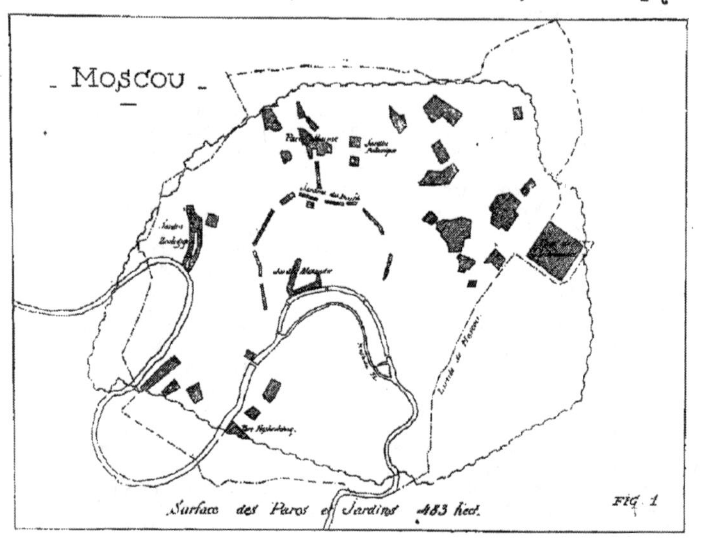

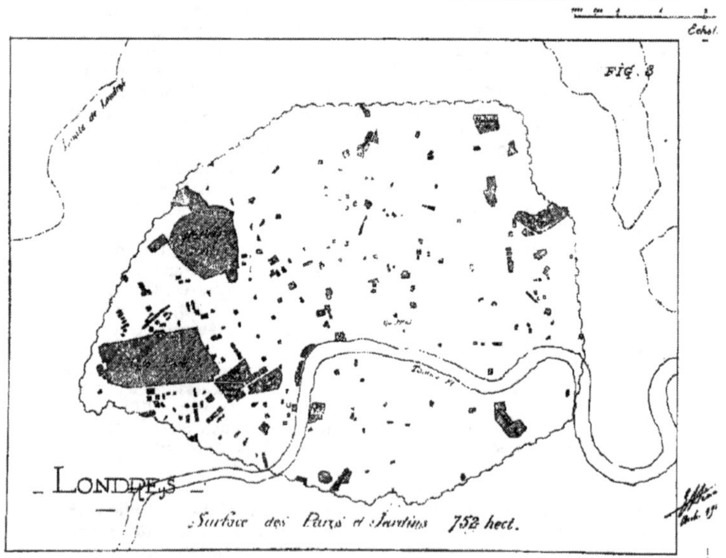

Les Surfaces indiquées ci-dessus représentent pour chaque Ville

occupée par les jardins, et dans lesquelles on aménagerait un immense parc central

Il y a là, à notre avis, un véritable contre-sens Dans l'intention très louable d'améliorer les cités, il faut s'en garder d'en détruire tous les avantages Une grande ville est un lieu d'activité intense, ce n'est pas un lieu de repos Mettre un parc au centre géométrique de l'agglomération, c'est simplement déplacer le centre des affaires qui se reportera un peu plus loin , donner à chaque habitant un carré de terre pour y cultiver ses légumes et y élever des poules, c'est revenir à la vie champêtre , il suffit, pour obtenir ce résultat, de retourner au village Il faut donc créer à l'intérieur des grandes villes un grand nombre de parcs bien placés et bien répartis, mais il ne faut pas dépasser une sage proportion qui risquerait, tout en devenant inutile à l'hygiène enfantine, de ralentir l'activité virile

La création de cités-jardins convient parfaitement, au contraire, à certains centres manufacturiers et industriels où l'ouvrier, en sortant de l'usine, trouve en sa propre maison un lieu de détente et de repos Mais cette conception ne peut s'appliquer qu'à des agglomérations relativement restreintes de quelques milliers d'habitants Elle ne saurait convenir à des capitales où se trouvent réunis des millions d'hommes, et où se trouve concentrée l'élite intellectuelle, artistique, scientifique, industrielle. commerciale et financière d'une nation

On peut, cependant, chercher un moyen de rendre moins compacte et plus hygiénique les masses serrées des maisons On a essayé d'obtenir ce résultat à Paris, notamment dans certains boulevards, en reculant l'alignement des maisons et en imposant aux propriétaires la servitude de laisser devant chaque façade un petit jardin de quelques mètres de largeur, planté d'arbres et d'arbustes et de fleurs Si de telles avenues ont un aspect satisfaisant, la servitude imposée a des résultats déplorables au point de vue de développement commercial , car aucune boutique ne peut alors prendre contact avec les passants La petite commune de Neuilly, au nord-ouest de Paris, construite sur ce plan, a démontré jusqu'à l'évidence l'inconvénient de ce système , c'est un charmant quartier de villas de plaisance, mais dont l'activité est presque nulle.

Le système que nous allons décrire est tout autre, et permet de concilier à la fois les nécessités commerciales et les nécessités hygiéniques d'une grande cité

Boulevards à Redans.

Pour qu'une voie publique rende tous les services qu'une circulation intensive est en droit d'exiger d'elle, il faut que sa chaussée carrossable soit correctement alignée, et que sa largeur soit uniforme, sans étranglement ni ressaut sur tout son parcours Cette vérité de toute évidence doit-elle entraîner l'alignement rigoureusement correspondant des édifices et des arbres qui bordent la chaussée ? Rien n'est moins démontré, et du moment que la partie utilitaire de la voie publique remplit les conditions requises, il n'y a aucune nécessité à maintenir la continuité d'alignement des autres éléments On pourrait donc substituer à la suite indéfinie et monotone des maisons et des arbres, des groupes alternés d'arbres et de maisons. On obtiendrait ainsi un type nouveau de boulevard offrant des avantages très appréciables sur les types actuels Voici quelle en serait la formule

La municipalité, en possession d'une bande de terrain de largeur suffisante, après avoir tracé et ouvert la chaussée centrale, établirait deux alignements parallèles et équidistants à droite et à gauche de cette chaussée Elle réserverait entre ces deux alignements des espaces vides et imposerait comme condition de vente aux propriétaires riverains d'enfermer les édifices à construire dans les limites du périmètre ainsi constitué. Les bâtiments en saillie borderaient la chaussée, comme dans

D D

les rues simples, sans aucun arbre devant les façades, les bâtiments en
retraite, au contraire, devraient subir la servitude indéfinie du voisinage
d'un certain nombre d'arbres bien déterminés, plantés et entretenus
par la municipalité, comme dans les boulevards actuels

Les acquéreurs, à titre de compensation, auraient le droit d'établir
une grille ou toute autre clôture à claire-voie, suivant l'alignement des
façades saillantes, et d'aménager, sous forme de jardins, les espaces ainsi
créés. Ils auraient la faculté soit de les conserver pour l'agrément de
leurs locataires, soit de les ouvrir au public

La seule réserve qui serait imposée serait de ne jamais couvrir ces
jardins et de laisser, autour des arbres, le sol sablé ou gazonné. Il deviendrait alors plus facile d'y faire pousser de belles essences. Les parois
de la voie publique se composeraient donc d'une série d'immeubles en
réalité continus, mais formant une suite de ressauts ou redans dont les
façades seraient séparées par des bouquets d'arbres qui en rompraient la
monotonie et en rehausseraient la valeur décorative   Au rez-de-chaussée de
vastes magasins, brillamment illuminés le soir, égayeraient et animeraient
la voie publique, comme dans nos boulevards actuels, mais avec des repos
réguliers de verdure tantôt fermés, tantôt largement ouverts   On réunirait
ainsi, tout le mouvement, la vie, l'éclairage brillant des rues commer-
çantes, à l'agrément des voies plantées d'arbres et bordées de jardins.

Nous donnons (Pl IV et V) le plan et la vue perspective d'un boulevard
à redans

Nous donnons à la chaussée de ce boulevard une largeur de 18 mètres.

Nous donnons aux trottoirs une largeur de 9 mètres   C'est la dimension des trottoirs du boulevard des Italiens, elle nous paraît suffisante,
puisqu'en réalité, les arbres étant rejetés entre les maisons, la circulation
à pied bénéficie d'un mètre de plus sur chaque rive

La largeur des corps de bâtiments en saillie serait de 36 mètres, leur
profondeur serait de 20 mètres, la largeur des jardins de 28 mètres

La cote de 20 mètres et de 28 mètres résulte de l'écartement des arbres,
qui est de 8 mètres, et de leur distance aux façades en retour, qui est de
10 mètres   Ces écartements sont nécessaires à leur complet développement   Ils ne sont écartés de la grille que de deux mètres, afin que leurs
branches débordent le plus possible au-dessus de celle-ci

Il va, sans dire, que ces cotes n'ont rien d'absolu et qu'elles peuvent
varier en plus ou en moins, selon la division qu'il sera possible de faire
entre deux coupures successives produites par la rencontre de deux rues
transversales

Ce n'est pas sans raison toutefois que nous avons choisi la cote de
36 mètres pour la largeur des façades en saillie. Dans son intégralité,
elle permet d'établir le plan d'un de ces grands immeubles de luxe où
chaque étage constitue une sorte d'hôtel de plain-pied

Si au contraire on divise la cote de 36 mètres en deux ou trois parties,
on obtient des maisons de 18 mètres ou de 12 mètres de façade, encore
suffisantes pour obtenir soit des appartements confortables de loyers
moyens, soit des appartements bon marché. Dans ces deux derniers
cas, on n'aurait plus des avant-corps d'un seul tenant, mais des groupes
d'immeubles formant avant-corps   Une subdivision analogue pourrait
s'effectuer dans l'espace réservé aux jardins. Nous supposons toutefois
que, dans la généralité des cas, la ligne mitoyenne passerait dans l'axe
de cet espace

On peut objecter à notre système que l'établissement de ces grands
redans fait perdre beaucoup de terrain à construire   La perte qui est
réelle n'est pas aussi grande qu'on pourrait le croire à première vue, et
elle est compensée d'ailleurs par d'autres avantages.

En effet, il suffit de remarquer que les enclaves de jardins sont des
cours ouvertes, plus gaies, plus aérées, plus hygiéniques que les cours
intérieures des immeubles actuels, que, par suite, toutes les chambres

To face p. 402.

PROJET DE BOULEVARD A REDANS
PL. IV.
COUPE DU BOULEVARD
Cour
Cour
Chaussée du Boulevard à Redans
Cour
Cour
Rue de 16 Mètres
DISPOSITION AU PREMIER ÉTAGE
DISPOSITION AU REZ-DE-CHAUSSÉE
PLAN D'UN FRAGMENT DE BOULEVARD
E. HÉNARD. Arc
1903.

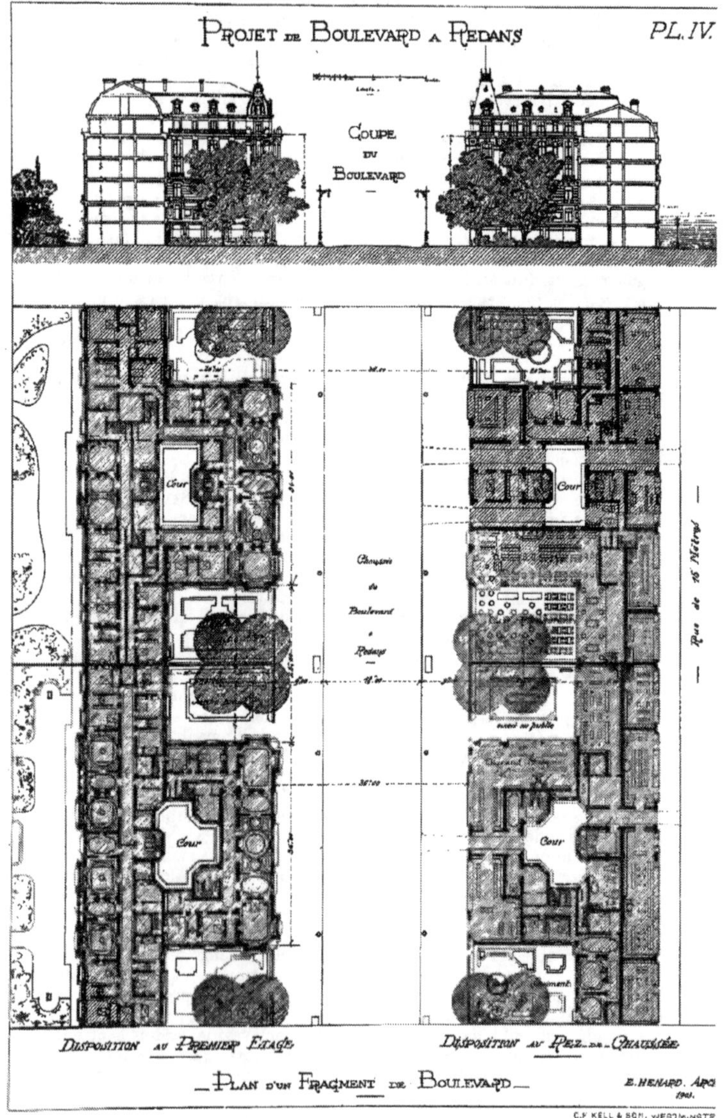

Nouveau Type de Boulevard à Redans : Alternance des Arbres et des Maisons.

habitables peuvent être établies sur les façades donnant soit sur le boulevard, soit sur ces jardins, ce qui permet de réduire les cours intérieures qui ne seraient plus destinées qu'à éclairer et à ventiler les divers locaux de service   Au surplus, le calcul est facile à faire.

Nous avons établi (Pl. VI.) deux plans de masse comparatifs, l'un représentant un fragment de boulevard à redans , l'autre un fragment de boulevard ordinaire.

Nous avons supposé, dans le second cas, des cours de surface moyenne telles qu'on les exécute aujourd'hui, et, dans le premier cas, des cours de surface réduites, telles qu'elles résultent de nos plans.

Le tracé ordinaire donne, pour une surface totale de 4,480 mètres carrés, une surface de constructions de 3,507 mètres carrés

Le tracé à redans donne une surface de constructions de 3,077 mètres carrés

La perte de terrain n'est que de 12 2 pour 100

Par contre, le développement des façades est de 208 mètres pour le tracé à redans, tandis qu'il n'est que de 128 mètres dans le tracé ordinaire   Soit un gain pour les façades de 62 5 pour 100, qui apporte une plus-value évidente à la masse des constructions   On voit que, au point de vue du rendement financier, la disposition que nous proposons n'est nullement inférieure à celle actuellement en usage.

Ce tracé présente de nombreux avantages

Le cube d'air de la voie publique, dont profitent les maisons riveraines, est notamment augmenté, et ce n'est plus un air stagnant comme celui des cours fermées, mais un air facilement renouvelé.

Les appartements ont des vues et des expositions variées, tantôt sur les façades leur faisant face, tantôt sur les jardins, tantôt obliquement sur la percée de la rue.

La présence des arbres plantés dans un terrain perméable, à une bonne distance des maisons, ce qui leur permet de se développer à l'aise, donne de la gaieté à l'ensemble, sans masquer la vue des édifices.

Les espaces réservés aux arbres se prêtent au niveau du sol à des combinaisons multiples   On peut y installer soit des massifs pour l'agrément des appartements à rez-de-chaussée, soit des terrasses sablées et ombragées pour des établissements de consommation, restaurants ou cafés, soit enfin des jardins spécialement aménagés en vue du commerce des magasins attenants

Ce nouveau type de boulevard à redans ne pourrait évidemment pas se généraliser pour toutes les nouvelles rues d'une ville, mais on pourrait en faire une application intéressante dans les voies nouvelles destinées à relier entre eux les parcs existants ou les parcs à créer.

Certaines grandes villes d'Amérique projettent de réunir leurs grands parcs par des promenades verdoyantes de faible largeur, mais ayant un grand développement kilométrique.   L'idée est très heureuse, mais elle serait trop coûteuse pour nos vieilles villes d'Europe, parce que sa réalisation exigerait l'expropriation de trop grandes surfaces qui n'auraient pas l'avantage hygiénique d'un grand parc abrité des poussières urbaines, ni l'avantage économique d'une grande voie commerciale.   Au contraire, la création de boulevards à redans avec l'alternance des maisons et des arbres formerait des voies de communication utiles et d'un aspect artistique entre les grands espaces libres

Projet de transformation de Paris.

Il nous reste à vous montrer, par un exemple, que les idées que nous venons de développer ne sont pas seulement théoriques, mais qu'il est possible de les appliquer à l'étude pratique du programme de transformation d'une grande ville   Pour cela, nous choisirons le plan de Paris, et nous ferons une première esquisse des améliorations qu'on pourrait y

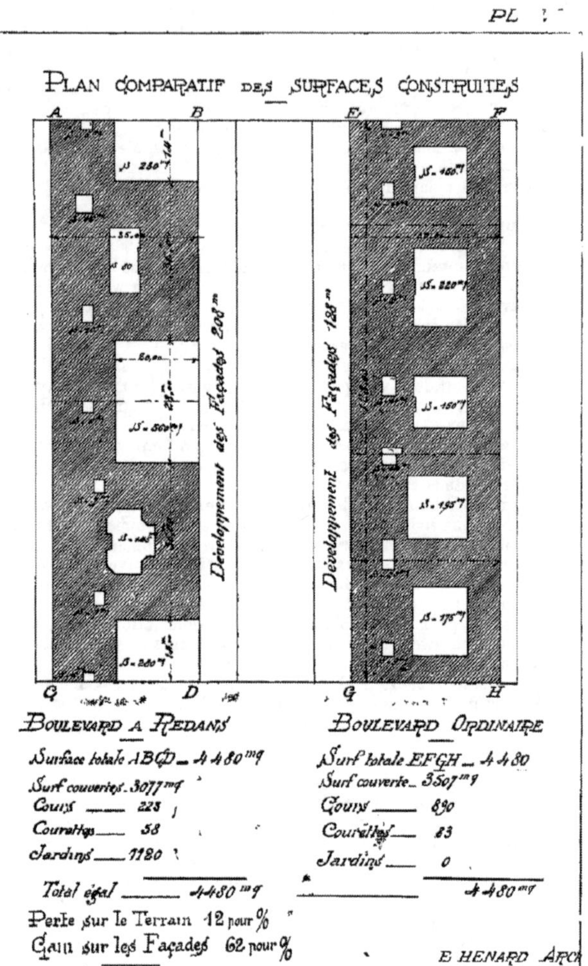
PL
PLAN COMPARATIF DES SURFACES CONSTRUITES
A   B   E   F
Développement des Façades 208ᵐ
Développement des Façades 188ᵐ
C   D   G   H
BOULEVARD A REDANS
Surface totale ABCD ___ 4.480 ᵐ9
Surf couvertes. 3077 ᵐ9
Cours ___ 225
Courettes ___ 58
Jardins ___ 1120
Total égal ___ 4480 ᵐ9
Perte sur le Terrain 12 pour %
Gain sur les Façades 62 pour %
BOULEVARD ORDINAIRE
Surf totale EFGH ___ 4.480
Surf couverte ___ 3507 ᵐ9
Cours ___ 890
Courettes ___ 83
Jardins ___ 0
4.480 ᵐ9
E. HENARD ARCH
1903

apporter au point de vue des voies de communication et des espaces libres

Nous donnons dans la Planche VIII le projet d'une transformation générale de Paris   Pour bien saisir la disposition projetée, reportons-nous à la figure 2 de la Planche II , qui nous donne le schéma des voies parisiennes de grande circulation, existant actuellement   Cette figure montre que Paris manque de grandes voies rayonnantes, que son noyau central manque de dégagements, et que son périmètre de rayonnement de 10 kilomètres de développement est trop étendu   Il est d'autant plus nécessaire de créer prochainement ces voies rayonnantes que la révolution qui s'opère chaque jour dans les moyens de transport, par les voitures automobiles, exige impérieusement l'ouverture des voies de pénétration plus larges et plus directes au centre, et de voies d'expansion plus allongées à la périphérie.

Il résulte, en outre, des observations relevées par la Préfecture de Police, qu'il existe à Paris huit directions principales de courants de circulation tendant au centre, et que ces huit courants suivent sensiblement les huit orientations principales (Nord, Nord-Ouest, Ouest, Sud-Ouest, Sud, Sud-Est, Est, Nord-Est), en se frayant un passage plus ou moins facile à travers le réseau des rues étroites de la ville

C'est en partant de ces données que nous proposons de créer un nouveau réseau de voies maîtresses, dont nous donnons (Planche VII) le schéma théorique

Le système se compose d'un noyau central de forme carrée, de 1 kilomètre de largeur dans les deux sens, entouré de larges voies, constituant un périmètre de rayonnement de 4 kilomètres, sur lequel viennent s'amorcer quatorze voies rayonnantes, qui sont

1	Avenue Richelieu (Nord)	Voie nouvelle
2.	Boulevard Sébastopol	Voie ancienne
3.	Avenue du Temple	Voie nouvelle
4	Avenue du Palais Royal (Est)	Voie nouvelle
5	Rue de Rivoli et Cours de Vincennes	Voies anciennes
6	Quai et route de Charenton	Voies anciennes
7	Avenue du Panthéon	Voie nouvelle
8.	Boulevard St Michel	Voie ancienne
9.	Avenue Richelieu (Sud)	Voie nouvelle
10.	Avenue du Carrousel	Voie nouvelle
11	Quai et route de Versailles	Voies anciennes
12	Avenue des Champs Elysées	Voie ancienne
13	Avenue du Palais Royal (Ouest)	Voie nouvelle
14.	Avenue de l'Opéra prolongée	Voie en partie nouvelle

Si l'on joint à ces quatorze voies quatre rues plus étroites, mais très passantes, et également rayonnantes, qui sont

15	La rue Montmartre	
16.	La rue Turbigo	Voies anciennes
17	La rue Gay-Lussac	
18.	La rue du Four .	

on obtient un total de 18 voies rayonnantes capables d'assurer pour un long avenir la circulation de Paris.

Dans le plan que nous donnons Planche VIII., toutes les voies nouvelles sont indiquées en rouge , cette figure ne donne plus un tracé schématique mais le tracé réel. L'alignement des nouvelles voies s'est courbé et assoupli dans la mesure des dérogations possibles, toutes les fois que l'alignement droit pouvait devenir dangereux pour l'existence des monuments où des sites connus   Nous n'avons employé l'alignement rectiligne que là où aucun monument ne pouvait être atteint.

En ce qui concerne les espaces libres, nous avons indiqué la création de 9 parcs périphériques sur des emplacements choisis, pris au dépens de l'enceinte fortifiée qui doit prochainement disparaître Ces neuf parcs nouveaux avec les 3 anciens parcs (Bois de Boulogne, Bois de Vincennes et Parc de Montsouris) donnent un total de 12 parcs périphériques. Nous proposons de les relier entre eux par un boulevard circulaire à redans qui constituerait pour Paris une couronne de verdure dont les grands parcs seraient les fleurons

Enfin, à l'intérieur même de la ville, nous prévoyons la création d'autres grands parcs et de jardins plus petits répartis de telle sorte qu'aucun habitant ne soit à plus d'un kilomètre de distance d'un grand parc, et à plus de 500 mètres de distance d'un jardin public

Dans notre plan, les parcs nouveaux sont indiqués en rouge, les parcs anciens en vert clair.

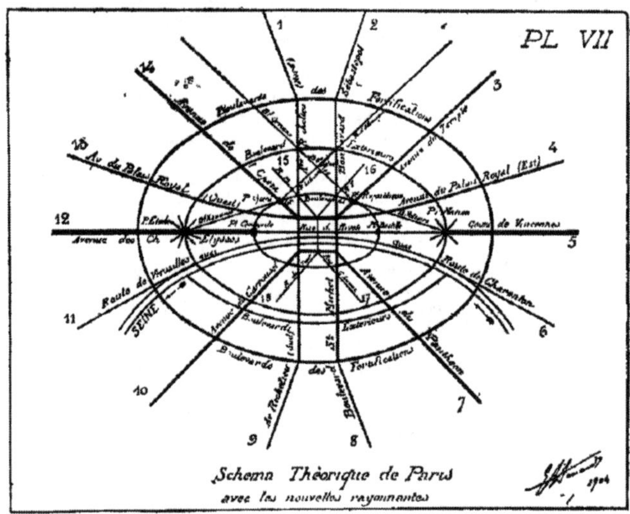

Un tel projet exigerait pour sa réalisation une somme considérable Elle ne dépasserait pas cependant celle qui a été dépensée par Haussmann, sous le Second Empire, pour l'embellissement de Paris.

De 1854 à 1870, Haussmann a dépensé un milliard et 430 millions (1,430,000,000), soit 84 millions par an, pour les grandes opérations de voirie, non compris les travaux d'adduction d'eau, d'égouts, de promenades, d'édifices divers, etc

L'évaluation du projet que nous proposons serait sensiblement équivalente Mais il ne s'agirait plus aujourd'hui comme autrefois de bouleverser Paris par des travaux hâtifs. On pourrait, au contraire, répartir les étapes d'une aussi vaste entreprise, en 40 ou 50 ans, et y consacrer une annuité de 30 millions par an   C'est là une charge qui n'a rien d'exagéré pour un budget qui dépasse 300 millions, surtout si l'on met en regard les bienfaits de toute sorte qu'une pareille transformation apporterait à la population, et le mouvement commercial et industriel qu'elle ferait naître

Conclusion

En achevant ce rapport, permettez-moi, Messieurs, de tirer une conclusion générale du travail trop incomplet que je vous ai présenté Vous avez pu constater, malgré les imperfections inévitables des figures qui vous ont été soumises, combien la comparaison des plans des grandes villes, ramenés à la même échelle, pouvait offrir d'intérêt

Il semble que s'il était possible de réunir des documents plus nombreux et moins incorrects embrassant les capitales ou les cités les plus importantes de tous les pays, on constituerait ainsi un ensemble technique de la plus grande valeur pour l'étude du développement des voies publiques et des espaces libres dans les villes

Cette proposition est en parfaite concordance avec celle que Sir Edwin Cornwall, président du County Council de Londres, a formulée dans une lettre publiée par le *Times* du 27 décembre, 1905

"Étant donné," disait-il, "que l'entente municipale entre Paris et Londres a déjà produit tant de bien, il m'a semblé que de meilleurs résultats encore suivraient, si l'exemple donné par Paris et Londres était développé Une façon d'atteindre ce but, et j'estime qu'elle sera la plus pratique, serait d'instituer un Congrès des capitales du monde civilisé. Le premier but de ce Congrès serait la discussion et l'examen des problèmes qui sont communs à toutes les grandes villes "

La proposition est séduisante. Mais pour que ce Congrès porte tous ses fruits, ne devrions-nous pas, nous architectes, entreprendre une tâche, fort lourde à la vérité, mais qui deviendrait plus légère si nous unissions nos efforts pour la mener à bonne fin ? Ne pourrions-nous pas réunir dans chaque pays, avec l'appui des administrations publiques, le dossier graphique des grandes villes, en le composant suivant une même méthode, avec des dessins à la même échelle et du même format ? On pourrait y joindre les vues photographiques des monuments, ou celles des sites intéressants et pittoresques On arriverait à créer ainsi l'histoire naturelle, l'anatomie comparée de ces grands organismes humains, et la masse de ces documents servirait de base solide aux embellissements que pourraient y apporter les gouvernements ou les municipalités. La constitution de ces dossiers aurait, d'ailleurs, une conséquence certaine En les comparant, en les étudiant, on finirait peut-être par comprendre que les transformations édilitaires ne sont pas seulement une œuvre de sèche géométrie, mais encore une véritable œuvre d'art, à laquelle doivent collaborer ceux qui, par leur éducation, leurs travaux et leur expérience, sont les défenseurs les plus autorisés de la beauté des villes La philosophie moderne a reconnu l'influence décisive des milieux sur l'évolution des êtres et des choses Il est donc de la plus haute importance de perfectionner sans cesse ces milieux, puisque les grandes capitales sont le laboratoire de tous les progrès, qui sont l'honneur des nations civilisées.

PLAN GÉNÉRAL
DES TRANSFORMATIONS
DE PARIS
PREMIÈRE ESQUISSE
Boulevard
Avenue
Rue du Maine
Boulevard
Boulevard
Avenue d'Orléans
Echelle
2000 m

3. By Dr J Stübben, Berlin

Entwerfen und Anlegen von Strassen und Freien Platzen in Stadten [1]

1 *Planning of Streets*

Verkehr—Richtung und Breite der Strassen mussen den Anforderungen des zu erwartenden Verkehrs entsprechen Der Verkehr muss überall und uberallhin einen ubersichtlichen, hindernisfreien Weg vorfinden Bei Hauptstrassen kann die erforderliche Breite 50 m und mehr betragen , in Nebenstrassen kann, wenn diese nur dem Verkehr der Anwohner dienen, die Breite auf 8 m. hinabgehen Alle Zwischenmaasse sind je nach den Umstanden gerechtfertigt

Die Steigungsverhaltnisse der Strassen sollen tunlichst flach sein In der Ebene sind starkere Steigungen als 1 · 70 nach Moglichkeit zu vermeiden, weil sie die Asphaltierung der Strassendecke hindern Im Hugelgelande sind fur Hauptstrassen Steigungen bis 1 : 20, fur Nebenstrassen solche bis 1 10 zulassig. Bei grosserer Steilheit sind Treppen oder Fusswege anzuordnen , letztere sollten uberhaupt an Berglehnen und zur Durchquerung langer Blocke mehr als bisher verwendet werden

Hygiene—Aus gesundheitlichen Gründen sind Strassen in reiner Westostlage nach Moglichkeit zu vermeiden, weil die Hauser an der Sudseite wahrend des grossten Teils des Jahres Sonnenstrahlen nicht empfangen. Die Strassenbreite soll mindestens gleich der Häuserhohe sein Breite Strassen sind mit Baumreihen und Gartenanlagen zu bepflanzen Vorgarten den Hausern entlang begunstigen Luft und Licht und gestatten oft die Einschrankung der Verkehrsbreite Sehr breite leere Strassenflachen sind wegen Staubtreibens und Schattenlosigkeit zu vermeiden , dasselbe gilt fur lange, gerade Strassen, besonders wenn sie in der herrschenden Windrichtung liegen.

Schonheit—Schonheitsgrunde sprechen im unbedingten Sinne ebensowenig gegen gerade als gegen krumme Strassen, und ebensowenig gegen regelmassige wie gegen unregelmassige Baufluchten Im hugeligen Gelande erleichtern gekrummte Strassen den Verkehr und die Aufteilung des Gelandes , in der Ebene sind gerade und krumme, regelmassige und unregelmassige Linien gerechtfertigt sowohl nach praktischen Erwagungen als nach kunstlerischen Absichten des Entwerfers Gerade Strassen von grosser Lange sind zu vermeiden , Gegenmittel sind Krummung oder Richtungsanderung, unter Umstanden auch Versetzung der Richtung oder der Baufluchten. Versetzungen sind indes nur insoweit zulassig, als sie eine ubersichtliche Verkehrsbahn frei lassen Convexe Gefallsbruche sind in geraden Strassen nach Moglichkeit zu vermeiden , das concave Nivellement ist zu bevorzugen Unvermeidliche Ruckenpunkte sind kunstlerisch als Endpunkte auszubilden Jede Strasse ist, soweit tunlich, individuell zu gestalten Auch in derselben Strasse kann der Wechsel in der Breite zur Verschonerung dienen Geschlossene Strassenbilder sind uberall anzustreben

2 *Planning of Open Spaces*

Verkehr.—Freie Platze fur den Ausgleich der Verkehrsrichtungen (*Verkehrsplatze*) sind am Zusammenfluss von Strassen, besonders an Bahnhofen, Brucken, Stadttoren u s w ein Bedurfnis. Aus Zweckmassigkeitsgrunden empfiehlt es sich, die verschiedenen Verkehrsrichtungen nicht in einem Punkte sich schneiden zu lassen Die Verkehrsplatze entbehren in der Regel einer kunstlerisch wichtigen Eigenschaft, namlich der geschlossenen Umrahmung, konnen aber dennoch ein schones Bild gewahren Der Mangel der geschlossenen Umrahmung wird gemildert durch eine

---

[1] Dr Stubben's Paper was illustrated by a large number of lantern-views

derartige Fuhrung der Strassen, dass der Blick uber den Platz hinweg
auf eine Platzwand trifft Unnotige Verkehrsplatze, hervorgerufen
durch willkurliche Zusammenfuhrung von Verkehrslinien, sind zu vermeiden

Marktplatze sollen an einer Hauptverkehrstrasse liegen, aber in ihrer
Hauptflache dem Fahrverkehr entzogen sein

Hygiene – Die Lufterneuerung verlangt eine reichliche Zahl freier
Platze ; sie sollen wenigstens 1/10 der Gesamtflache einnehmen Wichtig
fur die Gesundheit sind besonders die bepflantzen Plätze (*Gartenplatze* und
Spielplatze), sowie offentliche Parkanlagen und Promenaden

Schonheit —Die vornehmste kunstlerische Eigenschaft freier Plätze
ist ihre moglichst geschlossene Umrahmung Sie gilt als Forderung
für Markt und Gartenplatze, besonders aber fur reine *Architekturplatze*,
d h fur solche Platze, deren Zweck darin besteht, monumentale Gebäude
aufzunehmen Die Randstellung dieser Gebaude ist der Stellung auf
der freien Fläche vorzuziehen ; bei letzterer Stellung gilt die Forderung
der Umrahmung fur die verbleibenden Plat*zteile* Mittel zur Schliessung
des Rahmens sind Torbauten und Hallenanlagen, die uber die Strassen-
offnungen hinweg gefuhrt werden Massstabfehler, insbesondere uber-
trieben grosse Freiflachen, sind zu vermeiden. Die Convexitat der
Platzfläche ist unzulassig, die Concavität zu bevorzugen Jede Platzan-
lage ist, soweit tunlich, individuell zu gestalten

Combinationen von Platzen unterliegen je nach ihrer Bestimmung
den verschiedenartigen Anforderungen, z B des Verkehrs einerseits,
der monumentalen Gebaude andererseits Die *Gruppierung* mehrerer
getrennter Platze kann im kunstlerischen Sinne die schonsten Anordnungen ergeben

3. *Planning of Cities.*

Geschichtliche Entwickelung —Es ist lehrreich, einer Betrachtung zu
unterziehen

    die regelmassigen Stadte des alten Griechenland,

    die regelmassigen und unregelmassigen Stadte der Romer,

    die unregelmassigen Stadte des fruheren Mittelalters,

    die regelmassigen Stadtanlagen des spateren Mittelalters, der Renais-
sance und der Barockzeit,

    die schematischen Stadtanlagen Amerikas,

    die zumeist im geometrischen Sinne angelegten Stadtteile aus dem
19ten Jahrhundert,

    endlich die modernen Bestrebungen

Verkehr, Hygiene, Schonheit —Den modernen Bestrebungn liegen im
wesentlichen die Gesichtspunkte zu Grunde, welche vorstehend fur
das Entwerfen von Strassen und Plätzen angegeben sind Wir konnen
nicht die Stadte irgend einer fruheren Zeit einfach nachbilden, weil
besonders die Verkehrs- und hygienischen Forderungen andere geworden
sind. Die Uebersichtlichkeit des Stadtgrundrisses ist fur das Zurecht-
finden von Wichtigkeit. Die kunstlerische Aufgabe aber besteht in voller
Erfullung der Zweckmassigkeit unter schoner Formangebung , d.h
*in der schonheitlich befriedigenden Raumbildung unter freiem Himmel
bei gleichzeitiger, moglichst vollkommener Rucksichtnahme auf Verkehr
und Gesundheit*

Wirtschaftliche und soziale Anforderungen.—Zu den Anforderungen
des Verkehrs, der Gesundheit und der Schonheit treten wirtschaftliche
und soziale Erwägungen Die Strassen und Baublocke sollen nach
Ausstattung und Abmessungen den wirtschaftlichen und baulichen
Bedurfnissen der Bevölkerung entsprechen Breite Hauptstrassen sollen
den grossen Verkehr aufnehmen, schmalere Nebenstrassen (Wohn-
strassen) dienen zur Aufteilung des Bebauungsfeldes in einzelne Blocke
Nach ihrer Bestimmung zu geschlossener oder offener und halboffener

Bauweise, zu Miethausern oder zu Eigenhausern, zu herrschaftlichen,
Mittelstands- oder Arbeiterwohnungen, zu Ladengeschaften oder zu
kleingewerblichen und grossgewerblichen Betrieben sollen sich die Stadt-
teile schon im Entwurf unterscheiden Ihre Lage zum Stadtkern, zur
landschaftlichen Umgebung, zu Eisenbahn- und Hafenanlagen ist dabei
zu berucksichtigen

Wie fur die einzelnen Strassen und Plätze, so ist auch fur ganze Stadt-
teile die individuelle Gestaltung anzustreben

Denkmalpflege — Alte Baudenkmale aller Art, sowie bestehende
schone Strassen- und Landschaftsbilder sind nicht blos zu schonen,
sondern auch zur eigenartigen Ausgestaltung der Stadt im kunstlerischen
Sinne zu verwerten

---

4. Par B POLLÉS Y VIVÓ, J. MAJÓ Y RIBAS, M. BERTRAN DE QUINTANA.

La base fondamentale des connaissances de l'architecte est renfermée
dans les trois ordres d'idées suivantes : art, construction et hygiène, et,
sans contestation, le titre d'architecte porte avec lui celui d'hygiéniste
L'importance que ces connaissances ont entre elles, mieux, la suprématie
de l'une de ces connaissances sur les autres, dépend uniquement du genre
de construction à projeter   En effet, si le projet a pour but la construction d'un monument, il est évident que l'alpha de l'œuvre demande une
connaissance approfondie de l'art, tandis que s'il s'agit d'un chemin, d'un
canal, d'un acquéduc, c'est la science et les connaissances pratiques qui
serviront de guide   Enfin s'il s'agit de la construction d'une maison ou
appartement destiné à abriter une famille ou d'une habitation collective,
l'architecte ne doit pas oublier que sa mission consiste à offrir à l'homme
un local hygiénique afin que les êtres qui l'habitent puissent y vivre en de
saines conditions ; en un mot, l'architecte devra étudier à fond les préceptes
humanitaires de l'hygiène, car, permettez-nous cette comparaison, vrai
médecin des constructions il doit savoir reconnaître pour quel motif un
logement n'est pas hygiénique et, une fois reconnue, éviter les causes d'insalubrité, en d'autres termes, il doit avoir un coup d'œil sûr pour diagnos-
tiquer la maladie ou défauts de la construction, et connaître la théra-
peutique ou moyen pour corriger les causes perturbatrices de l'état
physiologique de l'habitation, et notez bien que l'architecte bien instruit
scientifiquement parlant se trouve pour cela dans des conditions plus
favorables que le médecin l'édifice pour ce dernier étant l'homme dont
l'organisme est sujet à des lois excessivement variables, et à des revire-
ments dont les causes restent souvent inconnues   Pour nous, au contraire, le bâtiment, corps complètement inerte, dont toutes les parties
nous sont connues, nous pouvons nous prononcer sûrement, tant sur les
éléments dont se compose la construction, que sur les causes qui peuvent
lui être préjudiciables, causes qui forcement doivent venir de l'extérieur
ou de l'intérieur de l'habitation et que, pour cette raison, nous classerons
en deux catégories, *celles extérieures* et *celles intérieures*   Les premières
dépendent de ce qui entoure la maison et sur quoi elle repose, c'est à dire
l'atmosphère et le sol. Les deuxièmes sont le résultat absolu de la présence
constante des êtres qui l'habitent, et de la qualité des matériaux employés
dans sa construction

Nous nous occuperons ici seulement des causes extérieures en vertu du
titre du thème que nous traitons.

Dans les grands centres l'homme est obligé de vivre dans des logements peu espacieux, et comme depuis sa naissance il absorbe par les poumons l'oxygène atmosphérique, l'air est vicié de ce fait, d'où il résulte que la civilisation attente à la pureté de l'atmosphère en créant les grandes agglomérations, cause originale de l'impureté de l'air. Il est évident que cet air que nous introduisons dans les dépendances habitées, et qui se renouvelle sans l'intermédiaire de la main de l'homme (ventilation naturelle), ou celui qui exige des moyens spéciaux (ventilation artificielle), provient uniquement de l'atmosphère qui entoure la construction De cette dernière considération se déduit la conséquence suivante l'air respiré dans l'intérieur d'un local sera plus ou moins pur suivant que le sera plus ou moins celui de l'endroit où il est situé

Comment peut-on resoudre ce problème ?

Ostensivement examinée, la question se présente sous deux aspects distincts le choix de l'emplacement pour la création d'un centre, et la disposition de celui-ci une fois l'emplacement choisi, mais en la pratique la chose ne se présente jamais ainsi , il s'agit généralement d'agrandir ou de modifier un centre de population existant, centre dont la création fut en principe très lente et sans être règlementée par aucun plan, comme le prouve clairement l'histoire de l'urbanisation.

L'aspect vrai et logique de la question est celui-ci . toute population est formée par une disposition plus ou moins complexe et plus ou moins rationnelle de voies de communication, rues, places, promenades, et jardins, dont l'ensemble des superficies nous donne le total des espaces libres.

Ces espaces libres doivent se tracer en tenant compte des circonstances multiples, de celles surtout qui se rattachent au climat de la localité , elles varieront en effet suivant la latitude, l'altitude, la direction des vents dominants, la plus ou moins grande distance de la mer ou de grands fleuves, la position des montagnes voisines, la fréquence des pluies, la nature du sol, etc Cependant de toutes ces circonstances celles qui ont une influence la plus prépondérante sont la direction des vents régnants et la latitude.

Ce que démontre évidemment l'importance de la direction des vents dominants, c'est qu'à ce facteur est subordonné l'emplacement des édifices classés dans la catégorie des bâtiments insalubres qui, à cause de multiples émanations viciant l'atmosphère, ne sauraient s'établir de façon que les courants d'air puissent apporter ces émanations malsaines aux espaces libres de la cité, convertissant ainsi en foyer d'infection l'air que nos habitations reçoivent du dehors ; en conséquence de ce qui précède, on devra étudier consciencieusement l'emplacement d'un cimetière, d'un four crématoire, d'un établissement destiné à l'épuration des eaux infectes, provenant d'un système d'égouts, d'un hôpital, d'un lazaret, de certaines industries, etc.

Relativement à la latitude, ou distance à l'équateur, à part les différences de température que suppose son plus ou moins grand éloignement des pôles, suivant les points géographiques que l'on considère, une des causes des plus importantes à la résolution du problème et sur laquelle nous devons fixer l'attention, c'est la considération de l'angle que forment les rayons solaires avec le plan de l'horizon de chaque localité, angle qui va diminuant à mesure qu'augmente la latitude

D'après les rapports des congrès internationaux de la tuberculose, et de la salubrité et hygiène des habitations, tenus récemment à Paris, il est hors de doute que l'une des mesures essentielles et *sine qua non* à prendre pour qu'un bâtiment soit placé dans des conditions hygiéniques c'est que ses façades soient exposées de façon à recevoir le plus long-temps possible les rayons solaires et l'air pur ; pour obtenir ce but on comprend que nous devrons orienter les rues, en déterminer la largeur et fixer la hauteur des maisons qui motiveront les voies, de manière que l'accès du soleil soit assuré.

Notre cadre restreint ne nous permettant pas de tracer graphiquement la marche des rayons solaires, pour chacune des latitudes correspondant à chaque degré (mode qui donnerait une idée précise de la chose), il nous suffira de considérer les distinctes latitudes correspondant à l'équateur latitude 0°, aux tropiques latitude 23° 27′ à un point intermédiaire—par exemple Madrid, latitude 40°, aux cercles pôlaires latitude 66° 33′ et aux pôles latitude 90°—pour démontrer clairement que les angles maximum que le rayon solaire, correspondant à 12 heures, soit l'heure à laquelle le soleil passe par le méridien de la localité, forme avec le plan de l'horizon aux époques des solstices d'été, des équinoxes et des solstices d'hiver, sont les suivants pour les dites latitudes —

	Latitude	S d'été	Equinoxes	S d'hiver
Equateur	0 0	113 27	90 0	66 33
Tropiques	23 27	90 0	63 33	41 33
Madrid	. 40 0	73 27	50 0	26 33
Cercles pôlaires .	61 33	46 54	23 27	0 0
Pôles . .	90 0	23 27	0 0	23 27

De ce qui précède il ressort clairement que les divers espaces libres pour chaque cité, rues, places, promenades etc, et par analogie ceux reservés sous forme de cour, pour faciliter dans les maisons l'accès de l'air et de la lumière, doivent augmenter de largeur à mesure qu'augmente la latitude de la localité, tandis que la hauteur des maisons devra décroite alors que la latitude sera plus grande, en d'autres termes, pour éviter qu'un parement projette son ombre sur un autre il faudra que la largeur des rues augmente proportionnellement à la latitude du lieu et que la hauteur des maisons décroisse dans les mêmes proportions.

Pour donner au sujet que nous venons légèrement d'esquisser tout le développement qu'il comporte, il faudrait tout un volume bourré d'explications scientifiques et doctorales, et comme ces notes sont destinées à un auditoire composé de professeurs compétents, nous voulons éviter de tomber dans ce ridicule et nous terminerons nos appréciations sur la partie du problème hygiénique, intimement lié avec le titre du thème que nous traitons, par les conclusions suivantes :

1. Que les voies de communication dans les cités devront être disposées de façon à ce qu'en aucun cas elles puissent servir de canal conducteur aux impuretés provenant des industries insalubres, qui nécessairement existent dans tous les centres de population, c'est à dire qu'on devra veiller à ce que l'emplacement de ces édifices soit situé de telle façon que les vents régnants ne puissent jamais apporter, dans les lieux habitées les émanations insalubres originaires de ces édifices

2. Que les dimensions des espaces libres dans une cité devront être subordonnées à la densité de la population ainsi qu'à sa latitude, en d'autres termes, plus une cité sera peuplée, plus grande devra être la surface des espaces libres, condition qu'on obtiendra avec les voies de communication et les cours faisant partie des bâtiments Considérant, en outre, que le soleil est l'élément dépurateur par excellence, afin d'obtenir sa présence le plus longtemps sur les façades des habitations, il conviendra d'augmenter la surface des espaces libres ou de diminuer la hauteur des constructions à mesure qu'augmentera la latitude de la cité.

5. Par Gaston Trélat (Paris).

Les rues devraient avoir, par rapport à la hauteur des maisons qui les bordent, une largeur qu'elles sont toutes loin d'atteindre en général Dans leur besoin de faire comme en Amérique, certaines nations d'Europe, s'attachant malheureusement aux moins bonnes choses, tendraient à élever leurs maisons à des hauteurs qui rappelassent les hauteurs démesurées qu'elles ont prises parfois aux Etats-Unis Ce qui pourrait être sans inconvénient dans des localités à espaces illimités devient, au contraire, des plus défectueux dans les villes du Continent où la largeur des voies est en général assez restreinte, relativement aux constructions en bordure et d'une hauteur moyenne Les maisons de 15 ou 20 étages peuvent en effet ne point présenter de gros inconvénients dans les villes du nouveau monde bénéficiant de plus grands territoires La pureté de l'atmosphère est de ce fait mise à la portée des habitants qui n'ont nullement à souffrir de concentrations telles que nous avons souvent à les subir Les espaces très étendus sont transformés en parcs, jardins, ou squares très accessibles aux habitants , et la superficie totale des agglomérations reste d'ordinaire évaluable à 200 mètres par tête. Et ce n'est pas trop. Je me souviens d'une étude récente où l'on rapprochait les superficies américaines de la centaine de mètres exigés, par unité d'occupant dans nos édifices d'assistance. On concluait par cette pensée que physiologiquement il n'y avait peut-être pas de raison déterminante pour ménager l'abondance et la pureté d'atmosphère à des organismes atteints par la maladie et réduits dans leur action vitale ; tandis que ceux, pourvus au contraire d'une plénitude d'activité en rapport avec les dépenses qu'une santé intacte peut autoriser, seraient moins bien partagés. Et cependant c'est seulement un peu plus de 20 mètres qui échoit, par exemple, à chaque unité de l'agglomération parisienne prise dans son ensemble C'est là une condition désas· treuse, comme les statistiques sanitaires ne le démontrent que trop , et les circonstances nouvelles, qui marquent le progrès dans le monde, sont destinées à transformer cet état de choses, en ménageant des espaces au centre même des cités agrandies

Sans plus nous attarder, occupons nous du phénomène contemporain sur lequel pareille question doit s'appuyer avant tout

La rapidité toujours croissante des moyens de communication se résume dans deux conséquences qu'il faut noter : d'une part l'embarras renouvelé et l'interception trop fréquente des voies de circulation, dans les vieux quartiers à habitations encombrées par leur superposition trop grande , par contre, la durée des trajets réduite jusqu'à pouvoir être considérée comme en voie d'apparence négligeable, relativement aux exigences d'activités présentes et aux souvenirs du passé.

Alors la santé publique voudrait que les municipalités étudiassent les moyens par lesquels il leur serait loisible de dégager les centres aujourd'hui trop encombrés. Les conditions nouvelles s'attacheront à faire passer une partie importante des habitants au-dehors de la périphérie actuelle, dans les territoires de banlieue qui sont appelés à être compris dans le domaine de l'agglomération sans, pour cela, entraîner aucune perte de temps appréciable, par suite des nouveaux modes de translation

Dès maintenant, il y aurait lieu de prévoir des espaces inoccupés et judicieusement ménagés ; de même que les rues projetées auraient à répondre à des règlements de voirie perfectionnés, par rapport aux anciens errements et conformément aux besoins contemporains On arriverait même ultérieurement—une fois le centre déplacé par suite de l'extension urbaine—à assainir les anciens quartiers. Ils seraient soustraits, aux dangers de trop grande superposition d'étages habités, par leur destruction partielle, suivant une idée émise, il y a déjà longtemps,

par M. Emile Trélat.   Ce serait d'une application heureuse dans cértaines
rues anciennes à bordure trop élevée par rapport à leur largeur.   Mais
il ne faudrait jamais procéder à semblable exécution, sans y faire intervenir
d'autres considérations que celles de l'hygiène   Aujourd'hui tout tend
à se confondre, et je veux, en ce moment, alléguer la question de beauté,
à laquelle l'intérêt de la collectivité est lié désormais   Rien ne se réaliserait
donc sans délibération préalable et spécialement compétente, en fait de
santé comme en fait de beauté.

Voilà déjà quelques unes des améliorations conséquentes de la rapidité
de translation, et qu'il serait permis d'affronter   Et la salubrité, qui
en résulterait pour les agglomérations, serait à considérer.   Il y a même
là un point de départ pour des modifications destinées à changer totalement les conditions de santé dans les villes.   Il semblerait même que
celles-ci fussent appelées, dans un temps assez proche, à ne plus donner
lieu à aucun des inconvénients sanitaires inhérents aux habitations comprimées qu'elles représentent encore   Il faudrait seulement que les
pouvoirs responsables s'attachassent aux applications d'un *traitement*
spécial en accord avec la conscience que veut notre temps et assurassent
partout un air pur, une lumière directe

Les espaces inhabités prendront une étendue comparable à celle
des Bois de Boulogne ou de Vincennes, au centre des cités assainies,
maintenant que l'électricité est venue se joindre à la vapeur pour assurer
la rapidité d'automobiles, de tramways, de toutes les communications,
qu'elles soient souterraines, à ciel ouvert, à fleur du sol ou en l'air

Quant aux rues, il est bien évident que l'extension périphérique les
dégagera en partie.   Encore faut-il que les nouvelles voies répondent
à des données différentes de celles que voulaient des temps où piétons,
cavaliers, véhicules traînés par des chevaux représentaient l'ensemble
des services auxquels les chaussées avaient à faire face, dans les villes.
Indépendamment des moyens de transport qui changent les conditions
élémentaires de l'activité urbaine, la science présente encore d'autres exigences   On ne peut oublier les obligations, que signalent les statistiques,
de lutter contre la mortalité   C'est un combat qui objective les premiers
devoirs des municipalités   Car elle est toujours menaçante, la mort ,
et les connaissances, comme les précautions qui en sont conséquentes à
notre époque, ont déjà réduit ses ravages de façon considérable.   Idéalement, on est bien conduit à envisager le temps où il n'y aura plus de
maladies transmissibles, par suite de la disparition d'ambiances favorables
à leur propagation.

Mais il ne devrait jamais y avoir de constatation, en fait d'insalubrité,
qui n'engageât la mise à l'ordre du jour de travaux répondant à la fois
aux dangers et aux maux envisagés, ainsi qu'à *l'idéal* même qu'il serait
loisible d'en déduire.   Il semblerait en conséquence que l'activité caractéristique de notre époque engage une activité correspondante dans la
supputation et la prévision des nécessités du lendemain.   Il serait urgent
que des projets d'ensemble s'y attachassent et missent au point technique
tout ce qui touche les nécessités courantes   C'est le seul procédé pour
assurer, un jour, les réalisations que la science permet dès maintenant
d'envisager   Rien alors ne serait exécuté qui ne fût subordonné à l'idéal
précis que les connaissances font concevoir et qui serait entretenu par
une mise au point journalière ou continue.

C'est là une idée générale qui s'appliquerait à toutes les conceptions
techniques, en ce qui touche la santé publique—et même la beauté publique.   Il convient de reconnaître que souvent les rues ne répondent
plus du tout aux nécessités de la circulation actuelle   Les lignes ferrées,
qui ne font encore qu'apparaître sur nos chaussées, sont appelées à
s'étendre à un plus grand nombre de voies   Elles engagent une direction
déterminée des véhicules qui perdent en conséquence la majeure partie
de leur souplesse à se subordonner aux nécessités d'une circulation différente.

Avec l'abondance du roulement, ce défaut de souplesse—dans une mobilité voulue des voitures—devient une cause nouvelle d'encombrement et d'interception. Les chaussées ne sont donc plus assez larges , elles devraient être considérablement agrandies Il n'y aurait, en conséquence que des avantages à procéder aussi amplement que possible à cet élargissement, pour toute rue nouvelle qu'il s'agirait de prévoir ou de créer La circulation comme la santé publique présentent l'une et l'autre un intérêt général qui, de notre temps, doit dominer toute autre pensée directrice en pareille occurrence.

Si nous en arrivons à envisager la réalisation, il semblerait bon de spécialiser la direction des roulements et d'avoir deux chaussées répondant chacune à un même sens de mouvement. Elles seraient distinctes du fait de refuges longitudinaux et réservés aux piétons, comme les trottoirs latéraux, ou même à des plantations Mais je dois rappeler, à titre de document, un travail qui intéresse la question. Voilà plus de vingt ans de cela, ce double point de vue de largeur des rues et de hauteur des maisons qui les bordent avait déjà donné lieu à une étude d'Adolphe Vogt. Elle faisait intervenir comme données · la latitude, l'angle d'incidence des rayons solaires au solstice d'hiver, l'angle que forme la direction de la rue par rapport au méridien. L'auteur en déduisait une division en rues méridiennes et en rues équatoriales Pour Paris, par exemple, le travail aboutissait, comme solution, à une largeur des voies méridiennes égale *à deux fois un tiers* la hauteur des maisons , tandis que celle des rues équatoriales comprenait *quatre fois* la hauteur des maisons C'était un repère intéressant à rappeler. Il fit à l'époque l'objet d'un article du Docteur Vallin dans la *Revue d'Hygiène*, et je le trouve rappelé, par M Emile Trélat, dans ses *Questions de Salubrité* Adolphe Vogt visait dans son étude les rez-de-chaussée, qui devaient bénéficier des rayons solaires pendant une heure au moins au jour le plus court de l'année C'était son *criterium*

La diffusion de la tuberculose et l'influence pernicieuse de l'absence de lumière, constatées dans nos grands centres, rendaient la solution, préconisée par le savant Allemand, particulièrement utile à rappeler en ce moment.

Résumé.—Les rues ne sont jamais assez larges pour que le mouvement de la chaussée s'y puisse développer sans exposer à des encombrements Ceux-ci occasionnent des pertes de temps en contradiction avec la rapidité que les moyens de locomotion tendent à assurer ; ils aboutissent encore à une confusion apparente de circulation, qui n'est pas en rapport avec la beauté objective des rues Cependant le fait dominant du jour est une rapidité de translation de plus en plus accentuée. Grâce à quoi, les anciennes banlieues des capitales ou des villes sont reliées ou peuvent être reliées instantanément aux centres des anciennes agglomérations La possibilité s'ensuivrait d'assimiler ces nouvelles localités aux anciens quartiers où se centralisent encore les activités urbaines On y reporterait donc, en partie, les habitations restées jusqu'ici encombrantes pour le centre des villes ; elles tendaient jusqu'ici à y propager toutes les maladies transmissibles et évitables

Les agglomérations élargies prendraient une salubrité considérable et un éclat de lumière, en opposition avec ces concentrations tellement défectueuses d'habitants resserrés et superposés sur des espaces relativement restreints et assombris par l'abondance des bâtiments.

Des superficies inhabitées prendraient la forme de parcs, de squares, de jardins, d'avenues plantées ; et même des squares privés pourraient être ménagés dans des terrains assez vastes, que les constructions borderaient sur les voies publiques. Et tout cela serait à projeter, à arrêter, pendant qu'il en est encore temps Cette œuvre préalable se poursuivrait sous le couvert des autorités municipales, indépendamment des exigences de l'exécution qui s'opérerait ensuite dans la mesure des possibilités et des volontés financières

Rien ne serait exécuté qui ne répondît aux ensembles qu'il convient d'entrevoir dès maintenant, pour assurer des réalités, telles que les connaissances présentes invitent à les considérer et à les prévoir

Il y aurait donc là une mise au point technique des progrès que la science envisage de nos jours. Il s'ensuivrait plus tard des réalisations ordonnées et répondant bien aux vues que notre vie intellectuelle peut bien comporter.

Il y a nécessité d'échapper aux errements surannés servant jusqu'ici de fond aux règlements de voirie Pour cela, il conviendrait de faire appel à des méditations et à des délibérations compétentes, ayant toutes pour objectif primordial la santé ou le bien-être des collectivités. Car c'est à son service exclusif que la réglementation doit répondre.

Conclusion —En conséquence, il y aurait lieu d'émettre le vœu que, pour toutes les agglomérations importantes, des projets fussent mis à l'étude sans retard. Ils auraient à tenir compte des conditions qui sont inspirées par la science et qui intéressent la santé comme la rapidité de translation Ces projets comporteraient donc une mise au point des solutions techniques à tirer de la science ou de l'expérience constatée par les statistiques Ils seraient mis à exécution dans la mesure des exigences locales et des possibilités budgétaires Mais rien alors ne se ferait qui ne répondît à un *idéal* en rapport avec les connaissances de l'époque.

---

6 THE PLANNING OF THE RESIDENTIAL DISTRICTS OF TOWNS.

By Raymond Unwin

In the section of town planning we in England have very much to learn from our Continental brethren. Owing largely to difference in national habits and sentiment, and, arising out of this, to the difference between the powers possessed by the local governing bodies here and on the Continent, there has been little scope in England for the laying out and development of town areas on any large scale Hence it is that we in England are only beginning to study this question, and have practically no literature, either permanent or periodical, dealing with it; and while our towns are growing as rapidly as those of other countries, we are behind them in the art of developing them In Germany, for example, we find that the art of city building has been widely studied for many years, that many able professional men devote themselves to this work, and that there is a valuable literature and at least one good periodical (*Der Stadtebau*) devoted entirely to it So far has development gone in Germany that since the time when many comprehensive town plans were laid down a new style almost has sprung up, and the school which we in England associate with the name of Camillo Sitte is exercising a predominating influence The Englishman who comes to know what his German brethren have been doing cannot but marvel at the scope of their work, the thoroughness with which it is done, and the zeal with which improvements are introduced, even after plans have been made; and he cannot but feel that the English system of allowing towns to grow in a haphazard and unordered manner, according to the interest or caprice of individual landowners, has only to be compared with the

German system of orderly development on a prearranged plan to stand utterly condemned

Public opinion is, however, rapidly becoming ripe for the adoption here of some system for controlling and guiding town development, and I hope we may effectively help in bringing this about. Probably the best plan would be to form small committees in each town to watch over the æsthetic side of development, to offer suggestions and criticisms on new proposals, and to secure as soon as possible the appointment by each municipality of an official whose special duty it should be to report on all improvement schemes from this point of view. This would bring the matter constantly before the public, and would help them to contrast what might be done under a properly ordered system with what actually is done under our lack of system

While this work is going forward it behoves us as architects to study the technical side of the subject and to learn what has already been done in other countries, so that when opportunities arise for similar work in England we may be prepared to take it up   For this would seem to be eminently the work for architects   No one else in quite the same way combines practical and artistic training, or is so accustomed, when laying down plans to meet practical requirements, to have always before his imagination the picture of what the effect of those plans will be when actually realised   Also to produce a successful result the buildings themselves must always be considered when planning roads, open spaces, and building sites.   One who is not—or at least has not been—accustomed to the designing of buildings will not be likely adequately to consider and weigh all the requirements when laying out their sites.

As, comparatively speaking, beginners in this country in the art of town planning, there is scope for much original work ; for while it would show gross insular prejudice not to study with the utmost respect and care what has been done abroad, it would be rash to an equal degree if we were to assume that what has been done and approved in Germany or in America will also be the best adapted to our own country.

It is in dealing with the vast growth of residential districts of all classes that we shall probably find it specially necessary to work on lines of our own, and it is to this problem that I propose to address myself.

There is probably no more pressing need in this country at the present time than the introduction of order and artistic consideration in the planning and laying out of such districts.   And in this branch of the work of city building, while much of such principles as Camillo Sitte evolves from the study of ancient Italian towns will be found most suggestive, many of his practical conclusions, and much of Continental practice generally, will be found hardly applicable   The Englishman's desire for privacy, his habit of living in self-contained houses and cottages on the outskirts of towns, and his general dislike of the flat system and block dwelling very materially modify the problem.   Indeed, there are not wanting signs that in the planning and arranging of residences our Continental brethren may be willing to learn much from us

In considering the development of a new suburban area one of the first suggestions of value which we get from ancient towns is the advantage of the limitation and definition of the area   If we compare the charm of the old walled-in town, where the country comes up clean and fresh right to the point where the town proper begins, with the ragged edges fringed with backyards and rubbish heaps which generally mark the limits of our modern town development, we shall at once realise the importance of finding some means of defining and limiting such new areas. Obviously we cannot ring in our towns with walls as of old, but some substitute may be found   Sometimes a broad walk and an avenue of trees may effectively circle the extremity of a newly laid out area.   In other cases a narrow belt of woodland, orchard, meadow, or park may be of great value, and at least some orderly line, a sunk fence or belt of shrubbery completing the gardens of the houses, may be secured (see Fig. 1). Should it be urged that it is impossible to define the areas in a town that is continually growing, I would reply that the continual growth only makes such definition of the greater importance, and that both the health of such a town and the pleasure of residence in it would be vastly increased if between areas of reasonable extent there were preserved those defining belts of woodland, park, or even of broad grass-lined walks or avenues of trees or shrubs.

Such limited suburban areas will often contain a few only of those public and business buildings which, in the central parts of towns, make possible the fine architectural effects due to the congregating of such buildings around an inclosed space or place. This, however, so far from being a reason why the entire effect of these few larger buildings should be lost by their being promiscuously scattered over the area, is a most potent reason why, in every suburban or new village area, special effort should be made to group together such public and other larger buildings as may be available, so that some definite effect may be produced, and some centre for the life of the district created   It must be remembered,

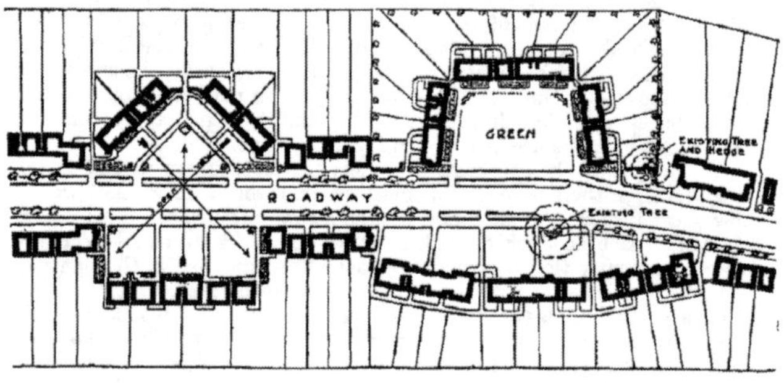

Fig. 1.

however, that where the buildings will be small in size, and perhaps often second-rate in character, it may be quite impossible successfully to create an inclosed place, particularly when the dimensions of the suburban roads which must necessarily enter such a place are considered   With this class of building, however, the architect may be greatly helped by the judicious use of trees and gardening, as buildings may be linked together into one whole by careful arrangement and careful planning Much as we may learn from beautiful Continental cities, we must not forget that in our own villages and older towns there is a wealth of suggestion, much of it more directly applicable to the conditions of the areas that we are now considering   Nor must we forget in planning such areas that we cannot afford to sacrifice to the production of some particular external effect the convenience and pleasure of those who are to occupy the houses, and for whom the district is created

This consideration will often lead us to arrange our buildings with a greater degree of openness than we might otherwise choose, and even to make great efforts to secure open views from the dwellings. The pleasure which such open glimpses will afford to the dwellers in a town house is not easily over estimated, and fully justifies their creation or preservation , but the growing desire for greater space and garden ground undoubtedly adds very much to the difficulty of producing fine architectural effects, which depend so much on the grouping of buildings and the inclosure of spaces. It is just this problem which we have to solve ; namely, to provide for the health and pleasure of the residents in new districts in a manner that will give to their lives a beautiful setting. Whether the development plan be made by a municipality, as in Germany, or by the ground landlord, as has been done in the few cases where such plans have been made in England, the guiding principles will be the same, and in each case the first consideration must, of course, be the site If the development is to be successful the site must be approached and studied in a spirit of great respect. Often we see the estate surveyor making for himself a clean sheet for his planning by clearing the ground of every tree and hedgerow, while the engineer makes a level site by toppling the hillocks into the hollows. But one who has been trained to know and love beauty will study his site with a thoroughness born of reverence, his intention being to take advantage of all its possibilities, to seize upon every feature of interest or beauty and turn it to account in the design. It is important, first of all, to prepare a contour plan of the ground , it will usually suffice if the contour lines represent five feet variation in level It is impossible properly to lay out the roads to the best advantage without such a plan To some owners the cost of this may seem an extravagance, but such cost may easily be saved many times over in one of the roads by its direction being more thoroughly adapted to the contour A survey should then be made of all the trees and other features on the estate that may be worth preservation. The cutting down of fine trees may in rare cases be justified where they would stand in the way of some necessary lines of development On the other hand, where the plan can be adapted to work in the existing trees as features, the cutting of them down becomes a positive crime, for the decoration they afford can only be reproduced after many generations. It is even possible at times to make effective use for street or garden decoration of well-grown existing hedgerows Anything, in fact, in a suburban district which will redeem or break the bare naked newness which for the first twenty or thirty years generally characterises such a district should be seized upon and made the most of Not only must the site be studied for its characteristics, but the direction of the roads and the placing of the centre above alluded to should also be studied on the site rather than in the office The plan, in fact, should be largely made in the fields and committed to paper afterwards.

It is the function of the architect who lays out a large tract of land,' in so far as he is an artist, to find expression, not for some preconceived ideas of his own, but for the needs and life of a rising community The details, the exact form, will express his own individuality, but in the main he must in imagination, standing on the ground, realise the community that is to come—must instinctively feel the natural lines of traffic and development that such community will take He must realise beforehand, as the result of careful study of all the conditions, where the land will become valuable, which spots will afford good business centres, and along which lines the main stream of life will naturally flow. There are limits within which the development of a community may be guided and induced to follow a plan , but if those limits are overstepped the natural growth of the district will eventually and inevitably set the plan aside. If, for example, we put our factories, with their noise and, alas ! their smoke, so that the prevailing wind carries these across our town, inevitably our residents will insist on passing beyond these factories and will build on the west of them There will arise certain focal points, such as the factory area, the railway station, the main town centre, and possibly municipal and educational centres, to and from which points one feels instinctively that the main lines of traffic will flow. Here roads should be provided, and so provided that they form a framework around which the secondary roads may be grouped, and a framework having some character, so that the general lie of the town may readily be grasped

For the purposes of making the plan of a town readily understood, some approach to symmetry, or rather definiteness of figure, in its frame may be very useful, though the actual and accurate symmetry which may appeal to one in a plan has little or no value in the actual town, for it is not possible there to recognise it. In the planning of a large site, there comes a time when, the realisation of the main lines of the plan having taken pretty clear shape in the mind, the whole swims a little indefinitely , then it becomes necessary to commit the plan to paper, and one returns with thankfulness to the definite points, such as bridges, roads, railways, or other existing features, to which the plan may be anchored, and from which it may be built up in definite position   Even the subsidiary roads, however, should be considered one by one upon the site itself ; it is wonderful how much may be done by such consideration to keep open pleasant views and take advantage of minor features in a way that would never occur to anyone working on a plan in the office   It is a first rule to do nothing without good reasons , the site will suggest plenty of such reasons, so that, instead of adopting some preconceived idea that roads should be straight or crooked, that they should be laid out on the basis of squares, diagonals, or circles, there will generally be found on the site some reason why in each case one or other form should be adopted   Existing roads, canals, rivers, railways, hills, or valleys will determine much of the plan One cannot make a rule and say that curved roads are always more beautiful than straight, or *vice versa*   Nor can we say in all cases that diagonal roads and focal points where several roads meet are to be avoided Camillo Sitte draws ingenious and alarming diagrams to show the possible collision points arising at different forms of road junctions , but such diagrams are misleading · a continuous stream of traffic is assumed which happens seldom in small towns, never in suburban areas No note is taken of the multiplication of minor risks at single junctions which the major risk at a multiple junction may displace, or of the difference of condition at busy junctions which police control of traffic produces. Certainly the less frequently the unwieldy tram or motor has to turn at right angles the better for the safety of all.   While agreeing generally as to the truth, and entirely as to the importance, of Sitte's contentions on this matter, it is probably also true that in each district there should be, for convenience of traffic, several centres to which more roads than two may converge with advantage

Either straight roads or curved may be adopted when our site suggests good reason, for there is one beauty of a curved road and another of a straight road.   A curved road, such as the High Street in Oxford, where the vista is constantly varying, towers and spires and other beautiful features one after the other coming into view and forming picturesque groups to close the street picture, has a beauty and charm which all can appreciate   But where there are no beautiful buildings, and where the road, as too often happens in a suburban district, simply meanders along in an aimless and meaningless wriggle, little of beauty can be claimed as resulting from its lack of straightness   On the other hand, where some prospect of great beauty, some wooded hillside, or the good view of a fine building can be kept open by the use of a straight road, such reason will more than justify its straightness , while the beauty of a straight avenue of trees is one that we can often with some certainty secure in a suburban area in cases where little else of beauty is with certainty to be depended on.   It seems to me that the great thing is that whether a particular road be straight or curved should be decided by some definite reason, and that some definite effect in each should be aimed at : straightness is at least better than aimless crookedness. I know of nothing much more monotonous than the meandering roads of some suburbs planned without any direct lines, centre, or framework, so that a stranger may wander about indefinitely and never know where he is or realise in the least the relationship of one part with another.

In the design and decoration of roads there is room for much individual variety   It is greatly to be desired that our local authorities would revise their by-laws as to width and character of streets.   No doubt this would follow from the extended powers to control town plans which we seek for them   To fix a width of forty, forty-five, or fifty feet as the minimum width for all streets, as is the common practice in England to-day, and to require that the whole of this width should be paved or macadamised, quite regardless of the probable requirements of traffic, is as absurd as the result it produces is monotonous   Grass margins, either between the footpath and the roadway, or between the footpath and the house, or house gardens, should be allowed.   Upon these might be planted avenues of trees, which would add much to the comfort and beauty of suburban roads ; in other cases shrubs, such as berberis, might be used, and by varying the detail, by planting some roads with heavy-foliaged trees of large growth, others with blossoming fruit trees, crab apple, almonds, and such like, not only would great variety and interest be introduced, but each suburban road would acquire a unity and dignity far beyond anything that is produced by planting all the roads with a miscellaneous collection of trees.   Many of the charming effects to be found in our villages with their greens or small grass margins offer useful suggestions for the treatment of road junctions and odd spaces in suburban areas.   Generally speaking, the gardening of roads and road spaces should be kept very simple and broad in character and somewhat formal in design   The dignity of many fine Continental streets has been destroyed by injudicious and trifling garden treatment · wriggling lines of path, beds of variegated foliage, and such like not only do not add any beauty to a street, but tend to destroy any dignity which it might have

It is very difficult in street decoration to improve on the effect produced by broad stretches of unbroken grass and groups or avenues of trees   The introduction of flowers requires great care, and simplicity of arrangement and breadth of effect are absolutely necessary in their use

Different views are held as to the best direction for building roads to take in residential districts, and there can be no doubt that in many ways the safest direction for roads is approximately from north to south, so that the buildings on each side of the road will secure a fair amount of sunshine on both sides.   A great many, perhaps the majority of people, however, prefer a south front to their houses   This can, of course, be obtained on a road running from north to south in the way that I have seen in France, where short rows of two or three houses are built with their end up to the road, and their south front facing small picturesque gardens, which sometimes, with a high wall at the end, and the back of the next row of houses, become inclosed courts of considerable beauty, but this is not always practicable   Where roads run from east to west, the houses on the north side of the road have the coveted south front : it is with the houses on the south side of the road that the difficulty arises , but this difficulty only exists because of a superstition that with small houses you must have to each house a tidy front to the road and an untidy back away from it   It is quite easy to give the houses on the south side of a road a southern aspect provided their north side is treated in a manner suitable for facing to the street (Fig. 2).   Where this can be arranged, and where there is reasonable chance that houses having their main living rooms on the south side will be designed, a fair proportion of roads giving a nearly due southern aspect would certainly be desirable   It is perhaps well that they should not run due east and west, but tend either to the

north or to the south, so that, at any rate in the summer months, all
sides of the houses may get a little sunshine.

The usual plan of fixing a building line and making all houses along
the street toe this line, if perhaps the simplest, is the least satisfactory
way of arranging them. The buildings are shown to least advantage:
they tend to be seen mainly on one side, the ends being so neglected
that they remind one of cakes cut from a bar of soap; and whether they
are built in terraces, in pairs, or singly, the effect is equally monotonous.
For dwelling houses it is most important to secure some little distance of

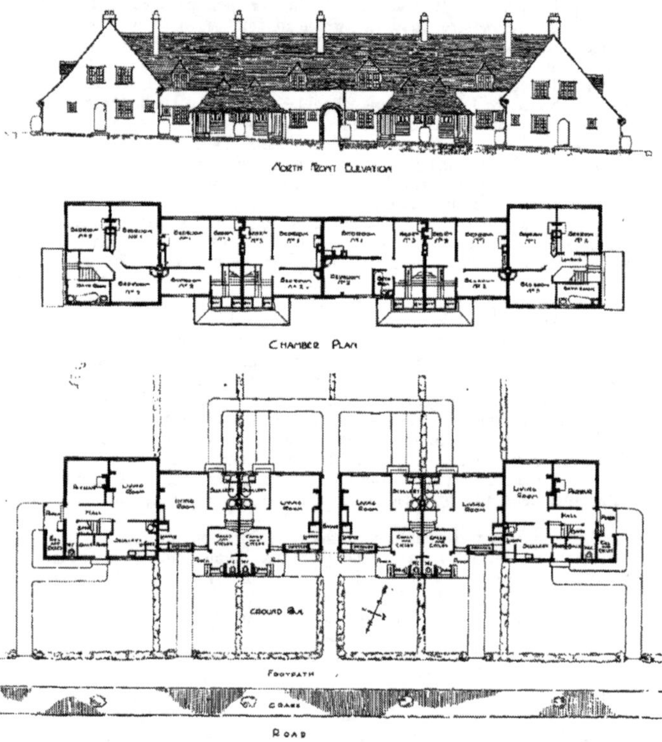

Fig. 2.

outlook; some relief from the oppression of gazing for ever at an unbroken
row of houses across the road. By breaking the building line, setting
some buildings further back from the road, and others further forwards;
by setting groups of buildings at an angle with the road instead of
parallel with it; by grouping buildings round two sides of a triangular
green, or three sides of a square, not only may a general sense of
openness of outlook be given to many of the houses, but vastly more
picturesque groups of buildings may be produced (Fig. 3). It is
particularly useful in the case of smaller houses, where the same design

must be repeated over and over again, to take advantage of such
grouping, for the endless multiplication of buildings too small in scale
to produce any effect in a road is one of the great difficulties we have
to contend with; the repetition of small or even of moderate-sized
detached residences soon becomes as hopelessly monotonous as the long
continuous row of cottages, and the monotony is only to a very small
extent relieved by variety in the individual buildings, variety, in
fact, being in itself not by any means necessarily a pleasing feature
Probably variety only gives pleasure when it is a variety within some
covering and governing unity   We shall produce little happy effect in
our suburban roads until we are able to group our smaller houses,

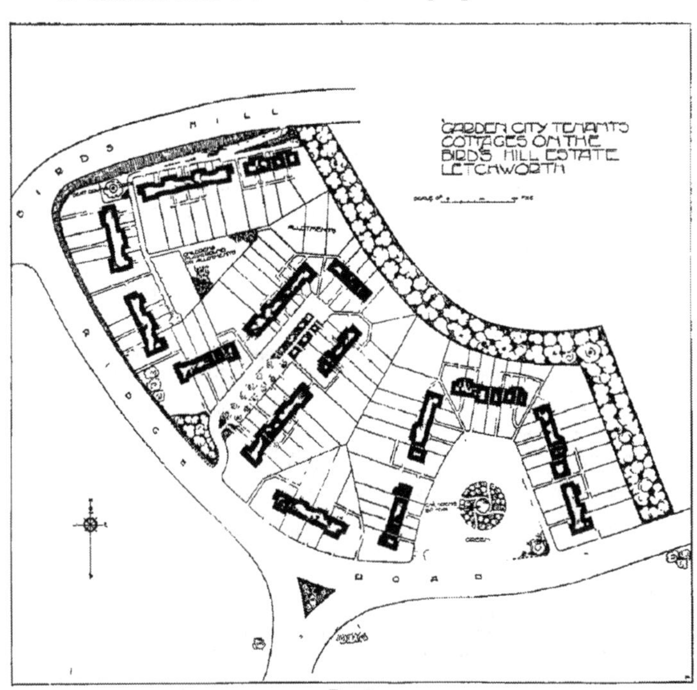

Fig 3

and, I believe, from the old village green, the college quadrangle,
and the cathedral close we may get our most fruitful suggestions   The
tendency of the modern individual is to build his house in such a way as to
emphasise its detachment and difference from all its neighbours   With
such a tendency it is exceedingly difficult to produce any totality of
effect, any sense of order or design in the whole appearance of a street.
No beauty can arise from the mere aggregation of detached units   The
endless multiplication of carefully fenced-in villas and rows of cottages,
each with its little cattle-pen-like garden securely railed from each, all
toeing the same building line, must be monotonous and devoid of beauty.
If we merely sweep away the railings and have a continuous strip of

grass, shrubs, or flowers open to the street, as has been so largely done in America, a great improvement is made, and by grouping the villas round some open green, gathering their little garden patches into one space sufficient to give a better outlook for all, some sense of dignity and design may even be produced. Most successful of all is the result when the buildings themselves can be grouped or linked together and designed not individually, but as groups, so that the unit in the street ceases to be the individual house or cottage, and becomes the group of four or six houses The scale of the unit in relation to the street is immediately improved, and by arranging such groups of buildings around greens, or in groves branching off the main road, a further improvement may be made.

And when the democratic tendencies of the age, about which we hear a great deal, shall enable us to dispense with the very complete sorting of houses, all one size, into one street, and to include in our roads houses of very different size and character, then, indeed, it will be possible to reproduce some of the picturesque grouping of buildings which is such a beautiful feature of our old villages (Fig. 1).

The desire for a sense of openness of outlook from the houses, desire also to escape the dust and noise of the road, so seriously aggravated by the increasing use of the motor car, is tending to set buildings further and further back from the road line, but much more complete seclusion from the main road, much greater sense of openness of outlook, may be obtained by the arrangements suggested above

Considerable economy may also be effected in the cost of road-making. A simple carriage drive is ample for giving access to such a group of dwellings, however large the houses may be, and both the dreariness and cost of useless expanses of roadway may well be saved

Obviously the proportions which are usually laid down between the width of a street and the height of the buildings which bound it are not applicable to such roads as we have been considering, and some quite different effects must be aimed at

In all town planning it is very important to understand clearly the difference between natural beauty and beauty of design Without attempting the difficult task of defining beauty, it will be generally agreed that both these kinds of beauty arise largely from order, adaptation to place and purpose, obedience to law. Does not the difference consist partly at least in this, that in natural beauty the obedience is perfect and the complexity of the laws obeyed infinite, while in the beauty of man's design the laws obeyed are few and simple, and the obedience is but imperfect? The form of a tree results from the absolute balance of complex fluid forces , these forces being what they are, the form of the tree could be none other than it is—unconsciously we recognise this. The same applies to the curve of the river bank or the mountain peak This style of beauty is for us to reverence, to cherish, and from it we should draw inspiration. But we cannot design it; far simpler and less complex are the few laws which we can obey in design. And the man who, requiring a path across his level front lawn, rules a straight line has probably a greater appreciation of that from which beauty springs than the one who makes his path meander across in what he likes to call a natural curve ! If, then, we cannot create natural beauty, we may at least be very careful not to destroy it; rather let us incorporate all we can into our design , let us gladly accept any reason that suggests to us the opportunity for bringing in the beauty of curved lines , but equally let us not be ashamed humbly to rule straight lines and squares when no valid reason suggests itself for doing otherwise

7.—DE LA DISPOSITION ET DES DÉVELOPPEMENTS DES RUES ET DES ESPACES LIBRES DANS LES VILLES.

Par Augustin Rey, Architecte de la Fondation Rothschild, Paris.

Comment créer nos Rues modernes ?
Méthodes réduisant pour l'Avenir les Frais d'Expropriation en vue de leur Elargissement.

Une des questions les plus importantes pour l'avenir de nos cités est la détermination de largeurs de rues qui puissent satisfaire à toutes les conditions qu'exigent à la fois l'hygiène publique et la circulation générale

Une largeur de voie publique serait dans des conditions parfaites si elle pouvait résoudre, dès le début, les conditions normales d'aération et d'éclairage des immeubles riverains en même temps que prévoir pour une très-longue période les meilleures dispositions pour éviter l'encombrement.

Satisfaire simultanément à deux questions si complexes semble presqu'une impossibilité.

Nous nous sommes efforcés, par une étude très attentive du sujet, de chercher une solution

Nous avons l'honneur de présenter, et de soumettre à l'appréciation du Congrès, les résultats de nos recherches

Qu'il nous soit permis de parler tout d'abord du noyau central de nos vieilles cités et de montrer à quelles difficultés se heurte aujourd'hui l'assainissement, par le tracé des voies publiques plus conformes aux nécessités modernes

Les rues étroites, tortueuses qui formait le réseaux de nos principales villes du Moyen Age et de la Renaissance, constituent une des difficultés les plus grandes que nous puissions rencontrer

Jusqu'à la fin du dix-septième siècle l'usage était d'entasser les habitations les unes contre les autres autour d'un point central, en général l'église Plus l'entassement était grand, plus les servitudes grevant les propriétés étaient nombreuses.

Ces servitudes, qui ont persisté pendant si longtemps, sont en grande partie la cause pour ces agglomérations d'une insalubrité parfois invraisemblable

La maison appartenait souvent à plusieurs propriétaires qui se partageaient soit plusieurs étages, soit partie même d'un étage. Cette propriété par tranches rendait très difficile, pour ne pas dire parfois impossible, toute modification de la maison. L'escalier et certaines parties restant seuls communs, comment décider des changements ou des améliorations dans de pareilles conditions ?

Aussi ne faut-il pas s'étonner que ces maisons, au centre de la ville, aient persisté dans leur plan ancien pendant de si longues périodes ? Nos pères, que l'on croit si " mal raisonneurs " du confort de l'habitation, ne sont pas en réalité responsables de cet état de choses ; ils se heurtaient à des difficultés à peu près insurmontables au point de vue légal Les lois de cette époque n'étaient que simples coutumes, appliquées trop souvent avec la partialité et les préjugés locaux. La main énergique d'un Napoléon Ier en France n'est venue que très tard mettre ordre à ce chaos.

Ces servitudes ne s'étendaient pas seulement à l'intérieur de la maison habitée, elles se répandaient sur les façades elles-mêmes ; certaines dispositions étaient de forme obligée, par suite d'obligations testamentaires empêchant les héritiers de toucher à l'héritage reçu Des familles

avaient entre elles des arrangements constituant un pacte irrévocable,
les obligeant à ne modifier en rien l'aspect esthétique des formes générales
quand ce n'était pas jusqu'aux plus petits détails de certaines maisons.

Pour être juste il faut dire aussi que les finances des villes n'étaient
pas assez prospères pour permettre des travaux d'expropriation et
d'élargissement des voies publiques   Ces villes furent trop longtemps
" taillables et corvéables à merci " pour présenter dans leur budget une
élasticité suffisante permettant de faire place à des ressources de quelque
importance à consacrer aux travaux d'assainissement.

———————— ·.·

Ce passé nous à légué de lourdes charges.   Le noyau central de nos
vieilles cités est très difficile à transformer, et les villes qui y sont parvenues
en partie, savent les sommes considérables qu'il a fallu y engloutir.

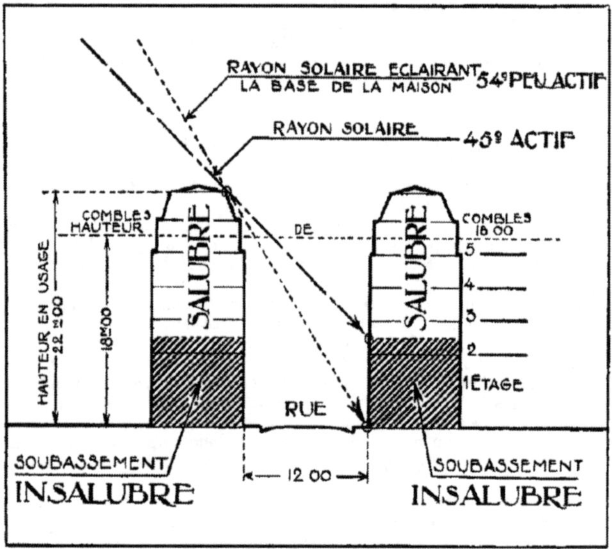

FIG 1—BÂTIMENTS DE CINQ ETAGES CONSTRUITS À L'ALIGNEMENT DES RUES DE
12 M DE LARGEUR

Solution autorisée à Paris par les règlements de voirie de 1902–1904

Si l'on considère que les rayons solaires inclinés à 45° ont encore une action active, on
voit que les soubassements de ces bâtiments sont insalubres

L'amélioration de la zone ancienne est cependant une nécessité de
premier ordre.   Nous ne pouvons négliger ce côté des obligations sociales ,
y créer, là surtout, des espaces libres est certes d'une importance qui ne
saurait être mise en doute dans un Congrès comme celui-ci

Contre cette solution cependant il faut le reconnaître s'accumulent des
difficultés de tous ordres qui augmentent singulièrement le prix d'expropriation   Nous sommes donc amenés à rechercher par toutes les
méthodes possibles à économiser l'argent des contribuables.   Dans cet
ordre d'idées cherchons à diminuer les sommes à consacrer aux expropriations futures des parties récemment créées, afin de faciliter l'amélioration
définitive des vieux quartiers légués par les générations passées.

C'est un vaste problème, notre intention est de n'en développer qu'un des côtés. La création, pour l'extension de nos villes, de voies nouvelles mérite non seulement une étude des plus approfondies des nécessités du présent mais encore de celles de l'avenir.

En nous contentant de tracer par à peu près, pour les besoins immédiats, les rues nouvelles nous sommes presques certains d'avoir à revenir plus tard sur un travail incomplètement établi

En dehors du problème de l'aération des voies publiques, celui absolument capital, qui domine les grandes lois de l'hygiène, l'éclairage des locaux habités, doit être avant tout résolu   Il n'est plus admissible qu'après les études qui ont été faites sur ce sujet, *nos voies publiques, qui constituent l'espace libre par excellence*, soient tracées à l'aventure de nécessités d'accès purement locales.

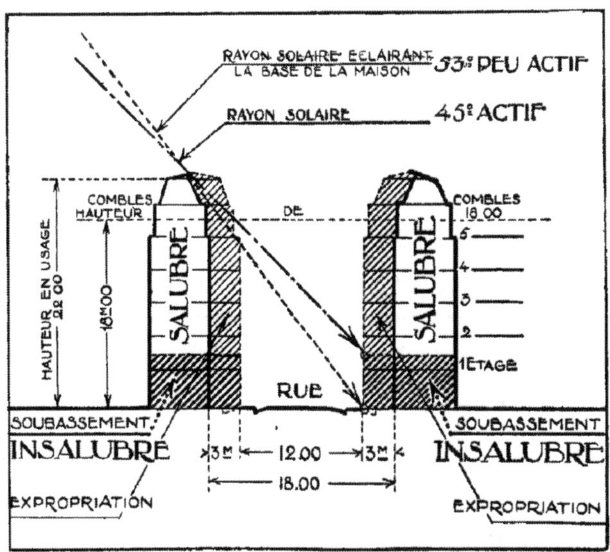

FIG 2 —BÂTIMENTS DE CINQ ÉTAGES CONSTRUITS A L'ALIGNEMENT D'UNE RUE DE 12 M DE LARGEUR

En cas d'expropriation pour élargissement de la rue passant de 12 à 18 m, les bâtiments riverains sont irrémédiablement perdus, et les indemnités à payer deviennent considérables

Il y a des lois pour la vie des habitants dont il faut se pénétrer, et qui trouvent leur source dans la direction même des rayons solaires ; l'éclairage et l'orientation rationnels des voies publiques doivent donc être à l'avenir la préoccupation dominante de toutes nos administrations

La voie publique bien orientée, la seconde question est de fixer sa largeur. Prévoir une largeur suffisante pour la circulation intense que l'avenir peut révéler est un point des plus délicats à fixer.

Les lourdes charges qu'ont pour nos grandes villes, qui seules ont à en supporter tout le poids, les expropriations pour élargissement de voies sont ruineuses pour leurs finances

Frapper de retrait d'alignement soit un côté, soit deux côtés d'une voie publique, sans délai pour les riverains, est la solution radicale, mais qui exige des capitaux immédiats.

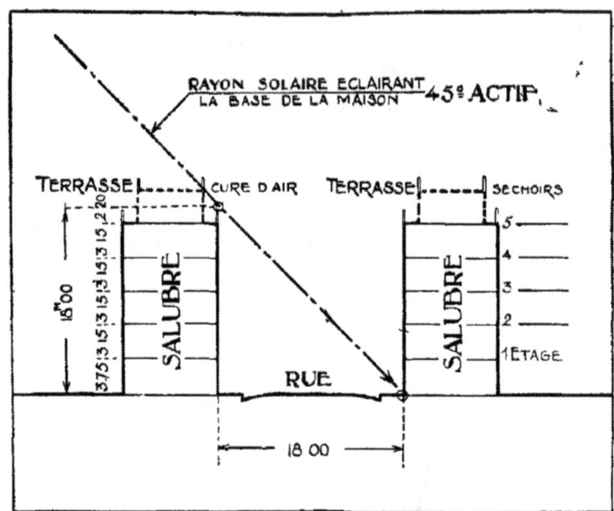

FIG 3.—BÂTIMENTS DE CINQ ÉTAGES CONSTRUITS À L'ALIGNEMENT D'UNE RUE DE
18 M DE LARGE
Les rayons à 45° viennent frapper la base des bâtiments   Leur salubrité est assurée.
C'est la solution idéale

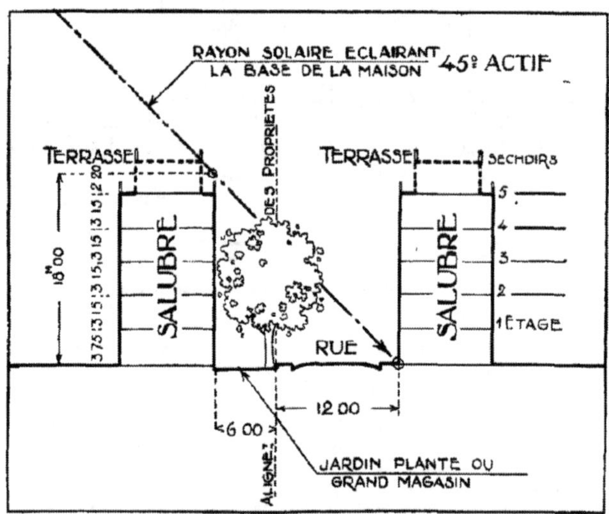

FIG 4—BÂTIMENTS DE CINQ ÉTAGES CONSTRUITS D'UN CÔTÉ À L'ALIGNEMENT
D'UNE RUE DE 12 M ET DE L'AUTRE EN RETRAIT DE 6 M DE CET ALIGNEMENT
L'espace au devant des bâtiments en retrait peut être planté ou converti en magasin
de la hauteur d'un rez de-chaussée
Les rayons à 45° venant frapper la base des bâtiments, leur salubrité est assurée

Lorsqu'ils font défaut la nécessité s'impose d'accorder aux propriétaires un très-long délai pour reculer leurs façades, délai qui n'expire qu'au moment où la vétusté dangereuse de l'immeuble le rend inhabitable L'opération n'est terminée qu'à très-longue échéance

.˙.

L'hygiène moderne a une tendance indéniable à réclamer l'élargissement des voies publiques. Pour élever un bâtiment à six étages, il y a cinquante ans, la largeur de la voie publique sur laquelle ce bâtiment était autorisé était moitié moindre dans les règlements d'alors que dans ceux actuels.   Cette largeur est cependant trop-souvent insuffisante

Or la nécessité d'expropriations pour élargissement des voies devient une charge écrasante pour le budget des États, des villes et des communes, la démolition généralement totale des immeubles expropriés oblige à des indemnités considérables et dépassant de beaucoup le service rendu à la communauté.   Est-il équitable que les contribuables, pris dans leur ensemble, voient de ce chef augmenter leurs impôts ?

Nous sommes d'un avis contraire, et il nous semble que ce serait gravement compromettre l'avenir que de surcharger d'une manière inconsidérée ces budgets déjà si obérés.

Faut-il alors se résigner à établir des rues insuffisamment larges ne prévoyant pas la circulation active à laquelle elles devront répondre dans l'avenir ?

En général on s'efforce, lors de la création de cet espace libre normal, qu'est la rue de calculer la circulation générale au moment de son établissement   Il est tout naturel que les contribuables participent aux frais d'entretien de la largeur strictement nécessaire aux besoins de la circulation, ceci est de toute équité   Vouloir étendre à une largeur plus grande cette contribution ne serait pas équitable.

Dans les voies principales d'une grande cité, boulevards, avenues, aucune difficulté ne peut se présenter, car l'hygiène de l'aération et de l'éclairage des maisons riveraines se trouve dès le début par les grandes largeurs fixées, assurée au-delà des nécessités.

Le cas le plus difficile est précisément celui où la largeur de la voie à créer pour les besoins actuels est insuffisante pour y élever à l'alignement des maisons, où la lumière et l'air ne pénétreront pas jusqu'aux soubassements mêmes de ces édifices.

Créera-t-on dans ce cas la voie d'une largeur supérieure aux nécessités de la circulation, et peut-on demander à la communauté des charges correspondantes ?   Ceci nous semble-t-il ne peut être soutenu

La largeur supplémentaire ne profitant qu'aux habitations elles-mêmes, c'est aux propriétaires riverains et non à la communauté à en assurer les charges

Si nous voulons conclure nous dirons qu'il est injuste de laisser à la charge des contribuables la création au début de voies plus larges que la circulation ne l'exige ; que les propriétaires riverains ayant besoin pour monter leurs immeubles de plus d'espace libre, c'est à eux que doit incomber les charges de cette largeur supplémentaire qui leur est nécessaire au point de vue de l'hygiène.

Dans la solution que nous proposons notre but est de régler plus équitablement les charges de chacun, et de préparer pour l'avenir l'élargissement possible de ces voies, en réduisant dans une proportion considérable les charges d'expropriations

Dans une série de figures nous montrons comment la question peut

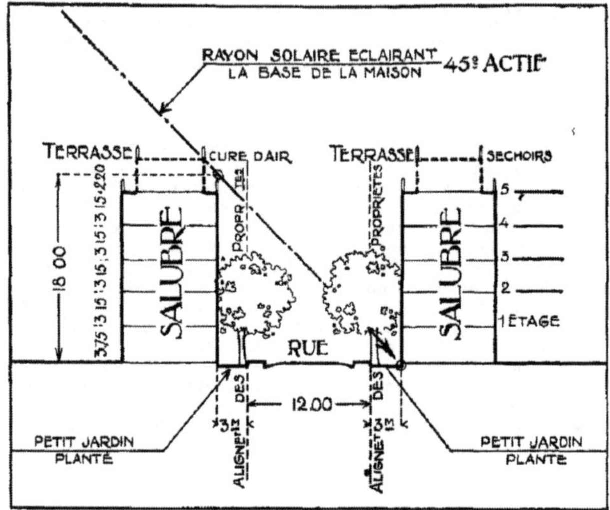

FIG 5—BÂTIMENTS DE CINQ ÉTAGES CONSTRUITS RESPECTIVEMENT EN RETRAIT
DE 3 M DE L'ALIGNEMENT DE LA RUE DE 12 M
L'espace au devant de ces bâtiments est occupé par des plantations
Les rayons à 45° venant frapper la base des bâtiments, leur salubrité est assurée

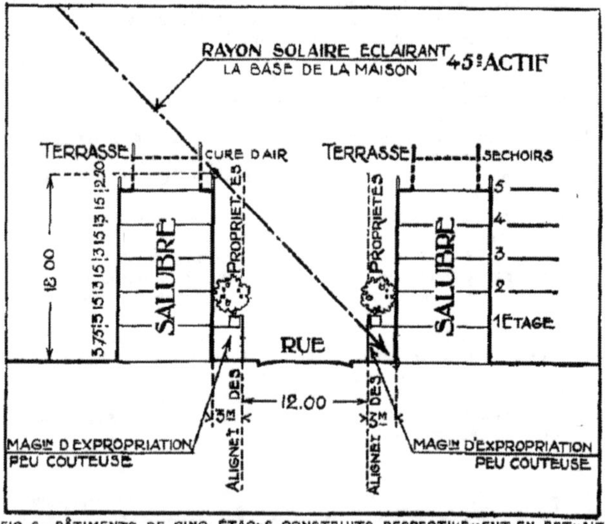

FIG. 6.—BÂTIMENTS DE CINQ ÉTAGES CONSTRUITS RESPECTIVEMENT EN RETRAIT
DE 3 M DE L'ALIGNEMENT DE LA RUE DE 12 M.
L'espace au devant de ces bâtiments est occupé par des magasins de la hauteur du
rez de chaussée, couverts en terrasses
Les rayons à 45° venant frapper la base des bâtiments, leur salubrité est assurée

être résolue pratiquement en satisfaisant aux conditions complexes du problème

Les légendes qui accompagnent chacune d'entre elles en font saisir clairement le sens.

La figure 1 expose l'état actuel qui aboutit sans espoir à l'insalubrité des soubassements des bâtiments ainsi créés

La figure 2 montre qu'au point de vue de l'expropriation aucune solution économique ne peut intervenir lorsque la rue de douze mètres de large a été créée avec bâtiments élevés à l'alignement dans toute leur hauteur

La figure 3 indique la solution à laquelle il faudrait recourir si l'on voulait, dès le début, assurer les conditions hygiéniques parfaites des habitations riveraines   L'excédant de largeur au moment de la création de la voie doit faire rejeter comme inacceptable cette solution.

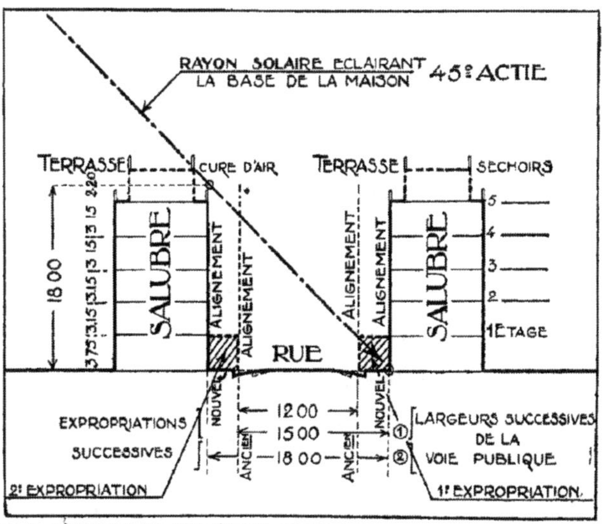

FIG 7 —BÂTIMENTS DE CINQ ÉTAGES CONSTRUITS RESPECTIVEMENT EN RETRAIT DE 3 M DE L'ALIGNEMENT DE LA RUE DE 12 M

Cette figure montre comment on peut procéder à deux expropriations successives   La première fait passer la rue de 12 m à 15 m , la deuxième, la rue de 15 m à 18 m de largeur   Cette solution respecte les bâtiments élevés à toutes hauteurs

La figure 4 montre, lorsque la rue créée n'a besoin dès le début, pour répondre à son trafic que d'une largeur de douze mètres, comment il est possible de réserver l'avenir en frappant de reculement les bâtiments construits sur un des côtés de cette rue

La figure 5 ainsi que la figure 6 donnent des solutions dérivées du même principe de recul des bâtiments à construire à toute hauteur, la partie réservée pouvant servir de jardin ou à l'édification d'un rez-de-chaussée.

Lorsque plusieurs années après la création d'une voie publique de douze mètres de large, dans les conditions fixées par les figures 4, 5 et 6, la circulation deviendra plus active, l'expropriation des bandes de terrain réservées à la construction de soubassement permettra de porter cette largeur successivement à 15 m , puis à 18 m , suivant la figure 7. On atteindra ainsi par étapes la largeur de 18 m , indiquée à la figure 3.

Le principe que nous avons appliqué ici à une rue qui aura définitivement 18 m. peut s'appliquer également à une largeur plus grande, et permettre à l'élargissement futur d'atteindre 21 m., ou 24 m.

La figure 8 et la figure 9 donnent le tracé des dispositions à imposer dans ces cas aux maisons riveraines.

Ces largeurs de 21 m et de 24 m nous semblent répondre à des cas extrêmes, et peuvent permettre la création soit d'un, soit de deux étages supplémentaires sur les maisons ainsi modifiées.

La partie de soubassement supprimée sera ainsi regagnée en hauteur, et le terrain qui peut avoir augmenté de valeur progressivement avec la largeur de la voie retrouvera équitablement avec ces étages supplémentaires une source de revenu. Cette faculté de surélévation contribuera ainsi à réduire encore les frais d'expropriation

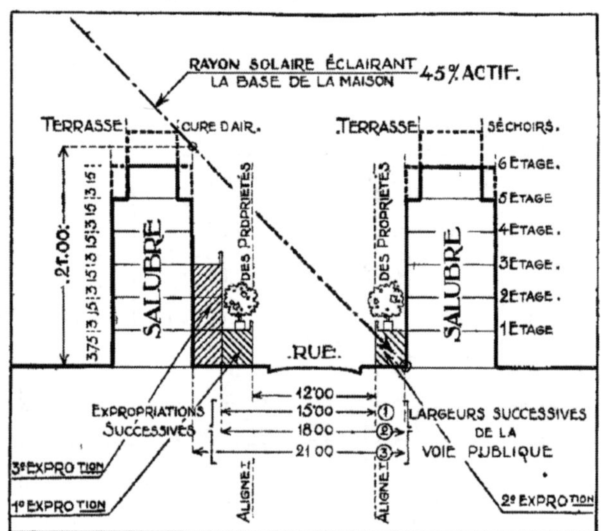

FIG 8 —BÂTIMENTS DE CINQ ÉTAGES CONSTRUITS EN RETRAIT D'UN COTÉ DE 3 M DE L'AUTRE DE 6 M DE L'ALIGNEMENT DE LA RUE DE 12 M

Cette disposition permet par trois expropriations successives d'arriver à une largeur de rue de 21 m en respectant les bâtiments, élevés à toute hauteur Un sixième étage peut être ajouté après la dernière expropriation

Les rayons à 45° venant frapper la base des bâtiments leur salubrité est assurée.

Ce principe du retrait progressif des étages, il faut le constater, est en opposition avec les méthodes actuelles de construction de nos bâtiments urbains.

Quand on veut bien y réfléchir, il est curieux de constater à quel point nos contemporains, insuffisamment éclairés sur les besoins d'hygiène de l'habitation, ont renversé les problèmes de la construction.

En effet, la mode dans les maisons à étages consiste à les doter de rotondités ventrues, lourdes et pantelantes, qui viennent, sous la forme de *bow window*, alourdir les façades.

L'origine des *bow windows* doit être recherchée dans ce pays hospitalier qui nous reçoit aujourd'hui en Congrès. C'est en effet dans les demeures rurales anglaises des 16° et 17e siècles que nous trouvons l'application

la plus charmante et la plus logique de ces délicieuses saillies dans des
maisons ayant deux étages au plus, là ces saillies étaient justifiées   Elles
ne le sont nullement dans des cages humaines de cinq et six étages,
quand ce n'est pas davantage. Avoir transporté ces formes si gracieuses,
qui conviennent si bien à des habitations peu élevées, à nos hauts immeubles urbains, comme l'ont fait certains règlements de voirie les plus
récents, et parmi ceux-là ceux de la ville de Paris, c'est faire preuve de
sentiments artistiques aussi contestables que de notions de construction
fâcheuses.

Au point de vue de l'hygiène ces saillies sont tout aussi défectueuses,
ayant pour conséquence principale d'assombrir les soubassements de nos
immeubles.

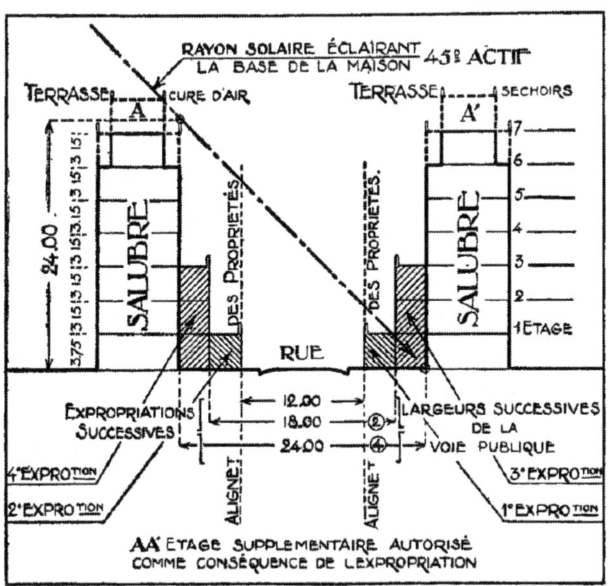

FIG 9 —BÂTIMENTS DE SIX ÉTAGES CONSTRUITS RESPECTIVEMENT EN RETRAIT DE
6 M, DE L'ALIGNEMENT DE LA RUE DE 12 M

Cette disposition par quatre expropriations successives d arriver à une largeur de rue
de 24 m, en respectant les bâtiments montant à toute hauteur   Un septième étage
peut être ajouté après la dernière expropriation
Les rayons à 45° viennent frapper la base des bâtiments   Leur salubrité est assurée

Au contraire, l'établissement de terrasses se succédant en retrait les
unes des autres par séries, non seulement crée la variété des saillies
par des changements successifs de plans, mais permet la pénétration
normale des rayons lumineux à tous les étages habités

Au fond, c'est au principe de construction du Moyen-âge, qui procédait
par encorbellements successifs, que nous faisons la guerre; le *bow
window* n'en est que la lourde et plus que médiocre réminiscence.   La
formule " plus d'air, plus de lumière," qui se pose si nettement de nos
jours, se trouve pleinement satisfaite par la méthode de construction par
retraits successifs.

La gaieté des terrasses est bien connue, elles peuvent se couvrir de végétation, à la belle saison s'agrémenter de tentes. Des balustrades, limites si gracieuses de l'habitation, les indiquent en façade de la manière la plus heureuse.

Ce genre de construction est un des éléments de succès dans cette guerre que nous devons entreprendre contre la platitude et la monotonie de nos façades modernes

---

Pour satisfaire aux nécessités de l'hygiène moderne, qui réclame l'élargissement des rues, il faut faciliter la tâche aux municipalités qui hésitent souvent devant des dépenses qui viennent grever lourdement leurs budgets.

Les expropriations successives de bandes de terrain seront relativement peu coûteuses, si nous les comparons aux expropriations désastreuses dans lesquelles les villes sont entraînées en rasant des immeubles entiers, construits à toutes hauteurs à l'alignement de rues trop etroites.

Les indemnités considérables qui résultent du système actuel sont trop souvent la source de spéculations qui, de nos jours, ne cherchent même plus à se dissimuler. C'est une véritable industrie que celle qui consiste à acheter en temps opportun des immeubles devant être atteints par l'expropriation Elle rapporte d'enormes profits à ceux qui s'y livrent, qui abusent de l'esprit de délicatesse dont sont inspirés les lois qui par intérêt général semblent porter atteinte au principe de la propriété.

Notre but de réduire les charges des expropriations pour l'avenir est atteint quand, par mesures de prévoyance, nous imposons à la construction des habitations des parties verticales pouvant se détacher successivement de l'immeuble principal sans porter atteinte à ses œuvres vives.

Ces expropriations ne comprendront dans le premier cas, d'une rue de 12 m passant à 18 m., que le paiement des deux bandes de terrain expropriées et l'indemnité relative à des constructions élevées seulement d'un rez-de-chaussée

Dans le second cas, le moins fréquent, d'une rue de 18 m. passant à 21 m , puis à 24 m., l'expropriation comprendra, outre les bandes de terrains, des constructions de deux étages sur rez-de-chaussée seulement, détachées du bloc principal, dont la construction aura été prévue de manière à n'être aucunement affectée comme solidité

Nous pensons avoir déterminé ainsi les bases de création rationnelle de nos voies publiques, qui à l'avenir permettront au budget d'expropriation pour élargissement de rues d'être réduit dans des proportions considérables

L'hygiène publique a assez de charges importantes à envisager dès maintenant pour ne négliger aucune occasion de diminuer certains chapitres de son budget au profit d'autres chapitres insuffisamment dotés

Il nous a semblé intéressant de présenter au septième Congrès International des Architectes les solutions, d'un caractère éminemment pratique, qui viennent de faire l'objet de cette communication, sur lesquelles nous attirons toute la bienveillante attention de nos Confrères.

DISCUSSION ON SUBJECT VII.

M. Buls said he took exception to M. Hénard's paper because he said it was not always convenient to have garden squares in cities   Certainly they prevailed in England, Germany, and Scandinavia, but in the formation of new centres, and in the reconstruction of others, it was important to note before the architect made his plans to what purpose the quarter was to be devoted   For instance, in a commercial centre garden squares would be out of place

Mr. Albert Kelsey (Philadelphia) said that the tendency throughout America where gardens were in front of houses was that when the locality changed the gardens were built over with shops

Sir W Emerson, in proposing a vote of thanks to the readers of the papers, said he regretted that time would not allow of a discussion   From the papers that had been read, it was evident that the writers had given great pains and attention to their tasks   The way in which large towns and cities should be laid out was a most interesting one at the present moment, and especially to Londoners, for the Metropolis was increasing every year, and was stretching out in all directions, and this question of the laying-out of extensions to large cities was one that met them every day.   They were exceedingly indebted to Dr Stubben for the time he must have taken in getting out the plans he had shown them, and they were also indebted to M Hénard for his most interesting paper   The remaining papers, which time had not permitted to be read, would appear in the printed proceedings of the Congress.

The resolution was carried with acclamation.

Mr Frank Miles Day, of Philadelphia, President of the American Institute of Architects, obtained the Chairman's permission to show a few plans of American cities.   He said that parks were a most important factor in the problem of the plan of the city, and, taking Cleveland as an example, he showed the relation which the park system bore to that portion of the city where the entrance from the new railway station was now being constructed.   The entrance occupies a central position, and the park system extends to the outskirts   A number of public buildings had to be constructed in Cleveland, and instead of scattering them about the city, it was found better to create a wide Mall, extending from the Union Station to the heart of the city, and to flank it with public buildings. The ground for the Mall and for several of the buildings had been purchased, plans for two of the larger buildings were completed, and the construction of the Government building was well advanced   The whole scheme was a very interesting one, especially in view of the fact that the arrangement of the buildings in this monumental fashion would cost only about ten per cent. more than if they had been scattered about the city   Many other cities in America had taken their cue from Cleveland and had proposed group plans.   In Buffalo a scheme had been perfected for placing such a group at the point of radiation of the street system.   St. Louis had need at the present time for the construction of several public buildings, and it had been proposed to carve out a central area for the purpose, placing at one end the public library and at the other certain municipal buildings.   The town-hall had already been constructed, facing the proposed Mall, and it was intended to place the court-house opposite to it.   The twin cities of St Paul and Minneapolis had an interesting park system, bordering rivers and lakes, which it was proposed to extend very largely.   It was intended to construct three wide avenues, converging at the new State capitol.   Mr Daniel Burnham was not long ago commissioned to study the plan of Manila, and he had made many important proposals, among which was one for overlaying a rectangular street system with a system of diagonal roads, such that the straight roads of one portion of the city became diagonal roads in other portions—an ingenious solution. Mr. Day then showed a picture of a recently completed scheme for the replanning of San Francisco, now under consideration. The present city was laid out upon a rectangular system, through which it was proposed to cut diagonal avenues to various centres and to make a great park extending from the high portion down to the sea. In Washington it was proposed to erect all the public buildings in accordance with a certain plan, buildings for legislative purposes being placed around the Capitol, those for executive work around the White House, and those for municipal purposes along the Mall. In the four years since that scheme had been proposed at least ten important buildings had been placed in accordance with it.

Mr. MAX CLARKE, in proposing a vote of thanks to the Chairmen, said they were especially indebted to those gentlemen for allowing Mr. Day to exhibit his photographs. Mr Day's contribution clearly brought home to them what could be done if this matter of planning of cities were taken in hand and treated in a large way.

The resolution was carried by acclamation, and having been acknowledged by the Chairman, the meeting terminated

M. AUGUSTIN REY, Architecte de la Fondation Rothschild, sends the following contribution to the discussion :—

La question des espaces libres à réserver dans nos grandes agglomérations modernes a fait l'objet d'importantes études depuis quelques années. Elle est devenue une véritable science et une de celles dont l'application exerce la plus haute influence sur la santé publique En Allemagne, en Angleterre, aux Etats-Unis, en Autriche, en Belgique, en Espagne, enfin en France, plusieurs Administrations Publiques, sous la pression de techniciens remarquables, Architectes et Ingénieurs, commencent à donner à cette question vitale, pour nos populations urbaines, la plus sérieuse attention. Un de nos confrères, M E Hénard, a notamment publié, en prenant comme base des statistiques irréfutables, le résultat de ses études sur la ville de Paris, comparée aux grandes capitales européennes

Nous désirons brièvement examiner dans cette discussion trois points Quel est l'espace libre par excellence que réclame l'habitation.—Pourquoi les espaces libres urbains doivent toujours être plantés d'arbres et couverts de végétation —La question de l'expropriation pour créations de voies publiques plus larges

Espace libre réclamé avant tout par l'habitation —Si l'on ne saurait trop encourager par tous les moyens possibles le maintien des espaces libres—places, squares, parcs boisés—lorsqu'ils n'existent pas en quantité suffisante, on n'envisage là qu'un des côtés de la question, mais non peut-être le plus important. *L'espace libre par excellence qu'il faut à l'habitation, c'est la voie publique, et cette portion de voie publique qu'on appelle la cour, sur laquelle la maison prend jour et air. C'est en définitive de la nature de cet espace que dépend, en réalité, la vie de la cité* L'influence profonde déterminante qu'exerce sur la santé urbaine la voie publique montre que c'est de ce côté qu'il faut porter la plus grande partie de l'effort pour réaliser de notables progrès Ces espaces, rues et cours, doivent être ménagés avec une science consommée. *Les bases salubres d'un quartier sont constituées avant tout par la large circulation de l'air et l'abondante pénétration des rayons solaires dans les blocs habités* Qu'à proximité soient situés des espaces libres, plantés d'arbres, ou l'air en grande masse se brasse avec celui des rues avoisinantes, l'amélioration sera certes considérable. Mais c'est en premier lieu à la voie publique à laquelle il faudra penser avant tout Pour purifier l'atmosphère contaminée qui sort des habitations par toutes les ouvertures, le mélanger à sa sortie avec de l'air en mouvement, est le problème primordial de la salubrité. *Aussi est-il essentiel que la cour et la rue soient formées d'espaces communiquant entre eux* Nous avons établi autre part les principales méthodes qui doivent nous permettre d'arriver à ce résultat, et avons été le premier à démontrer à quel point il est indispensable, si l'on veut satisfaire à l'hygiène de l'aération, qu'il en soit ainsi.   Nous ne pouvons prétendre faire avancer sérieusement la question des espaces libres dans la ville, si nous ne faisons l'important effort de modifier dans ce sens le plan de nos immeubles   L'hygiène publique doit placer au premier rang de ses préoccupations et de ses soucis la suppression des cours fermées et leur remplacement par des cours ouvertes   Dans le cas où cela serait même possible, nous allons jusqu'à préconiser d'éviter, pour les parties d'immeubles en bordure de la voie publique, les murs mitoyens de grande hauteur, les limitant aux soubassements de l'édifice, laissant ainsi au-dessus un espace vide, séparant deux propriétés voisines, pour la libre circulation de l'air. *Il est nécessaire, en effet, que l'on crée la demeure entourée de toute part et comme baignée d'air en mouvement* Ce que nous indiquons comme réformes est limité aux bâtiments servant à l'habitation urbaine, laissant de côté ceux d'autres catégories   Les bases de rénovation, dont nous venons de développer les grandes lignes, semblent à l'heure présente un peu comme des rêves   Elles s'imposeront dans l'avenir cependant peu à peu, et par étapes successives.   Les règlements de voirie, applicables aux extensions de toutes nos grandes cités, seront obligés d'y faire appel, car elles répondent aux besoins les plus impérieux de la vie humaine   Augmenter sans cesse le cube d'air en mouvement et les espaces situés dans le pourtour immédiat de la maison, ce qui permet en même temps une abondante lumière de pénétrer, faire une opposition de plus en plus énergique à tout ce qui tendrait à restreindre ces espaces, est le but vers lequel doivent tendre tous les efforts.

Pourquoi les espaces libres doivent toujours être plantés —L'importance des plantations dans tout espace libre suffisant, que ce soit dans les voies publiques ou dans les cours, a toujours été reconnue. Ces plantations ont une influence indéniable sur la santé du citadin Personne jusqu'ici n'a expliqué d'une manière satisfaisante les raisons de cette influence   A la suite de travaux sur ce sujet, nous sommes arrivés à des conclusions qui viennent confirmer d'une manière inattendue l'importance donnée jusqu'ici à la plantation des espaces libres.   Les études que nous avons entreprises se basent sur l'influence considérable que l'électricité exerce sur notre globe   La terre, domaine de l'électricité négative, filtre cette électricité par toutes les aspérités dont elle est recouverte   Les pointes végétales, les pointes minérales fonctionnent comme de véritables détenteurs de cette électricité du sol.   Celle-ci est en quantité colossale.   Des expériences récentes ont montré que rien ne pouvait contrarier la régularité de ces effluves, sauf dans un cas lorsque le sol était privé d'aspérités et se trouvait absolument plat   *Cet écoulement électrique, auquel on n'a jamais jusqu'ici attaché l'importance voulue, est peut-être une des lois de la nature qui exerce sur nos organismes la plus puissante influence*   L'électricité atmosphérique est en général de sens contraire à celle de la terre, et provient, comme on l'explique actuellement, de l'action des rayons solaires, peut être ceux du groupe obscur du spectre solaire sur l'éther et l'air   En temps normal la combinaison de ces deux électricités se fait dans les parties supérieures de l'atmosphère   La tension du fluide terrestre est parfois considérable, elle a été relevée dans les végétaux notamment comme dépassant toute attente   Comme nous venons de l'expliquer, ce fluide négatif du sol s'écoule avec une régularité absolue filtrant pour ainsi dire par toute aspérité, fonctionnant comme véritable détenteur. (L'eau est un filtreur naturel d'électricité dont rien ne peut venir contrarier l'action.) *En déboisant nos villes, par la suppression de tout espace libre couvert de*

*verdure, comme les jardins, en donnant à nos chaussées ces surfaces lisses,
et pour ainsi dire polies, nous substituons un espace plat et sans aspérités
qui empêche l'écoulement normal de l'électricité terrestre   Que se passe-
t-il alors?   L'homme en mouvement sur la voie publique macadamisée,
bitumée, pavée, arrive, comme détenteur subit de l'électricité considérable
accumulée à la surface du sol et qui ne pouvait s'écouler   Cette
électricité s'écoule par la surface extérieure de nos personnes   et ébranle
ainsi fatalement à la longue tout notre système nerveux   Les fatigues
si intenses que nous ressentons à la ville, en seraient la véritable cause
Pour nous remettre, il nous faut séjourner à la campagne, où cette
électricité qui s'écoule normalement par les innombrables aspérités du
sol ne passe plus par nous   Nous reprenons peu à peu notre équilibre,
notre système nerveux n'étant plus soumis à ces passages violents d'électricité terrestre.* Il ne suffit donc pas d'avoir des espaces libres, il est
indispensable de les boiser, et cela pour la raison capitale que le végétal-
brin d'herbe-arbuste-arbre est par essence un dés plus puissants
détenteurs de l'électricité du sol. Les hommes éminents qui se sont
occupés jusqu'ici de la question des espaces libres, et qui sont partisans
résolus de les voir toujours plantés, peuvent se rendre compte, par les
raisons d'ordre scientifique que nous venons pour la première fois de
mettre en lumière, de l'importance énorme que doivent avoir ces plantations

*La question des expropriations pour création de voies publiques plus
larges —*Une question délicate à laquelle vient de faire allusion notre Président, M Buls, et à laquelle M Hénard à donné une solution, est celle de
la voie publique avec ou sans magasins. La gaieté d'un quartier servant
à l'habitation est certainement augmentée par la présence de magasins
dans le soubassement des maisons   C'est là un fait qu'il faut reconnaître, et avec lequel il faut compter   Nous avons cherché, nous occupant
plus particulièrement de la question d'expropriation, à résoudre par une
formule simple ce problème complexe, que nous avons ainsi posé · *Comment
tracer une voie pour que, dans l'avenir, la circulation devenant intense,
la largeur de cette voie puisse être augmentée sans dépenses excessives
pour la communauté?   Voici la solution économique et pratique à
laquelle nous sommes parvenus   Si la largeur de 12 m. suffit pour les
besoins actuels, et qu'une largeur dans l'avenir de 18 m. soit moitié en
plus, soit considérée comme pouvant devenir nécessaire, en créant cette
voie de 12 m nous prévoyons le recul des façades de 3 m de chaque
côté, les propriétaires n'étant autorisés que dans la hauteur du soubassement de leurs maisons sur cette bande de 3 m de construire des
magasins jusqu'à l'alignement de la rue   Dans l'avenir, l'élargissement
de la rue devenant nécessaire, l'expropriation, en faisant disparaître une
première bande de maisons sur un des côtés de la rue, portera la largeur
de la rue à 15 m, et plus tard à 18 m. par l'expropriation de l'autre côté
C'est une méthode simple et qui permet toutes les variantes possibles
Sur cette base nouvelle les expropriations seront ramenées à des chiffres
très peu élevés   Elles ne comprendront, en effet, que le prix des bandes
de terrain et les indemnités ne porteront que sur la hauteur d'un soubassement, laissant indemne la maison tout entière* Les expropriations
pour élargissement des voies publiques sont celles qui grèvent le budget
d'une municipalité d'une manière régulière, et pour des chiffres considérables parfois   *Pour satisfaire aux charges croissantes de nos villes,
il faut ménager les dépenses d'avenir de nos cités et faire ce que n'ont
pas fait nos prédécesseurs, qui nous ont laissé les plus grandes difficultés
à résoudre.* Eviter, par la méthode que nous venons de donner, les expropriations désastreuses qui consistent à raser les immeubles de toute
hauteur qui entraînent à des indemnités considérables, est le but que
nous avons poursuivi. Cette réduction, dans de très grandes proportions
du budget futur de l'élargissement des voies publiques, est une mesure

de haute sagesse et sur laquelle nous attirons l'attention toute spéciale du Congrès et de grandes Administrations Municipales.

Résumé —L'espace libre par excellence est celui qui est immédiatement en communication avec l'habitation la rue et ce tronçon de rue qu'est la cour. C'est de lui surtout qu'il faut s'occuper, car il a en définitive sur la santé publique la plus grande influence

La cour fermée intérieure doit faire place à la cour ouverte. La Ville peut être comparée à un vaste organe sillonné de canaux, ou la cour fermée joue le rôle d'un réservoir isolé. Il faut le remettre en communication avec les canaux publics où l'air circule librement et en faire l'annexe obligée de la voie publique.

Nous rendrons ainsi à la maison d'habitation jusqu'en ses moindres replis, cet aliment de toute vie, l'air et la lumière, que l'avenir sanitaire exige et réclame de plus en plus

Boiser nos espaces libres, que ce soit nos cours, nos rues, nos squares, est une nécessité d'un ordre très élevé. Nous avons établi l'influence de la végétation sur l'équilibre nerveux de nos personnes Indépendamment d'autres raisons, qui ont été développées avec éloquence par quelques uns de nos éminents collègues, cette raison seule devrait nous guider

Une solution simple et économique, pour l'avenir de la circulation dans nos villes, nous a permis de dire un mot des expropriations pour cause d'élargissement de voies Ces espaces libres, que nous créons à si grands frais, peuvent être obtenus par la formule très souple dont nous avons fixé les bases et à laquelle il nous faudra inévitablement arriver dans la pratique

De quelque manière qu'on envisage la question, c'est à l'amélioration du tracé de nos voies publiques, à leur largeur, à leur orientation rationnelle, à la transformation radicale de nos cours fermées en cours ouvertes, que l'espace libre est destiné à exercer la plus puissante action sur la santé publique et sur l'avenir de nos cités surpeuplées

Subject VIII

TO WHAT EXTENT AND IN WHAT SENSE SHOULD THE ARCHITECT HAVE CONTROL OVER OTHER ARTISTS OR CRAFTSMEN IN THE COMPLETION OF A NATIONAL OR PUBLIC BUILDING ?

Thursday, 19th July —Institute Meeting-Room.

Chairmen   Mr R Boker (Russia) , Mr Leonard Stokes (England)
Hon Secretaries   Mr E Kirby (Liverpool) , Mr G Oakley Totten, jun
(United States)

1   By Sir WILLIAM RICHMOND, K C B , R A

A simple question is asked upon a very complicated subject, complicated because we live in times when artists come much more rarely into touch than formerly   Cities are bigger, life is less simple, distractions of various kinds are ever hindering any artistic intercourse   Above all, the State does not take much account of Art   Education is in all hands, superficially.   Hundreds of clever young fellows are taught the rudiments   How few of these gain permanent employment, or even make a living !   Yet notwithstanding, the Institute is always broadening its ground , the Royal Academy seeks to be more comprehensive   The Art Workers' Guild has accomplished much, and the " Arts and Crafts " have succeeded in gaining the interest of a section of the public.   Against the cold attitude of the Government towards Art may be set a growingly democratic bearing of artists to artists   Architecture, sculpture, and painting are getting only too slowly more closely into touch, and the professor of each separate art is gaining knowledge from the specialist   And yet there are great difficulties.   The great mother of Art, Architecture, is still shy of her children.   For this there must be a reason.   May it not be that though increased liberation from " Styles " finds a less pedantic outlook, still a really modern expression in architecture has not entirely overcome them ?   The rapidly increasing necessities of modern life, the almost innumerable and new problems which the architect has to solve, render him more or less an experimentalist.   And exactly, though less forcibly, an analogous uncertainty surrounds the inspiration of the sculptor and painter.

Modern costume does not lend itself to sculpturesque or pictorial art as monumental art, and only monumental design can find fellowship with architecture ; so that we are more or less in a dilemma, all of us.   It would seem a commonplace to say that a classic building should be embellished with classic stories told either in the round in relief or by painting of the same character, and the same applies to Gothic buildings.   And yet being done the average even instructed citizen is left cold.   He is aware of a certain anachronism ; and though he may admire, his admiration is without sympathy, and if he does not state it there is lurking in his mind some such sentence as this : " Is there nothing good enough, picturesque enough,

grand enough in modern life to create a style ? "   This leads one to the
conclusion that architecture must make the move , sculpture and painting
will follow   The divorce of the three arts has been destructive to the
highest art, which contains them all three   It is impossible to deny that
the Royal Academy is *per se* an academy of painting , it has fallen to be so
The architectural room there enlists but little of the public attention.
Why ?   The average public is neither interested in nor does it know
anything about that noble art, which is beyond its power of comprehension
because it appeals to the most abstract of our senses, beauty of line and of
proportion   Architecture is an art which appeals last, not first, to the
average individual.   Painting appeals first, first as portraiture, second as
anecdote , that painting which is the highest, which is abstract, and hence
in allegiance with architecture, appeals scarcely at all   The same may be
said of sculpture, though in a less degree than of painting   Regard for
the abstract beauty of form is very rare in England , thus architecture,
sculpture, and the higher forms of decorative painting have no market ,
they are not either of them, as it were, dealers' wares , their value is
intrinsic, not fluctuating, and it cannot be grouped in the sale-room
therefore neither architecture, sculpture, nor decorative painting is within
the market   So much the better !

Doubtless a combination of serious architects, sculptors, and painters
would be quite invaluable—a society, say, comprising a small number
of each section of the arts, perhaps six architects, six sculptors, and six
painters   The Institute is the very body to create this new departure
from specialism and all its narrowing effects

In my opinion no amount of " Papers," either for discussion at a Congress or for stimulating a pleasant chat at one of the evenings at the
Institute, will ever lead further than that evening's passing instruction and
pleasant pastime.   There are many men capable of writing able articles,
convincing also for the time being, but which very soon are found in that
limbo called forgetfulness   We must get practically into touch ; there
must be no priority.   Our several professions are full of difficulties, which
would be appreciated as soon as we could get to work together.   The
architect can learn much from the painter and sculptor, and *vice versa*
It is " touch " that is needed, not " shyness," and real " touch " can only
occur when practice follows precept in the initial stages of a great work
It is of little use for an architect to tell the sculptor or the painter .   Here I
want a statue, there a relief, here a wall painting, &c   At the very initial
the three should work together   There is nothing harder than the experience of an artist who is called to decorate a building with painting or
sculpture which is in a sense complete without either.   Surely the structure
must be designed to receive   A niche is nothing without its statue, a
sentry-box is a silly thing without its sentry, just as a framed panel seems
to ask for what it is framing, for something precious—marble, mosaic,
or colour   Incomplete is the monument to the Duke of Wellington in
St. Paul's   it looks like a pedestal without a reason ; it fails because it has
no culmination   There are plenty of arches, plinths, pedestals scattered
all over London which present the same absence in appearance of any
utility   If there is no money forthcoming to complete a scheme, why ask
us to imagine what all these pedestals, plinths, and arches mean ?   They
mean nothing, they are inadequate and senseless !   Surely we can imagine
a style of architecture the growth of necessity which shall ask for no
adornment save that of beauty of line and dignity of proportion   That
would be one thing, perfectly complete and quite comprehensive and
entirely satisfactory as far as it went   But when we see forms which are
not structural placed for purposes which they do not fulfil are we not
puzzled and dissatisfied ?   We are presented with shams.   Now, if the
architect, starting his design, says, I am going to design for sculpture
and painting, and calls in the best sculptor and painter to consult with him,

his hands will be strengthened , knowing how much money he has to
spend, he will be able to portion out the various costs of the various parts
of his scheme

My main contention is that, with a view to closer touch between the
architect, sculptor, and painter, a committee such as I have indicated
might be appointed by the Institute.   That committee might in time
become an advisory body to the Government and the London County Council, which both need assistance, not only in common sense, but good taste
also, in all that applies to Art

---

2   DES RAPPORTS PROFESSIONNELS ENTRE L'ARCHITECTE ET SES COLLABORATEURS PEINTRES ET SCULPTEURS

Par H P Nénot, Membre de l'Institut de France.

L'étude qui vous est soumise touche à un des points les plus délicats
de notre art , elle a pour sujet : " Des Rapports Professionnels entre
l'Architecte et ses Collaborateurs Peintres et Sculpteurs "

A toutes les époques antérieures de l'art une même pensée unissait tous
les artistes.   Peintres, architectes, sculpteurs avaient un même idéal, et le
maître de l'œuvre était sûr de trouver chez ses collaborateurs une interprétation décorative en parfaite communauté de sentiments avec sa propre
composition

Chez les Egyptiens les sculptures hiératiques font partie de l'architecture même, et les belles peintures des tombeaux des rois de Thèbes
indiquent qu'au point de vue décoratif pictural, comme au point de vue
sculptural, l'unité était parfaite

Les beaux monuments de la Grèce, où la sculpture jouait un rôle
considérable, quelquefois même prépondérant, comme à l'Erecthie, nous
montrent que les plus grands sculpteurs cherchaient avant tout cette
unité si désirable

A Pompéi, où nous retrouvons la vie intime des Romains, nous voyons
que dans leurs habitations particulières comme dans leurs constructions
monumentales les peintures et sculptures décoratives, quoique variées à
l'infini, sont toujours en communauté parfaite avec l'architecture

Au moyen-âge les charmantes basiliques latines, les splendides églises
byzantines, les belles cathédrales romanes et gothiques, malgré la très
grande liberté d'allures des sculpteurs et des peintres, indiquent bien
qu'une pensée commune, une même foi, animaient tous les artistes

A la Renaissance, architectes, peintres et sculpteurs avaient tous
ensemble modifié complètement leur esthétique, et le record de l'unité au
point de vue des trois arts appartient à Michel-Ange qui architecte était
son propre collaborateur comme peintre et sculpteur.

Avec le Louis XIII, le Louis XIV, le Louis XV, le Louis XVI et
l'Empire les architectes préfèrent les courbes ou les lignes très droites, et
peintres et sculpteurs en leurs œuvres tous ensemble s'adoptent à leurs
conceptions et sont gracieux et souples ou rigides et sévères suivant les
différentes époques.

Cette unité des différentes écoles était féconde pour les artistes , chacun
d'eux suivant son tempérament interprétait le sentiment d'art qui influen-
çait son époque et en suivait ou en dirigeait les fluctuations

Ils ignoraient les styles et passaient, comme notre grand confrère
Blondel, du Louis XIV au Louis XV sans s'en douter, simplement en
suivant la mode , peintres, sculpteurs et architectes étaient tous de la même
école , et cette école leur semblait bien supérieure à toutes celles des
époques antérieures ; ils avaient même un certain mépris pour les dites

époques, et cela devait être une grande joie et une grande force d'être sûr de la parfaite vérité de l'esthétique de son art

Combien étaient faciles et simples les rapports professionnels de l'architecte avec ses collaborateurs peintres et sculpteurs, ils parlaient toujours la même langue et cette pensée commune donnait à leurs mouvements cette belle unité si difficile à obtenir de nos jours.

Les paradis terrestre des belles époques unitaires nous est fermé · nous avons tous voulu mordre aux fruits de l'arbre de science critiques et archéologues nous ont appris l'histoire de l'art et des différents styles, et chacun de nous suivant ses préférences y a placé des apogées ou des décadences

Sans se douter que l'art est une langue que chaque génération ne doit modifier que légèrement, et qu'on ne peut se rendre compte de ces modifications et les juger qu'après au moins un demi-siècle, on nous a demandé quel style nous faisions ! Il nous aurait fallu répondre comme ces héros d'un drame populaire qui tirant leurs épées s'écriaient "Nous autres gentilshommes du moyen-âge", ceux-là au moins n'hésitaient pas à classer leur époque

On nous a, de plus, très gentiment dit que nous étions en pleine décadence, et alors au lieu de continuer à parler la langue que l'on avait apprise on a voulu remonter aux sources, mais il y a tant de délicieuses rivières et de charmants petits bras au fleuve de l'Art, quand on veut en remonter le courant, que les uns ont retrouvé la vraie source dans l'Inde, d'autres en Grèce, certains en Italie et beaucoup dans les pays romans et gothiques ou ailleurs

Chaque artiste ayant trouvé la vraie source s'y baignait délicieusement, ses adeptes affirmaient qu'il n'y avait pas d'eau plus pure, mais comme il y avait beaucoup de vraies sources, chaque groupement parlant une langue morte qu'il connaissait peu, les artistes cessèrent de se comprendre, comme jadis lors de la construction de la Tour de Babel

Dans cette confusion de belles individualités s'affirmèrent, mais toutes ces écoles rendaient la tâche de l'architecte très difficile quand il s'agissait de décorer un monument

Lors de la construction de la Sorbonne, dans le grand amphithéâtre, pour décorer la partie du fond qui porte la coupole, il avait été prévu une grande fresque de 26 mètres de développement Le succès dépendait de la tonalité de cette fresque. Puvis de Chavannes semblait indiqué ; avec lui le mur de pierre blanche presque entièrement recouvert continuerait à porter sa coupole, mais mon ami Benjamin Constant, désigné pour une autre décoration dans le même monument, ambitionnait cette fresque, et le Président de la République, M Grévy, fit savoir au Directeur des Beaux-Arts, M Kempfen, qu'il désirait vivement que la commande lui en fut faite La situation de l'architecte était pénible, résister au chef de l'Etat était chose difficile, mais d'autre part avec la palette puissante de Benjamin Constant la demi-coupole n'était plus supportée et l'harmonie générale était rompue Je fis savoir que si on m'imposait Benjamin Constant je renoncerais à la fresque et la remplacerais par un motif architectural On m'accorda Puvis de Chavannes

Il en devrait toujours être ainsi, au lieu d'imposer à l'architecte tel artiste on devrait lui laisser une grande liberté pour le choix de ses collaborateurs, et lui-même doit indiquer les artistes et suivre leurs travaux, sans autre préoccupation que l'harmonie générale de sa composition, et laisser aux peintres et sculpteurs responsables de leurs œuvres toute liberté de formes ou de couleurs, pourvu qu'ils ne portent pas atteinte à cette harmonie générale sans laquelle aucune œuvre architecturale ne peut réellement exister.

Paris · 28 avril 1906

3 By Gaston Trélat (Paris).

*Jusqu'à quel point et dans quel sens l'architecte doit-il avoir le contrôle sur
les autres artistes et sur les artisans dans l'édification complète des
monuments destinés à l'état ou au service public ?*

S'il n'y avait pas un contrôle permanent à exercer sur tous les artistes,
sur tous les artisans, dans l'édification des monuments destinés à l'Etat ou
aux municipalités, le rôle de l'architecte serait considérablement réduit,
et même jusqu'au point de supprimer la portée effective de l'art, en ce
qui concerne l'édification d'ensemble, sur laquelle repose l'architecture.

Les édifices d'un caractère national ou municipal sont des plus
nobles applications auxquelles il y ait à faire face.   Ils donnent donc
lieu à une mise-en-œuvre comprenant tous les caractères d'une exécution bien conçue et bien dirigée   La réalisation doit, en tous points,
répondre à la conception primitive, telle que l'Etat—ou une représentation
fondée de pouvoirs—se trouve en droit ne s'y attendre, de la part d'une
personnalité responsable, à qui l'on a montré sa confiance.   Quand il
s'agit de l'Etat ou de service public, les monuments, il faut bien le reconnaître, prennent en général plus d'ampleur qu'ils n'en auraient, s'il s'agissait
de services privés   Conséquemment, on se trouve en présence d'une complexité à laquelle il faut satisfaire.   Elle prend un accent encore plus
intense que dans toute autre condition.   Il est nécessaire d'assurer une
suite ininterrompue   Elle se continue avec une intelligence qui s'élargit
sans cesse, depuis les préoccupations du début, servant de point de départ
à la conception, jusqu'à l'extrême achèvement que l'exécution arrive à
parfaire.   Et si, d'autre part, on envisage l'harmonie que l'édifice devra
réaliser plastiquement, pour répondre de tout point à ce qui fut entrevu
et arrêté dans ses grandes lignes, au moment de la conception première,
on trouvera sans doute un nouvel argument en faveur du contrôle exclusif
de l'architecte, s'attachant par lui-même à l'achèvement final de l'œuvre
C'est du moins ce que pareille circonstance tendrait à exiger.

Je crois bien qu'une des *questions* précédentes m'a déjà fourni l'occasion de mettre en évidence la pensée   qu'un dessin, une étude, n'est pour
ainsi dire *rien du tout*, relativement à la réalisation entrevue par l'artiste
Les visions, qui guident l'auteur dans sa conception première ou dans
les étapes successives auxquelles l'élaboration donne lieu et qu'il pourrait
pousser indéfiniment, lui font sans cesse envisager un nouvel *au-delà*
L'exécution est seule à arrêter ces essais, d'accord avec la marche inquiète
de l'art   Et cette exécution elle-même demande, pour avoir une valeur
réelle, que l'auteur de l'ensemble, et aucun autre, exerce une sorte de
maestria jusqu'à l'extrême fin, qu'il soit seul à arrêter, à décider la figure et
le relief de tous les éléments pouvant intervenir dans la réalisation projetée.

Quant à la science mécanique assurant la stabilité de la construction,
le concepteur ne peut se désintéresser des moyens employés pour assurer
la durée des services qu'il aménage et dont il a une responsabilité publique.

Pour ce qui touche l'infinité d'éléments intervenant dans l'ordonnance
plastique d'un ensemble, il n'est pas permis à un architecte de s'en distraire ,
car ce serait s'exposer à compromettre l'œuvre conçue, amorcée en projet
et dont le mode d'exécution étudié en détail permet seulement d'affirmer la
valeur   S'agit-il de peinture et de sculptures décoratives ou même statu-
aires, c'est encore la même chose . aucune exécution ne peut, en l'espèce, être
tolérée sans avoir subi la mise au point qui appartient exclusivement au
chef de l'opération plastique   Il est seul à l'avoir *vue*, avant même que
l'exécution fût abordée , et il a vécu avec tous les éléments qu'il lui était
permis de prévoir en vue de l'harmonie plastique d'abord pressentie et que
ses premiers croquis repèraient déjà.   Et même, en ce qui concerne la
statuaire que nous venons déjà d'alléguer, l'équilibre *formel* doit encore être

subordonné au premier concept et ne jamais troubler le rythme de l'ensemble par un désaccord dans le *chant plastique*

L'expérience—dans le maniement des proportions et des reliefs qui font parler la matière—conduit à se rendre compte de toutes ces choses au moyen de croquis et de dessins. Mais quand il y a indécision, il ne faut pas hésiter à se renseigner par le modèle en relief, qui permet toujours à l'opinion définitive de s'établir

Résumé—En résumé je n'hésite pas à déclarer que l'architecte doit avoir un contrôle—sans autre limite que ses aptitudes et ses possibilités—sur tous les autres artistes, sur tous les artisans

Ce contrôle ne saurait être trop effectif, quant à la construction et quant à l'aménagement. C'est grâce à ce contrôle que les services pourront répondre à la volonté que le concepteur à mise au service du programme, d'accord avec le besoin social qu'il entre dans sa spécialité de remplir

Enfin, pour ce qui est du caractère que le motif plastique doit revêtir, l'architecte, en tant que compositeur, est seul à même de mûrir la conception qu'il a imaginée et rendue exécutable   Il n'y a que lui à être accommodé avec la multitude de formes dont il s'est rendu un compte précis par ses esquisses   C'est là tout un ordre d'idées que le crayon permet de comprendre et de sous-entendre   Cela, grâce à une incessante mise au point de l'intelligence, que les dessins et, au besoin, les modèles en relief guident jusqu'à l'exécution définitive   Et il s'ensuit une *maestria* —le mot que je repète là n'est pas trop fort !—qui appartient à l'architecte compositeur et qui l'attache de plus en plus à l'élaboration de l'œuvre qu'il a conçue

Conclusion.—Par conséquent c'est à l'architecte qu'il revient de contrôler tous les artistes comme tous les artisans, ayant à collaborer à l'édification de monuments destinés à l'Etat ou au service public   Et cela jusqu'à l'achèvement explicite de l'ensemble dont il s'agissait

---

4 By L. B Muller (Architekt), Dusseldorf

" Ist dem Architekten unumschränkte Gewalt über andere Künstler oder Handwerker bei der Vollendung eines nationalen oder öffentlichen Gebäudes zu erteilen ? "

Verfasser setzt voraus, dass bei Auftragserteilung an den betreffenden Architekten das *betätigte Können* (Sieg in einem Wettbewerb—oder bereits entworfene bezw nach eigenen Entwurfen ausgeführte *qualitativ* besonders hervorragende Bauten) massgebend war

Die *so* gefundenen Baukünstler *werden* und *sollen* soviel Geschmack besitzen, dass sie die Direktive für alle mitwirkenden Künstler erteilen können

Handelt es sich also darum, dass ein von *einem* Architekten ersonnenes öffentliches oder nationales Gebäude—oder auch ein Denkmal—mit Bildnissen oder Bildern geschmückt werden soll, so *ist der Architekt der Componist*

Er gestaltet den Rahmen des Bildes und giebt den Inhalt desselben an.

Die anderen Künstler sind die Mitwirkenden

Sie haben sich seinen Intentionen im Massstab, in der Betonung und im Farbenakkord zur Erzielung einer gewünschten Stimmung *unterzuordnen, oder* auf die Aufgabe zu *verzichten*

Handelt es sich um ein Denkmal, wo, sei es der Bildhauer oder der Maler (Innendenkmal) den Ton angiebt, so hat sich der *Architekt* den Intentionen des betreffenden Kunstlers *unterzuordnen* und hat so lange zu entwerfen, bis er die Stimmung im Sinne des betreffenden Kunstlers gefunden hat, oder *er muss* auf die Aufgabe *verzichten*

Nötigt man bei offentlichen und nationalen Gebäuden einem Architekten einen mitwirkenden Kunstler auf, oder notigt man umgekehrt bei Denkmalern einem anderen Kunstler einen Architekten auf, so *kommen sehr wahrscheinlich Antipoden zusammen*

Der Kräftigere siegt und "*das Werk wird ein Stuckwerk.*" Die Losung muss jedenfalls sein. "Der Componist hat die Wahl und Leitung seiner Mitwirkenden."

Der Componist darf aber kein falsches Ehrgefuhl haben

Er darf nicht etwas im Sinne seiner Composition " Verbessertes " nur darum ablehnen, weil *er* es nicht erfunden.

Er muss seinen Mitarbeitern, wenn sie mit Geschick im Sinne seiner Composition arbeiten, nicht alleine eine gewisse Freiheit, sondern auch einen berechtigten Teil der Ehre, " Nennung des Namens und Anerkennung einer Verbesserung," zugestehen

Er ehrt sich hierdurch selbst

Ist ein Vorstehenden nun schon vom mitwirkenden Kunstler die Unterordnung verlangt und begrundet, so soll sich der *Handwerker* umsomehr dem *Componisten unterordnen*

Der Architekt soll allerdings auch auf diesen Gebieten soviel Dilettant sein, dass er einen zweckentsprechenden Bestimmungsspruch bei verschiedenen Möglichkeiten abgeben kann

Er soll den Handwerker zum Vortrag uber etwas, das Gelingen des Baues Fordernde ermutigen

Er soll schlechte oder ohne Interesse ausgeführte Arbeiten ohne Erbarmen zur Verfugung stellen und hieruber schon im Verdingungsanschlag keinen Zweifel lassen

Der Architekt soll seine volle Aufmerksamkeit darauf richten, dass alles Notwendige in schonster Form gelost wird

Die Natur soll ihm hierin vorbildlich sein, in welcher alles Notwendige in schonster Form gegeben ist.

Eller, Dusseldorf Marz 1906

---

5. By OTTO WAGNER, Imp. and Roy Superintendent of Works, Vienna , Professor of the Imp and Roy Academy of the Plastic Arts

(On behalf of the Society of Austrian Architects)

Inwieweit und in welchem Sinne ist dem Architekten unumschränkte Gewalt uber andere Kunstler oder Handwerker bei der Vollendung eines internationalen oder öffentlichen Gebaudes zu erteilen, sind die vorgebrachten Ausfuhrungen noch durch Nachstehendes zu erganzen .

Die Qualitat und Quantität des Wissens des Architekten und gewiss in den meisten Fallen sein Können, uberragen, wie gezeigt wurde, sicher die gleichen Eigenschaften seiner Mitarbeiter, sie drängen dem Architekten also die Fuhrerrolle bei jeder Arbeitsausfuhrung geradezu auf Diese Fuhrerrolle ist, soll sie von Erfolg begleitet sein, mit unumschrankter Macht uber alle Beteiligten auszustatten, da ein richtiges, kunstlerisches und technisches Ineinandergreifen der einzelnen Herstellungen davon abhängt, und nur der Schöpfer der Arbeit, also der Architekt, in der Lage ist, diesbezüglich Anordnungen zu treffen

Hiezu kommt noch, dass viele Arbeiten und Materialverwendungen

vom Architekten selbst erfunden sind, er daher uber jede Bestimmung
bei auszufuhrenden Proben, Versuchen, Mustern etc. Herr bleiben muss.
Gewiss wird er sich uber Dinge, wenn sie vom breiten Wege der Gewohn-
lichkeit abweichen, mit den Unternehmern und Lieferanten beraten und
in Einvernehmen setzen, die endgiltige Entscheidung hieruber kann aber
nur ihm allein zustehen, weil nur er fur den Erfolg oder Misserfolg der
Allgemeinheit gegenuber verantwortlich bleibt

Bildet fur den Architekten eine richtige, von ihm vorzunehmende
Wahl von Personen, denen die Ausfuhrung der einzelnen Bauteile uber-
tragen werden soll, eine gewisse Sicherheit fur den anzustrebenden Erfolg
seines Werkes, so tritt die Bedeutung einer solchen Wahl in intensiverer
Weise zu Tage, wo es sich um die mitarbeitenden Kunstler handelt, da
hier ein neues Moment, namlich die Individualitat des Mitarbeitenden
schwer in die Wagschale fallt.   Jede kunstlerische Auffassung der Mitarbeiter hat sich den vom Architekten beabsichtigten Intentionen vollig
anzuschmiegen, so dass das entstehende Werk aus einem Gusse erscheint.
Nachdem der Schopfer des Werkes allein hieruber ein richtiges Urteil
abgeben kann, ist sicher nur er berufen, diese Mitarbeiter zu bestimmen.
Die Beantwortung der Frage 8 kann daher nur lauten :

Dem Architekten ist bei Ausfuhrung von Werken unumschrankte
Gewalt uber die mitwirkenden Handwerker, insbesondere aber uber die
mitwirkenden Kunstler einzuräumen.

---

6   Par Dr. P. J. H. Cuypers (Architecte), Amsterdam.

Pour répondre à la question 8 : " A quel point et dans quel sens
l'architecte doit-il avoir le contrôle sur les autres artistes et sur les
artisans jusqu'à l'édification complète des monuments destinés à l'Etat
ou au service public ? " nous n'avons qu'à voir le passé en étudiant les
manifestations architectoniques des differents époques.

Pendant l'antiquité chez les Grecs et les Romains l'architecte était
l'homme qui au moyen-âge était nommé "magister operum," le maître de
l'œuvre, l'artiste qui conçoit, le créateur de l'œuvre qui doit posséder,
dans la plus large mesure, les talents d'embrasser sous un coup d'œil
l'ensemble de son œuvre pour la diriger et la mener au but voulu.

L'architecte doit être le maître qui commande à tout ceux qui doivent
concourir par leur collaboration à effectuer le bâtiment, c'est lui qui
dirige le tout jusqu'à l'achèvement complet de l'édifice

C'est ainsi qu'on a travaillé dans l'antiquité ainsi qu'au moyen-âge,
c'est ainsi qu'il faut agir maintenant et à l'avenir, si l'on veut que le
monument nous offrira l'harmonie dans les détails et l'unité nécessaire dans
l'ensemble à toute œuvre architectonique.

On n'a qu'à consulter les cahiers de croquis des anciens maîtres, comme
par exemple le recueil de croquis de Villard de Honnecourt, pour constater
que les maîtres de l'œuvre au XIIIme siècle n'étaient pas seulement les
auteurs de leur projets mais ordonnaient le tout, la construction, la
structure, et donnaient également les dessins et détails pour la décoration,
la sculpture, la peinture dans tous les détails.

L'architecte, qui doit avoir dans sa tête son projet complet, peut, par
son imagination, le mieux juger de quelle manière l'harmonie peut être
obtenue par la coopération des différentes parties qui constituent le
monument

De même que pour une grande composition musicale il est nécessaire
que tous les exécutants se rangent et obéissent aux ordres du maître
(directeur), tout aussi il est nécessaire que les différents collaborateurs

d'un monument architectonique soient dirigés par l'architecte, sans quoi il est à craindre que le monument se ressentira de l'anarchie qui a sévi pendant la construction.

Nous ne savons que trop bien par l'expérience que le peintre, abandonné à sa propre volonté, considère probablement son travail pour le monument artistique le plus important du monument, et pour cela il tâchera de fixer l'attention sur son travail par tous les moyens qu'il aura à sa disposition, indifférent pour lui de nuire à l'unité et à l'harmonie de l'ensemble du monument, le sculpteur fera la même chose si l'on lui laisse la faculté d'agir à son gré.

Les exemples de cette nature sont abondants dans l'histoire de l'architecture des derniers siècles. On n'a qu'à regarder les monuments, et surtout les églises, dans lesquelles cette liberté d'agir aux collaborateurs de l'architecte a détruit toute l'unité et l'harmonie dans la conception architectonique

Ce sont les monuments dans lesquels l'architecte n'a pas su diriger avec une main forte et esprit ferme les différents éléments qui devaient concourir pour l'exécution de ses projets.

Rome nous donne un exemple frappant de ce genre. Qu'on se représente dans l'esprit la chapelle Sixtine. Michel-Ange, au lieu de faire servir ses tableaux à orner et compléter la structure du monument, a poussé l'indiscrétion si loin, qu'il a violé l'architecture du monument en faisant fermer les fenêtres par une maçonnerie et transformer la structure des voûtes Aussi cette peinture n'est nullement en harmonie avec la destination du monument, qui était de relever les cérémonies réligieuses qui devaient avoir lieu dans cette chapelle. Le peintre s'est soucié aussi peu de la destination du monument qu'on doit se coucher par terre pour voir convenablement son travail. La peinture est devenue l'objet principal ; l'architecture de la chapelle n'a pour le peintre (un des plus grands artistes de son temps) aucune signification ; la seule chose qui lui intéresse c'est d'avoir des pans de murs pour pouvoir exposer les produits de son talent particulier.

La tâche et la vocation de l'architecte sont exprimées par son nom : ἀρχι de ἄρχειν, commandeur, et τέκτων, artisans "L'architecte est l'artiste qui compose les édifices, en détermine les proportions, les distributions, les décorations, les fait exécuter sous ses ordres et en règle les dépenses." (Viollet-le-Duc.)

L'homme de métier était qualifié de "maître de l'œuvre," designation bien autrement positive du reste que celle d'architecte, car par " œuvre " on entendait tout ce qui constituait l'immeuble et le meuble d'un bâtiment depuis les fondations jusqu'aux tapisseries, aux flambeaux, aux menus objets mobiliers.

Si nous passons en revue les monuments qui ont été érigés pendant les siècles dans lesquels les architectes ont abandonné leur autorité et ont laissé aux différents artistes et artisans toute liberté d'exécution, nous voyons que la grandeur, l'unité et l'harmonie ont disparu par le manque d'équilibre et d'une organisation logique.

7. Par José Amargos, Salvador Oller y Padrol, P de
Miquelerena, et Salvador Valeri.

[Pour l'Association des Architectes de Catalogne]

Désignés par le Comité de Propagande de l'Association des Architectes
de Catalogne du Congrès que l'on célèbre actuellement dans cette grande
ville de Londres pour exposer les conclusions relatives au Thème VIII :
" L'architecte doit-il avoir l'autorité suprême sur tous les artistes et sur
tous les ouvriers jusqu'à l'édification complète des monuments, destinés
à l'État ou au service public ? " notre tâche accomplie, nous avons
l'honneur de soumettre à votre jugement supérieur le résultat de notre
labeur

Pendant la discussion du thème nous avons été saisis de la crainte de
n'en avoir peut-être bien interprété la portée et la transcendance, puisqu'il
est évident, et c'est chose pratique en Espagne, que l'autorité de l'architecte doit être suprême sur tous les autres artistes et sur les ouvriers jusqu'à
l'édification complète des monuments destinés à l'État ou au service
public. Si nous n'avions pas réussi, nous vous supplions de nous accorder
votre indulgence et toujours votre bienveillante attention pour une
affaire dont le résultat doit être notre propre défense afin d'obtenir le
respect de nos attributions et la suppression des pratiques abusives dont
nous pouvons être l'objet dans le noble exercice de notre profession.

Cette autorité suprême de l'architecte est nécessaire , laquelle indiscutable sur les ouvriers appartenant aux branches de la construction proprement dite, pourrait paraître à certains douteuse sur les personnes qui
exercent quelqu'un des beaux-arts et interviennent aussi dans l'exécution
des monuments de caractère public. La prétendue émancipation de cette
autorité de la part de certains artistes nous oblige encore d'avantage à
défendre nos droits, qui ne nous ont pas été concédés à titre gracieux,
mais bien reconnus par une loi sans appel de l'aptitude et de la distinction professionnelle ; droits qui doivent prévaloir autant pour rendre plus
facile, plus dégagée et plus correcte notre mission facultative que pour
atteindre le plus grand développement de l'œuvre architectonique.

Cela ne veut pas dire que cette autorité justifiée soit appliquée ou
exercée d'une manière absolue, puisque dans ce cas tous les ouvriers et
artistes se convertiraient en exécuteurs inconscients de l'œuvre. Cette
autorité doit s'exercer avec la plus grande discrétion en donnant les
instructions claires, précises et méthodiques aux ouvriers, en s'assurant
que ceux-ci ont compris la nature et l'importance du travail qui leur est
confié, dans le but que tous se surpassant contribuent par leur intelligence et
leur volonté à l'exécution complète de l'œuvre.

Des raisons puissantes d'ordre moral et matériel peuvent être allé-
guées en faveur du principe nécessaire de l'autorité suprême de l'architecte,
mais le caractère de ce travail et les prescriptions du règlement du Congrès nous défendent de nous étendre en argumentations qui justifieraient
pleinement notre jugement, lequel est de donner la plus formelle affirmation

L'architecte doit avoir l'autorité à laquelle se réfère le thème .

Premièrement Parce que l'architecte directeur doit transmettre sa
pensée par les moyens appropriés, graphiques, écrits ou verbaux, suivant
les cas à tous les artistes et ouvriers qui doivent intervenir dans l'exécution du monument, en leur expliquant les motifs qui le poussent à prendre
telle ou telle résolution , dans le cas contraire le monument en question
manquerait de l'harmonieuse variété dans l'unité que doit réunir toute
œuvre architectonique

Deuxièmement : Parce que dans toute édification est nécessaire et indispensable un architecte qui dirige des travaux pour que l'œuvre se réalise avec l'ordre convenable et sans interruptions, autrement cela occasionnerait des préjudices au monument et aux artistes et ouvriers qui contribuent à son exécution.

---

8 Par Modeste de Noyette, Directeur de la Section de la Flandre-Orientale (Société Centrale d'Architecture de Belgique)

Conclusions —Vœux déposés sur la VIIIme question :

" Jusqu'à quel point et dans quel sens l'architecte doit-il avoir le contrôle sur les autres artistes et sur les artisans jusqu'à l'édification complète des monuments destinés à l'Etat ou au service public ? "

L'architecte doit avoir le contrôle sur les autres artistes et sur les artisans jusqu'à l'achèvement complet des monuments ou édifices *dont les plans et détails d'exécution* lui ont été confiés.

L'architecte est *le maître de l'œuvre.* A l'idée d'élever un monument succède celle du choix de l'architecte, soit par voie de concours publics, ou qu'on tient compte de la valeur de la confiance pour le choix d'un artiste déterminé.

L'architecte est donc investi d'une mission : il assume la responsabilité de l'œuvre qu'il va élever ; il va de soi qu'il doit avoir l'autorité nécessaire. L'architecte est le créateur de l'œuvre : c'est son enfant ; c'est lui-même, et qui donc pourrait mieux interpréter ses idées, ses conceptions, que lui-même ? C'est donc bien lui qui a donné aux autres arts la place et l'importance qu'ils doivent occuper dans son œuvre.

Aujourd'hui on conteste trop souvent aux architectes leurs droits légitimes, et au détriment des monuments ou constructions, fussent-elles privées, qui leur ont été confiés. On dirait qu'il suffit de leur payer la note d'honoraires pour-échapper à leur autorité, et si l'on veut encore s'en souvenir c'est au point de vue de la responsabilité matérielle. C'est le code civil en main que, jusqu'à l'expiration des dix années de responsabilité, on examine si une crevasse ou une infiltration, un tassement irrégulier, ne saurait faire rentrer l'Etat ou le particulier dans les fonds consacrés à la création de l'œuvre, et pendant que l'architecte luttera contre les actes de vandalisme qu'on veut lui imposer, l'administration, représentée par des fonctionnaires incompétents, infligera une ou deux amendes pour avoir délivré les plans 24 heures après la date fixée.

On doit réagir contre ce système, et il ne faut pas seulement que dans les Congrès on exprime des vœux ; il ne suffit pas de constater la plaie— il faut réagir, il faut guérir.

Pour le moment il s'agit de s'adresser aux chefs d'Etat responsables ou chefs administratifs

Entre Partis —Des conditions doivent être stipulées d'avance quant à l'autorité à la direction artistique notamment L'architecte doit rester le maître de son œuvre, et ses collaborateurs doivent s'entendre et tenir compte de ses projets.

Si un différent surgit, si des modifications doivent se faire ou des économies être réalisées, *qu'il soit stipulé* que c'est à une commission des monuments, à des autorités artistiques, qu'on soumettra les propositions, et non à l'arbitraire de fonctionnaires incompétents

Mais quant à l'avenir, Messieurs, c'est à l'éducation artistique qu'on devra s'en prendre.

Il faut que l'architecte étudie davantage la peinture et la sculpture, et qu'il étudie avec plus de persistance les arts appliqués à l'industrie.

Il faut qu'il puisse connaître les couleurs et qu'il sache manier le pinceau. If faut qu'il sache modeler et plier le fer; Mais ce que nous demandons aussi c'est que l'on apprenne aux autres artistes les éléments de l'architecture, qu'ils puissent comprendre un plan et respecter les proportions, qu'ils connaissent les matériaux et leur résistance.

À quoi nos éducateurs de l'avenir doivent viser aussi, c'est un rapprochement des artistes et artisans spécialistes.

Il faut que les architectes créent des cercles où les peintres et les sculpteurs viennent les rejoindre et les connaître. Il faut que les sculpteurs et les peintres nous prouvent par leur conduite, par l'organisation de leurs expositions, par leurs écrits et par leurs rapports de tous les jours que l'architecture est la mère des arts, et qu'avec la peinture et la sculpture elle constitue une triplice où elle occupe la première place.

Un autre remède, Messieurs, c'est dans la réorganisation de nos musées publics.

Il faut que l'architecture y ait sa place légitime. Il faut que l'on rappelle par des expositions tous les chefs-d'œuvre que l'antiquité, que le moyen-âge, nous a laissés. Les peintres et les sculpteurs y puiseront des leçons pratiques ; ils connaîtront ce qu'a été la grandeur et la réussite de ces monuments, l'harmonie, l'entente entre les artistes, leur quasi-confusion. Vous voyez, Messieurs, que dans mon système je rapproche autant les œuvres que les artistes.

Il faut s'aimer, se respecter et travailler la main dans la main, et au lieu de se démolir, au lieu de vouloir dominer chacun dans sa branche, travailler à la réunion de l'œuvre et au progrès artistique. C'est dans cette voie que je vous convie à entrer Préparons par notre déjà longue expérience le chemin aux jeunes, c'est les laisser un bien beau patrimoine d'éducation artistique. Et s'il fallait, Messieurs, pour le moment encore protection pour l'artiste, que les architectes, autant que les peintres et les sculpteurs, tendent tous leurs efforts pour obtenir des lois qui nous mettent à l'abri des exploiteurs modernes.

DISCUSSION ON SUBJECT VIII

Mr. ELLICOTT (delegate from Baltimore) suggested that the control of the architect over the collaborating artist should be exercised with the utmost consideration In the case of an artist of transcendent genius this control might result in irreparable injury to the world in reducing him to the position of mere assistant. Ideal conditions are almost impossible of realisation, and to find that the highest aspirations of an artist of the first rank had been rendered abortive or only partially successful by the artificial restrictions thrown around him by the less sensitive and subtle architect would be a misfortune never to be retrieved. That the art of painting can and does lead to a higher sphere than does architecture cannot seriously be denied, that many noble works of art are partially or entirely lost to the world by the fact that they are unfortunately exhibited is certain, and wherever this is the case it is obvious that the conditions should be changed. What artist would begin by purchasing a frame for his picture ? And yet he is expected to conform his art to whatever contortions the architect may see fit to introduce into a given apartment! The architectural features and decoration of an interior should lead up to and not overwhelm the painting on wall or ceiling. *Enfin, il y a deux moyens* either confess that painting and sculpture are higher in the sphere of art than is architecture—that there is a point beyond which architecture should not go (for the reason that the same amount of effort expended in painting, sculpture, or tapestry can do a greater service to mankind)—give the artist his way, and only supply such features as will enhance the value of what he will evolve, or concede the point that his work is a mere accessory, which will inevitably tend to enslave and humiliate him, and so deprive the world of what he might have produced under happier conditions

M Rozet (Paris) contended that, whatever the calibre of the artist, he could not be given an absolutely free hand, and he must keep his own work in due subordination to the general design.

M Bonnier (Paris) supported M Rozet's contention He pointed out that the education and experience of the painter and the sculptor, as well as his scope in general, differ essentially from that of the architect. A sculptor, as a rule, does not allow himself to be hampered by any considerations of his site or the position his work will occupy. Similarly, a painting made in a studio often takes no account of the wall surface it is destined to cover, and so does not possess the necessary inherent qualities suitable, and indeed essential, for flat wall decoration. The architect, on the other hand, has carefully considered both painting and sculpture as adjuncts to architecture , and as he has assigned to each a certain function in the design, it is for him to decide whether each form of decoration does take its proper place in due subordination to the general scheme It is unusual to find either painter or sculptor who possesses a " sense of architecture "—*i.e.* who realises the essential differences which exist between an easel picture and a coloured wall, or a detached group and a tympanum And it is just the disregard of these inherent qualities which is so apt to mar the unity of a well-considered whole.

M Poupinel (Paris) spoke in support of M Bonnier, and laid great stress on the importance of the architect's advice to both painter and sculptor He further explained the system in vogue in Paris. When a large public building is to be carried out, the design has first to be approved by the Municipal Art Committee. Next, the preliminary sketches and models of both painters and sculptors have to be submitted to the Committee When completed, the painting and sculpture are again inspected, this time *in situ*, and if any work does not satisfy the Committee it is removed. The Art Committee possessing these powers consists partly of members of the municipality acting on behalf of the ratepayers, and partly of architects, painters, and sculptors of recognised ability, who ensure the best artistic criticism possible

The Chairman proposed the resolution in Herr Wagner's paper, viz :

> " *The architect in the construction of a building is to be given absolute power over the co-operating craftsmen, but in a special manner over the co-operating artists* "

Mr Howard Ince seconded the resolution, and it was carried.
The meeting then adjourned.

SUBJECT IX

THE RESPONSIBILITIES OF A GOVERNMENT IN THE CONSERVATION OF NATIONAL MONUMENTS

Thursday, 18th July.—Institute Meeting-Room

Chairmen   M E V Dahlerup (Denmark) , Mr Alexander Graham, F S A (England)
Hon Secretaries . Mr. C. A Cowper (Melbourne) , M Franz de Verstel (Belgium)

1. GOVERNMENT ACTION ON THE CONTINENT IN THE INTERESTS OF NATIONAL MONUMENTS.

By Professor G BALDWIN BROWN, M.A.

The question of the responsibilities of a Government in the Conservation of National Monuments may be treated from two points of view, the ideal and the practical   As a matter of principle the responsibility of a Government in this matter is unlimited.   The very term " National Monuments " implies that the Government as representing the nation has these monuments in charge.   A nation is not a thing of the moment. It has a past and a future as well as a present, and those responsible for the arrangements of the moment have also in their keeping the records of the nation's past, and are bound to take the widest possible outlook on the future   This great fact, the continuity of a nation's life, is not always present in people's minds, and they need to be reminded of it.   The example of the modern Japanese is in this respect instructive   Their complete, even aggressive modernness coexists with an idealistic view of the past, according to which the souls of the dead are invisible but interested witnesses of the proceedings of their successors of to-day.   To the finer spirits of the people these departed ancestors represent all the best elements of the national life, and the consciousness of their presence raises the moral standard and stimulates the efforts of the living.

Among European peoples the sense of historical continuity with the past is fed, not by ancestor-worship, but by the existence of tangible monuments and records in which history is enshrined   The value of such links with the past is sometimes lightly regarded by people who have grown up with these memorials all about them , but it is very instructive to see what attention is paid to them by those to whom they do not come naturally as an element in daily life.   Anyone who has conducted American acquaintances round one of the older British cities, such as York or Oxford or Edinburgh, must have felt that the sight of these historical memorials of the common race seemed to satisfy a natural hunger of the mind that had been hitherto deprived of its proper food.   Our American and our Colonial visitors open our eyes to the value of these elements in our own national life, and lead us to think more seriously of our duties in regard to their preservation.

A Government is accordingly bound to recognise the value to a nation of this sense of historical continuity, and to do what it can to keep it alive. Monumental records are for this service of even greater worth than written records, for they appeal to the general eye, and Continental Governments at any rate have generally recognised that the conservation of these records is a part of their duty A French official document on the subject of the preservation of ancient monuments lays down the principle in epigrammatic form —" To preserve the fabrics which testify to the glory of the land is to make its past live again for the profit of its present and of its future "

It was said at the outset that the responsibility thus laid upon government is in theory unlimited The most uncompromising statements of this doctrine in modern times were made in connection with the proposed Italian legislation on the subject in the year 1872 and following years Previous to the consolidation of the kingdom of Italy there had existed monument legislation of a somewhat drastic order in all the smaller States among which the peninsula was divided. After the union an attempt was made to consolidate these into a single national Act, and in the drafts of this Act, and the speeches of ministers and reporters on the subject of it, we find the claims of the State fearlessly asserted   " The State," it was said by the Minister in charge of the Act, " has a supreme interest in using all vigilance and care for the proper custody of the precious monuments of art and antiquity , its intervention is accordingly justified in all that concerns this great patrimony of the nation , " and among the provisions of the draft Act was one according to which any remains of ancient public buildings, such as temples or city walls, that might come to light in excavations on private ground, passed at once, *ipso facto*, into the possession of the State, the proprietor of the soil receiving an indemnity By another provision it was rigidly forbidden, under penalty, to destroy or alter objects of art or antiquity, even when these were in private proprietorship A member of the Committee of the Italian Senate that reported on the draft Act used the argument that there was an essential difference between the inexhaustible productions of nature and of human industry, which can be renewed at any moment, and the rare creations of the higher intelligence, that when once lost can never be repeated or restored , and that in the case of objects of this unique character absolute possession, the "jus utendi et abutendi," should not be conceded to irresponsible persons or bodies Another provision was that Committees of Preservation were to be constituted in each province under the Act, and that one function of these should be " to compile and to transmit to the Minister a complete artistic and archæo-logical inventory of the monuments, the collections, and the objects of art and archæology existing in each province, and belonging to the State, to corporate bodies, or to private individuals."

The Italian draft Act of 1872 has been quoted to show that attempts have been made in our own time to give practical effect to the principle that the State has complete responsibility for this portion of national assets. The Act in question, however, did not pass the Legislature, and it was not till 1902, thirty years afterwards, that Italy obtained a Monument Act. The same difficulty has been experienced in other countries where attempts have been made to embody in practical legislation the principle at stake It took France fifty years to pass in this way from principle to practice. In Austria the government has been at work for more than fifty years on the care of ancient monuments through the agency of its famous Central Commission, and has not yet advanced to legislation. The Prussian government was roused to take an active interest in the subject by a report drawn up by the well-known architect Schinkel in 1815, and various efforts made from that time to this have finally resulted in the drafting of a Monument Act that is believed to be

in an advanced state of preparation, though it has not yet been submitted
to the legislature.   The English Ancient Monuments Act, a measure of
very narrow scope, was discussed in Parliament for ten years, and was
only passed when the one provision that would have made it effective
was withdrawn.

The difficulty that besets Government action in this department,
and makes the difference between the practical and the ideal, is due
to the fact that adequate measures for the protection of ancient monuments cannot be enforced without interference with private interests.
Both Legislatures and Courts of Law are very sensitive on the subject of
the rights of private property, and consideration for these rights is carried
furthest in the most advanced and enlightened countries.   In despotically
governed lands the rights of the individual citizen count for very little ; and
if the ruler of such a country desire to protect from injury or destruction
the old buildings and works of art that are its glory, there is nothing
to prevent his carrying out his wish   The Government of a constitutional
country is in a very different position, for public opinion will only allow
it to override private rights to a very limited extent.

Now, the ancient monuments with which we are here concerned,
though they are in a true sense "national," in that they embody the
historical memories which we have claimed to be matters of public concern,
are yet in very many cases the property of individuals, who can exercise
over them all the rights of ownership   For example, Stonehenge is
undoubtedly a "national" monument, a monument one might almost say
which is the possession of the world , and yet at the same time it is so
absolutely under private control that the owner might destroy it to-morrow
by dynamite, and there is no power in the Crown or Parliament or the
Law Courts to stay his hand

The problem of monument administration in modern States is how
best to obtain control in the name of the public over works of art or
historical relics of national importance, while at the same time the rights
of private property are not unduly curtailed

The British Ancient Monuments Act, which was passed in 1882,
contained in its original draft a provision to the effect that if any private
owner possessed an ancient monument of national value and wished
to destroy it, he should be bound to give the State the option of purchasing
it at a fair valuation.   This clause was, however, objected to as an interference with these sacred rights of private property, and had to be withdrawn before the Act was allowed to pass.   In this respect the British
Act differs from those Acts which are in operation in France, Greece,
Hesse-Darmstadt, Hungary, Italy, Portugal, Roumania, and Switzerland.
In all these European Monument Acts, as well as in that which Lord
Curzon secured for India in 1904, the corner-stone of the protective
legislation is the power given to the public authorities to acquire by
compulsory purchase any monument of national importance that may
be in danger.   In countries where there is no such definite legislation
there is generally some little doubt as to how far expropriation on æsthetic
or historical grounds is actually legal.   It appears, however, that the
principle of its legality is established in Belgium, France, Greece, Hesse-
Darmstadt, Hungary, Portugal, Roumania, some of the Cantons of
Switzerland, and Turkey.   In Austria, in Prussia, in Spain, and in the
Scandinavian kingdoms the legality of the process seems in the present
state of legislation to be somewhat doubtful.   In Great Britain alone
it has been expressly decreed by Parliament that expropriation on artistic
or historical grounds shall *not* be allowed.

It is obvious that this process of compulsory purchase is the only
practical method which gives absolute legal security for a national monument in private hands.   It is, however, an expensive method and one
that can never be widely employed.   Those Governments that have

seriously taken up this matter as part of their duties have not been satisfied with the acquisition of this power, but have established machinery the object of which is to educate the private or corporate owner to a sense of the value of the possession which fortune has put into his hands, and to a recognition of himself in the matter as a trustee for the public, rather than as an absolute proprietor, who, as the saying goes, "can do as he likes with his own"

The means adopted have generally involved the establishment of Royal or State Commissions or Councils charged with the care of ancient monuments and served by a staff of inspectors and custodians. Such Commissions or Councils exist in Austria, Belgium, Denmark, Finland, France, Greece, Hesse-Darmstadt, Holland, Hungary, Italy, Norway, Portugal, Roumania, Russia, Saxony, Spain, Switzerland, Wurtemberg. Some, like the Commissions in Belgium, France, Austria, have been at work for more than half a century. In Russia the Imperial Archæological Commission was established in 1859. The Commission in Spain is of early date, and elaborate regulations for its working were promulgated in 1865. Other Commissions were first constituted within the last twenty years, and the most recent of all, that of Holland, began its work in 1903. In countries where there is no central commission there are State officials charged with the same duties. In Prussia there are fourteen Provincial and District Conservators of Ancient Monuments. In the Scandinavian kingdoms, where monuments are particularly well cared for, there are State antiquaries who have at their back the authority of the crown.

One work of essential value has been taken up in almost every European country, and this is the work of inventorisation It is obvious that the first step towards securing effective measures of protection for ancient monuments is to ascertain what objects of value in this department are actually in existence, where they are located, and what is their condition. In almost every Continental land Commissions and Conservators are endeavouring to answer these questions, and the results of the necessary surveys are being brought together in monumental publications, in most cases subsidised by the State. Nearly fifty separate works of the kind, each running to several volumes, are in progress in Germany alone.

Apart from this work of inventorisation the record of the labours of these Commissions and Conservators shows that they have been able to do much for the objects in view by moral means without direct legislative sanctions In some countries especially, their regulations have been generally obeyed by intelligent and docile citizens, though they may not have possessed the power of actually controlling the recalcitrant. It is, however, of great advantage that those responsible for monument administration should possess this power, though they may not often be called on to exercise it. Hence it is that Monument Acts, which will confer compulsory powers, are in preparation or contemplation in several of the leading European countries, such as Austria, Prussia, Bavaria, and Spain

What now is the condition of affairs in our own country ? The greater part of the work which on the Continent is in the hands of State Commissions is amongst ourselves carried on by private societies and by individuals. General Pitt Rivers, who was Government Inspector of Ancient Monuments under the Act of 1882, died in 1900, and no successor has been appointed to fill his place The only official agencies concerned in the matter are the Office of Works and the County Councils, to whom certain powers were granted in the year 1900. The functions of the Office of Works are very limited, while the efforts which may be made by County Councils and by Societies, such as the Society of Antiquaries and the National Trust, require to be supported and systematised. A generation ago the British Government showed its solicitude for one particular department of our national memorials by the appointment of the Historical Manuscripts Commission, which has been doing excellent work ever since in the survey and inventorisation of written records bearing upon the history of the country   Nothing of the kind has yet been attempted for works of art and for historical buildings. Is not the time come for the extension of this useful official work into the domain of the monumental records, for which an importance equally great may be claimed ?   There is a growing demand for some State action of the kind in the British Islands, and the International Congress of Architects would strengthen the hands of those who are working in this direction by a resolution in favour of a Government scheme for the survey and inventorisation of the vast treasures in ancient monuments and works of art which this country possesses, and for which now there is practically no legal protection. It is generally acknowledged that the British Government owes something in this department to the community, and the appointment of a Royal Commission for the purposes just indicated would be the most practical measure that could be adopted.

---

2. DE LA RESPONSABILITÉ DES GOUVERNEMENTS DANS LA CONSERVATION DES MONUMENTS NATIONAUX.

Par A. BESNARD, Architecte, Membre de la Société Centrale des Architectes Français

"Ce n'est pas en semant des statues qu'on récolte des hommes, c'est en respectant les pierres du sol natal."—RUSKIN.

S'il est une question qui, à un juste titre, doive préoccuper tous ceux qui sont épris d'art, c'est bien celle de la conservation des monuments du passé ; aussi, dans un noble souci de défense artistique, l'avez-vous inscrite à votre programme, marquant ainsi notre commun désir de sauvegarder ce qui reste encore du patrimoine où vont se fortifier nos aspirations.

Malheureusement, le "riche manteau de pierre," dont au moyen âge se couvrit la chrétienté, depuis longtemps se déchire, et nous connaissons tous maints morceaux violemment arrachés au plus grand dommage de l'histoire et de l'art.

Nombreuses ont été déjà les discussions auxquelles elle a donné lieu, sans que toutefois aucun résultat en ait été obtenu ; nous espérons que ce Congrès, outre les vœux qu'il pourra être amené à voter, prendra, avant de se séparer, les dispositions nécessaires pour les faire aboutir auprès des divers gouvernements

Tout d'abord, conviendrait-il de rappeler brièvement les différentes législations actuellement en vigueur sur la question qui nous occupe ?

En Angleterre la loi du 18 août 1882, votée sur les instances de sir John Lubbock, ne laisse aucune garantie pour le conservation des monuments anciens, le propriétaire d'un monument restant seul maître de demander à la Commission des travaux publics, soit l'acquisition amiable de son bien, soit de prendre les mesures utiles à sa conservation.

Les dispositifs de cette loi furent en 1892 étendus à l'Irlande et en 1900 à l'Ecosse   Un inventaire des richesses monumentales de la Grande-Bretagne fut dressé, mais à la fin de 1904, 189 monuments seulement étaient placés sous la protection des pouvoirs publics [1]

---

[1] Consulter sur ce sujet le livre récent de Mr. G Baldwin Brown, professeur des Beaux-Arts à l'Université d'Edimbourg (Cambridge, 1905), et du même auteur l'article paru dans le *Journal de l'Institut royal des Architectes britanniques* (vol. xii p. 70).

En Allemagne l'ordonnance prussienne du 4 octobre 1815 oblige à une autorisation préalable, le propriétaire se proposant d'apporter une modification à un monument lui appartenant. Quelques années avant 1870 il fut procédé à l'inventaire de toutes les richesses monumentales et artistiques antérieures à 1800 possédées par le royaume de Prusse, cet inventaire fut en 1880 étendu à tout l'empire

En Autriche une décision impériale du 31 décembre 1850 créa une Commission chargée de dresser un inventaire des monuments dont la conservation s'imposait, de veiller à leur rationnelle restauration et d'empêcher l'exportation des objets d'art pouvant s'y trouver. Cette commission, dont le rôle fut pendant vingt ans des plus utiles, se réorganisa en 1873 sous le nom de *Commission Centrale pour la recherche et la conservation des monuments artistiques et historiques.* Le mode de recrutement et de renouvellement de ses membres lui assure une grande influence, pour obtenir le résultat de défense recherchée.

En Hongrie la loi du 28 mai 1881 permet l'expropriation temporaire ou définitive envers tout propriétaire qui dégrade ou n'entretient pas le monument dont il a la garde, et, dans le même cas, lorsqu'il s'agit d'une commune, l'Etat est autorisé à se substituer à elle et à exécuter aux frais de celle-ci les restaurations et réfections utiles aux édifices anciens délaissés par la municipalité. Une sanction pénale atteint ceux qui ont contrevenu à la loi. L'État est de plus aidé dans sa tâche par une *Commission nationale des Monuments,* dont l'organisation et le fonctionnement diffèrent peu de ceux de la Commission française des Monuments historiques.

En Belgique l'article 108 de la Constitution et l'article 87 de la loi communale du 30 mars 1836, complétée par celle du 30 juin 1865 (articles 76 et 77), donnent au pouvoir royal le droit d'intervenir près des municipalités pour la défense des édifices publics ayant un caractère artistique, ou historique. De plus, les communes, lorsque leurs délibérations ont trait à des édifices publics ou à des monuments anciens, sont tenues à la publicité de leurs débats. Une circulaire du Ministre de la Justice, en date du 17 novembre 1882, ajoute aux lois précitées, en ce qui concerne les églises et les monuments appartenant à des hospices ou des associations d'assistance

Retenons au passage une disposition particulière de la loi du 30 mars 1836, portant à l'article 131 que l'entretien des bâtiments communaux est à la charge des communes et que les dites sont tenues de pourvoir aux grosses réparations des édifices consacrés au Culte ; au cas de refus des municipalités la dépense peut être inscrite d'office par la Députation du Conseil Provincial ou par le Roi

Une commission royale des Monuments, instituée en 1835, a charge d'examen et d'approbation des projets de restauration ou réparation des monuments

Au Danemark une ordonnance de 1752 prévoit la découverte d'objets d'art ayant un caractère artistique, et, depuis 1807, fonctionne une Commission royale pour la conservation des antiquités Cette assemblée, lors de sa constitution, dressa un inventaire des monuments qui furent déclarés nationaux, sans toutefois que les particuliers qui en étaient propriétaires aient été tenus d'abandonner leurs droits, la loi n'en ayant pas prévu l'expropriation Depuis 1848, un crédit est accordé annuellement à cette commission pour l'entretien des monuments classés Enfin, la loi du 19 février 1861 détermine le mode d'inspection, de conservation et de restauration des églises ainsi que de leur mobilier Le Code Danois et l'ordonnance de 1752 s'appliquent à la Norvège.

En Espagne les monuments anciens sont placés sous la protection du décret du 16 décembre 1878, rendu sur la proposition d'Emile Castelar, en vertu duquel les Gouverneurs de province peuvent s'opposer aux travaux que les assemblées municipales ou provinciales se disposeraient d'effectuer lorsque lesdits peuvent détériorer ou atteindre le caractère de l'édifice. A défaut du gouverneur, l'Académie de St Ferdinand peut de même s'opposer aux travaux Les municipalités ayant indûment engagé ces travaux sont tenues d'en supporter les dépenses.

La Grèce, qui, par son passé, apporte une si large contribution à l'histoire de l'art, a, par une loi du 10 mai 1834, accordé une grande protection aux monuments de l'antiquité, ainsi qu'à tout vestige de ces époques disparues En vertu de cette loi est considéré comme bien national, quoiqu'appartenant à un particulier, tout monument ancien , il ne peut être démoli, ni subir la moindre modification. Au cas de nécessité de réparation, cette dernière ne peut être exécutée qu'avec l'agrément de l'Etat, lequel, au cas de désaccord avec le particulier, peut procéder par voie d'expropriation.

En Roumanie la loi des 15 et 17 novembre 1892 assure la conservation et la restauration des monuments publics Un inventaire, révisé tous les cinq ans par une Commission pour la Conservation des Monuments publics, rend indestructible tout monument relevé par elle, et l'Etat est autorisé à exproprier le monument à restaurer pour lequel une entente n'a pu intervenir avec le propriétaire. Dans certains cas le délinquant peut être puni d'amende ou de prison

La Suède et la Finlande ont aussi, par les lois de 1867 et 1883, songé à la défense de leurs monuments anciens, mais ces lois s'appliquent surtout aux monuments anciens cultuels et à ceux élevés à la mémoire des morts

En France, depuis longtemps, cette question préoccupe les esprits clairvoyants, et la série de mesures édictées, si elles n'ont pas donné tout le résultat qu'on en attendait, ont néanmoins témoigné le vif désir que pouvoirs publics et particuliers avaient d'y parvenir.

Les quelques critiques que nous serons amené à formuler plus loin dans le cours de ce travail ne sauraient diminuer la valeur de leurs efforts

Dès 1790 et 1792 une Commission fut créée pour la conservation des monuments anciens et la réunion de tous les vestiges historiques et archéologiques qui, épars sur le sol de notre pays, menaçaient d'être dégradés ou vendus [1]

De là date la fondation du *Musée des Monuments français*. En 1830 les Chambres votèrent un crédit pour la conservation des monuments anciens qui ne fut moindre à 800,000 francs. En 1834 Monsieur Guizot créa le *Comité Historique des Arts et Monuments*. En 1837 fut instituée la *Commission des Monuments historiques* (réorganisée par le décret du 3 janvier 1889), et enfin, le 30 mars 1887, fut promulguée la loi relative à la Conservation des Monuments et objets d'art ayant un intérêt historique et artistique, dont nous rappelons le texte :

CHAPITRE PREMIER.—IMMEUBLES ET MONUMENTS HISTORIQUES
OU MÉGALITHIQUES.

ARTICLE PREMIER.—Les immeubles par nature ou par destination, dont la conservation peut avoir au point de vue *de l'histoire ou de l'art* un intérêt national, seront classés en totalité ou en partie par les soins du Ministre de l'Instruction Publique et des Beaux-Arts.

ART. 2.—L'immeuble appartenant à l'Etat sera classé par arrêté du Ministre de l'Instruction Publique et des Beaux-Arts, en cas d'accord avec le Ministre, dans les attributions duquel l'immeuble se trouve placé. Dans le cas contraire, le classement sera prononcé par un décret, rendu en la forme du règlement d'administration publique.

L'immeuble appartenant à un département, à une commune, à une fabrique ou à tout autre établissement public, sera classé par arrêté du Ministre de l'Instruction Publique et des Beaux-Arts, s'il y a consente-

---

[1] Consulter sur ce sujet l'ouvrage de Mr Louis Tuétey, *Procès-verbaux de la Commission des Monuments*, 1790–1794.

ment de l'établissement propriétaire et avis conforme du Ministre sous l'autorité duquel l'établissement est placé. En cas de désaccord, le classement sera prononcé par un décret, rendu en la forme de règlement d'administration publique

ART. 3.—L'immeuble appartenant à un particulier sera classé par arrêté du Ministre de l'Instruction Publique et des Beaux-Arts, mais ne pourra l'être qu'avec le consentement du propriétaire L'arrêté déterminera les conditions du classement

S'il y a contestation sur l'interprétation et sur l'exécution de cet acte, il sera statué par le Ministre de l'Instruction Publique et des Beaux-Arts, sauf recours au Conseil d'Etat statuant au contentieux.

ART. 4.—L'immeuble classé ne pourra être détruit, même en partie, ni être l'objet d'un travail de restauration, de réparation ou de modification quelconque, si le Ministre de l'Instruction Publique et des Beaux-Arts n'y a donné son consentement.

L'expropriation pour cause d'utilité publique d'un immeuble classé ne pourra être poursuivie qu'après que le ministre de l'Instruction Publique et des Beaux-Arts aura été appelé à présenter ses observations.

Les servitudes d'alignement et autres qui pourraient causer la dégradation des monuments ne sont pas applicables aux immeubles classés.

Les effets du classement suivront l'immeuble classé en quelques mains qu'il passe.

ART 5—Le Ministre de l'Instruction Publique et des Beaux-Arts pourra, en se conformant aux prescriptions de la loi du 3 mai 1841, poursuivre l'expropriation des monuments classés ou qui seraient, de sa part, l'objet d'une proposition de classement refusé par le particulier propriétaire

Il pourra, dans les mêmes conditions, poursuivre l'expropriation des monuments mégalithiques, ainsi que celle des terrains sur lesquels ces monuments seront placés.

ART. 6.—Le déclassement total ou partiel pourra être demandé par le ministre dans les attributions duquel se trouve l'immeuble classé, par le département, la commune, la fabrique, l'établissement public et le particulier propriétaire de l'immeuble.

Le déclassement aura lieu dans les mêmes formes et sous les mêmes distinctions que le classement.

Toutefois, en cas d'aliénation consentie à un particulier de l'immeuble classé appartenant à un département, à une commune, à une fabrique, ou à tout autre établissement public, le déclassement ne pourra avoir lieu que conformément au paragraphe 2 de l'article 2.

ART. 7—Les dispositions de la présente loi sont applicables aux monuments historiques régulièrement classés avant sa promulgation.

Toutefois, lorsque l'Etat n'aura fait aucune dépense pour un monument appartenant à un particulier, ce monument sera déclassé de droit dans le délai de six mois après la réclamation que le propriétaire pourra adresser au Ministre de l'Instruction Publique et des Beaux-Arts, pendant l'année qui suivra la promulgation de la présente loi.

CHAPITRE II —OBJETS MOBILIERS.

ART. 8.—Il sera fait, par les soins du Ministre de l'Instruction Publique et des Beaux-Arts, un classement des objets mobiliers appartenant à l'Etat, aux départements, aux communes, aux fabriques et autres établissements publics, dont la conservation présente au point de vue de l'histoire ou de l'art un intérêt national.

ART. 9.—Le classement deviendra définitif si le département, les communes, les fabriques et autres établissements publics n'ont pas réclamé, dans le délai de six mois à dater de la notification qui leur en sera faite. En cas de réclamation, il sera statué par décret rendu en la forme des règlements d'administration publique.

Le déclassement, s'il y a lieu, sera prononcé par le Ministre de l'Instruction Publique et des Beaux-Arts et à la Préfecture de chaque département, où le public pourra en prendre connaissance sans déplacements

ART 10.—Les objets classés et appartenant à l'Etat seront inaliénables et imprescriptibles

ART 11.—Les objets classés, appartenant aux départements, aux communes, aux fabriques ou autres établissements publics, ne pourront être restaurés, réparés, ni aliénés par vente, don ou échange, qu'avec l'autorisation du Ministre de l'Instruction Publique et des Beaux-Arts.

ART. 12 —Les travaux, de quelque nature qu'ils soient, exécutés en violation des articles qui précèdent, donneront lieu, au profit de l'Etat, à une action en dommages-intérêts contre ceux qui les auraient ordonnés ou fait exécuter.

Les infractions seront constatées et les actions intentées et suivies devant les tribunaux civils ou correctionnels, à la diligence du Ministre de l'Instruction Publique et des Beaux-Arts, ou des parties intéressées.

ART. 13 —L'aliénation faite en violation de l'article 11 sera nulle et la nullité en sera poursuivie par le propriétaire vendeur, ou par le Ministre de l'Instruction Publique et des Beaux-Arts, sans préjudice des dommages-intérêts qui pourraient être réclamés contre les parties contractantes et contre l'officier public qui aura prêté son concours à l'aide d'aliénation

Les objets classés qui auraient été aliénés irrégulièrement, perdus ou volés, pourront être revendiqués pendant trois ans, conformément aux dispositions des articles 2279 et 2280 du Code Civil. La revendication pourra être exercée par les propriétaires, et à leur défaut par le Ministre de l'Instruction Publique et des Beaux-Arts.

CHAPITRE III —FOUILLES.

ART. 14.—Lorsque, par suite de fouilles, de travaux ou d'un fait quelconque, on aura découvert des monuments, des ruines, des inscriptions ou des objets pouvant intéresser l'archéologie, l'histoire ou l'art, sur des terrains appartenant à l'Etat, à un département, à une commune, à une fabrique ou tout autre établissement public, le maire de la commune devra assurer la conservation provisoire des objets découverts et aviser immédiatement le préfet du département des mesures qui auront été prises

Le préfet en référera, dans le plus bref délai, au Ministre de l'Instruction Publique et des Beaux-Arts, qui statuera sur les mesures définitives à prendre. Si la découverte a lieu sur le terrain d'un particulier, le maire en avisera le préfet. Sur le rapport du préfet et après avis de la Commission des Monuments Historiques, le Ministre de l'Instruction Publique et des Beaux-Arts pourra poursuivre l'expropriation dudit terrain pour cause d'utilité publique, suivant les formes de la loi du 3 mai 1841.

ART. 15 —Les décisions prises par le Ministre de l'Instruction Publique et des Beaux-Arts, en exécution de la présente loi, seront rendues, après avis de la Commission des Monuments Historiques

Cette loi se complète aujourd'hui du titre III de la loi du 9 décembre 1905 concernant la séparation des Eglises et de l'Etat.

TITRE III —DES ÉDIFICES DES CULTES

ART. 12.—Les édifices qui ont été mis à la disposition de la nation et qui, en vertu de la loi du 18 germinal an X, servent à l'exercice public des cultes ou au logement de leurs ministres (cathédrales, églises, chapelles, temples, synagogues, archevêchés, presbytères, séminaires), ainsi que leurs dépendances immobilières et les objets mobiliers qui les garnissaient au moment où lesdits édifices ont été remis aux cultes, sont et demeurent propriétés de l'Etat, des départements et des communes.

Pour ces édifices, comme pour ceux postérieurs à la loi du 18 germinal an X, dont l'Etat, les départements et les communes seraient propriétaires, y compris les facultés de théologie protestante, il sera procédé conformément aux dispositions des articles suivants.

ART. 13.—Les édifices servant à l'exercice public du culte, ainsi que les objets mobiliers les garnissant, seront laissés gratuitement à la disposition des établissements publics du culte, puis des associations appelées à les remplacer auxquelles les biens de ces établissements auront été attribués par application des dispositions du titre II.

La cessation de cette jouissance, et, s'il y a lieu, son transfert, seront prononcés par décret, sauf recours au Conseil d'Etat statuant au contentieux

1°. Si l'association bénéficiaire est dissoute ;

2°. Si, en dehors des cas de force majeure, le culte cesse d'être célébré pendant plus de six mois consécutifs ,

3°. Si la conservation de l'édifice ou celle des objets mobiliers classés en vertu de la loi de 1887 et de l'article 16 de la présente loi est compromise par insuffisance d'entretien, et après mise en demeure dûment notifiée du Conseil Municipal ou, à son défaut, du préfet ;

4°. Si l'association cesse de remplir son objet ou si les édifices sont détournés de leur destination ;

5° Si elle ne satisfait pas soit aux obligations de l'article 6 ou du dernier paragraphe du présent article, soit aux prescriptions relatives aux monuments historiques

La désaffectation de ces immeubles pourra, dans les cas ci-dessus prévus, être prononcée par décret rendu en Conseil d'Etat. En dehors de ces cas, elle ne pourra l'être que par une loi.

Les immeubles autrefois affectés aux cultes et dans lesquels les cérémonies du culte n'auront pas été célébrées pendant le délai d'un an antérieurement à la présente loi, ainsi que ceux qui ne seront pas réclamés par une association cultuelle dans le délai de deux ans après sa promulgation, pourront être désaffectés par décret,

Il en est de même pour les édifices dont la désaffectation aura été demandée antérieurement au 1er juin 1905.

Les établissements publics du culte, puis les associations bénéficiaires, seront tenus des réparations de toute nature, ainsi que des frais d'assurance et autres charges afférentes aux édifices et aux meubles les garnissant,

ART. 14.—Les archevêchés, évêchés, les presbytères et leurs dépendances, les grands séminaires et facultés de théologie protestante seront laissés gratuitement à la disposition des établissements publics du culte, puis des associations prévues à l'article 13, savoir les archevêchés et évêchés pendant une période de deux années ; les presbytères dans les communes où résidera le ministre du culte, les grands séminaires et facultés de théologie protestante pendant cinq années à partir de la promulgation de la présente loi.

Les établissements et associations sont soumis, en ce qui concerne ces édifices, aux obligations prévues par le dernier paragraphe de l'article 13. Toutefois ils ne seront pas tenus de grosses réparations.

La cessation de la jouissance des établissements et associations sera prononcée dans les conditions et suivant les formes déterminées par l'article 13. Les dispositions des paragraphes 3 et 5 du même article sont applicables aux édifices visés par le paragraphe 1er du présent article.

La distraction des parties superflues des presbytères laissés à la disposition des associations cultuelles pourra, pendant le délai prévu au paragraphe 1er, être prononcée pour un service public par décret rendu en Conseil d'Etat.

A l'expiration des délais de jouissance gratuite, la libre disposition des édifices sera rendue à l'Etat, aux départements ou aux communes.

Les indemnités de logement incombant actuellement aux communes, à défaut de presbytère, par application de l'article 136 de la loi du 5 avril 1884, resteront à leur charge pendant le délai de cinq ans.   Elles cesseront de plein droit en cas de dissolution de l'association.

Art. 15 —Dans les départements de la Savoie, de la Haute-Savoie et des Alpes-Maritimes, la jouissance des édifices antérieurs à la loi du 18 germinal an X, servant à l'exercice des cultes ou au logement de leurs ministres, sera attribuée par les communes sur le territoire desquelles ils se trouvent aux associations cultuelles, dans les conditions indiquées par les articles 12 et suivants de la présente loi.   En dehors de ces obligations, les communes pourront disposer librement de la propriété de ces édifices

Dans ces mêmes départements les cimetières resteront la propriété des communes.

Art 16.—Il sera procédé à un classement complémentaire des édifices servant à l'exercice public du culte (cathédrales, églises, chapelles, temples, synagogues, archevêchés, presbytères, séminaires), dans lequel devront être compris tous ceux de ces édifices représentant, dans leur ensemble ou dans leurs parties, une valeur artistique ou historique.

Les objets mobiliers ou les immeubles par destination mentionnés à l'article 13, qui n'auraient pas encore été inscrits sur la liste de classement dressée en vertu de la loi du 30 mars 1887, sont, par l'effet de la présente loi, ajoutés à ladite liste   Il sera procédé par le Ministre de l'Instruction Publique et des Beaux-Arts, dans le délai de trois ans, au classement définitif de ceux de ces objets dont la conservation présenterait, au point de vue de l'histoire ou de l'art, un intérêt suffisant. A l'expiration de ce délai les autres objets seront déclassés de plein droit.

En outre les immeubles et les objets mobiliers, attribués en vertu de la présente loi aux associations, pourront être classés dans les mêmes conditions que s'ils appartenaient à des établissements publics.

Il n'est pas dérogé, pour le surplus, aux dispositions de la loi du 30 mars 1887.

Les archives ecclésiastiques et bibliothèques existant dans les archevêchés, évêchés, grands séminaires, paroisses, succursales et leurs dépendances seront inventoriées et celles qui seront reconnues propriété de l'Etat lui seront restituées.

Art. 17.—Les immeubles par destination classés en vertu de la loi du 30 mars 1887 ou de la présente loi sont inaliénables et imprescriptibles.

Dans le cas où la vente ou l'échange d'un objet classé serait autorisé par le Ministre de l'Instruction Publique et des Beaux-Arts, un droit de préemption est accordé : 1°, aux associations cultuelles ; 2°, aux communes, 3°, aux départements, 4°, aux musées et sociétés d'art et d'archéologie ; 5°, à l'Etat.   Le prix sera fixé par trois experts que désigneront le vendeur, l'acquéreur et le Président du Tribunal Civil.

Si aucun des acquéreurs visés ci-dessus ne fait usage du droit de préemption, la vente sera libre ; mais il est interdit à l'acheteur d'un objet classé de le transporter hors de France.

Nul travail de réparation, restauration ou entretien à faire aux monuments ou objets mobiliers classés ne peut être commencé sans l'autorisation du Ministre des Beaux-Arts, ni exécuté hors de la surveillance de son administration, sous peine, contre les propriétaires, occupants ou détenteurs qui auraient ordonné ces travaux, d'une amende de seize à quinze cents francs (16 à 1500 fr.).

Toute infraction aux dispositions ci-dessus, ainsi qu'à celles de l'article 16 de la présente loi et des articles 4, 10, 11, 12 et 13 de la loi du 30 mars 1887, sera punie d'une amende de cent à dix mille francs

(100 à 10000 fr.), et d'un emprisonnement de six jours à trois mois, ou de l'une de ces deux peines seulement.

La visite des édifices et l'exposition des objets mobiliers classés seront publiques , elles ne pourront donner lieu à aucune taxe ni redevance.

Enfin, nous donnons le dernier texte d'administration publique du 9 mars 1906, qui détermine sous le titre II les conditions d'application de la loi du 9 décembre 1905.

TITRE II —ÉDIFICES DES CULTES.

ART. 26.—Les édifices antérieurement affectés au culte et appartenant aux établissements ecclésiastiques sont attribués aux associations cultuelles dans les mêmes conditions et suivant les mêmes formes que les autres biens des dits établissements.

ART. 27.—L'entrée en jouissance par les associations cultuelles des édifices du culte mentionnés dans les articles 13, 14 et 15 de la loi susvisée, est constatée par un procès-verbal administratif dressé soit par le préfet, pour l'Etat et les départements, soit par le maire, pour les communes, contradictoirement avec les représentants des associations ou eux dûment appelés.

Il en est de même pour la mise à la disposition des associations des objets mobiliers appartenant à l'Etat, aux départements ou aux communes et garnissant ceux des édifices qui servent à l'exercice public du culte.

Le procès-verbal comporte un état de lieux si l'association en fait la demande, et dans tous les cas un état des dits objets mobiliers dressé d'après les indications de l'inventaire prévu à l'article 3 de la loi susvisée.

Il est établi en double minute et sur papier libre

ART. 28.—Les réparations incombant aux associations cultuelles en vertu des articles 13 et 14 de la loi du 9 décembre 1905 doivent être exécutées, sous réserve de l'application de la législation sur les monuments historiques, de manière a ne préjudicier sous aucun rapport aux édifices cultuels.

Les projets de grosses réparations doivent, un mois au moins avant leur exécution, être communiqués au préfet, pour les édifices appartenant à l'Etat ou au département, et au maire, pour ceux qui sont la propriété de la commune

ART. 29 —Le Ministre des Beaux-Arts est chargé d'assurer l'inspection des immeubles et objets mobiliers classés par application de la loi du 30 mars 1887 et de l'article 16 de la loi du 9 décembre 1905

Les associations cultuelles fixent, sous réserve de l'approbation du préfet, les jours et heures auxquels auront lieu, conformément à l'article 17 de la loi du 9 décembre 1905, la visite des édifices et l'exposition des objets mobiliers classés

Si l'association, bien que dûment mise en demeure par le préfet, n'a pris aucune disposition à cet effet, ou en cas de refus d'approbation, il est statué par le Ministre des Beaux-Arts

Quant à la Commission des Monuments Historiques, le décret l'instituant s'exprime ainsi .

Le Président de la République Française :

Sur le rapport du Ministre de l'Instruction Publique et des Beaux-Arts ,

Vu l'article 21 du décret du 3 janvier 1889 portant règlement d'administration publique pour l'exécution de la loi du 30 mars 1887, relative à la conservation des monuments et objets ayant un intérêt historique et artistique :

H H

DÉCRÈTE :

ARTICLE PREMIER.—La Commission des Monuments Historiques instituée près le Ministère de l'Instruction Publique et des Beaux-Arts a pour mission d'établir la liste des monuments et objets ayant un intérêt historique et artistique, de désigner ceux qu'il convient de restaurer, d'examiner les projets présentés pour leur restauration, de proposer au ministre la répartition des crédits ouverts pour la conservation des monuments classés.

ART. 2.—Le Ministre de l'Instruction Publique et des Beaux-Arts est Président de la Commission des Monuments Historiques Le directeur des Beaux-Arts est premier vice-président de droit. Un deuxième vice-président est désigné par le ministre. En l'absence du président et du vice-président, le doyen d'âge des membres présents remplit les fonctions de président.

ART. 3.—La Commission des Monuments Historiques est composée de membres de droit et de membres à la nomination du Ministère de l'Instruction Publique et des Beaux-Arts

ART 4—Sont membres de droit : le directeur des Beaux-Arts , le directeur des bâtiments civils et palais nationaux , le préfet de la Seine , le préfet de Police ; les inspecteurs généraux des monuments historiques , le directeur du Musée des Thermes et de l'Hôtel de Cluny ; le conservateur du Musée de Sculpture comparée.

ART. 5.—Les membres à la nomination du Ministre de l'Instruction Publique et des Beaux-Arts sont nommés par arrêtés ministériels.

Lorsqu'une vacance se produit, la Commission est invitée à présenter au ministre une liste de trois candidats

ART. 6.—La Commission peut constituer des sous-commissions chargées de préparer l'étude des questions qui lui sont soumises et de lui en faire un rapport.

ART. 7.—Le chef et le sous-chef de bureau des monuments historiques remplissent les fonctions de secrétaire et de secrétaire adjoint de la Commission

Des Sociétés particulières veillent aussi avec un soin jaloux à la conservation de nos antiquités nationales   A leur tête il convient de citer la *Société française d'Archéologie,* qui, depuis sa fondation, n'a pas dépensé moins d'un million de francs pour aider à cette œuvre de défense du patrimoine commun.

Mais c'est évidemment l'Italie, dont le premier acte de protection remonte à la bulle du pape Pie II du 28 avril 1462, qui semble être la mieux armée pour la défense de ses monuments, et la loi du 12 juin 1902, dont nous donnons le texte, édicte une série de mesures sages que nous livrons aux méditations du Congrès.

LOI DU 12 JUIN 1902.[1] N° 185,

Édictant des Dispositions sur la Protection et la Conservation des
Monuments et Objets ayant une Valeur d'Art et d'Antiquité

ARTICLE PREMIER.—Les dispositions de la présente loi s'appliquent aux monuments, aux immeubles et aux objets mobiliers ayant une valeur d'art ou d'antiquité. Elles ne visent pas les édifices et objets d'art dont les auteurs sont vivants ou dont l'exécution ne remonte pas au-delà de cinquante ans

ART. 2.—Les collections d'objets d'art ou d'antiquité, les monuments et les objets ayant une importance artistique et archéologique appartenant

---

[1] *Annuaire de Législation étrangère,* 2ᵉ série, 2ᵉ année (32ᵉ année de la collection), édit. 1903, pp. 227 et 289 , J. Constans, p. 111

Lepelletier, Prohibition d'exporter les Œuvres d'art, législation italienne (Clunet, 1896).

à des fabriques, confréries, à des personnes morales ecclésiastiques, de quelque nation que soient celles-ci, et ceux qui ornent des églises et leurs dépendances ou d'autres édifices publics, sont inaliénables Sont de même inaliénables aussi bien les collections que les objets isolés d'art ou d'antiquités ne faisant pas partie de collections, mais repris au catalogue prévu par l'article 23 ci-après et y qualifiés comme étant de la plus haute valeur, quand ces collections ou objets appartiennent à l'Etat, aux communes, aux provinces ou à d'autres personnes morales légalement reconnues, et qu'ils ne rentrent pas dans le premier paragraphe du présent article.

Art 3.—Le Ministre de l'Instruction Publique, sur l'avis de la Commission compétente, pourra autoriser la vente et l'échange des dites collections ou d'objets isolés, pourvu que ces aliénations aient lieu, soit entre les personnes morales dont il est question à l'article précédent, soit au profit de l'Etat.

L'interdiction de vente pourra faire l'objet d'un recours à la quatrième section du Conseil d'Etat, qui statuera même sur le fond

Art 4 —Les objets artistiques ou antiques non compris parmi ceux de la plus haute valeur par les catalogues institués par l'article 23, et ne faisant pas partie de collections, ne pourront, s'ils appartiennent à l'une des personnes morales énumérées à l'article 2, être aliénés sans l'autorisation du Ministre de l'Instruction Publique

La disposition de l'article précédent s'appliquera à la défense prononcée par le Ministère

Art 5.—Quiconque, soit comme propriétaire, soit aussi à titre de simple possesseur, sera détenteur d'un monument ou d'un objet artistique compris dans le catalogue prévu à l'article 23, sera tenu d'en déclarer à l'instant tout contrat d'aliénation ou toute mutation dans la possession

La même obligation pourra lui être imposée du fait de la notification de la valeur de l'objet ou du monument, quand, pour des raisons d'urgence, le Ministre de l'Instruction Publique, sur l'avis de la Commission compétente, procède à cette notification avant l'inscription au catalogue

L'effet de cette notification est provisoire et se prolonge au moins jusqu'à l'inscription au catalogue lui-même.

Dans l'acte même d'aliénation, le vendeur est tenu d'informer l'acheteur que le monument ou l'objet artistique ou antique est repris au catalogue ou qu'il a été procédé à la notification prévue au paragraphe précédent ; cette information a pour effet d'astreindre l'acheteur, sous la sanction édictée aux articles 26 et 27, à ne pas disposer du monument ou de l'objet sans déclaration préalable

Art 6 —Quand une personne aura l'intention de vendre un monument ou un objet artistique ou antique de la catégorie de ceux prévus à l'article précédent, le Gouvernement aura le droit de préemption à parité de conditions.   A quelque moment que soit effectuée la déclaration d'aliénation, ce droit devra être exercé dans les trois mois qui le suivent.   Ce délai pourra être prorogé jusqu'à l'expiration d'une période de six mois, lorsque, par suite de l'offre simultanée de nombreux objets antiques ou artistiques, le Gouvernement n'aura pas promptement à sa disposition toutes les sommes nécessaires aux acquisitions.

Lorsque le droit de préemption s'exerce sur un objet mobilier et sur la base d'une offre partie de l'étranger, qu'elle émane de particuliers ou d'institutions, le prix sera établi en déduisant de l'offre le montant de la taxe d'exportation établie par l'article 8 ci-dessous

Art 7 —Le droit de provoquer l'expropriation de monuments immeubles appartiendra, en outre des personnes morales indiquées dans l'article 83 de la loi du 25 juin 1865 (n° 2359), à toutes celles qui sont légalement reconnues et ont pour fin spéciale la conservation des monuments

Art. 8.—Indépendamment de ce qui est prescrit par les lois douanières, l'exportation de tout objet artistique et antique, à l'exclusion de ceux repris au paragraphe second de l'article premier, est assujettie à une taxe progressive applicable à la valeur de chaque objet, conformément au tableau annexé à la présente loi

La valeur est établie sur la base de la déclaration du propriétaire comparée avec l'estimation du service compétent

En cas d'écart entre la déclaration et l'estimation, le prix est déterminé par une commission d'experts nommée moitié par l'exportateur et moitié par le Ministère de l'Instruction

En cas de parité de voix, la décision sera remise à un arbitre choisi d'un commun accord.   Au cas où l'on ne pourrait s'entendre sur la nomination, celle-ci sera faite par le premier président de la Cour d'Appel

Le Gouvernement aura le droit d'acheter l'objet qu'on veut exporter au prix fixé, comme il vient d'être dit, diminué de la taxe d'exportation correspondante

L'acquisition devra être réalisée dans les deux mois de l'estimation définitive, sauf le cas exceptionnel prévu à l'article 6

ART 9.—La taxe d'exportation n'est pas applicable aux objets artistiques et antiques importés de l'étranger, pourvu que cette importation résulte de certificats authentiques conformes à ce qui sera prescrit au règlement

ART 10.—Sauf les précautions en cas d'urgence établie, il ne pourra être fait, sans autorisation du Ministère de l'Instruction Publique, de travaux aux monuments et aux objets artistiques et antiques repris aux articles 2, 3 et 4   Cette autorisation est également nécessaire s'il s'agit de monuments qui sont des propriétés privées, quand le propriétaire entend y exécuter des travaux de nature à modifier les parties de ces monuments exposées à la vue du public

ART. 11 —Il est interdit de démolir ou d'altérer les ruines monumentales existant même sur des propriétés privées , toutefois le propriétaire aura le droit de faire examiner par les fonctionnaires du Gouvernement si la ruine monumentale mérite d'être conservée

ART. 12 —Le Gouvernement a le droit d'exécuter les travaux nécessaires pour empêcher la détérioration des monuments.   Lorsque l'utilité financière de ces travaux sera établie, l'article 1144 du Code Civil sera applicable

ART 13 —Dans les communes dans lesquelles il existe des monuments assujettis aux dispositions de la présente loi, il pourra être prescrit, pour les cas de constructions nouvelles, de reconstructions, ou d'élévation d'édifices, l'observation de distances ou les mesures nécessaires, afin que les nouveaux ouvrages ne nuisent pas à la perspective ou à la lumière réclamées par la nature des monuments eux-mêmes, sauf une équitable compensation, selon les cas prévus par le règlement à édicter pour exécution de la présente loi

ART 14.—Quiconque voudra entreprendre des fouilles pour la recherche des antiquités devra présenter, à cet effet, une demande au Ministère de l'Instruction Publique, qui aura la faculté de les faire surveiller et de faire procéder à des études et des relevés, et pourra soit en faire différer le commencement, non toutefois au delà d'une durée de trois ans, soit encore les faire suspendre quand, par suite de demandes nombreuses et simultanées, il ne sera pas possible de surveiller en même temps toutes les fouilles, ou que ne seront pas observées les règles propres à la bonne direction scientifique des fouilles elles-mêmes

Les institutions ou citoyens étrangers qui, avec l'agrément du Gouvernement, ou dans les conditions à fixer pour chaque espèce, entreprendront des fouilles archéologiques, devront remettre gratuitement à une collection publique du royaume les objets retrouvés

Dans tous les autres cas l'Etat aura droit au quart des objets découverts ou à l'équivalence de ce quart.

Les conditions de l'exercice de ce droit seront indiquées dans le règlement à édicter pour l'exécution de la présente loi

ART. 15.—L'entrepreneur d'une fouille sera tenu de faire immédiatement la déclaration de la découverte de tout monument ou objet artistique ou antique   La même obligation incombe à l'inventeur fortuit   L'un et l'autre doivent veiller à la conservation des monuments mis au jour, et les laisser intacts jusqu'à ce qu'ils aient été visités par les autorités compétentes   Le Gouvernement a le devoir de les faire inspecter et étudier dans le plus bref délai.

Dans le cas de découverte de monuments ou d'objets dûs à l'art antique, découverte survenue au cours de fouilles de toute nature, les autorités administratives pourront prendre toutes les mesures de protection et de précaution qu'elles jugeront nécessaires ou utiles pour assurer la conservation et empêcher le détournement ou la dispersion des objets mis au jour

ART. 16 —Pour cause d'utilité publique scientifique le Gouvernement pourra exécuter des fouilles dans le terrain d'autrui.   Le propriétaire aura droit à une indemnité pour le gain manqué et pour le dommage qu'il aurait pu subir du fait des fouilles

L'utilité publique des fouilles est déclarée par un arrêté du Ministre de l'Instruction Publique, le Conseil d'Etat entendu   L'indemnité, lorsqu'elle ne peut etre fixée amiablement, est déterminée suivant les règles prescrites par les articles 65 et suivants de loi du 25 juin 1865 (n° 2359) pour autant qu'elles seront applicables.   Un quart des objets découverts dans les fouilles ou de leur équivalence en argent appartiendra alors au propriétaire du fonds et le reste à l'Etat

ART. 17.—Si l'on vient à découvrir des débris (*ruderi*) ou des monuments d'une importance telle que l'intérêt générale réclame qu'ils soient conservés et que l'accès en soit rendu possible au public, le Gouvernement pourra exproprier définitivement le terrain sur lequel se trouvent ces débris ou monuments et celui qui sera nécessaire pour étendre les fouilles et construire une voie d'accès.

La déclaration d'utilité publique de ces expropriations est faite par décret royal, après l'avis de la Commission compétente, sur la proposition du Ministre de l'Instruction Publique et suivant le mode indiqué dans l'article 12 de la loi du 25 juin 1865 (n° 2359).

ART. 18.—Le Ministre de l'Instruction Publique, après avis des Commissions spéciales et compétentes, et sous la réserve de s'en référer au règlement, est autorisé à opérer des échanges avec les musées étrangers et à vendre les répliques d'objets antiques ou artistiques qui sont sans intérêt pour les collections de l'Etat.   Il a également la faculté de mettre en vente les publications officielles relatives aux collections et aux monuments.

ART. 19 —La reproduction des monuments et des objets artistiques et antiques qui sont la propriété de l'Etat sera permise suivant les règles et aux conditions prévues au règlement et contre le paiement d'une redevance adéquates.

ART. 20,—Outre les fonds annuels qui seront inscrits à la partie ordinaire du budget des dépenses du Ministère de l'Instruction Publique, à l'effet de pourvoir à l'acquisition des œuvres de notable importance archéologique et artistique, et aux frais nécessaires à leur conservation, il sera inscrit dans le même but, au chapitre à ce destiné du même budget, une somme correspondante au montant total des rentrées obtenues au cours de l'exercice financier précédent, grâce aux ventes prévues à l'article 18, à l'application des taxes, peines pécuniaires et indemnités établies par la présente loi, et aux revenus éventuels mentionnés aux articles 14, 16 et 19.

ART 21.—La somme qui, aux termes de l'article 5 de la loi du 27 mai 1875, est annuellement inscrite au budget des dépenses du Ministère de l'Instruction Publique, sera divisée en deux parties, dont l'une restera affectée aux objets mentionnés dans cet article lui-même, et l'autre, constituée en un fonds unique, sera destinée à l'acquisition d'objets antiques et artistiques.   Ceux-ci seront attribués à des musées et galeries de la région à laquelle ils appartiennent, aux points de vue historique et artistique, ou encore à des musées et galeries d'autres régions, lorsque ces dernières manqueront d'objets dûs au même auteur ou à la même école.

Cette seconde partie (des crédits) correspondra à la moitié des produits de la taxe d'entrée dans les musées et galeries du royaume pendant le précédent exercice financier

Art. 22.—Le Gouvernement est autorisé à effectuer des acquisitions au moyen des sommes dont il est fait mention aux deux articles précédentes, sans être obligé de les faire spécifier par une loi, et quel que soit le montant de la dépense occasionnée par chaque opération.   Les sommes qui, à la fin de l'exercice financier, resteront disponibles sur lesdits fonds seront intégralement reportées au budget de l'exercice suivant, dont ils augmenteront les chapitres correspondants.

Art 23.—Le ministre de l'Instruction Publique procédera, dans les formes qui seront établies par le règlement, à la confection des catalogues des monuments et des objets artistiques et antiques.

Ces catalogues eux-mêmes seront divisés en deux parties, dont l'une comprendra les monuments et objets artistiques et antiques appartenant à des personnes morales, et l'autre ceux qui constituent des propriétés privées et y sont inscrites, soit à la suite de la déclaration des particuliers, soit d'office.   La première partie indiquera expressément les monuments et objets qui, par leur extrême importance, ne sont pas susceptibles d'être aliénés à des particuliers aux termes de la disposition de l'article 3. Les syndics (maires), présidents des députations provinciales, curés, recteurs des églises, et, en général, tous les administrateurs de personnes morales, présenteront au Ministère de l'Instruction Publique, dans les formes qui seront déterminées par le règlement, la liste des monuments, immeubles et des objets artistiques et antiques appartenant à la personne morale dont ils ont l'administration

L'inscription d'office au catalogue des objets artistiques et antiques constituant des propriétés privées, sera limitée à ceux de la plus haute valeur (*di somma valor*) et dont l'exportation hors du royaume constituerait un dommage grave pour le patrimoine artistique et pour l'histoire.

Art. 24.—Le Ministère de l'Instruction Publique, dans le mois qui suivra l'inscription au catalogue d'un objet artistique ou antique constituant une propriété privée, donnera communication de cette mesure au propriétaire lui-même aux fins de l'article 5 de la présente loi

Art 25.—Les aliénations faites au mépris de la défense édictée par les articles 2 et 3 sont nulles de plein droit.

Les fonctionnaires de l'Etat, des provinces et des communes et les administrations des personnes morales de toute nature qui auront contrevenu à ces dispositions seront punis d'une amende de 50 à 10000 lire. Les mêmes dispositions sont applicables aux violations de l'article 4, au moins en ce qui touche la nullité de la vente.

L'amende frappera également l'acheteur, s'il est à sa connaissance que l'objet artistique ou antique est compris parmi ceux mentionnés aux articles 2, 3 et 4

Art. 26.—L'omission de la déclaration prescrite à l'article 5 est punie d'une amende de 500 à 10000 lire.

Art 27.—Si, par l'effet de la violation des articles 2 à 5, l'objet artistique ou antique ne peut plus être recouvré ou a été exporté hors du royaume, ou, dans le cas de l'article 4, est devenue propriété privée, ces peines seront aggravées d'une indemnité égale à la valeur de l'objet.

Dans le cas du paragraphe final de l'article 25, l'acheteur sera tenu du paiement de l'indemnité solidairement avec le vendeur.

Art 28 —Sont applicables à l'exportation clandestine des œuvres antiques ou artistiques, les dispositions contenues dans le titre IX du texte unique de la loi douanière approuvé par le décret royal du 22 janvier 1896 (n° 20)   En conséquence, la confiscation aura lieu au bénéfice de l'Etat et la répartition des amendes sera effectuée dans les conditions que déterminera le règlement à édicter en exécution de la présente loi.

Art. 29.—Les peines portées en l'article 26 s'appliqueront à toutes violations des articles 10 et 11

Si le dommage est partiellement ou totalement irréparable, le contrevenant sera tenu d'une indemnité équivalant au monument ou à l'objet artistique ou antique perdu ou à la diminution de sa valeur

Art 30 —Les contraventions aux articles 14 et 15 sont punies d'une amende de 100 à 2000 lire ; en outre, dans le cas où le dommage serait en tout ou partie irréparable, on appliquera la disposition finale de l'article précédent.

Art. 31 —L'administrateur d'une personne morale qui, dans les six mois d'une mise en demeure à lui directement faite par le Ministère de l'Instruction Publique, ne présentera pas la liste des monuments et des objets artistiques et antiques appartenant à la personne morale qu'il administre, ainsi qu'il est prescrit à l'article 23, ou présentera une déclaration frauduleusement inexacte, sera puni d'une amende de 50 à 10000 lire.

Art 32.—Sont applicables aux anciens textes (*codici*), aux estampes et gravures rares et de prix, aux collections numismatiques appartenant aux personnes morales reprises aux articles 2 et 3, les dispositions de ces mêmes articles et le prescrit des articles 25, 27, 31 et du second paragraphe de l'article 23.

Si ces objets appartiennent à des particuliers, le Gouvernement, en ce qui touche ceux qui sont notoirement d'un grand prix et qui ont une valeur exclusivement historique ou artistique, pourra interdire au propriétaire d'en disposer autrement que dans les termes de l'article 5 et sous les sanctions édictées aux articles 25 et 27, sauf le droit de préemption de l'Etat, tel qu'il est réglé par l'article 6.   Sont également applicables dans ces cas les articles 8 et 28

Art 33.—Au cas de non-paiement des amendes édictées par la présente loi, on appliquera les dispositions de l'article 19 du Code pénal.

Art. 34 —Les prescriptions et sanctions légales de la présente loi ne seront pas applicables aux copies, reproductions ou imitations des objets artistiques ou antiques visés par elle

Art. 35.—Sont abrogés, du jour de la promulgation de la présente loi, toutes les prescriptions sur la matière en vigueur dans les diverses parties du royaume, sauf les dispositions de l'article 4 de la loi du 28 juin 1871 (n° 286, série 2), et des lois du 8 juillet 1883 (n° 1461, série 3) et du 7 février 1892 (n° 31).

Resteront en vigueur, pendant un an, au cours duquel le catalogue devra être dressé, à compter de la promulgation de la présente loi, les dispositions restrictives des lois en vigueur ayant trait à l'exportation des œuvres artistiques ou antiques

Art. 36.—Un règlement qui sera approuvé par décret royal, le Conseil d'Etat entendu, déterminera les mesures nécessaires pour l'exécution de la présente loi

Ce règlement pourra instituer, en sus de celles qui existent déjà, des commissions et services spéciaux qui donneront leur avis sur les matières de la présente loi et pour veiller à l'exécution de celle-ci.

Art. 37.—Les taxes d'exportation existant à ce jour sont abolies ou sont remplacées par celles du tableau ci-après

Tableau de la Taxe d'Exportation.

Sur les premiers 5000 lire	5 %
Sur les seconds 5000 lire	7 %
Sur les troisièmes 5000	9 %
Sur les quatrièmes 5000 lire	11 %

et ainsi de suite, jusqu'à ce que ces taxes égalent avec la taxe intérieure 20 % de la valeur de l'objet.

Comme on l'a vu par ce qui précède, notre pays semble être suffisamment défendu ; il n'en a malheureusement pas été toujours ainsi et souvent encore de regrettables abus se produisent, car, en France, tous les vestiges du passé, et particulièrement nos monuments d'architecture du moyen âge et de la Renaissance, nos vrais monuments nationaux, ceux que Viollet-le-Duc appelait " *nos gloires,*" parce qu'ils sont les produits de notre génie aussi bien que de notre labeur et de nos richesses, ont eu les destinées les plus étranges. Nés pour vivre jeunes et forts, faits pour rester les témoins fidèles des civilisations qui les ont enfantés, ils ont presque continuellement souffert, et autant des soins et des caresses de leurs amis que de l'abandon et des coups de leurs ennemis, ceux qui ont été sauvés ne l'ayant été, souvent, que pour subir de menteuses transformations.

"Le temps," dit J P. Schmit,[1] " ne s'est pas contenté de ses moyens ordinaires de destruction, si redoutables, si actifs, d'un effet si sûr ; il a armé la main de l'homme, il s'est donné l'art lui-même pour auxiliaire, en sorte que le progrès et l'ignorance, la piété et l'irréligion, la fureur de renverser et la prétention d'embellir, ont tous à tour de rôle ou simultanément produit des effets également funestes."

Alors que la Renaissance est encore dans tout son éclat, beaucoup de nos chefs-d'œuvre attendent encore leur achèvement ; d'autres l'ont à peine atteint, et déjà apparaît le vandalisme démolisseur, les protestants s'attaquant aux édifices religieux, aux bâtiments monastiques, décimant les cathédrales et les grandes églises abbatiales Deux siècles ne suffiront pas à réparer les ruines, et, à part quelques honorables exceptions, ils les répareront mesquinement et sans goût [2]

Le tour des fiers châteaux vient bientôt, pendant les guerres de la Ligue, puis sous les coups des édits de proscription fulminés par Richelieu et Mazarin.

Au dix-huitième siècle naît le vandalisme restaurateur, qui aussitôt s'arme en guerre contre les " colifichets gothiques," émonde, gratte, démeuble et travestit nos églises pour les ramener à des apparences plus classiques. Après lui, la Révolution par ses décrets imprudents et les mesures irréfléchies qui les suivent provoque d'effroyables dévastations qu'elle est la première à regretter et qu'elle s'efforce de réparer,[3] mais la plaie est trop profonde et trop large pour se cicatriser.

C'est à la Révolution que remonte, comme à son origine, la responsabilité des Gouvernements qui se sont succédé depuis. L'Etat, en se déclarant, le 2 novembre 1789, le propriétaire des biens du clergé, assumait l'obligation de prendre sur lui les soins de conservation, les dépenses de restauration et d'entretien qui avaient incombé aux anciens possesseurs Comment s'acquitta-t-il de ce devoir ? Des édifices consacrés au culte et des bâtiments qui en dépendaient, il désaffecta ou aliéna le plus grand

[1] *L'architecte des monuments religieux,* p 75   (Ouvrage trop peu connu, aujourd'hui disparu, et où se trouvent recueillis de nombreux éléments du problème qui aujourd'hui appelle notre attention)

[2] En Angleterre ce fâcheux état d'esprit n'eut pas cours. Le *Monasticon Anglicanum,* publié de 1655 à 1673 par sir William Dugdale, témoigne éloquemment du culte de cette époque pour les monuments du moyen-âge.

[3] Particulièrement sur les instances de l'abbé Grégoire et de David.

nombre, ce qui était livrer les uns aux remaniements qu'entraîne presque toujours un changement de destination, les autres à l'avidité et à l'ignorance des spéculateurs, autant dire à la destruction. Beaucoup d'édifices civils et militaires, confisqués ou expropriés, eurent un sort analogue. Et les édifices dont l'Etat garda la tutelle, au lieu de les administrer en bon père de famille, il ne s'en occupa guère que pour les laisser dépérir, les mutiler au dehors, les ravager au dedans, porter, pour le renversement des flèches gothiques, pour le brisement des statues et des tombeaux, des lois, des décrets qui fort heureusement ne furent que très rarement exécutés.[1]   Des monuments de toute nature avec la connivence et parfois sur l'initiative du pouvoir central, furent impitoyablement sacrifiés pour des besoins de voirie plus ou moins réels : en ceci on ne fit guère que préluder aux errements dans lesquels excellèrent le premier et le second Empire

Dès le premier Empire, cependant, on voulut bien s'apercevoir que des réparations sur une large échelle ne pouvaient être évitées   Le gouvernement, par le Conseil des Bâtiments civils, s'en attribua la haute main, et plus d'une fois il poussa ses allocations jusqu'à la prodigalité. Mieux que le clergé, les nobles et les municipalités du dix-huitième siècle, il avait pour.s'éclairer des hommes savants et habiles ; pour s'appuyer, le romantisme naissant, une sorte de retour instinctif vers le moyen âge , Chateaubriand célébrait les magnificences de l'art chrétien. Ce qu'avait été cet art, inspirateur, direct ou indirect, de tous les édifices pendant de longs siècles, cet art dont il fallait bien appliquer les principes pour maintenir ou rétablir ces édifices dans la pureté de leur style, l'Etat avait dès lors le devoir de le faire rechercher, il devait provoquer une étude méthodique et suivie des métamorphoses romane et gothique, et créer, lui, par des encouragements et des enseignements officiels, le mouvement qui devait venir, quelques temps après, des Gerville, des Caumont, qu'il n'aurait pas dû laisser à l'initiative privée, qui arriva trop tard pour beaucoup de monuments, et qui ne fut compris que très lentement par ceux qui s'y trouvaient le plus pratiquement intéressés [2]   Longtemps on crut ou on affecta de croire qu'il suffisait, pour bien restaurer nos vieux monuments français, d'avoir visité le Panthéon de Rome, le Parthénon d'Athènes, les ruines de Pæstum ou d'Agrigente, les Pyramides d'Egypte, et d'être capable d'élever une construction comme la Madeleine ou la Bourse

Aussi quel fut le chef-d'œuvre du règne de Napoléon, et, ajoutons-le, des règnes de ses deux successeurs ? La soi-disant restauration de la basilique de Saint-Denis, qui a justifié surabondamment le mot de Viollet-le-Duc : " *Restaurer, c'est une autre façon de détruire* " [3]   Avec les dix-huit millions engouffrés là, de 1805 à 1846, pour déformer et découronner (il fallut abattre la flèche, à peine reconstruite, et avec elle le clocher) un de nos plus précieux monuments, il y avait de quoi mettre sur pied, en attendant mieux, une douzaine de monuments.

Le Gouvernement de Louis-Philippe, il faut lui rendre justice, tint compte du mouvement d'études, de recherches et de protection dont, vers 1830, Arcise de Caumont fut le principal initiateur et propagateur Il fut fait un choix parmi les œuvres intéressantes du moyen âge; les œuvres désignées furent distraites des attributions du Conseil des Bâtiments Civils pour être confiées à des hommes spéciaux et animés envers

[1] Citons à titre d'exemple l'arrêté du 9 février 1794, pris par le district de Toulouse ordonnant la démolition des clochers jusqu'aux combles des bâtiments , le clocher de la Dalbade fut ainsi abattu.   Celui existant ne date que de 1875

[2] Faisons-nous devoir de rappeler que ce goût pour les monuments de notre architecture nationale fut dû, tout d'abord, au charme des charmantes vignettes des artistes anglais, tels que les frères Le Keux, Blore, Coke, Greig, qui, par les illustrations des monographies d'York et de Westminster, firent chercher et apercevoir aux Français qu'eux aussi possédaient des monuments dignes d'attention.]

[3] *Annales archéologiques*, t. vi. p. 300.

elles d'une sollicitude plus **particuliere**[1] Ainsi fut établie, en 1837, la
Commission des Monuments Historiques, institution nécessaire et excellente
qui a rendu d'immenses services et qui aurait pu en rendre de plus importants encore si parfois des influences tout à fait étrangères au but poursuivi n'étaient venus influer sur ses décisions   La politique, malheureusement, quelquefois s'abattit sur nos monuments, disgraciant les uns,
favorisant les autres, suivant que tel évêque, tel fonctionnaire, telle
municipalité, était contre ou était pour les opinions gouvernementales.
L'archevêque de Reims et l'évêque d'Evreux plurent à Napoléon III,
celui de Poitiers, trop peu courtisan, fut mis en pénitence ; aussi l'évêque
de Poitiers n'eut-il que des échafaudages qu'on laissa pourrir sur place ;
tandis que ses collègues eurent, celui-ci un million, celui-là deux millions,
qu'on ne. trouva le moyen d'employer qu'en dénaturant les deux
cathédrales   Des exemples récents témoigneraient qu'il a été apporté
peu de changements à ce mode de procéder, et l'Etat, qui demande aux
Chambres les crédits, qui en est le dispensateur, qui décide des travaux
à faire ou à différer, qui en patronne les principes bons ou mauvais, pré-
sidant aux restaurations, est seul responsable dans ce qu'il ordonne ou
tolère

Des restaurations qu'on a le droit de lui reprocher, il en est de trop
hâtives , il en est qui, trop radicales, cessent d'être des restaurations
Les restaurations prématurées ont eu deux inconvénients très graves
A l'époque où elles ont été entreprises, l'expérience manquait encore
pour s'en acquitter convenablement, et justement les édifices qui les ont
subies étaient de ceux qui, étudiés avec ensemble et méthode, pouvaient
le plus efficacement aider à cette expérience et fournir à la science des
données précieuses qu'on n'a laissé ni aux artistes ni aux érudits le temps
de recueillir.

Les restaurations radicales, achèvements, agrandissements, embellissements, ce que Schmit appelait des "*restaurations splendides,*" out en
elles aussi un double inconvénient   Si elles sont ostensiblement mal
faites, elles gâtent le monument, lui imprimant un cachet menteur d'importance ou de jeunesse qui le ridiculisent ; bien faites, en apparence,

---

[1] Citons à titre de souvenir la circulaire suivante qui montrera mieux que tout
autre exemple l'esprit de sollicitude éclairée de ce Gouvernement pour nos vieux
monuments ·

"Ministère de l'Intérieur, Paris ·
le 10 août 1837

"Monsieur le Préfet,—Le culte des souvenirs qui se rattachent à l'histoire des arts
aux annales du pays est malheureusement trop négligé dans les départements, on laisse
en oubli des monuments précieux ; on passe avec indifférence devant des vestiges qui
attestent la grandeur des peuples de l'antiquité , on cherche en vain les murs qui ont
vu naître les grands hommes dont s'honore la patrie, ou les tombes qui ont recueilli
leurs restes, et cependant tous ces souvenirs, tous ces debris vivants des temps qui
ne sont plus, font partie du patrimoine national et du trésor intellectuel de la
France Il importe de mettre un terme a cette insouciance Le Gouvernement et
les Chambres viennent de donner, à cet égard, une nouvelle preuve de leur solli-
tude , le fonds destiné aux monuments historiques a été augmenté , mais ce fonds
ne peut être considéré que comme un encouragement au zèle des départements , ils
doivent comprendre que la conservation des anciens monuments les intéresse autant
qu'elle les honore, en offrant un attrait de plus aux méditations de l'historien ou à
la curiosité du voyageur

"Je vous invite donc, Monsieur le Préfet, à recueillir tous les documents propres à
me faire connaître les anciens monuments qui existent dans votre département,
l'époque de leur fondation, le caractère de leur architecture, et les souvenirs historiques
qui s'y rapportent.

"Vous les classerez dans leur ordre d'importance, et vous indiquerez les sommes
qui seraient nécessaires pour les conserver ou remettre en bon état, sans oublier que les
secours que je puis donner ne sont qu'une prime au généreux empressement du Conseil
Général et des Conseils municipaux.

"Le fruit de vos recherches sera soumis à une Commission que je viens d'instituer,
et je me ferai un plaisir de diriger les fonds dont je puis disposer vers les départements
qui auront le mieux apprécié l'importance du travail "

elles trompent le spectateur et peuvent troubler l'archéologie par des
notions fausses Il en est qui ont été conduites avec une incroyable
désinvolture ; une ville, Rouen, en offre à elle seule des exemples fameux.
La cathédrale avait un clocher central dont les parties supérieures étaient
d'une Renaissance imposante et harmonieuse La foudre les ayant
ravagées en 1822, on les démolit ; on ne voulut pas, sous prétexte d'unité,
les reconstruire sur les mêmes dispositions, et on les remplaça par la
sèche et maigre flèche en fonte que personne n'admirera jamais, flagrant
mensonge qui ne sert pas plus l'art que l'histoire La Commission des
Monuments Historiques, hâtons-nous de le dire, ne figura que pour l'achèvement de cette malencontreuse entreprise A l'église Saint-Ouen il y
avait une souche de façade, style flamboyant, avec des dispositions uniques.
On pouvait la laisser indéfinitivement telle qu'elle était depuis près de
trois siècles et demi, ou bien la continuer en suivant exactement les projets
de l'architecte du quinzième siècle, projets dont il existe des dessins
précis et détaillés, et dont la réalisation ne souffrait aucune difficulté,
puisqu'il y avait de gros crédits à dépenser C'était trop simple on
aima mieux, en 1846, faire table rase des constructions en attente et
édifier, dans un style banal du quatorzième siècle, une façade qui détonne
sur tout ce qu'on a jamais vu à Rouen et dans la Normandie entière.
Enfin, rappelons comme mémoire la récente affaire de l'escalier du Palais
de Justice et du mur crénelé qui l'accompagne, engagée par la Direction
des Beaux-Arts sans que la Commission fût seulement consultée

Le second et peut-être principal inconvénient des "*restaurations
splendides,*" c'est celui auquel nous avons déjà fait allusion ; une seule
de ces restaurations absorbe souvent plus de dix fois ce qui suffirait à
consolider ou à restaurer sagement des édifices plus modestes dont les
besoins sont réels, parfois urgents, et pour lesquels bien souvent on ne
se dérange même pas. Ce manque d'équilibre est des plus préjudiciables.

Le vrai, c'est que, dès l'origine même, le classement aurait dû atteindre
neuf ou dix fois plus de monuments publics ou privés [1] et les diviser en
deux catégories ; les monuments susceptibles, autrement que par des
promesses platoniques, d'être subventionnés suivant leurs besoins réels ;
ensuite, pour le plus grand nombre, les monuments simplement sur-
veillés Les Gouvernements savent bien, quand ils le veulent, restreindre
les droits de propriété, et ici leur veto eut été des plus salutaires. Nous
posséderions encore, s'ils n'avaient fermé les yeux ou s'ils ne s'étaient
volontairement désarmés, les murs romains de Dax , la porte carlovingienne
d'Orléans, de précieuses abbayes cisterciennes épargnées par les protestants parce qu'elles étaient loin des routes fréquentées et dont la
plupart, il y a un demi-siècle, telles que Perseigne dans le Maine, Bonne-
font en Gascogne, laissaient encore des ruines très instructives ; nous
posséderions des ruines féodales non moins précieuses dont les unes ont
été utilisées comme carrières, les autres relevées, c'est-à-dire remplacées
par des pastiches dépourvus de vérité et de goût. Nous n'aurions pas
assisté à ces dépècements scandaleux des châteaux de la Renaissance,
tels que ceux de Coulanges-sur-l'Autise, la Batie, Montal et d'autres
encore.

En somme, le bilan de tout un siècle, à l'égard de nos vieux monuments et malgré de très louables efforts administratifs et particuliers,
aboutit à une situation qui ne laisse pas que d'être inquiétante. Aussi
conviendrait-il que les pouvoirs publics prissent d'énergiques mesures,
et il n'en est que temps, pour défendre et conserver ce qu'il nous reste
encore du patrimoine national Et ce que nous venons d'exposer pour
notre pays semble pouvoir s'appliquer à tous les Etats

Au surplus, les Congrès internationaux d'Architectes et d'Art Public,

---

[1] Aujourd'hui 2,700 monuments sont classés, dont 1,950 sous la rubrique de monuments historiques, et leur entretien se trouve assuré par un service de 37 architectes
ayant à leur disposition un crédit de 1,417,000 francs.

qui se sont succédés depuis plusieurs années, se sont-ils préoccupés de la question, montrant ainsi que le sujet qui nous arrête est commun à tous les pays dont l'histoire est écrite aux flancs des monuments

En premier lieu, ces Congrès ont été presque tous amenés à traiter la question des restaurations et leurs résolutions ont toujours été en faveur de la conservation la plus importante possible des vestiges des monuments à restaurer , les instructions données en France par la Direction des Cultes pour assurer la *conservation, l'entretien et la restauration des édifices diocésains*, semblent bien répondre à ce vœu [1] Notre confrère Selmersheim en a à Morienval donné un savant exemple , de même qu'appliquées à un édifice d'une autre époque notre vénéré Président,

[1] Voici quelques extraits de ces sages instructions que l'on serait heureux de voir dans la pratique, toujours strictement observées :

" Les architectes attachés au service des édifices diocésains, et particulièrement des cathédrales, ne doivent jamais perdre de vue que le but de leurs efforts est la *conservation* de ces édifices, et que le moyen d'atteindre ce but est de veiller constamment a leur *entretien*. Quelque habile que soit la restauration d'un édifice, cette restauration est toujours une nécessité fâcheuse, un entretien intelligent doit pouvoir la prévenir.

" La conservation des édifices ne dépend pas seulement du soin qu'on prend de les entretenir , elle peut être encore subordonnée à des causes extérieures que l'architecte doit étudier Tels sont l'isolement des constructions, l'assainissement du sol, l'écoulement facile des eaux. L'administration centrale ne négligera rien pour faire disparaître les causes de destruction et les inconvénients matériels que ses architectes auraient à lui signaler

" Dans les travaux de réparation et d'entretien, on ne remplacera que les parties des anciennes constructions qui seraient de nature a compromettre la solidité et la conservation du monument

" Tout fragment a enlever, s'il présente un certain intérêt, pour la forme, la matière ou quelque autre cause, sera étiqueté, classé et rangé en chantier ou en magasin.

" Les matériaux enlevés seront toujours remplacés par des matériaux de même nature, de même forme, et mis en œuvre suivant les procédés primitivement employés

" Toutes les pierres *incrustées* devront avoir le même volume que les pierres enlevées , elles seront *fichées* en mortier au *refouloir* , l'emploi du plâtre est interdit , il en est de même des mastics et ciments, qui ne seront adoptés que pour l'exécution de certains joints exposés directement à la pluie , les autres joints seront faits en mortier.

" Les jointoiements ne seront exécutés que quand ils seront jugés indispensables, et, dans ce cas, l'architecte devra les faire exécuter proprement, sans bavures sur les bords des pierres, légèrement enfoncés, de manière que l'appareil soit toujours visible et dessiné Si les pierres vieilles sont *épaufrées* par le temps sur leurs aretes, les joints en mortier ne devront pas couvrir ces *épaufrures*, mais les laisser visibles et ne remplir que l'intervalle entre les pierres.

" Tous les *refouillements* dans la vieille maçonnerie seront faits à la *masse* et au *poinçon*, jamais au *têtu* ou à la *pioche*. Les tasseaux nécessaires à la pose des pierres à incruster seront faits en bonnes billes de sapin ou de chêne , ils pourront être ordonnés en maçonnerie lorsque l'architecte le jugera convenable.

" Les cales nécessaires a la pose des pierres incrustées ne seront jamais faites en fer, mais en plomb ou en cœur de chêne, et toujours éloignées des parements.

" Toute pierre vieille portant moulure ou sculpture ne pourra être remplacée que lorsqu'elle aura été marquée par l'architecte ou ses agents.

" L'appareil des pierres neuves sera absolument semblable à l'appareil ancien Dans les édifices du moyen âge, les arcs seront extradossés, les parements neufs faits en assises de même hauteur que les anciennes.

" La plus grande attention sera portée à l'exécution des tailles des parements et moulures L'architecte devra observer à quelle époque et a quel style appartiennent ces tailles qui diffèrent entre elles , il remarquera que les tailles antérieures au XIIIᵉ siècle sont faites assez grossièrement et au *taillant droit*; celles du XIIIᵉ, a la *grosse bretture* et *layées* avec une grande précision ; celles du XIVᵉ, a la *bretture fine* et *layées* avec plus de netteté encore ; celles du XVᵉ, à la *bretture* et au *racloir*, etc etc. Sauf de rares exceptions qui peuvent contrarier ces usages, et dont on devra tenir compte, l'architecte fera exécuter les tailles des parties restaurées d'après ces indications On lui recommande de se défier des retailles, des grattages faits après coup, qui altèrent la physionomie des parements et la forme des profils ; il faut rechercher alors les tailles primitives conservées sur les points peu accessibles ou masqués. Il en est de même pour les modifications apportées par des restaurations plus ou moins anciennes aux formes primitives ; on devra examiner alors avec grand soin toutes les traces de ces formes, et dans le doute en référer à l'Administration

" L'emploi de l'outil appelé *boucharde* est rigoureusement interdit.

M. Daumet, nous en a, par sa belle monographie et sa si heureuse restauration du Château de Saint-Germain, fourni une fructueuse leçon de choses Notons en passant que ces vœux ne font que rappeler ce que préconisait déjà votre savant Ruskin, " *Consolider, non restaurer* "

De plus, une proposition de M le baron de Geymüller, faite en 1889 au Congrès tenu à Paris pour la protection des œuvres d'art, et par M Naef, architecte, membre de la Commission des Monuments Historiques suisses, en 1898 à Bruxelles, au premier Congrès de l'Art Public, et semblant avoir rallié tous les suffrages, voudrait que lorsqu'une restauration aura été exécutée, il en soit porté mention sur le monument lui-même à l'aide de signes conventionnels qui sont maintenant d'usage constant dans le pays de Vaud.   Ces signes sont au nombre de trois

1º. La date seule pour les parties entièrement modernes   Ex. 1906.

2º. La date et le signe R. L. pour les parties restaurées librement d'après des exemples analogues.   Ex. R. L 1906.

3º. La date et le signe R F S pour les parties remplacées, restaurées et reproduites exactement d'après le modèle original.   Ex. R. F S. 1906.

Au Congrès de Marseille, en 1904, notre regretté confrère Ch Lucas fut assez heureux pour faire voter les vœux suivants :

1º Que, outre les commissions administratives instituées auprès des gouvernements de la plupart des pays en vue de la conservation des monuments du passé, et sous le contrôle de ces commissions, il soit fait

"Les sculptures d'ornement à reproduire seront exécutées le plus possible d'après les fragments anciens eux-mêmes, et, à leur défaut, d'après des estampages ou des dessins modelés

"L'ornementation ancienne ne sera remplacée que lorsqu'il sera impossible de la conserver ; ainsi la sculpture fruste ou endommagée, toutes les fois que la construction à laquelle elle tiendra ne sera point mauvaise, devra être conservée avec soin

"Les sculptures de nos édifices anciens étant toujours exécutées sur le chantier avant la pose, chaque morceau de pierre portait son fragment d'ornement, et les joints ou les lits des pierres ne venaient pas contrarier la décoration. Ce système constant, auquel il n'est jamais dérogé du XIIe au XVe siècle, doit servir de guide a l'artiste qui restaurera ces édifices. Ainsi, dans les parties sculptées, il ne devra changer ni la hauteur des *lits*, ni l'écartement des joints verticaux, car il faudra qu'il retrouve sur chaque pierre l'ornement qui s'y voyait sculpté, qu'il observe même les irrégularités premières, afin que le travail neuf ne soit point en contradiction avec le système de construction et de décoration original.

"Il apportera dans l'exécution des sculptures d'ornement des soins tout particuliers ; non seulement il devra imiter scrupuleusement les formes anciennes, mais aussi le travail de la sculpture, qui varie à chaque époque Il s'attachera à distinguer les restaurations plus ou moins récentes, notera les originaux bien authentiques, les examinera avec soin, les étudiera, s'identifiera avec les formes anciennes

"S'il est nécessaire de refaire à neuf une partie complètement détruite, l'architecte cherchera des modèles d'ornementation dans des monuments de la même époque, dans une position analogue et dans la même contrée, il ne commencera l'exécution qu'après avoir fait approuver ses projets graphiques par l'Administration

"Il est rare que, dans des ornements courants a remplacer, il n'existe pas quelque partie en bon état, on devra la conserver en place ou la reposer comme un témoignage de l'état ancien

"On remarque, dans l'exécution de ces ornements, des différences qui proviennent du plus ou moins de talent des ouvriers, il est bien entendu que les fragments qui paraissent avoir servi de modèles, et qui sont probablement l'œuvre de *maîtres* habiles, doivent être conservés de préférence. En reproduisant des ornements courants l'architecte remarquera qu'ils sont toujours empreints d'une certaine variété qui, sans altérer l'unité d'aspect, exclut la froideur et la monotonie, il tâchera d'employer des sculpteurs habiles, intelligents, familiarisés déjà avec ces œuvres et sachant en comprendre l'esprit.

"La finesse des sculptures, leur fragilité ou leur mauvais état de conservation rendent toujours délicate, et quelquefois impossible, l'opération du moulage des sculptures. Peu d'artistes d'ailleurs sont assez adroits ou expérimentés pour exécuter ce travail sans causer plus ou moins de dommages, même dans les circonstances les plus favorables Les estampages ou moulages devront donc être formellement interdits, à moins d'une autorisation spéciale. L'architecte aura préalablement le soin de désigner les sculptures qu'il s'agira de mouler, et de faire connaître les motifs qui paraissent exiger une autorisation " appel aux sociétés régionales et locales d'architectes et d'archéologues, afin de faire bénéficier ces monuments des avantages qui découlent du droit moral, droit que l'opinion et la jurisprudence s'accordent de plus en plus, en France, à reconnaître aux auteurs sur leurs œuvres.

2° Que ces sociétés puissent, suivant le projet de loi sur le domaine public payant préparé par la Société des Gens de Lettres, percevoir une redevance sur les visites et sur les publications qui seraient faites des monuments du passé, afin de trouver dans cette redevance les ressources nécessaires à la conservation et à l'entretien de ces monuments, ainsi qu'à des publications spéciales destinées à les faire mieux connaître.

Ce même Congrès émit le vœu que dans chaque pays l'autorité arrêtât les mesures les plus efficaces à la conservation des monuments, en tenant compte des circonstances et de la législation locale

Aux Congrès de Madrid en 1904 et de Liège en 1905 notre savant confrère Cloquet, traitant la question de la *conservation et restauration des monuments d'architecture*, reprenait, en l'étendant, l'idée déjà émise par Schmidt,[1] de distinguer deux espèces de monuments, les monuments morts et les monuments vivants. Il obtenait, après une discussion à laquelle prenaient part de nombreux architectes, que la résolution suivante fut à l'unanimité adoptée par le Congrès.

1° Il y a lieu de distinguer deux espèces de monuments : les monuments morts (appartenant à une civilisation ou servant à des usages qui ne sont plus et ne seront plus), et les monuments vivants (continuant à servir à l'objet pour lequel ils ont été construits).

2°. Les monuments morts doivent seulement être conservés en consolidant les parties indispensables pour éviter qu'ils ne tombent en ruines, car l'importance d'un monument réside dans la valeur historique et technique, valeur qui disparaît avec le monument.

3°. Les monuments vivants, eux, doivent se restaurer, pour qu'ils puissent continuer à servir, car en architecture l'utilité est une des bases de la beauté.

4°. Cette restauration doit se faire dans le style primitif du monument, afin qu'il conserve son unité, l'unité de style étant aussi une des bases de la beauté en architecture, et les formes géométriques primitives étant parfaitement reproduisibles   On doit respecter les parties exécutées en un style différent de l'ensemble si ce style a du mérite en lui-même et s'il ne détruit pas l'équilibre esthétique du monument

5°. On ne chargera de la conservation et de la restauration des monuments que des architectes diplômés ou spécialement autorisés, agissant sous le contrôle artistique, archéologique et technique de l'Etat

6° On provoquera dans le pays où il n'en existe pas encore la création de sociétés de défense pour les monuments historiques et artistiques, dans le pays où il en existe on provoquera leur développement   Elles pourront se grouper pour un effort commun et collaborer à l'établissement de l'inventaire général des richesses nationales et locales.

A ce même Congrès de Madrid la question si délicate de l'expropriation fut reprise et après une longue discussion l'unanimité des suffrages fut obtenue sur ce texte.

" L'Etat a le droit d'exproprier toute œuvre artistique ou d'une valeur historique reconnue moyennant une indemnité fixée par des personnes compétentes, lorsqu'entre les mains du propriétaire elle se détruit ou ne se conserve pas dûment."

La même année, au Congrès de l'Art Public à Liège, les vœux suivants furent adoptés ·

" 1°. Que les municipalités puissent, par des mesures appropriées, assurer, notamment par des prêts consentis aux propriétaires de monuments du passé, la conservation et l'entretien de ces édifices [2]

---

[1] Ouvrage déjà cité (p. 56 et suivantes)

[2] " Il ne sera peut-être pas superflu de rappeler ici le mode ingénieux employé par

"2⁰. Que les municipalités, lorsqu'elles auront besoin de construire un édifice municipal, utilisent les monuments historiques ou artistiques susceptibles de recevoir l'affectation administrative destinée à en assurer la conservation.

"3⁰. Que, dans l'organisation actuelle des Etats, la protection de l'Art public soit efficacement assurée par tous les pouvoirs publics dans la sphère de leurs attributions respectives.

"4⁰. Que les diverses législations prennent les mesures nécessaires pour assurer la conservation des monuments du passé, celle des sites et paysages intéressants au point de vue artistique, scientifique, historique ou légendaire.

"5⁰. Que les objets trouvés ou découverts sur le territoire d'une commune soient placés de préférence dans le musée le plus proche de la localité, à moins que l'état de ce musée ou son entretien soit impossible

"6⁰. Que les pouvoirs publics, pour restreindre les abus de l'affichage, délimitent expressément les endroits où il sera permis d'afficher, et que l'affichage soit formellement interdit sur et autour des monuments et sites à défendre, qu'une pénalité vienne sanctionner ces décisions. [1]

"7⁰. Le Congrès estime qu'il est de la plus haute importance pour toutes les administrations publiques d'avoir un état des richesses artistiques des domaines qu'elles régissent.

"L'inventaire courant est actuellement dressé dans un ordre conventionnel quelconque, or, les fiches ne suffisent pas pour cela. L'inventaire reste une œuvre sèche et stérile, s'il ne présente un caractère didactique. En conséquence, le Congrès émet le vœu de voir dresser dans chaque administration un état méthodique au moyen de tableaux de classification rationnelle pouvant être utilisés pour la connaissance du passé comme pour celles des manifestations modernes de l'art intéressant les professions et les métiers."

Nous espérons par tout ce qui précède avoir rappelé l'état de la question à ce jour. Il nous reste maintenant à exposer ce que nous croyons devoir être applicable à tous les pays et que nous soumettons aux discussions du Congrès, trop heureux s'il peut y trouver les éléments des vœux à intervenir

Tout d'abord, il importe absolument que les Gouvernements soient armés pour obtenir l'expropriation obligatoire chaque fois qu'un monument présentant un intérêt historique, artistique ou archéologique ne sera pas entretenu comme il convient par son possesseur.

Que jamais, à moins d'une utilité absolue et immédiate, il ne soit permis à des administrations d'exécuter ou d'autoriser des particuliers à exécuter des ouvrages pouvant amener la disparition ou la ruine du monument dont l'intérêt historique et monumental est reconnu de tous [2]

Que partout où le site formera le cadre naturel du monument il soit interdit d'y toucher où quoi que ce soit.

Que dans les opérations de voirie les administrations soient tenues de respecter les monuments anciens, se trouvant sur le parcours des tracés, et que, dans certains cas, ces monuments soient pris pour bases des dits tracés. [3]

la ville de Bruxelles sur l'intelligente initiative de M. Ch. Buls pour la conservation des façades de la Grand' Place   En vertu d'une convention passée avec les différents propriétaires une servitude a été créée en faveur de l'Hotel de Ville imposant la conservation des façades   Pour mieux assurer ce résultat, la ville se charge elle-même des travaux de réparation et d'entretien nécessaires, et ce moyennant une légère redevance, elle intervient au contrat d'assurance des immeubles contre l'incendie" (extrait du *1ᵉʳ Congrès de l'Art Public,* p 38)

[1] En France une loi du 27 janvier 1902 porte interdiction de l'affichage sur les édifices et monuments ayant un caractère artistique

[2] En France l'existence d'une telle loi eût empêché la construction de la levée de Pontorson, ou tout au moins ne l'eût autorisée que dans des limites ne pouvant faire craindre pour la destinée de cette merveille qu'est le Mont-Saint-Michel

[3] Là encore c'est à cette lacune de la loi que nous devons a Creil la démolition

Qu'au cas d'impossibilité absolument reconnue de conservation d'un monument, les administrations soient tenues avant toute démolition de prendre des photographies, dresser des relevés exacts ainsi que des moulages pour être adressés aux musées locaux, et que les fragments d'architecture, de sculpture et de serrurerie d'art provenant de la démolition serait répartis dans les musées locaux ou régionaux.

Que des instructions particulières soient édictées sur le mode de procéder à ces démolitions.

Que des encouragements soient donnés aux municipalités pour arriver le plus rapidement possible à la suppression des constructions parasitaires qui trop souvent encore enserrent les monuments du passe.

Que partout où il sera possible, les monuments soient conservés avec leur affectation primitive et que, pour les autres, il soit pris les mesures d'hygiène et de salubrité qui permettront leur utilisation ; bon nombre de maisons anciennes intéressantes au point de vue monumental pourraient ainsi nous être conservées.

Que jamais les municipalités ne puissent être autorisées à confier ces travaux à des agents des services vicinaux, mais toujours à des architectes indiqués par le Gouvernement.

Qu'au cas d'agrandissement d'une ville, les pouvoirs publics soient tenus d'en conserver dans ses grandes lignes l'aspect primitif, ce qui permettra d'en perpétuer le caractère originaire.

Que l'affichage soit formellement interdit sur et autour des monuments.

Que des inventaires archéologiques établis sur un modèle unique soient partout dressés de manière à assurer la parfaite et complète connaissance de toutes les richesses nationales.

Que partout ou les crédits ne permettront pas l'exécution immédiate de travaux de restauration aux monuments, des mesures de protection soient imposées (particulièrement en ce qui concerne les sculptures), et, comme première conséquence, que dans tous les édifices cultuels les dalles tumulaires soient partout relevées et dressées contre les murs intérieurs des monuments.

Qu'au cas de restauration, des instructions basées sur un programme type soient la règle des architectes appelés à les exécuter. Parmi celles-ci nous citerons particulièrement l'obligation de conserver à chaque monument, pour toute partie de restauration, des témoins de l'état ancien. D'employer (chaque fois que cela sera possible) les matériaux originaires et de respecter les dispositions d'assises, ces dispositions étant l'un des éléments de la caractéristique des styles.[1]

Qu'avant toute restauration, un relevé très exact à grande échelle de l'état actuel soit dressé, avec moulage des sculptures et profils les plus caractéristiques.

Que des règles générales soient établies pour la dépose, l'entretien et la restauration des vitraux

Comme les Gouvernements ont pour mission non seulement de songer aux temps présents, mais aussi et surtout de préparer l'avenir, ils devront s'efforcer d'envelopper d'un sentiment d'art leurs programmes d'instruction générale des masses, de manière à obtenir de celles-ci pour les monu-

de Saint-Evremond et à Bordeaux la disparition de la porte d'Aquitaine, et ce malgré les vives protestations des amis des monuments bordelais. Voici comment s'exprimait Schmit (ouvrage cité, p. 5) à ce sujet :

" Il existe un autre fléau, non moins redoutable pour nos édifices que l'ignorance ou l'inexpérience c'est *l'alignement* qui renverse un monument comme une masure, un chef-d'œuvre d'architecture comme la chose la plus insignifiante, une antiquité précieuse comme une borne-fontaine , l'alignement qui a failli jeter bas Saint-Germain-l'Auxerrois , l'hôtel de Cluny, et qui, le plus souvent, n'est guère moins funeste à l'édifice qu'il conserve, qu'à celui qu'il detruit."

[1] On pourra sur ce sujet consulter avec intérêt les planches que l'architecte anglais Pugin y a consacrées dans son ouvrage *Les vrais principes de l'architecture ogivale.*

ments un respect qui trop souvent leur fait défaut. A titre d'exemple nous verrions avec plaisir de bonnes reproductions des chefs-d'œuvre de l'art monumental prendre place au rang des tableaux scolaires et l'établissement dans les grandes villes de musées de moulage établis sur le modèle de notre admirable musée du Trocadéro.

Les Gouvernements devront encourager avec le plus grand soin les écoles publiques ou privées d'apprentissage pour arriver à conserver le goût et l'habileté de l'ouvrier et de l'artisan, sans lesquels l'œuvre de l'architecte ne peut être qu'incomplète

Les Gouvernements auront aussi à encourager les Sociétés privées dont le but est la conservation et la défense des monuments, notamment en leur accordant les privilèges pouvant leur permettre d'exercer utilement leur mission

Ils devront de même encourager la publication et la diffusion des monographies particulières, telle celle en France *de l'Eglise de Notre-Dame, Cathédrale d'Amiens*, de G Durand, publiée sous les auspices de la Société des Antiquaires de Picardie , de même celles marquant les influences locales, comme *l'Architecture religieuse dans l'ancien diocese de Soissons au XIe et au XIIe siecle* de Lefèvre Pontalis, et enfin celles de documents d'ensemble comme la collection des *Archives de la Commission des Monuments Historiques*, publiées sous le patronage de l'Administration des Beaux-Arts par MM de Baudot et Perrault-Dabot, qui ne comprend pas moins de douze mille pièces et dont l'intérêt reconnu de tous en fait un document de tout premier ordre.

---

3 Par Gaston Trélat (Paris).

On assiste, de notre temps, à un mouvement dans le goût qui va s'accentuant chaque jour et qui accuse, de la part du public, des connaissances et des jugements correspondant à un affinement plus grand dont l'échelle sociale tout entière se montre l'objet   Le phénomène est frappant pour les hommes que leur âge permet de comparer des époques remontant seulement à une quinzaine d'années.

Alors on reste frappé par la différence qu'il est loisible de constater, par exemple, dans l'aménagement des magasins et des objets que l'on y montre au public de passage dans la rue.   Ils sont présentés avec un goût qui faisait certainement défaut, il n'y a pas longtemps.   De plus, on essaie bien des nouveautés intéressantes par les rapprochements de couleurs, dont on aime à garder l'impression   En vérité, le mouvement ne saurait être mis en doute ; il a déjà abouti à cette création que nous connaissons, de " l'art public," et de tout ce qui est de nature à le servir en développant les manifestations du goût qu'on voit à tous moments et, bien entendu, à combattre tout ce qui pourrait compromettre les beautés existantes ou propager des laideurs reconnues   Voilà où nous en sommes déjà   D'ailleurs, il faut rappeler encore, comme fait démonstratif, que les Etats ont été représentés au Congrès réuni, l'an dernier, à Liège pour s'occuper d'art public.   Nous avons eu la joie d'y constater un ensemble de volonté plus effective que nous ne l'espérions.   Ce fut un étonnement d'abord et, comme conséquence, un contentement pour ceux dont les pensées intimes, entretenues depuis la jeunesse, répondaient précisément au mouvement qui devait bien finir par se manifester dans les esprits et dont le succès du dernier Congrès *d'Art Public* est une confirmation.

J'ai déjà donné à entendre que les Etats y étaient officiellement représentés, c'est dire que l'art entre aujourd'hui dans les préoccupations inconsciemment répandues parmi les hommes. Et, si les Etats doivent être considérés comme des représentations supérieures d'intérêts nationaux, les Gouvernements sont comme des délégations effectives auxquelles en incomberait la responsabilité du service. Il leur appartiendrait donc de ne rien négliger de ce qui touche à ces grandes collectivités. Nous avons, en effet, à y penser souvent, quand ce ne serait que pour connaître et supputer les besoins généraux qui règlent les activités et qui restent le seul *criterium* d'utilité pour nos efforts.

Mais je ne voudrais pas que ma pensée s'égarât, et, pour serrer davantage la question qui est soumise au VIIᵉ Congrès, je rappellerai que la beauté publique, en s'attachant exclusivement aux solutions contemporaines, a déjà pu intéresser les Gouvernements ; *à fortiori* se trouve-t-on autorisé à leur demander de veiller, chacun chez eux, à la conservation des monuments nationaux. Il paraîtrait inexplicable que l'organisme exécutif des Etats, tel que nous l'avons précisé et défini, en vînt à se désintéresser de la conservation d'une propriété collective comme celle des monuments. Et il en serait ainsi, au moment même où l'aptitude à la compréhension des beautés monumentales est précisément en passe de grandir et de s'étendre aux masses sans distinction d'échelons sociaux.

En pareille circonstance, la conservation des monuments nationaux rentre donc essentiellement dans le rôle qui appartient aux Gouvernements comme aux autorités municipales. Certes, il y a là un élément intéressant l'art collectif. Déjà, celui-ci va jusqu'à vouloir conserver la beauté des sites, que les Gouvernements inclineraient même à protéger contre le *vandalisme*, cette forme d'inconscience humaine, qui arrive à se manifester par un aveuglement relatif à toute chose échappant à l'instantanéité de besoins matériels.

Nous nous trouvons donc ici en présence d'un des éléments du goût public. La beauté des édifices avait déjà sa place marquée dans la vieille classification des Beaux-Arts, mais il est bien possible que ceux-ci soient destinés a être remplacés par la série d'activités que le titre nouveau *d'art public* couvrirait très judicieusement. Tout était l'objet d'un effort en ce sens à ces époques reculées auxquelles les éléments originaires des Beaux-Arts ont été empruntés. Déjà l'art était donc public, puisqu'il y intéressait toute la société et qu'il s'étendait à tous les objets sans exception pouvant satisfaire des besoins sociaux ou individuels. La société d'alors était seulement représentée par les hommes libres. De nos jours, la société, qui comprend tout le monde pouvant concourir à la sélection d'élites, est appelée à développer également son art inclinant à témoigner des affinements de civilisation nouvelle.

Le cadre s'est peut-être élargi un peu plus que je ne l'aurais cru tout d'abord. Et cependant je n'ai rien à regretter si, comme je l'espère, la question s'y présente franchement dans le caractère qui lui appartient.

Ce caractère s'affirme dans le fait que les monuments font partie de l'art, auquel s'intéresse toute la société de nos jours. Les accusatifs, de plus en plus sensibles de compétence publique, veulent que les harmonies plastiques, créées ou laissées par le passé, soient servies dans un esprit considérablement élargi, par rapport à ce que l'on a pu voir jusqu'ici. La conservation des monuments entraîne d'autres aptitudes et d'autres modes—qu'on n'en a pu constater encore—à la conception harmonieuse des formes. Les archéologues des monuments historiques font souvent preuve d'inconscience en fait d'art. Ce qui explique les erreurs issues de recettes apprises en vue de *l'unité de style*. Il faut que les choses changent, pour répondre aux aspirations du peuple qui comprend tout le monde. On peut même s'attendre à une rectitude naïve de ses exigences. Et il y aurait à s'en applaudir si, comme il faut le croire, le bon sens des masses s'attachait avant tout à l'unité plastique se résumant en puissance d'harmonies de la matière mise en œuvre.

Résumé.—Si l'Etat est une haute synthèse des intérêts collectifs, le Gouvernement est l'agent effectif des mesures que ces intérêts réclament.

Or, les monuments sont des éléments importants de beauté nationale. A ce titre, ils font partie des préoccupations que, de nos jours, *l'art public* tendrait à couvrir de son titre et à faire entrer dans le champ de ses préoccupations

Cette institution nouvelle a déjà pris place dans les délibérations parlementaires à propos de la conservation des sites , et finalement les Gouvernements n'ont plus le droit de s'en désintéresser. Les monuments nationaux sont d'importants éléments de beauté publique Ils ont donc une place marquée, avec ce trait inhérent et distinctif qu'ils étaient compris dans l'ancienne classification des Beaux-Arts.

Si les Gouvernements se désintéressaient de leur conservation et de leur entretien, ce serait aller à l'encontre du grand fait qui s'accuse de mieux en mieux et qui prend un caractère de progression sociale, pour en venir à honorer notre temps

Conclusion—Les monuments sont une source de beauté publique, et leur conservation doit être soumise aux délibérations de personnalités compétentes représentant les collectivités intéressées Conséquemment elle engage au plus haut point la responsabilité des Gouvernements.

Pour faciliter la double opération comme pour renseigner effectivement le public sur les résultats entraînés par les travaux d'entretien, il y aurait lieu d'émettre le vœu que, chaque fois où l'utilité s'en montrerait, l'usage se répandît des modèles éphémères, avant toute exécution définitive.

---

4 Par Joseph Artigas y Ramoneda, Architecte
(Barcelone, Espagne).

L'intérêt légitime que l'architecte doit ressentir pour les monuments nationaux, considéré seulement au point de vue professionel, et la douleur naturelle qu'il doit éprouver devant la ruine plus ou moins proche qui les menace—si ce n'est déjà fait—sont des motifs suffisants pour élever sa voix autorisée, réclamant un remède efficace pour l'éviter, à qui peut et doit l'accorder.

Personne ne doit s'étonner donc qu'entre les questions intéressantes d'étude et de solutions soumises au Septième Congrès International des Architectes, figure celle qui est signalée dans le but de fixer la "responsabilité des Gouvernements dans la conservation des monuments nationaux."

Pour différentes raisons—la principale étant que ma nation est une de celles qui, je le dis avec douleur, ont le plus oublié le service de conservation de ses riches, nombreux et intéressants monuments architectoniques—je me suis imposé l'obligation de prêter mon humble concours à l'étude du sujet en question , et franchement je regrette vivement que ma compétence ne soit pas plus grande pour laisser clairement démontré —telle est mon intention—que ceux qui gouvernent les nations en négligeant la conservation des monuments nationaux sont responsables du crime de lèse-patrie , ou, en un mot plus doux, si l'on veut, que de tels hommes négligent par ignorance ou paresse des intérêts moraux et matériels de l'ordre le plus élevé et le plus transcendental

J'ai la certitude d'entendre dans ce Congrès des voix plus autorisées qui s'uniront à la mienne dans la démonstration de l'assertion consignée. s'élevant puissantes et à l'unisson afin qu'on les entende de l'enceinte des nations, réclamant toutes aux pouvoirs publics que les timbres nobiliaires que nous ont légués les générations éteintes, par les monuments qu'elles érigèrent un jour sur le sol de la patrie et que ceux que nous érigeons en notre temps, s'estiment à leur valeur et signification, en les conservant comme un héritage sacré que nous devons transmettre à ceux qui doivent venir après nous dans le chemin de la vie.

Demandant avec humilité à Dieu des lumières et à vous, mes chers collègues, de la bienveillance, j'entre en matière sans autre préambule.

Que sont les Monuments nationaux ?

Il va sans dire que je dois me rapporter aux architectoniques , à ceux qu'érige l'art par excellence, parce qu'il les résume tous : l'architecture monumentale.

Je ne réussis à les définir qu'en disant qu'ils sont des manifestations humaines d'ordre supérieur, élaborées avec le concours de connaissances scientifiques et artistiques de haute importance, dans le but de satisfaire des nécessités indispensables de l'ordre moral et matériel des nations, arrivées au bout par le courage des peuples et aidées par leur propre pécule. C'est en plus un blason de prix où se reflète leur état social dans les successifs moments historiques de leur existence.

Les croyances religieuses, le saint amour de la patrie, le souvenir des événements les plus importants et les plus glorieux arrivés dans la lutte éternelle pour vivre et prospérer, les faits sublimes des héros en prouesses vaillantes, en vertus civiques, en génies privilégiés qui arrachent au ciel ses mystères, à la nature ses secrets et au cœur des émotions ardentes et riantes, élevant tout et éternisant tout plastiquement dans le monument architectonique qui s'élève sur le sol de la patrie, répandant l'odorant encens que la reconnaissance des peuples élève sur les autels du temple de la civilisation, stimulant les âmes à vivre ensemble contentes et satisfaites dans la sainte paix sociale, contemplative en même temps qu'affective, les disposant pour le bien reçu à tâcher de les rendre toujours plus grand.

À qui appartiennent-ils ?

Le mot "nationaux" qu'ils portent pour les distinguer d'autres constructions architectoniques indique clairement ce qu'ils sont.

Ils appartiennent effectivement aux nations : ils constituent une partie très importante de leur patrimoine dans les manifestations les plus puissantes que produit la civilisation des peuples ; non seulement on a converti pour les ériger les deniers publics—et sous un tel aspect ils sont biens publics de l'Etat, de la région et de la municipalité—on peut dire aussi, et c'est plus fort, que le sang national y circule, que la sève de la nation nourrit leur existence puisque leurs sciences et leurs arts, leurs industries et leur commerce, leurs affections de tous genres concoururent à les former ; la foi religieuse et l'amour patriotique, les exigences sociales satisfaites donnant une pâture féconde à leur esprit et de l'éperon à leurs nobles soucis   A titre de gloire propre, elle les étale avec un légitime orgueil, offrant une notoire et éloquente preuve de l'ordre et une mesure où se développe leur vie sociale, et comme un héritage sacré elle veut les garder pour les générations futures

Tout ce qui reflue en bénéfice de la nation, tout ce qui sous une forme ou une autre constitue son patrimoine, doit être l'objet de l'attention et des soins de la part de ceux qui la gouvernent et la dirigent, naissant de ce devoir l'obligation sacrée dans tout pays civilisé—seul l'est celui qui est bien gouverné—de veiller pour la conservation de ses monuments ; obligation qui est en plus accentuée par la considération des hauts motifs et circonstances qui ont donné lieu à l'origine de son existence et y ont présidé, et par l'excellence et la nécessité des services qu'ils rendent.

Effectivement, en eux est contenue toute l'histoire civile et sociale des nations dans les phases successives de leur développement, en eux s'enracine le courage souverain qu'ils mirent dans leurs multiples entreprises, dirigées pour obtenir le bien social, synthèse vibrante de leurs souvenirs, de leur présent et de leur avenir. Une voix impérieuse, la voix du peuple pour la santé du peuple, réclame qu'on lui conserve ce qui lui appartient par droit et par raison, et devant la clameur publique les gouvernants doivent se rendre, fussent par ignorance ou par négligence qu'ils laissent les monuments nationaux dans l'abandon.

FRUITS QUE RAPPORTE LEUR CONSERVATION.

A part le maintien sans avarie de la valeur matérielle qu'ils ont par eux-mêmes et par les services publics qu'ils rendent; laissant même de côté la somptuosité qu'ils prêtent à l'ornement des villes, les monuments architectoniques sont une espèce de puissants phares lumineux qui éclairent les obscurités du passé en nous faisant connaître comment furent et vécurent les générations éteintes, être et vie qu'ils nous laissèrent consignés au moyen du bronze et du marbre qui perpétuent entre nous le souvenir de leur existence et nous font connaître les sentiers les plus profitables qui conduisent à la prospérité et à la gloire des peuples.

De combien de lumières ne leur sommes nous pas redevables!

Les temples, les palais, les maisons et les tombes, de l'Inde et de l'Egypte, de l'Assyrie et de la Perse, de la Grèce et de Rome, ceux du moyen-âge et ceux de la renaissance, vainquant les inclémences de la nature, les luttes de l'homme pour l'honneur parfois et souvent par sauvagerie, ont pu arriver jusqu'à nous, plus ou moins mutilés; que de vérités ignorées ils nous ont révélées! que d'utiles connaissances ils nous ont procurées! Combien en avons-nous utilisé pour nos entreprises?

Conservons donc un si riche patrimoine, héritage de nos ancêtres, augmentons-le avec celui que notre commun effort élève de nouveau, et il sera pour les générations suivantes une source savoureuse et abondante où l'on pourra boire les eaux pures et saines du savoir, thésaurisées par ceux qui nous précédèrent dans le chemin de la vie, adoucissant les ardeurs qu'allume dans l'âme le désir insatiable qui cherche de nouvelles vérités pour rehausser la créature et le Dieu immortel qui la créa à son image et à sa ressemblance.

Si, pour des fruits de tant de valeur et de signification, les peuples et les Gouvernements n'y attachent pas d'importance, mais bien, au contraire, regardent apathiques et indifférents leur destruction, les laissant périr sans les protéger et les soutenir; en vain ils prétendront, visionnaires, figurer dans les fastes de la civilisation; ils méritent seulement dans l'histoire un stigmate d'opprobre placé au lieu où figurent les "sauvageries illustres" pire mille fois que la sauvagerie naturel des déserts.

Conclusion —Illustres collègues et messieurs, de mes considérations déterminant la "nature des monuments nationaux," consignant "à qui ils appartiennent" et fixant les "fruits que rapporte leur conservation," on déduit logiquement que le devoir de les conserver incombe aux peuples et aux Gouvernements, ces derniers étant principalement les uniques responsables de leur perte, par la raison qu'ils sont les seuls aussi à disposer des moyens coercitifs pour l'éviter et du trésor public nécessaire pour les garder à couvert de la naturelle désorganisation que souffrent ses parties composées par l'action du temps et par la main destructive des hommes

Par mes moyens limités de connaissance et d'expression je n'ai pas pu vous présenter un mémoire instructif en droit, qui prouvera jusqu'à l'évidence l'assertion que je viens d'établir, et que je soumets à votre opinion savante; mais la force de l'amour que je professe pour l'art monumental a dirigé ma pensée, à la fin de louer à la façon d'un panégyrique les monuments nationaux et d'en démontrer leur haute valeur.

Dire d'une chose ce qu'elle vaut, c'est-à-dire ce qu'elle mérite; et si les monuments nationaux valent tant, il est juste et salutaire de réclamer énergiquement la protection que peuvent et doivent leur donner ceux qui gouvernent les nations.

5. THE PRESERVATION OF ANCIENT ARCHITECTURE.

By W R Lethaby.

In the course of the eighteenth and nineteenth centuries a great interest was developed in the ancient monuments of old lands, and the gradual and systematic study of ancient art has led to the perfecting of a second method of historical research, the history of civilisation by its monuments.

At the same time, while so much has been changing in the fashion of the world and of our lives, a conscious love of old works of art has been awakened in many minds, and a deep sentiment of communion with the men of the past through the works they have left to us has been aroused.

These, the historical and poetical aspects of old buildings, are, it is self-evident, very largely dependent upon their authenticity as handed down from age to age Such monuments, it must be realised, are not mere records—they are survivals—and a land in which they had been carefully conserved would carry on its past in actual being. We want, not mere models and abstract shapes of buildings, but the very handiwork of the men of old and the stones they laid On the historical side nothing else is a valid document to be reasoned on, and on the side of feeling and beauty nothing else can really touch our imaginations.

While the branch of archæology dealing with the science of old buildings was being built up, experts were naturally betrayed into mistakes by delight in their method of comparison, and the consciousness of learning by which they could see to some extent the completed form of fragmentary buildings. Their mistakes, however, were manifold. They did not in their eagerness think of the difference between the mere form of an old monument—a model at full size, as it were, of what it might have been—and the actual living building itself. They, as is well known, to bring the old and the new into harmony, often took away the oldness of the old part and made all new ; and when they did not do this, they refused to see how they wounded the old by placing their office-made conjectures by the side of the actual work of art which they thought they were improving. It is impossible to tell of the involutions of error and confusion which have followed—the maddening contradictions of learned ignorance, of careful violence, of loving destruction, which have arisen in the application of the method

Regrets for the past are vain, but in the present the charge, nay, the judgment against restorers is that they refuse to learn. They acknow-ledge the irreparable harm that was done in the past, that was being done yesterday, and then, with all professions of understanding and sympathy, they go and do likewise, often, indeed, taking the new words " necessary repair" for the discredited old words " thorough restoration," with an exactly similar result

Notwithstanding all the destruction wrought in the last century, restoration is going forward at an accelerated rate all over Europe, and of course it is precisely the most ancient, remarkable, and beautiful buildings which are laid hold of, passed through the mill of erudite restoration, and left desolate ghosts of themselves—ghosts to shudder at and pass on.

To tell of these things is too sadly absurd. Of St. Front, at Périgueux, which excited so much interest in France that they made it over again with learned correctness; of Charlemagne's wonderful chapel at Aachen, a riddle which has never been read, where they are covering over the fine old masonry with fashionable marbles and mosaics like those in the smoking-room of an hotel, and of Murano Cathedral, where the once mysterious and romantic apses now look as if they had been supplied from some cathedral factory in Chicago

At San Vitale, Ravenna, astounding things have been going on for years under the direction of a learned scholar, but again it is the trivial, the obvious, and the vulgar which result from all this arrogance of learning I say the trivial, and this may be illustrated by a point Everyone knows of the existence of a few wonderful old windows filled with sheets of translucent marble. The restorer simply cannot resist a chance like this of falling into a pitfall. Few and mysterious, are they? That is just what he wants. So with the help of a marble contractor he exploits them until they become a mere restorer's joke, and the Mausoleum of Galla Placidia looks like some grotto lit through yellow glass The mosaics of St Mark's, the west front of Reims, the porches of Chartres, the glass of Bourges, Chartres, and York—the great things of the world—all are being dealt with while we talk As for England, I could tell many stories, but I know too much to trust myself.

In every country protests have been made. In France Victor Hugo was stirred to passion by attacks on his Notre Dame, and lately a brilliant exposition of the method has been written by Emile Hovelaque Of Germany, Professor Strzygowski, of Gratz, has written an illuminating examination of the new splendours of the Dom of Aachen In Italy Cavaliere Boni has criticised the restorations at Parenzo.

Thus in one case an Austrian professor protests against what is done at Aachen, in the other an Italian protests against the Austrians I protest against the Italians and the French, and invite any foreign member of this Congress to protest against what we are doing in England, so as to complete a somewhat vicious circle of protestation, although undoubtedly each country has also had voices raised in its midst, as we have had Ruskin and Morris But for the most part it must be said that everywhere the custodians of ancient buildings and their architects make a few verbal concessions and go smiling on their predestined way, and subscriptions obtained for urgent repairs are as frequently transmuted into carvings and stained glass

In the recent report as to works said to be urgently required at St Mark's, £5,000 is allocated to structural work and nearly £1,000 to decorative restorations, including a sum of £432 for further restorations of the capitals, and proposals for restoring the pavement without estimate.

As to these capitals of St. Mark's, when in Venice I searched for three of the sixth century which had on them monograms of the emperor Justinian It happened that all three had been cut out and replaced by exquisitely mechanical copies of fresh white marble, and I know of half a dozen sixth-century capitals in a private collection in London which I believe to be from St. Mark's

None of us, I venture to say, could, without long research, say whether any of the old capitals of the ducal palace are still in place.

What is the alternative to this now customary method of dealing with old buildings? It is persistent care and repair, as of national treasure to be guarded. Instead of the long intervals of neglect alternating with great restoration campaigns, we need constant examination and minute reparations

You have noticed some masterpieces in our museums—the Venus of Milo at the Louvre, fragmentary sculptures from the Parthenon at the British Museum, the faded frescoes at the Brera—and felt that by the care taken of them, they seemed all the more precious for showing

history of antiquity, loss, and disintegration How precious must the
armless Venus be which is set in such a place of honour in the greatest
museum in the world! Why are tiny pieces of red and white pottery
brought from Greece and stuck together with such infinite pains, and
placed so carefully in costly cases ? They must surely have great historical
value and beauty So an old building, however much is lost, whatever
be its state, should be cared for in the spirit of proud guardianship, and
then no necessary process for strengthening and upholding will harm it

It is usual to object that old buildings are not in a museum and that
they have to be maintained in use All the better; use would not hurt
them. We must try to be honest here, and not let our pretences about
use lead up to their bedizenment. The use and stability of our cathedrals
have again and again been sacrificed for the caprices of ornamental restoration profuse in carvings, stained glass, and giant organs Why should
we call a building sacred as a preparation to making it a vulgar fraud ?
Or is it only we in England who do that ? If the principle is accepted
loyally, that our object, while being guardians of a national or a world's
treasure, is its integrity and obvious authenticity, we can hardly go wrong,
and the horrors of restoration would fall away naturally. Time does not
permit me to deal with detailed suggestions for the scientific protection
of ancient buildings, but much experience is stored up in the printed
matter issued by the Society I represent—the Society for the Protection
of Ancient Buildings.

The great difficulty of the case is caused by the natural enthusiasm
of the owners and architects of old buildings for their own views about
them They have found out this and that—they believe that it was
formerly so—and straightway they are anxious to make it so But their
theory is never a certainty. For instance, we know of the many supposed
correct restorations which have been suggested on paper for the Parthenon
and the Erechtheum, and of the continually shifting opinion on the
evidence

Think of the confusion which has resulted from encouraging modern
architects to *build* their theories of ancient buildings instead of embodying
them in a tract, where they might be properly exposed and laughed at
In a treatise they could point to what actually remained as evidence ,
in *building* their solid theories the evidence itself disappears, the validity
of the old work is destroyed, and the whole becomes a monument of con-
jecture, a tantalising mass of confusion which no one may read. They
violently impose their ideas on old buildings, and we have not even the
satisfaction of being able to show where they are wrong, for dead buildings
tell no tales

When I think of what is being done all over Europe, and being done
now faster than at any other time, I am indeed filled with astonishment
It is almost impossible to visit any famous monument without finding
it screened by scaffolding and resounding with hammer-strokes I wonder
here in England that it can still be done after all that has been said , I
wonder in Italy that they do not realise that their ancient buildings give
that country its pre-eminent value in the world ; I wonder in France
that their quick intelligence and artistic insight have not guided them
in this question ; but most of all I think I wonder at the things which are
being done in Germany, the land so justly famous for its historical criticism Baedeker's guides to North and South Germany are hardly any
longer indexes to old buildings so much as chronicles of restoration completed or in progress Unless this age of change and destruction is soon
followed by one of anxious preservation it is difficult to suppose that any,
more or less, authentic monuments will long remain on the earth,

6. Communicated by THE TUSCAN COLLEGE OF ENGINEERS AND
ARCHITECTS.

Il Comm Giovanni Pini, architetto delegato del Collegio degli
Architetti della Toscana, presente ed illustra le seguenti considerazioni
sul Tema :

Responsabilità del Governo nella Conservazione dei Monumenti Nazionali

Il defunto Ingegnero Architetto Prof Giuseppe Poggi di Firenze, Presidente onorario del Collegio Toscano degli Ingegneri e Architetti e Membro
del Reale Istituto degli Architetti Britannici, in alcune memorie ed articoli
che vengono ora raccolte in unico volume insieme ad altri documenti
d' arte, a cura della famiglia di lui, ebbe più volte ad esporre i propri
intendimenti, in merito alla Responsabilità del Governo nella Conservazione dei Monumenti Nazionali, e questo Collegio presenta ora al Settimo
Congresso Internazionale degli Architetti in Londra, insieme all' estratto
del volume riguardante tale soggetto, favoritogli dalla famiglia, il riassunto
dei criteri enunciati da persona di così riconosciuta competenza, facendoli
suoi in ogni sua parte.

Egli, che fin dal 1845 aveva scritto un articolo a stampa " Sul rispetto
che devesi ai Monumenti antichi," riassumeva in una Memoria letta alla
R Accademia dei Georgofili nel 1864, " Sul progetto di espropriazione
per conseguire la conservazione dei monumenti " le sue impressioni sulla
legge presentata al Parlamento Italiano, così concludendo ·

" Che provvido è lo spirito del Governo, il quale intende col mezzo
dell' espropriazione di conseguire la conservazione dei monumenti d' arte
e di storia nazionale che abbiano la natura d' immobili, e la cui conservazione pericolasse continuando ad esser posseduti dai privati e dai corpi
morali,

" Che, a parer nostro, una legge così larga e generica non può pro-
durre i suoi benefici effetti, per ragione della sua stessa eccessiva com-
prensione, perchè tanto lo Stato, quanto i Comuni, non potrebbero sop-
portare le ingenti gravezze che imporrebbe loro questa larga applicazione ;

" Che a fine di conseguire i desiderati resultati converrebbe, a parer
nostro, che la legge fosse coadiuvata da provvedimenti preventivi e da
disposizioni che ne rendessero men frequente l' applicazione ,

" Che fra queste disposizioni crederemmo di grande efficacia :

" 1°. La formazione di un elenco illustrativo che precisasse questi
monumenti d'interesse nazionale, compilandolo con tanto discernimento
da non registrare senza ragione in quel novero se non quegl' immobili
che realmente lo meritassero ,

" 2° Fare appello ai cittadini e corpi morali, possessori di detti immobili, con l' intento di risvegliare in loro l' antico sentimento del bello
e confortarli ai necessari sacrifizi ; eccitare poi l' intera nazione ed i Comuni
alla pubblica riconoscenza ed estimazione verso coloro che adempiono
così nobile e patriottico dovere ;

" 3°. Che nei casi in cui questo appello riuscisse infruttuoso, si dovrebbe .

" Per gl' immobili redditizi intimare il restauro dentro un dato tempo ;
e questo decorso senza frutto, farlo eseguire dal respettivo Comune a
spese del possessore ; oppure quando ciò paresse gravoso, dichiarare
l' espropriazione per quindi passar subito alla rivendita al pubblico incanto
con le prescrizioni opportune ,

" Per quelli privati addetti al culto, intimare la cessione del patronato
a famiglie disposte a mantenerli come si conviene ,

" Per quelli pure addetti al culto e spettanti ai corpi morali, imporre
il restauro od il mantenimento ; e provata l' impossibilità economica,
concedere dei soccorsi, e non decretare l' espropriazione se non quando si
abbia la certezza di conservazione migliore ;

" Per gli ultimi, infine, che non sono nel novero nè dei redditizi nè di quelli addetti al culto, si potrebbe, nel caso di cattiva conservazione, dichiarare per essi soli la permanente espropriazione, non potendo questa per le ragioni indicate riescire gravosa nè allo Stato, nè ai Comuni ;

" 4. Costituire infine un fondo, non tanto per l' acquisto degli immobili che possono essere colpiti dalla legge di espropriazione per conservarsi permanentemente, quanto per supplire alle perdite sul prezzo di quelli da riporsi subito all' incanto, e per sovvenire alle necessarie riparazioni "

In altra memoria letta al secondo Congresso degli Ingegneri e Architetti in Firenze nel 1875 dal titolo " Sulla Conservazione dei Monumenti d' Arte e d' Archeologia " concludeva nel tempo che faceva voti al Governo perchè affrettasse la legge per tale conservazione :

(*a*) Che sarebbe da rendere obbligatorio, in occasione di restauri importanti sui monumenti governativi, il preventivo giudizio delle Commissioni provinciali consultive ;

(*b*) Esser da sottoporre alla stessa legge di conservazione i monumenti di pertinenza dei privati, adottando il modo che sarà reputato più idoneo In ogni caso ordinare che i monumenti privati facciano parte dell' inventario generale dei monumenti della Nazione.

(*c*) Prima che funzionino le Commissioni provinciali consultive dovrebbero essere precedentemente trattate e stabilite da architetti ed altri artisti, archeologi e persone competentissime le basi e i criteri principali per la conservazione e restauro dei monumenti architettonici, e per la formazione degli inventari di quelli che debbono essere dichiarati d' interesse nazionale. I quali inventari dovrebbero avere a corredo le piante, sezioni e prospetti che fossero reputati necessari a dare chiara idea dello stato presente del monumento, e della necessità della sua riparazione e conservazione

(*d*) Doversi far voti allo stesso Governo, perchè provveda a costituire un patrimonio od una rendita che dia i mezzi d' applicare ed osservare la legge nei modi convenienti, sia facendo restituire al demanio quella parte che si fosse indebitamente appropriata, e che era devoluta alla conservazione delle opere e monumenti d' arte, sia prescrivendo quei provvedimenti che saranno reputati più idonei Ed essendoci fra questi provvedimenti quello (creduto opportuno) della tassa per la visita dei musei. gallerie, monumenti antichi, ecc., e da invocarsi che quel provento venga per intiero destinato al suddetto fine.

In posteriori occasioni il Poggi faceva voti che si preferisse impiegare i mezzi disponibili nel restauro e nella conservazione di tanti monumenti architettonici che soffrono e dei quali è nota l' importanza all' aprire nuovi scavi e all' andare in cerca di avanzi di monumenti Etruschi, Greci, Romani.

" L' Italia," scriveva egli, " è già riconosciuta grande nel mondo intero per i molti e svariati monumenti che ha in evidenza Dei resti sepolti non urge l' escavazione, essendo certi che nello stato in cui sono si troveranno ugualmente fra qualche secolo ; ma non possiamo dire lo stesso e lasciare passare molti lustri, senza il rammarico di vedere sempre più deperire quelli che sono visibile oggetto di ammirazione e di studio "

Il Congresso prende atto e fa sue queste conclusioni e le approva unanimamente.

DISCUSSION ON SUBJECT IX

At the opening of the meeting, prior to the reading of the papers, the Commendatore ALFREDO D' ANDRADE, rising on behalf of himself and Signor M. E. CANNIZZARO as delegates of the Italian Government, made the formal presentation of a gift from the Italian Government to the Royal Institute of British Architects, consisting of a series of works bearing upon the preservation of national monuments in Italy, including monographs of various ancient and historic buildings.

Commendatore D'ANDRADE said that he and Signor Cannizzaro (as Commissioners for the Preservation of Ancient Buildings) had asked the Italian Government to present the books, as they thought that Englishmen interested in the subjects involved would like to see what was happening in Italy, both as regards the existing laws and the methods of their enforcement.

The volumes presented were twenty-four in number, and include—

(*a*) The laws for the preservation of ancient buildings.

(*b*) A list of what were considered to be " ancient buildings," with an account of what had been done for their preservation.

(*c*) Works on classical antiquities

(*d*) Works on mediæval buildings.*

The Italian Government (continued Commendatore a Anarade) appointed Commissioners for the Inspection of Ancient Buildings For purposes of classification the country was divided into ten districts, and each had its own volume of reports   From these it was wonderful to see how much had been achieved at a comparatively trifling cost. Careful supervision was exercised over all items catalogued, and any instance of neglect or vandalism was immediately reported. It was found that by the exercise of much tact, and the expenditure of a little money, even peasant owners of interesting buildings could be persuaded to help the cause In fact, his opinion was that the best way of protecting ancient buildings was to limit the expenditure. Where money was scarce only essential repairs could be executed, and where money was plentiful it was sometimes difficult to discriminate between essential preservation and harmful restoration. In Italy buildings were classed as " dead " or " living " It was obvious that " living " buildings, still in use, had to be kept in a state of repair and efficiency suitable to the needs of the occupants. A " dead " building, on the other hand, admitted of more tender treatment ; and only such methods were adopted as prevented further decay.

In answer to Mr Lethaby's strictures on unnecessary restoration at St Mark's, Venice, Commendatore d'Andrade remarked that the fault must, partially at least, be laid at the door of the Austrian Government   When the Province of Venice was ceded to Italy in 1866 one of the clauses of the Treaty of Peace stipulated that a minimum sum of 100,000 francs (4,000*l*) a year was to be spent on the upkeep of St Mark's Of recent years an agreement had been arrived at whereby this sum was reduced to 2,000*l*., and Commendatore d'Andrade hoped that in future the action of the authorities would come under the heading of preservation rather than restoration.

Mr ALEXANDER GRAHAM, F.S A., Hon Secretary of the Royal Institute, formally accepted the present above mentioned* on behalf of the Institute, and begged the delegates to convey to the Italian Government an expression of the Institute's thanks and appreciation of the gift. Mr.

* The following is a list of the works presented

AVENA (ADOLFO)—Monumenti dell' Italia Meridionale, vol i   sm fo Rome 1902
BARNABEI (F)—La Villa Pompeiana di P Fannio Sinistore.   fo Rome 1905
BRIZIO (E)—Pitture e Sepolcri scoperti sull' Esquilino dalla Campagnia fondiaria Italiana nell' anno 1875   sm. fo Rome 1876
CAVALLARI (F S) & HOLM (A)—Topografia Archeologica di Siracusa   Text   fo Palermo 1883
  Plates   la fo Palermo 1883
EGIDI (P), GIOVANNONI (G.) & HERMANIN (F)—I Monasteri di Subiaco Notizie storiche L' Architettura Gli affreschi   8o. Rome 1904
FREOERICI (V)—I Monasteri di Subiaco   La Biblioteca e I' Archivio   la 8o. Rome 1904
GARVFI (C A)—Catalogo illustrato del Tabulario di S Maria Nuova in Monreale   la 8o. Palermo 1902
GENALA (F)—Il Palazzo di San Giorgio in Genova   sm fo Florence 1889
ITALY—SENATO DEL REGNO —Allegati al disegno di Legge Conservazione dei monumenti e degli oggetti di antichità e d' arte. Decreti-Legge dei cessati Governi d' Italia   4o Rome 1901
  MINISTERIO DELLA PUBBLICA ISTRUZIONE.—Elenco degli Edifizi Monumentali in Italia   4o Rome 1902
  Notizie intorno alle Scuole d' Arte e di Disegno Italiane.   la 8o Rome 1898
  L' Amministrazione delle Antichità e Belle Arti in Italia, Jan 1900–June 1902   2 vols. 8o. Rome 1901
  Sull' ordinamento del Servizio Archeologico   4o Rome 1885
  Regolamento per l' Esecuzione della Legge 12 Giugno 1902, No 185, Sulla Conservazione dei Monumenti   8o Rome 1904
UFFICIO TECNICO PER LA CONSERVAZIONE DEI MONUMENTI DI ROMA E PROVINCIA E DELLE PROVINCIE DI AQUILA E CHIETI.—Relazione dei Lavori eseguiti dall' Ufficio nel Quadriennio 1899-1902 8o. Rome 1903

Graham said that he hoped that in the near future the British Government would follow the excellent example of the Italian Government, and take steps to register and preserve the country's national monuments.

M. Besnard (Paris) moved .—" This Congress is of opinion that in every country the Government should be authorised to obtain, where necessary, the compulsory expropriation of any building which is of historical, artistic, or archæological interest where the building is not kept in a due state of preservation by its owner."

Commendatore D'Andrade seconded the motion. He considered M. Besnard's paper to be a most valuable one, and though he disagreed with a few of the conclusions, yet he very cordially endorsed the majority of them   He quoted the last two articles of the Italian law . " If a private individual allows a ' monument ' to fall into disrepair, the said building may be expropriated by the Government "; and the provincial and communal law, which obliges municipalities to look after their own ' monuments ' or ancient buildings.

M Adrien Delpy (Belgium) suggested that the resolution should be extended so as to include the façades of such interesting buildings as do not come under the strict designation of " Historical Monuments."   In Brussels a Royal Commission has made a catalogue of interesting buildings, yet they are not all classified as " Historical."   The Municipality of Brussels has bought the right to control any alteration proposed in the façades of the Grande Place   M. Adrien Delpy was also anxious that the Royal veto should be exercised where advisable for the protection of an ancient building

M Gaston Rozet (Paris) explained that in France façades do come under the designation of "Monuments Historiques " He instanced several streets and squares in Paris where the façade has to be left intact even where the interior may be gutted—*e.g.* the Rue de Rivoli, the Place Vendôme, &c.

Commendatore D'Andrade said that an Italian municipality can even take exception to the tint a house is colourwashed, and has full powers to prevent mischievous interference with the architectural features of a façade   He quoted the instance of a façade by Scammozzi in Verona : the owner wished to alter the arrangement of the upper windows to secure better lighting, but the municipality stepped in, and, supported by the law courts, would sanction no change in Scammozzi's design.

Signor Cannizzaro (Rome) remarked that the Society of the Cultori di Architettura had made an " Itinerario dei Rioni," a work which catalogues and describes the details and even the inscriptions on the façades of all the streets in Rome.   Thus any alteration can at once be detected, and the owner is obliged to keep to the original state of things. Façades are considered public property, to be carefully preserved as a heritage for future generations of citizens.

Various speakers urged that the powers given to a Government to deal with national monuments should be wide enough to include all objects of artistic interest, and refer equally to pictures, sculpture, furniture, silver, porcelain, &c., with powers of compulsory expropriation where the owners sought to dispose of such objects to foreigners.   It was acknowledged that considerable difficulties might be met with.

To give point to the contention, Commendatore d'Andrade instanced a fine palace in Genoa   Through the big entrance gateway the public gained an excellent view of the courtyard in general and of a beautiful " Andrea della Robbia " in particular.   When the Commendatore heard of the suggested removal of the Madonna, he at once went to the owners ; but all his persuasions in favour of its retention in its old place proved in vain. Although the Della Robbia had been as accessible to the public as the façade itself its position was not *on* the façade, and so, under this technicality, the municipality had not the legal right to interfere, and it proved impossible to save for the public the treasure which it had hitherto enjoyed so freely.

Mr. W D. Caröe, M.A Cantab , F S.A , said that the resolution was a very general one, and there could be no objection to it   If a monument were in bad hands and likely to be destroyed, somebody should step in and save it   Therefore he was very ready to support the proposition.

The resolution was carried.

Mr. Alex. Graham moved —" That this International Congress of Architects recommend that the British Government be approached with a view to appointing a Royal Commission to control and to extend the operations of the Ancient Monuments Protection Amendment Act of 1900, and to prepare an accurate catalogue of the ancient monuments of the British Islands, taking similar action to that of the Department of Ancient Manuscripts and in agreement with the measures adopted in other countries"

M Besnard raised the question of what was an ancient monument ?

Mr. W D Caröe said he had great pleasure in supporting the resolution, but would ask Mr. Graham to accept a slight modification.   The question had been asked what was an ancient monument, and as a matter of fact in England they were rather disposed to consider that an ancient monument belonged to the prehistoric period; therefore it was very necessary in the resolution to make it clear that they included not only prehistoric monuments, but also historic monuments, and he suggested that the resolution should read —" and prepare an accurate catalogue of all ancient monuments in the British Islands, whether historic or prehistoric."

Mr. Graham agreed to the reading suggested.

Mr Caröe said they were told, as Professor Lethaby had said, that their ancient monuments were being destroyed, and really the first thing they had to do before handing over their monuments to the Government was to educate the Government   Upon that point he must express himself frankly, and his feelings were entirely with Professor Lethaby when he said that so far on the Continent—and he begged the pardon of their visitors if he said anything that they might feel harsh—the result of placing monuments under Government had been disastrous.   It had not been intentionally so, but he felt it had been actually so.   Therefore, in seconding the resolution, which he believed was a necessary one, he felt they ought to act with caution and that their friends from across the seas should think with them a little as to what they felt over here of the restorations which had been going on in Europe.   It was very easy to give instances, and perhaps he might give one of a restoration taking place in their distinguished Chairman's own country   When he (the speaker) was a small boy of six or seven he was interested in ancient monuments, and he was travelling in Jutland and came to a little village called Thorsager, famous for its storks and its church, where he saw the first round church he had ever seen.   He did not know whether he was more interested in the storks than in the church, but at least he recollected the church.   He visited the place for the first time again about two years ago, and before going there he made for amusement a picture of the church as he remembered it as a little boy   He drew the tower, but when he got there his wife chaffed him and told him he could not rely on his memory, for the church had no tower   Well, they got hold of the old verger, and he told them that the tower was pulled down because the church belonged to the eleventh or twelfth century, and the tower belonged to the fifteenth century.   That was an excellent example of the kind of restoration which had been going on all over Europe.   He could give them other instances   He could tell them how he saw some beautiful ancient carvings pulled down because the figures were drawn out of proportion, and an admirable artist put back the same subjects revised to his own designs, which he thought worthy of the nineteenth and twentieth centuries.   That had been going on in many places. After all, it was not only the forms of their ancient monuments tha it was necessary to preserve if they were to be of value to them, but it was their spirit, and he could conceive no case where the form had been preserved and the spirit lost more completely than in that remarkable restoration which had taken place at Carcassonne in Southern France It seemed to give them everything that restoration ought not to be, and yet Viollet-le-Duc had produced the most remarkable monograph, which showed his extreme erudition in everything but the spirit of Gothic architecture, which he failed to understand, and had wiped out of the city He hoped that Professor Lethaby's paper would be translated into the various languages of those attending the Congress; and although they might not agree with it *in toto* (and he did not profess to do so himself), yet he trusted it would be read, marked, and digested, and considered by their friends across the seas.

Professor BALDWIN BROWN said that in supporting the resolution he thought they should not confuse the issue by saying too much about this great question of restoration It really did not depend upon the action of the Government They had committed the sins which Mr Caroe had spoken about in England just as they were committed all over Europe The present aspect of Salisbury front was as bad as that of Carcassonne or of the interior of Notre Dame What they wanted to do was to educate the public who were not official, and they had also to educate those who were in official charge He agreed very largely on what had been said as to restorations, although not to the full extent enunciated by Professor Lethaby in his paper. He did not mention the question of restoration in his paper, for he thought it stood apart from what they were really dealing with, which was the necessity of some Government care of monuments, and that did not necessarily take the form of restoration

Com D'ANDRADE and M BESNARD spoke in favour of passing a resolution in more general terms

Mr CAROE pointed out that they had already passed a general resolution, and they wanted this particular one to apply to the country in which the Congress was being held.

After some further conversation,

Professor BALDWIN BROWN said there appeared to be some feeling that the motion was not international enough because it concerned the British Government He thought it was international, for the International Congress asked the British Government to fall into line with other countries That he thought was an international matter, and was a demand which such a conference might make to one nation which was out of line with others It was a matter which affected the whole community, that all nations should be engaged in the common work of caring for these monuments.

Further discussion took place on the question of enlarging the scope of the resolution, but no amendment was moved, and the resolution was carried

A vote of thanks to the Chairman, on the proposition of Mr. Alexander Graham, concluded the sitting.

RESOLUTIONS

That in all countries the Governments should be authorised to obtain if necessary compulsory expropriation in every case where a monument possessing historical, artistic, or archæological interest is not kept in a proper state of preservation by its owner

That this International Congress of Architects recommends that the British Government be approached with a view to appointing a Royal Commission to control and extend the operations of the Ancient Monuments Protection (Amendment) Act of 1900, and to prepare an accurate catalogue of all ancient monuments, whether historic or prehistoric, taking similar action to that of the Department of Historical Manuscripts and in agreement with the measures adopted in other countries

SUBJECT X.

THE CONDUCT OF ARCHITECTURAL COMPETITIONS.

1. Par J. GUADET,

INSPECTEUR GÉNÉRAL DES BÂTIMENTS CIVILS, PROFESSEUR À L'ÉCOLE NATIONALE DES
BEAUX-ARTS, MEMBRE DU CONSEIL SUPÉRIEUR DE L'INSTRUCTION PUBLIQUE

DE L'ORGANISATION DES CONCOURS INTERNATIONAUX PUBLICS D'ARCHITECTURE

I.—DE L'OPPORTUNITÉ DES CONCOURS INTERNATIONAUX

Rien n'est plus simple—en apparence—que la théorie du concours . un pays, une province, une ville, une administration désire, pour un édifice à créer, la plus parfaite solution possible. On fait appel à toutes les lumières, pour pouvoir comparer et choisir C'est simple et limpide ; mais il faut se défier des idées simples dans des choses aussi complexes que les œuvres d'architecture Cela mérite donc étude, et si le concours est parfois très désirable, parfois aussi il est à déconseiller.

National ou international, le concours est parfaitement logique lorsqu'il a pour objet une expression monumentale ou artistique d'une pensée qui n'attend qu'une forme. Tel était entre tous le concours ouvert par l'Italie pour le monument à élever au roi Victor Emmanuel. La conception en est moins pratique lorsqu'il s'agit de construire un de ces édifices d'utilité qui exigent la combinaison patiente et successive, l'élaboration continue poursuivie en commun dans de nombreuses conférences entre l'architecte et les administrateurs, la recherche incessante non seulement du plan, mais souvent du programme lui-même ; que de fois voyons-nous une composition architecturale, conçue d'après des données qui paraissent certaines, se modifier profondément à l'épreuve des nécessités d'abord inaperçues et que révèle une étude ultérieure toujours nécessaire ?

Là comme partout, il ne peut exister de règles absolues , c'est à l'intelligence des administrateurs intéressés de peser prudemment le pour et le contre, d'apprécier si dans chaque cas spécial la méthode du concours est ou n'est pas celle à employer. Tout ce qu'on en peut dire, c'est qu'il serait toujours prudent, sur des questions aussi spéciales, de prendre avis et de s'entourer de conseils autorisés.

J'irai plus loin. Sauf dans le cas où—comme pour le concours du Palais de la Paix à la Haye—le monument à ériger est vraiment international, et où son caractère mondial prime la circonstance de lieu, le concours international ne m'apparaît comme légitime que dans les pays où l'on ne reconnaît pas dans le personnel des architectes la présomption de valeur suffisante en regard de l'œuvre à créer Un concours international est presque un affront pour les architectes du pays.

Et si la pratique s'en généralisait, s'il fallait que toute construction importante fût mise au concours entre toutes les nations, qui ne voit quel découragement ce serait pour les artistes d'un pays, qui se sentiraient capables de produire la composition requise, et se trouveraient ainsi réduits aux petits travaux, à ce qui est secondaire, aux miettes du métier au jour le jour, et mis à l'écart lorsqu'il s'agit d'une de ces grandes œuvres qui sont le rêve d'une vie d'artiste ? Mais, dira-t-on, qui les empêche de prendre part au concours, d'y lutter à armes égales, et d'en sortir vainqueurs ? Pure illusion : on ne veut pas s'exposer à une défaite dans son propre pays, et on s'abstient.

En France, nous déplorons un phénomène trop fréquent : les jeunes gens les mieux doués viennent faire leurs études à Paris, et y restent, privant ainsi leur région natale de l'apport du talent qu'ils ont acquis. Bien des fois j'ai demandé à d'anciens élèves pourquoi ils ne retournaient pas se fixer dans leur ville, où les attendaient sans doute des relations, au lieu d'encombrer de plus en plus Paris qui ne peut suffire à tous : il doit en être de même ailleurs aussi. Or, ils me répondaient entre autres raisons bonnes ou mauvaises : je végéterai à subir toutes les corvées du métier, puis si jamais il y a quelque chose d'un peu important à faire, on le mettra au concours. Mieux vaut rester à Paris , si un jour ce con‑ cours a lieu, je le ferai à Paris

C'est ici un côté très grave de la question ; un pays ne doit pas désespérer de ses artistes, sinon il arrête leur essor. Sans doute l'intérêt immédiat peut faire espérer que dans la circonstance on obtiendra un résultat plus satisfaisant en faisant appel à l'étranger. Mais il faut voir plus haut et plus loin. On ne fait pas un art national sans quelques tentatives malheureuses, mais c'est en mettant les artistes du pays aux prises avec les grands problèmes artistiques qu'on arrivera—après quel‑ ques échecs peut-être—à la possession incontestée d'un art national digne de ce beau nom.

Voyez les Etats-Unis d'Amérique. Leurs artistes ont osé, les Améri‑ cains ont eu foi dans leurs artistes, leur ont fait quelque crédit au début, et aujourd'hui il y a un art américain, qui marchera encore, mais qui s'affirme déjà Un jour, dans un banquet de jeunes Américains, je portais un toast à l'éclosion américaine d'un art américain : quelques années ont suffi pour l'assurer

Mais ceci n'est pas l'affaire des architectes, c'est celle des hommes d'état qui ont qualité pour méditer ces graves questions d'avenir. Notre rôle est plus modeste , ce n'est pas nous qui décidons s'il y aura ou non concours international. Il en est ouvert un, examinons quel en devra être le fonctionnement.

II—De l'Action possible des Concours

Et d'abord, que peut donner le concours, national ou international ? C'est ici qu'il faut relever les plus graves erreurs, non des architectes, mais des administrations Le concours produit des idées, des disposi‑ tions générales, entre lesquelles on choisit les plus heureuses ; il ne produit pas, il ne peut pas produire de projet définitif. Un projet de concours n'est et ne peut être que ce que nous appelons un *avant-projet*. Au con‑ traire, les administrations attendent trop souvent du concours la certitude d'une solution définitive, un projet arrêté *ne varietur*, et parfois jusqu'à de véritables *forfaits*. C'est là une erreur complète, grosse d'embarras sans issue, de mécomptes et de procès. C'est une erreur fréquente encore d'exiger des concurrents une quantité de dessins à de grandes échelles, par conséquent une grosse dépense, lorsque des plans, façades et coupes à des échelles pratiques permettent de distinguer les meilleures com‑ positions, sans que le concurrent soit obligé de recourir à de véritables *agences* dont l'intervention fausse le concours. On est allé parfois jusqu'à demander des détails d'exécution ; cela ne saurait en rien déterminer la valeur relative d'une composition.

Véritablement, pour quiconque sait un peu ce qu'est la préparation d'un projet d'architecture, il est incontestable qu'on ne peut à aucun

point de vue demander à un projet de concours une solution définitive.
On ne peut exiger que cinquante ou cent architectes fassent chacun
de leur côté l'énorme travail qu'exige l'étude complète d'un édifice jusque
dans ses derniers détails, étude qui dure aussi longtemps que la construction
elle-même. Puis, un programme, si clair et si détaillé qu'on le suppose,
ne suffira jamais à cet effet toujours, il faudra que l'architecte ait de
nombreuses conférences avec les administrateurs, chefs de service, etc.   ,
que chaque distribution, chaque aménagement soit passé au crible de la
discussion , toujours il y aura des modifications après coup, des remaniements ; les besoins même peuvent changer et changent souvent pendant
le cours de la construction S'il est nécessaire d'avoir dès le début un
ensemble certain et de s'y tenir avec fermeté, rien ne serait ni plus illusoire
ni plus dangereux qu'une prétendue invariabilité des détails et des mises
en œuvre ; et l'administration qui se flatterait d'avoir, par ces exigences
impérieuses, emprisonné l'architecte dans des barrières infranchissables,
s'y serait emprisonnée elle-même, à son très grand préjudice, sans recours
possible contre sa propre imprudence.

Si l'auteur du projet primé au concours, est ensuite chargé de l'exécution, il aura à établir avec tous les renseignements nécessaires un projet
définitif qui lui-même subira encore d'inévitables modifications, sans
parler de l'étude incessante de l'artiste.

Et de même que le projet de concours ne peut être qu'un *avant-projet*
l'évaluation de la dépense ne peut être qu'un *avant-devis*. C'est une
indication approximative qui se modifiera comme le projet lui-même.
J'ajouterai que *jamais*, je souligne ce mot, je n'ai vu dans un jugement
de concours le jury s'attacher au devis La seule chose vraie, c'est que
des hommes expérimentés peuvent, par comparaison, émettre des avis
relatifs sur les dispositions dispendieuses ou économiques du projet par
rapport aux autres ; mais chercher là une certitude est aussi illusoire que
de la chercher dans la présentation graphique du projet

Je voudrais ici poser un principe qui me paraît incontestable. Le
crédit du concours doit être absolument distinct du crédit de la construction. Une administration veut, au lieu de s'adresser à un architecte, en
consulter un grand nombre ; elle doit payer cette consultation , puis,
lorsqu'elle aura fait choix d'un architecte, celui-ci aura à faire tout ce que
comporte le mandat d'architecte . établissement d'un projet et d'un
devis, conduite des travaux, règlement des mémoires. Ce sont là deux
choses différentes, et après le concours, le travail de l'architecte choisi
restera aussi entier et devra conserver sa pleine rémunération Le concours doit donc avoir son crédit spécial, et bien doté, car les concurrents
ne seront nombreux que si l'enjeu est suffisant. Il faut que les administrations sachent qu'un concours engage pour elles une dépense sérieuse, en
regard de dépenses très considérables pour l'ensemble des architectes
qui y prennent part.

Est-il logique d'ailleurs que l'exécution soit garantie à l'auteur du
meilleur projet ? Dans tout concours, j'en doute, à moins qu'il ne s'agisse
que de concours restreints où l'on n'appelle que des architectes en qui on
a une confiance préalable. Trop de raisons d'âge ou de distance, de santé,
d'antécédents, voire même d'honorabilité, font que l'auteur du meilleur
projet peut n'être pas apte à remplir le rôle de l'architecte constructeur.
Mais c'est surtout dans les concours internationaux que le doute est
légitime. Certes, il peut se faire que ce lauréat soit à tous égards qualifié,
pour cette mission ultérieure. Mais que fera-t-il s'il ignore la langue du
pays, notamment la langue technique, si longue à acquérir, s'il n'a l'habitude
ni des mesures, ni des procédés de construction en usage ? Je ne
me vois pas quant à moi dirigeant une construction en Angleterre ou en
Allemagne, et je crois bien que nous sommes tous dans ce cas La difficulté ne pourrait être tournée que par des combinaisons de collaborations
qui ne peuvent être préjugées.

K K

Tout cela arrivera en somme à se résoudre, pourvu qu'on se pénètre bien de cette vérité que tout concours, et surtout tout concours international, est chose préparatoire et non définitive.

III —DE LA PRÉPARATION DU CONCOURS.

Tout concours suppose dès l'abord deux choses essentielles son règlement et le programme de l'édifice à projeter. Le plus souvent, il faut bien le dire, cela se fait un peu au hasard, et lorsque plus tard, dans le jury, des hommes compétents font ressortir les erreurs souvent graves qui ont vicié l'une ou l'autre de ces préparations, il est trop tard. J'ai vu bien souvent en pareil cas les administrateurs reconnaître ces erreurs, et s'en excuser sur leur inexpérience. Soit, l'inexpérience est trop naturelle pour n'être pas permise ; mais pourquoi ne s'étaient-ils pas entourés d'avis expérimentés ? Il faut le proclamer très énergiquement un concours ne peut être bien préparé, ni dans son règlement ni dans son programme, si l'administration ne fait pas appel aux lumières d'architectes, et j'ajouterai d'architectes ayant l'expérience des concours.

Certes, en principe il appartient à l'administration de poser les règles du concours auquel, à ses risques et périls, elle appelle les lutteurs, et de faire connaître les besoins de l'édifice à créer. Mais, en lui laissant le dernier mot, il est évident que nous pouvons lui faire connaître, par expérience, que les conditions qu'elle veut imposer écarteront les concurrents sérieux , ou que, dans son programme, elle demande une quantité de locaux que la capacité de l'emplacement ou les ressources financières ne pourront matériellement pas admettre. Et dans un concours international, cette consultation nécessaire doit être internationale. Sans doute cela prendra du temps, comportera des dépenses. Mais comme en toutes choses, c'est cette première préparation qui est le gage du succès, il ne faut pas regarder à faire ce qui est nécessaire.

Je pose donc en règle que dans la préparation d'un concours international, l'administration doit être éclairée par une commission consultative, et internationale, d'architectes dûment choisis, dont il est facile de demander la désignation par la voie diplomatique.

En ce qui concerne le *règlement* du concours, tout doit être fait en vue de la justice et de l'égalité, et cela demande quelques précautions.

Les principales conditions à observer sont les suivantes :

Un temps suffisant doit être laissé aux concurrents, et le même temps à tous. Pour cela, il importe que le programme du concours parvienne en même temps aux divers pays, soit que les envois de programmes soient échelonnés en conséquence, soit que les envois portent la mention " A ouvrir seulement le . ." et que cette mention soit uniforme, et les précautions nécessaires prises pour que la régularité de l'opération soit constatée.

Le programme doit être envoyé dans la langue où il a été rédigé, en laissant aux concurrents le soin de se le faire traduire s'il y a lieu   Lors du concours de Berkeley, j'avais rédigé le programme en français , il fut traduit en anglais ; puis de la traduction ainsi faite on fit des traductions pour les pays autres que ceux de langue anglaise, y compris la France Dans ce voyage aller et retour mon texte est revenu assez changé pour que le sens en fût altéré, et les concurrents induits en erreurs très préjudiciables

Après l'expédition des programmes, toute communication aux concurrents devrait être close. Si cependant sur demande de quelques-uns des explications ou éclaircissements sont donnés, ils doivent être adressés sans exception à tous ceux qui ont reçu le programme.

Pendant la durée du concours, il ne doit être rien changé ni à ses conditions, ni au nombre ou à l'échelle des dessins demandés, ni à la date de remise. Il est facile de comprendre que toute concession ainsi accordée à ceux qui se sont mis en retard est au préjudice de ceux qui n'ont pas perdu de temps

La date de terminaison doit s'entendre du moment où le concurrent fait remise de son projet, et ce moment doit être le même pour tous. La prescription fréquente qui fixe à une date déterminée la livraison des projets au siège du concours est injuste, car elle peut restreindre de deux semaines le temps concédé à un concurrent qui travaille de l'autre côté de l'Atlantique. Il doit donc être dit que tel jour, à telle heure, les projets devront être remis à un chemin de fer, bateau, ou autre mode de transport, ou à une légation ou consulat, et cette remise certifiée.

Il y a intérêt à ne pas demander un travail matériel exagéré comme on le fait souvent pour les grandeurs d'échelles, le nombre de dessins, ou des documents écrits que jamais un jury ne contrôle, tels que devis, mémoires descriptifs, calculs de résistance ou avant-métrés, etc. . On devra se rappeler que, comme il a été dit, un projet de concours ne peut être qu'un avant-projet, et un devis de concours une simple évaluation sommaire de la dépense Des conseils expérimentés sont ici indispensables.

Le budget du concours doit être complètement distinct du budget de l'exécution Les primes annoncées doivent être intégralement assurées aux concurrents. Il n'appartient ni au jury ni à l'administration d'en modifier la répartition si cette faculté n'a pas été stipulée dans le programme

Si l'un des lauréats est ultérieurement chargé de la rédaction d'un projet définitif et de l'exécution, la prime qu'il a reçue ne doit pas venir en déduction des honoraires qui seraient dûs à tout autre architecte investi de la même mission. Il y a intérêt à ce que les primes soient aussi importantes que possible.

Il est généralement spécifié que les projets primés seront la propriété de l'administration, mais cette acquisition ne doit pas comporter le droit de reproduction ni de publication sans le consentement de l'auteur. Il n'est pas licite non plus de se servir de l'un de ces projets pour une destination autre que celle qui a fait l'objet du concours ; ainsi, un concours ayant lieu en vue de la construction d'une église ou d'un théâtre dans la ville de . . . il serait délictueux de faire exécuter ce projet dans une autre ville, et surtout de le faire exécuter une seconde fois n'importe où.

Il doit être interdit de photographier les projets non primés, ou tout projet quelconque, avant les opérations du jury

Le droit de reproduction et de publication doit au contraire être réservé à l'auteur de tout projet envoyé, ainsi que la faculté de l'exposer dans les expositions universelles ou nationales.

L'auteur doit pouvoir rentrer en possession de ses dessins originaux, moyennant qu'il en délivre à l'administration une reproduction exacte

Les concours doivent donner lieu à une exposition avant et après les opérations du jury Ces expositions doivent être publiques. Toutefois, des réserves sont à faire en ce qui concerne les concours à deux degrés. Ce sujet sera traité en annexe, afin de ne pas alourdir le présent rapport

Les procès-verbaux des opérations du jury, et le rapport s'il en est fait, doivent être publiés

Il sera parlé plus loin de la formation et du fonctionnement des jurys

Le règlement du concours indiquera si les projets doivent être anonymes et reconnaissables seulement par une devise, ou s'ils doivent ou simplement peuvent être signés.

Il faut bien dire que l'anonymat est toujours illusoire, et nous n'assistons jamais à un jugement de concours sans que divers incidents démontrent que les auteurs de certains projets ne sont pas inconnus de tous les jurés Il en résulte une inégalité flagrante. Il est beaucoup plus loyal et plus correct que les projets soient signés. On objecte il est vrai que parfois un artiste éminent pourra affronter un concours ou, en cas d'échec, l'anonymat ne rendra pas cet échec public. Il serait facile de concilier les deux considérations en autorisant la signature par pseudonyme, le nom véritable étant consigné dans une enveloppe qui ne serait ouverte qu'en cas de succès.

Soit dans ce cas, soit dans le cas du concours anonyme, il ne peut être ouvert d'autres enveloppes que celles correspondant aux projets primés. Ainsi, les noms des auteurs distingués en dehors des primes par des mentions honorables ou des médailles ne doivent être connus qu'après autorisation de ces artistes

Passons au programme   C'est là une chose très difficile et qui doit être très sérieusement méditée   Un programme doit être très clair, et établi par grandes divisions   On se perd souvent dans les détails ou dans des descriptions puériles. Mais surtout, on demande souvent l'impossible : ainsi entre autres plus de choses que l'emplacement n'en peut contenir, ou des répartitions entre étages qui rendraient impraticable la superposition, si par exemple on demande au premier étage tout un ensemble double de ce qu'on demande au rez-de-chaussée   Et c'est fréquent   Un programme ne peut être établi qu'avec une expérience très sérieuse des difficultés de la composition. Je ne dis pas que le programme doive résulter d'un croquis préconçu   ce serait une mauvaise méthode, car il deviendrait trop rigide ; mais ses prescriptions doivent être pesées avec autant de prévoyance que possible · et prévoyance est synonyme d'expérience.

Evidemment, les besoins à satisfaire doivent être indiqués par l'administration · qu'il s'agisse par exemple d'un Palais de Justice, elle pourra seule décider combien il faut disposer de Chambres, quelles dépendances et quels services accessoires seront nécessaires. Mais cela fait, il restera une foule de questions pratiques, qui doivent être envisagées sinon résolues dès l'établissement du programme, et pour lesquelles les conseils de praticiens sont indispensables.

Je propose donc en y insistant encore de déclarer que pour tout ce qui concerne la préparation du concours—règlement et programme—l'élaboration en doit être confiée à une commission composée d'administrateurs et d'architectes expérimentés en matière de concours, et il serait bon que des architectes de plusieurs nations y fussent convoqués.

IV —Du Jugement du Concours

Un jury est constitué : par quels moyens ?   Question délicate surtout dans les concours internationaux.

Mais d'abord, voyons quel est le rôle du jury   Respectueux avant tout du programme, qui est le *contrat* inviolable et la *loi des parties*, il doit juger sans autre préoccupation que celle de la justice   Cela paraît évident, et cependant nous voyons parfois invoquer l'intérêt final de l'administration en faveur de projets qui, au mépris du programme, auront présenté une solution séduisante en sortant du terrain, ou en ajoutant tel ou tel service oublié par les rédacteurs du programme, parfois même en suggérant un autre emplacement, peut-être mieux choisi. Libre à l'administration d'acquérir amiablement ces projets, mais ils doivent être exclus du concours comme ayant violé le programme, obligatoire pour tous.

Un exemple : la Ville de Paris avait ouvert, pour la décoration de la Place de la République, des concours simultanés, l'un pour les mâts décoratifs, l'autre pour les balustrades, un autre pour les candélabres, etc . .   C'était une idée bizarre, mais enfin les concurrents avaient, par le programme, le droit de faire un seul de ces concours, ou deux, trois, ou tous. Au jury, un administrateur fit valoir que la Ville avait un intérêt évident à chercher une composition d'ensemble, où il y eût harmonie entre ces divers éléments. Il avait dix fois raison, mais trop tard. Je représentai qu'en opérant ainsi, on exclurait du concours les artistes qui, *sur la foi du programme*, c'est à dire du contrat, n'avaient traité qu'un seul sujet. Le jury me donna raison, chaque concours partiel fut jugé comme s'il n'y en avait pas d'autres, et dans le fait les mâts décoratifs qui seuls furent exécutés furent confiés à un artiste qui n'avait concouru que pour ce seul sujet.

Le programme, qui est la loi des concurrents, est aussi et au même titre la loi des juges.

Mais quelle doit être la composition du jury ? Au risque de paraître trop absolu, je réponds avec conviction . un jury d'architectes.

Pour juger une chose, il faut s'y connaître ; et l'idée ne viendrait pas de faire juger un concours de mathématiques par d'autres que des mathématiciens. Et surtout, il faut remarquer qu'il ne s'agit pas ici d'une œuvre réalisée, qui pourrait à la rigueur être appréciée par des hommes instruits et intelligents et non spécialistes, mais bien d'une œuvre représentée par une écriture qu'il faut savoir lire Qui donc peut lire des plans, des coupes, même des façades, apprécier les possibilités de construction, etc. . . . sinon des architectes ? Supposez un concours de composition musicale . s'il s'agit d'audition effective des œuvres, on comprendra un jury où figureront des amateurs ; mais s'il s'agit de prononcer entre des partitions simplement écrites, qui donc pourra le faire sinon des musiciens habitués à la lecture des partitions ? Le cas est certainement le même. Cependant, les administrateurs doivent être appelés à ce jugement, mais avec voix consultative. Il est nécessaire que le jugement émane de gens experts et, comme on dit au Palais, "*à ce connaissants.*"

Je n'ignore pas que cette conclusion, trop logique, n'a guère de chances d'être admise. Tout au moins, et subsidiairement, je demande que dans les jurys les hommes compétents—et il n'y en a pas d'autres que les architectes—soient en majorité.

Et cela est de toute justice. Que vient faire le jury ? Uniquement classer les projets, dire quel est le meilleur, toujours en regard du programme, puis lequel vient après, et ainsi de suite. L'administration fera ensuite ce que bon lui semblera, à ses risques et périls et sous sa responsabilité.

Le jury doit être maître de sa procédure. Cependant, il y a quelques données d'expérience qu'il est bon d'indiquer La meilleure méthode et la plus ordinairement suivie consiste à faire d'abord des éliminations de tout ce qui ne vaut pas la peine d'arrêter l'examen , puis une seconde, parfois une troisième élimination, de façon à conserver une sélection des meilleurs projets , enfin de voter entre ceux-ci au scrutin secret, par un seul numéro à la fois, jusqu'à l'obtention d'une majorité absolue pour le premier rang ; procéder de même pour la seconde prime, et ainsi de suite jusqu'à concurrence du nombre de primes allouées Si le jury se trouvant en nombre pair, l'égalité de voix est affirmée dans trois scrutins successifs, il doit y avoir de ce fait partage *ex æquo*. Dans ce cas, s'il s'agit par exemple du premier rang, il sera acquis aux deux projets également, et le total des deux premières primes sera partagé : ainsi, si la première prime est de 6,000 fr., la seconde de 4,000 fr , chacun recevra cinq mille francs, puis on passe au vote de la troisième prime, le nombre des projets primés restant invariable, sauf le cas où cette égalité se produirait pour la dernière prime.

Le vote par procuration est inadmissible. Tout juré absent perd son droit de vote. Le jugement du jury est sans appel.

Il est bon que les conditions matérielles, par exemple la configuration d'un terrain irrégulier, la concordance entre les divers dessins, l'observation des échelles imposées, soient au préalable vérifiées par des commissaires, membres du jury, qui feront un rapport et proposeront la mise hors de concours des délinquants, le jury restant appréciateur . souverain.

Le jury élit son président, son vice-président, et s'il y a lieu un rapporteur. Il est utile qu'un fonctionnaire ou employé soit mis à sa disposition pour la rédaction des procès-verbaux.

Reste la question très embarrassante, surtout dans les concours internationaux, de la désignation de ces architectes membres du jury. Un premier principe qui ne sera, je crois, contesté par personne, c'est qu'à un concours international il faut un jury international. Un tel concours n'est pas seulement un tournoi entre des personnes, mais aussi entre les diverses écoles artistiques représentées par leurs champions Mais la perfection est impossible, et telle nation qui n'aura qu'un seul concurrent ne pourra être représentée dans le jury comme celle qui en aura vingt. La formule vraie me paraît être *proportion, dans la mesure du possible*, entre les éléments du jury et ceux des concurrents.

Si ce principe est admis, une première conséquence sera que le nombre des jurés ne saurait être fixé *à priori* non plus que leur répartition par nationalité. Cela est sans inconvénients, pourvu que les concurrents soient informés, par le programme même, que leurs droits seront ainsi sauvegardés Je voudrais donc que tout programme de concours international spécifiât:

"Le jury se composera d'architectes désignés par chaque nation représentée au concours, et dans la proportion d'un juré par dix concurrents ou par fraction de dix à la suite des dizaines complètes. Toute nation qui sera représentée par moins de dix concurrents, et au moins par cinq, aura droit à la désignation d'un juré "

Il n'y aurait plus alors d'autre difficulté que la fixation effective du nombre de concurrents de chaque pays . question de mécanisme facile à régler, surtout avec l'intervention des agents diplomatiques. Il suffirait que, un concours étant ouvert, je suppose, par la Roumanie, les concurrents français, par exemple, fussent invités à déposer leurs projets à la Légation de Roumanie, qui en ferait connaître le nombre à son Gouvernement.

Voilà donc un premier point réglé · tel pays a, je suppose, 27 concurrents . il a droit à trois jurés. Qui les désignera ? Le Gouvernement ? Ce n'est guère son affaire. Une Académie, une Société d'Architectes ? Mais laquelle ? Et puis on dira volontiers qu'il y a tendance exclusive, favoritisme pour une école, etc.   . Le mode le plus juste et le plus libéral me paraît être l'élection par les concurrents

Mais pour cette élection, je récuse absolument le scrutin de liste On y voit trop souvent une minorité, qui se sera concertée, faire échec à une majorité qui n'aura pas pu s'entendre. Sur 30 votants, on fera ainsi passer une liste qui ne réunira que 10 voix, parce que les 20 autres votants, qui au fond sont d'accord, auront porté leurs voix sur douze ou quinze noms. Il faut ici encore le scrutin uninominal, et la majorité absolue des voix

En application de ces idées, la procédure serait la suivante :

A la date du . . les concurrents de la nation . . . font remise de leurs projets à la légation du pays ou le concours est ouvert, ou à une société d'architectes, déléguée à cet effet Il leur en est donné reçu, leurs noms et adresses sont pris.

D'après le nombre des projets déposés et le règlement du concours, la légation ou la société constate que les concurrents ont droit à un, deux, trois jurés ou plus ; on l'écrit à chacun des concurrents en l'invitant, par lettre recommandée, à se trouver quelques jours après à un lieu désigné, pour procéder à l'élection, en y apportant le récépissé de dépôt comme justification du droit de vote En cas d'empêchement, il pourra se faire représenter par un confrère, muni de son pouvoir et porteur du récépissé.

Au jour fixé pour l'élection, il est procédé sous la présidence de telle personne déléguée par la Légation ou par le Président de la Société accréditée, à l'élection à la majorité absolue d'un premier juré, puis d'un second, et ainsi de suite : chaque élection ne pouvant résulter que de la majorité absolue , en cas d'égalité de nombre de voix pendant trois scrutins consécutifs, les deux artistes qui se sont partagé les voix sont proclamés élus, à moins qu'il ne dût en résulter un excédant sur le nombre des jurés à élire ; dans ce cas il est tiré au sort entre eux.

Il est bon, pour parer d'avance au cas d'empêchement ou de non-acceptation de quelques jurés élus, que la réunion élise séance tenante et dans les mêmes formes un nombre égal de jurés suppléants, ainsi désignés d'avance pour combler les lacunes éventuelles

Après que les résultats des élections dans chaque pays ont été transmis à l'administration directrice du concours, avec notification de l'acceptation des jurés élus, la liste du jury définitif est arrêtée, et est notifiée à tous les concurrents, ainsi que les dates fixées pour l'exposition et pour le jugement Mais jusqu'à ce jugement, un juré acceptant venant à être empêché est remplacé par le premier juré suppléant restant disponible.

V —Conclusions

Telles sont les règles qui me paraissent devoir régir les concours internationaux. Je n'ignore pas que ce que je propose est assez compliqué ; mais il faut bien voir qu'un concours international n'est pas chose simple, et que les précautions doivent être minutieuses

J'ai l'honneur en conséquence de proposer au Congrès international la délibération suivante :

1 *Action possible des Concours*

Art. 1.—Un concours, international ou non, ne peut être qu'une œuvre préparatoire , il ne peut donner lieu qu'à des avant-projets et à de simples évaluations sommaires de dépenses.

Art. 2.—Ces projets et évaluations de dépenses sont absolument distincts du projet et du devis définitifs qui seront dressés ultérieurement, en s'inspirant plus ou moins des œuvres primées au concours

Art. 3 —Le crédit affecté au concours est en conséquence absolument distinct du crédit d'exécution de l'édifice Si cette exécution est confiée à l'un des concurrents, il ne peut être établi aucune confusion entre la prime qu'il aura méritée par le concours, et les honoraires auxquels il aura droit, ou auxquels tout autre architecte aurait droit, pour la rédaction du projet définitif et l'exécution de l'édifice.

Art. 4 —Dans les concours internationaux surtout, il serait imprudent et peu pratique de garantir la mission d'exécution à l'auteur du projet reconnu le meilleur

Art. 5.—Le crédit du concours doit être largement doté, en considération de la dépense très importante qu'il impose à la masse des concurrents.

2 *Préparation du Concours*

Art. 6.—La préparation du concours comporte deux éléments : le règlement du concours et son programme.

Pour tous deux, les conseils d'architectes expérimentés sont nécessaires. Le règlement et le programme doivent être élaborés par une commission composée d'administrateurs et d'architectes de divers pays

Art. 7.—Il doit être laissé aux concurrents un temps suffisant et le même pour tous Des dispositions sont à prendre pour que la délivrance des programmes ait lieu simultanément dans les divers pays.

Art. 8 —Le programme est envoyé partout dans la langue qui a servi à sa rédaction. Il appartient aux concurrents de le faire traduire à leurs risques et périls.

Art. 9.—Après l'expédition du programme, si des explications ou

renseignements complémentaires sont demandés, les réponses doivent
être communiquées à tous les concurrents qui ont reçu le programme

Art 10.—Pendant la durée du concours, il ne peut rien être changé
à ses dispositions matérielles, nombre ou échelle des dessins, prorogation
de la date de remise, etc   . :

Art 11 —La date de terminaison, devant être la même pour tous,
doit s'entendre de la remise du projet soit aux légations du pays qui
ouvre le concours, soit à une société d'architectes déléguée à cet effet

Ce mode est déterminé par le programme.

Art. 12 —Les projets primés deviennent la propriété de l'administra-
tration, mais sans que cela implique le droit de reproduction ou publication sans le consentement de l'auteur, ni le droit d'exécuter ailleurs le
même projet. Au contraire l'auteur peut rentrer en possession de ses
dessins originaux en délivrant à l'administration une expédition conforme.
Il ne peut être pris aucune photographie du projet.

Art. 13.—Il est fait une exposition du concours avant et après le
jugement. Les procès-verbaux et rapports du jury sont publiés.

Art. 14.—Le règlement du concours indique si les projets seront
anonymes et signalés par des devises, ou s'ils devront ou pourront être
signés. Il est préférable que le concours ne soit pas anonyme, mais que
les projets soient signés, avec autorisation toutefois du pseudonyme,
moyennant consignation du nom et de l'adresse de l'auteur dans une
enveloppe close

Art. 15 —Aucune enveloppe contenant l'indication d'un nom d'auteur
ne peut être ouverte sans son consentement, sauf s'il s'agit d'un projet
primé.

Art. 16 —Le programme technique doit être clair et précis et
établi avec les conseils d'architectes expérimentés , il doit éviter les prescriptions irréalisables   Il ne doit pas être imposé aux concurrents une
exagération de travail par la prescription de dessins inutiles ou à trop
grande échelle.   La dépense du concours doit être réduite au minimum
pour les concurrents.

3 *Jugement du Concours*

Art. 17 —Le jury a pour mission de juger le concours uniquement
au point de vue de la justice, en ne perdant pas de vue que le programme
est un véritable *contrat* faisant la loi des parties.   Il doit écarter les compositions, même séduisantes, qui auraient violé le programme.

Art. 18.—Le jury doit être composé d'architectes, seuls aptes
à lire les plans, façades, coupes, et à apprécier les possibilités de construction. Les administrateurs intéressés doivent être convoqués aux
opérations du jury, avec voix consultative.

Le jury décide quel est le meilleur projet, lequel vient ensuite , de
son jugement résulte l'allocation des primes ; ensuite l'administration
fait ce que bon lui semble, sous sa responsabilité.

Art. 19.—Le jury se composera d'architectes appartenant à
chaque nation représentée au concours, et dans la proportion d'un juré
par dix concurrents ou fraction de dix à la suite des dizaines complètes
Toute nation qui sera représentée par moins de dix concurrents, mais au
moins par cinq, aura droit à la désignation d'un juré

Art. 20.—Les jurés architectes sont nommés à l'élection par les
concurrents de chaque nation, au scrutin uninominal et à la majorité
absolue

Art 21 —En conséquence, à la date fixée pour tous les pays, les
concurrents remettent leurs projets à la légation du pays qui a ouvert le
concours ou à une société d'architectes déléguée pour les recevoir

D'après le nombre des projets déposés, la légation ou la société informe
les concurrents du nombre de jurés qu'ils ont à élire, du jour de cette
élection et du lieu où elle doit se faire   Au jour fixé pour l'élection, il

est procédé sous la présidence d'un délégué de la légation ou de la société à l'élection à la majorité absolue d'un premier juré, puis d'un second et ainsi de suite.

En cas de partage égal des voix pendant trois scrutins consécutifs, les deux artistes qui ont obtenu le même nombre de suffrages sont élus, jusqu'à concurrence du nombre de jurés auquel le pays a droit. Si cette élection *ex æquo* devait faire excéder ce nombre, il est recouru au tirage au sort.

ART. 22.—Pour parer à l'éventualité de non-acceptation ou d'empêchements, les concurrents élisent séance tenante et dans les mêmes formes autant de jurés suppléants que de jurés titulaires

ART. 23.—La constitution définitive du jury est notifiée aux concurrents, ainsi que les dates de l'exposition et du jugement

ART 24.—Le jury constitué élit son président, son secrétaire ou ses secrétaires, et s'il y a lieu son rapporteur.

ART. 25.—Le jury est juge et maître de sa procédure mais il ne peut ni modifier la répartition des primes, ni en augmenter ou en diminuer le total.

Le vote par procuration est interdit ; les jurés présents prennent seuls part au vote.

En dehors des administrateurs présents avec voix consultative, il peut être mis à la disposition du jury un employé chargé de la tenue des notes et proces-verbaux

ART 26.—Le jugement rendu par le jury est définitif et sans appel , il est obligatoire pour les concurrents et pour l'administration.

Proposé par le soussigné,
Inspecteur-Général des Bâtiments Civils, Professeur
à l'Ecole Nationale des Beaux-Arts de Paris.
J. GUADET.

ANNEXE

Concours à deux Degrés

La plus grande partie de ce qui vient d'être dit sur les concours en général s'applique aussi aux concours à deux degrés. Examinons maintenant ce qui peut leur être particulier.

Le concours à deux degrés impose aux concurrents choisis un double travail, et le plus souvent le second projet ne sera pas le simple développement du premier. Il faut donc tout d'abord que pour la première épreuve, considérée comme éliminatoire, on n'impose pas aux concurrents une surcharge inutile de dessins. Une grande esquisse suffit pour les éliminations.

Il est naturel aussi que les concurrents choisis soient tout d'abord, et avant la seconde épreuve, indemnisés de leurs frais, également et sans classement. Les primes variables récompenseront *en plus* les résultats du concours définitif

Tous les concurrents admis au concours définitif doivent s'y présenter dans des conditions identiques ; de là la nécessité de ne pas classer les esquisses retenues. Et je vais plus loin ; je voudrais que ce premier concours ne fût pas exposé, afin que les concurrents ne connussent pas respectivement leurs compositions. Seulement, comme il faut toujours que les opérations du jury soient contrôlées par l'opinion, toutes les esquisses devraient être conservées sous scellés, pour être finalement exposées en même temps que le concours définitif Et dès lors, liberté entière doit être laissée aux concurrents de conserver leur première composition ou d'en adopter une toute différente. La première épreuve ne doit être en effet considérée que comme une épreuve d'aptitude et une base de sélection.

Règlement du Concours

Il doit être porté dès le début à la connaissance de tous les concurrents éventuels .

Que le concours sera à deux degrés, cette décision ne devant pas être prise après coup, comme il y en a eu des exemples ;

Que les dates sont arrêtées d'ores et déjà, tant pour le premier concours que pour le concours définitif ,

Que le premier concours, donnant lieu à de simples esquisses, donnera lieu à un nombre *minimum* de concurrents agréés pour le concours définitif ;

Que chaque concurrent ainsi agréé recevra à l'issue du premier concours une indemnité fixe et uniforme de .   ,

Que le concours définitif sera récompensé par des primes de . . . de   de . . . sans qu'il puisse être établi de confusion entre ces primes et l'indemnité ci-dessus ,

Que à l'issue du concours définitif, il y aura exposition publique tant des esquisses du premier degré que des projets définitifs eux-mêmes ;

Que le jury du premier degré sera aussi le jury du concours définitif, sauf la latitude qui pourrait être laissée aux concurrents agréés de désigner des jurés en plus, à raison d'un par nationalité représentée ;

Que les indemnités et primes ne se confondront pas avec les honoraires d'architecte, si l'un des concurrents est chargé de l'exécution de l'édifice ;

Que le programme est actuellement donné pour le premier concours seulement, sous réserve de modifications pour le concours définitif. (Je reviendrai sur ce point.)

Le surplus du règlement emprunterait ses dispositions à ce qui a été proposé pour les concours en général.

Programme.

Il ne serait pas prudent de stipuler que le programme du premier concours restera invariablement celui du concours définitif. La vue même des esquisses, les avis du jury compétent, peuvent démontrer des erreurs , on peut s'apercevoir d'un manque de proportion entre les choses demandées, d'une insuffisance de terrain, d'oublis de services ; les circonstances elles-mêmes peuvent nécessiter des modifications de programmes.

J'estime donc que tout d'abord un premier programme doit être élaboré pour le premier concours , puis ensuite, que après le jugement de ce premier concours, il doit être élaboré, dans les délais annoncés, un nouveau programme pour le concours définitif, soit qu'il confirme simplement le premier, soit qu'il s'en écarte.

En résumé donc, je propose pour les concours internationaux à deux degrés ·

1 Tout ce que j'a proposé à l'égard des concours en général

2. Les dispositions particulières transcrites ci-dessus sous la rubrique " Règlement du Concours."

Ajoutant, ce qui est l'évidence même, que les administrations doivent bien comprendre que l'ouverture d'un concours à deux degrés doit nécessairement entraîner pour elles une dépense plus considérable

2 Par Gaston Trelat (Paris).

Il suffit d'avoir pris part à quelques concours pour se rendre compte de l'intérêt qu'ils présentent, relativement au service de la collectivité. Mais c'est seulement à la condition que ces concours, qui ont pour objet un édifice ou un monument, répondent directement à la tournure que les idées de l'artiste ont prise, si toutefois on veut assurer une portée fructueuse à l'épreuve.

Il était peut-être bon de rappeler, de montrer que, dans ces élaborations, il y avait lieu d'éviter toute restriction du champ offert à la pensée et devenant une gêne ou une entrave pour l'envergure des efforts A dire les choses telles qu'elles sont, sans craindre un peu de brutalité dans l'expression de pensées aussi délicates, il paraîtrait que toute considération d'intérêt immédiat soit de nature à diminuer l'étendue de nos conceptions Elles doivent toujours être libres et indépendantes de points de vue étroits. Et pourtant il se produit souvent qu'on en arrive à se borner à des recherches dans des publications, pour être au courant des partis répondant aux idées généralement admises et qu'une paresse, naturelle de l'homme, incite également les juges à choisir de préférence . . . Oui ! c'est ainsi que les choses se passent, mais c'est tout autrement qu'elles devraient être. Cependant il en est de la sorte Résultat d'une éducation fausse, ne poussant pas à contrôler suffisamment l'efficacité des solutions apprises Et les juges ont en général leurs idées toutes faites à l'avance ; il leur arrive rarement de s'efforcer à comprendre des partis ne répondant pas à ces idées issues des succès récents Les hommes sont toujours des hommes Et, dès qu'ils ont une détermination à prendre, on s'étonne d'avoir à constater jusqu'à quel point ils arrivent à être inconscients et peu scrupuleux. Ainsi, quand par hasard un *parti* présenté dans un concours est frappant d'audace et de franchise, il y a des chances pour que les juges tombent implicitement d'accord et empêchent cet *insolent* de passer La solution qu'il a élaborée était inattendue et contraire à ce qu'on apprend couramment En conséquence, la conception est l'objet de rigueurs répondant à pareille audace, qu'on ne qualifie même pas, se bornant à proclamer son absence de sagesse Oh ! que de neutralité intellectuelle, que d'inconscience des nécessités du jour ne couvre-t-on pas du mot de sagesse ! Cette pensée revient souvent à l'esprit dans les expositions où les châssis sont parfois dépourvus de toute recherche utilitaire ou même d'inspiration plastique. Les personnalités sont si fréquemment effacées dans une formule malheureuse d'école ! Quand on y pense un peu profondément, on s'aperçoit qu'il y a et qu'il y a eu vraiment trop d'écoles occupées à tuer les personnalités ; il n'y a donc pas à s'étonner si les choses ont pris semblable tournure. Et puis tant de gens sont là, qui prennent ces éducations ravalantes pour une force dont ils restent fiers Si nous revenons aux concours, ils sont la plupart du temps une occasion pour les juges de remettre à leur place les audacieux, se permettant de présenter une solution originale. Et pourtant l'originalité est toujours basée sur la logique d'enchaînement que comporte l'effort personnel.

Un ami me racontait son histoire dans un concours auquel il avait pris une double part puisqu'il y avait deux envois, dont il était particulièrement satisfait. Or ses deux envois furent également négligés et écartés par le jugement. Qu'était-ce donc à dire ? Il s'interrogeait, quand il rencontra l'un des juges et lui demanda s'il se souvenait du projet portant telle devise et ce qu'il en pensait " Oh, mais c'était très beau ! quel parti remarquable d'élévation ! C'était ce qu'il y avait de mieux comme façade, mais, ajouta-t-il, un parti aussi grandiose eût été ruineux." Voyant un autre juge qui était venu à son atelier, quelques jours plus tard, le même concurrent montra ses plans qu'il avait précisément alors sous la main. "Quels beaux partis de plans," fut-il dit ; et ce dernier juge d'ajouter : "Il fallait qu'il y eut de bien grosses fautes dans les façades." . . . Et voilà ! C'est souvent ainsi. J'insiste seulement sur la motion du premier des deux relative à la dépense qu'entraîne une *franchise de parti*. Oui ! Voilà où l'on peut en venir—par suite de quel mobile ?—je ne sais —Mais voyez-vous la franchise du parti, la rectitude en art, considérées comme des causes de dépense ! Qu'est-ce que cela peut bien vouloir dire ? Absolument rien pour tout homme tant soit peu compétent. Continuons. A propos d'un autre concours, j'entendais un membre du jury dire à l'un des concurrents · "Votre parti semblait un moment très bon, quand un de nous s'aperçut qu'il y avait un des murs portant à faux" . . . sic ! Un mur qui porte à faux ! qu'est-ce que cela devrait avoir à faire dans un concours ? Qu'est-ce que cela peut donc bien signifier de confondre ainsi cette chose sans portée avec la valeur d'un parti ? C'est elle seule qui aurait à servir de base aux jugements des concours, si la valeur spéciale des artistes en concurrence et la compétence des juges pouvaient répondre à ce que la situation peut réclamer. Mais les choses tournent autrement : on assiste souvent à des témoignages de capacité douteuse se retranchant ainsi derrière une expérience de conducteurs de chantier

Ce n'est pas tout Car, pour être sérieusement conduite, une étude comme celle-ci ne doit négliger aucun élément de nature à appuyer la solution. Je veux encore rapporter un fait, dont l'invraisemblance empêcherait tout d'abord d'y croire. Mais, des preuves irrécusables étant fournies, il fallut bien en tenir compte. Il s'agissait d'un concours portant spécialement sur un établissement d'assistance hospitalière, dont le titre exact m'échappe. Mais ce que je sais bien, c'est que le jury, comprenant trois membres, avait abouti à l'unanimité au même choix. Quand le nom de l'artiste choisi fut connu, l'un des juges se mit fort en colère, paraît-il : tellement en colère qu'il en vint à faire des articles de journaux contre le jugement, bien qu'il en fût responsable, et contre l'auteur qui n'était point honoré de son agrément. . . .

On le comprend de reste, des concours, permettant de tels exemples d'indiscipline morale ou mentale, ne sont pas précisément de nature à orienter sérieusement les administrations dans une bonne voie sociale, ni à étendre les horizons de l'art, à la mesure progressive de la science Au contraire, il y a là une source de désordre. On peut donc assurer qu'il y aurait tout à faire, et quant à la valeur de concurrence et quant à l'esprit du jugement C'est là surtout ce qui m'intéressait dans la dixième question. Aussi voudrais-je arriver à la servir dans la mesure de mon pouvoir, en m'efforçant d'amorcer la solution, d'accord avec tous les points que le problème soulève.

Je me souviens d'un temps où la science ne montrait pas toujours l'ampleur, qui, depuis, s'est généralisée, après l'étendue des conceptions de savants tels que Claude-Bernard, Pasteur, sans compter d'autres illustrations internationales, à la fin du XIX° siècle. A une époque déjà reculée, il suffisait que la jeunesse montrât des aptitudes au calcul pour que l'on y vît un don scientifique Les idées ont changé ; on reconnaît même qu'un grand mathématicien pourrait être un mauvais calculateur. Il est vrai qu'alors les sciences bornaient leur action à imprimer les intelligences d'allures comptables. Tandis que, aujourd'hui, il n'est pas de sciences qui ne tendent à comprendre à la fois une instruction et une éducation des cerveaux, qu'elles ne connaissaient point auparavant. Et cela est général. Mais c'est peut-être en art—et dans le nôtre spécialement—que cet esprit restreint de comptable se trouverait encore le plus répandu, du fait d'années trop longues passées à emmagasiner des recettes de portée limitée. Celles-ci sont restreignantes pour les complexités ou les variétés qui se résumeraient en richesse intellectuelle ; elles n'aboutissent qu'à masquer la pratique effective des choses, et finalement il s'ensuit une sorte de paralysie d'innovation pour les cerveaux

Pourquoi n'apprenons nous pas tous, maîtres et élèves, à mieux faire ? Par un généreux échange d'idées plus larges, plus étendues, plus vastes, il y aurait avantage à s'attacher à un *idéal* qui serait déduit de connaissances approfondies, en opposition avec cette instruction négative qui reste dépourvue de portée. Apprenons tous à aimer la franchise de conceptions pouvant être *insolentes* d'apparence, tellement elles seraient voulues. Que les *partis* accusent donc les personnalités de leurs auteurs, en contradiction avec ces neutralités pleines de sagesse. Celles-ci ne sont, en effet, que des valeurs trompeuses et nullement encourageantes pour l'art ni pour la société.

Alors les partis de plan s'inspireront des repères importants de la localité, conformément à une allusion déjà faite dans une communication précédente.

Alors les silhouettes demanderont à l'ambiance du site l'inspiration de leur contour dans l'atmosphère.

Alors tous les reliefs de l'ordonnance monumentale seront étudiés directement en vue de l'impression unitaire que toute œuvre plastique doit laisser dans l'esprit.

Alors les sites urbains ou campagnards, intelligemment questionnés, répondront avec générosité. Des traces s'en retrouveront dans tous les édifices ou monuments. Et ceux-ci ne s'élèveront que pour procurer au public le charme qu'il est en droit d'attendre.

Ce début n'était peut-être pas inutile. Je crois au contraire qu'il s'ensuivra des facilités d'argumentation. Mais il ne faudrait pas oublier le titre de la question que nous avons à traiter : " Des concours internationaux publics d'architecture." Déjà les idées émises répondraient à l'objectif.

Dans un temps où *l'art public* et la *santé publique* intéressent toutes les nationalités, ou bien, pour être plus correct dans l'expression de notre pensée, dans un temps où tous les territoires présentent une utilité d'observations, qu'ils mettent à portée des intelligences, nous ne saurions dire combien seraient entrevus d'avantages à ce que, sauf exception, tous les concours d'architecture fussent internationaux et publics.

Il y a plusieurs raisons pour qu'il en soit ainsi :

Le *temps* que l'on a bien suffisamment remonté pour en connaître tous les gestes plastiques, pour en étudier les mobiles, n'a plus grand'chose à nous apprendre aujourd'hui. Ce qui n'empêche le cadre d'idées, qui s'en puisse tirer, d'être d'autant plus utile à l'artiste que la préoccupation d'être moderne s'accentue davantage. Voilà pour le *temps*. Mais c'est *l'espace* dont nous avons aussi à nous occuper maintenant et qu'il faut traverser pour le mieux connaître. Il y a là un objet important qui s'impose à nos investigations, aujourd'hui qu'il n'y a, pourrait-on dire, aucun point de la surface du globe où la civilisation, pourvue des coutumes affinées que nous attachons à ce mot, ne se soit montrée pour suppléer à la barbarie. Il en résulte que, pour être intelligemment modernes et pour aboutir à la plastique des ordonnances qui serait de nature à créer l'impression généreuse de la beauté, il faudrait se tenir au fait de ce que l'espace peut bien, comme le temps, livrer à nos méditations.

Ce n'est pas un long exposé de doctrine Les lignes précédentes suffisent comme indication des avantages qu'il y aurait à se tenir en garde contre la restriction des points de vue locaux ou nationaux

En art, comme en tout autre déploiement d'activité humaine, on ne saurait donc plus se désintéresser de ce qui se fait au-delà des frontières. Je ne vois donc rien qui ne soit pas en faveur des concours d'architecture internationalisés.

L'abondance et la richesse des œuvres y gagneraient. Elles remplaceraient, on peut du moins l'espérer, cette pauvreté désespérante que la mesquinerie des doctrines, transmises de siècle à siècle, tendrait à entretenir. Pour ma part, je ne doute pas que, du fait de l'entraînement, on n'arrive, en moins de temps qu'il n'en fallait jusqu'ici, à ouvrir les esprits plus largement à l'art, à créer des personnalités toujours grandissantes par le fait des expériences qu'une vie intelligente réserve à la volonté.

Je sais bien que les avantages manifestes, de soustraire en partie les jugements de concours à ce que j'appellerai la mode locale, risqueraient d'être contrebalancés par un inconvénient équivalent et correspondant aux habitudes que l'ambiance crée généralement et qui aboutissent à une sorte d'aveuglement de la mentalité en présence de solutions particulières ou inattendues Et bien, mais, si cet inconvénient n'est pas entièrement évitable, il est au moins réductible de façon assez sensible dans ses effets On y arriverait par la manière de constituer le jury. Il devrait être attentivement formé pour assurer le triomphe de la solution la plus remarquable, à l'exclusion de toute autre préoccupation quelle qu'elle soit, comme celle qui s'attacherait, par exemple, au succès des nationalités ou au succès des personnes

De même que pour la santé publique, l'exemple de toutes les nations concourrait désormais aux solutions les plus remarquables, en fait de beauté générale ; et, si l'une participe à leur développement physique, l'autre n'a pas une moindre importance par rapport au déploiement des élégances morales qui se répercutent sur tout notre monde social Comme il y aurait avantage à ce que les artistes puissent, de toute contrée, apporter leurs idées dans toute recherche attachée à la beauté des sites ; de même une semblable collaboration aurait un effet considérable sur la rectitude d'aménagement des services que demandent les édifices et sur la santé, dont l'ambiance matérielle de l'homme doit toujours être pourvue L'art et le goût publics, tels que nos sociétés contemporaines amènent à les envisager, trouveraient leur compte dans cet usage généralisé des concours publics et internationaux, en fait *d'architecture*

Pour traiter la question comme elle le mérite, pour être en état d'aborder les solutions réellement effectives qu'elle comporterait, il n'y aurait rien autre à considérer que l'éclat du dénouement. C'est là une chose qu'il conviendrait de servir, à l'exclusion des personnes qui, en la circonstance, ne peuvent exister à l'état prédominant. Cette préoccupation et le but à atteindre font penser à notre grand maître Delacroix disant : " Je n'aime plus que les choses. . "

Les architectes entrant dans la lutte d'un concours—pour être foncièrement dignes d'intérêt mental, pour aboutir à l'honneur d'œuvres accomplies—échappent fatalement aux mesquineries égoïstes Sans cela, le choix du parti et les études qui s'ensuivent se ressentiraient toujours d'une telle cause d'abaissement. Il en est de même pour la composition des jurys ; ils doivent être tels que la volonté des compétences réunies soit largement respectée dans son esprit et qu'on ne puisse pas douter de leur indépendance dans le jugement rendu.

Je ne veux pas oublier que cette dixième question comprend le mot d'organisation. Dans ma pensée, les concours internationaux entraîneraient un nombre égal de juges appartenant à chacune des nations pouvant compter des concurrents J'insiste sur ce point · aucune nationalité ne serait représentée dans le jury par plus d'une ou deux personnalités. Et la nation spécialement intéressée ne ferait pas exception à la règle répondant à une ligne de conduite très déterminée Alors on échapperait peut-être aux préjugés, élevés à la hauteur de doctrines à défendre. On éviterait ces sortes de délégations représentant leur pays et leurs concurrents. Rien qui puisse ressembler à mandants et mandataires. Rien que des juges véritables, par leur indépendance, en face de la solution qui s'imposerait à leur conscience

" Cela peut être bon," dira-t-on, "pour le choix des partis, sans autoriser un choix convenable des personnes auxquelles reviendraient les études

ultérieures et la direction des travaux d'exécution. Et vous admettrez
bien que ceux-ci demandent une expérience locale, dont les conditions,
pressenties dans votre proposition, ne tiendraient pas compte, vos jugements ainsi compris n'y interviendraient pas."

A cela nous répondrons: l'expérience des réalités de la vie conduit à
une netteté qui s'accuse de plus en plus. On en vient à redouter toutes
les restrictions mentales, parce qu'elles couvrent des iniquités, auxquelles
l'absence de rectitude morale peut aboutir.

Continuons donc. En ce qui touche les arrangements et toutes les
études que pourrait comprendre l'ordonnance plastique d'un parti judicieux,
il est clair que personne ne serait indiqué pour s'en acquitter avec la même
portée, le même goût, le même entrain, la même volonté effective de
réalisation que l'auteur primitif d'une pensée initiale, qui continue à
le prédominer. Au cours des communications précédentes que je m'honore
d'avoir présentées au VIIe Congrès, je crois bien avoir déjà eu l'occasion
d'insister sur l'importance qu'il y avait, en égard à l'unité d'art, à suivre
une œuvre dans toutes les phases de son élaboration

Cette source de beauté qu'est l'*unité* veut donc une œuvre suivie
Et je me contente ici de rappeler et d'affirmer l'utilité d'une volonté
prédominante en fait d'art Ce que je dis là s'attache à tous les détails
des ordonnances plastiques ; mais cela s'étend également aux modes de
construction qui, en architecture, il faut le reconnaître, font *tout un* avec
le motif plastiquement conçu, dont la réalisation se poursuit, toujours la
même, quel que soit le métier appelé à y concourir.

Reste encore la direction des travaux, pour laquelle on ferait intervenir l'expérience locale Eh bien, je n'hésite pas a maintenir que c'est
le même artiste qui doit conserver la haute main L'auteur du parti,
lui seul, est en état d'accomplir le rêve dont on s'est épris et dont il a longuement médité la conception. Tout autre que lui montrerait une autre
discipline mentale dans la réalisation et compromettrait en conséquence
l'œuvre que l'on avait en vue. Comment voudrait-on, par exemple, que
personne apportât la même vigilance à redouter les exécutions préten-
tieuses, que la *maestria* d'une volonté conceptrice est naturellement
conduite à écarter ?

On le voit, c'est donc uniquement l'architecte, choisi pour son parti,
qui sera responsable de l'exécution et qui saura la subordonner à l'unité
de sa volonté en art Autrement il n'y aurait que désordre, en suite des
responsabilités multiples portant sur les mêmes points.

La détermination du directeur des travaux ne peut donc être considérée comme une volonté à part, mais comme une suite inhérente au
premier choix émis par les juges.

Résumé.—L'argumentation qui précède a porté, en premier lieu, sur
l'esprit en général prédominant chez les architectes Contrairement aux
volontés d'une application généreuse de l'art, l'architecte paraît souvent
trop préoccupé de ne point faire certaines choses. Et l'on passe bien du
temps à connaître ces choses qu'il faut éviter. Années perdues ! semble-t-
il. Au lieu de cela, combien serait préférable une éducation envisageant
les réalisations à déduire de la science contemporaine ! Ce qui s'accorderait
avec la mesure des intelligences autorisée par l'expérience.

Les concours, tels que nous les voyons pratiqués, n'ont pas la portée
qui leur reviendrait. Les conventions tiennent trop de place, on y sent
des choses apprises. Comptabilité d'un nouveau genre et dépourvue
d'influence éducatrice sur la mentalité des masses

La *beauté publique* correspond, comme la *santé publique*, au mouvement contemporain de démocratie, dont ces deux chapitres sont les
couronnements du moment. L'architecte n'a pas le droit de s'en distraire,
s'il veut remplir la fonction attendue de la compétence sociale qu'il a pour
devoir de montrer.

L'internationalité et la publicité donneront aux concours une jeunesse et une vie qu'ils n'avaient pas jusqu'ici et qui rentrent bien dans le mouvement des activités contemporaines

Ces concours auraient exclusivement en vue les services dont ils seraient l'objet   Il faut qu'il en soit ainsi, pour assurer à l'opération une rectitude normale, qui la tienne au-dessus de mesquineries trop connues et diminutrices de l'art   Causes amoindrissantes pour les concurrents comme pour les juges et desservant les solutions à recueillir.

Les concours étant internationaux, les nations y prenant part du fait de leurs artistes comprendront toutes le *même nombre de juges*

De cette façon les agents de concours, que les juges représentent, seront sans doute moins portés à se prendre pour une délégation ayant à représenter des intérêts de compatriotes ou l'idée de mode couramment admise dans leur pays.   Ce jury sera plus particulièrement préoccupé de choisir et de faire aboutir une solution, comme les concurrents eux-mêmes, en *l'absence de toute représentation autorisée des idées préconçues, s'attacheront à élaborer et à présenter des partis, à l'exclusion de tout esprit de coterie*   Et, si l'on veut respecter les personnalités utiles en art comme en science, on ne saurait assez se tenir en garde contre ces influences néfastes.   En effet, quel que soit l'intérêt de l'évolution contemporaine si abondante en observations curieuses, en comparaisons généreuses dans leurs intelligences, la malechance veut, comme contrepartie, que nous subissions les idées étroites de petits groupes, de petits clans, qui viennent mettre le désordre dans le service de la collectivité humaine.   C'est cependant à elle que tous nos efforts devraient se rapporter directement, en dehors de tout encombre, socialement très regrettable.

Pour en finir avec ce résumé, en ce qui concerne les concours, je dois dire encore que l'esprit de l'argumentation poursuivie dans ces lignes s'attache à assurer la souveraineté du jugement, en confondant le choix de l'œuvre et le choix de l'artiste chargé de son exécution   L'auteur de la conception première devra donc en parfaire les études et accomplir la réalisation   Et le même esprit, que le jugement a entendu mettre en évidence, se retrouvera dans l'œuvre accomplie. C'est ainsi que les choses doivent tourner, si l'on veut obéir à la rectitude que la situation comporte et respecter la responsabilité que le jugement impose au jury

Et l'organisation, telle qu'elle est indiquée ici dans ses traits caractéristiques, serait appelée à donner des résultats encore imprévus.   Mais ce serait à la condition de toujours rester dans la voie que l'on pourrait normalement en déduire, une fois l'accord fait sur les idées qui appuient la solution que je soumets au Congrès

Conclusion.—Sans conscience, point d'art ni d'artiste   C'est seulement par une large compréhension des choses aboutissant toutes à la conscience de son temps et de l'humanité, que l'artiste peut faire œuvre utile   Par le temps qui court, l'élargissement de la science sert de base à cette conscience.   Et les applications de l'art prennent un caractère spécial pour répondre aux besoins et aux aspirations de l'époque.

L'organisation de concours internationaux, montrant une plus grande ampleur d'horizon intellectuel, s'accorderait avec l'idéal du jour.

Ils auraient encore l'avantage d'étendre le caractère d'éducations resté jusqu'ici assez restreint par rapport aux exigences actuelles

Mais il y aurait des mesures à prendre, pour assurer l'entière liberté d'épanouissement intellectuel parmi les artistes entrant en concurrence, pour permettre une indépendance sans borne au jury et pour éclairer la conscience du verdict qu'il rendrait.

3 Propositions of the Society " Architectura et Amicitia "
(Amsterdam)

La Société " Architectura et Amicitia " (siège social à Amsterdam) propose au Comité du Septième Congrès International des Architectes le règlement suivant pour servir de base à " l'organisation des concours internationaux publics d'architecture " Ces propositions, ayant été formulées par une commission spéciale des membres de notre société, ont été arrêtées et approuvées définitivement dans la réunion du 18 avril 1906

Art 1.—Le Congrès International des Architectes arrête un règlement d'après lequel se constituent des Commissions permanentes de concours représentant les architectes d'un pays ou bien de différentes nationalités combinées, qui agiront comme représentant la profession d'architecture dans les mesures préparatoires aux concours internationaux La Commission du pays dans lequel le concours aura lieu prendra la direction des affaires. Les présidents de toutes ces Commissions constituent ensemble un Conseil Central, auquel est confié le contrôle du règlement international et les propositions éventuelles auprès du Congrès International concernant des changements à effectuer dans ce règlement

Art 2 —Les concours internationaux se feront de préférence en deux étapes Des concours préparatoires seront ouverts dans les différents pays, ou groupes de pays, par l'entremise des commissions permanentes des concours. L'admission au concours définitif est limitée aux lauréats des concours préparatifs ; un honoraire sera rétribué à tous les concurrents du concours définitif, dont le nombre est limité pour chaque pays ou groupe de nationalités par le Congrès International

Art 3 —Les conditions du concours sont les mêmes pour tous les concurrents Des conditions exceptionnelles, n'importe sous quelle forme, sont prohibées L'envoi des projets se fait anonymement

Art 4 —La date de l'expédition, constatée par le timbre de la station de départ, qui doit être remis au jury, compte comme terme final de clôture du concours Le programme du concours devra être publié et mis à la disposition des requérants dans tous les pays ou groupes de pays à la même date.

Art 5 —Le jury d'un concours international sera constitué en principe de la moitié, moins un, de membres de la nationalité du pays dans lequel le concours est ouvert Des architectes devront former la majorité des membres du jury. Les noms des membres du jury et de leurs remplaçants, avec une déclaration qui porte l'approbation de toutes les conditions, seront insérés dans le programme

Art. 6 —Le jury du pays dans lequel le concours se tient forme le bureau d'informations La publication de ces informations se fera de telle sorte qu'elle puisse être considérée comme ayant pu atteindre tous les intéressés. Ces informations auront la même valeur que les conditions du programme

Art 7.—Le programme doit exprimer en termes précis les conditions posées, en distinguant les exigences absolues et les désiderata facultatifs Il serait préférable toutefois que des désiderata facultatifs ne figurent pas dans le programme de concours.

Art. 8.—Le nombre de pièces des envois sera restreint à la quantité absolument nécessaire afin d'éviter tout travail inutile, tous les frais superflus Pour les concours provisoires des esquisses, éventuellement accompagnées d'estimations approximatives, seront demandées. Les pièces d'un envoi qui ne sont pas demandées par le programme ne seront pas soumis à l'appréciation du jury. Le programme prescrit une manière uniforme de traiter les pièces du concours Tout envoi devra être accompagné d'une déclaration que le projet est la propriété artistique du concurrent.

L L

Art. 9.—Au cas où la somme disponible pour l'exécution du projet de concours est prescrite d'une manière absolue, le programme devra indiquer les détails nécessaires pour l'élaboration uniforme de l'estimation, soit détaillée, soit approximative, les frais de fondations ne seront pas compris dans le chiffre de ces estimations Le programme devra contenir des indications bien précises concernant le caractère du sol, concernant le site, l'assiette et l'entourage.

Art. 10.—Le montant total de tous les prix à distribuer sera au moins égal au double des honoraires, qui seraient rétribués, pour la partie du travail architecturale exécutée, à un architecte, auquel le projet aurait été confié. Il faut admettre comme principe que l'exécution du projet soit confiée à l'architecte couronné, sous les conditions qui sont en vigueur dans le pays du concours. Le montant du prix ne sera pas déduit du montant des honoraires à payer En cas que la personne ou la corporation qui ouvre le concours désirait se réserver la faculté de pouvoir se passer de l'architecte classé premier, le programme devra contenir les conditions d'indemnité. Dans le cas qu'aucune exécution n'aurait lieu la même indemnisation lui serait due. Dans tous les cas les projets envoyés, resteront la propriété artistique des concurrents

Art 11.—Tous les projets seront exposés dans un endroit et assez longtemps que tous les concurrents soient en état de visiter cette exposition, qui devra être annoncée d'avance dans les publications architecturales Le rapport complet et raisonné du jury sera publié dans les journaux d'architecture avant l'ouverture de l'exposition, que tous les intéressés puissent en prendre connaissance. Le rapport des conclusions du jury des concours préparatoires devra être communiqué aux lauréats à temps avant le concours définitif

Le Comité

Joseph Th J Cuypers
W. Kromhout Czn.
J. H. W. Leliman.
H. P. Berlage,
Président Société Architectura et Amicitia.
Paul J. de Jongh,
Secrétaire Société Architectura et Amicitia.

Amsterdam 24 avril 1906.

---

4 Communicated by P A Weeldenburg (Rotterdam)
for the Society " Bouwkunst en Vriendschap."

La Société " Bouwkunst en Vriendschap " de Rotterdam (Hollande), tout en reconnaissant la grande valeur initiative de la proposition faite par la Société " Architectura et Amicitia " d'Amsterdam pour la réglementation des concours internationaux d'architecture, juge que la proposition faite par la susdite Société doit obtenir une plus grande extension

Ce jugement est fondé sur l'expérience acquise au dernier concours international d'architecture pour le Palais de la Paix à la Haye. Ce dernier concours a clairement prouvé qu'il est nécessaire de paraphraser les principaux devoirs du jury des concours d'architecture en général et des concours internationaux en particulier

La Société Bouwkunst en Vriendschap de Rotterdam est d'opinion qu'il est préférable que la nouvelle rédaction soit étudiée par une commission spéciale et qu'une conclusion sera présentée au prochain VIII Congrès International des Architectes

Afin de donner une plus grande extension à la proposition faite par la Société Architectura et Amicitia d'Amsterdam, la Société Bouwkunst en Vriendschap a l'honneur de présenter au VII⁰ Congrès la motion suivante .

" La proposition de la Société 'Architectura et Amicitia' d'Amsterdam présentée au VII⁰ Congrès International des Architectes demandant d'obtenir une plus grande extension · Le Bureau du VII⁰ Congrès International des Architectes choisira une commission préparatoire dans laquelle la Société 'Architectura et Amicitia' d'Amsterdam sera représentée. Cette commission se composera de sept membres "

DISCUSSION ON SUBJECT X

Signor M. E CANNIZZARO (Italy) seconded the motion

M GEORGES HARMAND (France) said the subject was a most important one, and he thought the various records ought to be collected and sent to the Permanent Committee of the Congress , that Committee might study them and present a report to the next Congress He moved, as an amendment, " That the papers be sent to the Permanent Committee of the Congress, who shall get out a special report on this topic for the next Congress "

Mr. TOTTEN seconded the amendment, and said he would like the Committee to be instructed to suggest the method of the selection of the jury

Signor CANNIZZARO spoke in favour of sending the matter to a special committee of seven members elected or to be elected by the nations who constitute the Congress He objected strongly to the matter being sent to the Central Committee, because that Committee was only at the beginning of its experience , it was a Committee started at the last Congress, and its real duty was the organisation of the Congress. It was not a Committee which had to go over the topics discussed at the Congress, or to deliberate on matters which affected the profession all over the world. He thought the Special Committee, as suggested, should be selected, and that they should get to work and prepare a report which might be sent to the Central Committee and printed and distributed all over the world.

M HARMAND said that the Permanent Committee was established at the Paris Congress to choose the place of conference, and also the topics which should come before the Conference If they chose a Special Committee in the manner suggested what would become of it ? They would only have until Saturday to do the work, and that was altogether too short a time in which to deal with it When the Congress was closed it was only the Permanent Committee which was left. He thought the matter should be sent to the Permanent Committee and dealt with by them, as proposed by his amendment

Mr. TOTTEN thought that the Committee to deal with the subject should not consist of seven but of one representative of each country associated with the Congress.

Signor CANNIZZARO pointed out that this was the same thing as asking the Permanent Committee to take the matter in hand. After some further discussion Signor Cannizzaro appealed to M. Harmand to accept his motion.

M HARMAND thought it would be better to discuss the question the following morning.

The CHAIRMAN said the original proposition was to elect a committee of seven members, and the amendment of M. Harmand was to transfer the work to the Permanent Committee. There was, however, a way of uniting both parties by allowing a selected committee of seven to do the work until the close of the Congress, and they could submit their work to the Congress on Saturday, and it could then be transferred to the Permanent Committee He suggested that this was the best thing to do.

M. HARMAND agreed to the suggestion

Mr G A T MIDDLETON said he thought the amendment of M Harmand was a very reasonable one, and they ought not to appoint any Special Committee to go over the Permanent Committee

The proposition was then put as follows, and carried " That the Congress, taking into consideration the reports submitted, recommends them to the examination of the Permanent Committee of the Congress in order that they may submit a special report to the next Congress."

A delegate asked if the Permanent Committee would appoint a Special Committee, or would they do the work themselves ?

The CHAIRMAN pointed out that they had just decided that the work be referred to the Permanent Committee, and it would be for that Committee to consider whether they would appoint a sub-committee.

M AUGUSTIN REY (Architecte de la fondation Rothschild, Paris).— Messieurs, les Concours Internationaux Publics d'Architecture constituent un moyen pratique très efficace d'intéresser la grande foule à l'architecture contemporaine C'est un puissant instrument d'instruction publique auquel nous ne faisons pas suffisamment appel Nous devons reconnaître qu'une tendance marquée existe actuellement pour demander aux Concours Publics Internationaux la solution de certains grands problèmes d'esthétique. Nous avons tout intérêt à encourager cette tendance *Or il faut constater que les Concours Publics Internationaux deviennent toujours davantage un gros risque pour le concurrent qui y prend part.* Ce risque ne cesse d'augmenter le travail matériel de plus en plus considérable que l'on exige et constitue un véritable et dangereux abus Il semble hors de proportion trop souvent avec le montant des primes allouées qui rationnellement devraient fixer les limites du travail à accomplir *Il y a là une réforme qui s'impose si l'on veut ne pas voir nos grands Concours Internationaux frappés de discrédit auprès des Architectes de valeur* Il est nécessaire que le prochain Congrès International soit en mesure, après une discussion approfondie—le sujet mérite plusieurs séances—de voter un code que tous les Architectes du monde entier attendent Les deux importants rapports présentés à ce Congrès—et nous ne savons auquel des deux, celui de M. Guadet, preuve de sa vaste expérience, celui de la Société Architectura et Amicitia, d'une fougue entraînante, donner notre plus entière approbation—ont fourni les plus précieuses indications Nous saluons ces deux importants travaux qui doivent faciliter dans la plus large mesure et la tâche de la commission et celle de son futur Rapporteur. Un second point, sur lequel nous désirons attirer l'attention toute spéciale des membres du Congrès, est beaucoup plus grave Il s'agit d'assurer aux concurrents des garanties morales de la part des membres du jury, qui donnent à leurs jugements la plus haute valeur Dans les concours publics le jugement rendu est sans appel Nous nous rattachons pleinement à cet égard à ce qu'a si bien défini M Guadet dans son rapport Nous admettons avec lui qu'aucune méthode à la fois simple et pratique ne peut être substituée à celle de rendre un jugement de Concours Public d'Architecture sans appel *Or le pouvoir redoutable d'être juge sans appel doit donner, à ceux qui en ont accepté le privilège, d'offrir, de par l'acceptation d'être jurés, des garanties d'impartialité absolue vis-à-vis des travaux mis au concours.* Que vise un Architecte en prenant part à un Concours Public International ? Est-ce la prime ? Non, car elle est la plupart du temps dépassée, s'il l'obtient, par les frais qu'il expose en faisant ce Concours. Est-ce l'honneur ? Oui, certainement, l'honneur d'être dans les premiers classés, ou le premier même, ne peut lui être indifférent *Mais enfin comme on n'en vit pas, il vise autre chose : il vise, s'il arrive en tête, d'être chargé de la construction du monument qui a fait l'objet du concours*   Que l'on entoure l'exécution d'un monument mis au concours de toutes les précautions que l'on voudra , que cette exécution ne soit pas formellement promise au premier lauréat par le programme, on peut le comprendre dans certains cas   Que dans les autres cette exécution constitue la vraie prime, il n'y a là rien qué de tout naturel   Le rapport de la Société de nos Confrères de Hollande propose à cet égard les plus sages mesures.   Mais promise ou non promise au premier lauréat, il est de la plus haute justice qu'un Architecte qui sera arrivé premier—vainqueur de cette rude bataille qu'est un concours— ne trouve jamais devant lui pour lui disputer l'exécution un des propres membres du jury.   Cela est trop évident pour être l'objet d'aucune contestation.   Et cependant il est nécessaire de l'indiquer formellement dans le programme   Des faits récents—ils ne sont pas nombreux heureusement—pourraient cependant par leur grand retentissement, étant donné le Concours International important dont il est question, faire le plus grand tort au principe des concours publics   Ce principe doit être défendu et maintenu, malgré les défaillances qui se sont produites parfois.

M REY, in conclusion, moved the following resolution

Le programme doit déclarer que les membres du jury, par le fait de leur acceptation, n'ont et n'auront directement ou indirectement aucun intérêt matériel dans l'exécution des travaux mis au concours

The resolution was adopted unanimously, and it was agreed that it should be added to the reports submitted by M. Guadet and the Society " Architectura et Amicitia," which are to form the basis of the special report to be presented on the subject at the VIIIth International Congress.

M. REY expressed the opinion that in order that a Code regulating the Conditions of Public International Competitions might be presented and put to the vote at the next Congress, a smaller committee would be desirable.   He supported the proposition of M Cannizzaro and moved the following resolution

Qu'un rapport sur la question des Concours Publics Internationaux d'Architecture soit présenté au prochain Congrès International de 1908 par les soins de la Commission permanente, qui nommera à cet effet une commission spéciale de sept membres

Mr. MIDDLETON said he could see no reason for such a motion.   If the matter was referred to the Permanent Committee he did not see how they could tie their hands as to the way in which they thought best to deal with the subject   At present they would be left a free hand as to what sub-committee they would appoint

The CHAIRMAN remarked that that was exactly his own view

Mr. HARE suggested that it would be better to send the matter forward as a recommendation from the meeting rather than as a resolution.

Mr. TOTTEN then moved that the motion be sent forward as a recommendation, and it was seconded by M. Harmand, and carried.

RESOLUTIONS.

That the Congress, taking into consideration the reports submitted, recommends them to the examination of the Permanent Committee of the Congress in order that they may submit a special report to the next Congress.

The competition programme should declare that the members of the jury by the fact of their acceptation of the office have not and will not have directly or indirectly any material interest in the execution of works put up to competition.

RECOMMENDATION

That the Permanent Committee nominate a special commission of seven members to study the question of international public competitions and report to the next Congress.

EXTRA PAPERS

I NOTICE SUR LE CHÂTEAU DE SAINT-GERMAIN

Par Honoré Daumet, Membre de l'Institut de France.

Nous ne connaissons pas d'une manière précise l'origine du château de Saint-Germain-en-Laye, l'un des plus importants que possède la France. Les rois des deux premières races vinrent probablement se livrer au plaisir de la chasse dans les vastes forêts qui couvraient les collines au pied desquelles coule la Seine, mais nous n'avons point la certitude qu'ils y possédaient une habitation. Le roi Robert Ier fonda au commencement du XIe siècle une église sur le plateau qui domine le village du Pecq. C'est seulement au XIIe siècle que l'on constate d'une manière certaine qu'il existait une résidence royale là où s'élève le château actuel. Louis VI, qui régna de 1108 à 1137, est le premier souverain dont un document authentique nous révèle la présence à Saint-Germain. Ses successeurs y firent des séjours nombreux : c'est d'abord Louis VII qui y habita en 1143 et y tint une conférence avec le roi d'Angleterre Henri II, c'est Philippe-Auguste qui y rédigea son testament et bâtit la première chapelle du château. Saint Louis y reçut en 1247 l'empereur latin de Constantinople, Baudoin II, qui lui fit présent de reliques de la Passion ; pour les abriter, le pieux monarque ordonna la construction de la Sainte Chapelle du Palais à Paris.

Le château de Saint-Germain était donc au XIIIe siècle une demeure royale déjà importante : il comprenait alors, outre un donjon, deux corps de bâtiments formant logis, placés à la suite l'un de l'autre, dont les fondations subsistent encore et que des fouilles ont permis de reconnaître. La chapelle de Philippe-Auguste, trouvée insuffisante, fut remplacée sous le règne de saint Louis, entre 1230 et 1240, par un édifice plus somptueux qui s'est conservé presqu'intact jusqu'à nos jours : c'est un exemple d'architecture d'une remarquable beauté dont il est peut-être permis d'attribuer le mérite à Pierre de Montereau qui bâtissait à la même époque une partie de l'église abbatiale de Saint-Denis, car certains détails des deux monuments sont identiques.

Habité successivement par Philippe le Hardi, Philippe le Bel et Philippe de Valois, entouré d'un parc dont la première mention se rencontre en 1331, le château fut brûlé lors de l'invasion anglaise de 1346, mais la destruction ne fut pas totale : la chapelle échappa heureusement aux flammes et des mesures furent bientôt prises pour relever de ses ruines et agrandir une résidence où les différents souverains qui se succédaient trouvaient tant d'agrément. Charles V semble s'y être complu particulièrement, et nous savons qu'il y fit faire des travaux considérables : c'est à lui que l'on doit l'enceinte actuelle qui comprend dans son périmètre le gros donjon de Louis VI et la chapelle de saint Louis. Cette enceinte, fortifiée, affectait la forme d'un pentagone irrégulier, elle servit plus tard de soubassement aux constructions élevées sous le règne de François Ier. Habité encore par Charles VI, le château fut occupé pendant quelques années par une garnison anglaise   Il resta abandonné ensuite durant la fin du XVe et le commencement du XVIe siècle

François Ier en ordonna la réédification en suivant l'enceinte de Charles V · les nouveaux bâtiments durent s'élever rapidement, on y employa les matériaux les plus simples   L'œuvre du moyen âge disparut presqu'entièrement, sauf la chapelle qui resta debout, mais fut en partie masquée du côté de l'abside par des constructions neuves, tandis que la rose était aveuglée et écrasée par le mur de la Salle des Fêtes, salle magnifique représentée dans le précieux livre de Du Cerceau, *Les plus excellents Bastiments de France*, dont les dessins originaux appartiennent aujourd'hui au British Museum.   Du Cerceau ne nomme point l'architecte qui travailla sous les ordres de François Ier, mais on peut affirmer que c'était un novateur, car il n'existe pas de type d'architecture analogue à l'œuvre qu'il produisit , il suffit pour s'en convaincre de considérer l'aspect si original de l'extérieur, la beauté des escaliers et des voûtes qui ont été conservées, la majesté et l'ampleur de proportions de la Salle des Fêtes, dite de Mars, où se tenaient les grandes assemblées royales et les fêtes rendues si brillantes par le luxe et l'élégance qui distinguaient la cour des Valois   Henri II, comme son père, affectionna Saint-Germain   Philibert Delorme modifia la disposition de la chapelle et Guillaume Marchant commença à bâtir le *Château Neuf*, d'où l'on avait sur la vallée de la Seine une admirable vue.   Du *Château Neuf* il ne subsiste qu'un pavillon, dit de Henri IV, qui contient au rez-de-chaussée une curieuse salle en architecture rustique   Pour mettre en communication aisée les deux édifices, on perça dans le bâtiment sud du *Vieux Château* une porte qui était surmontée d'une fort belle sculpture, déposée maintenant au musée du Louvre et qu'on a fidèlement reproduite au-dessus de l'entrée actuelle. Les derniers Valois habitèrent peu Saint-Germain, à ce qu'il semble , Louis XIV s'y réfugia pendant la Fronde et y passa presque toute sa jeunesse   D'après ses ordres Jules-Hardouin Mansart ajouta au château cinq gros pavillons qui en modifièrent complètement l'aspect extérieur. La belle et originale ordonnance imaginée par le maître d'œuvres de la Renaissance impressionna sans doute l'architecte du XVIIe siècle qui l'imita, fait très remarquable pour l'époque , des balcons en fer forgé supportés par d'opulentes consoles régnèrent tout autour et les chemins de ronde du moyen âge furent convertis en terrasses   Le château avec les ailes ainsi bâties fut doublé en surface et la cour d'un monarque fastueux, avec ses multiples services, put s'y loger   On s'y assemblait et c'est là que furent célébrées notamment les fêtes du baptême du Grand Dauphin dont la représentation précise est fournie par des gravures de l'époque

Délaissé pour Versailles, Saint-Germain servit depuis 1689 à abriter une infortune royale : la famille des Stuarts y reçut l'hospitalité de Louis XIV. C'est là que moururent Jacques II en 1701 et sa femme Marie d'Este en 1718

Depuis ce temps le *Vieux Château* ne compte plus que pour l'histoire . sa magnifique Salle des Fêtes servit parfois à des représentations théâtrales ; en 1803 on projeta d'y établir un hôpital de 800 lits ; on y mit successivement une école de cavalerie, une caserne et un pénitencier militaire   C'est seulement en 1862 que l'architecte Eugène Millet commença les travaux de restauration dont on poursuit encore l'achèvement.   Le musée des *Antiquités Nationales* qu'on a installé dans le château de Saint-Germain assure la conservation d'un monument précieux par les souvenirs qu'il rappelle et par les traces matérielles que, malgré les remaniements et les mutilations, l'art français des plus belles époques y a laissées.[1]

---

[1] M Daumet has since presented to the Institute Library a copy of the interesting and beautifully illustrated monograph of the Château, written by himself and M G Daumet (fo Paris, 1905) --ED

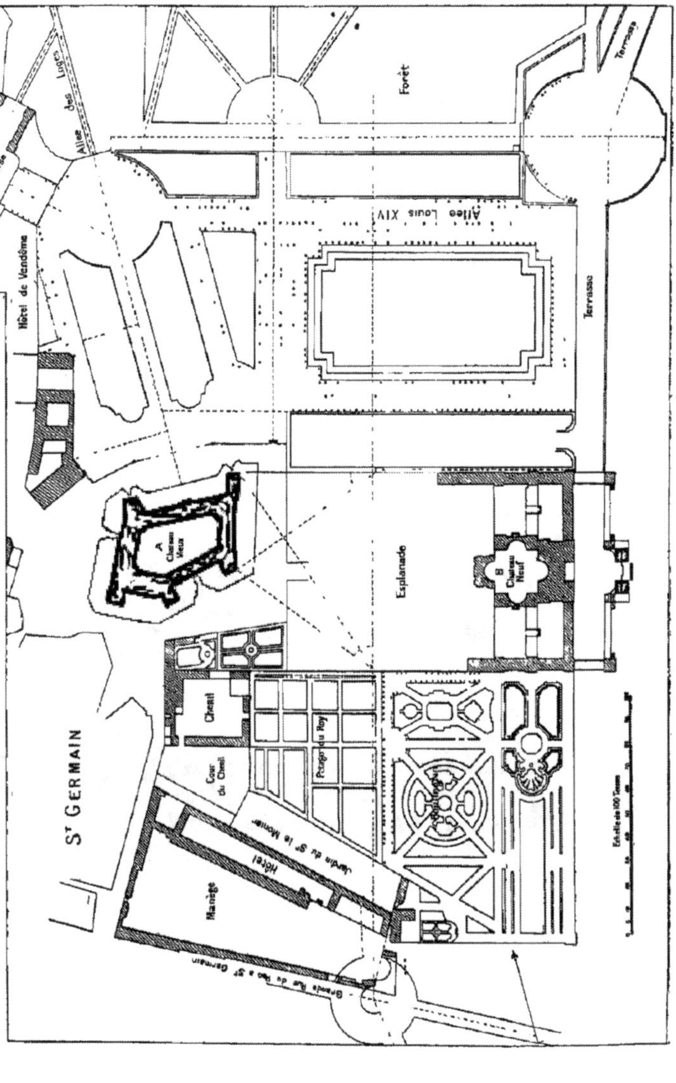

PLAN D'ENSEMBLE DES DEUX CHÂTEAUX DE SAINT-GERMAIN-EN-LAYE.

A Château Vieux de Charles V et de François Ier avec les Adjonctions de Louis XIV.
B Château Neuf commencé sous Henri II

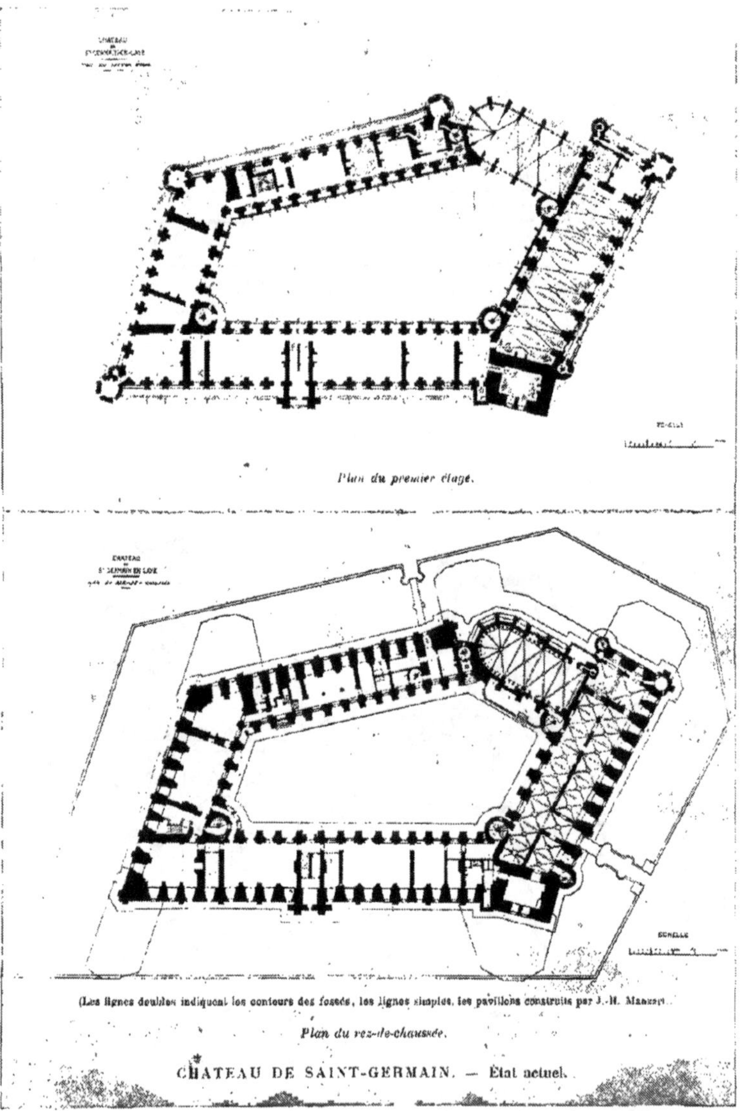

Plan du premier étage.

(Les lignes doubles indiquent les contours des fossés, les lignes simples, les pavillons construits par J.-H. Mansart.

Plan du rez-de-chaussée.

CHÂTEAU DE SAINT-GERMAIN. — État actuel.

From *Le Château de Saint-Germain-en-Laye*: by H. and G. Daumet [Paris 1905].

VOTE OF THANKS TO M. DAUMET.

The CHAIRMAN said they had listened to a most delightful paper, but he did not propose to detain them with any remarks of his own, for time was rather short and there were other papers to follow at eleven o'clock. Everyone would have liked to hear M. Daumet at greater length on a subject with which he was so thoroughly conversant.

Mr. R. PHENÉ SPIERS, speaking in French, said he had been asked to propose a vote of thanks to M. Daumet for the valuable paper he had prepared. It was not necessary that he should point to the fact, of which they had been able to judge themselves, that M Daumet had put his heart in this work, which he had had in hand for some years, and some of his life had been passed in working out the problems connected with the buildings and reconstruction and the various changes which had been made in it In the course of his work at the Château he had been able to make some remarkable discoveries—discoveries which would be of great interest, and he trusted it would be possible to publish a plan of what M Daumet had found. He had the advantage of going through the building some two years ago with M. Daumet, and seeing all the drawings illustrating it If a plan could be published it would render the description much more intelligible—a description which dealt with every historical point on which it was possible to throw any fresh light They owed M Daumet great thanks for coming there and giving them that discourse, and especially for the elaboration in it.

Signor CANNIZZARO seconded, and said that they all knew the work of M. Daumet at Saint-Germain. M. Daumet had given them the best example of what ought to be done in a work of restoration First of all he made himself familiar with the spirit of the time in which the building was erected, and thus, in carrying out the work of restoration, he was able to do the work as though it were being done by the original builders. That was the proper method to follow in restorations of this kind He thanked M. Daumet not only for his architectural work, but also for his archæological labours

Mr E. W. HUDSON supported the vote of thanks, and said he agreed with what Mr Spiers had said as to the one thing wanted to complete their satisfaction being a plan and some illustrations. It was very interesting to him to hear a description of this building, as he understood part of it was the work of Pierre de Montereau It seemed that there was some remarkable sculpture work in the keystones of the vaulting, especially the head of St Louis in stone , and it would be most interesting to have illustrations of the sculpture for the Institute *Journal*.

Lieut -Colonel PRENDERGAST said he desired to associate himself with what had been said by Mr Spiers. This was no ordinary occasion. It was an international congress of architects, and they were very grateful to those who had come long distances to help them in that which was the backbone of their existence—viz the love of architecture Naturally enough, the first paper came from our friends across the Channel, our nearest neighbours. We owed a great deal to France in our architectural work, and he associated himself with the thanks to M Daumet for his most interesting paper.

The vote of thanks was heartily agreed to.

M. DAUMET briefly replied, remarking that he was going to issue a work on Saint-Germain with illustrations.

The sitting then concluded.

II THE TOMB OF AGAMEMNON.

By Cecil Smith, LL D , Keeper of Greek and Roman Antiquities
at the British Museum.

The British Museum has recently become possessed of a monument—or
rather of part of a monument—of great interest in the history of Greek
architecture, and it is with much pleasure that I take the opportunity
kindly offered me by the Committee of the Architectural Congress of
presenting here the first published account of it   Through the generosity
of the Marquess of Sligo, three portions of shafts of the columns which
decorated the doorway.of the Treasury of Atreus at Mycenæ have been
presented to the nation. With the help of casts from portions existing
elsewhere, and with the addition of one or two fragments which were
already in the British Museum, we have been enabled to restore and set
them up, so that for the first time since the earthquake or vandalism
which overthrew them we can now see them once more approximately
in the form in which they stood at least 1,000 years B.c

Of course it must be understood that the re-discovery of the shafts
does not actually afford any new data for the restoration which were not
previously in existence. The portions of the columns which already
existed in different museums, compared with the traces left on the monument itself, were sufficient to permit of such a restoration, which has
indeed been more than once attempted on paper , but the new material
enables us to determine the true dimensions beyond all doubt, and makes
such a restoration more worth attempting.

The history of classical architecture has thus taken an important
step into the misty background which enshrouds its origins   Of these
origins we have been gradually learning to know something more in the
last twenty years, and particularly through the great discoveries of the
last seven years in Crete. The excavations of Dr Evans at Knossos
and of Prof Halbherr at Phæstos have shown us that it is here we must
look for the origins of all Hellenic culture. At present, however, the centre
of interest both at Knossos and Phæstos lies in a period which is far remote
from the classical age of Greece , before the first temple of classic order
arose on Greek soil, the age of Minos, from which that age descended, had
already passed into legend   The real connecting link between the two is
offered by the remains of Mycenæan populations on the mainland , above
all, the fortress towns of Mycenæ and Tiryns, of which the colossal "Cyclo-
pean " masonry of their walls has resisted the ravages of time. But
though the spade on these sites has revealed for us a marvellous picture
of the domestic life and thought of the Mycenæan world, of their architecture it has laid bare but little beyond the ground plans. Of the elevation of the Mycenæan palace or house our knowledge must still be based
largely on inference.   There is, however, one class of remains of which
the conditions of construction have favoured a more complete preservation,
and that is the so-called Treasuries or Tombs, which were intended to be
covered in earth, and which the kindly soil has preserved for us more or
less entire. Such buildings havé been discovered at Orchomenos in
Bœotia, at Menidi and Spata in Attica, and above all at Mycenæ, where
is the most famous of all, the " Treasury of Atreus " or " Tomb of Agamemnon "

Before the nineteenth century, such visitors as travelled in Argolis
regarded this building as the Tomb of Agamemnon. Peter Laurent in
his *Recollections of a Classical Tour made in* 1818–19, p. 146, says   " This
vault was for a long time denominated the Tomb of Agamemnon, and
Chateaubriand in his *Itinerary* mentions it as such   This traveller,"

he goes on to say, " certainly did stop in his hasty gallop across the Peloponnesus to look at Mycenæ through a spy-glass from the road, and to devote some moments to his romantic feelings, heated by so near a view of the kingdom of Agamemnon , but it should be recollected that Agamemnon and all those who were murdered at the banquet by Ægisthus are represented as having been buried within the citadel " That represents fairly well what was the accepted view at that period, a view which seemed to receive confirmation from the description of Pausanias, who mentions the " subterranean buildings belonging to Atreus and his children, where their treasures were kept." Comparison with other similar structures which have awaited the excavator more or less intact has shown that Chateaubriand was right and Pausanias was wrong , the buildings were tombs Moreover, they were, properly speaking, not usually subterranean.

The ordinary mode of construction was as follows Into the side of a hill a broad passage way (dromos) is driven, open to the sky and lined on each side with masonry, leading up to the doorway of the chamber itself This chamber is hollowed out of the earth (or sometimes partly built up and covered with heavy rocks and earth) in dome or " beehive " shape, and lined with regular concentric courses of squared masonry, narrowing gradually to a capstone at the summit A curious example of such a tomb in actual use occurs on an Attic vase in the British Museum, representing the beautiful myth of Glaukos and Polyeidos Here the beehive-shaped tomb chamber is shown in section, with the two figures inside, and a small tripod surmounting it as a kind of tomb monument This vase dates from the middle of the fifth century B C , it is hardly probable that the beehive tomb continued in use down to that date, but it shows at least that the tradition of it had survived, and indeed it is fairly certain that the Athenians of the time had access to some of the examples surviving from a previous age. For these tombs were not merely intended for the reception of the dead , the Greeks were from very early times devoted to ancestor-worship , by death they thought the mortal put on immortality, and the tomb was not only his resting-place, but a shrine at which his kinsfolk would at recurring intervals pay him semi-divine honours.

In two instances (the Treasury of Atreus and the similar tomb at Orchomenos) a smaller side chamber is added, at right angles to the axis of the tomb, and entered by a doorway in the centre of the right-hand side In the case before us this is excavated out of the rock, but the roughly hewn walls have probably been faced with a revetment, now lost Probably this side chamber was intended to receive the remains of less important members of the family, the poor relations, or the more precious of the offerings , in some of the later tombs the main receptacle is provided with a niche or pocket at one side to hold the offerings, possibly as a reminiscence of this custom

As the tomb chamber served the purpose of a shrine it was necessary that it should have a worthy passage and doorway ; but the " Treasury of Atreus " is the only example in which the architectural features are so imposing and the wealth of decoration so elaborate.

Before the beginning of last century the tomb was already rifled, and the upper part of the entrance was laid bare ; fragments of the richly sculptured decorations of the façade were still lying *in situ* , some small portions of these decorations have found their way into various museums , but the greater part has entirely disappeared It is possible, however, to reconstruct with more or less probability the main features of the architecture The doorway itself (measured from the floor, which is some four inches lower in the gangway than at the sides, probably owing to denudation) is eighteen feet one inch high and nine feet wide at the base, narrowing to eight feet three inches at the lintel The edge of the masonry immediately around it is enriched with two mouldings, of which the edges are curved , and on either side was a semi-column in dark-grey limestone, engaged, that is, with the flat or split surface attached to the wall.   It is these columns which are the principal subject of my paper this evening

In the years 1811-12 the second Marquess of Sligo visited Greece, and during his stay seems to have interested himself, as so many of the visitors of that time did, in acquiring a small collection of antiquities   Unfortunately no record appears to have been preserved in the family papers of the details of Lord Sligo's researches   The proceeds seem to have been, for the most part, at any rate, removed to the family estate of Westport, county Mayo, and it is only from an examination of these that an idea can be obtained of the field of his labours   There is, however, one mention in the literature of travel which associates him with the Treasury of Atreus   Laurent, in the work already quoted, p 145, describing that monument, says :

" During the stay of Lord Sligo in the Morea, excavations were made in this building under his direction and that of Veli, the Pasha of Tripolitza , we were informed that the result of these researches was the discovery of the shafts of two columns, without either capitals or bases , these were immediately presented to his lordship, who carefully transported the treasure to England."

Among the papers of Lord Elgin at Broomhall my colleague Mr Arthur Smith has recently found letters from Lusieri (the Neapolitan artist employed by Lord Elgin) which throw a somewhat different light on the affair.   In one of these, dated September 2, 1810, he says : " Veli Pacha de la Morée a fait excavation à Argos et Mycènes , il y a trouvé différents morceaux de sculpture, vendus à Messieurs Knight et Fazakerly, et deux colonnes données au marquis Sligo ; " and in another, dated September 4, 1811, " Veli Pacha de Tripolitza ayant entrepris des excavations dans la Morée a achevé celle du Tombeau d'Agamemnon, où il n'a pas trouvé que quelques morceaux de marbre   Dans un antre près de l'ancien théâtre d'Argos il trouva de petites statues d'un sculpture médiocre, qu'il fit vendre bien cher à M Fazakerly ; il fit présent d'autres marbres et vases à milord Sligo, qui lui coûtèrent aussi beaucoup, et qui valaient bien moins."

Veli Pasha's excavation does not appear to have amounted to very much, so far as the Treasury of Atreus was concerned   During the early years of the century the site was visited and described by several travellers , Dodwell was there in 1801-6, Gell at about the same time , Leake paid his second visit in 1806 ; and in 1801-5 the architect employed by Lord Elgin, Sébastien Ittar, of Catana, made drawings of what was then visible ; this last is also credited with an excavation, but this probably refers to some small clearing which was necessary for the purpose of making the drawings and plans.   One thing is certain from the evidence, that already before Lord Sligo's visit the columns were no longer in position , the space in front of the doorway and the whole of the dromos, or passage of approach, were still half choked with soil, which probably contained most of the remains of the decorative facing of the façade.   Leake in his *Morea*, ii p 374, says   "On my former visit to Mycenæ there were several large fragments of these semi-columns lying on the ground , I can now find only one or two very small pieces "   This was in 1806   Two small fragments came to the British Museum with the Elgin Collection, and are said by Dodwell to have been " found by the excavators of the Earl of Elgin " , two more from the Royal Institute of British Architects in 1843 , and a few others are scattered in European museums

A comparison of the views of the building drawn before and after Lord Sligo's visit seems to prove that Veli Pasha must have confined his attention possibly to the interior, but mainly at any rate to that part of the dromos immediately in front of the doorway.   In 1878 the

Archæological Society of Athens commissioned M Stamatakis to make a complete clearance of the entire soil and rubbish encumbering the monument, a drawing made shortly before this shows the condition much as in Gell's and the Elgin drawings, only on the sides near the entrance are traces of sinkings in the soil, which may very likely be those caused by Veli Pasha's excavation

The columns were each carved, as the marks of attachment show, in two solid blocks, each about eight feet long, joined together half-way up ; weighty objects such as these could not be easily moved, and when in the first disintegration of the building they fell forward from their place they would probably lie not far away from their original position   One half-column was quarried out probably by the builders of a Turkish mosque   In 1812 Baron Haller, the companion of Cockerell in the famous enterprise at Ægina, saw it at Argos lying outside the great mosque there ; subsequently Colonel Mure (1838) describes what was probably the same half-column as " forming the architrave of a building at Nauplia, formerly a Turkish mosque, in which the Courts of Justice held their sittings." It has now been rescued, and is worthily set up in the national museum at Athens

From 1812 onwards the remaining three halves of the columns remained *perdus*   It was only last year that the Earl of Altamont, son of the present Marquess of Sligo, in the course of studying the ancient monuments at Westport, was led to the conclusion that certain columns in the collection were of unusual importance , he made careful drawings and photographs of them, which were brought to the British Museum , the probability that the Westport objects were the missing decorations of the Treasury of Atreus was at once evident on a consideration of the facts above stated   Lord Altamont soon afterwards paid a visit to Mycenæ for the express purpose of comparing his measurements with the traces left *in situ*, and the result leaves hardly any doubt that the surmise is correct.   The credit of this interesting discovery is thus due to Lord Altamont

The reconstruction of the columns was a matter of some trouble, in which I was fortunate in having the assistance of the Messrs Pinker and Holcombe, our skilled masons at the Museum   The first question was to decide which shafts belonged to which side   for this purpose I asked Mr Carr Bosanquet, Director of the British School at Athens, who very kindly had drawings made for me of the bases which are still *in situ*.   These bases are formed out of bluish yellow breccia blocks which are sunk to the level of the lowest step and bedded with cement, the block being, as may be seen, considerably larger in plan than that part of it which forms the stepped base.   An instance of the absence of symmetry which obtains all through the construction of the Treasury is shown in the upper surface of the left-hand base, of which the plan, instead of being rectangular, takes the form of a trapezium.   Fortunately the same irregularity has been observed in making the cramp holes to receive the lower shafts of the columns , and, as we possess the lower edge of one shaft with its cramp holes, it was easy to decide that the two larger portions of shaft, forming nearly one entire column, must belong to the left-hand base.   This column is larger in section than the other by one inch all the way up   It has thus, with the ornamental pattern to help us, been possible to deduce with practical certainty the exact position of every fragment   The upper portion of the right-hand column is the part which has been already mentioned as built into a mosque at Argos , in the Athens Museum it is set up by the side of a partial restoration of the two capitals. Unluckily the Turkish architect, whether because he objected to a curved face of his lintel or for some other reason, has sliced off a wide strip of the front throughout the whole length.   The accompanying illustration also shows the two capitals, with the original fragments existing

at Athens inserted in a restoration , by the kindness of the authorities at
Berlin and Karlsruhe I was enabled to get casts of the important fragments there preserved   The Athenian restorations required some small
corrections, which the other fragments enabled us to make , and it then
became perfectly clear that one cap was of appreciably larger dimensions
than the other.   It was thus an easy matter to determine which capital
belonged to which column

In our restoration, as set up in the Archaic Room of the British Museum,
a distinction is observed throughout between pure restoration in plaster
and casts inserted from originals which still exist.   The latter are coloured
a slaty bluish tint, while the restoration is in buff.   In the illustration it
may be seen that, although all is in plaster, sufficient of the original is
represented to make the completion of the cap justifiable   As there was
no apparent variation in the pattern all round it was sufficient to ake a
squeeze of the original portion and repeat it as long as was required

In most of the former restorations of these capitals, it may be remembered, the angles of the pattern on the echinus are made to run outwards
from a diamond-shaped centre   Curiously enough, this error is not found
in the earliest, that of Lord Elgin s architect Ittar, but seems to have
begun with Donaldson, although he based his design on Ittar ; it has
continued, together with an entirely unworthy rendering of the charming
leaf pattern below the echinus, even down to that excellent work of
Puchstein, *Das Ionische Capitel* · now, I hope, it is laid for ever.

Here then are the columns as set up in the British Museum , the bases
have been reproduced as nearly as possible in a material which was the
closest approximation to the original procurable, a marble called " brèche
d'or "   The originals presented by Lord Sligo can be clearly distinguished
in the illustration ; what is not so clear is the small piece of the leaf pattern
under the right-hand echinus, which came to the Museum with the Elgin
Collection, and the fragment on the right-hand shaft presented in 1843
by the Royal Institute of British Architects   These little waifs have at
last returned to what I trust is their original home

I have already alluded to the absence of precision in the working of
these columns, which amounts almost to carelessness   Both in the
shafts and in the capitals an instance of this is to be seen in the way in
which the pattern is not worked out to the edges , on the shafts especially
the edges where they meet the wall are left altogether unworked, so that
a straight-edge can be passed along them and is perfectly true   This may
be partly due to the desire to strengthen a fragile part , but that does not
account for the neglect of the pattern, which sometimes extends as much as
four inches from the edge   It looks as if the columns had been sculptured
with the decoration after they were fixed in position , if that were so, on
the outer edges particularly it would be difficult to get this point of view,
and so the artist may have thought it of less importance

The shaft, which is 18 feet 3¾ ins high, is 1 ft 10 ins in diameter at the
lower extremity and 2 ft. at the upper, showing a taper downwards of 2 ins
This peculiarity, which is also found, of course, in the pillar of the well-
known Lion gate at Mycenæ, is of common occurrence in the Minoan
period in Crete, though not by any means universal   In the temple
fresco at Knossos no less than three such columns are shown, of slightly
varying forms , these columns may, for various reasons, be inferred to be of
wood, and hence their rather squat form and the base or socket in which
the central one rests   The Atreus columns are far more attenuated,
having in the shaft 9½ diameters against only 5½ at Knossos   This is only
what we might expect in the translation from wood into stone, and for the
same reason we may be prepared for the minute base at Mycenæ.   What is
the reason of the tapering form ?   Various theories have been suggested.
M. Perrot supposes that it came about through the necessity of pointing
the end of the wooden post in order to fix it in the ground, but he seems

to me to stultify his argument by an attempt to explain the base " Experience," he says, " taught men later to interpose a slab or cube of stone between the post and the rain-soaked soil " Surely if the slab of stone is there, the sharpening of the extremity is rather a drawback than otherwise ? I do not know that I can suggest a more satisfactory solution , certainly it is to Egypt that we must look, and in Egypt there is one form of column—that imitated from the bundle of reeds—which tapers towards the base. Whatever the origin, there is no doubt that the downward taper answers a special purpose here, where it serves to correct, as it were, to the eye the outward slope of the two sides of the doorway,

The practice of decorating the shafts of columns is, of course, native in Egypt , it is interesting to observe that in the palace of Tell el Amarna Mr Petrie found the fragment of a column shaft decorated with a pattern closely resembling that of the Atreus columns [1] Now there is evidence at Tell el Amarna of the influence of Cretan or Minoan artists having been at work there , and I think we may conclude that this style of decoration grew out of the contact of Cretans with Egypt The decoration of the echinus is unusual; the nearest parallel in later times is perhaps the series of Doric capitals at Pæstum, which are given in Schuchhardt's *Das Ionische Capitel*, pp. 48-9

The function of the columns here is probably mainly decorative, as they are not calculated to support much superincumbent weight beyond that of the lower projecting courses above the doorway

The question of the decoration of the façade above the doorway is one of considerable difficulty , we are bound, I think, to assume a revetment of sculptured slabs, but though several suitable fragments exist, it is only an assumption that these belong to this part of the building, and not one scrap remains in its original place. I hope before long to obtain casts of all these fragments, and after examination of them to visit Mycenæ and see whether any certain data can be laid down beyond what we already know

When Cockerell was in Athens, at the beginning of last century, a Turkish official one day asked him how Englishmen amused themselves in Greece His reply was, In examining antiquities and ancient cities celebrated in the accounts of historians. The next question was, Do those same historians in their accounts ever tell you where to find sequins ?

When we look back on the roll of distinguished names of Englishmen who played so prominent a part among the pioneers of archæology in Greece—Dodwell, Leake, Gell, Cockerell, and others—without hope of " sequins " but merely for the advancement of science—I think we may claim, before even an international audience, that England has done something to deserve the heritage of Greek originals which has fallen to her share, and of which the columns shown this evening are the latest and not the least important example.

DISCUSSION.

Sir Henry Howorth said that it was very seldom that one met with a student either of archæology or science who had the gift of describing with great precision of language and without useless rhetoric an admirable monument like that under discussion. It was Mr Smith's quick eye which first recognised the importance of these fragments, and they could hardly appreciate, unless they knew the history of the past few months at the Museum, the pains and care and skill which he had shown in restoring this gateway. One thing that struck him was, how it came about that archi-

[1] Cf Evans in *B S l* vii p 55

COLUMNS FROM THE DOORWAY
OF THE TREASURY OF ATREUS
AT MYCENAE

tects who had designed so many classical buildings, both in ancient and modern times, should have abandoned this most beautiful and graceful method of dealing with pillars. Pillars were very difficult things to ornament Here, however, they had a method of decorating pillars which to him seemed graceful, and which did not in the slightest degree appear to weaken them as supports. He hoped they might see someone attempt to imitate in a measure this method of treating pillars and pilasters.

Professor BALDWIN BROWN asked the lecturer whether he had made up his mind as to the reason for the tapering downwards of the columns, which, of course, was not the ordinary way for columns to taper in later architecture, and also whether he had formed any idea of the origin of the ornamentation of the columns—whether it was transferred from some other material, or whether it was developed on the stone itself. He had listened with great interest to the lecture. Not long ago he was on the spot, and it revived one's impressions to see the whole thing brought forward in a lucid manner.

Mr J D CRACE said he would like to know whether in the course of the many excavations which had been made any trace of the metal lining of the interior had been found

Mr. H. H. STATHAM proposed a hearty vote of thanks to Mr Cecil Smith for his exceedingly learned and interesting paper

Mr. FRANK T. BAGGALLAY seconded the motion.

Mr. R PHENÉ SPIERS, referring to Professor Baldwin Brown's question, said that there was no possible doubt whatever as to the columns tapering downwards in the frieze discovered at Knossos The frieze exhibited on the screen showed a decided tendency in that direction, and Dr. Evans had found traces of the ends of the columns still remaining, and also, in one or two cases, impressions of their form in places they used to occupy in portions of the palace He was therefore able at once to decide that these columns tapered downwards with a considerable diminution of diameter. As for the reason why the columns should be put into this position, it would seem that the Cretans, who were the first people they knew of to use them (because they are not found in Egypt), were sufficiently acquainted with the qualities of timber to know that the trunk of a tree, when cut off and utilised, would support an equal weight, whether put into the natural position or turned upside down They also found that when reversed it lasted twice as long, because the rain could not penetrate the outside There was another probable reason. The wooden architraves carried by these columns were rather large, and had to carry cross beams, and therefore as wide a support as possible was needed, given by the increased dimension of the upper diameter. The columns they found at Mycenæ followed in all respects the downward taper of those at Knossos, but there was this great difference, that the one was in wood and the other in stone. From the decorative point of view, and utilised as they were in the Tomb of Agamemnon, there was no reason why they should not follow the same custom ; but it was certain that if the column had been an isolated feature it would not have been strong enough to carry any such weight as that required. Therefore it was, he thought, as a decorative feature attached to the tomb that the column in stone was made to taper downwards. He had one apology to make. He would not have ventured to make a restoration had he not been absolutely obliged to do something of the sort. He found that there was not a single drawing of any kind which had the slightest resemblance to the actual features now set up in the British Museum. He found that the drawings made by Lord Elgin's artist were quite wrong. They were beautiful drawings, but the details were all wrong, and he was forced to make a restoration himself, to publish in a new edition of a work he had written.

The motion was then carried.

M M

Mr. CECIL SMITH, in reply, said he had tried to deal with the question of the tapering downwards of the columns in his paper   With regard to Mr. Grace's question he believed that no portion of the metal had been found at all, but a few of the nails which fastened the decoration had been known to exist. It was only assumption that the decoration was of metal, but there were reasons for supposing it was. As regards the origin of the decoration of the columns, he believed it extremely likely that the decoration also originated in metal   It was necessary in a climate which was very bad in the winter that wooden columns should be protected as far as possible, and this spiral decoration was the commonest form of decoration of all Mycenæan metal work   He thought it very likely that the wooden column had first been covered with a coating of metal , and that subsequently, in imitating the wooden column in stone, they also imitated the metal covering of the wood in the stone. He should be glad to assist anyone in the gathering who would care to visit the British Museum and see the restoration.

[*Note*.—Since the above paper was written, the cast of a fragment of one of the columns preserved in the Munich Museum has been received, which modifies the reconstruction as here given. Mr. Cecil Smith proposes to deal with the new material in a more detailed study of the Tomb of Agamemnon, which will shortly appear in the JOURNAL of the Royal Institute of British Architects.—ED]

III MÉTHODE POUR RELEVER LES MONUMENTS D'ARCHITECTURE PAR LA MÉTROPHOTOGRAPHIE.

Par MARCEL LE TOURNEAU,
Architecte Diplômé par le Gouvernement Français, Boursier de Voyage du Ministère de l'Instruction Publique et des Beaux-Arts , Chargé de Missions.

HISTORIQUE.

La métrophotographie a été étudié et créée par le colonel Laussedat, un illustre savant français, membre de l'Institut, ancien directeur du Conservatoire National des Arts et Métiers. Sa méthode est maintenant appliquée dans tous les pays du globe.

Au moment de la découverte de la photographie les savants français ont prévu son utilisation au relevé des monuments   Arago, notamment, en 1839, prévoyait cette utilisation en termes explicites, dans des communications à la Chambre des Députés et à l'Académie.   Jomard et Caristie déduisaient des géométraux d'après des vues prises à la chambre claire et les publiaient dans le grand ouvrage sur l'expédition d'Egypte. Enfin, en 1850, après les perfectionnements apportés à la construction des appareils photographiques, on effectuait sur une vue photographique de l'église de Santa-Maria delle Grazie de Milan la transformation des perspective en géométraux   Depuis ces travaux les architectes français, et M. Lebon, ont souvent utilisé les propriétés géométriques des photographies pour leurs besoins personnels   Mais ces travaux n'ont jamais été faits systématiquement et avec des appareils spéciaux, du moins en France

En 1903, au moment où une mission m'était confiée, j'ai été mis en rapport avec le colonel Laussedat, et j'ai été convaincu des avantages de la métrophographie.   Ayant fait transformer mes appareils, j'ai effectué plusieurs voyages en 1903, 1904, 1905 en Grèce, en Turquie et en Macédoine. J'ai rapporté de ces voyages plus de 200 vues du format 13/18 pour une vingtaine de monuments ; et j'ai fait les géométraux de deux églises, l'un exposé au Salon de 1904, l'autre, très important, au Salon de cette année.

AVANTAGES DE LA MÉTROPHOTOGRAPHIE.

Ces avantages sont les suivants

On obtient des documents d'une exactitude absolue et incontestable, sans crainte d'erreur de cote, sans intervention de la personnalité de l'artiste, avec des contrôles ultérieurs possibles, puisque les clichés subsistent.

On peut relever exactement des monuments inaccessibles, en totalité, ou en partie, grâce aux différentes combinaisons d'objectifs.

Les opérations sur le terrain sont réduites au minimum, pour être reportées au bureau du dessinateur Il suffit, en effet, de prendre des clichés méthodiquement, soit en ceinturant l'édifice. Les autres opérations se font où et quand il plaît à l'artiste, et elles peuvent être exécutées par un opérateur et un dessinateur connaissant la perspective

EXPOSÉ DE LA METHODE.

Elle est basée sur l'emploi des propriétés géométriques des photographies de monuments convenablement prises avec des appareils de précision Ces photographies représentent en perspective, sur un tableau plan vertical, les monuments à restituer. Pour faire cette restitution il est nécessaire de retrouver la ligne d'horizon, le point de fuite principal, la distance du point de vue au tableau, et de connaître la dimension réelle d'un des objets représentés. On détermine facilement ces éléments avec un appareil photographique de précision, et un mètre donne la grandeur réelle d'un des éléments photographiés. Quand ces éléments sont déterminés la restitution des dimensions réelles du monument s'obtient en résolvant le problème inverse de la perspective

APPAREILS À EMPLOYER

Il faut donc employer un appareil de précision donnant une image plane, verticale, sans déformation, et tenant sur cette image la ligne d'horizon, la ligne principale, permettant de connaître la distance du point de vue au tableau

Mon appareil donne tous ces éléments Il se compose d'une chambre en bois, à tirage du format 13/18, montée sur pieds, au moyen d'un support à 3 vis calantes et à cercle horizontal Elle est munie de deux niveaux en croix et le châssis porte 4 pointes déterminant 2 lignes à angle droit. Les déplacements de l'objectif et du châssis sont mesurés au moyen de règles graduées et de verniers. La position du point nodal, pour chaque objectif, est connue.

Un dispositif spécial, applicable en cas de besoin, permet de donner une position inclinée à la chambre, et d'obtenir encore des perspectives coniques pouvant servir de base à des restitutions géométrales. Ce dispositif consiste essentiellement dans un cadre en forme de ⊔ vissé sur le pied, lequel cadre supporte au moyen de pivots deux branches en croix formant un plan vertical. Ces branches reçoivent la chambre photographique. Le dispositif a été combiné de telle façon que l'axe de rotation est horizontal et parallèle à la droite horizontale formée par l'intersection du plateau et de la planchette porte-objectif. L'angle d'inclinaison se voit à simple lecture par la position d'un index mobile sur un cercle divisé fixe

USAGE DES APPAREILS

La métrophotographie doit être employée avec ordre et méthode, faute de quoi on ne retrouverait plus pour chaque cliché les éléments nécessaires à son utilisation Chaque cliché doit donc avoir son dossier, dans lequel on a noté : 1° le n° du cliché ; 2° le n° du châssis employé, 3° la combinaison d'objectif employée ; 4° le tirage de la chambre, 5° et 6° les déplacements de l'objectif, 7° l'angle d'inclinaison, 8° l'angle de visée horizontale par rapport au cliché précédent près du même point ; 9' le diaphragme employé, 10' le temps de pose, 11° le sujet photographié, avec les différentes remarques

Le cliché doit être le meilleur possible au point de vue optique et au point de vue géométrique   Pour cela la chambre doit être stable et bien horizontale.

Les clichés doivent être fins dans toute leur profondeur et sans opposition, c.-à-d. pris avec de faibles ouvertures et légèrement surexposés, et en diminuant les contrastes dans le monument à photographier

Il importe surtout de ne laisser échapper aucun détail intéressant, et de relier entre eux tous le clichés. de façon à n'avoir aucune interruption dans le relevé du monument.

CRITIQUE DE LA METHODE.

La plaque sensible étant une surface gauche, le cliché obtenu présente des déformations

Le gauchissement de la plaque est, par rapport à la distance focale (surtout en employant des objectifs à long foyer), d'un ordre tel que les déformations de l'image sont nulles. On pourrait, d'ailleurs, avoir des plaques sensibles absolument planes, en faisant étendre l'émulsion sensible sur des glaces

Le cliché et l'épreuve varient à chaque instant de surface. Cette variation empêcherait, en effet, de déduire les dimensions réelles et fixes des édifices, si l'élément mesuré ne variait pas dans la même proportion que l'ensemble du cliché et du papier   Or ce n'est pas le cas. Ses variations sont proportionnelles. Par conséquent chaque épreuve est une perspective de surface variable, il est vrai, mais qui permet de restituer avec exactitude les dimensions réelles du monument

CATALOGUE

OF THE

EXHIBITION OF BRITISH ARCHITECTURE (INCLUDING WATER-COLOURS, MEASURED DRAWINGS, PLANS, PHOTOGRAPHS), FURNITURE AND SILVERWORK,

held in the Grafton Galleries, 16–21 July

[NOTE.—*The Catalogue, which has been slightly abridged for the purposes of the present publication, was prepared by Mr. Ralph Straus, B.A., late Scholar of Pembroke College, Cambridge, who acted as Secretary of the Exhibition Sub-Committee*]

PREFACE TO THE CATALOGUE.

" The Exhibition is divided into eight sections, of which six deal with purely architectural subjects, one with British furniture, which is generally allowed to be closely connected with architecture, and one with British silver-work   Of the first six sections four go to make up what may be termed a fair representation, arranged chronologically, of British architecture.   These are entirely confined to the long galleries Having decided that the exhibition most interesting to architects would take the form of a collection of plans and measured drawings, supplemented by photographs, the Committee have endeavoured to illustrate in this way such buildings as appeared most representative of their particular type.   The period so covered begins at the Norman Conquest and ends in 1860, the year in which Sir Charles Barry, R A, died.   It will be noted that, where possible, original drawings have been secured, although it was found necessary to include certain reproductions to complete the scheme of the Exhibition

" The large galleries contain a small collection of water-colour paintings dealing with British architectural subjects

" In the lower gallery a series of photographs forms a more or less representative exhibition of the work of living British architects

" It was never the Committee's intention to bring together what might be termed properly a representative collection of British furniture   Very much more space than that allowed by a single room in the galleries would have to be filled if the collection were to be representative in the fullest sense.   But in assigning a certain portion of the Exhibition to furniture the Committee have been actuated by a desire to show some few specimens of British work more or less illustrative of their own particular school or period.   The pieces shown all come out of private collections now in London.   The same may be said of the silver-work, exhibited with the furniture, in the lower gallery.   There are very few pieces of silver, but each is of great individual interest, and some are now exhibited for the first time.

" The Committee desire to take this opportunity of expressing their thanks to all those who have in one way or another helped them in their work.   " RALPH STRAUS "

NORMAN AND EARLY GOTHIC SECTION
First Long Gallery.

In this and the next Section certain photographs by S Gardner, Esq., were lent by the Architectural Association and the remainder by Messrs S. B Bolas & Co.

P = Photograph   M D = Measured Drawing   GEN VIEW = General View

1–9 DURHAM CATHEDRAL, DURHAM —1 P The Galilee, looking S E 2 P Exterior, N side 3 P Nave, looking E 4 Plan showing ancient arrangements (based on plan by J Carter, 1801) 5 Plan of Monastic Buildings 6. P. Interior, looking W., showing Choir Vaulting. 7 P. View inside S Triforium of Choir 8 M.D N aisle of Choir, Plan of Vault. 9. M.D Elevation of Bay of Choir, N side, and half section of Choir. *See also* Nos 199–203 (Nos 4 and 5 *lent by W. St John Hope, Esq , F.S.A* Nos. 8 and 9 *lent by John Bilson, Esq , F S A*)

10 BARFRESTON CHURCH, KENT —P South Doorway

11 BRISTOL CATHEDRAL, SOMERSET —P. Chapter House, looking W *See also Nos.* 206–209

12–14. IFFLEY CHURCH, OXON —12. P W Doorway 13 P S. Doorway 14 P Exterior from N W

15–27 ST ALBANS CATHEDRAL, HERTS.—15 M D Longitudinal Section, looking N. 16 M.D S Elevation 17 M D E Elevation. 18 M D Ground Plan 19. P Crossing, looking W 20 Perspective View, from S E 21 P View in Nave, looking N 22 M D Bay of Choir, and Bay in S Transept. 23 M D Elevation of Tower 24 M D Section through Saint's Chapel 25. M.D Section through N. Aisle of Sanctuary 26 M D. Bay of Nave, S. side 27 M.D Bay of Nave, N side *See also* Nos 273–281 (Nos 15–18, 20, and 22–27 *lent by Jas Neale, Esq , F S A*)

28–35 PETERBOROUGH CATHEDRAL, NORTHANTS —28 M.D S Aisle of Choir, Plan of Vault. 29. M D Historical Ground Plan R W Paul 30 P. View of S Aisle, showing Vaulting 31 P View of Aisle, S. side, looking W 32 P View of Exterior from W 33 P. Interior, looking W 34 P. Triforium of Choir, N. side. 35 P View into N. Transept from Crossing *See also* Nos 242–243 (No 28 *lent by J. Bilson, Esq , F S A* No. 29 *lent by " The Builder* ")

36–39 NORWICH CATHEDRAL, NORFOLK —36 P Exterior, E end 37 P View from S W 38 P. The Presbytery, looking E 39 M D Historical Ground Plan J Repton *Lent by " The Builder"* *See also* Nos 174–175.

40–41 GLOUCESTER CATHEDRAL, GLOS —40 P Nave Arcade, N side 41 M D Historical Ground Plan · F S Waller *Lent by " The Builder"* *See also* Nos 300–306

42–52A CANTERBURY CATHEDRAL, KENT —42 P Exterior, Transepts, S side 43 P Exterior, S E end 44 Historical Ground Plan G Smith 45. P Vault of Ambulatory 46 P Piers of Choir, S side 47 P Interior, the Choir looking E 48 P The Apse 49 P. View of Eastern Transepts looking S across Choir 50 P Triforium 51 P Staircase of King's School 52 P The Crypt 52A. Crypt of Trinity Chapel (No. 44 *lent by " The Builder"* *See also Nos.* 216–221)

53 MALMESBURY ABBEY, GLOUCESTER —M D S Aisle of Nave, Plan of Vault John Bilson, Esq , F S A

54–55. ROMSEY ABBEY, HANTS —54 P Interior, Arcade on N side of Nave 55 P Exterior view of N side

57 LUDLOW CASTLE, SHROPSHIRE P Doorway to Round Chapel in Courtyard W Wonnacott

58–63 ROCHESTER CATHEDRAL, KENT —58. P. Vaulting of Choir 59 P Nave Arcade, N side 60 P The Transepts, N side, exterior 61 M D Historical Ground Plan of Church and Monastery. W St John Hope 62 P Nave, looking W 63 P Western Entrance (No 61 *lent by W H. St. John Hope, Esq , F S A*)

64–65. FOUNTAINS ABBEY, YORKS —64 M D Historical Ground Plan Harold Brakspear, F S A 65 M D One Bay of Choir, Interior and Exterior, and Plan, W end of Nave · Edmund Sharpe (No. 64 *lent by Harold Brakspear, Esq , F S A.*)

66 BEAULIEU ABBEY, HANTS —M D. Historical Ground Plan. Harold Brakspear, F S A *Lent by the Author*

67 WAVERLEY ABBEY, SURREY —M D Historical Ground Plan. Harold Brakspear, F S A *Lent by the Author*

68. GLASTONBURY ABBEY, SOMERSET.—M.D Ground Plan of Church   W. St. John Hope, F S A   *Lent by the Author*

69. WATTON PRIORY, YORKS —M D. Historical Ground Plan   Harold Brakspear, F S A , and W St John Hope   *Lent by the Authors*

70 HAYLES ABBEY, GLOUCESTER —M D Ground Plan   Harold Brakspear, F S A   *Lent by the Author.*

71. BURNHAM ABBEY, BUCKS —M D. Site Plan   Harold Brakspear, F S A   *Lent by the Author*

72 MOUNT GRACE CHARTERHOUSE, YORKS —M D Historical Ground Plan   W St John Hope, F S A   *Lent by the Author*

73-74 FURNESS ABBEY, LANCASHIRE —73 M D Historical Ground Plan   W St John Hope, F S A   74 M D Six Bays of Nave.   Edmund Sharpe   (No. 73 *lent by W. St. John Hope, Esq , F.S.A*)

75 CASTLE ACRE PRIORY, NORFOLK —M D Historical Ground Plan   W. St John Hope, F S A   *Lent by the Author.*

76 LACOCK ABBEY, WILTS —M D Ground Plan   Harold Brakspear, F S A   *See also* No. 342

77 HEDON CHURCH, YORKS —M D Elevation of N Transept   C de Gruchy

78-79 RIEVAULX ABBEY, YORKS —78 M.D. Longitudinal Section of Choir   79. M.D. South Elevation of Choir   Edmund Sharpe

80-85 WELLS CATHEDRAL, SOMERSET —80 M D. Plan of Nave and Cloisters   J T Irvine (1875)   83 Historical Plan (after Professor Willis, 1851)   84 P W Front   85 P Western Entrance   *See also* No 210-215   (Nos 80 and 83 *lent by the Dean and Chapter of Wells*)

81-82 WHITBY ABBEY, YORKS —81 M D Ground Plan   Roland W Paul   82 M D. Transverse Section of Choir   Edmund Sharpe   (No 81 *lent by* " *The Builder* ")

86 ELY CATHEDRAL, CAMBRIDGE —P West Doorway and Galilee Porch   W Wonnacott   *See also* Nos 176-188

87-90 SOUTHWELL CATHEDRAL, NOTTS —87 P Exterior, view from N W   88 P Interior, Nave looking E   89 P Choir looking E   90 P North Porch

91-93 HEXHAM ABBEY, NORTHUMBERLAND —91 M D Choir, Longitudinal Section   92 M D Two Bays of North Transept, east side   93 M D North Elevation   *Lent by C C Hodges, Esq*

94-98 STEWKLEY CHURCH, BUCKS —94 M D Ground Plan   95 M D S Elevation   96 Sketch of Interior   97 M D Longitudinal Section   98 End Elevations and Section   *Lent by W A Forsyth, Esq*

{ 99-103 CHRISTCHURCH PRIORY, HANTS —99 M D Longitudinal Section   100 M D Ground Plan   101 M D North Elevation   102 M D Elevations and Sections   103 Various details   *Lent by C J Coombs, Esq   See also* Nos 148 and 149

104-110. BEVERLEY MINSTER, YORKS —104 M D Historical Ground Plan   John Bilson, F.S A   105 P. Interior looking E.   W. Wonnacott   106 P Exterior View of St Transept   107. P Nave looking E   W Wonnacott   108 P. Triforium of Transept   109 M D S Transept Doorway   Edward Healey   *See also* Nos. 170-173   (No 140 *lent by J Bilson, Esq , F S A*)

111 SKELTON CHURCH, YORKS —M D Plan, Elevations, and Sections   *Lent by Arthur Stratton, Esq*

112 WARMINGTON CHURCH, NORTHANTS —M D Plan, Elevation, and details of Vault and one Bay of Nave   *Lent by C D Oliver, Esq*

113-123 LINCOLN MINSTER, LINCOLN —113 M D Ground Plan   A B Pite   114 P West Front   115 P Nave looking W   116 P Choir looking E   117 P. Chapter House   118 P Exterior S side of Choir   119 P Triforium of N Transept   120 P Triforium of Nave   121 P Triforium of Angel Choir   122 P Wall of Angel Choir   123 M D One Bay of the Angel Choir   *Lent by Sydney Vacher, Esq   See also* Nos 144-146

124-130 SALISBURY CATHEDRAL, WILTS —124 M.D Historical Ground Plan   R W Paul   125 P Western Entrance   126 P View of West Front   127. P Interior of Nave   128 P N Aisle looking W   129 P View from Choir looking W   130 P Choir looking W   (No 124 *lent by* " *The Builder* ")

131-141 WESTMINSTER ABBEY, LONDON —131 Water-colour Drawing, Spandrils of Chapter House Doorway   T M Rooke   132 Ground Plan showing dates of work.   133 P S Transept and View into Choir.   134. P The Apse   135 P View across Transepts showing Choir   136 P View in Nave looking E   137 P Triforium of N Transept.   138 P Triforium of S Transept   139 P S. side of Nave with Cloister   140 P Triforium of S Transept   141 M D One Bay of Sacrarium, N side   E Emlyn White   *See also* Nos 228-232, 312-323, and 333-335   (No 131 *lent by the Artist   No 132 lent by J T. Micklethwaite, Esq , F S A   No 141 lent by the Architectural Association*)

MIDDLE AND LATE GOTHIC SECTION.

First Long Gallery.

142-143 SNETTISHAM CHURCH, NORFOLK —142 P Gen View 143 P West Window

144-147. LINCOLN CATHEDRAL —144 P Bishop Longland's Chantry. 145 P Cloisters. 146. P Central Tower 147 Sketch. Central Tower and Galilee Porch · C. E. Mallows *Lent by the Artist.* (*See also* Nos 113-123, and 731.)

148-149 CHRISTCHURCH PRIORY —148 P Gen View from E. 149 P. Interior of Choir (*See also* Nos 99-103)

150-152 CHICHESTER CATHEDRAL —150. Plan *Lent by " The Builder "* 151 P E. end of Lady Chapel 152 P Cloisters and End of Nave

153-159 WINCHESTER CATHEDRAL —153, 154 M D F C Nash. 155 Plan *Lent by " The Builder "* 156 P Arcading at back of Reredos. 157 P. Nave looking E 158 P South Aisle looking W 159. P W Door York Cathedral

160-164 YORK CATHEDRAL.—160 P View from W. 161 P Nave looking W 162 P. Chapter House 163, 164 M D Bay of Chapter House and of N. Aisle C Spooner

165. CHESTER CATHEDRAL.—P. Tower (*See also* No. 795)

166 LICHFIELD CATHEDRAL.—P E End

167-169 ST MARY, BEVERLEY —M D N Aisle of Choir and Plan C. de Gruchy

170-173. BEVERLEY MINSTER.—170, 171 P Percy Shrine 172 P Screen 173. P Transept (*See also* Nos 104-110, and 732)

174-175 NORWICH CATHEDRAL —174 P Flying Buttresses of Choir 175 P Corner of Cloister (*See also* Nos 36-39.)

176-189. ELY CATHEDRAL —176 M D Presbytery Arcade 177-179 M D Prior Crawden's Chapel C. Spooner. 180. Plan. *Lent by " The Builder."* 181-182 P Interior, looking W , and Interior of Crossing and Choir. 183 Sketch of Central Tower and Transept : A N Wilson. 184 P N. Aisle of Choir 185-186. M D Lady Chapel : L Stokes. 187, 188. Sketches, Lady Chapel J J Joass 189 P Lady Chapel Arcading. (*See also* Nos 86, 760, 764, 805, and 806)

190-198. EXETER CATHEDRAL —190 P Vaulting in Nave 191 P W Front, Details 192 P Tower from Palace Garden 193 P. E. End 194 Plan *Lent by " The Builder "* 195 Sketch · A N Wilson 196. P. Nave, looking W. 197 P Choir Screen 198. P Choir, looking E

199-203 DURHAM CATHEDRAL —199 M D East Wall of Nine Altars Chapel . C Spooner 200 P Gen View from S E 201. P. Bishop's Throne 202. P Central Tower, &c. 203 P Arcade in Central Tower (*See also* Nos. 1-9)

204-205 ELEANOR CROSS, NORTHAMPTON 204. P. Gen. View 205 M D. South Elevation W A Forsyth *Lent by Northampton County Council*

206-209 BRISTOL CATHEDRAL —206 P Door in Retro Choir. 207. Plan *Lent by " The Builder "* 208. P Vaulting in Berkeley Chapel Vestibule 209 P. Retro-Choir, looking E (*See also* No. 11)

210-215 WELLS CATHEDRAL —210 P Exterior, N. side 211. P Interior of Choir, E End 212 Plan *Lent by " The Builder."* 213 P E End of Choir. 214 P Bridge to Vicar's Close 215 P Interior of Lady Chapel (*See also* Nos 80-85)

216-221. CANTERBURY CATHEDRAL.—216 P Tombs of Archbishops Peckham and Warham 217 P Cloisters 218 P Gen View from S W 219 P. Nave looking E 220. P S Aisles and Transept 221. M.D Plan · G Smith. *Lent by the Dean and Chapter.* (*See also* Nos 42-52A.)

222-227 WORCESTER CATHEDRAL —222. P S. Choir Transept 223 P N Cloister 224 Plan. *Lent by " The Builder "* 225 P Cloisters and Tower 226. P Prince Arthur's Chantry 227 P Nave, looking E

228-231 WESTMINSTER ABBEY.—228-231 M D S E Angle of Cloisters . F. Winton Newman (*See also* Nos 131-141, 312-323, 333-335, and 804.)

232 DORCHESTER ABBEY, OXFORD —P. Interior

233 SHERINGHAM CHURCH, NORFOLK —P. Rood Loft

234-240. PARTINGTON CHURCH, NORTHANTS.—234-237. M D Plan, N. Elevation, Section, and Details 238. P Gen. View 239 P Interior 240. M D E Elevation. *Lent by Messrs Paley and Austin*

241. BOSTON CHURCH, LINCOLNSHIRE —P Tower from West.

242-243. PETERBOROUGH CATHEDRAL —242 P Retro-Choir Interior 243. P East End (*See also* Nos 28-35)

244-245. HECKINGTON CHURCH, LINCOLNSHIRE, Sedilia.—244 M D Gen. Drawing.
　　　245 M D Details　J J Cresswell
　　246. KNAPTON CHURCH, NORFOLK —M D Roof of Nave　J J Joass.
247-248　HOUGHTON-LE-DALE, NORFOLK —247 P Gen View　248 M D. Elevation
　　　and Details · J. J Joass
　　249　CROMER CHURCH —P Gen View
　　250　SHOTTESBROOKE CHURCH, BERKS.—M D A. B Mitchell
251-253　EDINGTON CHURCH, WILTS —M.D C E Ponting　*See also* 439.
　　254　SALISBURY CATHEDRAL —P Spire
255-256　CARLISLE CATHEDRAL —255 P Choir Interior.　256 P N Aisle
257-258　WALSOKEN CHURCH, NORFOLK —257 P Bench Ends　258 P Porch and
　　　Clerestory
259-262. GREYFRIARS CHURCH, STIRLING —259, 260, and 262 M D　J J. Joass.
　　　261 Sketch of Exterior.
　　263. OXBURGH HALL, NORFOLK —P. Three views *lent by Editor of " Country
　　　Life."*
　　264　HOREHAM HALL, ESSEX —Two views *lent by Editor of " Country Life."*
　　265　ST CROSS HOSPITAL, HANTS —P Tower
266-267　ATHELHAMPTON, DORSET —266 P The E Gable.　267 Exterior of Parlour.
268-269. EAST BARSHAM —P Two Doorways　*See also* No 800
270-272. COMPTON WYNYATES, WARWICK —270 P South Front　271 S W. View.
　　　272. Gateway　(Nos. 266-272 *lent by the Editor of " Country Life "*)
273-281　ST ALBANS CATHEDRAL —273 P St Alban's Shrine　274, 275, 276 M D
　　　Chantrey of Abbot Ramryge　C de Gruchy　277 M D Roof of Choir.
　　　J J Joass　278 P Watch in Loft and Shrine of St Alban　279 P.
　　　Reredos　280 P Lady Chapel　281 P Organ Screen　*See also* Nos.
　　　15-27
282-285　SELBY ABBEY —282 P S Side.　283. P. E. End　284 P Gen View.
　　　285 S Aisle of Nave
286-290　HEREFORD CATHEDRAL.—286. P. Exterior from N W.　287. Plan.　*Lent
　　　by " The Builder."*　288 P N Porch　289 P Bishop Stanbury's
　　　Chantry　290 P S Transept
　　291. LAVENHAM CHURCH, NORFOLK —P S Side
　　292　BLYTHBURGH CHURCH, NORFOLK —M D Roof of Nave and Choir · J J
　　　Joass　*See also* No 807.
293-294. TRUNCH CHURCH, NORFOLK —293 Sketch of Baptistery　Sir C A Nicholson,
　　　Bart　294 M D Detail of Chancel Screen · J J Joass
　　295　WALSINGHAM CHURCH, NORFOLK —P Font
　　296　SOUTHWOLD CHURCH —M D Detail of Chancel Screen · J J Joass.
　　297　MAGDALEN COLL , OXFORD —P Tower
298-299　CHRIST CHURCH CATHEDRAL, OXFORD —298 P Interior of Choir　299 P
　　　Detail of Vault of Choir　*See also* No 810
300-306. GLOUCESTER CATHEDRAL —300 P Sedilia.　301. P. Cloisters　302 P Tower
　　　and S Porch　303. P Choir, looking E　304 P. Lady Chapel, looking
　　　W.　305, 306 Sketches, Cloisters　C E Mallows　*See also* Nos 40-41.
307-311. KING'S COLL CHAPEL, CAMB —307 P. Porch　308 P Detail of Interior.
　　　309. P Gen View Interior　310 P Exterior, S　311 P Exterior, W
312-323　WESTMINSTER ABBEY —312 P Ground Plan　313 Bishop Islip's Chantry
　　　314 M D Henry V's Chantry　G T McCombie　Henry VII Chapel
　　　315. P S Aisle.　316 P. Interior, looking W　317 Tomb　318 P
　　　Interior, looking W　319 P Interior, showing Vaulting　320. P. Detail
　　　of Gates　321 Exterior, N E Side.　322 M D Screen of Henry VII
　　　Tomb · H O. Cresswell　323. M D. Plan of Chantry of Henry V. : G T
　　　McCombie.　*See also* Nos 131-141, 228-231, 333-335, and 804

EARLY RENAISSANCE SECTION.

Second Long Gallery.

A number of photographic views, &c., were lent by B T Batsford, Esq

　　324　OCKELLS, BERKSHIRE (early 16th cent)
　　325　HOLBEIN GATE, WHITEHALL, LONDON.—Erected by Henry VIII (c 1535)
　　　From a design attributed to Hans Holbein　Original drawing by George
　　　Vertue (1648-1756)　*Lent by Walter Spiers, Esq*
　　326　HATFIELD, HERTFORDSHIRE —P Old Palace
　　327　EAST BARSHAM HALL, NORFOLK (1500-15) —P Gen View.
　　328. MELCOMBE BINGHAM, DORSET.—P. Gen View
　　329　THORNBURY CASTLE, GLOS —P. Gen. View
　　330　HARGRAVE HALL, SUFFOLK.—P Entrance.

LATER RENAISSANCE' SECTION.

Second Long Gallery.

A number of photographic views &c were lent by B T. Batsford, Esq.

516–521 RAYNHAM HALL, NORFOLK (1630) —516 M D E Front   517 Plans 518. E and W Elevations, M.D   519 M D W. Front · H Inigo Trigge 520 P Entrance Front   521. P Entrance.
522 BANQUETING HALL, WHITEHALL —P. Inigo Jones.
523 WILTON HOUSE, WILTS —P S Front   Inigo Jones
524–527 DESIGNS FOR A PALACE (WHITEHALL) —W Kent   *Lent by the R I B A (Burlington Collection)*
528–529 YORK WATER GATE, THAMES EMBANKMENT —Inigo Jones M D F W Newman
530–534 ASHBURNHAM HOUSE, WESTMINSTER —530–532. M D Staircase and Drawing Room H Sirr   533 D Staircase W Wonnacott   *Lent by the Artist.* 534 P Staircase
535–536 ELEVATIONS BY J WEBB —*Lent by the R I B A. (Burlington Collection)*
537–538 THORPE HALL, PETERBOROUGH —537 P S Front   538 P Staircase
539 TYTTENHANGER, HERTS —P. S Front
540 WIDCOMBE, BATH —P Gen View
541 ASHMOLEAN MUSEUM, OXFORD —P Entrance
542 TOWN HALL, ABINGDON —Christopher Kempster   P General View.
543 THE CASTLE, NOTTINGHAM —P. E Front
544 ASHDOWN, BERKS —P Gen View
545 GROOMBRIDGE PLACE, SUSSEX —P W Front
546 CHAPEL, KING CHARLES THE MARTYR, TUNBRIDGE WELLS —P The Ceiling.
547 HOUSE AT ELTHAM —P Staircase
548 THE CUSTOMS HOUSE, KING'S LYNN —P Gen. View
549–556 GREENWICH HOSPITAL —Sir Christopher Wren and others   549 M D W. Elevation 550. M D King Charles's Palace   551 M D King Charles's Palace, River Front.   552 M D Detail of Dome and portion of Colonnade   553 M D Portion of River Front to half-inch Scale C J Macdonald. 554 P Colonnade   555 P View of Main Building   556 P Gen View
557 TRINITY COLLEGE, OXFORD —P Interior of Chapel
558 ST LAWRENCE JEWRY —P Vestry
559 ORIGINAL SKETCH.—Sir Christopher Wren
560. TEMPLE BAR.—P Gen View (as re-erected at Theobald's Park, Herts). *Lent by W H Watts, Esq*
561. ST STEPHEN, WALBROOK —Sir C Wren M D Transverse Section looking E W Grellier   *Lent by the Victoria and Albert Museum*
562 GREENWICH HOSPITAL —Original Sketch for Dome Sir C Wren   *Lent by the R I B A*
563–573 ST PAUL'S CATHEDRAL —Sir C Wren   563, 564 M D Design for the first Cathedral, measured from the Model E C. Sayer. *See also Nos 565–568* M D Morning Chapel: T H Watson *Lent by the Victoria and Albert Museum.* 569 P S Aisle   570 P View from the Steeple of St Martin's, Ludgate   571 P View from N.W.   572 Choir Stalls   573 P. Interior
574–575. ST JAMES'S, PICCADILLY —574 M D Sections L Wilkinson   *Lent by the Victoria and Albert Museum*
576 ST VEDAST, FOSTER LANE.—P Steeple
577 ST DUNSTAN-IN-THE-EAST —P Steeple
578 ST MARTIN, LUDGATE —P View from S W
579 ST MAGNUS, LONDON BRIDGE —P Steeple.
580–581. ST MARY-LE-BOW —580 P Steeple. 581 M D Tower and Spire . J T Christopher
582 ST STEPHEN, WALBROOK —P Steeple.
583 ST MICHAEL, CORNHILL —P Tower
584 CHRIST CHURCH, NEWGATE —P Steeple
585 ST CLEMENT DANES —P Steeple.
586 ST BRIDE, FLEET STREET —P Steeple
587. ST MICHAEL, PATERNOSTER ROYAL —P Steeple
588–592 HAMPTON COURT PALACE —Sir C Wren   588–590 M D River and Garden Fronts H P. G Maule   591. P Fountain Court   592 P River Front
593 CHELSEA HOSPITAL —P Interior of Chapel.
594–596 CHRIST'S HOSPITAL—594, 595. M D S Front : F. J. Wass   596 P. S Front
597 HOUSE IN WEST STREET, CHICHESTER —P Gen View
598–603 MORDEN COLLEGE, BLACKHEATH —598–602. M D T F Green   603. P Entrance and Portion of Court
604 ALL SAINTS', NORTHAMPTON —P. Portico
605–607 WOLVESLEY HOUSE, WINCHESTER —605, 606 M D Screen in Chapel and Garden Front. L G Detmar   607 P Parts of N and S Front.
608 KENSINGTON GARDENS —P Alcove and Banqueting Hall
609 ROCHESTER CATHEDRAL —P. Gen. View

610-611. TRINITY COLLEGE, CAMBRIDGE, LIBRARY.—610 P. Interior. 611 P Exterior.
   612. GATEHOUSE, MIDDLE TEMPLE LANE —M D Elevation to Fleet Street. A E Richardson
613-615 GUILDFORD GUILDHALL —613, 614 M D Front and Side Elevations : R. W Schultze and H Read *Lent by the Victoria and Albert Museum.* 615 P. Gen View
   616 HAM HOUSE, PETERSHAM —P Entrance Front.
   617. MELTON CONSTABLE, NORFOLK —P. Garden Front.
   618 LUCAS ASYLUM, WOKINGHAM.—P Gen View
   619 HONINGTON HALL, WILTS —P Gen View
   620. STAMFORD —P. Houses near St George's Church.
   621 CLARE COLLEGE, CAMBRIDGE —P Gen View.
622-623 NEW RIVER OFFICES, CLERKENWELL —M.D. Woodwork, Withdrawing Room T F Green
624-625. SALISBURY —House in the Close   624. M D Entrance Front · R S Balfour. 625 P Gen. View
   626 SENATE HOUSE, CAMBRIDGE —P Interior
   627 ST MARY-LE-STRAND.—P. Gen. View from W.
   628. CASTLE HOWARD, YORKS.—P Gen View.
   629. RADCLIFFE LIBRARY, OXFORD —P Exterior
   630 ST. MARTIN-IN-THE-FIELDS, LONDON —P View from N W
631-633 HOUGHTON HALL, NORFOLK —631, 632 M D Plan and Elevations S Towse 633 P. Entrance Front
   634 HORSE GUARDS.—W Kent P W Front
635-637 BLENHEIM PALACE, OXON.—635 P Principal Entrance   636 P E Front. 637. P N. Front
   638 SEATON DELAVAL, NORTHUMBERLAND —P Entrance and Garden Front.
   639 CHRIST CHURCH, SPITALFIELDS —P. View of W End
   640 ST GEORGE, BLOOMSBURY —P View from S E
641-643 ST MARY WOOLNOTH (1716) —Nicholas Hawksmoor. M.D. Plan and Sections. A C. Blossom
   644 ST GILES-IN-THE-FIELDS —P Steeple.
   645 ST PHILIP'S, BIRMINGHAM Aldrich P W Trout.
   646. ST. CATHARINE'S HALL, CAMBRIDGE —P. Gen View
   647 PRIOR PARK, BATH.—P Garden Front
   648 HOUSES IN CAVENDISH SQUARE, LONDON —P Gen View
   649 TREASURY BUILDINGS.—W Kent P Gen. View
650-651 SOMERSET HOUSE —650 P View in Courtyard   651 P. Water Gate.
   652 BOODLE'S CLUB —P Gen View
653-654 CUSTOMS HOUSE, DUBLIN —James Gandon M D River Front and Detail of Dome H. H Hill.
   655 ELY HOUSE, DOVER STREET, LONDON —P. Gen View
   656 CORPUS CHRISTI COLLEGE, OXFORD.—656 P Peckwater Quad
657-658 ALL SAINTS, OXFORD —657. P Steeple   658 View from High Street.
659-660 THE WELLINGTON ARCH.—Decimus Burton   659. P Gen View   660 P Screen, Hyde Park Corner
   661. ELMES' DESIGN FOR ASSIZE COURTS, LIVERPOOL.—Redrawn by R. P Jones
662-667 ST GEORGE'S HALL, LIVERPOOL —662, 663. M D Section through Great Hall and S. Elevation · R P Jones 664 W. Elevation Sketch · R. P. Jones 665 Original Drawing by H. L Elmes. *Lent by the R.I.B.A.* 666. P View from S.W   667. P View from S E.
   668. TAYLOR AND RANDOLPH BUILDINGS, OXFORD —C R Cockerell P. Gen View.
   669 BANK OF ENGLAND, Liverpool Branch —C. R Cockerell P Gen View
   670 CLIEFDEN —E M Barry, R A , from designs by Sir Charles Barry, R A Drawing by E M. Barry, R A *Lent by W Bottomley, Esq.*
   671. PALACE OF WESTMINSTER.—Elevation of River Front. Sir Charles Barry, R.A *Lent by W. Bottomley, Esq.*

A COLLECTION OF OLD ENGRAVINGS LENT BY HERBERT BATSFORD, ESQ

672-673. PERSPECTIVE VIEW OF ST MARTIN'S CHURCH AND INTERIOR.

674-675 MONTAGUE HOUSE, GREAT RUSSELL STREET, LONDON.

   676. MARLBOROUGH HOUSE, ST. JAMES'S PARK

677-678 BUCKINGHAM HOUSE.

   679 ST MARY-LE-STRAND

   680 BOW CHURCH

681 St George's, Hanover Square
682-683 St Paul's Cathedral
684 St Clement Danes
685 Hampton Court
686 Royal Hospital, Chelsea
687 Powis House
688 Covent Garden Piazza.
689-690 Royal Hospital, Greenwich
691 Somerset House.
692 Tutsham Hall.
693 Orchard Portman, Somerset
694 Brympton, Somerset
695 Staunton Harold, Leicester
696 Lees Court

697 Newby, Yorks
698 Waldershare
699 Nottingham from E
700 Wentworth Castle, Yorks.
701 Bethlehem Hospital
702 Sandywell
703 Mount Morris.
704 Acklam, Yorks
705 King's Western
706 Southwick, Southampton
707 Nibley
708 Miserden
709 Lowther, Westmorland
710 Lupiatt

MODELS.

711 Model of the Palace of Westminster.
712 Model of Stonehenge

WATER-COLOUR SECTION.

Octagon Gallery.

713-714 Claydon House, Bucks —Drawings R Adam. *Lent by Sir Edmund Verney, Bart.*

715 Painting showing Various Buildings and Designs of Inigo Jones — Sir W. Tite *Lent by the R I B A*

716 Palace of Westminster Elevation of River Front.—Sir Charles Barry, R.A *Lent by W. Bottomley, Esq*

717-718 Castle Rising, Norfolk Whitby, Yorkshire —E Guy Dawber *Lent by the Artist.*

719-720 Oil Paintings —John O'Connor, R I 719 Ruins of Tower, St John's, Chester 720 Windsor *Lent by Mrs O'Connor*

721. Customs House, King's Lynn —Alfred B Yeates *Lent by the Artist*

722. The Station, Newcastle —John Dobson *Lent by the Trustees of the Laing Art Gallery, Newcastle*

723 Lincoln —John O'Connor, R I *Lent by T W Cutler, Esq.*

724-725 Cowdray House 724 Ruins. 725 Entrance to Back of Hall —W Flockhart. *Lent by the Artist.*

726 Old Tower, West Gate, Gloucester —Joseph Braddon *Lent by S G Saunders, Esq*

727 Old Town Hall, Leominster —Joseph Braddon *Lent by S G Saunders, Esq*

728 Louth Church Steeple —Sir G. G. Scott, R.A. *Lent by J. O. Scott, Esq*

Large Gallery.

729 Queens' College, Cambridge —John O'Connor, R.I.
730 Chesham House.—John O'Connor, R.I.
 The pair lent by Mrs O'Connor

731 Lincoln Cathedral.—South-East View —J. K Colling.
732 Beverley Minster —The Percy Tomb —J. K Colling.
 The pair lent by the R I B A

733-735. Drawings by H C Corlette —733 New College, Oxford —Stained Glass Window in ante-chapel 734, 735. St. Albans Abbey.—Decorations on Ceiling of Choir and on Vaulting of Sanctuary. *Lent by the Artist.*

736 Abbey Church of St. Albans.—Decoration of the Choir Ceiling —Jas Neale, F S A *Lent by the Artist.*

737 Middle Temple Hall,—The Screen J Turner *Lent by the R I B A*

738 Garden House —Artist Unknown (Early British School). *Lent by Alfred B Yeates, Esq*

739-740 St Paul's Cathedral —T Malton *Lent by the R.I B.A.*

741 St Stephen's, Walbrook —Pulpit R Phené Spiers. *Lent by the Victoria and Albert Museum.*

742 St Stephen's, Walbrook.—Transverse Section, looking east. *Lent by the R I B.A*

743 PARK GATE (WELLINGTON ARCH), HYDE PARK —*Lent by the R I B A*
744 A VIEW OF THE EXAMINATION ROOMS, BURLINGTON GARDENS —W. Flockhart	*Lent by the Artist.*
745 TEWKESBURY ABBEY —West Front	H H Statham	*Lent by the Artist*
746 INTERIOR OF OLD HOUSE, EXETER —Solomon Hart, R A
747 ENTRANCE TO CRYPT, GLASGOW CATHEDRAL.
748 COURTYARD OF FORD'S HOSPITAL AT COVENTRY —(?) G L J. Pretty.
749 INTERIOR OF VICARS' COLLEGE, EXETER.—Solomon Hart, R.A. (1833)
	The four lent by R Phené Spiers, Esq
750. THE ABBOT'S CHAPEL, WESTMINSTER.—N Aisle of Choir	T M. Rooke
	Lent by Rev J A Sedgwick.
751 ST BARTHOLOMEW THE GREAT, SMITHFIELD —With Rahere's Tomb	T M.
	Rooke	*Lent by the Artist*
752. CHAPTER HOUSE DOORWAY, WESTMINSTER ABBEY —T M. Rooke	*Lent
	by H W Birks, Esq*
753 KNOLE HOUSE, KENT —Interior	John O'Connor, R I	*Lent by Mrs
	O'Connor*
754 WINCHFIELD CHURCH, HANTS —Chancel Arch.	Sir C A Nicholson, Bart
	Lent by the Artist.
755 THE PRIOR'S DOOR, ELY —C J. Watson	*Lent by the Artist*
756 ST STEPHEN'S, WALBROOK —Interior	John Fulleylove, R.I
757. THE MONUMENT AND ST MAGNUS' CHURCH —Fish Street Hill, London
	John Fulleylove, R I
758 ST PAUL'S CATHEDRAL —Interior, looking E.	John Fulleylove, R.I
	The three lent by the Artist.
759 WESTMINSTER ABBEY, EAST CLOISTER —T M Rooke	*Lent by the Artist*
760 THE LANTERN, ELY —C. J Watson	*Lent by the Artist.*
761. HAMPTON COURT —Great Bow Window of Hall	R Phené Spiers.	*Lent
	by the Artist*
762 ST MICHAEL ROYAL, COLLEGE HILL, LONDON —J Ogilvy.	*Lent by the
	Artist.*
763 KNOLE HOUSE, KENT —Cartoon Gallery	C Essenhigh Corke	*Lent by
	the Artist*
764. ELY CATHEDRAL —W Front	C J Watson	*Lent by the Artist*
765 ONE OF "THE TWA BRIGS O' AYR "—Ernest George
766. THE BRIDGE, DURHAM —Ernest George
767. THE OLD BRIDGE, STIRLING.—Ernest George
	The Three lent by the Artist.
768–769. TWO SKETCHES —A W Pugin	*Lent by C Sibeth, Esq*
770 MUCHELNEY, SOMERSET —W Haywood
771 SHERBORNE ABBEY —W. Haywood
772. MONTACUTE HOUSE, SOMERSET —W Haywood.
	The three lent by the Artist
773–784. A SET OF DRAWINGS, by George Devey (1820–1886) —773–774 Two Lodges.
	775 House at Newport, Monmouth, for G Hooper, Esq	776 Wilcote,
	Oxon , for Chas. Sartoris, Esq	777–778 Macharioch House, for H R H.
	the Princess Louise.	779–780 Wickwar Rectory, for the Earl of Ducie.
	781 Hall Place, Tonbridge, for Sam Morley, Esq	782 First Sketch
	for " Goldings," Herts, for R Souter, Esq	783. Heathfield Lodge
	784 Schoolhouse
	The set lent by Jas Williams, Esq
785–790 A SET OF DRAWINGS, by R. Phené Spiers —785 Pinkie House, N B , the
	Fountain	786 Haddon Hall, Entrance Courtyard.	787 Netley Abbey,
	S Transept.	788 Winchester Cathedral, S Transept and Tower
	789 Christ Church Priory, Lady Chapel	790 Dunblane Cathedral
	The Nave before addition of new roof
791 OLD MAGDALEN HALL, OXFORD —J K Colling
	Nos 785–791 *lent by R Phené Spiers, Esq*
792. CRATHES CASTLE, N B —W Flockhart	*Lent by the Artist*
793 CHARTERHOUSE CHAPEL —Sir C A Nicholson, Bart.	*Lent by the Artist*
794. IRTHLINGBOROUGH CHURCH, NORTHANTS —Tower and W End.	George
	Sidney Shepherd (*worked* 1821–1860)
795 CHESTER CATHEDRAL —View from S W	Charles Wild (1781–1835)
796 REDCLIFF CHURCH, BRISTOL —View from S E end of Churchyard	Charles
	Wild (1781–1835)
	The three lent by the Victoria and Albert Museum
797 SWANHURST FARM, HALL GREEN, WARWICK —J A. Swan
798 MANOR HOUSE, HAMPTON-IN-ARDEN —J A Swan
	The pair lent by the Artist.
799. OLD BUILDINGS AT HIGH WYCOMBE —Henry de Cort (1801).	*Lent by
	T. W. Cutler, Esq.*

800-803 FOUR DRAWINGS OF NORFOLK HOUSES —W Millard   800   East Barsham
House   801. Oxburgh Hall   802 Barningham Hall   803. Blickling
Hall.
No 801 *lent by C A Millard, Esq , the others by the Artist.*

804. WESTMINSTER ABBEY —Interior   J. M. W Turner, R A (1775-1851)
Lent by T. W Cutler, Esq

805. ELY CATHEDRAL.—Interior   J M W. Turner, R.A. (1775-1851) *Lent by
Mrs Winkworth*

806-809 DRAWINGS —W Millard   806. S.E Angle of Lady Chapel, Ely   807
Blythburgh   808 Chipping Campden, Glos   809. Layer Marney Church,
Essex
Nos. 806, 807, 809 *lent by the Artist* , No. 808 *by C A. Millard, Esq*

810-813 A SET OF DRAWINGS BY JOSEPH NASH (1808-1878)   810 Christ Church
Cathedral, Oxford, View of Interior, Looking East from Nave. 811
Hampton Court Palace, Presence Chamber. 812 Hall of Christ Church,
Oxford   813 St John's College, Oxford
Nos 810-812 *lent by the Victoria and Albert Museum* ; No. 813 *by
R Phené Spiers, Esq*

814. HEADINGTON CHURCH, OXON —Sir C. A Nicholson, Bart *Lent by the
Artist.*

815 THE ROWS, CHESTER —John O'Connor, R.I.

816 COTTAGES —John O'Connor, R I.
The pair lent by Mrs O'Connor.

CONTEMPORARY WORK

Lower Gallery.

817-818 ST PETER'S CHURCH (LOWDER MEMORIAL BAPTISTERY), LONDON DOCKS —
CENTRAL LIBRARY, ACTON   (*Maurice B Adams*)

819-821 ROYAL VICTORIA PAVILION, RAMSGATE   Main Entrance , Tea Room
Proscenium Detail   (*S D. Adshead*)

822-824 BRITISH LINEN Co 's BANK   Entrance Doorway —MESSRS. COUTTS &
Co 's BANK, STRAND Exterior and Interior. (*J Macvicar Anderson*)

825. LIVERPOOL & LONDON & GLOBE INSURANCE CO   (*J. Macvicar Anderson*
and *H. L Anderson*)

826-829 THE WODEHOUSE, WOMBOURNE, for Col Shaw Holier —THE MAGPIE &
STUMP, 38-39 Cheyne Walk, CHELSEA —72, 73, 74 CHEYNE WALK,
CHELSEA —75 CHEYNE WALK, CHELSEA, for Mrs Hunt. (*C R
Ashbee.*)

830 HEATH END, CHECKENDEN, READING   (*Maxwell Ayrton.*)

831-834. ST ANSELM'S CHURCH, DAVIES STREET, LONDON: Interior View.—
CAMPDEN HOUSE CHAMBERS, W.: Dining Room —COTTAGE AT GUILD-
FORD —HOUSE IN PARK LANE, for Alfred Beit, Esq (*Balfour &
Turner*)

835-838. BRYN TEG, FOUR OAKS —CORHAMPTON HOUSE, FOUR OAKS —HAWKES-
FORD, FOUR OAKS —REDLANDS, FOUR OAKS   (*C E. Bateman*)

839 ELECTRA HOUSE, FINSBURY PAVEMENT, E.C. (*John Belcher, A.R A ,
Pres. R.I B.A.*)

840-841 HOLLINGTON HOUSE, NEWBURY. Exteriors and Interiors (*Sir A.
Blomfield & Sons*)

842 NATIONAL DEBT OFFICE, OLD JEWRY, E C : Entrance Doorway. (*Arthur
C Blomfield*)

843-845 6 GROSVENOR PLACE · New Hall, Upper Part New Main Stairs and Dining
Room —SALTCOTE PLACE, PLAYDEN, SUSSEX.—Entrance Front and
Garden Front.—LEASOM, RYE, SUSSEX Entrance Hall and Corridor
and Garden Front. (*Reginald Blomfield, A R.A*)

846. LONDON HOUSE, for Viscount Ridley (in course of construction) (*Detmar
Blow* and *Termand Bullerey*)

848 INGRAM HOUSE, STOCKWELL ROAD, S W —Part of S.W. Front   Interior
of Library   Interior of Lounge   Corner of Waiting Room   Chimney-
piece in Dining Room Wing.   Central Portion of Dining Room   (*Arthur
T. Bolton*)

849. DITTON PLACE, BALCOMBE.—Loggia, Entrance, West and South Fronts
and Gallery   (*Cecil C Brewer*)

850-852. NEW COURT HOUSE AND POLICE STATION, BEDALE, YORKS   Exterior
View and Interior of Court House —THORPE UNDERWOOD HALL, near
YORK View of Porch, Hall, and Fireplace.—WELBURN HALL, KIRBY-
MOORSIDE, YORKS · View of House, Interior of Long Gallery (*Walter
H Brierley, F S A.*)

853–854 HEAD OFFICES OF THE NATIONAL TELEPHONE CO, TEMPLE AVENUE AND VICTORIA EMBANKMENT, LONDON (*A M Bromley*)
SKISKEN CHURCH, ARRAN —GARDNER MEMORIAL CHURCH, BRECHIN —ELDER PUBLIC LIBRARY, GOVAN —ATHENÆUM BUILDINGS, ST. GEORGE'S PLACE FRONT, GLASGOW —ATHENÆUM BUILDINGS, BUCHANAN STREET FRONT, GLASGOW.—CLYDE TRUST OFFICES, GLASGOW —CHARING CROSS MANSIONS, GLASGOW —FINE ART INSTITUTE, GLASGOW. (*John Burnet & Son.*)

855–858. BUSINESS PREMISES, NORTHUMBERLAND STREET, NEWCASTLE-ON-TYNE —DELAVAL ARMS PUBLIC HOUSE TRUST, NEWCASTLE.—ENTRANCE LAING ART GALLERY, NEWCASTLE-ON-TYNE.—TOWER LAING ART GALLERY, NEWCASTLE-ON-TYNE (*Cackett & Burns Dick.*)

859–860. ST. DAVID'S CHURCH, EXETER.—LYTCHETT MANOR, DORSET. (*W. D Caroe, F S A*)

861. MESSRS BECHSTEIN'S: Fireplace to Showroom and Entrance New Premises.—LITTLECOURT, FARTHINGSTONE · Dining Room and South Terrace (*Walter Cave.*)

862–866 IMPERIAL INSTITUTE. General View, Main Hall, Staircase —LLOYD'S REGISTRY.—SAVOY HOTEL. (*T. E Collcutt.*)

867 ENGINEERING WORKSHOPS AND POWER STATION, QUEENSFERRY, FLINT (*H Bulkeley Creswell*)

868–870 NEW HALL AND CLASS ROOMS, COMMERCIAL TRAVELLERS' SCHOOLS, PINNER Exterior and Interior —A PAIR OF COTTAGES AT PINNER FOR THE COMMERCIAL TRAVELLERS' SCHOOLS. (*H. O. Cresswell.*)

871–872. WOOD GREEN ALMSHOUSES (*Alfred W S. Cross*)

873 QUEEN'S HOTEL, SOUTHSEA —ITALIAN HOSPITAL, FROM DEVONSHIRE STREET —ITALIAN HOSPITAL, QUEEN SQUARE, LONDON.—HÔTEL MÉTROPOLE, FOLKESTONE Part of Lounge, Billiard Room (*T W Cutler*)

874. HOUSES AT NORTHWOOD (*F M Elgood.*)

875 COURT-HOUSE, BROADWAY —PARR'S BANK, WOODFORD. Exterior and Doorway.—SOLOMS COURT, SURREY · Three Views (*E. Guy Dawber.*)

876. SHOTTON CHURCH, NORTH WALES.—BATH STREET, CHESTER —MEMORIAL SCREEN, PARISH CHURCH, WARRINGTON.—ECCLESTON HILL LODGE, EATON ESTATE —NORTHGATE STREET, CHESTER.—DEGANWY CHURCH, NORTH WALES —ST. WERBURGH'S STREET, CHESTER.—GROSVENOR PARK ROAD, CHESTER.—COTTAGES, PORT SUNLIGHT, CHESHIRE —"OAKMERE," CHESHIRE —ABBEYSTEAD, LANCASHIRE for the Rt Hon Earl Sefton (*John Douglas*)

877 COUNCIL SCHOOLS, MERTON, SURREY.—COTTAGES AT MITCHAM —EAST WINDOW AND DECORATION, ST BARNABAS MISSION CHURCH, MITCHAM. (*H Burke Downing*)

878–879 BUSINESS PREMISES, 21–22 GREAT CASTLE STREET, W.—49 HARLEY STREET, W. (*F. M. Elgood*).

880 COUNTRY HOUSE Entrance Corridor, Hall, Drawing Room, Garden Front, and First Floor Corridor. (*Norman Evill*)

881 NEW LONDON OFFICES FOR N E RAILWAY (*Horace Field.*)

882–887 ST PAUL'S PRESBYTERIAN CHURCH HOUSE AND SOCIAL HOME, WESTBOURNE GROVE, W. HOUSES AT HARROW —FREE LIBRARY, NOTTING HILL —"THE WABE," HAMPSTEAD HEATH Exterior, View in Hall —GENERAL OFFICES, CITY AND SOUTH LONDON RAILWAY, FINSBURY PAVEMENT, E C (*T P Figgis*)

888–891 DODDINGS FARM, BERE REGIS, DORSET —THE MILL HOUSE, TADWORTH, SURREY Additions, Staircase in Living Room, Exterior and Fireplace in Dining Room —SHERFORD FARM, BERE REGIS, DORSET —SEVEN BARROWS FARM, WAREHAM, DORSET —THE STOOKS, WITTERSHAM, KENT Stable and Greenhouse. (*Forsyth & Maule.*)

892–896 ELM BANK, KETTERING.—THE GABLES, PETERBOROUGH: Garden Front; Entrance Hall —LONDON CITY AND MIDLAND BANK, KETTERING —PARK ROAD SCHOOLS, KETTERING —CORBY HOUSE, NORTHANTS (*Gotch and Saunders*)

897. CRATHORNE HALL, YORKS —FOXCOMBE, OXON. : Interior and Exterior Views —MOTOR HOUSE, FOXCOMBE. (*Ernest George & Yeates*)

898–899 MAPPIN ART GALLERY, SHEFFIELD Exterior and Interior (*Gibbs & Flockton.*)

900–901 PUBLIC LIBRARY, HARROGATE —COUNTY BUILDING, STAFFORD (*Henry T Hare.*)

902. EAGLE INSURANCE BUILDINGS, CROSS STREET, MANCHESTER. (*O Heathcote & Sons*)

903 "FRAMEWOOD," STOKE POGES · View from Drive, Garden Front, Hall, and Dining Room (*Gerald C Horsley*)

N N

904-906   "GREYSTOCK," WIMBLEDON —THE GATE HOUSE, SHACKLEFORD, SURREY.
—REMODELLING NEWTOWN LODGE, HUNGERFORD, BERKS   (*Hubbard & Moore*)

907-908.   PUBLIC OFFICES AND FIRE STATION, ALDERSHOT   (*C E. Hutchinson.*)

909-914.   TERRACE HOUSES, HUNSTANTON, NORFOLK —BAPTIST MEETING HOUSE, CHORLEY WOOD, HERTS —THE HUT, HUNSTANTON, NORFOLK.—ROOD SCREEN, HATFIELD BROAD OAK, HARLOW, ESSEX —Ditto, Rood Screen, Details of Ornament —COTTAGE AND STABLES, HUNSTANTON, NORFOLK   (*Herbert G Ibberson*)

915-917.   NEW CHAPEL, GIGGLESWICK, YORKS —RUSHTON HALL, NORTHANTS — NEW BUILDINGS FOR THE UNIVERSITY OF CAMBRIDGE   (*T G Jackson, R.A*)

918-919   KINGSGATE CHAPEL, HOLBORN —PREMISES IN BOND STREET   (*Arthur Keen*)

920   DEPTFORD TOWN HALL.—*Lanchester* and *Rickards.*

921   HALLYBURTON, COUPAR-ANGUS —Alterations for W G. Graham-Menzies, Esq   (*R. S Lorimer, A R.S.A*)

922   "FRITHWOOD" HOUSE, NORTHWOOD —WELDERS, CHALFONT ST GILES   (*Mervyn Macartney*)

923-924   MARISCHAL COLLEGE, UNIVERSITY OF ABERDEEN · View from Broad Street —MITCHELL TOWER, MARISCHAL COLLEGE, UNIVERSITY OF ABERDEEN   (*A. Marshall Mackenzie*)

925.   THE ORCHARD, HARROW-ON-THE-HILL   Drawing-room, Entrance Door, Garden Front, Entrance Front, Entrance Gate, and Dining-room   (*Arnold Mitchell.*)

926.   HOUSE IN KENSINGTON PALACE GARDENS: For Wm. Willett, Esq.   (*E J May*)

927-930.   VICARAGE, LINDFIELD, SUSSEX.—HOUSE, THE PARK, PETERBOROUGH   For J. E S Perkins, Esq —HOUSE, WYMONDLEY ROAD, HITCHIN, HERTS   (*Walter Millard*)

931   ALL SAINTS', TOOTING   Interior and Exterior Views.—ST MARK'S, MANSFIELD —ST CUTHBERT'S, MIDDLESBRO' · Interior View — ALVESTON VICARAGE, STRATFORD-ON-AVON —CARLTON-IN-CLEVELAND —ST MARY'S, SLEDMERE . Interior and Exterior Views —SCREEN IN ALL SAINTS', DRIFFIELD —HIGHFIELD HOUSE, DRIFFIELD   Interior and Exterior Views —ST JOHN'S, HENDON   (*Temple Moore.*)

932-933   HINTON HOUSE, NORTHANTS —SAVOY CROFT, AYR   (*James A Morris*)

934-936   NEW CENTRAL CRIMINAL COURT   View —"CROSSWAYS," BUSBRIDGE, NEAR GODALMING —LIVERPOOL TECHNICAL SCHOOL, LECTURE HALL.   (*E W Mountford*)

937-938   ROYAL NAVAL HOSPITAL, CHATHAM   (*J. C T Murray, J E Newberry*)

939-943   MARTIN'S BANK, BROMLEY, KENT —RED COURT, HASLEMERE: Garden Front —STEEP HILL, JERSEY · Entrance Hall —ST. SWITHIN'S CHURCH, INTERIOR, HITHER GREEN . (*Ernest Newton.*)

944   ALL SOULS' CHURCH, LOUDOUN ROAD, HAMPSTEAD, N   New West Front —YIEWSLEY CHURCH, WEST DRAYTON   West End and Interior Views —THE CHOIR SCHOOLS, NEW COLLEGE, OXFORD —ST. ALBAN'S CHURCH, WESTCLIFF-ON-SEA, ESSEX: Interior.   (*Nicholson & Corlette*)

945-947.   HARRIETSHAM MANOR HOUSE, HARRIETSHAM, KENT —"HILLINGTON," WALTON-ON-THAMES —SCANDINAVIAN   SAILORS'   HOME   Annexe   (*Niven & Wigglesworth*)

948   EYWOOD HALL   Exterior, Porch, and Hall —TECHNICAL SCHOOL, WARRINGTON —CHRIST CHURCH, PORT SUNLIGHT   Interior and Exterior   (*William & Segar Owen.*)

949-951.   LONDON HOMŒOPATHIC HOSPITAL.—VICARAGE, EALING —ETHELBURGA, EALING —THE PERCEVAL MEMORIAL CHURCH, EALING   (*William A Pite*)

952.   VIEWS OF CHAPELWOOD MANOR, SUSSEX.   (*A N Prentice.*)

953-954.   NEW PLACE, HORSHAM, SUSSEX   External and Interior Views —LYCH GATE, BOLNEY, SUSSEX   (*Edward Turner Powell*)

955   REREDOS, CHURCH OF SS PHILIP AND JAMES, LECKHAMPTON.—GREAT HALL, GOODRICH COURT, HEREFORDSHIRE —CHELTENHAM COLLEGE CHAPEL —LYCH GATE, PAINSWICK —CHALICE, CHELTENHAM COLLEGE CHAPEL —LECKHAMPTON   COURT,   CHELTENHAM —"WHITESHOOTS," GLOUCESTERSHIRE   (*H. A. Prothero* (*Prothero & Phillott*))

956-959.   ALL SAINTS' CHURCH, ELLAND —ST NEOT'S CHURCH, CORNWALL   New Rood Screen and Restored Chancel —GIFFORD HOUSE, ROEHAMPTON, S W   Exterior and Interiors   (*George H Fellowes Prynne*)

960   TOWN HALL, LYNTON, DEVON —HOUSE AT HASLEMERE, SURREY.— HOUSE AT BUCKLAND, SURREY —BUSINESS PREMISES, TOTTENHAM COURT ROAD, W —HOUSE, KENSINGTON PALACE GARDENS, W — BUSINESS PREMISES, OXFORD STREET.   (*Read & Macdonald.*)

961 RHINEFIELD, FROM UPPER TERRACE Various views.—DANESFIELD, SOUTH-WEST VIEW —ABBEY COTTAGES, MEDMENHAM —MEDMENHAM ABBEY AS RESTORED (*W H Romaine-Walker & S Besant.*)

962 PORT SUNLIGHT Terrace of Seven Cottages (*Chas. H Reilly*)

963–965. ROYAL ARMY MEDICAL CORPS MEMORIAL, ALDERSHOT —PICKENHAM HALL, NORFOLK —"BEAUMONTS," EDENBRIDGE, KENT —HOW GREEN, HEVER, KENT (*Robert Weir Schultz.*)

966–971. COTTAGES, GARDEN CITY View from N E —COTTAGES, GARDEN CITY: Interior of Kitchen —HOUSE AT WINDERMERE Entrance Front; The Hall, Drawing-room Fireplace —HOUSE AT KNUTSFORD Porch and Corridor (*M H Baillie-Scott.*)

972–976. ST ALBANS CATHEDRAL, BISHOP'S THRONE —ST JOHN'S CHURCH, PALMER'S GREEN, N —ST MARK'S CHURCH, HARROGATE (*J. Oldrid Scott & Sons*)

977. VARIOUS WORKS IN GLOUCESTERSHIRE AND OXFORDSHIRE (*Seth Smith & Monro*)

978–980. CARDIFF PUBLIC LIBRARY View of Central Portion, Entrance Doorway, Flank View (*Edwin Seward*)

981. NEWTOWN GRANGE, NEWBURY The Studio (*J W Simpson & Maxwell Ayrton*)

982–986 "THE GABLES," ORFORD, SUFFOLK Ditto, Entrance Hall —TOWN HALL, ORFORD, SUFFOLK Interiors. (*Harry Sirr*)

987–991 ST ETHELDREDA'S CHURCH, FULHAM PALACE ROAD, S W View from Chancel, looking West Exterior and Interiors —PULPIT, ST. ALBAN'S CHURCH, TEDDINGTON. (*A. H Skipworth*)

992–993. LITTLE BARLEY END Laundry and Cottage Farmhouses —MOWER HILL AND THE FIVES COURT, PINNER (*Smith & Brewer.*)

994 OFFICE OF "THE BUILDER," CATHERINE STREET, LONDON. (*H H. Statham*)

995 ALL SAINTS' CONVENT, COLNEY CHAPEL, ST ALBANS (*Leonard Stokes*)

996–998 WOOLWICH TOWN HALL Entrance Hall, Interior of Council Chamber, and Chair —BELFAST CITY HALL (*Sir A Brumwell Thomas*)

999–1000 22 CAVENDISH SQUARE, LONDON: View of the Gardens and Outside of Consulting-room, Corridor, Inside of Consulting-room —CHURCH OF ST CHRISTOPHER, HASLEMERE, SURREY The Figure of the Patron Saint by *Mrs M. D Spooner* (*Charles Spooner, Esq*)

1001 OCEANIC HOUSE, COCKSPUR STREET, CHARING CROSS (*H Tanner, jun*)

1003–1004 BISHOPSGATE INSTITUTE, LONDON —INTERIOR OF ST MARTIN'S, WONERSH, SURREY (*C Harrison Townsend*)

1005–1006 THREE COTTAGES, LINGFIELD, SURREY —HOUSE AT SAXLINGHAM, NETHERGATE (*F W Troup*)

1007 BEDFORD COURT MANSIONS, LONDON (*Allan F Vigers*)

1008 THE ORCHARD, CHORLEY WOOD, HERTS —HOUSE AT SHACKLEFORD, SURREY —HOUSE ON HOG'S BACK, SURREY —PERRYCROFT, COLWALL, HEREFORDSHIRE.—WALNUT TREE FARM, CASTLEMORTON, WORCESTER. (*C F A Voysey*)

1009 HALL AND SUNDAY SCHOOLS, VICTORIA ROAD, HENDON, N W (*F W Troup*)

1010–1012 TOWN HOUSE FOR THE EARL OF PLYMOUTH, MOUNT STREET Exterior and Interior Views —SHERFIELD MANOR, HAMPSHIRE Entrance Front Cottages. (*Fairfax B Wade.*)

1013. TOWNSEND HOUSE, REGENT'S PARK —ESTCOURT HOUSE, KENSINGTON PALACE GARDENS —HANOVER HOUSE, REGENT'S PARK (*Edward Warren*)

1014–1015 VARIOUS WORKS AT NEWLAND, BUCKS —STAIRCASE, MOUNT MELVILLE, ST ANDREWS (*Paul Waterhouse*)

1016. WELSH UNIVERSITY, REGISTRY OFFICE, CARDIFF (*Messrs Wills & Anderson*)

1017–1019. BRITANNIA ROYAL NAVAL COLLEGE, DARTMOUTH General View from Kingswear, A portion of the Front with Terraces and Gardens, Principal Entrance · Centre of Main Front. (*Sir Aston Webb, R A*)

1020–1022 CHURCH OF THE CHRISTIAN SCIENTISTS, MANCHESTER.—WESLEYAN CHAPEL, MIDDLETON —HOUSE AT EDGERTON, HUDDERSFIELD (*Edgar Wood*)

1023 MESSRS. THURSTONS' PREMISES, LEICESTER SQUARE (*Edmund Wimperis & East.*)

1024. THE NEW WAR OFFICE Staircase (*The late Wm. Young*)

1025 THE INDIAN HALL, ELVEDEN (*Clyde Young*)

1026. THE NEW WAR OFFICE, WHITEHALL (*The late Wm Young*)

1027–1029. No 139 PICCADILLY —TYLNEY HALL, HANTS · Tower Garden and Loggia, Carriage Court, Garden Pavilions. (*R. Selden Wornum*)

1030 INNER HALL, 10 DE VERE GARDENS, S W · For Capt Osborne —
LIBRARY DOOR AND CHIMNEY PIECES, 9 HYDE PARK TERRACE · for
E S Montefiore, Esq —HOUSE AT HADLEY COMMON.—SATINWOOD
ROOM, 11 HILL STREET, MAYFAIR. (*J Leonard Williams.*)
1031. GLASGOW MUNICIPAL BUILDINGS (*The late Wm Young.*)

FURNITURE.

1032 LADY'S CHAIR.—In Oak About 1535 *Lent by Percy Macquoid, Esq*
1033 OAK STOOL —Gothic Early 16th Cent *Lent by Seymour Lucas,
Esq , R.A*
1034 JOINT STOOL
1035 JOINT STOOL —Early 17th Cent *Lent by Seymour Lucas, Esq , R A*
1036. CHESTNUT CHAIR —Late 17th Cent *Lent by Seymour Lucas, Esq , R A*
1037 OAK ARMCHAIR.—Inlaid with Holly and Ebony Late 16th Cent *Lent
by Seymour Lucas, Esq., R A*
1038 WALNUT CHAIR. Period Charles II *Lent by T W Cutler, Esq*
1039 OAK GATE TABLE —Late 17th Cent *Lent by Seymour Lucas, Esq , R A.*
1040 WALNUT CHAIR —Late 17th Cent. *Lent by Seymour Lucas, Esq , R A*
1041 · QUEEN ANNE CHAIR WITH INLAID BACK —Early 18th Cent. *Lent by
Seymour Lucas, Esq , R A*
1043-1044 A PAIR OF QUEEN ANNE CHAIRS —Early 18th Cent. *Lent by David
Murray, Esq , R A*
1045 QUEEN ANNE CHAIR.—Early 18th Cent *Lent by R S. Balfour, Esq*
1046-1047 PAIR OF QUEEN ANNE CHAIRS, CABRIOLE LEGS.—Early 18th Cent
Lent by F F Burghard, Esq , F R C S
1048 CHAIR —Early 18th Cent *Lent by E. Guy Dawber, Esq*
1049 EARLY 18TH CENT LACQUER CHAIR *Lent by W Reynold Stephens, Esq.*
1050. QUEEN ANNE LACQUERED CABINET.
1051. MAHOGANY SETTEE.—1st quarter 18th Cent *Lent by R S Balfour, Esq.*
1052-1053 ARMCHAIR AND SINGLE CHAIR —Early Georgian. *Lent by E Guy Dawber,
Esq*
1054-1055 ARMCHAIRS —Mahogany 18th Cent *Lent by E Guy Dawber, Esq*
1056-1057 PAIR OF MAHOGANY CHAIRS —18th Cent *Lent by E Guy Dawber Esq*
1058-1060 CHIPPENDALE ARMCHAIR — CHIPPENDALE CIRCULAR TABLE. — CHIP-
PENDALE MAHOGANY CARVED TABLE. *Lent by Ernest Blake, Esq*
1061 CHIPPENDALE LONG CASE CLOCK —Latter half of 18th Cent *Lent by
Alfred Davis, Esq , 37 Ladbroke Grove, W*
1062 CIRCULAR TOPPED TABLE —With Tripod Support carved as Dolphins
Lent by Ernest Blake, Esq.
1063 CLAVICHORD —Latter half of 18th Cent *Lent by Mr C Heath.*
1064. CHIPPENDALE STOOL —In Mahogany with Clustered Column Legs. *Lent
by F F. Burghard, Esq , F R C S*
1065 HEPPLEWHITE ARMCHAIR.—With Shield Back *Lent by Alfred Davis,
Esq , 37 Ladbroke Grove, W*
1066 SPINET —Thomas Hitchcock, maker about 1710 *Lent by Messrs John
Broadwood & Sons*
1067 HEPPLEWHITE ARMCHAIR —With Interlaced Back and Prince of Wales's
Feathers *Lent by Alfred Davis, Esq , 37 Ladbroke Grove, W*
1068 EARLY ADAM ARMCHAIR.—With Lyre Back. *Lent by Alfred Davis,
Esq , 37 Ladbroke Grove, W*
1069 STANDARD BAROMETER.—By Adam *Lent by Alfred Davis, Esq , 37 Ladbroke Grove, W*
1070-1071 PAIR OF GLOBES —Celestial and Terrestrial Adam Period The Carved
Heads are Symbolical of the Four Quarters of the Globe *Lent by
F. F. Burghard, Esq , F R C S*
1072 DRESSING TABLE —With tambour top, by Shears *Lent by Alfred Davis,
Esq , 37 Ladbroke Grove, W*
1073. SHERATON PEMBROKE TABLE —In Harewood and inlaid *Lent by Alfred
Davis, Esq , 37 Ladbroke Grove, W*
1074 HARPSICHORD —Maker, Burkat Shudi, 1771 *Lent by Messrs John
Broadwood & Sons*
1075. SQUARE PIANOFORTE —Maker, Johannes Broadwood, 1774. *Lent by
Messrs John Broadwood & Sons*
1076. KIDNEY-SHAPED MAHOGANY WRITING TABLE.—Sheraton. *Lent by F. F
Burghard, Esq., F R C S.*
1077-1078. SHERATON CARD TABLE —In Decorated Satinwood *Lent by Alfred
Davis, Esq , 37 Ladbroke Grove, W*

1079 SETTEE —Painted Satinwood, Sheraton.   *Lent by T. W Cutler, Esq.*
1080–1081 PAIR OF ARMCHAIRS —With Cane Back and Sides, painted Satinwood.
       Lent by T W Cutler, Esq.
1082 ARMCHAIR.—In painted Satinwood   *Lent by T W Cutler, Esq*
1083 CLOCK.—Decorated Satinwood, Sheraton   *Lent by T. W Cutler, Esq*
1084 SATINWOOD PEMBROKE TABLE —With painted decoration, Sheraton
       Lent by T W Cutler, Esq.
1085. WINDOW SEAT.—In Satinwood, painted decoration, Sheraton.   *Lent by*
       T. W Cutler, Esq
1086 ARMCHAIR.—In Mahogany   End of 18th Cent   *Lent by David Murray,*
       Esq , R A
1087–1088. ARMCHAIR AND SINGLE CHAIR.—End of 18th Cent.   *Lent by R S*
       Balfour, Esq
1089 INLAID MAHOGANY LONG-CASE CLOCK —Sheraton   *Lent by Alfred Davis,*
       Esq , 37 Ladbroke Grove, W

OLD ENGLISH SILVER

Lent by Sir Samuel Montagu, Bart.—Collection of plate, by Paul Lamerie, a celebrated silversmith who worked between 1712 and 1751. During this period his mark was three times changed, L A, 1712, P L. 1733, P L. 1739.   His work usually fetches about £5 per ounce, and is greatly sought after

Lent by Mr Pierpont Morgan.—A large Pilgrim Bottle, nearly two feet high, Queen Anne.—A smaller Pilgrim Bottle, gilt —Monteith, with engraving in the Chinese taste of 1685 —Peg Tankard, covered with engraved floral design on pomegranate feet   The scrolled handle forms a whistle and has a purchase of two pomegranates (1659) —Set of four richly cut, rectangular, 18th cent Spirit Bottles, each enclosing within the solid glass two biscuit medallion portraits by the celebrated James and William Tassie, of Edinburgh

Lent by Mrs. Percy Macquoid —Pair of fluted and gadrooned Candlesticks of large size on octagonal feet

Lent by Mr B S Straus, M P—Set of three Covered Vases, chased, fluted spirally and repoussé with flowers (1755) —Helmet-shaped Milk Jug on three feet with lions' masks, repousse, in the style of Louis XV (1750) —Helmet-shaped Milk Jug on foot, repousse and gadrooned (1741) —Coffee Pot, finely repoussé with floral designs and ivory handle (1749) —A plain covered tankard (1724).—A plain ovate covered tea-caddy (1728) —Cream jug decorated with repoussé shell and foliage spirally disposed (1767)

Lent by Sir Samuel Montagu, Bart.—A trellis pattern Cake Basket, engraved with the Royal arms and richly chased —A finely modelled Oval Bowl on foot enriched with dolphins, the bowl with shell handles and garlands in relief —A two-handled Cup with cover, with scroll handles and flowers embossed in relief.—Two Candlesticks, balustered and chased —*All by Paul Lamerie.*

Lent by Mr Pierpont Morgan —A collection of 40 Spoons, arranged chronologically, and dating from 1560 to 1698 —Steeple Cup of large size, gilt, made from the Great Seal of Ireland (1604) —Covered Pedestal Salt, cylindrical, richly embossed with masks and garlands, fruit, &c , gilt, on lion feet, surmounted by a warrior in Roman armour   Elizabethan —Covered Cup on balustered stem, gilt, the bowl engraved with scrolled foliage, the cover and foot richly embossed with fruit and flowers in medallions on matted ground.   Elizabethan

Lent by Sir Samuel Montagu, Bart.—Set of 3 Casters and a single Castor, by Paul Lamerie.

Lent by Mr. B. S. Straus, M.P.—A small Bowl with repoussé flowers (1665).

Lent by Mr. Leopold de Rothschild —A magnificent Steeple Cup and Cover, gilt, James I.—A Beaker, boldly embossed, of the time of Elizabeth.—A Pedestal Salt and Cover, rectangular body, embossed with masks and fruit, of the time of Elizabeth —Tankard and Cover, gilt, embossed with fruit and flowers in medallions, of the time of Elizabeth

RESOLUTIONS ADOPTED BY THE CONGRESS

SUBJECT I.—THE EXECUTION OF IMPORTANT GOVERNMENT AND MUNICIPAL ARCHITECTURAL WORK BY SALARIED OFFICIALS.

That in the future, in the interests of administrative bodies and the public, and in the higher interests of the art of architecture, public bodies (whether Governmental, provincial, or municipal) should entrust important architectural works only to professionally qualified architects, either by competition or otherwise

SUBJECT II.—ARCHITECTURAL COPYRIGHT AND OWNERSHIP OF DRAWINGS.

(a) *Ownership of Drawings.*

That this Congress is of opinion that the architect is employed to produce a building, and that all drawings and papers prepared by him to that end are undoubtedly his property

(b) *Artistic Copyright.*

This Seventh International Congress of Architects assembled at London in 1906,

Recalling, on the one hand, the resolutions passed during the past twenty-eight years by the International Congresses of Architects and by the International Congress of Artistic Copyright, as well as by the International Congresses of the Association Littéraire et Artistique Internationale, notably at Madrid in 1904 ; Recalling, on the other hand, the " Protocole de Clôture " of the Diplomatic Conference held at Paris in 1896, which upholds the principle of complete protection of works of architecture, Recalling, finally, the Spanish law of 1879 and the French law of 1902, both of which expressly protect works of architecture

Is of opinion

(1) That architectural designs comprise designs of façades, exterior and interior, together with the plans, sections, and elevations, and they constitute the first manifestation of the architect's idea and the work of architecture.

(2) That the building is but a reproduction, on the site, of the architectural drawings.

And this Congress again expresses the desire that works of architecture be protected in all legislative enactments and in all international conventions equally with every other kind of artistic work.

SUBJECT III.—STEEL AND REINFORCED-CONCRETE CONSTRUCTION.

(a) THE GENERAL ASPECT OF THE SUBJECT. (b) WITH SPECIAL REFERENCE TO ÆSTHETIC AND HYGIENIC CONSIDERATIONS IN THE CASE OF VERY HIGH BUILDINGS

(1) That this Congress considers it desirable that an inquiry should be made as to what failures have taken place in reinforced-concrete buildings, and as to the causes of the failures

RÉSOLUTIONS ADOPTÉES PAR LE CONGRÈS.

Thème I —De l'Exécution des Edifices importants destinés a l'État et aux Municipalités des Fonctionnaires salariés (agents voyers etc).

Qu'à l'avenir, dans les intérêts des administrations et du public et dans les intérêts les plus hauts de l'art d'architecture, les administrations publiques (Gouvernementales, provinciales et communales) ne chargent de travaux importants d'architecture que des architectes professionnels qualifiés soit par le concours ou d'ailleurs.

Thème II —La Propriété artistique des Œuvres d'Architecture et la Propriété des Dessins d'Architecture.

(a) La Propriété des dessins d'Architecture

Que ce Congrès est d'opinion que l'architecte est employé pour produire un édifice, et que tous les dessins et papiers préparés par lui à cet effet sont indubitablement sa propriété.

(b) La Propriété artistique des Œuvres d'Architecture.

Ce Septième Congrès International des Architectes réuni à Londres en 1906,

Rappelant, d'une part, les vœux émis depuis vingt-huit ans dans les Congrès Internationaux des Architectes et de la Propriété Artistique, ainsi que dans les Congrès Internationaux de l'Association Littéraire et Artistique Internationale, et notamment à Madrid en 1904 , et rappelant d'autre part le Protocole de clôture de la Conférence diplomatique tenue à Paris en 1896, lequel consacre le principe de la protection complète des œuvres d'architecture , Rappelant enfin la loi espagnole de 1879 et la loi française de 1902, lesquelles protègent expressément les œuvres d'architecture,

Est d'avis :

1° Que les dessins d'architecture comprennent les dessins des façades extérieures et intérieures, les plans, coupe et élévation, et constituent la première manifestation de la pensée de l'architecte et l'œuvre d'architecture ,

2° Que l'édifice n'est qu'une reproduction, sur le terrain, des dessins d'architecture ;

Et renouvelle le vœu que les œuvres d'architecture soient protégées dans toutes les législations et dans toutes les conventions internationales à l'égal de toutes les autres œuvres artistiques.

Thème III —Les Constructions en Acier et en Ciment Armé.

(a) Considérations Générales. (b) Questions spéciales relatives a l'Esthétique et a l'Hygiène dans les Constructions à grande hauteur.

1) Que le Congrès est d'opinion qu'il est à désirer qu'on fasse une enquête pour établir le nombre des cas où les constructions en béton armé n'ont pas répondu à l'attente et les causes de la non-réussite.

(2) That this Congress is of opinion that, where reinforced concrete is intended to be fire-resisting, the greatest possible care should be taken as to the nature of the aggregate and its size, and also as to the protection of the steel

SUBJECT IV.—THE EDUCATION OF THE PUBLIC IN ARCHITECTURE

No resolution proposed.

SUBJECT V.—A STATUTORY QUALIFICATION FOR ARCHITECTS.

That this Congress considers it desirable, in the interests of the public of all nations and of the profession of architecture, that all practitioners should have a statutory qualification

SUBJECT VI.—THE ARCHITECT-CRAFTSMAN HOW FAR SHOULD THE ARCHITECT RECEIVE THE THEORETICAL AND PRACTICAL TRAINING OF A CRAFTSMAN?

That this Congress, considering that the architect, the master of the works, having under his immediate direction workmen and artisans of the most varied bodies of the State, and utilising the services of the most varied industries, has no means of acquiring in each of these trades and in each of these industries the complete knowledge of a specialist, expresses the desire that the opportunity should be given to architectural students to acquire in a general but exact manner the technical part of the various trades and industries of the building trades without claiming to practise these trades and industries. It also expresses the wish that international and continuous relations may be established between the schools.

SUBJECT VII.—THE PLANNING AND LAYING-OUT OF STREETS
AND OPEN SPACES.

No resolution proposed.

SUBJECT VIII.—TO WHAT EXTENT AND IN WHAT SENSE SHOULD THE ARCHITECT HAVE CONTROL OVER OTHER ARTISTS OR CRAFTSMEN IN THE COMPLETION OF A NATIONAL OR PUBLIC BUILDING?

That this Congress is of opinion that the architect in the construction of a building should be given absolute power over the co-operating craftsmen, but in a special manner over the co-operating artists.

SUBJECT IX.—THE RESPONSIBILITIES OF A GOVERNMENT IN THE
CONSERVATION OF NATIONAL MONUMENTS.

(1) That in all countries the Governments should be authorised to obtain if necessary compulsory expropriation in every case where a monument possessing historical, artistic, or archæological interest is not kept in a proper state of preservation by its owner

(2) That this International Congress of Architects recommends that the British Government be approached with a view to appointing a Royal Commission to control and extend the operations of the Ancient Monuments Protection (Amendment) Act of 1900 and to prepare an

(2) Que ce Congrès est d'opinion que là où le béton armé est destiné à
résister au feu il est nécessaire de prendre le plus grand soin par
égard à la nature de la masse et de son volume, comme aussi à la
protection de l'acier

THÈME IV.—L'EDUCATION DU PUBLIC EN ARCHITECTURE.
Pas de conclusion.

THÈME V.—LE TITRE ET LE DIPLÔME D'ARCHITECTE

Que ce Congrès est d'avis que, dans l'intérêt du public de tous les pays
et dans l'intérêt de la profession d'architecture, tous les architectes
doivent avoir une qualification reconnue par la loi.

THÈME VI.—DE L'ARCHITECTE-ARTISAN JUSQU'À QUEL POINT L'ARCHI-
TECTE DOIT-IL RECEVOIR L'EDUCATION THÉORIQUE ET PRATIQUE
DE L'ARTISAN ?

Ce Congrès, considérant que l'architecte, le maître des travaux, ayant
sous ses ordres immédiats des ouvriers et des artisans des classes les
plus différentes de la population, et faisant usage des services des
industries les plus variées, n'a aucun moyen d'acquérir dans chacun
de ces métiers et dans chacune de ces industries les connaissances
complètes d'un spécialiste, exprime l'opinion qu'il serait désirable
de donner aux étudiants d'architecture l'occasion d'acquérir d'une
manière générale et pourtant exacte la partie technique des différents métiers et industries de la profession du bâtiment sans prétendre
de vouloir exercer ces métiers et industries   Le Congrès exprime
également le désir qu'entre ces écoles des relations internationales
et soutenues soient établies

THÈME VII.—DE LA DISPOSITION ET DU DÉVELOPPEMENT DES RUES
ET DES ESPACES LIBRES DANS LES VILLES.
Pas de conclusion

THÈME VIII —JUSQU À QUEL POINT ET DANS QUEL SENS L'ARCHITECTE
DOIT-IL AVOIR LE CONTRÔLE SUR LES AUTRES ARTISTES ET SUR LES
ARTISANS JUSQU'A L'ÉDIFICATION COMPLÈTE DES MONUMENTS
DESTINÉS À L'ETAT OU AU SERVICE PUBLIC ?

Le Congrès émet le vœu 'que dans l'exécution des travaux on doit
accorder à l'architecte un contrôle absolu sur les artisans collaborateurs, mais surtout sur les artistes qui y contribuent

THÈME IX —DE LA RESPONSABILITÉ DES GOUVERNEMENTS DANS LA
CONSERVATION DES MONUMENTS NATIONAUX.

(1) Que dans tous les Etats les Gouvernements soient autorisés pour obtenir,
si cela est nécessaire, l'expropriation obligatoire chaque fois qu'un
monument présentant un intérêt historique, artistique ou archéologique ne sera pas entretenu comme il convient par son possesseur.
(2) Ce Congrès International des Architectes émet le vœu qu'on s'adresse
au Gouvernement britannique pour qu'on nomme une Commission
Royale pour contrôler et étendre l'opération de la loi de 1900 sur la
Conservation des Anciens Monuments et de préparer un catalogue

accurate catalogue of all ancient monuments, whether historic or prehistoric, taking similar action to that of the Department of Historical Manuscripts and in agreement with the measures adopted in other countries.

SUBJECT X —THE CONDUCT OF ARCHITECTURAL COMPETITIONS

(1) That the Congress, taking into consideration the reports submitted, recommends them to the examination of the Permanent Committee of the Congress in order that they may submit a special report to the next Congress

(2) The competition programme should declare that the members of the jury by the fact of their acceptation of the office have not and will not have directly or indirectly any material interest in the execution of works put up to competition.

Recommendation

That the Permanent Committee nominate a special commission of seven members to study the question of international public competitions and report to the next Congress.

exact de tous les monuments anciens dans les Iles britanniques,
soit historiques ou préhistoriques, suivant les mêmes lignes que le
Département des Manuscrits historiques et pour se mettre d'accord
avec les mesures mises dans les autres pays.

THÈME X —DE L'ORGANISATION DES CONCOURS INTERNATIONAUX
PUBLICS D'ARCHITECTURE.

(1) Que ce Congrès, prenant en considération les rapports soumis, recommande au Comité Permanent du Congrès de les examiner, pour qu'un rapport spécial soit soumis au prochain Congrès.

(2) Le programme doit déclarer que les membres du jury par le fait de leur acceptation n'ont et n'auront directement ou indirectement aucun intérêt matériel dans l'exécution des travaux mis au concours

Recommandation

Qu'un rapport sur la question des Concours Publics Internationaux d'Architecture soit présenté au prochain Congrès International de 1908 par les soins de la Commission permanente, qui nommera à cet effet une commission spéciale de sept membres

SEVENTH INTERNATIONAL CONGRESS

INCOME AND

Dr.   EXPENDITURE.

	£	s	d	£	s	d
Visits	756	10	9			
Dinner	557	0	7			
				1,313	11	4
General Printing .				551	1	6
Hire of Hall				274	14	0
Staff and Extra Assistance .				499	19	0
Exhibition and Meetings				240	19	9
Badges				210	6	11
Stamps and Petty Expenses				129	17	3
Stationery				24	11	0
Cleaning				42	17	6
'Transactions' · Printing and Illustrations				408	0	6
Balance *				58	14	7
				£3,754	13	4

* This balance will be applied to defray the cost of binding and issuing the 'Transactions' Any surplus will be handed to the Council of the Architects' Benevolent Society, in aid of the funds of that institution.

OF ARCHITECTS, LONDON, 1906.

EXPENDITURE ACCOUNT.

	Income.		£	s	d	Cr.
Subscriptions and Donations	.		2,479	2	2	
Visits and Dinners	. . . . .		1,248	17	7	
Amount received from Advertisements	. . . .		20	0	0	
Interest on Deposit	. . .		6	13	7	

£3,754 13 4

Audited by JOHN W SIMPSON,
Member of the Executive Committee

JOHN BELCHER, A R.A.,   W. J. LOCKE,
      President.   *Secretary.*

www.ingramcontent.com/pod-product-compliance
Lightning Source LLC
LaVergne TN
LVHW011137210726
843642LV00017B/2863